Riverside/San Bernardino Counties

D0780359

2011-2012
SOCIAL SERVICE RAINBOW RESOURCE DIRECTORY

The Comprehensive Resource and Referral Guide to "People Who Can Help"
in Every Community in Riverside/San Bernardino Counties. A Book Dedicated to "Connecting People With People."

www.ResourceDirectory.com

Acknowledgements

All Rainbow Resource Directory publications are kept accurate as a result of the tremendous cooperation and support of the nonprofit agency staff throughout our research and update process. We are grateful for the assistance of the agency staff in responding to our fax, mail and telephone update requests. Without this help our efforts would not be possible.

Staff

Managing Editor:	Alisa Driscoll
Research Manager:	Justine Wiggans
Advertising:	Ryan Kerby
Art Director:	Sara Eisenbach
Research Assistant:	Sharikia Martin

TABLE OF CONTENTS

FREQUENTLY ASKED QUESTIONS

How Do I Add My Agency to the Rainbow Referral Guide?

Nonprofit agencies may submit information to receive a complimentary basic listing. Information about adding your agency is available on the page titled "Getting in the Guide" or online at (www.resourcedirectory.com/listing.htm). Private service providers that deliver services that are relevant and appropriate for the Rainbow Referral Guides may also be listed in the Guides for a fee. Information about adding your business to the Guides is also available online (www.resourcedirectory.com/advertising.htm). Resource Directory reserves the right to make any and all editorial decisions regrading both complimentary and paid listings.

What Is Included in This Referral Guide?

A comprehensive list of resources in 44 topical chapters covering everything from adoption services to senior services throughout Riverside and San Bernardino Counties.

Is the Information Correct?

To ensure accuracy, all information was updated by fax, online, or telephone during the weeks just before publishing. When you contact an agency, you should reconfirm the services and cost before making your selection. If you discover an inaccuracy, we would appreciate if you would bring it to our attention.

Unfortunately, it is impossible to compile a Guide without a single error. Since agencies move and change telephone numbers from time to time; the information could have been completely accurate at the time of publishing, but a few weeks later the address, phone number or services offered may have changed.

Who Can Get a Copy of This Guide?

Anyone can purchase a copy of the Guide and we commonly sell directories to public nonprofit agencies, government agencies, and private organizations, as well as individuals wanting a personal copy. The Guide was designed primarily for professionals trying to help other people. This Guide includes referral agencies and information that is particularly useful for: social workers, educators, law enforcement, religious leaders, medical professionals, recreation leaders, college students, senior service center directors, employee assistance staff, hospitals, hotlines, referral staff and, of course, the nonprofit agency staff who are on the front lines helping those who are most in need.

How Do I Order Copies of the Guide?

You can order online (www.resourcedirectory.com), by telephone (800) 440-4780, by fax (714) 751-2709 or by regular mail (Resource Directory, 3505 Cadillac Ave., Suite H, Costa Mesa, CA 92626). An order form is provided at the back of this Directory. Prepaid orders are preferred, however, government agencies and school districts may use a Purchase Order. Phone orders can be placed with a credit card (Visa, MasterCard, or American Express) and are generally shipped the same day. Please make checks payable to: James Publishing, Inc. For current brochures, additional order forms, quotes on large quantities or any other questions please do not hesitate to call us at (800) 440-4780.

Why Did You Decide to Include Display Ads in the Guide?

Due to the response by our readers, we have begun accepting display advertising from selected private service providers in the community. It is important for us to maintain the editorial quality and integrity of the Guides therefore we have worked to ensure that the display ads we accept are both relevant and appropriate for our readers. We are confident that many of you will find these private service providers to be valuable resources when seeking high quality services.

HOW TO USE THIS REFERRAL GUIDE

How to Find the Agency You Need

The Riverside/San Bernardino Rainbow Resource Guide is divided into 44 chapters by topic. These subject groupings cluster agencies providing similar services into separate lists. If you are not sure of the agency name, the best place to begin your search is the "Table of Contents." Look through the topics and identify the subject you feel is closest to your service need. Remember that many agencies offer a wide range of services and may be listed in several chapters with different descriptions.

Locating the Agency

If you know the specific name of an agency or you know what type of services you are interested in, use the "EZ-Index" at the front of this Guide. All agency names appear in alphabetical order along with the page numbers on which they appear. If you do not know the name of the agency, look in the front of the book at the table of contents. After reviewing each of the chapter names, select the one where you feel the service you want is most likely to be listed.

Agency Names and Addresses

Many agencies have more than one name, sometimes they indicate the name of their program as the primary name and other listings may appear under the heading of the parent organization. Whenever possible, we strive for uniformity in the directory listings in order to assist you in locating similar services, or in identifying all of the listings for a certain agency.

Description of Services

The *Description of Services* for the same agency may be different because of the special programs that are featured in various chapters. Look under the topic you feel is closest to the kind of resource you are seeking for the description of those specific services. The description also includes: funding sources, eligibility criteria, geographic area served, foreign languages spoken, etc. Individuals wishing to refer non-English speaking clients to one of the agencies listed are encouraged to make the initial call to the agency on the person's behalf and confirm the presence of a staff member speaking the desired language.

Cost of Service – Most agency descriptions indicate the type of payment options at the end of the description. Wide variations exist in sliding fee scales from free to full price (most agencies use income and family size as factors in determining the rate for a given person). You will want to check with the agency for details. If the agency accepts Medi-Cal, it is included in the agency description.

What Do the Abbreviations Mean?

ADM REQ	Admission Requirement for the program
ADOL	Adolescent
ASSN	Association
CO.	County
COMM	Community
DEV.	Developmental or Developmentally
EVAL.	Evaluation
FUNDING	Funding sources for the agency
INFO	Information
INTERNATL	International
NATL.	National
OFC HRS	Regular office hours or business hours
PVT.	Private
SERVES	Geographic area served by this agency
SO.	South/Southern
SLIDING SCALE	In most cases, fees are assessed on the basis of family size and income

GETTING IN THE GUIDE

Adding a Nonprofit Agency

The correct procedure for submitting a prospective agency is as follows:

- Review the listings in the Rainbow Referral Guide chapter where the agency services are most likely to appear.

- Write a brief note asking to be considered for the next edition of the directory. There is no guarantee that the agency will be included just because a request is received. Each agency is reviewed based on current listings in the directory and how the proposed agency services fit within the guidelines of the directory.

- Type the agency listing in the same format as those in the Guide. Try to keep the text as objective as possible. List the actual services provided by the agency instead of providing a mission statement or subjective narrative about the agency. Readers of the Rainbow Guides want to know what specific services are offered by the agency, what geographic areas the agency serves, what languages are spoken by the staff, who is eligible to use the services and whether there is a fee for the services. Please do not simply mail a brochure or reference your website for information. You must describe your own services in a brief summary if you wish to be considered for this directory.

- Submit a copy of the proposed agency description along with a copy of the agency 501(c)(3) to:

RESOURCE DIRECTORY
Attn: New Listings
3505 Cadillac Ave., Suite H
Costa Mesa, CA 92626

Or submit by fax to: (714) 755-2983

Or sumbit online at: www.ResourceDirectory.com

Private Service Providers

Private for-profit agencies and service providers that wish to be included in the Directories should contact our advertising department at (714) 755-5463. You can also visit us online at (www.resourcedirectory.com/advertising.htm) for more information and to download a copy of our media kit.

!

1 (800) GAMBLER . . . . (800)426-2537
Pg 196
1-800-ALCOHOL . . . . (800)252-6465
Pg 94
1-800-RELAPSE . . . . (800)729-6686
Pg 94,196
1-888-MARIJUANA . . . . (800)662-4357
Pg 94
1736 FAMILY CRISIS CENTER . . . . (323)737-3900
Pg 12,47,129,151,185,318,341,343
24-HR HOTLINES . . . . (323)737-3900
Pg 196
4-H CLUB . . . . (909)387-2171
Pg 333
4-H CLUB/RIVERSIDE COUNTY . . . . (951)683-6491
Pg 20,333

A

A & A HEARING AIDS . . . . (323)588-0742
Pg 71,283
A BETTER WAY . . . .
Pg 12,216
A GIFT FROM WITHIN . . . . (207)236-8858
Pg 259
A HOME WITHIN . . . . (888)898-2249
Pg 1,318
A IS 4 ADOPTION . . . . **(714)556-0220**
Pg 1
A NOTE ABOUT THIS CHAPTER . . . .
Pg 151
A WINDOW BETWEEN WORLDS . . . . (310)396-0317
Pg 12,47
A.V. DOMESTIC VIOLENCE COUNCIL . . . . (661)945-5509
Pg 12,196
A.Y.S.O. . . . .
Pg 333
AAA . . . .
Pg 301
AARP/AMER ASSN/RETIRED PERSONS . . . . . (866)448-3615
Pg 283
AARP/PHARMACY SERVICE . . . . (877)422-7719
Pg 159,283
ABA CENTER/CHILDREN & LAW . . . . (202)662-1720
Pg 24,216
ABC CASKETS FACTORY . . . . (866)369-5457
Pg 61
ABC FOSTER FAMILY AGENCY . . . . (714)545-2046
Pg 1
ABILITY AWARENESS . . . . (714)277-4330
Pg 71,210,306,312
ABILITY COUNTS, INC. . . . . (951)734-6595
Pg 71,129
ABILITYFIRST/CAMP PAIVIKA . . . . (909)338-1102
Pg 20,71
ABILITYFIRST/CLAREMONT CTR . . . . (909)621-4727
Pg 71,333
ABILITYFIRST/CORPORATE HDQTRS . . . . (626)396-1010
Pg 20,71
ABODE COMMUNITIES . . . . (213)629-2702
Pg 185,210,278
ABORTION RECOVERY INTERNATL NTWK . . . (949)679-9276
Pg 47,144,253
ABRAHAM LOW SELF-HELP SYSTEMS . . . . . . (866)221-0302
Pg 259
ACADEMY FOR EATING DISORDERS . . . . (847)498-4274
Pg 111
ACCESS FOR INFANTS/MOTHERS (AIM) . . . . . (800)433-2611
Pg 144,159,242,253
ACLU/SOUTHERN CALIFORNIA . . . .
Pg 216
ACORN NATURALISTS CTR FOR SCIENCE . . . (800)422-8886
Pg 333
ACTION PARENT & TEEN SUPPORT . . . . (818)763-9556
Pg 242,259,318
ACTS/ADVENTIST COMM TEAM SRVS . . . .
Pg 115,301

ADDUS HEALTHCARE . . . . (760)770-9490
Pg 71,276
ADECCO . . . . (909)464-0810
Pg 129
ADOBE VILLAS APTS . . . . (760)367-2966
Pg 210
ADOPTION CONNECTION . . . . (415)359-2494
Pg 1
ADOPTION INFORMATION CENTER . . . . (424)757-5170
Pg 1
ADOPTIONS UNLIMITED, INC. . . . . (909)902-1412
Pg 1
ADULT ABUSE REPORTING . . . . (800)491-7123
Pg 196,283
ADULT CHILDREN OF ALCOHOLICS (ACA) . . . (310)534-1815
Pg 94,259
ADULTS MOLESTED AS CHILDREN . . . . (760)340-2336
Pg 259
ADVANCE ENTERPRISE-BEAUMONT . . . .
Pg 71
ADVENT GROUP MINISTRIES . . . . (408)281-0708
Pg 47,94,318
ADVENTIST COMM TEAM SRVS (ACTS) . . . . . (909)796-8357
Pg 115,185,301
ADVOCATE SCHOOL . . . .
Pg 71
AEROBICS/FITNESS ASSN OF AMER . . . . (877)968-7263
Pg 159
AFDC . . . .
Pg 115,151,185
AGAPE GROUP HOMES . . . . (805)937-5475
Pg 318,341,343
AGAPE HOME CARE . . . . (909)949-7666
Pg 276
AGRICULTURAL LABOR RELATIONS BOARD . . (916)653-3699
Pg 129,141
AIDS ASSISTANCE PROGRAM . . . . (760)325-8481
Pg 7,115
AIDS CLEARINGHOUSE . . . .
Pg 7
AIDS CLINICAL TRIAL INFO SRV . . . .
Pg 7,196
AIDS CLINICAL TRIALS UNIT SUBSITE . . . . . . (310)222-3848
Pg 7
AIDS EDU & GLOBAL INFO SYSTEM . . . . (949)495-1952
Pg 7
AIDS HEALTHCARE FNDN/UPLAND . . . . (909)579-0708
Pg 7
AIDS HOTLINE . . . .
Pg 7
AIDS INFO . . . . (800)448-0440
Pg 7,196
AIDS RESEARCH ALLIANCE OF AMERICA . . . . (310)358-2423
Pg 7
AIDS/HIV NIGHTLINE . . . . (800)273-2437
Pg 196
AIRLINES SERVING ORANGE COUNTY . . . . . .
Pg 301
AL-ANON FAMILY GROUP HEADQUARTERS . . (888)425-2666
Pg 94,259
AL-ANON FAMILY GROUP, INC. . . . . (909)824-1516
Pg 94,259
ALANO CLUB/RIVERSIDE . . . . (951)351-0100
Pg 94
ALANO CLUB/SAN BERNARDINO . . . . (909)885-9643
Pg 94
ALARA ADVOCACY FOUNDATION . . . . (877)292-5272
Pg 71,283
ALATEEN . . . . (757)563-1600
Pg 94,259
ALCOHOL 24-HR HELPLINE . . . . (800)334-0394
Pg 196
ALCOHOL ABUSE 24-HR HELPLINE . . . . (954)972-7014
Pg 196
ALCOHOL AND DRUG HELPLINE . . . . (800)821-4357
Pg 94,196
ALCOHOLICS ANONYMOUS/ADMIN . . . . (323)936-4343
Pg 94,259
ALCOHOLICS ANONYMOUS/DESERT . . . . (760)324-4880
Pg 94,259

ALCOHOLICS ANONYMOUS/I.E. . . . . (909)825-4700	AMERICAN ASSN/INTELLECTUAL & DEVELOPMENTAL DISABI (202)387-1968
Pg 94,196,259	Pg 71
ALCOHOLICS ANONYMOUS/POMONA . . . . (909)629-0493	AMERICAN ASSN/MARRIAGE & FAM . . . . (703)838-9808
Pg 94	Pg 47
ALCOHOLICS ANONYMOUS/RIVERSIDE . . . . (951)695-1535	AMERICAN ASSN/PEOPLE/DISABILITIES . . . . (800)840-8844
Pg 95	Pg 71
ALCOHOLICS ANONYMOUS/VICTOR VLY . . . . (760)242-9292	AMERICAN BOARD/MED SPECIALTIES . . . . (312)436-2600
Pg 95,259	Pg 159
ALISA ANN RUCH BURN FOUNDATION . . . . (800)242-2876	AMERICAN BRAIN TUMOR ASSN . . . . (847)827-9910
Pg 159,259	Pg 159
ALIVE AND WELL . . . . (818)780-1875	AMERICAN CAMPING ASSN (ACA) . . . . (800)428-2267
Pg 7,159,260	Pg 20
ALLERGY & ASTHMA NETWORK . . . . (800)878-4403	AMERICAN CANCER SOCIETY . . . . (760)568-2691
Pg 159	Pg 160,301
ALLIANCE FOR DONATION & TRANSPLANTATION . . . . . . (951)689-2822	AMERICAN CHRONIC PAIN ASSN (ACPA) . . . . (916)632-0922
Pg 260	Pg 160,260
ALLIANCE ON MENTAL ILLNESS	AMERICAN CIVIL LIBERTIES UNION . . . . (213)977-9500
Pg 260	Pg 216
ALLIANCE/EATING DISORDERS AWARENESS . . . . (866)662-1235	AMERICAN COLL/ALLERGY/IMMUN . . . . (800)842-7777
Pg 111	Pg 160
ALPHA LEARNING CENTERS . . . . (951)328-1020	AMERICAN COUNCIL FOR HEADACHE EDU . . . . (856)423-0043
Pg 1,318	Pg 160
ALPHA TREATMENT CENTERS . . . . (951)369-5282	AMERICAN COUNCIL OF THE BLIND . . . . (800)424-8666
Pg 1	Pg 71,237
ALS ASSOCIATION/NATIONAL . . . . (818)880-9007	AMERICAN COUNCIL ON ALCOHOLISM . . . . (800)527-5344
Pg 71,159,260,283	Pg 95
ALTA VISTA HEALTHCARE . . . . (951)688-8200	AMERICAN DIABETES ASSOCIATION . . . . (800)342-2383
Pg 71	Pg 20,160,260
ALTERNATE AVENUES . . . . (909)621-4800	AMERICAN DIETETIC HOTLINE . . . .
Pg 144,242,253	Pg 111,160
ALTERNATIVE SENTENCING . . . . (760)863-8420	AMERICAN FNDN FOR SUICIDE PREV . . . . (888)333-2377
Pg 12,24,242	Pg 47,260
ALTERNATIVES TO DOMESTIC VIOL . . . . (951)320-1370	AMERICAN HEART ASSOCIATION . . . . (213)291-7000
Pg 12,24	Pg 160
ALTURA CREDIT UNION . . . . (951)684-6414	AMERICAN HOLISTIC HEALTH ASSN. . . . . (714)779-6152
Pg 151	Pg 160,260
ALWAYS IN MY HEART SUPPORT GROUP . . . . (909)558-7261	AMERICAN HOSP ASSN/RESOURCE . . . . (312)422-3000
Pg 61,260	Pg 192
ALZHEIMER'S ASSN/COACHELLA VALLEY . . . . (760)328-6767	AMERICAN HUMANE ASSN . . . . (800)227-4645
Pg 260,283	Pg 24
ALZHEIMER'S ASSN/NATIONAL. . . . . (800)272-3900	AMERICAN INST/CANCER RESEARCH. . . . . (800)843-8114
Pg 260,283	Pg 160,260
ALZHEIMER'S DISEASE EDU & REFERRAL . . . . (800)438-4380	AMERICAN KIDNEY FUND (AKF) . . . . (800)638-8299
Pg 159,283	Pg 160
ALZHEIMER'S DISEASE RES/TREATMT CTR . . . . (949)824-2382	AMERICAN LEGION . . . .
Pg 159,283	Pg 306
ALZHEIMER'S FOUNDATION OF AMERICA . . . . (866)232-8484	AMERICAN LEGION POST #106. . . . . (909)792-4523
Pg 196	Pg 306
ALZHEIMER'S SUPP GRP/CALIMESA . . . . (909)798-1667	AMERICAN LEGION POST #112. . . . . (909)984-3811
Pg 260	Pg 306
ALZHEIMER'S SUPP GRP/CORONA . . . . (951)736-2363	AMERICAN LEGION POST #14 . . . . (909)885-4090
Pg 260	Pg 306
ALZHEIMER'S SUPP GRP/RIVERSIDE . . . . (951)509-2500	AMERICAN LEGION POST #155. . . . . (909)825-2985
Pg 260	Pg 306
ALZHEIMER'S SUPP GRP/TEMECULA . . . . (951)672-9536	AMERICAN LEGION POST #200. . . . . (951)678-7777
Pg 260	Pg 306
AMBULANCE/EMERGENCY DIAL 911.	AMERICAN LEGION POST #229. . . . . (760)246-6054
Pg 192	Pg 306
AMC CANCER RESEARCH CENTER . . . . (800)321-1557	AMERICAN LEGION POST #262. . . . . (909)823-8061
Pg 196	Pg 306
AMEILA'S LIGHT TRANSITIONAL HOUSE . . . . (951)656-6020	AMERICAN LEGION POST #289. . . . . (951)520-8551
Pg 185	Pg 306
AMER-I-CAN FNDN FOR SOCIAL CHANGE . . . . (310)652-7884	AMERICAN LEGION POST #299. . . . . (909)628-2080
Pg 316,318	Pg 306
AMERICAN ACAD OF FAM PHYSICIANS . . . . (800)274-2237	AMERICAN LEGION POST #324. . . . . (760)252-8369
Pg 159	Pg 306
AMERICAN ACAD OF PEDIATRICS . . . . (847)434-4000	AMERICAN LEGION POST #328. . . . . (951)371-9108
Pg 159	Pg 306
AMERICAN ANOREXIA BULIMIA ASSN	AMERICAN LEGION POST #360. . . . . (909)336-7745
Pg 111	Pg 306
AMERICAN ASSN OF KIDNEY PATIENTS. . . . . (800)749-2257	AMERICAN LEGION POST #421. . . . . (909)862-8225
Pg 159	Pg 306
AMERICAN ASSN OF RETIRED PERSONS.	AMERICAN LEGION POST #422. . . . . (909)874-0433
Pg 283	Pg 306
AMERICAN ASSN OF SUICIDOLOGY. . . . . (202)237-2280	AMERICAN LEGION POST #426. . . . . (909)790-4030
Pg 260	Pg 306
AMERICAN ASSN OF SUICIDOLOGY (AAS) . . . . (202)237-2280	AMERICAN LEGION POST #466. . . . . (760)665-9308
Pg 47	Pg 306
AMERICAN ASSN/GERIATRIC PSYCH . . . . (301)654-7850	AMERICAN LEGION POST #497. . . . . (909)877-9871
Pg 283	Pg 306

AMERICAN LEGION POST #500	(951)685-4257	Pg 306
AMERICAN LEGION POST #519	(619)325-6229	Pg 306
AMERICAN LEGION POST #574	(909)653-1590	Pg 306
AMERICAN LEGION POST #584	(909)866-4845	Pg 306
AMERICAN LEGION POST #650	(909)792-6783	Pg 306
AMERICAN LEGION POST #710	(909)880-1336	Pg 306
AMERICAN LEGION POST #751	(760)257-3173	Pg 306
AMERICAN LEGION POST #763	(760)329-9332	Pg 306
AMERICAN LEGION POST #772	(909)829-9490	Pg 306
AMERICAN LEGION POST #777	(909)882-3110	Pg 306
AMERICAN LEGION POST #797	(760)254-2545	Pg 306
AMERICAN LEGION POST #800	(951)659-3517	Pg 306
AMERICAN LEGION POST #848	(951)487-1664	Pg 307
AMERICAN LEGION POST #883	(951)243-8567	Pg 307
AMERICAN LEPROSY MISSIONS	(800)543-3135	Pg 160
AMERICAN LIVER FNDN/SAN DIEGO	(619)291-5483	Pg 160,196,261
AMERICAN LIVER FOUNDATION	(800)465-4837	Pg 160,196,261
AMERICAN LUNG ASSN/INLAND CO	(909)884-5864	Pg 160,261
AMERICAN PAIN FOUNDATION	(888)615-7246	Pg 161
AMERICAN PARKINSON DISEASE ASSN	(800)908-2732	Pg 161,196
AMERICAN PREGNANCY ASSOCIATION	(972)815-2337	Pg 144,196,253
AMERICAN PREGNANCY HELPLINE	(866)942-6466	Pg 144,196,253
AMERICAN PSYCHIATRIC ASSN (APA)	(888)357-7924	Pg 47
AMERICAN PSYCHOLOGICAL ASSN	(800)374-2721	Pg 47
AMERICAN RED CROSS/29 PALMS	(760)830-6685	Pg 115,307,312
AMERICAN RED CROSS/FT. IRWIN	(760)380-3697	Pg 115,307,312
AMERICAN RED CROSS/HIGH DESERT	(760)245-6511	Pg 307
AMERICAN RED CROSS/MORONGO BASIN	(760)365-5501	Pg 307
AMERICAN RED CROSS/ONTARIO	(909)481-2835	Pg 115,307,312
AMERICAN RED CROSS/RIVERSIDE CO	(888)831-0031	Pg 307
AMERICAN RED CROSS/SAN BRDO	(909)888-1481	Pg 115,307,312
AMERICAN SIDS INSTITUTE	(239)431-5425	Pg 61
AMERICAN SLEEP APNEA ASSN	(202)293-3650	Pg 161,261
AMERICAN SOC/DERM SURGERY	(847)330-0230	Pg 161
AMERICAN SOC/PLASTIC SURGEONS	(888)475-2784	Pg 161
AMERICAN SOCIAL HEALTH ASSN	(919)361-8400	Pg 197
AMERICAN SOCIETY OF YOUNG MUSICIANS	(310)358-8301	Pg 333
AMERICAN SOCIETY ON AGING (ASA)	(415)974-9600	Pg 283
AMERICAN SPEECH LANG/HEAR ASSN	(800)498-2071	Pg 72
AMERICAN STROKE ASSN/HEART ASSN	(888)478-7653	Pg 161,261
AMERICAN TINNITUS ASSN	(800)634-8978	Pg 161
AMERICAN TRAUMA SOCIETY (ATS)	(800)556-7890	Pg 161
AMERICAN WOMEN VETERANS	(202)436-0678	Pg 307
AMERICAN YOUTH SOCCER/AYSO	(951)242-2976	Pg 333
AMPUTEE CONNECTION/REDLANDS	(951)735-7963	Pg 72,261
AMTRAK PASSENGER STATION	(800)872-7245	Pg 301
AMYOTROPHIC LATERAL SCLEROSIS		Pg 72
ANAD NATL OFFICE		Pg 111,261
ANASAZI ORGANIZATION	(800)678-3445	Pg 316,318
ANGEL FLIGHT WEST	(310)390-2958	Pg 301
ANGEL VIEW CRIPPLED CHILDREN'S FNDN	(760)329-6471	Pg 72
ANONYMOUS CRIME HOTLINE-WE TIP	(800)782-7463	Pg 197
ANXIETY DISORDERS ASSN OF AMER	(240)485-1001	Pg 47
AOK/ECOWAYS	(909)477-6530	Pg 283
APLASTIC ANEMIA & MDS INTNL FNDN	(800)747-2820	Pg 161
APPLE CANYON CENTER	(951)659-4609	Pg 20,333
APPLE VALLEY CARE CENTER	(760)240-5051	Pg 278
APPLE VALLEY HEAD START/PRESCH	(760)247-6955	Pg 32
APPLE VALLEY SENIOR CITIZEN CLUB	(760)247-3155	Pg 283
APPLE VALLEY UNIFIED SCHOOL DIST	(760)247-8001	Pg 72
APPLE VALLEY USD STATE PRESCHOOL PRGM	(760)247-2052	Pg 232
APPLIED PRINCIPLES FOR SERVICE, INC	(909)486-3775	Pg 318
APU COMMUNITY COUNSELING CENTER	(626)815-5421	Pg 47,72,242
AQUARIUM OF THE PACIFIC	(562)590-3100	Pg 333
ARC/MORENO VALLEY	(951)688-5141	Pg 72
ARC/RIVERSIDE	(951)845-3385	Pg 72,129
ARC/SAN BERNARDINO	(909)884-6484	Pg 72,129
ARLANZA HEAD START	(951)352-7984	Pg 32
ARLINGTON GARDENS	(951)689-2340	Pg 72
ARLINGTON SDA COMMUNITY SRVS	(951)688-6632	Pg 115
ARLINGTON TEMPORARY ASSISTANCE	(951)689-5620	Pg 115
ARMY NATIONAL GUARD	(951)684-1713	Pg 129
ARROWHEAD CREDIT UNION	(800)743-7228	Pg 151 - 152
ARROWHEAD VISTA	(323)930-2300	Pg 210
ARSON HOTLINE-WE TIP	(800)472-7766	Pg 197
ARTHRITIS FNDN/COACHELLA VLY	(760)773-3076	Pg 161,261
ARTHRITIS FNDN/INFO LINE	(800)283-7800	Pg 161
ARTHRITIS FNDN/INLAND EMPIRE	(949)585-0201	Pg 161
ASCOT PARK APARTMENTS	(909)884-5575	Pg 210
ASIAN AMERICAN ECONOMIC DEVELOP	(626)572-7021	Pg 129,141

ASIAN PACIFIC RESIDENTIAL PRGM. . . . . (323)731-3534 Pg 47	BARSTOW SENIOR CENTER . . . . (760)256-5023 Pg 284
ASISTENCIA VILLA REHAB & CARE CTR. . . . . (909)793-1382 Pg 278	BASIC OCCUPATIONAL TRAINING CTR . . . . (951)788-2349 Pg 73
ASPO/LAMAZE . . . . Pg 144	BATTEN DISEASE SUPP/RESEARCH ASSN . . . . (800)448-4570 Pg 162,261
ASSIST LEAGUE/FOOTHILL COMMUNITIES . . . . (909)987-2813 Pg 66,115,318	BAZELON CENTER/MENTAL HLTH LAW . . . . (202)467-5730 Pg 48,216
ASSIST LEAGUE/HEMACINTO . . . . (951)652-8307 Pg 115,318	BEACH CITIES BRAILLE GUILD, INC.. . . . . (714)969-7992 Pg 73,237
ASSIST LEAGUE/PALM SPRINGS/DESERT . . . . (760)321-1990 Pg 115,318	BEAR HAWK EDUCATION SERVICES . . . . (760)329-4457 Pg 7,48,197
ASSIST LEAGUE/REDLANDS . . . . (909)792-2675 Pg 66,115,318	BEAR VALLEY COMMUNITY HOSPITAL . . . . (909)878-8268 Pg 192
ASSIST LEAGUE/RIVERSIDE . . . . (951)682-3445 Pg 115,319	BEAR VALLEY SENIOR CTR. . . . . (909)584-0323 Pg 284
ASSIST LEAGUE/SAN BERNARDINO . . . . (909)885-2045 Pg 66,116,319	BEARSKIN MEADOW CAMP. . . . . (925)680-4994 Pg 20
ASSIST LEAGUE/TEMECULA VALLEY . . . . (951)694-8018 Pg 116,319	BEAUMONT CARE CENTER. . . . . (951)845-1166 Pg 278
ASSIST LEAGUE/VICTOR VALLEY . . . . (760)961-2468 Pg 116,319	BEAUMONT EARLY HEAD START. . . . . (951)769-7025 Pg 32
ASSN FOR RETARDED CITIZENS. . . . . Pg 72	BEAUMONT HEAD START . . . . (951)826-4500 Pg 32
ASSN OF REGIONAL CTR AGENCIES . . . . (916)446-7961 Pg 7,72	BEAUMONT LIBRARY DISTRICT . . . . (951)845-1357 Pg 225
ASTHMA & ALLERGY FNDN OF AMER . . . . (800)624-0044 Pg 161	BEAUMONT PRESBYTERIAN CHURCH . . . . (951)845-1506 Pg 116
ASTHMA INFO & REFERRAL LINE . . . . (800)822-2762 Pg 162,197	BEAUMONT SENIOR CENTER . . . . (951)769-8539 Pg 284
ASTROCAMP. . . . . (909)625-6194 Pg 20	BEAUMONT-CHERRY VALLEY REC/PARK . . . . (951)845-9555 Pg 333
AT NETWORK. . . . . (800)390-2699 Pg 72	BEAUTIFUL LIGHT INN. . . . . (909)884-4033 Pg 278
ATTENTION DEFICIT DISORDER ASSN . . . . (800)939-1019 Pg 162	BEAUTY FOR ASHES WOMEN'S CENTER . . . . (909)477-2781 Pg 41,95,312
AUA FOUNDATION . . . . (860)746-4282 Pg 162	BECKSTRAND CANCER FOUNDATION . . . . (949)955-0099 Pg 162
AUDIO VISION READING FOR THE BLIND . . . . (909)797-4336 Pg 72,237	BEHAVIORAL SYSTEMS SOUTHWEST . . . . (949)492-3574 Pg 41,95
AURORA LAS ENCINAS HOSPITAL . . . . **(800)792-2345** **Pg 95**	BEREAVEMENT SUPP GRP/MORONGO . . . . (760)366-1308 Pg 61,261
AUTO CLUB OF SO CALIF (AAA) . . . . (800)390-2699 Pg 301	BEST BUDDIES. . . . . (888)682-8339 Pg 73
AXIS RESIDENTIAL TREATMENT. . . . . **(760)636-5427** **Pg 95**	BETA CENTER HUNGER PROGRAM . . . . Pg 116
	BETHANY CHRISTIAN SRVS/NATL . . . . (800)238-4269 Pg 1,144

B.R.I.D.G.E.S., INC.. . . . . (909)623-6651 Pg 47,95,185	BETHANY CHRISTIAN SRVS/SO CAL. . . . . (877)465-0057 Pg 1,144,253
BABY CARE AND NUTRITION . . . . (800)233-2468 Pg 242	BETHANY LUTHERAN CHILD CARE . . . . (951)737-1173 Pg 32
BABY SAFE. . . . . (877)222-9723 Pg 144,197,253	BETHEL CHRISTIAN FELLOWSHIP . . . . (909)823-1198 Pg 116,185
BABY STEP INN . . . . Pg 95	BETTER HEARING INSTITUTE (BHI) . . . . (800)327-9355 Pg 162
BALLARD REHABILITATION HOSPITAL. . . . . (909)473-1200 Pg 73,192	BETTY FORD CENTER. . . . . (800)434-7365 Pg 95
BANNING HEALTHCARE. . . . . (951)849-4723 Pg 278	BIENVENIDOS FOSTER FAMILY . . . . (626)919-3579 Pg 1
BANNING HIGH ADULT EDUCATION . . . . (951)922-2740 Pg 129,232	BIG BROTHERS/BIG SISTERS/DESERT . . . . (760)568-3977 Pg 319
BANNING PUBLIC LIBRARY . . . . (951)849-3192 Pg 225,232	BIG BROTHERS/SISTERS/GTR L.A. & I.E. . . . . (213)481-3611 Pg 242,312,319,333
BANNING SENIOR CENTER . . . . (951)922-3250 Pg 284	BIG ROCK CREEK CAMP . . . . (661)944-9005 Pg 20
BARBARA SINATRA CHILDREN'S CENTER . . . . (760)340-2336 Pg 24	BILINGUAL FAMILY COUNSELING. . . . . (909)986-7111 Pg 48,95,319
BARKER MANAGEMENT, INC.. . . . . (714)533-3450 Pg 210,278	BILL'S SPECIAL KIDS . . . . (951)242-7261 Pg 73
BARSTOW AREA TRANSIT . . . . (760)256-0311 Pg 301	BINGE EATING DISORDER ASSN. . . . . (443)597-0066 Pg 111
BARSTOW COMMUNITY COLLEGE. . . . . (760)252-2411 Pg 73,129,307	BIO SCRIP . . . . (800)584-0265 Pg 162,276
BARSTOW HEAD START/STATE PRESCH . . . . (760)253-2956 Pg 32	BIRTH CHOICE . . . . (760)744-1313 Pg 48,116,162,242,253
BARSTOW LITERACY COALITION . . . . (760)256-4847 Pg 232	BIRTH CHOICE OF TEMECULA . . . . (951)699-9808 Pg 144,242,312
	BIRTH CONTROL INFO FOR STATE . . . . (800)942-1054 Pg 144,197,253

BIRTH CONTROL INFO LINE	(800)722-4777
Pg 144,197,253	
BIRTH DEFECT RESEARCH FOR CHILDREN	(407)895-0802
Pg 73,242	
BLACK AIDS INSTITUTE	(213)353-3610
Pg 7	
BLACK INFANT HEALTH PRGM	(951)210-1392
Pg 141,162,253	
BLACK RESOURCE CENTER	(310)538-3350
Pg 141,225	
BLIND CHILDREN'S CENTER	(323)664-2153
Pg 73,237	
BLIND INFORMATION AND SERVICES	(909)424-0392
Pg 73	
BLIND YOUTH CAMP	
Pg 20	
BLINDED VETERANS ASSN OF SO CALIF	(310)235-6125
Pg 237,307	
BLINDED VETERANS ASSOCIATION	(800)669-7079
Pg 237,307	
BLINDNESS SUPPORT SERVICES	(951)341-9244
Pg 73,242	
BLOOMINGTON HEAD START	(909)876-6342
Pg 32	
BLYTHE NURSING CARE CENTER	(760)922-8176
Pg 278	
BLYTHE SENIOR CENTER	(760)922-8830
Pg 284	
BOBBY BONDS HEAD START/ST PRESCH	(951)784-3293
Pg 32	
BOBBY BONDS PARK/COMMUNITY CTR	(951)826-5746
Pg 333	
BOBBY SOX SOFTBALL-NATL HQTRS	(714)522-1234
Pg 333	
BONNIE BAKER SENIOR CENTER	(760)665-2667
Pg 284	
BOOT CAMP FOR NEW DADS	(949)754-9067
Pg 242,261	
BOY SCOUTS OF AMER/INLAND EMP	(909)793-2463
Pg 20,333	
BOY SCOUTS OF AMER/OLD BALDY	(909)983-4534
Pg 334	
BOY SCOUTS OF AMERICA	
Pg 334	
BOYS & GIRLS CLUB/BARSTOW	(760)255-2422
Pg 32,334	
BOYS & GIRLS CLUB/CAMPING	
Pg 20	
BOYS & GIRLS CLUB/CATHEDRAL CITY	(760)324-5844
Pg 32,319,334	
BOYS & GIRLS CLUB/COACHELLA VLY	(760)398-5287
Pg 32,334	
BOYS & GIRLS CLUB/DESERT HOT SP	(760)329-1312
Pg 319,334	
BOYS & GIRLS CLUB/FONTANA	(909)822-4988
Pg 32,334	
BOYS & GIRLS CLUB/HIGH DESERT	(760)365-5437
Pg 32,334	
BOYS & GIRLS CLUB/INDIO	(760)347-5712
Pg 33,316,334	
BOYS & GIRLS CLUB/MTN COMM	(909)338-0418
Pg 319,334	
BOYS & GIRLS CLUB/MURRIETA	(951)698-3838
Pg 33,334	
BOYS & GIRLS CLUB/PALM SPRINGS	(760)327-1304
Pg 334	
BOYS & GIRLS CLUB/REDLANDS	(909)798-4599
Pg 33,334	
BOYS & GIRLS CLUB/SAN BERNARDINO	(909)888-6751
Pg 129,319,335	
BOYS & GIRLS CLUB/TEMECULA	(951)699-1526
Pg 20,33,335	
BOYS HOPE GIRLS HOPE OF SO CALIF	(949)515-8833
Pg 24,319,341	
BOYS REPUBLIC	(909)628-1217
Pg 41,319	
BOYS TOWN NATL HOTLINE	(197)
Pg 197	
BOYS TOWN OF SO CALIF	
Pg 1	

BRADLEY GARDENS, THE	(951)654-9347
Pg 278	
BRAILLE INSTITUTE	(760)321-1111
Pg 73,237	
BRAILLE INSTITUTE OF AMERICA	**(800)272-4553**
Pg 73	
BRAIN INJURY ASSOCIATION/USA	(703)761-0750
Pg 73	
BRAIN INJURY FOUNDATION	(949)250-5727
Pg 73	
BRASWELL'S COMM CONVALESCENT CTR	(909)795-2421
Pg 278	
BRASWELL'S HAMPTON MANOR	(909)790-2273
Pg 278	
BRASWELL'S IVY RETREAT	(909)794-1189
Pg 73	
BRASWELL'S YUCAIPA VALLEY CONV	(909)795-2476
Pg 278	
BREAST CANCER ANGELS	(562)795-0100
Pg 152,162	
BREAST CANCER NET OF STRENGTH	(714)361-2106
Pg 162,261	
BREAST CANCER SOLUTIONS	(866)960-9222
Pg 116,152,162	
BREAST CANCER SUPPORT GROUP	(909)865-9555
Pg 261	
BREAST FEEDING ADVOCACY	
Pg 144	
BREAST FEEDING SUPPORT GROUPS	
Pg 261	
BRIARWOOD MANOR APARTMENTS	(909)624-5041
Pg 278	
BROOKSIDE HEALTHCARE CENTER	(909)793-2271
Pg 278	
BRYANT PARK HEAD START/ST PRESCH	(951)509-1932
Pg 33	
BUDDHIST PEACE FELLOWSHIP	(510)655-6169
Pg 41	
BUDDHIST TZU CHI FREE CLINIC	(626)281-3383
Pg 66,162	
BUSINESS, TRANSPORT/HOUSING AGENCY	(916)323-5400
Pg 152	
B'NAI B'RITH	(202)857-2785
Pg 284	

C

C.A.R.E. PROGRAM	
Pg 284	
C.P.A.F. SHELTER & HOTLINE	
Pg 197	
CA ASSOCIATION OF FOOD BANKS	(510)272-4435
Pg 116	
CABAZON COMMUNITY CENTER	
Pg 284	
CAL POLY POMONA ENNIS W. COSBY	(909)869-3799
Pg 48	
CAL-SAFE/APPLE VALLEY	(760)247-7206
Pg 253	
CAL-SAFE/BIG BEAR LAKE	(909)866-4631
Pg 253	
CAL-SAFE/CHINO	(909)628-1201
Pg 253	
CAL-SAFE/CORONA-NORCO UNIFIED SCHOOL DISTRICT	(951)739-5670
Pg 253	
CAL-SAFE/FONTANA	(909)357-5000
Pg 253	
CAL-SAFE/HESPERIA	(760)948-3999
Pg 254	
CAL-SAFE/REDLANDS	(909)307-5380
Pg 254	
CAL-SAFE/RIVERSIDE CO.	(951)826-6464
Pg 254	
CAL-SAFE/UPLAND UNIFIED SCHOOL DISTRICT	(909)985-1864
Pg 254	
CAL-SAFE/YUCAIPA	(909)790-8550
Pg 254	
CALICO GHOST TOWN	(760)254-2122
Pg 335	

CALIF ACUPUNCTURE BOARD . . . . (916)445-3021 Pg 162	CALIF DEPT HEALTH SRVS . . . . (916)449-5900 Pg 7,95,163,192
CALIF ADOPTION & FOSTER CARE . . . . (800)543-7487 Pg 1	CALIF DEPT HLTH SRVS/FOOD/DRUG . . . . (800)495-3232 Pg 163
CALIF ADVOCATES/NURSING HOME REF . . . . (800)474-1116 Pg 216,284	CALIF DEPT INDUSTRIAL RELATIONS . . . . (213)620-6330 Pg 130
CALIF AIDS CLEARINGHOUSE . . . . (916)558-1784 Pg 7	CALIF DEPT MOTOR VEHICLES Pg 301 - 302
CALIF ALCOHOLIC BEV CONTROL . . . . (951)782-4400 Pg 95	CALIF DEPT OF CORRECTIONS . . . . (800)374-8474 Pg 41
CALIF APARTMENT LAW INFO FOUNDATION . . . . (213)251-9665 Pg 206,216	CALIF DEPT OF CORRECTIONS/REHAB . . . . (760)246-3328 Pg 41
CALIF ASSN/HOMES/SRVS FOR AGING . . . . (916)392-5111 Pg 278,284	CALIF DEPT OF JUSTICE . . . . (800)222-3463 Pg 24,319
CALIF ASSN/SCHOOL PSYCHOLOGISTS . . . . (916)444-1595 Pg 48,242	CALIF DEPT OF SOCIAL SRVS . . . . (323)981-1730 Pg 1,12,24
CALIF ATHLETIC COMMISSION . . . . (916)263-2195 Pg 335	CALIF DEPT REHAB/ADMIN . . . . (916)558-5300 Pg 74,130
CALIF BOARD OF OPTOMETRY . . . . (866)585-2666 Pg 237	CALIF DEPT REHAB/BARSTOW. Pg 74,130
CALIF BOARD/BARBERS/COSMETOLOGY . . . . (800)952-5210 Pg 129	CALIF DEPT REHAB/BLYTHE . . . . (760)922-2118 Pg 74,130
CALIF BOARD/BEHAVIORAL SCIENCES . . . . (916)574-7830 Pg 48	CALIF DEPT REHAB/HEMET Pg 74,130
CALIF BOARD/DISPENSING OPTICIANS . . . . (916)263-2382 Pg 237	CALIF DEPT REHAB/JOSHUA TREE . . . . (760)366-2681 Pg 74,130
CALIF BOARD/GUIDE DOGS FOR BLIND. . . . . (916)574-7825 Pg 74,237	CALIF DEPT REHAB/PALM DESERT . . . . (760)674-0262 Pg 74,130
CALIF BOARD/MEDICAL ASSISTANT . . . . (916)263-8382 Pg 130,162	CALIF DEPT REHAB/RIVERSIDE . . . . (951)782-6650 Pg 74,130
CALIF BOARD/MEDICAL LICENSING . . . . (800)633-2322 Pg 162	CALIF DEPT REHAB/SAN BERNARDINO . . . . (909)383-4401 Pg 74,130
CALIF BOARD/PHARMACY . . . . (916)574-7900 Pg 162	CALIF DEPT REHAB/TEMECULA . . . . (951)693-4451 Pg 74,130
CALIF BOARD/PHYSICAL THERAPY . . . . (916)561-8200 Pg 163	CALIF DEPT REHAB/UPLAND . . . . (909)948-6050 Pg 74,130
CALIF BOARD/PODIATRIC MEDICINE . . . . (916)263-2647 Pg 163	CALIF DEPT REHAB/VICTORVILLE . . . . (760)243-6024 Pg 74,130
CALIF BOARD/PSYCHOLOGY. . . . . (916)263-2699 Pg 48	CALIF DEPT TRANSPORTATION . . . . (916)324-1700 Pg 130,302
CALIF BOARD/REGISTERED NURSING . . . . (916)322-3350 Pg 163	CALIF DEPT VETERANS AFFAIRS . . . . (951)774-0102 Pg 206,307
CALIF BOARD/RESPIRATORY CARE . . . . (916)323-9983 Pg 163	CALIF DIABETES & PREGNANCY PRGM. . . . . Pg 163
CALIF BOARD/VICTIM COMPENSATION . . . . (800)777-9229 Pg 12,216	CALIF FAMILY LIFE CENTER . . . . (951)654-2352 Pg 2,131,320
CALIF BOARD/VOC NURSE/PSYCH TECH . . . . . . (916)263-7800 Pg 130,163	CALIF FRANCHISE TAX BOARD . . . . Pg 206
CALIF CEMETERY/FUNERAL BUREAU. . . . . (916)574-7870 Pg 61	CALIF HIGHWAY INFORMATION . . . . (800)427-7623 Pg 197,302
CALIF CHILDREN & FAMILIES COMM . . . . (916)263-1050 Pg 144,243	CALIF HIGHWAY PATROL/FWY SRVS . . . . (213)897-7275 Pg 302
CALIF CHILDREN'S SERVICES (CCS) . . . . (951)358-5401 Pg 74,163	CALIF HIV/AIDS INFO & REFERRAL . . . . Pg 7
CALIF COALITION FOR BATTERED WOMEN . . . . Pg 12	CALIF HOSPICE ASSN (CHAPCA) . . . . (916)925-3770 Pg 61,163
CALIF COALITION FOR WOMEN PRISONERS . . . . (415)255-7036 Pg 41	CALIF HOUSING FINANCE AGENCY . . . . (310)342-1250 Pg 206
CALIF COMMISSION ON AGING . . . . (916)419-7591 Pg 284	CALIF HOUSING LAW PROJECT . . . . (916)446-9241 Pg 185
CALIF CONSERVATION CORPS. . . . . (909)594-4206 Pg 130	CALIF HOUSING/COMMUNITY DEV . . . . (800)952-8356 Pg 206
CALIF COUNCIL OF THE BLIND. . . . . (800)221-6359 Pg 74,197,237	CALIF INDIAN MANPOWER CONSORTIUM . . . . . . (800)499-2462 Pg 131
CALIF COUNCIL ON PROBLEM GAMBLING . . . . . . (714)765-5804 Pg 197	CALIF INDUSTRIAL RELATIONS DEPT . . . . (909)383-4522 Pg 131
CALIF DEAF/BLIND SRVS . . . . (800)822-7884 Pg 74,237	CALIF INDUSTRIAL RELATIONS DEPT. . . . . (951)782-4269 Pg 131
CALIF DEAF/DISABLED/TELE PRGM . . . . (800)806-1191 Pg 74	CALIF INSTITUTION FOR MEN . . . . (909)597-1821 Pg 42
CALIF DENTAL ASSOCIATION. . . . . (800)232-7645 Pg 66	CALIF INSTITUTION FOR WOMEN . . . . (909)597-1771 Pg 42
CALIF DEPT AGING . . . . (916)419-7500 Pg 284	CALIF MAJOR RISK MED INSURANCE . . . . (916)324-4695 Pg 163
CALIF DEPT ALCOHOL & DRUG PRGMS. . . . . (800)879-2772 Pg 95	CALIF MEDICAL ASSOCIATION . . . . (800)786-4262 Pg 163
CALIF DEPT CORRECTIONS . . . . (760)772-3157 Pg 41	CALIF MEDICAL REVIEW, INC. (CMRI) . . . . Pg 163
CALIF DEPT FAIR EMPLOY/HOUSING . . . . (800)884-1684 Pg 130,206,216	CALIF NURSING & REHAB CTR . . . . (760)325-2937 Pg 75,278

CALIF OFC OF EMERGENCY SRVS .... (800)550-5234		CAMP CONRAD/CHINNOCK .... (310)751-3057		

CALIF OFC OF EMERGENCY SRVS .... (800)550-5234
Pg 197

CALIF OFC OF FAMILY PLANNING .... (800)942-1054
Pg 144,197

CALIF OFC OF SMALL BUSINESS .... (800)559-5529
Pg 131

CALIF PARALYZED VETERANS ASSN ...... (562)826-5713
Pg 307

CALIF PARTNERSHIP TO END DOMESTIC VIOLENCE ..... (916)444-7163
Pg 12

CALIF POISON CONTROL SYSTEM .... (800)222-1222
Pg 95,163,197

CALIF PUBLIC UTILITIES COMMISSION ...... (800)848-5580
Pg 302

CALIF RECOVERY CLINICS .... (951)549-8888
Pg 95

CALIF REHABILITATION CENTER .... (951)737-2683
Pg 42

CALIF RELAY SERVICE .... (800)735-2929
Pg 75

CALIF RURAL LEGAL ASSISTANCE .... (760)398-7261
Pg 141,214,216

CALIF SCH FOR THE DEAF/RIVERSIDE ...... (951)782-6500
Pg 75

CALIF SMOKERS' HELPLINE .... (800)662-8887
Pg 95,163

CALIF STATE ATTORNEY GENERAL .... (800)952-5225
Pg 216

CALIF STATE BAR ASSN. .... (213)765-1000
Pg 216

CALIF STATE COUNCIL ON DEVELOPMENTAL DISABILITIES . (916)322-8481
Pg 75

CALIF STATE DISABILITY INSURANCE ...... (800)480-3287
Pg 75

CALIF UNEMPLOYMENT INS APPEALS ...... (909)987-2212
Pg 131

CALIF YOUTH AUTHORITY ....
Pg 42

CALIF YOUTH CONNECTION .... (800)397-8236
Pg 2

CALIF YOUTH CRISIS LINE .... (800)843-5200
Pg 24,197,254,320

CALIF-HAWAII ELKS MAJOR PROJECT, INC. ... (559)255-4531
Pg 237

CALIF-HAWAII ELKS VISION SCREENING ..... (951)672-0667
Pg 237

CALIFORNIA KIDS .... (818)755-9700
Pg 243

CALIFORNIA MENTOR FOUNDATION .... (415)789-1007
Pg 316,320,335

CALIFORNIA PRISON FOCUS .... (510)836-7222
Pg 42

CALIFORNIA VOLUNTEERS .... (888)567-7378
Pg 312

CALIFORNIAKIDS HEALTH INSURANCE ......
Pg 163

CALIFORNIANS FOR DISABILITY RIGHTS ..... (909)343-1327
Pg 75,216

CALIMESA SEVENTH DAY ADVENTIST CHURCH ..... (909)795-9741
Pg 116

CALJOBS .... (714)518-2323
Pg 131

CALMA .... (877)225-6202
Pg 75,163,284

CALTRANS HIGHWAY INFORMATION ....
Pg 302

CALVARY PRESBYTERIAN CHURCH .... (951)686-0761
Pg 116,185

CALWORKS ....
Pg 116,131,152

CAMEO HOUSE .... (415)703-0600
Pg 42

CAMP AZALEA TRAILS ....
Pg 20

CAMP BLOOMFIELD .... (323)295-4555
Pg 20

CAMP CHINNOCK ....
Pg 20

CAMP CONNECT CALIFORNIA .... (650)866-4080
Pg 2,21

CAMP CONRAD/CHINNOCK .... (310)751-3057
Pg 21,75

CAMP DEL CORAZON, INC. .... (818)754-0312
Pg 21

CAMP ESPERANZA .... (323)954-5750
Pg 21

CAMP GOOD GRIEF .... (909)558-4073
Pg 21,261

CAMP JCA SHALOM .... (818)889-5500
Pg 21

CAMP LAUREL .... (626)683-0800
Pg 7,21

CAMP MOUNTAIN CHAI .... (858)499-1330
Pg 21

CAMP QUEST ....
Pg 21,75

CAMP TAUTONA ....
Pg 21

CAMP-A-LOT & CAMP-A-LITTLE .... (619)685-1175
Pg 75

CAMPESINOS UNIDOS CHILD DEV. .... (760)344-6300
Pg 33

CAMPESINOS UNIDOS CHILD DEV CTR ..... (760)398-3689
Pg 33

CANCER CARE .... (800)813-4673
Pg 164

CANCER CARE CENTER .... (909)865-9555
Pg 164

CANCER CONTROL SOCIETY .... (323)663-7801
Pg 164

CANCER FEDERATION .... (951)849-4325
Pg 164

CANCER HELPLINE .... (800)748-6722
Pg 197

CANCER LEGAL RESOURCE CENTER ...... (866)843-2572
Pg 164,197,216

CANCER PREVENTION COALITION .... (310)457-5176
Pg 164,261

CANCER RECOVERY FNDN OF AMERICA ..... (800)238-6479
Pg 164

CANCER RESEARCH INSTITUTE .... (800)992-2623
Pg 164

CANCER SOCIETY ....
Pg 164

CANCER SUPPORT GROUP .... (951)353-4755
Pg 261

CANCER SUPPORT GROUPS ....
Pg 262

CANCER/YOUTH CAMPS ....
Pg 21

CANCER411 .... (818)842-1504
Pg 262

CANDLELIGHTERS CHILDHOOD CANCER FNDN ...... (909)558-3419
Pg 262

CANINE COMPANIONS FOR INDEPENDENCE ...... (800)572-2275
Pg 75

CANINE SUPPORT TEAMS, INC. .... (951)301-3625
Pg 75

CANYON ACRES CHILDREN & FAMILY SRVS ...... (714)383-9401
Pg 2,24,48,243,320

CARE CONNEXXUS, INC. .... (951)509-2500
Pg 75,284

CARE LEARNING CTR/PSYCH SRVS. .... (951)288-6835
Pg 48,320

CARE-A-VAN TRANSIT SYSTEM .... (951)791-3572
Pg 302

CAREGIVER SUPPORT GROUP .... (909)506-7733
Pg 262

CARING CONNECTIONS .... (800)658-8898
Pg 61

CAROLYN E. WYLIE CTR FOR CHILDREN ...... (951)784-0020
Pg 75

CARRIER ALERT PROGRAM ....
Pg 284

CASA ....
Pg 24,216

CASA BLANCA CHILD CARE CENTER ...... (951)689-7891
Pg 33

CASA BLANCA HOME OF NEIGHBORLY SRV ...... (951)688-3043
Pg 116,284,320

CASA COLINA CENTERS FOR REHABILITATION . . . . (866)724-4127 Pg 75	CENTER FOR LIVING AND LEARNING . . . . (818)781-1073 Pg 131
CASA COLINA HOSPITAL CHILDREN'S SRVS . . . . (909)596-7733 Pg 76	CENTER FOR NONPROFIT MGMT . . . . (213)687-9511 Pg 312
CASA COLINA OUTDOOR ADVENTURES . . . . (909)596-7733 Pg 76	CENTER FOR SUBSTANCE ABUSE PREV . . . . (800)967-5752 Pg 97
CASA COLINA PADUA VILLAGE . . . . (760)248-6245 Pg 76	CENTER FOR THE IMPROVEMENT OF CHILD CARING . . . . (818)980-0903 Pg 243
CASA COLINA RETURN TO WORK SRV . . . . (909)596-7733 Pg 76,131	CENTER FOR THE PACIFIC ASIAN FAMILY . . . . (800)339-3940 Pg 13,24
CASA DE SAN BERNARDINO, INC. . . . . (909)381-5507 Pg 96	CENTER FOR THE PARTIALLY SIGHTED . . . . (310)988-1970 Pg 76,237
CASA LAS PALMAS RECOVERY HOME . . . . (760)347-9442 Pg 96	CENTER FOR UNIVERSAL DESIGN . . . . (919)515-3082 Pg 76
CASA MARIA APTS . . . . (760)398-0011 Pg 210	CENTER ON DEAFNESS INLAND EMPIRE . . . . (951)275-5000 Pg 76
CASA RAMONA CHILD DEV CENTER . . . . (909)889-0011 Pg 33	CENTER/COMMUNICATIVE DISORDER . . . . Pg 76
CASA RAMONA DROP-IN CENTER . . . . (909)889-0011 Pg 33	CENTERFORCE . . . . (415)456-9980 Pg 42
CASA YOUTH SHELTER . . . . (562)594-6825 Pg 312,320,341	CENTRAL CITY LUTHERAN MISSION . . . . (909)381-6921 Pg 8,185,320
CATHEDRAL CITY SENIOR HOUSING . . . . (800)500-7725 Pg 278	CENTRAL CO. UNITED WAY. . . . . (951)929-0423 Pg 285,312
CATHEDRAL CITY/OFC OF HOUSING ASSIST . . . . (760)770-0376 Pg 206	CENTRAL COUNTY UNITED WAY . . . . Pg 117
CATHEDRAL OF PRAISE CHURCH . . . . (909)874-8676 Pg 116	CESAR CHAVEZ HEAD START/ST P.S. . . . . (760)398-0619 Pg 33
CATHOLIC CHARITIES USA . . . . (703)549-1390 Pg 116	CESAR E. CHAVEZ FOUNDATION . . . . (213)362-0260 Pg 141,320
CATHOLIC CHARITIES/COMMUNITY SRVS . . . . (951)924-9964 Pg 7,42,48,116 - 117,152,185,206,214,285,302	CHADD/NATL . . . . (800)233-4050 Pg 197
CATHOLIC CHARITIES/COUNSELING . . . . (909)763-4970 Pg 12,24,48,96,320	CHAFFEY ADULT SCHOOL . . . . (909)983-7102 Pg 232
CATHOLIC CHARITIES/IMMIGRATION SRVS. . . . . (909)388-1243 Pg 214	CHAFFEY COLLEGE . . . . (909)652-7675 Pg 76
CDC NATL AIDS HOTLINE . . . . (800)232-4636 Pg 8,197	CHAFFEY COLLEGE/EOPS . . . . (909)652-6349 Pg 131,320,343
CDC NATL PREVENTION INFO NETWORK. . . . . (800)458-5231 Pg 8	CHAPMAN CONVALESCENT HOSPITAL . . . . (951)683-7111 Pg 278
CEDAR HOUSE REHAB CENTER . . . . (909)421-7120 Pg 96	CHAPMAN HOSPICE . . . . (951)784-1388 Pg 61
CEDAR LAKE CHRISTIAN CAMP . . . . (909)866-5714 Pg 21	CHAPMAN HOUSE, INC. . . . . (714)288-9779 Pg 97
CEDARBROOK CAMP SO CALIF . . . . (909)866-9366 Pg 21	CHARGE SYNDROME FOUNDATION, INC.. . . . . (516)684-4720 Pg 164
CEDARS-SINAI MEDICAL CENTER . . . . (310)423-3896 Pg 8	CHARIS YOUTH CENTER . . . . (530)477-9800 Pg 320
CEDARS-SINAI PSYCH/MENTAL HLTH . . . . (800)233-2771 Pg 48,96	CHARITY CARS. . . . . (800)242-7489 Pg 117,152,302
CELEBRATE RECOVERY . . . . (951)359-1123 Pg 12,96 - 97,111,262 - 263	CHEMO ANGELS . . . . Pg 164,312
CELEBRATE WHOLENESS . . . . (909)796-0222 Pg 97,111,263	CHERRY VALLEY HEALTHCARE . . . . (951)845-1606 Pg 279
CELIAC DISEASE FOUNDATION . . . . (818)990-2354 Pg 164	CHICANO RESOURCE CENTER . . . . (323)263-5087 Pg 141,225
CELIAC SPRUE ASSN CSA/USA . . . . (714)750-9543 Pg 164	CHILD ABUSE HOTLINE/HIGH DESERT . . . . (760)375-7100 Pg 198
CENTER AGAINST SEXUAL ASSAULT . . . . (951)652-8300 Pg 12,24	CHILD ABUSE PREVENTION COUNCIL . . . . (951)686-5581 Pg 25
CENTER FOR AUTO SAFETY (CAS) . . . . (202)328-7700 Pg 302	CHILD ABUSE REPORTING HOTLINE . . . . (800)442-4918 Pg 25,198
CENTER FOR CRIMINALITY & ADDICTION RESEARCH, TRAIN (858)334-4600 Pg 42,97	CHILD ADVOCACY PROGRAM, INC. . . . . Pg 25
CENTER FOR EMPLOYMENT TRAINING . . . . (909)478-3818 Pg 131,232	CHILD BIRTH . . . . Pg 144,254
CENTER FOR ENFORCEMENT/FAM SUP . . . . (310)417-4141 Pg 216	CHILD CARE ADVOCATES/SO CALIF. . . . . (619)767-2249 Pg 33
CENTER FOR FAMILY LIVING . . . . (951)734-8831 Pg 48,243	CHILD CARE AWARE . . . . (800)424-2246 Pg 33
CENTER FOR FAMILY SOLUTIONS . . . . (760)353-6922 Pg 13,49	CHILD CARE DEVELOPMENT PRGM . . . . (800)822-5777 Pg 33
CENTER FOR HEALING CHILDHOOD TRAUMA . . . . (909)875-5288 Pg 13,49,243	CHILD FIND OF AMERICA, INC . . . . (800)426-5678 Pg 198
CENTER FOR HEALTH PROMOTION . . . . (909)558-4594 Pg 97,111,164	CHILD FIND OF AMERICA, INC. . . . . (800)426-5678 Pg 25,320
CENTER FOR INDEPENDENT LIVING . . . . (510)841-4776 Pg 76	CHILD PROTECTIVE SRVS/RIVERSIDE CO. . . . . (800)448-4969 Pg 25
CENTER FOR INDIVIDUAL DEVELOPMENT . . . . (909)384-5426 Pg 76	CHILD PROTECTIVE SRVS/SAN BRDO. . . . . (909)388-1900 Pg 25

CHILD QUEST INTERNATIONAL . . . . (888)818-4673
Pg 25,320

CHILD WELFARE INFORMATION GATEWAY . . . . (800)394-3366
Pg 2

CHILDHELP INC. . . . . (909)335-1164
Pg 2

CHILDHELP USA/BEAUMONT . . . . (951)845-3155
Pg 25

CHILDHELP USA/HOTLINE . . . . (800)422-4453
Pg 25,198,243

CHILDHELP/WESTERN REGL OFC . . . . (323)465-4016
Pg 2

CHILDNET YOUTH & FAMILY SRVS. . . . . (562)498-5500
Pg 2,25,341

CHILDREN AFFECTED BY AIDS FNDN . . . . (310)258-0850
Pg 8

CHILDREN NOW . . . . (510)763-2444
Pg 321

CHILDREN OF THE NIGHT . . . . (800)551-1300
Pg 25,198,321

CHILDREN'S BURN FOUNDATION . . . . (818)907-2822
Pg 164

CHILDREN'S CRANIOFACIAL ASSOC. . . . . (800)535-3643
Pg 198

CHILDREN'S FUND. . . . . (909)387-4949
Pg 25,117,321

CHILDREN'S HEALTH ACCESS PRGMS . . . . (888)747-1222
Pg 144,165,243,254

CHILDREN'S HOPE . . . . (909)949-8181
Pg 321

CHILDREN'S HOSP L.A. . . . . (323)660-2450
Pg 192

CHILDREN'S HOSP OF O.C. (CHOC) . . . . (714)532-8481
Pg 49

CHILDREN'S HOSPICE INTERNATIONAL . . . . (800)242-4453
Pg 61

CHILDREN'S HUNGER FUND . . . . (818)899-5122
Pg 117

CHILDREN'S INTERAGENCY PRGM . . . . (951)413-5678
Pg 49

CHILDREN'S MUSEUM AT LA HABRA . . . . (562)905-9793
Pg 335

CHILDREN'S TUMOR FOUNDATION . . . . (310)216-9570
Pg 76,165

CHILDREN'S WISH FOUNDATION INTNL. . . . . (800)323-9474
Pg 61

CHILDTIME CHILD CARE . . . . (909)591-9169
Pg 33

CHINESE AMERICAN MUSEUM. . . . . (213)485-8567
Pg 141,335

CHINESE CONSULATE GENERAL . . . . (213)807-8088
Pg 141,214

CHINESE HISTORICAL SOCIETY OF SO CALIF . . . . (323)222-0856
Pg 141

CHINO COMMUNITY ADULT SCHOOL . . . .
Pg 131,232

CHINO COMMUNITY SERVICES . . . . (909)591-9822
Pg 13,25,49,97,243,254,263,285,316,321

CHINO HILLS COMM SRVS DEPT. . . . . (909)364-2710
Pg 285,321

CHINO NEIGHBORHOOD HOUSE. . . . . (909)628-5608
Pg 117

CHINO SENIOR CENTER . . . . (909)591-9836
Pg 285

CHINO VALLEY ADULT SCHOOL . . . . (909)627-9613
Pg 131,232

CHINO VALLEY MEDICAL CENTER . . . . (909)464-8600
Pg 192

CHINO VALLEY TYKES PROGRAM . . . . (909)590-5562
Pg 33,243

CHRISTIAN FAMILY COUNSELING . . . . (951)682-7138
Pg 49,97,321

CHRISTIAN HERITAGE CARE CTRS . . . . (909)949-4887
Pg 165,279

CHRISTIAN HERITAGE GARDENS . . . . (909)946-5757
Pg 279

CHRISTOPHER REEVE FNDN. . . . . (949)673-8474
Pg 76,165

CHRISTOPHER WAHL YOUTH CENTER . . . . (562)693-2247
Pg 8,97,321

CHRONIC FATIGUE IMMUNE DYSFUNCTION . . . . (704)365-2343
Pg 165,198,263

CHURCH OF RELIGIOUS SCIENCE. . . . . (760)365-2205
Pg 49

CIRCLE OF HOPE FAMILY SHELTER . . . . (951)278-2215
Pg 185

CITIZENS OF INGLEWOOD TENANT ASSN . . . . (310)677-7294
Pg 206,216

CITIZENSHIP & IMMIGRATION SRVS . . . . (800)870-3676
Pg 198

CITRUS NURSING CENTER . . . . (909)823-3481
Pg 279

CITY LIBRARY LITERACY CENTER . . . .
Pg 232

CITY OF FONTANA . . . . (909)349-6900
Pg 335

CITY OF HOPE . . . .
Pg 61,165,263

CITY OF HOPE NATL MEDICAL CTR . . . . (800)826-4673
Pg 165,192

CITY OF RIVERSIDE PUBLIC LIBRARY . . . . (951)826-5201
Pg 225,232,321,335

CLAREMONT ADULT SCHOOL . . . . (909)398-0609
Pg 131,232,243

CLARK TERRACE APTS . . . . (951)738-9712
Pg 279

CLEANING FOR HEROES . . . . (401)732-7856
Pg 307

CLEANSLATE, INC. . . . . (562)945-9111
Pg 42,49,263,316,321

CLINICAS DE SALUD DEL PUEBLO, INC . . . . (760)922-4981
Pg 8,165

CLINICAS DE SALUD DEL PUEBLO, INC.. . . . . (760)396-1249
Pg 144,243

CLOVERLEAF HEALTHCARE CENTER . . . . (951)658-9441
Pg 77

CLUTTERERS ANONYMOUS (CLA) . . . . (310)281-6064
Pg 263

CO-ABODE . . . .
Pg 210,243,263

CO-ANON FAMILY GROUPS WORLD SRVS . . . . (800)898-9985
Pg 263

COACH AMERICA . . . . (800)642-3287
Pg 303

COACHELLA COMMUNITY HOMES . . . . (760)398-6411
Pg 210

COACHELLA SENIOR CENTER . . . . (760)398-0104
Pg 285

COACHELLA VALLEY ADULT SCHOOL . . . . (760)398-6302
Pg 132,232

COACHELLA VALLEY HOUSING COALITION. . . . . (760)347-3157
Pg 34,206

COACHELLA VALLEY RESCUE MISSION. . . . . (760)347-3512
Pg 117,186

COACHELLA VALLEY U.S.D.. . . . . (760)399-5137
Pg 34

COACHELLA VALLEY USD. (760)399-8129
Pg 49,66,244

COALINGA STATE HOSPITAL . . . . (559)935-4300
Pg 42

COALITION TO ABOLISH SLAVERY/TRAFFICKING . . . . . (213)365-1906
Pg 13,214,216

COCAINE ANONYMOUS . . . . (800)347-8998
Pg 97,263

COCAINE ANONYMOUS WORLD SRVS . . . . (310)559-5833
Pg 98,263

COLLEGE OF THE DESERT . . . . (760)346-8041
Pg 232

COLLEGE OF THE DESERT/EOPS . . . . (760)773-2539
Pg 132,321,343

COLLETT HEAD START . . . . (951)826-4221
Pg 34

COLORADO RIVER MEDICAL CENTER. . . . . (760)326-4531
Pg 192

COLORADO RIVER SENIOR COMM CENTER . . . . (760)922-6133
Pg 285

COLTON COMMUNITY SRVS DEPT. . . . . (909)370-6153
Pg 34,321,335

COLTON EARLY CHILDHOOD EDUCATION . . . . (909)370-6171
Pg 34,244

COLTON HEAD START/STATE PRESCH . . . . (909)876-4240 Pg 34	CONGRESS OF CALIFORNIA SENIORS . . . . (800)543-3352 Pg 285
COLTON NEIGHBORHOOD SRVS DEPT . . . . (909)370-6153 Pg 141,198,285	CONSEJO DE LATINOS UNIDOS . . . . (800)474-7576 Pg 141,214
COLTON PUBLIC LIBRARY . . . . (909)370-5083 Pg 225,232	CONSUMER CREDIT COUNSELING SRVS. . . . . (800)213-2227 Pg 153
COMMUNITY ACCESS CENTER . . . . (760)347-4858 Pg 77	CONSUMER HOME MORTGAGE INFO . . . . Pg 206
COMMUNITY ACCESS NETWORK . . . . (951)279-3222 Pg 2,49	CONSUMER NUTRITION INFO LINE . . . . (800)877-1600 Pg 112,166
COMMUNITY ACTION EAP . . . . (800)777-9376 Pg 132	COOLEY'S ANEMIA FOUNDATION . . . . (800)522-7222 Pg 166
COMMUNITY ACTION PARTNERSHIP . . . . (951)955-6418 Pg 117,132,152 - 153,186,206	COOPER-BURKHART HOUSE. . . . . Pg 285
COMMUNITY ANTI-DRUG COALITIONS . . . . (703)706-0560 Pg 98	COPE (COMM OUTREACH PARENT ED) . . . . Pg 77
COMMUNITY ASSISTANCE PRGM (CAP). . . . . (909)803-1059 Pg 117,198	COPPER MOUNTAIN COLLEGE/EOPS . . . . (760)366-3791 Pg 132,322,343
COMMUNITY BAPTIST CHURCH . . . . (909)945-5001 Pg 263	COPPER MOUNTAIN HEAD START . . . . (760)366-9762 Pg 34
COMMUNITY CARE & REHAB CENTER . . . . (951)680-6500 Pg 279	COPS FOR KIDS, INC. . . . . (951)245-3389 Pg 285,322,335
COMMUNITY CARE LICENSING . . . . (916)651-6040 Pg 2,34,77,285	CORAZON DE VIDA FOUNDATION . . . . (949)476-1144 Pg 313,316
COMMUNITY CENTER AT TIERRA DEL SOL . . . . (760)321-1548 Pg 285	CORNELIA DE LANGE SYNDROME FNDN . . . . (800)223-8355 Pg 166
COMMUNITY COUNSELING CENTER . . . . (760)949-4357 Pg 49	**CORNERSTONE HOSPICE** . . . . **(866)872-8102** **Pg 62,63**
COMMUNITY COUNSELING CTR/CSUSB . . . . (909)537-5040 Pg 13,26,49,61,321	CORONA COMMUNITY TOWERS . . . . (323)930-2300 Pg 210,279
COMMUNITY DEV & HOUSING . . . . (909)388-0800 Pg 206,210	CORONA COMMUNITY VILLAS/ELDERLY . . . . (323)930-2300 Pg 279
COMMUNITY EXTENDED CARE HOSPITAL . . . . (909)621-4751 Pg 77	CORONA ECONOMIC DEVELOPMENT . . . . (951)736-2297 Pg 206
COMMUNITY FOOD PANTRY . . . . (760)364-3957 Pg 118	CORONA NORCO SETTLEMENT HOUSE . . . . (951)737-3504 Pg 118,186
COMMUNITY HEALTH CHARITIES . . . . (714)502-9153 Pg 165	CORONA PARKS/REC/COMM SRVS DEPT. . . . . (951)736-2241 Pg 285,335
COMMUNITY HEALTH RESOURCE CENTER . . . . (909)888-7881 Pg 153,165,206,217	CORONA PUBLIC LIBRARY . . . . (951)736-2381 Pg 225
COMMUNITY HEALTH SYSTEMS, INC. . . . . (951)224-8220 Pg 8,66,145,165,238,254	CORONA SENIOR CENTER . . . . (951)736-2363 Pg 286
COMMUNITY HELPLINE . . . . (310)793-1415 Pg 198,312	CORONA VET CENTER . . . . (951)734-0525 Pg 50,307
COMMUNITY HOME HEALTH . . . . (909)887-6333 Pg 61,77,166,285	CORONA-NORCO ADULT SCHOOL. . . . . (951)736-3325 Pg 132,232
COMMUNITY HOSPICE CARE. . . . . (760)321-2273 Pg 61	CORPORATE ANGEL NETWORK . . . . (914)328-1313 Pg 303
COMMUNITY HOSPICE OF VICTOR VALLEY. . . . . (760)946-4730 Pg 61	COSA NATL SERVICE ORGANIZATION . . . . (763)537-6904 Pg 264
COMMUNITY OUTREACH MINISTRY . . . . (951)698-7650 Pg 118	COUNCIL/SIZE/WEIGHT DISCRIMINATION. . . . . (845)679-1209 Pg 217
COMMUNITY OUTREACH PROGRAM . . . . (951)736-2381 Pg 118,132	COUNSELING/PSYCHOTHERAPY REFERRAL. . . . . . . (800)638-8799 Pg 50
COMMUNITY PANTRY . . . . (951)929-1101 Pg 118	COUNTRY VILLA BELLA VISTA HLTHCARE . . . . (909)985-2731 Pg 286
COMMUNITY SERVICES DEPARTMENT . . . . Pg 118,153,186,206	COUNTRY VILLA HACIENDA HEALTHCARE . . . . (909)882-3316 Pg 286
COMMUNITY SETTLEMENT ASSOCIATION . . . . (951)782-2336 Pg 98,118,285	COUNTRY VILLA RANCHO MIRAGE . . . . (760)340-0053 Pg 279
COMPASSION NETWORK, THE . . . . (714)924-0223 Pg 118	COUNTRY VILLA REDLANDS . . . . (909)793-2678 Pg 279
COMPASSIONATE FRIENDS/MORONGO. . . . . (877)969-0010 Pg 263	COURT APPOINTED SPECIAL ADV. . . . . (760)863-7539 Pg 26,217,313
COMPASSIONATE FRIENDS/NATL . . . . (877)969-0010 Pg 61,263	COURT APPOINTED SPECIAL ADV/NATL . . . . (800)628-3233 Pg 26,217,313
COMPREHENSIVE YOUTH SERVICES . . . . (909)466-8685 Pg 26,321	COVENANT HOUSE NINELINE . . . . (800)999-9999 Pg 198,254,322,341
COMPULSIVE EATERS ANONYMOUS . . . . (562)342-9344 Pg 112	CRAFTON HILLS COLLEGE/EOPS . . . . (909)389-3239 Pg 132,322,343
CONCEPT 7 FAMILY SUPPORT CTRS . . . . (877)864-4448 Pg 2	CREDIT COUNSELING. . . . . Pg 153
CONCEPT 7 FOSTER FAMILY . . . . (877)424-2369 Pg 3	CREST FOREST SENIOR CITIZENS CLUB . . . . (909)338-5036 Pg 286
CONCERNED UNITED BIRTHPARENTS (CUB). . . . . . . (800)822-2777 Pg 3,264	CRESTVIEW CONVALESCENT HOSP . . . . (909)877-1361 Pg 77
CONCILIO/CENTRO DE NINOS . . . . (951)683-8935 Pg 34	CRIME SURVIVORS . . . . (949)872-7895 Pg 13,313
CONGENITAL HEART INFO NETWORK. . . . . (609)822-1572 Pg 153,166,264	CRIME VICTIMS UNITED OF CALIF . . . . (530)885-9544 Pg 13,264

CRISIS HOTLINE . . . . (760)240-8255
Pg 198
CRISIS LINE . . . .
Pg 13
CRISIS MINISTRY . . . . (760)247-6494
Pg 118
CRISIS PREGNANCY CENTER . . . . (760)568-2200
Pg 145,254,313
CROHN'S & COLITIS FNDN OF AMER . . . . (800)932-2423
Pg 166
CROHN'S & COLITIS FNDN/GREATER L.A. . . . . . (310)478-4500
Pg 166,264
CROHN'S & COLITIS SUPPORT GROUP . . . . (800)932-2423
Pg 264
CROSSLIGHT FAMILY MINISTRIES . . . . (909)980-6939
Pg 118
CROSSROADS CHRISTIAN CHURCH . . . . (951)737-4664
Pg 264
CROSSROADS CHURCH . . . . (951)541-8574
Pg 50,244,264
CROSSROADS, INC. . . . . (909)626-7847
Pg 42
CRYSTAL CATHEDRAL/COUNSELING CTR . . . . . . (714)971-4222
Pg 50
CRYSTAL METH ANONYMOUS . . . . (213)488-4455
Pg 98,264
CSAT HOTLINE . . . . (800)729-6686
Pg 8,98,198
CSP WORKPLACE HELPLINE . . . .
Pg 98
CTAP . . . . (800)806-1191
Pg 77
CTIS PREGNANCY RISK INFO LINE . . . . (800)532-3749
Pg 145,166,254
CUCAMONGA HEAD START . . . . (909)948-6979
Pg 34
CUCAMONGA PRESCHOOL/ELEM . . . . (909)980-1318
Pg 34
CYPRESS GARDENS REHAB CARE CTR . . . . (951)688-3636
Pg 279
CYSTIC FIBROSIS FOUNDATION . . . . (714)938-1393
Pg 166,264

D

D.A.R.T. . . . .
Pg 77,132
D.O.V.E.S. OF BIG BEAR VALLEY . . . . (909)866-1546
Pg 13,198
DALES SENIOR CENTER . . . . (951)826-5303
Pg 286
DALTON & ASSOCIATES. . . . . (760)241-1777
Pg 98
DASH, INC. (909)798-1667
Pg 279
DAVID & MARGARET YOUTH & FAMILY SRVS . . . . (909)596-5921
Pg 3,98,322,341,343
DE ANZA COMMUNITY & TEEN CENTER . . . . . . (909)395-2030
Pg 335
DEAF KID'S KAMP . . . . (661)657-3323
Pg 21
DEBT COUNSELING . . . .
Pg 153
DEBTORS ANONYMOUS/SO CALIF. . . . . (781)453-2743
Pg 153,264
DEL ROSA VILLA . . . . (909)885-3261
Pg 77
DELANCEY STREET FOUNDATION. . . . . (415)512-5104
Pg 13,42,98,316,322
DELMANN HEIGHTS COMM CENTER . . . . (909)384-5417
Pg 118,286,335
DENTAL BOARD OF CALIF . . . . (877)729-7789
Pg 66
DENTI-CAL BENEFICIARIES SRVS DEPT . . . . . . (800)322-6384
Pg 66
DENTI-CAL DENTIST. . . . . (909)364-0030
Pg 66 - 67
DEPRESSED ANONYMOUS . . . . (502)569-1989
Pg 50,264

DEPRESSION & BIPOLAR SUPPORT ALLIANCE . . . . (714)744-8718
Pg 264
DEPRESSION AWARENESS. . . . . (800)421-4211
Pg 50
DEPRESSIONRECOVERYGROUPS.COM . . . .
Pg 50,264
DEPT OF FAIR EMPLOYMENT/HOUSING . . . .
Pg 207
DEPT OF MOTOR VEHICLES . . . .
Pg 303
DEPT OF REHABILITATION . . . .
Pg 132
DEPT OF VETERANS AFFAIRS . . . .
Pg 308
DEPT OF VETERANS AFFAIRS EDUCATION. . . . . . . (888)442-4551
Pg 198,308
DEPT. OF WORKFORCE DEV . . . . (909)382-0440
Pg 132
DES ACTION USA . . . . (800)337-9288
Pg 166,198
DESERT AIDS PROJECT. . . . . (760)323-2118
Pg 8,166,264
DESERT AREA EARLY INTERVENTION . . . .
Pg 77
DESERT AREA ENTERPRISE . . . .
Pg 77
DESERT AREA RESOURCES/TRAINING . . . . (760)375-9787
Pg 77,132,166
DESERT AREA SUPPORTED LIVING . . . .
Pg 77
DESERT BLIND/HANDICAPPED ASSN . . . . (760)318-2882
Pg 77,303
DESERT HIGHLAND EVEN START . . . . (760)416-6000
Pg 232
DESERT HOSPITAL MEDICAL DIRECTORY . . . . (760)323-6511
Pg 166
DESERT HOT SPRINGS FAMILY RESOURCE CTR . . . . . (760)288-3313
Pg 118,132,244,308
DESERT HOT SPRINGS SENIOR SRVS . . . . (760)329-0222
Pg 286
DESERT MANNA/EMERGENCY HOUSING . . . . (760)256-7797
Pg 118,186,207
DESERT MANOR . . . . (760)365-0717
Pg 279
DESERT MOUNTAIN SELPA CHILDREN'S CTR . . . . . (760)242-6336
Pg 50
DESERT RECREATION DISTRICT. . . . . (760)347-3484
Pg 21,34,335
DESERT REHABILITATION SERVICES . . . .
Pg 98
DESERT S.O.S. . . . . (760)327-4394
Pg 118,186
DESERT SANCTUARY/HALEY HOUSE . . . . (760)256-3441
Pg 13,26,118,199,217
DESERT SANDS UNIFIED SCHOOL DIST . . . . (760)771-8678
Pg 34
DESERT SIERRA PARTNERSHIP . . . . (951)241-8723
Pg 167
DESERT VALLEY HOSPITAL. . . . . (760)241-8000
Pg 192
DESERT/MOUNTAIN EARLY START PRGM. . . . . . . (760)244-1083
Pg 34
DESERTARC . . . . (760)346-1611
Pg 77
DEV DISABILITIES AREA BOARD #12 . . . . (909)890-1259
Pg 77,217
DEVELOPING AGING SOLUTIONS/HEART. . . . . . . (909)798-1667
Pg 286
DEVONSHIRE CARE CENTER . . . . (951)925-2571
Pg 279
DIABETES ASSOCIATION . . . .
Pg 167
DIABETES INFO CLEARINGHOUSE . . . .
Pg 167
DIABETES SUPPORT GROUPS . . . . (909)558-3022
Pg 264
DIABETES/PREGNANCY PRGM/CAL . . . .
Pg 167
DIABETIC HELP LINE/SUPPORT GRP . . . . (714)992-3037
Pg 167,264

DIABETIC YOUTH CAMPS . . . . Pg 21	
DIAL-A-RIDE/BANNING . . . . (951)922-3252 Pg 303	
DIAL-A-RIDE/BARSTOW . . . . (760)256-0311 Pg 303	
DIAL-A-RIDE/BEAUMONT/CHERRY VLY . . . . (951)769-8532 Pg 303	
DIAL-A-RIDE/BIG BEAR LAKE . . . . (909)878-5200 Pg 303	
DIAL-A-RIDE/CORONA-NORCO . . . . (951)734-7220 Pg 303	
DIAL-A-RIDE/JURUPA . . . . (800)795-7887 Pg 303	
DIAL-A-RIDE/LAKE ELSINORE . . . . (800)795-7887 Pg 303	
DIAL-A-RIDE/MORENO VALLEY . . . . (800)795-7887 Pg 303	
DIAL-A-RIDE/MURRIETA . . . . (800)795-7887 Pg 303	
DIAL-A-RIDE/PERRIS . . . . (800)795-7887 Pg 303	
DIAL-A-RIDE/RIVERSIDE METRO . . . . (951)687-8080 Pg 303	
DIAL-A-RIDE/SOUTHWEST RIVERSIDE . . . . (800)795-7887 Pg 303	
DIAL-A-RIDE/TEMECULA . . . . (800)795-7887 Pg 303	
DIAL-A-RIDE/YUCCA VALLEY . . . . (800)794-6282 Pg 304	
DIETETICS ASSOCIATION . . . . Pg 167	
DIGESTIVE DISEASE INFO . . . . Pg 167	
DINO PAPA VERO SENIOR CENTER . . . . (909)350-0575 Pg 279	
DISABILITIES MINISTRIES . . . . (951)737-4664 Pg 77	
DISABILITY INSURANCE . . . . Pg 132	
DISABILITY RIGHTS ADVOCATES . . . . (510)665-8644 Pg 78,217	
DISABILITY RIGHTS CALIFORNIA . . . . (213)427-8747 Pg 78,217	
DISABILITY RIGHTS EDU/DEFENSE FUND . . . . . (510)644-2555 Pg 78,217	
DISABLED AMERICAN VETERANS . . . . (877)426-2838 Pg 78,98,308	
DISABLED DEALER . . . . (800)588-5099 Pg 78	
DISABLED SERVICES . . . . (909)384-4443 Pg 78	
DISABLED SPORTS USA . . . . (949)460-6969 Pg 78,336	
DISABLED YOUTH CAMPS . . . . Pg 21,78	
DISCOVERY SCIENCE CENTER . . . . (714)542-2823 Pg 336	
DISTRICT ATTORNEY . . . . Pg 217	
DIVERSIFIED INDUSTRIES/OPARC . . . . Pg 78	
DIVISION OF JUVENILE JUSTICE . . . . (916)262-1396 Pg 8,42 - 43	
DIVORCE CARE SUPPORT GROUP . . . . (909)606-4848 Pg 265	
DOGS FOR THE DEAF, INC. . . . . (541)826-9220 Pg 78	
DOHENY EYE INSTITUTE . . . . (323)442-7100 Pg 238	
DOLPHINS MOBILE HEALTH VAN OUTREACH . . . (760)922-1349 Pg 167,244,254	
DOMESTIC ABUSE HELPLINE . . . . (888)743-5754 Pg 13,199	
DOMESTIC VIOLENCE EDU SERVICES . . . . Pg 13	
DOMESTIC VIOLENCE HELPLINE . . . . (800)978-3600 Pg 13,199	
DOMESTIC VIOLENCE HOTLINE . . . . (909)381-3471 Pg 199	

DOMESTIC VIOLENCE/SEXUAL ASSAULT . . . . (800)339-3940
Pg 199
DON A. TURNER LAW LIBRARY . . . .
Pg 217,225
DOUBLE CHECK RETREAT . . . . (951)927-2567
Pg 98
DOWN SYNDROME CONGRESS . . . .
Pg 78
DREAM STREET FOUNDATION . . . . (424)248-0696
Pg 21
DRUG & ALC TREATMENT REFERRAL . . . . (866)716-3460
Pg 98,199,322
DRUG & ALCOHOL ABUSE INFO/REF . . . . (800)729-6686
Pg 98,199
DRUG ABUSE PROGRAMS . . . .
Pg 98
DRUG ABUSE PROGRAMS/RIV CO. . . . .
Pg 98
DRUG ENDANGERED CHILDREN PRGM. . . . . . . (877)955-6384
Pg 98,322
DRUG STRATEGIES . . . . (202)289-9070
Pg 98,316
DUAL RECOVERY ANONYMOUS . . . . (877)883-2332
Pg 50,265
DYSLEXIA AWARE/RESOURCE CTR . . . . (805)963-7339
Pg 265
DYSLEXIA FOUNDATION . . . . (949)642-7303
Pg 78
DYSLEXIA SOCIETY . . . .
Pg 78
DYSLEXIA SUPPORT GROUP . . . .
Pg 78
DYSTONIA MEDICAL RESEARCH FNDN . . . . (800)377-3978
Pg 167

E

EAR FOUNDATION (THE) . . . . (615)248-8828
Pg 167
EARLY START FAMILY RESOURCE NTWK . . . . . . (800)890-4794
Pg 78,244
EAST L.A. HOTLINE/SHELTER . . . . (800)548-2722
Pg 14,199
EAST VALLEY CHARLEE . . . . (909)307-5777
Pg 26,50,322
EAST WEST ADOPTIONS, INC. . . . . (888)242-9604
Pg 3
EASTER SEALS/CHILD CARE CENTER . . . . (909)981-4668
Pg 35,78
EASTER SEALS/NATIONAL . . . . (800)221-6827
Pg 78
EASTER SEALS/SO CALIF . . . . (714)834-1111
Pg 78,265
EASTFIELD MING QUONG CHILDREN/FAM . . . . . (909)266-2700
Pg 3,322
EATING DISORDER FOUNDATION OF O.C. . . . . . (800)342-8793
Pg 50,112,244
EATING DISORDER REFERRAL & INFO CTR . . . . (858)792-7463
Pg 112
EATING DISORDERS ANONYMOUS (EDA) . . . . . . (218)339-2500
Pg 112,265
EATING DISORDERS COALITION . . . . (202)543-9570
Pg 112
ECCLESIA CHRISTIAN FELLOWSHIP . . . . (909)881-5551
Pg 50
ECHOES OF FAITH CHRISTIAN CTR . . . . (909)627-0927
Pg 118
EDDIE DEE SMITH SENIOR CENTER . . . . (951)275-9975
Pg 286
EDGEWOOD CTR FOR CHILDREN & FAMILIES . . (415)681-3211
Pg 322,343
EDUCATION OPTIONS CTR/STATE PRESCH . . . . (951)276-7670
Pg 35
EDUCATIONAL OPTIONS CENTER . . . . (951)276-7670
Pg 133,233
EDWARD-DEAN MUSEUM . . . . (951)845-2626
Pg 336
EF FNDN FOR FOREIGN STUDY . . . . (800)992-1892
Pg 336

EISENHOWER MED CTR FIVE STAR CLUB . . . . (760)836-0232	FAMILY CAREGIVER ALLIANCE. . . . . (800)445-8106
Pg 286	Pg 265
EISENHOWER MEDICAL CENTER . . . . (760)773-1403	FAMILY PACT . . . . (916)650-0414
Pg 167,192	Pg 145
EL CENTRO REGIONAL MEDICAL CENTER . . . . (760)339-7100	FAMILY PLANNING (CALIF INFO/REF) . . . .
Pg 192	Pg 145,199
ELDER ABUSE	**FAMILY PLANNING ASSOCIATES** . . . .
Pg 286	**Pg 145,147**
ELDERCARE LOCATOR . . . . (800)677-1116	FAMILY SELF-SUFFICIENCY . . . .
Pg 276,286	Pg 79,210,279
ELSINORE HEALTH CENTER	FAMILY SERVICE AGENCY/FONTANA . . . . (909)822-3533
Pg 167	Pg 199
EMERSON STATE PRESCHOOL . . . . (951)788-7462	FAMILY SERVICE AGENCY/SAN BRDO. . . . . (909)338-4689
Pg 35	Pg 14,26,50,119,244,323
EMMANUEL TEMPLE CME CHURCH . . . . (760)245-4973	FAMILY SERVICE ASSN/CORONA . . . . (951)737-8410
Pg 119	Pg 14,26,51,244
EMMANUEL UNIQUE OUTREACH PARTNERS . . . . . . (951)279-0031	FAMILY SERVICE ASSN/REDLANDS . . . . (909)793-2673
Pg 244,286,336	Pg 67,119,153,207,238
EMOTIONS ANONYMOUS . . . . (909)873-2273	FAMILY SERVICE ASSN/WEST RIVERSIDE . . . . (951)274-7940
Pg 265	Pg 35,51,119,244 - 245,265,286,297
EMPLOYMENT & BUSINESS RESOURCE CTR . . . . . . (760)949-8526	FAMILY SERVICE ASSOCIATION . . . . (951)686-3706
Pg 133	Pg 35,51,286
EMPLOYMENT DEV DEPT/DISABILITY . . . . (800)480-3287	FAMILY SERVICE ASSOCIATION OF REDLANDS . . . . (909)792-2673
Pg 79,133	Pg 119,186
EMPLOYMENT DEV DEPT/JOB SRVS . . . . (909)948-6606	FAMILY SERVICES . . . . (951)304-1623
Pg 79,133,308	Pg 35,245
EMPOWERTECH COMPUTER ACCESS CTR . . . . (310)338-1597	FAMILY SERVICES OF THE DESERT . . . . (760)347-2398
Pg 79,133,244	Pg 14,26,51,99,245 323
ENDOMETRIOSIS ASSOCIATION . . . . (800)992-3636	FAMILY SOLUTIONS . . . . (909)418-6923
Pg 167	Pg 168,245
ENGLISH AS A SECOND LANGUAGE.	FATHERS NETWORK . . . . (425)653-4286
Pg 233	Pg 245
EPILEPSY FNDN OF AMERICA . . . . (800)332-1000	FEDERAL CITIZEN INFORMATION CENTER . . . . (888)878-3256
Pg 79,167	Pg 214
EPILEPSY FNDN OF GREATER L.A. . . . . (800)564-0445	FEDERAL IDENTIFICATION THEFT HOTLINE . . . . (877)438-4338
Pg 79,167,265	Pg 199,265
EPILEPSY FNDN OF SAN DIEGO . . . . (619)296-0161	FEDERAL INFORMATION CENTER . . . . (800)333-4636
Pg 21,79,167	Pg 199
EQUAL RIGHTS ADVOCATES . . . . (415)621-0672	FEDERAL PUBLIC DEFENDER . . . . (951)276-6346
Pg 133,217	Pg 218
EQUIFAX CREDIT INFO . . . . (800)685-1111	FEDERAL RES BANK. . . . . (888)851-1920
Pg 199	Pg 153
ESCORT/MIGRANT EDUCATION . . . . (800)451-8058	FEDERATION/CHILDREN/SPECIAL NEEDS . . . . (617)236-7210
Pg 199,214	Pg 79
ESSENCE OF LIGHT . . . . (323)779-2727	FEINGOLD ASSN OF THE UNITED STATES . . . . (631)369-9340
Pg 186	Pg 79
ESTELLE DOHENY EYE FOUNDATION.	FELLOWSHIP BAPTIST CHURCH . . . . (951)684-8071
Pg 238	Pg 119
ETTIE LEE YOUTH & FAMILY SERVICES . . . . (626)960-4861	FEMA FOR KIDS . . . .
Pg 3,50,98,316,322,343	Pg 245,336
EXCEPTIONALLY EXCITED KIDS (EEK) . . . . (951)375-6906	FIELDS COMPREHENSIVE YOUTH SRVS . . . . (909)945-1318
Pg 79,244,265	Pg 316,323,343
EXECUTIVE WOMEN INTERNATL. . . . . (801)355-2800	FIESTA EDUCATIVA, INC. . . . . (323)221-6696
Pg 265	Pg 79,141,245
EXTENDED CARE HOSP OF RIVERSIDE. . . . . (951)687-3842	FIFTH STREET SENIOR CENTER. . . . . (909)384-5430
Pg 279	Pg 287
EYE CARE CLINIC . . . . (714)449-7444	FINANCIAL CRISIS . . . .
Pg 238	Pg 119,153
EYE DOG FOUNDATION FOR THE BLIND . . . . (661)831-1333	FINANCIAL FRAUD ENFORCE TASK FORCE . . . . (202)514-2000
Pg 79	Pg 153
EYE FOUNDATION	FIND (FOOD IN NEED OF DISTRIBUTION) . . . . (760)775-3663
Pg 238	Pg 119
EYECARE AMERICA . . . . (877)887-6327	FIND THE CHILDREN . . . . (888)477-6721
Pg 167,238,286	Pg 27,199,323
	FIRST 5 CALIFORNIA . . . . (916)263-1050
	Pg 245
F	FIRST BAPTIST CHURCH OF YUCAIPA . . . . (909)790-1971
	Pg 225,336
FACIAL PLASTIC SURGERY INFO . . . . (800)332-3223	FIRST CALL FOR HELP . . . . (760)243-9646
Pg 167	Pg 14,27,51,79 119,168,199,323
FAIR HOUSING COUNCIL/RIVERSIDE CO. . . . . (760)864-1540	FIRST CANDLE/SIDS ALLIANCE . . . . (800)221-7437
Pg 207,218	Pg 62,266
FAITH'S HOPE FOUNDATION . . . . (714)871-4673	FIRST CHRISTIAN CHURCH NURSERY SCHL . . . . . . (951)683-5780
Pg 153,313	Pg 35
FAMILIES ANONYMOUS . . . . (800)736-9805	FIRST CONGREGATIONAL CHURCH . . . . (951)684-2494
Pg 99	Pg 119
FAMILY AND FRIENDS OF MURDER VICTIMS	FIRST FINANCIAL CREDIT UNION . . . . (800)537-8491
Pg 62,265	Pg 153
FAMILY CARE CENTER	FIRST FIVE/RIALTO . . . . (909)421-4201
Pg 167	Pg 254

FIRST STEPS CHILD DEVELOPMENT CTR	(909)793-7856
Pg 35	
FISH/LOWER COACHELLA VALLEY.	(760)398-1600
Pg 119	
FLOWERS HERITAGE FOUNDATION	(510)587-2668
Pg 8,153,168	
FNDN FOR AFFORDABLE HOUSING	(949)443-9101
Pg 210	
FONTANA ADULT SCHOOL	(909)357-5490
Pg 214,233	
FONTANA FAMILY HEALTH CENTER	(909)422-8029
Pg 168	
FONTANA HIGH SCHOOL	(909)357-5500
Pg 133	
FONTANA REHAB WORKSHOP	(909)428-3833
Pg 79,134	
FONTANA VICTIM SERVICES CENTER.	(909)356-6406
Pg 218	
FOOD ADDICTS ANONYMOUS	(561)967-3871
Pg 112	
FOOD ADDICTS IN RECOVERY ANONYMOUS	(781)932-6300
Pg 112,266	
FOOD NOW	(760)329-4100
Pg 119	
FOOD STAMPS	
Pg 119	
FOOTHILL AIDS PROJECT	(909)884-2722
Pg 8	
FOOTHILL FAMILY SHELTER	(909)920-5568
Pg 186	
FOOTHILL FAMILY SHELTER HOMELESS COURT.	(909)608-2865
Pg 186,218,266	
FOREST HOME.	(909)389-2300
Pg 22	
FOSTER FAMILY NETWORK.	
Pg 3	
FOUNDATION FIGHTING BLINDNESS	(310)207-2089
Pg 79,168,238	
FOUNDATION FOR MEXICAN AMERICAN SRVS	(951)485-3394
Pg 80,218	
FOUNDATION FOR RECOVERY, INC..	(702)257-8199
Pg 99,225	
FOUNTAIN OF LIFE TEMPLE	(951)849-1517
Pg 119	
FOUNTAINS AT THE CARLOTTA	(760)346-5420
Pg 279	
FRAGILE X ASSN OF SO CALIF	(818)754-4227
Pg 168,266	
FRAZEE COMMUNITY CENTER.	(909)889-4424
Pg 119,186	
FREE ANNUAL CREDIT REPORT SRVS	
Pg 153	
FREE INDEED CHRISTIAN FELLOWSHIP	(951)657-2449
Pg 99,186,266	
FREE SPIRIT SHELTER	(323)937-1312
Pg 14	
FREEDOM FROM FEAR	(718)351-1717
Pg 51,266	
FRESH START SURGICAL GIFTS	(760)944-7774
Pg 168	
FRIDAY NIGHT LIVE/ADMIN	(559)733-6496
Pg 99,323	
FRIDAY NIGHT LIVE/RIVERSIDE CO.	(951)782-5004
Pg 99,323	
FRIDAY NIGHT LIVE/SAN BERNARDINO CO.	(800)387-6623
Pg 99,323	
FRIENDS OUTSIDE/ESPERANZA VISITOR.	(760)922-5300
Pg 43	
FRIENDS OUTSIDE/FRONTERA	(909)597-0234
Pg 43	
FRIENDS OUTSIDE/SAN BRDO CO.	(909)597-5428
Pg 43	
FRIENDSHIP HOUSE ASSN/AMER INDIANS	(415)865-0964
Pg 99	

G

G.A.I.N. PROGRAMS	
Pg 134	

G.A.P. FOOD BANK.	(909)945-1020
Pg 119	
GAIN/CALWORKS PROGRAMS	
Pg 119,134	
GALLAUDET UNIVERSITY	(202)651-5000
Pg 80	
GAM-ANON HOTLINE	(818)377-5144
Pg 199	
GAM-ANON INTERNATL	(718)352-1671
Pg 99	
GAMBLERS ANONYMOUS	(760)325-2808
Pg 199	
GAMBLING HELPLINE	(888)277-3115
Pg 199	
GARDEN OF ANGELS	(909)797-8599
Pg 145,255	
GARRETSON HEAD START/ST PRESCH	(951)279-4231
Pg 35	
GATEWAYS COMM CORRECTIONS CTR.	(323)644-2020
Pg 43	
GAY & LESBIAN MEDICAL ASSOCIATION	(202)600-8037
Pg 168	
GAY & LESBIAN NATIONAL HOTLINE.	(888)843-4564
Pg 199,266	
GAY MEN'S DOMESTIC VIOLENCE PROJECT	(617)354-6056
Pg 14,199	
GAY STRAIGHT ALLIANCE NETWORK	(415)552-4229
Pg 323,336	
GAY, LESBIAN, STRAIGHT EDU NETWORK	(212)727-0135
Pg 313,323	
GED HOTLINE	(800)626-9433
Pg 134	
GED INFO	(916)445-9438
Pg 200	
GENERATIONS UNITED	(202)289-3979
Pg 287,323	
GENESIS SHELTER	
Pg 119,186	
GENETIC & RARE DISEASES INFO CTR	(301)402-0911
Pg 168	
GENETIC ALLIANCE	(202)966-5557
Pg 168,266	
GENETICALLY HANDICAPPED PERSONS	(800)639-0597
Pg 80,168	
GEORGE GIBSON SENIOR CENTER	(909)981-4501
Pg 287	
GET ON THE BUS	(818)980-7714
Pg 43,266	
GILDA'S CLUB DESERT CITIES	(760)770-5678
Pg 266	
GIRL SCOUTS OF USA	
Pg 22,336	
GIRL SCOUTS/SAN GORGONIO CNCL	(909)307-6555
Pg 22,336	
GIRLS & BOYS TOWN NATL HOTLINE	(800)448-3000
Pg 200	
GIRLS CLUBS	
Pg 35,336	
GIVE AN HOUR	
Pg 51,308,313	
GLAUCOMA FOUNDATION	(212)285-0080
Pg 168	
GLBT NATIONAL HELP CENTER	(415)355-0003
Pg 8,323	
GLEN AVON SENIOR CENTER	
Pg 287	
GLENVIEW HEAD START/PRESCH	(951)940-8530
Pg 35	
GOD'S FAMILIES INTL ADOPTION SRVS.	(949)858-7621
Pg 3	
GOD'S HELPING HAND	(951)653-2529
Pg 119 - 120	
GOLDEN RAINBOW SENIOR CENTER	(760)416-7790
Pg 287,313	
GOLDEN SHARE FOODS	(909)873-5380
Pg 120	
GOLDEN STATE MOBILE HOME OWNERS	(714)826-4071
Pg 207	
GOOD SHEPHERD COUNSELING	(951)678-1642
Pg 51,62	

GOOD SHEPHERD SHELTER . . . . (323)737-6111 Pg 14	HANMI FAMILY COUNSELING CENTER . . . . (714)892-9910 Pg 51,141,245,324
GOODWILL INDUSTRIES/INLAND CO. . . . . (760)951-5572 Pg 80,134	HANNAH'S CHILDRENS HOMES . . . . (909)483-2552 Pg 3,27,324
GOODWILL INDUSTRIES/SAN BRDO . . . . (909)885-3831 Pg 80,134	HANNAH'S CHILDREN'S HOMES . . . . (714)516-1077 Pg 3,27,324
GOODWILL INDUSTRIES/SO CALIF. . . . . (323)223-1211 Pg 80,134	HANSEN'S DISEASE . . . . Pg 168
GOT RECOVERY, INC. . . . . **(951)328-8778** **Pg 99**	HAPPY TRAILS CHILDREN'S FNDN. . . . . (760)240-3330 Pg 27
GRANDPARENT INFORMATION CENTER . . . . (866)227-7457 Pg 245,287	HARMONY SOUP KITCHEN . . . . (760)921-4508 Pg 186
GRANDPARENTS RAISING GRANDCHILDREN . . . . . . (800)303-0001 Pg 245,287	HARRIS EATING DISORDERS CENTER . . . . (617)726-8470 Pg 112
GREATER HOPE FOUNDATION . . . . (760)256-0432 Pg 3	HART COMMUNITY HOMES . . . . (714)526-2729 Pg 27,134,324,344
GREATER L.A. AGENCY ON DEAFNESS . . . . (323)478-8000 Pg 8,80	HAVEN HOUSE . . . . (626)564-8880 Pg 14
GREENLEAF BATON TWIRLING ACADEMY . . . . (949)768-4664 Pg 336	HEADACHE FOUNDATION . . . . Pg 168
GRIEF RECOVERY GROUP . . . . (909)558-7261 Pg 62,266	HEALING ODYSSEY . . . . (949)951-3930 Pg 168,266
GRIEF RECOVERY INSTITUTE . . . . (818)907-9600 Pg 62	HEALTH GUARD INLAND . . . . (909)920-1165 Pg 287
GRIEF RECOVERY SUPPORT GROUP . . . . (909)425-1777 Pg 266	HEALTH INFO CLEARINGHOUSE . . . . (301)565-4167 Pg 200
GRIEF SHARE . . . . (760)328-3313 Pg 62,266	HEALTH INFO LINE/RIVERSIDE CO. . . . . (951)358-5000 Pg 9,168
GRIEF SHARE RECOVERY GROUP . . . . (760)772-8462 Pg 62,266	HEALTH INSURANCE PLAN/CALIF . . . . Pg 168
GROVE APTS . . . . (909)983-3525 Pg 80,279	HEALTH RESOURCES & SRVS ADMIN . . . . (888)275-4772 Pg 168
GUARDIAN SCHOLARSHIP PRGM . . . . (657)278-4900 Pg 3,344	HEALTHY FAMILIES . . . . Pg 169
GUIDE DOG FOUNDATION FOR BLIND . . . . (800)548-4337 Pg 80,238	HEALTHY FAMILY CLINIC . . . . (760)776-1600 Pg 145,169,245
GUIDE DOGS FOR THE BLIND . . . . (800)295-4050 Pg 80,238	HEAR NOW . . . . (800)648-4327 Pg 80
GUIDE DOGS OF AMERICA . . . . (818)362-5834 Pg 80,238	HEARING AID DISPENSER BOARD . . . . (916)574-7990 Pg 80,287
GUIDE DOGS OF THE DESERT . . . . (760)329-6257 Pg 80,238	HEARING AID HELPLINE . . . . (734)522-7200 Pg 80,287
GUIDED DISCOVERIES, INC. . . . . (909)625-6194 Pg 22,336	HEARING LOSS SUPPORT GROUP . . . . (760)343-3828 Pg 81,266
GUIDING LIGHT HOME FOR BOYS . . . . (951)485-0423 Pg 323	HEART ASSOCIATION . . . . Pg 169
	HEART TOUCH PROJECT . . . . (310)391-2558 Pg 9,62,169,287
## H	HEARTLINE MINISTRIES . . . . Pg 145
H.E.A.R.T., INC. FOUNDATION. . . . . (951)506-4488 Pg 27,51,245	HEARTLINE PREGNANCY COUNSELING CTR. . . . . . . (951)682-2400 Pg 145,255
H.E.A.T.H. RESOURCE CENTER . . . . Pg 80	HEATH RESOURCE CENTER . . . . Pg 81
H.E.L.P. INC. . . . . (951)922-2305 Pg 120,186	HELEN HUNT JACKSON ALT SCHOOL . . . . (951)765-5193 Pg 324
H.U.D. (HUD) . . . . Pg 210	HELEN WOODWARD ANIMAL CENTER. . . . . (858)756-4117 Pg 81,287
HABITAT FOR HUMANITY/HEMET . . . . (951)658-0235 Pg 210,313	HELPING HANDS MINISTRY OF MOUNT ZION . . . . (909)983-2411 Pg 120
HABITAT FOR HUMANITY/PALM DESERT . . . . (760)770-3723 Pg 210,313	HELPING OUR PEOPLE IN ELSINORE . . . . (951)245-7510 Pg 120
HABITAT FOR HUMANITY/RIVERSIDE . . . . (951)787-6754 Pg 210,313	HELPLINE CRISIS HOTLINE. . . . . Pg 200
HABITAT FOR HUMANITY/SAN GORGONIO . . . . (951)922-3944 Pg 211,314	HELPLINE INFO & REFERRAL . . . . Pg 51,120
HACIENDA CHRISTIAN LIFE CAMPUS . . . . (951)657-3041 Pg 43,99	HEMET ADULT SCHOOL. . . . . (951)765-5190 Pg 134,233
HACIENDA VALDEZ . . . . Pg 99	HEMET ESTATES. . . . . (951)925-5222 Pg 211
HACIENDA VILLAGE . . . . (951)683-4056 Pg 51	HEMET PUBLIC LIBRARY . . . . (951)765-2440 Pg 226,233
HADASSAH SOUTHERN CALIFORNIA . . . . (310)234-8300 Pg 233,266,314	HEMET VALLEY MENTAL HEALTH CTR. . . . . (951)652-2811 Pg 200
HAEMOSTASIS & THROMBOSIS . . . . (213)742-6509 Pg 168	HEMOPHILIA COUNCIL OF CALIF. . . . . (916)498-3780 Pg 314
HALEY HOUSE . . . . Pg 14	HEMOPHILIA FNDN OF SO CALIF. . . . . (800)371-4123 Pg 9,169
HANDS ON INLAND EMPIRE . . . . (909)980-2857 Pg 43,134,314,316,323	HEMOPHILIA TREATMENT CENTER . . . . Pg 169

HEP C CONNECTION	(303)860-0800	HOME OF GUIDING HANDS	(619)938-2850
Pg 267		Pg 81	
HEPATITIS C SUPPORT GROUP	(760)200-2766	HOME OF NEIGHBORLY SERVICE	(909)885-3491
Pg 267		Pg 36,120,233,316,336	
HEPATITIS FOUNDATION INTERNATIONAL	(800)891-0707	HOME START NORTH COUNTY	(760)439-7513
Pg 200,267		Pg 14	
HERITAGE GARDENS RETIREMENT	(909)796-0216	HOMEAID AMERICA	(949)258-0850
Pg 280		Pg 186	
HERITAGE PARK CARE CTRS.	(909)949-4887	HOMEAID/INLAND EMPIRE	(951)686-0628
Pg 280		Pg 187	
HERMANDAD MEXICANA NACIONAL.	(714)541-0250	HOMECARE WORKERS UNION	(909)373-3018
Pg 120,214,218		Pg 81,276	
HERNANDEZ COMMUNITY CENTER	(909)384-5420	HOMELESS VETERANS STAND DOWNS.	
Pg 120,336		Pg 187,308	
HERPES RESOURCE CENTER	(800)227-8922	HOMEOWNER/RENTER ASSISTANCE	(800)868-4171
Pg 9,267		Pg 81,207,288	
HESPERIA HEAD START.	(760)948-4411	HOMEOWNERSHIP PRESERVATION FNDN	(888)995-4673
Pg 35		Pg 207,211	
HESPERIA REC & PARK SENIOR CTR	(760)244-1680	HOMES OF HOPE FOSTER FAMILY	(626)814-9085
Pg 287		Pg 4,344	
HESPERIA REC & PARKS DISTRICT	(760)244-5488	HOPE LUTHERAN CHURCH.	(951)676-6262
Pg 81,336		Pg 120	
HI-DESERT MEDICAL CENTER	(760)366-3711	HOSPICE LINK	(800)331-1620
Pg 169,192		Pg 62	
HICAP	(800)434-0222	HOSPICE OF THE DESERT COMMUNITIES	(760)323-6642
Pg 169,287		Pg 62	
HIGH DESERT CENTER		HOSTELLING INTNL/ADMIN OFC	(301)495-1240
Pg 99		Pg 337	
HIGH DESERT CHILD/ADOL/FAM SRVS	(760)243-7151	HOTLINE OF SOUTHERN CALIFORNIA	(562)596-5548
Pg 99,324		Pg 200	
HIGH DESERT DOMESTIC VIOLENCE PRGM	(760)843-0701	HOUSE EAR INSTITUTE	(213)483-4431
Pg 14,27,200,267		Pg 81,169,245	
HIGH DESERT HOME HEALTH & HOSPICE	(760)366-6424	HOUSE OF HOPE/SOROPTIMIST	(951)849-9491
Pg 62,276		Pg 99	
HIGH DESERT HOMELESS SERVICES	(760)245-5991	HOUSE OF RUTH/CLAREMONT.	(909)623-4364
Pg 186,341,344		Pg 14,200	
HIGH DESERT VET CENTER	(760)261-5925	HOUSING & URBAN DEV	(800)669-9777
Pg 51,308		Pg 200,211	
HIGH DESERT YOUTH CENTER	(760)245-7103	HOUSING CALIFORNIA	(916)447-0503
Pg 336		Pg 211	
HIGH HOPES HEAD INJURY PRGM.	(949)733-0044	HUD USER CLEARINGHOUSE	(800)245-2691
Pg 81		Pg 207	
HIGHGROVE HEAD START/ST PRESCH	(951)352-8290	HUMAN GROWTH FOUNDATION	(800)451-6434
Pg 35		Pg 81,169	
HIGHLAND HEAD START	(909)425-0785	HUNTINGTON DISEASE SOCIETY	(888)443-7252
Pg 35		Pg 169,267	
HIGHLAND PALMS HEALTHCARE CTR	(909)862-0611	HUNTINGTON'S DISEASE SOCIETY/NATL	(800)345-4372
Pg 280		Pg 169	
HIGHLAND SENIOR CENTER	(909)862-8104		
Pg 287			
HIGHLAND STATE PRESCHOOL	(951)788-7292		
Pg 36			
HIGHLANDER CHILDREN'S SRVS	(951)343-2536	**I**	
Pg 43,324			
HIGHWAY REPORTS.		I AM NEW LIFE RANCH	(951)767-2575
Pg 200		Pg 100	
HILL-BURTON FREE MED CARE PRGM	(301)443-5656	I CAN COPE.	(951)683-6415
Pg 169,192		Pg 267	
HILLVIEW ACRES CHILDREN'S HOME	(909)628-1272	I CAN COPE EDUCATION SERIES	(915)353-4755
Pg 324		Pg 267	
HISTIOCYTOSIS ASSOCIATION.	(856)589-6606	IBS COMMUNITY HEALTH CARE CLINIC	(909)881-6146
Pg 169		Pg 169	
HOLLYHOCK HOUSE	(323)644-6269	IDEAL CARE & HEALTH SRVS, INC.	(909)865-0191
Pg 336		Pg 100	
HOLY FAMILY CATHOLIC CHURCH.	(760)244-9180	IDYLLWILD PINES CAMP & CONFERENCE CTR.	(951)659-2605
Pg 120		Pg 22	
HOLY FAMILY SERVICES	(714)528-6300	IDYLLWILD RANGER STATION	(909)382-2921
Pg 3,255		Pg 22	
HOME DELIVERED MEALS/ADELANTO	(760)246-7736	IMMIGRATION & NATURALIZATION SVC	
Pg 297		Pg 214	
HOME DELIVERED MEALS/LUCERNE VLY.	(760)248-2248	IMMIGRATION CENTER FOR WOMEN/CHILDREN	(213)614-1165
Pg 297		Pg 15,27	
HOME DELIVERED MEALS/TRONA.	(760)372-5889	IMMIGRATION EXPRESS	(800)985-1234
Pg 297		Pg 141,214	
HOME ENERGY ASSIST PRGM (HEAP)	(916)576-7109	IMPACT	(877)322-7299
Pg 120,153		Pg 81,245	
HOME GARDENS HEAD START/ST PRESCH	(951)549-8492	IMPACT DRUG/ALCOHOL TREATMNT CTR	(626)798-0884
Pg 36		Pg 100	
HOME IMPROVEMENT PROGRAM	(951)351-0700	IMPOTENCE/URINARY INCONTINENCE	(800)843-4315
Pg 207,287		Pg 169	
		INA ARBUCKLE HEAD START/ST PRESCH	
		Pg 36	

INCEST SURVIVORS ANONYMOUS	(562)428-5599
Pg 15,27	
INCREDABLES SPECIAL NEEDS PROGRAM	(909)477-2782
Pg 81,245,314,337	
INDIAN CHILD & FAMILY SERVICES	
Pg 4,27,51,141	
INDIAN HEALTH, INC.	(951)849-4761
Pg 288,297	
INDIAN RESERVATION NUTRITION PRGM	(951)676-6810
Pg 297	
INDIO COMMUNITY CENTER	(760)347-4263
Pg 337	
INDIO NURSING & REHAB CENTER	(760)347-0750
Pg 81	
INDIO SENIOR CENTER	(760)391-4170
Pg 288	
INFANT DEVELOPMENT ASSN OF CALIF	(916)453-8801
Pg 81,245	
INFANT FAMILY SERVICES	
Pg 81,246	
INLAND AGENCY.	(951)241-8723
Pg 169,288,316,324	
INLAND AIDS PROJECT	(951)224-8314
Pg 9,267	
INLAND BEHAV & HEALTH SERVICES	(909)881-6146
Pg 52,100,169,187,246,324	
INLAND CAREGIVER RESOURCE CENTER	(909)514-1404
Pg 81	
INLAND CHRISTIAN HOME	(909)983-0084
Pg 280	
INLAND COUNTIES HEALTH SYSTEMS	
Pg 169,288	
INLAND COUNTIES LEGAL SRVS/INDIO	(800)226-4257
Pg 218	
INLAND COUNTIES LEGAL SRVS/R.C.	(909)980-0982
Pg 218	
INLAND COUNTIES LEGAL SRVS/RIV	(951)368-2555
Pg 218	
INLAND COUNTIES LEGAL SRVS/SAN BRD	(909)884-8615
Pg 218	
INLAND COUNTIES LEGAL SRVS/V VLY	(760)241-7073
Pg 218	
INLAND EMPIRE CREDIT UNION	(909)865-2655
Pg 154	
INLAND EMPIRE HEALTH PLAN	**(800)440-4347**
Pg 170,171	
INLAND EMPIRE LATINO LAWYERS ASSOC.	(951)369-3009
Pg 218	
INLAND EMPIRE LIGHTHOUSE FOR THE BLIND	(909)884-3121
Pg 82,238	
INLAND EMPIRE SMALL BUSINESS DEV.	(760)864-1311
Pg 154	
INLAND EMPIRE UNITED WAY	(909)888-9011
Pg 154,246,314	
INLAND EMPIRE WEST CONSERV DIST	(909)799-7407
Pg 337	
INLAND FAIR HOUSING & MEDIATION	(760)256-7779
Pg 207,219	
INLAND HOSPICE ADULT PRGM	(909)399-3289
Pg 62,246,267	
INLAND REGIONAL CENTER	(909)890-3000
Pg 82	
INLAND TEMPORARY HOMES	(909)796-6381
Pg 120,187	
INLAND VLY DRUG/ALCOHOL RECOVERY	(909)932-1069
Pg 43,100,324	
INSIGHT COUNSELING	(949)707-5100
Pg 52,100,112,246	
INSPECTOR GENERAL'S HOTLINE	
Pg 200	
INSTITUTE FOR BLACK PARENTING	(951)274-2800
Pg 4,141,246	
INSTITUTE FOR FAMILIES.	(323)361-4649
Pg 82,238	
INSTITUTE OF MULTISENSORY LEARNING	(916)418-5100
Pg 134	
INSTITUTE ON DOMESTIC VIOLENCE	(877)643-8222
Pg 15	
INSTITUTE/STUDY OF ADULT LITERACY	(814)863-3777
Pg 233	

INTEGRATED LEARNING INSTITUTE.	(760)772-9019
Pg 82,316	
INTEGRATED NURSING	(951)657-2135
Pg 280	
INTER VALLEY HEALTH PLAN.	(800)500-7018
Pg 288	
INTERNAL REVENUE SERVICE (IRS).	(949)389-4002
Pg 154,288	
INTERNATIONAL CHILD ABUSE NETWORK	(888)224-4226
Pg 15,27,246	
INTERNATL ASSN EATING DISORDER	(800)800-8126
Pg 112	
INTERNATL CHRISTIAN ADOPTION	(951)695-3336
Pg 4	
INTERNATL DYSLEXIA ASSN	(410)296-0232
Pg 82,200,233	
INTERNATL SOUNDEX REUNION REGISTER	(888)886-4777
Pg 246	
IRS HELPLINES.	(800)829-1040
Pg 154	

J

JACKSON TERRACE APARTMENTS	(760)347-1718
Pg 211	
JAMBOREE HOUSING CORPORATION.	(949)263-8676
Pg 211,280	
JAMES A. VENABLE COMMUNITY CENTER	(951)922-1097
Pg 288	
JAMES L. BRULTE SENIOR CTR	(909)477-2782
Pg 120,288	
JANET GOESKE CENTER	(951)351-8800
Pg 207,288	
JAPAN BUSINESS ASSN/SO CALIF	(310)515-9522
Pg 142	
JEFFEREY OWENS COMMUNITY CENTER	
Pg 267,324	
JEFFERSON HEAD START/ST PRESCH	(951)340-1526
Pg 36	
JEFFERSON TRANSITIONAL PROGRAMS	(951)686-5484
Pg 82,134	
JENESSE CENTER.	(800)479-7328
Pg 15	
JEWELS FOR KIDS.	(888)770-7456
Pg 246,314	
JEWISH FAMILY SERVICE OF THE DESERT	(760)325-4088
Pg 52,63,288	
JOB ACCOMMODATION NETWORK	(800)526-7234
Pg 82,134	
JOB CORPS INFORMATION HOTLINE	(510)832-2549
Pg 134,324	
JOB OPPORTUNITIES FOR THE BLIND	(410)659-9314
Pg 82,134	
JOBS AND EMPLOY SRVS/ONE-STOP	
Pg 134	
JOBS AND EMPLOYMENT SERVICES	(909)854-4000
Pg 134 - 135,324	
JOHN TRACY CLINIC	(800)522-4582
Pg 82	
JOHN WAYNE AIRPORT/O.C.	(949)252-5200
Pg 304	
JORDAN OUTREACH MINISTRIES INTERNATL	(760)398-3352
Pg 120	
JOSHUA TREE COMMUNITY CENTER	(760)366-8415
Pg 120	
JOSHUA TREE KID'S CLUB	(760)366-0378
Pg 337	
JOSHUA TREE NATL PARK ASSOC.	(760)367-5525
Pg 337	
JOSLYN SENIOR CTR/COVE COMM	(760)340-3220
Pg 288	
JOSLYN SENIOR CTR/REDLANDS	(909)798-7550
Pg 288	
JTPA.	
Pg 135	
JTPA/JOBS AND EMPLOYMENT SRVS	
Pg 135	
JULIAN YOUTH ACADEMY	(800)494-2200
Pg 324	

JUNIOR ACHIEVEMENT OF SO CALIF . . . . (323)957-1818
Pg 337
JURUPA ADULT EDUCATION . . . . (951)222-7739
Pg 135,233
JURUPA MOUNTAINS CULTURAL CENTER . . . . (951)685-5818
Pg 337
JURUPA UNIFIED SCHOOL DIST . . . . (951)360-4149
Pg 36
JUST FOR SENIORS . . . . (909)558-6618
Pg 288
JUVENILE DIABETES RESEARCH FNDN . . . . (800)533-2873
Pg 170,200,246
JUVENILE JUSTICE CLEARINGHOUSE . . . . (800)851-3420
Pg 43,219,317,325

K

KAIROS PRISON MINISTRY & KAIROS OUTSIDE . . . . (760)772-0330
Pg 43,267
KAISER PERMANENTE . . . . (951)248-4000
Pg 112
KAISER PERMANENTE/CARES FOR KIDS . . . .
Pg 170
KAISER PERMANENTE/CHEMICAL DEP . . . . (909)427-5128
Pg 100
KAISER PERMANENTE/HOME HEALTH . . . . (951)358-2600
Pg 276
KAISER PERMANENTE/HOSPICE . . . . (909)609-3838
Pg 63
KAISER PERMANENTE/MEDICAL CTR . . . . (909)427-5000
Pg 192 - 193
KAY CENICEROS SENIOR CENTER . . . .
Pg 288
KEYSTONE SCHOOLS . . . . (951)785-0504
Pg 82
KIDNEY & UROLOGIC DISEASES FNDN . . . .
Pg 170
KIDNEY FNDN YOUTH CAMP . . . .
Pg 22
KIDNEY FOUNDATION . . . .
Pg 170
KIDS WISH NETWORK . . . . (727)937-3600
Pg 246
KIDSAID . . . .
Pg 63,267,337
KIDSNCARE/CHILD DEV SRVS . . . . (909)384-1492
Pg 36,246
KIDSPEACE . . . . (800)257-3223
Pg 52,200,247
KINECTA FEDERAL CREDIT UNION . . . . (800)854-9846
Pg 154
KINSHIP CENTER . . . . (909)798-9547
Pg 4,52,247
KNOTTS FAMILY AGENCY . . . . (909)880-0600
Pg 4,27,255,325
KOINONIA FOSTER HOMES, INC. . . . . (909)890-2381
Pg 4,27
KRISTIE'S PLACE . . . . (714)408-9781
Pg 170,247,267,337

L

L.A. CO. INFO/OPERATOR . . . . (213)974-1234
Pg 200
L.A. FAMILY HISTORY LIBRARY . . . . (310)474-9990
Pg 226
L.A. INTERNATIONAL AIRPORT . . . . (310)646-5252
Pg 304
L.A. ZOO . . . . (323)644-4200
Pg 337
L.I.F.T. . . . . (714)749-4283
Pg 325,337
L.U.N.A. RECOVERY . . . . (562)693-0400
Pg 325
LA LECHE LEAGUE . . . .
Pg 146,247,267
LA LECHE LEAGUE INTERNATL . . . . (800)525-3243
Pg 146,247,267

LA QUINTA COMMUNITY CENTER . . . . (760)564-9921
Pg 337
LA QUINTA SENIOR CENTER . . . . (760)564-0096
Pg 121,288
LA VISTA ALCOHOL/DRUG RECOVERY CTR . . . . (877)316-9477
Pg 100
LA VISTA WOMEN'S RECOVERY HOME . . . . (951)925-8450
Pg 100
LAKE ELSINORE SENIOR CTR . . . . (951)674-2526
Pg 289
LAKEVIEW APARTMENTS . . . . (951)674-6004
Pg 211
LAMAZE INTERNATIONAL . . . . (800)368-4404
Pg 146
LATINO COMMISSION COUNSELING . . . . (760)398-9000
Pg 52
LAUBACH LANGUAGE DEVELOPMENT CLASSES . . . . . (760)247-6494
Pg 233
LAURA'S HOUSE . . . . (949)361-3775
Pg 15,28,52,247
LAUREL CONVALESCENT CENTER . . . . (909)822-8066
Pg 82
LAW ENFORCEMENT CANCER SUPPORT FNDN . . . . . . (888)456-5327
Pg 170
LAW LIBRARY FOR SAN BERNARDINO CO. . . . . (909)944-5106
Pg 219,226
LAW OFFICES OF THE PUBLIC DEFENDER . . . . (951)358-4134
Pg 219
LAWS SUPPORT CENTER . . . . (323)294-5204
Pg 43,325
LAWYER REFERRAL SERVICE . . . . (909)483-0548
Pg 200,219
LAZY CREEK RECREATIONAL CENTER . . . . (951)679-8092
Pg 337
LDS FAMILY SERVICES . . . . (909)824-0480
Pg 4,52,146,255
LEAD POISONING . . . .
Pg 170
LEAGUE OF WOMEN VOTERS/CLAREMONT . . . . (909)624-9457
Pg 267
LEE/SHARIKIABOYS & GIRLS CLUB/HEAD START . . . . . (909)381-4294
Pg 36
LEGACY POST ACUTE REHAB CENTER . . . . (909)885-0268
Pg 82
LEGAL PROTECTION FOR WOMEN . . . . (323)721-9882
Pg 15,219
LESBIAN & GAY PSYCH ASSN OF SO CALIF . . . . (310)288-3465
Pg 52
LEUKEMIA & LYMPHOMA SOCIETY, THE . . . . (888)535-9300
Pg 170
LIBERTY GODPARENT HOME . . . . (888)760-5433
Pg 4,146,255
LIFE ADOPTION SERVICES . . . . (714)838-5433
Pg 4
LIFE CENTER PREGNANCY COUNSELING . . . . (714)835-5433
Pg 146,255
LIFE CHOICE OF HEMET . . . . (951)652-3111
Pg 146,255,268
LIFE SERVICES, INC. . . . . (818)547-0585
Pg 154,289
LIFEHOUSE CARE CONVALESCENT . . . . (951)685-1531
Pg 280
LIFELINE SYSTEMS, INC. . . . . (800)380-3111
Pg 170,289
LIGHTHOUSE FOR THE BLIND . . . .
Pg 82
LIGHTHOUSE INTERNATIONAL . . . . (800)829-0500
Pg 82,200,239
LILLY HILL APTS . . . . (760)326-2433
Pg 211
LINCOLN DEVELOPMENT CENTER . . . . (909)983-9803
Pg 82
LINCOLN INFANT CENTER . . . . (951)684-3082
Pg 36,255
LINDA VALLEY CARE CENTER . . . . (909)796-0235
Pg 280
LITERACY NETWORK OF GREATER L.A. . . . . (323)761-8888
Pg 233,314
LITTLE PEOPLE OF AMERICA . . . . (888)572-2001
Pg 83

LIVING BANK, THE . . . . (800)528-2971
Pg 170

LIVING IN THE HERE AND NOW . . . . (909)865-9555
Pg 268

LIVING WATERS . . . . (760)247-6488
Pg 121

LOCKS OF LOVE . . . . (561)833-7332
Pg 83,170

LOMA LINDA BEHAV HEALTH CTR. . . . . (800)752-5999
Pg 100,101

LOMA LINDA CHILDREN'S CENTER . . . . (909)558-4568
Pg 36

LOMA LINDA CTR/HEALTH PROMOTION. . . . .
Pg 170

LOMA LINDA OUTPATIENT SURGERY CTR . . . . . . (909)558-2867
Pg 170

LOMA LINDA UNIV MEDICAL CTR. . . . .
Pg 63,193,276

LOMA LINDA UNIV PSYCH SRVS CLINIC. . . . . . . (909)558-8576
Pg 52,325

LOMA LINDA UNIV SCH/DENTISTRY . . . . (909)558-4222
Pg 67

LOMA LINDA UNIV/MARRIAGE/FAMILY . . . . (909)558-4934
Pg 15,28,52,63,100

LONG-TERM CARE OMBUDSMAN . . . . (800)334-9473
Pg 280

LONG-TERM CARE OMBUDSMAN/CRISIS . . . . . . (714)479-0107
Pg 280,289

LONGFELLOW HEAD START/ST PRESCH . . . . (951)788-7335
Pg 36

LORD OF LIFE LUTHERAN CHURCH . . . . (951)924-4887
Pg 100

LOU GEHRIG'S DISEASE . . . .
Pg 83,170

LOUISIANA CENTER FOR THE BLIND . . . . (800)234-4166
Pg 83,239

LUCERNE VALLEY SENIOR CENTER. . . . . (760)248-2248
Pg 289

LUCERNE VLY DOMESTIC VIOL OUTREACH . . . . . (760)248-2064
Pg 15

LUGGAGE OF LOVE . . . . (805)804-5952
Pg 4,344

LUMETRA (FORMERLY CMRI). . . . . (800)841-1602
Pg 170

LUNG ASSOCIATION. . . . .
Pg 170

LUNG DISEASE SUPPORT GROUP. . . . .
Pg 268

LUNG LINE INFORMATION SERVICE. . . . . (877)225-5654
Pg 170

LUPUS FOUNDATION OF AMERICA, INC. . . . . . . (202)349-1155
Pg 170,268

LUPUS FOUNDATION OF SO. CALIF . . . . (858)278-2788
Pg 171,268

LUPUS INTERNATIONAL. . . . . (949)833-2121
Pg 171,268

LUPUS SUPPORT NETWORK. . . . . (909)874-9257
Pg 171,268

LUQUE COMM & SENIOR CENTER. . . . . (909)370-5087
Pg 289

LUTHER VILLAGE & LUTHER GLEN . . . . (909)797-9183
Pg 22

LUTHERAN SOCIAL SRVS. . . . . (909)866-5721
Pg 52,83

LUTHERAN SOCIAL SRVS/SHELTER PRGM . . . . . (951)689-7847
Pg 121,187

LYMPHOMA RESEARCH FNDN . . . . (310)204-7040
Pg 171

L'TANYA JAMES MINISTRIES . . . . (661)265-9784
Pg 120

M

M-2 MATCH-TWO PRISONER OUTREACH . . . . . . (909)606-5036
Pg 43,314

M.A.D.D.. . . . . (714)838-6199
Pg 101

MAMMOGRAPHY/LOW COST . . . .
Pg 171

MANAGED RISK MEDICAL INSURANCE BOARD . . . . (916)324-4695
Pg 171

MANOR CARE NURSING AND REHAB . . . . (951)925-9171
Pg 83

MANORCARE HEALTH SERVICES . . . . (760)341-0261
Pg 83

MARCH A.F.B./FAMILY SUPPORT . . . . (951)655-5350
Pg 52,121,135,154,308

MARCH OF DIMES BIRTH DEFECTS FNDN . . . . . . (213)637-5050
Pg 146,171,255

MARINE CORP AIR GROUND COMBAT CTR. . . . . . (760)830-7225
Pg 135,308

MARINE CORPS AIR GROUND COMBAT CTR. . . . . (760)830-6323
Pg 121,308

MARTA BIG BEAR LAKE . . . . (909)878-5200
Pg 304

MARTHA'S VILLAGE & KITCHEN, INC. . . . . (760)347-4741
Pg 121,172,187

MARY MAGDALENE PROJECT, INC. . . . . (818)988-4970
Pg 15,341

MARY PHILLIPS SENIOR CENTER . . . . (951)694-6464
Pg 289

MARYGOLD GARDENS APARTMENTS . . . . (909)822-8046
Pg 211

MARY'S MERCY CENTER . . . . (909)889-2558
Pg 121,187

MARY'S SHELTER . . . . (714)730-0930
Pg 255

MASADA HOMES. . . . . (909)428-2366
Pg 52

MASONIC HOME FOR CHILDREN . . . . (626)251-2231
Pg 28

MASTER'S TABLE FOOD MINISTRY . . . . (951)686-5233
Pg 121

MATERNITY INFORMATION . . . . (909)980-2229
Pg 146,247

MATRIX INSTITUTE ON ADDICTIONS . . . . (310)478-8305
Pg 101

MAVERICK HOUSE FOUNDATION INC.. . . . . (626)841-8259
Pg 101

MAYOR'S COMMISSION ON AGING . . . . (951)826-5372
Pg 289

MAYWOOD MANOR COOPERATIVE SRVS. . . . . . . (323)773-5175
Pg 280

MCGEORGE SCHOOL OF LAW . . . .
Pg 15,219

MCKINLEY CHILDREN'S CENTER . . . . (909)599-1227
Pg 5,28,325,341

MCNEAL NUTRITIONAL . . . . (800)522-8243
Pg 172

MEAD VALLEY COMMUNITY CENTER . . . .
Pg 289

MEAD VALLEY COMMUNITY COMPLEX . . . . (951)657-0686
Pg 247,297,337

MEALS ON WHEELS . . . .
Pg 289

MEALS ON WHEELS/BIG BEAR LAKE . . . . (909)866-5233
Pg 297

MEALS ON WHEELS/PALM DESERT . . . . (760)340-3220
Pg 297

MEALS ON WHEELS/RIVERSIDE . . . . (951)683-7151
Pg 297

MEALS ON WHEELS/SUN CITY . . . . (951)679-0119
Pg 297

MEALS ON WHEELS/UPLAND. . . . . (909)981-0377
Pg 297

MECCA STATE PRESCHOOL . . . . (760)396-2800
Pg 36

MEDI-CAL DENTIST . . . . (909)483-1177
Pg 67 - 70

MEDI-CAL FIELD OFFICE . . . . (909)383-4192
Pg 172

MEDI-CAL OPTICAL SURGERY . . . . (909)982-8846
Pg 239

MEDI-CAL OPTOMETRIST. . . . . (951)849-2020
Pg 239 - 240

MEDIATION RESOURCES . . . . (909)621-0092
Pg 219

MEDIC ALERT FOUNDATION, INTL . . . . (888)633-4298
Pg 289

MEDICAL BOARD OF CALIFORNIA . . . . (916)263-2382	MO VAN FRIENDS-MORENO VALLEY . . . . (951)358-9202
Pg 146,172	Pg 304
MEDICAL CTR CONVALESCENT HOSPITAL . . . . (909)884-4781	MOBILE HOME OMBUDSMAN. . . . . (800)952-5275
Pg 83	Pg 207
MEDICAL SOCIETY.	MODERN TECHNOLOGY SCHOOL . . . . (714)418-9100
Pg 9,172	Pg 135
MEDICALLY INDIGENT SERVICES	MODEST NEEDS FOUNDATION. . . . . (212)463-7042
Pg 172	Pg 121,268
MEDICARE & MEDICAID INFO SRVS . . . . (415)744-3602	MOJAVE VALLEY VOLUNTEER HOSPICE . . . . (760)256-5706
Pg 172,289	Pg 63,172
MEDICARE TELEPHONE HOTLINE . . . . (800)633-4227	MONTCLAIR COMMUNITY CENTER . . . . (909)399-3173
Pg 172,200,289	Pg 172,289,337
MEDICARE/MEDICAID COMPLAINTS. . . . . (800)447-8477	MONTCLAIR HUMAN SRVS DIVISION . . . . (909)625-9460
Pg 201	Pg 121,247,297
MENIERE'S DISEASE NETWORK	MONTCLAIR MANOR CARE CENTER . . . . (909)626-1294
Pg 172	Pg 83
MENIFEE STATE PRESCHOOL . . . . (951)672-6478	MONTE VISTA PARK REC CTR . . . . (909)627-7577
Pg 36	Pg 338
MENIFEE VALLEY COMMUNITY CUPBOARD . . . . (951)301-4414	MONTEREY PALMS HEALTHCARE CENTER. . . . . (760)776-7700
Pg 121	Pg 83
MENIFEE VALLEY MEDICAL CENTER . . . . (951)679-8888	MORENO VALLEY ADULT SCHOOL. . . . . (951)571-4790
Pg 193	Pg 233
MENTAL HEALTH AMERICA . . . . (800)969-6642	MORENO VALLEY CITY LIBRARY. . . . . (951)413-3880
Pg 53	Pg 233
MENTAL HEALTH SYSTEMS, INC. . . . . (909)433-9824	MORENO VALLEY COMMUNITY ASSIST . . . . (951)485-7792
Pg 101	Pg 121,154
MENTORING PROGRAM.	MORENO VALLEY SENIOR CENTER . . . . (951)413-3430
Pg 325,337	Pg 289
MEN'S HEALTH NETWORK . . . . (202)543-6461	MORONGO BASIN ADULT HEALTH SRVS . . . . (760)365-9661
Pg 172	Pg 83,172,289
MERCY AIRLIFT . . . . (800)637-2945	MORONGO BASIN COALITION/ADULT LIT . . . . (760)367-1146
Pg 121,304,314	Pg 233
MERCY HOUSE. . . . . (909)391-2630	MORONGO BASIN COUNSELING & RECOVERY . . . . (760)365-3022
Pg 121,187	Pg 53,102,172
MERCY HOUSE TRANSITIONAL LIVING . . . . (714)836-7188	MORONGO BASIN UNITY HOME . . . . (760)366-9663
Pg 9,187	Pg 15
MERCYCARE, INC.. . . . . (888)776-3729	MORONGO INDIAN NUTRITION PRGM. . . . .
Pg 172	Pg 297
MERRI MIXERS . . . . (909)384-5426	MOSES HOUSE MINISTRIES . . . . (866)606-6737
Pg 83	Pg 5,121,146,256
MESA COUNSELING CENTER . . . . (909)421-9200	MOTHERS AGAINST DRUNK DRIVERS . . . . (760)772-6237
Pg 53,325	Pg 63,102
METASTIC CANCER SUPPORT GROUP . . . . (951)353-4755	MOTHERS AGAINST DRUNK DRIVING . . . .
Pg 268	Pg 63,102
METH RESOURCES . . . . (916)324-5523	MOUNT RUBIDOUX MANOR. . . . . (951)684-3154
Pg 9,101,247,268,325	Pg 280
METRO TRANSIT AUTHORITY . . . . (213)626-4455	MOUNTAIN COMMUNITIES SENIOR CTR . . . . (909)337-1824
Pg 304	Pg 289
METROLINK . . . . (800)371-5465	MOUNTAIN VIEW CLINIC . . . . (951)658-1253
Pg 304	Pg 15,28,53
MEXICAN AMER LEGAL DEFENSE & EDU . . . . (213)629-2512	MOUNTAIN VIEW COMMUNITY CHURCH . . . . (909)357-9377
Pg 214,219	Pg 122
MICHAEL'S HOUSE . . . . (760)320-5486	MOURNING STAR . . . .
Pg 101	Pg 64,247
MICHELLE'S PLACE . . . . (866)304-1280	MOURNING STAR CENTER, THE . . . . (760)836-0360
Pg 172,268,314	Pg 53,64,268,326
MICROREAD/LITERACY PROGRAM	MT. RUBIDOUX CONV HOSPITAL. . . . . (951)681-2200
Pg 233	Pg 83
MID-STEP ASSISTED LIVING	MT. SAN JACINTO CHILDREN'S SRVS . . . . (951)487-2674
Pg 280	Pg 53,247,326
MILESTONES RESIDENTIAL FACILITY . . . . (760)347-4347	MT. SAN JACINTO COLLEGE/EOPS . . . . (951)487-3295
Pg 53,193	Pg 135,326,344
MILHOUS CHILDREN'S SERVICES . . . . (530)265-9057	MT. SAN JACINTO COMMUNITY COLLEGE . . . . (951)487-3255
Pg 5,325	Pg 135
MILL CHILD DEVELOPMENT CENTER . . . . (909)885-0789	MT. VIEW STATE PRESCH. (951)788-7433
Pg 36	Pg 36
MINORITY HEALTH OUTPATIENT . . . . (562)987-7522	MULTICULTURAL AIDS RESOURCE CTR . . . . (415)777-3229
Pg 9	Pg 9
MIRAVILLA CARE CENTER . . . . (951)845-3194	MULTIPLE SCLEROSIS CLINIC/LLU. . . . . (909)558-2880
Pg 280	Pg 83,172
MISSING CHILDREN INTERNATL, INC. . . . . (714)542-8083	MULTIPLE SCLEROSIS FOUNDATION . . . . (800)441-7055
Pg 28,247,325	Pg 201
MISSION BELL PRESCHOOL	MULTIPLE SCLEROSIS GREATER RIVERSIDE . . . . (951)544-1441
Pg 36	Pg 268
MISSION NURSING CENTER . . . . (951)688-2222	MULTIPLE SCLEROSIS SOCIETY. . . . .
Pg 280	Pg 172
MISSION VILLAS . . . . (951)276-1952	MULTIPLE SCLEROSIS SUPPORT GRP . . . . (909)596-7733
Pg 280	Pg 268
MIZELL SENIOR CENTER . . . . (760)323-5689	MURRIETA COMMUNITY SRVS DEPT . . . . (951)304-7275
Pg 289	Pg 338

MURRIETA HEAD START/ST PRESCH	. . . .	(951)600-5680
Pg 37		
MURRIETA PUBLIC LIBRARY	. . . .	(951)304-2665
Pg 226		
MUSICIANS WORKSHOP ARTS & MUSIC	. . . .	(951)678-2517
Pg 338		
MYASTHENIA GRAVIS FNDN/CALIF	. . . .	(323)887-0056
Pg 172		
MYASTHENIA GRAVIS FNDN/NATL	. . . .	(877)596-1491
Pg 173		

N

NAACP	. . . .	
Pg 142		
NAADAC (ASSN FOR ADDICTION PROF)	. . . .	(800)548-0497
Pg 102		
NAMI-CHINO VALLEY	. . . .	(909)923-7517
Pg 268		
NAMI-COACHELLA VALLEY	. . . .	(888)881-6264
Pg 268		
NAMI-LOS ANGELES	. . . .	(310)889-7200
Pg 53,247,269		
NAMI-LOS ANGELES COUNTY	. . . .	(562)435-2264
Pg 269		
NAMI-MT. SAN JACINTO	. . . .	(951)765-1850
Pg 53,269		
NAMI-NATIONAL OFFICE	. . . .	(800)950-6264
Pg 53,269		
NAMI-SAN BERNARDINO	. . . .	(909)824-8060
Pg 269		
NAMI-TEMECULA VALLEY	. . . .	(951)672-2089
Pg 269		
NAMI-WESTERN REGION	. . . .	(951)369-1913
Pg 269		
NAR-ANON/FAMILY/HEADQUARTERS	. . . .	(310)534-8188
Pg 102,201,269		
NARCONON INTERNATIONAL	. . . .	(323)962-2404
Pg 102,201,247		
NARCONON SAN DIEGO COUNTY	. . . .	(760)782-0471
Pg 102		
NARCONON SOUTHERN CALIF.	. . . .	(949)675-8988
Pg 102		
NARCOTIC EDU FNDN OF AMERICA	. . . .	(661)775-6960
Pg 102,269		
NARCOTICS ANONYMOUS	. . . .	(626)359-0084
Pg 102,201,269		
NATIONAL CENTER ON LIFE PLANNING	. . . .	(888)881-8113
Pg 83		
NATIONAL CENTER ON SENIOR TRANSPORTATION	. . . . .	(866)528-6278
Pg 290,304		
NATIONAL FNDN FOR CREDIT COUNSELING	. . . .	(800)388-2227
Pg 154,207,211		
NATIONAL GUARD FAMILY PROGRAM	. . . .	(703)607-5411
Pg 154,308		
NATL ADOPTION CENTER.	. . . .	(215)735-9988
Pg 5		
NATL AGING INFORMATION CENTER	. . . .	(800)677-1116
Pg 290		
NATL AIDS HOTLINE	. . . .	
Pg 9		
NATL ALLIANCE FOR HISPANIC HEALTH	. . . .	(866)783-2645
Pg 64,142,146,173		
NATL ALLIANCE ON MENTAL ILLNESS	. . . .	
Pg 269		
NATL ASSN FOR CONTINENCE	. . . .	(843)377-0900
Pg 173		
NATL ASSN FOR HISPANIC ELDERLY	. . . .	(626)564-1988
Pg 142,290		
NATL ASSN FOR MALES WITH EATING DISORDERS	. . . .	(877)780-0080
Pg 112		
NATL ASSN FOR SHOPLIFTING PREVENTION	. . . . . .	(800)848-9595
Pg 102,269		
NATL ASSN FOR THE DUALLY DIAGNOSED	. . . .	(800)331-5362
Pg 53,83		
NATL ASSN OF ANOREXIA NERVOSA & ASSOCIATED DISORDE		
. . . .	(630)577-1330
Pg 112,269		

NATL ASSN OF HEARING LOSS	. . . .	(301)657-2248
Pg 83		
NATL ASSN/ADVANCE/COLORED PEOPLE	. . . .	(909)887-7411
Pg 142,219		
NATL ASSN/CHILDREN/ALCOHOLICS	. . . .	(888)554-2627
Pg 103		
NATL ASSN/EDU OF YOUNG CHILDREN	. . . .	(800)424-2460
Pg 37		
NATL ASSN/FOR HOME CARE	. . . .	(202)547-7424
Pg 276,290		
NATL ASSN/PARENTS OF CHILDREN WITH VISUAL IMPAIRME	(800)562-6265
Pg 84,240		
NATL ASYLEE INFO & REFERRAL LINE	. . . .	(800)354-0365
Pg 201,214		
NATL BIPOLAR FOUNDATION.	. . . .	
Pg 53		
NATL BLACK UNITED FUND, INC..	. . . .	(973)643-5122
Pg 142		
NATL BRAIN INJURY ASSOCIATION	. . . .	
Pg 84		
NATL BRAIN TUMOR FOUNDATION	. . . .	(800)934-2873
Pg 201,269		
NATL BREAST CANCER COALITION	. . . .	(800)622-2838
Pg 173		
NATL CENTER FOR PTSD	. . . .	(802)296-6300
Pg 53,308		
NATL CENTER FOR STUTTERING	. . . .	(800)221-2483
Pg 201		
NATL CENTER FOR SUBSTANCE ABUSE	. . . .	(800)662-4357
Pg 103,201		
NATL CENTER FOR VICTIMS OF CRIME	. . . .	(800)394-2255
Pg 15,219		
NATL CENTER ON DEAFNESS	. . . .	(818)677-2054
Pg 84		
NATL CHILD ABUSE HOTLINE.	. . . .	
Pg 28		
NATL CHILD CARE INFORMATION CTR	. . . .	(800)616-2242
Pg 37		
NATL CHILD SAFETY COUNCIL	. . . .	(800)222-1464
Pg 28,326		
NATL CHILDHOOD CANCER FNDN	. . . .	(800)458-6223
Pg 173,248,269		
NATL CLEARINGHOUSE/ALCOHOL/DRUG	. . . .	(800)729-6686
Pg 103		
NATL CLEARINGHOUSE/CHILD ABUSE	. . . .	(800)394-3366
Pg 28		
NATL CNCL ON CHILD ABUSE/FAM VIOL	. . . .	(202)429-6695
Pg 201		
NATL COMM/PRESERVE SOCIAL SECURITY AND MEDI-CAL	(800)998-0180
Pg 290		
NATL COMM/PREVENT CHILD ABUSE	. . . .	
Pg 28		
NATL COMMUNITY RENAISSANCE	. . . .	(909)483-2444
Pg 211		
NATL COUNCIL ON ALCOHOL/DRUG DEP	. . . .	(800)622-2255
Pg 103		
NATL COUNCIL ON THE AGING.	. . . .	(202)479-1200
Pg 290		
NATL CRIMINAL JUSTICE REFERENCE	. . . .	(800)851-3420
Pg 15,103,219		
NATL CTR FOR CHRONIC DISEASE PREV AND HEALTH PROMO	
. . . .	(800)232-4636
Pg 173		
NATL CTR FOR COMP/ALTERNATIVE MED	. . . .	(888)644-6226
Pg 173		
NATL CTR FOR STUTTERING	. . . .	(212)532-1460
Pg 84		
NATL CTR/MISSING AND EXPLOITED CHILDREN	. . . . .	(800)843-5678
Pg 28,326		
NATL CTR/MISSING/EXPLOIT/CHILDREN	. . . .	(714)508-0150
Pg 28,326		
NATL DAIRY COUNCIL.	. . . .	(847)803-2000
Pg 112		
NATL DIABETES INFO CLEARINGHOUSE	. . . .	(800)860-8747
Pg 173		
NATL DIGESTIVE DISEASE INFO	. . . .	(866)569-1162
Pg 173		
NATL DISSEMINATION CTR FOR CHILDREN WITH DISABILIT	(800)695-0285
Pg 84		

NATL DOMESTIC VIOLENCE HOTLINE	(800)799-7233	
Pg 16,201		
NATL DOWN SYNDROME CONGRESS	(800)232-6372	
Pg 84		
NATL DOWN SYNDROME SOCIETY	(800)221-4602	
Pg 84		
NATL EATING DISORDERS ASSN.	(206)382-3587	
Pg 112		
NATL EYE CARE PROJECT		
Pg 240		
NATL FAMILY PARTNERSHIP (NFP)	(305)856-4886	
Pg 103		
NATL FIBROMYALGIA ASSN.	(714)921-0150	
Pg 173,270		
NATL HEAD INJURY FOUNDATION		
Pg 84		
NATL HEADACHE FOUNDATION	(888)643-5552	
Pg 173		
NATL HEALTH FEDERATION	(626)357-2181	
Pg 173		
NATL HEALTH INFORMATION CENTER	(800)336-4797	
Pg 173		
NATL HEALTH LAW PRGM.	(310)204-6010	
Pg 219		
NATL HEART, LUNG & BLOOD INSTITUTE	(301)592-8573	
Pg 173		
NATL HIV/AIDS CLINICIANS CONSULT CTR	(415)206-8700	
Pg 173		
NATL HUMAN TRAFFICKING RESOURCE CTR	(888)373-7888	
Pg 16,201		
NATL HYDROCEPHALUS FOUNDATION	(888)857-3434	
Pg 174,270		
NATL IMMUNIZATION INFO HOTLINE.	(800)232-4636	
Pg 174,201		
NATL INDIAN COUNCIL ON AGING, INC.	(951)369-8581	
Pg 135,290		
NATL INHALANT PREVENTION COALITION	(800)269-4237	
Pg 103		
NATL INST ALLERGY/INFECTIOUS DISEASES	(301)496-5717	
Pg 174		
NATL INST DEAFNESS/COMM DISORDERS	(800)241-1044	
Pg 174		
NATL INST FOR LITERACY HOTLINE.	(800)228-8813	
Pg 233		
NATL INST OF CHILD HEALTH & HUMAN DEV	(800)370-2943	
Pg 201		
NATL INST OF ENVIRONMTL HLTH SCI	(919)541-3345	
Pg 174		
NATL INSTITUTE FOR JEWISH HOSPICE	(800)446-4448	
Pg 64,142		
NATL INSTITUTE OF MENTAL HEALTH	(301)443-4513	
Pg 53		
NATL INSTITUTE ON AGING.		
Pg 174		
NATL INSTITUTES OF HEALTH	(301)496-4000	
Pg 174		
NATL KIDNEY FNDN HOTLINE	(800)622-9010	
Pg 174,201		
NATL KIDNEY FNDN OF SO CALIF	(800)747-5527	
Pg 22,174		
NATL KIDNEY/UROLOGIC DISEASES INFO	(800)891-5390	
Pg 174		
NATL LATINO ALLIANCE FOR THE ELIMINATION	(505)224-9080	
Pg 16,142		
NATL LEAD INFO CENTER/U.S. EPA	(800)424-5323	
Pg 174,201		
NATL LEGAL STUDIES INSTITUTE & LEGAL CTR	(951)653-4240	
Pg 219		
NATL LIBRARY SRVS FOR THE BLIND & PHYSICALLY HANDI	(888)657-7323	
Pg 84,226		
NATL LIFE CENTER	(800)848-5683	
Pg 147,256		
NATL LYMPHEDEMA NETWORK	(800)541-3259	
Pg 174		
NATL MARROW DONOR PROGRAM	(800)627-7692	
Pg 174		
NATL MULTIPLE SCLEROSIS SOCIETY	(212)463-7787	
Pg 84,174 - 175		
NATL NETWORK FOR YOUTH.	(202)783-7949	
Pg 103,326		

NATL ORG DISORDERS/CORPUS CALLOSUM	(714)747-0063	
Pg 175		
NATL ORG RARE DISORDERS (NORD)	(203)744-0100	
Pg 175		
NATL ORGANIZATION/VICTIM ASSISTANCE.	(800)879-6682	
Pg 16,201,220		
NATL OSTEOPOROSIS FNDN.	(800)223-9994	
Pg 201		
NATL PARENTING INSTITUTE.	(951)694-8910	
Pg 248		
NATL PARKINSON FNDN/O.C. CHAPTER	(949)764-6998	
Pg 175		
NATL PARKINSON FOUNDATION HDQR	(800)327-4545	
Pg 175		
NATL PATIENT TRAVEL CENTER	(800)296-1217	
Pg 175		
NATL PSORIASIS FOUNDATION	(800)723-9166	
Pg 175		
NATL REFERENCE/BIOETHICS LIT.	(202)687-3885	
Pg 226		
NATL REHABILITATION INFO CENTER	(800)346-2742	
Pg 84,226		
NATL RETINITIS PIGMENTOSA FNDN		
Pg 240		
NATL REYE'S SYNDROME FNDN	(800)233-7393	
Pg 175		
NATL RUNAWAY SWITCHBOARD.	(800)786-2929	
Pg 202,326,341		
NATL SENIOR CITIZENS LAW CENTER	(202)289-6976	
Pg 220		
NATL SEXUAL ASSAULT HOTLINE	(800)656-4673	
Pg 202		
NATL SOCIETY/PREVENT BLINDNESS.		
Pg 84		
NATL SPASMODIC TORTICOLLIS ASSN	(800)487-8385	
Pg 84,175,270		
NATL SPINAL CORD INJURY ASSN.	(800)962-9629	
Pg 84,175		
NATL STROKE ASSN.	(800)787-6537	
Pg 175		
NATL STUTTERING ASSOCIATION	(800)937-8888	
Pg 84,270		
NATL SUBSTANCE ABUSE PROFESSIONALS NETWORK	(800)879-6428	
Pg 103		
NATL SUICIDE PREVENTION LIFELINE	(800)784-2433	
Pg 202		
NATL TECHNICAL INFO SERVICE.	(703)605-6050	
Pg 226		
NATL TEEN DATING ABUSE HELPLINE	(866)331-9474	
Pg 16,202		
NATL VETERANS FOUNDATION	(888)777-4443	
Pg 308		
NATL WOMEN'S HEALTH INFO CENTER.	(800)994-9662	
Pg 202		
NATL WOMEN'S HEALTH RESOURCE CTR	(877)986-9472	
Pg 175		
NAVAL HOSPITAL CAMP PENDLETON	(760)725-0063	
Pg 103,308		
NCADD/NATL CNCL ALC/DRUG DEP		
Pg 103		
NEEDLES HEAD START/STATE PRESCH	(760)326-5221	
Pg 37		
NEEDLES HOUSING AUTHORITY.	(760)326-5740	
Pg 208		
NEEDLES REGIONAL SENIOR CENTER	(760)326-4789	
Pg 290		
NEIGHBORHOOD HEALTHCARE	(951)694-9449	
Pg 175		
NEIGHBORHOOD HOUSING SRVS.	(909)884-6891	
Pg 208		
NEIGHBORHOOD PARTNERSHIP.	(909)988-5979	
Pg 280		
NEIGHBORWORKS AMERICA.	(202)220-2300	
Pg 208,211		
NEUROFIBROMATOSIS FOUNDATION		
Pg 175		
NEUROFIBROMATOSIS, INC	(800)942-6825	
Pg 175,202		
NEW DIRECTIONS, INC.	(310)914-5966	
Pg 187,309		

NEW HAVEN YOUTH & FAMILY SRVS . . . . (760)630-4035	OLIVE CREST TREATMENT CENTER. . . . . (951)686-8500
Pg 28,85	Pg 5,28,54,326 - 327
NEW HOPE CRISIS COUNSELING . . . . (714)639-4673	OLIVE GROVE MANOR I & II. . . . . (951)687-2241
Pg 54,202,270,314	Pg 280
NEW HOPE MINISTRIES. . . . . (951)845-2693	OMBUDSMAN PROGRAM . . . .
Pg 122	Pg 85,202,290
NEW HOPE VILLAGE, INC. . . . . (760)256-3656	OMNILINK/YUCAIPA . . . . (800)990-2406
Pg 122,187	Pg 304
NEW HOPE/MORENO VALLEY . . . . (951)247-6542	OMNITRANS . . . . (909)379-7100
Pg 54,64,112,248,326	Pg 304
NEW HOUSE INC. (909)881-0390	ON THE MOVE ADULT DEV CENTER. . . . . (951)779-9665
Pg 103	Pg 85
NEW LIFE BEGINNINGS . . . . (562)590-1538	ONE-STOP CENTER . . . .
Pg 187	Pg 135
NEW WINE CHURCH RETREAT, INC.. . . . . (760)248-7315	ONE-STOP CENTER/SAN BERNARDINO . . . . (909)888-7881
Pg 103	Pg 135
NEWBERRY SPRINGS SENIOR SRVS ASSN. . . . . . . (760)257-3284	ONE-STOP KIOSK/JOB BOARD . . . . (951)955-3100
Pg 290	Pg 135 - 136
NEWPORT SPORTS MUSEUM . . . . (949)721-9333	ONELEGACY . . . . (909)801-3701
Pg 338	Pg 176,240
NICOTINE ANONYMOUS/SO CALIF. . . . . (800)642-0666	ONTARIO CARE CENTER . . . . (909)984-6713
Pg 103,270	Pg 280
NICOTINE ANONYMOUS/WORLD SRVS . . . . (415)750-0328	ONTARIO CHRISTIAN CENTER . . . . (909)983-5269
Pg 104	Pg 122
NIGHTLIGHT CHRISTIAN ADOPTIONS . . . . (714)693-5437	ONTARIO CITY LIBRARY. . . . . (909)395-2004
Pg 5	Pg 226
NIKKEI HELPLINE . . . . (213)473-3030	ONTARIO HOUSING AGENCY. . . . . (909)395-2006
Pg 54,142	Pg 208
NORCO PARKS, RECREATION & SRVS . . . . (951)270-5632	ONTARIO INTERNATIONAL AIRPORT . . . . (909)937-2700
Pg 338	Pg 304
NORCO SENIOR CENTER. . . . . (951)270-5647	ONTARIO MAPLE HEAD START . . . . (909)984-4117
Pg 85	Pg 37
NORRIS COMPREHENSIVE CANCER CTR.	ONTARIO SENIOR CENTER . . . . (909)395-2021
Pg 193	Pg 290
NORTH TOWN COMMUNITY CENTER . . . . (909)941-7465	OPARC/ADULT DEVELOPMENT CTR . . . . (909)625-0213
Pg 122	Pg 85,136,290
NORTHERN CALIF TRANSLATORS ASSN . . . . (510)845-8712	OPARC/DIVERSIFIED INDUSTRIES . . . . (909)982-4090
Pg 142	Pg 85
NORTHTOWN HOUSING DEVELOPMENT . . . . (909)930-0465	OPEN DOORS SUPPORT GROUPS. . . . . (951)358-6858
Pg 122,135,208,234,338	Pg 248,270
NORTON YOUNGLOVE SENIOR CENTER . . . . (909)795-2287	OPERATION GRACE. . . . . (909)382-8540
Pg 290	Pg 187,208
NURSEFINDERS/SAN BERNARDINO . . . . (909)890-2286	OPERATION HOMEFRONT . . . . (866)424-5210
Pg 276	Pg 309
NURSING HOME HOTLINE	OPERATION PROVIDER . . . . (909)337-8585
Pg 280,290	Pg 122,154
NUTRITION FOR SENIORS	OPERATION SAFEHOUSE. . . . . (951)351-4418
Pg 297	Pg 327,342,344
NUTRITION HOTLINE	OPTIMIST YOUTH HOMES/FAMILY SRVS . . . . (323)443-3175
Pg 175	Pg 5,54,327
NUVIEW UNION SCHOOL DISTRICT . . . . (951)928-3570	OPTION HOUSE/DV INTERV & PREV. . . . . (909)381-3471
Pg 37	Pg 16,28,202
	OPTOMETRY BOARD . . . .
	Pg 240
	ORANGE EMPIRE RAILWAY MUSEUM . . . . (951)657-2605
O	Pg 338
	ORANGETREE CONVALESCENT HOSPITAL. . . . . (951)785-6060
O-ANON GENERAL SERVICE OFFICE	Pg 85
Pg 113	ORTHOPAEDIC HOSPITAL L.A. . . . . (213)742-1000
OAK GROVE CENTER . . . . (951)677-5599	Pg 85,176,193
Pg 85,104,326	ORTON DYSLEXIA SOCIETY . . . .
OASIS STATE PRESCHOOL . . . . (760)397-1000	Pg 85,234
Pg 37	OUR HOUSE . . . .
OBSESSIVE COMPULSIVE ANONYMOUS . . . . (516)739-0662	Pg 104
Pg 104	OUR LADY OF GUADALUPE. . . . . (760)396-2717
OBSESSIVE-COMPULSIVE FNDN, INC. . . . . (617)973-5801	Pg 122
Pg 54,175	OUR LADY OF HOPE FOOD PANTRY. . . . . (909)884-6375
ODYSSEY HEALTHCARE . . . . **(877)637-9432**	Pg 122
Pg 64,65	OUR LADY OF MT. CARMEL CHURCH . . . . (909)987-2717
OFFICE ON AGING/RIVERSIDE CO.	Pg 122
Pg 290	OUR LADY OF PERPETUAL HELP . . . . (951)689-8921
OFFICE ON SMOKING & HEALTH. . . . . (800)232-4636	Pg 122
Pg 176	OUR LADY OF PERPETUAL HELP/MEALS . . . .
OFFICE/MINORITY HEALTH RESOURCE. . . . . (800)444-6472	Pg 122,187
Pg 142,176	OUR LADY OF THE DESERT CATHOLIC . . . . (760)242-4427
OLD TIMERS FNDN/FONTANA . . . . (909)829-4543	Pg 122
Pg 297	OUR LADY OF VLY CATHOLIC CHURCH . . . . (951)929-6131
OLD TOWN TEMECULA SENIOR CTR	Pg 304
Pg 290	OUTREACH CONCERN, INC. . . . . (714)547-1163
OLIVE BRANCH COUNSELING CTR, INC. . . . . (909)989-9030	Pg 327
Pg 16,54,113,326	

OVERCOMERS IN CHRIST . . . . (402)573-0966
    Pg 113
OVERCOMER'S OUTREACH . . . . (800)310-3001
    Pg 104,270
OVEREATERS ANONYMOUS/HDQR . . . . (505)891-2664
    Pg 113,270
OVEREATERS ANONYMOUS/I.E. . . . . (951)715-2080
    Pg 113,270

P

P.A.D.R.E. FOUNDATION. (714)532-8330
    Pg 85,270
PACHAPPA HEAD START/ST PRESCH . . . . (951)788-7355
    Pg 37
PACIFIC AIDS EDU & TRAINING CTR. . . . . (415)597-8198
    Pg 9,176
PACIFIC AVENUE HEAD START. . . . .
    Pg 37
PACIFIC CLINICS. . . . . (626)254-5000
    Pg 54,104,188
PACIFIC CLINICS/TBS . . . . (760)416-1753
    Pg 85
PACIFIC LIFELINE . . . . (909)931-2624
    Pg 188
PACIFIC MARINE CREDIT UNION. . . . . (800)736-4500
    Pg 154 - 155
PACIFIC TRUST BANK. . . . . (951)352-5980
    Pg 155
PAL CAMP. . . . . (714)505-4692
    Pg 317
PAL COMPREHENSIVE CHILD DEV CTR . . . . (909)887-3975
    Pg 37
PALM DESERT COMMUNITY CENTER . . . . (760)568-9697
    Pg 338
PALM GROVE HEALTHCARE . . . . (951)845-3125
    Pg 281
PALM SPRINGS HEALTH CARE & REHAB . . . . . . (760)327-8541
    Pg 281
PALM SPRINGS PARKS & RECREATION . . . . (760)323-8265
    Pg 338
PALM SPRINGS PUBLIC LIBRARY . . . . (760)322-7323
    Pg 226,234
PALM SPRINGS REDEVELOP AGENCY . . . . (760)323-8264
    Pg 86,208
PALM SPRINGS SENIOR HOUSING. . . . . (800)500-7725
    Pg 281
PALM SPRINGS UNIFIED SCHOOL DIST . . . . (760)416-8090
    Pg 37,234
PALM SPRINGS USD/HEAD START/ST PRESCH/ . . . . (760)416-8090
    Pg 37
PALM TERRACE CONVALESCENT CENTER. . . . . (951)687-7330
    Pg 86
PALM VIEW STATE PRESCHOOL . . . . (760)391-9362
    Pg 37
PALO VERDE COLLEGE CHILD DEV CTR . . . . (760)922-8714
    Pg 37
PALO VERDE COMMUNITY COLLEGE . . . . (760)922-6168
    Pg 234
PALO VERDE COMMUNITY COLLEGE/EOPS . . . . (760)921-5402
    Pg 136,327,344
PALO VERDE HEAD START . . . . (760)922-8454
    Pg 37
PALO VERDE VALLEY LIBRARY DISTRICT. . . . . . . (760)922-5371
    Pg 226
PANORAMA RECOVERY RANCH . . . . (760)366-9100
    Pg 104
PAPA DIDOS IDEALS FOUNDATION . . . . (949)500-3030
    Pg 234,327
PARALYZED VETERANS ASSN/CALIF . . . .
    Pg 309
PARENT INFANT PROGRAM . . . . (760)244-1083
    Pg 86
PARENTS ANONYMOUS, INC.. . . . . (909)621-6184
    Pg 29,248,270
PARENTS OF MURDERED CHILDREN . . . .
    Pg 64,270
PARENTS OF SPECIAL NEEDS KIDS. . . . .
    Pg 86

PARENTS WITHOUT PARTNERS (ADMIN) . . . . (800)637-7974
    Pg 248,270
PARKINSON'S CENTER . . . . (760)340-3911
    Pg 176
PARKINSON'S DISEASE. . . . .
    Pg 176
PARKINSON'S EDUCATIONAL PRGM. . . . . (800)457-6676
    Pg 176,202
PARTNERSHIP FOR PRESCRIPTION ASSIST . . . . (877)777-7815
    Pg 155,248,290,309
PARTNERSHIP/PRESERVE INDEP LIVING . . . . (951)867-3800
    Pg 86,290
PASSPORT AGENCY. . . . . (877)487-2778
    Pg 214
PATH OF LIFE FAMILY SHELTER . . . . (951)275-8755
    Pg 104,136,188
PATH OF LIFE MINISTRIES . . . . (951)786-9048
    Pg 43,104,188
PATHFINDER RANCH . . . . (951)659-2455
    Pg 22
PATTON STATE HOSPITAL . . . . (909)425-7000
    Pg 44
PEACE CORPS . . . .
    Pg 136
PEACE IN THE VALLEY . . . . (909)355-2008
    Pg 104
PECHANGA INDIAN HEALTH CLINIC . . . . (951)676-6810
    Pg 9,54,147,176
PEDIATRIC CANCER RESEARCH FNDN . . . . (949)859-6312
    Pg 176
PEOPLE WITH DISABILITIES SUPPORT . . . . (951)274-0358
    Pg 270
PEPPERMINT RIDGE . . . . (951)273-7320
    Pg 86
PERRIS HEAD START/EARLY/ST PRESCH. . . . . (951)943-5815
    Pg 37
PERRIS HILL SENIOR CENTER . . . . (909)384-5436
    Pg 290
PERRIS SCHOOL DISTRICT. . . . . (951)657-3118
    Pg 86
PERRIS SENIOR CITIZENS CENTER . . . . (951)657-7334
    Pg 290
PERRIS UNION HIGH SCHOOL DISTRICT . . . . (951)943-6369
    Pg 136
PERRIS VALLEY FAMILY RESOURCE CENTER . . . . (951)443-1158
    Pg 122,147,234,317
PERRIS VALLEY RECOVERY PRGMS, INC. . . . . (951)657-2960
    Pg 104
PHILIP ALLRED CHILD DEV CTR . . . . (909)388-6307
    Pg 38,188
PHOENIX SERVICES. . . . .
    Pg 54,327
PHYSICIAN REFERRAL SERVICE. . . . . (760)340-3911
    Pg 176,202
PIC JOB TRAINING. . . . .
    Pg 136
PILGRIM PINES CAMP & CONF CTR . . . . (909)797-1821
    Pg 22
PINE SPRINGS RANCH . . . . (951)659-3173
    Pg 22
PIONEER PARK PLAZA . . . . (909)885-5773
    Pg 281
PLANET YOUTH . . . . (951)471-8415
    Pg 136,327
PLANNED PARENTHOOD . . . . (800)230-7526
    Pg 147,256
PLANNED PARENTHOOD/INDIO CENTER . . . . (760)674-0040
    Pg 147,256
PLANNED PARENTHOOD/MORENO VLY. . . . . (951)601-2322
    Pg 147,256
PLANNED PARENTHOOD/RIVERSIDE . . . . (888)743-7526
    Pg 9,147
PLANNED PARENTHOOD/SAN BRDO . . . . (909)890-5511
    Pg 147,256
PLANNED PARENTHOOD/UPLAND . . . . (909)890-5511
    Pg 147,256
PLASTIC SURGERY INFO . . . .
    Pg 176
PLOTT NURSING HOME. (909)984-8629
    Pg 86

PLYMOUTH TOWER . . . . (951)636-8202
Pg 281
PLYMOUTH VILLAGE . . . . (909)793-9195
Pg 281
PLYMOUTH VILLAGE ASSISTED LIVING . . . . (909)793-1233
Pg 281
PLYMOUTH VILLAGE HEALTH CENTER . . . . (909)793-9195
Pg 281
POINT OF GRACE CHRISTIAN FELLOWSHIP . . . . (909)944-9909
Pg 104,122,271,290
POISON INFORMATION . . . . (800)222-1222
Pg 104,176
POLARIS RESEARCH & DEVELOPMENT. . . . .
Pg 9
POLICE ACTIVITIES LEAGUE/PALM SPRINGS. . . . . (760)318-1226
Pg 317,327,338
POLICE WATCH . . . . (213)387-3325
Pg 220
POLISH AMERICAN CONGRESS/SO CAL . . . . (562)426-9830
Pg 142
POLLY KLAAS FOUNDATION . . . . (800)587-4357
Pg 29,327
POMONA COMMUNITY CRISIS CTR . . . . (909)623-1588
Pg 104
POMONA VALLEY HOSPITAL MED CTR . . . . (909)620-6663
Pg 148,176,248,271
POMONA VALLEY WORKSHOP . . . . (909)624-3555
Pg 86,136
POMONA/INLAND VLY COUNCIL/CHURCH . . . .
Pg 122,188
POSSABILITIES PROGRAM . . . . (877)558-6248
Pg 86,271
POSTPARTUM SUPPORT INTERNATL . . . . (503)894-9453
Pg 148,248,271
PRECIOUS BLOOD. . . . . (951)849-2434
Pg 122
PREGNANCY COUNSELING CENTER . . . . (909)948-6702
Pg 148,256
PREGNANCY HELPLINE. . . . .
Pg 256
PREMIER CARE & REHAB/PALM SPRINGS . . . . . (760)323-2638
Pg 281
PREVENT BLINDNESS AMERICA. . . . . (800)331-2020
Pg 86,240
PREVENT CHILD ABUSE/AMERICA. . . . . (312)663-3520
Pg 29
PREVENTIVE HEALTH FOR ADULTS . . . .
Pg 176
PRISON FELLOWSHIP MINISTRIES . . . . (800)245-9998
Pg 44
PRO LITERACY WORLDWIDE. . . . . (888)528-2224
Pg 234
PROJECT CUDDLE, INC. . . . . (888)628-3353
Pg 29,104,256
PROJECT CUIDAR . . . . (909)537-5945
Pg 248,256
PROJECT GET SAFE. (714)834-0050
Pg 16,86
PROJECT INFORM . . . . (415)558-8669
Pg 9,176,202
PROJECT SISTER . . . . (909)623-1619
Pg 16,29,54,271
PROSTATE & SKIN CANCER SCREENING . . . .
Pg 176
PROSTATE CANCER SUPPORT GOUP. . . . . (951)682-2753
Pg 271
PROVIDENCE SPEECH/HEARING CENTER . . . . (714)639-4990
Pg 86,291
PROVISIONAL EDUCATIONAL SRVS . . . . (909)887-7002
Pg 104,136,317,327
PUBLIC DEFENDER . . . .
Pg 220
PUENTE PROJECT. . . . . (510)987-9548
Pg 317,327
PULMONARY HYPERTENSION SUPPORT GROUP . . . . . . (909)883-5508
Pg 271

Q

QUEEN OF ANGELS CHURCH . . . . (951)689-3674
Pg 123
QUICKCAPTION, INC. . . . . (951)779-0787
Pg 86

R

R.A.P. COMMUNITY RECOVERY SRVS. . . . . (909)350-0278
Pg 105,248
R.E.A.C.H. . . . . (909)875-1360
Pg 123
R.O.P. PROGRAMS. . . . .
Pg 136
RAINBOW PRIDE YOUTH ALLIANCE . . . .
Pg 271,327
RAINBOW SPRINGS HEAD ST/ST PS. . . . . (951)571-4710
Pg 38
RAINBOW TO THE FUTURE . . . .
Pg 38
RAMONA HOME HEALTH/HOSPICE . . . .
Pg 64
RAMONA MANOR CONVALESCENT HOSP. . . . . (951)652-0011
Pg 281
RAMONA VNA AND HOSPICE . . . . (951)658-9288
Pg 64
RANCHO & MILL APTS. . . . . (909)889-8417
Pg 211
RANCHO COMMUNITY CHURCH . . . . (951)303-6789
Pg 105,113,271
RANCHO CUCAMONGA PUBLIC LIBRARY . . . . (909)477-2720
Pg 226,234
RANCHO CUCAMONGA RESOURCE CENTER . . . . (909)477-2781
Pg 16,123,234,248
RANCHO CUCAMONGA TEEN CENTER . . . . (909)477-2760
Pg 338
RANCHO CUCAMONGA VOLUNTEER PRGM . . . . (909)477-2760
Pg 314
RANCHO DAMACITAS . . . . (951)302-2317
Pg 5,29,327
RANCHO MESA CARE CENTER. . . . . (909)987-2501
Pg 86
RANCHO MIRAGE PUBLIC LIBRARY . . . . (760)341-7323
Pg 226
RANCHO PHOENIX . . . . (951)929-1968
Pg 105
RANCHO SANTA ANA BOTANIC GARDEN . . . . (909)625-8767
Pg 338
RANCHO SANTA ANA BOTANIC GARDEN LIBRARY. . . . . . (909)625-8767
Pg 227
RANDALL PEPPER SCHOOL . . . . (909)357-5730
Pg 234
RAPE CRISIS CENTER/RIVERSIDE AREA . . . . (951)686-7273
Pg 202
RAPE CRISIS CENTER/SAN BRDO . . . .
Pg 16
RAPE CRISIS HOTLINE . . . . (760)568-9071
Pg 202
RCC EARLY CHILDHOOD PRESCHOOL . . . . (951)222-8068
Pg 38
RCC MORENO VLY HEAD START/ST PS . . . . (951)924-6974
Pg 38
RCC NORCO HEAD START/ST PRESCH . . . . (951)270-0060
Pg 38
REACH OUT WEST END. . . . . (909)982-8641
Pg 105,328
REBUILDING MOUNTAIN HEARTS & LIVES . . . . (909)337-9922
Pg 123
REBUILDING TOGETHER SO CALIF COUNCIL . . . . . . (714)657-8174
Pg 208,314
RECHE CANYON REHAB & HEALTH CTR . . . . (909)370-4411
Pg 86
RECORDING FOR THE BLIND & DYSLEXIC . . . . (866)732-3585
Pg 86,240
RECOVERY, INC. . . . . (323)651-2170
Pg 271
REDLANDS ADULT SCHOOL . . . . (909)748-6930
Pg 38,87,136,234,248

REDLANDS CITY LIBRARY . . . . (909)798-7565
    Pg 227,234

REDLANDS COMMUNITY CENTER. . . . . (909)798-7572
    Pg 291,338

REDLANDS COMMUNITY HOSPITAL. . . . . (909)335-5520
    Pg 193,194

REDLANDS COMMUNITY SENIOR CTR . . . . (909)798-7579
    Pg 291

REDLANDS DAY NURSERY . . . . (909)792-2463
    Pg 38

REDLANDS DAY NURSERY II . . . . (909)792-9717
    Pg 38

REDLANDS EMPLOYMENT RESOURCE CTR . . . . (909)798-1795
    Pg 136

REDLANDS HEALTHCARE CENTER . . . . (909)793-2609
    Pg 87

REDLANDS NORTH HEAD START/ST PRESCH . . . . (909)793-7181
    Pg 38

REDLANDS POLICE DEPT RECREATION BUREAU . . . . . . (909)798-7572
    Pg 38

REDLANDS SOUTH HEAD START . . . . (909)798-2690
    Pg 38

REECE'S RAINBOW . . . .
    Pg 5

REFUGEE PROGRAMS BUREAU . . . . (916)654-4356
    Pg 214

REHAB INSTITUTE OF SO CALIF (RIO). . . . . (714)633-7400
    Pg 87

RELIANT PROFESSIONAL SERVES. . . . . (909)793-4011
    Pg 276,291

RENCK COMMUNITY CTR AT HUNT PARK. . . . . (951)351-6132
    Pg 291,338

RENU HOPE FOUNDATION . . . . (951)845-3816
    Pg 38

RESEARCH & TRAINING CTR ON FAMILY FOR PATHWAYS . . (503)725-4040
    Pg 55,328

RESEARCH TO PREVENT BLINDNESS. . . . . (800)621-0026
    Pg 240

RESIDENTIAL TREATMENT CENTERS . . . . (866)495-8406
    Pg 317,328

RESOLVE . . . . (703)556-7172
    Pg 148

REST MINISTRIES, INC. . . . . (888)751-7378
    Pg 271

RESTLESS LEGS SYNDROME SUPPORT GRP . . . . (760)285-2231
    Pg 271

RETINITIS PIGMENTOSA INTERNATL . . . . (800)344-4877
    Pg 241

RETIRED & SENIOR VOLUNTEER PRGM . . . . (909)482-0355
    Pg 291,314 - 315

RIALTO ADULT SCHOOL. . . . . (909)879-6010
    Pg 136,234

RIALTO RECREATION/COMMUNITY SRVS. . . . . (909)421-4949
    Pg 291,338

RIALTO SENIOR CENTER . . . . (909)877-9706
    Pg 291

RICHARD NIXON LIBRARY/BIRTHPLACE . . . . (714)993-5075
    Pg 227,338

RIDGECREST COMMUNITY HEALTH CENTER . . . . (760)446-7978
    Pg 148,176

RIDGECREST REGIONAL HOSPITAL . . . . (760)499-3615
    Pg 176

RIM FAMILY SRVS, INC. . . . . (909)336-1800
    Pg 16,55,105,328

RIMROCK VILLA CONVALESCENT HOSP . . . . (760)252-2515
    Pg 281

RIO (REHAB INST OF SO. CALIF) . . . .
    Pg 87

RITA PROJECT, INC. (866)775-7482
    Pg 55,248,271,328

RIVER RANCH MOBILE HOME PARK . . . . (760)245-9831
    Pg 211,281

RIVERSIDE ADULT SCHOOL . . . . (951)788-7185
    Pg 234

RIVERSIDE AREA RAPE CRISIS CENTER . . . . (951)686-7273
    Pg 16,29,55

RIVERSIDE CITY MISSION . . . . (951)341-5055
    Pg 123,188

RIVERSIDE CITY PARK/RECREATION . . . . (951)826-2000
    Pg 338

RIVERSIDE CITY PUBLIC UTILITIES . . . . (951)782-0330
    Pg 155,291,339

RIVERSIDE CO. BAR ASSOCIATION . . . . (951)682-7520
    Pg 202,220

RIVERSIDE CO. CHILD SUPPORT SRVS . . . . (866)901-3212
    Pg 155,220,248 - 249

RIVERSIDE CO. COMM HEALTH AGENCY . . . . (951)358-5438
    Pg 177,249,276

RIVERSIDE CO. CRISIS/REFERRAL . . . .
    Pg 202

RIVERSIDE CO. DEPT OF PUBLIC HEALTH . . . . (951)358-4977
    Pg 249

RIVERSIDE CO. DEPT/MENTAL HEALTH . . . . (951)955-2105
    Pg 9,17,29,55,105,188,249,291,328

RIVERSIDE CO. DIST ATTORNEY. . . . . (951)922-7130
    Pg 220

RIVERSIDE CO. DRUG COURT . . . . (760)770-2241
    Pg 105

RIVERSIDE CO. ECONOMIC DEV AGENCY . . . . (951)955-3100
    Pg 136

RIVERSIDE CO. FAMILY CONCILIATION CT . . . .
    Pg 5

RIVERSIDE CO. HOUSING AUTHORITY . . . . (951)351-0700
    Pg 87,211,281

RIVERSIDE CO. HUMAN RESOURCES DEPT . . . . (951)955-3500
    Pg 136

RIVERSIDE CO. INFO SRVS. . . . . (951)955-1000
    Pg 202

RIVERSIDE CO. JAIL . . . . (951)955-4500
    Pg 44

RIVERSIDE CO. LATINO COMMISSION. . . . . (760)398-2008
    Pg 105

RIVERSIDE CO. LAW LIBRARY . . . . (760)863-8316
    Pg 220,227

RIVERSIDE CO. LIBRARY LITERACY PRGM . . . . (951)657-0796
    Pg 234 - 235

RIVERSIDE CO. LIBRARY SYSTEM. . . . . (951)763-4216
    Pg 227 - 228,235

RIVERSIDE CO. LITERACY NETWORK . . . . (951)697-4700
    Pg 235

RIVERSIDE CO. MEDICAL ASSN . . . . (951)686-3342
    Pg 177

RIVERSIDE CO. MENTAL HEALTH . . . . (760)770-2222
    Pg 29,44,55 - 56,87,136,249,328

RIVERSIDE CO. OFFICE ON AGING . . . . (951)867-3800
    Pg 137,291,315

RIVERSIDE CO. OFFICE/EDUCATION . . . . (800)442-4927
    Pg 38,44,105,137,249,256,328

RIVERSIDE CO. PROBATION DEPT. . . . . (951)922-7200
    Pg 44,328

RIVERSIDE CO. PUBLIC DEFENDER . . . . (951)922-7230
    Pg 220 - 221

RIVERSIDE CO. PUBLIC GUARDIAN . . . . (951)341-6440
    Pg 221,291

RIVERSIDE CO. PUBLIC HEALTH DEPT . . . . (951)272-5445
    Pg 10,106,123,148 - 149,177 - 178,249,256 - 257,297,315,328

RIVERSIDE CO. PUBLIC SOCIAL SRVS . . . . (951)413-5000
    Pg 5,29 - 30,87,123 - 124,137,155 - 156,178 - 179,188 - 189,249 -
    250,257,276,292,344

RIVERSIDE CO. REGL PARKS/OPENSPACE . . . . (951)955-4310
    Pg 339

RIVERSIDE CO. SHERIFF'S DEPT . . . . (800)950-2444
    Pg 202

RIVERSIDE CO. SUBSTANCE ABUSE . . . . (951)791-3350
    Pg 106

RIVERSIDE CO. SUPERIOR COURT . . . . (951)922-7145
    Pg 221

RIVERSIDE CO. VETERANS SRVS . . . . (951)766-2566
    Pg 309

RIVERSIDE COMMUNITY COLLEGE . . . . (951)222-8000
    Pg 235

RIVERSIDE COMMUNITY COLLEGE/EOPS . . . . (951)222-8045
    Pg 137,329,344

RIVERSIDE COMMUNITY HEALTH FNDN . . . . (951)788-3471
    Pg 292,329

RIVERSIDE HOSPICE . . . . (951)274-0710
    Pg 64,272

RIVERSIDE HOUSING DEVELOP CORP . . . . (951)341-6511
    Pg 208

RIVERSIDE LIFE SRVS . . . . (951)784-2422
Pg 149,257

RIVERSIDE METROPOLITAN MUSEUM . . . . (951)826-5273
Pg 339

RIVERSIDE RECOVERY RESOURCES . . . . (951)658-4466
Pg 106,329

RIVERSIDE SUPERIOR COURT . . . . (951)955-4600
Pg 221

RIVERSIDE TRANSIT AGENCY . . . . (951)565-5002
Pg 304

RIVERSIDE WORKFORCE DEV CENTER . . . .
Pg 137

RIVERSIDE/SAN BERN INDIAN HLTH CLINIC . . . . (760)397-4476
Pg 70,106,179

RIVERSIDE/SAN BRDO CO. INDIAN HLTH . . . . (800)732-8805
Pg 10,56,106,149,179

ROAD CONDITIONS . . . .
Pg 304

ROBERT E. BUSH NAVAL HOSPITAL . . . . (760)830-2190
Pg 193

RODEO DRIVE APTS. . . . . (760)245-2922
Pg 212

ROLLING START, INC. . . . . (909)884-2129
Pg 87,106,292

ROMOLAND HEAD START. . . . . (951)928-2924
Pg 38

RONALD MCDONALD HOUSE/LOS ANGELES . . . . (310)268-8488
Pg 22

ROP/BALDY VIEW . . . . (909)980-6498
Pg 137

ROP/COLTON-REDLANDS-YUCAIPA . . . . (909)793-3115
Pg 137

ROP/RIVERSIDE COUNTY. . . . . (951)826-6797
Pg 137

ROP/SAN BRNDO CO. SUPT OF SCHOOLS . . . . (909)252-4550
Pg 137,329

ROP/VICTORVILLE . . . . (760)955-3201
Pg 138

ROSE OF SHARON LIFE CENTER . . . . (760)243-5006
Pg 149

ROSEMARY KENNEDY HEAD START/PRESCH . . . . (951)688-5660
Pg 38

ROY'S DESERT RESOURCE CENTER . . . . (760)676-5200
Pg 124,189

RSVP . . . .
Pg 292,315

RUBEN CAMPOS COMMUNITY CENTER. . . . . (909)384-5421
Pg 339

RUBIDOUX COMMUNITY RESOURCE CTR . . . . (951)328-1575
Pg 138,235,250

RURAL INFORMATION CENTER . . . . (800)633-7701
Pg 229

S

S. COACHELLA VLY COMM SRVS DIST . . . . (760)396-1014
Pg 202

S.A.F.E./SUBSTANCE ABUSE/ED . . . . (714)505-4692
Pg 106,329

S.C.O.R.E./SMALL BUSINESS ADMIN. . . . .
Pg 138,315

S.P.A.R.E. MINISTRIES COUNSELING . . . . (714)345-4938
Pg 56

SAC HEALTH SYSTEM. . . . . (909)382-7100
Pg 179

SACRED HEART CHURCH . . . . (951)685-5058
Pg 124

SAFE AT HOME. . . . . (714)435-9992
Pg 17

SAFE HARBOR . . . . (951)279-4477
Pg 106,113,272

SAFE KIDS INLAND EMPIRE COALITION. . . . . (909)558-8118
Pg 250,329

SAFE SITTER . . . . (800)255-4089
Pg 203

SAFETY & EMERG EDUCATOR'S COUNCIL . . . . (619)692-2011
Pg 106,179

SALEM CHRISTIAN HOMES . . . . (909)614-0575
Pg 87

SALVATION ARMY/ADULT REHAB . . . . (951)940-5790
Pg 106,138

SALVATION ARMY/CATHEDRAL CITY . . . . (760)324-2275
Pg 124,189

SALVATION ARMY/FAMILY SRVS . . . . (951)656-1822
Pg 124,189

SALVATION ARMY/HEMET. . . . . (951)766-2020
Pg 124,298

SALVATION ARMY/HOSPITALITY HOUSE . . . . (909)888-1336
Pg 189

SALVATION ARMY/MISSING PERSONS . . . . (800)698-7728
Pg 215

SALVATION ARMY/ONTARIO . . . . (909)986-6748
Pg 22,124,339

SALVATION ARMY/REDLANDS CORPS. . . . . (909)792-6868
Pg 124,156,189,208

SALVATION ARMY/RIVERSIDE CORPS. . . . . (951)784-3571
Pg 124,189

SALVATION ARMY/VICTORVILLE CORPS . . . . (760)245-2545
Pg 124,156,189

SALVATION ARMY/VICTORY PLACE . . . . (310)478-3711
Pg 106,309

SALVATION ARMY/YUCCA VLY SRVS. . . . . (760)228-0114
Pg 124,156,189,208

SAMARITAN COUNSELING CENTER . . . . (909)985-0513
Pg 56

SAMARITAN'S HELPING HAND . . . . (760)243-5933
Pg 124

SAMHSA . . . . (240)276-2000
Pg 56,107

SAMHSA CTR FOR SUBSTANCE ABUSE PREV . . . . . . (800)967-5752
Pg 203

SAMHSA'S NATL MENTAL HLTH INFO CTR . . . . (800)789-2647
Pg 56

SAN BERNARDINO ADULT SCHOOL . . . . (909)388-6000
Pg 138

SAN BERNARDINO CHILD ADVOCACY . . . . (909)881-6760
Pg 30,329

SAN BERNARDINO CITY MISSION . . . . (909)889-2700
Pg 125,189

SAN BERNARDINO CITY PARKS & REC . . . . (909)384-5233
Pg 292,339

SAN BERNARDINO CITY U.S.D. . . . . (909)880-6701
Pg 10,190

SAN BERNARDINO CO. AGING/ADULT. . . . . (760)256-5544
Pg 87 - 88,138,277,292 - 293

SAN BERNARDINO CO. ALCOHOL/DRUG . . . . (760)326-4590
Pg 56,107

SAN BERNARDINO CO. BAR ASSN. . . . . (909)885-1986
Pg 221

SAN BERNARDINO CO. BEHAV HEALTH . . . . (909)423-0750
Pg 45,56 - 57,125,179,190,221,293,317,329

SAN BERNARDINO CO. CHILD ABUSE REPORTING . . . . . (800)827-8724
Pg 30,250

SAN BERNARDINO CO. CHILD SUPPORT . . . . (866)901-3212
Pg 156,221,250

SAN BERNARDINO CO. CHILDREN'S SRVS . . . .
Pg 30,250

SAN BERNARDINO CO. CLERK. . . . . (909)384-1888
Pg 5

SAN BERNARDINO CO. DIST ATTORNEY . . . . (760)256-4810
Pg 221 - 222

SAN BERNARDINO CO. HIV CLINIC . . . .
Pg 10

SAN BERNARDINO CO. HOUSING AUTH . . . . (909)983-1318
Pg 88,208,212,281

SAN BERNARDINO CO. HUMAN SRVS SY . . . . (909)891-3300
Pg 5 - 6,30,39,125,138,156,179,190,193,250,257,293,309,329

SAN BERNARDINO CO. INFO SRVS . . . . (909)388-5500
Pg 203

SAN BERNARDINO CO. LAW LIBRARY. . . . .
Pg 222,229

SAN BERNARDINO CO. LIB/LITERACY . . . . (909)337-5420
Pg 215,235

SAN BERNARDINO CO. LIBRARY. . . . . (760)246-5661
Pg 229 - 230

SAN BERNARDINO CO. MEDICAL SOCIETY . . . . (951)787-7700
Pg 10,179

SAN BERNARDINO CO. MENTAL HEALTH . . . . (909)580-1000
Pg 193

SAN BERNARDINO CO. OFC/AGING . . . .
    Pg 293
SAN BERNARDINO CO. OMBUDSMAN . . . . (909)891-3928
    Pg 88,203,293
SAN BERNARDINO CO. PROBATION DEPT . . . . (909)387-7359
    Pg 45
SAN BERNARDINO CO. PUBLIC ADMIN . . . . (909)387-2481
    Pg 222,293
SAN BERNARDINO CO. PUBLIC DEFNDR . . . . (760)256-4722
    Pg 222
SAN BERNARDINO CO. PUBLIC HEALTH . . . . (800)722-4777
    Pg 10 - 11,30,88,107,125,149 - 150,156,179 - 181,250,257 -
    258,293,329
SAN BERNARDINO CO. PUBLIC SOC SRVS . . . .
    Pg 30,125,329
SAN BERNARDINO CO. PVT IND COUNCIL . . . . (909)387-9835
    Pg 138
SAN BERNARDINO CO. SUPERIOR CRT. . . . . (909)580-1812
    Pg 57,222 - 223
SAN BERNARDINO CO. VET AFFAIRS . . . . (909)465-5241
    Pg 309
SAN BERNARDINO CO/FIRST 5. . . . . (909)386-7706
    Pg 6,250
SAN BERNARDINO COMM/WOMEN . . . . (909)387-5543
    Pg 272
SAN BERNARDINO PARK/REC HDSTRT . . . . (909)887-3349
    Pg 39
SAN BERNARDINO PUBLIC LIB/LITERACY . . . . (909)381-8205
    Pg 235
SAN BERNARDINO PUBLIC LIBRARY . . . . (909)381-8201
    Pg 231
SAN BERNARDINO VALLEY COLLEGE. . . . . (909)384-4440
    Pg 39
SAN BERNARDINO VET CENTER. . . . . (909)801-5762
    Pg 57,309
SAN BERNARDINO VILLAGE GREEN APTS . . . . (909)888-3001
    Pg 212
SAN BERNARDINO VLY COLLEGE/EOPS . . . . (909)384-4412
    Pg 138,329,344
SAN FRANCISCO AIDS FOUNDATION . . . . (800)367-2437
    Pg 11
SAN GORGONIO CHILD CARE CONSRTM . . . . (951)849-2930
    Pg 39
SAN GORGONIO MEMORIAL HOSPITAL . . . . (951)845-1121
    Pg 193
SAN JACINTO HEAD START/STATE PRESCH . . . . (951)654-1531
    Pg 39
SAN SALVADOR HEAD START . . . .
    Pg 39
SBC ACCESS RESOURCES. . . . .
    Pg 88
SCAN HEALTH PLAN. . . . . (562)989-5100
    Pg 293
SCHOEPE SCOUT RESERVATION/LOST VLY . . . . (714)546-4990
    Pg 22
SCHULZ, CHRISTINA H. - LMFT (MFC43973) . . . . (909)815-9009
    Pg 57
SCLERODERMA FNDN. . . . . (800)722-4673
    Pg 181
SCLERODERMA FNDN/SO CALIF. . . . . (310)477-8225
    Pg 181
SCORE/S.C.O.R.E. . . . .
    Pg 315
SCREENING FOR MENTAL HEALTH, INC. . . . . (781)239-0071
    Pg 57,113
SEARLES VALLEY COMM SRV SENIOR CTR . . . . (760)372-5889
    Pg 293
SECOND HARVEST FOOD BANK . . . . (951)359-4757
    Pg 125
SEEKING PEACEFUL SOLUTIONS, INC. . . . . (323)753-1314
    Pg 17,57,107
SELPA/DESERT/MOUNTAIN . . . . (760)242-6333
    Pg 88
SELPA/FONTANA. . . . . (909)357-5000
    Pg 88
SELPA/MORANGO UNIFIED . . . . (760)367-9191
    Pg 88
SELPA/MORENO VALLEY . . . . (951)571-7500
    Pg 88

SELPA/RIVERSIDE COUNTY . . . . (951)826-6687
    Pg 88
SELPA/RIVERSIDE USD . . . . (951)788-7142
    Pg 89
SELPA/SAN BERNARDINO . . . . (909)880-6616
    Pg 89
SELPA/WEST END . . . . (909)476-6188
    Pg 89
SEMINOLE GARDEN APARTMENTS . . . . (760)328-5913
    Pg 212
SENECA CTR FOR CHILDREN & FAMILIES . . . . (510)481-1222
    Pg 6,57
SENIOR CARE ACTION NETWORK (SCAN) . . . .
    Pg 294
SENIOR COMMUNITY SERVICE EMPLOYMENT . . . . (909)891-3913
    Pg 138,294
SENIOR COMPANION PROGRAM. . . . . (909)384-5430
    Pg 89,277,294
SENIOR HOME AND HEALTH CARE . . . .
    Pg 294
SENIOR INFO & ASSISTANCE. . . . . (760)256-5544
    Pg 203,294
SENIOR MEALS . . . .
    Pg 294
SENIOR NUTRITION PRGM . . . . (951)867-3800
    Pg 298
SENIOR NUTRITION SITE . . . . (760)367-1678
    Pg 294,298 - 300
SENIORS EYECARE PROGRAM . . . .
    Pg 181,241,294
SERENITY ALANO CLUB . . . . (909)881-0170
    Pg 107
SERENITY OUTREACH . . . . (909)464-0400
    Pg 107
SET FREE CHRISTIAN FELLOWSHIP. . . . . (760)241-9428
    Pg 107
SEVENTH DAY ADVENTIST COMM SRVS . . . . (951)682-9810
    Pg 125,190
SEX ADDICTS ANONYMOUS (S.A.A.). . . . . (213)896-2964
    Pg 272
SEXAHOLICS ANONYMOUS (S.A.) . . . . (615)370-6062
    Pg 45,107,272
SEXUAL ASSAULT SRVS/REDLANDS . . . . (909)335-8777
    Pg 17,30,57
SEXUAL ASSAULT SRVS/SAN BRDO. . . . . (909)885-8884
    Pg 17,30,57,203
SEXUAL ASSAULT SRVS/VICTORVILLE . . . . (760)952-0041
    Pg 17,57
SEXUAL ASSAULT SRVS/YUCAIPA . . . . (909)790-9374
    Pg 17,30,57,223
SEXUAL COMPULSIVES ANONYMOUS/SCA. . . . . (800)977-4325
    Pg 272
SEXUALITY INFO & EDU COUNCIL OF THE U.S. . . . . . . (212)819-9770
    Pg 150
SHANDIN HILLS BEHAV THERAPY CTR . . . . (909)886-6786
    Pg 58,193
SHANDIN HILLS REHABILITATION CTR . . . . (909)886-6786
    Pg 89
SHEEPFOLD, THE . . . . (877)743-3736
    Pg 17,190
SHELTER FOR THE HOMELESS . . . . (714)897-3221
    Pg 190
SHELTER FROM THE STORM, INC.. . . . . (760)674-0400
    Pg 17
SHELTER WINGS CORP DAY PRGM . . . . (760)922-0399
    Pg 89
SHRINERS HOSPITALS FOR CHILDREN/L.A. . . . . (213)388-3151
    Pg 193
SICKLE CELL DISEASE ASSN OF AMER . . . . (800)421-8453
    Pg 181
SICKLE CELL DISEASE FNDN OF CALIF . . . . (310)693-0247
    Pg 23
SICKLE CELL ORGANIZATION/INLAND CO. . . . . (800)992-6722
    Pg 181
SIDS INFORMATION CLEARINGHOUSE . . . . (866)866-7437
    Pg 64,181
SIDS NETWORK . . . .
    Pg 272
SIERRA CLUB/SAN GORGONIO. . . . . (951)684-6203
    Pg 250,339

SIERRA VISTA REHABILITATION CTR . . . . (909)862-6454 Pg 89	SPINA BIFIDA ASSN OF AMERICA . . . . (202)944-3285 Pg 90,181
SILBY GARDENS . . . . Pg 212	SPINAL CORD INJURY NETWORK INTL . . . . (800)548-2673 Pg 90,181
SILVER LAKES COMMUNITY CHURCH. . . . . (760)952-1485 Pg 250,272	SPINAL CORD SOCIETY . . . . (218)739-5252 Pg 90
SIMON FOUNDATION FOR CONTINENCE . . . . (800)237-4666 Pg 181,294	SPONDYLITIS ASSN OF AMERICA . . . . (800)777-8189 Pg 90,181
SIMPSON CENTER. . . . . (951)765-2390 Pg 208,294	SPRINGBOARD CONSUMER CREDIT MGMT . . . . (800)947-3752 Pg 156 - 157
SINGLE PARENT . . . . (626)294-3211 Pg 251,272	SPRINGBOARD CONSUMER CREDIT MGT . . . . (877)947-3752 Pg 157
SINGLE PARENTS OF POWER EMLAC HEALTH SRVS . . . . . (310)753-7860 Pg 17,31,107	ST. ANNE'S . . . . (213)381-2931 Pg 6,258
SK MANAGEMENT COMPANY. . . . . (323)930-2300 Pg 212	ST. ANN'S CATHOLIC OUTREACH . . . . (760)326-2721 Pg 125,215
SKY HARBOR CARE CENTER. . . . . (760)365-4870 Pg 89	ST. BERNARDINE MEDICAL CENTER. . . . . (909)883-8711 Pg 193
SMALL BUSINESS ADMINISTRATION . . . . (800)827-5722 Pg 203	ST. BERNARDINE PLAZA . . . . (909)888-0153 Pg 282
SMALL CLAIMS ADVISORY PRGM . . . . (951)683-3700 Pg 223	ST. CATHERINE OF SIENA CHURCH . . . . (909)875-1360 Pg 125
SMITH CORRECTIONAL FACILITY . . . . (951)922-7300 Pg 45	ST. CHRISTOPHER'S CHURCH . . . . (951)924-1968 Pg 125,190
SMOKENDERS . . . . (800)828-4357 Pg 107,272	ST. ELIZABETH CHURCH . . . . (760)329-8794 Pg 126,190
SMOKING CESSATION. . . . . Pg 272	ST. GEORGE CATHOLIC CHURCH . . . . (909)983-2637 Pg 126
SO CALIF ALCOHOL & DRUG PRGM . . . . Pg 17,107,203	ST. JOAN OF ARC . . . . (760)241-2043 Pg 126
SO CALIF ASSN NONPROFIT HOUSING . . . . (213)480-1249 Pg 208	ST. JUDE CHILDREN'S RESEARCH HOSP . . . . (800)227-6737 Pg 11,193
SO CALIF ASSN OF GOVERNMENTS . . . . (213)236-1800 Pg 208,304	ST. MARTHA'S THRIFT STORE . . . . (951)677-6347 Pg 126
SO CALIF COLLEGE OF OPTOMETRY/LIB . . . . (714)449-7440 Pg 231	ST. MARY MEDICAL CENTER . . . . (760)242-2311 Pg 194
SO CALIF EDISON/LOW INCOME PRGM . . . . (800)736-4777 Pg 156,294	ST. MEL'S FOOD PANTRY . . . . (951)737-7144 Pg 126
SO CALIF GENEALOGICAL SOCIETY LIBR. . . . . (818)843-7247 Pg 231	ST. MICHAEL'S CAMP FOR BOYS. . . . . (949)858-0222 Pg 23
SO CALIF INDIAN CENTER, INC. . . . . (714)962-6673 Pg 6,58,125,138,142,251	ST. THERESA'S CHURCH . . . . (760)323-2669 Pg 126
SO CALIF LIBRARY LITERACY NETWORK . . . . (951)279-3789 Pg 235	STALKING RESOURCE CENTER . . . . (202)467-8700 Pg 17
SOBOBA INDIAN HEALTH CLINIC. . . . . (800)851-5816 Pg 11,58,107,150,181	STARLIGHT CHILDREN'S FOUNDATION . . . . (310)479-1212 Pg 90,182,251,272,330
SOCIAL SCIENCE SRVS-CEDAR HOUSE . . . . Pg 108	STARSHINE TREATMENT CENTERS . . . . (909)882-7978 Pg 330
SOCIAL SECURITY ADMINISTRATION . . . . (800)772-1213 Pg 89 - 90,294 - 295	STD EDUCATION & INFO . . . . Pg 11
SOCIAL SECURITY BENEFITS INFO . . . . (800)772-1213 Pg 203	STEELWORKERS OLDTIMERS FNDN . . . . (909)829-0384 Pg 295,300
SOCIAL SERVICES . . . . Pg 125	STEELWORKERS OLDTIMERS II . . . . (909)829-0384 Pg 282
SODEXHO . . . . (951)827-3613 Pg 300	STEELWORKS OLDTIMERS . . . . Pg 282
SOLDIER'S ANGELS . . . . (626)529-5114 Pg 309,315	STOMP OUT BULLYING . . . . (877)602-8559 Pg 17,251,330
SOROPTIMIST HOUSE OF HOPE . . . . Pg 108	STRIVING TO REDUCE YOUTH VIOLENCE . . . . Pg 317
SOS (SECULAR ORGANIZATION FOR SOBRIETY) . . . . . . (323)666-4295 Pg 108,272	STROKE ASSOCIATION OF SO CALIF . . . . (310)575-1699 Pg 182,272
SOUTH ASIAN HELPLINE & REFERRAL AGENCY . . . . (562)402-4132 Pg 58,203,223,295	STROKE INFO & REFERRAL . . . . Pg 272
SOUTH COAST COMMUNITY SRVS . . . . (909)980-6700 Pg 17,58,181,330,344	STROKE REHABILITATION GROUP. . . . . (760)322-3995 Pg 272
SOUTHERN CALIF YOUTH FOR CHRIST . . . . (562)424-0775 Pg 339	STUDENT ASSISTANCE PROGRAM . . . . (951)736-5106 Pg 108,330
SOUTHERN CALIFORNIA . . . . Pg 58	STUMPS 'R US . . . . (925)952-4408 Pg 272
SOUTHLAND FARMERS' MARKET ASSN. . . . . (310)455-0181 Pg 125	STURGE-WEBER FOUNDATION, THE . . . . (800)627-5482 Pg 182
SOUTHPOINTE VILLA . . . . (909)874-9110 Pg 281	STUTTERING FOUNDATION OF AMERICA. . . . . (800)992-9392 Pg 90
SPAN CALIFORNIA. . . . . (760)753-4565 Pg 64,295,330	STUTTERING/NATIONAL CENTER . . . . Pg 90
SPANISH ASSEMBLY OF GOD/HLTH PRG . . . . (760)324-1471 Pg 181	SUICIDE HOTLINES . . . . Pg 203
SPECIAL OLYMPICS/SO CALIF . . . . (562)354-2600 Pg 90	SUICIDE PREVENTION CENTER . . . . (877)727-4747 Pg 58,203,330

SUICIDE PREVENTION LIFELINE . . . . (800)273-8255
    Pg 203,309
SUICIDE SURVIVORS . . . . (909)393-2563
    Pg 273
SUMMIT PAYEE SRVS, INC. . . . . (909)884-5299
    Pg 90,157,295
SUN CITY CONCERN, INC. . . . . (951)679-2374
    Pg 203,295
SUN CITY CONVALESCENT CENTER . . . . (951)679-6858
    Pg 282
SUN RAY ADDICTIONS . . . . **(951)652-3560**
    Pg 108
SUN WEST VILLAS . . . .
    Pg 212
SUNLINE TRANSIT AGENCY . . . . (760)343-3456
    Pg 90,304
SUNRISE APTS. . . . . (760)591-9737
    Pg 212
SUNSHINE EARLY CHILDHOOD CTR. . . . . (951)352-8488
    Pg 39,90
SUPPORT GROUPS . . . . (951)571-9090
    Pg 273
SURVIVE FOOD BANK . . . .
    Pg 126
SURVIVORS OF INCEST ANONYMOUS (SIA) . . . . . (410)893-3322
    Pg 18
SURVIVORS OF TORTURE INTERNATL . . . . (619)278-2400
    Pg 18,142,215,273
SUSAN B. KREVOY EATING DISORDERS PRGM . . . (310)277-2682
    Pg 58,113
SUSAN G. KOMEN BREAST CANCER FNDN. . . . . . (714)957-9157
    Pg 182,273,315
SWEET RELIEF MUSICIANS FUND . . . . (714)846-3030
    Pg 126,157
SWEET SUCCESS . . . . (909)558-3996
    Pg 182
SYCAMORE TERRACE APARTMENTS . . . . (909)946-2811
    Pg 282

T

TAIPEI ECONOMIC & CULTURAL OFFICE . . . . (323)782-8765
    Pg 142
TALK ABOUT CURING AUTISM (TACA) . . . . (949)640-4401
    Pg 90,251,273
TALK IT OVER WITH MAMA . . . . (323)525-1393
    Pg 251,273
TANF
    Pg 126,157,190
TARGET COMMUNITY SCHOOLS. . . . . (909)798-5391
    Pg 91
TARJAN CTR FOR DEV DISABILITIES . . . . (310)825-0170
    Pg 91
TEAM OF ADVOCATES FOR SPECIAL KIDS . . . . . . (714)533-8275
    Pg 91,251
TEEN CHALLENGE INTERNATIONAL. . . . . (714)835-8822
    Pg 108,317,330
TEEN CHALLENGE INTERNATL/SO CALIF . . . . (951)682-8990
    Pg 108,330
TEEN CRISIS LINE . . . . (800)914-2272
    Pg 203
TEEN IMPACT . . . . (323)361-4660
    Pg 182,273
TEEN LINE . . . . (310)855-4673
    Pg 203
TEEN RESCUE, INC. . . . . (800)494-2200
    Pg 58,330
TEEN SAVERS . . . . (714)288-9779
    Pg 108
TELACU VILLA . . . . (951)486-9842
    Pg 91,282
TEMECULA FAMILY HEALTH CENTER . . . .
    Pg 182
TEMECULA HEAD START/ST PRESCH . . . . (951)506-4105
    Pg 39
TEMECULA VALLEY USD . . . . (951)695-7153
    Pg 235
TEMECULA VET CENTER . . . . (951)296-5608
    Pg 58,309

TEMECULA VLY SENIOR SERVICE CTR . . . . (951)600-9557
    Pg 126,295
TEXT4BABY . . . .
    Pg 251,258
THE AMPUTEE COALITION OF AMERICA . . . . (888)267-5669
    Pg 91,273
THE BRIDGE SCHOOL. . . . . (650)696-7295
    Pg 23,91
THE CALIFORNIA ENDOWMENT . . . . (800)449-4149
    Pg 182
THE CHICAGO SCHOOL OF PROFESSIONAL PSYCHOLOGY . (213)615-7200
    Pg 58
THE CHILDREN'S VILLAGE OF SONOMA CO. . . . . . (707)566-7044
    Pg 6,345
THE CHURCH FOR WHOSOEVER . . . . (760)242-3191
    Pg 126
THE CLOSET . . . . (909)466-7789
    Pg 126
THE COMPASSIONATE FRIENDS . . . .
    Pg 65,273
THE ELISA PROJECT . . . . (214)369-5222
    Pg 113
THE ERIC ALLEN GROUP . . . . (866)217-0777
    Pg 317,330
THE FACIAL PAIN ASSN . . . . (800)923-3608
    Pg 182
THE FRIENDSHIP LINE . . . . (415)752-3778
    Pg 58,203,295
THE GOLDEN 1 CREDIT UNION. . . . . (877)465-3361
    Pg 157
THE GOODEN CENTER . . . . (626)356-0078
    Pg 45,108
THE GROVE COMMUNITY CHURCH . . . . (951)571-9090
    Pg 59,108,113,273
THE JACQUELINE SIDMAN HEALTH FNDN . . . . . . (949)251-9550
    Pg 59,108,113,273
THE JOHN HENRY FOUNDATION. . . . . (714)554-8906
    Pg 59,182,194
THE LIGHTHOUSE, INC. . . . .
    Pg 91,204,241
THE MENTOR NETWORK . . . . (909)483-2505
    Pg 91
THE MENTORING NETWORK . . . . (909)483-2505
    Pg 91
THE NAMES PROJECT FOUNDATION . . . . (404)688-5500
    Pg 11,65
THE OPHELIA PROJECT. . . . . (760)776-1600
    Pg 330
THE OTHER BAR NATIONAL HOTLINE . . . . (800)222-0767
    Pg 108,204,273
THE PAINTED TURTLE. . . . . (310)451-1353
    Pg 23
THE RECOVERY CENTER . . . . (909)949-4667
    Pg 108
THE RELATIONAL CENTER . . . . (323)935-1807
    Pg 59,273
THE SALVATION ARMY . . . .
    Pg 126
THE SOLUTIONS ALCOHOL/DRUG RECOVERY. . . . (323)731-4981
    Pg 59,108
THE TREVOR PROJECT. . . . . (866)488-7386
    Pg 204,330
THE TRINITY HOUSE . . . . (619)477-7158
    Pg 108,139,190
THE U.S. UNINSURED HELPLINE. . . . . (800)234-1317
    Pg 157,182,204
THE UNFORGETTABLES FOUNDATION . . . . (951)680-9996
    Pg 65,251
THE WAY . . . . (714)906-9097
    Pg 109
THE WELL IN THE DESERT . . . . (760)327-8577
    Pg 126,300
THE 'I AM' FOUNDATION. . . . . (619)297-7010
    Pg 236,330
THERAPY/HANDI-CAPABLE EQUESTRIANS . . . . . . (951)658-7790
    Pg 91
THESSALONIKA FAMILY SERVICES . . . . (951)302-2317
    Pg 6
THOUSAND PINES CHRISTIAN CAMP . . . . (909)338-2705
    Pg 23

TLC TEEN MOMS & DADS . . . . (562)429-1782 Pg 258	U.S. FEDERAL TRADE COMMMISSION . . . . (888)382-1222 Pg 204
TOLL-FREE NUMBER INFORMATION . . . . (800)555-1212 Pg 204	U.S. IMMIGRATION/CUSTOMS ENFORCE . . . . (562)980-3170 Pg 204
TOPS (TAKE OFF POUNDS SENSIBLY) . . . . (800)932-8677 Pg 113,273	U.S. IMMIGRATION/NATURALIZATION . . . . (800)375-5283 Pg 215
TOTALLY KIDS SPECIALTY HEALTHCARE . . . . (909)796-6915 Pg 91	U.S. INTERNAL REVENUE SERVICE/TDD . . . . (800)829-1040 Pg 91
TOURETTE SYNDROME ASSOCIATION . . . . (718)224-2999 Pg 182	U.S. PASSPORT OFFICE . . . . Pg 215
TRAGEDY ASSIST PRGM FOR SURVIVORS . . . . (202)588-8277 Pg 65,309	U.S. PEACE CORPS . . . . (800)424-8580 Pg 139,315
TRANS UNION CREDIT INFO . . . . (800)838-4213 Pg 204	U.S. PROBATION/PAROLE SERVICE . . . . (213)894-3600 Pg 45
TRANS YOUTH FAMILY ALLIES . . . . (888)462-8932 Pg 251,331	U.S. RAILROAD RETIREMENT BOARD . . . . (626)339-9993 Pg 295
TRANSCRIBERS OF ORANGE COUNTY . . . . (714)731-5899 Pg 91	U.S. SMALL BUSINESS ADMINISTRATION . . . . (714)550-7420 Pg 139
TRANSPORTATION ACCESS PROGRAM . . . . Pg 305	U.S. VETS . . . . (951)656-6892 Pg 310
TRI-COUNTY DENTAL SOCIETY . . . . (800)287-8237 Pg 70	UCI MEDICAL CTR . . . . (714)456-7890 Pg 194
TRI-COUNTY MEM FUNERAL SOCIETY . . . . (714)962-1917 Pg 65	UCI WOMEN'S HEALTHCARE CENTER . . . . (714)456-7002 Pg 150,182
TRINITY COMM OUTREACH CORP . . . . (951)601-0253 Pg 157,251	UCLA MEDICAL CENTER . . . . (310)825-9111 Pg 194
TRINITY EVANGELICAL CHURCH . . . . (909)335-7333 Pg 65,109,273	UCLA NEUROPSYCHIATRIC HOSPITAL . . . . (800)825-9989 Pg 59,113,194,295
TRUESDAIL SPEECH CENTER . . . . (909)748-8061 Pg 91	UCLA PARENT TRAINING PRGM . . . . (310)825-0142 Pg 251,331
TRUSTLINE . . . . (800)822-8490 Pg 31,251	UCR/CALIF MUSEUM OF PHOTOGRAPHY . . . . (951)827-4787 Pg 339
TUBEROUS SCLEROSIS ALLIANCE . . . . (800)225-6872 Pg 182	UHS KEYSTONE SCHOOLS . . . . (909)783-8400 Pg 91
TUBEROUS SCLEROSIS ASSOCIATION . . . . Pg 182	UMBRELLA MINISTRIES . . . . (760)775-0296 Pg 273
TURNING POINT COUNSELING . . . . (800)998-6329 Pg 59	UN LIBRO, MIL MUNDOS . . . . (951)233-6160 Pg 143,236
TWENTYNINE PALMS COMMUNITY FOOD PANTRY . . . . . . (760)361-3663 Pg 126	UNEMPLOYMENT COMPENSATION . . . . (800)494-4944 Pg 204
TWENTYNINE PALMS PARKS/REC . . . . (760)367-7562 Pg 295,339	UNEMPLOYMENT INSURANCE CLAIMS . . . . (800)300-5616 Pg 139
TWIN PALMS ADULT EDUCATION . . . . (760)922-4884 Pg 236	UNITED CANCER RESEARCH SOCIETY . . . . (800)222-1533 Pg 182
TWIN PINES RANCH . . . . (951)849-4131 Pg 45	UNITED CEREBRAL PALSY ASSN . . . . (760)321-8184 Pg 23,91 - 92,182
	UNITED LAW CENTERS/WOMENS LAW CTR . . . . (714)667-1038 Pg 18,223

U

U.S. AIRFORCE . . . . (760)245-7680 Pg 310	UNITED METHODIST CHILDREN'S CTR . . . . (760)245-4250 Pg 39
U.S. ATTORNEY'S OFFICE . . . . (213)894-2434 Pg 223	UNITED MITOCHONDRIAL DISEASE FNDN . . . . (412)793-8077 Pg 183
U.S. BANKRUPTCY COURT . . . . (951)774-1000 Pg 223	UNITED OSTOMY ASSN OF AMERICA . . . . (800)826-0826 Pg 274
U.S. CONSUMER PRODUCT SAFETY HOTLINE . . . . (800)638-2772 Pg 204	UNITED WAY OF THE DESERT . . . . (760)323-2731 Pg 126
U.S. CTR FOR DISEASE CONTROL/PREVENTION . . . . . . (888)246-2675 Pg 204	UNITED WAY/ARROWHEAD . . . . (909)884-9441 Pg 126
U.S. CUSTOMS DRUG SMUGGLING . . . . (800)232-5378 Pg 204	UNITED WAY/CENTRAL COUNTY . . . . (951)929-9691 Pg 126
U.S. DEPT OF AIR FORCE . . . . (951)655-4137 Pg 310	UNITED WAY/CORONA/NORCO . . . . (951)736-0620 Pg 126
U.S. DEPT OF HEALTH & HUMAN SRVS . . . . (800)447-8477 Pg 204	UNITED WAY/DESERT COMMUNITIES . . . . (760)242-5370 Pg 127
U.S. DEPT OF HOUSING/URBAN DEV . . . . (888)827-5605 Pg 212 - 213,295	UNITED WAY/INLAND EMPIRE . . . . (888)435-7565 Pg 204
U.S. DEPT OF INTERIOR/SO. CALIF AGENCY . . . . . . (951)276-6624 Pg 142	UNITED WAY/INLAND VALLEYS . . . . (951)697-4700 Pg 18,127,339
U.S. DEPT OF LABOR/OSHA . . . . (877)889-5657 Pg 139	UNITED WAY/MOJAVE VALLEY . . . . (760)256-8789 Pg 127
U.S. DEPT OF TRANSPORTATION . . . . (202)366-2220 Pg 305	UNITY HOME . . . . Pg 18
U.S. DEPT OF VETERANS AFFAIRS . . . . (800)827-1000 Pg 310	UNIV OF CALIF-RIVERSIDE . . . . (951)827-7344 Pg 315
U.S. ELDER CARE REFERRAL AGENCY . . . . (800)848-1008 Pg 282	UNIV OF CALIF-RIVERSIDE/LIBRARY . . . . (951)827-1012 Pg 231
U.S. FAIR HOUSING/EQUAL OPPORT . . . . Pg 213	UNIVERSITY OF CALIF COOP EXT . . . . (951)683-6491 Pg 157
	UNIVERSITY OF LA VERNE/LAW LIBRARY . . . . (909)460-2070 Pg 231

UNIVERSITY OF REDLANDS LIBRARY . . . . (909)335-4021
    Pg 231

UNO MAS! DOWN SYNDROME ONLINE
    Pg 92,251,274

UPLAND CITY HOUSING AUTHORITY . . . . (909)982-2649
    Pg 209

UPLAND COMMUNITY COUNSELING . . . . (909)579-8100
    Pg 59,331

UPLAND HEAD START/STATE P.S. . . . . (909)931-0147
    Pg 39

UPLAND PUBLIC LIBRARY . . . . (909)931-4200
    Pg 231,236

UPLAND RECREATION DEPT . . . . (909)931-4280
    Pg 339

UPLAND REHAB & CARE CENTER . . . . (909)985-1903
    Pg 92

URBAN EDUCATIONAL PARTNERSHIP . . . . (213)622-5237
    Pg 252,331

USA FEDERAL CREDIT UNION . . . . (888)842-6328
    Pg 157

USC NORRIS COMP CANCER CTR. . . . . (800)872-2273
    Pg 183,194

V

V.A. HEALTH ADMIN CLINIC . . . . (760)341-5570
    Pg 183,310

V.A. HEALTH ADMINISTRATION . . . . (562)826-8000
    Pg 183,310

V.A. MEDICAL CENTER/LOMA LINDA . . . . (909)825-7084
    Pg 183,190,194,310

V.A. MEDICAL CENTER/WEST L.A. . . . . (310)478-3711
    Pg 70

V.I.P. TOTS . . . . (951)652-7611
    Pg 39,92

VA HEALTH CARE BENEFITS . . . . (877)222-8387
    Pg 204,310

VA LIFE INSURANCE HELPLINE . . . . (800)669-8477
    Pg 204

VA MAMMOGRAPHY HELPLINE . . . . (888)492-7844
    Pg 310

VALENCIA PALMS NURSING CENTER . . . . (760)347-6000
    Pg 282

VALLEY HEALTHCARE CENTER . . . . (909)886-5291
    Pg 282

VALLEY IMPROVEMENT PROGRAMS, INC. . . . . (909)983-3665
    Pg 109

VALLEY OASIS ACCESS CENTER . . . . (661)942-2758
    Pg 190

VALLEY OASIS SHELTER . . . .
    Pg 18

VALLEY ORTHOPAEDIC CLINIC . . . . (760)357-3931
    Pg 183

VALLEY RESOURCE CENTER . . . . (760)345-3830
    Pg 92,139

VALLEY RESTART CENTER . . . . (951)766-7476
    Pg 127,190

VALLEY STAR CHILDREN & FAMILY SRVS . . . . (909)388-2222
    Pg 59,331

VALLEY-WIDE COUNSELING SRVS. . . . . (951)654-2026
    Pg 109

VAN BUREN HEAD START . . . .
    Pg 39

VAN HORN YOUTH CENTER (VHYC) . . . . (951)358-4400
    Pg 45

VARP, INC. . . . . (760)922-8625
    Pg 109,310

VCF COMMUNITY SERVICES . . . . (951)789-8514
    Pg 127,139,191,209

VEHICLE SAFETY HOTLINE . . . . (888)327-4236
    Pg 204

VERDUGO PINES BIBLE CAMP . . . . (760)249-3532
    Pg 23

VERONICA'S HOME OF MERCY . . . . (909)888-9064
    Pg 18,31,127,191,258

VETERANS HOME OF CALIF/BARSTOW . . . . (760)252-6200
    Pg 310

VETERANS HOME OF CALIF/CHULA VISTA . . . . (888)857-2146
    Pg 310

VETERANS OF FOREIGN WARS . . . .
    Pg 311

VICTIM SERVICES CENTER . . . . (909)370-5164
    Pg 223

VICTIM-WITNESS ASSISTANCE . . . . (760)256-4810
    Pg 18,31,223 - 224

VICTIMS OF CRIME PROGRAM . . . .
    Pg 224

VICTIMS OF CRIME RESOURCE CTR . . . . (800)842-8467
    Pg 18,224

VICTOR HEADSTART/ST PRESCH . . . . (760)245-9147
    Pg 39

VICTOR VALLEY COLLEGE LIBRARY . . . . (760)245-4271
    Pg 231

VICTOR VALLEY RESCUE MISSION . . . . (760)955-5958
    Pg 127,191

VICTOR VALLEY TRANSIT AUTHORITY . . . . (760)948-3030
    Pg 305

VICTOR VLY COMM COLLEGE/EOPS . . . . (760)245-4271
    Pg 139,331,345

VICTOR VLY COMMUNITY HOSPITAL . . . . (760)245-8691
    Pg 195

VICTOR VLY COMMUNITY SRVS COUNCIL . . . . (760)243-9646
    Pg 127,315

VICTOR VLY DOMESTIC VIOLENCE, INC. . . . . (760)955-8010
    Pg 19,224,252

VICTORIA HEIGHTS APTS . . . . (951)687-2070
    Pg 213

VICTORVILLE SENIOR CITIZENS CLUB . . . . (760)245-5018
    Pg 295

VICTORY OUTREACH/HELENDALE . . . . (760)245-0042
    Pg 109

VICTORY OUTREACH/INLAND ADMIN . . . . (909)884-1921
    Pg 109,317

VICTORY OUTREACH/INTERNATL . . . . (909)599-4437
    Pg 45,109

VICTORY OUTREACH/RIVERSIDE . . . . (951)784-6313
    Pg 109

VICTORY OUTREACH/SANTA ANA . . . . (714)245-2580
    Pg 110

VILLA DE NINOS . . . . (909)484-1903
    Pg 39

VILLA HEALTH CARE CENTER . . . . (951)689-5788
    Pg 282

VILLA MESA CONV HOSPITAL . . . . (909)985-1981
    Pg 92

VILLA MIRAGE II . . . . (760)328-6005
    Pg 213

VILLAGE COUNSELING . . . . (760)773-0669
    Pg 59,110,331

VILLAGE HEALTHCARE CENTER, THE . . . . (951)766-5116
    Pg 282

VILLAGE OF CHILDHELP . . . .
    Pg 31

VINEYARD ANAHEIM . . . . (714)777-4777
    Pg 110,274

VINEYARD OF THE NEW WINE . . . . (951)973-3582
    Pg 127

VIP, INC. . . . . (760)948-1312
    Pg 92,139

VIRGINIA TERRACE APTS . . . . (760)256-0341
    Pg 213

VISITING HOME NURSES INC. . . . . (909)484-7881
    Pg 183

VISITING NURSE ASSN/INLAND . . . .
    Pg 65,92,277

VISTA COMM COUNSELING CTR . . . . (909)854-3420
    Pg 59

VISTA PACIFICA CENTER . . . . (951)682-4833
    Pg 92,296

VISTA PACIFICA CONVALESCENT . . . . (951)682-4833
    Pg 282

VISTA PARK CHINO . . . . (909)591-4212
    Pg 213

VISTERRA CREDIT UNION . . . .
    Pg 157

VITAS SUPPORT GROUP SRVS. . . . . (800)394-6774
    Pg 274

VITILIGO SUPPORT INTERNATL . . . . (818)752-9002
    Pg 183,274

VOLUNTEER CENTER/RIVERSIDE CO. . . . . (951)329-4709	WOMEN'S HEALTH AMERICA . . . . (800)558-7046
Pg 45,59,127,204,213,282,305,315	Pg 205
VOLUNTEER CENTER/VICTOR VALLEY . . . . (760)245-8592	WOMEN'S LAW CENTER . . . .
Pg 46,315	Pg 19,224
VOLUNTEERMATCH . . . . (415)241-6868	WOMEN'S RESOURCE CENTER . . . . (760)757-3500
Pg 315	Pg 19
VOLUNTEERS OF AMERICA/SOUTHWEST CC . . . . . . (909)562-0901	WOMEN'S SPORTS FOUNDATION . . . . (516)542-4700
Pg 252	Pg 339

W

	WONDER VALLEY FIRE STATION . . . . (760)367-3761
	Pg 128
WATERMAN CONVALESCENT . . . . (909)882-1215	WOOD-HAVEN MANOR . . . . (909)980-3106
Pg 282	Pg 213
WAY STATION/YUCCA VALLEY . . . . (760)366-8088	WORKFORCE DEVELOPMENT CENTER . . . . (760)863-2500
Pg 127,191	Pg 140
WE CAN HELP . . . . (760)375-7100	WORKING WONDERS . . . . (760)324-7586
Pg 31,204	Pg 11
WE CARE HOME CARE . . . . (909)792-5096	WORLD INSTITUTE ON DISABILITY . . . . (510)225-6400
Pg 277	Pg 93
WE TIP CRIME HOTLINE. . . . . (800)782-7463	WORLD LITERACY CRUSADE INTERNATL . . . . (310)537-2273
Pg 31,204,317	Pg 236
WEB WISE KIDS . . . . (866)932-9473	WORLD RESEARCH FOUNDATION . . . . (928)284-3300
Pg 252,339	Pg 183,231
WELFARE	WORTHWHILE REFERRAL SOURCES . . . . (818)995-6646
Pg 127,157,191	Pg 224,274
WELL SPOUSE ASSOCIATION . . . . (800)838-0879	WOUNDED WARRIOR RESOURCE CTR . . . . (800)342-9647
Pg 92,274	Pg 205,311
WESCOM CREDIT UNION . . . . (888)493-7266	WWW.ADVOCATESFORYOUTH.ORG. . . . . (202)419-3420
Pg 157 - 158	Pg 11,331
WEST END FAMILY COUNSELING . . . . (909)983-2020	WWW.AGING-PARENTS-AND-ELDER-CARE.COM . . . .
Pg 59,331	Pg 93,252,274,296
WEST END HUNGER PROGRAM/SOVA . . . . (909)391-4882	WWW.BEFRIENDERS.ORG . . . .
Pg 127	Pg 60,205,274
WEST RIVERSIDE HEAD START/ST PRESCH	WWW.CALMEDICARE.ORG . . . . (800)434-0222
Pg 39	Pg 93,158,296
WESTCARE FOUNDATION, INC. . . . . (702)385-2090	WWW.DEAFQUEER.ORG . . . .
Pg 110,331	Pg 93
WESTERN EAGLE FOUNDATION . . . . (951)695-7206	WWW.DUIFOUNDATION.ORG . . . .
Pg 127	Pg 110
WESTMINSTER HEAD START. . . . . (909)983-0600	WWW.GIRLSHEALTH.GOV . . . .
Pg 39	Pg 252,339
WESTSIDE ANNEX HEAD START . . . . (909)383-3442	WWW.GLBTNEARME.ORG . . . .
Pg 39	Pg 274
WESTSIDE CHILD/ADULT TRTMT CTR	WWW.GRANDPARENTING.ORG . . . .
Pg 59,331	Pg 252,296
WESTSIDE COUNSELING CENTER	WWW.GRANDPARENTS.COM . . . . (646)839-8800
Pg 59	Pg 252,274
WESTSIDE PLAZA HEAD START . . . . (909)884-6036	WWW.GRIEFNET.ORG . . . .
Pg 39	Pg 65,274
WESTVIEW FIELD ADULT DEV CTR . . . . (951)699-0047	WWW.HEALTHFINDER.GOV. . . . .
Pg 93	Pg 183,274
WESTVIEW SERVICES, INC. . . . . (714)517-6606	WWW.HELPMYRESUME.ORG. . . . .
Pg 93,139	Pg 140
WESTVIEW TERRACE . . . . (951)849-4333	WWW.HIVDENT.ORG. . . . .
Pg 213	Pg 11,70
WHEELCHAIR TENNIS INFO LINE . . . . (310)208-3838	WWW.HUD.GOV/FORECLOSURE/ . . . .
Pg 93	Pg 158,213
WIA	WWW.IMMUNESUPPORT.COM . . . . (805)564-3064
Pg 139	Pg 93,274
WIC/WOMEN, INFANT AND CHILDREN.	WWW.INCRISIS.NET . . . .
Pg 128,150,258	Pg 46,60,252,331
WIGS FOR KIDS . . . . (440)333-4433	WWW.INSPOT.ORG . . . .
Pg 93,183	Pg 11
WILDOMAR SENIOR LEISURE COMM . . . . (951)678-1555	WWW.LDONLINE.ORG. . . . .
Pg 282	Pg 93
WISR MINISTRIES, INC. . . . . (951)897-5560	WWW.NARCOLEPSYNETWORK.ORG . . . . (888)292-6522
Pg 59,110,331	Pg 275
WOMEN AGAINST GUN VIOLENCE. . . . . (310)204-2348	WWW.NCTEQUALITY.ORG . . . . (202)903-0112
Pg 274	Pg 252,275
WOMEN FOR SOBRIETY . . . . (215)536-8026	WWW.NURSETOWN.COM . . . . (877)282-2416
Pg 110,274	Pg 140
WOMEN HELPING WOMEN NEWSLETTER	WWW.OEFOIF.VA.GOV. . . . .
Pg 274	Pg 60,183,311
WOMEN HELPING WOMEN SRVS . . . . (323)651-2930	WWW.TALKINGWITHKIDS.ORG . . . . (800)244-5344
Pg 60,252,274	Pg 252,331
WOMEN IN TECHNOLOGY INTERNATL . . . . (818)788-9484	WWW.TEENGETGOING.COM . . . . (866)435-7999
Pg 139	Pg 331
WOMEN'S CANCER NETWORK . . . . (800)444-4441	WWW.TRANSPLANTLIVING.ORG . . . . (888)894-6361
Pg 183,274	Pg 183,275
	WWW.VETSPREVAIL.COM . . . .
	Pg 60,311

WWW.WECONNECT.NET . . . .
    Pg 158
WWW.YOUNGSURVIVAL.ORG . . . . (877)972-1011
    Pg 183,275

Y

Y-ME NATIONAL BREAST CANCER ORGN . . . . (312)986-8338
    Pg 184
YELLOW CAB COMPANY . . . . (909)622-1313
    Pg 305
YMCA/CAMP EDWARDS . . . . (909)794-1702
    Pg 23
YMCA/CAMP OAKES . . . . (909)585-2020
    Pg 23
YMCA/CORONA/NORCO . . . . (951)736-9622
    Pg 23,339
YMCA/DESERT . . . . (760)341-9622
    Pg 23,40,340
YMCA/EAST VALLEY . . . . (909)881-9622
    Pg 40,296,340
YMCA/GREATER LONG BEACH . . . . (562)279-1630
    Pg 23
YMCA/HIGHLAND . . . . (909)425-9622
    Pg 340
YMCA/INDIO . . . . (760)347-6698
    Pg 40
YMCA/JURUPA . . . . (951)685-5241
    Pg 40
YMCA/LA QUINTA . . . . (760)564-2848
    Pg 40
YMCA/ONTARIO/MONTCLAIR . . . . (909)986-5847
    Pg 340
YMCA/PALM DESERT . . . . (760)902-1748
    Pg 40,296
YMCA/PALM SPRINGS . . . . (760)320-6430
    Pg 340
YMCA/REDLANDS . . . . (909)798-9622
    Pg 40,340
YMCA/RIVERSIDE CAMP . . . . (951)685-5241
    Pg 23
YMCA/RIVERSIDE FAMILY . . . . (951)689-9622
    Pg 340
YMCA/RIVERSIDE/CHILDCARE . . . . (951)689-4863
    Pg 40
YMCA/THE DESERT . . . . (760)341-9622
    Pg 40
YMCA/UPLAND . . . . (909)946-6120
    Pg 40,340
YOUNG VISIONARIES . . . . (909)881-3382
    Pg 317,331
YOUTH CHANGE . . . . (800)545-5736
    Pg 252,332
YUCAIPA ADULT SCHOOL . . . . (909)790-8580
    Pg 140,215,236
YUCAIPA HEADSTART/ST PRESCHOOL . . . . (909)797-3585
    Pg 40
YUCAIPA TEEN CENTER . . . . (909)797-3662
    Pg 340
YWCA LIVING FREE . . . . (951)530-8127
    Pg 110
YWCA/RIVERSIDE . . . . (951)687-9922
    Pg 31,252,275,340
YWCA/RIVERSIDE CO.. . . . . (951)530-8280
    Pg 110,150,191
YWCA/WINGS SHELTER . . . . (626)338-3123
    Pg 19,205

Z

ZERO TO THREE . . . . (202)638-1144
    Pg 252

A HOME WITHIN

2500 18th Street
San Francisco, CA 94110
(888) 898-2249
(415) 621-6548 FAX

Pairs foster children and youth with private practice therapists who provide free long-term psychotherapy. Provides direct srvs & training and is active in public awareness and advocacy. Fostering Art prgm seeks to provide an avenue for foster youth to express themselves through photography and writing. Branch offices located in various states. Visit (www.ahomewithin.org) for more info. FUNDING: Nonprofit. OFC HRS: M-F 9am-5pm. Spanish spoken. SERVES: U.S.A.

A IS 4 ADOPTION

151 Kalmus Dr.
Costa Mesa, CA 92626
(866) 569-2229

Provide support for women with an unplanned pregnancy. Free services to birth parents. Immediate birth parent assistance with living expenses, relocation, housing, medical & legal needs. We take the worry out of adoption. Visit (www.ais4adoption.com). OFC HRS: M-F 9am-6pm. On call 24 hours, 7 days. Spanish spoken. SERVES: California.

ABC FOSTER FAMILY AGENCY

1520 Brookhollow Dr., Ste 35
Santa Ana, CA 92705
(714) 545-2046
(800) 595-2007
(714) 545-4064 FAX

Recruits and trains foster parents and places children ages birth-18 yrs into certified foster homes. Social work srvs to foster parents and foster children. FUNDING: Govt, nonprofit. OFC HRS: M-F 8:30am-5pm. Korean & Spanish spoken. Foster parents must be ages 21 yrs+. Fees set by state. SERVES: Orange, Riverside & San Bernardino Counties.

ADOPTION CONNECTION

Jewish Family and Child Srvs
1710 Scott St.
San Francisco, CA 94115
(415) 359-2494
(415) 359-2490 FAX

Adoption srvs and parent support group. For after hours emerg, call (800) 972-9225. For adoptive parents, call (415) 359-2494. FUNDING: Nonprofit. OFC HRS: M-F 8:30am-5pm. ADM REQ: Dependent of the court due to abuse or neglect. SERVES: U.S.A.

ADOPTION INFORMATION CENTER

1327 Post Ave., Ste K
Torrance, CA 90501
(424) 757-5170
(424) 757-5172
(424) 757-5181 FAX

Comprehensive adoption info and srvs. Resource and referral agency that addresses the concerns of individuals and families interested in adoption. Assist to birth mothers in a crisis pregnancy, facilitation srvs. FUNDING: Nonprofit. OFC HRS: M-F 9am-5pm. Spanish spoken. SERVES: U.S.A.

ADOPTIONS UNLIMITED, INC.

4091 Riverside Dr., Ste 115
Chino, CA 91710
(909) 902-1412
(888) 923-2229
(909) 902-1414 FAX

Available 24 hrs, 7 days to meet with birth parents, answer questions, discuss srvs, provide counseling & support. Confidential srvs. FUNDING: Nonprofit. OFC HRS: M-Th 9am-5pm. Spanish spoken. Set fees. Free srvs to birth parents. SERVES: L.A., San Bernardino, Riverside, Ventura, Orange, Santa Barbara, Kern, San Diego, San Luis Obispo & Imperial Counties.

ALPHA LEARNING CENTERS

5053 LaMart Dr., Ste 104
Riverside, CA 92507
(951) 328-1020
(951) 784-4123 FAX

Through the Riverside County Office of Education, the learning center provides free tutoring to foster children. Tutoring to non-foster children for a nominal fee. FUNDING: Nonprofit. OFC HRS: M-F 9am-5pm. Tutors available Sat & Sun. Spanish spoken. SERVES: Riverside, Moreno Valley & Perris.

ALPHA TREATMENT CENTERS

Foster Family Agency
5053 La Mart Dr., Ste 107
Apple Valley, CA 92307
(951) 369-5282
(877) 955-2122
(951) 369-1753 FAX

Adoption agency that provides in-home foster family prgm for children who have been neglected, abused or abandoned. Ongoing therapy & case mgmt. FUNDING: State, fed, donations, nonprofit. OFC HRS: M-F 8am-5pm. Spanish spoken. ADM REQ: Child must be dependent of the court. Must be ages 25 yrs+. SERVES: So. Calif.

ALPHA TREATMENT CENTERS

Foster Family Agency
14176 Armagosa Rd., Ste F
Victorville, CA 92392
(760) 955-2122
(760) 955-1331 FAX

In-home residential foster family prgm for neglected, abandoned or abused children. Therapy & case mgmt. FUNDING: Donations, nonprofit. OFC HRS: M-F 8am-5pm. Spanish spoken. ADM REQ: Child must be dependent of court. SERVES: High Desert area.

BETHANY CHRISTIAN SRVS/NATL

Headquarters
P.O. Box 294
901 Eastern Ave., NE
Grand Rapids, MI 49501-0294
(800) 238-4269
(616) 224-7595
(616) 224-7611 FAX

Domestic & internatl adoption (traditional, private or open adoption), foster home placement, pregnancy counseling, assist during pregnancy, special needs children's fund, refugee resettlement, child & family counseling. More than 75 offices in U.S. 800# open 7 days a wk. FUNDING: Fees, donations, churches, nonprofit. OFC HRS: M-F 8:30am-5pm. SERVES: U.S.A.

BETHANY CHRISTIAN SRVS/SO CAL

14125 Telephone Rd., Ste 12
Chino, CA 91710
(877) 465-0057
(909) 465-0057
(909) 628-8294 FAX

Pregnancy counseling, pre-adoptive foster care, adoption srvs. FUNDING: Church, donations, fees, nonprofit. OFC HRS: M-F 9am-5pm. ADM REQ: Adoptive couples must be Christian. Sliding fee scale for adoptive parents. Free pregnancy counseling & srvs for birth parents. SERVES: So. Calif.

BIENVENIDOS FOSTER FAMILY

Agency Headquarters
9736 E. Garvey Ave., 2nd Fl.
South El Monte, CA 91733
(626) 919-3579
(626) 919-2660 FAX

Matches abandoned, abused (sexual, drugs, physical, etc.) and neglected children who are dependents of the court to foster families. In-home support to families, natural family reunification, community referrals, training, support groups & psych assessments. Also offices in Whittier, Riverside, Northridge & Montclair. FUNDING: Donations, govt, nonprofit. OFC HRS: M-F 8:30am-5pm. Spanish spoken. ADM REQ: Children under 18 yrs. SERVES: So. Calif.

BOYS TOWN OF SO CALIF

Look in the index for "Girls & Boys Town of So Calif" for listings for this agency.

CALIF ADOPTION & FOSTER CARE

Referral Line (Kids For Us)
744 P Street, M/S 14-78
Sacramento, CA 95814
(800) 543-7487
(916) 574-1313 FAX

Offers info & referral for adoption srvs by county for Calif residents. FUNDING: State, govt. OFC HRS: M-F 9am-5pm. Spanish spoken. SERVES: Calif.

CALIF DEPT OF SOCIAL SRVS

Adoption Agency
1000 Corporate Center Dr., Ste 630
Monterey Park, CA 91754
(323) 981-1730
(323) 981-1785 FAX

Independent adoption prgm. Also investigates set-aside adoption petitions for finalized adoptions in either the agency or independent adoption prgms. Does not cover agency adoption, but provides resources to find children in agency adoption prgm. Provides info for and helps facilitate interstate and inter-country adoptions. FUNDING: Govt. OFC HRS: M-F 8am-5pm. SERVES: Calif.

CALIF DEPT OF SOCIAL SRVS

Calif Ombudsman for Foster Care
744 P Street, MS 9-025, Rm. 900
Sacramento, CA 95814
(877) 846-1602

(916) 651-6568 FAX

Representatives for each Calif county record and investigate complaints regarding foster care, placement and srvs. Educates foster youth and the public on foster care rights and supports foster youth rights. FUNDING: Govt. OFC HRS: M-F 8am-5pm. 24-hr hotline. Spanish spoken. Free srvs. SERVES: Calif.

CALIF FAMILY LIFE CENTER
Foster Family Agency
930 N. State St.
Hemet, CA 92543
(951) 654-2352

Foster family agency serving infants & children ages birth-18 yrs. Residential care & treatment for abused, neglected, delinquent girls ages 13-17 yrs. For intake, call (951) 765-6955. Youth employment & training prgms for males & females ages 16-21 yrs. Responds to referral within one working day. Licensed facilities. FUNDING: Grants, govt, donations, nonprofit. OFC HRS: M-F 9am-5pm. Spanish spoken. ADM REQ: Referral by county worker, Probation or Social Srvs Depts. SERVES: Riverside County.

CALIF YOUTH CONNECTION
S. Regional Office
901 Corporate Center Dr., Ste 205
Monterey Park, CA 91754
(800) 397-8236
(323) 267-0720
(323) 267-0620 FAX

Advocacy, youth leadership organization run by current and former foster youth with 23 county-based chapters that work in policy development and legislative change targeted to improve the foster care system. FUNDING: Nonprofit. OFC HRS: Varied. ADM REQ: Ages 14-24 yrs. SERVES: Calif.

CAMP CONNECT CALIFORNIA
Aspira Foster & Family Srvs
400 Oyster Point Blvd., Ste 501
South San Francisco, CA 94080
(650) 866-4080
(650) 866-4081 FAX

Week-long summer camp for siblings who are separated by out-of-home foster care. Sibling enhancement, therapeutic art, life seminar. FUNDING: Nonprofit, donations. ADM REQ: Ages 10-18 yrs. SERVES: Calif.

CANYON ACRES CHILDREN & FAMILY SRVS
1845 W. Orangewood Ave., Ste 300
Orange, CA 92868
(714) 383-9401
(714) 383-9300 FAX

Serves children & families through a comprehensive list of community prgms. The mental health clinic includes individual, family, & group therapy, psych medication support, and parent edu classes. The therapeutic afterschool prgm contains an array of structured group activities and a therapeutic horse riding prgm for children that have been identified as needing additional support for a mental health issue. The Creating Family Connections prgm works to find family or kin for dependent youth and engage them in the child's life. Foster care and adoption srvs prgm helps find kids forever families. FUNDING: AFDC-FC, EPSDT, County of Orange Health Care Agency, donations. OFC HRS:

M-F 7am-5pm. Sat appts also available. Spanish spoken. Accepts Medi-Cal. Pvt insurance and cash pay for select srvs. SERVES: Orange Co (all prgms). Select prgms in L.A., Riverside, San Bernardino, & San Diego Counties.

CHILD WELFARE INFORMATION GATEWAY
Formerly Natl Adoption Clearinghouse
1250 Maryland Ave., SW 8th Fl.
Washington, DC 20024
(800) 394-3366
(703) 385-7565
(703) 385-3206 FAX

Provides access to info and resources to help protect children and strengthen families. Child abuse, out-of-home care, adoption referrals available. FUNDING: Govt, nonprofit. OFC HRS: M-F 8:30am-5:30pm, EST. Spanish spoken. SERVES: U.S.A.

CHILDHELP INC.
Foster Family Agency
1743-A Orange Tree Ln.
Redlands, CA 92374
(909) 335-1164
(877) 702-4453
(909) 793-7466 FAX

Foster family agency for placement of children in So. Calif counties, operated under the direction of the Village of Childhelp for children of all ages. Info on how to become a foster parent and certification requirements available upon request. Provides training, support, and financial reimbursement for foster families. FUNDING: AFDC, nonprofit. OFC HRS: M-F 8:30am-5pm. ADM REQ: Foster parents must be ages 21 yrs+. SERVES: So. Calif.

CHILDHELP/WESTERN REGL OFC
Foster Family Agency
1345 El Centro Ave.
Hollywood, CA 90028
(323) 465-4016
(877) 702-4453
(323) 466-4432 FAX

Foster family placement of children of all ages in all So. Calif counties. Info on how to become a foster parent and certification requirements. FUNDING: Nonprofit, AFDC. OFC HRS: M-F 9am-5pm. Spanish spoken. SERVES: U.S.A.

CHILDNET YOUTH & FAMILY SRVS
Formerly Long Beach Youth Centers, Inc.
P.O. Box 4550
5150 E. Pacific Coast Hwy., Ste 365
Long Beach, CA 90804
(562) 498-5500
(562) 498-5501 FAX

ChildNet consists of 5 divisions: Vista Ridge & Zinsmeyer Academies, state-certified, non-public schools for severely emotionally disturbed and learning-disabled children; Foster Family Network recruits, trains, certifies and supports foster homes for children, with 24-hr counseling support; Behavioral Health Srvs provides mental health srvs to low income youth; Wraparound prgm is aimed at keeping at-risk teens out of psychiatric and probation facilities; and adoption srvs. FUNDING: Donations, grants, govt, nonprofit. OFC HRS: M-F 8:30am-5pm. Spanish & Khmer spoken. ADM REQ: Ages birth-17 yrs. Family support srvs extend to entire family, regardless of age. Free srvs for those who qualify. SERVES: L.A., Or-

ange, Riverside, San Bernardino, Kern & Fresno Counties.

CHILDNET YOUTH & FAMILY SRVS
Foster Family Network
12712 Heacock, Ste 9-B
Moreno Valley, CA 92553
(951) 247-6064
(951) 242-6201 FAX

See Long Beach address for srvs. OFC HRS: M-F 8am-5pm. Spanish spoken.

CHILDNET YOUTH & FAMILY SRVS
Foster Family Network
1845 Business Center Dr. #127
San Bernardino, CA 92408
(909) 890-9620
(877) 244-5437
(909) 890-9623 FAX

See Long Beach address for srvs. OFC HRS: M-F 8:30am-5pm. Spanish spoken.

COMMUNITY ACCESS NETWORK
Foster Family Agency/Counseling Ctr
2791 Green River Rd., Ste 101
Corona, CA 92882
(951) 279-3222
(951) 279-5222 FAX

Srvs provided to infants and children ages birth-18 yrs. Residential care & treatment for abused and dependent children. Supportive srvs: weekly social worker contact, foster parent training, crisis response. FUNDING: Nonprofit. OFC HRS: M-F 9am-5:30pm. Spanish spoken. ADM REQ: Court placement. SERVES: Orange, Riverside & San Bernardino Counties.

COMMUNITY CARE LICENSING
Statewide Children's Residential Prgms Office
744 P Street, MS 9-14-48
Sacramento, CA 95814
(916) 651-6040
(916) 651-0515 FAX

Licenses and monitors group homes, foster homes & small family homes, foster family agencies, adoption agencies. FUNDING: Govt. OFC HRS: M-F 8am-5pm. SERVES: Calif.

CONCEPT 7 FAMILY SUPPORT CTRS
Family Support & Treatment Centers
5675 Telegraph Rd., Ste 260
Commerce, CA 90040
(877) 864-4448
(323) 838-9566
(323) 838-9573 FAX

Social work srvs provided to foster parents and foster children. Offers therapeutic and support-related foster srvs for boys and girls. Offers support and guidance for parents who wish to adopt/foster. FUNDING: Govt grants, AFDC, nonprofit. OFC HRS: M-F 8am-5pm. Spanish spoken. SERVES: So. Calif.

CONCEPT 7 FAMILY SUPPORT CTRS
Family Support & Treatment Centers
625 N Main St., Ste 200
Orange, CA 92868
(800) 888-1699
(714) 966-9743 FAX

Social work srvs provided to foster and adoptive parents and foster children. Offers therapeutic and support-related foster srvs for boys and girls. Offers support and guidance for parents who wish to adopt/foster. FUNDING: Nonprofit.

OFC HRS: M-F 8am-5pm. Spanish spoken. SERVES: So. Calif.

CONCEPT 7 FOSTER FAMILY
2990 Inland Empire Blvd., Ste 100
Ontario, CA 91764
(877) 424-2369
(909) 483-2081 FAX

Social work srvs provided to foster and adoptive parents and foster children. Offers therapeutic and support-related foster srvs for boys and girls. Offers support and guidance for parents who wish to adopt/foster. FUNDING: Nonprofit. OFC HRS: M-F 8am-5pm. Spanish spoken. SERVES: So. Calif.

CONCERNED UNITED BIRTHPARENTS (CUB)
P.O. Box 341442
Los Angeles, CA 90034
(800) 822-2777
(858) 712-3317 FAX

Support, search & edu for those affected by the separation of family by adoption, divorce, family feud, etc. Free support meetings & search workshops. Meets 4th Sat of the month at Mesa Vista Hospital, Day Wing, 7850 Vista Hill Ave., San Diego, CA. FUNDING: Donations, nonprofit. New member fee $40. SERVES: Orange, Riverside & San Bernardino Counties, referral to other areas.

DAVID & MARGARET YOUTH & FAMILY SRVS
1350 3rd Street
La Verne, CA 91750
(909) 596-5921
(909) 596-7583 FAX

Residential treatment prgm and specialized non-public school for girls ages 11-18 yrs. Shelter care for children ages 11-18 yrs. Foster family agency and adoption srvs serving children ages birth-18 yrs. Learning enhancement ctr for youth and adults with LD, ADHD, ADD. Community-based edu prgms including self-injury, alcohol and drug intervention, anger mgmt courses. Social srvs, probation and mental health agency referrals. Serves children and families. Provides transitional housing for youth ages 18-25 yrs who are at-risk of homelessness. Provides mentoring prgm for foster youth and pvt counseling on a sliding scale basis. FUNDING: State, county, donations, nonprofit. OFC HRS: M-F 8:30am-5pm. Spanish spoken. Accepts insurance, Medicare, Medi-Cal. Sliding fee scale. Set fee to public. SERVES: So. Calif.

EAST WEST ADOPTIONS, INC.
56 E. Mill St.
Porterville, CA 93267
(888) 242-9604

Internatl adoptions only. Prgm countries include Ethiopia, Russia, China, Ukraine and India. Home studies, post adopt reports, and online education courses available to client families. Adoption grant info available to client families. FUNDING: Nonprofit. OFC HRS: By appt. ADM REQ: Ages 25 yrs+. SERVES: All Calif counties. Interntl prgm avail to residents of other states who have an approved home study & to all U.S. citizens living abroad.

EASTFIELD MING QUONG CHILDREN/FAM
Program UPLIFT
572 N. Arrowhead Ave., Ste 200

San Bernardino, CA 92401
(909) 266-2700
(909) 266-2708
(909) 266-2710 FAX

Residential group home for youth ages birth-18 yrs. Long-term care, short-term emerg care, family reunification, mental health srvs, srvs for abused children and wards of the court, substance abuse prgm, accepts emotionally disturbed children. FUNDING: Nonprofit. OFC HRS: M-F 8am-5pm. Spanish spoken. ADM REQ: Referral from Children's Srvs, Dept of Behavioral Health, or Probation Dept. Accepts Medicare, Medi-Cal, insurance, sliding fee scale. SERVES: San Bernardino County.

ETTIE LEE YOUTH & FAMILY SERVICES
P.O. Box 339
5146 N. Maine Ave.
Baldwin Park, CA 91706-0339
(626) 960-4861
(626) 337-2621 FAX

Family-style homes for severely emotionally disturbed young men ages 8-18 yrs. 24-hr care by trained staff. Individua & group therapy, gang intervention srvs, independent living skills training, case mgmt, family counseling, therapeutic recreation, 12-Step prgms, substance abuse treatment & on-site school. Licensed treatment foster family agency for boys & girls ages birth-18 yrs. Mental health therapy, case mgmt & family counseling. FUNDING: Nonprofit. OFC HRS: M-F 8am-5pm. Spanish spoken. ADM REQ: County referral for group home & foster care. SERVES: So. Calif.

FOSTER FAMILY NETWORK
See "ChildNet Youth & Family Srvs"

GOD'S FAMILIES INTERNATL ADOPTION SRVS
P.O. Box 320
Trabuco Canyon, CA 92678
(949) 858-7621
(949) 858-5431 FAX

Full-srv, Christian state-licensed agency offers home studies and post placement & counseling srvs for internatl adoption. Specializes in adoption placements in Guatemala, Kazakhstan, Russia, Ukraine, Krygyzstan, & Ethiopia. Hague-accredited. FUNDING: Nonprofit. OFC HRS: M-F 10am-5pm. SERVES: Los Angeles, Orange, San Diego, Riverside, Ventura, Santa Barbara & San Bernardino Counties.

GREATER HOPE FOUNDATION
P.O. Box 544
231 E. Main St.
Barstow, CA 92311
(760) 256-0432
(760) 256-3024 FAX

Foster family agency provides srvs to abused, abandoned, neglected children. Foster parent training. FUNDING: Nonprofit, donations, fundraising. OFC HRS: M-Th 8:30am-5pm. Spanish spoken. ADM REQ: Ages birth-18 yrs. SERVES: San Bernardino County.

GUARDIAN SCHOLARSHIP PRGM
Cal State University Fullerton
P.O. Box 6828
800 State College Blvd., Ste C120
Fullerton, CA 92834-6828
(657) 278-4900

Srvs to young men and women ages 17-23 yrs emancipating from foster care or seeking to live

independent of their guardians. Guardian Scholarship Prgm provides academic & living financial assist. Assists with on-campus housing, info & referral, counseling, mentoring, job search and professional networking. Helps youth navigate campus life and gives social support. OFC HRS: M-F 8am-5pm. ADM REQ: Foster youth admitted to Cal State Fullerton with FAFSA form, and no family or benefactor financial support. SERVES: Calif.

HANNAH'S CHILDREN'S HOMES
1045 W. Katella Ave., Ste 330
Orange, CA 92867
(714) 516-1077
(866) 736-8434
(714) 516-1080 FAX

Foster and adoption agency provides out-of-home care for abused and neglected children, ages birth-18 yrs. FUNDING: Nonprofit. OFC HRS: M-F 9am-5pm. Spanish spoken. SERVES: L.A., Orange, Riverside, San Bernardino and San Diego Counties.

HANNAH'S CHILDRENS HOMES
9229 Utica Ave., Ste 140
Rancho Cucamonga, CA 91730
(909) 483-2552
(909) 483-2532 FAX

Foster and adoption agency that provides out-of-home care to abused and neglected children, ages birth-18 yrs. FUNDING: Nonprofit. OFC HRS: M-F 9am-5pm. Spanish spoken. SERVES: Riverside, San Bernardino Counties.

HOLY FAMILY SERVICES
Adoption & Foster Care
P.O. Box 9
701 W. Kimberley Ave., Ste 115
Placentia, CA 92870
(714) 528-6300
(800) 464-2367
(714) 528-6305 FAX

HFS is an accredited California state-licensed, non-denominational adoption and foster care agency. Srvs are provided to birth parents and prospective adoptive parents, adult adoptees (adopted through HFS), and those who wish to become temporary, short-term foster parents. Provides birth parent counseling to those working with other adoption providers and conducts home studies for prospective adoptive parents involved in international and other state adoptions. FUNDING: Nonprofit, fees, grants, donations. OFC HRS: M-F 8:30am-5:30pm. Spanish spoken. ADM REQ: Must be a resident of the 5 county srv area. SERVES: L.A., Ventura, Orange, San Bernardino & Riverside Counties.

HOLY FAMILY SERVICES
Inland Empire
1441 North D Street, Ste 201
San Bernardino, CA 92405-4738
(909) 885-4882
(800) 464-2367
(909) 888-7065 FAX

HFS is an accredited California state-licensed, non-denominational, adoption and foster care agency. Srvs are provided to birth parents and prospective adoptive parents, adult adoptees (adopted through HFS), and those who wish to become temporary, short-term foster parents. Provides birth parent counseling to those working with other adoption providers and conducts home studies for prospective adoptive parents involved in internatl and other state adoptions. FUNDING: Donations, adoption fees, United Way, fndns, guilds, nonprofit. OFC HRS: M-Th 8:30am-5:30pm; F 8:30am-1pm, by appt after hours; 24-hr pager for birth parents who require immediate help. Spanish spoken. Birth parents receive free srvs. Adoptive parents srvs on a sliding fee scale. SERVES: L.A., Orange, Riverside, San Bernardino & Ventura Counties.

HOMES OF HOPE FOSTER FAMILY

Foster Care
1107 S. Glendora Ave.
West Covina, CA 91790
(626) 814-9085
(626) 814-2276 FAX

Recruits and certifies foster families to care for boys and girls ages birth-17 yrs who are under the protection of Children's Srvs. Srvs include: PRIDE training, weekly social worker contact, KIDS fund, counseling, tutoring, transportation, emancipation srvs, and newsletter. 24-hr phone support. FUNDING: Nonprofit. OFC HRS: M-F 8:30am-5pm. Spanish spoken. SERVES: So. Calif.

INDIAN CHILD & FAMILY SERVICES

See "So Calif Indian Center, Inc."

INDIAN CHILD & FAMILY SERVICES

P.O. Box 2269
29377 Rancho California Rd., Ste 200
Temecula, CA 92591
(800) 969-4237
(951) 676-8832
(951) 676-3950 FAX

Counseling referrals for abused children, foster placements, adoptive placements. Tribal Kinship Model used to intervene in the cycle of child abuse. CASA prgm. Spirit Prgm is a prevention/intervention parenting prgm. FUNDING: Bureau of Indian Affairs. OFC HRS: M-F 8am-5pm. ADM REQ: Must be enrolled or eligible for federally recognized tribe. No fees. SERVES: Riverside, San Diego, San Bernardino Counties.

INSTITUTE FOR BLACK PARENTING

Adoption, Foster Care, Family Preservation
3120 Chicago Ave., Ste 130
Riverside, CA 92507
(951) 274-2800
(877) 367-8858
(951) 782-9768 FAX

Adoption and foster care agency specializing in recruiting African-American families for special needs children. Culturally sensitive, personalized free srvs, streamlined application, edu training process. Open to all ethnic groups. FUNDING: Nonprofit. OFC HRS: M-F 8am-5pm. ADM REQ: Foster children ages birth-17 yrs, adults ages 21 yrs+. SERVES: So. Calif.

INTERNATL CHRISTIAN ADOPTION

Institute for Children's Aid
41745 Rider Way, Ste 2
Temecula, CA 92590
(951) 695-3336
(951) 308-1753 FAX

Adoption & relief srvs to U.S. & foreign countries. Assists birth parents who are placing their children for adoption with counseling & support srvs. Provides counseling prgms, reunification srvs, and respite care for foster children. Provides counseling, support, and training srvs for adoptive parents. FUNDING: Donations, fees, nonprofit. OFC HRS: M-F 9am-5pm. Spanish spoken. Other languages vary depending on prgm and country involved. SERVES: Calif.

KINSHIP CENTER

Adoption & Foster Care
414 Tennessee St., Ste Y
Redlands, CA 92373
(909) 798-9547
(800) 454-6744
(909) 798-4138 FAX

Provides adoption and foster family care, parent & professional edu, child dev & mental health clinics, parent recruitments, support and counseling. Conducts child placement studies. Individual, family & group counseling in areas of adjustment to adoption, attachment issues, depression, grief, anxiety, ADHD, behavior difficulties & anger mgmt. FUNDING: Nonprofit. OFC HRS: M-Th 9am-5pm; F 9am-3:30pm. ADM REQ: Ages 20 yrs+. Free birth parent counseling. SERVES: So. Calif.

KINSHIP CENTER

Seedling Project
1504 Brookhollow Dr., Ste 117
Santa Ana, CA 92705
(714) 432-8584
(714) 432-8588 FAX

Early intervention srvs to help decrease children's dev delays. Provides dev & behavioral screenings for children in their homes, in-home support, psychological testing, occupational therapy eval. FUNDING: Nonprofit. OFC HRS: M-F 8am-5pm. Spanish spoken. ADM REQ: Ages birth-6 yrs and have Orange Co. Medi-Cal. SERVES: Orange, Riverside & San Bernardino Counties.

KNOTTS FAMILY AGENCY

1505 W. Highland Ave., Ste 19
San Bernardino, CA 92411
(909) 880-0600
(909) 473-1918 FAX

Residential care facility providing long-term srvs for pregnant & parenting teens & their infants/toddlers. Srvs to troubled adol girls whose lives are complicated by pregnancy or single parenthood. Also srvs to non-pregnant, abused, neglected or abandoned girls ages 12-17 yrs. Adol girls in Juvenile Probation or DPSS. Foster care agency, parenting prgm for parents with children ages birth-5 yrs. FUNDING: Private, nonprofit. OFC HRS: 24 hrs, 7 days. SERVES: Riverside, San Bernardino Counties.

KOINONIA FOSTER HOMES, INC.

Southern California Regional Office
1881 S. Business Center Dr., Ste 10-A
San Bernardino, CA 92408
(909) 890-2381
(877) 244-5374
(909) 890-0580 FAX

Recruits & trains foster and adoptive parents to care for children who are dependents of the juvenile court. Provides child placement services and conducts home studies. Social worker is assigned to provide counseling and other support srvs. Prgm serves children ages birth-18 yrs who have a history of abuse, neglect or delinquency. Foster to Adopt Prgm for those interested in adopting a child. FUNDING: Nonprofit.

OFC HRS: M-F 8am-5pm. Spanish spoken. SERVES: Riverside, San Bernardino Counties.

LDS FAMILY SERVICES

Unwed Pregnancy Options Counseling
791 N. Pepper Ave.
Colton, CA 92324
(909) 824-0480
(909) 824-0487 FAX

No pressure, confidential counseling to unwed parents & their families. A safe, comfortable place provided to discuss various options. Licensed adoption srvs. Individual, marital, and family counseling. Community outreach to interested agencies and organizations. FUNDING: Nonprofit. OFC HRS: M-F 8am-5pm. Spanish & German spoken. Free counseling srvs. SERVES: So. Calif.

LDS FAMILY SERVICES

Adoption Service
13042 Burbank Blvd.
Van Nuys, CA 91401-5409
(818) 781-5511
(800) 537-2229
(818) 781-5595 FAX

Free pregnancy planning and adoption counseling for birth parents, regardless of denomination. Adoptive parents must be LDS members. Satellite clinics in Menifee, Murrieta, Palm Desert, Yucca Valley, Hesperia, Victorville, Corona, Ridgecrest, Arcadia and Ventura. FUNDING: Nonprofit. OFC HRS: M-F 8am-5pm. Spanish spoken. SERVES: So. Calif.

LIBERTY GODPARENT HOME

P.O. Box 4199
124 Liberty Mountain Dr.
Lynchburg, VA 24502
(888) 760-5433
(434) 845-3466
(434) 845-1751 FAX

Christian, residential maternity home offers housing, edu, medical care & counseling for single, pregnant young women who either parent their child or place their child up for adoption. Also network with over 1,300 referrals in U.S.A. & Canada. Srvs for women ages 10-21 yrs. Client must intake by the 24th week of pregnancy. 24-hr helpline. FUNDING: Thomas Road Baptist Church, Lynchburg, Virginia, other churches, donations, nonprofit. OFC HRS: M-F 8am-4:30pm. ADM REQ: Arrangements must be made for medical portion of prgm through admissions coordinator. Free srvs. SERVES: U.S.A. & Canada.

LIFE ADOPTION SERVICES

Adoption & Foster Family Srvs
440 W. Main St.
Tustin, CA 92780
(714) 838-5433
(714) 838-1160 FAX

Hague accredited through COA, Russian accredited agency. Full service domestic & internatl adoption agency providing homestudy and post-placement srvs. FUNDING: Adoption fees, nonprofit. OFC HRS: M-F 9am-4pm. Spanish spoken. ADM REQ: Must be U.S. citizen. Free counseling to birth mothers. SERVES: U.S.A.

LUGGAGE OF LOVE

295 Willis Ave., Ste E
Camarillo, CA 93010

(805) 804-5952
(805) 482-1665 FAX

Organization that is dedicated to providing children in shelters and foster care with a brand new piece of luggage so that their belongings are safe during transition. FUNDING: Nonprofit SERVES: Calif.

MCKINLEY CHILDREN'S CENTER
762 W. Cypress St.
San Dimas, CA 91773
(909) 599-1227
(909) 592-3841 FAX

Level 12 residential care and non-public school for 44 boys ages 7-15 yrs with serious behavioral and emotional problems related to histories of abuse, neglect and inadequate parenting. Specialized residential treatment prgm is designed to meet individual and family needs. FUNDING: State, county, govt. OFC HRS: M-F 8am-5pm. Spanish spoken. SERVES: So. Calif.

MILHOUS CHILDREN'S SERVICES
24077 State Hwy. 49
Nevada City, CA 95959-8519
(530) 265-9057
(530) 292-3803 FAX

Residential group home for boys ages 8-17 yrs. Long-term care, family reunification, mental health srvs. Serves abused children and wards of the court, accepts emotionally disturbed children. FUNDING: Nonprofit. OFC HRS: M-F 8am-4:30pm. Spanish spoken. County-paid services. SERVES: Calif.

MOSES HOUSE MINISTRIES
P.O. Box 2033
15180 Anacapa Rd.
Victorville, CA 92393
(866) 606-6737
(760) 955-1895
(760) 955-1303 FAX

Private Christian family homes offer pregnant young women and teens housing during their pregnancy. Case mgmt, assists with family reunification, edu, employment, parenting, or placing their babies for adoption. Transportation srvs available. Emerg assist prgm for prenant or parenting moms with children ages birth-5 yrs offers bottles, formula, and other necessary supplies. Resource ctr for single moms. FUNDING: Nonprofit, United Way, donations. OFC HRS: M-F 9am-4pm. SERVES: San Bernardino County.

NATL ADOPTION CENTER
1500 Walnut St., Ste 701
Philadelphia, PA 19102
(215) 735-9988
(800) 862-3678
(215) 735-9410 FAX

Expands adoption opportunities throughout the United States, particularly for children with special needs and minorities. Visit (www.adopt.org) to see photos and descriptions of children and adoption info. FUNDING: Donations, nonprofit. OFC HRS: M-F 9am-5pm, EST. SERVES: U.S.A.

NIGHTLIGHT CHRISTIAN ADOPTIONS
Formerly Christian Adopt/Family Srvs
4430 E. Miraloma Ave., Ste B
Anaheim Hills, CA 92807
(714) 693-5437
(888) 933-2237

(714) 693-5438 FAX

Home studies for adopting parents. Assists birth mothers in identifying an adoptive family for their baby. Also internatl adoptions from Taiwan, Kyrgyzstan, Kazakhstan, and Russia. Also offers "Snowflakes" prgm for frozen embryo adoptions. FUNDING: Donations, fees, nonprofit. OFC HRS: M-F 8am-5pm. 24-hr pager srvs. Spanish & Russian spoken. ADM REQ: Varies with prgm. Free counseling for birth parents. Fees for adopting parents. SERVES: U.S.A.

OLIVE CREST TREATMENT CENTER
555 Technology Ct., Ste 300
Riverside, CA 92507
(951) 686-8500
(951) 369-3037 FAX

Intense residential treatment prgm for adolescents experiencing emotional problems, using a medical model with nursing srvs. Centers are accredited and available to children through most health insurance plans. Occupational therapy, dietitian assessment, individual, group and family therapy. Residential care for boys & girls ages 13-17 yrs. Also licensed as a foster care and adoption agency, recruits, trains, provides respite care & network srvs for foster & adoptive families. This prgm places children ages birth-18 yrs in certified foster homes & provides placement srvs for adoptive families. FUNDING: Grants, nonprofit. OFC HRS: M-F 8:30am-5pm. SERVES: So. Calif.

OPTIMIST YOUTH HOMES/FAMILY SRVS
P.O. Box 41-1076
6957 N. Figueroa St.
Los Angeles, CA 90041-1076
(323) 443-3175
(323) 443-3264 FAX

24-hr residential mental health treatment srvs for male adolescents ages 12-18 yrs. Main campus in Highland Park. Four (2 male, 2 female) 6-bed group homes in L.A. County. Non-public school, foster family agency and adoptions prgms, mental health srvs, after care prgms. Referrals through the courts & probation. Limited pvt placements. Accredited by the Council on Accreditation (C.O.A.). FUNDING: Donation, grants, govt, nonprofit. OFC HRS: M-F 9am-5pm. Spanish, Vietnamese & Farsi spoken. Accepts Medi-Cal. SERVES: Calif.

RANCHO DAMACITAS
P.O. Box 890326
Temecula, CA 92589
(951) 302-2317
(951) 302-7015 FAX

Residential prgm providing treatment & srvs for juvenile victims of child abuse. Also operates a foster family agency which certifies, trains & supports foster families. FUNDING: State, county, pvt donations. OFC HRS: M-F 8:30am-4:30pm. ADM REQ: Ages 6-18 yrs. Most children are dependents of the court. SERVES: Orange, Imperial, Riverside, San Bernardino & San Diego Counties.

REECE'S RAINBOW
P.O. Box 4024
Gaithersburg, MD 20885

International adoption agency that specializes in matching American adoptive parents to international children who have Down Syndrome. E-mail Andrea (bamaroberts@comcast.net) or

visit (www.reecesrainbow.com) for more info. FUNDING: Nonprofit. Spanish spoken. ADM REQ: Various adoption parent requirements, see website for more info. SERVES: U.S.A.

RIVERSIDE CO. FAMILY CONCILIATION CT
See, "Thessalonika Family Services"

RIVERSIDE CO. PUBLIC SOCIAL SRVS
Foster Parent Training
23119 Cottonwood Ave., Bldg. A
Moreno Valley, CA 92553
(951) 413-5000
(951) 413-5650 FAX

Support & training for foster parents. Places foster children in approved homes. Call (951) 413-5176 to speak to foster care director. OFC HRS: M-F 8am-5pm SERVES: Riverside County.

RIVERSIDE CO. PUBLIC SOCIAL SRVS
Placement Support Services
10281 Kidd St., 2nd Fl.
Riverside, CA 92503
(800) 665-5437
(951) 358-7001
(951) 358-7640 FAX

Placement support srv & foster parent recruitment. OFC HRS: M-F 8am-5pm. SERVES: Riverside County.

RIVERSIDE CO. PUBLIC SOCIAL SRVS
Adoption Services
10769 Hole Ave., Ste 200
Riverside, CA 92505
(951) 358-3645
(951) 358-3555
(951) 358-6061 FAX

Social workers assist parents who are considering adoption as a plan for their child. Home studies completed on families wishing to adopt a child through this agency. FUNDING: Federal, state, county. OFC HRS: M-F 8am-5pm. Spanish spoken. SERVES: Riverside County.

SAN BERNARDINO CO. CLERK
Adoptions and Free From Custody
351 N. Arrowhead Ave.
San Bernardino, CA 92415-0063
(909) 384-1888
(909) 387-3000 FAX

OFC HRS: M-F 8am-4pm. Spanish spoken. SERVES: San Bernardino County.

SAN BERNARDINO CO. HUMAN SRVS SY
Dept Children's Srvs/Adoption Srvs
412 W. Hospitality Lane, 2nd Fl.
San Bernardino, CA 92415
(909) 891-3300
(909) 891-3399 FAX

Public agency providing relinquishment adoption srvs to children, birthparents and potential adoptive parents. Pregnancy counseling provided at no charge to any person who asks to discuss the alternatives in a non-pressured, relaxed manner. Counseling srvs are also available to birthfathers. Birthparents may select and meet adoptive parents and participate in "Open Adoptions." When it is not possible or practical for children to live with their birth parents, permanent families interested in adopting are educated about the adoption process and the adopted child. All adoptive families participate in the "home study" process prior to being considered for placement of an adoptive child or siblings. Child abuse hotline (800) 827-8724.

FUNDING: County, state, federal. OFC HRS: M-F 8am-5pm. Spanish spoken. SERVES: San Bernardino County.

SAN BERNARDINO CO. HUMAN SRVS SY
Transitional Assistance
150 S. Lena Rd.
San Bernardino, CA 92415
(909) 388-0245
(909) 388-0233 FAX

Social Srvs Administrative Office, transitional assist. Child abuse hotline (800) 827-8724, Adoption Srvs (909) 891-3300. FUNDING: Govt. OFC HRS: M-F 8:30am-4:30pm. Spanish spoken. ADM REQ: Low income. SERVES: San Bernardino County.

SAN BERNARDINO CO. HUMAN SRVS SY
Dept Children's Srvs/Adoption Srvs
15480 Ramona Ave.
Victorville, CA 92392
(760) 243-6640
(760) 843-4211 FAX

See San Bernardino address for description. OFC HRS: M-F 8am-5pm. Spanish spoken.

SAN BERNARDINO CO/FIRST 5
Kelly Torres Resource Center
330 North D Street
San Bernardino, CA 92401
(909) 386-7706
(909) 386-7703 FAX

Parent edu, resource ctr, child dev & child health srvs. FUNDING: Govt. OFC HRS: M-F 8:30am-4:30pm. Spanish, Vietnamese, Tagalog, Chinese spoken. SERVES: San Bernardino County.

SENECA CTR FOR CHILDREN & FAMILIES
Admin Office
2275 Arlington Dr.
San Leandro, CA 94578
(510) 481-1222
(510) 481-1605 FAX

Residential treatment, intensive treatment foster care, day, in-home & outpatient srvs for children with emotional, behavioral & learning problems. Center for Living Skills works with public schools in conflict resolution, leadership, drug & alcohol edu. FUNDING: Nonprofit. OFC HRS: M-F 8am-5:30pm. Spanish speaker by arrangement. ADM REQ: Ages 3-18 yrs. SERVES: Calif.

SO CALIF INDIAN CENTER, INC.
Corporate Office
10175 Slater Ave., Ste 150
Fountain Valley, CA 92708-4702
(714) 962-6673
(714) 962-6343 FAX

Edu, cultural, economic & recreational prgms for American Indians. Indian Child & Family Srvs (counseling, parenting, foster parents, etc.), WIA (employment assist & voc training), edu tutoring for Indian students in grades K-12. Emerg shelter, food, clothing, referral srvs. FUNDING: United Way, govt, nonprofit. OFC HRS: M-F 8am-5pm. ADM REQ: American-Indian verification. SERVES: So. Calif.

ST. ANNE'S
155 N. Occidental Blvd.
Los Angeles, CA 90026-4641
(213) 381-2931
(213) 381-7804 FAX

Residential care prgm provides a safe haven for teenagers, ages 13-18 yrs, and their babies where they can grow to be caring and nurturing parents. Transitional housing prgm for single mothers available for up to 24 months. Residents receive edu and vocational srvs, medical care, psychiatric counseling, social srvs, parenting training, substance abuse counseling, life skills dev, info & referral srvs. Family-based srvs prgm offers in-home care to at-risk young women and their families. FUNDING: Donation, grants, govt, nonprofit. OFC HRS: M-F 9am-6pm; 24-hr facility. Spanish spoken. SERVES: Calif.

THE CHILDREN'S VILLAGE OF SONOMA CO.
1321 Lia Lane
Santa Rosa, CA 95404
(707) 566-7044
(707) 566-7105 FAX

Provides nurturing, stable family homes in a multi-generational, enriched environment for children and their siblings in foster care. Goals: to establish stability for foster children, opportunity for siblings to remain together and allow children to develop healthy emotional attachments in a nurturing environment. FUNDING: Grants, donations. OFC HRS: M-F 8:30am-5pm. SERVES: Nationwide.

THESSALONIKA FAMILY SERVICES
P.O. Box 890326
Temecula, CA 92589
(951) 302-2317
(951) 302-7015 FAX

Provides long-term care for children in a group home. Staff and therapists develop individualized treatment plan for each child. FUNDING: DPSS, adoption assist, AB2627. OFC HRS: M-F 8am-4:30pm. ADM REQ: Ages 6-18 yrs. Call first. SERVES: Riverside, San Bernardino, Orange, San Diego, & Imperial Counties.

AIDS ASSISTANCE PROGRAM

P.O. Box 4182
1276 N. Palm Cyn., Ste 108
Palm Springs, CA 92262
(760) 325-8481
(760) 325-1893 FAX

Food vouchers to low income people who are HIV+ or are living with AIDS. Bilingual website (www.aidsassistance.org). FUNDING: Nonprofit. OFC HRS: M-F 8am-3pm. Spanish by arrangement. ADM REQ: Must have lived in the area one year, proof of income, valid ID, application. Must meet income level. No cost to client. SERVES: Desert communities.

AIDS CLEARINGHOUSE

See "Calif AIDS Clearinghouse"

AIDS CLINICAL TRIAL INFO SRV

See "AIDS Info"

AIDS CLINICAL TRIALS UNIT SUBSITE

UCLA School of Medicine
1124 W. Carson St., Bldg N-24
Torrance, CA 90502
(310) 222-3848
(310) 533-0447 FAX

HIV/AIDS testing, treatment, edu & prevention, info & referral, counseling & research. FUNDING: Govt. OFC HRS: M-F 7am-6pm. Spanish spoken. ADM REQ: HIV+ diagnosis. SERVES: U.S.A.

AIDS EDU & GLOBAL INFO SYSTEM

P.O. Box 184
32302 Alipaz St. #267
San Juan Capistrano, CA 92693
(949) 495-1952
(949) 443-1755 FAX

Open access website contains HIV prevention, testing and comprehensive treatment info, and a variety of interactive srvs. Visit (www.aegis.org). FUNDING: Nonprofit. OFC HRS: 24-hr srvs. SERVES: Internatl.

AIDS HEALTHCARE FNDN/UPLAND

8263 Grove Ave., Ste 201
Rancho Cucamonga, CA 91730
(909) 579-0708
(800) 243-2101
(909) 579-0778 FAX

Full range of medical srvs for people with HIV. Open to all, even if not covered by health insurance. ADAP enrollment site. OFC HRS: Tu, Th 8:30am-5pm. Night clinic: Open Tu until 8pm. Spanish spoken. SERVES: Riverside, San Bernardino Counties.

AIDS HOTLINE

See "CDC Natl AIDS Hotline"

AIDS INFO

P.O. Box 6303
Rockville, MD 20849-6303
(800) 448-0440
(301) 318-2818 FAX

Current info on federally & privately sponsored clinical trials for adults and children at all stages of HIV infection. Provides contacts for open clinical trials, printouts, custom database searches, press releases and relevant pamphlets and booklets via mail, fax, etc. Phone reference srvs for people with HIV, their families and health care providers. Offers treatment info. TTY/TDD (888) 480-3739. Web chat 12noon-4pm, EST (www.aidsinfo.nih.gov). FUNDING: Govt. OFC HRS: M-F 12noon-5pm, EST. Spanish reference specialist available. Free srvs. SERVES: U.S.A.

AIDS RESEARCH ALLIANCE OF AMERICA

1400 S. Grand Ave., Ste 701
Los Angeles, CA 90015
(310) 358-2423
(310) 358-2431 FAX

Conducts research and clinical trials to find and accelerate the dev of effective HIV treatments. Partners with the pharmaceutical industry and others to create a link to disease research. Volunteer opportunities available. For the clinic, call (310) 358-2429. FUNDING: Donations. SERVES: U.S.A.

ALIVE AND WELL

AIDS Alternatives
11684 Ventura Blvd.
Studio City, CA 91604
(818) 780-1875
(877) 922-5483
(818) 780-7093 FAX

Support, edu, and advocacy network. Free monthly events, distributes free info packets upon request. Also provides referrals and resources. Please e-mail (info@aliveandwell.org) or visit website (www.aliveandwell.org). FUNDING: Nonprofit, donations. Spanish and Italian spoken. SERVES: U.S.A.

ASSN OF REGIONAL CTR AGENCIES

915 L Street, Ste 1440
Sacramento, CA 95814
(916) 446-7961
(916) 446-6912 FAX

21 regional centers offer support srvs for people with dev disabilities. Also HIV/AIDS edu & prevention. FUNDING: Nonprofit. OFC HRS: M-F 8:30am-5pm. Spanish spoken. Free srvs. SERVES: Calif.

BEAR HAWK EDUCATION SERVICES

100 S. Sunrise Way, PMB 292
Palm Springs, CA 92262
(760) 329-4457
(800) 367-2437
(760) 329-7803 FAX

HIV & outreach srvs to high-risk populations. Pre- and post- HIV test referral srvs, hotline info, mental health & shelter facilities. Srvs provided at 65861 Pearson St., Ste C, Desert Hot Springs. FUNDING: Nonprofit. OFC HRS: M 9am-5pm; Tu-Th 9am-3pm. SERVES: Blythe to Banning.

BLACK AIDS INSTITUTE

Formerly African American HIV Univ
1833 W. 8th Street, Ste 200
Los Angeles, CA 90057
(213) 353-3610
(213) 989-0181 FAX

HIV/AIDS edu, prevention prgm, info & referral srvs. FUNDING: Nonprofit. OFC HRS: M-F 9am-5:30pm. Spanish spoken. Free srvs. SERVES: U.S.A.

CALIF AIDS CLEARINGHOUSE

Calif Office on AIDS
1616 Capitol Ave., Ste 616
Sacramento, CA 95814
(916) 558-1784

Targets Calif Dept of Health Srvs, Office of AIDS funded community edu & prevention prgms & HIV test sites. Offers materials, info & communication regarding HIV/AIDS & bulk purchasing and printing to allow prgms to join together for lower cost. Pre-printed materials, fact sheet originals and self-customized materials with prgm's logo & local contact numbers. Currently undergoing an operational transition. E-mail (CACTransitionInfo@cdph.ca.gov) for more specific info. FUNDING: State, nonprofit. OFC HRS: M-F 8am-5pm. Spanish spoken. SERVES: Calif.

CALIF DEPT HEALTH SRVS

Prevention Srvs Division
1616 Capitol Ave., Ste 616
Sacramento, CA 95814
(916) 449-5900
(916) 449-5909 FAX

Drug assist, HIV/AIDS srvs. Mailing address: P.O. Box 997426, Sacramento, CA 95899-7426. FUNDING: Govt. OFC HRS: M-F 8am-5pm. Spanish spoken. Free srvs. SERVES: Calif.

CALIF HIV/AIDS INFO & REFERRAL

See "San Francisco AIDS Foundation"

CAMP LAUREL

75 S. Grand Ave.
Pasadena, CA 91105
(626) 683-0800
(626) 683-0890 FAX

Year-round residential camps for children living with HIV/AIDS. Horseback riding, swimming, mountain bike riding, rock climbing, canoeing, archery, arts & crafts, ropes course, overnight trips. One-week camps, several times during the year. FUNDING: Nonprofit, donations, grants. OFC HRS: M-F 9am-6pm. Spanish spoken. Free for eligible children. SERVES: U.S.A.

CATHOLIC CHARITIES/COMMUNITY SRVS

Inland Valleys Regional Center
23623 Sunnymead Blvd., Ste E
Moreno Valley, CA 92553
(951) 924-9964
(951) 924-9997 FAX

Emerg srvs for low income. Assists with food, utility, rental assist & motel vouchers (when funding is available). Info & referral, immigration & citizenship prgm, HIV/AIDS housing assist. For counseling, call (909)763-4970 or (951)801-5282. FUNDING: Nonprofit. OFC HRS: M-Th 8:30am-4:30pm. By appt only. Spanish spoken. Most srvs free. SERVES: Moreno Valley, Riverside, Perris, Hemet, San Jacinto, Sun City, Corona, Lake Elsinore, Banning, Beaumont, Cherry Valley.

CATHOLIC CHARITIES/COMMUNITY SRVS

Administration
1450 North D Street
San Bernardino, CA 92405
(909) 388-1239
(909) 384-1130 FAX

Psychological counseling for individuals & family, case mgmt, emerg food, diapers, clothing, furniture (when available), utility assist, holiday baskets, transportation, advocacy, HIV/AIDS srvs, info & referrals. Emerg housing for needy transients with pre-arranged motel accommodations (as funds allow). Refugee & immigration srvs, parolee reintegration. FUNDING: Donations, nonprofit. OFC HRS: M-F 8:30am-4:30pm. Spanish, Chinese, Filipino, Vietnamese, Russian Sliding fee scale. SERVES: San Bernardino & Riverside Counties.

CDC NATL AIDS HOTLINE
English or Spanish
(800) 232-4636
(888) 282-7681 FAX

24-hr hotline offering AIDS & STD info, nationwide referrals and free literature for anyone in the U.S. TTY (888) 232-6348. Free srvs. SERVES: U.S.A.

CDC NATL PREVENTION INFO NETWORK
P.O. Box 6003
Rockville, MD 20849-6003
(800) 458-5231
(888) 282-7681 FAX

Provides primary reference, referral & publications for HIV and AIDS info. Helps identify organizations, clinics, hospitals, external care, HIV/AIDS conferences, public health depts, private, community-based agencies with HIV and AIDS related srvs. Locates hard to find edu materials, teaching guides and sources of funding for HIV/AIDS prgms. For AIDS clinical trials info, call (800) TRIALS-A. For treatment info, call (800) HIV-0440. TTY/TDD (800) 243-7012. OFC HRS: M-F 9am-6pm, EST. Spanish spoken. SERVES: U.S.A.

CEDARS-SINAI MEDICAL CENTER
AIDS & Immune Disorder Center
8700 Beverly Blvd., Ste B-220
Los Angeles, CA 90048
(310) 423-3896
(800) 233-2771
(310) 423-4599 FAX

32-bed inpatient unit for patients with HIV/AIDS. FUNDING: Donations, grants, nonprofit. SERVES: So. Calif.

CENTRAL CITY LUTHERAN MISSION
1354 North G Street
San Bernardino, CA 92405
(909) 381-6921
(909) 884-5104 FAX

Transitional housing for homeless persons with HIV. Edu & prevention, info & referral, outreach srvs. FUNDING: Nonprofit. OFC HRS: M-F 9am-5pm. Spanish spoken. Free srvs. SERVES: San Bernardino County.

CHILDREN AFFECTED BY AIDS FNDN
6033 W. Century Blvd., Ste 603
Los Angeles, CA 90045
(310) 258-0850
(310) 258-0851 FAX

Works to improve the lives of children infected or affected by AIDS. Direct srvs to families with children under age 13 yrs, Camp Network, Dial-A-Kid, Play Areas Initiative. Visit (www.caaf4kids.org). FUNDING: Donations, corps, fndns, grants. SERVES: U.S.A.

CHRISTOPHER WAHL YOUTH CENTER
12401 Slauson Ave., Ste G
Whittier, CA 90606

(562) 693-2247
(562) 954-7264 FAX

Offers free HIV testing and prevention edu. Houses various support groups and 12-Step prgms including Celebrate Recovery. FUNDING: Nonprofit. OFC HRS: M-F 9am-5pm. Free srvs. SERVES: L.A. County, San Bernardino County.

CLINICAS DE SALUD DEL PUEBLO, INC
Blythe Family Health Center
321 W. Hobson Way, Ste C
Blythe, CA 92225
(760) 922-4981
(760) 922-4442 FAX

Primary health care for all ages. AIDS/STD, pediatrics. FUNDING: BPHC site, donations, nonprofit. OFC HRS: M-F 8am-5pm. Spanish spoken. ADM REQ: Low income. Accepts insurance, Medicare, Medi-Cal, sliding fee scale. SERVES: Blythe & nearby.

COMMUNITY HEALTH SYSTEMS, INC.
Eastside Health Ctr
1970 University Ave.
Riverside, CA 92507
(951) 224-8220
(951) 328-9574 FAX

Primary health care for all ages. Prenatal, HIV testing, AIDS/STD screenings, teen clinic, family planning, immunizations, counseling. Enrollment assist for Medi-Cal, Healthy Families, Healthy Kids. FUNDING: BPHC site, donations, nonprofit. OFC HRS: M-F 8am-5:30pm. Spanish spoken. ADM REQ: Low income. Accepts insurance, Medicare, Medi-Cal, sliding fee scale. SERVES: Riverside County.

COMMUNITY HEALTH SYSTEMS, INC.
Arlanza Family Health Ctr
8856 Arlington Ave.
Riverside, CA 92503
(951) 353-2702
(951) 353-2976 FAX

Primary care for all ages. Family planning, HIV/AIDS, STD testing, Teenage Edu to Avoid Motherhood (T.E.A.M.), Child Health and Disability prgm. Also dental clinic. FUNDING: Nonprofit. OFC HRS: M-F 8am-5:30pm. Accepts Medi-Cal, Medicare, insurance, sliding fee scale. SERVES: Riverside County.

CSAT HOTLINE
(800) 729-6686

CSAT (Center for Substance Abuse Treatment) answers questions about drug abuse & AIDS as it relates to IV drug users. Referrals to support groups & drug treatment prgms. TDD (800)487-4889. Spanish (877) 767-8432. FUNDING: Govt. OFC HRS: 24 hrs, 7 days. Spanish spoken. SERVES: U.S.A.

DESERT AIDS PROJECT
P.O. Box 2890
1695 N. Sunrise Way
Palm Springs, CA 92263-2890
(760) 323-2118
(866) 331-3344
(760) 323-9865 FAX

HIV health center (outpatient specialty clinic), support groups for HIV positive, caregivers, partners or family. Anonymous testing for HIV & syphilis. Counseling, in-home care, pro bono legal clinic, prevention & edu, case mgmt, "friend-to-friend" & admin volunteer prgm, sub-

stance abuse srvs, transportation, food, child care. ADAP enrollment site. For satellite ofc, call(760) 342-4197. TDD (760) 969-1796. FUNDING: Nonprofit. OFC HRS: M-F 8am-5pm. Spanish spoken. ADM REQ: HIV positive. Free srvs or sliding fee scale. SERVES: Eastern Riverside Co. & upper desert of San Bernardino County.

DIVISION OF JUVENILE JUSTICE
Calif Dept of Corrections Healthcare Srvs
4241 Williamsborough Dr., Ste 217
Sacramento, CA 95823
(916) 262-1396
(916) 262-1087 FAX

HIV/AIDS awareness edu and prevention, info and referral. FUNDING: Govt. OFC HRS: M-F 8am-5pm. Free srvs. SERVES: Calif.

FLOWERS HERITAGE FOUNDATION
Bridge the Gap Program
200 Webster St., Ste 200
Oakland, CA 94607
(510) 587-2668
(510) 587-2794 FAX

Prgm helps people with HIV/AIDS and low incomes to afford their medications. Also offers health edu, advocacy, and community grants for nonprofit agencies. FUNDING: Nonprofit. Free srvs. SERVES: Calif.

FOOTHILL AIDS PROJECT
362 Orange Show Lane
San Bernardino, CA 92408
(909) 884-2722
(909) 884-2732 FAX

HIV testing, counseling, case mgmt, support groups, financial assist, housing, edu & prevention, info & referral, outreach. Offers 3 additional offices in Riverside/San Bernardino Counties. FUNDING: Nonprofit. OFC HRS: M-F 9am-5pm. Spanish spoken. Free srvs. SERVES: San Bernardino County.

GLBT NATIONAL HELP CENTER
2261 Market St., PMB #296
San Francisco, CA 94114
(415) 355-0003
(415) 552-5498 FAX

Hotlines and online chat support for the GLBT population including emotional support with coming out, info on HIV/AIDS, relationships, and safe sex. Gay & Lesbian National Hotline: (888) 843-4564, email (glnh@glbtnationalhelpcenter.org). Gay & Lesbian Youth Talkline: (800) 246-7743, email (youth@glbtnationalhelpcenter.org). FUNDING: Nonprofit. OFC HRS: M-F 1pm-9pm; Sat 9am-2pm. Free srvs. SERVES: U.S.A.

GREATER L.A. AGENCY ON DEAFNESS
Administrative Office
2222 Laverna Ave.
Los Angeles, CA 90041
(323) 478-8000
(323) 550-4205 FAX

Srvs for deaf and hard-of-hearing persons include: interpreter referral, info & referral, advocacy, document and phone assist, job placement, ASL classes for people who are HOH or late deaf, facility rental. Tobacco control prgm, AIDS/HIV edu srvs, family health edu and bookstore, life signs, interpreting referral srvs. TTY (323) 550-4226. FUNDING: Nonprofit. OFC HRS: M-F 8:30am-5pm. ASL available. Free srvs. SERVES: So. Calif.

HEALTH INFO LINE/RIVERSIDE CO.

Riverside Co. Dept of Health
4065 County Circle Dr.
Riverside, CA 92503
(951) 358-5000
(951) 358-4529 FAX

A comprehensive health info and referral line to help the public access the county health system. For TDD, call (951) 358-5124. OFC HRS: M-Th 7:30am-5pm. Spanish spoken. SERVES: Riverside County.

HEART TOUCH PROJECT

3400 Airport Ave., Ste 42
Santa Monica, CA 90405
(310) 391-2558
(310) 391-2168 FAX

Compassionate & healing touch therapy provided by professional therapists & volunteers to persons with AIDS, non-ambulatory persons, senior citizens, persons receiving hospice care, infants & children. FUNDING: Nonprofit. OFC HRS: M-F 10am-6pm. ADM REQ: Must have approval of primary health provider to ensure that the massage is allowed for the patient's condition. Accepts donations. Free srvs. SERVES: So. Calif.

HEMOPHILIA FNDN OF SO CALIF

6720 Melrose Ave., Ste 102
Hollywood, CA 90038
(800) 371-4123
(323) 525-0440
(323) 525-0445 FAX

Info & referral srvs related to hemophilia, HIV/AIDS and hepatitis C, summer camp, youth Medic-Alert sponsorships, scholarships, resource library, info seminars, family retreats, holiday parties, and counseling referrals. FUNDING: Donations, grants, nonprofit. OFC HRS: M-F 10am-5pm. Spanish spoken. ADM REQ: All ages with hemophilia & other bleeding disorders, & their families. Free srvs. SERVES: So. Calif.

HERPES RESOURCE CENTER

CDC National STI Hotline
P.O. Box 13827
Research Triangle Park, NC 27709
(800) 227-8922
(919) 361-8488
(919) 361-8425 FAX

ASHA (American Social Health Assn) provides a network of over 90 herpes (HELP) and HPV support groups throughout the U.S. Write to request a complete list of groups or call (919) 361-8400. Visit (www.ashastd.org) for info & counseling about any aspect of the herpes simplex virus. 24-hr hotline for STDs/AIDS (800) 342-2437. Natl herpes hotline (916) 361-8488. FUNDING: Nonprofit. Hotline hrs: M-F 9am-6pm, EST. Free srvs. SERVES: U.S.A.

INLAND AIDS PROJECT

3767 Elizabeth St.
Riverside, CA 92506
(951) 224-8314
(951) 683-2965 FAX

Case mgmt for HIV-infected persons, counseling, support groups, emerg food and shelter, utility assist, relapse prevention counseling, edu outreach, advocacy and medical referrals. Counseling available for significant others. FUNDING: Nonprofit. OFC HRS: M-F

8:30am-5pm. ADM REQ: HIV+. SERVES: Riverside County.

MEDICAL SOCIETY

See "San Bernardino Co. Medical Society"

MERCY HOUSE TRANSITIONAL LIVING

P.O. Box 1905
730 Garfield St.
Santa Ana, CA 92702
(714) 836-7188
(714) 836-7901 FAX

Operates 3 transitional living centers in Santa Ana. Joseph House serves single, employable men; Regina House serves single, employable mothers and their children, ages 10 yrs and under; Emmanuel House serves single adults living with HIV or AIDS; Guadalupe House and Assisi House in Ontario offer supportive housing for single mothers, single men and single women. Also offers Trinity House for men; case mgmt, life skills classes, job dev, & referrals. All prgms require sobriety. Also offers rental assist and cold weather shelters (Fullerton and Santa Ana) during winter months (714) 836-7188. FUNDING: Grants, donations, nonprofit. Spanish spoken. ADM REQ: Homeless, drug and alcohol free; employed, readily employable or going to school. Other criteria vary by program. SERVES: Southern California.

METH RESOURCES

www.methresources.gov
(916) 324-5523

Visit website to find various resources and prgms in the fight against meth. FUNDING: Govt. SERVES: U.S.A.

MINORITY HEALTH OUTPATIENT

Substance Abuse Foundation
3125 E. 7th Street
Long Beach, CA 90804
(562) 987-7522
(562) 434-7463 FAX

Licensed staff provide free mental health srvs to HIV+ individuals and their families. Address above is for residential office. 24-hr hotline: (888) 476-2743. FUNDING: Nonprofit. OFC HRS: M-F 8am-4pm. Spanish spoken. SERVES: So. Calif.

MULTICULTURAL AIDS RESOURCE CTR

Polaris Research & Development
390 4th Street
San Francisco, CA 94107
(415) 777-3229
(415) 512-9625 FAX

AIDS research & public awareness. AIDS edu, prevention, info & referral. FUNDING: Nonprofit. OFC HRS: M-F 9am-5pm. Spanish & Tagalog spoken. Sliding fee scale. SERVES: Calif.

NATL AIDS HOTLINE

See "CDC Natl AIDS Hotline"

PACIFIC AIDS EDU & TRAINING CTR

50 Beale St., Ste 1300
San Francisco, CA 94105-0361
(415) 597-8198
(415) 897-9213 FAX

AIDS/HIV training, edu & info srvs provided to health care providers. Various locations in Calif. OFC HRS: M-F 8am-5pm. SERVES: U.S.A.

PECHANGA INDIAN HEALTH CLINIC

12784 Pechanga Rd.

Temecula, CA 92592
(951) 676-6810
(951) 676-0744 FAX

Comprehensive health care, mental health (individual and family counseling), nutrition, pharmacy, lab, nursing, AIDS testing, family planning, patient transportation srvs. FUNDING: Fed, state, county. OFC HRS: M-Th 8am-5pm; F 8am-2pm. ADM REQ: Eligible American Indian dependents only. Must have appt. Accepts Medi-Cal for eligible patients only. Sliding fee scale. Free srvs to qualified Indians.

PLANNED PARENTHOOD/RIVERSIDE

3772 Tibbetts St., Ste A
Riverside, CA 92506
(888) 743-7526
(951) 682-7904 FAX

Birth control, pap smear, gynecology exams, breast exams, morning-after pill, pregnancy testing, option counseling, pregnancy termination, diagnosis and treatment of STDs for men and women, sterilization for men and women, HIV testing, counseling. Health educator offers presentations to community groups on issues relating to reproductive health care. Wait varies. FUNDING: State (Office of Family Planning), donations. Surgical Srvs Hrs: M-F 8am-7:30pm; Sat 8:30am-5pm. Spanish spoken. Accepts Medi-Cal, sliding fee scale. Annual exams $0-66 (based on income). Donations requested. SERVES: Riverside, San Diego Counties.

POLARIS RESEARCH & DEVELOPMENT

See "Multicultural AIDS Resource Ctr"

PROJECT INFORM

1375 Mission St.
San Francisco, CA 94103
(415) 558-8669
(415) 558-0684 FAX

Fights for an HIV and HCV cure by advancing national research agenda to generate optimal treatments; helps secure expanded access to quality health care for low income individuals. Provides free, reliable info on living with HIV through its natl HIV treatment and care benefits hotline: (866) HIV-INFO, M-F 10am-4pm. FUNDING: Nonprofit. OFC HRS: M-F 9am-5pm. Spanish spoken. SERVES: Internatl.

RIVERSIDE CO. DEPT/MENTAL HEALTH

Substance Abuse Treatment
1827 Atlanta Ave., Ste D-1
Riverside, CA 92507
(951) 955-2105
(951) 955-8060 FAX

Srvs provided to substance abusers and their families. Outpatient counseling, referral to residential treatment and detox, prevention edu, pregnant addicts and women's prgms. Outpatient day prgm for men, women, youth, transgendered and parolees. Non-medical detox, co-occurring srvs. HIV certified counselor, pre-test and post-test counseling, HIV tests. Lectures on AIDS edu and prevention. For detox, call (951) 955-2100. State ID: 330023CN. FUNDING: Nonprofit. OFC HRS: M-Th 8am-6pm. Spanish spoken. ADM REQ: Ages 13 yrs+ and Medi-Cal eligible. Call for more info. Accepts Medi-Cal, sliding fee scale. SERVES: Riverside County.

RIVERSIDE CO. PUBLIC HEALTH DEPT

Corona Health/Family Care Center
505 S. Buena Vista Ave., Ste 101
Corona, CA 92882-1901
(951) 272-5445
(951) 272-5489 FAX

Primary care srvs, family planning, pregnancy testing, STD testing, diagnosis and treatment, OB/GYN, family planning, pediatric, treatment of non-emerg medical problems. Wait: Varies. For an appt, call (800) 720-9553. FUNDING: Govt. OFC HRS: M-F 7:30am-5pm. Spanish spoken. Accepts Medi-Cal/MIA, ability to pay, insurance, pvt pay. Fee scale based on family size, income, & srv provided. SERVES: Corona, Norco.

RIVERSIDE CO. PUBLIC HEALTH DEPT

Hemet Health/Family Care Center
880 N. State Street
Hemet, CA 92543
(951) 766-2450
(951) 766-2479 FAX

Family srvs include: treatment of non-emerg medical problems, nutrition info & counseling, STD testing with diagnosis and treatment, family planning srvs, public health nursing assist to families in maintaining good health and promoting wellness in the home. Srvs for children include: immunizations, preventive health, family planning edu for teens, assist to pregnant teens, referral for medical care and rehab for physically disabled up to age 21 yrs. Srvs for women include: pregnancy testing, breast cancer screening, pap smears, WIC supplemental food & prenatal care. FUNDING: Nonprofit. OFC HRS: M-F 7:30am-5pm. Spanish spoken. ADM REQ: Low income. Accepts insurance, Medicare, Medi-Cal. SERVES: Riverside County.

RIVERSIDE CO. PUBLIC HEALTH DEPT

Lake Elsinore Health/Family Care Ctr
2499 E. Lakeshore Dr.
Lake Elsinore, CA 92530
(951) 471-4200
(951) 471-4205 FAX

Primary care, family planning, comprehensive perinatal care, cancer screening, STDs, immunizations, TB clinic & skin tests, pregnancy testing & counseling, teen clinic, well-child care, nutrition, WIC, public health nursing, AFLP. FUNDING: BPHC site, donations, nonprofit. Clinic hrs: M-F 7:30am-5pm. Spanish spoken. ADM REQ: Low income. Accepts insurance, Medicare, Medi-Cal, sliding fee scale. SERVES: Riverside Co.

RIVERSIDE CO. PUBLIC HEALTH DEPT

Palm Springs Health/Family Care Ctr
1515 N. Sunrise Way
Palm Springs, CA 92262
(760) 778-2210
(760) 778-2214 FAX

HIV/STD testing, diagnosis and treatment, well-child care, prenatal care, women's health care, family planning, teen clinic, primary care treatment of non-emerg medical problems. For an appt, call (800) 720-9553. FUNDING: BPHC site, donations, nonprofit. OFC HRS: M-F 7:30am-5pm. Children's clinic Sat 8am-5pm. Spanish spoken. ADM REQ: Low income. Accepts Medi-Cal, insurance. Fees based on family size, income, & srvs provided. SERVES: Riverside County.

RIVERSIDE CO. PUBLIC HEALTH DEPT

HIV/AIDS Program
P.O. Box 7600
6370 Magnolia Ave.
Riverside, CA 92503
(800) 243-7275
(909) 358-5307
(951) 358-5407 FAX

Edu, testing srvs, HIV primary care, and surveillance activities. Outreach activities are targeted to high-risk individuals: men who have sex with men, women of childbearing age, IV drug users and other drug abusers, sex workers, and youth. HIV primary care is available at Riverside Neighborhood Health Center. Edu sessions provided to community groups, schools, jails, and others upon request. Classes ordered by the courts are provided on scheduled dates at sites throughout the county. OFC HRS: M-F 8am-5pm. Spanish spoken. Free testing srvs. SERVES: Riverside County.

RIVERSIDE CO. PUBLIC HEALTH DEPT

Riverside Neighborhood Family Health Ctr
7140 Indiana Ave.
Riverside, CA 92504
(951) 358-6000
(951) 358-6044 FAX

Well-child exams, adult physicals, teen clinic, prenatal care, family planning, treatment of non-emerg medical problems. Wait: Varies. FUNDING: BPHC site, donations, nonprofit. OFC HRS: M-F 7:35am-5pm. OB/GYN, HIV/STD testing: M 8am-5pm; Tu 1pm-5pm; Th 8am-12noon. Spanish spoken. ADM REQ: Medi-Cal/MIA, sliding fee scale. Accepts Medi-Cal, Medicare, pvt pay. Sliding fee scale based on family size, income & srvs provided. SERVES: Riverside County.

RIVERSIDE CO. PUBLIC HEALTH DEPT

Rubidoux Family Care Center
5256 Mission Blvd.
Riverside, CA 92509
(951) 955-0840
(951) 955-5317 FAX

Primary care, perinatal care, immunizations, cancer screening, STD tests, TB tests, well-child care, nutrition. FUNDING: County. OFC HRS: M-F 7:30am-5pm. Spanish spoken. Accepts Medi-Cal, Medicare, insurance, sliding fee scale. SERVES: Riverside County.

RIVERSIDE/SAN BRDO CO. INDIAN HLTH

Morongo Indian Health Clinic
11555 1/2 Potrero Rd.
Banning, CA 92220
(800) 732-8805
(951) 849-4761
(951) 849-5612 FAX

Outpatient alcohol & drug treatment prgm, AA meetings, parenting classes, counseling. Comprehensive health care: medical, dental, vision, mental health (individual & family counseling), pharmacy, lab, nursing, family planning, AIDS testing, WIC prgm, transportation. Serves all ages. FUNDING: Govt. OFC HRS: M, W, Th 8am-5pm; Tu 8am-7pm; F 8am-2pm. ADM REQ: Must have appt. Accepts Medi-Cal. Free srvs to qualified Indians. SERVES: Riverside & San Bernardino Counties.

SAN BERNARDINO CITY U.S.D.

School Link Services
1535 W. Highland Ave.
San Bernardino, CA 92411
(909) 880-6701
(909) 880-6702 FAX

Homeless liason, HIV & health srvs, family resource center. FUNDING: Donations. OFC HRS: M-F 8am-4:30pm. Spanish spoken. SERVES: San Bernardino USD.

SAN BERNARDINO CO. HIV CLINIC

See "San Bernardino Co. Public Health"

SAN BERNARDINO CO. MEDICAL SOCIETY

3993 Jurupa Ave.
Riverside, CA 92506
(951) 787-7700
(951) 787-8795 FAX

Free health edu info to the residents of San Bernardino County, including a physician speaker's bureau of over 200 current health topics. Medical museum. Up-to-date legislative and edu info on health and medical policy issues from the Calif Medical Assn and American Medical Assn. FUNDING: Pvt, nonprofit. OFC HRS: M-F 8:30am-5pm. SERVES: San Bernardino County.

SAN BERNARDINO CO. PUBLIC HEALTH

Reproductive Health Centers
303 E. Mountain View
Barstow, CA 92311
(800) 722-4777
(760) 256-4715
(760) 256-4909 FAX

Reproductive health exams for men & women. STD testing & treatment, HIV testing & referral to care. Edu srvs, pregnancy testing, counseling, lab testing, young adult clinics. FUNDING: Dept of Public Health. OFC HRS: Tu-Th 9am-4pm. ADM REQ: Must have appt. Accepts Medi-Cal. Fees based on srvs provided. SERVES: Barstow.

SAN BERNARDINO CO. PUBLIC HEALTH

Reproductive Health Centers
P.O. Box 2835
477 Summit Blvd.
Big Bear Lake, CA 92315
(800) 722-4777
(909) 866-0177

Reproductive health exams for men & women. STD testing & treatment, HIV testing & referral to care. Edu srvs, pregnancy testing, counseling, lab testing, young adult clinic. FUNDING: Calif Office of Family Planning, govt. OFC HRS: F 9am-4pm. Spanish spoken. ADM REQ: Must have appt. Accepts Medi-Cal, F-PACT, sliding fee scale, no one turned away for lack of funds. SERVES: San Bernardino Mtns.

SAN BERNARDINO CO. PUBLIC HEALTH

Reproductive Health Centers
16453 Bear Valley Road
Hesperia, CA 92345
(800) 722-4777
(760) 956-4465
(760) 956-4450 FAX

Reproductive health exams for men & women. STD testing & treatment, HIV testing & referral to care. Edu srvs, pregnancy testing, counseling, lab testing, young adult clinics. For HIV testing, call (909) 383-3060 W 9am-3pm. FUNDING: Dept Public Health. OFC HRS: M-F

9am-4pm. Spanish spoken. ADM REQ: Must have appt. Accepts Medi-Cal. Sliding fee scale. No one denied srvs due to lack of funds. SERVES: Victor Valley area.

SAN BERNARDINO CO. PUBLIC HEALTH

Reproductive Health Centers
P.O. Box 1066
1406 Bailey Ave., Ste D
Needles, CA 92363
(800) 722-4777
(760) 326-9230
(760) 326-9235 FAX

Reproductive health exams for men & women. STD testing & treatment, HIV testing & referral to care. Edu srvs, pregnancy testing, counseling, lab testing, young adult clinics. FUNDING: Dept Public Health. OFC HRS: Tu-Th 7am-4:30pm. Accepts Medi-Cal, insurance. Fees based on srv. SERVES: Amboy, Big River, Essex, Needles, Havasu Landing, Parkers Dam.

SAN BERNARDINO CO. PUBLIC HEALTH

Reproductive Health Centers
1647 E. Holt Blvd.
Ontario, CA 91764
(800) 722-4777
(909) 458-9716
(909) 458-9729 FAX

Reproductive health exams for men & women. STD testing & treatment, HIV testing & referral to care. Edu srvs, pregnancy testing, counseling, lab testing, young adult clinics. For HIV testing, call (909) 383-3060 F 8am-3:30pm. FUNDING: Dept Public Health. OFC HRS: M-F 8am-5pm. Spanish spoken. ADM REQ: Must have appt. Sliding fee scale. No one denied srvs due to lack of funds. SERVES: Ontario.

SAN BERNARDINO CO. PUBLIC HEALTH

Reproductive Health Centers
800 E. Lugonia Ave., Ste F
Redlands, CA 92374
(800) 722-4777
(909) 793-6399

Reproductive health exams for men & women. STD testing & treatment, HIV testing & referral to care. Edu srvs, pregnancy testing, counseling, lab testing, young adult clinics. FUNDING: Govt. OFC HRS: M-F 8am-5pm. Spanish spoken. ADM REQ: Must have appt. Accepts Medi-Cal, F-PACT, sliding fee scale. No one denied srvs due to lack of funds. SERVES: San Bernardino County.

SAN BERNARDINO CO. PUBLIC HEALTH

Administrative Office
385 Arrowhead Ave.
San Bernardino, CA 92415-0120
(909) 387-7020
(909) 387-6228 FAX

Administers branch offices at various locations throughout San Bernardino Co. including: Barstow, Big Bear, Chino, Fontana, Joshua Tree, Needles, Ontario, Redlands, San Bernardino, Trona, Victorville & Twin Peaks. Edu, alcohol & drug prevention, animal control, birth & death certificates, Calif Children's Srvs, epidemiology, family planning, high-risk infant prgm, immunizations, nutrition, WIC, public health nursing, school health, senior health, VD control, TB, HIV/AIDS control. TDD (909) 397-6354. OFC HRS: M-F 8am-5pm; clinic hrs may vary. SERVES: San Bernardino County.

SAN BERNARDINO CO. PUBLIC HEALTH

AIDS Program
799 E. Rialto Ave.
San Bernardino, CA 92415
(909) 755-6560
(909) 383-3212 FAX

HIV clinic provides medical exam, eval & treatment, psychological eval & counseling, nutrition assessment & counseling, prevention edu & behavior change support, medication adherance edu support, case mgmt & benefits. Counseling for persons with HIV, referral for substance abuse counseling, dental care & other srvs, edu & prevention prgms for any community group requesting srvs. Clinic hrs: M, W 8am-11:30am; Tu 5pm-6 30pm; Th 8am-11:30am, 1pm-4pm. Walk-ins taken M, W, Th 8am-9am. Other locations in Ontario & Victorville. ADAP enrollment site. FUNDING: State, federal. OFC HRS: M-F 8am-4:30pm; Tu until 6:30pm. Spanish spoken. Accepts Medi-Cal. SERVES: San Bernardino County.

SAN BERNARDINO CO. PUBLIC HEALTH

Reproductive Health Centers
799 E. Rialto Ave.
San Bernardino, CA 92415-0011
(800) 722-4777
(909) 885-9962
(909) 387-3340 FAX

Birth control, male & female exams, pregnancy testing, counseling, referrals, verification, HIV & sexually transmitted infection (STI) testing and counseling, male sterilization. Srvs are confidential and low-cost. Call individual clinic to schedule appt. Weekly young adult clinics (YAC) on a walk-in basis at Fontana, Ontario, Redlands, San Bernardino and Hesperia sites. FUNDING: Calif Office of Family Planning. OFC HRS: M-F 8am-5pm. Spanish spoken. Accepts Medi-Cal, managed care plans, pvt pay through sliding fee scale. SERVES: San Bernardino County.

SAN FRANCISCO AIDS FOUNDATION

AIDS/HIV Hotline
1035 Market St., Ste 400
San Francisco, CA 94103
(800) 367-2437
(415) 487-3000
(415) 487-3009 FAX

Volunteers offer HIV/STD info, support and referral. FUNDING: Donations, grants, govt, nonprofit. OFC HRS: M,W-F 9am-5pm; Tu 9am-9pm. Spanish spoken. Free srvs. SERVES: Calif.

SOBOBA INDIAN HEALTH CLINIC

607 Donna Way
San Jacinto, CA 92583
(800) 851-5816
(951) 654-0803
(951) 487-9634 FAX

Comprehensive health care: medical, dental, vision, mental health (indivual & family counseling), pharmacy, lab, AIDS testing, nursing, family planning, well-baby, pediatric, health edu, transportation srvs. FUNDING: Fed, state, county. OFC HRS: M, Tu, Th 8am-5pm; W 8am-7pm; F 8am-2pm. ADM REQ: American Indian. Accepts Medi-Cal. Free to qualified Indians. SERVES: Riverside County.

ST. JUDE CHILDREN'S RESEARCH HOSP

12365 Lewis St., Ste 101

Garden Grove, CA 92840
(800) 227-6737
(714) 663-7200
(714) 663-7222 FAX

Unique institution dedicated to research & treatment for children with cancer, pediatric AIDS and other catastrophic childhood diseases. FUNDING: Fundraisers, donations, nonprofit. OFC HRS: M-F 8am-4:30pm. Spanish spoken. Accepts Medi-Cal, no one turned away for lack of funds. Free srvs to terminally ill children ages 18 yrs or under. SERVES: So. Calif.

STD EDUCATION & INFO

See also "CDC Natl AIDS Hotline"

THE NAMES PROJECT FOUNDATION

AIDS Memorial Quilt
204 14th Street NW
Atlanta, GA 30318-4315
(404) 688-5500
(404) 688-5552 FAX

Sponsors and displays the AIDS Memorial Quilt. Goal is to provide remembrance and healing, illustrate the enormousness of the AIDS epidemic, increase public awareness, assist with community fundraising. FUNDING: Nonprofit. OFC HRS: M-F 8am-5pm, EST. Spanish spoken. Accepts donations. SERVES: U.S.A.

WORKING WONDERS

34100 Shifting Sands Trail
Cathedral City, CA 92234
(760) 324-7586
(760) 324-6909 FAX

HIV testing, referrals, family & individual case mgmt, support groups, prevention edu, community outreach, advocacy, youth dev prgm, and a resource & referral network. Visit (www.workingwonders4u.org). Mailing address: P.O. Box 3698, Cathedral City 92235. FUNDING: Nonprofit. OFC HRS: M-Th by appt only. Spanish spoken. ADM REQ: Women, children, youth & families. Free srvs. Donations accepted. SERVES: Cathedral City, Mecca, Thermal, Coachella, Indio, Palm Desert, Rancho Mirage, Palm Springs, Banning.

WWW.ADVOCATESFORYOUTH.ORG

2000 M Street, NW, Ste 750
Washington, DC 20036
(202) 419-3420
(202) 419-1448 FAX

Informational website aimed at teens on STDs, sex edu, and pregnancy prevention. FUNDING: Nonprofit. Free srvs. SERVES: U.S.A.

WWW.HIVDENT.ORG

Coalition of health care professionals committed to ensuring access to quality oral health care srvs for persons living with HIV. Individuals as well as professionals can communicate via e-mail with experts in the field of dentistry on a variety of subjects, such as pediatric health, dental treatment, medications, mental health, nutrition, etc. FUNDING: Nonprofit. SERVES: U.S.A.

WWW.INSPOT.ORG

Website that allows users to anonymously send e-mail notifications to past partners informing them of a potential STD they may have acquired. Also offers a clinic locator to find resources near you. SERVES: U.S.A.

1736 FAMILY CRISIS CENTER

Homeless Resources & Prgms
2116 Arlington Ave., Ste 200
Los Angeles, CA 90018
(323) 737-3900
(323) 737-3993 FAX

Outpatient counseling and case mgmt for adults, families and children. Battered women's support groups, community edu, outreach. Also shelter, counseling, food, clothing, advocacy and other 24-hr srvs free of charge to battered women and their children and to runaway and homeless adols. Operates five shelters: four for battered women and their children (ages birth-17 yrs) for 1-24 months offering a comprehensive survival and job dev prgm to promote long-term safety, survival, and success; one emerg shelter for runaways (two-week crisis-oriented shelter). 24-hr hotlines in South Bay (310) 379-3620, (310) 370-5902; Long Beach (562) 388-7652; South L.A. (213) 222-1237, (213) 745-6434. 24-hr drop-in center at 1736 Monterey Blvd., Hermosa Beach. May call collect if needed. FUNDING: Grants, donations, govt, nonprofit. OFC HRS: M-F 8:30am-5pm. Spanish spoken. ADM REQ: Vary by prgm. Free srvs. SERVES: So. Calif.

1736 FAMILY CRISIS CENTER

Admin Office
2116 Arlington Ave., Ste 200
Los Angeles, CA 90018
(323) 737-3900
(323) 737-3993 FAX

This location is one of the 21 Family Source Centers in L.A. County providing the One e-App system for financial assist, case mgmt, and high-risk youth/young adult employment and edu srvs. 24-hr srvs provided to runaway and homeless adols, including: counseling, food, clothing, advocacy and other basic needs. 2-week emerg youth shelter for adols 10-17 yrs who need short-term, crisis-oriented shelter. Also operates four shelters for battered women and their children (ages birth-17 yrs) for 1-24 months offering a comprehensive survival and job dev prgm to promote long-term safety, survival & success. 24-hr hotlines in South Bay (310) 379-3620; (310) 370-5902; Long Beach (562) 388-7652; South L.A. (213) 222-1237, (213) 745-6434. May call collect if needed. 24-hr drop-in center at 1736 Monterey Blvd., Hermosa Beach. FUNDING: Donations, grants, govt, CDBG, nonprofit. OFC HRS: M-F 8:30am-5pm. Spanish spoken. Free srvs. SERVES: So. Calif, Southwest L.A.

A BETTER WAY

See "Victor Vly Domestic Violence, Inc."

A WINDOW BETWEEN WORLDS

710 4th Avenue, Ste 5
Venice, CA 90291
(310) 396-0317
(310) 396-9698 FAX

Trains shelter staff in conducting art expression & empowerment workshops. Art Circle offers art expression workshop outside the shelter. Available to any agency or org wanting to use art as a healing tool for domestic abuse survivors. FUNDING: Nonprofit. OFC HRS: M-F 10am-6pm. Hours do vary. Spanish spoken. SERVES: U.S.A.

A.V. DOMESTIC VIOLENCE COUNCIL

Valley Oasis Shelter
P.O. Box 2980
Lancaster, CA 93539
(661) 945-5509
(661) 945-5726 FAX

24-hr domestic violence phone support, shelter for domestic violence victims (men and women), clothing, food, individual & group counseling, edu classes, budgeting, parenting, job search & readiness, self-assertiveness & related referrals. Some transportation. Outreach srvs, transitional housing prgm and legal srvs to clients in prgm. For admin, call (661) 949-1916. FUNDING: Nonprofit, grants, donations. Spanish spoken. ADM REQ: Max stay of 60 days. Free srvs. SERVES: So. Calif.

ALTERNATIVE SENTENCING

Indio Probation Department
47-940 Arabia St.
Indio, CA 92201
(760) 863-8420
(760) 863-8916 FAX

Provides domestic violence, sexual deviance, anger mgmt, parenting, child batterer classes, community srv provider, referrals for home monitoring and administers court-ordered vehicle ignition interlock prgm. FUNDING: Nonprofit. OFC HRS: M-Th 8am-4pm; F 8am-3pm. Spanish spoken. ADM REQ: Assigned by court, probation, parole or DPSS depts. Fees vary by service; accepts money orders only. SERVES: Coachella Valley.

ALTERNATIVES TO DOMESTIC VIOLENCE

P.O. Box 910
Riverside, CA 92502
(951) 320-1370
(951) 320-1381 FAX

Outreach prgm for victims of domestic violence and their children. One-on-one counseling, support groups, children's prgm (offered in Spanish & English), community edu, court accompaniment, TRO assist, shelter, info & referral. 24-hr crisis line (951) 683-0829. FUNDING: Govt, donations, nonprofit. OFC HRS: M-F 8am-5pm. Spanish spoken. Free srvs. SERVES: Western Riverside County.

CALIF BOARD/VICTIM COMPENSATION

Government Claims Board
P.O. Box 3035
Sacramento, CA 95812-3035
(800) 777-9229
(916) 327-2933 FAX

If you are a victim of a crime of violence which occurred in Calif (or were a Calif resident victimized outside of the state) and you cooperated with the police investigation of the crime, you may apply to the state for compensation for qualifying unreimbursed expenses. Local victim witness center can help file. Hearing impaired, call California Relay Service (800) 735-2929 FUNDING: Govt. OFC HRS: M-F 8am-5pm. Spanish spoken. $25 filing fee and a surcharge paid by state agencies on approved claims. SERVES: Calif.

CALIF COALITION FOR BATTERED WOMEN

See "Calif Partnership End Domestic Viol"

CALIF DEPT OF SOCIAL SRVS

Ofc of Child Abuse Prevention
744 P Street, MS 11-82
Sacramento, CA 95814
(916) 651-6960
(916) 651-6328 FAX

Access website to locate srvs & providers; download forms, report abuse, file a complaint, etc. Visit (www.dss.cahwnet.gov). FUNDING: State. OFC HRS: M-F 8am-5pm. SERVES: Calif.

CALIF PARTNERSHIP TO END DOMESTIC VIOLENCE

P.O. Box 1798
Sacramento, CA 95812-1798
(916) 444-7163
(800) 524-4765
(916) 444-7165 FAX

Statewide membership-based domestic violence coalition of domestic violence srv providers & others. Combined with So. Calif Coalition for Battered Women & Calif Alliance Against Domestic Violence. Offers on-site, regional & statewide technical assist & training opportunities, statewide info, referral & resources to member prgms & allied professionals. No direct srvs. FUNDING: Nonprofit. OFC HRS: M-F 9am-5pm. Spanish spoken. Training fees vary. SERVES: Calif.

CATHOLIC CHARITIES/COUNSELING

Caritas Counseling Srvs
1441 N. D St., Ste 4
San Bernardino, CA 92405
(909) 763-4970
(909) 763-4977 FAX

Professional counseling without regard to race, creed, sex, or age. Marriage, family, child counseling for a wide range of issues such as child abuse, anger mgmt, relationships, parent edu. Counseling provided days, eve & Sat in various locations. FUNDING: Nonprofit. OFC HRS: M-F 10am-4:30pm. Spanish spoken. Sliding fee scale. Some free srvs. SERVES: San Bernardino & Riverside Counties.

CELEBRATE RECOVERY

Bethel Christian Center
2425 Van Buren Blvd.
Riverside, CA 92503
(951) 359-1123
(951) 359-3372 FAX

Christ-centered 12-Step recovery prgm. Support groups for all types of problems & addictions, including: food, sex, or relationship addictions, co-dependency and chemical dependency. Meets F at 7pm. Contact: Jerry or Julia Thromson. FUNDING: Nonprofit. OFC HRS: M-F 9am-5pm. SERVES: Riverside & nearby.

CENTER AGAINST SEXUAL ASSAULT

P.O. Box 2564
Hemet, CA 92546
(951) 652-8300
(951) 652-0944 FAX

Crisis intervention support resource, referral & advocacy for victims of sexual assault, family & friends. Counseling, exams, judicial system and law enforcement accompaniment, support group for adolescents and adults, community edu, rape prevention presentation, and srvs. Nationwide 24-hr srv line (866) 373-8300. FUNDING: State (OES), community, nonprofit. OFC HRS: M-F 8am-5pm. Spanish spoken. Free srvs. SERVES: Hemet, San Jacinto & nearby.

CENTER FOR FAMILY SOLUTIONS

Formerly Womanhaven, Inc.
P.O. Box 2219
741 Main St.
El Centro, CA 92244
(760) 353-6922
(760) 353-8530
(760) 353-8441 FAX

Domestic violence srvs, HIV prevention prgm, bullying prgm, individual & group counseling, outreach, emerg shelter, legal assist, drop-in center, TROs, crisis srvs, transitional housing, prevention & edu prgm, info & referral, batterer's treatment prgm. 24-hr hotline (760) 353-8530. FUNDING: Nonprofit. OFC HRS: M-F 8am-5pm. Spanish spoken. Fees apply for divorce cases & lawyer srvs. SERVES: So. Calif.

CENTER FOR HEALING CHILDHOOD TRAUMA

101 S. Olive Ave.
Rialto, CA 92376
(909) 875-5288
(909) 875-0608 FAX

Counseling for children, adolescents and adult victims of sexual abuse. Also family resource ctr offering a wide range of parenting curricula. Parents United certified providers. Also has an office in O.C. at 1420 E. Chapman Ave., Orange 92866, (949) 348-1717. FUNDING: Nonprofit. OFC HRS: M-Th 9am-7pm; F 10am-5pm. Spanish spoken. Accepts pvt pay, Victims of Crime. SERVES: Orange, Riverside & San Bernardino Counties.

CENTER FOR THE PACIFIC ASIAN FAMILY

543 N. Fairfax Ave., Ste 108
Los Angeles, CA 90036
(800) 339-3940
(323) 653-4045
(323) 653-7913 FAX

Confidential emerg and transitional shelters, 24-hr hotline and crisis intervention, counseling, TRO assist, case mgmt, victim advocacy throughout the medical, legal and criminal justice and social srv systems for victims of domestic violence, sexual assault, child abuse, and their families. Call first. FUNDING: United Way, state, nonprofit. OFC HRS: M-F 9am-5pm. Various Pacific Asian languages spoken. ADM REQ: Willing to abide by house rules. No fee to victims. SERVES: L.A. County (Orange, Riverside & San Bernardino Counties as needed).

CHINO COMMUNITY SERVICES

Counseling Srvs
13201 Central Ave.
Chino, CA 91710
(909) 591-9822
(909) 628-4093 FAX

Low-cost outpatient family and individual counseling. Community outreach for residents of Chino. Domestic violence prgms. FUNDING: State, county, school, city, nonprofit. OFC HRS: M-Th 8am-8pm; F 8am-6pm. Spanish spoken. Free srvs for juveniles & low income residents of Chino. School-based counseling free. Outpatient family treatment $26 per visit. SERVES: Western San Bernardino County.

COALITION TO ABOLISH SLAVERY/ TRAFFICKING (CAST)

5042 Wilshire Blvd., Ste 586
Los Angeles, CA 90036
(213) 365-1906
(213) 365-5257 FAX

CAST is a multi-ethnic, multilingual human rights organization dedicated exclusively to serving survivors of trafficking. CAST has become a pioneering leader in the U.S. anti-trafficking movement. Comprehensive social srvs & legal assist is provided to trafficking survivors. Promotes policy advocacy at the state & national levels. The shelter prgm has become a model prgm for victim srvs around the country. FUNDING: Nonprofit. OFC HRS: M-F 8:30am-5pm. Korean, Mandarin, Russian, Spanish & Tagalog spoken. SERVES: U.S.A.

COMMUNITY COUNSELING CTR/CSUSB

Dept of Psychology, Calif State Univ
5500 State University Pkwy.
San Bernardino, CA 92407
(909) 537-5040
(909) 537-7061 FAX

Graduate students in 2-yr M.S. counseling psychology prgm provide low-cost, long-term individual psychotherapy. Student therapists are supervised by Ph.D level psychologists on CSUSB faculty. FUNDING: CSUSV, govt. OFC HRS: M, Th, F 8am-5pm. Tu, W 8am-7pm. ADM REQ: CSUSB student or connected to student, not suicidal, abusive, drug dependent or violent. Cost covered by tuition. SERVES: San Bernardino County.

CRIME SURVIVORS

P.O. Box 54552
Irvine, CA 92619-4552
(949) 872-7895
(775) 245-4798 FAX

The mission of Crime Survivors is to ensure that the public knows of victim rights. Provides resources, support and information to empower crime victims to survive and thrive. Visit (www.crimesurvivors.com). FUNDING: Donations, nonprofit. SERVES: Calif.

CRIME VICTIMS UNITED OF CALIF

11400 Atwood Rd.
Auburn, CA 95603
(530) 885-9544
(530) 885-4608 FAX

Political action committee. Works to enhance public safety using edu & political action. Endorses political candidates who share in this mission. FUNDING: Nonprofit. OFC HRS: M-F 9am-5pm. SERVES: Calif.

CRISIS LINE

See also listings in the "Counseling" and "Hotlines" chapters.

D.O.V.E.S. OF BIG BEAR VALLEY

P.O. Box 3646
41943 Big Bear Blvd., Ste 1
Big Bear Lake, CA 92315

(909) 866-1546
(800) 851-7601
(909) 866-8580 FAX

24-hr hotline (800) 851-7601. Long-term (180-day) shelter offers an intense prgm for victims of domestic violence. Professional counseling for men, women & children. Legal assist & advocacy, women's support groups. FUNDING: Nonprofit. OFC HRS: M-F 8:30am-5pm. Shelter 24 hrs, 7 days. Spanish spoken. Free srvs. SERVES: So. Calif.

DELANCEY STREET FOUNDATION

600 Embarcadero
San Francisco, CA 94107
(415) 512-5104
(415) 512-5141 FAX

Rehab prgm provides assist to ex-felons, substance abusers, gang members, perpetrators, and victims of abuse to assist them with skills to rebuild their lives. Literacy, homeless issues, anger mgmt, edu & voc mentoring. Does not accept people with mental disorders, people on medication or with disabilities, arsonists, or sex offenders. FUNDING: Nonprofit, donations. OFC HRS: 24/7. ADM REQ: Ages 18 yrs+. Free srvs. SERVES: Calif.

DESERT SANCTUARY/HALEY HOUSE

P.O. Box 1781
703 E. Main St.
Barstow, CA 92312
(760) 256-3441
(760) 256-3733
(760) 256-4002 FAX

16-bed shelter for battered women & their children up to 6 mos. Also outreach for community & area victims in need of srvs not inclusive of shelter. Outreach srvs include: rent/utility assist, anger mgmt, therapy, sexual assault srvs, court-ordered supervised visitation, legal aid, housing stabilization. 24-hr hotline: (800) 982-2221. FUNDING: Nonprofit. OFC HRS: Hotline 24 hrs. Outreach M-F 9am-5pm. German & Spanish spoken. ADM REQ: Women in abusive surroundings. Free srvs. SERVES: So. Calif.

DOMESTIC ABUSE HELPLINE

For Men and Women
P.O. Box 252
Harmony, ME 04942
(888) 743-5754

24-hr helpline for victims of domestic violence, specializing in male victim domestic abuse. Refers callers to resources in their area and if applicable, "male friendly" facilities. FUNDING: Nonprofit. Free srvs. SERVES: U.S.A.

DOMESTIC VIOLENCE EDU SERVICES

See 'D.O.V.E.S. of Big Bear..."

DOMESTIC VIOLENCE HELPLINE

Multilingual Info & Srvs
(800) 978-3600
(800) 799-7233

Helpline is a single point of entry system that links callers directly to the domestic violence shelter nearest to them based on their language needs. 24-hr toll free helpline provides a safe way out to all victims of domestic violence in all areas. M-Th 8am-6pm for literature & referral to county-funded shelters. FUNDING: Nonprofit. OFC HRS: 24 hrs, 7 days. Multiple languages spoken. Free srvs. SERVES: U.S.A.

Battered Persons/Victim/Adult Abuse

EAST L.A. HOTLINE/SHELTER
Chicana Service Action Center
3601 E. 1st Street
Los Angeles, CA 90063
(800) 548-2722
(323) 268-5669 FAX

24-hr hotline and shelter for women and children. The shelter is described separately under "Free Spirit Shelter," which can be found in the Battered Persons/Victim/Adult Abuse chapter. FUNDING: Nonprofit. Spanish spoken. ADM REQ: Domestic violence, homeless. Free srvs. SERVES: So. Calif.

FAMILY SERVICE AGENCY/SAN BRDO
Crest Forest Family Srvs
P.O. Box 4484
23406 Crest Forest Dr.
Crestline, CA 92325
(909) 338-4689
(909) 338-8230 FAX

Counseling and mental health treatment for child sexual abuse, dysfunctional families. Anger diversion classes, court-ordered batterer's intervention prgm, high-risk youth prgms, limited utility asst. 24-hr suicide and crisis hotline (800) 832-9119. Food bank available F 9am-12noon, 1pm-5:30pm; call ahead to get more info. FUNDING: United Way, client fees, nonprofit. OFC HRS: M-Th 8:30am-6pm. ADM REQ: Varies per prgm. Ages 5 yrs+. Accepts Medi-Cal, sliding fee scale. SERVES: San Bernardino County.

FAMILY SERVICE AGENCY/SAN BRDO
Outpatient Mental Health Srvs
1669 North E Street
San Bernardino, CA 92405
(909) 886-6737
(909) 881-3871 FAX

Info & referral, counseling & mental health treatment for child sexual abuse, domestic violence intervention counseling, dysfunctional families, parenting classes, anger diversion classes, high-risk youth prgms. S.N.A.A.P. (narcotics/alcohol abuse prgm for teens). State ID: 360044AN. FUNDING: United Way, client fees, nonprofit. OFC HRS: M-Th 9am-9pm. Spanish spoken. ADM REQ: Varies per prgm. Ages birth-21 yrs. Accepts Medi-Cal for youth only, sliding fee scale. SERVES: San Bernardino County.

FAMILY SERVICE ASSN/CORONA
Alternatives to Domestic Violence
Outreach Office
515 S. Corona Mall
Corona, CA 92879
(951) 737-8410
(951) 737-3517 FAX

Counseling for individuals, marriages & familes. Anger mgmt, edu, child abuse prevention & treatment. Employee assist prgm, mental health advocacy, social mentorship & family life edu. Anonymous shelter, advocacy for domestic violence. 24-hr crisis line (800) 339-SAFE or (951)683-0829. Riverside outreach and admin office (951) 320-1370. Hemet outreach office (951)929-3079. OFC HRS: M-F 9am-5pm. Spanish spoken. ADM REQ: Victim of domestic violence. Sliding fee scale for therapeutic srvs and anger mgmt. SERVES: West Riverside County.

FAMILY SERVICES OF THE DESERT
81-711 Highway 111, Ste 101
Indio, CA 92201
(760) 347-2398
(800) 536-4357
(760) 347-6468 FAX

Family, individual and group counseling. Locations in Indio, Desert Hot Springs and Blythe. FUNDING: United Way, donations, client fees, nonprofit. OFC HRS: M-F 9am-5pm. Eve & weekend by appt. Spanish spoken. SERVES: Coachella Valley.

FIRST CALL FOR HELP
Volunteer Center of Victor Valley
P.O. Box 1992
16692 Mojave Dr.
Victorville, CA 92393
(760) 243-9646
(760) 243-4762 FAX

Info & referral for people seeking srvs or info on community agencies. Interaction with individuals in crisis situations in order to reduce tension and stress, allowing that person to utilize available resources more effectively. FUNDING: Donations, grants, nonprofit. OFC HRS: M-Th 9am-2:45pm. Spanish spoken. SERVES: San Bernardino County.

FREE SPIRIT SHELTER
Chicana Service Action Center
P.O. Box 23309
Los Angeles, CA 90023
(323) 937-1312
(213) 430-0657 FAX

Shelter for battered women and children. Stay can be up to 45 days. It is a closed shelter; participants in the prgm may not leave while there. No teenage boys accepted. Intake through 24-hr hotline. OFC HRS: M-F 8am-5pm. Spanish spoken. SERVES: So. Calif.

GAY MEN'S DOMESTIC VIOLENCE PROJECT
955 Massachusetts Ave., PMB 131
Cambridge, MA 02139
(617) 354-6056
(617) 354-6072 FAX

Provides crisis intervention, support, and resources to gay victims and survivors of domestic violence. 24-hr hotline: (800) 832-1901. FUNDING: Nonprofit. SERVES: U.S.A.

GOOD SHEPHERD SHELTER
Administrative Office
P.O. Box 19487
Los Angeles, CA 90019
(323) 737-6111
(323) 737-6113 FAX

Non-emerg, long-term treatment and edu-oriented shelter for battered women with children under age 11 yrs. Women & children attend school on campus. Classes in personal dev, health, parenting, home mgmt, and computer skills. Individual & group counseling for mothers. Average length of stay is 6-12 mos. FUNDING: Donations, nonprofit. OFC HRS: M-F 9am-4:30pm. Spanish, Vietnamese, Cantonese & Tagalog spoken. ADM REQ: Applicants are usually referred by emerg domestic violence shelters. Prgm fee $70 a month & utilities for the family's apartment. SERVES: So. Calif.

HALEY HOUSE
See "Desert Sanctuary/Haley House"

HAVEN HOUSE
P.O. Box 50007
Pasadena, CA 91115
(626) 564-8880
(626) 564-9348 FAX

Shelter for battered women and their children. Food, clothing, counseling & advocacy srvs. Outreach prgm provides counseling for community clients. Training and edu on domestic violence. No waiting list for shelter: immediate entry or referral out. State ID: 190024AN. FUNDING: Donations, grants, nonprofit. OFC HRS: M-F 8:30am-4pm. Hotline 24 hrs, 7 days. Spanish spoken & Korean available upon request. ADM REQ: Victim of domestic violence, clean & sober, able to care for self & children. No one turned away for lack of funds. SERVES: So. Calif.

HIGH DESERT DOMESTIC VIOLENCE PRGM
Battered Women's Shelter
P.O. Box 284
15075 7th Street
Victorville, CA 92392
(760) 843-0701
(760) 843-9551 FAX

Confidential emerg shelter for battered women and their children, hotline, emerg food, clothing. Counseling and support groups, assist with restraining orders & local resource referrals. Utility and rental assist program. Monitored visitation by appt only. 24-hr hotline (760) 949-4357. FUNDING: San Bernardino County, United Way, nonprofit. OFC HRS: M-F 8am-5pm, admit to shelter on 24-hr basis. Spanish spoken. ADM REQ: Victim of domestic violence. SERVES: Victor Valley, will take referrals from other areas.

HOME START NORTH COUNTY
Coastal
1320 Union Plaza Court
Oceanside, CA 92054
(760) 439-7513
(760) 439-5625 FAX

Comprehensive home-based srvs for victims of crime & their families. Promotes healing in children & adults who have experienced rape, assault, sexual or physical abuse & domestic violence. FUNDING: Nonprofit. OFC HRS: M-F 8:30am-5pm. Spanish spoken. Free srvs. SERVES: San Diego County.

HOUSE OF RUTH/CLAREMONT
P.O. Box 459
Claremont, CA 91711
(909) 623-4364
(909) 629-9581 FAX

Advocates for and provides assist to battered women and their children. Srvs include: 24-hr hotline (909) 988-5559, 30-day emerg safe shelter, individual counseling, support groups for women, children and teens, transitional living shelter, career, edu & housing assist, TRO clinics, community outreach, edu, and teen dating violence prgm. FUNDING: United Way, CDBG, donations, nonprofit. OFC HRS: M-F 9am-5pm. Shelter 24 hrs, 7 days. Spanish spoken. ADM REQ: Women abused by intimate partner. Free srvs. SERVES: L.A., San Bernardino & Riverside Counties.

IMMIGRATION CENTER FOR WOMEN/ CHILDREN

634 S. Spring St., Ste 727
Los Angeles, CA 90014
(213) 614-1165
(213) 624-1163 FAX

Immigration srvs for abused, abandoned or neglected children. Also, women and children who are victims of trafficking, domestic violence and sexual assaults. FUNDING: Nonprofit. OFC HRS: M-F 9am-5pm. Spanish spoken. ADM REQ: Intake by phone, appt. required. SERVES: Southern Calif.

INCEST SURVIVORS ANONYMOUS

World Service Office
P.O. Box 17245
Long Beach, CA 90807-7245
(562) 428-5599

Literature for survivors of incest as well as info on groups meeting in area. 12-Step & 12-Tradition. Send a self-addressed, stamped envelope for info in English or Spanish. Cassette tapes & packets available for small fee; ISA e-mail, family letter also available at no charge. Srvs for men, women and older teens. FUNDING: Donations. OFC HRS: M-F 9am-5pm. ADM REQ: Survivors only, no perpetrators. Accepts donations. Free srvs. SERVES: U.S.A. & internatl.

INSTITUTE ON DOMESTIC VIOLENCE IN THE AFRICAN AMERICAN COMMUNITY

290 Peters Hall
1404 Gortner Ave.
Saint Paul, MN 55108-6142
(877) 643-8222
(612) 624-9201 FAX

Focuses on the unique circumstances of African Americans as they face issues related to domestic violence. Works with African-American communities to build the knowledge base within the population and develop strategies to meet service needs. FUNDING: Nonprofit. SERVES: U.S.A.

INTERNATIONAL CHILD ABUSE NETWORK

P.O. Box 155
7657 Winnetka Ave.
Canoga Park, CA 91306-2677
(888) 224-4226
(818) 716-0658 FAX

Online-facilitated chat rooms for child abuse and domestic violence survivors. Visit (www.yesican.org). FUNDING: Nonprofit. OFC HRS: M-F 8am-5pm. SERVES: Internatl.

JENESSE CENTER

P.O. Box 8476
Los Angeles, CA 90008
(800) 479-7328
(323) 299-9496
(323) 299-0699 FAX

24-hr hotline for battered women and men, two shelters (emerg & transitional) for victims of domestic violence and their children. Psych & peer counseling for individuals & groups. Referrals for comm srvs. Comm outreach, consultation & edu. Drop-in center provides food, clothes, counseling & edu. Intake screening by hotline. Legal srvs & advocacy. For the Inglewood legal clinic, call Don at (310) 419-6788. FUNDING: Donations, nonprofit. OFC HRS: M-F 9am-5pm. 24-hr hotline and shelter. Spanish spoken. SERVES: So. Calif.

LAURA'S HOUSE

Emergency Shelter
999 Corporate Dr., Ste 225
Ladera Ranch, CA 92694
(949) 361-3775
(949) 361-3548 FAX

Emergency shelter prgm for battered women with or without children; pregnant women accepted. Emergency shelter provides case mgmt, counseling and legal advocacy. Counseling & resource center for men, women & child victims of domestic violence. 24-hr hotline (866) 498-1511. Counseling hrs: M-F 9am-5pm, eve by appt. Shelter: 24 hrs, 7 days. Spanish & Farsi spoken. Language line available. Sliding fee scale. No one turned away for lack of funds. SERVES: Southern California. Able to refer out of area if needed

LEGAL PROTECTION FOR WOMEN

5300 E. Beverly Blvd., Ste D
Los Angeles, CA 90022
(323) 721-9882
(323) 721-7731 FAX

Paralegal srvs, including prep of family law forms for divorce, legal separation, nullity, TRO, civil harassment order, modification of child custody, support of visitation, alimony, name change, wage assignment for unpaid support, paternity and step-parent adoption. FUNDING: Nonprofit. OFC HRS: Tu-F 9am-5pm; Sat 10am-2pm, by appt only. Spanish spoken. Sliding fee scale, $20-$550 depending on action. SERVES: Calif.

LOMA LINDA UNIV/MARRIAGE/FAMILY

Marriage & Family Therapy Clinic
1686 Barton Rd.
Redlands, CA 92373
(909) 558-4934
(909) 558-0334 FAX

Individual, group, marriage, family, child & adol counseling. Srvs for child abuse prevention, grief counseling, domestic violence, chemical addiction and other issues. FUNDING: Nonprofit. OFC HRS: Sun 9am-5pm; M-Th 9am-8pm; F 9am-2:30pm. Spanish spoken. Sliding fee scale starts at $25 per session. Medi-Cal not accepted. Will not bill insurance. SERVES: San Bernardino, Riverside Counties.

LUCERNE VLY DOMESTIC VIOLENCE OUTREACH

P.O. Box 2003
32649 Highway 18
Lucerne Valley, CA 92356
(760) 248-2064
(760) 248-9194 FAX

Domestic violence hotline & outreach srvs. Counseling for individuals, families & children. Anger mgmt, court-ordered batterer's treatment prgm. Transport to shelters out of area, TRO, court support. Referrals to other Victor Valley resources. FUNDING: Nonprofit. OFC HRS: M-F 9am-2pm. SERVES: Lucerne Valley & unincorp areas of Apple Valley.

MARY MAGDALENE PROJECT, INC.

P.O. Box 8396
7136 Haskell Ave., Ste 125
Van Nuys, CA 91409
(818) 988-4970
(818) 947-3923 FAX

Residential prgm helps street prostitutes rebuild their lives and become contributing members of society. Medical and psychological eval, counseling, edu assist. FUNDING: Donations, grants, nonprofit. OFC HRS: M-F 9am-4pm. Limited Spanish spoken. ADM REQ: Prostitutes ages 18 yrs+ with a strong desire for lifestyle change. Free srvs. SERVES: So. Calif.

MCGEORGE SCHOOL OF LAW

See "Natl Criminal Justice Reference"

MORONGO BASIN UNITY HOME

P.O. Box 1662
61740 29 Palms Hwy.
Joshua Tree, CA 92252
(760) 366-9663
(760) 366-2643 FAX

Safe, confidential shelter for women & children who are victims of abuse. 30-bed emerg shelter (up to 45 days), group & individual counseling, parenting classes, court support, legal advocacy, tutoring for school children, supervised visitation, substance abuse prgm, transitional housing, teen prgm. Outreach srvs in Joshua Tree & Needles. Wait: 1st come, 1st served. FUNDING: Govt, grants, donations, nonprofit. HRS: Outreach M-F 8am-5pm; Sat 10am-2pm for supervised visitation only. 24-hr hotline, 24-hr shelter. Swedish, Italian, German & Spanish spoken. ADM REQ: Victim of domestic violence. No charge for srvs, $20 per hr for supervised visitation. SERVES: San Bernardino County, Morongo Basin to Needles.

MOUNTAIN VIEW CLINIC

1001 N. State St.
Hemet, CA 92543
(951) 658-1253
(951) 658-1253 FAX

Counseling srvs for married couples, families, individuals, adolescents, children. Hypnotherapy also available. OFC HRS: Tu-F 10am-7pm; Sat 10am-4pm. SERVES: Riverside County.

NATL CENTER FOR VICTIMS OF CRIME

2000 M Street, NW, Ste 480
Washington, DC 20036
(800) 394-2255
(202) 467-8700
(202) 467-8701 FAX

A nationwide helpline offering info and referral for victims of crime. Assist with accessing victim compensation, developing personalized safety plans, legal referrals, and accessing social srvs. TTY (800) 211-7996. FUNDING: Nonprofit. OFC HRS: M-F 10am-6pm, EST. Hotline: M-F 8:30am-8:30pm, EST. Serves victims in any language through the language line. Spanish, French, Japanese & English speakers on staff. Free srvs. SERVES: U.S.A.

NATL CRIMINAL JUSTICE REFERENCE

Office of Justice Programs
P.O. Box 6000
Rockville, MD 20849-6000
(800) 851-3420
(301) 519-5500
(301) 519-5212 FAX

Access to criminal justice library. Product & online srvs, info specialists available. TTY (877) 712-9279 or (301) 947-8374. FUNDING: U.S. Dept of Justice, Office for Victims of Crime. OFC HRS: M-F 10am-6pm, EST. SERVES: U.S.A. & internatl.

NATL DOMESTIC VIOLENCE HOTLINE
P.O. Box 161810
Austin, TX 78716-3074
(800) 799-7233
(512) 453-8541 FAX

Info & referral for victims of domestic violence and those who assist victims. Also provides crisis intervention, resource materials, bilingual advocates and a nationwide database of resources. TDD/TTY (800) 787-3224, e-mail (deafhelp@ndvh.org). FUNDING: Grants, fed, nonprofit. OFC HRS: M-F 8:30am-5:30pm, CST. 24-hr hotline. Spanish spoken. Over 170 other languages available. Free srvs. SERVES: U.S.A.

NATL HUMAN TRAFFICKING RESOURCE CTR
U.S. Admin of Children & Families
370 L'Enfant Promenade, S.W.
Washington, DC 20447
(888) 373-7888

24-hr hotline number for reporting potential victims of human trafficking within the U.S. Also answers questions from community members and distributes info. OFC HRS: 24 hrs, 7 days. Free srvs. SERVES: U.S.A.

NATL LATINO ALLIANCE FOR THE ELIMINATION OF DOMESTIC VIOLENCE
P.O. Box 7886
Albuquerque, NM 87194
(505) 224-9080
(505) 224-9079 FAX

Provides culturally sensitive training, tech assist, resources, community edu, and outreach srvs to Latino communities regarding domestic violence. FUNDING: Nonprofit. SERVES: U.S.A.

NATL ORGANIZATION/VICTIM ASSISTANCE (NOVA)
510 King St., Ste 424
Alexandria, VA 22314
(800) 879-6682
(703) 535-6682
(703) 535-5500 FAX

Crisis counseling, advocacy, and referral srvs to crime victims and their families. Also crisis response team. Refers victims & survivors to nearby srvs. FUNDING: Nonprofit. OFC HRS: M-F 9am-6pm, EST. SERVES: U.S.A.

NATL TEEN DATING ABUSE HELPLINE
www.loveisrespect.org
P.O. Box 16180
Austin, TX 78716
(866) 331-9474

Phone or Internet info & referral for teen victims of domestic violence and those who assist victims. Provides crisis intervention, resource materials, bilingual advocates and a nationwide database of resources. Chat online from 4pm-2am, CST. TTY (800) 331-8453. FUNDING: Grants, fed, nonprofit. OFC HRS: M-F 8:30am-5:30pm, CST. Hotline 24 hrs. Spanish spoken. Over 170 other languages available. SERVES: U.S.A.

OLIVE BRANCH COUNSELING CTR, INC.
9033 Baseline Rd., Ste H
Rancho Cucamonga, CA 91730
(909) 989-9030
(909) 466-4594 FAX

Counseling services for individuals, families, couples & groups including: anger mgmt, eating disorders, grief recovery, domestic violence, sexual abuse, victims of crime. Pre-marital, divorce recovery, parenting classes. Court certified for anger mgmt, domestic violence (DV), parenting & co-parenting classes. Certified visitation. All programs available for high-risk youth and adults. Locations in Claremont, Riverside, and Rancho Cucamonga. FUNDING: Nonprofit. OFC HRS: M-F 9am-8pm; Sat 9am-5pm. Spanish spoken. Accepts insurance, sliding fee scale. SERVES: San Bernardino County.

OLIVE BRANCH COUNSELING CTR, INC.
4041 Brockton Ave.
Riverside, CA 92501
(951) 369-8534
(951) 369-1145 FAX

Counseling services for individuals, families, couples & groups including: anger mgmt, eating disorders, grief recovery, domestic violence, sexual abuse, victims of crime. Pre-marital, divorce recovery, parenting classes. Court certified for anger mgmt, domestic violence (DV), parenting & co-parenting classes. Certified visitation. All programs available for high-risk youth and adults. Locations in Claremont, Riverside, and Rancho Cucamonga. FUNDING: Nonprofit. OFC HRS: M-F 9am-5pm; Sat 8:30am-5pm. Evening counseling avail by appt. Spanish spoken. Accepts insurance, sliding fee scale. SERVES: Riverside.

OPTION HOUSE/DV INTERV & PREV
Domestic Violence Interv & Prev Agency
P.O. Box 970
San Bernardino, CA 92401
(909) 381-3471
(909) 889-7312 FAX

Confidential emerg & temporary shelter, 24-hr crisis intervention hotline. One-on-one advocacy, emotional support, resource & referrals to female victims of domestic violence & their children. Six-week in-house prgm for residents in shelter, 18-month transitional housing, legal assist for TROs, child custody, court & mediation accompaniment, women's support groups for non-shelter victims (English & Spanish), teen relationship, violence prevention workshops, children's prgm, speakers bureau, community edu, training & workshops. For Tri-City DV Prevention Outreach Ctr, courthouse family violence outreach srvs & teen dating violence prevention srvs, call (909) 884-4802. FUNDING: Donations, grants, nonprofit. OFC HRS: M-F 8am-5pm. Spanish spoken. ADM REQ: Women, children & teens who are victims of domestic violence. SERVES: San Bernardino & nearby.

PROJECT GET SAFE
17602 17th Street, Ste 259
Tustin, CA 92780
(714) 834-0050
(714) 834-0070 FAX

Specializes in personal safety, sexual assault intervention, self-defense, and violence prev for children, women, men & persons with dev disabilities. FUNDING: Nonprofit. OFC HRS: Vary. Sliding fee scale. SERVES: So. Calif.

PROJECT SISTER
Sexual Assault Crisis & Prev Srvs
P.O. Box 1369
Pomona, CA 91769-1369

(909) 623-1619
(909) 622-8389 FAX

24-hr sexual assault crisis hotline; personal accompaniment to hospital, police station and court; in-person counseling; support groups for rape. AMAC (Adults Molested As Children) and incest survivors, referrals to other agencies, community edu (including sexual harassment) and teen date rape awareness & self-protection classes. Srvs for seniors also available. 24-hr helpline (909) 626-4357 and (626) 966-4155. FUNDING: United Way, Office of Emerg Srvs, donations, CDBG grants, nonprofit. OFC HRS: M-F 8am-5pm. Spanish spoken. Free srvs, except for counseling & groups on a sliding fee scale. No one turned away for lack of funds. SERVES: East San Gabriel Valley, Pomona Valley & West San Bernardino County.

RANCHO CUCAMONGA RESOURCE CENTER
9791 Arrow Route
Rancho Cucamonga, CA 91730
(909) 477-2781
(909) 919-2625 FAX

Resource center provides access to various srvs provided to the community. Prgms include: emerg needs (food and clothing), domestic abuse prevention workshops and counseling, ESL classes, parenting classes, youth socialization prgms, room rentals, info & referral srvs. FUNDING: Govt, city, donations. OFC HRS: M-F 8am-10pm. Spanish spoken. ADM REQ: Residents, however no one will be turned away. SERVES: Riverside, San Bernardino Counties.

RAPE CRISIS CENTER/SAN BRDO
See "Sexual Assault Srvs/San Brdo"

RIM FAMILY SRVS, INC.
P.O. Box 578
28545 Highway 18
Skyforest, CA 92385
(909) 336-1800
(909) 336-0990 FAX

Individual, group and family counseling, trauma recovery for victims of crime, domestic violence, etc. Community edu prgm. Info & referral; prevention & edu; outpatient counseling; DUI 1st offender & multiple (18-month) prgms; outpatient drug & alcohol treatment prgm. PC-1000, Strengthening Family Prgm, mobile resource center, aftercare prgm. State ID: 360036AN. FUNDING: Nonprofit. OFC HRS: M-Th 8am-6pm; F 8am-5pm; Sat 8am-2pm. Spanish spoken. Interpreter as needed. ADM REQ: Counseling for all ages. DUI prgm for ages 16 yrs+. Accepts Medi-Cal for drug/alcohol srvs, sliding fee scale for others. SERVES: San Bernardino County.

RIVERSIDE AREA RAPE CRISIS CENTER
1845 Chicago Ave., Ste A
Riverside, CA 92507
(951) 686-7273
(951) 686-0839 FAX

Crisis line. Hospital, law enforcement & court accompaniment, info & referral, community edu, child abuse prev, senior outreach prgm, support group, follow-up. Outreach prgm available in Spanish. Southwest County, call (866) 686-7273. FUNDING: OCJP, county, city, fndns, donors, United Way, nonprofit. OFC HRS: M-F 8am-5pm. Crisis line and hospital advocacy 24/7. Some Spanish spoken. ASL available. ADM REQ: Victim of sexual assault, family member or significant other. Free srvs. SERVES: Western Riverside County.

RIVERSIDE CO. DEPT/MENTAL HEALTH
Administrative Office
P.O. Box 7549
4095 County Circle Dr.
Riverside, CA 92513
(951) 358-4500
(951) 358-4513 FAX

Overall planning, implementation, direction, co-ordination and eval of the Dept of Mental Health prgms in Riverside County. Treatment for adults: residential, outpatient, day care, socialization ctrs, crisis srvs, case mgmt, continuing care, etc. Children's prgms: outpatient, case mgmt, foster home placement, etc. Also main admin office for drug abuse and alcohol control prgms. No actual srvs available at this location. FUNDING: Govt. Spanish spoken. Accepts Medi-Cal SERVES: Riverside County.

SAFE AT HOME
Calif Secretary of State
1500 11th Street
Sacramento, CA 95814
(714) 435-9992
(877) 322-5227

Gives victims of domestic violence an official, substitute address in place of their real home address. Mail goes directly to the main office in Sacramento and is forwarded to you directly. Also helps participants register to be a confidential voter, apply for a confidential name change, and suppress DMV records. Visit (www.casafeathome.org) for more info and to find an enrolling agency near you. FUNDING: Govt. ADM REQ: Referral from an enrolling agency. Free srvs. SERVES: Calif.

SEEKING PEACEFUL SOLUTIONS, INC.
8724 S. Vermont Ave.
Los Angeles, CA 90047
(323) 753-1314
(323) 753-6619 FAX

Conflict and dispute resolution srvs that assist in the reduction and prevention of violence among youth, adolescents, adults and communities at large. These srvs provided in partnership with schools, law enforcement, businesses, communities and within families. FUNDING: Nonprofit. OFC HRS: M-F 8:30am-7:00pm; Sat 9am-3:30pm; Sunday by appointment only. Spanish spoken. SERVES: L.A., Orange, Riverside & San Bernardino Counties.

SEXUAL ASSAULT SRVS/REDLANDS
Redlands Outreach
30 Cajon Street
Redlands, CA 92373
(909) 335-8777
(909) 335-4768 FAX

Support for victims of sexual assault and significant others through individual and group counseling, hospital and court accompaniment. Community edu prgms and self-defense. 24-hour natl crisis hotline (800) 656-4673. FUNDING: Nonprofit. OFC HRS: M-F 8am-5pm. Free srvs. SERVES: San Bernardino County.

SEXUAL ASSAULT SRVS/SAN BRDO
444 N. Arrowhead Ave., Ste 101-104
San Bernardino, CA 92401-1221

(909) 885-8884
(800) 656-4673
(909) 383-8478 FAX

Support for victims of sexual assault and significant others. Individual and group counseling, hospital & court accompaniment, community edu prgms and self-defense. Rape crisis ctr has support groups for adolescents, adults molested as children, etc. Coachella Valley (760) 568-9071. Morongo Basin (760) 369-3353. FUNDING: United Way, Ofc of Emergency Services, nonprofit. OFC HRS: M-Th 8am-5pm; F 8am-2pm. Spanish spoken. ADM REQ: Victims of sexual assault. Free srvs. SERVES: San Bernardino County.

SEXUAL ASSAULT SRVS/VICTORVILLE
15437 Anacapa Rd., Ste 8
Victorville, CA 92392
(760) 952-0041
(760) 383-8478 FAX

Individual & group counseling, outreach, crisis srvs, prevention & edu prgms, referrals for legal assist and parenting resources. 24-hr natl crisis line (800) 656-4673. FUNDING: Nonprofit. OFC HRS: M-Th 8am-5pm; F 8am-2pm. Spanish spoken. ADM REQ: Victims of sexual assault. Free srvs. SERVES: San Bernardino County.

SEXUAL ASSAULT SRVS/YUCAIPA
Yucaipa Outreach/Domestic Viol Prgm
34282 Yucaipa Blvd.
Yucaipa, CA 92399
(909) 790-9374
(909) 790-3111 FAX

Srvs to survivors of domestic violence. Individual & group counseling, community edu, referrals, court accompaniment & 24-hr hotline (800) 656-4673. FUNDING: Members, donations, nonprofit. OFC HRS: M-F 8am-5pm. Spanish spoken. Free srvs. SERVES: Inland Empire.

SHEEPFOLD, THE
P.O. Box 4487
Orange, CA 92863
(877) 743-3736
(714) 237-1444
(714) 237-1440 FAX

Shelter for homeless and abused women with children. Christian atmosphere, daily Bible studies. FUNDING: Donations, nonprofit. OFC HRS: M-F 9am-4pm. ADM REQ: Must attend church on Sunday. SERVES: Orange & Riverside Counties.

SHELTER FROM THE STORM, INC.
For Victims Of Domestic Violence
73555 Alessandro Dr., Ste D
Palm Desert, CA 92260
(760) 674-0400
(760) 674-0440 FAX

72-bed domestic violence shelter. 60-day prgm. Evening groups, parenting class, legal advocacy, one-to-one counseling, TRO assist, Walk in or call. Outreach Centers in Indio, Palm Desert, Palm Springs, Desert Hot Springs. 24-hr crisis hotline (760)328-7233 or (800)775-6055. FUNDING: Grants, donations, nonprofit. OFC HRS: M-F 8am-5pm. 24-hr shelter. Spanish spoken. ADM REQ: Battered women & their children. Free emerg shelter. Sliding fee scale for other srvs. SERVES: East Riverside County.

SINGLE PARENTS OF POWER EMLAC HEALTH SRVS
P.O. Box 452602
1620 Centinela Ave, Ste 202
Inglewood, CA 90302
(310) 753-7860

Counseling services include: mental health, sexual abuse, anger mgmt, parenting, alcohol and drug abuse. Advocacy and counseling for victims of violent crimes and post-traumatic counseling for veterans. FUNDING: Nonprofit. OFC HRS: M-F 9am-9pm; Sat 10am-3pm. Spanish, Swahili spoken. Free counseling for victims of domestic violence. All other srvs on a sliding fee scale. SERVES: L.A. & San Bernardino Counties.

SO CALIF ALCOHOL & DRUG PRGM
Angel Step Inn
11500 Paramount Blvd.
Downey, CA 90241
(323) 780-7235 FAX

30-bed emerg shelter for women ages 18 yrs+ and their children (up to age 17 yrs) with co-occuring domestic violence & substance abuse issues. Max 45-day prgm. Also serves pregnant women. 24-hr hotline (323) 780-4357. Address above is for admin only, call for specific prgm site. FUNDING: Donation, nonprofit, state, county, United Way, SCADP, O.C. Health Care Agency. Spanish spoken. SERVES: L.A., Ventura, Orange, San Bernardino & Riverside Counties.

SOUTH COAST COMMUNITY SRVS
San Bernardino Co. Srvs Office
2930 Inland Empire Blvd., Ste 120
Ontario, CA 92764
(909) 980-6700

Provides life-essential srvs to troubled children, youth and families. Offers 4 group homes for abused, neglected and abandoned children ages 10-18 yrs and 2 group homes for young adults ages 18-25 yrs in need of short-term assist. Wraparound prgm offers family intervention srvs. Children's intensive srvs prgm provides outpatient counseling for individuals, children, teens and their families. Eval, assessment, testing, therapy, medication support, crisis intervention, case mgmt. Offers mental health clinics in Redlands (909) 792-0747 & Yucaipa (909) 790-0210. FUNDING: Nonprofit. Accepts Medi-Cal and pvt pay; sliding fee scale available. SERVES: San Bernardino County.

STALKING RESOURCE CENTER
National Center for Victims of Crime
2000 M Street NW, Ste 480
Washington, DC 20036
(202) 467-8700
(202) 467-8701 FAX

Provides srvs including training, tech assist, website, and info clearinghouse on stalking. Visit (www.ncvc.org/src/) or e-mail (src@ncvc.org) for more info. FUNDING: Nonprofit. Spanish SERVES: U.S.A.

STOMP OUT BULLYING
www.stompoutbullying.org
(877) 602-8559

Anti-bullying and cyberbullying prgm for kids and teens. Website provides info and prevention techniques regarding bullying. FUNDING: Nonprofit. SERVES: U.S.A.

Battered Persons/Victim/Adult Abuse

SURVIVORS OF INCEST ANONYMOUS (SIA)
P.O. Box 190
Benson, MD 21018
(410) 893-3322
(410) 893-3322 FAX

SIA is a 12-Step, self-help recovery prgm modeled after Alcoholics Anonymous. Internatl support groups, literature, penpals, speakers and newsletters. Incest defined very broadly; individuals learn that they are not alone and not to blame. Send a self-addressed, stamped envelope & $3 (if possible) for a directory of meetings. FUNDING: Nonprofit. OFC HRS: Vary. Various languages spoken. ADM REQ: Ages 18 yrs+ and not abusing any child. Are a victim of child abuse and want to recover. No dues or fees. SERVES: Internatl.

SURVIVORS OF TORTURE INTERNATL
P.O. Box 151240
San Diego, CA 92175-1240
(619) 278-2400
(619) 294-9405 FAX

Case mgmt srvs & referrals for psych, medical, & social srvs for survivors of torture and their families. For emerg, call (619) 278-2403; intake (619) 278-2404. Info provided for So. Calif, assist primarily for San Diego. FUNDING: Nonprofit. OFC HRS: M-F 8am-5pm. Chaldean, Kurdish, Arabic, Cambodian, Farsi, French & Spanish spoken. Interpretation for all languages available. Free srvs. Insurance utilized where applicable. Referrals to Medi-Cal providers. Accepts workers' compensation. SERVES: So. Calif.

UNITED LAW CENTERS/WOMEN'S LAW CTR
950 W. 17th Street, Ste D
Santa Ana, CA 92706-3573
(714) 667-1038
(714) 667-2388 FAX

Legal srvs for men & women for about half the cost of traditional lawyers. Flat rate fees and payment plans. Family law, divorce, custody, domestic violence, TRO, paternity, child support, criminal law, and immigration. FUNDING: Grants, nonprofit. OFC HRS: M-F 8am-5pm. Spanish, Vietnamese spoken. Sliding fee scale according to income. Free adoption srv to birth mothers includes free medical care. Free consultation. SERVES: Court Srvs in L.A., Orange & Riverside Counties.

UNITED WAY/INLAND VALLEYS
Southwest Co. Regional Office
5109 Jefferson Ave., Ste 225-A
Murrieta, CA 92562
(951) 697-4700
(951) 656-8210 FAX

Partners with donors to support many nonprofit health & human srv agencies. Prgms include: srvs for battered women, child care, youth, low-cost counseling, medical srvs, senior prgms, homeless srvs, emerg assist, volunteer srvs, etc. FUNDING: Donations, grants, nonprofit. OFC HRS: Vary. SERVES: Inland Valley.

UNITY HOME
See "Morongo Basin Unity Home"

VALLEY OASIS SHELTER
See "A.V. Domestic Violence Council"

VERONICA'S HOME OF MERCY
1495 W. Victoria St.
San Bernardino, CA 92411
(909) 888-9064
(909) 888-7390 FAX

Long-term, faith-based residential home (room for up to 20 women) for adult pregnant women & children or women with small children, as an alternative to domestic violence, addictions, abortion and/or homelessness. Women must be involved with the prgm and be willing to continue their education. Not an emergency shelter. FUNDING: Nonprofit. OFC HRS: M-F 8am-4pm. Spanish spoken. ADM REQ: Ages 18 yrs+ or emancipated by court. SERVES: So. Calif.

VICTIM-WITNESS ASSISTANCE
San Bernardino Co. District Attorney
235 E. Mountain View
Barstow, CA 92311
(760) 256-4810
(760) 256-4869 FAX

Apply for Victim of Violent Crimes Funds (via State Board of Control), crisis counseling, crime victims counseling, brochures, and referrals to providers and court support witnesses and victims. Explains criminal justice system, gives feedback on what is happening with court. Walk in or call. FUNDING: State and county district attorney's office. OFC HRS: M-F 8am-5pm. ADM REQ: Victim or witness of crime. Free srvs. SERVES: Barstow, Daggett, Hinkley, Lenwood, Baker, Needles and surrounding area.

VICTIM-WITNESS ASSISTANCE
Riverside Co. District Attorney
82-675 Hwy. 111, 4th Fl.
Indio, CA 92201
(760) 863-8216
(760) 863-8987 FAX

Crisis intervention, emerg assist, info & referral, court support & assist in filing for victim of crime compensation. FUNDING: State. OFC HRS: M-F 8am-5pm. Spanish spoken. Free srvs. SERVES: Riverside County.

VICTIM-WITNESS ASSISTANCE
San Bernardino Co. District Attorney
P.O. Box 6602
6527 White Feather Rd.
Joshua Tree, CA 92252
(760) 366-4120
(760) 366-4126 FAX

Apply for Victim of Violent Crimes Funds (via State Board of Control), crisis & crime victims counseling, brochures, referrals to providers and court support witnesses and victims. Explains criminal justice system, gives feedback on what is happening with court. Also assists after sentencing with regard to release date, etc. Works with victim upon contact. Walk in or call. FUNDING: State and county district attorney's office. OFC HRS: M-F 8am-5pm. ADM REQ: Victim or witness of crime. Free srvs. SERVES: Morongo Basin.

VICTIM-WITNESS ASSISTANCE
Riverside Co. District Attorney
30123 Technology Dr., Ste 130
Murrieta, CA 92563
(951) 304-5500
(951) 677-9326 FAX

Info, guidance and support to victims of crime. Assist victims with the application for the Victims of Crime prgm. FUNDING: Govt. OFC HRS: M-F 8am-5pm. Spanish spoken. SERVES: Southwest Riverside County.

VICTIM-WITNESS ASSISTANCE
San Bernardino Co. District Attorney
8303 Haven Ave., 4th Fl.
Rancho Cucamonga, CA 91730
(909) 945-4241
(909) 945-4035 FAX

Prgm assists victims of violent crimes with reimbursement process for medical bills, loss of wages, psychological fees and funeral and burial expenses not covered by insurance. Assists in criminal justice process including trial process. Referral to comm agencies for counseling. FUNDING: State. OFC HRS: M-F 8am-5pm. Spanish spoken. ADM REQ: Cooperation with investigation and prosecution. Free srvs. SERVES: West San Bernardino County.

VICTIM-WITNESS ASSISTANCE
Riverside Co. District Attorney
3960 Orange St.
Riverside, CA 92501
(951) 955-5400
(951) 955-5682 FAX

Direct and referral assist provided to victims of violent crimes and their families. Srvs include: emerg assist, crisis intervention, crime victim compensation, orientation to criminal justice system, court info, accompaniment, and restraining order assist. Walk in or call. FUNDING: State grants. OFC HRS: M-F 7am-5pm. SERVES: Riverside County.

VICTIM-WITNESS ASSISTANCE
Bureau of Victim Srvs/Dist Attorney
303 W. 3rd Street, 5th Fl.
San Bernardino, CA 92415
(909) 382-7671
(909) 382-7676 FAX

Prgm is designed to assist victims by providing emerg assist for short-term needs, referral to community agencies for counseling, special srvs to victims of sexual assault and domestic violence, elder orientation to criminal system, and for victims of violent crimes, assist in applying for financial compensation from State Victim Compensation Prgm. Call for info. FUNDING: State. OFC HRS: M-F 8am-5pm. Some Spanish spoken. Free srvs. SERVES: San Bernardino County.

VICTIM-WITNESS ASSISTANCE
Victorville Victim Srvs Center
15371 Civic Dr., 2nd Fl.
Victorville, CA 92392
(760) 552-6944
(760) 552-6941 FAX

Prgm is designed to assist the victims and witnesses by providing emerg assist for short-term needs, referrals to community agencies for counseling, special srvs to victims of sexual assault and domestic violence & elder abuse, orientation to criminal system. Assists victims of violent crimes apply for financial compensation from State Victim Compensation Prgm. FUNDING: State. OFC HRS: M-F 8am-5pm. Some Spanish spoken. Free srvs. SERVES: San Bernardino County.

VICTIMS OF CRIME RESOURCE CTR
Univ of Pacific/McGeorge School of Law

3200 5th Avenue
Sacramento, CA 95817
(800) 842-8467
(916) 739-7395 FAX

Info & referral srvs to crime victims in Calif. Referrals to counselors or legal assist who provide info concerning crime victims' rights in the justice system, state funds available for certain crime-related expenses, and civil lawsuit. FUNDING: State Office of Criminal Justice Planning, nonprofit. OFC HRS: M-F 8am-6pm. Spanish spoken. Free srvs. SERVES: Calif.

VICTOR VLY DOMESTIC VIOLENCE, INC.

A Better Way/Outreach Office
P.O. Box 2825
14114 Hesperia Rd.
Victorville, CA 92393
(760) 955-8010
(760) 955-8248 FAX

18-bed shelter for abused women and their children. Outreach, TRO assist, children's prgms, parenting classes, When Love Hurts prgm, peer support groups, anger mgmt, health, nutrition, basic budgeting. Max stay is 90 days. Counseling, transitional housing. 24-hr hotline (760) 955-8723. FUNDING: Donations, nonprofit. OFC HRS: M-F 8am-4pm. Some Spanish spoken. ADM REQ: Victim of domestic violence. SERVES: High Desert.

WOMEN'S LAW CENTER

See "United Law Centers/..."

WOMEN'S RESOURCE CENTER

1963 Apple St.
Oceanside, CA 92054
(760) 757-3500
(760) 757-0680 FAX

24-hr hotline and shelter for women & children. This prgm is located in the Oceanside area but serves all of So. Calif. Counseling, parenting classes & other srvs for families & individuals victimized by sexual assault & domestic violence. FUNDING: Nonprofit. OFC HRS: M-F 9am-5pm. Spanish spoken. Sliding fee scale for counseling. SERVES: So. Calif.

WOMEN'S RESOURCE CENTER

Univ of Calif, Riverside
900 University Ave., 260 Costo Hall
Riverside, CA 92521
(951) 827-3337
(951) 827-5199 FAX

Sexual harassment & rape prevention edu prgm is a resource, a learning tool and a support system. Emphasis is on edu to help women and men learn the most effective means of avoiding personally violating behavior. Also support for survivors, their families and friends. Walk in or call for appt. FUNDING: Nonprofit. OFC HRS: M-F 8am-5pm. Free srvs. SERVES: Riverside County.

YWCA/WINGS SHELTER

For Battered Women
P.O. Box 1464
West Covina, CA 91793
(626) 338-3123
(626) 338-5419 FAX

24-hr helpline (626) 967-0658, with crisis intervention & referrals. 45-day shelter prgm for women and their children who are victims of domestic violence. Legal referrals, restraining order clinic, support groups, community edu, substance abuse counseling. Accompaniment to court, DPSS, and medical srvs. FUNDING: State, county, United Way, CSBC, donations, nonprofit. OFC HRS: M-F 8am-5pm; 24-hr shelter. Spanish & Mandarin spoken. ADM REQ: Battered women & their children. Free srvs. SERVES: Calif, will shelter women from outside the area.

4-H CLUB/RIVERSIDE COUNTY

Univ of Calif Coop Ext-Riverside Co.
21150 Box Springs Rd., Ste 202
Moreno Valley, CA 92557-8718
(951) 683-6491
(951) 788-2615 FAX

Community-based clubs offering a wide variety of edu projects and activities for youth ages 5-19 yrs. 4-H clubs are lead by adult volunteers who are screened and oriented. Annual prgm fee approx $25 covers accident insurance, newsletter, awards, incentives prgms & defrays the cost of camps & training prgms for leaders & youth. Additional offices in Indio (760) 863-8293, fax (760)775-0600; Blythe (760) 921-7884, fax (760) 921-7887. FUNDING: USDA, state, county. OFC HRS: M-F 9am-5pm. Spanish spoken. SERVES: Riverside County.

ABILITYFIRST/CAMP PAIVIKA

P.O. Box 3367
600 Playground Dr.
Cedarpines Park, CA 92322
(909) 338-1102
(909) 338-2502 FAX

Residential camp for children & adults with physical & dev disabilities. Camp operates June-Aug each year with adaptive recreation and sports activities. Winter weekend respite prgms also available. FUNDING: United Way, donations, Regional Ctrs, nonprofit. ADM REQ: Ages 7 yrs+. SERVES: San Bernardino County.

ABILITYFIRST/CORPORATE HDQTRS

Formerly Crippled Children's Society
1300 E. Green St.
Pasadena, CA 91106
(626) 396-1010
(877) 768-4600
(626) 396-1021 FAX

Programs and srvs for children and adults with physical & dev disabilities throughout So. Calif. Workforce srvs, after-school prgms, adult day prgms, socialization, recreation, aquatic therapy, affordable & accessible housing, residential & day camps, infant & toddler prgms, info & referral to outside community resources for the disabled. Contact Kelly Privitt. FUNDING: Donors, Regional Ctrs, fundraising, United Way, Dept of Rehab, nonprofit. OFC HRS: M-F 8am-5:30pm. Spanish spoken. SERVES: So. Calif.

AMERICAN CAMPING ASSN (ACA)

P.O. Box 712218
Los Angeles, CA 90071-7218
(800) 428-2267
(765) 342-2065 FAX

Publishes "Accredited Camps and Approved Sites in So. Calif & Hawaii." Guide includes camps for youths & adults, plus a list of group retreat rentals. The guide is free; call or write to above address for a single copy. Visit (www.ACAsocal.org). OFC HRS: M-F 9am-5pm, voicemail after hrs. SERVES: So. Calif & Hawaii.

AMERICAN DIABETES ASSOCIATION

1701 N. Beauregard St.
Alexandria, VA 22311
(800) 342-2383
(703) 549-6995 FAX

Natl call center for persons seeking diabetes info, support or prgms. Online camp directory listing American Diabetes Assn affiliated camps for diabetic children and teens. Visit (www.diabetes.org). FUNDING: Nonprofit. OFC HRS: M-F 8:30am-8pm, EST. 24-hr recording. Spanish spoken. SERVES: U.S.A.

APPLE CANYON CENTER

P.O. Box 35
56400 Apple Canyon Rd.
Mountain Center, CA 92561-0035
(951) 659-4609
(951) 659-4710 FAX

Facility available for camping, conferences, family reunions, retreats. Youth camp & edu, teamwork & challenge course, outdoor edu. FUNDING: Nonprofit. ADM REQ: Call for reservations and more info. SERVES: Calif.

ASTROCAMP

P.O. Box 1360
Claremont, CA 91711
(909) 625-6194
(909) 625-7305 FAX

Co-ed camp for ages 8-14 yrs. Three-week sessions are offered June-July. School prgms during the school year. Astronomy, rocketry, hands-on laboratories in physical & earth sciences, rock climbing, wall, high ropes course, hiking and much more. ACA accredited. FUNDING: Nonprofit. OFC HRS: M-F 8am-4:30pm. SERVES: Calif.

BEARSKIN MEADOW CAMP

Diabetic Youth Foundation
5167 Clayton Rd., Ste F
Concord, CA 94521
(925) 680-4994
(925) 680-4863 FAX

Residential co-ed camp with prgms for children, teens and young adults with diabetes. Also family prgms. Medical staff available at all times. Camps located in Sequoia Natl Forest from mid-June to late Aug. Swimming, arts & crafts, hiking, rock climbing, archery, sports, backpacking, campfires, performing arts, nature activities & diabetes edu. Sessions fill quickly, sign up early. ACA accredited. FUNDING: Donations, fees. OFC HRS: M-F 9am-5pm. Spanish spoken. Scholarships available. SERVES: Calif.

BIG ROCK CREEK CAMP

P.O. Box 66
18101 Paradise Dr.
Valyermo, CA 93563
(661) 944-9005
(661) 944-9011 FAX

Christian camp in the San Gabriel mountains on 145 acres of forest. Swimming, basketball, volleyball, tennis, fishing, petting zoo, hiking, horseshoes, horseback riding, rock climbing, snow play in the winter. Outdoor science edu, survival training, ropes challenge. Prgms for all ages. FUNDING: Nonprofit. OFC HRS: M-F 8am-5pm. SERVES: So. Calif.

BLIND YOUTH CAMP

See "Camp Bloomfield"

BOY SCOUTS OF AMER/INLAND EMP

Calif Inland Empire Council (CIEC)

1230 Indiana Court
Redlands, CA 92374-2896
(909) 793-2463
(877) 732-1450
(909) 793-0306 FAX

One-week resident camp for youth ages 8 yrs+. Activities include: archery, arts & crafts, camping skills/outdoor living, hiking, nature/environmental studies, riflery, instructional swimming, recreational swimming. Based on scout activities & ideals, prgm seeks to develop youth & prevent future social costs for rehab or detention. Adult volunteers provide youth with various prgms, club meetings, campouts, comm involvement, social & recreational activities. ACA accredited. FUNDING: United Way, donations, fundraising, nonprofit. OFC HRS: M-F 9:30am-5:30pm. ADM REQ: Boys ages 7-20 yrs and girls ages 15-20 yrs, adults all ages. Membership dues vary with unit. Cost for camp is $76-$200 per week. SERVES: Riverside, San Bernardino Counties.

BOYS & GIRLS CLUB/CAMPING

Many Boys & Girls Clubs sponsor day camp and resident camp activities at various times throughout the year. Contact your local club for full details about their camping prgms. FUNDING: Nonprofit.

BOYS & GIRLS CLUB/TEMECULA

P.O. Box 892349
28790 Pujol St.
Temecula, CA 92589-2349
(951) 699-1526
(951) 699-4273 FAX

Youth srvs for boys & girls. Recreation, informal guidance, league sports, edu prgms, computer skills training, health & life skills. Homework & tutorial srvs, transportation, delinquency prevention prgm. Day camp, before & after school care for grades 1-8. Roller hockey, sports for toddlers, Tae Kwon Do. FUNDING: United Way, nonprofit. OFC HRS: M-F 6:30am-7pm; Sat 9am-2pm. Spanish spoken. ADM REQ: Ages 6-17 yrs. Annual membership $20. SERVES: Temecula, Murrieta.

CAMP AZALEA TRAILS

See "Girl Scouts/San Gorgonio Cncl"

CAMP BLOOMFIELD

Foundation for the Junior Blind
5300 Angeles Vista Blvd.
Los Angeles, CA 90043
(323) 295-4555
(800) 352-2290
(323) 296-0424 FAX

Co-ed residential camp for blind or visually impaired infants, children & young adults ages 6-21 yrs & their families. Camp site is in Malibu. Annual camps are one week or longer between June & Aug. Register before June for summer camps. ACA accredited. FUNDING: Donations, grants, nonprofit. OFC HRS: M-Th 8am-4:30pm; F 8am-4pm. Spanish spoken. Registration fee $25 per camper. SERVES: U.S.A.

CAMP CHINNOCK

See "Camp Conrad/Chinnock"

CAMP CONNECT CALIFORNIA
Aspira Foster & Family Srvs
400 Oyster Point Blvd., Ste 501
South San Francisco, CA 94080
(650) 866-4080
(650) 866-4081 FAX

Week-long summer camp for siblings who are separated by out-of-home foster care. Sibling enhancement, therapeutic art, life seminar. FUNDING: Nonprofit, donations. ADM REQ: Ages 10-18 yrs. SERVES: Calif.

CAMP CONRAD/CHINNOCK
Diabetic Youth Srvs
12045 E. Waterfront Dr.
Los Angeles, CA 90094
(310) 751-3057
(888) 800-4010 FAX

Srvs & facilities are shared with health-based assns, schools & community organizations looking to promote self-esteem, spiritual awareness & moral character in children, including those living with chronic illness, physical disability or economic hardship. Camp located in the San Bernardino Natl Forest. Recreational, social & edu opportunities for youth & families with diabetes. Campers are taught diabetes self-mgmt skills in a fun, interactive and safe environment. Also water activities, rock climbing, canoeing, hiking, arts/crafts, volleyball, basketball, mountain biking, along with medical edu & self-knowledge. Family & youth camps, multiple youth sessions. FUNDING: Donations, nonprofit. OFC HRS: M-F 9am-3pm. Spanish spoken. Financial aid available for qualifying families. SERVES: So. Calif.

CAMP DEL CORAZON, INC.
Corp Ofc
11615 Hesby St., North
North Hollywood, CA 91601-3620
(818) 754-0312
(888) 621-4800
(818) 754-0842 FAX

Residential summer camp for children ages 7-17 yrs who are living with heart disease. FUNDING: Nonprofit. OFC HRS: M-F 8:30am-5pm. Free srvs. SERVES: Internatl.

CAMP ESPERANZA
Arthritis Fndn/Youth
800 W. 6th Street, Ste 1250
Los Angeles, CA 90017
(323) 954-5750
(800) 954-2873
(323) 954-5790 FAX

Co-ed residential camp for children ages 8-17 yrs with any type of rheumatic disease. Medical staff are present. Three sessions; each 5 days and 4 nights. Camp site is at Fawnskin, near Big Bear. Register at least 12 weeks prior to camp date. Camps usually held in mid-August. FUNDING: Donations, govt, nonprofit. OFC HRS: M-Th 8:30am-5pm; F 8:30am-4:30pm. Spanish spoken. Camp fee. Scholarships available. SERVES: So. Calif.

CAMP GOOD GRIEF
Loma Linda Univ Children's Hospital
11234 Anderson St., Rm. 2816
Loma Linda, CA 92354
(909) 558-4073
(800) 825-5437

Three-day camp for children and teens who have had a sibling or parent die. Also have Spe-

cial Victims Prgm sponsored by the San Bernardino Co. Dist Atty's office. Held at various locations. FUNDING: Loma Linda Univ Children's Hospital Fndn. ADM REQ: Must make reservation and fill out application. Ages 10-16 yrs. Free srvs. SERVES: So. Calif.

CAMP JCA SHALOM
34342 Mulholland Hwy.
Malibu, CA 90265
(818) 889-5500
(818) 889-5132 FAX

Residential camps with 4 sessions in summer, weekend camp in the fall and a weekend in the spring. Winter camp held in Dec. Registration starts in October and continues until sessions are full. All faiths are welcome. Camperships based on financial need. ACA accredited. FUNDING: Nonprofit. OFC HRS: M-F 9:30am-5pm. Hebrew & Russian spoken. SERVES: So. Calif., Arizona, Nevada & New Mexico.

CAMP LAUREL
75 S. Grand Ave.
Pasadena, CA 91105
(626) 683-0800
(626) 683-0890 FAX

Year-round residential camps for children living with HIV/AIDS. Horseback riding, swimming, mountain bike riding, rock climbing, canoeing, archery, arts & crafts, ropes course, overnight trips. One-week camps, several times during the year. FUNDING: Nonprofit, donations, grants. OFC HRS: M-F 9am-5pm. Spanish spoken. Free for eligible children. SERVES: U.S.A.

CAMP MOUNTAIN CHAI
Admin Office
4950 Murphy Canyon Rd.
San Diego, CA 92123
(858) 499-1330
(858) 499-1331 FAX

ACA accredited Jewish residential and day summer camp serving children entering grades 3-11. Camp is located in the San Bernardino Mountains. Scholarships available. SERVES: San Bernardino County.

CAMP QUEST
See "Epilepsy Fndn of San Diego"

CAMP TAUTONA
See "Girl Scouts/San Gorgonio Cncl"

CANCER/YOUTH CAMPS
See "Ronald McDonald House/Los Angeles"

CEDAR LAKE CHRISTIAN CAMP
P.O. Box 1568
Big Bear Lake, CA 92315
(909) 866-5714
(909) 866-5715 FAX

Families, single adults or seniors. Pvt rooms, meeting rooms, lakeside chapel, food srv. One-to 2-week sessions. ACA accredited. FUNDING: Nonprofit. SERVES: Calif.

CEDARBROOK CAMP SO CALIF
P.O. Box 400610
Hesperia, CA 92340
(909) 866-9366
(909) 752-5337 FAX

Summer and year-round camps with a Christian emphasis. Camps for girls & boys ages 6-18 yrs, co-ed ages 6-13 yrs. Summer camp location is 3191 Radford Rd in Angelus Oaks. CCI

member. Women's retreat, parent-child weekends. ACA accredited. FUNDING: Nonprofit. OFC HRS: M-F 9am-5pm. Camps in June-August. Fee $275. Some camperships available. SERVES: So. Calif.

DEAF KID'S KAMP
Sproul Ranch, Inc.
42263 50th Street, West, Ste 610
Quartz Hill, CA 93536
(661) 657-3323

ACA-accredited free summer camp provided to deaf children. Held in Big Bear, CA. FUNDING: Nonprofit, fundraising. ADM REQ: Deaf children ages 6-17 yrs. Must meet requirements. Processing fee $100, non-refundable. SERVES: U.S.A.

DESERT RECREATION DISTRICT
Formerly Coachella Vly Rec & Park Dist
45-305 Oasis St.
Indio, CA 92201
(760) 347-3484
(760) 347-4660 FAX

This is not a day care facility. Preschool Tiny Tot Prgm M-Th 9am-11:30am. Prgms held at three community centers. Swimming, cultural prgms, summer day camp, kid's club, licensed after school care for grades K-6 in Indio, La Quinta and Palm Desert, two gyms with basketball, volleyball, racquetball. FUNDING: Nonprofit, donations. OFC HRS: M-F 8am-5pm. Spanish spoken. Low fees. SERVES: Palm Desert, Indian Wells, La Quinta, Indio, Coachella, Thousand Palms, Rancho Mirage, Bermuda Dunes, Thermal, Oasis, Mecca, and the Salton Sea.

DIABETIC YOUTH CAMPS
See "Bearskin Meadow..." or "Camp Conrad..."

DISABLED YOUTH CAMPS
The Camps chapter includes many camps for children with disabilities including: "AbilityFirst/...," "American Diabetes Association," "Bearskin Meadow Camp," "Camp Conrad/Chinnock," "Camp Laurel," "Dream Street Foundation," "Epilepsy Fndn...," "Girl Scouts of USA," "Natl Kidney Fndn...," "Sickle Cell Disease... ."

DREAM STREET FOUNDATION
Camp Dream Street
433 N. Camden Dr., Ste 600
Beverly Hills, CA 90212
(424) 248-0696
(800) 553-7326
(310) 951-1233 FAX

Camping prgms for children with chronic & life-threatening illnesses. Medical staff on hand for children who require medication or special attention. Completely volunteer operated. No child sits on the sidelines or has to worry about being different. Also has young adult prgm. FUNDING: Nonprofit. ADM REQ: Ages 4-24 yrs. Free for those attending camp. SERVES: Calif, Arizona, Arkansas, New Jersey & Mississippi.

EPILEPSY FNDN OF SAN DIEGO
Camp Quest
2055 El Cajon Blvd.
San Diego, CA 92104-1092
(619) 296-0161
(619) 296-0802 FAX

A medically supervised summer camp for children with seizure disorders. Camp Quest is held for one week in July at a mountain camp. Agency provides individual, family & group counseling, employment prgms, info & referral, advocacy, epilepsy edu. FUNDING: Donations, United Way, nonprofit. OFC HRS: M-F 9am-5pm. ADM REQ: Camp for children ages 8-12 yrs. Application deadline is June 1st. SERVES: Calif.

FOREST HOME

Forest Home Christian Conference Ctr
40000 Valley of the Falls Dr.
Forest Falls, CA 92339
(909) 389-2300
(909) 389-2330 FAX

Co-ed residential Christian camp in summer for elementary, junior high and high school families. Crafts, swimming, hiking, sport fishing, zipline, wall, ropes, skateboard park for grades 5-6, mini-golf and obstacle courses. Site is located in San Bernardino Mountains. Session themes vary. Camp is a member of CCI & ACA accredited. FUNDING: L.A. Times scholarships, nonprofit. OFC HRS: M-F 8am-4:30pm. Fees vary per prgm. SERVES: So. Calif.

GIRL SCOUTS OF USA

Most Girl Scout troops sponsor day and residential camps at various times during the year. Contact local Girl Scout Council for details about their camping.

GIRL SCOUTS/SAN GORGONIO CNCL

Youth Organization/Camps
1751 Plum Lane
Redlands, CA 92374-4505
(909) 307-6555
(800) 400-4475
(909) 307-6526 FAX

Girl Scouts offers an informal edu prgm for girls. Prgms support self-worth, values and contributing to the community in an all-girl environment. Resident & day camps offered to girls throughout the summer in various areas. Camps include Camp Azalea Trails which is held in the San Jacinto Mountains near Idyllwild, and Camp Tautona. Summer hrs vary. FUNDING: United Way, donations, product sales. OFC HRS: M-W 8am-6:30pm; Th 8am-6pm. Spanish spoken. ADM REQ: Girls ages 5-18 yrs. $10 annual membership fee. Financial assist available. SERVES: Riverside Co. & most of San Bernardino County.

GUIDED DISCOVERIES, INC.

P.O. Box 1360
Claremont, CA 91711
(909) 625-6194
(800) 645-1423
(909) 625-7305 FAX

Summer resident camps and school prgms. Visit (www.guideddiscoveries.org). FUNDING: Nonprofit. OFC HRS: M-F 8am-5pm. ADM REQ: Ages 8-14 yrs. Fees vary per prgm. SERVES: U.S.A.

IDYLLWILD PINES CAMP & CONFERENCE CTR

P.O. Box 425
26375 State Highway 243
Idyllwild, CA 92549
(951) 659-2605
(951) 659-5195 FAX

Christian camp & center available to rent for Christian groups. Meeting halls, lodging, activities. Call for group rates. FUNDING: Nonprofit. OFC HRS: M-F 8am-5pm. SERVES: Calif.

IDYLLWILD RANGER STATION

San Bernardino Natl Forest
P.O. Box 518
54270 Pine Crest
Idyllwild, CA 92549
(909) 382-2921

Info on camping, wilderness use, and local fishing areas. TTY: (800) 877-8339. OFC HRS: M-W, F-Sun 8:am-4pm. SERVES: So. Calif.

KIDNEY FNDN YOUTH CAMP

See "Natl Kidney Fndn of So Calif"

LUTHER VILLAGE & LUTHER GLEN

Lutheran Retreats, Camps & Conferences
39136 Harris Rd.
Yucaipa, CA 92399
(909) 797-9183
(800) 464-2417
(909) 797-9184 FAX

Christian 1-week residential co-ed camp for ages 7 yrs+ located in Oak Glen. Camps run during July & August. Also adult retreat and elder hostel prgms. Camps serve all denominations. Archery, arts and crafts, camping skills, outdoor living, challenge rope courses, hiking, leadership dev, nature, religious study, recreational swimming. ACA accredited. FUNDING: Nonprofit. OFC HRS: M-F 9am-5pm. Contact for fees. Some camperships available. SERVES: So. Calif.

NATL KIDNEY FNDN OF SO CALIF

Camping Programs
15490 Ventura Blvd., Ste 210
Sherman Oaks, CA 91403
(800) 747-5527
(818) 783-8153
(818) 783-8160 FAX

Camps for children and families whose lives have been affected by kidney disease. Summer camp at Camp Whittle for children ages 9-14 yrs with all treatment modalities related to end-stage renal disease. Teenage camp designed specifically for patients ages 15-21 yrs. Family camp prgm allows adult kidney patients a unique and rare opportunity to partake in two family camp weekends in the wilderness. FUNDING: Nonprofit. OFC HRS: M-F 9am-5pm. Spanish spoken. Free srvs. SERVES: So. Calif.

PATHFINDER RANCH

35510 Pathfinder Rd., Ste 104
Mountain Center, CA 92561
(951) 659-2455
(951) 659-0351 FAX

Year-round facility. Dorms, meeting rooms, dining hall, picnic area, outdoor campfire area. ACA accredited. FUNDING: Nonprofit, donations. SERVES: Calif.

PILGRIM PINES CAMP & CONF CTR

39570 Glen Rd.
Yucaipa, CA 92399
(909) 797-1821
(800) 616-6612
(909) 797-2691 FAX

One-week residential camp for youth in grades 1-12. Archery, swimming, crafts, music. 5 one-week summer camps July & Aug. Co-ed resident camps with separate cabins. Mini-camps for grades 1-3, junior camps for grades 4-6, junior high camps & senior high camp. Camps for dev challenged youth (ages 10-14 yrs), teens (ages 15-21 yrs) and adults. Register early. Group rates & partial camperships available. ACA accredited. FUNDING: Nonprofit. OFC HRS: M-Sun 8am-5pm. Some Spanish spoken. Fee $350 per week. SERVES: So. Calif.

PINE SPRINGS RANCH

P.O. Box 37
Mountain Center, CA 92561
(951) 659-3173
(951) 659-5692 FAX

Seven-day residential camp for ages 8-16 yrs, sponsored by the Seventh Day Adv Church. Discounts for church members. Ropes Course Assn and Certified Horsemanship Assn. Camp site in Idyllwild area. ACA accredited, member of CCI. For summer camp, call (951) 509-2266. FUNDING: Donations, client fees, nonprofit. OFC HRS: M-F 8am-5pm. Spanish spoken. SERVES: So. Calif.

RONALD MCDONALD HOUSE/LOS ANGELES

Camp Ronald McDonald for Good Times
1954 Cotner Ave.
Los Angeles, CA 90025-5602
(310) 268-8488
(800) 625-7295
(310) 473-3338 FAX

Co-ed camps for ages 7-18 yrs who have presently or previously been diagnosed with cancer. Six summer camps (1-week residential camps), as well as four winter sessions, each four days in length. Family camps for children ages 6 yrs and younger. Also sibling camps. Medical staff available at all times. Camp site at Mountain Center (Idyllwild). ACA-accredited. FUNDING: Nonprofit. OFC HRS: M-F 9am-5:30pm. Spanish spoken. ADM REQ: Ages birth-18 yrs. Free to eligible children. SERVES: Calif.

SALVATION ARMY/ONTARIO

P.O. Box 408
1412 S. Euclid Ave.
Ontario, CA 91762
(909) 986-6748
(909) 986-9979 FAX

Emerg short-term assist to resident families and transients including food and lodging assist. Case mgmt is also provided. Salvation Army Ontario Corps serves Western San Bernardino County. This regional office will provide referrals for needed srvs at various srv locations. Also provides youth prgms and women's srvs. Shelter when funding is available, disaster relief, summer camp, scouting activities for children, and an after school prgm. FUNDING: FEMA, United Way, donations. OFC HRS: M-F 8:30am-4:30pm. Spanish spoken. ADM REQ: Photo ID, proof of income, address verification. SERVES: Ontario, Fontana, Upland, Rialto, Chino, Chino Hills & Rancho Cucamonga.

SCHOEPE SCOUT RESERVATION/LOST VLY

O.C. Council of Boy Scouts
1211 E. Dyer Rd.
Santa Ana, CA 92705
(714) 546-4990
(714) 546-0415 FAX

One-week summer residential camp for Boy Scout members in July & August located in San Diego mountains. ACA accredited. FUNDING: Nonprofit. OFC HRS: M-F 8:30am-5pm. Spanish, Armenian, Russian & Mandarin spoken. Fee: $205. Camperships available. SERVES: So. Calif.

SICKLE CELL DISEASE FNDN OF CALIF
Camp Crescent Moon
6133 Bristol Pkwy., Ste 240
Culver City, CA 90230
(310) 693-0247
(877) 288-2873
(310) 693-0266 FAX

Co-ed camp for children ages 8-14 yrs who have sickle cell disease. One-week camp in July. Registration fee. FUNDING: Donations, grants, nonprofit. OFC HRS: M-F 8:30am-5pm. Spanish spoken. SERVES: So. Calif.

ST. MICHAEL'S CAMP FOR BOYS
Norbertine Fathers of Orange, Inc.
24361 El Toro Rd., Ste 220
Silverado 92637
(949) 858-0222
(949) 273-5451
(949) 858-4583 FAX

Residential camp for boys ages 7-12 yrs. Five 1-week resident camps in July & August. Swimming, team sports, hiking, camp fire events, character building, arts & crafts. The site is a 30-acre campground in South Orange County with dorm sleeping facilities. Registration is by mail. ACA accredited. FUNDING: Nonprofit. Fee per week. SERVES: U.S.A.

THE BRIDGE SCHOOL
545 Eucalyptus Ave.
Hillsborough, CA 94010-6404
(650) 696-7295
(650) 342-7598 FAX

School for individuals with severe speech and physical impairments. Augmentative & alternative means of communication & assistive technology is used. Summer camp for ages 5-17 yrs. Call for more info. FUNDING: Nonprofit, donations, fundraising. OFC HRS: M-F 8am-4pm. Campers who are residents of Calif and clients of Regional Centers may be eligible to receive partial funding. Some scholarships available. SERVES: Calif.

THE PAINTED TURTLE
1300 4th Street, Ste 300
Santa Monica, CA 90401
(310) 451-1353
(310) 451-1357 FAX

Camp for seriously ill children. FUNDING: Nonprofit. OFC HRS: M-F 9am-5pm. Free to eligible children. SERVES: So. Calif.

THOUSAND PINES CHRISTIAN CAMP
P.O. Box 3288
359 Thousand Pines Road
Crestline, CA 92325
(909) 338-2705
(888) 423-2267
(909) 338-3511 FAX

One-week co-ed residential Christian camp for ages 6 yrs+. Camps throughout the year, three to six day camps with crafts, aquatic activities, archery, ceramics, pottery, counselor training (CIT), religious study, hiking, rope challenge course, climbing wall, paintball course. Registration is on first come basis. Camp site in San Bernardino mountains. ACA accredited. FUNDING: Fees, donations, nonprofit. OFC HRS: M-F 8am-4:30pm. ADM REQ: Grades 1-12. SERVES: So. Calif.

UNITED CEREBRAL PALSY ASSN
Dennis James Center
35325 Date Palm Dr., Ste 136
Cathedral City, CA 92234
(760) 321-8184
(760) 321-8284 FAX

Info & referral, family resource center, in-home respite care, recreation & camping prgms, parent support groups. "Skillbuilders" after school prgm for ages 8-18 yrs. "Little Bridges" recreation prgm for ages 3-6 yrs. FUNDING: Nonprofit. OFC HRS: M-F 8:30am-4:30pm. Spanish spoken. Srvs paid through Inland Regional Center. SERVES: San Bernardino, Riverside Counties.

VERDUGO PINES BIBLE CAMP
P.O. Box 1989
22400 Big Pines Hwy.
Wrightwood, CA 92397
(760) 249-3532
(888) 226-7482
(760) 249-4447 FAX

One-week residential camp for youth. Aquatic activities and counselor training (CIT). ACA accredited. ADM REQ: Grades 3-12. Fee $100-$250 per week. SERVES: So. Calif.

YMCA/CAMP EDWARDS
P.O. Box 277
42842 Jenks Rd. E
Angelus Oaks, CA 92305
(909) 794-1702
(909) 794-3157 FAX

Residential camp for ages 7-17 yrs. ACA accredited. FUNDING: Nonprofit. OFC HRS: Vary seasonally. Financial assist available to those who qualify. SERVES: So. Calif.

YMCA/CAMP OAKES
P.O. Box 452
47400 Monte Vista Dr.
Big Bear City, CA 92314
(909) 585-2020
(800) 642-2014
(909) 585-8038 FAX

Open year-round. Astronomy, crafts, nature, boating, swimming, archery, horseback riding, ropes challenge course, seasonal hiking. Primarily serves ages 7-14 yrs. Summer long-term camp runs three 1-week sessions. Outdoor edu for school district. FUNDING: Nonprofit. OFC HRS: M-F 9am-5pm. SERVES: So. Calif.

YMCA/CORONA/NORCO
Youth Services
1331 River Road
Corona, CA 92880
(951) 736-9622
(951) 736-6759 FAX

A variety of prgms including: karate, swimming lessons, preschool, before & after school care (also evening child care), day & resident camp, sports, drama classes, Bingo adventure guides, senior aerobics. OFC HRS: M-F 6am-6pm. Spanish, Portuguese, Tagalog spoken. Limited scholarships available. SERVES: Corona, Norco & Home Gardens.

YMCA/DESERT
43-930 San Pablo Ave.
Palm Desert, CA 92260
(760) 341-9622
(760) 779-9651 FAX

Recreation prgms, camping, licensed child care, youth sports, martial arts, yoga, aquatics, summer resident and day camps, teen prgms & special events. Walk in or call. FUNDING: United Way, donors, fees, nonprofit. OFC HRS: M-F 8am-7pm; Sat 9am-12noon. Spanish spoken. Sliding fee scale. Scholarships available. SERVES: Coachella Valley.

YMCA/GREATER LONG BEACH
Office of Camping Srvs
P.O. Box 90995
3605 Long Beach Blvd., Ste 210
Long Beach, CA 90809-0995
(562) 279-1630
(562) 425-1169 FAX

Camping throughout the year. Annual summer camp prgm with 1- to 6-week sessions. Traditional activities as well as special activities, aquatics, and horseback riding. Open to children ages 8-14 yrs. Leadership training for ages 15-17 yrs. Labor Day, New Year's Day and other family residential camping. Rents camp facilities to others. ACA accredited. FUNDING: Nonprofit. OFC HRS: M-F 8:30am-5pm. Fee varies per session length. SERVES: U.S.A.

YMCA/RIVERSIDE CAMP
9254 Galena Street
Riverside, CA 92509
(951) 685-5241
(951) 689-7543 FAX

Residential camp for youth. Aquatic activities, biking, canoeing, climbing/rapelling, counselor training (CIT), fishing, recreational swimming, team building. ACA accredited. FUNDING: Nonprofit. OFC HRS: M-F 9am-5pm. ADM REQ: Grades 3-9. Fee $385+; registration fee $35. Scholarships to needy children. SERVES: Riverside County.

ABA CENTER/CHILDREN & LAW

740 15th Street, NW, 9th Fl.
Washington, DC 20005-1019
(202) 662-1720
(800) 285-2221
(202) 662-1755 FAX

Info, tech assist, consulting & training on legal issues related to child welfare & protection, publications on issues. Sponsored by the American Bar Assn. Voicemail after hours. FUNDING: Nonprofit. OFC HRS: M-F 9am-5pm, EST. SERVES: U.S.A.

ALTERNATIVE SENTENCING

Indio Probation Department
47-940 Arabia St.
Indio, CA 92201
(760) 863-8420
(760) 863-8916 FAX

Domestic violence, sexual deviance, anger mgmt, parenting, child batterer classes, community srv provider, referrals for home monitoring and administers court-ordered vehicle ignition interlock prgm. FUNDING: Nonprofit. OFC HRS: M-Th 8am-4pm; F 8am-3pm. Spanish spoken. ADM REQ: Assigned by court, probation, parole or DPSS depts. Fees vary by service; only accepts money orders. SERVES: Coachella Valley.

ALTERNATIVES TO DOMESTIC VIOLENCE

P.O. Box 910
Riverside, CA 92502
(951) 320-1370
(951) 320-1381 FAX

Outreach prgm for victims of domestic violence and their children. One-on-one counseling, support groups, children's prgm (offered in Spanish & English), community edu, court accompaniment, TRO assist, shelter, info & referral. 24-hr crisis line: (951) 683-0829. FUNDING: Govt, donations, nonprofit. OFC HRS: M-F 8am-5pm. Spanish spoken. Free srvs. SERVES: Western Riverside County.

AMERICAN HUMANE ASSN

Children's Srvs
63 Inverness Dr., East
Englewood, CO 80112-5117
(800) 227-4645
(303) 792-9900
(303) 792-5333 FAX

Info on child abuse and neglect, research & eval, newsletter, sponsors special meetings, training for professionals in the area of child abuse & child protection srvs. Operates natl resource center on the link between violence to people & animals. FUNDING: Donations, grants, nonprofit. OFC HRS: M-F 8am-5pm, MST. SERVES: U.S.A.

BARBARA SINATRA CHILDREN'S CENTER

Eisenhower Medical Center
39000 Bob Hope Dr.
Rancho Mirage, CA 92270
(760) 340-2336
(760) 340-1851 FAX

Outpatient therapy center for children who have been physically or sexually abused, adults molested as children (AMAC). FUNDING: Nonprofit. OFC HRS: M-F 8am-5pm. Spanish spoken. Sliding fee scale. SERVES: Coachella Valley.

BOYS HOPE GIRLS HOPE OF SO CALIF

1041 W. 18th Street, Ste A101
Costa Mesa, CA 92627
(949) 515-8833
(949) 515-8844 FAX

Long-term, family-like residential group homes for capable, needy youth. Serves academically capable boys and girls who have been abused, neglected or abandoned, or who have come from dysfunctional families. Provides safe, stable, long-term alternative living environment; youth must be free of significant emotional or learning difficulties. This is a voluntary placement. Focus is at-risk children with academic ability who are determined to go to college. FUNDING: Donations, grants, nonprofit. OFC HRS: M-F 9am-5pm. ADM REQ: Clear need for long-term out-of-home placement, at least an average IQ. Ages 10-14 yrs can remain through graduation from high school. Free srvs. SERVES: So. Calif.

CALIF DEPT OF JUSTICE

Missing & Unidentified Persons Unit
P.O. Box 903387
Sacramento, CA 94203-3870
(800) 222-3463
(916) 227-3290
(916) 227-3270 FAX

Assists law enforcement and other criminal agencies to locate missing persons. Helps parents of missing children work with law enforcement. Distributes missing child posters, publishes a quarterly missing persons bulletin. Online bulletin updated quarterly. FUNDING: State, nonprofit. OFC HRS: 24 hrs, 7 days. Spanish, Japanese, Cantonese spoken. SERVES: Calif.

CALIF DEPT OF SOCIAL SRVS

Ofc of Child Abuse Prevention
744 P Street, MS 11-82
Sacramento, CA 95814
(916) 651-6960
(916) 651-6328 FAX

Access website to locate srvs & providers, download forms, report abuse, file a complaint, etc. Visit (www.dss.cahwnet.gov). FUNDING: State. OFC HRS: M-F 8am-5pm. SERVES: Calif.

CALIF YOUTH CRISIS LINE

Calif Coalition for Youth
P.O. Box 161448
Sacramento, CA 95816
(800) 843-5200
(916) 340-0505
(916) 340-0510 FAX

Statewide, 24-hr crisis intervention counseling for youth ages 12-24 yrs & their families on a wide range of mental health, drug & alcohol, peer, family and relationship issues. Youth-to-parent message srv, phone connections to srv providers & families, info & referrals. Rides provided to youth who cannot afford transportation home. FUNDING: Nonprofit, donations. OFC HRS: 24 hrs, 7 days. Spanish spoken. Translation srvs available. Free srvs. SERVES: Calif.

CANYON ACRES CHILDREN & FAMILY SRVS

1845 W. Orangewood Ave., Ste 300
Orange, CA 92868
(714) 383-9401
(714) 383-9300 FAX

Serves children & families through a comprehensive list of community prgms. The mental health clinic includes individual, family, & group therapy, psych medication support, and parent edu classes. The therapeutic afterschool prgm contains an array of structured group activities and a therapeutic horse riding prgm for children that have been identified as needing additional support for a mental health issue. The Creating Family Connections prgm works to find family or kin for dependent youth and engage them in the child's life. Foster care and adoption srvs prgm helps find kids forever families. FUNDING: AFDC-FC, EPSDT, County of Orange Health Care Agency, donations. OFC HRS: M-F 7am-5pm. Sat appts also available. Spanish spoken. Accepts Medi-Cal; pvt insurance and cash pay for select srvs. SERVES: Orange Co. Select prgms in L.A., Riverside, San Bernardino, & San Diego Counties.

CASA

See "Court Appointed Special Adv"

CATHOLIC CHARITIES/COUNSELING

Caritas Counseling Srvs
1441 N. D Street, Ste 4
San Bernardino, CA 92405
(909) 763-4970
(909) 763-4977 FAX

Professional counseling without regard to race, creed, sex, or age. Marriage, family, child counseling for a wide range of issues such as child abuse, anger mgmt, relationships, parent edu. Counseling provided days, eve & Sat in various locations. FUNDING: Nonprofit. OFC HRS: M-F 10am-4:30pm. Spanish spoken. Sliding fee scale. Some free srvs. SERVES: San Bernardino & Riverside Counties.

CENTER AGAINST SEXUAL ASSAULT

P.O. Box 2564
Hemet, CA 92546
(951) 652-8300
(951) 652-0944 FAX

Crisis intervention support resource, referral & advocacy for victims of sexual assault and their family & friends. Counseling, exams, judicial system and law enforcement accompaniment, support group for adolescents and adults, community edu, rape prevention presentation, and srvs. Nationwide 24-hr srv line (866) 373-8300. FUNDING: State (OES), community, nonprofit. OFC HRS: M-F 8am-5pm. Spanish spoken. Free srvs. SERVES: Hemet, San Jacinto & nearby.

CENTER FOR THE PACIFIC ASIAN FAMILY

543 N. Fairfax Ave., Ste 108
Los Angeles, CA 90036
(800) 339-3940
(323) 653-4045
(323) 653-7913 FAX

Confidential emerg and transitional shelters, 24-hr hotline and crisis intervention, counseling, TRO assist, case mgmt, victim advocacy throughout the medical, legal and social srv systems for victims of domestic violence, sexual assault, child abuse, and their families. Call first. FUNDING: United Way, state, nonprofit. OFC HRS: M-F 9am-5pm. Various Pacific Asian languages spoken. ADM REQ: Willing to abide by house rules. No fee to victims. SERVES: L.A. County (Orange, Riverside & San Bernardino Counties as needed).

CHILD ABUSE PREVENTION COUNCIL

Prevent Child Abuse - Southwest
1945 Chicago Ave., South, Ste B
Riverside, CA 92507
(951) 686-5581
(951) 686-5654 FAX

Coalition of agencies, social srvs, educators, mental health, medical professionals, law enforcement and community members. Mission is the elimination of child abuse through leadership, edu, advocacy & srv. Leadership, prevention & awareness. No direct srvs provided. Meets 2nd W of each month 12noon-1:30pm at 28720 Via Montezuma in Temecula. FUNDING: Nonprofit. OFC HRS: M-F 8am-5pm. Spanish spoken. Free srvs. SERVES: Riverside County.

CHILD ABUSE REPORTING HOTLINE

Riverside Co. Public Social Srvs
(800) 442-4918
(951) 413-5122 FAX

Report actual or suspected physical or sexual child abuse, neglect, or exploitation 24 hrs, 7 days. SERVES: Riverside County.

CHILD ABUSE REPORTING HOTLINE

Human Social Srvs
412 W. Hospitality Lane
San Bernardino, CA 92415-0029
(800) 827-8724
(909) 384-9233
(909) 891-3545 FAX

Report actual or suspected physical or sexual child abuse, neglect or exploitation. FUNDING: Nonprofit. OFC HRS: 24 hrs. Spanish spoken. Free srvs. SERVES: San Bernardino County.

CHILD ADVOCACY PROGRAM, INC.

See "San Bernardino Child Advocacy"

CHILD FIND OF AMERICA, INC.

P.O. Box 277
New Paltz, NY 12561-0277
(800) 426-5678
(845) 883-6614 FAX

Registers & helps locate missing children (800) I-AM-LOST (Child Find Hotline). Helps to recover parentally abducted children through crisis mediation, and preventing parental abduction (800) A-WAY-OUT (Parent Abduction Hotline). Dissemination of photos of missing children, safety info, Natl Missing Children's Day (845) 883-6060. FUNDING: Donors, corp, frdn, nonprofit. OFC HRS: M-F 9am-5pm, EST. Spanish spoken. ADM REQ: Child to be registered must be under age 17 yrs. Free srvs. SERVES: U.S.A.

CHILD PROTECTIVE SRVS/RIVERSIDE CO.

Dept Public Social Srvs
23119 Cottonwood Ave., Bldg. B, 2nd Fl.
Moreno Valley, CA 92553
(800) 448-4969
(951) 413-5000
(951) 413-5122 FAX

Child Protective Services (CPS) investigates all reports regarding children who are in danger of death, injury, sexual abuse, neglect, or exploitation. Case work, group work, emerg placement, supervision & coordination with other community resources to meet the needs of the family. Persons desiring to make a referral for this srv should contact the numbers listed above. To report child abuse 24 hrs a day, call, call (800) 442-4918. FUNDING: County. OFC HRS: M-F 8am-5pm. Free srvs. SERVES: Riverside County.

CHILD PROTECTIVE SRVS/SAN BRDO

Human Social Srvs/Dept Children's Srv
P.O. Box MC-0084
128 Carousel Mall
San Bernardino, CA 92415
(909) 388-1900
(909) 383-1901 FAX

Child Protective Srvs (CPS) investigates all reports regarding children who are in danger of death, injury, sexual abuse, neglect, or exploitation. Case work, group work, emerg placement, supervision and coordination with other community resources to meet the needs of the family. 24-hr hotline (909) 384-9233. TDD (909) 387-5036. Within Calif only (800) 827-8724. SERVES: San Bernardino County.

CHILD QUEST INTERNATIONAL

1060 N. 4th Street, Ste 200
San Jose, CA 95112
(888) 818-4673
(408) 287-4673
(408) 287-4676 FAX

Search for missing children including those abducted by non-custodial parents or guardians, and runaways. Also for recovery of abused and exploited children. Our Kids Are Safe Kids prgm provides on-site presentations to elem school children. FUNDING: Nonprofit, donations, fundraisers. OFC HRS: M-F 9am-4pm, 24-hr emerg sighting line. Spanish spoken. Free srvs. Sliding fee scale for some. SERVES: U.S.A. & Internatl.

CHILDHELP USA/BEAUMONT

Village of Childhelp West
P.O. Box 247
14700 Manzanita Rd.
Beaumont, CA 92223
(951) 845-3155
(951) 845-8412 FAX

Residential treatment srvs for emotionally disturbed children ages 6-12 yrs who are dependents of the court because of abuse or neglect. Referrals are made through Dept of Children's Srvs and Community Mental Health. Non-public school for special ed children in grades K-12. FUNDING: Govt, donations, nonprofit. OFC HRS: M-F 8am-5pm; Sat, Sun 9am-6pm. Spanish & Zulu spoken. SERVES: So. Calif.

CHILDHELP USA/HOTLINE

National Child Abuse Hotline
15757 N. 78th Street, Ste B
Scottsdale, AZ 85260
(800) 422-4453
(480) 922-8212
(480) 922-7061 FAX

Professional hotline counselors available 24 hrs, 7 days to respond to crisis calls regarding child abuse & related issues. Crisis intervention & contact for mandated reporters, concerned

citizens or worried friends & family. Info & referral. Visit (www.childhelpusa.org). FUNDING: Nonprofit. Communication available in 140 different languages. Free srvs. SERVES: U.S.A. & Canada.

CHILDNET YOUTH & FAMILY SRVS

Formerly Long Beach Youth Centers, Inc.
P.O. Box 4550
5150 E. Pacific Coast Hwy., Ste 365
Long Beach, CA 90804
(562) 498-5500
(562) 498-5501 FAX

ChildNet consists of 5 divisions: Vista Ridge & Zinsmeyer Academies, state-certified, non-public schools for severely emotionally disturbed and learning-disabled children; Foster Family Network recruits, trains, certifies and supports foster homes for children, with 24-hr counseling support; Behavioral Health Srvs provides mental health srvs to low income youth; Wraparound prgm is aimed at keeping at-risk teens out of psychiatric and probation facilities; and adoption srvs. FUNDING: Donations, grants, govt, nonprofit. OFC HRS: M-F 8:30am-5pm. Spanish & Khmer spoken. ADM REQ: Ages birth-17 yrs. Family support srvs extend to entire family, regardless of age. Free srvs for those who qualify. SERVES: L.A., Orange, Riverside, San Bernardino, Kern & Fresno Counties.

CHILDREN OF THE NIGHT

14530 Sylvan St.
Van Nuys, CA 91411
(800) 551-1300
(818) 908-4474
(818) 908-1468 FAX

Assist for children forced into prostitution. Natl 24-hr hotline; shelter home & school receives child prostitutes 24 hrs a day from every state. Structured prgm, includes transportation. FUNDING: Nonprofit, donations, grants. Spanish spoken. ADM REQ: Ages 11-17 yrs involved in prostitution. Free srvs. SERVES: U.S.A.

CHILDREN'S FUND

County Government Center
825 E. Hospitality Lane, 2nd Fl.
San Bernardino, CA 92415-0132
(909) 387-4949
(909) 383-9758 FAX

Provides for the needs of children (ages birth-18 yrs) who are at-risk because of abuse, poverty, neglect. Accessed through case mgrs from any of the 19 Children's Network agencies in the county. Other resources must be explored before requesting assist from Children's Fund, as its mission is to provide for those things that "fall through the cracks." FUNDING: Nonprofit. OFC HRS: M-F 8am-5pm. SERVES: San Bernardino County.

CHINO COMMUNITY SERVICES

Counseling Srvs
13201 Central Ave.
Chino, CA 91710
(909) 591-9822
(909) 628-4093 FAX

Low-cost outpatient family and individual counseling. Community outreach for residents of Chino. Domestic violence prgms. FUNDING: State, county, school, city, nonprofit. OFC HRS: M-Th 8am-8pm; F 8am-6pm. Spanish spoken. Free srvs for juveniles & low-income residents of Chino. School-based counseling is free. Out-patient family treatment $26 per visit. SERVES: Western San Bernardino County.

COMMUNITY COUNSELING CTR/CSUSB

Dept of Psychology, Calif State Univ
5500 State University Parkway
San Bernardino, CA 92407
(909) 537-5040
(909) 537-7061 FAX

Graduate students in 2-yr M.S. counseling psychology prgm provide low-cost, long-term individual psychotherapy. Student therapists are supervised by Ph.D. level psychologists on CSUSB faculty. FUNDING: CSUSV, govt. OFC HRS: M, Th, F 8am-5pm; Tu, W 8am-7pm. ADM REQ: CSUSB student or connected to student. Not suicidal, abusive, drug dependent or violent. Cost covered by tuition. SERVES: San Bernardino County.

COMPREHENSIVE YOUTH SERVICES

8780 19th Street, Ste 196
Alta Loma, CA 91701
(909) 466-8685
(909) 466-4815 FAX

Residential group home for boys ages 13-17 yrs. Long-term care, short-term emerg care, mental health srvs, family reunification, parenting edu, computer training, substance abuse prevention prgm. Serves abused children & wards of the court. Transportation to school. Counseling for individuals & groups. FUNDING: Nonprofit. OFC HRS: 24 hrs. Spanish spoken. Accepts insurance, Medicare, Medi-Cal, sliding fee scale. SERVES: Calif.

COURT APPOINTED SPECIAL ADV

Indio Center
P.O. Box 3008
44-199 Monroe St.
Indio, CA 92202-3008
(760) 863-7539
(760) 863-7431 FAX

CASA consists of trained community volunteers appointed by the Juvenile Court of Riverside County to act as advocates for dependent, abused or neglected children. Represents the child's needs, provides second point of view during the dependency process. Supportive & positive adult model for the abused or neglected child. The volunteer has weekly contact with the child. Walk in or call to apply. For Spanish, call (760) 863-7424. FUNDING: Nonprofit. OFC HRS: M-F 8:30am-4:30pm. Spanish spoken. Free srvs. SERVES: Riverside County.

COURT APPOINTED SPECIAL ADV

Southwest Justice Center
30755-D Auld Rd., Ste 1226
Murrieta, CA 92563
(951) 304-5220
(951) 304-5210 FAX

CASA consists of trained community volunteers appointed by the Juvenile Court of Riverside County to act as advocates for dependent, abused or neglected children. Represents the child's needs, provides second point of view during the dependency process. Supportive and positive adult model for the abused or neglected child. The volunteer has weekly contact with the child. Walk in or call to apply. FUNDING: Nonprofit. OFC HRS: M-F 8:30am-4:30pm. Spanish spoken. Free srvs. SERVES: Riverside County.

COURT APPOINTED SPECIAL ADV

437 N. Riverside Ave., Ste 10
Rialto, CA 92376
(909) 881-6760
(909) 881-6764 FAX

CASA recruits, screens and trains community volunteers to act as advocates for dependent, abused or neglected children. Volunteers represent the child's needs, provide a second point of view during the dependency process. Supportive and positive adult model for the abused or neglected child. The volunteer has regular contact with the child. Call to apply. FUNDING: Nonprofit. OFC HRS: M-F 8am-5pm. Spanish spoken. Free srvs. SERVES: San Bernardino County.

COURT APPOINTED SPECIAL ADV

Riverside Office
9991 County Farm Rd.
Riverside, CA 92503
(951) 358-4305
(951) 358-4302 FAX

CASA consists of trained community volunteers appointed by the Juvenile Court of Riverside County to act as advocates for dependent, abused or neglected children. Represents the child's needs, provides second point of view during the dependency process. Supportive and positive adult model for the abused or neglected child. The volunteer has weekly contact with the child. Walk in or call to apply. For Spanish, call (951) 358-4343. FUNDING: Nonprofit. OFC HRS: M-F 8:30am-4:30pm. Free srvs. SERVES: Riverside County.

COURT APPOINTED SPECIAL ADV/NATL

National CASA Assn
100 W. Harrison St., North Tower, Ste 500
Seattle, WA 98119
(800) 628-3233
(206) 270-0078 FAX

Supports a nationwide network of CASA prgms that train & support community volunteers to act as advocates for dependent, abused or neglected children. Represents the child's needs, provides a second point of view during the dependency process. Supportive and positive adult model for the abused or neglected child. FUNDING: Nonprofit. OFC HRS: M-F 8am-5pm. Spanish spoken. Free srvs. SERVES: U.S.A.

DESERT SANCTUARY/HALEY HOUSE

P.O. Box 1781
703 E. Main St.
Barstow, CA 92312
(760) 256-3441
(760) 256-3733
(760) 256-4002 FAX

16-bed shelter for battered women & their children up to age 6 mos. Also outreach for community & area victims in need of srvs not inclusive of shelter. Outreach srvs include: rent/utility assist, anger mgmt, therapy, sexual assault srvs, court-ordered supervised visitation, legal aid, housing stabilization. 24-hr hotline: (800) 982-2221. FUNDING: Nonprofit. OFC HRS: Hotline 24 hrs. Outreach M-F 9am-5pm. German & Spanish spoken. ADM REQ: Women in abusive surroundings. Free srvs. SERVES: So. Calif.

EAST VALLEY CHARLEE

440 Cajon St.

Redlands, CA 92373
(909) 307-5777
(909) 307-5776 FAX

County-funded prgm providing sexual abuse prevention for all minors accepted into the prgm. Also offers individual, family & child counseling. FUNDING: Dept of Social Srvs, San Bernardino Mental Health, nonprofit. OFC HRS: M-F 8:30am-5pm. Spanish available upon request. ADM REQ: Referrals by SSA or Dept Mental Health. Accepts Medi-Cal, insurance. SERVES: San Bernardino metro.

FAMILY SERVICE AGENCY/SAN BRDO

Crest Forest Family Srvs
P.O. Box 4484
23406 Crest Forest Dr.
Crestline, CA 92325
(909) 338-4689
(909) 338-8230 FAX

Counseling and mental health treatment for child sexual abuse, dysfunctional families. Anger diversion classes, court-ordered batterer's intervention prgm, high-risk youth prgms, limited utility asst. 24-hr suicide and crisis hotline (800) 832-9119. Food bank available F 9am-12noon, 1pm-5:30pm; call ahead to get more info. FUNDING: United Way, client fees, nonprofit. OFC HRS: M-Th 8:30am-6pm. ADM REQ: Varies per prgm. Ages 5 yrs+. Accepts Medi-Cal, sliding fee scale. SERVES: San Bernardino County.

FAMILY SERVICE AGENCY/SAN BRDO

Outpatient Mental Health Srvs
1669 North E Street
San Bernardino, CA 92405
(909) 886-6737
(909) 881-3871 FAX

Info & referral, counseling & mental health treatment for child sexual abuse, domestic violence intervention counseling, dysfunctional families, parenting classes, anger diversion classes, high-risk youth prgms. S.N.A.A.P. (narcotics/alcohol abuse prgm for teens). State ID: 360044AN. FUNDING: United Way, client fees, nonprofit. OFC HRS: M-Th 9am-9pm. Spanish spoken. ADM REQ: Varies per prgm. Ages birth-21 yrs. Accepts Medi-Cal for youth only, sliding fee scale. SERVES: San Bernardino County.

FAMILY SERVICE ASSN/CORONA

Alternatives to Domestic Violence
Outreach Office
515 S. Corona Mall
Corona, CA 92879
(951) 737-8410
(951) 737-3517 FAX

Counseling for individuals, marriages & familes. Anger mgmt, edu, child abuse prevention & treatment. Employee assist prgm, mental health advocacy, social mentorship & family life edu. Anonymous shelter, advocacy for domestic violence. 24-hr crisis line (800) 339-SAFE or (951)683-0829. Riverside outreach and admin office (951) 320-1370. Hemet outreach office (951)929-3079. OFC HRS: M-F 9am-5pm. Spanish spoken. ADM REQ: victim of domestic violence Sliding fee scale for therapeutic srvs and anger mgmt. SERVES: West Riverside County.

FAMILY SERVICES OF THE DESERT

81-711 Highway 111, Ste 101

Indio, CA 92201
(760) 347-2398
(800) 536-4357
(760) 347-6468 FAX

Family, individual and group counseling. Locations in Indio, Desert Hot Springs and Blythe. FUNDING: United Way, donations, client fees, nonprofit. OFC HRS: M-F 9am-5pm. Eve & weekend by appt. Spanish spoken. SERVES: Coachella Valley.

FIND THE CHILDREN

2656 29th Street, Ste 203
Santa Monica, CA 90405
(888) 477-6721
(800) 843-5678
(310) 314-3169 FAX

Dedicated to the prevention and recovery of missing & abducted children. Srvs include photo & flyer distribution, contact with law enforcement, safety materials, school safety prgms, community outreach prgms & referrals. FUNDING: Nonprofit. OFC HRS: M-F 9am-4pm. Spanish spoken. Free srvs. SERVES: U.S.A.

FIRST CALL FOR HELP

Volunteer Center of Victor Valley
P.O. Box 1992
16692 Mojave Dr.
Victorville, CA 92393
(760) 243-9646
(760) 243-4762 FAX

Info & referral for people seeking srvs or info on community agencies. Interaction with individuals in crisis situations in order to reduce tension and stress, allowing that person to utilize available resources more effectively. FUNDING: Donations, grants, nonprofit. OFC HRS: M-Th 9am-2:45pm. Spanish spoken. SERVES: San Bernardino County.

H.E.A.R.T., INC. FOUNDATION

Heart For The Children
P.O. Box 1922
Temecula, CA 92593-1922
(951) 506-4488
(760) 723-1116 FAX

Underwrites therapy, counseling funding and child care tuition for abused children and families in crisis. Assist is usually provided on a short-term basis (three months) and is given to families who have no other financial resources available to them. Additional counseling may be available depending on case evaluation, waiting list, and available funds. Tax exempt ID#: 33-00787074. FUNDING: Nonprofit. SERVES: Southwest Riverside County.

HANNAH'S CHILDREN'S HOMES

1045 W. Katella Ave., Ste 330
Orange, CA 92867
(714) 516-1077
(866) 736-8434
(714) 516-1080 FAX

Foster and adoption agency provides out-of-home care for abused and neglected children ages birth-18 yrs. FUNDING: Nonprofit. OFC HRS: M-F 9am-5pm. Spanish spoken. SERVES: L.A., Orange, Riverside, San Bernardino and San Diego Counties.

HANNAH'S CHILDRENS HOMES

9229 Utica Ave., Ste 140
Rancho Cucamonga, CA 91730
(909) 483-2552

(909) 483-2532 FAX

Foster and adoption agency that provides out-of-home care to abused and neglected children, ages birth-18 yrs. FUNDING: Nonprofit. OFC HRS: M-F 9am-5pm. Spanish spoken. SERVES: Riverside, San Bernardino Counties.

HAPPY TRAILS CHILDREN'S FNDN

10755 Apple Valley Rd.
Apple Valley, CA 92308
(760) 240-3330
(760) 240-1458 FAX

Sponsors Cooper Home for abused & neglected children ages 9-15 yrs. Raises money for the dev and building of homes for abused children. No direct srvs at this address. FUNDING: State, county, donors, nonprofit. OFC HRS: M-F 8am-5pm. ADM REQ: All referrals via Dept of Social Srvs. Free srvs. SERVES: So. Calif.

HART COMMUNITY HOMES

208 N. Lemon
Fullerton, CA 92832
(714) 526-2729
(714) 526-2653 FAX

Residential treatment for foster care youth ages 13-18 yrs. Treatment model is tailored to meet individual needs. Prgm focuses on emancipation and has a vocational center providing a life skills workforce dev prgm. Also offers Monkey Business Cafe which provides paid work experience in a cafe setting for foster care youth in and emancipating out of the foster care system. Visit (www.hartcommunityhomes.org). FUNDING: Nonprofit. OFC HRS: M-F 9am-5pm. Cafe open M-F 7am-3pm. Spanish, Korean spoken. ADM REQ: Abused and abandoned boys ages 13-18 yrs. SERVES: L.A., Orange & San Bernardino Counties.

HIGH DESERT DOMESTIC VIOLENCE PRGM

Battered Women's Shelter
P.O. Box 284
15075 7th St.
Victorville, CA 92392
(760) 843-0701
(760) 843-9551 FAX

Confidential emerg shelter for battered women and their children, hotline, emerg food, clothing. Counseling and support groups, assist with restraining orders & local resource referrals. Utility and rental asst program. Monitored visitation by appt only. 24-hr hotline (760) 949-4357. FUNDING: San Bernardino County, United Way, nonprofit. OFC HRS: M-F 8am-5pm, admits to shelter on 24-hr basis. Spanish spoken. ADM REQ: Victim of domestic violence. SERVES: Victor Valley, will take referrals from other areas.

IMMIGRATION CENTER FOR WOMEN/CHILDREN

634 S. Spring St., Ste 727
Los Angeles, CA 90014
(213) 614-1165
(213) 624-1163 FAX

Immigration srvs for abused, abandoned or neglected children. Also for women and children who are victims of trafficking, domestic violence and sexual assaults. FUNDING: Nonprofit. OFC HRS: M-F 9am-5pm. Spanish spoken. ADM REQ: Intake by phone, appt. required. SERVES: Southern Calif.

INCEST SURVIVORS ANONYMOUS

World Service Office
P.O. Box 17245
Long Beach, CA 90807-7245
(562) 428-5599

Literature for survivors of incest as well as info on groups meeting in area. 12-Step & 12-Tradition. Send a self-addressed, stamped envelope for info in English or Spanish. Cassette tapes & packets available for small fee; ISA e-mail, family letter also available at no charge. Srvs for men, women and older teens. FUNDING: Donations. OFC HRS: M-F 9am-5pm. ADM REQ: Survivors only, no perpetrators. Accepts donations. Free srvs. SERVES: U.S.A. & Internatl.

INDIAN CHILD & FAMILY SERVICES

P.O. Box 2269
29377 Rancho California Rd., Ste 200
Temecula, CA 92591
(800) 969-4237
(951) 676-8832
(951) 676-3950 FAX

Counseling referrals for abused children, foster placements, adoptive placements. Tribal Kinship Model used to intervene in the cycle of child abuse. CASA prgm. Spirit Prgm is a prevention/intervention parenting prgm. FUNDING: Bureau of Indian Affairs. OFC HRS: M-F 8am-5pm. ADM REQ: Must be enrolled or eligible for federally recognized tribe. No fees. SERVES: Riverside, San Diego, San Bernardino Counties.

INTERNATIONAL CHILD ABUSE NETWORK

P.O. Box 155
7657 Winnetka Ave.
Canoga Park, CA 91306-2677
(888) 224-4226
(818) 716-0658 FAX

Online-facilitated chat rooms for child abuse and domestic violence survivors. Visit (www.yesican.org). FUNDING: Nonprofit. OFC HRS: M-F 8am-5pm. SERVES: Internatl.

KNOTTS FAMILY AGENCY

1505 W. Highland Ave., Ste 19
San Bernardino, CA 92411
(909) 880-0600
(909) 473-1918 FAX

Residential care facility providing long-term srvs for pregnant & parenting teens & their infants/toddlers. Srvs to troubled adol girls whose lives are complicated by pregnancy or single parenthood. Also srvs to non-pregnant, abused, neglected or abandoned girls ages 12-17 yrs. Adol girls in Juvenile Probation or DPSS. Foster care agency, parenting prgm for parents with children ages birth-5 yrs. FUNDING: Private, nonprofit. OFC HRS: 24 hrs, 7 days. SERVES: Riverside, San Bernardino Counties.

KOINONIA FOSTER HOMES, INC.

Southern California Regional Office
1881 S. Business Center Dr., Ste 10-A
San Bernardino, CA 92408
(909) 890-2381
(877) 244-5374
(909) 890-0580 FAX

Recruits & trains foster and adoptive parents to care for children who are dependents of the juvenile court. Provides child placement services and conducts home studies. Social worker is assigned to provide counseling and other support srvs. Prgm serves children ages birth-18 yrs who have a history of abuse, neglect or delinquency. Foster to Adopt Prgm for those interested in adopting a child. FUNDING: Nonprofit. OFC HRS: M-F 8am-5pm. Spanish spoken. SERVES: Riverside, San Bernardino Counties.

LAURA'S HOUSE
Emergency Shelter
999 Corporate Dr., Ste 225
Ladera Ranch, CA 92694
(949) 361-3775
(949) 361-3548 FAX

Emergency shelter prgm for battered women with or without children; pregnant women accepted. Emergency shelter provides case mgmt,counseling and legal advocacy. Counseling & resource center for men, women & child victims of domestic violence. 24-hr hotline (866) 498-1511. Counseling hrs: M-F 9am-5pm, eve by appt. Shelter: 24 hrs, 7 days. Spanish & Farsi spoken. Language line available. Sliding fee scale. No one turned away for lack of funds. SERVES: So Calif. Able to refer out of area if needed

LOMA LINDA UNIV/MARRIAGE/FAMILY
Marriage & Family Therapy Clinic
1686 Barton Rd.
Redlands, CA 92373
(909) 558-4934
(909) 558-0334 FAX

Individual, group, marriage, family, child & adol counseling. Srvs for child abuse prevention, grief counseling, domestic violence, chemical addiction and other issues. FUNDING: Nonprofit. OFC HRS: Sun 9am-5pm; M-Th 9am-8pm; F 9am-2:30pm. Spanish spoken. Sliding fee scale starts at $25 per session. Medi-Cal not accepted. Will not bill insurance. SERVES: San Bernardino, Riverside Counties.

MASONIC HOME FOR CHILDREN
1650 E. Old Badillo St.
Covina, CA 91724
(626) 251-2231
(626) 251-2326 FAX

Pvt placement residential facility for abused, neglected, abandoned, financially distressed children & children with moderate behavior problems, ages 4-17 yrs of age. Can accommodate sibling groups. Prgm focuses on teaching appropriate social, academic and independent living skills. FUNDING: Private, nonprofit. OFC HRS: M-F 9am-4pm. SERVES: So. Calif.

MCKINLEY CHILDREN'S CENTER
762 W. Cypress St.
San Dimas, CA 91773
(909) 599-1227
(909) 592-3841 FAX

Level 12 residential care and non-public school for 44 boys ages 7-15 yrs with serious behavioral and emotional problems related to histories of abuse, neglect and inadequate parenting. Specialized residential treatment prgm is designed to meet individual and family needs. FUNDING: State, county, govt. OFC HRS: M-F 8am-5pm. Spanish spoken. SERVES: So. Calif.

MISSING CHILDREN INTERNATL., INC.
1905 E. 17th Street, Ste 110
Santa Ana, CA 92705-8628
(714) 542-8083

(800) 339-4357
(714) 210-1163 FAX

State-by-state search for missing persons. 24-hr hotline: (714) 323-6730. FUNDING: Nonprofit. OFC HRS: M-F 8am-5pm. SERVES: U.S.A. & Internatl.

MOUNTAIN VIEW CLINIC
1001 N. State St.
Hemet, CA 92543
(951) 658-1253
(951) 658-1253 FAX

Counseling srvs for married couples, families, individuals, adolescents, children. Hypnotherapy also available. OFC HRS: Tu-F 10am-7pm; Sat 10am-4pm. SERVES: Riverside County.

NATL CHILD ABUSE HOTLINE
See "Childhelp USA/Hotline"

NATL CHILD SAFETY COUNCIL
P.O. Box 1368
4065 Page Ave.
Jackson, MI 49204-1368
(800) 222-1464
(517) 764-3068 FAX

Child safety edu materials & drug prevention provided to law enforcement agencies & schools. FUNDING: Donors, nonprofit. OFC HRS: M-F 8am-4:30pm, EST. SERVES: U.S.A.

NATL CLEARINGHOUSE/CHILD ABUSE
Clearinghouse on Child Abuse & Neglect
1250 Maryland Ave., SW 8th Fl.
Washington, DC 20024
(800) 394-3366
(703) 385-7565
(703) 385-3206 FAX

The largest natl resource for acquisition, organization and dissemination of info on child abuse, neglect & child welfare. Info and prgm specialists at toll-free number. Bibliographies, custom searches, documents and referrals available. Maintains Internet-accessible database of child abuse and neglect prevention prgms. FUNDING: Govt, nonprofit. OFC HRS: M-F 8:30am-5:30pm, EST. Spanish spoken. SERVES: U.S.A.

NATL COMM/PREVENT CHILD ABUSE
See "Prevent Child Abuse/America"

NATL CTR/MISSING AND EXPLOITED CHILDREN
699 Prince St.
Alexandria, VA 22314
(800) 843-5678
(703) 224-2150
(703) 224-2122 FAX

Acts as a clearinghouse for missing & exploited children. Activities include assisting in the distribution of photos of missing children. Accepts calls from people who believe they have seen missing children. Families may receive tech assist. Training prgms are offered for law enforcement staff. Assists in locating children worldwide. Also provides an online location (www.cybertipline.com) for reporting Internet child pornography, prostitution, molestation, Internet-related exploitation & child sex tourism. FUNDING: Nonprofit. OFC HRS: 24 hrs, 7 days. Language line available. Publications & child safety brochures available free of charge by calling the hotline. SERVES: U.S.A.

NATL CTR/MISSING/EXPLOIT/CHILDREN
18111 Irvine Blvd.
Tustin, CA 92780
(714) 508-0150
(714) 508-0154 FAX

Safety edu prgm (promotes child safety & confidence), family srvs (advocacy for exploited children & their families), training & speakers. FUNDING: Nonprofit. OFC HRS: M-F 8am-5pm. Spanish spoken. Accepts donations. Free srvs. SERVES: Western U.S.A.

NEW HAVEN YOUTH & FAMILY SRVS
P.O. Box 1199
216 W. Los Angeles Dr.
Vista, CA 92083
(760) 630-4035
(760) 630-4030 FAX

Assists children facing emotional & dev challenges. 72-bed residential treatment prgm, special edu, vocational schools. FUNDING: Nonprofit. OFC HRS: M-F 8am-5pm. ADM REQ: Boys ages 8-17 yrs, referred by DMH, DPSS or Probation Dept. SERVES: San Diego, L.A., & Riverside Counties.

OLIVE CREST TREATMENT CENTER
Corporate Office
2130 E. 4th Street, Ste 200
Santa Ana, CA 92705
(714) 543-5437
(714) 543-5463 FAX

Residential homes serving children, ages birth-18 yrs, victimized by neglect, abuse and/or abandonment. Full continuum of srvs, child abuse prevention & family intervention. Individual, residential treatment & family style homes in residential areas. Licensed foster family agency recruits, trains, offers respite care & network for foster families. Also independent living prgm for youth emancipating from foster care prgms. FUNDING: Donations, grants, govt, nonprofit. OFC HRS: M-F 8:30am-5pm. Spanish & Vietnamese spoken. SERVES: So. Calif; also Seattle, Tacoma, Spokane & Las Vegas.

OPTION HOUSE/DV INTERV & PREV
Domestic Violence Interv & Prev Agency
P.O. Box 970
San Bernardino, CA 92401
(909) 381-3471
(909) 889-7312 FAX

Confidential emerg & temporary shelter, 24-hr crisis intervention hotline (909) 381-3471. One-on-one advocacy, emotional support, resource & referrals to female victims of domestic violence & their children. Six-week in-house prgm for residents in shelter, 18-month transitional housing, legal assist for TROs, child custody, court & mediation accompaniment, women's support groups for non-shelter victims (English & Spanish), teen relationship/violence prevention workshops, children's prgm, speakers bureau, community edu & training. For Tri-City DV Prevention Outreach Ctr, Courthouse Family Violence Outreach Srvs & Teen Dating Violence Prevention Srvs, call (909) 884-4802. FUNDING: Donations, grants, nonprofit. OFC HRS: M-F 8am-5pm. Spanish spoken. ADM REQ: Women, children & teens who are victims of domestic violence. SERVES: San Bernardino & nearby.

PARENTS ANONYMOUS, INC.
675 W. Foothill Blvd., Ste 220
Claremont, CA 91711
(909) 621-6184
(909) 625-6304 FAX

Child abuse prev organization. Free weekly on-going community-based support groups. FUNDING: Donations, govt, nonprofit. OFC HRS: M-F 8am-5pm. Spanish spoken. SERVES: U.S.A.

POLLY KLAAS FOUNDATION
Missing Child Agency
P.O. Box 800
Petaluma, CA 94953
(800) 587-4357
(707) 769-1334
(707) 769-4019 FAX

Hotline, 24 hrs, 7 days, to assist parents and families of missing children. Public edu and info about child safety and Internet safety, child ID kits. Advocates for legislation supporting children & a safer community. FUNDING: Non-profit, donations, corporations. OFC HRS: M-F 8am-5:30pm. Hotline open 24/7. Free srvs. SERVES: U.S.A.

PREVENT CHILD ABUSE/AMERICA
228 S. Wabash Ave., 10th Fl., Ste 200
Chicago, IL 60604
(312) 663-3520
(312) 939-8962 FAX

Large number of publications on child abuse issues. Works for the prevention of child abuse and neglect through state & national public awareness, education & advocacy efforts with state chapters disseminating info & serving as a strong voice for children. FUNDING: Contributions, nonprofit. OFC HRS: M-F 9am-5pm, CST. SERVES: U.S.A.

PROJECT CUDDLE, INC.
2973 Harbor Blvd., Ste 326
Costa Mesa, CA 92626
(888) 628-3353
(714) 432-9681
(714) 433-6815 FAX

24-hr, toll-free hotline for pregnant women or women contemplating abandoning their children. Support & edu for those caring for drug-exposed babies and children. Training for birth parents and caregivers. Speakers and lectures for teens on drugs during pregnancy. FUNDING: Donations, grants, nonprofit. OFC HRS: M-F 9am-4pm. Spanish spoken. Free srvs. SERVES: U.S.A.

PROJECT SISTER
Sexual Assault Crisis & Prev Srvs
P.O. Box 1369
Pomona, CA 91769-1369
(909) 623-1619
(909) 622-8389 FAX

24-hr sexual assault crisis hotline; personal accompaniment to hospital, police station and court; in-person counseling; support groups for rape. AMAC (Adults Molested As Children) and incest survivors groups, referrals to other agencies, community edu (including sexual harassment) and teen date rape awareness & self-protection classes. Srvs for seniors also available. 24-hr helpline (909) 626-4357 and (626) 966-4155. FUNDING: United Way, Office of Emerg Srvs, donations, CDBG grants, nonprofit. OFC HRS: M-F 8am-5pm. Spanish spo-

ken. Free srvs, except for counseling & groups on a sliding fee scale. No one turned away for lack of funds. SERVES: East San Gabriel Valley, Pomona Valley & West San Bernardino County.

RANCHO DAMACITAS
P.O. Box 890326
Temecula, CA 92589
(951) 302-2317
(951) 302-7015 FAX

Residential prgm providing treatment & srvs for juvenile victims of child abuse. Also operates a foster family agency which certifies, trains & supports foster families. FUNDING: State, county, pvt donations. OFC HRS: M-F 8:30am-4:30pm. ADM REQ: Ages 6-18 yrs. Most children are dependents of the court. SERVES: Orange, Imperial, Riverside, San Bernardino & San Diego Counties.

RIVERSIDE AREA RAPE CRISIS CENTER
1845 Chicago Ave., Ste A
Riverside, CA 92507
(951) 686-7273
(951) 686-0839 FAX

Crisis line. Hospital, law enforcement & court accompaniment, info & referral, community edu, child abuse prev, senior outreach prgm, support group, follow-up. Outreach prgm available in Spanish. For Southwest County, call (866) 686-7273. FUNDING: OCJP, county, city, fndns, donors, United Way, nonprofit. OFC HRS: M-F 8am-5pm. Crisis line and hospital advocacy 24/7. Some Spanish spoken. ASL available. ADM REQ: Victim of sexual assault, family member or significant other. Free srvs. SERVES: Western Riverside County.

RIVERSIDE CO. DEPT/MENTAL HEALTH
Administrative Office
P.O. Box 7549
4095 County Circle Dr.
Riverside, CA 92513
(951) 358-4500
(951) 358-4513 FAX

Overall planning, implementation, direction, coordination and eval of the Dept of Mental Health prgms in Riverside County. Treatment for adults: residential, outpatient, day care, socialization ctrs, crisis srvs, case mgmt, continuing care, etc. Children's prgms: outpatient, case mgmt, foster home placement, etc. Also main admin office for drug abuse and alcohol control prgms. No actual srvs available at this location. FUNDING: Govt. Spanish spoken. Accepts Medi-Cal SERVES: Riverside County.

RIVERSIDE CO. MENTAL HEALTH
Mental Health/Substance Abuse Srvs
61297 W. Hobson Way
Blythe, CA 92225
(760) 770-2222

County sponsored mental health counseling and crisis intervention, children's therapy groups. Walk in or call. Wait: 3-6 months. FUNDING: County. OFC HRS: M-Th 8am-6pm. Spanish spoken. Accepts Medi-Cal. Sliding fee scale. SERVES: Riverside County.

RIVERSIDE CO. PUBLIC SOCIAL SRVS
Children's Protective Srvs
1225 W. Hobson Way
Blythe, CA 92225
(760) 921-5800
(760) 921-7715 FAX

24-hr emerg response, protective srvs for children in danger of abuse, exploitation, neglect, etc. Call to report incidents or suspicions of child abuse or neglect. Full range of srvs from emerg shelter to investigation. 24-hr hotline (800) 442-4918. Walk in or call. FUNDING: State, county, fed. OFC HRS: M-Th 7am-5:30pm; F 8am-5pm. Spanish spoken. SERVES: Desert area.

RIVERSIDE CO. PUBLIC SOCIAL SRVS
In-Home Support/Child Protective Srvs
68-625 Perez Rd., Ste 2
Cathedral City, CA 92234
(760) 773-6700
(760) 770-2450
(760) 773-6793 FAX

IHSS provides frail elderly and disabled with outreach and in-home support srvs. Also CPS (Children's Protective Srvs). To report child abuse/neglect call, (800) 442-4918. FUNDING: County, state, fed. OFC HRS: M-F 8am-5pm. Spanish & Tagalog spoken. Free srvs. SERVES: Coachella Valley.

RIVERSIDE CO. PUBLIC SOCIAL SRVS
Adult & Child Protective Srvs
505 S. Buena Vista, 3rd Fl., Ste 312
Corona, CA 92282
(951) 272-5564
(888) 877-3985
(951) 272-5583 FAX

24-hr hotline (800) 491-7123. FUNDING: Govt. OFC HRS: M-Th 8am-5pm. Spanish spoken. Free srvs. SERVES: Riverside County.

RIVERSIDE CO. PUBLIC SOCIAL SRVS
Children's Protective Srvs
547 N. San Jacinto Ave.
Hemet, CA 92543
(951) 791-3200
(800) 442-4918
(951) 791-3210 FAX

24-hr emerg response, protective srvs for children in danger of abuse, exploitation, neglect, etc. Call to report incidents or suspicions of child abuse or neglect. Full range of srvs from emerg shelter to investigation. Walk in or call. FUNDING: County, state, fed. OFC HRS: M-F 8am-5pm. Spanish spoken. SERVES: Riverside County.

RIVERSIDE CO. PUBLIC SOCIAL SRVS
Child Protective Srvs
48113 Jackson St.
Indio, CA 92201
(760) 863-7210
(800) 442-4918
(760) 863-7225 FAX

24-hr emerg response, protective srvs for children in danger of abuse, exploitation, neglect, etc. Call to report incidents or suspicions of child abuse or neglect. Full range of srvs from emerg shelter to investigation. Walk in or call. FUNDING: County, state, fed. OFC HRS: M-F 8am-5pm. Spanish spoken. SERVES: Coachella Valley.

RIVERSIDE CO. PUBLIC SOCIAL SRVS
Children's Srvs/Child Protection
23119 Cottonwood Ave., Bldg. A, 2nd Fl.
Moreno Valley, CA 92553
(951) 413-5000
(951) 413-5016 FAX

Children's prgm provides preventive and protective srvs to victims of child abuse and their families, emerg response, investigation, out-of-home placement, info & referral, sex abuse treatment, and case mgmt (voluntary or Juvenile Court related) to link families with counseling, parent edu, drug treatment, testing, child care and respite care. 24-hr hotline for reporting child abuse (800) 442-4918. OFC HRS: M-F 8am-5pm. Spanish spoken. SERVES: Mid-County area.

RIVERSIDE CO. PUBLIC SOCIAL SRVS
County Administrative Offices
4060 County Circle Dr.
Riverside, CA 92503
(951) 358-3000
(951) 358-3036 FAX

CalWORKs offers financial assist to families with children who are deprived of support due to incapacity, unemployment or continued absence of one or more parents. Food stamps prgm offers an increased food purchase power for low-income families. Medical assist prgm (Medi-Cal). General Relief Prgm: assist to indigent individuals & families in temporary need of housing, food or transportation (this is a loan prgm and recipients are to repay benefits). In-Home Supportive Srvs (IHSS) provides household and personal care to allow elderly and disabled to remain in their own home. For adult abuse, call (800) 491-7123. FUNDING: County, state, fed, govt. OFC HRS: M-Th 7:30am-5:30pm Spanish spoken. Interpreters available in local offices by appointment. ADM REQ: Varies with prgm & srvs. SERVES: Riverside County.

RIVERSIDE CO. PUBLIC SOCIAL SRVS
27464 Commerce Center Dr., Ste E
Temecula, CA 92590
(951) 955-3450

Child protection srvs. Child abuse hotline: (800) 442-4918. FUNDING: Govt. OFC HRS: M-F 8am-5pm. Spanish, Chinese spoken. SERVES: Riverside County.

SAN BERNARDINO CHILD ADVOCACY
555 North D Street, Ste 100
San Bernardino, CA 92405
(909) 881-6760
(909) 881-6764 FAX

Recruits, screens and trains volunteers, CASA (Court Appointed Special Advocates) guardians advocate for the best interests of abused children in the court system. Volunteers provide advocacy srvs for abused children during court process. Mentoring prgms. Wait: varies depending on number of volunteers available. FUNDING: Grants, donations. OFC HRS: M-F 8am-5pm. Spanish spoken. ADM REQ: Children must be in the juvenile court system. Free srvs to children. SERVES: San Bernardino County.

SAN BERNARDINO CO. CHILD ABUSE REPORTING
Dept of Children's Srvs
170 N. Yucca Ave., 2nd Fl., Ste D
Barstow, CA 92311
(800) 827-8724
(760) 255-5400
(760) 255-1501 FAX

24-hr emerg response. Protective srvs for children in danger of abuse, exploitation, neglect, etc. Call to report incidents or suspicions of child abuse or neglect. Full-range of emerg srvs

including shelter and investigations. OFC HRS: M-F 8am-5pm. Spanish spoken. SERVES: San Bernardino County.

SAN BERNARDINO CO. CHILDREN'S SRVS
See "San Bernardino Co. Human Srvs Sy"

SAN BERNARDINO CO. HUMAN SRVS SY
Children's Srvs/Child Protective Srvs
1300 Bailey Ave.
Needles, CA 92363
(760) 326-9293
(800) 827-8724
(760) 326-9340 FAX

24-hr emerg response. Protective srvs for children in danger of abuse, exploitation, neglect, etc. Call to report incidents or suspicions of child abuse or neglect. Full-range of emerg srvs including shelter and investigations. SERVES: Needles.

SAN BERNARDINO CO. HUMAN SRVS SY
Children's Srvs/Child Protective Srvs
P.O. Box 1088
9638 7th Street
Rancho Cucamonga, CA 91730
(909) 945-3762
(909) 945-3784
(909) 945-3785 FAX

24-hr emerg response. Protective srvs for children in danger of abuse, exploitation, neglect etc. Call to report incidents or suspicions of child abuse or neglect. Full-range of emerg srvs including shelter and investigations. OFC HRS: M-F 8am-5pm. Hindi, Spanish & Vietnamese spoken. SERVES: West San Bernardino County.

SAN BERNARDINO CO. HUMAN SRVS SY
Children's Srvs/Child Protective Srvs
1504 Gifford
San Bernardino, CA 92415
(909) 386-1100
(909) 386-1913 FAX

Child protection after hours (909) 384-9233. Hotline: within Calif (800) 827-8724. OFC HRS: M-F 8am-5pm. Spanish spoken. SERVES: San Bernardino County.

SAN BERNARDINO CO. HUMAN SRVS SY
Transitional Assistance
150 S. Lena Rd.
San Bernardino, CA 92415
(909) 388-0245
(909) 388-0233 FAX

Social Srvs Administrative Office, transitional assist. Child abuse hotline (800) 827-8724, Adoption Srvs (909) 891-3300. FUNDING: Govt. OFC HRS: M-F 8:30am-4:30pm. Spanish spoken. ADM REQ: Low income. SERVES: San Bernardino County.

SAN BERNARDINO CO. HUMAN SRVS SY
Children's Srvs/Child Protective Srvs
15400 Civic Dr., Ste 250
Victorville, CA 92392
(760) 243-5227
(800) 827-8724
(760) 843-4932 FAX

24-hr emerg response. Protective srvs for children in danger of abuse, exploitation, neglect, etc. Call to report incidents or suspicions of child abuse or neglect. Full-range of emerg srvs including shelter and investigations. OFC HRS: M-F 8am-5pm. Spanish spoken. SERVES: Victorville & nearby.

SAN BERNARDINO CO. HUMAN SRVS SY
Children's Srvs/Child Protective Srvs
56311 Pima Trail
Yucca Valley, CA 92284
(760) 228-5300
(800) 827-8724
(760) 228-5321 FAX

24-hr emerg response. Protective srvs for children in danger of abuse, exploitation, neglect, etc. Call to report incidents or suspicions of child abuse or neglect. Full-range of emerg srvs including shelter and investigations. OFC HRS: M-F 8am-5pm. Spanish spoken. SERVES: Morongo Basin.

SAN BERNARDINO CO. PUBLIC HEALTH
Health Nursing
120 Carousel Mall
San Bernardino, CA 92415-0048
(800) 722-3777
(909) 388-0401 FAX

Services include: physical, psychosocial and environmental assessments with focus on capacity to meet own needs and needs of the child. Info & referral and dev of support systems. Call first and referral will be sent out. FUNDING: County. OFC HRS: M-F 8am-5pm. Spanish spoken. ADM REQ: High-risk for child abuse. SERVES: San Bernardino County.

SAN BERNARDINO CO. PUBLIC SOC SRVS
See "San Bernardino Co. Human Srvs Sy"

SEXUAL ASSAULT SRVS/REDLANDS
Redlands Outreach
30 Cajon St.
Redlands, CA 92373
(909) 335-8777
(909) 335-4768 FAX

Support for victims of sexual assault and significant others through individual and group counseling, hospital and court accompaniment. Community edu prgms and self-defense. 24-hour natl crisis hotline: (800) 656-4673. FUNDING: Nonprofit. OFC HRS: M-F 8am-5pm. Free srvs. SERVES: San Bernardino County.

SEXUAL ASSAULT SRVS/SAN BRDO
444 N. Arrowhead Ave., Ste 101-104
San Bernardino, CA 92401-1221
(909) 885-8884
(909) 383-8478 FAX

Support for victims of sexual assault and significant others. Individual and group counseling, hospital & court accompaniment, community edu prgms and self-defense. Rape Crisis Ctr has support groups for adolescents, adults molested as children, etc., 24-hr crisis line: (800) 656-4673. Coachella Valley (760) 568-9071. Morongo Basin (760) 369-3353. FUNDING: United Way, Ofc of Emergency Services, nonprofit. OFC HRS: M-Th 8am-5pm; F 8am-2pm. Spanish spoken. ADM REQ: Victims of sexual assault. Free srvs. SERVES: San Bernardino County.

SEXUAL ASSAULT SRVS/YUCAIPA
Yucaipa Outreach/Domestic Viol Prgm
34282 Yucaipa Blvd.
Yucaipa, CA 92399
(909) 790-9374
(909) 790-3111 FAX

Srvs to survivors of domestic violence. Individual & group counseling, community edu, referrals, court accompaniment & 24-hr hotline (800) 656-4673. FUNDING: Members, donations, nonprofit. OFC HRS: M-F 8am-5pm. Spanish spoken. Free srvs. SERVES: Inland Empire.

SINGLE PARENTS OF POWER EMLAC HEALTH SRVS

P.O. Box 452602
1620 Centinela Ave, Ste 202
Inglewood, CA 90302
(310) 753-7860

Counseling services include: mental health, sexual abuse, anger mgmt, parenting, alcohol and drug abuse. Advocacy and counseling for victims of violent crimes and post-traumatic counseling for veterans. FUNDING: Nonprofit. OFC HRS: M-F 9am-9pm; Sat 10am-3pm. Spanish, Swahili spoken. Free counseling for victims of domestic violence. All other srvs on a sliding fee scale. SERVES: L.A. & San Bernardino Counties.

TRUSTLINE

Calif Child Care Resource/Referral Network
111 New Montgomery St., 7th Fl.
San Francisco, CA 94105
(800) 822-8490
(415) 882-0234
(415) 882-6233 FAX

Conducts background checks on child care providers exempt from licensing, babysitters and nannies. FUNDING: Govt, nonprofit. OFC HRS: M-F 9am-5pm. Spanish spoken. SERVES: Calif.

VERONICA'S HOME OF MERCY

1495 W. Victoria St.
San Bernardino, CA 92411
(909) 888-9064
(909) 888-7390 FAX

Long-term, faith-based residential home (room for up to 20 women) for adult pregnant women & children or women with small children, as an alternative to domestic violence, addictions, abortion and/or homelessness. Women must be involved with the prgm and be willing to continue their education. Not an emergency shelter. Transitional living. FUNDING: Nonprofit. OFC HRS: M-F 8am-4pm. Spanish spoken. ADM REQ: Must be aged 18 yrs+ or emancipated by court. SERVES: So. Calif.

VICTIM-WITNESS ASSISTANCE

San Bernardino Co. District Attorney
235 E. Mountain View
Barstow, CA 92311
(760) 256-4810
(760) 256-4869 FAX

Apply for Victim of Violent Crimes Funds (via State Board of Control), crisis counseling, crime victims counseling, brochures, and referrals to providers and court support witnesses and victims. Explains criminal justice system, gives feedback on what is happening with court. Walk in or call. FUNDING: State and county district attorney's office. OFC HRS: M-F 8am-5pm. ADM REQ: Victim or witness of crime. Free srvs. SERVES: Barstow, Daggett, Hinkley, Lenwood, Baker, Needles and surrounding area.

VICTIM-WITNESS ASSISTANCE

Riverside Co. District Attorney
82-675 Hwy. 111, 4th Fl.
Indio, CA 92201
(760) 863-8216

(760) 863-8987 FAX

Crisis intervention, emerg assist, info & referral, court support & assist in filing for victim of crime compensation. FUNDING: State. OFC HRS: M-F 8am-5pm. Spanish spoken. Free srvs. SERVES: Riverside County.

VICTIM-WITNESS ASSISTANCE

San Bernardino Co. District Attorney
P.O. Box 6602
6527 White Feather Rd.
Joshua Tree, CA 92252
(760) 366-4120
(760) 366-4126 FAX

Apply for Victim of Violent Crimes Funds (via State Board of Control), crisis & crime victims counseling, brochures, referrals to providers and court support witnesses and victims. Explains criminal justice system, gives feedback on what is happening with court. Also assists after sentencing with regard to release date, etc. Works with victim upon contact. Walk in or call. FUNDING: State and county district attorney's office. OFC HRS: M-F 8am-5pm. ADM REQ: Victim or witness of crime. Free srvs. SERVES: Morongo Basin.

VICTIM-WITNESS ASSISTANCE

San Bernardino Co. District Attorney
8303 Haven Ave., 4th Fl.
Rancho Cucamonga, CA 91730
(909) 945-4241
(909) 945-4035 FAX

Prgm assists victims of violent crimes with reimbursement process for medical bills, loss of wages, psychological fees and funeral & burial expenses not covered by insurance. Assists in criminal justice process including trial process. Referral to comm agencies for counseling. FUNDING: State. OFC HRS: M-F 8am-5pm. Spanish spoken. ADM REQ: Cooperation with investigation and prosecution. Free srvs. SERVES: West San Bernardino County.

VICTIM-WITNESS ASSISTANCE

Riverside Co. District Attorney
3960 Orange St.
Riverside, CA 92501
(951) 955-5400
(951) 955-5682 FAX

Direct and referral assist provided to victims of violent crimes and their families. Srvs include: emerg assist, crisis intervention, crime victim compensation, orientation to criminal justice system, court info, accompaniment, and restraining order assist. Walk in or call. FUNDING: State grants. OFC HRS: M-F 7am-5pm. SERVES: Riverside County.

VICTIM-WITNESS ASSISTANCE

Victorville Victim Srvs Center
15371 Civic Dr., 2nd Fl.
Victorville, CA 92392
(760) 552-6944
(760) 552-6941 FAX

Prgm is designed to assist the victims and witnesses by providing emerg assist for short-term needs, referrals to community agencies for counseling, special srvs to victims of sexual assault and domestic violence & elder abuse, orientation to criminal system. Assists victims of violent crimes with applying for financial compensation from State Victim Compensation Prgm. FUNDING: State. OFC HRS: M-F 8am-5pm. Some Spanish spoken. Free srvs. SERVES: San Bernardino County.

VILLAGE OF CHILDHELP

See "Childhelp USA/..."

WE CAN HELP

(760) 375-7100

Hotline to report child abuse or to assist stressed parents. Sponsored by the High Desert Child Abuse Prevention Council. FUNDING: Nonprofit. Free srvs. SERVES: San Bernardino County.

WE TIP CRIME HOTLINE

P.O. Box 1296
Rancho Cucamonga, CA 91729
(800) 782-7463
(909) 987-2477 FAX

Takes info from anonymous informants about all major crimes (drug traffic, arson, murder, rape, fraud, etc.) and passes it to law enforcement agencies. Callers remain anonymous. Calls taken 24 hrs a day. Additional phone numbers: (800) 78-CRIME, (800) 47-ARSON, (800) 87-FRAUD, (800) 47-DRUGS. Visit (www.wetip.com). See actual photos of criminals wanted in every state. See photos of missing and kidnapped children throughout the nation. Info can be provided on crime or criminals on WeTip-encrypted e-mail at (wetiphome@wetip.com). Possible reward of up to $1,000 upon conviction. SEEK prgm: Support Enforcement Enriching Kids, new prgm for O.C. available through any of the toll-free numbers. This prgm invites the callers to turn in parents not paying their child support. FUNDING: Nonprofit. OFC HRS: 24 hrs, 7 days. Spanish spoken. Free srvs. SERVES: U.S.A.

YWCA/RIVERSIDE

8172 Magnolia Ave.
Riverside, CA 92504
(951) 687-9922
(951) 688-5270 FAX

Program offers parenting skills classes which meet or exceed current Calif state guidelines governing parenting classes. The YWCA also offers numerous support groups for parents, and anger mgmt. Also women's sobriety, TOPS, & AA meetings. Twinges in the Hinges prgm for Arthritis patients. Also offers teen pregnancy prevention classes. Sober living house. FUNDING: Nonprofit, class fees, donations, United Way. OFC HRS: M-F 8am-8pm; Sat 9am-1pm. Spanish spoken. Fees for classes. Y members receive discount of $10. SERVES: Riverside County.

CHILD CARE

APPLE VALLEY HEAD START/PRESCH
Preschool Srvs Dept
13589 Navajo Rd., Ste 104-109
Apple Valley, CA 92308
(760) 247-6955
(760) 247-9605 FAX

Part-day classes are 3.5 hrs a day, 4 days a week for children ages 3-4 yrs. Also full-day prgm 7am-5pm, 5 days a week. FUNDING: Federal, state. OFC HRS: M-F 7:30am-5pm. Spanish spoken. ADM REQ: Low income & special needs children. Free for eligible children. SERVES: Apple Valley.

ARLANZA HEAD START
Riverside Co. Office of Edu
5891 Rutland
Riverside, CA 92503
(951) 352-7984
(951) 352-7985 FAX

DIR: Jill Wilson. Head Start Prgm for low income children between 3.9-5 yrs of age Classes are 3.5 hrs, 4 days per week. Children with special needs are welcome. FUNDING: Govt. OFC HRS: M-F 8am-4:30pm. Sessions operate from M-Th 8:10am-11:40am, 12:20pm-3:50pm (half day) or M-F 8:10am-2:40pm (full day). Spanish spoken. Free to eligible children. SERVES: Riverside County.

BARSTOW HEAD START/STATE PRESCH
Preschool Srvs Dept
25757 Agate Rd.
Barstow, CA 92311
(760) 253-2956
(760) 253-4941 FAX

Prgm for ages 3-5 yrs, usually 3.5 hrs a day, 5 days a wk. CAP: 168. FUNDING: Govt. OFC HRS: M-F 7:30am-4:30pm. Spanish spoken. ADM REQ: Low income and special needs children. Sliding fee scale. SERVES: Barstow and nearby.

BEAUMONT EARLY HEAD START
Riverside Co. Ofc of Ed/Child/Family Srvs
P.O. Box 868
600 E. 8th Street
Beaumont, CA 92223
(951) 769-7025
(866) 766-4500
(951) 769-7026 FAX

DIR: Barbara Esther. Head Start Prgm for low income children between ages 3.9-5 yrs. Classes are 3.5 hrs, 4 days per week. Children with special needs welcome. Head Start & Early Head Start offer a full-day transition class as well as a home-based prgm. FUNDING: Federal govt. OFC HRS: M-F 8am-4:30pm. Spanish spoken. Free to eligible families.

BEAUMONT HEAD START
Riverside Co. Ofc of Ed/Child/Family Srvs
P.O. Box 868
1141 Beaumont Ave.
Beaumont, CA 92223
(951) 826-4500
(866) 766-4500
(951) 826-4525 FAX

DIR: Barbara Esther. Head Start Prgm for low income children ages 3.9-5 yrs. Classes are 3.5 hrs, 4 days per week. Children with special needs are welcome. Classes include part-day classes M-Th or full-day class M-F. FUNDING: Federal govt. OFC HRS: M-F 8am-4:30pm. Spanish spoken. Free to eligible families. SERVES: Mid-County area.

BETHANY LUTHERAN CHILD CARE
1609 Hamner Ave.
Norco, CA 92860
(951) 737-1173
(951) 734-4432
(951) 734-3355 FAX

Child care for ages 2-5 yrs. FUNDING: Nonprofit. OFC HRS: M-F 6am-6pm. Spanish spoken. SERVES: Norco.

BLOOMINGTON HEAD START
Preschool Srvs Dept
18829 Orange St.
Bloomington, CA 92316
(909) 876-6342
(909) 428-8597
(909) 423-0622 FAX

Supervisor: Teresa Negrete. Prgm for low income or special needs children between ages 3-5 yrs. Most prgms are 3.5 hrs, 5 days a week. FUNDING: Govt. OFC HRS: M-F 8am-4pm. Spanish spoken. ADM REQ: Low income. Free to eligible children. SERVES: Bloomington.

BOBBY BONDS HEAD START/ST PRESCH
Riverside Co. Ofc of Ed/Child/Family Srvs
P.O. Box 868
2060 University Ave., Ste 300
Riverside, CA 92507
(951) 784-3293
(951) 784-3298 FAX

DIR: Aja Bradley. Head Start Prgm for low income children ages 3.9-5 yrs. Classes are 3.5 hrs, 4 days per week. Children with special needs are welcome. Classes include part-day classes M-Th or full-day class M-F. FUNDING: Federal, state. OFC HRS: M-F 8am-4:30pm. Spanish spoken. Free for eligible children.

BOYS & GIRLS CLUB/BARSTOW
P.O. Box 204
120 Avenue G
Barstow, CA 92312
(760) 255-2422
(760) 255-2422 FAX

Youth srvs for boys & girls. Recreation, informal guidance, league sports, edu prgms, computer skills training, health & life skills, homework & tutorial srvs, after school child care, parent edu. FUNDING: Nonprofit. OFC HRS: M-F 11am-6pm. Spanish spoken. ADM REQ: Youth ages 6-17 yrs. Membership: school yr $15, summer $30. SERVES: San Bernardino County.

BOYS & GIRLS CLUB/CATHEDRAL CITY
32141 Whispering Palms Trail
Cathedral City, CA 92234
(760) 324-5844
(760) 321-2464 FAX

After school, summer, and holiday vacation child care srvs. Offers special assist with homework. Some transportation provided. Walk in. FUNDING: Nonprofit. OFC HRS: M-F 7:30am-5:30pm. Spanish spoken. ADM REQ: Ages 6-19 yrs. Annual membership $10. Scholarships & free srvs to low income families. Sliding fee scale. SERVES: Cathedral City, Rancho Mirage.

BOYS & GIRLS CLUB/COACHELLA VLY
Coachella Clubhouse
85-350 Bagdad Ave.
Coachella, CA 92236
(760) 398-5287
(760) 398-8468 FAX

Youth srvs for boys & girls. Recreation, informal guidance, league sports, edu prgms, computer skills training, homework assist, health & life skills, homework & tutorial srvs, parent edu. FUNDING: Nonprofit. OFC HRS: Summer M-F 7:30am-5:30pm. School yr: M-F 2pm-8pm. Spanish spoken. ADM REQ: Youth ages 7-18 yrs. Annual membership $20. SERVES: Coachella.

BOYS & GIRLS CLUB/COACHELLA VLY
La Quinta Clubhouse
49-995 Park Ave.
La Quinta, CA 92253
(760) 564-5555
(760) 564-5527 FAX

Youth srvs for boys & girls, recreation, informal guidance, league sports, edu prgms, computer skills training, homework assist, health & life skills, parent edu. FUNDING: Nonprofit. OFC HRS: Summer M-F 7:30am-5:30pm; school yr: M-F 2pm-8pm. Spanish spoken. ADM REQ: Ages 6-17 yrs. Annual membership $140 school yr, $120 summer. SERVES: La Quinta.

BOYS & GIRLS CLUB/FONTANA
Almeria Middle School Clubhouse
P.O. Box 3712
7723 Almeria Ave.
Fontana, CA 92336
(909) 822-4988
(909) 355-8663 FAX

Youth srvs for boys & girls. Recreation, informal guidance, league sports, edu prgms, computer skills training, health & life skills, homework & tutorial srvs, after school child care, delinquency prevention prgm, parent edu. Teen clubs, cyber cafe. FUNDING: Donations, nonprofit. OFC HRS: M-F 10am-5pm. Spanish spoken. ADM REQ: Ages 6-17 yrs. Annual membership $30 per yr per child. SERVES: San Bernardino County.

BOYS & GIRLS CLUB/HIGH DESERT
56525 Little League Dr.
Yucca Valley, CA 92284
(760) 365-5437
(760) 228-3017 FAX

Youth srvs for boys & girls. Recreation, informal guidance, league sports, edu prgms, computer skills training, health & life skills, homework & tutorial srvs, before & after school child care, transportation, delinquency prevention prgm, parent edu. For mail, P.O. Box 402 Yucca Valley, CA 92284. FUNDING: Donations, nonprofit. OFC HRS: M-F 10am-6pm; summer hrs: M-F 10am-5pm. ADM REQ: Ages 7-17 yrs. Annual membership $50 during the school year. Summer $30 every two weeks. SERVES: Yucca Valley.

BOYS & GIRLS CLUB/INDIO

Indio Clubhouse
83-100 Date St.
Indio, CA 92201
(760) 347-5712
(760) 347-1192 FAX

Youth srvs for boys & girls, recreation, informal guidance, league sports, edu prgms, computer skills training, health & life skills, homework & tutorial srvs, after school child care, transportation, delinquency prevention prgm. FUNDING: Nonprofit. OFC HRS: Winter: M-F 2pm-8pm. Summer: M-F 7:30am-5:30pm. Spanish spoken. ADM REQ: Ages 7-18 yrs. Annual membership fee $20. SERVES: Indio.

BOYS & GIRLS CLUB/MURRIETA

P.O. Box 892349
40550 California Oaks Rd.
Murrieta, CA 92562
(951) 698-3838
(951) 461-1774 FAX

Youth srvs for boys & girls. Recreation, informal guidance, league sports, edu prgms, computer skills training, health & life skills. Homework & tutorial srvs, before & after school child care, transportation, delinquency prevention prgm, guest speakers. FUNDING: Donations, nonprofit. OFC HRS: M-F 6:30am-7pm. Spanish spoken. ADM REQ: Ages 6-17 yrs. Annual membership fee $20. SERVES: Southwest Riverside County.

BOYS & GIRLS CLUB/REDLANDS

P.O. Box 8416
1251 Clay St.
Redlands, CA 92374
(909) 798-4599
(909) 798-1684 FAX

Youth srvs for boys & girls. Recreation, informal guidance, league sports, edu prgms, computer skills training, health & life skills, homework & tutorial srvs, after school child care, transportation, parent edu, delinquency prevention prgm. FUNDING: Donations, nonprofit. OFC HRS: M-F 9am-6pm. Spanish spoken. ADM REQ: Ages 6-17 yrs. Annual membership fee $12. SERVES: Redlands USD.

BOYS & GIRLS CLUB/TEMECULA

P.O. Box 892349
28790 Pujol St.
Temecula, CA 92589-2349
(951) 699-1526
(951) 699-4273 FAX

Youth srvs for boys & girls. Recreation, informal guidance, league sports, edu prgms, computer skills training, health & life skills. Homework & tutorial srvs, transportation, delinquency prevention prgm. Day camp, before & after school care for grades 1-8. Roller hockey, sports for toddlers, Tae Kwon Do. FUNDING: United Way, nonprofit. OFC HRS: M-F 6:30am-7pm; Sat 9am-2pm. Spanish spoken. ADM REQ: Ages 6-17 yrs. Annual membership fee $20. SERVES: Temecula, Murrieta.

BRYANT PARK HEAD START/ST PRESCH

Riverside Co. Office of Edu
7940 Philbin Ave.
Riverside, CA 92503
(951) 509-1932
(951) 509-1936 FAX

DIR: Barbara Esther. Head Start Prgm for low income children ages 3.9-5 yrs. Classes are 3.5 hrs, 4 days per week. Children with special needs are welcome. Part-day classes M-Th as well as a home-based prgm. FUNDING: Federal. OFC HRS: M-F 8am-4:30pm. Spanish spoken. Free to eligible children. SERVES: Riverside County.

CAMPESINOS UNIDOS CHILD DEV

Headquarters
P.O. Box 39
1005 C Street
Brawley, CA 92227
(760) 344-6300
(760) 344-0322 FAX

Child care for ages birth-5 yrs, capacity of 450. Also serves special needs children. Four locations. FUNDING: Federal, state. HRS: M-Th 8am-5pm; F 8am-4pm (Sept-June). Spanish spoken. ADM REQ: Low income migrant. Sliding fee scale. SERVES: Riverside & Imperial Counties.

CAMPESINOS UNIDOS CHILD DEV CTR

51996 Tyler Ave.
Coachella, CA 92236
(760) 398-3689
(760) 398-8598 FAX

Child care for ages 3-5 yrs for children of migrant workers and low-income families. FUNDING: State, federal govt. OFC HRS: M-F 6am-5pm. Spanish spoken. ADM REQ: Low income families. Sliding fee scale. SERVES: Coachella Valley.

CAMPESINOS UNIDOS CHILD DEV CTR

47-155 Van Buren St., Ste 252
Indio, CA 92201
(760) 342-7784
(760) 342-9694 FAX

Child care for children ages 18 mos-5 yrs from low-income migrant families. FUNDING: Fed, state. OFC HRS: M-F 6am-4pm. Spanish spoken. Sliding fee scale. SERVES: Indio, Palm Springs & nearby.

CASA BLANCA CHILD CARE CENTER

3020 Madison St.
Riverside, CA 92504
(951) 689-7891
(951) 689-9941 FAX

Srvs shown under "Concilio/Centro de Ninos" OFC HRS: M-F 7am-5:30pm. Spanish spoken. SERVES: Riverside & nearby.

CASA RAMONA CHILD DEV CENTER

1633 W. 5th Street
San Bernardino, CA 92411
(909) 889-0011
(909) 381-2871 FAX

Prgm for children ages 3-5 yrs from low income families. CAP: 48 children. FUNDING: State, govt. OFC HRS: M-F 7am-5:30pm. Spanish spoken. Free to qualifying families. Sliding fee scale. SERVES: San Bernardino County.

CASA RAMONA DROP-IN CENTER

1622 W. 5th Street
San Bernardino, CA 92411
(909) 889-0011
(909) 381-2871 FAX

Child care center and charter school. OFC HRS: M-F 8am-5pm. Spanish spoken. Sliding scale for child care center. SERVES: San Bernardino.

CESAR CHAVEZ HEAD START/ST P.S.

Coachella Valley USD
49601 Avenida De Oro
Coachella, CA 92236
(760) 398-0619

Head Start and State Preschool prgms for low income children who are 3.9-5 yrs of age. 10% of their enrollment is also reserved for special needs children. Most prgms are 3 to 3.5 hrs long, 5 days a week. Prgm serves approx 24 children. FUNDING: State, federal. OFC HRS: M-F 8:30am-4:30pm. Spanish spoken. SERVES: Coachella.

CHILD CARE ADVOCATES/SO CALIF

Stephanie Anderson c/o Calif Dept Soc Srvs
7575 Metropolitan Dr., Ste 110
San Diego, CA 92108
(619) 767-2249
(619) 767-2200
(619) 767-2203 FAX

Assists the efforts in improving the child care delivery system by providing info & resources to parents, employers, govt agencies, schools and child protective agencies regarding licensing regulations, current legislation and child care info. Accepts complaints about child care providers. FUNDING: State. OFC HRS: M-F 8am-5pm. Free srvs. SERVES: So. Calif, parts of Central Calif.

CHILD CARE AWARE

1515 N. Courthouse Rd., 11th Fl., Ste 350
Arlington, VA 22201
(800) 424-2246
(703) 341-4101 FAX

Info for finding quality child care & resources. Refers parents to local child care resource & referral agencies (CCR&Rs). Publications, newsletter. Visit (www.childcareaware.org). TTY: (866) 278-9428. FUNDING: Govt. OFC HRS: M-F 8am-7pm, EST. Free srvs. SERVES: U.S.A.

CHILD CARE DEVELOPMENT PRGM

Pomona USD
1460 E. Holt Ave., Ste 130
Pomona, CA 91767-5864
(800) 822-5777
(909) 397-4740
(909) 620-5267 FAX

Referrals to parents for child care in 21 cities in East L.A. Co. and West San Bernardino Co. Also alternative payment prgm for low income families. Free child care referrals & tech assist to child care providers, toy loan prgm. FUNDING: Calif Dept of Edu, nonprofit. OFC HRS: M-F 8am-4:30pm. Spanish spoken. Free srvs. SERVES: San Bernardino & L.A. Counties.

CHILDTIME CHILD CARE

3656 Riverside Dr.
Chino, CA 91710
(909) 591-9169
(909) 591-9160 FAX

Pvt prgm serving children ages 6 wks-11 yrs. CAP: 129. OFC HRS: M-F 6am-6pm. Spanish spoken. Fees: $42-$210 per week depending on the number of days and ages. SERVES: Chino, Chino Hills, Montclair, Diamond Bar, Pomona, Phillips Ranch area.

CHINO VALLEY TYKES PROGRAM

13220 Central Ave.
Chino, CA 91710
(909) 590-5562
(909) 590-1803 FAX

School readiness for ages birth-5 yrs. Also, parenting classes, edu workshops, case mgmt srvs. FUNDING: County, city. OFC HRS: M-F 9am-5pm; 1st Sat each month 9am-1pm. Spanish spoken. SERVES: Chino.

COACHELLA VALLEY HOUSING COALITION
45-701 Monroe St., Ste G
Indio, CA 92201
(760) 347-3157
(800) 689-4663
(760) 342-6466 FAX

Developer of affordable housing to low and very low income people. Also child care, community dev, self-help. Equal housing opportunity. Walk in or call. Wait: Varies. FUNDING: State, fed, city, county, nonprofit. OFC HRS: M-F 8:30am-5pm. Spanish spoken. ADM REQ: Must meet federal low income guidelines. Free srvs. SERVES: Riverside County.

COACHELLA VALLEY U.S.D.
Head Start/State Preschool Prgm
P.O. Box 847
87225 Church St.
Thermal, CA 92274
(760) 399-5137
(760) 399-1389 FAX

This district sponsors Head Start and State Preschool Prgms for low income children who are ages 4 yrs+. Most prgms are 3 to 3.5 hrs long, 5 days a wk. Prgms at Mecca, Oasis, Palm View, Peter Pendleton, Valley View, Westside Cesar Chavez, Tlaquepaque & John Kelley schools. The Child dev prgms at John Kelley, Palm View, Las Casas, Pie De La Cuesta and Nueva Vista serve children ages 2-5 yrs. Mecca Childcare serves infants 9 mos-2 yrs as well as child care for ages 2-5 yrs. Teen Parent at Coachella Valley High School provides child care for children ages 6 wks-4 yrs whose parents are going to high school. OFC HRS: M-F 8am-4:30pm. SERVES: Riverside County.

COLLETT HEAD START
Riverside Co. Office of Edu
10850 Collett Ave.
Riverside, CA 92505
(951) 826-4221
(951) 352-0184 FAX

DIR: Janis Arnold. Head Start Prgm for low income children ages 3.9-5 yrs. Classes are 3.5 hrs, 4 days per week. Children with special needs are welcome. Classes include part-day classes M-Th or full-day class M-F. FUNDING: Federal, state. OFC HRS: M-F 8am-4:30pm. Spanish spoken. Free to eligible children.

COLTON COMMUNITY SRVS DEPT
670 Colton Ave.
Colton, CA 92324
(909) 370-6153
(909) 777-3351 FAX

Recreation division, youth, family & seniors division. Senior outreach, counseling, tutoring, child care, summer youth, and youth intervention. Walk in or call. FUNDING: Govt. OFC HRS: M-F 7am-8pm; Sat 8am-5pm. Spanish spoken. SERVES: Colton, Grand Terrace & Bloomington.

COLTON EARLY CHILDHOOD EDUCATION
Community Srvs
660 Colton Ave.
Colton, CA 92324

(909) 370-6171
(909) 370-6173 FAX

Program for grades K-6. Four elementary school sites, two preschool sites, state preschool for ages 3-5 yrs. Curriculum-based, no-cost psychological srvs, NSACA accreditation, parenting classes. Capacity varies by site. FUNDING: State, city, parent fees, GAIN, CDBG. OFC HRS: M-F 7am-6pm. Spanish spoken. ADM REQ: State income requirements. Sliding fee scale. Parents may qualify for subsidized srvs. SERVES: Colton & nearby.

COLTON HEAD START/STATE PRESCHOOL
San Salvador School
471 Agua Mansa Rd.
Colton, CA 92324
(909) 876-4240
(909) 824-7406 FAX

DIR: Kathleen McGinn. Sponsored by the Preschool Srvs Dept. Prgm for children 3 yrs of age. 3.5 hrs a day, also full-day prgm M-F 6:30am-5:30pm. Extended day for kindergarten M-F 12noon-5:30pm. Special day for special needs children M-F partial days. Waiting list. FUNDING: Federal, state. OFC HRS: M-F 6:30am-5:30pm. Spanish spoken. ADM REQ: Low income & special needs children. Free prgm for eligible children. SERVES: San Bernardino County.

COMMUNITY CARE LICENSING
Calif Dept of Social Srvs
3737 Main St., Ste 700
Riverside, CA 92501
(951) 782-4200
(951) 782-4985 FAX

Licenses, monitors, investigates complaints on all child care centers and family day care homes. Inland Empire child care office. FUNDING: Govt. OFC HRS: M-F 8am-5pm. Spanish spoken, other languages if advance request. SERVES: Riverside & San Bernardino Counties.

CONCILIO/CENTRO DE NINOS
Child Care
2010 Martin Luther King Blvd.
Riverside, CA 92507
(951) 683-8935
(951) 683-6557 FAX

Licensed bilingual, bicultural preschool for children ages 3-5 yrs. Center provides a learning environment that supports social, emotional, physical, cognitive and language dev which will prepare the children for successful opportunities. Wait: 6 mos. FUNDING: State. OFC HRS: M-F 8:30am-5:30pm; child care hrs: 7am-5:30pm. Spanish spoken. ADM REQ: State-funded child care for parents who are working or in school. Sliding fee scale. Free to eligible children. SERVES: Riverside County.

COPPER MOUNTAIN HEAD START
Preschool Srvs Dept
P.O. Box HCI 699
6334 Rotary Way
Joshua Tree, CA 92252
(760) 366-9762
(760) 366-7350 FAX

170-day prgm for children ages 3.9-5 yrs. Most classes 3-3.5 hrs a day, 5 days a week. Wait list. FUNDING: Govt. OFC HRS: M-F 7:30am-4:30pm. Spanish spoken. ADM REQ: Low income and special needs children. Prgm

is free to eligible children. SERVES: San Bernardino County.

CUCAMONGA HEAD START
Preschool Srvs Dept
P.O. Box 1073
9324 San Bernardino Rd.
Rancho Cucamonga, CA 91730-1073
(909) 948-6979
(909) 944-0574 FAX

DIR: Eldoris Jackson. Federally funded prgm for 3-5 yr old low income and special needs children. Prgms are usually 3.5 hrs a day, four days a week. CAP: 90 children in part-day prgms. OFC HRS: M-F 7:30am-4:30pm. Spanish spoken. Free to eligible children. SERVES: San Bernardino County.

CUCAMONGA PRESCHOOL/ELEM
8677 Archibald Ave.
Rancho Cucamonga, CA 91730
(909) 980-1318

Preschool to 5th grade. FUNDING: Nonprofit. OFC HRS: M-F 7:30am-4pm. SERVES: Rancho Cucamonga.

DESERT RECREATION DISTRICT
Formerly Coachella Vly Rec & Park Dist
45-305 Oasis St.
Indio, CA 92201
(760) 347-3484
(760) 347-4660 FAX

This is not a day care facility. Preschool Tiny Tot Prgm M-Th 9am-11:30am. Prgms held at three community centers. Swimming, cultural prgms, summer day camp, kid's club, licensed after school care for grades K-6 in Indio, La Quinta and Palm Desert, two gyms with basketball, volleyball, racquetball. FUNDING: Nonprofit, donations. OFC HRS: M-F 8am-5pm. Spanish spoken. Low fees. SERVES: Palm Desert, Indian Wells, La Quinta, Indio, Coachella, Thousand Palms, Rancho Mirage, Bermuda Dunes, Thermal, Oasis, Mecca, and the Salton Sea.

DESERT SANDS UNIFIED SCHOOL DIST
Early Childhood Education Admin Head Start/State Preschool/Parent Edu
47-950 Dune Palms Rd.
La Quinta, CA 92253
(760) 771-8678
(760) 771-8725
(760) 771-8505 FAX

Program for low income children who are 3.9-5 yrs of age. 10% of their enrollment is also reserved for special needs children. Most programs are 3-3.5 hrs long and meet 4 days a wk, M-Th. DSUSD sponsors Head Start prgms, state preschool, fee-based preschool, child development center, and a parent education resource center. OFC HRS: M-F 8am-5pm. ADM REQ: Low income. SERVES: Indio, Palm Desert, La Quinta, Rancho Mirage, Bermuda Dunes, Indian Wells.

DESERT/MOUNTAIN EARLY START PRGM
Lucy Siegrist School
15922 Willow St.
Hesperia, CA 92345
(760) 244-1083
(760) 244-6508 FAX

Early intervention prgm for children ages birth-3 yrs, who are deaf, blind, orthopedically impaired, delayed in gross motor/fine motor language dev, social dev, self-help skills, and other health impairment. Srvs are provided in the home by a credentialed teacher on a scheduled basis. FUNDING: Nonprofit. OFC HRS: M-F 8am-4pm. Spanish spoken. ASL available. Free srvs. SERVES: Hesperia, Victorville, Apple Valley, Barstow, Ft. Irwin, Big Bear, Adelanto, Phelan, Silver Valley, Helendale, Oro Grande.

EASTER SEALS/CHILD CARE CENTER
Child Development Center
531 W. 8th Street
Upland, CA 91786
(909) 981-4668
(909) 608-0147 FAX

Infant, toddler and preschool prgm. Scholarships available for pregnant moms and income eligible families with parents seeking employment, working, or attending school. In-home and center-based srvs available. Srvs include: breakfast, lunch, snacks and full-year prgm. FUNDING: Fed, state; sponsored by the Easter Seals. OFC HRS: M-F 7:30am-5:30pm. Spanish spoken. ADM REQ: Low income or disabled children. SERVES: San Bernardino County.

EDUCATION OPTIONS CTR/STATE PRESCHOOL
Riverside USD
6401 Lincoln Ave.
Riverside, CA 92506
(951) 276-7670
(951) 276-7685 FAX

Head Start & State Preschool for low income and/or special needs children ages 3.9-5yrs. Most prgms are 3-3.5 hrs, 5 days a week. State preschool prgm is similar but is state funded. FUNDING: Govt. OFC HRS: M-F 7:30am-3:30pm. Spanish spoken. Free to eligible children. SERVES: Riverside.

EMERSON STATE PRESCHOOL
Riverside Co. Office of Edu
4660 Ottawa Ave.
Riverside, CA 92507
(951) 788-7462
(951) 788-1100 FAX

State preschool prgm for low income and/or special needs children ages 3.9-5yrs. Prgms are 3 hrs, 5 days a week. FUNDING: State. Free to eligible children. SERVES: Riverside County.

FAMILY SERVICE ASSN/WEST RIVERSIDE
Rubidoux Child Care Center
5765 42nd Street
Rubidoux, CA 92509
(951) 274-7940
(951) 274-7943 FAX

Infant, preschool & school-age care. OFC HRS: M-F 6:30am-6:30pm. Spanish spoken. Sliding fee scale. SERVES: Riverside County.

FAMILY SERVICE ASSOCIATION
Mental Health Clinic
21250 Box Springs Rd., Ste 201
Moreno Valley, CA 92557
(951) 686-3706
(951) 686-7267 FAX

Full-srv marriage, family, child, individual and group counseling. Medi-Cal prgm for children. Counseling office in Riverside. Senior nutrition/home-delivered meals in Sun City & Mead Valley San Jacinto, Hemet, Reno Valley, Cabazon, Banning, Calimesa, Desert Hot Springs. Child dev prgm with child care sites in La Sierra,

Mead Valley, Rubidoux. Adult day srvs in Hemet, (951)791-3556. FUNDING: State, grants, contracts, United Way, donations, nonprofit. OFC HRS: M-F 8am-5pm. Clinic M-Th 8pm-9pm; F 8am-5pm. Spanish spoken. Sliding fee scale. SERVES: West & Mid-Riverside County.

FAMILY SERVICES
Parent Center
24300 Las Brisas Road, North
Murrieta, CA 92562
(951) 304-1623
(951) 304-1627 FAX

Edu & personal support srvs to parents & educators. Classes & workshops: Parent Project, Parent & Me, Child Health & Safety. Support groups including: Al-Anon, Families & Friends of Murder Victims, Special Ed Parent Advisory Council, Mommy & Me. For parenting center, call (951) 304-1624. For Head Start/state preschool, call (915) 304-1625. FUNDING: Nonprofit. OFC HRS: M-Th 9am-1pm, 2pm-4:30pm; F 9am-1pm, 2pm-4pm. Prgm hrs vary. Spanish spoken. SERVES: Southwest Riverside County.

FIRST CHRISTIAN CHURCH NURSERY SCHL
4055 Jurupa Ave.
Riverside, CA 92506
(951) 683-5780
(951) 683-5780 FAX

Child care for children ages 6 wks-5 yrs. FUNDING: Pvt fees, nonprofit. OFC HRS: M-F 6:30am-6pm. SERVES: Riverside

FIRST STEPS CHILD DEVELOPMENT CTR
821 Sun Ave.
Redlands, CA 92374
(909) 793-7856
(909) 798-4987 FAX

DIR: Tammy Ellis. Prgm for low income families with infants and children up to 5 yrs of age. FUNDING: Govt, United Way, fees, nonprofit. OFC HRS: M-F 7:30am-5:30pm. Spanish spoken. Sliding fee scale. SERVES: Redlands area.

FIRST STEPS CHILD DEVELOPMENT CTR
10510 Hole Ave.
Riverside, CA 92505
(951) 689-2811
(951) 689-2877 FAX

DIR: Sherri Embry. Infant and toddler prgm for low income families. FUNDING: State, federal, United Way. OFC HRS: M-F 7:30am-5:30pm. Spanish spoken. ADM REQ: Ages birth-3 yrs. Sliding fee scale. SERVES: Riverside.

FIRST STEPS CHILD DEVELOPMENT CTR
Waterman Gardens
382 Crestview Ave.
San Bernardino, CA 92410
(909) 884-9766

DIR: Gloria Lopez. Prgm for children ages 2-5 yrs. Also serves CalWORKs & GAIN families. OFC HRS: M-F 7:30am-5:30pm. Spanish spoken. SERVES: San Bernardino County.

GARRETSON HEAD START/ST PRESCH
Riverside Co. Office of Edu
1650 Garretson Ave.
Corona, CA 92879
(951) 279-4231
(951) 272-2065 FAX

DIR: Francis Lee. Head Start Prgm for low income children ages 3.9-5 yrs. Classes are 3.5 hrs, 4 days per week. Children with special needs are welcome. Classes include part-day classes M-Th or full-day class M-F. FUNDING: Federal. OFC HRS: M-F 8am-4:30pm. Free to eligible children. SERVES: Riverside County.

GIRLS CLUBS
The "Youth/Recreation" chapter in this directory will help you locate some of these clubs. Most of the clubs have after school recreational activities for children. The membership cost for one year varies per site, a positive option to latchkey children who are often left unattended in the afternoons. Many prgms are not licensed child care ctrs. Girls Clubs may be shown as "Boys and Girls Clubs."

GLENVIEW HEAD START/PRESCH
Val Verde USD
16820 Via Pamplona
Moreno Valley, CA 92551
(951) 940-8530
(951) 940-8535 FAX

Principal: Julie Singletary. Federally funded Head Start prgm serving children ages 3.9-5yrs with priority given to low income and special needs children. Also receives state funds for state preschool. Open Sept-June with morning and afternoon classes. CAP: 200 children. FUNDING: Federal. OFC HRS: M-F 7:45am-3:15pm. Spanish spoken. Free to eligible children. SERVES: Perris.

HESPERIA HEAD START
Preschool Srvs Dept
9352 E Avenue
Hesperia, CA 92345
(760) 948-4411
(760) 948-8071 FAX

DIR: Frances Flowers. Head Start prgm for low income and special needs children ages 3.9-5yrs. FUNDING: Federal. OFC HRS: M-F 8am-4pm. Spanish spoken. SERVES: Hesperia.

HIGHGROVE HEAD START/ST PRESCH
Riverside USD
690 Center St.
Riverside, CA 92507
(951) 352-8290
(951) 276-7642 FAX

Early childhood program for low income children ages 3.9-5 yrs. 10% of enrollment reserved for special needs children. Most prgms are 3-3.5 hrs long, 5 days a week. CAP: 34 children. A.M. class meets M-F 7:30am-11am and P.M. class meets M-F 12noon-3:30pm. FUNDING: Federal, state. OFC HRS: M-F 7:30am-3:30pm. Spanish spoken. SERVES: Riverside.

HIGHLAND HEAD START
Preschool Srvs Dept
26887 5th Street
Highland, CA 92346
(909) 425-0785
(909) 425-0210 FAX

DIR: Lisa Simmons. Prgm for low income and/or special needs children ages 3.9-5 yrs. Most prgms are 3-3.5 hrs, 4 days a week. FUNDING: State. OFC HRS: M-F 7am-5pm. Free to eligible children. SERVES: Highland.

Child Care

HIGHLAND STATE PRESCHOOL
700 Highlander Dr.
Riverside, CA 92507
(951) 788-7292
(951) 788-7576 FAX

Prgm for low income and/or special needs children ages 3.5-5 yrs.. All prgms are 3.5 hrs, 5 days a week. FUNDING: State. HRS: Morning session 8am-11am; afternoon 11:45am-2:45pm. Spanish spoken. SERVES: Riverside County.

HOME GARDENS HEAD START/ST PRESCH
Riverside Office Of Education
13550 Tolton Ave.
Corona, CA 92879
(951) 549-8492
(951) 272-2051 FAX

DIR: Janis Arnold. Head Start Prgm for low income children ages 3.9-5 yrs. Classes are 3.5 hrs, 4 days per week. Children with special needs are welcome. Part-day classes M-Th. FUNDING: Federal. HRS: M-F 8am-4:30pm. Spanish spoken. SERVES: Riverside County.

HOME OF NEIGHBORLY SERVICE
839 N. Mt. Vernon Ave.
San Bernardino, CA 92411
(909) 885-3491
(909) 884-0181 FAX

After school enrichment prgm for children in first grade and up. Recreation, youth skill building, counseling groups, gang intervention & prevention, homework assist/tutoring for youth, Boy & Girl Scouts, nutrition classes for adults, ESL for adults, children's clothes closet, Narcotics Anonymous meetings, parenting support groups, sewing for adults, boxing, hip hop dancing, aerobics & emerg food srv, resource & referrals. OFC HRS: M-Th 8am-5:30pm; F 8am-5pm. Spanish spoken. Free srvs & referrals. SERVES: San Bernardino County.

INA ARBUCKLE HEAD START/ST PRESCH
See "Jurupa Unified School Dist"

JEFFERSON HEAD START/ST PRESCH
Riverside Co. Office of Edu
1040 S. Vicentia Ave.
Corona, CA 92882
(951) 340-1526
(951) 340-2035 FAX

DIR: Francis Lee. Head Start Prgm for low income children ages 3.9-5 yrs. Classes are 3.5 hrs, 4 days per week. Children with special needs are welcome. Classes include part-day classes M-Th or full-day class M-F. FUNDING: Federal, state. OFC HRS: M-F 8am-4:30pm. Spanish spoken. Free to eligible children.

JURUPA UNIFIED SCHOOL DIST
Head Start/Preschool
4850 Pedley Rd.
Riverside, CA 92509
(951) 360-4149
(951) 360-4155 FAX

Admin office for Head Start & State Preschool prgms located at various sites throughout Jurupa School Dist. Part-day edu experience for children, ages 3.9-5 yrs, from low income families. Prgms are 3-3.5 hrs. 10% of enrollment is reserved for special needs children. FUNDING: Fed, state. OFC HRS: M-F 8am-4:30pm. Spanish spoken. Free to eligible children. SERVES: Jurupa USD.

KIDSNCARE/CHILD DEV SRVS
San Bernardino Co. Supt of Schools
1111 E. Mill St., Ste 100
San Bernardino, CA 92408
(909) 384-1492
(800) 722-1091
(909) 384-8030 FAX

Resource & referral for child care centers and licensed family child care home settings and Livescan (fingerprint) site. Assists in starting a child care prgm. Child Care Food Prgm (CCFP) for family child care providers. Alternative Payment Prgm (APP) to assist low income families with child care costs. APP also serves other counties where parents are employed. Walk in or call. FUNDING: Donations, grants, state, nonprofit. OFC HRS: M-F 8am-4:30pm. Spanish spoken. Free srvs. SERVES: Riverside & San Bernardino Counties (except the west end).

KIDSNCARE/CHILD DEV SRVS
San Bernardino Co. Supt of Schools
14397 Amargosa Rd.
Victorville, CA 92392
(760) 245-0770
(760) 245-1072 FAX

Resource & referral for child care centers and licensed family child care home settings and Livescan (fingerprint) site. Assists in starting a child care prgm. Child Care Food Prgm (CCFP) for family child care providers. Alternative Payment Prgm (APP) to assist low income families with child care costs. APP also serves other counties where parents are employed. Walk in or call. FUNDING: Donations, grants, state, nonprofit. OFC HRS: M-F 7:30am-4:30pm. Spanish spoken. Free srvs. SERVES: High Desert area.

LEE/SHARIKIABOYS & GIRLS CLUB/HEAD START
Preschool Srvs Dept
1180 W. 9th Street
San Bernardino, CA 92411
(909) 381-4294
(909) 386-7585 FAX

Federally funded prgm for 3-5 yr old low income and/or special needs children. Prgm 3.5 hrs a day, 5 days a week. FUNDING: Nonprofit. OFC HRS: M-F 7:30am-4:30pm. Spanish spoken. Free to eligible children. SERVES: San Bernardino County.

LINCOLN INFANT CENTER
Riverside Co. Office of Edu
4341 Victoria Ave.
Riverside, CA 92507
(951) 684-3082
(951) 788-1182 FAX

Cal-SAFE prgm on site at Lincoln Continuation High School. Public edu for pregnant & parenting teens. Info on nutrition, child dev, pre-natal & child birth classes, career edu. FUNDING: State. OFC HRS: Vary. Free child care for children ages birth-5 yrs of teen parents. SERVES: Riverside.

LOMA LINDA CHILDREN'S CENTER
25228 Shepardson Dr.
Loma Linda, CA 92354
(909) 558-4568
(909) 558-4720 FAX

Child care for ages 3 mos-6 yrs. CAP: 158. FUNDING: Tuition plus some subsidy, non-

profit. OFC HRS: M-F 6am-6pm. ADM REQ: Priority to Loma Linda Univ & Medical Ctr employees, church members & students, then the community. Fees depend on days and age of child. SERVES: Inland Empire.

LONGFELLOW HEAD START/ST PRESCH
Riverside USD
3610 Eucalyptus Ave.
Riverside, CA 92507
(951) 788-7335
(951) 369-3346 FAX

Head Start prgm is for low income and/or special needs children ages 3.9-5 yrs. Most prgms are 3-3.5 hrs, 5 days a week. The state preschool is similar but state funded. FUNDING: Federal, state. OFC HRS: M-F 7:45am-3:45pm. Free to eligible children. SERVES: Riverside County.

MECCA STATE PRESCHOOL
Coachella Valley USD
65-250 Cahuilla St.
Mecca, CA 92254
(760) 396-2800
(760) 399-5137
(760) 396-0463 FAX

Serves low income children ages 3.9-5 yrs. 10% of enrollment reserved for special needs children. Most prgms are 3 to 3.5 hrs long, 5 days a week. Serves about 40 children per site. This site also has a prgm for infants & a day care. OFC HRS: M-F 8:30am-11:30am. Spanish spoken. SERVES: Riverside County.

MENIFEE STATE PRESCHOOL
Menifee USD
30465 Evans Rd.
Menifee, CA 92584
(951) 672-6478
(951) 672-6479 FAX

DIR: Jeanne Bargman. State Preschool prgm for low income and/or special needs children ages 3.9-5yrs. Prgms are 3 hrs, 5 days a week. FUNDING: State, contract. OFC HRS: M-F 8:30am-3pm. Free to eligible children. SERVES: Menifee.

MILL CHILD DEVELOPMENT CENTER
Preschool Srvs Dept
503 E. Central Ave.
San Bernardino, CA 92408
(909) 885-0789
(909) 890-1198 FAX

DIR: Luz Gonzales. Head Start, State Preschool, child dev center. Funded prgms for ages 3-5 yrs, low income and special needs children. CAP: 198 children in the child dev center in part-day and full-day, morning & afternoon prgms. FUNDING: State, fed. HRS: M-F 7am-5pm. Indonesian, Spanish spoken. SERVES: San Bernardino County.

MISSION BELL PRESCHOOL
See "Jurupa Unified School Dist"

MT. VIEW STATE PRESCHOOL
Riverside USD
6180 Streeter Ave.
Riverside, CA 92504
(951) 788-7433
(951) 276-7640 FAX

State preschool serves low income children ages 3.9-4.9 yrs. 10% of enrollment reserved for special needs children. Most prgms are 3.5 hrs long and meet 5 days a week. CAP: 34.

State preschool is a similar prgm but is state funded. FUNDING: Federal, state. OFC HRS: M-F 7:45am-10:45am, 11:15pm-2:15pm. SERVES: Riverside.

MURRIETA HEAD START/ST PRESCH

Riverside Co. Office of Edu
24980 Las Brisas Rd.
Murrieta, CA 92562
(951) 600-5680
(951) 600-5689 FAX

DIR: Cami Mann. Head Start Prgm for low income children ages 3.9-5 yrs. Classes are 3.5 hrs, 4 days per week. Children with special needs are welcome. Classes include part-day classes M-Th or full-day class M-F. FUNDING: Federal, state. HRS: M-F 8am-4:30pm. Spanish spoken. Free for eligible children. SERVES: Riverside County.

NATL ASSN/EDU OF YOUNG CHILDREN

NAEYC
1313 L Street, NW, Ste 500
Washington, DC 20005
(800) 424-2460
(202) 232-8777
(202) 328-1846 FAX

Prof assn for early childhood educators. Annual conference and public awareness activities concerning the edu of children ages birth-8 yrs. Complete catalog online. Visit (www.naeyc.org) for a list of local NAEYC-accredited early childhood prgms. FUNDING: Nonprofit. OFC HRS: M-F 9am-5pm, EST. SERVES: U.S.A.

NATL CHILD CARE INFORMATION CTR

9300 Lee Hwy.
Fairfax, VA 22030
(800) 616-2242
(800) 716-2242 FAX

Natl clearinghouse & tech assist center. Info for parents, providers, policy makers & researchers on finding & providing quality child care. TTY (800) 516-2242. FUNDING: Govt. OFC HRS: M-F 8am-5pm, EST. SERVES: U.S.A.

NEEDLES HEAD START/STATE PRESCH

Preschool Srvs Dept
1404 M Street
Needles, CA 92363
(760) 326-5221
(760) 326-6117 FAX

DIR: Judy Thornton. Federally funded Head Start prgm for 3-5 yr olds, low income or special needs children. Prgms usually 3.5 hrs a day, 5 days a week. State preschool funded by the state. CAP: 76 children in a part-day prgm. Mailing address: 1900 Erin Dr. FUNDING: Federal, state. OFC HRS: M-F 8am-3:30pm. Spanish spoken. Free to eligible children. SERVES: Needles.

NUVIEW UNION SCHOOL DISTRICT

Child Development Prgm
29780 Lakeview Ave.
Nuevo, CA 92567
(951) 928-3570
(951) 928-0066
(951) 928-2982 FAX

State preschool for ages 3-5 yrs. General child care ages birth-5 yrs. EvenStart Family Literacy Prgm. Preschool 4 All prgm for ages 4 yrs+ who are residents of Nuevo. Early Reading First Prgm. FUNDING: Govt. OFC HRS: M-F 8:15am-11:15am, 12:15pm-3:15pm. Child care

M-F 7:30am-5:30pm. Spanish spoken. SERVES: Riverside County.

OASIS STATE PRESCHOOL

Coachella Valley USD
88775 Avenue 76
Thousand Palms, CA 92276
(760) 397-1000

For low income children ages 3.9-5 yrs. 10% of enrollment reserved for special needs children. Most prgms are 3 hrs long, 5 days a week. CAP: 24 children (double session). Also 6.5 hr day prgm. FUNDING: State. OFC HRS: M-F 8am-4:30pm. Spanish spoken. SERVES: Thermal.

ONTARIO MAPLE HEAD START

Preschool Srvs Dept
555 W. Maple St.
Ontario, CA 91761
(909) 984-4117
(909) 988-2015 FAX

DIR: Cheryl Soars. Federally funded prgm for 3-5 yr old low income and special needs children. Prgms are usually 3.5 hrs a day, 5 days a week. Children also attend a designated center twice a month for socialization. CAP: 340 children in South Ontario area in a part day and home-based prgm. Also 6-hr prgm, 5 days a wk. FUNDING: Govt. OFC HRS: M-F 7am-5pm. Spanish, Vietnamese spoken. SERVES: San Bernardino County.

PACHAPPA HEAD START/ST PRESCH

Riverside USD
6200 Riverside Ave.
Riverside, CA 92506
(951) 788-7355
(951) 276-7643 FAX

Head Start prgm for low income and/or special needs children between ages 3.9-5yrs. Most prgms are 3-3.5 hrs, 5 days a week. State preschool is similar but state funded. FUNDING: Federal, state. OFC HRS: M-F 7:30am-4pm. Free to eligible children. SERVES: Riverside.

PACIFIC AVENUE HEAD START

See, "Jurupa Unified School Dist"

PAL COMPREHENSIVE CHILD DEV CTR

P.O. Box 7100
1686 W. 19th Street
San Bernardino, CA 92411
(909) 887-3975
(909) 887-5745 FAX

Subsidiary of the Provisional Edu Learning Center. Prgms for ages 2-5 yrs and before & after school prgm for ages 6-12 yrs. FUNDING: Client fees, nonprofit. OFC HRS: M-F 6am-6pm. Spanish spoken. ADM REQ: Open to the public. Some sliding fee scale. SERVES: San Bernardino County.

PALM SPRINGS UNIFIED SCHOOL DIST

Early Childhood Edu Prgms
1000 E. Tahquitz Canyon Way, Ste C
Palm Springs, CA 92262
(760) 416-8090
(760) 416-8413 FAX

This office provides Head Start/State Preschool Prgms: Agua Caliente, Julius Corsini, Cielo Vista, Cathedral City, Cahuila, United Methodist Church, Two Bunch Palms, Sunny Sands, Rio Vista, Desert Highland, Coyote Run, Bubbling Wells, Della Lindley. 3 child care centers located at Coyote Run, Cielo Vista and Della

Lindley. In addition to prgms for low income preschool children they sponsor before and after school prgms for school-aged children including prgms during the winter, spring and summer recesses. ECE is located at 15 sites. FUNDING: State, federal. OFC HRS: M-F 7:30am-5pm. Spanish spoken. ADM REQ: Serves ages 3-5 yrs, from low income families. Child care based on sliding fee scale. No fee for Head Start/Preschool, Even Start prgms. SERVES: Palm Springs USD.

PALM SPRINGS USD/HEAD START/ST PRESCH/

First 5 Programs District Office
1000 E. Tahquitz Canyon Way
Palm Springs, CA 92262
(760) 416-8090
(760) 416-8413 FAX

Serves children ages 2.5-5 yrs with priority given to low income and special needs children. 23 sites. FUNDING: State, fed. OFC HRS: M-F 8am-3:45pm. Spanish spoken. ADM REQ: Low income applicants must apply through Palm Springs USD and will then be sent to the appropriate site. Free to eligible children. SERVES: Riverside County.

PALM VIEW STATE PRESCHOOL

Coachella Valley USD
1390 7th Street
Coachella, CA 92236
(760) 391-9362
(760) 398-2592 FAX

Prgm for low income children who are ages 3.9-5 yrs. Most prgms are 3 to 3.5 hrs long, 5 days a week. CAP: 36 children. OFC HRS: M-F 7:30am-11am, 11:40am-3:30pm. Spanish spoken. SERVES: Riverside County.

PALO VERDE COLLEGE CHILD DEV CTR

1 College Dr.
Blythe, CA 92225
(760) 922-8714
(760) 922-8714 FAX

Child care prgm for ages 2.9-5 yrs. Capacity 60 children. Call for info. FUNDING: Nonprofit, State. OFC HRS: M-F 7:30am-5:30pm. Spanish spoken. ADM REQ: Both parents working, in training or students. Sliding fee scale based on income & family size. SERVES: Palo Verde Valley.

PALO VERDE HEAD START

Palo Verde USD
295 E. Chanslor Way
Blythe, CA 92225
(760) 922-8454
(760) 922-1390
(760) 922-3204 FAX

Prgm Dir: Suzanne Kuykendall. Prgm for children ages 3-5 yrs. Head Start classes are 3.5 hrs a day, 4 days a week. Day care M-F 7:30am-5:30pm. Extended day prgm M-F 7:30am-5:30pm. 10% of enrollment is reserved for special needs children. Morning & afternoon sessions. FUNDING: Fed, state. OFC HRS: M-F 7:30am-5:30pm. Spanish spoken. ADM REQ: Low income families. Free prgm. SERVES: Ripley, Palo Verde.

PERRIS HEAD START/EARLY/ST PRESCH

Riverside Co. Ofc of Ed/Child/Family Srvs
P.O. Box 868
148 Avocado Ave.
Perris, CA 92571

(951) 943-5815
(951) 943-1384 FAX

DIR: Barbara Esther. Head Start Prgm for low income children ages 3.9-5 yrs. Classes are 3.5 hrs, 4 days per week. Children with special needs are welcome. Classes include part-day classes M-Th or full-day classes M-F. Prgm is open Sept-June with full day classes. Head Start for Perris only. Early Head Start in Perris & Moreno Valley. FUNDING: Federal, state. OFC HRS: M-F 8am-4:30pm. Spanish spoken. Free to eligible families. SERVES: Perris & Moreno Valley.

PHILIP ALLRED CHILD DEV CTR
San Bernardino City USD
303 South K Street
San Bernardino, CA 92410
(909) 388-6307
(909) 885-4068 FAX

Srvs to children ages birth-5 yrs whose parents are receiving public assist, or are below 75% of the state median income, adjusted for family size, homeless families, and children in need of protective srvs. Walk in or call for info. FUNDING: Govt. OFC HRS: M-F 7am-5:30pm. Spanish spoken. ADM REQ: Parents need to be working or going to school to be qualified. Sliding fee scale. SERVES: San Bernardino City USD.

RAINBOW SPRINGS HEAD ST/ST PS
Moreno Valley USD
23990 Eucalyptus Ave., Ste 1
Moreno Valley, CA 92553
(951) 571-4710
(951) 571-4715 FAX

Prgm for children ages 3.9-5 yrs. Classes are 3-5 hrs, 4 or 5 days a week. Serves 316 children at 6 locations. Eligibility list. FUNDING: Federal, state. OFC HRS: M-F 8am-4pm. Spanish spoken. ADM REQ: Low income and special needs children. Free to eligible children. SERVES: Moreno Valley USD.

RAINBOW TO THE FUTURE
See "Easter Seals/Child Care..."

RCC EARLY CHILDHOOD PRESCHOOL
4800 Magnolia Ave.
Riverside, CA 92506
(951) 222-8068
(951) 222-8690 FAX

Dev appropriate edu prgm for preschool and early primary children ages 6 wks-5 yrs. Emphasis is on developing a child's self-esteem & self-concept. FUNDING: Tuition, state, Riverside Comm College. OFC HRS: M-F 9am-5pm. Child care M-F 6:30am-5:30pm. Some Spanish spoken. ADM REQ: First come, first served. SERVES: Riverside.

RCC MORENO VLY HEAD START/ST PS
Riverside Co. Office of Edu
16130 Lasselle St.
Moreno Valley, CA 92551
(951) 924-6974
(951) 924-6936 FAX

DIR: Melvin Rasberry. Head Start Prgm for low income children ages 3.9-5 yrs. Classes are 3.5 hrs, 4 days per week. Children with special needs are welcome. Classes include part-day classes M-Th or full-day class M-F. FUNDING: Federal. OFC HRS: M-F 8am-4:30pm. Spanish

spoken. Free to eligible children. SERVES: Moreno Valley.

RCC NORCO HEAD START/ST PRESCH
Riverside Co. Office of Edu
1980 3rd Street
Norco, CA 92860
(951) 270-0060
(951) 735-0851 FAX

DIR: Perla Leyvas. Head Start Prgm for low income children ages 3.9-5 yrs. Classes are 3.5 hrs, 4 days per week. Children with special needs are welcome. Classes include part-day classes M-Th or full-day classes M-F. FUNDING: Federal, state. OFC HRS: M-F 8am-4:30pm. Spanish spoken. Free to eligible children.

REDLANDS ADULT SCHOOL
Redlands USD
P.O. Box 3008
10568 California St.
Redlands, CA 92373-1508
(909) 748-6930
(909) 307-5324 FAX

Parent edu classes and parent participation preschool. Call for waiting list availability. OFC HRS: M-Th 9am-8pm; F 9am-4:30pm. Summer Hrs: M-F 9am-4:30pm. Closed at 12noon 1st F each month. Spanish spoken. SERVES: Redlands.

REDLANDS DAY NURSERY
Subsidized Infant/Toddler Prgm/Preschool
1041 E. Brockton Ave.
Redlands, CA 92374
(909) 792-2463
(909) 792-5822 FAX

Day care for children ages 3 mos-5 yrs. FUNDING: State, United Way, fees, nonprofit. OFC HRS: M-F 6:45am-5:45pm. Spanish spoken. ASL available. Sliding fee scale. SERVES: San Bernardino County.

REDLANDS DAY NURSERY II
1643 Plum Lane
Redlands, CA 92374
(909) 792-9717
(909) 307-5605 FAX

Site Dir: Milly Lara. Prgm Dir: Deborah Wasbotton. Subsidized child care for ages 3 mos-5 yrs. CAP: 140. FUNDING: State, nonprofit. HRS: M-F 6:45am-6pm. Spanish spoken. Sliding fee scale. SERVES: Redlands & East Valley.

REDLANDS NORTH HEAD START/ST PRESCH
Preschool Srvs Dept
1321 6th Street
Redlands, CA 92374
(909) 793-7181
(909) 793-4621 FAX

DIR: Nancy Roth. Federally funded Head Start prgm for 3-5 yr old low income and special needs children. Prgms usually 3.5 hrs a day, 4 days a wk. CAP: 64 children in a part-day prgm. OFC HRS: M-F 7:30am-4:30pm. Spanish spoken. Free to eligible children. SERVES: San Bernardino County.

REDLANDS POLICE DEPT RECREATION BUREAU
Ready, Set, Grow Preschool Prgm
111 W. Lugonia Ave.
Redlands, CA 92374
(909) 798-7572

(909) 798-1349 FAX

Students explore letters, sounds, colors, shapes and numbers through stories, art, music, and play. Children must be potty trained. FUNDING: City, donations. OFC HRS: M-F 10am-7pm. Fees. Full scholarships are offered for qualified children. SERVES: Redlands, Loma Linda, San Bernardino, Colton, Inland Empire.

REDLANDS SOUTH HEAD START
Preschool Srvs Dept
15 N. Center St.
Redlands, CA 92373
(909) 798-2690
(909) 798-6730 FAX

Site Supervisor: Daniella Vargas. Federally funded Head Start prgm for ages 3-5 yrs, low income and special needs children. Prgms usually 3.5 hrs a day, 4 days a week. CAP: 128 children in a part-day prgm, 24 children in home-based prgm. FUNDING: Nonprofit. OFC HRS: M-F 7:30am-4:30pm. Spanish spoken. Free to eligible children. SERVES: Loma Linda, Redlands & Mentone.

RENU HOPE FOUNDATION
802 Beaumont Ave.
Beaumont, CA 92223
(951) 845-3816
(951) 845-0286 FAX

State preschool and private nursery for children ages 3-5 yrs. State preschool prgm is 3-7 hrs daily. Breakfast or lunch is served. FUNDING: State, nonprofit. OFC HRS: M-F 7:30am-5:30pm. Spanish spoken. ADM REQ: Low income and special needs children. State preschool prgms are free to qualifying families. SERVES: Beaumont, Banning, Cherry Valley, Cabazon & Perris.

RIVERSIDE CO. OFFICE/EDUCATION
Children's Srvs Unit
2300 Market St.
Riverside, CA 92501
(800) 442-4927
(951) 826-6626
(951) 826-4478 FAX

Child care resource & referral, subsidized child care, parenting edu, brochures, early childhood conferences & trainings, toy loan prgm. FUNDING: State Dept of Edu, govt. OFC HRS: M-F 8am-5pm. Spanish spoken. ADM REQ: Income eligibility for child care, none for other srvs. Free srvs except sliding fee scale for child care based on state median income level. SERVES: Riverside County.

ROMOLAND HEAD START
Romoland School Dist
25890 Antelope Rd.
Romoland, CA 92585
(951) 928-2924
(951) 928-2923 FAX

Head Start prgm for low income children ages 3-5 yrs. 10% of enrollment reserved for special needs children. CAP: 60. Prgms are 3.5 hrs long, 4 days a week. FUNDING: Govt. OFC HRS: M-F 8am-4pm. Spanish spoken. SERVES: Romoland, Homeland, Sun City.

ROSEMARY KENNEDY HEAD START/ PRESCHOOL
Riverside Co. Office of Edu
10353 Gramercy Ave.
Riverside, CA 92505

(951) 688-5660
(951) 688-0126 FAX

DIR: Jill Wilson. Head Start Prgm for low income children ages 3.9-5 yrs. Classes are 3.5 hrs, 4 days per week. Children with special needs are welcome. Classes include part-day classes M-Th or full-day class M-F. FUNDING: Fed, state. OFC HRS: M-F 8am-4:30pm. Spanish spoken. Free for eligible children.

SAN BERNARDINO CO. HUMAN SRVS SY

HSS Administration
385 N. Arrowhead Ave., 5th Fl.
San Bernardino, CA 92415-0515
(909) 357-4717
(909) 387-5430 FAX

HSS is composed of the following depts: Aging & Adult Srvs, Behavioral Health, Children's Srvs, Community Srvs, Preschool Srvs, Public Health, Transitional Assist, and Veterans Affairs. OFC HRS: M-F 7:30am-5pm. SERVES: San Bernardino County.

SAN BERNARDINO PARK/REC HEAD START

Delmann Heights Community Center
2969 N. Flores St.
San Bernardino, CA 92407
(909) 887-3349

Sponsored by the Preschool Srvs Dept. Head Start is a federally funded prgm for 3-4 yr old low income and special needs children. Prgms are usually 3.5 hrs a day, 5 days a week. CAP: 60 children. OFC HRS: M-F 7:30am-4:30pm. Spanish spoken. Free to eligible children. SERVES: San Bernardino County.

SAN BERNARDINO VALLEY COLLEGE

Campus Child Care Center
701 South Mt. Vernon
Colton, CA 92324
(909) 384-4440
(909) 824-3442 FAX

Child care prgm serving children ages birth-5 yrs. Exceptional needs referrals. FUNDING: State, college, parent fees, nonprofit. HRS: M-F 8am-4pm. Spanish spoken. Sliding fee scale based on income and family size. SERVES: San Bernardino Community College District.

SAN GORGONIO CHILD CARE CONSRTM

P.O. Box 1629
671 N. Florida, Ste A
Banning, CA 92220
(951) 849-2930
(951) 849-2262 FAX

Low-cost child care for working parents. Targets special needs children, child protective srvs as well as coordinated child care for ages birth-12 yrs. Wait: Depends on enrollment. Walk in or call. FUNDING: State, pvt funds, United Way, nonprofit. OFC HRS: M-F 7am-5:30pm. Spanish spoken. ADM REQ: Must have current immunizations. Sliding fee scale. SERVES: Pass Area, Cherry Valley, Banning, Beaumont, Cabazon.

SAN JACINTO HEAD START/STATE PRESCHOOL

San Jacinto Unified School Dist
257 Grand Army
San Jacinto, CA 92583
(951) 654-1531
(951) 654-5549 FAX

DIR: Denise Carver. Head Start prgm for low income and special needs children who are ages

3-5 yrs. Prgms are 3.5 hrs long, 5 days a wk. 40 6.5 hr slots available. State preschool is similar to the Head Start prgm but is funded by the state. Serves approximately 223 children. OFC HRS: M-F 7:30am-4pm. Spanish spoken. Free to eligible children. SERVES: Riverside County.

SAN SALVADOR HEAD START

See "Colton Head Start/State Preschool"

SUNSHINE EARLY CHILDHOOD CTR

Riverside Unified School Dist
9390 California Ave.
Riverside, CA 92503
(951) 352-8488
(951) 689-6876 FAX

Project M.O.V.E. integrates Head Start with special edu. Walk in or call. FUNDING: State, nonprofit. OFC HRS: M-F 7:30am-4pm. Spanish spoken. Free srvs if children qualify. SERVES: Riverside area.

TEMECULA HEAD START/ST PRESCH

Riverside Co. Office of Education
41951 Moraga Rd., Rm. 61
Temecula, CA 92591
(951) 506-4105
(951) 587-6395 FAX

DIR: Cami Mann. Head Start Prgm for low income children ages 3.9-5 yrs. Classes are 3.5 hrs, 4 days per week. Children with special needs are welcome. Classes include part-day classes M-Th or full-day class M-F. FUNDING: Fed, state. OFC HRS: M-F 8am-4:30pm. Spanish spoken. Free to eligible children.

UNITED METHODIST CHILDREN'S CTR

15150 La Paz Dr.
Victorville 92395
(760) 245-4250

Part or full-day prgm for children ages 6 wks-5 yrs. CAP: 91. Full-day prgm is open from 6am-6pm. FUNDING: Tuition, nonprofit. OFC HRS: M-F 6am-6pm. Spanish spoken. ADM REQ: Must have current immunization. Enrollment fee $60. State subsidized. SERVES: Victor Valley area.

UPLAND HEAD START/STATE P.S.

Preschool Srvs Dept
732 N. 3rd Avenue
Upland, CA 91786
(909) 931-0147
(909) 920-0857 FAX

DIR: Anita Delatorre. Head Start is a federally funded prgm for 3-5 yr old low income and special needs children. Prgms are 3.5 hrs a day, 4 days a week. CAP: 128 children. FUNDING: Nonprofit. OFC HRS: M-F 7:30am-4:30pm. Spanish spoken. Free to eligible children. SERVES: San Bernardino County.

V.I.P. TOTS

Early Intervention and Child Care
41915 E. Acacia Ave.
Hemet, CA 92544
(951) 652-7611
(951) 925-0288 FAX

Preschool and child care facility providing a dev based curriculum to normally developed and special needs children. Early intervention for children with disabilities. Srvs include: edu therapy, parent support, inclusion settings. Serving children in home-based prgms ages birth-3 yrs, center-based prgms ages 18 mos-6 yrs. Child care prgm is for ages 18 mos-5 yrs, including

children with disabilities. FUNDING: Reg Center, school district, CSU, DPSS, fees, nonprofit. OFC HRS: M-F 7am-6pm. Spanish spoken. No charge to parents for special needs prgm. SERVES: Hemet, Temecula, Perris, Lake Elsinore, San Jacinto, Murrieta.

VAN BUREN HEAD START

See also, "Jurupa Unified School Dist"

VICTOR HEADSTART/ST PRESCHOOL

Preschool Srvs Dept
14029 Amargosa Rd., Ste C
Victorville, CA 92392
(760) 245-9147
(760) 245-2054 FAX

DIR: Debra Brewer. Head Start is a federally funded prgm for 3-5 yr old low income & special needs children. Prgms are usually 3.5 hrs, 4 days a week. FUNDING: Federal. OFC HRS: M-F 7am-5pm. Spanish spoken. ADM REQ: Low income. Free to eligible children. SERVES: Victorville.

VILLA DE NINOS

Mexican American Opportunity Foundation
9999 Feron Blvd., Ste B
Rancho Cucamonga, CA 91730
(909) 484-1903
(909) 481-0051 FAX

Licensed bilingual, bicultural preschool for ages 3-5 yrs. FUNDING: Govt. OFC HRS: M-F 7am-5:30pm. Spanish spoken. ADM REQ: Must be toilet-trained. SERVES: Rancho Cucamonga.

WEST RIVERSIDE HEAD START/ST PRESCH

See "Jurupa Unified School Dist"

WESTMINSTER HEAD START

Preschool Srvs Dept
720 N. Sultana Ave.
Ontario, CA 91764
(909) 983-0600
(909) 983-4213 FAX

DIR: Anna Aguirre. Head Start is a federally funded prgm for 3-5 yr old low income and/or special needs children. Prgm is 3.5 hrs, 4 days per week. OFC HRS: M-F 7am-4:30pm. Spanish, Arabic spoken. ADM REQ: Must meet income criteria. Free to eligible children. SERVES: Ontario.

WESTSIDE ANNEX HEAD START

Preschool Srvs Dept
1584 W. Baseline, Ste 107
San Bernardino, CA 92411
(909) 383-3442
(909) 383-1132 FAX

Head Start is a federally funded prgm for low income and/or special needs children ages 3-5 yrs. Prgms are usually full day, 7am-5pm. FUNDING: Federal. OFC HRS: M-F 8am-5pm. Spanish spoken. Free to eligible children. SERVES: San Bernardino County.

WESTSIDE PLAZA HEAD START

Preschool Srvs Dept
1558 W. Baseline, Bldg. F, Ste 101
San Bernardino, CA 92411
(909) 884-6036
(909) 384-0383 FAX

DIR: Victoria Bucchino. Head Start prgm for low income and/or special needs children ages 3.9-5yrs. Most prgms are 3-3.5 hrs, 5 days a week. FUNDING: Federal. OFC HRS: M-F 7am-4:30pm. Spanish spoken. ADM REQ:

Child Care

Must meet age & income requirements. Free to eligible children. SERVES: San Bernardino County.

YMCA/DESERT
Ford School Site
44-210 Warner Trail
Palm Desert, CA 92260
(760) 902-1754

Before & after school child care for grades K-5. FUNDING: Nonprofit, donations. OFC HRS: M-F 7am-6pm. Spanish spoken. SERVES: Palm Desert, Indian Wells.

YMCA/DESERT
Jean Benson Child Care Center
75-433 Orange Blossom Lane
Palm Desert, CA 92211
(760) 836-3336
(760) 836-0096 FAX

Before & after school child care for ages 2.5-5 yrs. FUNDING: Nonprofit, donations. OFC HRS: M-F 7am-6pm. SERVES: Riverside County.

YMCA/DESERT
Family YMCA/Carter YMCA Child Care Ctr
74-251 Hovley Lane
Palm Desert, CA 92260
(760) 346-7171

Before & after school child care for grades K-5, homework & tutorial srvs. Open during summer, Christmas break & spring break. FUNDING: Nonprofit, donations. OFC HRS: M-F 7am-6pm. SERVES: Riverside County.

YMCA/EAST VALLEY
San Bernardino Branch
808 E. 21st Street
San Bernardino, CA 92404
(909) 881-9622
(909) 886-3151 FAX

Active aquatics prgm with swim team. Twinges in the Hinges prgm, aquagym, swim lessons, gymnastics, karate, Itty Bitty Sports, basketball, day camp for off-track elementary. Summer resident camp. Off-site after school care. Walk in or call. ACA accredited. FUNDING: Nonprofit. OFC HRS: M-F 5am-9:30pm; Sat 8am-6pm; Sun 1pm-5pm. Spanish spoken. SERVES: San Bernardino County.

YMCA/INDIO
Doris Mechanick Preschool
44-700 Arabia
Indio, CA 92201
(760) 347-6698
(760) 775-3606 FAX

Two half-day 3-hr prgms for ages 3-5 yrs, 9am-12noon or 1pm-4pm. FUNDING: Nonprofit, donations. OFC HRS: M-F 7:30am-5:30pm. Spanish spoken. SERVES: Coachella Valley.

YMCA/INDIO
Amelia Earheart Elementary
45-250 Dune Palms Rd.
Indio, CA 92201
(760) 902-1746

Before & after school child care for grades 1-7. FUNDING: Nonprofit, donations. OFC HRS: M-F 7am-6pm. SERVES: Indio, La Quinta.

YMCA/JURUPA
Child Care Program
9254 Galena St.
Riverside, CA 92509

(951) 685-5241
(951) 681-7910 FAX

Before & after school child care prgms for grades K-6. Holiday and summer camps. Toddler (ages 18 mos-2 yrs) & preschool children (ages 3-5 yrs) socialization prgm. Fee $365-$390 per month for full-time. Part-time hrs are available. Wide range of recreational activities for all ages including sports for preschool children aimed at "everyone is a winner," called Bitty Sports. Walk-in or call. FUNDING: United Way, nonprofit. OFC HRS: M-F 9am-7pm. Spanish spoken. Fees vary with prgm. Scholarships available for needy children. SERVES: Jurupa & nearby.

YMCA/LA QUINTA
La Quinta YMCA Child Care Center
49-955 Park Ave.
La Quinta, CA 92253
(760) 564-2848
(760) 564-2768 FAX

Before & after school child care for grades K-5. Homework & tutorial srvs, preschool for ages 2.5-5 yrs. FUNDING: Nonprofit. OFC HRS: M-F 7am-6pm. SERVES: Riverside County.

YMCA/LA QUINTA
77-800 Calle Tampico
La Quinta, CA 92253
(760) 902-0752

Sports and fitness programs for youth. Aquatics and senior programs. FUNDING: Nonprofit, donations. SERVES: La Quinta.

YMCA/PALM DESERT
Lincoln Elementary School
74-100 Rutledge Way
Palm Desert, CA 92260
(760) 902-1748

Sports and fitness programs, aquatics. Family nights, programs for seniors. Child care for grades K-12. FUNDING: Nonprofit, donations. OFC HRS: M-F 7am-6pm. SERVES: Palm Desert.

YMCA/REDLANDS
500 E. Citrus Ave.
Redlands, CA 92373
(909) 798-9622
(909) 335-2007 FAX

Youth sports, basketball, aerobics, swimming, fitness centers for men and women, indoor and outdoor pools, camping prgms, roller hockey rink, gymnastics circus, racquetball courts and teen & senior center. Full-day child care at this site, for toddlers through middle school. Prime time afternoon prgm held at 16 elementary school campuses. FUNDING: Nonprofit. OFC HRS: M-F 5am-9:30pm; Sat 8am-6pm; Sun 1pm-8pm. Spanish spoken. SERVES: East Valley.

YMCA/RIVERSIDE/CHILDCARE
4020 Jefferson St.
Riverside, CA 92504
(951) 689-4863
(951) 689-7543 FAX

Nonprofit preschool for children ages 2.5-5 yrs. Extended day prgms for grades K-6 at Moreno Valley, Riverside, Jurupa. Evening care for ages 2-10 yrs at Riverside & Jurupa sites. Weekend care available at Jurupa site. FUNDING: United Way, donations, parent fees. OFC HRS: M-Th 8am-8pm; F 8am-7pm. Spanish

spoken. Sliding fee scale. SERVES: Riverside, Moreno Valley, Jurupa.

YMCA/THE DESERT
Administrative Office
43-930 San Pablo Ave.
Palm Desert, CA 92260
(760) 341-9622
(760) 779-9651 FAX

Before & after school child care for gradesK-5 at seven sites from Rancho Mirage to Indio. Also sport prgms for ages 6-14 yrs. FUNDING: United Way, donations, fees, nonprofit. OFC HRS: M-F 7am-6pm. Spanish spoken. Financial aid available. SERVES: Coachella Valley, East Riverside County.

YMCA/UPLAND
1325 San Bernardino Rd.
Upland, CA 91786-4930
(909) 946-6120

Child care & youth sports prgms. OFC HRS: M-F 8am-5pm. Farsi, Spanish spoken. ADM REQ: Members, ages 2 yrs+. SERVES: Upland.

YUCAIPA HEADSTART/ST PRESCHOOL
Preschool Srvs Dept
12236 California St.
Yucaipa, CA 92399
(909) 797-3585
(909) 797-3877 FAX

Federally funded Head Start prgm for low income & special needs children ages 3-5 yrs. Prgms usually 3.5 hrs a day, 4 days a week. CAP: 128 children in a part-day prgm. FUNDING: Federal. OFC HRS: M-F 7:30am-4:30pm. Spanish spoken. SERVES: Yucaipa.

BEAUTY FOR ASHES WOMEN'S CENTER
Aftercare Program
9791 Arrow Route
Rancho Cucamonga, CA 91730
(909) 477-2781

BFA provides training, education, support and spiritual guidance for life following treatment and/or incarceration. 12-Step prgms, personal development courses, and job training. Volunteer opportunities available. Located at R.C. Family Resource Center. FUNDING: Nonprofit. Spanish spoken. ADM REQ: Adult women ages 18 yrs+, in crisis. SERVES: L.A., Riverside & San Bernardino Counties.

BEHAVIORAL SYSTEMS SOUTHWEST
118 Avenida Victoria
San Clemente, CA 92672
(949) 492-3574
(949) 492-6798 FAX

Residential treatment prgms for offenders released from federal and state prison. Outpatient counseling for individuals convicted of drunk driving. FUNDING: Federal Bureau of Prisons, Calif Dept of Corrections, nonprofit. OFC HRS: M-F 8am-4:30pm. ADM REQ: Approved by fed, state or county for placement. SERVES: So. Calif.

BOYS REPUBLIC
1907 Boys Republic Dr.
Chino Hills, CA 91709
(909) 628-1217
(909) 627-9222 FAX

Residential and day treatment for adjudicated wards or dependents. Residential prgm serves 212 boys and 8 girls, ages 13-18 yrs. Non-residential prgm is co-ed & serves 30 youth. FUNDING: Govt. OFC HRS: M-F 8am-4:30pm. Spanish spoken. ADM REQ: Primarily adjudicated wards or dependents. SERVES: Calif.

BUDDHIST PEACE FELLOWSHIP
Prison Programs
P.O. Box 3470
Berkeley, CA 94703-9906
(510) 655-6169
(510) 655-1369 FAX

Turning Wheel Inside prgm sends the Turning Wheel magazine to inmates for free. The Dharma Companions prgm offers Buddhist books, pamphlets, used magazines, and some tapes for inmates who are considering Buddhism. Dharma Companions also offers a mentoring correspondence prgm for inmates who are practicing Buddhism in prison without a teacher. There may be a waiting list for this service. Dharma Companions can be reached at P.O. Box 762, Cotati, CA 94931. FUNDING: Nonprofit, donations. OFC HRS: M-F 8am-5pm. SERVES: Calif.

CALIF COALITION FOR WOMEN PRISONERS
1540 Market St., Ste 490
San Francisco, CA 94102
(415) 255-7036
(415) 552-3150 FAX

Public edu, info, referral & outreach, newsletter, support for former prisoners, addresses the needs of incarcerated survivors of domestic vi-

olence. Visits women at Central Calif women's facilities. FUNDING: Donations. SERVES: Calif.

CALIF DEPT CORRECTIONS
Parole & Community Srvs Division
79-687 Country Club Dr., Ste 101
Bermuda Dunes, CA 92201
(760) 772-3157
(760) 772-3165 FAX

Protection for the community by monitoring parolees' behavior. Assists those parolees who are attempting to make a successful adjustment to the community and remove those parolees from the community who present a danger or a threat to the public. OFC HRS: M-F 8am-5pm. Spanish spoken. SERVES: Bermuda Dunes.

CALIF DEPT CORRECTIONS
Parole & Community Srvs Division
279 S. Waterman Ave., Ste F
El Centro, CA 92243
(760) 352-7524
(760) 352-8854 FAX

Assist and referrals to parolees released from state prison. Assists parolees and their families in locating social srvs. OFC HRS: M-F 8am-5pm. SERVES: Calif.

CALIF DEPT CORRECTIONS
Adult Parolee Operations
8621 Juniper Ave., Ste 106
Fontana, CA 92335
(909) 357-1153
(909) 357-1159 FAX

Protection for the community by monitoring parolees' behavior. Assists parolees who are attempting to make a successful adjustment to the community and removes parolees from the community who present a danger or a threat to the public. OFC HRS: M-F 8am-5pm. Spanish spoken. ASL available. SERVES: Fontana, Rialto, Loma Linda.

CALIF DEPT CORRECTIONS
Parole & Community Srvs Division
1511 E. Holt Blvd.
Ontario, CA 91761
(909) 983-0692
(909) 984-1502 FAX

Assist and referrals to parolees released from state prison. Assists parolees and their families in locating social srvs. OFC HRS: M-F 8am-5pm. SERVES: Ontario.

CALIF DEPT CORRECTIONS
Parole & Community Srvs Division
1777 Atlanta Ave., Ste G-3
Riverside, CA 92507
(951) 782-4479
(951) 782-4491 FAX

Links ex-offenders with community resources for food, clothing, shelter, edu, health and therapy. Funds can be provided for emerg shelter, based on availability. This division serves in a law enforcement capacity to determine if conditions of parole are met through supervision and assessment. Clients are limited to adult parolees/releasees from state correctional facilities. Walk in. Supervision of parolees. Assists with food, shelter & transportation. FUNDING:

State. OFC HRS: M-F 8am-5pm. ADM REQ: Parolees or releasees from state correctional institutions or those residing in community correctional facilities. SERVES: Riverside County.

CALIF DEPT CORRECTIONS
Parole & Community Srvs Division
303 W. 5th Street
San Bernardino, CA 92401
(909) 806-3516
(909) 384-7403 FAX

Links ex-offenders with community resources for food, clothing, shelter, edu, health and therapy. Funds can be provided for emerg shelter, food and transportation, based on availability. This division serves in a law enforcement capacity to determine if conditions of parole are met through supervision and assessment. Clientele is limited to adult parolees & releasees from state correctional institutions or those residing in community correctional facilities. OFC HRS: M-F 8am-5pm. SERVES: Bryn Mawr, Bloomington, Colton, Grand Terrace, Loma Linda, and Rialto.

CALIF DEPT CORRECTIONS
Dept of Adult Parole Operations
14040 Park Ave.
Victorville, CA 92392
(760) 241-3744
(760) 241-0443 FAX

Protection for the community by monitoring parolees' behavior. Assist parolees who are attempting to make a successful adjustment to the community and remove parolees from the community who represent a danger or a threat to the public. Also assists parolees and their families in locating social srvs. OFC HRS: M-F 8am-5pm. SERVES: Victor Valley to Needles.

CALIF DEPT OF CORRECTIONS
Visitor Infoline
P.O. Box 1841
5th and Western
Norco, CA 92860
(800) 374-8474

Hospitality for visitors, emerg help, clothing exchange, inmate dress out, inmate notary, transportation, children's prgm, motel reservations, transportation discount with Greyhound. FUNDING: Centerforce, C.N., United Way, nonprofit. OFC HRS: F 1pm-8pm; Sat, Sun 8am-3pm. Some Spanish spoken. ADM REQ: Visitor to state institution. Accepts donations. SERVES: Calif.

CALIF DEPT OF CORRECTIONS
Division of Juvenile Justice
Executive Office
4241 Williamsbourgh Dr., Ste 201
Sacramento, CA 95823
(916) 262-1470
(916) 262-1767 FAX

Works with law enforcement, the courts, probation and any other agencies providing srvs to youth. Provides training and treatment srvs to youth offenders. FUNDING: Govt. OFC HRS: M-F 7:30am-4:30pm. ADM REQ: Prison prgm. SERVES: Calif.

CALIF DEPT OF CORRECTIONS/REHAB
Adelanto Comm Correctional Facility

10450 Rancho Rd.
Adelanto, CA 92301
(760) 246-3328
(760) 246-6420 FAX

Men's correctional facility. FUNDING: Govt. OFC HRS: M-F 8am-5pm. Spanish spoken. SERVES: Calif.

CALIF INSTITUTION FOR MEN
P.O. Box 128
14901 S. Central Ave.
Chino, CA 91710
(909) 597-1821
(909) 597-4983 FAX

Prison for about 6,000 male felons with 4 physically separated facilities including 3 reception units. Vocational training prgms and a full array of academic prgms. FUNDING: Govt. SERVES: Calif.

CALIF INSTITUTION FOR WOMEN
P.O. Box 6000
16756 Chino-Corona Rd.
Corona, CA 92880-9508
(909) 597-1771
(909) 606-4902 FAX

State prison for women. FUNDING: Govt. OFC HRS: M-F 8am-4:30pm. SERVES: Calif.

CALIF REHABILITATION CENTER
Calif Dept of Corrections
P.O. Box 1841
5th & Western
Norco, CA 92860
(951) 737-2683
(951) 273-2310 FAX

State prgm for inmates who are addicted to drugs. FUNDING: Govt. OFC HRS: M-F 7am-4:30pm. Spanish spoken. ADM REQ: Court referrals only. SERVES: Calif.

CALIF YOUTH AUTHORITY
See "Division of Juvenile Justice"

CALIFORNIA PRISON FOCUS
1904 Franklin St., Ste 507
Oakland, CA 94612
(510) 836-7222
(510) 836-7333 FAX

Dignity campaign working to ensure the defense of the rights of female prisoners. Advocacy and research. Publishes "Prison Focus" newsletter by and for prisoners and their families. Newsletter is distributed free to SHU prisoners. Info and referrals given to prisoners. Volunteers welcome. Visit (www.prisons.org). FUNDING: Nonprofit., donations. OFC HRS: M-F 8am-5pm. Fee for newsletter to prisoners not in SHU. SERVES: California.

CAMEO HOUSE
Transitional Housing for Women/Children
424 Guerrero St.
San Francisco, CA 94110
(415) 703-0600
(415) 703-0550 FAX

Srvs provided to offenders and ex-offenders. Transitional housing, substance abuse counseling, rehab, job dev & placement, social srvs, life skills training. Also has opportunities for volunteers and interns. FUNDING: Nonprofit, donations, fndns. OFC HRS: 9am-5pm. ADM REQ: Single women in or out of the Calif Prison System; may have two children up to age 6 yrs. SERVES: Calif.

CATHOLIC CHARITIES/COMMUNITY SRVS
Administration
1450 North D Street
San Bernardino, CA 92405
(909) 388-1239
(909) 384-1130 FAX

Psychological counseling for individuals & family, case mgmt, emerg food, diapers, clothing, furniture (when available), utility assist, holiday baskets, transportation, advocacy, HIV/AIDS srvs, info & referrals. Emerg housing for needy transients with pre-arranged motel accommodations (as funds allow). Refugee & immigration srvs, parolee reintegration. FUNDING: Donations, nonprofit. OFC HRS: M-F 8:30am-4:30pm. Spanish, Chinese, Filipino, Vietnamese, Russian spoken. Sliding fee scale. SERVES: San Bernardino & Riverside Counties.

CENTER FOR CRIMINALITY & ADDICTION RESEARCH, TRAINING
UCSD School of Medicine
5060 Shoreham Pl., Mail Code 0980, Ste 200
San Diego, CA 92122
(858) 334-4600
(858) 334-4601 FAX

University of Calif, San Diego School of Medicine facilitates a variety of science-based edu, training & networking events annually addressing substance abuse prevention, treatment & publishing related materials. The Criminal Justice Institute provides those involved in substance abuse treatment with the most up-to-date knowledge & skills. The purpose is to enhance the knowledge, skills, & attitudes of those engaged (or preparing to be) in the delivery of treatment & recovery srvs, or for those performing health & social srvs to patients & clients who may be troubled by alcohol & other drug use. FUNDING: Nonprofit, grants. SERVES: Calif.

CENTERFORCE
2955 Kerner Blvd., 2nd Fl.
San Rafael, CA 94901
(415) 456-9980
(415) 456-2146 FAX

Visitor srvs provided at various county jails, state prisons & federal facilities. Comprehensive edu & support to those who are incarcerated & their families. Children & family srvs, prisoner srvs, transitional srvs, info srvs. Fresno office (559) 276-1656. FUNDING: Calif Dept of Corrections contracts. OFC HRS: M-F 9am-5pm. SERVES: Calif.

CLEANSLATE, INC.
Gang Recovery Group & Tattoo Removal
12401 Slauson Ave., Ste G
Whittier, CA 90606
(562) 945-9111

CleanSlate is a gang violence recovery, rage resolution and tattoo removal prgm that helps to erase the visible signs of gang involvement while working with gang members to reconnect with their emotions. Individual counselors give one-on-one support. Gang recovery group every F 7:30pm-9pm at the So. Calif. Counseling Ctr. 5615 W. Pico Blvd., L.A. 90019. No appt needed for F groups. Tattoo removal prgm is at different locations one Sat a month. Address above is mailing address only. Visit (www.cleanslatela.org) for tattoo removal

dates. FUNDING: Nonprofit. Spanish spoken. Groups $5 donation. SERVES: So. Calif.

COALINGA STATE HOSPITAL
P.O. Box 5000
24511 W. Jayne Ave.
Coalinga, CA 93210-5000
(559) 935-4300

Treatment facility for sexually violent predators. Behavioral & relapse prevention training. Substance abuse treatment, vocational training, pharmacological treatments, surveillance upon discharge. TTY (559) 935-7120. FUNDING: Calif Dept of Mental Health. OFC HRS: M-F 8am-5pm. SERVES: Calif.

CROSSROADS, INC.
Re-Entry Prgms
P.O. Box 15
Claremont, CA 91711
(909) 626-7847
(909) 626-7867 FAX

Re-entry home for women on parole in Calif. Provides room and board, counseling, and support to women as they re-establish themselves within the community. All women participate in a structured prgm, attend 12-Step meetings in the community & work. Crossroads works to empower women. Info & referral srvs for anyone. Substance abuse prgm. Also 12-bed residential home. State ID: 190205AN/BN. FUNDING: Govt contract, grants, donations, nonprofit. OFC HRS: M-F 8am-5pm. ADM REQ: Women on parole, ages 18 yrs+. SERVES: Calif.

DELANCEY STREET FOUNDATION
600 Embarcadero
San Francisco, CA 94107
(415) 512-5104
(415) 512-5141 FAX

Rehab prgm provides assist to ex-felons, substance abusers, gang members, perpetrators, and victims of abuse to assist them with skills to rebuild their lives. Literacy, homeless issues, anger mgmt, edu & voc mentoring. Does not accept people with mental disorders, people on medication or with disabilities, arsonists, or sex offenders. FUNDING: Nonprofit, donations. OFC HRS: 24/7. ADM REQ: Ages 18 yrs+. Free srvs. SERVES: Calif.

DIVISION OF JUVENILE JUSTICE
Herman G. Stark Youth Correctional Fac
15180 S. Euclid Ave.
Chino, CA 91710-9148
(909) 606-5000
(909) 606-5001 FAX

1500-bed state institution for males ages 18-25yrs committed by the courts. 30 vocational trades, remedial classes, high school classes & a college prgm. Specialized counseling srvs dealing with substance abuse and aggressive behavior. OFC HRS: 24 hrs. SERVES: Calif.

DIVISION OF JUVENILE JUSTICE
Juvenile Parole Regional Office
741 Glenvia St., 2nd Fl.
Glendale, CA 91206
(818) 543-4713
(818) 543-4725 FAX

Parole supervision srvs & resources for offenders released from Youth Authority correctional facilities. Liaison srvs to courts, probation & law enforcement agencies. Victim srvs referrals &

comm srvs prgm referrals. FUNDING: Govt. OFC HRS: M-F 8am-5pm. Spanish spoken. SERVES: So. Calif.

DIVISION OF JUVENILE JUSTICE
Inland Parole Unit
5700 Division St., 2nd Fl.
Riverside, CA 92506
(951) 782-3214
(951) 782-4918 FAX

Parole supervision and employment referrals for parolees only. FUNDING: Govt. OFC HRS: M-F 8am-5pm. ADM REQ: Court order. SERVES: Riverside & San Bernardino Counties.

FRIENDS OUTSIDE/ESPERANZA VISITOR
Chuckawalla Valley State Prison
P.O. Box 2289
Blythe, CA 92226
(760) 922-5300
(760) 922-6855 FAX

Hospitality srvs for families of prisoners coming for prison visits, including info, clothing, food, child care, transportation. Walk in. FUNDING: State, nonprofit. OFC HRS: M, Tu, Th, F 8am-1pm; Sat, Sun 8am-4pm. Spanish spoken. ADM REQ: Family of prisoner at Chuckawalla State Prison. Free srvs. SERVES: Calif.

FRIENDS OUTSIDE/FRONTERA
Casa Frontera/Calif Inst for Women
12345 Mountain Ave., Ste N-234
Chino, CA 91710
(909) 597-0234

Supportive srvs offered to family members of women at the Calif Institution for Women. Srvs may include transportation and emerg assist, etc. FUNDING: Nonprofit. OFC HRS: Sat 8am-12noon; Sun 12:30pm-8pm. SERVES: Calif.

FRIENDS OUTSIDE/SAN BRDO CO.
Calif Institution for Men
P.O. Box 393
Chino, CA 91710
(909) 597-5428
(909) 597-6989 FAX

Supportive srvs to family members of inmates (visitor center located at CIM). Info & referral, limited transportation, drop-in emerg child care. 24-hr answering machine. Referrals to visitor centers serving prisons in Calif. FUNDING: Donations, nonprofit. OFC HRS: Sat, Sun 8am-3:30pm. Free srvs. SERVES: Calif.

GATEWAYS COMM CORRECTIONS CTR
1801 Lakeshore Ave.
Los Angeles, CA 90026
(323) 644-2020
(323) 644-2044 FAX

Court-mandated residential and outpatient treatment and supervision srvs for adult men and women, ages 18-59 yrs, who are released from federal prison, are under U.S. probation or parole supervision, or are directly committed to the prgm through U.S. and L.A. County courts. Also residential treatment to CONREP patients. FUNDING: Nonprofit. Spanish spoken. ADM REQ: Must be referred by the court. SERVES: U.S.A.

GET ON THE BUS
5411 Camelia Ave.
North Hollywood, CA 91601
(818) 980-7714

(818) 980-7702 FAX

Transportation, counseling and support srvs for children visiting their mothers and/or fathers incarcerated in the Calif prison system. For Northern Calif, call (925) 335-9314; central Calif, call (805) 544-2357 ext. 32. FUNDING: Nonprofit. OFC HRS: M-F 9am-5pm. ADM REQ: Must sign up. Free srvs. SERVES: Calif.

HACIENDA CHRISTIAN LIFE CAMPUS
God's Helping Hand
1040 Tepee Lane
Perris, CA 92570
(951) 657-3041
(951) 657-0426 FAX

Christian residential substance abuse prgm. Men's discipleship prgm for drug addicts, alcoholics & homeless men coming out of prison. Vocational training, anger mgmt, domestic violence counseling. FUNDING: Nonprofit. OFC HRS: M-F 9am-5pm. ADM REQ: One year prgm. Phone for intake interview. Prgm does not accept those who have been convicted of a sex crime or arson. Cannot be on any psych medication. Non-smoking facility. Free srvs. SERVES: Riverside County.

HANDS ON INLAND EMPIRE
9624 Hermosa Ave.
Rancho Cucamonga, CA 91730
(909) 980-2857
(909) 980-2957 FAX

The Alternative Sentencing Prgm acts as the referral agency for adult and juvenile residents of San Bernardino Co. who are assigned community srv work by the court or probation dept. The prgm provides referral follow-up, monitoring & reports on individuals referred to complete community srv hours. FUNDING: Fees. OFC HRS: M-F 8am-4pm. Spanish spoken. Prgm fee of $75 is charged for each referral payable by money order only. SERVES: San Bernardino County.

HIGHLANDER CHILDREN'S SRVS
Residential Treatment Program
10001 County Farm Rd.
Riverside, CA 92503
(951) 343-2536
(951) 729-3309 FAX

30-bed residential treatment prgm for sex offenders with on-site school. Prgm serves adjudicated males only, ages 13-18 yrs. Offers AA, NA, Pathways prgm, licensed therapist. FUNDING: Nonprofit. OFC HRS: M-F 8am-4:30pm, 24-hr care. Spanish spoken. SERVES: Riverside, Orange, San Diego, San Bernardino & L.A. Counties.

INLAND VLY DRUG/ALCOHOL RECOVERY
Administration/Residential
916 N. Mountain Ave., Ste A
Upland, CA 91786
(909) 932-1069
(909) 932-1087 FAX

Residential substance abuse treatment for single or parenting adults. Outpatient and court-referred DUI, anger mgmt srvs, domestic violence batterer's treatment, parent project classes. Sub-acute detox prgm also available. State ID: 360001BN. FUNDING: CalWORKs, CPS, PSN, SASCA, county, resident fees, nonprofit. OFC HRS: M-F 8am-5pm; 24-hr facility. Spanish spoken. Accepts most insurance and pvt pay.

Sliding fee scale. SERVES: L.A., Riverside & San Bernardino Counties.

JUVENILE JUSTICE CLEARINGHOUSE
Natl Criminal Justice Reference Srvs
P.O. Box 6000
Rockville, MD 20849-6000
(800) 851-3420
(301) 519-5212 FAX

A link between the Office of Juvenile Justice and Delinquency Prev (OJJDP) and the community at-large interested in juvenile justice, delinquency prev and missing and exploited children. The clearinghouse offers publications, references and referrals, conference support and attendance, online resources and other outreach activities. TDD (877) 712-9279 or (301) 712-9279. FUNDING: Govt. SERVES: U.S.A. & Internatl.

KAIROS PRISON MINISTRY & KAIROS OUTSIDE
Palm Desert, CA 92211
(760) 772-0330

Faith-based outreach program for incarcerated men and women throughout the world. 3 open and running locations in the area. Contact Harry for more info. Support for women with incarcerated loved ones. Contact Audrey for more info. SERVES: Riverside County, Coachella Valley.

LAWS SUPPORT CENTER
Outpatient Alcohol & Drug Treatment Prgm
2707 W. 54th Street
Los Angeles, CA 90043
(323) 294-5204
(323) 294-4758 FAX

Six-month to one-year outpatient drug-free prgm. Edu classes, individual, group and family counseling. Based on 12-Step philosophy. Individuals are presented with the knowledge and skills necessary for their recovery. Their family and significant others are given info and guidance to understand and support continued recovery. FUNDING: Nonprofit. OFC HRS: M-F 9am-6pm. ADM REQ: Ages 18 yrs+. Referrals from Dept of Corrections, Dept of Health Srvs, and other community organizations. Free srvs for those with Medi-Cal. SERVES: L.A. & San Bernardino Counties.

M-2 MATCH-TWO PRISONER OUTREACH
Southern Regional Office
P.O. Box 1350
15180 Euclid Ave.
Chino, CA 91710
(909) 606-5036
(909) 597-4824 FAX

Matches community volunteer mentors for supportive one-to-one visitation of incarcerated men, women and youth in Calif & Utah state prisons who receive few or no visits. Assists with basic needs and referrals. Wait: 30-60 days. FUNDING: State, donations, nonprofit. OFC HRS: M-F 8:30am-5:30pm. ADM REQ: Person receiving no visits while incarcerated. Free srvs. SERVES: Calif & Utah.

PATH OF LIFE MINISTRIES
Men's Recovery Home
P.O. Box 1445
Riverside, CA 92501
(951) 786-9048
(951) 786-9049 FAX

Christian residential prgm addressing the needs of dysfunction, addiction and incarceration by means of a holistic approach to rebuilding lives. Goal is to help individuals identify the root cause of their problem, train in life values, both practically and spiritually and to give necessary tools to obtain and maintain gainful employment. Homeless food prgm and three homeless centers. FUNDING: Donations, nonprofit. OFC HRS: M-F 9am-6pm. Spanish spoken. ADM REQ: One year prgm. SERVES: Riverside County.

PATTON STATE HOSPITAL
3102 E. Highland Ave.
Patton, CA 92369-0001
(909) 425-7000
(909) 425-7520 FAX

Inpatient forensic psychiatric hospital which srvs long-term committed (court-committed under the Penal Code) mentally disordered persons. Chemical dependency, geriatric unit, voluntary and involuntary placement. FUNDING: Govt. OFC HRS: 24 hrs, 7 days. Spanish spoken. ADM REQ: Must be ordered by Superior Court. Accepts insurance, Medicare, Medi-Cal. SERVES: Calif.

PRISON FELLOWSHIP MINISTRIES
P.O. Box 452152
Los Angeles, CA 90045
(800) 245-9998
(310) 671-5463
(310) 671-3015 FAX

Prison ministry sponsored by a large number of local churches. Ministry to inmates, ex-offenders and their families by working with volunteers from local churches. Trains volunteers from churches to conduct in-prison Bible studies and seminars. No direct srvs from this office, which works with churches from Mojave to San Diego. Key goal is to provide effective aftercare and family ministry. FUNDING: Donations, nonprofit. OFC HRS: M-F 8am-4pm. Free srvs. SERVES: So. Calif.

RIVERSIDE CO. JAIL
Robert Presley Detention Center
P.O. Box 710
4000 Orange St.
Riverside, CA 92501
(951) 955-4500

Visiting appointments are scheduled daily from 9am-5pm by calling (951) 341-8888. SERVES: Riverside County.

RIVERSIDE CO. MENTAL HEALTH
Mental Health Detention Srvs
4275 Lemon St., Ste 207
Riverside, CA 92501
(951) 955-8540
(951) 955-8542 FAX

Psychiatric eval, medication, individual counseling for clients incarcerated in Riverside County Jail and post-release planning. OFC HRS: 24 hrs. Language line available. SERVES: Riverside County.

RIVERSIDE CO. OFFICE/EDUCATION
Alternative Education
P.O. Box 868
3939 13th Street
Riverside, CA 92502-0868
(951) 826-6320
(951) 826-6906 FAX

OFC HRS: M-F 8am-5pm. SERVES: Riverside, Hemet, Murietta, Moreno Valley, Banning, Indio, Blythe, Temecula, Perris.

RIVERSIDE CO. PROBATION DEPT
135 N. Alessandro
Banning, CA 92220
(951) 922-7200
(951) 922-7210 FAX

Supervises adult & juvenile probationers. OFC HRS: M-F 8am-5pm. SERVES: Beaumont, Banning, Cabazon, Calimesa, Cherry Valley, Poppet Flats & Whitewater.

RIVERSIDE CO. PROBATION DEPT
240 N. Broadway St.
Blythe, CA 92225
(760) 921-5860
(760) 921-5886 FAX

Supervision of adult & juvenile probationers and court investigative reports. Walk in. OFC HRS: M-F 8am-5pm. ADM REQ: Court order. SERVES: Blythe, Ripley, Desert Center.

RIVERSIDE CO. PROBATION DEPT
505 S. Buena Vista Ave., Ste 102
Corona, CA 92882
(951) 272-5671
(951) 272-5687 FAX

This office is under the supervision of the Juvenile Probation Director. Serves juvenile and adult probationers in the Corona area through investigations, reports to the courts and supervision of clients. Wait: 1-2 weeks. OFC HRS: M-F 8am-5pm. Spanish spoken. ADM REQ: Court referral. SERVES: Corona.

RIVERSIDE CO. PROBATION DEPT
47-940 Arabia
Indio, CA 92201
(760) 863-8221
(760) 863-8916 FAX

Juvenile and adult probation srvs. Wait: 2 weeks+. Srvs are subject to court-ordered fees. OFC HRS: M-F 8am-5pm. Spanish spoken. ADM REQ: Court-referrals. SERVES: East Riverside County, Palm Springs to Colorado River.

RIVERSIDE CO. PROBATION DEPT
Indio Juvenile Hall
47665 Oasis St.
Indio, CA 92201-6950
(760) 863-7600
(760) 863-7615 FAX

OFC HRS: M-F 8am-5pm. 24-hr facility SERVES: Indio.

RIVERSIDE CO. PROBATION DEPT
Southwest Juvenile Hall
30755-C Auld Rd.
Murrieta, CA 92563-2599
(951) 600-6750
(951) 600-6767 FAX

OFC HRS: M-F 8am-5pm. SERVES: Murrieta.

RIVERSIDE CO. PROBATION DEPT
3255 E. Tahquitz Canyon Way, Ste 101
Palm Springs, CA 92262
(760) 778-2120
(760) 778-2140 FAX

Supervision of juvenile & adult offenders. OFC HRS: M-F 8am-5pm. Spanish spoken. ADM REQ: Referrals by the court. Free srvs. SERVES: Cathedral City, Rancho Mirage, Desert Hot Springs, Palm Desert, Palm Springs & Thousand Palms.

RIVERSIDE CO. PROBATION DEPT
P.O. Box 219
2560 N. Perris Blvd., Bldg. N1

Perris, CA 92572
(951) 443-2250
(951) 443-2255 FAX

OFC HRS: M-F 8am-5pm. SERVES: Perris.

RIVERSIDE CO. PROBATION DEPT
Juvenile Hall
3933 Harrison St.
Riverside, CA 92503-3523
(951) 358-4200
(951) 358-4213 FAX

OFC HRS: M-F 8am-5pm; 24- hr srvs. Spanish spoken. SERVES: Riverside County.

RIVERSIDE CO. PROBATION DEPT
Juvenile Division
9889 County Farm Rd.
Riverside, CA 92503-3504
(951) 358-4310
(951) 358-4353 FAX

Intake, court, filing of petitions, probation supervision, informal probation, civil investigations for court, marriage consent, court-ordered placement srvs. Wait: 2-3 weeks. OFC HRS: M-F 8am-5pm. Spanish spoken. ASL available. ADM REQ: Court referrals only. SERVES: Riverside Metro, Moreno Valley, Norco, Corona, Perris.

RIVERSIDE CO. PROBATION DEPT
Admin Office
3960 Orange St., Ste 600
Riverside, CA 92501
(951) 955-2830
(951) 955-2843 FAX

OFC HRS: M-F 8am-5pm. Spanish spoken. SERVES: Riverside County.

RIVERSIDE CO. PROBATION DEPT
Youth Accountability Board
4168 12th Street
Riverside, CA 92501
(951) 275-8783
(951) 275-8784 FAX

Mentoring prgm is one of several youth prgms available. Team mentoring and one-to-one. OFC HRS: M-F 8am-5pm. ADM REQ: At-risk youth, and 1st time offenders. SERVES: Riverside County.

RIVERSIDE CO. PROBATION DEPT
Adult Office
P.O. Box 1086
3021 Franklin St.
Riverside, CA 92501
(951) 358-7500
(951) 358-7585 FAX

OFC HRS: M-F 8am-5pm. SERVES: Riverside County.

RIVERSIDE CO. PROBATION DEPT
San Jacinto Probation Office
1330 S. State St., Ste A
San Jacinto, CA 92583
(951) 487-2650
(951) 487-2660 FAX

Supervision of juvenile & adult probationers in the greater Hemet, San Jacinto area. OFC HRS: M-F 8am-5pm. Spanish, Tagalog, Japanese, Guamanian spoken. ADM REQ: Court referral. SERVES: Mountain Center, Garner Valley, Aguanga, Anza, Sage, Idyllwild, Pine Cove, Hemet, Green Acre, Homeland.

RIVERSIDE CO. PROBATION DEPT
Southwest Services Division

41002 County Center Dr., Bldg. A 225, Rm. 42
Temecula, CA 92591-2037
(951) 600-6282
(951) 600-6280 FAX

OFC HRS: M-F 8am-5pm. SERVES: Perris, Murrieta, Temecula, Lake Elsinore, Menifee, Canyon Lake, Romoland, Homeland, Sun City, Quail Valley, Lakeview and Nuevo.

SAN BERNARDINO CO. BEHAV HEALTH
Supervised Treatment After Release
1330 E. Cooley Dr.
Colton, CA 92324
(909) 423-0750
(909) 423-0760 FAX

Mental health referrals are usually given to inmates while in a county detention center. Case mgmt, residential placement, drug & alcohol treatment & periodic court reviews. Intake while in jail. FUNDING: County. OFC HRS: M-F 8am-5pm. ADM REQ: Court referrals only. SERVES: Bloomington, Colton, Fontana, Grand Terrace, Loma Linda, Redlands, Rialto, San Bernardino.

SAN BERNARDINO CO. BEHAV HEALTH
9478 Etiwanda Ave.
Rancho Cucamonga, CA 91739
(909) 463-7624
(909) 463-7625 FAX

Juvenile eval & treatment srvs. Counseling srvs for minors in West Valley Juvenile Hall. Screening, assessment, brief psychotherapy, crisis intervention, medications, aftercare planning & referral. FUNDING: County. OFC HRS: M-F 8am-5pm. Spanish spoken. SERVES: San Bernardino County.

SAN BERNARDINO CO. BEHAV HEALTH
Jail Services
9500 Etiwanda Ave.
Rancho Cucamonga, CA 91739
(909) 463-5234

Mental health srvs provided to incarcerated persons in San Bernardino Co. detention facilities. Some therapy, case mgmt, medication support, crisis intervention & aftercare referrals for inmates awaiting trial at West Valley Detention or serving sentence at Glen Helen Rehab Center. FUNDING: County. OFC HRS: M-F 8am-5pm. Spanish, Mandarin spoken. ADM REQ: Ages 18 yrs+. SERVES: San Bernardino County.

SAN BERNARDINO CO. PROBATION DEPT
Regional Youth Educational Facility
900 E. Gilbert St.
San Bernardino, CA 92415-0940
(909) 387-7359
(909) 387-7364 FAX

40-bed treatment prgm for male & female "602" offenders ages 16-18 yrs (6-9 month residential prgm) and substance abuse prgm. Wait: 30 days. Kuiper Youth Ctr for Girls facility is now served at this location. Center for girls (909) 387-0471; center for boys (909) 387-6965. FUNDING: Govt. OFC HRS: M-F 8am-5pm. Spanish spoken. ADM REQ: Referral by court and/or probation officer. Sliding fee scale based on ability to pay. SERVES: San Bernardino, Riverside Counties.

SAN BERNARDINO CO. PROBATION DEPT
Psychiatry Dept.
900 E. Gilbert St.
San Bernardino, CA 92415

(909) 387-6940
(909) 387-7087 FAX

Psychological srvs for high-risk offenders. Specialty is juvenile sex offenders. Assessment of biochemical and mental toxics. Srvs available to those in juvenile hall and those referred out-of-custody. FUNDING: Govt. OFC HRS: M-F 8am-5pm. Nursing 24 hrs except for 3 days a week.

SAN BERNARDINO CO. PROBATION DEPT
Central Adult Division
401 N. Arrowhead Ave.
San Bernardino, CA 92415
(909) 386-1810
(909) 387-4956 FAX

OFC HRS: M-F 8am-5pm. SERVES: San Bernardino County.

SAN BERNARDINO CO. PROBATION DEPT
Central Juvenile Division
150 W. 5th Street
San Bernardino, CA 92415
(909) 383-2700
(909) 383-2936 FAX

OFC HRS: M-F 8am-5pm. Spanish, Tagalog spoken. SERVES: San Bernardino County.

SEXAHOLICS ANONYMOUS (S.A.)
Central Office
P.O. Box 3565
Brentwood, TN 37024-3565
(615) 370-6062
(866) 424-8777
(615) 370-0882 FAX

12-Step recovery prgm for those who want to stop sexually self-destructive thinking and behavior. This prgm is also available to sexaholics in correctional institutions (literature srv, sponsor-by-mail srvs where inmates are linked with members outside who can help them work the 12-Step prgm, support for starting SA meetings at the prisons, connection srv that helps parolees find the nearest SA contact). FUNDING: Nonprofit. OFC HRS: M-F 9am-5pm. SERVES: U.S.A.

SMITH CORRECTIONAL FACILITY
Programs Unit
1627 S. Hargrave
Banning, CA 92220
(951) 922-7300
(951) 922-7310 FAX

Inmate prgms unit structured to prepare inmates for their return to society by providing edu and counseling srvs. OFC HRS: M-F 8am-5pm. ADM REQ: County inmates. Free srvs. SERVES: Riverside County.

THE GOODEN CENTER
Formerly Bishop Gooden Home
191 N. El Molino Ave.
Pasadena, CA 91101
(626) 356-0078
(800) 931-9884
(626) 795-2844 FAX

Licensed and C.A.R.F. accredited drug and alcohol treatment prgm for men offering residential day treatment and IOP levels of care. Sober living also available. FUNDING: Donations, grants, client fees, nonprofit. OFC HRS: M-F 8am-7pm. ADM REQ: Men ages 18 yrs+. Must interview and be sober. Financial assist available. Insurance friendly. 3 partial scholarships available for those in need. SERVES: So. Calif.

TWIN PINES RANCH
Riverside Co. Probation Dept
49500 Twin Pine Ranch Rd.
Banning, CA 92220-9681
(951) 849-4131
(951) 849-2951 FAX

24-hr residential treatment prgm for delinquent male wards of the court ages 15-18 yrs. Capacity for 70 wards. Young men participate in aftercare probation supervision following graduation from the Ranch. Accredited high school. Individual and group drug counseling. Individual and group counseling for gang members. FUNDING: County. OFC HRS: M-F 7am-3pm vocational instruction. ADM REQ: Male, wards of juvenile court, court-ordered placement. Fees based on ability to pay. SERVES: Riverside & partial San Bernardino Counties.

U.S. PROBATION/PAROLE SERVICE
312 N. Spring St., Ste 600
Los Angeles, CA 90012
(213) 894-3600
(213) 894-3627 FAX

Presentencing investigations, probation & parole. OFC HRS: M-F 8am-4:30pm. Spanish spoken. SERVES: So. Calif.

U.S. PROBATION/PAROLE SERVICE
290 North D Street, Ste 700
San Bernardino, CA 92401
(909) 383-5521
(909) 383-5602 FAX

Probation & parole srvs for U.S. Courts and U.S. Parole Commission. OFC HRS: M-F 8am-4:30pm. Spanish spoken. SERVES: San Bernardino & Riverside Counties.

VAN HORN YOUTH CENTER (VHYC)
Riverside Co. Probation Dept
10000 County Farm Rd.
Riverside, CA 92503-3508
(951) 358-4400
(951) 358-4420 FAX

24-hr residential boot camp treatment center for boys (ages 13-16 yrs) and girls (ages 13-18 yrs) who are wards of the court. Call for info. FUNDING: Govt. OFC HRS: M-F 8am-4pm. Spanish spoken. ADM REQ: Court-ordered placements only. Youth must be under age 18 yrs. SERVES: Riverside County.

VICTORY OUTREACH/INTERNATL
Admin Office
P.O. Box 3760
250 W. Arrow Hwy.
San Dimas, CA 91773
(909) 599-4437
(909) 599-6244 FAX

Men and women are given spiritual guidance and are encouraged to stay involved with various church-related activities until they are able to completely re-enter mainstream society. Victory Outreach sponsors 328 prgms in the U.S. and other countries including: prison and jail ministry (counseling and after release placement), drug and assist prgms. Sponsors several 24-hr residential prgms. FUNDING: Donations, nonprofit. OFC HRS: M-F 9am-5pm. SERVES: U.S.A.

VOLUNTEER CENTER/RIVERSIDE CO.
Alternative Sentencing
P.O. Box 5376
2060 University Ave., Ste 212

Riverside, CA 92507
(951) 329-4709

Placement for people assigned community srv hours by the courts. Monitoring srv for cases on court probation that require monitoring, i.e. inter-lock ignition device. Anger mgmt prgm, youth drunk driving prgm, and victim impact prgm for DUI. FUNDING: United Way. OFC HRS: M-F 8am-5pm. Spanish translation service available. Free srvs. SERVES: Riverside County.

VOLUNTEER CENTER/VICTOR VALLEY

16692 Mojave Dr., Ste A
Victorville, CA 92392
(760) 245-8592
(760) 243-9646
(760) 243-4762 FAX

Recruits community members interested in giving their time and talent and then refers them to over 50 nonprofit agencies that have specific volunteer needs. Court referral prgm an alternative prgm for court clients, in lieu of fines or jail time. Clients can serve community volunteer hours. Works with the courts of San Bernardino. Community Srvs Network; monthly meeting with nonprofit agencies, churches, schools to offer support, info & opportunity to network. Human Race is annual walk-a-thon to raise money for agencies. FUNDING: Nonprofit. OFC HRS: M-Th 9am-3pm. Spanish spoken. SERVES: High Desert area.

WWW.INCRISIS.NET

Online Behavioral Screening & Reports
965 NE Wiest Way, No. 2
Bend, OR 97701

Online mental health screening software that generates reports with analysis and treatment suggestions for teens who may have mental or addictive disorders. Reports are used to share with professionals in seeking help for troubled youth. Free public srv for parents, caregivers, educators, and youth professionals. Contact agency via website (www.incrisis.net). FUNDING: Nonprofit, Mentor Research Institute. SERVES: U.S.A.

1736 FAMILY CRISIS CENTER
Homeless Resources & Prgms
2116 Arlington Ave., Ste 200
Los Angeles, CA 90018
(323) 737-3900
(323) 737-3993 FAX

Outpatient counseling and case mgmt for adults, families and children. Battered women's support groups, community edu, outreach. Also shelter, counseling, food, clothing, advocacy and other 24-hr srvs free of charge to battered women and their children and to runaway and homeless adol. Operates five shelters: four for battered women and their children (ages birth-17 yrs) for 1-24 months offering a comprehensive survival and job dev prgm to promote long-term safety, survival, and success; one emerg shelter for runaways (two-week crisis-oriented shelter). 24-hr hotlines in South Bay (310) 379-3620, (310) 370-5902; Long Beach (562) 388-7652; South L.A. (213) 222-1237, (213) 745-6434. 24-hr drop-in center at 1736 Monterey Blvd., Hermosa Beach. May call collect if needed. FUNDING: Grants, donations, govt, nonprofit. OFC HRS: M-F 8:30am-5pm. Spanish spoken. ADM REQ: Vary by prgm. Free srvs. SERVES: So. Calif.

A WINDOW BETWEEN WORLDS
710 4th Avenue, Ste 5
Venice, CA 90291
(310) 396-0317
(310) 396-9698 FAX

Trains shelter staff in conducting art expression & empowerment workshops. Art Circle offers art expression workshop outside the shelter. Available to any agency or org wanting to use art as a healing tool for domestic abuse survivors. FUNDING: Nonprofit. OFC HRS: M-F 10am-6pm. Hours do vary. Spanish spoken. SERVES: U.S.A.

ABORTION RECOVERY INTERNATL NTWK
5319 University Dr., Ste 252
Irvine, CA 92612
(949) 679-9276
(866) 469-7326
(949) 551-9771 FAX

Srvs provided to those touched by the abortion experience. Support and guidance for those mourning the loss of a terminated pregnancy. Helps wounded women, men and their families find peace and victory from their past. Also provides edu opportunities to increase abortion awareness. Public speaking for schools, universities, companies or groups. 24-hr hotline, (800) 395-4357 to assist those in crisis. FUNDING: Nonprofit. OFC HRS: M-F 8am-5pm. SERVES: So. Calif.

ADVENT GROUP MINISTRIES
90 Great Oaks Blvd., Ste 108
San Jose, CA 95119
(408) 281-0708
(408) 281-2658 FAX

Faith-based social service agency serving at-risk children and their families since 1986. Founded as a residential treatment program for adolescents, they have since grown to include an outpatient recovery program, horse therapy, a comprehensive family counseling center and

a foster care program for children of all ages. FUNDING: Nonprofit. OFC HRS: M-F 8:30am-5pm. SERVES: Northern Calif, San Bernardino County.

AMERICAN ASSN OF SUICIDOLOGY (AAS)
5221 Wisconsin Ave., NW
Washington, DC 20015
(202) 237-2280
(202) 237-2282 FAX

Promotes research, edu, training of suicide prevention for professionals and volunteers. Provides edu materials, newsletters, pamphlets, conferences, a support group directory and referrals. FUNDING: Nonprofit. OFC HRS: M-F 9am-5pm. Membership fee. SERVES: U.S.A.

AMERICAN ASSN/MARRIAGE & FAM
Association of Marriage & Family Therapy
112 S. Alfred St.
Alexandria, VA 22314
(703) 838-9808
(703) 838-9805 FAX

AAMFT offers info to the public about the field of marriage and family therapy. Also publishes the Journal of Marital and Family Therapy and Family Therapy Magazine. FUNDING: Nonprofit. OFC HRS: M-F 8:30am-5pm, EST. Spanish spoken. SERVES: U.S.A.

AMERICAN FNDN FOR SUICIDE PREV
120 Wall St., 22nd Fl.
New York, NY 10005
(888) 333-2377
(212) 363-3500
(212) 363-6237 FAX

Works to prevent suicide through research, edu, training and support. Srvs include: literature, conferences and a directory of support groups nationwide. FUNDING: Nonprofit. OFC HRS: M-F 9am-5pm, EST. Free srvs. SERVES: U.S.A.

AMERICAN PSYCHIATRIC ASSN (APA)
1000 Wilson Blvd., Ste 1825
Arlington, VA 22209-3901
(888) 357-7924
(703) 907-1085 FAX

Resources on mental illness, including videos, fact sheets on mental illnesses APA library, publications and referrals. Many Spanish materials available. FUNDING: Nonprofit. OFC HRS: M-F 8:30am-6pm EST. Spanish & French spoken. SERVES: U.S.A.

AMERICAN PSYCHOLOGICAL ASSN
750 1st Street., NE, 6th Fl.
Washington, DC 20002-4242
(800) 374-2721
(202) 336-5500
(202) 336-5502 FAX

Info on psychological issues and mental health to consumers. TDD/TTY (202) 336-6123. FUNDING: Nonprofit. OFC HRS: M-F 8:30am-5pm, EST. Spanish spoken. SERVES: U.S.A.

ANXIETY DISORDERS ASSN OF AMER
8730 Georgia Ave.
Silver Spring, MD 20910
(240) 485-1001
(240) 485-1035 FAX

ADAA offers edu materials to professionals and consumers regarding anxiety disorders. Free materials include pamphlets, self-help books and a newsletter. FUNDING: Nonprofit. OFC HRS: M-Th 9am-5pm; F 9am-2pm. Spanish, French & Chinese spoken. SERVES: U.S.A

APU COMMUNITY COUNSELING CENTER
Formerly Child and Family Dev Center
P.O. Box 7000
918 E. Alosta Ave.
Azusa, CA 91702
(626) 815-5421
(626) 633-0651 FAX

Community-based counseling facility featuring a therapeutic staff that provides quality counseling and consulting srvs in a variety of locations throughout the east San Gabriel Valley. The clinicians at the CCC provide a broad range of cutting-edge treatment srvs for individuals, couples, and families including support for life transition dilemmas, crisis-related issues, and disorders of depression and anxiety. Counseling and edu srvs are provided by licensed professionals, interns, and trainees, depending on the need. Also offers the Pediatrics Neurodevelopment Institute (PNI) which works with a spectrum of disorders including mental retardation. Testing, treatment, and eval available. Affliated with Azusa Pacific Univ Dept of Graduate Psychology, APA approved. OFC HRS: M-Th 9am-9pm; F 9am-6pm; Sat 10am-2pm. Low cost srvs, sliding fee scale, insurance reimbursement. SERVES: L.A., Orange, San Bernardino and Riverside Counties.

ASIAN PACIFIC RESIDENTIAL PRGM
1665 W. Adams Blvd.
Los Angeles, CA 90007
(323) 731-3534
(323) 731-5618 FAX

Serves Asian Pacific clients with chronic mental illness (adults ages 18-59 yrs) in partnership with a nearby residential facility. Structured transitional prgm to assist in acquiring skills for independent living, community resources, recreational activities, pre-vocational assessment. FUNDING: SSI, Short Doyle, govt funds, nonprofit. OFC HRS: M-F 7:30am-4:30pm. Korean, Vietnamese, Mandarin & Cantonese spoken. ADM REQ: Asian descent, adult, history of chronic mental illness. SERVES: So. Calif.

B.R.I.D.G.E.S., INC.
Adminstrative Office
1977 N. Garey Ave., Ste 6
Pomona, CA 91767
(909) 623-6651
(909) 623-0455 FAX

L.A. County Dept of Mental Health contract provider focusing on serving individuals with mental illness. Residential and outpatient prgms; 5 social rehabilitation facilities (6-14 beds each) with stay up to 18 months. Residential prgms offered in San Fernando Valley and San Gabriel Valley. Outpatient prgm in SFV offers individual and group specialized mental health counseling, substance abuse support, case mgmt, medication and psychiatry. Wellness & Recovery Ctr in El Monte provides mental health counseling, recreational and vocational support, peer support, medication, and other srvs. FUNDING: Nonprofit. OFC HRS: M-F 8am-4:30pm. Spanish spoken. ADM REQ: Intake (626) 350-5304. Residential prgms house clients ages 18-59 yrs with mental illness and co-occurring disorders; outpatient up to age 21 yrs. Accepts Medi-Cal, SSI. Limited beds may be available without any funding. SERVES: Los Angeles & San Bernardino Counties.

BAZELON CENTER/MENTAL HLTH LAW

1101 15th Street, NW, Ste 1212
Washington, DC 20005
(202) 467-5730
(202) 223-0409 FAX

Supports the legal rights of mentally disabled people through litigation & policy reform. Also offers advocacy manuals & consumer publications. Does not provide individual legal representation. For TDD, call (202) 223-0409. FUNDING: Donations, grants, nonprofit. OFC HRS: M-F 9am-5pm, EST. SERVES: U.S.A.

BEAR HAWK EDUCATION SERVICES

100 S. Sunrise Way, PMB 292
Palm Springs, CA 92262
(760) 329-4457
(800) 367-2437
(760) 329-7803 FAX

HIV & outreach srvs to high-risk populations. Pre- and post-HIV testing srvs, edu, referral srvs, hotline info, mental health & shelter facilities. Srvs provided at 65861 Pearson St., Ste C, Desert Hot Springs. FUNDING: Nonprofit. OFC HRS: M 9am-5pm; Tu-Th 9am-3pm. SERVES: Blythe to Banning.

BILINGUAL FAMILY COUNSELING

317 West F Street
Ontario, CA 91762
(909) 986-7111
(909) 986-0941 FAX

County-funded center offers outpatient drug/alcohol and child abuse treatment. Prgms for adults, adolescents & children (including play therapy). Prevention prgms include: school & community presentations, and parent edu. Also crisis intervention, OTP Jag prgm, individual, family & group counseling, referrals for suicide intervention and post-intervention srvs. FUNDING: Ofc of Alcohol/Drug Prgms, Human Srvs System, nonprofit. OFC HRS: M-Th 9am-8pm. Spanish spoken. Accepts Medi-Cal for drug/alcohol treatment, pvt fees. SERVES: San Bernardino County.

BIRTH CHOICE

277 S. Rancho Santa Fe Rd., Ste S
San Marcos, CA 92069-2343
(760) 744-1313

Counseling, supportive services, info and referrals to medical professionals. Financial aid prgms, post-abortion counseling and adoption srvs. FUNDING: Nonprofit. OFC HRS: M 9am-6pm; Tu-Th 9am-8pm; F 8am-12noon; Sat 10am-12noon. Spanish spoken. Free srvs. SERVES: San Marcos.

CAL POLY POMONA ENNIS W. COSBY

Child & Family Services Friend Mobile
300 W. 2nd Street
Pomona, CA 91766
(909) 869-3799
(909) 469-0174 FAX

Child, adolescent, adult, family counseling. Tutoring, and mentoring for children ages 5-18 yrs, psychological assessment of academic, cognitive, emotional, & social functioning. FUNDING: Pvt fndn grants. OFC HRS: Counseling by appt only. Call for current tutoring/mentoring hrs. Some Spanish spoken. ADM REQ: Low income. Free srvs. SERVES: Pomona, La Verne, San Dimas, Chino & Upland.

CALIF ASSN/SCHOOL PSYCHOLOGISTS

1020 12th Street, Ste 200
Sacramento, CA 95814
(916) 444-1595
(916) 444-1597 FAX

Statewide membership organization for school psychologists in Calif. Provides professional dev, acts as a liaison with state boards & commissions. The goal is to ensure schools are responsive to psych needs of students. Fact sheets are available online. OFC HRS: M-F 8:30am-5pm. SERVES: Calif.

CALIF BOARD/BEHAVIORAL SCIENCES

1625 N. Market Blvd., Ste S-200
Sacramento, CA 95834
(916) 574-7830
(916) 574-8625 FAX

Agency licenses edu psychologists, clinical social workers, marriage & family therapists. FUNDING: Govt. OFC HRS: M-F 8am-5pm. Spanish spoken. SERVES: Calif.

CALIF BOARD/PSYCHOLOGY

Dept of Consumer Affairs
2005 Evergreen St., Ste 1400
Sacramento, CA 95815
(916) 263-2699
(866) 503-3221
(916) 263-2697 FAX

Regulates psychology professionals. FUNDING: Govt. OFC HRS: M-F 8am-5pm. SERVES: Calif.

CANYON ACRES CHILDREN & FAMILY SRVS

1845 W. Orangewood Ave., Ste 300
Orange, CA 92868
(714) 383-9401
(714) 383-9300 FAX

Serves children & families through a comprehensive list of community prgms. The mental health clinic includes individual, family, & group therapy, psych medication support, and parent edu classes. The therapeutic afterschool prgm contains an array of structured group activities and a therapeutic horse riding prgm for children that have been identified as needing additional support for a mental health issue. The Creating Family Connections prgm works to find family or kin for dependent youth and engage them in the child's life. Foster care and adoption srvs prgm helps find kids forever families. FUNDING: AFDC-FC, EPSDT, County of Orange Health Care Agency, donations. OFC HRS: M-F 7am-5pm. Sat appts also available. Spanish spoken. Accepts Medi-Cal. Pvt insurance and cash pay for select srvs. SERVES: Orange Co (all prgms). Select prgms in L.A., Riverside, San Bernardino, & San Diego Counties.

CARE LEARNING CTR/PSYCH SRVS

27715 Jefferson Ave., Ste 112
Temecula, CA 92592
(951) 288-6835

(951) 506-9113 FAX

Edu & psych organization made up of professional educators, licensed psychologists, therapists, and counselors. Provides edu srvs including tutoring, edu therapy, counseling for individuals and families, and academic coaching for children. FUNDING: Nonprofit. OFC HRS: M-F 9am-9pm. Spanish spoken. SERVES: Riverside, northern San Diego Counties.

CATHOLIC CHARITIES/COMMUNITY SRVS

Administration
1450 North D Street
San Bernardino, CA 92405
(909) 388-1239
(909) 384-1130 FAX

Psychological counseling for individuals & family, case mgmt, emerg food, diapers, clothing, furniture (when available), utility assist, holiday baskets, transportation, advocacy, HIV/AIDS srvs, info & referrals. Emerg housing for needy transients with pre-arranged motel accommodations (as funds allow). Refugee & immigration srvs, parolee reintegration. FUNDING: Donations, nonprofit. OFC HRS: M-F 8:30am-4:30pm. Spanish, Chinese, Filipino, Vietnamese, Russian spoken. Sliding fee scale. SERVES: San Bernardino & Riverside Counties.

CATHOLIC CHARITIES/COUNSELING

Caritas Counseling Srvs
1441 N. D St., Ste 4
San Bernardino, CA 92405
(909) 763-4970
(909) 763-4977 FAX

Professional counseling without regard to race, creed, sex, or age. Marriage, family, child counseling for a wide range of issues such as child abuse, anger mgmt, relationships, parent edu. Counseling provided days, eve & Sat in various locations. FUNDING: Nonprofit. OFC HRS: M-F 10am-4:30pm. Spanish spoken. Sliding fee scale. Some free srvs. SERVES: San Bernardino & Riverside Counties.

CEDARS-SINAI PSYCH/MENTAL HLTH

Dept of Psychiatry & Mental Health
8730 Alden Dr., Plaza Level
Los Angeles, CA 90048
(800) 233-2771
(310) 423-0428 FAX

Adult & geriatric inpatient and partial hospitalization & day treatment. Adult, geriatric, adol, child, infant and family outpatient mental health srvs. Dual-diagnosis, IOP srvs, psych and chemical dep srvs. Day treatment & intensive outpatient chemical dependency treatment. For TDD, call (310) 423-2655. FUNDING: Nonprofit. OFC HRS: 24-hr for emerg. Accepts Medi-Cal, Medicare, insurance. SERVES: U.S.A.

CENTER FOR FAMILY LIVING

1128 E. 6th Street, Ste 8
Corona, CA 92879
(951) 734-8831
(951) 734-8518 FAX

Multi-disciplinary group (MFTs) offering srvs to children, adolescents and adults. Specialties include: family, marital, court-ordered co-parenting counseling, PTSD (post traumatic stress disorder), children's behavior problems, depression, anxiety, personal growth. FUND-

ING: Client fees. OFC HRS: M-F 8:30am-5:30pm; Sat 9am-3pm. Spanish spoken. ADM REQ: Call for appt. Accepts insurance, sliding fee scale. SERVES: Riverside County.

CENTER FOR FAMILY SOLUTIONS
Formerly Womanhaven, Inc.
P.O. Box 2219
741 Main St.
El Centro, CA 92244
(760) 353-6922
(760) 353-8530
(760) 353-8441 FAX

Domestic violence srvs, HIV prevention prgm, bullying prgm, individual & group counseling, outreach, emerg shelter, legal assist, drop-in center, TROs, crisis srvs, transitional housing, prevention & edu prgm, info & referral, batterer's treatment prgm. 24-hr hotline (760) 353-8530. FUNDING: Nonprofit. OFC HRS: M-F 8am-5pm. Spanish spoken. Fees apply for divorce cases & lawyer srvs. SERVES: So. Calif.

CENTER FOR HEALING CHILDHOOD TRAUMA
101 S. Olive Ave.
Rialto, CA 92376
(909) 875-5288
(909) 875-0608 FAX

Counseling for children, adolescents and adult victims of sexual abuse. Also family resource ctr offering a wide range of parenting curricula. Parents United certified providers. Also has an office in O.C. at 1420 E. Chapman Ave, Orange 92866, (949) 348-1717. FUNDING: Nonprofit. OFC HRS: M-Th 9am-7pm; F 10am-5pm. Spanish spoken. Accepts pvt pay, Victims of Crime. SERVES: Orange, Riverside & San Bernardino Counties.

CHILDREN'S HOSP OF O.C. (CHOC)
Pediatric Psychology Dept
455 S. Main St.
Orange, CA 92868
(714) 532-8481
(714) 532-8756 FAX

Specializes in working with medically fragile children. This dept provides child psychiatry, psychological & neuropsychological eval, assessment testing, consultation & treatment of children, adol & their families. FUNDING: Nonprofit. OFC HRS: M-F 8am-5pm. Spanish spoken. Accepts Medi-Cal. SERVES: Orange County, parts of Riverside, San Bernardino & L.A. Counties.

CHILDREN'S INTERAGENCY PRGM
23119 Cottonwood Ave., Ste 110
Moreno Valley, CA 92553-9661
(951) 413-5678
(951) 413-5660 FAX

Outpatient mental health srvs. FUNDING: Govt. OFC HRS: M-Th 8am-5:30pm. Spanish spoken. ADM REQ: Children ages 17 yrs or younger. SERVES: Riverside County.

CHINO COMMUNITY SERVICES
Counseling Srvs
13201 Central Ave.
Chino, CA 91710
(909) 591-9822
(909) 628-4093 FAX

Low-cost outpatient family and individual counseling. Community outreach for residents of Chino. Domestic violence prgms. FUNDING: State, county, school, city, nonprofit. OFC HRS: M-Th 8am-8pm; F 8am-6pm. Spanish spoken. Free srvs for juveniles & low income residents of Chino. School-based counseling free. Outpatient family treatment $26 per visit. SERVES: Western San Bernardino County.

CHINO COMMUNITY SERVICES
Human Services
13271 Central Ave.
Chino, CA 91710
(909) 591-9822
(909) 628-4093 FAX

Professional counseling srvs to low income children ages 5-18 yrs and their families. Youth & teen counseling srvs. Parenting classes, anger mgm, court referrals and PC-1000 drug diversion prgm are offered throughout the year. Speakers are available for schools and other associations on a variety of subjects. Call for info. FUNDING: Chino Community Srvs Dept, Chino Valley USD, govt. OFC HRS: M-Th 8am-8pm; F 8am-6pm. Family counseling is free. Fees vary per prgm. SERVES: San Bernardino County.

CHRISTIAN FAMILY COUNSELING
6117 Brockton Ave., Ste 100
Riverside, CA 92506
(951) 682-7138
(877) 777-0755
(951) 686-2271 FAX

Marriage, individual, family teen, adol, drug & alcohol counseling. FUNDING: Donations, nonprofit. OFC HRS: M-F 9am-8pm, Sat 10am-5pm. $45 per session. SERVES: Riverside, San Bernardino Counties.

CHURCH OF RELIGIOUS SCIENCE
7434 Bannock Trail
Yucca Valley, CA 92284
(760) 365-2205

General counseling on practical issues by the minister. Not intended for people with mental health problems. Call for appt. Also OA and Al-Anon meetings. FUNDING: Nonprofit. OFC HRS: Tu-Th 10am-1pm. Accepts fees based on ability to pay. SERVES: Morongo Basin.

CLEANSLATE, INC.
Gang Recovery Group & Tattoo Removal
12401 Slauson Ave., Ste G
Whittier, CA 90606
(562) 945-9111

CleanSlate is a gang violence recovery, rage resolution and tattoo removal prgm that helps to erase the visible signs of gang involvement while working with gang members to reconnect with their emotions. Individual counselors give one-on-one support. Gang recovery group every F 7:30pm-9pm at the So. Calif. Counseling Ctr. 5615 W. Pico Blvd., L.A. 90019. No appt needed for F groups. Tattoo removal prgm is at different locations one Sat a month. Address above is mailing address only. Visit (www.cleanslatela.org) for tattoo removal dates. FUNDING: Nonprofit. Spanish spoken. Groups $5 donation. SERVES: So. Calif.

COACHELLA VALLEY USD
School Readiness Program Center
83800 Airport Blvd.
Thermal, CA 92274
(760) 399-8129
(760) 399-4421 FAX

Medical, dental, vision, mental health counseling & special needs assessments & treatment. OFC HRS: M-F 8am-4pm. ADM REQ: Low income families with children ages birth-5 yrs. SERVES: East Valley Riverside County.

COMMUNITY ACCESS NETWORK
Foster Family Agency/Counseling Ctr
2791 Green River Rd., Ste 101
Corona, CA 92882
(951) 279-3222
(951) 279-5222 FAX

Srvs provided to infants and children ages birth-18 yrs. Residential care & treatment for abused and dependent children. Supportive srvs: weekly social worker contact, foster parent training, crisis response. FUNDING: Nonprofit. OFC HRS: M-F 9am-5:30pm. Spanish spoken. ADM REQ: Court placement. SERVES: Orange, Riverside & San Bernardino Counties.

COMMUNITY ACCESS NETWORK
Community Counseling Center
2791 Green River Rd., Ste 101
Corona, CA 92882
(951) 279-3222
(951) 279-5222 FAX

Outpatient counseling for individuals, couples, families and children. Medication support srvs for children receiving therapy at the agency. FUNDING: Nonprofit. OFC HRS: By appt. Spanish spoken. ADM REQ: Referral from Riverside Co. DPSS. Accepts Medi-Cal, sliding fee scale. SERVES: Riverside County.

COMMUNITY COUNSELING CENTER
High Desert Domestic Violence Program
15075 7th Street
Victorville, CA 92392
(760) 949-4357
(866) 770-7867
(760) 843-9551 FAX

Non-emergency outpatient psychotherapy for children, youth, teens, adults, seniors, individuals, couples and families. All treatment provided by volunteer interns and masters level students, supervised by a licensed clinician. No emergency psychiatric or medication srvs available. No court mandated classes, such as anger management. Outreach Office, M-Th 8am-5pm, (760)843-0701. Must call first to make an appointment. No walk in for info. FUNDING: Nonprofit, fees, donations. OFC HRS: T, W evenings with sessions at 5pm and 6pm. Clients leave at 7pm when clinical supervision begins. Spanish spoken. ADM REQ: Must have appt. Low income and/or are unable to access mental health services elsewhere. No actively psychotic clients. No CPS clients at this time. Sliding fee scale from $1-$45. SERVES: High desert area.

COMMUNITY COUNSELING CTR/CSUSB
Dept of Psychology, Calif State Univ
5500 State University Pkwy.
San Bernardino, CA 92407
(909) 537-5040
(909) 537-7061 FAX

Graduate students in 2-yr M.S. counseling psychology prgm provide low-cost, long-term individual psychotherapy. Student therapists are supervised by Ph.D. level psychologists on CSUSB faculty. FUNDING: CSUSV, govt. OFC HRS: M, Th, F 8am-5pm; Tu, W 8am-7pm.

ADM REQ: CSUSB student or connected to student. Not suicidal, abusive, drug dependent or violent. Cost covered by tuition. SERVES: San Bernardino County.

CORONA VET CENTER
Dept of Veterans Affairs
800 Magnolia Ave., Ste 110
Corona, CA 92879
(951) 734-0525
(800) 523-7052
(951) 734-0063 FAX

Mental health counseling for all combat veterans, Vietnam era veterans, and for any sexual harassment or assault victims during any time while on active duty. Also assist in filing a claim for srv-connected disability. Counseling for couples, children of veterans, substance abuse, and combat-related emotional trauma. Referrals for benefits, medical, employment, etc. FUNDING: Govt. OFC HRS: M-F 8am-4:30pm. Free srvs. SERVES: Riverside County.

COUNSELING/PSYCHOTHERAPY REFERRAL
Natl Assn of Social Workers
750 1st Street, NE, Ste 700
Washington, DC 20002-4241
(800) 638-8799
(202) 408-8600
(202) 336-8395 FAX

Professional assn of social workers. Offices in all 50 states. Year-round depression screenings. Clinical registry lists licensed clinical social workers practicing as mental health professionals. FUNDING: Nonprofit. OFC HRS: M-F 8:30am-5:30pm, EST. Spanish spoken. SERVES: U.S.A.

CROSSROADS CHURCH
S.M.U.R.F.
31805 Temecula Pkwy., Ste 389
Temecula, CA 92592
(951) 541-8574
(951) 541-0886 FAX

Address listed above is for mailing only. Single Moms United in Rewarding Fellowship meets Sun at 5pm. Support group for single mothers & their children. Free child care and a Sun night meal. Meets at 28753 Via Montezuma in Temecula. Subject to change. FUNDING: Nonprofit, donations. OFC HRS: By appointment. ADM REQ: Single mothers & their children. SERVES: Southwest County.

CRYSTAL CATHEDRAL/COUNSELING CTR
Professional Counseling Srvs
13280 Chapman Ave.
Garden Grove, CA 92840
(714) 971-4222

Outpatient individual psychotherapy (adult, adol, children), couple and family counseling. Call for appt. FUNDING: Fees, nonprofit. OFC HRS: M-Th 9am-9pm; F 9am-3pm; Sat 10am-6pm. Arabic, Spanish spoken. Accepts pvt pay. Sliding fee scale may be available, (from $50-$95). SERVES: Orange, L.A., Riverside & San Bernardino Counties.

DEPRESSED ANONYMOUS
P.O. Box 17414
Louisville, KY 40217
(502) 569-1989

Resources for depressed individuals of all ages, printed info, support groups, referrals, advocacy, education. Website contains info on books and support groups. Visit (www.depressedanon.com). FUNDING: Nonprofit. SERVES: U.S.A.

DEPRESSION AWARENESS
(800) 421-4211

Call to request up to three free brochures about the general symptoms of depression, student info, elderly depression & treatment for all types of depression. Sponsored by the National Institute of Mental Health. For TTY, call (301) 443-8431. FUNDING: Nonprofit. OFC HRS: 24-hr message machine. Spanish spoken. SERVES: U.S.A.

DEPRESSIONRECOVERYGROUPS.COM

Website that hosts several support groups for depression each day. Users only need a microphone and computer to participate. Facilitated by Dr. Vincent Caimano, Ph.D. Donations accepted, no one turned away for lack of funds. SERVES: U.S.A.

DESERT MOUNTAIN SELPA CHILDREN'S CTR
17800 Highway 18
Apple Valley, CA 92307
(760) 242-6336
(760) 242-6339 FAX

Counseling center designed to meet the therapeutic needs of children and adolescents. Provides individual, group counseling. Ages birth-21 yrs. FUNDING: Nonprofit. OFC HRS: M-F 8am-4:30pm, Summer Hrs vary. Spanish spoken. Accepts Medi-Cal, IEHP, TriCare, Pacific Care, Molina & cash payments. SERVES: San Bernardino County.

DUAL RECOVERY ANONYMOUS
World Service Central Office
P.O. Box 8107
Prairie Village, KS 66208
(877) 883-2332
(913) 991-2703

12-Step fellowship of men & women who meet to support each other in a common recovery from two no-fault illnesses: an emotional or psychiatric illness and chemical dependency. Meetings in Northern, Central & So. Calif. FUNDING: Nonprofit. OFC HRS: M-F 9am-5pm, CST. 24-hr recorded info. SERVES: U.S.A.

EAST VALLEY CHARLEE
440 Cajon St.
Redlands, CA 92373
(909) 307-5777
(909) 307-5776 FAX

County-funded prgm providing sexual abuse prevention for all minors accepted into the prgm. Also offers individual, family & child counseling. FUNDING: Dept of Social Srvs, San Bernardino Mental Health, nonprofit. OFC HRS: M-F 8:30am-5pm. Spanish spoken upon request. ADM REQ: Referrals by SSA or Dept Mental Health. Accepts Medi-Cal, insurance. SERVES: San Bernardino metro.

EATING DISORDER FOUNDATION OF O.C.
23232 Peralta Dr., Ste 211
Laguna Hills, CA 92653
(800) 342-8793
(949) 285-9827
(949) 488-2418 FAX

Dedicated to the awareness and prevention of eating disorders by providing edu to local schools, businesses, and youth organizations. Community outreach, edu, teacher in-service training, consultations, eating disorder assessments, counseling, fitness and nutrition referrals, support groups, group presentations for youth sports, individual assessments for athletes and coaches. FUNDING: Nonprofit. OFC HRS: M-Th 8am-9pm; F 8am-7pm; Sat 9am-2pm. Spanish spoken. SERVES: Orange, Riverside & San Bernardino Counties.

ECCLESIA CHRISTIAN FELLOWSHIP
Cornerstones Christian Counseling
1314 Date St.
San Bernardino, CA 92404
(909) 881-5551
(909) 881-0199 FAX

Counseling from a Christian view point. Includes: addictions, anger management, anxiety, bipolar, blended family issues, child/adolescent, chronic illness, conflict resolution, courtship/relationship, depression, family, gender issues, grief, intimacy, life changes, marital, meaning and purpose, pastoral, premarital, school problems, sexual issues, spiritual issues, stress management, unspecified. Contact for more information. Contact Brenda. FUNDING: Nonprofit. OFC HRS: M-Th 8am-5pm. Sliding fee scale. Usually $60 for 6 weeks. SERVES: San Bernardino County.

ETTIE LEE YOUTH & FAMILY SERVICES
P.O. Box 339
5146 N. Maine Ave.
Baldwin Park, CA 91706-0339
(626) 960-4861
(626) 337-2621 FAX

Family-style homes for severely emotionally disturbed young men ages 8-18 yrs. 24-hr care by trained staff. Individual & group therapy, gang intervention srvs, independent living skills training, case mgmt, family counseling, therapeutic recreation, 12-Step prgms, substance abuse treatment & on-site school. Licensed treatment foster family agency for boys & girls ages birth-18 yrs. Mental health therapy, case mgmt & family counseling. FUNDING: Nonprofit. OFC HRS: M-F 8am-5pm. Spanish spoken. ADM REQ: County referral for group home & foster care. SERVES: So. Calif.

FAMILY SERVICE AGENCY/SAN BRDO
Crest Forest Family Srvs
P.O. Box 4484
23406 Crest Forest Dr.
Crestline, CA 92325
(909) 338-4689
(909) 338-8230 FAX

Counseling and mental health treatment for child sexual abuse, dysfunctional families. Anger diversion classes, court-ordered batterer's intervention prgm, high-risk youth prgms, limited utility asst. 24-hr suicide and crisis hotline (800) 832-9119. Food bank available F 9am-12noon, 1pm-5:30pm; call ahead to get more info. FUNDING: United Way, client fees, nonprofit. OFC HRS: M-Th 8:30am-6pm. ADM REQ: Varies per prgm. Ages 5 yrs+. Accepts Medi-Cal, sliding fee scale. SERVES: San Bernardino County.

FAMILY SERVICE AGENCY/SAN BRDO
Outpatient Mental Health Srvs
1669 North E Street
San Bernardino, CA 92405
(909) 886-6737

(909) 881-3871 FAX

Info & referral, counseling & mental health treatment for child sexual abuse, domestic violence intervention counseling, dysfunctional families, parenting classes, anger diversion classes, high-risk youth prgms. S.N.A.A.P. (Narcotics/alcohol abuse prgm for teens). State ID: 360044AN. FUNDING: United Way, client fees, nonprofit. OFC HRS: M-Th 9am-9pm. Spanish spoken. ADM REQ: Varies per prgm. Ages birth-21 yrs. Accepts Medi-Cal for youth only. sliding fee scale. SERVES: San Bernardino County.

FAMILY SERVICE ASSN/CORONA
Alternatives to Domestic Violence
Outreach Office
515 S. Corona Mall
Corona, CA 92879
(951) 737-8410
(951) 737-3517 FAX

Counseling for individuals, marriages & familes. Anger mgmt, edu, child abuse prevention & treatment. Employee assist prgm, mental health advocacy, social mentorship & family life edu. Anonymous shelter, advocacy for domestic violence. 24-hr crisis line (800) 339-SAFE or (951)683-0829. Riverside (951) 320-1370. Hemet (951)929-3079. OFC HRS: M-F 9am-5pm. Spanish spoken. ADM REQ: Victim of domestic violence. Sliding fee scale for therapeutic srvs and anger mgmt. SERVES: West Riverside County.

FAMILY SERVICE ASSN/WEST RIVERSIDE
JND/Family Counseling
21250 Box Springs Rd., Ste 106
Moreno Valley, CA 92557
(951) 686-3706
(951) 686-7267 FAX

Full-srv marriage, family, child, individual & group counseling. Parenting groups. Call for times & locations. FUNDING: Nonprofit. OFC HRS: M-F 8am-5pm. Spanish spoken. Sliding fee scale $30-$120. Some srvs free for those who qualify. SERVES: Western Riverside County.

FAMILY SERVICE ASSN/WEST RIVERSIDE
La Sierra Clinic
11290 Pierce St.
Riverside, CA 92505
(951) 509-8733
(951) 509-8479 FAX

Individual, family counseling, anger mgmt classes. OFC HRS: M-Th 1pm-9pm. Sliding fee scale. SERVES: Riverside County.

FAMILY SERVICE ASSOCIATION
Mental Health Clinic
21250 Box Springs Rd., Ste 201
Moreno Valley, CA 92557
(951) 686-3706
(951) 686-7267 FAX

Full-srv marriage, family, child, individual and group counseling. Medi-Cal prgm for children. Counseling office site in Riverside. Senior nutrition/home-delivered meals in Sun City & Mead Valley San Jacinto, Hemet, Reno Valley, Cabazon, Banning, Calimesa, Desert Hot Springs. Child dev prgm with child care sites in La Sierra, Mead Valley, Rubidoux. Adult day srvs in Hemet, (951)791-3556. FUNDING: State, grants, contracts, United Way, donations, nonprofit. OFC HRS: M-F 8am-5pm.

Clinic M-Th 8pm-9pm; F 8am-5pm. Spanish spoken. Sliding fee scale. SERVES: West & Mid-Riverside County.

FAMILY SERVICES OF THE DESERT
81-711 Highway 111, Ste 101
Indio, CA 92201
(760) 347-2398
(800) 536-4357
(760) 347-6468 FAX

Family, individual and group counseling. Locations in Indio, Desert Hot Springs and Blythe. FUNDING: United Way, donations, client fees, nonprofit. OFC HRS: M-F 9am-5pm. Eve & weekend by appt. Spanish spoken. SERVES: Coachella Valley.

FIRST CALL FOR HELP
Volunteer Center of Victor Valley
P.O. Box 1992
16692 Mojave Dr.
Victorville, CA 92393
(760) 243-9646
(760) 243-4762 FAX

Info & referral for people seeking srvs or info on community agencies. Interaction with individuals in crisis situations in order to reduce tension and stress, allowing that person to utilize available resources more effectively. FUNDING: Donations, grants, nonprofit. OFC HRS: M-Th 9am-2:45pm. Spanish spoken. SERVES: San Bernardino County.

FREEDOM FROM FEAR
Anxiety & Depression Resource Org
308 Seaview Ave.
Staten Island, NY 10305
(718) 351-1717
(718) 980-5022 FAX

Agency seeks to impact the lives of those affected by anxiety, depression and related disorders through advocacy, edu, research, and community support. Also offers a free anxiety and depression screening prgm. Visit (www.freedomfromfear.org) for more info. FUNDING: Nonprofit. Free srvs. SERVES: U.S.A.

GIVE AN HOUR
P.O. Box 5918
Bethesda, MD 20824

Matches volunteer mental health counseling providers with troops and families involved with current conflicts in Iraq and Afghanistan. Volunteers provide one hour of free therapy to client. For more info, e-mail (info@giveanhour.org) or visit (www.giveanhour.org). FUNDING: Nonprofit. Free srvs. SERVES: U.S.A.

GOOD SHEPHERD COUNSELING
30713 Riverside Dr., Ste 203
Lake Elsinore, CA 92530
(951) 678-1642

Outpatient counseling with locations in Tustin and Lake Elsinore. Grief recovery specialist. Trauma recovery (EMDR certified). Depression and anxiety. Individual, family, child and teen. Contact Susan Kell. FUNDING: Nonprofit. OFC HRS: by appt. Accepts insurance, sliding fee scale. SERVES: Riverside, San Bernardino Counties.

H.E.A.R.T., INC. FOUNDATION
Heart For The Children
P.O. Box 1922
Temecula, CA 92593-1922

(951) 506-4488
(760) 723-1116 FAX

Underwrites therapy, counseling funding and child care tuition for abused children and families in crisis. Assist is usually provided on a short-term basis (three months) and is given to families who have no other financial resources available to them. Additional counseling may be available depending on case evaluation, waiting list, and available funds. Tax exempt ID#: 33-00787074. FUNDING: Nonprofit. SERVES: Southwest Riverside County.

HACIENDA VILLAGE
1435 University Ave.
Riverside, CA 92507-4496
(951) 683-4056
(951) 788-5352 FAX

Residential board & care center for chronically mentally ill men & women ages 18-59 yrs. FUNDING: Nonprofit. OFC HRS: 24 hrs. Tagalog spoken. ADM REQ: Recommendation from the county. Accepts SSI, Medicare & Medi-Cal. SERVES: Inland Empire.

HANMI FAMILY COUNSELING CENTER
Formerly Korean American Counseling Ctr
12362 Beach Blvd., Ste 1
Stanton, CA 90680
(714) 892-9910
(714) 892-9927 FAX

Serves the Korean American community. Counseling, referrals, community edu, support groups for gamblers, parenting edu, alternative high school on site. FUNDING: Private for profit. OFC HRS: M-F 9am-5pm. Korean spoken. Sliding fee scale. SERVES: U.S.A.

HELPLINE INFO & REFERRAL
See "Volunteer Center/Riverside Co."

HIGH DESERT VET CENTER
Dept of Veterans Affairs
15095 Amargosa Rd., Ste 107
Victorville, CA 92394
(760) 261-5925
(760) 241-7828 FAX

Provides individual and group counseling for veterans and their families. Also offers assessment and info & referral srvs for substance abuse, employment, various medical conditions, and VBA benefits. Bereavement counseling also offered to families of soldiers who experienced an active duty death. FUNDING: Govt. OFC HRS: M-F 8am-4:30pm. ADM REQ: Must be a veteran or family member of a veteran. Free srvs. SERVES: San Bernardino Co.

INDIAN CHILD & FAMILY SERVICES
P.O. Box 2269
29377 Rancho California Rd., Ste 200
Temecula, CA 92591
(800) 969-4237
(951) 676-8832
(951) 676-3950 FAX

Counseling referrals for abused children, foster placements, adoptive placements. Tribal Kinship Model used to intervene in the cycle of child abuse. CASA prgm. Spirit Prgm is a prevention/intervention parenting prgm. FUNDING: Bureau of Indian Affairs. OFC HRS: M-F 8am-5pm. ADM REQ: Must be enrolled or eligible for federally recognized tribe. Free srvs. SERVES: Riverside, San Diego, San Bernardino Counties.

INLAND BEHAV & HEALTH SERVICES
Westside Counseling Ctr
1963 North E Street
San Bernardino, CA 92405
(909) 881-6146
(909) 881-0111 FAX

Comprehensive health care, substance abuse, mental health and homeless support srvs. Offers crisis intervention, primary prevention edu, PC-1000 classes, anger mgmt, parenting STEP classes. Perinatal prgm for expectant and parenting mothers who are addicted to drugs with both pre- and post-natal srvs. Provides transportation as well as child care. State ID: 360015AN. FUNDING: Govt, contracts, grants, nonprofit. OFC HRS: M-Th 8am-6pm; F 8am-5pm. Spanish spoken. ADM REQ: Ages 13 yrs+, referrals & walk in. Accepts Medicare, Medi-Cal. SERVES: San Bernardino County.

INSIGHT COUNSELING
23232 Peralta Dr., Ste 211
Laguna Hills, CA 92653
(949) 707-5100
(949) 488-2418 FAX

Comprehensive individual, family, couples and group therapy. Edu classes in anger mgmt and parenting. Therapists specialize in: Drug/alcohol treatment; interventions; eating disorders; anxiety; panic attacks; depression; teen, family and couples issues. FUNDING: Nonprofit. OFC HRS: M-Th 9am-9pm; F 7am-9pm; Sat 9am-1pm. Spanish spoken. Accessible and affordable srvs. SERVES: Orange, Riverside & San Bernardino Counties.

JEWISH FAMILY SERVICE OF THE DESERT
Palm Springs-Desert Area
801 E. Tahquitz Canyon Way, Ste 202
Palm Springs, CA 92262
(760) 325-4088
(760) 778-3781 FAX

Counseling, senior case mgmt, info & referral srvs for individuals, couples and families. Specialized support groups based on need (i.e., group for widowed persons, people in divorce process and resolving problems of everyday living), case mgmt srvs for frail, elderly adults. Project Outreach provides volunteer srvs to older persons in residential and skilled nursing facilities, including friendly visitors. Shabbat welcome and celebration of Jewish holidays. Wait: within one week. FUNDING: Jewish Federation, United Way, fndn, donations, fees, nonprofit. OFC HRS: M-Th 8:30am-5pm; F 8am-4pm. Spanish spoken upon request. Accepts Medi-Cal/Medicare combined and many insurance plans. Sliding fee scale for counseling & case mgmt. SERVES: Coachella Valley.

KIDSPEACE
KidsPeace Helpline
4085 Independence Dr.
Schnecksville, PA 18078
(800) 257-3223
(610) 799-8900 FAX

Hotline provides counseling, info & referral srvs to children & parents in crisis. Also mental health & behavioral health srvs, children's psychiatric hospital, residential, foster care, juvenile justice & outpatient. FUNDING: Nonprofit. OFC HRS: 24 hrs, 7 days. Free helpline. SERVES: U.S.A.

KINSHIP CENTER
Seedling Project
1504 Brookhollow Dr., Ste 117
Santa Ana, CA 92705
(714) 432-8584
(714) 432-8588 FAX

Early intervention srvs to help decrease children's dev delays. Provides dev & behavioral screenings for children in their homes, in-home support, psychological testing, occupational therapy eval. FUNDING: Nonprofit. OFC HRS: M-F 8am-5pm. Spanish spoken. ADM REQ: Ages birth-6 yrs and have Orange Co. Medi-Cal. SERVES: Orange, Riverside & San Bernardino Counties.

LATINO COMMISSION COUNSELING
Formerly Aguas del Desierto Counseling
1612 1st Street, Ste 1
Coachella, CA 92236
(760) 398-9000
(760) 398-9790 FAX

Marriage counseling srvs for individuals, families & groups. Parenting classes & youth self-esteem and communication seminars. FUNDING: Nonprofit. OFC HRS: M-F 9am-9pm; Sat 9am-3pm. Spanish spoken. SERVES: San Bernardino & Riverside Counties.

LAURA'S HOUSE
Emergency Shelter
999 Corporate Dr., Ste 225
Ladera Ranch, CA 92694
(949) 361-3775
(949) 361-3548 FAX

Emergency shelter prgm for battered women with or without children; pregnant women accepted. Emergency shelter provides case mgmt, counseling and legal advocacy. Counseling & resource center for men, women & child victims of domestic violence. 24-hr hotline (866) 498-1511. Counseling hrs: M-F 9am-5pm, eve by appt. Shelter: 24 hrs, 7 days. Spanish & Farsi spoken. Language line available. Sliding fee scale. No one turned away for lack of funds. SERVES: So Calif. Able to refer out of area if needed

LDS FAMILY SERVICES
Unwed Pregnancy Options Counseling
791 N. Pepper Ave.
Colton, CA 92324
(909) 824-0480
(909) 824-0487 FAX

No pressure, confidential counseling to unwed parents & their families. A safe, comfortable place provided to discuss various options. Licensed adoption srvs. Individual, marital, and family counseling. Community outreach to interested agencies and organizations. FUNDING: Nonprofit. OFC HRS: M-F 8am-5pm. Spanish & German spoken. Free counseling srvs. SERVES: So. Calif.

LESBIAN & GAY PSYCH ASSN OF SO CALIF
P.O. Box 34142
Los Angeles, CA 90034
(310) 288-3465
(310) 838-6769 FAX

Provides referrals and an online directory of therapists and counselors who are committed to providing a safe space for the LGBT population to receive treatment for various mental health issues. Also sponsors professional dev and edu courses. Visit (www.lagpa.org) for more info. FUNDING: Nonprofit. SERVES: Southern California.

LOMA LINDA UNIV PSYCH SRVS CLINIC
11130 Anderson St., Ste 117
Loma Linda, CA 92354
(909) 558-8576
(909) 558-0413 FAX

Specializes in the treatment of children, adolescents, students, adults, couples, families and seniors. Low-cost therapy and assessment srvs. FUNDING: Nonprofit. OFC HRS: M-Th 8am-6pm. Spanish spoken. ADM REQ: Ages 4 yrs+. Fee for srvs. SERVES: San Bernardino, Riverside Counties.

LOMA LINDA UNIV/MARRIAGE/FAMILY
Marriage & Family Therapy Clinic
1686 Barton Rd.
Redlands, CA 92373
(909) 558-4934
(909) 558-0334 FAX

Individual, group, marriage, family, child & adol counseling. Srvs for child abuse prevention, grief counseling, domestic violence, chemical addiction and other issues. FUNDING: Nonprofit. OFC HRS: Sun 9am-5pm; M-Th 9am-8pm; F 9am-2:30pm. Spanish spoken. Sliding fee scale starts at $25 per session. Medi-Cal not accepted. Will not bill insurance. SERVES: San Bernardino, Riverside Counties.

LUTHERAN SOCIAL SRVS
Family Counseling Center
P.O. Box 1927
41945 Big Bear Blvd., Ste 200
Big Bear Lake, CA 92315
(909) 866-5721

Individual, group, family & crisis intervention sessions. Ongoing psychotherapy with medication intervention as needed, no outpatient drug or alcohol. AB2726. School counseling for special edu students. FUNDING: County, pvt, nonprofit. OFC HRS: M-F 8am-7pm. Spanish spoken. ADM REQ: Clients who require sustained therapeutic intervention for acute and/or ongoing psychiatric distress. Ages 18 yrs+. Accepts Medi-Cal. SERVES: Bear Valley residents.

MARCH A.F.B./FAMILY SUPPORT
1261 Graeber St., Bldg. 2313, Rm. 1A
March Air Base, CA 92518-1775
(951) 655-5350
(951) 655-4719 FAX

Info & referral. Assessment and referral assist to families in crisis, support during family separation, relocation assist, skill workshops as needed on family issues and job search skills. FUNDING: Govt. OFC HRS: M-F 7:30am-4pm (some weekends). ADM REQ: Military staff or family member. SERVES: March Air Reserve area.

MASADA HOMES
8485 Tamarind Ave., Ste C
Fontana, CA 92335
(909) 428-2366
(909) 428-2363 FAX

Foster family agency and mental health srvs (individual, family, and group therapy psychological testing, psychiatric srvs, TBS). FUNDING: Nonprofit. OFC HRS: M-F 8:30am-5:30pm. ADM REQ: L.A. Medi-Cal eligible youth, dependents and wards of the court, ages 4-18 yrs. SERVES: L.A., Riverside and San Bernardino Counties.

MENTAL HEALTH AMERICA

Formerly Natl Mental Health Assn
2000 N. Beauregard St., 6th Fl.
Alexandria, VA 22311
(800) 969-6642
(703) 684-7722
(703) 684-5968 FAX

NMHA Resource Center provides treatment & srvs referrals to approx 6,000 organizations & free literature on more than 60 topics related to mental health & mental illness. TTY (800) 433-5959. FUNDING: Nonprofit. OFC HRS: 9am-5pm, EST. Spanish spoken. SERVES: U.S.A.

MESA COUNSELING CENTER

San Bernardino Co. Behavorial Health
850 E. Foothill Blvd.
Rialto, CA 92376
(909) 421-9200
(909) 421-9219 FAX

Coordinates srvs for severely emotionally disabled children ages 5-17 yrs who are in residential placement or who require intensive treatment. Includes: hospital discharge planning, residential placement, intensive treatment, wilderness prgms, specialized case mgmt, AB3632, assessment and referral, OT & recreational therapy, individual, family and group therapy, medication eval & monitoring, and crisis intervention. Also, eval for conservatorship and residential placement. Continuing care srvs for minors in state hospitals also provided. FUNDING: County, nonprofit. OFC HRS: M-F 8am-5pm. Walk-ins accepted M-F 8am-10am. Outpatient hrs: M-F 8am-2pm. Spanish spoken. ADM REQ: Resident of Rialto or nearby. Accepts Medi-Cal, some insurances. Sliding fee scale used by all state-funded agencies: $0-full cost. Free referrals. SERVES: San Bernardino County.

MILESTONES RESIDENTIAL FACILITY

82485 Miles Ave.
Indio, CA 92201-4249
(760) 347-4347
(760) 342-7829 FAX

Residential mental health srvs for adults ages 18-59 yrs. Substance abuse treatment, counseling. FUNDING: Govt. OFC HRS: 24-hr srvs. Spanish spoken. ADM REQ: Ages 18 yrs+. SERVES: Riverside County.

MORONGO BASIN COUNSELING & RECOVERY

Services
55475 Santa Fe Trail
Yucca Valley, CA 92284
(760) 365-3022
(760) 365-3513 FAX

Services in mental health, substance abuse recovery & treatment and recovery. Individual & group therapy for children & adults. School counseling available. Specialized prgms for DUI court referrals, Welfare-to-Work transition prgms. Inpatient & outpatient drug & alcohol counseling prgm. FUNDING: Nonprofit. OFC HRS: M-F 8am-5pm. Crisis walk-in clinic 24 hrs, 7 days. Spanish spoken. ADM REQ: Ages 18 yrs+. Children with legal guardian/parent. SERVES: Morongo Basin, San Bernardino County.

MORONGO BASIN COUNSELING & RECOVERY

55475 Santa Fe Trial
Yucca Valley, CA 92284
(760) 365-3022
(760) 248-3389 FAX

Outpatient mental health srvs. Behavioral health screening, medication assist & support srvs. Counseling, group therapy, vocational srvs. FUNDING: County. OFC HRS: M-F 8am-5pm. Spanish spoken. ADM REQ: Children under 18 yrs. SERVES: San Bernardino County.

MOUNTAIN VIEW CLINIC

1001 N. State St.
Hemet, CA 92543
(951) 658-1253
(951) 658-1253 FAX

Counseling srvs for married couples, families, individuals, adolescents, children. Hypnotherapy also available. OFC HRS: Tu-F 10am-7pm; Sat 10am-4pm. SERVES: Riverside County.

MOURNING STAR CENTER, THE

42600 Cook St., Ste 210
Palm Desert, CA 92211
(760) 836-0360
(760) 776-1612 FAX

Open-ended support groups for children and teens, ages 3-19 yrs, and their families, who are grieving due to a death. Trained volunteers and professionals facilitate groups. Also extended support, edu srvs, free grief camp and community outreach. Visit www.mourningstar.org for more information about srvs and locations. FUNDING: Donations, nonprofit. OFC HRS: Vary. Spanish spoken. Accepts donations. Free srvs. SERVES: Riverside County.

MT. SAN JACINTO CHILDREN'S SRVS

950 Ramona Blvd., Ste 2
San Jacinto, CA 92582
(951) 487-2674
(951) 487-2679 FAX

Info & referral srvs, intake assessments, psychiatric evaluations & treatment, case mgmt. In-home behavioral srvs, 5150 evaluations, transportation srvs, individual therapy, group therapy & family therapy to seriously disturbed children & adolescents. FUNDING: County. OFC HRS: M-Th 8am-5pm. Spanish spoken. ADM REQ: Ages birth-18 yrs. Must meet county criteria. Accepts Medi-Cal and Healthy Families. SERVES: Riverside County.

NAMI-LOS ANGELES

Natl Alliance on Mental Illness
824 Moraga Dr.
Los Angeles, CA 90049
(310) 889-7200

NAMI is a natl organization that provides families of mentally ill persons with edu support and resources. Click the "Find Support" tab on the website for srvs in your area (www.nami.org). FUNDING: Nonprofit. OFC HRS: M-F 8am-6pm. Spanish spoken. SERVES: U.S.A.

NAMI-MT. SAN JACINTO

National Alliance on Mental Illness
P.O. Box 716
San Jacinto, CA 92581
(951) 765-1850

Advocacy group formed to help combat stigma faced by the mentally ill and their family members. Provides educational prgms & promotes awareness of mental issues in the community. Support group & info meetings 1st W each month, 6pm-8:30pm, in Hemet & San Jacinto Valley. Meetings held at the Camelot Retirement Community, 800 W. Oakland Ave., Hemet, CA, 92543. FUNDING: Nonprofit, dues, fundraising, donations. OFC HRS: M-Sat 9am-5pm. SERVES: L.A., Orange & Riverside Counties.

NAMI-NATIONAL OFFICE

National Alliance on Mental Illness
3803 N. Fairfax Dr., Ste 100
Arlington, VA 22201-3042
(800) 950-6264
(703) 524-7600
(703) 524-9094 FAX

Helpline provides info about mental illness & referral to community resources. NAMI is the country's leading grassroots advocacy organization dedicated solely to improving the lives of persons with severe mental illness, including schizophrenia, bipolar disorder (manic-depressive illness), major depression, obsessive-compulsive disorder, and severe anxiety disorders. More than 1,200 state & local affiliates, Calif office (916) 567-0163, Fax (916) 567-1757. FUNDING: Nonprofit. OFC HRS: M-F 10am-6pm, EST. Spanish spoken. SERVES: U.S.A.

NATL ASSN FOR THE DUALLY DIAGNOSED

132 Fair St.
Kingston, NY 12401
(800) 331-5362
(845) 331-4336
(845) 331-4569 FAX

Membership assn established for professionals, care providers and families to promote understanding for individuals who have both dev disabilities and mental illness. FUNDING: Nonprofit.

NATL BIPOLAR FOUNDATION

111 S. Highland, Ste 129
Memphis, TN 38111

Mission is to reduce the stigma, educate the public, and seek afforable healthcare treatment for those with the bipolar condition. Also offers the Jericho Project, a prgm designed to help those with mental illness divert the justice system. Visit (www.nationalbipolarfoundation.org). FUNDING: Nonprofit. SERVES: U.S.A.

NATL CENTER FOR PTSD

U.S. Dept. of Veterans Affairs
810 Vermont Ave., N.W.
Washington, DC 20420
(802) 296-6300

Center aims to help U.S. veterans, professionals, and community members through research, edu, and training on trauma and PTSD. Website includes VA PTSD prgm locator. Visit (www.ptsd.va.gov). FUNDING: Govt. ADM REQ: Must be a veteran in order to obtain clinical srvs. SERVES: U.S.A.

NATL INSTITUTE OF MENTAL HEALTH

MSC 9663
P.O. Box MSC 9663
6001 Executive Blvd., Rm. 8184
Bethesda, MD 20892-9663

(301) 443-4513
(866) 615-6464
(301) 443-4279 FAX

Federal research institute conducts & supports research that focuses on the causes, diagnosis, prevention & treatment of severe mental illness. Public inquiries line is staffed with trained specialists who respond to info requests from the lay public, clinicians & scientific community. TTY (301) 443-8431 or (866) 415-8051. FUNDING: Govt. OFC HRS: M-F 8:30am-5pm, EST. Spanish spoken. SERVES: U.S.A.

NEW HOPE CRISIS COUNSELING
Crystal Cathedral
12141 Lewis St.
Garden Grove, CA 92840
(714) 639-4673
(714) 971-4327 FAX

24-hr phone counseling and online counseling in a pvt chat room for all types of problems: crisis intervention, suicide prev, info & referral. Srvs provided by trained & caring volunteers. To learn about training classes & the benefits of volunteering, e-mail (quinnw@crystalcathedral.org) or call (714) 971-4123.. Hotline (714) NEW-HOPE. Teenline: M-F 4pm-10pm, (714) 639-TEEN. Visit (www.newhopenow.org). FUNDING: Church, donations, nonprofit. OFC HRS: M-F 9am-5pm. Crisis helplines 24 hrs, 7 days. Spanish spoken. Free srvs. SERVES: U.S.A.

NEW HOPE/MORENO VALLEY
12818 Heacock St., Ste C-6
Moreno Valley, CA 92553
(951) 247-6542
(951) 247-9819 FAX

Christian counseling center. Serves as a training facility for those in the counseling profession. Psychological testing, child abuse counseling, crisis eval, parenting issues, school problems, teenage issues such as suicide, runaway, depression, eating disorders and substance abuse, bereavement counseling, adult abuse issues, pain mgmt and a host of other adult counseling needs. FUNDING: Donations, fees, nonprofit. OFC HRS: By appt. ADM REQ: Low income. Accepts insurance in most cases, Victim-Witness Program, recovery assistance foundation. Sliding scale basis upon request. SERVES: So. Calif.

NIKKEI HELPLINE
231 E. 3rd Street, Ste G-106
Los Angeles, CA 90013
(213) 473-3030
(800) 645-5341
(213) 473-3031 FAX

Helpline, info & referrals. Trained volunteers listen to all types of problems; some referrals are made for counseling in L.A. Co. only. FUNDING: Nonprofit. OFC HRS: M-F 9:30am-5:30pm. Japanese & Korean spoken. SERVES: So. Calif.

OBSESSIVE-COMPULSIVE FNDN, INC.
P.O. Box 961029
112 Water St., Ste 501
Boston, MA 02129
(617) 973-5801

Internatl organization composed of people with obsessive-compulsive disorder (OCD) and related disorders, their families, friends, professionals and others. Individual membership is

$45 per yr and includes bi-monthly newsletter with latest research, resources and recovery, conferences, research awards, related support groups, etc. FUNDING: Nonprofit. OFC HRS: M-F 9am-5pm, EST. Spanish spoken. ADM REQ: Membership. SERVES: U.S.A. & Internatl.

OLIVE BRANCH COUNSELING CTR, INC.
9033 Baseline Rd., Ste H
Rancho Cucamonga, CA 91730
(909) 989-9030
(909) 466-4594 FAX

Counseling services for individuals, families, couples & groups including: anger mgmt, eating disorders, grief recovery, domestic violence, sexual abuse, victims of crime. Pre-marital, divorce recovery, parenting classes. Court-certified for anger mgmt, domestic violence (DV), parenting & co-parenting classes. Certified visitation. All programs available for high-risk youth and adults. Locations in Claremont, Riverside, and Rancho Cucamonga. FUNDING: Nonprofit. OFC HRS: M-F 9am-8pm; Sat 9am-5pm. Spanish spoken. Accepts insurance, sliding fee scale. SERVES: San Bernardino County.

OLIVE BRANCH COUNSELING CTR, INC.
4041 Brockton Ave.
Riverside, CA 92501
(951) 369-8534
(951) 369-1145 FAX

Counseling services for individuals, families, couples & groups including: anger mgmt, eating disorders, grief recovery, domestic violence, sexual abuse, victims of crime. Pre-marital, divorce recovery, parenting classes. Court-certified for anger mgmt, domestic violence (DV), parenting & co-parenting classes. Certified visitation. All programs available for high-risk youth and adults. Locations in Claremont, Riverside, and Rancho Cucamonga. FUNDING: Nonprofit. OFC HRS: M-F 9am-5pm; Sat 8:30am-5pm. Evening counseling available by appt. Spanish spoken. Accepts insurance, sliding fee scale. SERVES: Riverside.

OLIVE CREST TREATMENT CENTER
555 Technology Ct., Ste 300
Riverside, CA 92507
(951) 686-8500
(951) 369-3037 FAX

Intense residential treatment prgm for adolescents experiencing emotional problems, using a medical model with nursing srvs. Centers are accredited and available to children through most health insurance plans. Occupational therapy, dietitian assessment, individual, group and family therapy. Residential care for boys & girls ages 13-17 yrs. Also licensed as a foster care and adoption agency; recruits, trains, provides respite care & network srvs for foster & adoptive families. This prgm places children ages birth-18 yrs in certified foster homes & provides placement srvs for adoptive families. FUNDING: Grants, nonprofit. OFC HRS: M-F 8:30am-5pm. SERVES: So. Calif.

OPTIMIST YOUTH HOMES/FAMILY SRVS
P.O. Box 41-1076
6957 N. Figueroa St.
Los Angeles, CA 90041-1076
(323) 443-3175
(323) 443-3264 FAX

24-hr residential mental health treatment srvs for male adolescents ages 12-18 yrs. Main campus in Highland Park. Four (2 male, 2 female) 6-bed group homes in L.A. County. Non-public school, foster family agency and adoptions prgms, mental health srvs, after care prgms. Referrals through the courts & probation. Limited pvt placements. Accredited by the Council on Accreditation (C.O.A.). FUNDING: Donation, grants, govt, nonprofit. OFC HRS: M-F 9am-5pm. Spanish, Vietnamese & Farsi spoken. Accepts Medi-Cal. SERVES: Calif.

PACIFIC CLINICS
Administration
800 S. Santa Anita Ave.
Arcadia, CA 91006
(626) 254-5000
(877) 722-2737

Outpatient mental health srvs to seriously ill children, youth, adults and seniors regardless of ability to pay. Prgms include: day treatment for children & adol, homeless mentally ill outreach, geriatric outreach and Asian-Pacific srvs. Adult clubhouse drop-in prgms at some sites. Multilingual prgms. APA-accredited intern prgm. Most referrals are through county health care agencies. For child & adol srvs, call (626) 441-4221. Also outpatient & residential alcohol & drug treatment prgm at various sites. Locations in L.A., Orange, Riverside, San Bernardino and Ventura countries. State ID: 190254EN. FUNDING: County, state, United Way, donations, nonprofit. OFC HRS: M-F 8am-5pm. Multiple languages spoken. Accepts Medi-Cal SERVES: L.A., Orange & Riverside Counties.

PECHANGA INDIAN HEALTH CLINIC
12784 Pechanga Rd.
Temecula, CA 92592
(951) 676-6810
(951) 676-0744 FAX

Comprehensive health care, mental health (individual and family counseling), nutrition, pharmacy, lab, nursing, AIDS testing, family planning, patient transportation srvs. FUNDING: Fed, state, county. OFC HRS: M-Th 8am-5pm; F 8am-2pm. ADM REQ: Eligible American Indian dependents only. Must have appt. Accepts Medi-Cal for eligible patients only. Sliding fee scale. Free srvs to qualified Indians.

PHOENIX SERVICES
See "San Bernardino Co. Behav Health"

PROJECT SISTER
Sexual Assault Crisis & Prev Srvs
P.O. Box 1369
Pomona, CA 91769-1369
(909) 623-1619
(909) 622-8389 FAX

24-hr sexual assault crisis hotline; personal accompaniment to hospital, police station and court; in-person counseling; support groups for rape. AMAC (Adults Molested As Children) and incest survivors, referrals to other agencies, community edu (including sexual harassment) and teen date rape awareness & self-protection classes. Srvs for seniors also available. 24-hr helpline (909) 626-4357 and (626) 966-4155. FUNDING: United Way, Office of Emerg Srvs, donations, CDBG grants, nonprofit. OFC HRS: M-F 8am-5pm. Spanish spoken. Free srvs, except for counseling & groups on a sliding fee scale. No one turned away for lack of funds. SERVES: East San Gabriel Valley, Pomona Valley & West San Bernardino County.

RESEARCH & TRAINING CTR ON FAMILY FOR PATHWAYS TO POSITIVE FUTURES

Portland State University
P.O. Box 751
1600 SW 4th Avenue, Ste 900
Portland, OR 97201
(503) 725-4040
(503) 725-4180 FAX

Supports successful transition for youth and young adults with serious mental health conditions. Srvs include rigorous research, Focal Point (natl publication), and effective training and dissemniation. FUNDING: Govt, grants. OFC HRS: M-F 8am-5pm. Spanish spoken. Most publications free, some mailed at cost. SERVES: U.S.A.

RIM FAMILY SRVS, INC.

P.O. Box 578
28545 Highway 18
Skyforest, CA 92385
(909) 336-1800
(909) 336-0990 FAX

Individual, group and family counseling, trauma recovery for victims of crime, domestic violence, etc. Community edu prgm. Info & referral; prevention & edu; outpatient counseling; DUI 1st offender & multiple (18-month) prgms; outpatient drug & alcohol treatment prgm. PC-1000, strengthening family prgm, mobile resource center, aftercare prgm. State ID: 360036AN. FUNDING: Nonprofit. OFC HRS: M-Th 8am-6pm. F 8am-5pm. Sat 8am-2pm. Spanish spoken. Interpreter as needed. ADM REQ: Counseling for all ages. DUI for ages 16 yrs+. Accepts Medi-Cal for drug/alcohol, sliding fee scale. SERVES: San Bernardino County.

RITA PROJECT, INC.

Mailing Address
2046 Hillhurst Ave.
Los Angeles, CA 90027
(866) 775-7482

Rita (Sanskrit for truth) is a global movement to stop suicide and celebrate life. Devoted to using the arts to help survivors of suicide connect with the power of creation, and in doing so, foster transformation. Prgms offered through Rita Studios, Rita Workshops & Rita Exhibitions. Assist with healing, suicide prev, edu and public awareness on the importance of the arts to mental health. Visit (www.ritaproject.org). Rita Studios are held weekly at the Bergamot Cafe, 2525 Michigan Ave., #A-3, Santa Monica, CA 90404. Please call to register. FUNDING: Nonprofit. OFC HRS: 24 hrs. ADM REQ: Ages 18 yrs+. SERVES: So. Calif.

RIVERSIDE AREA RAPE CRISIS CENTER

1845 Chicago Ave., Ste A
Riverside, CA 92507
(951) 686-7273
(951) 686-0839 FAX

Crisis line. Hospital, law enforcement & court accompaniment, info & referral, community edu, child abuse prev, senior outreach prgm, support group, follow-up. Outreach prgm available in Spanish. Southwest County (866) 686-7273. FUNDING: OCJP, county, city, fndns, donors, United Way, nonprofit. OFC

HRS: M-F 8am-5pm. Crisis line and hospital advocacy 24/7. Some Spanish spoken. ASL available. ADM REQ: Victim of sexual assault, family member or significant other. Free srvs. SERVES: Western Riverside County.

RIVERSIDE CO. DEPT/MENTAL HEALTH

Administrative Office
P.O. Box 7549
4095 County Circle Dr.
Riverside, CA 92513
(951) 358-4500
(951) 358-4513 FAX

Overall planning, implementation, direction, coordination and eval of the Dept of Mental Health prgms in Riverside County. Treatment for adults: residential, outpatient, day care, socialization ctrs, crisis srvs, case mgmt, continuing care, etc. Children's prgms: outpatient, case mgmt, foster home placement, etc. Also main admin office for drug abuse and alcohol control prgms. No actual srvs available at this location. FUNDING: Govt. Spanish spoken. Accepts Medi-Cal SERVES: Riverside County.

RIVERSIDE CO. DEPT/MENTAL HEALTH

Open Doors Parent Group/Phone Support
4020 Jefferson St.
Riverside, CA 92504
(951) 358-3622

Community support group open to families & caregivers who are experiencing difficulties raising children with mental health, emotional and/or behavioral challenges. The meeting objective is to provide families an opportunity to meet, speak and join with other families who are experiencing similar challenges in order to share support, info, resources & solutions that will empower one another. Helpline for community info (800) 464-1123. 24-hr suicide helpline (909) 686-4357. FUNDING: Riverside Co. Dept/Mental Health Children's Srvs. OFC HRS: M-Th 8am-6pm. SERVES: Riverside County.

RIVERSIDE CO. MENTAL HEALTH

Desert Regional Srvs
1330 W. Ramsey Blvd., Ste 100
Banning, CA 92220
(951) 849-7142
(951) 849-1762 FAX

Dual-diagnosis srvs for adults, case mgmt, medication, group activities, crisis srvs. Outpatient srvs for children. Walk in or call. FUNDING: Govt. OFC HRS: M-Th 8am-5pm. 24-hr crisis line. Spanish spoken. ADM REQ: Severely, persistently & acutely mentally ill who do not have resources to be treated in the private sector. Accepts Medi-Cal, sliding fee scale. SERVES: Riverside County.

RIVERSIDE CO. MENTAL HEALTH

Hemet Mental Health Clinic
650 N. State St.
Hemet, CA 92543
(951) 791-3300
(909) 791-3333 FAX

Family advocate prgm provides info & support to families of the mentally ill. Outpatient medication clinic for the mentally ill. Homeless department. Substance abuse department. FUNDING: Govt. OFC HRS: M-Th 8am-5:30pm. Spanish, Tagalog spoken. ADM REQ: Severely mentally ill. Accepts Medi-Cal, Medicare, indigent prgms. SERVES: Hemet, San Jacinto, Idyllwild, Anza, Winchester.

RIVERSIDE CO. MENTAL HEALTH

Indio Mental Health Srvs
47-825 Oasis St.
Indio, CA 92201
(760) 863-8455
(760) 863-8587 FAX

Admin office for Desert Region Mental Health Srvs. Plans, coordinates & oversees several mental health prgms in Eastern Riverside County. Outpatient & residential prgms for severely mentally ill or severe crisis (suicidal). FUNDING: Govt. OFC HRS: M-Th 8am-6pm. Srvs for crisis or severely ill 24 hrs. Spanish spoken. Accepts Medi-Cal, sliding fee scale. SERVES: Desert & Eastern Riverside County.

RIVERSIDE CO. MENTAL HEALTH

Perris Mental Health Clinic
1688 N. Perris Blvd., Ste L7- L11
Perris, CA 92571-4709
(951) 443-2200
(951) 443-2230 FAX

Plans, coordinates and administers the mental health srvs for Riverside Mid-County Region. Branch offices in Hemet and Temecula; vocational center in San Jacinto. The prgms at this location include: crisis srvs, children's srvs, case mgmt, medications, socialization, dual-diagnosis, assessment & a variety of treatment modalities. FUNDING: Govt sponsored, Short Doyle, Medi-Cal, County. OFC HRS: M-Th 8am-6pm. Spanish spoken. ADM REQ: People experiencing acute or persistent mental illness. Accepts Medi-Cal only. SERVES: Riverside County.

RIVERSIDE CO. MENTAL HEALTH

Children's Treatment Srvs Admin
9990 County Farm Rd., Ste 5
Riverside, CA 92503
(951) 358-4840
(951) 358-4881

Support and edu groups, trainings relating to mental health. Parent-to-parent support line, call (888) 358-3622. FUNDING: Govt. OFC HRS: M-Th 8am-6pm Spanish spoken. SERVES: Riverside County.

RIVERSIDE CO. MENTAL HEALTH

Van Horn Counseling Center
10000 County Farm Rd.
Riverside, CA 92503
(951) 358-4390
(951) 358-4472 FAX

Placement is court-ordered only. Not a public outpatient facility. Intensive residential treatment providing individual, group and family counseling. FUNDING: Govt. OFC HRS: M-F 8am-5pm. Spanish spoken. ADM REQ: Adolescent wards of the court from Riverside Co. SERVES: Riverside County.

RIVERSIDE CO. MENTAL HEALTH

Blaine Street Clinic
769 Blaine St., Ste B
Riverside, CA 92507
(951) 358-4705
(951) 358-4719 FAX

Crisis and outpatient srvs. TTY (951) 358-4728. FUNDING: Govt. OFC HRS: M-Th 8am-6pm. Spanish spoken. ADM REQ: Crisis or eligible mental illness. Accepts Medi-Cal only. SERVES: Riverside County.

RIVERSIDE CO. MENTAL HEALTH
Children's Treatment Srvs
9990 County Farm Rd., Ste 5
Riverside, CA 92503
(951) 358-4840
(951) 358-4848 FAX

Intensive prgms designed for children who need more intervention than a 1-2 hour outpatient prgm. Designed to increase coping skills and reduce their symptomology. FUNDING: Govt. OFC HRS: M-Th 8am-5:30pm. Spanish spoken. ADM REQ: Ages 5-18 yrs. Accepts Medi-Cal, Healthy Kids. SERVES: City of Riverside.

RIVERSIDE CO. MENTAL HEALTH
Jefferson Wellness Center
1827 Atlanta Ave., Ste D-3
Riverside, CA 92507
(951) 955-8000
(951) 955-8010 FAX

Develops life skills including: socialization, job skills, time mgmt, specialized skills (computer classes, math, woodwork), health-related skills, food prep, independent living and various other skills. FUNDING: County. OFC HRS: M-Th 9am-6pm. Spanish spoken. ADM REQ: Diagnosed as mentally disabled. SERVES: West Riverside County from Corona to Moreno Valley.

RIVERSIDE CO. MENTAL HEALTH
Children's Case Management
9707 Magnolia Ave.
Riverside, CA 92503
(951) 358-6858
(951) 687-3478 FAX

Case mgmt srvs for seriously emotionally disturbed adol & children ages 6-18 yrs. Includes screening, referral, placement and follow-up for minors in residential and hospital treatment. FUNDING: Govt. OFC HRS: M-Th 8am-6pm. Spanish spoken. ASL available. ADM REQ: Pre-eval required. Accepts Medi-Cal. Sliding fee scale. SERVES: Riverside County.

RIVERSIDE CO. MENTAL HEALTH
Mental Health Detention Srvs
4275 Lemon St., Ste 207
Riverside, CA 92501
(951) 955-8540
(951) 955-8542 FAX

Psychiatric eval, medication, individual counseling for clients incarcerated in Riverside County Jail and post-release planning. OFC HRS: 24 hrs. Language line available. SERVES: Riverside County.

RIVERSIDE CO. MENTAL HEALTH
Mid-County Temecula
41002 County Center Dr., Ste 320
Temecula, CA 92591
(951) 600-6355
(951) 600-6365 FAX

Case mgmt, medication, crisis srvs. Outpatient for children. FUNDING: Govt. OFC HRS: M-Th 8am-6pm. Spanish spoken. ADM REQ: Serious mental illness and do not have resources to be treated in the pvt sector. Accepts Medi-Cal only. SERVES: Riverside County.

RIVERSIDE/SAN BRDO CO. INDIAN HLTH
Morongo Indian Health Clinic
11555 1/2 Potrero Rd.
Banning, CA 92220
(800) 732-8805
(951) 849-4761
(951) 849-5612 FAX

Outpatient alcohol & drug treatment prgm, AA meetings, parenting classes, counseling. Comprehensive health care: medical, dental, vision, mental health (indiv & family counseling), pharmacy, lab, nursing, family planning, AIDS testing, WIC prgm, transportation. Serves all ages. FUNDING: Govt. OFC HRS: M, W, Th 8am-5pm; Tu 8am-7pm; F 8am-2pm. ADM REQ: Must have appt. Accepts Medi-Cal. Free srvs to qualified Indians. SERVES: Riverside & San Bernardino Counties.

S.P.A.R.E. MINISTRIES COUNSELING
Society Providing Assist, Rehab & Edu
1215 W. Imperial Hwy., Ste 223
Brea, CA 92821
(714) 345-4938

Offers counseling srvs to individuals, couples, families and other groups to address life issues facing both Christian and non-religious communities. Goal is to cultivate emotional, physical, and spiritual healing that will allow clients to increase their ability to be in a relationship with others. FUNDING: Nonprofit. OFC HRS: M-Sat 9am-5pm. Accepts some insurance. Sliding fee scale. SERVES: Orange, L.A., and San Bernardino Counties.

SAMARITAN COUNSELING CENTER
869 N. Euclid Ave.
Upland, CA 91786
(909) 985-0513
(909) 985-7193 FAX

Marriage and family counseling, therapy for all age groups; individual therapy for depression, anxiety, stress, self-esteem, emotional abuse, divorce, vocational change, etc. FUNDING: Donations, nonprofit. OFC HRS: M-F 8:30am-5:30pm; eve by appt. Sliding fee scale depending on funding. SERVES: San Bernardino County.

SAMHSA
Substance Abuse & Mental Hlth Srvs Admin
P.O. Box 2345
1 Choke Cherry Rd.
Rockville, MD 20857
(240) 276-2000
(240) 276-2010 FAX

Established to provide info on prevention, diagnosis & treatment srvs for substance abuse and mental illness. Clearinghouse for prevention & treatment info (800) 729-6686. For mental health info, call (877) SAMHSA7. FUNDING: Govt. OFC HRS: M-F 8am-5pm, EST. Spanish spoken. SERVES: U.S.A.

SAMHSA'S NATL MENTAL HLTH INFO CTR
Center for Mental Health Srvs Info
P.O. Box 42557
Washington, DC 20015
(800) 789-2647
(240) 221-1295 FAX

Publications on a variety of mental health topics such as depression, anxiety, stress, self-help, support groups, treatment and research. Consumers can order these publications by calling the number above or through the website which also enables users to search for srvs. Visit (www.samhsa.gov). Materials available in Spanish. TDD (866) 889-2647. Publications can also be ordered via fax or e-mail. FUND-

ING: Govt. OFC HRS: M-F 8:30am-12midnight, EST. Spanish spoken. Free srvs. SERVES: U.S.A.

SAN BERNARDINO CO. ALCOHOL/DRUG
Needles Center for Change
300 H Street
Needles, CA 92363
(760) 326-4590
(888) 743-1478
(760) 326-3154 FAX

Alcohol & drug outpatient, info & referral, outpatient counseling, DUI 1st offender & 2nd offender (18-month) prgms, individual and group therapy, PC-1000, drug court. Walk in or call. State ID: 360033IN. FUNDING: Nonprofit. OFC HRS: M-Th 8am-12noon, 1pm-6pm. ADM REQ: Ages 18 yrs+. SERVES: San Bernardino County.

SAN BERNARDINO CO. BEHAV HEALTH
Outpatient Services - Central Valley
See "Family Service Agency/Fontana"

SAN BERNARDINO CO. BEHAV HEALTH
Outpatient Services - West Valley
See "West End Family Counseling"

SAN BERNARDINO CO. BEHAV HEALTH
Outpatient Mental Health/Substance Abuse
805 E. Mt. View
Barstow, CA 92311
(760) 256-5026
(760) 256-5092 FAX

Counseling for children, adolescents, transitional age youth, adults & elderly; dual-diagnosis srvs. FUNDING: Govt. OFC HRS: M, W, F 8am-5pm; Tu, Th 8am-6:30pm. Spanish spoken. ADM REQ: Must meet county requirement; chronic mental illness. Sliding fee scale. SERVES: Barstow, Helendale, Lucerne Valley to Baker.

SAN BERNARDINO CO. BEHAV HEALTH
Agewise Program
850 E. Foothill Blvd.
Rialto, CA 92376
(909) 421-9470
(909) 873-4461 FAX

County-sponsored outreach mental health srvs for older adults using professionals and senior peer counselors, support groups and professional training. FUNDING: Dept of Behav Health, county, govt. OFC HRS: M-F 8am-5pm. ADM REQ: Ages 60 yrs+, in need of counseling. Free srvs. SERVES: San Bernardino County.

SAN BERNARDINO CO. BEHAV HEALTH
Adult Resident Srvs
850 E. Foothill Blvd.
Rialto, CA 92376
(909) 421-9475
(909) 421-9392 FAX

Augmented boarding care placement (36 beds, with waiting list), IMD instution placement. Dual-diagnosis residential treatment based on referral only. Portals long-term program, by referral, for patients with long-term stability. Info and referral. No direct residential srvs. Contact: Dr. Pfau. Visit (www.ccld.ca.gov) for licensed board & care facilities. Contact CWIK clinic for crisis intervention, (909)421-9494. FUNDING: Govt. OFC HRS: M-F 8am-5pm. ADM REQ: By referral only. Sliding fee scale. SERVES: Rialto, Fontana, Bloomington.

SAN BERNARDINO CO. BEHAV HEALTH

Patient's Rights Office
850 E. Foothill Blvd.
Rialto, CA 92376
(800) 440-2391

This office protects the patient, consumer and human rights of all recipients of psychiatric srvs. Consultation and training are available to providers of psychiatric srvs. Advocates investigate complaints concerning behavioral health srvs, monitor mental health facilities, provide training and edu regarding mental health law, and ensure that recipients of mental health srvs are notified of their rights. FUNDING: Govt. OFC HRS: M-F 8am-5pm. Spanish SERVES: San Bernardino County.

SAN BERNARDINO CO. BEHAV HEALTH

Phoenix Community Counseling
820 E. Gilbert St.
San Bernardino, CA 92415-0920
(909) 387-7200

Crisis and referral srvs, assessment, individual, family, group counseling, psychological testing. Intensive case mgmt, home contacts, rehab training. Wait: max of 2 hrs for assessment. Walk in or call. FUNDING: County agency, pvt insurance. OFC HRS: M-F 8am-5pm. Assessment hrs vary on appt. Spanish spoken. Hearing-impaired interpreter available. Other languages by request. ADM REQ: Some limitations based upon severity of problems. Must have ID. Accepts Medi-Cal. Sliding fee scale. Free referrals to community resources. SERVES: San Bernardino County.

SAN BERNARDINO CO. BEHAV HEALTH

Mentally Ill Homeless Program
237 W. Mill St.
San Bernardino, CA 92408
(909) 388-4133
(909) 388-4190 FAX

Shelter provided to the mentally ill homeless adults in San Bernardino County. Clients must have a major mental diagnosis. Prgm utilizes intensive case mgmt and assists clients in obtaining SSI, temporary housing and employment. Walk-in clients and call referrals are accepted. Limited availability for 30 days. FUNDING: Govt. OFC HRS: M-F 8am-5pm. Spanish spoken. Free srvs. SERVES: San Bernardino County.

SAN BERNARDINO CO. BEHAV HEALTH

Victor Valley Behavioral Health Center
12625 Hesperia Rd.
Victorville, CA 92392
(760) 955-1777
(760) 955-2356 FAX

Outpatient treatment of clients with mental illness. Medical, social, psychiatric, psychological support srvs. Crisis intervention, prevention prgms. FUNDING: OADP, nonprofit. OFC HRS: M-F 8am-5pm. Spanish spoken. Accepts Medi-Cal. Sliding fee scale. SERVES: San Bernardino County.

SAN BERNARDINO CO. SUPERIOR CRT

Mental Health Counselors/AR Health Bldg.
400 N. Pepper St.
Colton, CA 92324
(909) 580-1812
(909) 580-1827 FAX

Field eval for involuntary psychiatric hospitalization (i.e. 5150-5200) and referrals to appro-

priate resources. FUNDING: County, govt. OFC HRS: M-F 8am-5pm. Foreign languages available for court proceedings. ADM REQ: Probability for meeting legal criteria. Free srvs. SERVES: San Bernardino County.

SAN BERNARDINO CO. SUPERIOR CRT

Mental Health Counselors
400 N. Pepper Ave.
Colton, CA 92324
(909) 580-1812
(909) 580-2165 FAX

70-bed psychiatric hospital. Screening eval & consultations for involuntary psychiatric hospitalization. Edu presentation to promote community awareness of mental health laws and resources. FUNDING: Govt. OFC HRS: 24 hrs. Spanish spoken. SERVES: San Bernardino County.

SAN BERNARDINO VET CENTER

Dept of Veterans Affairs
1325 E. Cooley Dr., Ste 101
Colton, CA 92324
(909) 801-5762
(909) 801-5767 FAX

Provides individual and group counseling for veterans and their families. Also offers assessment and info & referral srvs for substance abuse, employment, various medical conditions, and VBA benefits. Bereavement counseling also offered to families of soldiers who experienced an active duty death. FUNDING: Govt. OFC HRS: M-F 8am-4:30pm. ADM REQ: Must be a veteran or a family member of a veteran. Free srvs. SERVES: San Bernardino Co.

SCHULZ, CHRISTINA H. - LMFT (MFC43973)

313 N. Second Ave.
Upland, CA 91786
(909) 815-9009

Individuals, couples, and group counseling for all ages, genders, and sexual orientations. Counselor experienced in relationship issues, divorce, parenting or adoption, depression, anxiety and grief recovery. Are you affected by a loved one with a health impairment or mental illness? Together we can explore solutions to manage these issues in a safe, confidential, compassionate and professional manner. Visit my website www.uplandcounseling.com. OFC HRS: M-F 9am-9pm, Sat/Sun 9am-5pm. Payments: various insurance/sliding scale/PayPal.

SCREENING FOR MENTAL HEALTH, INC.

One Washington St., Ste 304
Wellesley Hills, MA 02481-1706
(781) 239-0071
(781) 431-7447 FAX

Coordinates nationwide mental health screening prgms: Natl Depression Screening Day, Natl Alcohol Screening Day and Natl Eating Disorders Screening prgm, Signs of Suicide prgm. Crisis line: (800) 273-8255. FUNDING: Nonprofit. OFC HRS: M-F 9am-6pm, EST. Spanish spoken. SERVES: U.S.A, Canada, Bermuda & Virgin Islands.

SEEKING PEACEFUL SOLUTIONS, INC.

8724 S. Vermont Ave.
Los Angeles, CA 90047
(323) 753-1314
(323) 753-6619 FAX

Conflict and dispute resolution srvs that assist in the reduction and prevention of violence among youth, adolescents, adults and communities at large. These srvs provided in partnership with schools, law enforcement, businesses, communities and within families. FUNDING: Nonprofit. OFC HRS: M-F 8:30am-7:00pm; Sat 9am-3:30pm; Sun by appt only. Spanish spoken. SERVES: L.A., Orange, Riverside & San Bernardino Counties.

SENECA CTR FOR CHILDREN & FAMILIES

Admin Office
2275 Arlington Dr.
San Leandro, CA 94578
(510) 481-1222
(510) 481-1605 FAX

Residential treatment, intensive treatment foster care, day, in-home & outpatient srvs for children with emotional, behavioral & learning problems. Center for Living Skills works with public schools in conflict resolution, leadership, drug & alcohol edu. FUNDING: Nonprofit. OFC HRS: M-F 8am-5:30pm. Spanish speaker by arrangement. ADM REQ: Ages 3-18 yrs. SERVES: Calif.

SEXUAL ASSAULT SRVS/REDLANDS

Redlands Outreach
30 Cajon St.
Redlands, CA 92373
(909) 335-8777
(909) 335-4768 FAX

Support for victims of sexual assault and significant others through individual and group counseling, hospital and court accompaniment. Community edu prgms and self-defense. 24-hour natl crisis hotline (800) 656-4673. FUNDING: Nonprofit. OFC HRS: M-F 8am-5pm. Free srvs. SERVES: San Bernardino County.

SEXUAL ASSAULT SRVS/SAN BRDO

444 N. Arrowhead Ave., Ste 101-104
San Bernardino, CA 92401-1221
(909) 885-8884
(909) 383-8478 FAX

Support for victims of sexual assault and significant others. Individual and group counseling, hospital & court accompaniment, community edu prgms and self-defense. Rape Crisis Ctr has support groups for adolescents, adults molested as children, etc., 24-hr crisis line: (800) 656-4673. Coachella Valley (760) 568-9071. Morongo Basin (760) 369-3353. FUNDING: United Way, Ofc of Emergency Services, nonprofit. OFC HRS: M-Th 8am-5pm; F 8am-2pm. Spanish spoken. ADM REQ: Victims of sexual assault. Free srvs. SERVES: San Bernardino County.

SEXUAL ASSAULT SRVS/VICTORVILLE

15437 Anacapa Rd., Ste 8
Victorville, CA 92392
(760) 952-0041
(760) 383-8478 FAX

Individual & group counseling, outreach, crisis srvs, prevention & edu prgms, referrals for legal assist and parenting resources. 24-hr natl crisis line (800) 656-4673. FUNDING: Nonprofit. OFC HRS: M-Th 8am-5pm; F 8am-2pm. Spanish spoken. ADM REQ: Victims of sexual assault. Free srvs. SERVES: San Bernardino County.

SEXUAL ASSAULT SRVS/YUCAIPA

Yucaipa Outreach/Domestic Viol Prgm

34282 Yucaipa Blvd.
Yucaipa, CA 92399
(909) 790-9374
(909) 790-3111 FAX

Srvs to survivors of domestic violence. Individual & group counseling, community edu, referrals, court accompaniment & 24-hr hotline (800) 656-4673. FUNDING: Members, donations, nonprofit. OFC HRS: M-F 8am-5pm. Spanish spoken. Free srvs. SERVES: Inland Empire.

SHANDIN HILLS BEHAV THERAPY CTR
4164 N. 4th Avenue
San Bernardino, CA 92407
(909) 886-6786
(909) 886-2953 FAX

47-bed psychiatric institute providing residential care for those with mental disease. 6-9 month prgm. Discharge planning goal is lower level care. FUNDING: County of San Bernardino. OFC HRS: 24-hr srvs. Some Spanish spoken. ADM REQ: Referral by San Bernardino County Mental Health. Accepts Medi-Cal. SERVES: San Bernardino County.

SINGLE PARENTS OF POWER
Emlac Health Srvs
P.O. Box 452602
1620 Centinela Ave, Ste 202
Inglewood, CA 90302
(310) 753-7860

Counseling services include: mental health, sexual abuse, anger mgmt, parenting, alcohol and drug abuse. Advocacy and counseling for victims of violent crimes and post-traumatic counseling for veterans. FUNDING: Nonprofit. OFC HRS: M-F 9am-9pm; Sat 10am-3pm. Spanish, Swahili spoken. Free counseling for victims of domestic violence. All other srvs on a sliding fee scale. SERVES: L.A. & San Bernardino Counties.

SO CALIF INDIAN CENTER, INC.
Corporate Office
10175 Slater Ave., Ste 150
Fountain Valley, CA 92708-4702
(714) 962-6673
(714) 962-6343 FAX

Edu, cultural, economic & recreational prgms for American Indians. Indian Child & Family Srvs (counseling, parenting, foster parents, etc.), WIA (employment assist & voc training), edu tutoring for Indian students in grades K-12. Emerg shelter, food, clothing, referral srvs. FUNDING: United Way, govt, nonprofit. OFC HRS: M-F 8am-5pm. ADM REQ: American Indian verification. SERVES: So. Calif.

SOBOBA INDIAN HEALTH CLINIC
607 Donna Way
San Jacinto, CA 92583
(800) 851-5816
(951) 654-0803
(951) 487-9634 FAX

Comprehensive health care: medical, dental, vision, mental health (individual & family counseling), pharmacy, lab, AIDS testing, nursing, family planning, well-baby, pediatric, health edu, transportation srvs. FUNDING: Fed, state, county. OFC HRS: M, Tu, Th 8am-5pm; W 8am-7pm; F 8am-2pm. ADM REQ: American Indian. Accepts Medi-Cal. Free to qualified Indians. SERVES: Riverside County.

SOUTH ASIAN HELPLINE & REFERRAL AGENCY (SAHARA)
17100 S. Pioneer Blvd., Ste 260
Artesia, CA 90701
(562) 402-4132
(562) 402-6093 FAX

Serves the South Asian community by providing them with info, referrals, skills dev and other culturally sensitive support srvs including mental health, health care, legal assist, transitional living ctrs, client advocacy, case mgmt, financial assist, job training and placement, community edu prgms, and senior srvs. FUNDING: Nonprofit. OFC HRS: M-F 8am-5pm. Hindi, Gujarati, Bengali, Urdu, Nepali, Tamil & Telugu spoken. Free srvs. SERVES: Southern California.

SOUTH COAST COMMUNITY SRVS
San Bernardino Co. Srvs Office
2930 Inland Empire Blvd., Ste 120
Ontario, CA 92764
(909) 980-6700

Provides life-essential srvs to troubled children, youth and families. Offers 4 group homes for abused, neglected and abandoned children ages 10-18 yrs and 2 group homes for young adults ages 18-25 yrs in need of short-term assist. Wraparound prgm offers family intervention srvs. Children's intensive srvs prgm provides outpatient counseling for individuals, children, teens and their families. Eval, assessment, testing, therapy, medication support, crisis intervention, case mgmt. Offers mental health clinics in Redlands (909) 792-0747 & Yucaipa (909) 790-0210. FUNDING: Nonprofit. Accepts Medi-Cal and pvt pay; sliding fee scale available. SERVES: San Bernardino County.

SOUTHERN CALIFORNIA
See "So Calif..."

SUICIDE PREVENTION CENTER
(877) 727-4747
(310) 398-5690 FAX

24-hr crisis hotline. AAS Certified. Crisis counseling & referrals to resources. Also Survivors After Suicide bereavement support groups to help cope with loss. Prevention speakers for schools & other community outreach. Toll-free (877) 727-4747 for L.A. & Orange Counties only. FUNDING: Govt, United Way, donations, nonprofit. OFC HRS: 24 hrs, 7 days. Free srvs. SERVES: So. Calif.

SUSAN B. KREVOY EATING DISORDERS PRGM
Wright Institute Los Angeles
9911 W. Pico Blvd., Ste 720
Los Angeles, CA 90035
(310) 277-2682
(310) 277-8903 FAX

Low fee individualized outpatient prgm. Individual, group & family therapy. Nutritional counseling to differentiate between physical & psychological hunger; art therapy, yoga, meditation. Cognitive behavior groups on topics such as self-esteem, body image & communication skills. Free comprehensive assessment. Case mgr will devise a three or four evening/week prgm structured to meet the patient's needs. When the patient is ready to leave the prgm, an aftercare group provides continued support for adolescents and adults. FUNDING: Nonprofit. OFC HRS: M-F 8am-5pm. Accepts

most insurance, sliding fee scale. SERVES: So. Calif.

TEEN RESCUE, INC.
Family Advocate Counseling
P.O. Box 2167
11800 Central Ave., Ste 121
Chino, CA 91710
(800) 494-2200
(909) 590-7030
(909) 590-7040 FAX

Christian faith-based agency specializing in working with adols and their families. Offers child, adol, individual, couple, and family therapy dealing with issues like adoption, anger, communication, depression, divorce, family issues, and anxiety. FUNDING: Nonprofit. OFC HRS: M-F 9am-5pm, evenings by appt. Sliding fee scale from $5 to $100. Insurance not accepted. SERVES: San Bernardino, Riverside, and L.A. Counties.

TEMECULA VET CENTER
Dept of Veterans Affairs
40935 County Center Dr., Ste A & B
Temecula, CA 92591
(951) 296-5608
(951) 296-0598 FAX

Provides individual and group counseling for veterans and their families. Also offers assessment and info & referral srvs for substance abuse, employment, various medical conditions, and VBA benefits. Bereavement counseling also offered to families of soldiers who experienced an active duty death. FUNDING: Govt. OFC HRS: M-F 8am-4:30pm. ADM REQ: Must be a veteran or a family member of a veteran. Free srvs. SERVES: Riverside Co.

THE CHICAGO SCHOOL OF PROFESSIONAL PSYCHOLOGY
617 W. 7th Street
Los Angeles, CA 90017
(213) 615-7200
(800) 721-8072

Nonprofit graduate school dedicated exclusively to psychology and related fields. Accredited by the Higher Learning Commission and an active member of the National Council of Schools and Programs of Professional Psychology. Areas of study: applied behavior analysis, child and adol. Psych, clinical psych, and forensic psych, general psych, gerontology, health psych, I/O and business psych, international psych, MFT, organizational leadership, psychodynamic psych, school psych, school and exercise psych, abuse and addiction. Campuses in Los Angeles, Orange County, Washington D.C., Chicago and online. FUNDING: Nonprofit. OFC HRS: M-F 9am-5pm. SERVES: U.S.A.

THE FRIENDSHIP LINE
Center for Elderly Suicide Prevention
3626 Geary Blvd.
San Francisco, CA 94118
(415) 752-3778

Free and supportive telephone counseling for seniors who are bereaved, depressed, isolated, or abused. Also offers srvs for their caregivers and advocates; grief support groups available in the San Francisco area. FUNDING: Nonprofit. OFC HRS: 24 hrs, 7 days. Free srvs. SERVES: Calif.

THE GROVE COMMUNITY CHURCH
19900 Grove Community Dr.
Riverside, CA 92508
(951) 571-9090
(951) 571-9091 FAX

Celebrate Recovery, a faith-based 12-Step support group dealing with anger mgmt, chemical dependency, co-dependency, eating disorders and sexual addictions, meets M at 7pm. Recovery Worship Service F at 7pm. Pre-marital, individual & family counseling and various support groups available. FUNDING: Nonprofit. OFC HRS: M-F 8am-5pm. Sat sessions by appt. Must call to register for counseling. Fees vary. $40 before 5pm, $50 after 5pm. No one turned away due to lack of funds. SERVES: Riverside.

THE JACQUELINE SIDMAN HEALTH FNDN
4199 Campus Dr., Ste 550
Irvine, CA 92612
(949) 251-9550
(949) 509-6599 FAX

An effective, drug-free treatment for the recovery of behavioral and physical health, from addiction, through the use of the subconscious mind. FUNDING: Nonprofit. OFC HRS: M-Sun 11:30am-6:30pm. SERVES: Calif.

THE JOHN HENRY FOUNDATION
403 N. Susan St.
Santa Ana, CA 92703
(714) 554-8906
(714) 554-8770 FAX

Provides a safe, welcoming and clinically supervised long-term, residential community for adults with schizophrenia spectrum disorders. JHF provides a home, medical and psychiatric care, a therapeutic community, family support & edu, recreational activities, and a supported work prgm to promote stabilization and healing for the individual and their family. FUNDING: Nonprofit. OFC HRS: 24 hrs, 7 days. SERVES: Southern Calif.

THE RELATIONAL CENTER
Formerly "The Center for Relational Studies"
5486 Wilshire Blvd.
Los Angeles, CA 90036
(323) 935-1807
(323) 935-1171 FAX

Affordable counseling/mental health srvs. Comprehensive assessment, resource coordination, individual, couple, family and group psychotherapy. All care srvs are designed and delivered in a way that is culturally sensitive and respectful of differences. Assist consumers to organize self-advocacy groups. Harm reduction approach is used when dealing with addiction issues. FUNDING: Nonprofit. OFC HRS: M, Th 9am-8pm; Tu 9am-5pm; W 9am-8:30pm; F 9am-5:30pm; Sat 9am-2pm. Spanish spoken. SERVES: L.A. & San Bernardino Counties.

THE SOLUTIONS ALCOHOL/DRUG RECOVERY
The Solutions Foundation, Inc.
3210 W. Jefferson Blvd.
Los Angeles, CA 90018
(323) 731-4981
(323) 731-4958 FAX

Collaborates with individuals, communities and agencies to break down barriers based on illiteracy, substance abuse, unemployment, crime and homelessness. Assists the recovering addict in rebuilding their lives & creating responsible environments through partnerships that positively impact their lives, their families and communities. FUNDING: Nonprofit. OFC HRS: M-F 8am-8pm, Sat 8am-4pm. SERVES: L.A., Ventura, Orange, Riverside & San Bernardino Counties.

TURNING POINT COUNSELING
915 W. Imperial Hwy., Ste 150
Brea, CA 92821
(800) 998-6329
(714) 784-2945 FAX

Christian outpatient counseling for individuals, families, couples, children & adol. Has several offices throughout Southern Calif, call for more info on those locations. FUNDING: Client fees, donations, nonprofit. OFC HRS: M-F 9am-5pm. SERVES: L.A., Orange, Riverside, San Bernardino, Ventura & San Diego Counties.

UCLA NEUROPSYCHIATRIC HOSPITAL
150 UCLA Medical Plaza
Los Angeles, CA 90095
(800) 825-9989
(310) 825-9111
(310) 267-0376 FAX

Comprehensive inpatient & outpatient srvs for a wide variety of psychiatric, emotional and dev disorders. Prgms in geriatric, adult child & adol psychiatry. Spanish-speaking psychosocial clinic. Individual prgms target: eating disorders, depression, obsessive compulsive disorder, schizophrenia & seizure disorders, anxiety. Matrix UCLA Alcoholism and Addiction Medicine Srv: (310) 206-7518. FUNDING: Nonprofit. OFC HRS: M-F 8am-5pm. Multilingual staff. Accepts insurance, Medicare, Medi-Cal. SERVES: So. Calif.

UPLAND COMMUNITY COUNSELING
934 N. Mountain Ave., Ste C
Upland, CA 91786-3659
(909) 579-8100
(909) 579-8149 FAX

Outpatient mental health srvs for all ages. Psychiatric evaluations, school-based prevention prgm, support groups. Walk-ins on Tu-Th 8am-10am for those without insurance. For Medi-Cal, call and make an appt. FUNDING: Govt. OFC HRS: M-F 8am-5pm. Spanish, Vietnamese spoken. Accepts Medi-Cal, sliding fee scale. SERVES: San Bernardino County.

VALLEY STAR CHILDREN & FAMILY SRVS
1585 South D Street, Ste 101
San Bernardino, CA 92408
(909) 388-2222
(909) 388-2220 FAX

Mental health srvs for troubled children, adolescents and families. In-home, clinic-based & school-based srvs. FUNDING: County. OFC HRS: M-F 8:30am-4:30pm. ADM REQ: Referrals from SB County Dept of Behavioral Health, Children's Srvs, Probation, foster family agencies, schools, counselors, family. Accepts Medi-Cal only. SERVES: San Bernardino County.

VILLAGE COUNSELING
Breaking Free
73302 Highway 111
Palm Desert, CA 92260
(760) 773-0669
(760) 773-0569 FAX

Outpatient drug & alcohol treatment prgm, parenting classes, marriage & family counseling, adol and individual counseling, anger mgmt. trauma & abuse counseling, life transitions, etc. State ID: 330052AP. FUNDING: Nonprofit. OFC HRS: Tu-F 9am-5pm. ADM REQ: Open to all ages SERVES: Riverside County.

VISTA COMM COUNSELING CTR
San Bernardino Co. Behavioral Health
17216 Slover Ave., Bldg. L
Fontana, CA 92335
(909) 854-3420
(909) 428-8437 FAX

Outpatient srvs for chronic mental illness. Behavioral health screening, help with medication, support srvs. Counseling, group therapy, dual-diagnosis, vocational skills. FUNDING: County. OFC HRS: M-F 8am-5pm. Spanish spoken. ADM REQ: Serves all ages. SERVES: Bloomington, Colton, Fontana.

VOLUNTEER CENTER/RIVERSIDE CO.
Crisis/Suicide Prevention
P.O. Box 5376
Riverside, CA 92517
(951) 686-4357
(951) 686-7417 FAX

24-hr crisis/suicide intervention hotline staffed by trained volunteers. Spanish counseling available. Speakers promote community awareness & edu for suicide prevention. FUNDING: United Way, nonprofit. OFC HRS: 24 hrs. Spanish spoken. Free srvs. SERVES: Riverside County.

WEST END FAMILY COUNSELING
Headquarters & Clinic
855 N. Euclid Ave.
Ontario, CA 91762
(909) 983-2020
(909) 983-6847 FAX

Outpatient mental health psychotherapy for adolescents, children and adults. Individual, family and group therapy. School-based counseling prgm, parent edu, elder outreach, info and referral. FUNDING: United Way, DBH contract, fees, nonprofit. OFC HRS: M 9am-8pm; Tu 9am-7pm; W 9am-6pm; Th 9am-5pm. Spanish spoken. Accepts Medi-Cal, sliding fee scale. SERVES: West Valley of San Bernardino County.

WESTSIDE CHILD/ADULT TRTMT CTR
See "San Bernardino Co. Behav Health"

WESTSIDE COUNSELING CENTER
See "Inland Behav & Health Services"

WISR MINISTRIES, INC.
13800 Heacock St., Ste C242
Moreno Valley, CA 92553
(951) 897-5560
(951) 653-9084 FAX

WISR is an outpatient facility that specializes in spiritual recovery. Individual and group counseling for substance abuse, anger mgmt, domestic violence, sexual assault; parenting edu. Intervention, prevention for teens. FUNDING: Nonprofit, donations. OFC HRS: W, F 12noon-8pm; Sat 10am-6pm. More hours likely to be added. Spanish spoken. ADM REQ: No one will be discriminated against based on disability, religion, sexual orientation, race or ability to pay. Counseling fee based on sliding scale. Accepts Drug Medi-Cal and Medi-Cal. SERVES: Riverside, Moreno Valley, Perris.

WOMEN HELPING WOMEN SRVS

543 N. Fairfax Ave.
Los Angeles, CA 90036
(323) 651-2930
(323) 651-5348 FAX

Callers receive emotional support and practical info on any issue. Support groups dealing with issues such as divorce, single parenting, domestic violence, self-esteem, individual counseling, case mgmt and volunteering. Talkline counselor training, specialized srvs for residents of CIPA3, including case mgmt, counseling, workshops & resources. Also offers edu scholarships. Talkline:(877)655-3807. FUNDING: Natl Council of Jewish Women, fndn, donations, nonprofit. Talkline hrs: M, Tu, Th 10am-12:30pm; W 6pm-8pm. 24-hr voicemail, calls returned. For srvs at this physical location, must have an appt. Spanish, Hebrew & French spoken. Free srvs or on low sliding fee scale. SERVES: So. Calif.

WWW.BEFRIENDERS.ORG

Offers anonymous, non-immediate, supportive email srvs for those having thoughts of suicide. This is not an emergency service. Trained volunteers answer emails on a daily basis and all go by the pseudonym "Jo." Email (jo@samaritans.org). Website also offers a directory of emotional distress centers throughout the U.S.A. and internatl. FUNDING: Nonprofit. OFC HRS: 24 hrs, 7 days. Free srvs. SERVES: Internatl.

WWW.INCRISIS.NET

Online Behavioral Screening & Reports
965 NE Wiest Way, No. 2
Bend, OR 97701

Online mental health screening software that generates reports with analysis and treatment suggestions for teens who may have mental or addictive disorders. Reports are used to share with professionals in seeking help for troubled youth. Free public srv for parents, caregivers, educators, and youth professionals. Contact agency via website. FUNDING: Nonprofit, Mentor Research Institute. SERVES: U.S.A.

WWW.OEFOIF.VA.GOV

Resource website by the Dept. of Veterans Affairs for newly returning service members (OEF/OIF). Topics include health care eligibility, life insurance benefits, edu/training, and prgms that specialize in the treatment of PTSD. If you are an OEF/OIF veteran and have not been contacted by VA about your health care benefits, call (866) 606-8216.

WWW.VETSPREVAIL.COM

P.O. Box 619101
Chicago, IL 60661

Website allows vets to connect with other vets through forums, blogs and multimedia. Also offers a 6-week mental health prgm to assist with life after deployment and transition back into civilian life. For more info, e-mail (team@vetsprevail.com). SERVES: U.S.A.

ABC CASKETS FACTORY

1705 N. Indiana St.
Los Angeles, CA 90063
(866) 369-5457
(323) 268-1783
(323) 265-5215 FAX

Casket manufacturer open to the public. Staff will guide you through the buying and planning process and show you how to cut costs. Free local delivery to funeral homes. OFC HRS: M-Th 7am-5pm; F 7am-3:30pm; Sun by appt. Prices are lower than traditional options and staff are trained to assist buyers of all income levels. SERVES: So. Calif.

ALWAYS IN MY HEART SUPPORT GROUP

Loma Linda Univ Medical Center
11234 Anderson St.
Loma Linda, CA 92354
(909) 558-7261

Support groups for parents who have suffered a miscarriage, stillbirth, or infant death. Meets 2nd M from 7pm-8:30pm, in room 129A (South Entrance) at Loma Linda Univ Rehab Institute, 11406 Loma Linda Dr. Also 4th Tu 9:30-11am at Mt. View Plaza Suite 10 (south end), 11255 Mountain View Ave., Loma Linda. For questions or more info call Cheri Moreno. No child care available. Welcome to attend one or both meetings. SERVES: San Bernardino County.

AMERICAN SIDS INSTITUTE

528 Raven Way
Naples, FL 34110
(239) 431-5425
(239) 431-5530 FAX

Aggressive, comprehensive natl prgm of research, edu and family support aimed at conquering SIDS. Dedicated to the prevention of Sudden Infant Death and the promotion of infant health. FUNDING: Grants, donations, nonprofit. OFC HRS: M-F 9am-5pm, EST. 24-hr hotline. SERVES: U.S.A.

BEREAVEMENT SUPP GRP/MORONGO

Hospice of Morongo Basin
61675 Twenty Nine Palms Hwy.
Joshua Tree, CA 92252
(760) 366-1308
(760) 366-1935 FAX

Bereavement support group. Meetings 1st & 3rd Th 1:30pm-3:30pm or 5pm-7pm. SERVES: Morongo Basin.

CALIF CEMETERY/FUNERAL BUREAU

Calif Dept of Consumer Affairs
1625 N. Market Blvd., Ste S-208
Sacramento, CA 95834
(916) 574-7870
(800) 952-5210
(916) 574-8620 FAX

Receives complaints about funeral directors, funeral facilities, embalmers, cemeteries, apprentice embalmers, funeral arrangement trusts, crematories, cemetery brokers & salespersons & cremated remains disposers. E-mail complaints online (www.cfb.ca.gov). For licensing info, call (916) 327-3219. FUNDING: Govt. OFC HRS: M-F 8am-5pm. SERVES: Calif.

CALIF HOSPICE ASSN (CHAPCA)

3841 N. Freeway Blvd., Ste 225
Sacramento, CA 95834
(916) 925-3770
(888) 252-1010
(916) 925-3780 FAX

Represents hospice & palliative care providers, residential facilities for the elderly and healthcare professionals. Advocates for those facing life-threatening illness, promotes availability and access to quality care. Also provides info & referral srvs to people interested in hospice. FUNDING: Nonprofit. OFC HRS: M-F 8am-5pm. SERVES: Calif & Nevada.

CARING CONNECTIONS

Washington, DC 20042-6058
(800) 658-8898

Natl consumer website and helpline providing info for end-of-life care. Provides state-specific free resources including: grief support, paying for long-term care, caring for seriously ill children, talking to a doctor, etc. Spanish (877) 658-8896. Visit (www.caringinfo.org). FUNDING: Grant, donations. Spanish spoken. Free srvs. SERVES: U.S.A.

CHAPMAN HOSPICE

6736 Palm Ave.
Riverside, CA 92506
(951) 784-1388
(951) 683-2359 FAX

Medical care and counseling for terminally ill individuals and grief support to family members. TDD (800) 735-2929. FUNDING: Nonprofit. OFC HRS: M-F 8am-4:30pm. Spanish spoken. ADM REQ: Srvs ordered by M.D. Accepts insurance, Medicare, Medi-Cal. SERVES: Riverside County.

CHILDREN'S HOSPICE INTERNATIONAL

1101 King St., Ste 360
Alexandria, VA 22314
(800) 242-4453
(703) 684-0330
(703) 684-0226 FAX

Info for health care professionals, families and networking organizations offering hospice care to children living with life-threatening conditions. FUNDING: Donations, grants, govt, client fees, nonprofit. OFC HRS: M-F 9am-5pm, EST. SERVES: U.S.A. & internatl.

CHILDREN'S WISH FOUNDATION INTNL

8615 Roswell Rd.
Atlanta, GA 30350-7526
(800) 323-9474
(770) 393-9474
(770) 393-0683 FAX

Internatl organization provides wishes for children with life-threatening illnesses. Serves children under 18 yrs of age. FUNDING: Nonprofit. OFC HRS: M-F 8:30am-5pm. SERVES: U.S.A. & internatl.

CITY OF HOPE

Duarte Campus
1500 E. Duarte Rd.
Duarte, CA 91010
(626) 256-4673

Contact the community srvs dept for more info on the various support and edu srvs offered to patients, their families, local community and health care professionals. Also visit (www.cityofhope.org). OFC HRS: M-F 8am-5pm. SERVES: U.S.A.

COMMUNITY COUNSELING CTR/CSUSB

Dept of Psychology, Calif State Univ
5500 State University Pkwy.
San Bernardino, CA 92407
(909) 537-5040
(909) 537-7061 FAX

Graduate students in 2-yr M.S. counseling psychology prgm provide low-cost, long-term individual psychotherapy. Student therapists are supervised by Ph.D. level psychologists on CSUSB faculty. FUNDING: CSUSV, govt. OFC HRS: M, Th, F 8am-5pm; Tu, W 8am-7pm. ADM REQ: CSUSB student or connected to student. Not suicidal, abusive, drug dependent or violent. Cost covered by tuition. SERVES: San Bernardino County.

COMMUNITY HOME HEALTH

1805 Medical Center Dr.
San Bernardino, CA 92411
(909) 887-6333
(877) 966-3066
(909) 806-1059 FAX

Skilled health care to homebound patients, RN, home health aide, PT, OT, speech pathology, medical social srvs, mental health, perinatal & pediatric care. JCAHO accredited. FUNDING: Nonprofit. OFC HRS: M-F 8am-4:30pm. Spanish spoken. ADM REQ: Physician order, medical necessity, homebound. Accepts Medi-Cal, Medicare, HMO, pvt pay, insurance. SERVES: East San Bernardino County.

COMMUNITY HOSPICE CARE

Vitas Health Care Corp of Calif
35325 Date Palm Dr., Ste 204
Cathedral City, CA 92234
(760) 321-2273
(760) 321-7149 FAX

Comfort and care provided for terminally ill patients and families in their own home, in a residential or care center. OFC HRS: 24 hrs. ADM REQ: Certification of terminal illness. Accepts Medicare, Medi-Cal, insurance. SERVES: Desert communities.

COMMUNITY HOSPICE OF VICTOR VALLEY

16147 Kamana Rd.
Apple Valley, CA 92307
(760) 946-4730
(760) 242-0566 FAX

Medical care and counseling for terminally ill individuals and grief support to family members. FUNDING: Nonprofit. OFC HRS: M-F 8am-5pm, 24-hr srvs. Spanish spoken. ADM REQ: Srvs ordered by M.D. Accepts insurance, Medicare. SERVES: San Bernardino County.

COMPASSIONATE FRIENDS/NATL

The Compassionate Friends, Inc.
P.O. Box 3626
Oak Brook, IL 60522-3696
(877) 969-0010
(630) 990-0246 FAX

Natl self-help organization will refer you to over 550 local chapters in U.S.A. Provides support and understanding to families who have experienced the death of a child, grandchild or siblings of any age, from any cause. The goal is positive resolution of grief. Brochures, videos, newsletters and helpful materials are available. All inquiries can be sent to above address. FUNDING: Donations, nonprofit. OFC HRS: M-F 9am-4pm, CST. 24-hr voicemail. Free group srvs. SERVES: U.S.A.

CORNERSTONE HOSPICE
(See Display Ad on Page 63)
1461 E. Cooley Dr., Ste 220
Colton, CA 92324
(866) 872-8102
(909) 872-8106 FAX

Cornerstone Hospice is dedicated to providing a special form of care for people with a life-limiting illness. When medical treatments can no longer offer a cure, Cornerstone Hospice's team of caring professionals partner with the family as well as the patient to control pain and reduce stress and anxiety. Cornerstone provides medical, spiritual, emotional comfort and bereavement srvs to patients and their families. Our passion is to bring you comfort! JCAHO accredited. OFC HRS: 24 hrs, 7 days. Accepts most insurance, Medicare, Medi-Cal. SERVES: San Bernardino and Riverside Counties.

FAMILY AND FRIENDS OF MURDER VICTIMS
P.O. Box 11222
San Bernardino, CA 92423-1222
(909) 387-6384
(909) 798-6273 FAX

Info, support & friendship to those who have experienced the murder of a loved one, as well as those who are victims of attempted murder. So. Calif. chapters in Riverside & San Bernardino Counties. Call for meeting times. FUNDING: Nonprofit, donations. Spanish spoken. Free srvs. SERVES: Calif.

FAMILY AND FRIENDS OF MURDER VICTIMS
Bilingual Meeting
Upland, CA 91786
(909) 215-7063

Support group for those who have lost a loved one through homicide. Meets 2nd Th each month 7pm-9pm. St. Anthony's Catholic Church in Upland CA . Spanish spoken. SERVES: Riverside County.

FIRST CANDLE/SIDS ALLIANCE
National Headquarters
1314 Bedford Ave., Ste 210
Baltimore, MD 21208
(800) 221-7437
(410) 653-8226
(410) 653-8709 FAX

SIDS (Sudden Infant Death Syndrome) group provides emotional support to families. Educates the public and financially supports research. Will send a free packet of info on SIDS and assist families in finding local resources and support groups. After hrs emerg referrals to on-call counselors. For Orange County, contact the "Guild for Infant Survival" at (714) 973-8417 or (800) 247-4370. FUNDING: Nonprofit. OFC HRS: M-F 9am-5pm, EST. Spanish spoken. Free srvs. SERVES: U.S.A.

GOOD SHEPHERD COUNSELING
30713 Riverside Dr., Ste 203
Lake Elsinore, CA 92530
(951) 678-1642

Outpatient counseling with locations in Tustin and Lake Elsinore. Grief recovery specialist. Trauma recovery (EMDR certified). Depression and anxiety. Individual, family, child and teen. Contact Susan Kell. FUNDING: Nonprofit. OFC HRS: by appt. Accepts insurance, sliding fee scale. SERVES: Riverside, San Bernardino Counties.

GRIEF RECOVERY GROUP
Loma Linda University Med Center
11406 Loma Linda Dr., Ste 129 A
Loma Linda, CA 92354
(909) 558-7261
(909) 558-4000

Bereavement support group for parents who have lost a baby. Various bereavement support programs available. Call or see website for info. Visit (www.lomalindahealth.org). SERVES: San Bernardino County.

GRIEF RECOVERY INSTITUTE
P.O. Box 6061-382
Sherman Oaks, CA 91413
(818) 907-9600
(818) 907-9329 FAX

Answers questions about loss and recovery from loss. Not limited to death; includes major change or loss, moving, divorce, financial changes, etc. Grief recovery educators encourage callers to complete relationships to improve the quality of their lives. 12-wk outreach prgms, 3-day seminars, etc. FUNDING: Donations, client fees, nonprofit. OFC HRS: M-F 9am-5pm. Free phone srvs. SERVES: U.S.A.

GRIEF SHARE
Victory Christian Church
P.O. Box 5060
34-500 Bob Hope Dr.
Palm Springs, CA 92263
(760) 328-3313

Designed to support those who are suffering the loss of a loved one through death or for those dealing with long-term illness. Coping skills and sharing are offered in a caring environment. Meets W at 7pm. Call for dates. FUNDING: Nonprofit. OFC HRS: M-F 10am-5pm Free srvs. SERVES: Coachella Valley.

GRIEF SHARE RECOVERY GROUP
Southwest Community Church
77-701 Fred Waring Dr., Rm. 209
Indian Wells, CA 92210
(760) 772-8462
(760) 902-2678

Support for those who have experienced the death of a loved one. Meets Tu 6:30pm-8:30pm. No child care available. Contact facilitator Ealeene Reynolds at (760) 772-7053. ADM REQ: Must call first. SERVES: Riverside County.

HEART TOUCH PROJECT
3400 Airport Ave., Ste 42
Santa Monica, CA 90405
(310) 391-2558
(310) 391-2168 FAX

Compassionate & healing touch therapy provided by professional therapists & volunteers to persons with AIDS, non-ambulatory persons, senior citizens, persons receiving hospice care, infants & children. FUNDING: Nonprofit. OFC HRS: M-F 10am-6pm. ADM REQ: Must have approval of primary health provider to ensure that the massage is allowed for the patient's condition. Accepts donations. Free srvs. SERVES: So. Calif.

HIGH DESERT HOME HEALTH & HOSPICE
6601 White Feather Rd., Ste A-2
Joshua Tree, CA 92252
(760) 366-6424
(760) 366-9818 FAX

Home health & hospice srvs. FUNDING: Nonprofit. OFC HRS: M-F 8:30am-5pm. ADM REQ: Srvs ordered by M.D. Homebound. Accepts Medicare, Medi-Cal, SSI, insurance. SERVES: Morongo Basin.

HOSPICE LINK
Hospice Education Institute
P.O. Box 98
Three Unity Square
Machiasport, ME 04655-0098
(800) 331-1620
(207) 255-8800
(207) 255-8008 FAX

General info about hospice and palliative care and referrals to local prgms nationwide. Does not offer medical advice or personal counseling. FUNDING: Donations, nonprofit. OFC HRS: M-F 9am-4:30pm, EST. Free srvs. SERVES: U.S.A.

HOSPICE OF MORONGO BASIN
61675 29 Palms Hwy.
Joshua Tree, CA 92252
(760) 366-1308
(760) 366-1935 FAX

Hospice volunteer srvs to seriously ill patients and their families. In-home srvs, bereavement and support. Walk in or call. FUNDING: Local donations, nonprofit. OFC HRS: M-F 8:30am-4:30pm. Free srvs. SERVES: Morongo Basin.

HOSPICE OF THE DESERT COMMUNITIES
P.O. Box 2739
1150 N. Indian Canyon Drive
Palm Springs, CA 92262
(760) 323-6642
(760) 327-8086 FAX

Supportive srvs for the terminally ill and their families in the patient's home or an inpatient facility. Nurse on call 24 hrs. Grief support group every W 2pm-3:30pm. FUNDING: United Way, donations, fees, nonprofit. OFC HRS: M-F 8am-4:30pm. Spanish spoken. ADM REQ: Referral by doctor. SERVES: Palm Springs area, Coachella Vly from Beaumont to 29 Palms to Thermal.

INLAND HOSPICE ADULT PRGM
233 W. Harrison Ave.
Claremont, CA 91711
(909) 399-3289
(909) 626-4369 FAX

Volunteers & staff tend to the physical, emotional & spiritual needs of the terminally ill, the frail & elderly & their families. Adult bereavement groups offered at various locations, open to those who are experiencing the loss of a loved one. The Common Threads Project, bereavement support for children & youth ages 6-17 yrs & their families. Call to register. FUNDING: United Way, fundraisers, nonprofit. OFC HRS: M-F 9am-5pm. ADM REQ: Must register for Common Threads. Free srvs. SERVES: East L.A. & West San Bernardino.

JEWISH FAMILY SERVICE OF THE DESERT

Palm Springs-Desert Area
801 E. Tahquitz Canyon Way, Ste 202
Palm Springs, CA 92262
(760) 325-4088
(760) 778-3781 FAX

Counseling, senior case mgmt, info & referral srvs for individuals, couples and families. Specialized support groups based on need (i.e., group for widowed persons, people in divorce process and resolving problems of everyday living), case mgmt srvs for frail, elderly adults. Project Outreach provides volunteer srvs to older persons in residential and skilled nursing facilities, including friendly visitors. Shabbat welcome and celebration of Jewish holidays. Wait: within one week. FUNDING: Jewish Federation, United Way, fndn, donations, fees, nonprofit. OFC HRS: M-Th 8:30am-5pm; F 8am-4pm. Spanish spoken upon request. Accepts Medi-Cal/Medicare combined and many insurance plans. Sliding fee scale for counseling & case mgmt. SERVES: Coachella Valley.

KAISER PERMANENTE/HOSPICE

9961 Sierra Ave., Bldg. 3A
Fontana, CA 92335
(909) 609-3838

Hospice, infusion therapy, PT, OT, home care, skilled nursing, medical social srvs, perinatal & pediatric srvs. JCAHO accredited. FUNDING: Nonprofit. OFC HRS: M-F 8:30am-5pm. Spanish spoken. ADM REQ: Srvs ordered by M.D. Accepts Medi-Cal, Medicare, Kaiser insurance. SERVES: Riverside, San Bernardino Counties.

KIDSAID

2 Kids 4 Kids by Kids
P.O. Box 3272
Ann Arbor, MI 48106-3272

Website with resources for kids dealing with grief or loss. E-mail support groups, bookstore. A safe place for kids to share experiences with other kids. Visit (www.kidsaid.com). FUNDING: Nonprofit, donations. SERVES: U.S.A.

LOMA LINDA UNIV MEDICAL CTR

11234 Anderson St.
Loma Linda, CA 92354
(909) 558-4006
(909) 588-4000
(909) 558-0149 FAX

The only state-designated, 797-bed, level 1 Regional Trauma Center for the four Inland Counties of Riverside, San Bernardino, Inyo & Mono. Up to 35 percent of the Medical Center's patients served in nine ICUs: surgical & trauma, neurosurgical, cardio-thoracic, pediatric cardio-thoracic, respiratory, coronary, medical, neonatal, and pediatric. Hosts various bereavement groups. Spanish speaking srvs (909) 558-4367. SAFE KIDS prgm at (909) 558-4704. Facilities include: acute rehab, Total Care Birthing Center, computerized tomography, MRI, lithotripsy, and hospital-based proton accelerator for the treatment of cancer, and a children's hospital. Also HIV/AIDS treatments & therapies. Wait: varies. Many languages spoken. Accepts Medi-Cal, Medicare, pvt insurance. SERVES: Riverside, San Bernardino, Inyo, Mono Counties.

LOMA LINDA UNIV/MARRIAGE/FAMILY

Marriage & Family Therapy Clinic
1686 Barton Rd.
Redlands, CA 92373
(909) 558-4934
(909) 558-0334 FAX

Individual, group, marriage, family, child & adol counseling. Srvs for child abuse prevention, grief counseling, domestic violence, chemical addiction and other issues. FUNDING: Nonprofit. OFC HRS: Sun 9am-5pm; M-Th 9am-8pm; F 9am-2:30pm. Spanish spoken. Sliding fee scale starts at $25 per session. Medi-Cal not accepted. Will not bill insurance. SERVES: San Bernardino, Riverside Counties.

MOJAVE VALLEY VOLUNTEER HOSPICE

Elder Haven
P.O. Box 504
516 E. Williams St.
Barstow, CA 92312-0504
(760) 256-5706
(760) 256-5197 FAX

Volunteer-driven organization with a coordinated prgm of supportive srvs for terminally ill patients and their families. Senior day care prgm. FUNDING: United Way, donations, nonprofit. OFC HRS: M, Tu, Th, F 9am-1pm. Spanish spoken. ADM REQ: Srvs ordered by M.D. Member should be mobile with assistance of a cane/walker or wheelchair and usually continent. Free srvs. SERVES: Barstow, Newberry, Daggett, Helendale.

MOTHERS AGAINST DRUNK DRIVERS

77-760 Country Club #I
Palm Desert, CA 92211
(760) 772-6237
(760) 772-0710 FAX

Awareness of drunk driving issues and underage drinking through presentations, literature, media campaigns & youth prgms. Offers statistics, publishes a quarterly newsletter, support groups for survivors and victims families. FUNDING: Nonprofit. OFC HRS: M-F 8am-4pm. Victim srvs 24 hrs. SERVES: Riverside County.

MOTHERS AGAINST DRUNK DRIVING

California State Office
4629 Whitney Ave., Ste 7
Sacramento, CA 95821
(916) 481-6233
(800) 426-6233
(916) 485-9623 FAX

MADD is a volunteer-based natl nonprofit organization. Membership is free and open to all who claim solidarity with the MADD mission to stop drunk driving. Supports the victims of this violent crime and prevents underage drinking. Members & volunteers work collectively to enact mission through edu, public awareness, legislative action & victim advocacy. FUNDING: Donations, nonprofit. OFC HRS: M-F 9am-5pm. Spanish spoken. Free srvs. SERVES: Calif.

MOTHERS AGAINST DRUNK DRIVING

242 Airport Dr., Ste 200
San Bernardino, CA 92408
(909) 888-6233
(909) 885-1503 FAX

MADD is a natl organization that helps victims of drunk or drugged drivers and promotes legislation that will help victims of traffic crashes related to alcohol and drugs. Provides victim support srvs & advocacy, active in building pub-

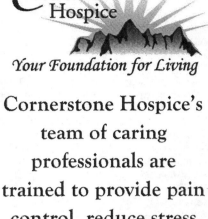
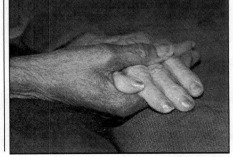

lic awareness of substance abuse & its cost to society. 24-hr grief counselors available at (877) MADD-HELP. FUNDING: Nonprofit. OFC HRS: M, W, F 8:30am-4pm. SERVES: San Bernardino County.

MOURNING STAR
Bereavement Support for Children
6235 River Crest Dr.
Riverside, CA 92507
(951) 413-1317

Bereavement support for children and teens who have experienced the death of a loved one. Prgm provided by the Visiting Nurses Assn. Also parent group. FUNDING: Nonprofit, grants. ADM REQ: Call for appt. Free srvs. SERVES: Riverside County.

MOURNING STAR CENTER, THE
VNA of the Inland Counties
18169 Bear Valley Rd.
Hesperia, CA 92345
(760) 948-7249

Support center for grieving children their families or caregivers. Also has locations in Palm Desert, Riverside, Banning, and Murrieta. FUNDING: Nonprofit, donations, fndns, corps, grants, fundraising. ADM REQ: Ages 3-18 yrs. Referrals from schools, hospices, hospitals, physicians, volunteers. Free srvs. SERVES: Inland Empire.

MOURNING STAR CENTER, THE
42600 Cook St., Ste 210
Palm Desert, CA 92211
(760) 836-0360
(760) 776-1612 FAX

Open-ended support groups for children and teens, ages 3-19 yrs, and their families, who are grieving due to a death. Trained volunteers and professionals facilitate groups. Also extended support, edu srvs, free grief camp and community outreach. Visit www.mourningstar.org for more information about srvs and locations. FUNDING: Donations, nonprofit. OFC HRS: Vary. Spanish spoken. Accepts donations. Free srvs. SERVES: Riverside County.

NATL ALLIANCE FOR HISPANIC HEALTH
Su Familia (Family Health Helpline)
1501 16th Street, NW
Washington, DC 20036
(866) 783-2645
(202) 797-4353 FAX

Bilingual health helpline and website. Callers are referred to health care providers in their area. For prenatal info, call La Linea Nacional Prenatal Hispana (800) 504-7081. For hospice info, call (877) 658-8896. Visit (www.hispanichealth.org). FUNDING: Grants, donations. OFC HRS: M-F 9am-6pm, EST. Spanish spoken. SERVES: U.S.A.

NATL INSTITUTE FOR JEWISH HOSPICE
732 University St.
North Woodmere, NY 11581
(800) 446-4448

Nationwide helpline. Serves terminally ill patients, families, professional health caregivers and volunteers. Offers counseling and referral srv for Jewish hospice care and support, database with natl references. Variety of publications on issues of the terminally ill, their families and caregivers. NIJH gives accreditation to hospices across the country. FUNDING: Dona-

tion, nonprofit. OFC HRS: 24 hrs, 7 days. Free referrals, counseling. SERVES: U.S.A.

NEW HOPE/MORENO VALLEY
12818 Heacock St., Ste C-6
Moreno Valley, CA 92553
(951) 247-6542
(951) 247-9819 FAX

Christian counseling center. Serves as a training facility for those in the counseling profession. Psychological testing, child abuse counseling, crisis eval, parenting issues, school problems, teenage issues such as suicide, runaway, depression, eating disorders and substance abuse, bereavement counseling, adult abuse issues, pain mgmt and a host of other adult counseling needs. FUNDING: Donations, fees, nonprofit. OFC HRS: By appt. ADM REQ: Low income. Accepts insurance in most cases, Victim-Witness Program, recovery assistance foundation. Sliding scale basis upon request. SERVES: So. Calif.

ODYSSEY HEALTHCARE
Serving San Bernardino County, Riverside County, the High Desert and the Desert Cities.
(See Display Ad on Page 65)
(877) 637-9432

Odyssey hospice provides srvs to terminally ill patients with a wide range of diagnoses. Srvs are available 24/7 and include medications, equipment, expert physician, nursing care and counseling srvs. Visit (www.odyssey-healthcare.com). OFC HRS: 24 hrs, 7 days. Spanish spoken. SERVES: Riverside County, San Bernardino and Desert Cities.

PARENTS OF MURDERED CHILDREN
Inland Empire Chapter
P.O. Box 9413
Alto Loma, CA 91701
(909) 987-6164
(909) 652-0188 FAX

Three meeting locations: 1st Th, Preciado Funeral Home 923 W. Mill St. San Bernardino; 2nd Th at St. Paul's Episcopal Church 242 E. Alvarado St. Pomona; 3rd Th at St. Mark's Episcopal Church, 330 E. 16th Street, Upland. All meeting times begin at 7pm. Spanish available at all meetings. Help available over the phone as well. FUNDING: Nonprofit. OFC HRS: Call anytime. Spanish spoken. Free srvs. SERVES: Inland Empire.

PARENTS OF MURDERED CHILDREN
National Headquarters
100 E. 8th Street, Ste 202
Cincinnati, OH 45202
(513) 721-5683
(888) 818-7662
(513) 345-4489 FAX

Info, advocacy & newsletters to survivors. Crisis calls taken 24 hrs. FUNDING: Donation, nonprofit. OFC HRS: M-F 8am-5pm, EST. Free srvs. SERVES: U.S.A.

RAMONA HOME HEALTH/HOSPICE
See "Visiting Nurse Assn/Hospice"

RAMONA VNA AND HOSPICE
890 W. Stetson Ave., Ste A
Hemet, CA 92543
(951) 658-9288
(951) 765-6229 FAX

Assist with end of life care through physical, emotional and spiritual support. Our team helps

make every moment as pain, symptom and anxiety free as possible. FUNDING: Nonprofit. OFC HRS: M-Sun 8am-5pm. ADM REQ: Physician order, medical necessity. Accepts Medi-Cal, Medicare, pvt insurance. SERVES: Southwestern Riverside County.

RIVERSIDE HOSPICE
6052 Magnolia Ave.
Riverside, CA 92506
(951) 274-0710
(951) 274-9551 FAX

In-home support and care for terminal patients and their families, assist with practical needs, personal care and edu, volunteer prgm, bereavement groups in English and in Spanish, grief counseling referrals to hospices nationwide. Some printed materials in Spanish. Companion Connection for elderly. FUNDING: United Way, donations, grants. OFC HRS: M-F 9am-5pm. Spanish spoken. ADM REQ: Terminal diagnosis. Accepts Medi-Cal & pvt insurance. SERVES: Riverside, Moreno Valley, Corona, Norco, and parts of San Bernardino County.

SAN BERNARDINO CO. PUBLIC HEALTH
Maternal Health Program
505 N. Arrowhead Ave., 3rd Fl.
San Bernardino, CA 92415-0048
(800) 227-3034
(909) 388-5755 FAX

AFLP prgm provides case mgmt to pregnant and parenting teens. Srv coordination for pregnant and parenting teens and their families. Also counseling and info for families who have had an infant die from SIDS. Prenatal mgmt care to low income residents of San Bernardino Co. Call for prenatal referrals. FUNDING: Govt. OFC HRS: M-F 8am-5pm. Spanish spoken. Accepts Medi-Cal, pvt pay.

SIDS INFORMATION CLEARINGHOUSE
National SIDS Resource Center
Georgetown University
2115 Wisconsin Ave., NW, Ste 601
Washington, DC 20007-2292
(866) 866-7437
(202) 687-7466
(202) 784-9777 FAX

NSIDRC produces and provides professional & consumer edu materials, makes referrals to natl, state, and local organizations, publishes the "Information Exchange" newsletter, and maintains an in-house bibliographical database of public awareness and medical research materials. Resource center staff provides resources, referrals and technical assist to health care professionals, counselors, legal professionals & emerg medical personnel. Also assists parents, families, and the general public in acquiring info on SIDS and related topics. FUNDING: Nonprofit. OFC HRS: M-F 8:30am-5pm, EST. SERVES: U.S.A.

SPAN CALIFORNIA
Suicide Prevention Advocacy Network
P.O. Box 235260
Encinitas, CA 92023
(760) 753-4565

Creates awareness regarding suicide prevention. Advocates legislative policy. No direct srvs. Volunteers work throughout the state speaking at events & conferences. Visit (www.span-california.org). FUNDING: State. SERVES: Calif.

THE COMPASSIONATE FRIENDS

See "Compassionate Friends/..."

THE NAMES PROJECT FOUNDATION

AIDS Memorial Quilt
204 14th Street NW
Atlanta, GA 30318-4315
(404) 688-5500
(404) 688-5552 FAX

Sponsors and displays the AIDS Memorial Quilt. Goal is to provide remembrance and healing, illustrate the enormousness of the AIDS epidemic, increase public awareness, assist with community fundraising. FUNDING: Nonprofit. OFC HRS: M-F 8am-5pm, EST. Spanish spoken. Accepts donations. SERVES: U.S.A.

THE UNFORGETTABLES FOUNDATION

7197 Brockton Ave., Ste 5
Riverside, CA 92506
(951) 680-9996
(951) 680-9981 FAX

Burial assist prgm for families who have lost a child ages 18 yrs or younger. Also CPR training. FUNDING: Nonprofit. OFC HRS: M-F 8am-5pm. Spanish spoken. ADM REQ: Low income. SERVES: Riverside, San Bernardino Counties.

TRAGEDY ASSIST PRGM FOR SURVIVORS (TAPS)

1777 F Street, NW, Ste 600
Washington, DC 20006
(202) 588-8277
(800) 959-8277
(202) 509-8282 FAX

Organization offers tragedy assist to anyone who has suffered the loss of a military loved one regardless of relationship. Provides srvs including peer-based emotional network, case mgmt, crisis intervention, and grief & trauma resources. Also offers Good Grief camps for children and teens to teach coping skills in dealing with death. Visit (www.taps.org) to participate in an active online community including real-time chats. FUNDING: Nonprofit. Free srvs. SERVES: U.S.A.

TRI-COUNTY MEM FUNERAL SOCIETY

P.O. Box 114
Midway City, CA 92655-0114
(714) 962-1917

Assist with pre-death planning for economical funerals. FUNDING: Nonprofit. OFC HRS: M-F 9am-5pm. SERVES: Orange, Riverside & San Bernardino Counties.

TRINITY EVANGELICAL CHURCH

Pathways Support Group Ministries
1551 Reservoir Rd.
Redlands, CA 92373
(909) 335-7333
(909) 798-7096 FAX

Offers a variety of support groups including: divorce care groups for adults and children ages 5-12 yrs, grief share group, group for caregivers, struggling relationships. Also offers "Every Man's Challenge" prgm for men who battle sexually compulsive issues and special prgms for women who have gone through an abortion, struggle with sexual matters, or have been sexually abused. See website for more information, including session times and dates. Child care available by arrangement for children 12 yrs and under. FUNDING: Nonprofit. OFC HRS: M-F 8am-5pm. ADM REQ: Some classes require pre-registration, call ahead. SERVES: San Bernardino County.

VISITING NURSE ASSN/INLAND

Homecare/Hospice
264 N. Highland Springs, Bldg. 4, Ste A
Banning, CA 92220
(951) 769-1419
(951) 769-9873 FAX

Home health and support srvs, including nursing, PT, OT, speech therapy, respite care, medical social srvs, mental health, perinatal & pediatric care, enterostomal therapy, hospice srvs. For hospice, call (951) 845-8439 or fax (951) 769-1038. FUNDING: Nonprofit. OFC HRS: M-F 8am-5pm. Spanish interpreter available. ADM REQ: Physician's referral in need of homecare. Accepts insurance, Medicare, Medi-Cal. SERVES: Riverside & San Bernardino Counties.

VISITING NURSE ASSN/INLAND

6235 Rivercrest Dr., Ste L
Riverside, CA 92507
(951) 656-3153
(951) 656-4795 FAX

Full range of health care srvs for in-home and hospice care. Nursing, assist with daily activities, home infusion, rehab therapies, nutrition counseling, medical social srvs. Wait: none. Free info & referral, some professional srvs based on need. JCAHO accredited. FUNDING: United Way, nonprofit. OFC HRS: M-F 8am-5pm, nursing on call 24 hrs. Spanish & Tagalog spoken. ADM REQ: Physician order, medical necessity. Fee for srv. Accepts Medicare, Medi-Cal, insurance. SERVES: Riverside & San Bernardino Counties.

VISITING NURSE ASSN/INLAND

56300 Twenty Nine Palms Hwy., Ste 105
Yucca Valley, CA 92284
(760) 365-4271
(760) 365-1754 FAX

Home health srvs including nursing, PT, speech therapy, etc. FUNDING: Nonprofit. OFC HRS: M-F 8am-5pm. Spanish spoken. ADM REQ: Physician's referral in need of homecare. Accepts Medicare, Medi-Cal, insurance. SERVES: San Bernardino County.

WWW.GRIEFNET.ORG

P.O. Box 3272
Ann Arbor, MI 48106-3272

Website with resources for adults dealing with grief or loss. E-mail support groups, bookstore. Companion site for kids (www.kidsaid.com). FUNDING: Nonprofit, donations. Donation of $5 per month for each support group; no one turned away due to lack of funds. SERVES: U.S.A.

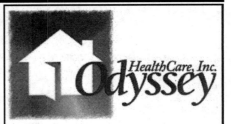

DENTAL CARE

ASSIST LEAGUE/FOOTHILL COMMUNITIES
P.O. Box 927
Upland, CA 91785
(909) 987-2813
(909) 484-0504 FAX

Three main areas of srv: (1) Operation School Bell is a prgm that provides clothing for needy children in grades K-6 when referrals are made through the school districts; (2) Dental prgm is co-sponsored with San Antonio Community Hospital for children in grades K-8 whose parents are not on welfare, do not have insurance and are low income. Referrals are made through the school district and (3) A-LUV prgm provides teddy bears to fire and police staff to give to victims of accidents, crimes, or trauma who need this special srv. Also ASK (Assault Survivor Kit) provides clothing, hygiene kits, and A-Luv Bear for assault victims through San Antonio Emerg Hospital. FUNDING: Donations, nonprofit. OFC HRS: Vary, this is a volunteer-staffed prgm. ADM REQ: Call first. Varies with prgm. SERVES: Upland, Montclair, Rancho Cucamonga, Alta Loma, Ontario, Fontana, Etiwanda.

ASSIST LEAGUE/REDLANDS
506 W. Colton Ave.
Redlands, CA 92374-3054
(909) 792-2675
(909) 798-0436 FAX

Operation School Bell (clothing for needy children in Redlands School District). Dental center for children in grades K-12 (must be referred by family srvs). Assault survivor kit and stuffed animals for traumatized children provided through the police dept. FUNDING: Nonprofit. OFC HRS: M-F 9am-3pm; Sat 10am-1pm. Spanish spoken. SERVES: Redlands & nearby.

ASSIST LEAGUE/SAN BERNARDINO
Children's Dental Center
580 W. 6th Street
San Bernardino, CA 92410
(909) 885-2045

Dental care provided to low income children. Also Operation School Bell provides clothing to needy children. FUNDING: Nonprofit. OFC HRS: M-F 8:30am-4pm. ADM REQ: Must attend SBUSD and meet income guidelines. SERVES: San Bernardino County.

BUDDHIST TZU CHI FREE CLINIC
1000 S. Garfield Ave.
Alhambra, CA 91801
(626) 281-3383
(626) 281-5303 FAX

Clinic provides one-stop medical srvs, including treatment, medicine, lab srvs, X-Rays, alternative and dental care to residents who have no other access to medical care. FUNDING: Nonprofit, donations, grants. OFC HRS: Tu-Sat 9am-11:30am, 1pm-5pm. Spanish, Vietnamese & Chinese spoken. ADM REQ: Under 200% of federal poverty guideline & no other health insurance. All ages welcome. Free srvs. SERVES: Southern Calif.

CALIF DENTAL ASSOCIATION
Resource Center
1201 K Street
Sacramento, CA 95814

(800) 232-7645
(916) 443-3382
(916) 443-2943 FAX

Info on background of dentists. "Senior-Dent" referral to dentists who offer at least 15% discount to ages 60 yrs & up. Also accepts complaints about dentists. FUNDING: Nonprofit. OFC HRS: M-F 8:30am-5pm. SERVES: Calif.

COACHELLA VALLEY USD
School Readiness Program Center
83800 Airport Blvd.
Thermal, CA 92274
(760) 399-8129
(760) 399-4421 FAX

Medical, dental, vision, mental health counseling & special needs assessments & treatment. OFC HRS: M-F 8am-4pm. ADM REQ: Low income families with children ages birth-5 yrs. SERVES: East Valley Riverside County.

COMMUNITY HEALTH SYSTEMS, INC.
I.E. Community Health Center
18601 Valley Blvd.
Bloomington, CA 92316
(909) 877-0510
(909) 877-1818
(909) 877-5468 FAX

Primary health care for all ages. OB/GYN, prenatal, dental srvs, optometry, referrals, pediatrician, internal medicine. No cost dental screenings offered to clients, must provide proof of income or unemployment. FUNDING: Donations, nonprofit. OFC HRS: M-F 8am-5:30pm. Spanish spoken. ADM REQ: Low income. Accepts insurance, Medicare, Medi-Cal, sliding fee scale, I.E.H.P., Molina. SERVES: San Bernardino County.

COMMUNITY HEALTH SYSTEMS, INC.
Eastside Dental Clinic
1970 University Ave.
Riverside, CA 92507
(951) 224-8230
(951) 328-9574 FAX

Dental clinic for adults and children. Pediatric dentist on staff. Medi-Cal, Healthy-Families (Delta Dental), CHDP Referrals. FUNDING: Nonprofit. OFC HRS: M-F 8am-5:30pm. Spanish spoken. Limited free srvs. Sliding fee scale (for those without dental insurance and who qualify). SERVES: Riverside.

COMMUNITY HEALTH SYSTEMS, INC.
Arlanza Family Health Ctr
8856 Arlington Ave.
Riverside, CA 92503
(951) 353-2702
(951) 353-2976 FAX

Primary care for all ages. Family planning, HIV/AIDS, STD testing, Teenage Edu to Avoid Motherhood (T.E.A.M.), Child Health and Disability prgm. Also dental clinic. FUNDING: Nonprofit. OFC HRS: M-F 8am-5:30pm. Accepts Medi-Cal, Medicare, insurance, sliding fee scale. SERVES: Riverside County.

DENTAL BOARD OF CALIF
Dept of Consumer Affairs
2005 Evergreen St., Ste 1500
Sacramento, CA 95815
(877) 729-7789

(916) 263-2300
(916) 263-2140 FAX

Accepts written complaints regarding fraud, misrepresentation, unprofessional conduct & negligence by dentists. FUNDING: Govt. OFC HRS: M-F 8am-5pm. Telephone hrs: 9am-12noon, 1pm-4pm. Closed 2nd, 3rd, 4th F of each month due to furloughs. Spanish spoken. SERVES: Calif.

DENTI-CAL BENEFICIARIES SRVS DEPT
P.O. Box 15539
Sacramento, CA 95852-1539
(800) 322-6384

Will make referrals to Denti-Cal (Medi-Cal Dentist) by ZIP code. Can also check on the status of a claim and benefits available. The best time to call is 8am-9am. Very busy line. FUNDING: State, govt. OFC HRS: M-F 8am-5pm. Spanish spoken. SERVES: Calif.

DENTI-CAL DENTIST
Western Dental Centers
12400 Central Ave.
Chino, CA 91710
(909) 364-0030
(909) 591-8779 FAX

OFC HRS: M-Th 9am-7:30pm; F 9am-7pm; Sat 8am-4:30pm. Vietnamese, Spanish spoken.

DENTI-CAL DENTIST
Beauchamp/Western Dental Center
740 S. Indian Hill Blvd., Ste B
Claremont, CA 91711
(800) 579-3783

OFC HRS: M-F 9am-7pm; Sat 8am-4:30pm. Spanish spoken.

DENTI-CAL DENTIST
Western Dental Center
9765 Sierra Ave.
Fontana, CA 92335
(800) 579-3783

OFC HRS: M-Th 8am-8pm; F 8am-7pm; Sat 8am-4:30pm. Spanish spoken.

DENTI-CAL DENTIST
Beauchamp/Western Dental Center
3027 W. Florida Ave.
Hemet, CA 92545
(951) 929-2222
(951) 929-2793 FAX

OFC HRS: M-F 9am-7pm; Sat 8:30am-4:30pm. Spanish spoken.

DENTI-CAL DENTIST
Western Dental
23185 Hemlock Ave.
Moreno Valley, CA 92553
(951) 243-1000
(951) 924-7384 FAX

OFC HRS: M-Th 9am-8pm; F 9am-7pm; Sat 8am-4:30pm. Indonesian, Spanish spoken.

DENTI-CAL DENTIST
Beauchamp/Western Dental Center
3485 Madison St.
Riverside, CA 92504
(951) 966-5555
(951) 688-6417 FAX

OFC HRS: M-F 8am-7pm; Sat 8am-4:30pm. Spanish spoken.

DENTI-CAL DENTIST
Beauchamp/Western Dental Center
1199 North E Street
San Bernardino, CA 92410
(909) 381-9337
(909) 381-9517 FAX

OFC HRS: M-Th 8am-8pm; F 8am-7pm; Sat
8am-4:30pm. Spanish spoken.

DENTI-CAL DENTIST
Beauchamp Western Dental Centers
15290-B Bear Valley Rd., Ste B
Victorville, CA 92392
(760) 951-7777
(760) 951-1582 FAX

OFC HRS: M-F 8am-7pm; Sat 8am-4:30pm.
Spanish spoken.

FAMILY SERVICE ASSN/REDLANDS
612 Lawton St.
Redlands, CA 92374
(909) 793-2673
(909) 793-7324 FAX

Srvs provided to low income and homeless
families. Case mgmt, food, clothing, utility and
rental assist, cold weather motel vouchers,
screening for dental & vision, prescription assist, and edu prgms. Home Again Project is a
long-term comprehensive prgm helping homeless families into permanent housing and employment. Client srv M-W, F 9am-12noon,
1:30pm-7pm. Surplus food avail on walk-in basis, all other srvs require appt. FUNDING: Donations, United Way, grants, nonprofit. OFC
HRS: M-W 8am-7pm; Th 8am-12noon; F
8am-4:30pm. Spanish spoken. ADM REQ: Low
or no income. Free srvs. SERVES: Redlands,
East Valley area.

LOMA LINDA UNIV SCH/DENTISTRY
11092 Anderson St.
Loma Linda, CA 92350
(909) 558-4222
(909) 558-4822 FAX

General dentistry for anyone, performed by
dental students (exams, cleanings, fillings, root
canals, x-rays, etc.). Some special srvs by resident dentist and interns: Orthodontics,
endontics, periodontics, oral surgery,
implantology, TMJ (jaw specialist). Special
prgm for medically compromised patients and
disabled. FUNDING: Tuition, client fees, nonprofit. OFC HRS: M-Th 8am-5pm; F 8am-12pm.
ADM REQ: Screening appt approved. Accepts
Medi-Cal. Fixed fees but lower than most pvt
practices. SERVES: San Bernardino, Riverside
Counties.

MEDI-CAL DENTIST
Sparkle Family Dentistry
8750 19th Street
Alta Loma, CA 91701
(909) 483-1177
(909) 483-1179 FAX

OFC HRS: M 2pm-6pm; Tu, W 9am-6:30pm; F
7:30am-1pm. (24-hr emerg). Spanish spoken.

MEDI-CAL DENTIST
Apple Valley Dental Associates
20162 Highway 18, Ste L
Apple Valley, CA 92307
(760) 946-1466
(760) 946-1956 FAX

OFC HRS: M-F 9am-5pm. Korean, Vietnamese
and Spanish spoken.

MEDI-CAL DENTIST
Banning Dental Center
471 N. San Gorgonio Ave.
Banning, CA 92220
(951) 849-2888
(951) 849-1454 FAX

OFC HRS: M-Th 8:30am-5:30pm; F
8:30am-4:30pm. Spanish, Lau spoken.

MEDI-CAL DENTIST
Banning Family Dentistry
1035 W. Ramsey St., Ste B2
Banning, CA 92220
(951) 922-2322
(951) 922-2319 FAX

OFC HRS: M-F 9am-5pm; Th 10am-6pm.
Spanish spoken.

MEDI-CAL DENTIST
Dr. Salman, DDS
927 Armory Rd.
Barstow, CA 92311
(760) 252-4488
(760) 252-3222 FAX

OFC HRS: M-Th 9am-5pm; F 9am-1pm. Spanish spoken.

MEDI-CAL DENTIST
Jack Ackerman, DDS
19059 Valley Blvd., Ste 103
Bloomington, CA 92316
(909) 877-3660
(909) 877-3682 FAX

OFC HRS: M-F 8:30am-4pm. Spanish spoken.

MEDI-CAL DENTIST
Family Dentistry/Dr Cherukuri
12850 10th Street, Ste B-2
Chino, CA 91710
(909) 627-6699
(909) 627-6975 FAX

OFC HRS: M-W 9am-6pm; Th 10am-7pm; F by
appt. Spanish spoken. ADM REQ: Accepts
Medi-Cal for ages 21 yrs or under.

MEDI-CAL DENTIST
Adult & Child Toothcare/John Ramos DDS
5250 E. Philadelphia St., Ste O
Chino, CA 91710
(909) 613-1300
(909) 613-1302 FAX

OFC HRS: Tu,Th 10am-6pm; W 9am-6pm; Sat
9am-2pm. Spanish spoken. SERVES: Western
San Bernardino County, Eastern L.A. County.

MEDI-CAL DENTIST
Dr. Cruz
5814 Riverside Dr.
Chino, CA 91710
(909) 548-4844
(909) 548-0774 FAX

OFC HRS: M-F 9:30am-6:30pm. Spanish
spoken.

MEDI-CAL DENTIST
Dr. Castandeda
14652 Pipeline Ave., Ste A-2
Chino, CA 91710
(909) 393-5501
(909) 393-0781 FAX

OFC HRS: Tu, Th, F 10am-7pm; W 8am-5pm;
Sat 8am-3pm for emerg only. Spanish, Tagalog
spoken. SERVES: L.A. & San Bernardino
Counties.

MEDI-CAL DENTIST
Group Dental Ctr/S. Ou & E. Chan

5480 Philadelphia, Ste D
Chino, CA 91710
(909) 464-2398
(909) 464-2398 FAX

OFC HRS: M-F 9am-5pm, alt Sat 9am-3pm.
Chinese, Spanish spoken.

MEDI-CAL DENTIST
California Dental
4200 Chino Hills Pkwy., Ste 880
Chino Hills, CA 91709
(909) 393-5456
(909) 393-2051 FAX

OFC HRS: M-Th 8am-7pm; F 8am-5pm; Sat
8am-1pm. Spanish, Tagalog, Korean spoken.

MEDI-CAL DENTIST
Corona Dental Plaza/Dr. Desai
1222 Magnolia Ave., Ste 101
Corona, CA 92881
(951) 371-1337
(951) 371-8843 FAX

OFC HRS: M-F 9am-7pm; Sat 8am-12noon.

MEDI-CAL DENTIST
Family Dentistry
675 E. Grand Blvd., Ste 104
Corona, CA 92879
(951) 272-1233
(951) 272-0576 FAX

OFC HRS: M-F 9:30am-6:30pm. Spanish
spoken.

MEDI-CAL DENTIST
Harry Hart, DDS
11523 Palm Dr.
Desert Hot Springs, CA 92240
(760) 329-6713
(760) 329-1088 FAX

OFC HRS: M-Th 8am-5pm; F 8am-3pm.

MEDI-CAL DENTIST
Family Dentistry
12526 Palm Dr.
Desert Hot Springs, CA 92240
(760) 251-2666
(760) 251-7655 FAX

OFC HRS: M-F 9am-6pm. Spanish spoken.

MEDI-CAL DENTIST
Heritage Dental Group
13677 Foothill Blvd., Ste L & M
Fontana, CA 92335
(909) 899-8040
(909) 463-7424 FAX

OFC HRS: M-F 10am-6pm. Spanish spoken.

MEDI-CAL DENTIST
Dr. Kim, DDS
9261 Sierra Ave.
Fontana, CA 91744
(909) 822-2212

OFC HRS: M-F 9am-6pm; Sat 9am-3pm. Spanish spoken.

MEDI-CAL DENTIST
Area Dental Center
560 N. San Jacinto St.
Hemet, CA 92544
(951) 765-3174
(951) 658-1146 FAX

OFC HRS: M-F 8:30am-5:30pm. Spanish
spoken.

MEDI-CAL DENTIST
Dr. Lam Family Dentistry
17137 Main Street

Dental Care

Hesperia, CA 92345
(760) 244-0781
(760) 244-1748 FAX

OFC HRS: M-Th 9am-5pm. Vietnamese, Spanish spoken.

MEDI-CAL DENTIST
Golden Dental Group
11949 Hesperia Rd., Ste A
Hesperia, CA 92345
(760) 244-1212
(760) 244-2009 FAX

OFC HRS: M-F 9am-5pm. Arabic, Farsi, Spanish spoken.

MEDI-CAL DENTIST
Highland Village Dentistry
7291 Boulder Ave., Ste 2B
Highland, CA 92346
(909) 425-8980
(909) 425-2684 FAX

OFC HRS: M, Tu, Th 9am-6pm; W 8am-4pm; F 8am-5pm; Sat 8am-1pm. Spanish, Vietnamese spoken. SERVES: San Bernardino County.

MEDI-CAL DENTIST
Universal Dental Care
4160 E. Highland Ave., Ste 6-C
Highland, CA 92346
(909) 425-2700
(909) 425-2727 FAX

OFC HRS: Tu-F, alt Sat 9am-6pm. By appt. Spanish, Tagalog spoken.

MEDI-CAL DENTIST
Desert Dental Services
81-955 Hwy 111, Plaza Center
Indio, CA 92201
(760) 347-2332
(760) 347-0492 FAX

OFC HRS: M, Tu, Th 8am-6pm; W 8am-5pm. Spanish spoken.

MEDI-CAL DENTIST
Dr. Baek & Dr. Lee
61325 Twenty Nine Palms Hwy, Ste A
Joshua Tree, CA 92252
(760) 366-0420
(760) 366-0520 FAX

OFC HRS: M, W 9am-5pm. Korean spoken.

MEDI-CAL DENTIST
Anita C. Singh, DDS
31641 Auto Center Dr., Ste 2A
Lake Elsinore, CA 92530
(951) 674-6889
(951) 674-6880 FAX

OFC HRS: M-F 8:30am-5pm. Spanish spoken.

MEDI-CAL DENTIST
Arafiles Alvin, DDS
25227 Redlands Blvd.
Loma Linda, CA 92354
(909) 799-9194
(909) 799-0564 FAX

OFC HRS: M-Th 9am-7pm. Spanish spoken.

MEDI-CAL DENTIST
James Patrick Caley, DDS
1856 Mentone Blvd., Ste B
Mentone, CA 92359
(909) 794-7310
(909) 335-3056 FAX

OFC HRS: W, Th 1pm-4pm; F 8am-11pm. Spanish spoken.

MEDI-CAL DENTIST
Montclair Plaza Dental Group
5182 N. Montclair Plaza Lane
Montclair, CA 91763
(909) 626-3566
(909) 626-6112 FAX

OFC HRS: M 7am-7pm; Tu, Th 9am-6pm; W 8am-5pm; F 7am-3pm. Hindu, Spanish spoken. Accepts children's Medi-Cal only for those under ages 18 yrs.

MEDI-CAL DENTIST
Sumana Anun, DDS
5467 Moreno, Ste A
Montclair, CA 91763
(909) 946-6771
(909) 946-6851 FAX

OFC HRS: Tu-Sat 9am-5pm. Spanish, Thai Spoken.

MEDI-CAL DENTIST
First Dental Group
9804 Central Ave.
Montclair, CA 91763
(909) 625-9100
(909) 625-9200 FAX

OFC HRS: M-F 9am-6pm; Sat 8am-3pm. Spanish spoken.

MEDI-CAL DENTIST
Sparkle Family Dentistry
12264 Perris Blvd.
Moreno Valley, CA 92557
(951) 485-2800
(951) 485-2802 FAX

OFC HRS: M-F 9am-5pm; Sat 9am-1pm. Spanish, Tagalog, Hindi spoken.

MEDI-CAL DENTIST
Plaza Dental
23767 Sunnymead Blvd., Ste D
Moreno Valley, CA 92553
(951) 924-2433
(951) 924-2899 FAX

OFC HRS: Tu 9am-3:30pm; W, Th 11am-5:30pm; F, Sat 9am-2pm. Spanish, Tagalog spoken.

MEDI-CAL DENTIST
Mission Dental Care
941 W. Mission Blvd., Ste H
Ontario, CA 91762
(909) 984-7883
(909) 984-3463 FAX

OFC HRS: M, Tu, Th, F 8am-6pm; W 3pm-8pm. Spanish spoken.

MEDI-CAL DENTIST
Chong I. Lee, DDS
1739 S. Euclid Ave., Ste A
Ontario, CA 91762
(909) 983-9325
(909) 467-9956 FAX

OFC HRS: M-F 9am-5pm; Sat 9am-2pm. Spanish, Korean spoken.

MEDI-CAL DENTIST
Vineyard Family Dentistry
1857 E. 4th Street
Ontario, CA 91764
(909) 984-2255
(909) 988-4800 FAX

OFC HRS: M, Tu, Th, F 9am-7pm; Sat 8am-2pm. Spanish, Armenian spoken.

MEDI-CAL DENTIST
Ontario-Chino Dental Center

203 W. Francis St.
Ontario, CA 91762
(909) 984-2476
(909) 625-3603 FAX

OFC HRS: M, Tu 9am-12noon; W-F 3pm-6pm, alt Sat 9am-1pm. Spanish, Hindi, Telugu spoken.

MEDI-CAL DENTIST
Mehta Shubhada, DDS
1128 W. Mission Blvd., Ste D
Ontario, CA 91762
(909) 984-9333
(909) 984-9143 FAX

OFC HRS: M, Th 9am-6pm; Tu 9:30am-6pm; F 9am-1pm; Sat 9am-1pm. Spanish spoken.

MEDI-CAL DENTIST
Dr. Hip & Linh Nguyen
2409 S. Vineyard Ave., Ste D
Ontario, CA 91768
(909) 923-9557
(909) 923-9946 FAX

OFC HRS: M 12noon-7pm; Tu, Th, F 9am-6pm; Sat 9am-2pm. Spanish, Vietnamese spoken.

MEDI-CAL DENTIST
Jogi Dental
2242 S. Mountain Ave.
Ontario, CA 91762
(909) 391-1549
(909) 391-1540 FAX

OFC HRS: M-Th 9am-6pm. Spanish, Hindi spoken.

MEDI-CAL DENTIST
Prime Dental Office
1049 W. Philadelphia
Ontario, CA 91762
(909) 391-2324
(909) 391-4722 FAX

OFC HRS: M-F 9am-6pm. Spanish spoken.

MEDI-CAL DENTIST
Dr. Juan Camarena
452 N. Mountain
Ontario, CA 91762-3513
(909) 983-7707
(909) 984-2261 FAX

OFC HRS: M-F 9am-5pm. Spanish spoken.

MEDI-CAL DENTIST
Ontario Village Dental/L. Paniagua
533 West Holt Blvd., Ste B
Ontario, CA 91762
(909) 988-1992
(909) 988-0542 FAX

OFC HRS: M 10am-7pm; Tu, Th 9am-6pm; F 8am-5pm. Spanish spoken.

MEDI-CAL DENTIST
Dr. Fransico Enverga
2598 S. Archibald, Ste C
Ontario, CA 91761
(909) 923-7776

OFC HRS: M-F 9am-7pm. Spanish, Tagalog spoken.

MEDI-CAL DENTIST
Gentle Family Dentistry
2217 S. Mountain Ave.
Ontario, CA 91761
(909) 395-5090
(909) 988-4270 FAX

OFC HRS: Tu-F 8:30am-5pm; Sat 8:30am-2pm. Spanish spoken.

MEDI-CAL DENTIST
Perris Family Dentistry
391 Wilkerson Ave., Ste B
Perris, CA 92570
(951) 943-4007
(951) 943-1037 FAX
OFC HRS: M, Th 9am-6:30pm; W 9am- 5pm; F 9am-4pm; Sat by appt. Spanish spoken.

MEDI-CAL DENTIST
Akkera Reddy, DDS
4361 Phelan Rd.
Phelan, CA 92371
(760) 868-2244
(760) 868-1542 FAX
OFC HRS: M, Th, F 10am-6pm. Spanish spoken.

MEDI-CAL DENTIST
Paul H. Jung, DDS
10570 Foothill Blvd., Ste 240
Rancho Cucamonga, CA 91730
(909) 948-2000
(909) 948-2003 FAX
OFC HRS: M-W, F 9am-6pm; Sat 9am-1pm. German, Korean, Spanish spoken.

MEDI-CAL DENTIST
Foothill Family Dentistry
9724 Foothill Blvd.
Rancho Cucamonga, CA 91730
(909) 481-7876
(909) 481-1187 FAX
OFC HRS: M-F 9:30am-6:30pm, one Sat per month 9:30am-6:30pm. Hindi, Spanish spoken.

MEDI-CAL DENTIST
James Patrick Caley, DDS
419 Brookside
Redlands, CA 92373
(909) 798-5117
(909) 335-3056 FAX
OFC HRS: M, Tu 8am-4pm; W, Th 8am-10pm. Spanish spoken.

MEDI-CAL DENTIST
Orange Plaza Dentistry
470 Orange St.
Redlands, CA 92374
(909) 793-4585
(909) 307-8031 FAX
OFC HRS: Tu-F 9am-6pm. Indonesian, Spanish spoken.

MEDI-CAL DENTIST
Redlands Dental Surgery Group
1180 Nevada St., Ste 100
Redlands, CA 92374
(909) 335-0474
(909) 335-0477 FAX
Outpatient surgery center. OFC HRS: M-W 7am-4pm; Th 8am-4pm, F by appt. Spanish, Arabic spoken.

MEDI-CAL DENTIST
Renaissance Dental Center
1374 W. Foothill Blvd., Ste 2E
Rialto, CA 92376
(909) 874-7444
(909) 874-7458 FAX
OFC HRS: M, Tu, Th 10am-5pm. Spanish, Hindi spoken.

MEDI-CAL DENTIST
Wendell Bond, DDS
3845 La Sierra Ave., Ste 101B
Riverside, CA 92505
(951) 359-7544
(951) 359-4125 FAX
OFC HRS: M-F 8:30am-5:30pm. Spanish spoken.

MEDI-CAL DENTIST
Tyler Dental Center/M.J. Savani, DDS
4080 Tyler, Ste D
Riverside, CA 92503
(951) 359-0149
(951) 359-6408 FAX
OFC HRS: M, Tu, Th, F 9am-5pm. Spanish, Indonesian spoken.

MEDI-CAL DENTIST
Riverside West Dental Group
6945 Streeter Ave.
Riverside, CA 92504
(951) 687-7300
(951) 687-2092 FAX
OFC HRS: M, Tu, Th, F 9am-6pm; Sat 8am-12noon. Spanish, Korean spoken.

MEDI-CAL DENTIST
Central City Dental Group
8880 Limonite Ave.
Riverside, CA 92509
(951) 360-3800
(951) 360-8949 FAX
OFC HRS: M-F 9am-6pm; Sat 9am-2pm. Spanish, Chinese, Korean spoken.

MEDI-CAL DENTIST
Riverside Family Dentistry
3667 Arlington Ave.
Riverside, CA 92506
(951) 684-6600
(951) 684-3631 FAX
OFC HRS: M-F 8am-6pm, alt Sat by appt. Tagalog, Spanish, Vietnamese spoken.

MEDI-CAL DENTIST
Stephen Oh, DDS
3568 Adams St.
Riverside, CA 92504
(951) 354-7664
(951) 354-7605 FAX
OFC HRS: Tu, Th 9am-6pm; Sat 9am-1pm. Korean, Spanish spoken.

MEDI-CAL DENTIST
Seong K. Cho, DDS
9295 Magnolia, Ste 103
Riverside, CA 92503
(951) 354-2000
(951) 354-0029 FAX
OFC HRS: M-F 9:30am-5:30pm. Spanish, Korean spoken.

MEDI-CAL DENTIST
Riverside Dentistry
1857 University Ave.
Riverside, CA 92507
(951) 781-3021
(951) 781-2900 FAX
OFC HRS: M-F 9am-6pm. Spanish, French, Vietnamese spoken.

MEDI-CAL DENTIST
Newport Dental
3560 Arlington Ave.
Riverside, CA 92506
(951) 680-1200
(951) 680-1299 FAX
OFC HRS: M 11am-8pm; Tu 9am-6pm; Th 11am-8pm; W 9am-6pm; Sat 8am-4pm. Spanish spoken.

MEDI-CAL DENTIST
Newport Dental
3724 La Sierra Blvd., Ste F-1
Riverside, CA 92505
(951) 688-2400
(951) 354-5070 FAX
OFC HRS: M 10am-8pm; Tu 9am-7pm; Th 10am-7pm; W 10am-8pm; F 9am-6pm; Sat 8am-4pm. Spanish spoken.

MEDI-CAL DENTIST
Nat Shain, DDS
4151 Brockton Ave.
Riverside, CA 92501
(951) 788-4500
OFC HRS: M-Th 9am-5:30pm; F 9am-12noon.

MEDI-CAL DENTIST
Vivian Kwon, DDS
2955 Van Buren Blvd., Ste H4
Riverside, CA 92503
(951) 689-8544
(951) 689-2465 FAX
OFC HRS: M-Th 9am-6pm. Spanish, Korean spoken.

MEDI-CAL DENTIST
Robert E. Peters
6180 Clay St., Ste A
Riverside, CA 92509
(951) 685-3355
(951) 685-0241 FAX
OFC HRS: M-Th 8:30am-5pm. Spanish spoken.

MEDI-CAL DENTIST
Central City Dental Group
6005 Arlington Ave.
Riverside, CA 92504
(951) 352-8318
(951) 352-8319 FAX
OFC HRS: M, W, F 9am-6pm; Tu 10am-7pm. Spanish spoken.

MEDI-CAL DENTIST
Today Dental
4000 Tyler St.
Riverside, CA 92503
(951) 687-4155
(951) 687-7448 FAX
OFC HRS: M,Th 10am-7pm; Tu, W 8am-5pm; F 8am-3pm. Spanish, Vietnamese spoken.

MEDI-CAL DENTIST
Van Buren Dental
3993 Van Buren Blvd.
Riverside, CA 92503
(951) 637-0808
(951) 637-1986 FAX
OFC HRS: M-F 9am-6pm. Spanish, Korean spoken.

MEDI-CAL DENTIST
Citrus Dental
242 E. Airport Dr., Ste 100
San Bernardino, CA 92408
(909) 890-0050
(909) 890-0042 FAX
OFC HRS: M-Th 8am-7pm. Spanish spoken.

MEDI-CAL DENTIST
Peter Lee & Tina Park-Lee, DDS
1063 North D Street
San Bernardino, CA 92410
(909) 888-5499
(909) 888-5611 FAX

OFC HRS: M, Tu, Th 9am-5pm. Korean, Spanish spoken.

MEDI-CAL DENTIST
James M. Sumilat, DDS
2035 E. Highland Ave., Ste B
San Bernardino, CA 92404
(909) 864-7200

OFC HRS: M, W, Th 8:30am-5pm; Tu 9am-6pm, alt Sun by appt only. Korean, Cantonese, Mandarin, Indonesian, Spanish, Vietnamese spoken.

MEDI-CAL DENTIST
Melquiades Fronda, DDS
2102 N. Arrowhead, Ste B
San Bernardino, CA 92405
(909) 882-3706
(909) 882-3707 FAX

OFC HRS: M, Tu, Th, F 9am-4pm; alt W, Sat 9am-1pm.

MEDI-CAL DENTIST
Highland Family Dental Center
1063 W. Highland Ave.
San Bernardino, CA 92405
(909) 881-2679

OFC HRS: M, W, Th 9am-5pm; Tu 9am-1pm; Sat by appt only. Spanish, Hindi spoken.

MEDI-CAL DENTIST
Lee W. Sulaeman, DDS
25054 E. Baseline St.
San Bernardino, CA 92410
(909) 889-9591
(951) 354-0029 FAX

OFC HRS: M-Th 8am-6pm; F 8am-5pm. Spanish, Indonesian, Mandarin spoken.

MEDI-CAL DENTIST
Dental Care of San Bernardino
322 North H Street
San Bernardino, CA 92410
(909) 888-1301
(909) 884-4697 FAX

OFC HRS: M 8am-5pm; Tu, W 10am-7pm; Th 9am-6pm; F 7:45am-2:30pm. Spanish, Swahili, Chinese spoken. Accepts Medi-Cal for children only.

MEDI-CAL DENTIST
D Street Dental Group
1579 North D Street
San Bernardino, CA 92405
(909) 889-1977
(909) 889-3989 FAX

OFC HRS: M, Th 8am-5pm; Tu 8am-4pm; W 9am-6pm; F 8am-12noon. Spanish, Korean spoken.

MEDI-CAL DENTIST
Central City Dental Group
189 North E Street
San Bernardino, CA 92401
(909) 383-8328
(909) 383-8332 FAX

OFC HRS: M-F 9:30am-6:30pm; Sat 8am-2pm. Spanish spoken.

MEDI-CAL DENTIST
University Heights Family Dental
985 Kendall Dr., Ste B
San Bernardino, CA 92407
(909) 882-8882
(909) 882-2382 FAX

OFC HRS: M-W 9am-5pm; F 9am-1pm, alt Sat 9am-12noon. Spanish spoken.

MEDI-CAL DENTIST
Waterman Dental Center
1428 N. Waterman, Ste A
San Bernardino, CA 92404
(909) 889-1111
(909) 386-3667 FAX

OFC HRS: M, W, F 8am-5pm; Tu, Th 1:30pm-7pm. Spanish spoken.

MEDI-CAL DENTIST
Arrowhead Family Dentistry
407 South E Street
San Bernardino, CA 92401
(909) 889-3300
(909) 885-4444 FAX

OFC HRS: M 11am-8pm; Tu, Th 9am-6pm; F 8am-5pm; Sat 8am-2pm. Spanish, Hindi, Arabic, Vietnamese spoken.

MEDI-CAL DENTIST
Taufik F. Iskaq, DDS
495 N. Central Ave., Ste A
Upland, CA 91786
(909) 931-2600
(909) 931-2605 FAX

OFC HRS: M 11am-8pm; Tu-F 9am-6pm. Spanish, Chinese, Indonesian spoken.

MEDI-CAL DENTIST
Surinder Sharma, DDS
1493 E. Foothill Blvd.
Upland, CA 91786
(909) 946-6891
(909) 946-1361 FAX

OFC HRS: Tu-Th 10am-6:30pm; Sat 10am-5pm. Spanish, Hindi spoken.

MEDI-CAL DENTIST
Victor Valley Dental Plaza
14707 7th Street
Victorville, CA 92392
(760) 245-1015
(760) 245-1146 FAX

OFC HRS: M, Th, F 8am-5pm; Tu, W 9am-6pm.

MEDI-CAL DENTIST
Victor Valley Dental Group
14689 Valley Center Dr., Ste E101
Victorville, CA 92392
(760) 245-0151
(760) 245-8414 FAX

OFC HRS: M-F 8am-4pm. Spanish spoken. ADM REQ: Must have Calif ID and Medi-Cal card.

MEDI-CAL DENTIST
Valley Dental Practice
15080 7th Street, Ste 7
Victorville, CA 92392
(760) 243-5410
(760) 243-1459 FAX

OFC HRS: M-Th 8:30am-5pm; F 9am-5pm; Sat 8am-2pm, closed alt Th. Spanish, Chinese, Korean spoken.

MEDI-CAL DENTIST
Dr. Shin Dental Office
17100 Bear Valley Rd., Ste N
Victorville, CA 92392
(760) 245-7083
(760) 245-7083 FAX

OFC HRS: M-W 9am-6pm; Th 9am-7pm; F 9am-5pm. Spanish, Korean, Vietnamese spoken.

MEDI-CAL DENTIST
Stephen Oh, DDS

33040 Simpson Rd.
Winchester, CA 92596
(951) 926-2489
(951) 926-1537 FAX

OFC HRS: M, W, F 9am-6pm. Japanese, Korean, Spanish spoken.

RIVERSIDE/SAN BERN INDIAN HLTH CLINIC
P.O. Box 1098
66-735 Martinez Rd.
Thermal, CA 92274
(760) 397-4476
(800) 717-4476
(760) 397-0066 FAX

Free clinic for Native American families residing in Riverside or San Bernardino Counties. Mental health, substance abuse, nutrition, dental, general medicine. State ID: 330057DN. FUNDING: Federal, govt, nonprofit. OFC HRS: M-Th 8am-5pm; F 8am-2pm. Spanish spoken. ADM REQ: Proof of Indian heritage, linkage, proof of residency. SERVES: Riverside & San Bernardino Counties.

TRI-COUNTY DENTAL SOCIETY
952 S. Mt. Vernon, Ste A
Colton, CA 92324
(800) 287-8237
(909) 370-2112

Referrals for dental treatment, conducts dental health edu prgms for schools. FUNDING: Nonprofit. OFC HRS: M-F 9am-5pm. SERVES: San Bernardino County.

V.A. MEDICAL CENTER/WEST L.A.
Dental Prgms
11301 Wilshire Blvd.
Los Angeles, CA 90073
(310) 478-3711
(310) 268-3182 FAX

Dental srvs: M, W, Th, F 8am-11am & 1pm-3:30pm; Tu 10am-11am, 1pm-3:30pm. Walk in. FUNDING: Govt. ADM REQ: Eligible veterans only. Free srvs. SERVES: U.S.A.

WWW.HIVDENT.ORG

Coalition of health care professionals committed to ensuring access to quality oral health care srvs for persons living with HIV. Individuals as well as professionals can communicate via e-mail with experts in the field of dentistry on a variety of subjects, such as pediatric health, dental treatment, medications, mental health, nutrition, etc. FUNDING: Nonprofit. SERVES: U.S.A.

A & A HEARING AIDS
Formerly Internatl Hearing Aid Services
7720 Pacific Blvd.
Huntington Park, CA 90255
(323) 588-0742
(323) 588-6805 FAX

Answers questions about hearing aids: in-the-ear, behind-the-ear, earmolds, sound suppressors, assistive listening devices, batteries & repair srv. 100% digital technology available. Hearing Aid Assist Prgm. TDD assist. OFC HRS: M-F 9am-5pm. Spanish spoken. SERVES: U.S.A.

ABILITY AWARENESS
1440 E. 1st Street, Ste 107
Santa Ana, CA 92701
(714) 277-4330
(714) 277-3743 FAX

Natl organization dedicated to enhancing the quality of life for people with disabilities through housing, employment, edu, media and volunteer opportunities. Ability House, developed in partnership with Habitat for Humanity affiliates, is an accessible home built for low income families to which one or more members have a health condition or disability. A unique aspect of this prgm is the outreach to volunteers with disabilities during all phases of construction. FUNDING: Nonprofit. OFC HRS: M-F 8:30am-5:30pm. SERVES: U.S.A.

ABILITY COUNTS, INC.
775 Trademark Cir., Ste 101
Corona, CA 92879
(951) 734-6595
(951) 734-5574 FAX

Job training & opportunities for dev disabled. Open entry & exit prgm. FUNDING: Nonprofit. OFC HRS: M-F 8am-4:30pm. ADM REQ: Ages 18 yrs+, developmentally disabled, can deal with own personal needs, active interest and motivation to work 8-hr days, eligible for Regional Center or State Dept of Rehab srvs. Exceptions on individual basis. SERVES: Riverside & Orange Counties.

ABILITYFIRST/CAMP PAIVIKA
P.O. Box 3367
600 Playground Dr.
Cedarpines Park, CA 92322
(909) 338-1102
(909) 338-2502 FAX

Residential camp for children & adults with physical & dev disabilities. Camp operates June-Aug each year with adaptive recreation and sports activities. Winter weekend respite prgms also available. FUNDING: United Way, donations, Regional Ctrs, nonprofit. ADM REQ: Ages 7 yrs+. SERVES: San Bernardino County.

ABILITYFIRST/CLAREMONT CTR
480 S. Indian Hill Blvd.
Claremont, CA 91711
(909) 621-4727
(909) 624-8388 FAX

Center offers after school prgms for children & adults with physical & dev disabilities. Prgms include: socialization, recreational, & dev activities. Weekend recreation prgm offered for adults ages 18 yrs+, on F nights & Sat mornings. Aquatic therapy available M-F. FUNDING: United Way, regional ctr, pvt, nonprofit. OFC HRS: M-F 9am-6pm. Spanish spoken. ADM REQ: Must be able to participate in prgms. SERVES: Claremont & nearby.

ABILITYFIRST/CORPORATE HDQTRS
Formerly Crippled Children's Society
1300 E. Green St.
Pasadena, CA 91106
(626) 396-1010
(877) 768-4600
(626) 396-1021 FAX

Programs and srvs for children and adults with physical & dev disabilities throughout So. Calif. Workforce srvs, after-school prgms, adult day prgms, socialization, recreation, aquatic therapy, affordable & accessible housing, residential & day camps, infant & toddler prgms, info & referral to outside community resources for the disabled. Contact Kelly Privitt. FUNDING: Donors, Regional Ctrs, fundraising, United Way, Dept of Rehab, nonprofit. OFC HRS: M-F 8am-5:30pm. Spanish spoken. SERVES: So. Calif.

ADDUS HEALTHCARE
35-325 Date Palm Dr., Ste 235
Cathedral City, CA 92234-7015
(760) 770-9490
(866) 601-0163
(760) 770-9401 FAX

Homecare for seniors & disabled. Respite care, homemaker srvs, companionship, eldercare mgmt. FUNDING: Nonprofit. OFC HRS: M-F 7:30am-5:30pm; 24-hr srvs Spanish spoken. ADM REQ: Srvs ordered by M.D. Accepts Medicare, Medi-Cal, pvt pay. SERVES: Riverside County.

ADDUS HEALTHCARE
2627 W. Florida, Ste 103
Hemet, CA 92543
(951) 652-1000
(951) 658-9981 FAX

Homecare for seniors & disabled. Skilled nursing, respite care, homemaker srvs companionship, elder care mgmt. FUNDING: Nonprofit. OFC HRS: M-F 7:30am-5:30pm. Spanish spoken. ADM REQ: Call home support srvs for criteria, (951) 413-5050. Accepts Medicare, Medi-Cal, pvt pay. SERVES: Riverside County.

ADDUS HEALTHCARE
1660 Chicago Ave., Ste N11
Riverside, CA 92507-2048
(951) 784-5222
(951) 784-5610 FAX

Homecare for seniors & disabled. Homemaker srvs, companionship, elder care mgmt. FUNDING: Nonprofit. OFC HRS: M-F 7:30am-5:30pm. Spanish spoken. ADM REQ: Srvs ordered by M.D. Accepts Medicare, Medi-Cal, pvt pay. SERVES: Riverside County.

ADVANCE ENTERPRISE-BEAUMONT
See "ARC/Riverside"

ADVOCATE SCHOOL
See "Keystone Schools"

ALARA ADVOCACY FOUNDATION
P.O. Box 3415
Culver City, CA 90231
(877) 292-5272
(818) 337-2181 FAX

Provides vital srvs for disabled persons and the elderly including: housing assist, medical devices, assist applying for Medi-Cal & Medicaid, food clothing, disaster kits, gifts for special occasions, bathroom equipment, pharmaceutical assist, & college entrance & financial worksops. Tailors srvs to the individual needs of client. FUNDING: Nonprofit. OFC HRS: M-F 9am-5pm. SERVES: L.A., Orange, & Riverside Counties.

ALS ASSOCIATION/NATIONAL
National Office (Lou Gehrig's disease)
27001 Agoura Rd., Ste 250
Calabasas Hills, CA 91301-5104
(818) 880-9007
(818) 880-9006 FAX

Info, resource and referral srv for ALS patients & families. Public awareness and research support to find the cause and cure of ALS (Lou Gehrig's disease). Support groups, patient srvs prgms. Patient hotline (800) 782-4747. FUNDING: Donations, nonprofit. OFC HRS: M-F 7:30am-4pm. Free srvs. SERVES: U.S.A.

ALTA VISTA HEALTHCARE
Skilled Nursing Facility
9020 Garfield St.
Riverside, CA 92503
(951) 688-8200
(951) 688-0386 FAX

99-bed, serves all ages; ambulatory, non-ambulatory, Alzheimer's. OFC HRS: M-F 8am-5pm. Spanish spoken. Accepts Medi-Cal, Medicare, SSI, insurance. SERVES: Riverside County.

AMERICAN ASSN/INTELLECTUAL & DEVELOPMENTAL DISABILITIES
501 3rd Street, Ste 200
Washington, DC 20001
(202) 387-1968
(800) 424-3688
(202) 387-2193 FAX

Promotes dev and dissemination of policies, research, practices & rights for people with intellectual disabilities. FUNDING: Nonprofit. OFC HRS: M-F 9am-5pm, EST. Spanish spoken. Free srvs. SERVES: U.S.A.

AMERICAN ASSN/PEOPLE/DISABILITIES
1629 K Street, NW, Ste 950
Washington, DC 20006
(800) 840-8844
(202) 457-0046
(202) 457-0473 FAX

Membership organization for people with disabilities. Annual fee $15. Prgm srvs: Disability Vote Project, National Disability Mentoring Day, leadership dev. For more info, please visit (www.aapd-dc.org). FUNDING: Nonprofit. OFC HRS: M-F 9am-5pm, EST. SERVES: U.S.A.

AMERICAN COUNCIL OF THE BLIND
2200 Wilson Blvd., Ste 650
Arlington, VA 22201
(800) 424-8666
(202) 467-5081
(703) 465-5085 FAX

Membership group for blind and visually impaired persons. Info on blindness, referrals to clinics, rehabs, research centers & local chapters. Publishes resource lists & monthly magazine. Hotline M-F 2pm-5pm, EST. FUNDING: Donations, nonprofit. OFC HRS: M-F 9am-5pm, EST. Free srvs. SERVES: U.S.A.

AMERICAN SPEECH LANG/HEAR ASSN

National Office
2200 Research Blvd.
Rockville, MD 20850-3289
(800) 498-2071
(800) 638-8255
(301) 571-0457 FAX

ASHA offers info on communication disorders for members & consumers. Referrals for audiologists & speech pathologists certified by ASHA. FUNDING: Nonprofit. OFC HRS: M-F 8:30am-5pm, EST. SERVES: U.S.A.

AMPUTEE CONNECTION/REDLANDS

Redlands Community Hospital
350 Terracina Blvd.
Redlands, CA 92373
(951) 735-7963
(909) 423-0562

Support group for amputees meets 3rd Sun from 2pm-4pm at the Weisser Pavilion (follow signs). Pot luck snacks. Contact: Bert at the above number or Bill at (909)423-0562.

AMYOTROPHIC LATERAL SCLEROSIS

See "ALS Association/National"

ANGEL VIEW CRIPPLED CHILDREN'S FNDN

12379 Miracle Hill Rd.
Desert Hot Springs, CA 92240
(760) 329-6471
(760) 329-9024 FAX

Residential, therapeutic environment for disabled children and young adults, long-term rehab for head injury victims. Wait: 3-6 weeks. FUNDING: Nonprofit. OFC HRS: M-F 8am-4:30pm. Spanish spoken. Accepts Medi-Cal, sliding fee scale.

APPLE VALLEY UNIFIED SCHOOL DIST

22974 Bear Valley Rd.
Apple Valley, CA 92308
(760) 247-8001
(760) 247-7063 FAX

Special edu, speech, psychological testing, counseling, vision and hearing screening, referrals for srvs. FUNDING: Govt. OFC HRS: M-F 7am-3:30pm. ADM REQ: State qualification criteria. SERVES: Apple Valley residents.

APU COMMUNITY COUNSELING CENTER

Formerly Child and Family Dev Center
P.O. Box 7000
918 E. Alosta Ave.
Azusa, CA 91702
(626) 815-5421
(626) 633-0651 FAX

Community-based counseling facility featuring a therapeutic staff that provides quality counseling and consulting srvs in a variety of locations throughout the east San Gabriel Valley. The clinicians at the CCC provide a broad range of cutting-edge treatment srvs for individuals, couples, and families including support for life transition dilemmas, crisis-related issues, and disorders of depression and anxiety. Counseling and edu srvs are provided by licensed pro-

fessionals, interns, and trainees, depending on the need. Also offers the Pediatrics Neurodevelopment Institute (PNI) which works with a spectrum of disorders including mental retardation. Testing, treatment, and eval available. Affliated with Azusa Pacific Univ Dept of Graduate Psychology, APA approved. OFC HRS: M-Th 9am-9pm; F 9am-6pm; Sat 10am-2pm. Low cost srvs, sliding fee scale, insurance reimbursement. SERVES: L.A., Orange, San Bernardino and Riverside Counties.

ARC/MORENO VALLEY

Moreno Valley Resource Center
8130 Mar Vista Court
Riverside, CA 92504
(951) 688-5141
(951) 688-7207 FAX

Advocates for persons with dev disabilities. FUNDING: Private, nonprofit. OFC HRS: M-F 8am-4:30pm. SERVES: Riverside County.

ARC/RIVERSIDE

Ray Strebe Resource Ctr
702 E. 11th Street
Beaumont, CA 92223-1909
(951) 845-3385
(951) 769-1706 FAX

Dedicating to improving the welfare of those with developmental disabilities and their families. Expert training in self-help skills, activities of daily living, vocational skills, community awareness, and social interaction skills. Also advocacy and info. See "Pass Resource Center" for info on activity center srvs for disabled. FUNDING: Inland Regional Center, Depts of Rehab. OFC HRS: M-F 8am-4:30pm. Spanish spoken. ADM REQ: Ages 18 yrs+, primary diagnosis of mental retardation, free from behavioral and medical conditions posing hazard to self, others, and/or association property, able to tolerate 6-hr day prgm. Referred by Inland Regional Center. Free srvs if approved by Dept of Rehab. SERVES: Moreno Valley, Beaumont, Banning, Redlands, Hemet, Cinta Cino, Yucaipa.

ARC/RIVERSIDE

Administrative Office
8138 Mar Vista Court
Riverside, CA 92504
(951) 688-5141
(951) 688-7207 FAX

Work centers, prgms & srvs for adults with dev disability. Packaging and assembly for moderate and mild mental retardation. Day activity centers for severe mental retardation. Also advocacy and info. Minimal wait if openings; if no openings, may be placed on waiting list. FUNDING: Inland Regional Center, Depts of Rehab & Dev Srvs. OFC HRS: M-F 8am-5pm. Spanish spoken. ADM REQ: Adults with mental retardation assessed as appropriate for prgms. Free srvs. SERVES: West Riverside County, including Corona, Norco, Moreno Valley, Beaumont, Banning, San Jacinto, Hemet, Calimesa, Yucaipa.

ARC/RIVERSIDE

Riverside Resource Center
5105 Jurupa Ave.
Riverside, CA 92504
(951) 788-0747
(951) 788-0754 FAX

Arts & crafts, life skills and activities for the severely mentally retarded. OFC HRS: M-F 7:30am-4pm. SERVES: Greater Riverside area.

ARC/RIVERSIDE

Brockton Resource Center
6900 Brockton Ave., Ste 7
Riverside, CA 92506
(951) 367-0856
(951) 367-0858 FAX

Advocates for persons with dev disabilities, restricted healthcare available. FUNDING: Private, nonprofit. OFC HRS: M-F 8am-3pm. SERVES: Riverside County.

ARC/SAN BERNARDINO

796 E. 6th Street
San Bernardino, CA 92410
(909) 884-6484
(909) 885-3111 FAX

Work, training, and activities for dev disabled adults ages 18 yrs+. Receive referrals through Inland Regional Center. OFC HRS: M-F 9am-3:30pm. Spanish spoken, ASL available. SERVES: San Bernardino area.

ARLINGTON GARDENS

Skilled Nursing Facility
3766 Nye Ave.
Riverside, CA 92505
(951) 689-2340
(951) 358-0831 FAX

28-bed facility, ages 18 yrs+; ambulatory, non-ambulatory, Alzheimer's. OFC HRS: M-F 9am-5:30pm. Accepts Medi-Cal, Medicare, SSI, HMO, pvt pay.

ASSN FOR RETARDED CITIZENS

See also "ARC..." or "OPARC..."

ASSN OF REGIONAL CTR AGENCIES

915 L Street, Ste 1440
Sacramento, CA 95814
(916) 446-7961
(916) 446-6912 FAX

21 regional centers offer support srvs for people with dev disabilities. Also HIV/AIDS edu & prevention. FUNDING: Nonprofit. OFC HRS: M-F 8:30am-5pm. Spanish spoken. Free srvs. SERVES: Calif.

AT NETWORK

1029 J Street, Ste 120
Sacramento, CA 95814
(800) 390-2699
(916) 325-1690
(916) 325-1699 FAX

Info & referral on assistive technology devices, srvs and funding sources for the disabled. TTY (800) 900-0706. Info line operators available M-F 9am-5pm. FUNDING: Grants, govt, nonprofit. OFC HRS: M-F 8:30am-4:30pm. Spanish spoken. Language line for any language. Free srvs. SERVES: Calif.

AUDIO VISION READING FOR THE BLIND

Audio Vision Radio Reading
35242 Yucaipa Blvd., Ste C
Yucaipa, CA 92399
(909) 797-4336
(909) 797-3516 FAX

Radio reading srvs for the blind. 24 hrs, 7 days. FUNDING: Donation, grants, nonprofit. OFC HRS: M-F 8am-2pm; Sat-Sun 8am-12noon. ADM REQ: Blindness or disability preventing reading or understanding print. Sign up for radio. Free srvs. SERVES: So. Calif.

BALLARD REHABILITATION HOSPITAL

1760 W. 16th Street
San Bernardino, CA 92411
(909) 473-1200
(909) 473-1276 FAX

Comprehensive physical rehab srvs for adults and pediatric patients diagnosed with brain injury, spinal cord injuries, multiple trauma, amputation, stroke, neurological disorders or orthopedic injuries. Complete inpatient and outpatient medical rehab prgms & srvs. Specialty areas include: indoor therapeutic pool, transitional living suites, mobility court, outpatient workers' comp, pain mgmt prgm & orthopedic srvs. Offers OT, PT, speech and language pathology, therapeutic recreation, respiratory therapy, rehab nursing, neuropsychology case mgmt, pharmacy, rehab nursing and physician, dietary, lab, radiology, social srvs, case mgmt & community re-entry. Forms in English and Spanish. FUNDING: Nonprofit. OFC HRS: M-F 8am-5pm. Spanish, Tagalog, Thai, German, Polish, Russian, Slovac, French spoken. Accepts pvt insurance HMO, PPO, Medicare, Medi-Cal. SERVES: So. Calif.

BARSTOW COMMUNITY COLLEGE

2700 Barstow Rd.
Barstow, CA 92311
(760) 252-2411
(760) 252-1875 FAX

Institution of higher edu offers counseling, testing, vocational edu & rehab srvs, financial aid, veteran srvs, servicemen's opportunity college srvs, extended opportunity prgms, disabled student prgm, scholarship awards, etc. TTY (760) 252-6759. FUNDING: Govt. OFC HRS: M-F 8am-5pm. Foreign languages available upon request. SERVES: Barstow & nearby.

BASIC OCCUPATIONAL TRAINING CTR

1044 E. La Cadena Dr.
Riverside, CA 92507
(951) 788-2349

Adult day care prgm providing daytime supervison, behavior modification & activities for dev disabled. FUNDING: Nonprofit. OFC HRS: M-F 8am-3pm. SERVES: Riverside County.

BEACH CITIES BRAILLE GUILD, INC.

P.O. Box 712
Huntington Beach, CA 92648
(714) 969-7992
(714) 960-1815 FAX

Volunteer transcription into Braille. Jumbo Braille for the touch-impaired blind. Counseling resources for blind or visually impaired. FUNDING: Donations, nonprofit. OFC HRS: M-F 9am-5pm. Fees for cost of materials only. Free counseling. SERVES: U.S.A.

BEST BUDDIES

California Headquarters
5711 W. Slauson Ave., Ste 170
Culver City, CA 90230
(888) 682-8339
(310) 642-2620
(310) 642-2630 FAX

Works to enhance the lives of individuals with dev disabilities by providing opportunities to form one-on-one friendships through integration in schools, the workplace & community.

Provides person-centered supported employment srvs to individuals with dev disabilities. FUNDING: Regional Ctrs, Dept of Rehab, donations, nonprofit. OFC HRS: M-F 9am-6pm. Free srvs. SERVES: Calif.

BILL'S SPECIAL KIDS

25392 Jaclyn Ave.
Moreno Valley, CA 92557
(951) 242-7261

Social and recreational prgms for children with disabilities. FUNDING: Nonprofit. OFC HRS: M-F 9am-5pm. ADM REQ: Ages 5-18 yrs. Must be enrolled in special class, call for info. Fees vary per prgm. SERVES: Moreno Valley.

BIRTH DEFECT RESEARCH FOR CHILDREN

976 Lake Baldwin Ln., Ste 104
Orlando, FL 32814
(407) 895-0802

Free info for families of children with birth defects. Referral to local support groups. Visit (www.birthdefects.org). FUNDING: Nonprofit. OFC HRS: M-F 9am-5pm. EST. Birth defect info free to parents & expectant parents. Memberships avail. SERVES: U.S.A.

BLIND CHILDREN'S CENTER

4120 Marathon St.
Los Angeles, CA 90029
(323) 664-2153
(800) 222-3567
(323) 665-3828 FAX

Diversified srvs which meet special needs of visually impaired or multi-handicapped blind children, ages birth-5yrs and their families. Infant and preschool prgms, extended day care M-F, family support & training, publications, info & referral. Call first. FUNDING: Nonprofit. OFC HRS: M-F 8am-4pm. Spanish spoken. Free srvs. SERVES: Internatl.

BLIND INFORMATION AND SERVICES

Riverside Braille Club
2275 Cordillera Ave.
Colton, CA 92324
(909) 424-0392

Phone assist & referral srv for the visually impaired. Executive Director: Kim Kahler. Meets Tu 10am-2pm. SERVES: Riverside & Orange Counties.

BLINDNESS SUPPORT SERVICES

3696 Beatty Dr., Ste A
Riverside, CA 92506
(951) 341-9244
(951) 341-6335 FAX

Actively works to improve housing, daily living conditions and consumer independence for the visually impaired. Offers info & referral, Braille transcription, affordable housing assist, public transportation assist, independent living skills, orientation and mobility, computer training, health and wellness srvs, employment prep & job placement, senior prgms. FUNDING: State, nonprofit. OFC HRS: M-F 8am-5pm. Spanish spoken. Free for blind or visually impaired persons. SERVES: So. Calif.

BLINDNESS SUPPORT SERVICES

Children's Division
3696 Beatty Dr., Ste A
Riverside, CA 92506
(951) 341-9244
(951) 341-6335 FAX

Prgms for blind or visually impaired children. Provider training for licensed preschool and family day care. FUNDING: First 5, nonprofit. OFC HRS: M-F 8am-5pm. Spanish spoken. ADM REQ: Children ages birth-5 yrs. SERVES: Riverside County.

BRAILLE INSTITUTE

Desert Center
70-251 Ramon Rd.
Rancho Mirage, CA 92270
(760) 321-1111
(760) 321-9715 FAX

Library srvs, visual aids consultation, counseling, as well as classes for training for independence in the areas of orientation, mobility, sensory awareness, independent living skills, home mgmt, etc. FUNDING: Donations, grants, nonprofit. OFC HRS: M-F 8:30am-5pm. ADM REQ: Blind or visually impaired. No certificate needed. Free srvs. SERVES: Riverside & San Bernardino Counties.

BRAILLE INSTITUTE OF AMERICA

(800) 272-4553

Call (800) BRAILLE. Edu & counseling srvs for people of all ages who are blind and visually impaired, talking book library for So. Calif, braille & recording srvs, low vision consultations. Free srvs. Visit (www.brailleinstitute.org). OFC HRS: M-F 8:30am-5pm. Spanish spoken. SERVES: L.A., Ventura, San Luis Obispo, Riverside, San Bernardino, San Diego, Imperial, Santa Barbara, & Orange Counties.

BRAIN INJURY ASSOCIATION/USA

Information & Resource Dept
1608 Spring Hill Rd., Ste 110
Vienna, VA 22182
(703) 761-0750
(703) 761-0755 FAX

Hotline (800) 444-6443, dedicated to improving the quality of life of people with brain injury and their families as well as increasing understanding of brain injury and prevention efforts. Info, referral and support groups. FUNDING: Donation, grants, nonprofit. OFC HRS: M-F 9am-5pm, EST. Spanish spoken. Free srvs. SERVES: U.S.A.

BRAIN INJURY FOUNDATION

Sea Star School/Neurological Center
16662 Hale Ave.
Irvine, CA 92606
(949) 250-5727
(949) 250-5734 FAX

Non-public school for the edu, rehab, neurorehab, behavior mgmt and school reintegration of students ages 5-21 yrs who are survivors of a brain injury. Certified by the Calif Dept of Edu. FUNDING: Nonprofit. OFC HRS: M-F 8:30am-3pm. ADM REQ: Accepts children who have sustained or who have been diagnosed with a brain injury due to, but not limited to: accidents, brain tumor, seizure disorder, hypoxia, anoxia, infectious disorders, meningitis, encephalitis, stroke, or aneurysm. SERVES: U.S.A.

BRASWELL'S IVY RETREAT

Skilled Nursing Facility
2278 Nice Ave.
Mentone, CA 92359
(909) 794-1189
(909) 794-7868 FAX

50-bed, serves ages 18 yrs+, ambulatory, hospice, Alzheimer's, rehab srvs. OFC HRS: M-F 9am-5pm. Spanish spoken. Accepts Medi-Cal, Medicare, SSI, HMO. SERVES: San Bernardino County.

CALIF BOARD/GUIDE DOGS FOR BLIND

Dept of Consumer Affairs
1625 N. Market Blvd., Ste S-202
Sacramento, CA 95834
(916) 574-7825
(866) 512-9103
(916) 324-9340 FAX

State agency regulates schools & instructors that provide guide dogs for the blind. No dogs are provided directly through this office. FUNDING: Govt. OFC HRS: M-F 9am-5pm. SERVES: Calif.

CALIF CHILDREN'S SERVICES (CCS)

Riverside Co. Dept of Health
10769 Hole Ave., Ste 220
Riverside, CA 92505
(951) 358-5401
(951) 358-5198 FAX

State-sponsored specialized medical & rehab care for disabled children whose families are unable to provide such srvs. Referrals based on medical, residential & financial criteria. Provides case mgmt & reimbursement for care. PT & OT to children with neuromuscular or musculoskeletal conditions. FUNDING: State, county. OFC HRS: M-Th 8am-5pm. ADM REQ: Ages birth-21 yrs. SERVES: Riverside County.

CALIF COUNCIL OF THE BLIND

Executive Office
1510 J Street, Ste 125
Sacramento, CA 95814
(800) 221-6359
(916) 441-2100
(916) 441-2188 FAX

Info & referral to legally blind, visually impaired, those experiencing loss of vision and parents/caregivers. Low-cost loans for adaptive equip & referrals. 32 chapters & 8 statewide affiliates in Calif. "California Connection" weekly news line. Advocacy for the blind community, financial scholarships for blind Calif residents going to a Calif vocational or academic institution. Crisis loan fund for members only. Adm ofc Calif only, (800) 221-6359, M-F 10am-4pm. After 4pm, call this number to hear recorded news updated weekly. FUNDING: Nonprofit. OFC HRS: M-F 10am-4pm. ADM REQ: Calif residents who are blind or interested in blindness issues. Member dues vary per chapter. SERVES: Calif.

CALIF DEAF/BLIND SRVS

2001 Junipero Serra Blvd., 7th Fl.
Daly City, CA 94014
(800) 822-7884
(415) 405-7560
(415) 405-7562 FAX

Srvs available to personnel from public & pvt schools & public agencies, family members & care providers of individuals who are deaf-blind. Voice/TTY (415) 239-8089 ext. 23. FUNDING: U.S. Dept of Ed Special Edu Prgms. ADM REQ: Ages birth-21 yrs. SERVES: Calif.

CALIF DEAF/DISABLED/TELE PRGM

California Telephone Access Prgm
P.O. Box 30310
81 March Lane
Stockton, CA 95213

(800) 806-1191
(800) 889-3974 FAX

State-mandated prgm for individuals who have medical certification of a hearing, vision, speech, mobility, or cognitive impairment which limits the use of their standard phone equipment & are eligible to receive specialized equipment and/or srvs at no extra charge to monthly phone bill. TTY (800) 806-4474. Spanish (800) 949-5650; Mandarin (866) 324-8747; Cantonese (866) 324-8754; Hmong (866) 880-3394. OFC HRS: M-F 7am-6pm; Sat 9am-4pm (Call Center). SERVES: Calif.

CALIF DEPT REHAB/ADMIN

State Headquarters
721 Capitol Mall
Sacramento, CA 95814
(916) 558-5300

Works in partnership with consumers and other stakeholders to provide srvs and advocacy resulting in employment, independent living and equality for individuals with disabilities. TTY (916) 558-5302. OFC HRS: M-F 8am-5pm. Closed first three F of the month. Must live in California. Citizenship or valid work permit. Free srvs. SERVES: Calif.

CALIF DEPT REHAB/BARSTOW

See "Calif Dept Rehab/Victorville"

CALIF DEPT REHAB/BLYTHE

Blythe Branch
1277 W. Hobson Way
Blythe, CA 92225
(760) 922-2118
(760) 922-8678 FAX

Assists people with all types of disabilities to retain employment and live independently. Srvs include: vocational rehab (training, edu, transportation, job placement), assistive technology, deaf & hearing srvs, blind srvs, and tech assist. FUNDING: State, govt. OFC HRS: M-F 8am-5pm. Spanish spoken. ADM REQ: Eligible disability. SERVES: Blythe.

CALIF DEPT REHAB/HEMET

See "Calif Dept Rehab/Temecula"

CALIF DEPT REHAB/JOSHUA TREE

Copper Mountain College
6162 Rotary Way
Joshua Tree, CA 92252
(760) 366-2681
(760) 365-4569 FAX

Assists people with all types of disabilities to retain employment and live independently. Srvs include: vocational rehab (training, edu, job placement, transportation), assistive technology, deaf & hearing srvs, blind srvs and tech assist. FUNDING: State, govt. OFC HRS: M-F 8am-5pm. ADM REQ: Eligible disability. SERVES: High Desert.

CALIF DEPT REHAB/PALM DESERT

73-720 Fred Waring Dr., Ste 102
Palm Desert, CA 92260
(760) 674-0262
(760) 674-0268 FAX

Assists people with all types of disabilities to retain employment and live independently. Srvs include: vocational rehab (training, edu, transportation, job placement), assistive technology, deaf & hearing srvs, blind srvs, tech assist, college, orthotic and prosthetic devices. Wait: varies. TTY (760) 674-0266. FUNDING: State,

federal. OFC HRS: M-F 8am-5pm. Spanish spoken. ASL available. ADM REQ: Eligible disability. Free srvs. SERVES: Coachella Valley.

CALIF DEPT REHAB/RIVERSIDE

Inland Empire District Office
3130 Chicago Ave.
Riverside, CA 92507-3445
(951) 782-6650
(951) 782-6676 FAX

Assists people with all types of disabilities to retain employment and live independently. Srvs include: vocational rehab (training, edu, transportation, job placement), assistive technology, deaf & hearing srvs, blind srvs, and tech assist. For TTY, call (951) 682-0143, (951) 320-2061 or (951) 782-4277. FUNDING: State, federal. OFC HRS: M-F 8am-5pm. Spanish spoken, ASL available. ADM REQ: Eligible disability. SERVES: Riverside, San Bernardino, Imperial Counties.

CALIF DEPT REHAB/SAN BERNARDINO

San Bernardino District Office
464 W. 4th. Street, Ste 152
San Bernardino, CA 92401-1419
(909) 383-4401
(909) 383-6880 FAX

Assists people with all types of disabilities to retain employment and live independently. Srvs include: vocational rehab (training, edu, job placement), assistive technology, deaf & hearing srvs, blind srvs, and tech assist. For TTY, call (909)885-0028. FUNDING: State, govt. OFC HRS: M-F 8am-5pm. Spanish spoken. ASL available. ADM REQ: Eligible disability. SERVES: East San Bernardino County.

CALIF DEPT REHAB/TEMECULA

27555 Ynez Rd., Ste 310
Temecula, CA 92591-4678
(951) 693-4451
(951) 693-4462 FAX

Assists people with all types of disabilities to retain employment and live independently. Srvs include: vocational rehab (training, edu, transportation, job placement), assistive technology, deaf & hearing srvs, blind srvs, & tech assist. TTY (951) 693-4468. FUNDING: State, govt. OFC HRS: M-F 8am-5pm. Spanish spoken. ASL available. ADM REQ: Eligible disability. SERVES: Riverside County.

CALIF DEPT REHAB/UPLAND

3585 E. Inland Empire Blvd., Bldg. 4
Ontario, CA 91764
(909) 948-6050

Assists people with all types of disabilities to retain employment and live independently. Srvs include: vocational rehab (training, edu, job placement), assistive technology, deaf & hearing srvs, blind srvs, and tech assist. Call first. FUNDING: State, govt. OFC HRS: M-F 8am-5pm. Spanish spoken. ADM REQ: Eligible disability. Majority of srvs are free. SERVES: Western San Bernardino County.

CALIF DEPT REHAB/VICTORVILLE

15415 W. Sand St., 2nd Fl.
Victorville, CA 92392
(760) 243-6024
(760) 243-0522 FAX

Assists people with all types of disabilities to retain employment and live independently. Srvs include: vocational rehab (training, edu, job placement), assistive technology, deaf & hearing srvs, blind srvs, and tech assist. For TTY, call (760) 245-4127. FUNDING: State, govt. OFC HRS: M-F 8am-5pm. Spanish spoken, ASL available. ADM REQ: Eligible disability. SERVES: Victorville, Southern San Bernardino.

CALIF NURSING & REHAB CTR
Skilled Nursing Facility
2999 N. Indian Ave.
Palm Springs, CA 92262
(760) 325-2937
(760) 322-7250 FAX

80-bed, ages 18 yrs+; ambulatory, non-ambulatory, Alzheimer's. OFC HRS: 24 hrs, 7 days. Spanish, Tagalog spoken. Accepts Medi-Cal, Medicare, SSI. SERVES: Palm Springs & nearby.

CALIF RELAY SERVICE
6436 Oakdale Rd.
Riverbank, CA 95367-9648
(800) 735-2929
(877) 432-9624 FAX

This prgm enables people who use text telephones (TTYs) or personal computers (PCs) to communicate with people who use voice phones, and vice versa. This allows the deaf and hard-of-hearing or speech-disabled to use TTY/PC to communicate with family, friends & business assoc through trained relay operators. Non-TTY users call customer srvs (800) 735-0373. FUNDING: Nonprofit. SERVES: U.S.A.

CALIF SCH FOR THE DEAF/RIVERSIDE
Calif Dept of Edu/Special Schools
3044 Horace St.
Riverside, CA 92506
(951) 782-6500
(951) 782-6509 FAX

Psych testing & therapy srvs for children ages 3-21 yrs attending Calif School for the Deaf, Riverside. Comprehensive edu prgm serves children, preschool through high school grad. Most students are day students but residential srvs available for those who do not live in the Riverside area. School enrollment is over 500 children. TTY (951) 782-6501. FUNDING: State agency, nonprofit. OFC HRS: M-F 8am-4:30pm. Spanish spoken, ASL available. ADM REQ: Deaf or deaf with other disabling conditions. Must be referred and meet eligibility. SERVES: So. Calif.

CALIF STATE COUNCIL ON DEVELOPMENTAL DISABILITIES
1507 21st Street, Ste 210
Sacramento 95811
(916) 322-8481
(866) 802-0514
(916) 443-4957 FAX

Established to ensure that disabled individuals and their families get the support and srv they need. Assists in planning, coordinating, monitoring and evaluating srvs. FUNDING: Govt. OFC HRS: M-F 8am-5pm. SERVES: Calif.

CALIF STATE DISABILITY INSURANCE
P.O. Box 781
371 West 3rd Street, Ste 280
San Bernardino, CA 92402-0781
(800) 480-3287
(909) 383-6840 FAX

Spanish (866) 658-8846. TTY (800) 563-2441. SERVES: Calif.

CALIFORNIANS FOR DISABILITY RIGHTS
Chapter #34
5567 Peacock Lane
Riverside, CA 92505
(909) 343-1327

Volunteer advocacy organization with a goal of influencing legislation that impacts physically disabled, including getting legislation passed to improve lifestyle of the disabled. Monthly meetings. President: Leslie Robinson. FUNDING: Membership dues, donations. OFC HRS: Vary. SERVES: San Bernardino, Riverside Counties.

CALMA
Calif Advocates for Long-Term Care and Medi-Cal Assist
17130 Van Buren Blvd., Ste 181
Riverside, CA 92504
(877) 225-6202

Serves older adults and persons with disabilities at risk throughout Calif. Mission is to promote adult empowerment, prevent abuse and advocate for the rights and dignity of those experiencing health and aging issues. Dedicated to serving the needs of vulnerable adults. FUNDING: Nonprofit. Free srvs. SERVES: Calif.

CAMP CONRAD/CHINNOCK
Diabetic Youth Srvs
12045 E. Waterfront Dr.
Los Angeles, CA 90094
(310) 751-3057
(888) 800-4010 FAX

Srvs & facilities are shared with health-based assns, schools & community organizations looking to promote self-esteem, spiritual awareness & moral character in children, including those living with chronic illness, physical disability or economic hardship. Camp located in the San Bernardino Natl Forest. Recreational, social & edu opportunities for youth & families with diabetes. Campers are taught diabetes self-mgmt skills in a fun, interactive and safe environment. Also water activities, rock climbing, canoeing, hiking, arts/crafts, volleyball, basketball, mountain biking, along with medical edu & self-knowledge. Family & youth camps, multiple youth sessions. FUNDING: Donations, nonprofit. OFC HRS: M-F 9am-3pm. Spanish spoken. Financial aid available for qualifying families. SERVES: So. Calif.

CAMP QUEST
See "Epilepsy Fndn of San Diego"

CAMP-A-LOT & CAMP-A-LITTLE
The ARC of San Diego
3080 Market St.
San Diego, CA 92102
(619) 685-1175
(619) 234-3759 FAX

Traditional one week summer resident camp for children, teens and adults with dev disabilities. Swimming, hiking, crafts, team sports, dance, hockey. FUNDING: Nonprofit. OFC HRS: M-F 8am-4:30pm. Call for more information. SERVES: Calif.

CANINE COMPANIONS FOR INDEPENDENCE
P.O. Box 446
Santa Rosa, CA 95402
(800) 572-2275

Organization trains srv dogs for people with disabilities. TTY (760) 901-4326. FUNDING: Nonprofit. OFC HRS: M-F 8am-5pm. ADM REQ: Persons with disability. SERVES: U.S.A.

CANINE SUPPORT TEAMS, INC.
P.O. Box 891767
Temecula, CA 92589-1767
(951) 301-3625
(951) 301-3605 FAX

Trains assist dogs for persons with disabilities other than blindness. Srv dogs assist with a variety of daily tasks. Social dogs may also be placed with individuals in nursing homes or in group care facilities. All staff except the trainer are volunteers. Qualified persons receive the dogs at no cost. Average wait is 2-3 yrs. Assists the disabled in training their own dog. FUNDING: Donations, grants, United Way Employee Campaign, sponsors, nonprofit. OFC HRS: M-F 9am-3pm. ADM REQ: Disabled, approval of health care provider and pass the screening process. SERVES: Calif.

CARE CONNEXXUS, INC.
Adult Day Srvs Center
4130 Adams St., Ste B
Riverside, CA 92504
(951) 509-2500
(951) 509-2578 FAX

Day care for adults ages 18 yrs+ with memory impairment. Support srvs include: counseling, family support groups, info & referral, case mgmt. Walk in or call. FUNDING: United Way, county, state, fees, nonprofit. OFC HRS: M-F 8am-5pm; prgm hrs: M-F 8:30am-2pm. Spanish spoken. ADM REQ: Must complete physician's health assessment form. Accepts SCAN, Medi-Cal, VA, pvt pay. Flat rate ADCP $51 per day, ADHC $77 per day, financial assist may be available. SERVES: Riverside County.

CAROLYN E. WYLIE CTR FOR CHILDREN
Youth & Families
7177 Potomac St.
Riverside, CA 92504
(951) 784-0020
(951) 784-7062 FAX

Intervention prgm of edu & therapy for children with and without disabilities ages birth-6 yrs. Day care & early childhood prgms. Family edu, counseling, referral, coordination with other agencies. FUNDING: Pvt, public, nonprofit. Child Care Hrs: M-F 7am-6pm. Spanish spoken. ASL available. Pvt pay, 3rd party providers. SERVES: Western Riverside County, some from San Bernardino County.

CASA COLINA CENTERS FOR REHABILITATION
P.O. Box 6001
255 E. Bonita Ave.
Pomona, CA 91769-6001
(866) 724-4127
(909) 596-7733
(909) 593-0153 FAX

Acute inpatient, outpatient, physical med and rehab for children and adults diagnosed with brain injury, spinal cord injury, stroke, back and pain disorders, chronic pulmonary disease, neurological and neuromuscular disorders and other disabling conditions. Outpatient clinics: audiology, hand, orthotics, prosthetics, driver training/eval, amputee and pulmonary. Return to work, long-term residential and post rehab support prgms. Adaptive sports and outdoor adventures, adapted fitness center. Support groups open to community members. Also provides: adult day health care, imaging, sports medicine, and various medical specialty prgms. TDD/TTY (909) 596-3646. FUNDING: Donations, client fees, insurance, nonprofit. OFC HRS: Outpatient M-F 7am-7pm, 24-hr hospital. Spanish spoken. ADM REQ: Doctor referral for therapy prgms. Ability to participate in and benefit from srvs. Accepts Medicare, Medi-Cal, contracts with most insurance & managed care. Set fees. SERVES: So. Calif.

CASA COLINA HOSPITAL CHILDREN'S SRVS
P.O. Box 6001
255 E. Bonita Ave.
Pomona, CA 91769-6001
(909) 596-7733
(909) 596-3548 FAX

Outpatient therapy srvs for children ages one month-15 yrs; clinical srvs for children with brain injury, orthopedic conditions, dev delay and other disabling conditions. Early intervention prgms for at-risk children ages birth-3 yrs, specialized early intervention prgm for children with autism spectrum disorders. FUNDING: CCS, United Way, nonprofit, insurance, regional ctrs, school districts. OFC HRS: M-F 8am-7pm. Spanish spoken. ADM REQ: Physician's referral or call for info; ability to benefit from srvs. Accepts Medi-Cal, HMO, PPO. SERVES: So. Calif.

CASA COLINA OUTDOOR ADVENTURES
P.O. Box 6001
255 E. Bonita Ave.
Pomona, CA 91769-6001
(909) 596-7733
(800) 926-5462
(909) 593-0153 FAX

Year-round recreational, outdoor high adventure for physically or dev disabled children and adults. FUNDING: Pvt, nonprofit. OFC HRS: M-F 8am-5pm. SERVES: So. Calif & Western U.S.

CASA COLINA PADUA VILLAGE
Rancho Pino Verde
11981 Midway Rd.
Lucerne Valley, CA 92356
(760) 248-6245
(760) 248-2245 FAX

Long-term care for disabled adults. Residents participate in ranch life & community activities. Srvs include room & board, transportation, edu, employment & recreational opportunites. Range of operations from structured daily activity to semi-independent living. Ages 18-59 yrs. FUNDING: Pvt, nonprofit. OFC HRS: 24 hrs. Spanish spoken. ADM REQ: Must have TBI or neurological disorder. SERVES: San Bernardino County.

CASA COLINA RETURN TO WORK SRV
Vocational Evaluation Facility
P.O. Box 6001
255 E. Bonita Ave.
Pomona, CA 91769
(909) 596-7733
(866) 724-4127
(909) 596-7845 FAX

Vocational eval, work hardening and clerical training for disabled adults. Call for locations.

FUNDING: Nonprofit. OFC HRS: M-F 9am-5pm.

CENTER FOR INDEPENDENT LIVING
2539 Telegraph Ave.
Berkeley, CA 94704
(510) 841-4776
(510) 841-6168 FAX

Srvs to people with disabilities. Housing assist, employment asst, advocacy, peer counseling, benefits counseling, deaf & blind srvs, personal assistance, and advice on Dept. of Rehab & federal rehab prgms. Travel training, ramps modification for accessibility. Call for Independent Living Ctrs anywhere in Calif. TDD (510) 848-3101. FUNDING: Nonprofit. OFC HRS: M-F 9am-5pm. Spanish, Cantonese, Vietnamese & Japanese spoken. ASL available. Free srvs. SERVES: Northern Alameda County, referral to prgms throughout Calif.

CENTER FOR INDIVIDUAL DEVELOPMENT
San Brdo City Parks, Rec & Comm Srvs
8088 Palm Lane
San Bernardino, CA 92410
(909) 384-5426
(909) 384-5427 FAX

Regional recreation center serving people with disabilities ages 3-80 yrs old. Therapeutic recreation, social, recreational and daily living skills. Walk in. Call first before faxing. FUNDING: City & County. OFC HRS: M-F 8am-5pm. Spanish spoken. ADM REQ: People with disabilities and their friends. Free aquatic prgms. Most prgms have a nominal fee. Donations accepted. SERVES: San Bernardino Metro.

CENTER FOR THE PARTIALLY SIGHTED
6101 W. Centinela Ave., Ste 150
Culver City, CA 90230
(310) 988-1970
(310) 988-1980 FAX

Low vision srvs for the partially sighted and/or legally blind. Training with prescribed visual devices, psych counseling, diabetes edu & support group, HIV & vision loss prgm, pediatric vision assessments, orientation & mobility instruction, independent living skills classes & independent living aids, home safety assessments. Technology assessments including intro to specific devices for work or school such as computer software, telescopic lenses. Transportation for appts in L.A. area. Wait: 1-3 weeks. FUNDING: Corp, grants, donors, state, fees, nonprofit. OFC HRS: M-F 8:30am-5pm, by appt. Spanish spoken. ASL available. Other languages available upon request. ADM REQ: Visually impaired, including legally blind. Accepts Medicare & Medi-Cal to cover portion of exams. Sliding fee scale. SERVES: U.S.A.

CENTER FOR UNIVERSAL DESIGN
North Carolina State Univ. College of Design
P.O. Box 8613
Raleigh, NC 27695-8613
(919) 515-3082
(919) 515-8951 FAX

Evaluates, develops, and promotes accessible and universal design for housing and public buildings. Works to improve quality and availability of universal products and environments for persons of all abilities. Assist & info provided to individuals with disabilities and professionals through research and collaborative efforts with manufacturers, training and info srvs. For publi-

cations and fact sheets, call (800) 647-6777 M-F 10:30am-4pm, EST. FUNDING: Grants, donations, nonprofit. OFC HRS: M-F 9am-5pm, EST. SERVES: U.S.A. & internatl.

CENTER ON DEAFNESS INLAND EMPIRE
3576 Arlington Ave., Ste 211
Riverside, CA 92506
(951) 275-5000
(951) 275-5065 FAX

Srvs provided for the deaf & hard-of-hearing. Advocacy, employment, counseling, workshops, interpreting, independent living skills, resources. TTY (951) 275-0640. FUNDING: Pvt nonprofit, state. OFC HRS: M-F 8:30am-5pm. SERVES: Riverside County.

CENTER/COMMUNICATIVE DISORDER
See "Truesdail Speech Center"

CHAFFEY COLLEGE
Learning Development Center
9375 9th Street
Rancho Cucamonga, CA 91730
(909) 652-7675
(909) 652-7682 FAX

Vocational and academic prgm leading to competitive employment for students with various learning styles including dev learning and physical disabilities. Referral to other srvs for the disabled. Call for info. FUNDING: Title V. OFC HRS: M-F 7:30am-4:30pm. Summer Hrs: M-Th 7am-5pm; F 7:30am-11:30am. ADM REQ: Any disability. SERVES: San Bernardino County.

CHILDREN'S TUMOR FOUNDATION
Calif Regional Office
8939 S. Sepulveda Blvd., Ste 516
Los Angeles, CA 90045
(310) 216-9570
(800) 323-7938
(310) 216-7789 FAX

Dedicated to finding the treatment & cure of Neurofibromatosis. Refers individuals to genetic counseling, medical diagnosis and care; connects them with local support groups, supplies, edu brochures; provides professional and public edu, public awareness, health professional edu packets, speakers, resources & referrals. FUNDING: Dues, donations, nonprofit. OFC HRS: M-F 9am-5pm. SERVES: Calif.

CHRISTOPHER REEVE FNDN
Formerly American Paralysis Association
2113 Seville Ave.
Newport Beach, CA 92661
(949) 673-8474
(800) 225-0292
(949) 723-4818 FAX

Raises funds for research to develop a cure for paralysis. Grants given to improve the quality of life for people with disabilities. Info & referral. FUNDING: Donors, nonprofit. OFC HRS: M-F 9am-5pm. SERVES: Western U.S.A.

CHRISTOPHER REEVE FNDN
Resource Center
636 Morris Turnpike, Ste 3A
Short Hills, NJ 07078
(800) 225-0292
(973) 467-2870
(973) 467-9845 FAX

Natl clearinghouse for info, referral and edu materials on paralysis. FUNDING: Nonprofit. OFC HRS: M-F 9am-5pm, EST. SERVES: U.S.A.

CLOVERLEAF HEALTHCARE CENTER
Skilled Nursing Facility
275 N. San Jacinto St.
Hemet, CA 92543
(951) 658-9441
(951) 766-1908 FAX

99-bed facility for ages 18 yrs+; ambulatory, non-ambulatory, Alzheimer's. OFC HRS: 24 hrs. Spanish, Tagalog spoken. Accepts Medi-Cal, Medicare, HMO, pvt pay. SERVES: Riverside County.

COMMUNITY ACCESS CENTER
83-233 Indio Blvd., Ste 3
Indio, CA 92201
(760) 347-4858
(760) 347-0722 FAX

Many srvs offered for the disabled. Info & referral, sign language interpretation, independent living assist, housing info, peer support groups, job registry, ombudsman, etc. TTY (951) 274-0834. FUNDING: Nonprofit. OFC HRS: M-F 8:30am-5pm. Spanish spoken, ASL available. SERVES: Riverside County.

COMMUNITY ACCESS CENTER
6848 Magnolia Ave., Ste 150
Riverside, CA 92506
(760) 274-0358
(760) 274-0833 FAX

Many srvs offered for the disabled. Info & referral, sign language interpretation, independent living assist, housing info, peer support groups, job registry, ombudsman, etc. TTY (760) 347-6802. FUNDING: Nonprofit. OFC HRS: M-F 8:30am-5pm. ASL available. SERVES: Riverside County.

COMMUNITY CARE LICENSING
Statewide Children's Residential Prgms Office
744 P Street, MS 9-14-48
Sacramento, CA 95814
(916) 651-6040
(916) 651-0515 FAX

Licenses and monitors group homes, foster homes & small family homes, foster family agencies, adoption agencies. FUNDING: Govt. OFC HRS: M-F 8am-5pm. SERVES: Calif.

COMMUNITY EXTENDED CARE HOSPITAL
Skilled Nursing Facility
9620 Fremont Ave.
Montclair, CA 91763
(909) 621-4751
(909) 621-5410 FAX

140-bed, serves ages 20 yrs+, ambulatory, non-ambulatory. OFC HRS: M-F 8am-4:30pm. Spanish, Indonesian, Vietnamese, Tagalog spoken. Accepts Medi-Cal, Medicare, SSI. SERVES: San Bernardino County.

COMMUNITY HOME HEALTH
1805 Medical Center Dr.
San Bernardino, CA 92411
(909) 887-6333
(877) 966-3066
(909) 806-1059 FAX

Skilled health care to homebound patients, RN, home health aide, PT, OT, speech pathology, medical social srvs, mental health, perinatal & pediatric care. JCAHO accredited. FUNDING: Nonprofit. OFC HRS: M-F 8am-4:30pm. Spanish spoken. ADM REQ: Physician order, medical necessity, homebound. Accepts Medi-Cal,

Medicare, HMO, pvt pay, insurance. SERVES: East San Bernardino County.

COPE (COMM OUTREACH PARENT ED)
See "ARC/..."

CRESTVIEW CONVALESCENT HOSP
Skilled Nursing Facility
1471 S. Riverside Ave.
Rialto, CA 92376
(909) 877-1361
(909) 877-0854 FAX

201-bed facility, serves ages 16 yrs+; ambulatory, non-ambulatory, Alzheimer's. OFC HRS: M-Th 8am-5pm; F 7:30am-4pm. Spanish, Tagalog, Urdu spoken. Accepts Medi-Cal, Medicare, SSI, HMO, pvt pay. SERVES: San Bernardino County.

CTAP
Walk in Center
6370 Magnolia Ave., Ste 310
Riverside, CA 92506
(800) 806-1191
(800) 806-4474
(800) 889-3974 FAX

Customized telephone equipment for mobility, vision, speech or hearing impaired persons. Field manager may make visit to homes when there is a need for special equipment design. TTY (800) 806-4474. OFC HRS: M-F 9am-6pm. Spanish spoken, ASL available. SERVES: Inland Empire.

D.A.R.T.
See "Desert Area Resources/..."

DEL ROSA VILLA
Skilled Nursing Facility
2018 N. Del Rosa Ave.
San Bernardino, CA 92404
(909) 885-3261
(909) 888-3871 FAX

104-bed facility, serves ages 30 yrs+; ambulatory, non-ambulatory, Alzheimer's. Spanish, Chinese, Tagalog spoken. Accepts Medi-Cal, Medicare, SSI. SERVES: San Bernardino County.

DESERT AREA EARLY INTERVENTION
See "Desert Area Resources/..."

DESERT AREA ENTERPRISE
See "Desert Area Resources/..."

DESERT AREA RESOURCES/TRAINING
Inform/Employ/Supported Living
201 E. Ridgecrest Blvd.
Ridgecrest, CA 93555
(760) 375-9787
(760) 375-1288 FAX

Multi-srv agency serving special needs individuals. Prgms include: INFORM: a centrally located resource lab with info & resources open to anyone. Community Employment Srvs offers a variety of ways to increase vocational skills through on-the-job training, pre-vocational training skills, and supported job placement. CREST (Crafts, Recreation, Exercise & Socialization Together) provides recreation and social opportunities for persons living in the Indian Wells Valley, ages 7 yrs+. Supported living provides adults with disabilities an opportunity to live in their own homes, via srvs & support from agencies, families and friends. DART also provides early childhood srvs from ages birth-3 yrs; in-home and group settings. Preschool for ages

3-5 yrs. FUNDING: Nonprofit. OFC HRS: M-F 7:30am-4:30pm. Spanish spoken. SERVES: Ridgecrest, Trona & Rand, Inyo & Kern Counties.

DESERT AREA RESOURCES/TRAINING
Early Intervention
201 E. Ridgecrest Blvd.
Ridgecrest, CA 93555
(760) 375-8494
(760) 375-1288 FAX

Promotes the physical, emotional, social and cognitive dev of children from ages birth-3 yrs, who are dev delayed, high-risk and premature. Encourages active involvement of parents in their child's prgm and provides support srvs to the families. FUNDING: Nonprofit. OFC HRS: M-F 7:30am-4:30pm. Spanish spoken. SERVES: Ridgecrest & nearby.

DESERT AREA SUPPORTED LIVING
See "Desert Area Resources/..."

DESERT BLIND/HANDICAPPED ASSN
777 E. Tahquitz Canyon Way, Ste 200-28
Palm Springs, CA 92262
(760) 318-2882
(760) 770-1722 FAX

Transportation for blind, elderly & disabled. Info & referral srvs. FUNDING: Nonprofit, donations. OFC HRS: M-Sat 9am-4pm. ADM REQ: Member organization must fill out application and pay $30 annual fee. Must live in the service area. Accepts donations from $2-$4 or coupons. Coupon books can be purchased from drivers or by calling. SERVES: Palm Springs, Cathedral City, Desert Hot Springs, Eisenhower Medical Ctr.

DESERT ARC
73-255 Country Club Dri.
Palm Desert, CA 92260
(760) 346-1611
(760) 773-0933 FAX

Wide range of srvs for mentally retarded and dev disabled adults: adult day care facility, work training prgm & supported employment. Walk in or call. FUNDING: State, United Way, thrift shops, donations. OFC HRS: M-F 8am-4:30pm. Spanish spoken. ADM REQ: Ages 18 yrs+ whose primary diagnosis is mental retardation. Free srvs for those who qualify. SERVES: Coachella Vly.

DEV DISABILITIES AREA BOARD #12
650 E. Hospitality Ln., Ste 280
San Bernardino, CA 92408
(909) 890-1259
(909) 890-1635 FAX

Advocates for people with dev disabilities, conducts public info prgms, encourages the dev of needed srvs and reviews the policies and practices of publicly funded agencies serving people with dev disabilities. FUNDING: Govt. OFC HRS: M-F 8am-5pm. ADM REQ: Must have a dev disability (mental retardation, cerebral palsy, epilepsy, autism). Free srvs. SERVES: Riverside, San Bernardino, Inyo, Mono Counties.

DISABILITIES MINISTRIES
Crossroads Christian Ch/Beyond Limits
2331 Kellogg Ave.
Corona, CA 92881
(951) 737-4664
(951) 278-3176 FAX

Wide range of activities for dev disabled including: outings, special events, recreation prgm, camping, bible ministries/choir, Special Olympics, & support groups. Sun transportation for physically disabled. Spanish church at 1pm. FUNDING: Nonprofit. OFC HRS: Vary. Free srvs. SERVES: Inland Empire.

DISABILITY RIGHTS ADVOCATES
2001 Center St., 4th Fl.
Berkeley, CA 94704-1204
(510) 665-8644
(510) 665-8716 FAX

Legal representation & advocacy of people with disabilities whose civil rights have been violated. TTY (510) 665-8716. FUNDING: Nonprofit. OFC HRS: M-F 9am-5:30pm. Spanish spoken. SERVES: U.S.A.

DISABILITY RIGHTS CALIFORNIA
Formerly Protection and Advocacy, Inc.
3580 Wilshire Blvd., Ste 902
Los Angeles, CA 90010-2512
(213) 427-8747
(213) 427-8767 FAX

Legal assist to people with physical, dev & psychiatric disabilities. Srvs include: info & referral to other sources of assist; peer and self-advocacy training; representation in admin and judicial proceedings; investigations of abuse, neglect & legislative advocacy. For TTY/TDD, call (800) 776-5746. FUNDING: Fed, nonprofit. OFC HRS: M-F 9am-5pm. Intake M-F 9am-3pm. Vietnamese, Chinese, Spanish & Korean spoken. ADM REQ: Must go through an intake process. Free srvs. SERVES: So. Calif.

DISABILITY RIGHTS EDU/DEFENSE FUND
3075 Adeline St., Ste 210
Berkeley, CA 94703
(510) 644-2555
(800) 348-4232
(510) 841-8645 FAX

Info, advocacy, training and referral srvs for people with disabilities & parents of children with disabilities on a full-range of disability civil rights laws. Wait: 1-2 wks for special edu tech assist. FUNDING: Donations, grants, nonprofit. OFC HRS: M-F 9am-5pm. Spanish, Mandarin & Cantonese spoken. Most srvs are free, copy costs for some info. SERVES: U.S.A. for some trainings & Calif for parent trainings.

DISABLED AMERICAN VETERANS
National Headquarters
3725 Alexandria Pike
Newport, KY 41076
(877) 426-2838
(859) 441-7300

Helps with benefits assist from the Dept. of Veterans Affairs, provides a network of volunteers who offer rides to and from VA medical facilities for veterans, grassroots advocacy & srvs. Also offers special prgms for homeless vets and those suffering from substance abuse issues. Visit (www.dav.org) for more info and to find a chapter near you. Free srvs. SERVES: U.S.A.

DISABLED DEALER
23941 Nomar St.
Woodland Hills, CA 91367
(800) 588-5099
(818) 884-3472 FAX

Publishes the "Disabled Dealer Magazine" where individuals buy, sell and trade adaptive resources and equipment. Visit

(www.disableddealer.com) for a free copy. FUNDING: Private for profit. OFC HRS: M-F 9am-5pm. SERVES: Calif & Nevada.

DISABLED SERVICES
San Bernardino Valley College
701 S. Mt. Vernon Ave.
San Bernardino, CA 92410
(909) 384-4443
(909) 381-2444 FAX

Director: Rebecca Warren-Marlatt. Edu srvs for disabled community college students. Call first. FUNDING: State. OFC HRS: M-Th 8am-7pm; F 8am-4:30pm. Summer M-Th 8am-6pm. Some Spanish spoken, ASL available. ADM REQ: Assessment for learning disabilities group. SERVES: San Bernardino, Riverside Counties.

DISABLED SPORTS USA
P.O. Box 10502
Fullerton, CA 92838
(949) 460-6969
(714) 526-8360 FAX

Recreation and socialization including monthly ski weekends at Mammoth (Dec-May). Serves blind, deaf, cerebral palsy, paraplegics, spina bifida, children and adults with any disability. FUNDING: Donations, dues. Annual dues are $15 (includes monthly newsletter). SERVES: So. Calif.

DISABLED YOUTH CAMPS
The Camps chapter includes many camps for children with disabilities including: "AbilityFirst/ ...," "American Diabetes Association," "Bearskin Meadow Camp," "Camp Conrad/ Chinnock," "Camp Laurel," "Dream Street Foundation," "Easter Seals/So Calif," "Epilepsy Fndn...," "Girl Scouts of USA," "Natl Kidney Fndn...," "Sickle Cell Disease... ."

DIVERSIFIED INDUSTRIES/OPARC
See "OPARC/...."

DOGS FOR THE DEAF, INC.
10175 Wheeler Rd.
Central Point, OR 97502
(541) 826-9220
(541) 826-6696 FAX

Rescues and trains dogs from shelters to assist and enhance the lives of hearing impaired and deaf individuals. Average wait from being placed on waiting list and qualifying is approx one year. FUNDING: Donations, nonprofit. OFC HRS: M-F 8am-4:30pm. ASL available. $25 application fee. SERVES: U.S.A. & Canada.

DOWN SYNDROME CONGRESS
See "Natl Down Syndrome Congress"

DYSLEXIA FOUNDATION
833 Dover Dr., Ste 27
Newport Beach, CA 92663
(949) 642-7303
(949) 642-0689 FAX

Personalized srvs and enrichment prgms for individuals with learning disabilities and their families, professionals working with dyslexics and the medical community. Lending library, annual symposium and lecture series. Outreach prgms and literacy classes sponsored. FUNDING: Nonprofit. OFC HRS: M-F 9am-6pm. Some Spanish spoken. Sliding fee scale $1 & up. SERVES: U.S.A. & Canada.

DYSLEXIA SOCIETY
See "Internatl Dyslexia Assn"

DYSLEXIA SUPPORT GROUP
See "Internatl Dyslexia Assn"

EARLY START FAMILY RESOURCE NTWK
P.O. Box 6127
1425 S. Waterman Ave.
San Bernardino, CA 92412-6127
(800) 890-4794
(909) 890-4709 FAX

Resource center for families with children ages birth-36 months, born medically at-risk or having dev delays or disabilities. Parent support groups, newsletters, resource library. Call for location. FUNDING: Donations, govt, nonprofit. OFC HRS: M-F 8am-5pm. Spanish spoken, ASL available. ADM REQ: Call for appt. SERVES: Inland Empire.

EASTER SEALS/CHILD CARE CENTER
Child Development Center
531 W. 8th Street
Upland, CA 91786
(909) 981-4668
(909) 608-0147 FAX

Infant, toddler and preschool prgm. Scholarships available for pregnant moms and income eligible families with parents seeking employment, working, or attending school. In-home and center-based srvs available. Srvs include: breakfast, lunch, snacks and full-year prgm. FUNDING: Fed, state; sponsored by the Easter Seals. OFC HRS: M-F 7:30am-5:30pm. Spanish spoken. ADM REQ: Low income or disabled children. SERVES: San Bernardino County.

EASTER SEALS/NATIONAL
National Administrative Office
233 S. Wacker Dr., Ste 2400
Chicago, IL 60606-4802
(800) 221-6827
(312) 726-1494 FAX

Helps children & adults with disabilities gain greater independence. Provides medical rehab, job training & employment, inclusive child care, adult day srvs, camping & recreation, info and referral. Publications and resource catalog available upon request. Website lists all 409 sites, prgms and srvs provided, disability info and employment resources. Visit (www.easterseals.com). OFC HRS: M-F 8:30am-5pm, CST. Spanish spoken. SERVES: U.S.A.

EASTER SEALS/SO CALIF
Inland Counties Regional Office
1800 E. Edinger Ave., Ste 190
Santa Ana, CA 92705
(714) 834-1111
(909) 834-1128 FAX

Prgms and srvs for children and adults with disabilities: socialization, recreation. Support groups for stroke, head injury and post-polio syndrome. Resident summer camping and social recreation bowling. Disability awareness for preschool and elementary students. Info & referral for disabled. Upland Child Dev Center. Riverside Adult Dev Prgm. Call (909) 888-4125 (TDD or voice). Riverside Ofc (909) 248-4873. FUNDING: Donations, grants, nonprofit. OFC HRS: M-F varies. SERVES: Riverside & San Bernardino Counties.

EMPLOYMENT DEV DEPT/DISABILITY

Disability Insurance
P.O. Box 781
371 W. 3rd Street
San Bernardino, CA 92402-0781
(800) 480-3287

Disability insurance coverage for workers who become ill, injured or pregnant. This is coverage for off-the-job injuries (Workers' Comp covers job-related). Wait: 7 days. Spanish line (866) 658-8846. See website for additional language lines [www.edd.ca.gov]. FUNDING: Earnings, contributions. OFC HRS: M-F 8am-5pm. Spanish spoken. Free srvs. SERVES: San Bernardino County.

EMPLOYMENT DEV DEPT/JOB SRVS

Rancho Employment Resource Center
9650 9th Street, Ste A
Rancho Cucamonga, CA 91730
(909) 948-6606
(909) 941-6500
(909) 941-1676 FAX

EDD offers employment srvs to employers & job seekers. Srvs include: employer recruitment, workshops & access to computers, fax machines & the Internet. EDD provides priority srvs to veterans & personalized assist to persons with disabilities & youth ages 15-21 yrs with employment barriers. FUNDING: State. OFC HRS: M-F 8am-5pm. Spanish spoken. Free srvs. SERVES: San Bernardino County.

EMPOWERTECH COMPUTER ACCESS CTR

Empowering & Educating People with Disabilities
6234 W. 87th Street
Los Angeles, CA 90045
(310) 338-1597
(310) 338-9318 FAX

Provides children and adults who have physical and dev disabilities with edu and training to lead independent and productive lives utilizing assistive technology. Open Access prgm available free of charge every W 3:30pm-6:30pm. FUNDING: Donations, nonprofit. OFC HRS: M-F 9am-5pm. Spanish & French spoken. SERVES: L.A., Orange & Riverside Counties.

EPILEPSY FNDN OF AMERICA

National Office
8301 Professional Pl.
Landover, MD 20785-7223
(800) 332-1000
(301) 459-3700
(301) 577-4941 FAX

Represents people with epilepsy. Devoted to helping create a better world for people with epilepsy. Provides info on local and natl levels for everything from technical info to finding another person to talk to. Answers questions and discusses caller's concerns about seizure disorders and treatments. Prof library (800) 332-4050. FUNDING: Donation, grants, govt, nonprofit. OFC HRS: M-Th 9am-5pm; F 9am-3pm, EST. Spanish spoken. Free srvs. SERVES: U.S.A.

EPILEPSY FNDN OF GREATER L.A.

5777 W. Century Blvd., Ste 820
Los Angeles, CA 90045
(800) 564-0445
(310) 670-2870
(310) 670-6124 FAX

Info & referral, self-help groups, edu outreach, residential and family camps, parent phone network, conferences, medical ID bracelets and necklaces, seizure first aid training, advocacy, literature and written edu guides. Srvs for persons with seizure disorders, their family members and the community. FUNDING: Donations, grants, nonprofit. OFC HRS: M-F 9am-4:30pm. Spanish spoken. Free srvs. SERVES: So. Calif.

EPILEPSY FNDN OF SAN DIEGO

Camp Quest
2055 El Cajon Blvd.
San Diego, CA 92104-1092
(619) 296-0161
(619) 296-0802 FAX

A medically supervised summer camp for children with seizure disorders. Camp Quest is held for one week in July at a mountain camp. Agency provides individual, family & group counseling, employment prgms, info & referral, advocacy, epilepsy edu. FUNDING: Donations, United Way, nonprofit. OFC HRS: M-F 9am-5pm. ADM REQ: Camp for children ages 8-12 yrs. Application deadline is June 1st. SERVES: Calif.

EXCEPTIONALLY EXCITED KIDS (EEK)

P.O. Box 185
San Jacinto, CA 92581
(951) 375-6906
(951) 491-5598

Mission is to provide latest in exercise science to those with special needs through play, fitness, games, nutrition, etc. Online support, education and resources for special needs children and adults ages 2-25 yrs. Down Syndrome, Autism, Cerebral Palsy, etc. Visit (www.eekandfriends.com/) FUNDING: Nonprofit. SERVES: Inland Empire.

EYE DOG FOUNDATION FOR THE BLIND

Administrative Office
P.O. Box 519
415 Foothill Blvd., Ste 126
Claremont, CA 91711
(661) 831-1333
(800) 393-3641
(661) 831-0681 FAX

Training in the use of the guide dogs to blind persons in the U.S. and most foreign countries. The training center is located at 8252 S. 15th Avenue, Phoenix, AZ, 85011, (602) 276-0051. Donations accepted & are tax exempt. FUNDING: Donations, legacies left in wills and trusts, nonprofit. OFC HRS: M-F 8am-4pm. Free srvs to the blind. SERVES: U.S.A.

FAMILY SELF-SUFFICIENCY

See "Riverside Co. Housing Authority"

FEDERATION/CHILDREN SPECIAL NEEDS

National Parent Information Ctr
1135 Tremont St., Ste 420
Boston, MA 02120
(617) 236-7210
(617) 572-2094 FAX

Info, support & assist to parents of children with disabilities, their professional partners & their communities. FUNDING: Donations, grants, nonprofit. OFC HRS: M-F 9am-5pm. Spanish & Portuguese spoken. SERVES: U.S.A.

FEINGOLD ASSN OF THE UNITED STATES

37 Shell Rd., 2nd Fl.
Rocky Point, NY 11778
(631) 369-9340
(800) 321-3287
(631) 369-2988 FAX

Teaches a dietary mgmt prgm that will help to identify and remove offending foods and additives that affect hyperactive & learning disabled children and chemically sensitive adults. Membership provides researched brand name food and medication lists (continually updated). Provides materials, one-on-one counseling and monthly support group meetings to ensure success of this prgm. Call for info or visit (www.feingold.org). FUNDING: Membership, donation, nonprofit. Varies depending on pgrm. SERVES: So. Calif, Nevada, Arizona, Hawaii & Guam.

FIESTA EDUCATIVA, INC.

161 S. Avenue 24, Ste 201
Los Angeles, CA 90031
(323) 221-6696
(323) 221-6699 FAX

Info, edu seminars, training & referral srvs to Latino families with disabled children. "Fiesta Familiar" in-home training held in L.A., Orange County, Imperial Valley, San Jose, Sacramento & San Diego Counties. FUNDING: Nonprofit. OFC HRS: M-F 8am-5pm. Spanish spoken. Free srvs. SERVES: Calif.

FIRST CALL FOR HELP

Volunteer Center of Victor Valley
P.O. Box 1992
16692 Mojave Dr.
Victorville, CA 92393
(760) 243-9646
(760) 243-4762 FAX

Info & referral for people seeking srvs or info on community agencies. Interaction with individuals in crisis situations in order to reduce tension and stress, allowing that person to utilize available resources more effectively. FUNDING: Donations, grants, nonprofit. OFC HRS: M-Th 9am-2:45pm. Spanish spoken. SERVES: San Bernardino County.

FONTANA REHAB WORKSHOP

Industrial Support Systems
P.O. Box 848
8333 Almeria Ave.
Fontana, CA 92335
(909) 428-3833
(800) 755-4755
(909) 428-3835 FAX

Vocational training & eval, job dev and placement, supported employment srvs, consulting. Wait: depends on needed paperwork from other agencies. FUNDING: Fed, state, pvt, industry, nonprofit. OFC HRS: M-F 7:30am-4:15pm. Spanish spoken. ADM REQ: Medically documented disabling condition, ages 16 yrs+ and set for third party sponsorship. SERVES: Inland Empire.

FOUNDATION FIGHTING BLINDNESS

Southern California
11900 W. Olympic Blvd., Ste 560
Los Angeles, CA 90064
(310) 207-2089
(310) 207-2039 FAX

Info on retinal degenerative diseases including RP & macular degeneration. FUNDING: Nonprofit. OFC HRS: M-F 9am-5pm. SERVES: So. Calif.

FOUNDATION FOR MEXICAN AMERICAN SRVS

P.O. Box 702
Moreno Valley, CA 92556
(951) 485-3394
(951) 485-6804 FAX

Represents families at IEP, IFSP, & IPP meetings. Special edu, regional center & fair hearings. In-home supportive srvs. Suspension & expulsion hearings. Parent workshops & training. FUNDING: Nonprofit. OFC HRS: Vary by appt. Spanish spoken. SERVES: So. Calif.

GALLAUDET UNIVERSITY

800 Florida Ave., NE
Washington, DC 20002-3695
(202) 651-5000

Private, nonprofit, 4-yr liberal arts univ for students who are deaf or hard of hearing. Over 50 undergrad & graduate prgms. Also provides a clearinghouse of resources for the deaf.

GENETICALLY HANDICAPPED PERSONS

Calif Dept of Health Srvs
P.O. Box 997413
MS 8105
Sacramento, CA 95899-7413
(800) 639-0597
(916) 327-1112 FAX

Helps pay medical cost of enrolled persons with hemophilia, sickle-cell, cystic fibrosis, Huntington's disease, PKU, etc. FUNDING: State, nonprofit. OFC HRS: M-F 8am-5pm. Spanish spoken. ADM REQ: Resident of state, medical eligibility restricted to specific inherited diseases. Accepts Medi-Cal. Enrollment fees based on sliding fee scale. SERVES: Calif.

GOODWILL INDUSTRIES/INLAND CO.

Vocational Services
14580 7th Street, Ste Q-1
Victorville, CA 92394
(760) 951-5572
(760) 951-5350
(760) 951-5679 FAX

Supported employment for the dev or physically challenged adult and includes job placement assist, employment prep srvs, career resource center. OFC HRS: M-Th 9am-5pm; F 9am-12noon. Spanish spoken. ADM REQ: Referral from Dept of Rehab. SERVES: San Bernardino County.

GOODWILL INDUSTRIES/SAN BRDO

8120 Palm Lane
San Bernardino, CA 92410
(909) 885-3831
(909) 386-6251 FAX

Voc eval, skill training, job placement, and supported employment for people with disabilities and other major barriers to employment. Wait: 1-2 weeks. FUNDING: Retail sales, fees, nonprofit. OFC HRS: M-F 7:30am-4:30pm. Spanish spoken. ADM REQ: Ready to pursue vocational prgm leading to competitive employment. Free to those who qualify. SERVES: San Bernardino County.

GOODWILL INDUSTRIES/SO CALIF

Corporate Office
342 N. San Fernando Rd.
Los Angeles, CA 90031
(323) 223-1211
(323) 343-9927 FAX

Srvs to physically, mentally and emotionally disabled and other disadvantages such as illiteracy, homelessness, former gang member, etc. Job training & placement prgms, career counseling, WIA, training in food srvs, janitorial, & retail. Metro North Work Source Ctr, Career Evaluation Ctr. Vintage Fashion show for business, club or groups (323) 223-1211, ext 2329. FUNDING: Self-funded, VR, WIA, VA, nonprofit. OFC HRS: M-F 8am-5pm. Spanish spoken. ADM REQ: Ages 18 yrs+, barrier to employment. Youth prgm available. Free srvs. SERVES: L.A. & San Bernardino Counties.

GREATER L.A. AGENCY ON DEAFNESS

Administrative Office for GLAD
2222 Laverna Ave.
Los Angeles, CA 90041
(323) 478-8000
(323) 550-4205 FAX

Srvs for deaf and hard-of-hearing persons include: interpreter referral, info & referral, advocacy, document and phone assist, job placement, ASL classes for people who are HOH or late deaf, facility rental. Tobacco Control Prgm, AIDS/HIV edu srvs, family health edu and GLAD Bookstore, life signs, interpreting referral srvs. TTY (323) 550-4226. FUNDING: Nonprofit. OFC HRS: M-F 8:30am-5pm. ASL available. Free srvs. SERVES: So. Calif.

GROVE APTS

Forest City Residential Mgmt
227 West H Street
Ontario, CA 91762-2748
(909) 983-3525
(909) 983-6062 FAX

Rental housing for disabled, Section 236 & seniors, Section 202. FUNDING: HUD subsidized. OFC HRS: M-F 9am-5pm. ADM REQ: Low income ages 62 yrs+ or disabled. SERVES: San Bernardino County.

GUIDE DOG FOUNDATION FOR BLIND

371 E. Jericho Turnpike
Smithtown, NY 11787-2976
(800) 548-4337
(631) 930-9000
(631) 930-9009 FAX

Increased mobility through the use of guide dogs. The blind applicant and guide dog train together as a team for 25 days at campus at no cost to the recipient. Transportation provided to and from the fndn within North America. Emerg calls 24 hrs. FUNDING: Nonprofit. OFC HRS: M-F 8am-5pm, EST. ADM REQ: Applicants must be legally blind. Free srvs. SERVES: U.S.A.

GUIDE DOGS FOR THE BLIND

350 Los Ranchitos Rd.
San Rafael, CA 94903
(800) 295-4050
(415) 499-4035 FAX

Provides highly trained guide dogs & training in their use to qualified blind men and women. More than 8,000 people have received guide dogs & in-residence training. FUNDING: Donors, nonprofit. OFC HRS: M-F 8am-5pm. Free srvs. SERVES: U.S.A. & Canada.

GUIDE DOGS OF AMERICA

An Internatl Guiding Eyes Prgm
13445 Glenoaks Blvd.
Sylmar, CA 91342
(818) 362-5834

(800) 459-4843
(818) 362-6870 FAX

Guide dog prgm includes training guide dogs and providing instruction to legally blind people in the use of a guide dog (28-day training in residence). In-home training prgm. FUNDING: Donations, nonprofit. OFC HRS: M-F 8:30am-12noon, 12:45pm-4:30pm. ADM REQ: Must be ages 16 yrs+, physically and mentally able to complete training. Free srvs. SERVES: U.S.A. & Canada.

GUIDE DOGS OF THE DESERT

P.O. Box 1692
Palm Springs, CA 92263
(760) 329-6257
(760) 329-2866 FAX

Trains guide dogs for the blind and multi-handicapped blind and instructs them in their use during a 28-day in-residence training class at facility. Wait: 4 months. FUNDING: Donations, nonprofit. OFC HRS: M-F 8:30am-5pm. ADM REQ: Legally blind ages 16 yrs+. Free srvs. SERVES: U.S.A., Canada & Mexico.

H.E.A.T.H. RESOURCE CENTER

See "Heath Resource Center"

HEAR NOW

Hearing Aid Assistance
9440 Santa Monica Blvd., Ste 708
Beverly Hills, CA 90210
(800) 648-4327
(310) 691-1411
(310) 691-1450 FAX

Hearing aids for the hearing impaired who do not have the financial resources to purchase these devices. Collects used hearing aids. Applications for assist available. For individual assist, call M-F 8:30am-4pm, CST. Leave recorded message. FUNDING: Nonprofit. OFC HRS: M-F 9am-4pm, CST. ADM REQ: Low income or meet financial criteria; permanent legal resident of U.S. Processing fee $60 per aid. SERVES: U.S.A.

HEARING AID DISPENSER BOARD

Department of Consumer Affairs
1625 N. Market Blvd., Ste S-202
Sacramento, CA 95834
(916) 574-7990
(916) 574-8645 FAX

State agency that licenses individuals to fit and sell hearing aids. Provides info to consumers on licensed hearing aid dispensers regarding license status and a 30-day warranty on hearing aids and other laws. Accepts and processes consumer complaints relating to hearing aids. Provides consumer info. TDD (916) 322-1700. OFC HRS: M-F 8am-5pm. ADM REQ: Ages 18 yrs+ & HS diploma or equivalent. Complaint & mediation srvs at no charge. SERVES: Calif.

HEARING AID HELPLINE

International Hearing Society
16880 Middlebelt Rd., Ste 4
Livonia, MI 48154
(734) 522-7200
(800) 521-5247
(734) 522-0200 FAX

Internatl source for general info on hearing aids and referrals to local hearing aid specialists who are members of the Internatl Hearing Aid Society. FUNDING: Membership, nonprofit.

OFC HRS: M-F 8am-5pm, EST. SERVES: U.S.A.

HEARING LOSS SUPPORT GROUP

Tri-Palms Club House
32700 Desert Moon Dr.
Thousand Palms, CA 92276-3713
(760) 343-3828

Meets last F each month at 1pm, October-March at the Tri-Palms Country Club in clubhouse. Call for more information. SERVES: Coachella Valley.

HEATH RESOURCE CENTER

George Washington University
2134 G Street, NW
Washington, DC 20037
(202) 994-3365 FAX

Clearinghouse for info on higher edu for individuals with disabilities. This is a prgm of the American Council on Edu funded by the U.S. Dept of Edu. Does not offer telephone srvs. FUNDING: U.S. Dept of Edu. OFC HRS: M-F 9am-5pm, EST. Free srvs. SERVES: U.S.A.

HELEN WOODWARD ANIMAL CENTER

P.O. Box 64
6461 El Apajo Rd.
Rancho Santa Fe, CA 92067
(858) 756-4117
(858) 756-1466 FAX

Dog & cat adoptions, humane edu, AniMeals for pets of the homebound elderly, Pet Encounter Therapy for people in institutions, therapeutic horseback riding for the physically and mentally challenged, animal hospital, pet boarding. FUNDING: Nonprofit. OFC HRS: M-Sun 11am-6pm. SERVES: San Diego, Riverside & Orange Counties.

HESPERIA REC & PARKS DISTRICT

P.O. Box 401055
Hesperia, CA 92340
(760) 244-5488
(760) 244-2513 FAX

Recreational activities for adults and children including: swimming, special interest classes, equestrian events, youth & adult sports, preschool prgms. Sponsors the Mojave River Valley Special Olympics. OFC HRS: M-F 8:30am-5pm. SERVES: San Bernardino County.

HIGH HOPES HEAD INJURY PRGM

2953 Edinger Ave.
Tustin, CA 92780
(949) 733-0044
(949) 733-0041 FAX

Rehab of head-injured adults. Day treatment, physical conditioning, cognitive and vocational retraining, speech therapy, physical therapy, etc. Wait: completion of application and interview. Scholarships available. FUNDING: Fees, donations, grants, nonprofit. OFC HRS: M-Th 8am-3pm. Some Spanish spoken. ADM REQ: Ages 18 yrs+. SERVES: So. Calif.

HOME OF GUIDING HANDS

1825 Gillespie Way, Ste 200
El Cajon, CA 92020-0501
(619) 938-2850
(619) 938-3050 FAX

Round-the-clock residential and training srvs for people with dev disabilities, (mental retardation, autism, cerebral palsy, epilepsy and neurological handicaps) through 27 homes located in San Diego's East County area. Also offers in-home respite for children with dev disabilities who reside with their families, and community living srvs for adults with dev disabilities who live independently in an apartment or home of their own. Prgms & srvs emphasize self-sufficiency & maximize individual choice. FUNDING: Nonprofit. OFC HRS: M-F 8am-4:30pm. Spanish spoken. ADM REQ: Ages 18 yrs+, ages 6 yrs+ for residential prgm. Referral from San Diego Regional Ctr required. Accepts Medi-Cal, Medicare, Military & pvt insurance. SERVES: So. Calif.

HOMECARE WORKERS UNION

SEIU, Local 434B
195 N. Arrowhead Ave.
San Bernardino, CA 92408
(909) 373-3018
(909) 386-7739 FAX

Free referrals for in-home supportive srvs. Helps low income seniors and the disabled remain in their home. Will match needs and find a worker in your area. FUNDING: Nonprofit. OFC HRS: M-F 8am-5pm. Spanish, Russian, Armenian spoken. SERVES: San Bernardino County.

HOMEOWNER/RENTER ASSISTANCE

Calif Franchise Tax Board
(800) 868-4171
(916) 845-0484 FAX

Assists homeowners and renters ages 62 yrs+, blind or disabled, with low income. Eligible recipients receive annual refund TDD (800) 822-6268. FUNDING: Govt OFC HRS: M-F 8am-5pm. Spanish spoken. Free srvs. SERVES: Calif.

HOUSE EAR INSTITUTE

House Ear Clinic
2100 W. 3rd Street
Los Angeles, CA 90057
(213) 483-4431
(800) 388-8612
(213) 483-8789 FAX

Research, edu, and clinical srvs for deaf and hard-of-hearing children & their families. Srvs include: outpatient infant screenings, diagnostic testing, auditory rehab with referrals to edu prgms and therapy, pre- and post- evaluations for Cochlear Implant srvs. Also camp for families and children with parent workshops and fun activities for children. TDD (213) 484-2642; L.A. appts, call (213) 483-5706; Orange County appts, call (714) 516-9570; Care Children's Center, call (213) 353-7005. TDD (213) 483-2226. FUNDING: Nonprofit, donations. OFC HRS: M-F 8:30am-5pm. ADM REQ: Must pre-register for family camp. SERVES: U.S.A.

HUMAN GROWTH FOUNDATION

National Office
997 Glen Cove Ave., Ste 5
Glen Head, NY 11545
(800) 451-6434
(516) 671-4041
(516) 671-4055 FAX

Edu materials & mutual support. Supports research & promotes public awareness of physical & emotional problems of growth abnormalities and adult growth hormone deficiency. Free edu material for families. FUNDING: Donations, grants, nonprofit. OFC HRS: M-F 9am-5pm, EST. SERVES: U.S.A.

IMPACT

34130 Gannon Terrace
Fremont, CA 94555
(877) 322-7299

Volunteer group of professionals and parents working for quality prgms, and advocacy for students who are deaf and/or hard of hearing. Visit (www.deafkids.org). Also support for parents. FUNDING: Nonprofit. Spanish spoken. SERVES: Calif.

INCREDABLES SPECIAL NEEDS PROGRAM

Rancho Cucamonga Civic Center
10500 Civic Center Dr.
Rancho Cucamonga, CA 91730
(909) 477-2782
(909) 477-2848 FAX

Recreational programs offered to residents and non-residents with special needs. Sports, singing, dancing, cooking, etc. Call for more info. Volunteers welcome. FUNDING: City. OFC HRS: M-Th 7am-6pm. ADM REQ: Ages 5-22 yrs, no one turned away. Fees for some activities. SERVES: Rancho Cucamonga.

INDIO NURSING & REHAB CENTER

Skilled Nursing Center
47763 Monroe St.
Indio, CA 92201
(760) 347-0750
(760) 347-9322 FAX

99-bed facility serves ages 20 yrs+; ambulatory, non-ambulatory, Alzheimer's. Spanish spoken. Accepts Medi-Cal, Medicare, SSI. SERVES: Riverside County.

INFANT DEVELOPMENT ASSN OF CALIF

P.O. Box 186550
3210 24th Street
Sacramento, CA 95818-9550
(916) 453-8801
(916) 453-0627 FAX

Advocates for children, ages birth-3 yrs, with disabilities & those at risk for dev disabilities & their families. Workshops, training, public forums, etc. Chapters in Alameda, Yolo/Sacramento, San Diego/Imperial, L.A. areas. Visit (www.idaofcal.org). FUNDING: Nonprofit. SERVES: Calif.

INFANT FAMILY SERVICES

5855 E. Naples Plaza, Ste 103
Long Beach, CA 90803

In-home early intervention prgm serving children ages birth-3 yrs with special needs and at-risk for dev delays. Support srvs to child & families during transition to center and/or school prgms. Assists families in accessing community resources, home visitation, parent-child play groups, OT consultation, speech & language consultation, infant massage instruction, lending library, newsletter. OFC HRS: M-F 8:30am-5pm. ADM REQ: Referral from regional center. SERVES: L.A., Orange & San Bernardino Counties.

INLAND CAREGIVER RESOURCE CENTER

1420 E. Cooley Dri.
Colton, CA 92324
(909) 514-1404
(800) 675-6694
(909) 514-1613 FAX

Serves the caregivers of brain impaired adults ages 18 yrs+. Info & referral to community resources, respite care, family consultation, case planning, legal consultation, support groups, short-term counseling, training and conferences. FUNDING: State Dept of Mental Health, govt. OFC HRS: M-F 9am-5pm. Spanish spoken. ADM REQ: Patient must have sustained brain impairment after the age of 18 yrs. Most srvs are free, sliding fee scale for respite care and counseling. SERVES: San Bernardino, Riverside, Inyo, Mono Counties.

INLAND EMPIRE LIGHTHOUSE FOR THE BLIND

762 N. Sierra Way
San Bernardino, CA 92410
(909) 884-3121
(909) 884-2964 FAX

Teaches independent daily living skills and provides recreational and social prgms to the legally and totally blind. Classes Tu-Th 10am-2pm. Health screening 4th Tu 9:30-11:30am, appt required. FUNDING: Donations, nonprofit. OFC HRS: M-F 8am-5pm. Spanish spoken. ADM REQ: Must be legally blind with certificate signed by a doctor. Free srvs. SERVES: Inland Empire.

INLAND REGIONAL CENTER

P.O. Box 6127
1365 S. Waterman Ave.
San Bernardino, CA 92408
(909) 890-3000
(909) 890-3001 FAX

Eval and diagnosis, case mgmt, info & referral to those suspected of being dev disabled (mental retardation, autism, epilepsy, cerebral palsy & disabilities found to be related to mental retardation). Conditions must originate before age 18 yrs and continue or expect to continue indefinitely and constitute a substantial disability. Other srvs include: advocacy, day prgm placement, early intervention, parent training, etc. FUNDING: State. OFC HRS: M-F 8am-5pm. Spanish spoken. SERVES: San Bernardino & Riverside Counties.

INSTITUTE FOR FAMILIES

4650 Sunset Blvd., MS 111
Los Angeles, CA 90027
(323) 361-4649
(323) 665-7869 FAX

Counseling for families of children who have visual impairments and other anomolies. Referrals for visually impaired children. FUNDING: Grants, donors, nonprofit. OFC HRS: M-F 8am-4pm. Spanish spoken. ADM REQ: Visually impaired child. Free srvs. SERVES: So. Calif.

INTEGRATED LEARNING INSTITUTE

43-875 Washington St., Ste F
Palm Desert, CA 92211
(760) 772-9019
(760) 772-9610 FAX

Help for students of all ages to overcome learning problems and equip them for a lifetime of independent learning. Scholarships available. Agency has plans to move location, please call to confirm address. FUNDING: Nonprofit. OFC HRS: M-F 7am-5pm. SERVES: Coachella Valley.

INTERNATL DYSLEXIA ASSN

Formerly Orton Dyslexia Society
40 York Rd., 4th Fl.
Baltimore, MD 21204
(410) 296-0232

(800) 222-3123
(410) 321-5069 FAX

Clearinghouse with 47 branches providing info on testing, tutoring and effective teaching methods used to aid people with dyslexia. Call to confirm address. FUNDING: Nonprofit. OFC HRS: M-F 8:30am-4:30pm, EST. SERVES: U.S.A.

INTERNATL DYSLEXIA ASSN

Formerly Orton Dyslexia Society
P.O. Box 308
5225 Canyon Crest Dr., Ste 71
Riverside, CA 92507-6301
(951) 686-9837

Provides info & referrals. Call or check website (www.dyslexia-ca.org) for meeting info. Conferences 2-3 times a yr with member discounts. Free meetings and info packet. FUNDING: Nonprofit. Member fee $80 per yr, student $60 per yr, family $135 per yr. SERVES: South Orange, San Bernardino & Riverside Counties.

JEFFERSON TRANSITIONAL PROGRAMS

3839 Brockton Ave.
Riverside, CA 92501
(951) 686-5484
(951) 686-6630 FAX

Vocational & support living prgms for mentally ill and dually diagnosed individuals. Supported housing prgm for men & women, life mgmt skills, one-to-one sessions, house meetings. FUNDING: Nonprofit. OFC HRS: M-F 8am-4pm. ADM REQ: Ability to meet prgm goals & objectives. SERVES: Riverside County.

JOB ACCOMMODATION NETWORK

West Virginia University
P.O. Box 6080
Morgantown, WV 26506-6080
(800) 526-7234
(304) 293-5407 FAX

Ideas for accommodating disabled persons in the workplace & info on availability of accommodation aids & procedures. Answers questions about Americans With Disabilities Act, etc. TTY (877) 781-9403. FUNDING: Govt, nonprofit. OFC HRS: 9am-6pm, EST. Recording accepts messages after hours. Spanish spoken. Free srvs. SERVES: U.S.A.

JOB OPPORTUNITIES FOR THE BLIND

Natl Federation of the Blind
200 E. Wells St.
Baltimore, MD 21230
(410) 659-9314
(410) 685-5653 FAX

Organization of blind people working together to improve opportunities for the blind and the understanding of blindness by the general public. Special prgms and srvs include: job opportunities for the blind (free job search prgm & training for job-ready blind clients); internatl Braille and technology center; newsline talking newspaper; as well as info and literature on all aspects of blindness including aids, appliances, and special items for the blind. FUNDING: Donations, govt. OFC HRS: M-F 8am-5pm, EST. Spanish spoken. SERVES: U.S.A.

JOHN TRACY CLINIC

806 W. Adams Blvd.
Los Angeles, CA 90007-2505
(800) 522-4582
(213) 748-5481

(213) 749-1651 FAX

Family-centered edu facility serving deaf preschool children ages birth-5 yrs. For families in the L.A. area, srvs include: audiological eval, parent & infant prgms, preschool prgms, parent classes & support groups and a three-week intensive summer session. Also provides correspondence courses to parents of hearing-impaired children and deaf/blind children, and a Master's Degree in Deaf Edu through USC. For TTY srv, call (213) 747-2924. Long Beach Center (562) 426-2257. FUNDING: Pvt donations, grants, nonprofit. OFC HRS: M-F 8am-4pm. Spanish spoken. Free srvs. SERVES: Intl.

KEYSTONE SCHOOLS

9994 County Farm Rd.
Riverside, CA 92503
(951) 785-0504
(951) 785-0106 FAX

Non-public school for students who have special needs. Referrals through the school districts only, no pvt placements. Goal is to return the child to the public school setting. HRS: M-F 7:30am-3:30pm. Spanish spoken. Fees paid by school dist. SERVES: Riverside & San Bernardino Counties.

LAUREL CONVALESCENT CENTER

Skilled Nursing Facility
7509 N. Laurel Ave.
Fontana, CA 92336
(909) 822-8066
(909) 822-6282 FAX

97-bed facility serves ages 18 yrs+, ambulatory, non-ambulatory, Alzheimer's. OFC HRS: M-F 8am-4:30pm. Spanish, Tagalog spoken. Accepts Medi-Cal, Medicare, SSI.

LEGACY POST ACUTE REHAB CENTER

Skilled Nursing Facility
1335 N. Waterman Ave.
San Bernardino, CA 92404
(909) 885-0268
(909) 888-5982 FAX

120-bed facility; ambulatory, non-ambulatory, sub-acute unit, rehab unit. OFC HRS: M-F 8am-6:30pm. Spanish spoken. Accepts Medi-Cal, Medicare, SSI, most HMO. SERVES: San Bernardino County.

LIGHTHOUSE FOR THE BLIND

See "Inland Empire Lighthouse For The Blind"

LIGHTHOUSE INTERNATIONAL

Info & Resource Service
111 E. 59th Street
New York, NY 10022-1202
(800) 829-0500
(212) 821-9705 FAX

Free literature on eye diseases, resource lists, etc. A guide to reading options, intro to assistive computer tech, financial aid resource list for persons with impaired vision. Referrals to low vision srvs, rehab agencies, support groups, state agencies and advocacy groups. TDD (212) 821-9713. FUNDING: Donations, nonprofit. OFC HRS: M-F 9am-8pm, EST. Spanish & Chinese spoken. SERVES: Internatl.

LINCOLN DEVELOPMENT CENTER

440 N. Allyn Ave.
Ontario, CA 91764
(909) 983-9803
(909) 459-2865 FAX

School for the severely handicapped and for regular edu. FUNDING: Govt. OFC HRS: M-F 8:45am-3pm. Spanish spoken. ADM REQ: Referrals by PPS. SERVES: Ontario, Montclair, Chino, Upland, Rancho areas.

LITTLE PEOPLE OF AMERICA

National Office
250 El Camino Real, Ste 201
Tustin, CA 92780
(888) 572-2001
(714) 368-3689
(714) 368-3367 FAX

Dedicated to helping people with dwarfism. Provides resources, social opportunities, referrals and support to persons with dwarfism, including average height parents of children with dwarfism. Info on employment, edu, disability rights, adoption of short-statured children, medical issues, clothing, adaptive devices, parenting tips. Natl magazine, "LPA Today." 62 chapters & 14 districts each offering newsletters & other srvs. FUNDING: Donations, grants, client fees, nonprofit. OFC HRS: M-F 8:30am-4:30pm. Spanish spoken. ADM REQ: Membership with annual dues $50. Lifetime membership $500, senior membership $10. SERVES: U.S.A.

LOCKS OF LOVE

234 Southern Blvd.
West Palm Beach, FL 33405
(561) 833-7332
(561) 833-7962 FAX

Accepts donated hair to provide hairpieces to low income children ages birth-18 yrs who have lost their hair due to a medical condition. FUNDING: Donations, nonprofit. OFC HRS: M-F 8:30am-5pm, EST. Spanish spoken. Each case reviewed for financial circumstance. SERVES: U.S.A. & Canada.

LOU GEHRIG'S DISEASE

See "ALS Association/National"

LOUISIANA CENTER FOR THE BLIND

101 S. Trenton St.
Ruston, LA 71270
(800) 234-4166
(318) 251-2891
(318) 251-0109 FAX

Residential rehab for adults who are legally blind. Adult orientation to blindness and adjustment training, employment assist, training in computer literacy and adaptive technology, summer training and employment project for teens, summer buddy prgm for blind children, special seminars, outreach and referral srvs, internships & training for rehab professionals. Prgm for persons over age 55 yrs who are losing their vision. FUNDING: Nonprofit. OFC HRS: M-F 8am-5pm, CST. SERVES: U.S.A.

LUTHERAN SOCIAL SRVS

Family Counseling Center
P.O. Box 1927
41945 Big Bear Blvd., Ste 200
Big Bear Lake, CA 92315
(909) 866-5721

Individual, group, family & crisis intervention sessions. Ongoing psychotherapy with medication intervention as needed, no outpatient drug or alcohol. AB2726. School counseling for special edu students. FUNDING: County, pvt, nonprofit. OFC HRS: M-F 8am-7pm. Spanish spoken. ADM REQ: Clients who require sustained therapeutic intervention for acute and/or

ongoing psychiatric distress. Ages 18 yrs+. Accepts Medi-Cal. SERVES: Bear Valley residents.

MANOR CARE NURSING AND REHAB

Skilled Nursing Facility
1717 W. Stetson Ave.
Hemet, CA 92545
(951) 925-9171
(951) 925-8186 FAX

178-bed facility for ages 30 yrs+; ambulatory, non-ambulatory, OT, ST & PT. OFC HRS: M-F 7:30am-7pm. Spanish spoken. Accepts Medi-Cal, Medicare, pvt insurance. SERVES: Riverside County.

MANORCARE HEALTH SERVICES

Skilled Nursing Facility
74-350 Country Club Dr.
Palm Desert, CA 92260
(760) 341-0261
(760) 779-1563 FAX

178-bed facility, ambulatory, non-ambulatory rehab, Alzheimer's. Accepts Medi-Cal, Medicare, SSI. SERVES: Riverside County.

MEDICAL CTR CONVALESCENT HOSPITAL

Skilled Nursing Facility
467 E. Gilbert St.
San Bernardino, CA 92404
(909) 884-4781
(909) 381-3162 FAX

99-bed facility, serves ages 25 yrs+; ambulatory, non-ambulatory, Alzheimer's. OFC HRS: 24 hrs. Spanish spoken. Accepts Medi-Cal, Medicare, SSI. SERVES: San Bernardino County.

MERRI MIXERS

8088 Palm Lane
San Bernardino, CA 92410
(909) 384-5426
(909) 384-5427 FAX

Social recreational and living skills for dev disabled adults. FUNDING: Nonprofit. OFC HRS: M-W, F 8am-5pm; Th 8am-8pm. Spanish spoken. ADM REQ: Must be toilet trained. Resident fee $20 per month; $22 for non-residents. SERVES: San Bernardino County.

MONTCLAIR MANOR CARE CENTER

Skilled Nursing Facility
5119 Bandera St.
Montclair, CA 91763
(909) 626-1294
(909) 626-4005 FAX

59-bed facility, serves ages 65 yrs+; ambulatory, non-ambulatory, Alzheimer's. OFC HRS: M-F 8am-5pm. Spanish, Tagalog Indonesian spoken. Accepts Medi-Cal, Medicare, SSI. SERVES: San Bernardino County.

MONTEREY PALMS HEALTHCARE CENTER

Skilled Nursing Facility
44-610 Monterey Ave.
Palm Desert, CA 92260
(760) 776-7700
(760) 776-7756 FAX

99-bed facility, ages 18 yrs+; ambulatory, non-ambulatory. OFC HRS: M-F 8:30am-8:30pm. Spanish, Tagalog spoken. Accepts Medicare. SERVES: Riverside County.

MORONGO BASIN ADULT HEALTH SRVS

P.O. Box 106
57121 Sunnyslope Dr.
Yucca Valley, CA 92284

(760) 365-9661
(760) 994-1337 FAX

Prgms include a senior center and pool to help keep our friends in their own homes by helping them stay healthy and fit. For applications and payment info, visit (www.mbahs.org). FUNDING: Client fees, grants, insurance, donations, nonprofit. OFC HRS: M-F 8am-4pm; F 8am-2pm. SERVES: Morongo Basin.

MT. RUBIDOUX CONV HOSPITAL

Skilled Nursing Facility
6401 33rd Street
Riverside, CA 92509
(951) 681-2200
(951) 681-4402 FAX

143-bed facility serves ages 18 yrs+, ambulatory, non-ambulatory, Alzheimer's. OFC HRS: M-F 9am-5:30pm. Spanish spoken. Accepts Medi-Cal, Medicare, SSI. SERVES: Riverside County.

MULTIPLE SCLEROSIS CLINIC/LLU

Loma Linda Univ Medical Center
Neurology Clinic
11370 Anderson St., Ste 2400
Loma Linda, CA 92354
(909) 558-2880
(888) 558-8705
(909) 558-2237 FAX

Diagnosis, eval, medical advice, clinical follow-up and info. FUNDING: Donations, nonprofit. OFC HRS: M-Th 8am-5pm; F 8am-2pm; MS Clinic on Tu afternoon. Spanish spoken. ADM REQ: Diagnosed or suspected multiple sclerosis. Accepts pvt insurance. SERVES: U.S.A.

NATIONAL CENTER ON LIFE PLANNING FOR PERSONS WITH DISABILITIES

19029 Nordhoff St., Ste 204
Northridge, CA 91324-4804
(888) 881-8113
(818) 709-1990 FAX

Assists families who have loved ones with a disability with a comprehensive life plan at the lowest possible cost. Srvs include: special needs trusts, living trusts, conservatorships, funding specialists. NCLP provides edu & info seminars to all support groups at no cost. All materials are also in Spanish. FUNDING: Nonprofit. OFC HRS: M-F 9am-7pm, by appt. Spanish spoken. Set fees. SERVES: Calif.

NATL ASSN FOR THE DUALLY DIAGNOSED

132 Fair St.
Kingston, NY 12401
(800) 331-5362
(845) 331-4336
(845) 331-4569 FAX

Membership assn established for professionals, care providers and families to promote understanding for individuals who have both dev disabilities and mental illness. FUNDING: Nonprofit.

NATL ASSN OF HEARING LOSS

7910 Woodmont Ave., Ste 1200
Bethesda, MD 20814
(301) 657-2248
(301) 913-9413 FAX

Dedicated to the well-being of people who do not hear well. Natl membership offers a bi-monthly journal on hearing loss, discount on publications and resource materials, and support of various prgms promoting awareness, edu, employment & communication access. Extensive network of chapters and groups across the country. An annual convention in June. TTY (301) 657-2249. FUNDING: Donations, client fees, nonprofit. OFC HRS: M-F 9am-5pm. SERVES: U.S.A.

NATL ASSN/PARENTS OF CHILDREN WITH VISUAL IMPAIRMENTS

P.O. Box 317
Watertown, MA 02471
(800) 562-6265
(617) 972-7441
(617) 972-7444 FAX

Members receive help immediately after child is diagnosed. Connections to families who have children with similar conditions, practical suggestions, info & referral, advocacy, research info, related publications etc. 24-hr recording asks for an address to have info mailed or callers may leave a phone number for a return call. FUNDING: Donations, grants, nonprofit. OFC HRS: M-F 9am-5pm, EST. Spanish spoken. SERVES: U.S.A.

NATL BRAIN INJURY ASSOCIATION

See "Brain Injury Association/USA"

NATL CENTER ON DEAFNESS

Cal-State University Northridge
18111 Nordhoff St.
Chisholm Hall, Mail Drop 8267
Northridge, CA 91330-8267
(818) 677-2054
(818) 677-7192 FAX

NCOD is provided for prospective deaf and hard-of-hearing students to provide communication access, tutoring, scholarships, academic advisement, etc. Also provides training and outreach to edu institutions throughout the country and houses one of the largest libraries dedicated to the deaf and hard-of-hearing. FUNDING: Grants, state, donations. ADM REQ: Prospective students are encouraged to e-mail NCOD prior to enrollment; include name, year and semester you are applying for: (aileen.rolon@csun.edu). SERVES: U.S.A.

NATL CTR FOR STUTTERING

200 E. 33rd Street, Ste 17-C
New York, NY 10016
(212) 532-1460
(800) 221-2483
(212) 683-1372 FAX

Info for people who stutter, parents of young children showing early symptoms and professionals seeking training. FUNDING: Nonprofit. OFC HRS: M-F 10am-5pm, EST. French spoken. ADM REQ: Ages 7 yrs+. Fees vary. SERVES: U.S.A.

NATL DISSEMINATION CTR FOR CHILDREN WITH DISABILITIES

P.O. Box 1492
1825 Connecticut Ave., NW, Ste 700
Washington, DC 20013
(800) 695-0285
(202) 884-8441 FAX

Info for anyone involved with children and youth with disabilities. Info given by personal responses to specific questions, referrals to other organizations and sources of help (publication, prepared info packets). Wait: 1-10 days depending on volume. Phone number listed above also serves as a TTY. FUNDING: Non-

profit, govt. OFC HRS: M-F 9am-5pm, EST. Spanish spoken. Free srvs, some publications have a small fee. SERVES: U.S.A.

NATL DOWN SYNDROME CONGRESS

1370 Center Dr., Ste 102
Atlanta, GA 30338-4132
(800) 232-6372
(770) 604-9500
(770) 604-9898 FAX

Responds to questions concerning all aspects of Down Syndrome. "Down Syndrome News" is published and available to all members. Also refers to organizations throughout the U.S. Info available in Spanish. FUNDING: Donations, membership. OFC HRS: M-F 9am-5:30pm, EST. SERVES: U.S.A.

NATL DOWN SYNDROME SOCIETY

666 Broadway, 8th Fl.
New York, NY 10012-2317
(800) 221-4602
(212) 460-9330
(212) 979-2873 FAX

Info about Down Syndrome, referrals to local resources and parent groups. Free packet of info and free newsletter. Booklets, manuals, videos at small cost. FUNDING: Donors, fndn, corporate, nonprofit. OFC HRS: M-F 9am-5pm, EST. Spanish spoken. SERVES: U.S.A.

NATL HEAD INJURY FOUNDATION

See "Brain Injury Association/USA" or "Brain Injury Foundation"

NATL LIBRARY SRVS FOR THE BLIND & PHYSICALLY HANDICAPPED

1291 Taylor St., NW
Washington, DC 20542
(888) 657-7323
(202) 707-5100
(202) 707-0712 FAX

Network of regional and subregional libraries. Provides free library srvs to the blind or visually impaired. Recorded or braille books & magazines, specially designed phonographs & cassette players on loan. TDD (202) 707-0744. FUNDING: Govt. HRS: M-F 8am-4:30pm, EST. Free srvs. SERVES: U.S.A.

NATL MULTIPLE SCLEROSIS SOCIETY

Headquarters
733 3rd Avenue, 3rd Fl.
New York, NY 10017
(212) 463-7787
(800) 344-4867
(212) 986-7981 FAX

Publications regarding MS and living with MS. Info & referrals. OFC HRS: M-F 9am-5pm, EST. Free srvs. SERVES: U.S.A.

NATL MULTIPLE SCLEROSIS SOCIETY

Coachella Valley Branch
73710 Fred Waring Dr., Ste 103
Palm Desert, CA 92260
(760) 776-5740
(760) 776-5742 FAX

Current info and research data on MS. Referral to support groups, srvs, health professionals and other community resources. Call for schedule of prgms appropriate for individuals, family members or friends. Materials available in Spanish. FUNDING: Nonprofit. OFC HRS: M-F 9am-5pm. SERVES: Coachella Valley, Morongo Basin and Palo Verde Valley.

NATL MULTIPLE SCLEROSIS SOCIETY

Inland Empire Field Office
869 E. Foothill Blvd., Ste I
Upland, CA 91786
(800) 752-1773
(909) 949-1363

General info & research data on multiple sclerosis. Referral to support groups and srvs. FUNDING: Donations, grants, nonprofit. OFC HRS: M-F 9am-5pm. Spanish spoken. SERVES: Riverside & San Bernardino Counties.

NATL REHABILITATION INFO CENTER

8201 Corporate Dr., Ste 600
Landover, MD 20785
(800) 346-2742
(301) 459-5900
(301) 459-4263 FAX

Library and info center on disability and rehab. Quick reference and referral; REHABDATA searches bibliographic database of more than 70,000 documents, both federally funded and commercially produced. Doc delivery provides photocopies of docs in their collection. TTY (301) 459-5984. Visit (www.NARIC.com). FUNDING: Natl Inst on Disability, rehab research, nonprofit. HRS: M-F 9am-5pm, EST. Small charge for REHABDATA searches. SERVES: U.S.A.

NATL SOCIETY/PREVENT BLINDNESS

See "Prevent Blindness America"

NATL SPASMODIC TORTICOLLIS ASSN

ST also known as Cervical Dystonia
9920 Talbert Ave.
Fountain Valley, CA 92708
(800) 487-8385
(714) 378-9837
(714) 378-7830 FAX

Resources and info for physicians who treat this debilitating neurological movement disorder. Also offers support group contacts. FUNDING: Nonprofit. OFC HRS: M-F 8am-5pm. SERVES: U.S.A.

NATL SPINAL CORD INJURY ASSN

Natl Office Resource Center
1 Church St., Ste 600
Rockville, MD 20850
(800) 962-9629
(866) 387-2196 FAX

Info, data, local resources & referrals to persons with SCI. Health care staff. Various fact sheets provide valuable info to individuals with SCI. Local chapters offer seven rehab centers, visitation and peer counseling to those with SCI. FUNDING: Donations, grants, nonprofit. OFC HRS: M-F 8:30am-5pm, EST. Spanish spoken. SERVES: U.S.A.

NATL STUTTERING ASSOCIATION

119 W. 40th Street, 14th Fl.
New York, NY 10018
(800) 937-8888
(212) 944-8244 FAX

Info & referral srvs regarding stuttering. FUNDING: Nonprofit. OFC HRS: M-F 8am-5pm, EST. SERVES: U.S.A.

NATL STUTTERING ASSOCIATION

Formerly Natl Stuttering Project
Riverside, CA 92522
(909) 790-2363
(909) 790-0074 FAX

Supportive, tension-free environment for people who stutter. Call or write for info on meetings. Contact Ron Mitchell at the number above or e-mail: (ron.mitchell3@verizon.net). Group meets on the 2nd Sun of each month at 6pm in the edu trailers at Kaiser Hospital in Riverside. SERVES: Inland Empire.

NEW HAVEN YOUTH & FAMILY SRVS

P.O. Box 1199
216 W. Los Angeles Dr.
Vista, CA 92083
(760) 630-4035
(760) 630-4030 FAX

Assists children facing emotional & dev challenges. 72-bed residential treatment prgm, special edu, vocational schools. FUNDING: Nonprofit. OFC HRS: M-F 8am-5pm. ADM REQ: Boys ages 8-17 yrs, referred by DMH, DPSS or Probation Dept. SERVES: San Diego, L.A., & Riverside Counties.

NORCO SENIOR CENTER

Party Partners Program
2690 Clark Ave.
Norco, CA 92860
(951) 270-5647
(951) 371-5622 FAX

Socialization for dev disabled adults. Meets 2nd & 4th F 6:30pm-9pm. Entertainment, activities, refreshments. FUNDING: City, Corona CDBG, nonprofit. OFC HRS: M-F 7am-5pm. SERVES: Corona, Norco.

OAK GROVE CENTER

Formerly Oak Grove Institute
24275 Jefferson Ave.
Murrieta, CA 92562
(951) 677-5599
(951) 698-0461 FAX

Residential treatment for children and adol, ages 8-18 yrs experiencing social, emotional and behavioral disorders, neurological problems, chronic medical problems with concurrent behavioral difficulties, school problems, family dysfunction and secondary alcohol or substance abuse. Partial hospitalization & day treatment. Nonpublic school on grounds. Also offers an autism center for children with mild to severe autism. FUNDING: Dept of Children's Srvs, school districts, Regional Ctr, nonprofit. OFC HRS: M-F 8am-5pm. ADM REQ: Clinically appropriate for residential or day treatment & funding available. SERVES: So. Calif.

OMBUDSMAN PROGRAM

See "San Bernardino Co. Ombudsman"

ON THE MOVE ADULT DEV CENTER

3351 Chicago Ave.
Riverside, CA 92507
(951) 779-9665

Adult day care prgm provides daytime supervision & activities for dev disabled. FUNDING: Nonprofit. OFC HRS: M-F 8am-5pm. Spanish spoken. ADM REQ: Ages 22-62 yrs. SERVES: Riverside County.

OPARC/ADULT DEVELOPMENT CTR

Adult Dev Center/Montclair
4650 Arrow Hwy., Ste G-21
Montclair, CA 91763
(909) 625-0213
(909) 625-7375 FAX

Voc skills for the dev disabled adult, including janitorial and yard crews. FUNDING: Nonprofit.

OFC HRS: M-F 8am-4pm. Spanish spoken. ADM REQ: Referral from regional center. SERVES: Pomona Valley & Inland Empire.

OPARC/ADULT DEVELOPMENT CTR

Administrative Offices
9029 Vernon Ave.
Montclair, CA 91763
(909) 985-3116
(909) 985-8579 FAX

Oversees five different prgms for dev disabled adults including day care prgms in Montclair, Rancho Cucamonga and Ontario; Summit Behavioral Mgmt prgm in Upland; voc training & supported employment prgm in Montclair. Recreational prgm for seniors with disabilities. FUNDING: Govt, nonprofit. OFC HRS: M-F 8:15am-4:45pm. Spanish spoken. ADM REQ: Adults 21 yrs+, dev disabled or have mental illness. SERVES: Pomona Valley & Western San Bernardino County.

OPARC/ADULT DEVELOPMENT CTR

Adult Dev Center/Monte Vista
9160 Monte Vista Ave.
Montclair, CA 91763
(909) 621-3884
(909) 621-9614 FAX

Community life training for dev disabled adults. VTDD machines at each site for the hearing impaired. FUNDING: Nonprofit. OFC HRS: M-F 8am-4pm. Spanish spoken. ADM REQ: Referral from Regional Center. SERVES: Pomona Valley & Inland Empire.

OPARC/ADULT DEVELOPMENT CTR

Adult Dev Center/Ontario
1235 E. Francis St., Ste A
Ontario, CA 91761
(909) 923-5355
(909) 923-8477 FAX

Community life training for dev disabled adults. VTDD machines at each site for the hearing impaired. FUNDING: Nonprofit. OFC HRS: M-F 8am-4pm. Some Spanish spoken. ADM REQ: Referral from Regional Center. SERVES: Pomona Valley & Inland Empire.

OPARC/ADULT DEVELOPMENT CTR

Passport Senior Srvs
8333 Rochester Ave., Ste 12
Rancho Cucamonga, CA 91730
(909) 948-5592
(909) 980-4682 FAX

Community life training for dev disabled adults. VTDD machines at each site for the hearing impaired. FUNDING: Pvt donations. OFC HRS: M-F 8am-5pm. Spanish spoken. ADM REQ: Dev disability. SERVES: Pomona Valley & Inland Empire.

OPARC/ADULT DEVELOPMENT CTR

Adult Dev Center/Summit Srvs
436 S. Sultana Ave.
Upland, CA 91786
(909) 920-5204
(909) 920-0604 FAX

Community life training for dev disabled adults. VTDD machines at each site for the hearing impaired. FUNDING: Dept of Rehab, nonprofit. OFC HRS: M-F 8am-4pm. Spanish spoken. ADM REQ: Regional Center referral. SERVES: Pomona Valley & Inland Empire.

OPARC/DIVERSIFIED INDUSTRIES

9029 Vernon Ave.

Montclair, CA 91763
(909) 982-4090
(909) 982-5180 FAX

Adults with voc and dev disabilities learn work skills in an industrial setting. For TDD srv, call (909) 982-5000. FUNDING: Dept of Rehab, nonprofit. OFC HRS: M-F 8:15am-4:45pm. Spanish spoken. ADM REQ: Ages 18 yrs+. Free srvs. SERVES: Pomona Valley & Inland Empire.

ORANGETREE CONVALESCENT HOSPITAL

Skilled Nursing Facility
4000 Harrison St.
Riverside, CA 92503
(951) 785-6060
(951) 785-6710 FAX

146-bed facility serves ages 20 yrs+; ambulatory, non-ambulatory, Alzheimer's. Spanish, Tagalog spoken. Accepts Medi-Cal, Medicare. SERVES: Riverside County.

ORTHOPAEDIC HOSPITAL L.A.

2400 S. Flower
Los Angeles, CA 90007
(213) 742-1000
(800) 339-6784
(213) 742-1137 FAX

100 outpatient clinics for children with wide range of problems: spina bifida, scoliosis, cerebral palsy, bone tumor, arthritis, osteogenesis imperfecta, and muscle disease. For adult orthopaedic physician referrals, call (213) 742-6509. For the children's clinic, call (213) 742-1300. Provides orthopaedic care for children under 18 yrs of age, regardless of ability to pay. FUNDING: Nonprofit. OFC HRS: M-F 8am-5pm. Spanish spoken. Accepts Medi-Cal for children's clinic. SERVES: Western U.S.A.

ORTON DYSLEXIA SOCIETY

See "Internatl Dyslexia Assn"

P.A.D.R.E. FOUNDATION

Diabetic Support for Kids
455 S. Main St.
Orange, CA 92868
(714) 532-8330
(714) 532-8398 FAX

PADRE (Pediatric Adol Diabetes Research & Edu). Provides numerous edu & support prgms which are open to children with diabetes and their families regardless of medical provider or where they are located. Prgms include: Kids Klub (ages 5-12 yrs), Tadpoles (ages birth-5 yrs), and Parents of Children with Diabetes. Support groups meet the 2nd Tu of the month at CHOC. Also provides edu classes for caregivers, carb counting, pediatric edu, as well as family retreats, teen retreats and other events for children. For Kaiser Bellflower, RSVP to (562) 461-6184, meets 3rd Tu 7pm-8pm. DIR: Heather Speer. FUNDING: Fndn, corp, nonprofit. OFC HRS: M-F 9:30am-5:30pm. Spanish translators available. Free srvs. SERVES: L.A., Orange, Riverside & San Diego Counties.

PACIFIC CLINICS/TBS

Therapeutic Behavioral Srvs
400 S. El Cielo, Ste I
Palm Springs, CA 92262-6757
(760) 416-1753
(626) 254-5000
(760) 416-0263 FAX

A supplemental srv for seriously emotionally disabled children and youth who need additional short-term support to prevent out-of-home placement. Also provides one-to-one behavior modification intervention in the home or school setting. FUNDING: Nonprofit. OFC HRS: M-F 8am-5pm. Spanish spoken. ADM REQ: Referral from RCDMH. Accepts Medi-Cal only. SERVES: Riverside County.

PALM SPRINGS REDEVELOP AGENCY
City of Palm Springs
P.O. Box 2743
3200 E. Tahquitz Canyon Way
Palm Springs, CA 92263-2743
(760) 323-8264
(760) 322-8325 FAX

Owner-occupied home repair grants to very low income Palm Springs homeowners. FUNDING: CDBG. OFC HRS: M-F 8am-5pm. ADM REQ: Must meet income guidelines. Free srvs. SERVES: Palm Springs.

PALM TERRACE CONVALESCENT CENTER
Skilled Nursing Facility
11162 Palm Terrace Lane
Riverside, CA 92505
(951) 687-7330
(951) 687-0322 FAX

75-bed facility serves ages 18 yrs+; ambulatory, non-ambulatory, Alzheimer's. Spanish, Tagalog spoken. Accepts Medi-Cal, Medicare, SSI. SERVES: Riverside County.

PARENT INFANT PROGRAM
15922 Willow St.
Hesperia, CA 92345
(760) 244-1083

Education prgm for children with dev delays. Staff make home visits to work with infants ages birth-3 yrs. Ages 3-22 yrs receive srvs at school site. FUNDING: Nonprofit, govt. OFC HRS: M-F 8am-3:15pm. Spanish spoken. ADM REQ: Dev disabled. Free srvs for those who qualify. SERVES: High Desert.

PARENTS OF SPECIAL NEEDS KIDS
See "Team of Advocates For Special Kids"

PARTNERSHIP/PRESERVE INDEP LIVING
6296 Rivercrest Dr., Ste K
Riverside, CA 92507
(951) 867-3800
(951) 867-3831 FAX

Info & referral srvs to seniors & persons with disabilities. Quarterly newsletter. Edu health videos. FUNDING: Nonprofit. OFC HRS: M-Th 7:30am-5:30pm. Spanish spoken. ADM REQ: Ages 18 yrs+ with disability. SERVES: Riverside County.

PEPPERMINT RIDGE
825 Magnolia Ave.
Corona, CA 92879
(951) 273-7320
(951) 737-0726 FAX

Residential community for dev disabled adults. Provides support to more than 100 persons in on-campus & neighborhood homes, independent living situations. FUNDING: SSI, United Way, Medi-Cal, donations, nonprofit. OFC HRS: M-F 8am-5pm. ASL available. ADM REQ: Ages 18 yrs+, disabled at birth or before age 18 yrs. SERVES: Inland Empire, Orange & L.A. Counties.

PERRIS SCHOOL DISTRICT
Special Education Dept
143 E. 1st Street
Perris, CA 92570
(951) 657-3118
(951) 940-5115 FAX

Walk in or call for info. FUNDING: Public, govt. OFC HRS: M-F 8am-4:30pm. Spanish spoken. SERVES: Perris.

PLOTT NURSING HOME
Skilled Nursing Facility
800 E. 5th Street
Ontario, CA 91764
(909) 984-8629
(909) 984-1182 FAX

216-bed facility serves ages 18 yrs+, ambulatory, non-ambulatory, Alzheimer's. OFC HRS: 24 hrs. Spanish spoken. Accepts Medi-Cal, Medicare, SSI. SERVES: San Bernardino County.

POMONA VALLEY WORKSHOP
4650 Brooks St.
Montclair, CA 91763
(909) 624-3555
(909) 624-5675 FAX

Senior work activity, voc edu, supported employment & adult socialization provided to persons with dev disabilities. OFC HRS: M-F 7:30am-4pm. Fixed fees. SERVES: Eastern L.A. County, western San Bernardino County.

POSSABILITIES PROGRAM
Loma Linda University Med Ctr
East Campus
25333 Barton Rd.
Loma Linda, CA 92354
(877) 558-6248
(909) 558-6384 FAX

A community outreach prgm for persons with physical disabilities. Peer mentoring, social and recreational activities, support groups, discount prescriptions, wheelchair sports, etc. Free membership. SERVES: San Bernardino County.

PREVENT BLINDNESS AMERICA
211 W. Wacker Dr., Ste 1700
Chicago, IL 60606
(800) 331-2020
(312) 363-6052 FAX

Eye health and safety organization dedicated to fighting blindness and preserving sight. Serves millions of people each year through public & community prgms, patient srvs & research. FUNDING: Donations, nonprofit. OFC HRS: M-F 8:30am-5pm, CST. Free srvs except quantity brochure orders. SERVES: U.S.A.

PROJECT GET SAFE
17602 17th Street, Ste 259
Tustin, CA 92780
(714) 834-0050
(714) 834-0070 FAX

Specializes in personal safety, sexual assault intervention, self-defense, and violence prev for children, women, men & persons with dev disabilities. FUNDING: Nonprofit. OFC HRS: Vary. Sliding fee scale. SERVES: So. Calif.

PROVIDENCE SPEECH/HEARING CENTER
1301 Providence Ave.
Orange, CA 92868
(714) 639-4990
(714) 744-3841 FAX

Mission is to enrich life through the gifts of speech and hearing. Strives to continually provide the highest standard of srvs in the identification, diagnosis, treatment and prevention of speech, language and hearing disorders for persons of all ages, races and economic backgrounds. Complete testing for speech and hearing problems for all ages. Hearing tests and speech therapy for seniors. Hearing aids & repairs, info & listening devices, newborn hearing screening, swim molds and musician's earplugs. Also licensed day care and Providence Therapeutic Preschool and clinical school for children ages 2-6 yrs. FUNDING: Nonprofit. OFC HRS: M-F 8am-5:30pm. Spanish spoken. Accepts Medicare, Medi-Cal, CalOptima, insurance, grants and financial aid. SERVES: L.A., Orange & Riverside Counties.

QUICKCAPTION, INC.
4927 Arlington Ave.
Riverside, CA 92504
(951) 779-0787
(951) 779-0980 FAX

Transcription, proofreading, video captioning, and remote real-time captioning srvs for the deaf and hearing-impaired community. OFC HRS: M-F 8:30am-5:30pm. Accepts sliding fee scale. SERVES: So. Calif.

RANCHO MESA CARE CENTER
Skilled Nursing Facility
9333 La Mesa Dr.
Alta Loma, CA 91701
(909) 987-2501
(909) 987-0282 FAX

59-bed facility, ambulatory, non-ambulatory, Alzheimer's. OFC HRS: 24 hrs. Spanish spoken. ADM REQ: Ages 65 yrs+. Accepts Medi-Cal, Medicare, SSI. SERVES: San Bernardino County.

RECHE CANYON REHAB & HEALTH CTR
Skilled Nursing Facility
1350 Reche Canyon Rd.
Colton, CA 92324
(909) 370-4411
(909) 370-1846 FAX

156-bed facility, serves ages 16 yrs+; ambulatory, non-ambulatory, Alzheimer's. Also, subacute unit. OFC HRS: M-F 8:30am-5pm. Spanish & Tagalog spoken. Accepts Medi-Cal, Medicare, insurance, pvt pay. SERVES: San Bernardino County.

RECORDING FOR THE BLIND & DYSLEXIC
National Headquarters
20 Roszel Rd.
Princeton, NJ 08540
(866) 732-3585
(800) 221-4792
(609) 520-7990 FAX

Recorded & computerized textbooks of all academic levels to people who cannot read standard print because of visual, learning, or physical disability. 32 studios & offices across the U.S. FUNDING: Nonprofit. OFC HRS: M-F 8:30am-4:45pm, EST. ADM REQ: Blind or dyslexic. SERVES: U.S.A.

RECORDING FOR THE BLIND & DYSLEXIC
Inland Empire/Orange County
1844 W. 11th Street, Ste C
Upland, CA 91786
(909) 949-4316
(909) 981-8457 FAX

Natl volunteer srv organization records academic texts for loan to persons having a visual, physical, or perpetual print reading disability. Srvs for individual and institutional members after registration. Individual borrowers, $65 one time registration fee. $35 annually (1st yr, total $100). Works with schools to provide recorded texts for students with print reading disabilities. FUNDING: Donations, grants, nonprofit. OFC HRS: Upland Studio: M, Tu 8am-9pm; W, Th 8am-5pm; F 8am-3pm; Sat 8am-12noon. ADM REQ: Volunteers ages 18-90 yrs. SERVES: Inland Empire and Orange County.

REDLANDS ADULT SCHOOL

Redlands Unified School District
P.O. Box 3008
10568 California St.
Redlands, CA 92373
(909) 748-6930
(909) 307-5324 FAX

Adults with dev disabilities prgm, traffic school, ESL, nursing prgm, GED, parent education. FUNDING: Fees. OFC HRS: M,Tu 9am-8pm; W,Th 9am-5pm; F 9am-4:30pm. Summer Hrs: M-F 9am-4:30pm. Spanish spoken. SERVES: Redlands.

REDLANDS HEALTHCARE CENTER

Skilled Nursing Facility
1620 W. Fern Ave.
Redlands, CA 92373
(909) 793-2609
(909) 793-2196 FAX

78-bed facility, serves all ages; ambulatory, non-ambulatory, Alzheimer's. OFC HRS: M-F 8am-4pm. Spanish and various Asian languages spoken. Accepts Medi-Cal, Medicare, insurance, pvt pay. SERVES: San Bernardino County.

REHAB INSTITUTE OF SO CALIF (RIO)

Comprehensive Services
1800 E. La Veta Ave.
Orange, CA 92866
(714) 633-7400
(714) 633-0738 FAX

Comprehensive therapeutic srvs and prgms for physically disabled persons of all ages. Child care, early intervention, adult day care (& health daycare), aquatics, independent living skills training, social srvs, PT, OT, speech and voc srvs. Walk in or call. FUNDING: Fees, donations, contracts, insurances, nonprofit. OFC HRS: M-F 7:30am-4pm. Spanish spoken. ASL available. ADM REQ: Varies by prgm. Accepts Medi-Cal, pvt pay. SERVES: So. Calif.

RIO (REHAB INST OF SO. CALIF)

See "Rehab Institute of So Calif (RIO)"

RIVERSIDE CO. HOUSING AUTHORITY

Housing Assistance Information
5555 Arlington Ave.
Riverside, CA 92504
(951) 351-0700
(800) 655-4228
(951) 354-6324 FAX

Housing prgms include: Section 8 tenant-based aqssist which provides rental assist to low & moderate income seniors and disabled. Tenants pay between 30% and 40 % of their adjusted income; a Housing Choice Voucher is given to eligible participants. Affordable housing prgm allows families to live in selected HUD housing units. The Planning & Dev Dept is responsible for formulation, processing & implementation of new construction projects and maintenance of all the existing housing units. Also have a senior home repair prgm. Application is free. FUNDING: Govt. OFC HRS: M-Th 8am-5pm. Spanish spoken. SERVES: Riverside County.

RIVERSIDE CO. MENTAL HEALTH

Jefferson Wellness Center
1827 Atlanta Ave., Ste D-3
Riverside, CA 92507
(951) 955-8000
(951) 955-8010 FAX

Develops life skills including: socialization, job skills, time mgmt, specialized skills (computer classes, math, woodwork), health-related skills, food prep, independent living and various other skills. FUNDING: County. OFC HRS: M-Th 9am-6pm. Spanish spoken. ADM REQ: Diagnosed as mentally disabled. SERVES: West Riverside County from Corona to Moreno Valley.

RIVERSIDE CO. PUBLIC SOCIAL SRVS

In-Home Support/Child Protective Srvs
68-625 Perez Rd., Ste 2
Cathedral City, CA 92234
(760) 773-6700
(760) 770-2450
(760) 773-6793 FAX

IHSS provides frail elderly and disabled with outreach and in-home support srvs. Also CPS (Children's Protective Srvs). To report child abuse/neglect, call (800) 442-4918. FUNDING: County, state, fed. OFC HRS: M-F 8am-5pm. Spanish & Tagalog spoken. Free srvs. SERVES: Coachella Valley.

RIVERSIDE CO. PUBLIC SOCIAL SRVS

Adult Protective Services
68625 Perez Rd., Ste 2
Cathedral City, CA 92234
(760) 770-2450
(800) 582-9893
(760) 770-2260 FAX

Srvs for adults in danger of abuse & exploitation. Emerg shelter investigation and in-home support. Provides frail elderly and disabled with outreach and in-home support. To report elder abuse, call (800) 491-7123. FUNDING: County, state, fed. OFC HRS: M-Th 8am-5pm. Spanish spoken. SERVES: Coachella Valley.

RIVERSIDE CO. PUBLIC SOCIAL SRVS

Adult Protective Srvs/In-Home Srvs
541 N. San Jacinto St.
Hemet, CA 92543
(951) 791-3250
(800) 331-6742
(951) 791-3255 FAX

24-hr emerg response, protective srvs for adults in danger of abuse, exploitation, neglect, etc. Call to report incidents or suspicions of abuse or neglect. Also provides frail elderly and disabled outreach and in-home support srvs. 24-hr hotline (800) 491-7123. FUNDING: County, state, fed. OFC HRS: M-Th 8am-5pm. Spanish spoken. ADM REQ: Varies per prgm. SERVES: Hemet, San Jacinto, Menifee & nearby.

RIVERSIDE CO. PUBLIC SOCIAL SRVS

Adult Protective Services
23119 Cottonwood Ave., Bldg. A, 1st Fl.
Moreno Valley, CA 92553
(951) 413-5050
(800) 345-6083
(951) 413-5107 FAX

Srvs for adults in danger of abuse, exploitation, etc. with full range of srvs from emerg shelter to investigation and in-home support srvs. Provides frail elderly and disabled with outreach and in-home support srvs. Walk in or call. Call, (800) 345-6083 to report any actual or suspected abuse. FUNDING: Govt. OFC HRS: M-Th 8am-5pm. ADM REQ: Varies with prgm. SERVES: Riverside County.

ROLLING START, INC.

570 W. 4th Street, Ste 107
San Bernardino, CA 92401
(909) 884-2129
(909) 386-7446 FAX

Independent living skills training, attendant referral, housing referral, info & referral, advocacy, deaf srvs, helpline, peer counseling for seniors and disabled. ADA tech assist, free workshops. Assistive technology, computer classes. For TDD, call (909) 884-7396. FUNDING: Govt, county, city. OFC HRS: M-F 8am-5pm. ASL available. ADM REQ: Ages 18 yrs+, county resident with disability. Free srvs except helpline. SERVES: San Bernardino County.

ROLLING START, INC.

15400 Cholame Rd., Ste B
Victorville, CA 92392
(760) 843-7959
(909) 384-2129
(760) 241-8787 FAX

Assists individuals with disabilities in their effort to achieve and maintain an independent lifestyle. FUNDING: Nonprofit. OFC HRS: M-F 8am-5pm. SERVES: Inland Empire.

SALEM CHRISTIAN HOMES

6921 Edison Ave., Bldg. 1
Chino, CA 91710
(909) 614-0575
(909) 614-0595 FAX

Residential care & training for dev disabled adults. Wait: up to 2 yrs. Free counseling & referral. Fee scale set by Regional Center. FUNDING: Regl Centers, donations. OFC HRS: M-F 8:30am-4:30pm. ADM REQ: Primary diagnosis of mental retardation. SERVES: Western U.S.A.

SAN BERNARDINO CO. AGING/ADULT

In-Home Supportive Services
536 E. Virginia Way
Barstow, CA 92311
(760) 256-5544
(760) 256-1435
(760) 256-1605 FAX

Social workers will make an assessment of need for in-home care and authorize payments for domestic and personal srvs in order to keep elderly, blind, and disabled in their own homes and thus avoid institutionalization. OFC HRS: M-F 8am-5pm. SERVES: Barstow area & Trona.

SAN BERNARDINO CO. AGING/ADULT

Adult Protective Srvs
536 E. Virginia Way
Barstow, CA 92311
(760) 256-1435
(760) 256-1605 FAX

For older adults or disabled and dependent adults in danger of abuse, exploitation, etc. Full range of srvs from emerg shelter to investigation of suspected abuse. 24-hr crisis line (877) 565-2020. OFC HRS: M-F 8am-5pm. SERVES: Barstow, Trona.

SAN BERNARDINO CO. AGING/ADULT
Adult Protective Srvs
1300 Bailey Ave.
Needles, CA 92363
(760) 326-9274
(760) 326-9340 FAX

For older adults or disabled and dependent adults in danger of abuse, exploitation, etc. Full range of srvs from emerg shelter to investigation of suspected abuse. Hotline (877) 565-2020. OFC HRS: M-F 8am-5pm, closed alt F. SERVES: Needles.

SAN BERNARDINO CO. AGING/ADULT
In-Home Supportive Srvs
1300 Bailey Ave.
Needles, CA 92363
(760) 326-9328
(760) 326-9340 FAX

Social workers will make an assessment of a need for in-home care and authorize payments for domestic and personal srvs in order to keep elderly, blind, and disabled in their own homes and thus avoid institutionalization. Hotline (877) 565-2020. OFC HRS: M-F 8am-5pm, closed alt F. SERVES: Needles.

SAN BERNARDINO CO. AGING/ADULT
Adult Protective Srvs
686 E. Mill St.
San Bernardino, CA 92415-0640
(909) 891-3900
(909) 388-6718 FAX

Protects and supports the rights of adults. Social workers provide case work srvs to adults in danger of neglect, abuse, or exploitation to alleviate danger, correct hazardous living, prevent unnecessary institutionalizations. Referral srvs for domestic violence and sexual assault prgms. FUNDING: County, state, federal. OFC HRS: 24 hrs, 7 days. Spanish spoken. SERVES: San Bernardino County.

SAN BERNARDINO CO. AGING/ADULT
DAAS/In-Home Supportive Srvs Prgm
686 E. Mill St.
San Bernardino, CA 92415-0640
(909) 891-3900
(909) 891-3919 FAX

IHSS is designed to enable eligible blind and disabled individuals to remain safely in their own home by paying someone to assist with those tasks needed for basic day-to-day home life. Tasks for the IHSS may include essential housekeeping, meal prep, non-medical personal srvs under a physician's supervision, paramedical srvs. Other locations: Barstow, Joshua Tree, Needles, Victorville, Rancho Cucamonga. FUNDING: County, state, federal. OFC HRS: M-F 8am-5pm. Spanish spoken. SERVES: San Bernardino County.

SAN BERNARDINO CO. AGING/ADULT
Administration
686 E. Mill St.
San Bernardino, CA 92415-0640
(909) 891-3900
(909) 891-3919 FAX

Admin office only, administers prgms and funding to provide srvs to seniors and at-risk individuals to improve or maintain choice, independence, and quality of life. DAAS works to ensure seniors and adults with disabilities the right to age in a place with the least restrictive environment. Aging adult infoline (800) 510-2020, will direct caller to an agency in their area. FUNDING: Fed, state. OFC HRS: M-F vary. Spanish spoken. Translation srv available. SERVES: U.S.A.

SAN BERNARDINO CO. AGING/ADULT
In-Home Supportive Srvs Prgm
17270 Bear Valley Rd., Ste 108
Victorville 92395
(760) 843-5100
(760) 843-5105 FAX

Social workers make an assessment of need for in-home care & authorize payments for domestic & personal srvs in order to keep elderly, blind, & disabled in their own homes & avoid institutionalization. FUNDING: County, state, fed, nonprofit. OFC HRS: M-F 8am-5pm. Spanish spoken. Low income srvs available for those who qualify. SERVES: High Desert.

SAN BERNARDINO CO. HOUSING AUTH
424 N. Lemon Ave.
Ontario, CA 91764
(909) 983-1318
(909) 381-3052 FAX

Housing Choice Voucher prgm. Assist for very low income families, seniors, & the disabled. TTY (909) 391-5058. FUNDING: County. OFC HRS: M-Th 7:30am-5:30pm; alt F 7:30am-4:30pm. ADM REQ: Low income, poverty level. SERVES: Fontana, Rialto, Pomona Valley, Unicorp Areas, West Side San Bernardino County.

SAN BERNARDINO CO. HOUSING AUTH
Administrative Office
715 E. Brier Dr.
San Bernardino, CA 92408-2841
(909) 890-0644
(909) 890-4618 FAX

Administers two rental assist prgms for low income families, seniors, and disabled. Public housing prgm comprised of 2,500+ units owned or managed by Housing Authority, and scattered throughout 23 cities in San Bernardino Co. Housing Choice Voucher Prgm provides rental subsidy to very low income individuals by providing subsidy payments directly to the owners on behalf of participant, who is required to pay at least 30% of their income toward rent. TTY (909) 388-9279. FUNDING: U.S. Dept of HUD. OFC HRS: M-Th 7:30am-5:30pm; alt F 7:30am-4:30pm. ADM REQ: Gross yearly income within HUD guidelines. SERVES: San Bernardino County, except the cities of Needles and Upland.

SAN BERNARDINO CO. HOUSING AUTH
15465 Seneca Rd.
Victorville, CA 92392
(760) 243-1043
(760) 243-2123 FAX

Housing Choice Voucher Prgm. Assist for very low income families, seniors & the disabled. TTY (760) 951-7872. FUNDING: County. OFC HRS: M-Th 7:30am-5:30pm; alt F 7:30am-4:30pm. ADM REQ: Low income, pov-

erty level. SERVES: High Desert, Mid Desert, Mountains

SAN BERNARDINO CO. OMBUDSMAN
686 E. Mill St.
San Bernardino, CA 92415-0640
(909) 891-3928
(866) 229-0284
(909) 891-3957 FAX

Investigates complaints, problems of long-term care facilities for the elderly and dev disabled adults in licensed facilities. FUNDING: Federal, state. OFC HRS: M-F 8am-5pm. Free srvs. SERVES: San Bernardino County.

SAN BERNARDINO CO. PUBLIC HEALTH
California Children's Srvs
150 Carousel Mall
San Bernardino, CA 92415
(909) 387-8400
(909) 387-8401 FAX

Assists families with payment of medical bills for children ages birth-21 yrs, who have serious injury, disability or illness. Also provides PT & OT. FUNDING: Govt. OFC HRS: M-F 8am-5pm. Spanish spoken. ADM REQ: Must meet medical financial and residential criteria. SERVES: San Bernardino County.

SBC ACCESS RESOURCES
See "CTap"

SELPA/DESERT/MOUNTAIN
Special Education Local Plan Area
17800 Highway 18
Apple Valley, CA 92307
(760) 242-6333
(760) 242-5363 FAX

Special education for ages birth-21 yrs. Call for info. FUNDING: Fed, state & local. OFC HRS: M-F 8am-5pm. ADM REQ: Eligibility for special edu srvs. Free srvs. SERVES: Desert & mountain areas of San Bernardino County.

SELPA/FONTANA
9680 Citrus Ave., Ste 33
Fontana, CA 92335-5594
(909) 357-5000
(909) 357-5250 FAX

Early childhood classes, special day classes, classes for the visually impaired or deaf/hard-of-hearing, etc. FUNDING: Govt. OFC HRS: M-F 8am-5pm. SERVES: Fontana.

SELPA/MORANGO UNIFIED
P.O. Box 1209
5715 Utah Trail
Twentynine Palms, CA 92277
(760) 367-9191
(760) 361-0749 FAX

Single district SELPA. With rare exceptions, the district handles all of its own special edu students in grades K-12. ROP prgm. OFC HRS: M-F 8am-4:30pm. SERVES: 29 Palms, Joshua Tree, Yucca Valley, Landers, Morongo Valley.

SELPA/MORENO VALLEY
25634 Alessandro Blvd.
Moreno Valley, CA 92553
(951) 571-7500

Early intervention srvs for the disabled, evaluations, assessments, dev of IFSPs. OFC HRS: M-F 8am-4pm. Spanish spoken. SERVES: Riverside County.

SELPA/RIVERSIDE COUNTY
P.O. Box 868

3939 13th Street
Riverside, CA 92502
(951) 826-6687
(951) 826-6943 FAX

Education services for individuals with disabilities. Works cooperatively with 21 school districts and other public & private agencies. FUNDING: County. OFC HRS: M-F 8am-5pm. SERVES: Riverside County.

SELPA/RIVERSIDE USD

P.O. Box 2800
3380 14th Street
Riverside, CA 92501
(951) 788-7142
(951) 276-7634 FAX

CONTACT: Dr. Steven Morford, SELPA Director. FUNDING: Govt. OFC HRS: M-F 8am-5pm. SERVES: Riverside County.

SELPA/SAN BERNARDINO

Harmon Preschool
4865 State St.
San Bernardino, CA 92407
(909) 880-6616
(909) 880-4236 FAX

Early intervention srvs for the disabled, evaluations, assessments, dev of IFSPs. OFC HRS: M-F 8pm-4pm. Spanish spoken. SERVES: San Bernardino City.

SELPA/WEST END

8265 Aspen Ave., Ste 200
Rancho Cucamonga, CA 91730
(909) 476-6188
(909) 987-2279 FAX

CONTACT: Joann Reilly. Early intervention srvs for the disabled, evaluations, assessments, dev of IFSPs. OFC HRS: M-F 8am-4pm. Spanish spoken. SERVES: West San Bernardino County.

SENIOR COMPANION PROGRAM

600 W. 5th Street
San Bernardino, CA 92410
(909) 384-5430
(909) 889-9801 FAX

Personal in-home srvs to homebound adults. Respite care to caregivers. Also disabled, isolated adults ages 21 yrs+. Walk in. FUNDING: Federal, city. OFC HRS: M-Th 7:30am-5pm. ADM REQ: Ages 21 yrs+, low income bracket, companions must over be 55 yrs+ & low income. Free srvs. SERVES: Morongo Basin, Victor Valley, San Bernardino, Fontana, Rialto, Loma Linda.

SHANDIN HILLS REHABILITATION CTR

Skilled Nursing Facility
4164 N. 4th Avenue
San Bernardino, CA 92407
(909) 886-6786
(909) 886-2953 FAX

78-bed facilities, serves ages 11-65 yrs; ambulatory. OFC HRS: M-F 8am-5pm. Accepts Medi-Cal, Medicare, SSI. SERVES: San Bernardino County.

SHELTER WINGS CORP DAY PRGM

1503 E. Hobson Way
Blythe, CA 92225
(760) 922-0399
(760) 922-0360 FAX

Adult day care prgm provides daytime supervision & activities for dev disabled. FUNDING: Nonprofit. OFC HRS: M-F 9am-3:30pm. Spanish spoken. ADM REQ: Ages 22-53 yrs. SERVES: Riverside County.

SIERRA VISTA REHABILITATION CTR

Skilled Nursing Facility/Mental Health Rehab
3455 E. Highland Ave.
Highland, CA 92346
(909) 862-6454
(800) 729-6600
(909) 862-6474 FAX

116-bed facility for ages 18 yrs+. 71-bed mental health unit for residents from Dept of Mental Health. 45-bed mental health, mental retardation unit for residents of Regional Centers. Integrated deaf srvs. FUNDING: Regional Ctrs, Medi-Cal, Dept of Mental Health. OFC HRS: M-F 8am-5pm. 24-hr srvs. Spanish & Tagalog spoken. ASL available. ADM REQ: Referral & certification approval from Dept of Mental Health and/or Regional Centers. Accepts Medi-Cal, pvt insurance. SERVES: Calif.

SKY HARBOR CARE CENTER

Skilled Nursing Facility
57333 Joshua Lane
Yucca Valley, CA 92284
(760) 365-4870
(760) 369-1407 FAX

99-bed facility serves ages 18 yrs+, ambulatory, non-ambulatory. OFC HRS: 24 hrs. Spanish spoken. ADM REQ: Srvs ordered by M.D. Accepts Medi-Cal, Medicare, pvt pay. SERVES: Desert Hot Springs, Joshua Tree, Yucca Valley, Palm Springs, Indio, 29 Palms, Landers, San Bernardino.

SOCIAL SECURITY ADMINISTRATION

720 E. Main St.
Barstow, CA 92311
(800) 772-1213
(760) 256-9294 FAX

Info on Social Security and SSI benefits, SS cards, Medicare benefits & sign-up, survivor and burial benefits. For TTY, call (800) 325-0778. OFC HRS: M-F 9am-4:30pm. Spanish spoken by phone. SERVES: San Bernardino County.

SOCIAL SECURITY ADMINISTRATION

874 E. Hobson Way
Blythe, CA 92225
(800) 772-1213
(760) 922-5718 FAX

Assist with Social Security benefits including retirement, survivors' benefits & disability, SSI for those who are blind, disabled and age 65 yrs+. TTY (800) 325-0778. FUNDING: Fed, govt. OFC HRS: M-F 9am-4:30pm. Spanish spoken. Free srvs. SERVES: Riverside County.

SOCIAL SECURITY ADMINISTRATION

2191 Sampson Ave., Ste 105
Corona, CA 92879
(800) 772-1213
(951) 272-0423 FAX

Assists with Social Security benefits including: retirement, survivors' benefits, & disability, SSI for those who are blind, disabled and ages 65 yrs+. TTY (800) 325-0778. FUNDING: Govt. OFC HRS: M-F 9am-4:30pm. Spanish spoken. Free srvs. SERVES: Riverside County.

SOCIAL SECURITY ADMINISTRATION

10668 Sierra Ave.
Fontana, CA 92337
(800) 772-1213
(909) 829-0119 FAX

Info on Social Security and SSI benefits, SS cards, Medicare benefits & sign-up, survivor and burial benefits. For TTY, call (800) 325-0778. FUNDING: Fed, govt. OFC HRS: M-F 9am-4:30pm. Spanish spoken. SERVES: Fontana, Colton.

SOCIAL SECURITY ADMINISTRATION

3095 W. Devonshire Ave.
Hemet, CA 92545
(800) 772-1213
(951) 766-1968 FAX

Assists the blind, disabled & seniors ages 65 yrs+, with Social Security benefits including: retirement, survivors' benefits, disability, & supplemental security income. TTY (800)325-0778. OFC HRS: M-F 9am-4:30pm. Spanish spoken. Free srvs. SERVES: Riverside County.

SOCIAL SECURITY ADMINISTRATION

46845 Monroe St., Ste 2
Indio, CA 92201
(800) 772-1213
(760) 342-2972 FAX

Info on Social Security, SSI benefits, SS cards, Medicare benefits & sign-up, survivor and burial benefits. For TTY, call (800) 325-0778. FUNDING: Fed, govt. OFC HRS: M-W, F 9am-4:30pm; Th 9am-4pm. Spanish spoken. Free srvs. SERVES: Riverside County.

SOCIAL SECURITY ADMINISTRATION

1096 E. Broadway
Needles, CA 92363
(760) 326-4460
(760) 326-4029 FAX

Info on Social Security and SSI benefits, SS cards, Medicare benefits & sign-up, survivor and burial benefits. For TTY, call (800) 325-0778. FUNDING: Fed, govt. OFC HRS: Tu-F 9am-4:30pm. SERVES: Needles area.

SOCIAL SECURITY ADMINISTRATION

1533 E. Holt Blvd.
Ontario, CA 91761
(866) 331-2216
(909) 986-1369 FAX

Assists with Social Security benefits including: retirement, survivors' benefits, disability, SSI for those who are blind, disabled and ages 65 yrs+. TTY (800) 325-0778. OFC HRS: M-F 9am-4pm. Spanish spoken by phone. Free srvs. SERVES: San Bernardino County.

SOCIAL SECURITY ADMINISTRATION

4201 E. Ramon Rd.
Palm Springs, CA 92264
(800) 772-1213
(760) 327-8935 FAX

Assists with Social Security benefits including: retirement, survivors' benefits, and disability. Supplemental security income for the blind, disabled and ages 65 yrs+. Social security numbers and replacement cards. TTY (800) 325-0778. FUNDING: Fed, govt. OFC HRS: M-F 9am-4:30pm. Spanish spoken. Free srvs. SERVES: Riverside County.

SOCIAL SECURITY ADMINISTRATION

1449 W. Redlands Blvd.
Redlands, CA 92373
(909) 798-2669
(909) 307-9949 FAX

Info on Social Security and SSI benefits, SS cards, Medicare benefits & sign-up, survivor and burial benefits. For TTY, call (800) 325-0778. FUNDING: Fed, govt. OFC HRS: M-F 9am-4:30pm. Spanish spoken. SERVES: Redlands.

SOCIAL SECURITY ADMINISTRATION
7880 Mission Grove Park, South
Riverside, CA 92508
(866) 931-4495
(951) 789-7340 FAX

Info on Social Security, SSI benefits, SS cards, Medicare benefits & sign-up, survivor and burial benefits. Call anywhere in the U.S. for info on srvs or local offices. For TTY, call (800) 325-0778. Phone hrs: M-F 7am-7pm. FUNDING: Fed, govt. OFC HRS: M-F 9am-4:30pm. Spanish spoken. SERVES: Riverside County.

SOCIAL SECURITY ADMINISTRATION
605 N. Arrowhead Ave., Ste 101
San Bernardino, CA 92401
(866) 331-7132
(800) 772-1213

Assists with Social Security benefits including retirement, survivors' benefits, disability, SSI for the blind, disabled and ages 65 yrs+. TTY (800) 325-0778. OFC HRS: M-F 9am-4:30pm. Spanish spoken by phone. Free srvs. SERVES: San Bernardino County.

SOCIAL SECURITY ADMINISTRATION
13955 Park Ave., Ste 110
Victorville, CA 92392
(760) 241-5009
(760) 241-2189 FAX

Info on Social Security and SSI benefits, SS cards, Medicare benefits & sign-up, survivor and burial benefits. For TTY, call (800) 325-0778. FUNDING: Govt. OFC HRS: M-F 9am-4:30pm. Spanish spoken. SERVES: Victorville area.

SOCIAL SECURITY ADMINISTRATION
57019 Yucca Trail
Yucca Valley, CA 92284
(760) 369-6535
(760) 369-6533 FAX

Info on Social Security and SSI benefits, SS cards, Medicare benefits & sign-up, survivor and burial benefits. Call anywhere in the U.S. for info on srvs or local offices. For TTY, call (800) 325-0778. FUNDING: Fed, govt. OFC HRS: M-F 9am-4:30pm. Spanish spoken. SERVES: Morongo Basin.

SPECIAL OLYMPICS/SO CALIF
6730 W. Carson St.
Long Beach, CA 90808
(562) 354-2600
(562) 938-7671 FAX

This is the admin office for all So Calif prgms. Each county has many sports training prgms & sporting events for children & adults with mental disabilities. All athletes welcome. Minimum age to compete is 8 yrs. FUNDING: Nonprofit. OFC HRS: M-F 8am-5pm. Spanish spoken. Free srvs. SERVES: So. Calif.

SPINA BIFIDA ASSN OF AMERICA
Research/Support/Awareness
4590 MacArthur Blvd., NW, Ste 250
Washington, DC 20007-4226
(202) 944-3285
(800) 621-3141

(202) 944-3295 FAX

Fosters and promotes the rights and well-being of persons with spina bifida. Promotes research into the causes, treatment, and prevention of spina bifida and promotes public awareness. Toll-free info & referral srv, bi-monthly newsletter offers insights to members and serves as a liaison to other organizations sharing similar goals. Also a professional advisory council on edu, medicine, legislation. 60 chapters nationwide. Free info packets. Annual natl conference. FUNDING: Donations, grants, govt, client fees, nonprofit. OFC HRS: M-F 9am-5pm, EST. Free srvs. SERVES: U.S.A.

SPINAL CORD INJURY NETWORK INTL
3911 Princeton Dr.
Santa Rosa, CA 95405-7013
(800) 548-2673
(707) 577-8796
(707) 577-0605 FAX

Member of the Natl Network of Libraries of Medicine. Dedicated to providing high quality info srvs. The library maintains a collection of 500 volumes, 50 journals, and numerous publications worldwide about spinal cord injury and/or diseases. A lending prgm of over 200 info videotapes. Contact SCINI for registration info. Various topics include exercise, health issues, sports, and travel. FUNDING: Donations, grants. OFC HRS: M-Th 9am-4pm. SERVES: U.S.A.

SPINAL CORD SOCIETY
19501 County Hwy 1
Fergus Falls, MN 56737-7609
(218) 739-5252
(218) 739-5261
(218) 739-5262 FAX

Research to find a cure. Offers info & referral srvs all over the U.S. FUNDING: Nonprofit. OFC HRS: 24 hrs, 7 days. Dutch spoken. Newsletter $30 per year. SERVES: U.S.A.

SPONDYLITIS ASSN OF AMERICA
P.O. Box 5872
Sherman Oaks, CA 91413
(800) 777-8189
(818) 892-1616
(818) 981-9826 FAX

Natl membership organization focusing attention solely on a family of arthritic conditions that primarily affect the spine. Includes: ankylosing; spondylitis; reactive arthritis/Reiter's Syndrome; psoriatic arthritis; inflammatory bowel disease (IBD); undifferentiated spondyloarthritis and juvenile spondyloarthritis. Printed info & videos available. Bi-monthly newsletter for members. FUNDING: Dues, donations, nonprofit. OFC HRS: M-F 8am-5pm. SERVES: U.S.A.

STARLIGHT CHILDREN'S FOUNDATION
5757 Wilshire Blvd., Ste M-100
Los Angeles, CA 90036
(310) 479-1212
(800) 315-1212
(310) 479-1235 FAX

When a child or teenager has a serious medical condition, everyone in the famliy is affected. The Starlight Fndn has dedicated itself to helping seriously ill children and their families cope with pain, fear and isolation through entertainment, edu, and family activities. Starlight's prgms have been proven to distract children

from their pain, help them better understand and manage their illness. Connect families facing similar challenges so that no one feels alone. Outpatient, hospital-based and web offerings. To learn more, visit (www.starlight.org). FUNDING: Nonprofit. OFC HRS: M-F 8am-5pm. Accepts donations. SERVES: U.S.A., Canada, Australia, UK & Japan.

STUTTERING FOUNDATION OF AMERICA
P.O. Box 11749
3100 Walnut Grove Rd., Ste 603
Memphis, TN 38111-0749
(800) 992-9392
(901) 761-0484 FAX

Resources, srvs and support to those who stutter & their families as well as support for research into the cause of stuttering. 28 books, 40 videotapes, & 19 free brochures on stuttering. FUNDING: Donations, nonprofit. OFC HRS: M-F 8am-4pm, CST. French spoken. SERVES: Internatl.

STUTTERING/NATIONAL CENTER
See "Natl Ctr for Stuttering"

SUMMIT PAYEE SRVS, INC.
1361 North E Street
San Bernardino, CA 92405
(909) 884-5299
(951) 263-9527
(909) 885-2859 FAX

Approved representative payee srvs through the Social Security Administration. FUNDING: Nonprofit. OFC HRS: M-F 9am-4pm. ADM REQ: Inability to manage financial resources. SERVES: Inland Empire. Srvs also available in limited areas throughout So Calif.

SUNLINE TRANSIT AGENCY
32-505 Harry Oliver Trail
Thousand Palms, CA 92276
(760) 343-3456
(800) 347-8628
(760) 343-3845 FAX

Fixed route transportation and door-to-door van equipped with wheelchair lift. OFC HRS: M-F 8am-5pm (srv from 4:40am-11:19pm). Spanish spoken. Adult fare $1; ages 5-17 yrs $.85; seniors, disabled or on Medicare $.50. Transfer $.25. SERVES: Coachella Valley.

SUNSHINE EARLY CHILDHOOD CTR
Riverside Unified School Dist
9390 California Ave.
Riverside, CA 92503
(951) 352-8488
(951) 689-6876 FAX

Project M.O.V.E. integrates Head Start with special edu. Walk in or call. FUNDING: State, nonprofit. OFC HRS: M-F 7:30am-4pm. Spanish spoken. Free srvs if children qualify. SERVES: Riverside area.

TALK ABOUT CURING AUTISM (TACA)
3070 Bristol Ave., Ste 340
Costa Mesa, CA 92626
(949) 640-4401
(949) 640-4424 FAX

Info and connection to improve the quality of life of people with autism and their families. For families who have just received the autism diagnosis, TACA aims to speed up the cycle time that gets them from the diagnosis to the appropriate info that will lead to effective treatment and support. TACA builds the autism community by connecting people with each other & the professionals who can help them. FUNDING: Nonprofit. OFC HRS: M-F 9am-5pm. SERVES: So. Calif.

TARGET COMMUNITY SCHOOLS
940 Stillman Ave., Ste B
Redlands, CA 92374
(909) 798-5391
(909) 798-8071 FAX

Non-public school for seriously emotionally disturbed boys ages 6-14 yrs. Wait: depends on capacity. FUNDING: IEP, LEP contract. OFC HRS: M-F 8am-3pm. ADM REQ: Interview & acceptance. Placement by IEP only. Fees: $127.50-$131 per day. SERVES: Redlands & nearby.

TARJAN CTR FOR DEV DISABILITIES
UCLA's Semel Institute
760 Westwood Plaza, Ste 67-467
Los Angeles, CA 90095-1759
(310) 825-0170
(310) 794-1143 FAX

Interdisciplinary training, exemplary srv, tech asst, info dissemination, and research to enhance the lives of persons with dev disabilities and their families. Three key functions: early intervention (severe and challenging behavior), family support & community inclusion. Advocates for srvs for dev disabled, independence and inclusion in the community. Resource and referral info for consumers, families & care providers. Pre- and post-doctoral training fellowships in the field of dev disabilities. OFC HRS: M-F 9am-5pm. Spanish spoken. SERVES: Calif.

TEAM OF ADVOCATES FOR SPECIAL KIDS
TASK
100 W. Cerritos Ave.
Anaheim, CA 92805
(714) 533-8275
(866) 828-8275
(714) 533-2533 FAX

Parent training and info center serving families of children with disabilities. Support, legal rights info, phone advocacy, workshops and referral srvs. Conducts eval & tech explorations with reports for ages 12 mos+. Workshops on adapted toys, adaptive hardware and specialized software. Phone assist advocacy. Minimal cost for workshops, seminars, in-office IEP consulting, IEP attendance & tech consultation. Also offices in San Diego & L.A. FUNDING: Donations, fed, fndn, nonprofit. OFC HRS: M-F 8am-4pm. Spanish & Vietnamese spoken. SERVES: So. Calif.

TELACU VILLA
Telacu Residential Mgmt
25105 Fir Ave.
Moreno Valley, CA 92553-2300
(951) 486-9842
(323) 485-1710 FAX

Rental housing for seniors, Section 202. Disabled, Section 236. Wait: 6 mos-1.5 yrs. OFC HRS: M-F 8am-5pm. ADM REQ: Low income ages 62 yrs+, or disabled ages 18 yrs+. SERVES: Riverside County.

THE AMPUTEE COALITION OF AMERICA
(www.amputee-coalition.org)
900 E. Hill Ave., Ste 205
Knoxville, TN 37915-2566
(888) 267-5669

(865) 525-7917 FAX

Online community lists resources for amputees. Support groups, edu, advocacy, annual conference. For TTY, call (865) 525-4512. FUNDING: Nonprofit. SERVES: U.S.A.

THE BRIDGE SCHOOL
545 Eucalyptus Ave.
Hillsborough, CA 94010-6404
(650) 696-7295
(650) 342-7598 FAX

School for individuals with severe speech and physical impairments. Augmentative & alternative means of communication & assistive technology is used. Summer camp for ages 5-17 yrs. Call for more info. FUNDING: Nonprofit, donations, fundraising. OFC HRS: M-F 8am-4pm. Campers who are residents of Calif and clients of Regional Centers may be eligible to receive partial funding. Some scholarships available. SERVES: Calif.

THE LIGHTHOUSE, INC.
See "Lighthouse International"

THE MENTOR NETWORK
Family Behavioral Srvs
9166 Anaheim Place, Ste 200
Rancho Cucamonga, CA 91730
(909) 483-2505
(909) 481-1984 FAX

Parent edu prgm for children served by Inland Regional Center. Classes & behavioral consultation for children exhibiting challenging behaviors. Alternative living options to adults with dev disabilities. SERVES: San Bernardino County.

THE MENTORING NETWORK
Early Intervention Prgm
9166 Anaheim Place, Ste 200
Rancho Cucamonga, CA 91730
(909) 483-2505
(909) 481-1984 FAX

In-home early intervention srvs. Home visits arranged. Call for info. FUNDING: Public school contracts, regional centers. OFC HRS: M-F 8am-5pm. Some Spanish spoken. Early intervention free to families with regional center or public school referral. SERVES: Riverside & San Bernardino Counties & parts of L.A. County.

THERAPY/HANDI-CAPABLE EQUESTRIANS
T.H.E. Center, Inc.
P.O. Box 5337
27260 Girard St.
Hemet, CA 92544
(951) 658-7790
(951) 765-6001 FAX

Accredited therapeutic horseback riding prgm for physically and mentally disabled people of all ages. Scholarships available. Students ride once a week for one hour. FUNDING: Donations, nonprofit, fundraisers, community sponsors, United Way, Riverside CDBG, Hemet CDBG. OFC HRS: Tu-Th 8am-2pm; F 8am-5:30pm; Sat 7am-5pm. Spanish spoken. ASL available. ADM REQ: Must have a signed parental and physician release form. Fees based on income. SERVES: Riverside County.

TOTALLY KIDS SPECIALTY HEALTHCARE
Skilled Nursing Facility
1720 Mountain View Ave.
Loma Linda, CA 92354-1727
(909) 796-6915

(909) 799-6205 FAX

59-bed sub-acute facility for ages birth-21 yrs; ambulatory. OFC HRS: M-F 8am-5pm. Chinese, Spanish, Tagalog, and Vietnamese spoken. Accepts Medi-Cal, Medicare, SSI. SERVES: San Bernardino County.

TRANSCRIBERS OF ORANGE COUNTY
10982 Paddock Lane
Santa Ana, CA 92705
(714) 731-5899

Transcribes books, song lyrics, recipes, menus, instructions, letters, cards, etc. for blind children or adults. For info, ask for Alice Schultz. FUNDING: Donations, nonprofit. OFC HRS: M-F 8am-5pm. ADM REQ: Any blind person. Free srvs, only charge for materials. SERVES: So. Calif.

TRUESDAIL SPEECH CENTER
University of Redlands
P.O. Box 3080
1200 E. Colton Ave.
Redlands, CA 92373-0999
(909) 748-8061
(909) 335-5192 FAX

Professional training prgm for students of speech & language pathology at the Univ of Redlands. Diagnosis & treatment of speech, lang, hearing & other communicative disorders. FUNDING: Nonprofit, client fees, donations. OFC HRS: M-F 9am-12noon, 1pm-5pm. Fees: $125 eval, $250 treatment per semester (20-21 fifty min. visits). SERVES: Inland Empire.

U.S. INTERNAL REVENUE SERVICE/TDD
(800) 829-1040
(703) 368-9694 FAX

Using this nationwide TDD system, deaf and hearing impaired taxpayers can get answers to their federal income tax questions. Topics covered include: medical deductions, TDDs, hearing aids, trained hearing ear dogs and questions about sending deaf children to special schools. Orders for the publication "Tax Information for Disabled Individuals" and other free IRS publications are accepted. TDD HRS: M-F 5am-3:45pm(Jan 1-Apr 15); M-F 5am-1:30pm (Apr 16-Dec 31). Spanish spoken. SERVES: U.S.A.

UHS KEYSTONE SCHOOLS
Administrative Office
11980 S. Mt. Vernon Ave.
Grand Terrace, CA 92313
(909) 783-8400
(909) 783-7754 FAX

Non-public special edu schools available only by referral from school districts. No pvt placements. Serves severe emotionally disturbed and learning disabled students ages 6-20 yrs. Schools located in Riverside, Victorville, Grand Terrace, Hemet, Ventura, Carmichael, Vallejo, Yucca Valley, Rancho Cucamonga, San Rafael, Santa Rosa & Cotati. FUNDING: Public funds, nonprofit. OFC HRS: M-F 8am-4:30pm. ADM REQ: Public school referral. Free srvs. SERVES: L.A., Riverside, Ventura, San Bernardino, San Diego, Sacramento, Solano, Yolo, Napa & West Contra Costa Counties.

UNITED CEREBRAL PALSY ASSN
Dennis James Center
35325 Date Palm Dr., Ste 136
Cathedral City, CA 92234
(760) 321-8184

(760) 321-8284 FAX

Info & referral, family resource center, in-home respite care, recreation & camping prgms, parent support groups. "Skillbuilders" after school prgm for ages 8-18 yrs. "Little Bridges" recreation prgm for ages 3-6 yrs. FUNDING: Nonprofit. OFC HRS: M-F 8:30am-4:30pm. Spanish spoken. Srvs paid through Inland Regional Center. SERVES: San Bernardino, Riverside Counties.

UNITED CEREBRAL PALSY ASSN
1660 L Street, NW, Ste 700
Washington, DC 20036
(800) 872-5827
(202) 776-0406
(202) 776-0414 FAX

Info & referral and free literature about cerebral palsy, legislative advocacy, public policy, edu. Model projects that demonstrate best practice in areas related to technology, early intervention, edu, employment, and homeownership. No direct srvs from this office. FUNDING: Donations, grants, nonprofit. OFC HRS: M-F 9am-5:30pm, EST. SERVES: U.S.A.

UNO MAS! DOWN SYNDROME ONLINE
Mailing Address
40485 Murrieta Hot Springs Rd., Ste 207
Murrieta, CA 92563

Online sharing and support for parents of children born with Down Syndrome: activities, bulletin & message board, share stories, etc. Visit (www.unomas21.com). Donations accepted to maintain the site. SERVES: Riverside County.

UPLAND REHAB & CARE CENTER
Skilled Nursing Facility
1221 E. Arrow Highway
Upland, CA 91786
(909) 985-1903
(909) 949-4975 FAX

206-bed facility, serves non-ambulatory. 24-hr nursing care. Spanish & Tagalog spoken. ADM REQ: Ages 19 yrs+. Skill requirement. Accepts Medi-Cal, Medicare, HMOs. SERVES: San Bernardino County.

V.I.P. TOTS
Early Intervention and Child Care
41915 E. Acacia Ave.
Hemet, CA 92544
(951) 652-7611
(951) 925-0288 FAX

Preschool and child care facility providing a dev based curriculum to normally dev and special needs children. Early intervention for children with disabilities. Srvs include: edu therapy, parent support, inclusion settings. Serving children in home-based prgms for ages birth-3 yrs, center-based prgms for ages 18 mos-6 yrs. Child care prgm is for ages 18 mos-5 yrs, including children with disabilities. FUNDING: Reg Center, school district, CSU, DPSS, fees, nonprofit. OFC HRS: M-F 7am-6pm. Spanish spoken. No charge to parents for special needs prgm. SERVES: Hemet, Temecula, Perris, Lake Elsinore, San Jacinto, Murrieta.

VALLEY RESOURCE CENTER
EXCEED Program
79-733 Country Club Dr., Ste 2
Bermuda Dunes, CA 92203
(760) 345-3830
(800) 689-7552
(760) 345-7634 FAX

Vocational, living skills and job placement for dev disabled. Srvs provided on an individual basis. FUNDING: State & fed rehab, regional ctrs, pvt funds, donations, grants, contracts. OFC HRS: M-F 8am-5pm. Spanish spoken. ADM REQ: Ages 18 yrs+, able to take care of personal needs. SERVES: Desert communities.

VALLEY RESOURCE CENTER
Sheltering Wings Corp
721 E. Hobson Way
Blythe, CA 92225
(760) 922-3139
(760) 922-6630 FAX

Day prgm, vocational and job placement for dev disabled. Thrift store open M-F 9am-5pm. FUNDING: Dept of Rehab, pvt funds, contracts, nonprofit. OFC HRS: M-F 8am-3pm. Spanish spoken. ADM REQ: Ages 18 yrs+, able to take care of personal needs. SERVES: Desert communities.

VALLEY RESOURCE CENTER
EXCEED Program
1285 N. Santa Fe
Hemet, CA 92543
(951) 766-8659
(800) 647-3451
(951) 929-9758 FAX

Vocational, living skills, training and job placement for dev disabled. Wait for funding to be authorized. Call first. FUNDING: Dept of Rehab, Regional Center, pvt funds, contracts, nonprofit. OFC HRS: M-F 8am-5pm. Spanish spoken. ASL available. ADM REQ: Ages 18 yrs+, able to take care of personal needs. SERVES: Riverside & San Bernardino Counties.

VALLEY RESOURCE CENTER
EXCEED Program
P.O. Box 1773
2050 Trumble Rd.
Perris, CA 92572
(951) 657-0609
(800) 423-1227
(951) 657-2277 FAX

Vocational, living skills and job placement for dev disabled. Wait for funding to be authorized. Fee scale as funding source. FUNDING: Regional Ctr/Dept of Rehab, pvt funds, contracts. OFC HRS: M-F 8am-5pm. Spanish spoken. ADM REQ: Ages 18 yrs+, able to take care of personal needs. SERVES: Riverside & San Bernardino Counties.

VILLA MESA CONV HOSPITAL
Skilled Nursing Facility
867 E. 11th Street
Upland, CA 91786
(909) 985-1981
(909) 982-2885 FAX

99-bed facility; ambulatory, non-ambulatory, Alzheimer's. OFC HRS: M-F 9am-5pm. Spanish spoken. Accepts Medi-Cal, Medicare, SSI. SERVES: San Bernardino County.

VIP, INC.
Formerly J.O.B., Inc.
17292 Eucalyptus St.
Hesperia, CA 92345
(760) 948-1312
(760) 948-0993 FAX

Sheltered workshop for dev disabled adults. FUNDING: Dept of Rehab, donations, grants, contracts, nonprofit. OFC HRS: M-F

7:30am-4pm. Spanish spoken. ADM REQ: Certifiable disability. SERVES: Victor Valley area.

VISITING NURSE ASSN/INLAND
222 E. Main St., Ste 112
Barstow, CA 92311
(760) 256-2016
(760) 256-2302 FAX

Full range of health care srvs in the home. Nursing, assist with daily living activities, rehab therapies, OT, PT, nutrition counseling & medical social srvs. Free info & referral. FUNDING: United Way, nonprofit. OFC HRS: M-F 8am-4:30pm, nursing on call 24 hrs for high-tech. Spanish spoken. ADM REQ: Physician order, medical necessity. Accepts Medicare, Medi-Cal. Fees for srv. SERVES: Barstow & nearby.

VISITING NURSE ASSN/INLAND
42-600 Cook St., Ste 202
Palm Desert, CA 92211
(760) 346-3982
(866) 333-1424
(760) 779-9162 FAX

Full range of health care srvs in the home. Nursing, assist with daily living activities, rehab therapies, nutrition counseling and medical social srvs. Free info & referral, some professional srvs based on need. JCAHO accredited. FUNDING: Fees, United Way, nonprofit. OFC HRS: M-F 8am-5pm, nursing on call 24 hrs for high-tech. Spanish spoken. ADM REQ: Physician order, medical necessity. Accepts Medicare, Medi-Cal, insurance, pvt pay. SERVES: Palm Springs, Coachella Valley to the Salton Sea.

VISITING NURSE ASSN/INLAND
12421 Hesperia Rd., Ste 11
Victorville 92395
(760) 241-1966
(760) 241-7055 FAX

Home health care professionals provide personalized health care to patients in their own homes. Teaches patients, family & friends about medications, injections, oxygen use, ostomy care, intravenous and tube feedings, special diets or other aspects of care. Wait: none. FUNDING: Srv fees, donations, nonprofit. OFC HRS: M-F 8am-5pm, nursing on call 24 hrs. Spanish spoken. ADM REQ: Physician order, medical necessity. Sliding fee scale. SERVES: Victor Valley area south & east of Lucerne Valley.

VISTA PACIFICA CENTER
Skilled Nursing Facility
3674 Pacific Ave.
Riverside, CA 92509
(951) 682-4833
(951) 274-2742 FAX

108-bed facility, long-term care, locked gero-psych skilled nursing facility. FUNDING: Medi-Cal. OFC HRS: M-F 8am-5pm. Spanish spoken. ADM REQ: Ages 65 yrs+, mental illness diagnosis with behavioral problems (hitting, yelling, resistant to care, hallucinations, delusions). Accepts Medi-Cal, Medicare, SSI. SERVES: Riverside County.

WELL SPOUSE ASSOCIATION
63 W. Main St., Ste H
Freehold, NJ 07728
(800) 838-0879
(732) 577-8899

(732) 577-8644 FAX

Volunteer-based natl organization focused on providing emotional support to husbands, wives and partners caring for spouses with chronic illnesses and/or long-term disabilities. FUNDING: Fees, donations, grants, nonprofit. OFC HRS: M-F 10am-3pm, EST. SERVES: U.S.A.

WESTVIEW FIELD ADULT DEV CTR
27576 Commerce Center Dr., Ste 103
Temecula, CA 92590
(951) 699-0047

Adult day care prgm provides daytime supervision & activities for dev disabled. FUNDING: Nonprofit. Prgm Hrs: M 8:30-2:30pm. Spanish, Tagalog spoken. ADM REQ: Must have approval from Inland Regional Ctr counselor. SERVES: Lake Elsinore, Wildomar, Temecula, Sun City.

WESTVIEW SERVICES, INC.
Administrative Office
10522 Katella Ave.
Anaheim, CA 92804
(714) 517-6606
(714) 517-6613 FAX

Srvs designed to help the disabled realize their potential. Dev employment skills, social interaction, self-advocacy, & daily living skills. Offices in Costa Mesa, Lakewood, Fountain Valley, Covina, Fullerton, Garden Grove, Gardena, Glendale, Long Beach, Los Angeles, Riverside, Santa Ana, Temecula, Torrance, Ventura, Westchester & Westminster, as well as Arizona & Nevada. FUNDING: Nonprofit. OFC HRS: M-F 8am-4:30pm. Spanish, Tagalog & Vietnamese spoken. Accepts Medi-Cal, regional ctr, pvt pay. SERVES: So. Calif, Arizona & Nevada.

WESTVIEW SERVICES, INC.
Westview Vocational Srvs
11728 Magnolia, Ste D
Riverside, CA 92503
(951) 343-8730
(951) 343-8732 FAX

Supported employment prgm for disabled. Job training, placement, self-advocacy, behavior mgmt, vocational assessments. FUNDING: Regional Center, Dept of Rehab, nonprofit. OFC HRS: M-F 8am-4:30pm. Spanish spoken, ASL available. ADM REQ: Referral by Regl Ctr or Dept of Rehab. No cost to applicants. SERVES: Inland Empire.

WHEELCHAIR TENNIS INFO LINE
So Calif Tennis Association
P.O. Box 240015
420 Charles Young Dr., W
Los Angeles, CA 90024
(310) 208-3838
(310) 824-7691 FAX

Info & referrals to junior wheelchair tennis prgms for disabled youth. Contact Annette Buck. FUNDING: Nonprofit. OFC HRS: M-F 9am-5pm. SERVES: So. Calif.

WIGS FOR KIDS
24231 Center Ridge Rd., Ste 26
Westlake, OH 44145
(440) 333-4433
(440) 835-1084 FAX

Accepts donated hair to provide hairpieces to low income children who have lost their hair due to a medical condition. FUNDING: Donations,

nonprofit. ADM REQ: Children under 18 yrs of age. SERVES: Calif.

WORLD INSTITUTE ON DISABILITY
3075 Adeline St, Ste 280
Berkeley, CA 94703
(510) 225-6400
(510) 225-0477 FAX

Internationally recognized public policy ctr organized by & for people with disabilities. Conducts research, training, advocacy & public edu so that people with disabilties can gain increased opportunities to live independently. TTY (510) 225-0478. FUNDING: Nonprofit. OFC HRS: M-F 9am-5pm Spanish spoken. ASL available. SERVES: U.S.A. & internatl.

WWW.AGING-PARENTS-AND-ELDER-CARE .COM
950 Tower Lane, 6th Fl.
San Mateo, CA 94404

Helpful website for caregivers. Free referral srv, newsletter. SERVES: U.S.A.

WWW.CALMEDICARE.ORG
Medicare Info
5380 Elvas Ave.
Sacramento, CA 95819
(800) 434-0222
(916) 231-5114 FAX

Visit (www.calmedicare.org) or call for info on prescription drugs, Medicare coverage, counseling, fraud, low income help. FUNDING: Calif Healthcare Fndn, nonprofit. OFC HRS: M-F 8am-4pm. SERVES: Calif.

WWW.DEAFQUEER.ORG
Volunteer-run site with resources and info for the deaf LGBT community. FUNDING: Nonprofit. SERVES: U.S.A.

WWW.IMMUNESUPPORT.COM
ProHealth
2040 Alameda Padre Serra
Santa Barbara, CA 93103
(805) 564-3064
(800) 366-6056
(805) 965-0042 FAX

Website listing info and resources for those who suffer from chronic fatigue syndrome and fibromyalgia. FUNDING: Nonprofit. OFC HRS: M-F 7am- 5pm SERVES: U.S.A.

WWW.LDONLINE.ORG
2775 S. Quincy St.
Arlington, VA 22206
(703) 998-2060 FAX

World's leading website on learning disabilities and ADHD serving more than 200,000 parents, teachers, and other professionals. FUNDING: Fndns, grants. SERVES: U.S.A.

1-800-ALCOHOL
345 W. Foothill Blvd.
Monrovia, CA 91016
(800) 252-6465
(800) 281-5133 FAX

Private agency providing referrals for alcohol & drug treatment prgms. FUNDING: Private for profit. OFC HRS: M-F 6:30am-10pm. SERVES: U.S.A.

1-800-RELAPSE
U.S. Department of Health Srvs
(800) 729-6686

Info and referral to substance abuse prgms. 24-hr hotline. Natl Substance Abuse Treatment Center. TDD (800) 487-4889. Spanish (877) 767-8432. FUNDING: Govt. Free srvs. SERVES: U.S.A.

1-888-MARIJUANA
(800) 662-4357
(800) 729-6686
(301) 468-6433 FAX

1 (888) Marijuana is no longer in service. Info and referral for support groups and treatment for marijuana and any other drug or alcohol abuse issue may be obtained from the 800# shown above at the Natl Clearing House for Alcohol & Drug Info. 24-hr hotline. FUNDING: Govt. Spanish spoken. SERVES: U.S.A.

ADULT CHILDREN OF ALCOHOLICS (ACA)
ACA World Service Organization, Inc.
P.O. Box 3216
Torrance, CA 90510
(310) 534-1815

Self-help, 12-Step prgm of recovery for individuals who grew up in an alcoholic or dysfunctional household. Send self-addressed, stamped, business-sized envelope to the above address for info. Write for meeting times & places. FUNDING: Donations, nonprofit. OFC HRS: Volunteer staffed, no physical office location. Spanish & Chinese spoken. Suggested donation $5. SERVES: U.S.A. & internatl.

ADVENT GROUP MINISTRIES
90 Great Oaks Blvd., Ste 108
San Jose, CA 95119
(408) 281-0708
(408) 281-2658 FAX

Faith-based social service agency serving at-risk children and their families since 1986. Founded as a residential treatment program for adolescents, we have since grown to include an outpatient recovery program, horse therapy, a comprehensive family counseling center and a foster care program for children of all ages. FUNDING: Nonprofit. OFC HRS: M-F 8:30am-5pm. SERVES: Northern Calif, San Bernardino County.

AL-ANON FAMILY GROUPS HEADQUARTERS
1600 Corporate Landing Pkwy.
Virginia Beach, VA 23454-5617
(888) 425-2666
(757) 563-1600
(757) 563-1655 FAX

Support & community groups for relatives & friends of those with drinking problems. Also provides printed materials specifically aimed at helping families deal with problems of alcoholism. Referrals to local meetings & chapters throughout the U.S.A. & Canada. Alateen support prgm for younger family members. Meeting info in English, Spanish & French. Visit (www.al-anon.alateen.org). FUNDING: Member donations, sale of literature, nonprofit. OFC HRS: M-F 8am-7pm, EST.

AL-ANON FAMILY GROUPS, INC.
Inland Empire Ctr
1016 E. Cooley Dr., Ste C2
Colton, CA 92324
(909) 824-1516
(909) 824-1515 FAX

More than 200 Al-Anon group meetings throughout Riverside & San Bernardino Counties every week. Above phone number will refer you to the meeting location in your area and provide a list of times, days, etc. Al-Anon is a self-help group for family or friends of problem drinkers. Groups for adults as well as groups for teens (Alateen for ages 13-19 yrs) and groups for children (Pre-Alateen for ages 8-12 yrs). FUNDING: Nonprofit. OFC HRS: M-F 12noon-4pm; Sat 9am-1pm. Spanish spoken. ADM REQ: Family member or friend who is a problem drinker. No fees. Donations accepted. SERVES: Inland Empire.

AL-ANON FAMILY GROUPS, INC.
Palm Desert AIS/LDC
P.O. Box 1364
73-441 Fred Waring Dr. 92260, Ste 2
Palm Desert, CA 92261
(760) 674-9554
(760) 416-9736 FAX

Mutual support groups for family & friends of those with drinking problems. Call for meeting days, times & locations. Also Alateen prgm. For literature, Alateen, and more info, call (760) 341-6202. Hotline, (888) 512-0061. FUNDING: Donations, nonprofit. OFC HRS: Tu, Th 10am-4pm; call for hrs on W. SERVES: Riverside County.

ALANO CLUB/RIVERSIDE
7620 Cypress Ave.
Riverside, CA 92503
(951) 351-0100

Recreational activities and support to members of Alcoholics Anonymous. FUNDING: Nonprofit. OFC HRS: M-Th, Sun 7am-10pm; F 7am-12noon; Sat 8am-10pm. Free srvs. SERVES: Moreno Valley, March AFB, Riverside, Jurupa.

ALANO CLUB/SAN BERNARDINO
449 W. 10th Street
San Bernardino, CA 92410
(909) 885-9643

Sober & clean atmosphere for recovering alcoholics & drug addicts. Meeting place for AA. Walk in. OFC HRS: 6:30am-9pm

ALATEEN
Al-Anon Family Group, Inc.
1600 Corporate Landing Pkwy.
Virginia Beach, VA 23454-5617
(757) 563-1600
(888) 425-2666
(757) 563-1655 FAX

Meeting resource for young people whose lives have been affected by someone else's drinking. Based on 12-Step prgm. Referrals to local meetings and chapters throughout the U.S. and Canada. Includes Alateen support prgm for younger family members. Meeting info in English, Spanish & French. FUNDING: Member donations, sale of literature, nonprofit. OFC HRS: M-F 8am-6pm, EST. SERVES: U.S.A.

ALCOHOL AND DRUG HELPLINE
7309 South 180 West
Midvale, UT 84047
(800) 821-4357
(801) 567-1490 FAX

General info, AA groups & treatment prgm referrals for any drug and/or alcohol issue. FUNDING: Private for profit. OFC HRS: 24 hrs, 7 days.

ALCOHOLICS ANONYMOUS/ADMIN
Southern Calif Central Office
P.O. Box 70159
4311 Wilshire Blvd., Ste 104
Los Angeles, CA 90010
(323) 936-4343
(323) 936-8729 FAX

24-hr self-help info for alcoholics. Will help anyone who wants to stop drinking. This is an original 12-Step self-help group. AA meeting info. Spanish (323) 735-2089. FUNDING: Nonprofit. OFC HRS: M-F 8am-7:30pm; Sat, Sun, holidays 9am-4:30pm. Spanish & Russian spoken. Free srvs. SERVES: So. Calif.

ALCOHOLICS ANONYMOUS/DESERT
Central Office of the Desert
35-325 Date Palm Dr., Ste 134
Cathedral City, CA 92234
(760) 324-4880
(760) 324-4851 FAX

Help for the alcoholic who still suffers from the disease of alcoholism. Referral to meetings. For east valley, call (760) 568-4004. FUNDING: Nonprofit. OFC HRS: M-F 9am-8pm; Sat, Sun 10am-2pm. Free srvs except for printed material. SERVES: Desert communities to Blythe.

ALCOHOLICS ANONYMOUS/I.E.
Inland Empire Central Office
897 Via Lata, Ste AA
Colton, CA 92324
(909) 825-4700
(909) 825-7370 FAX

Helps anyone with an alcohol problem who wants to stop drinking by putting them in touch with sober members of AA or directing them to AA meetings. Primary purpose is to stay sober and help other alcoholics achieve sobriety. FUNDING: Self-supported by AA members. OFC HRS: M-F 9am-5pm; Sat 9am-1pm. Spanish spoken upon request. ADM REQ: Desire to stop drinking. Free srvs. SERVES: Riverside Metro, Corona, Norco, Banning, Beaumont, Moreno Valley, Hemet, Perris, Lake Elsinore, Temecula, San Bernardino Metro, Ontario, Upland, Pomona Valley and mountain areas.

ALCOHOLICS ANONYMOUS/POMONA
Oficina Intergrupal de Chino
898 N. Garey Ave.
Pomona, CA 91767
(909) 629-0493

Self-help meetings in Spanish for men and women who want to stop drinking. Referrals to meeting locations, support materials, literature. FUNDING: Donations, nonprofit. Spanish spoken. SERVES: San Bernardino County.

ALCOHOLICS ANONYMOUS/RIVERSIDE
Central Srvs Office, Inc.
28636 Old Town Front St., Ste 106
Temecula, CA 92590
(951) 695-1535
(951) 695-2265 FAX

Self-help meetings for men & women who want to stop drinking. Referral to meeting locations in Temecula, Hemet, Sun City, Lake Elsinore, Murrietta, Perris, Moreno Valley, Wildomar, Fallbrook, Anza. Support materials & literature also in Spanish. FUNDING: Donations, nonprofit. OFC HRS: M-F 10am-5:30pm; Sat 9am-12noon. SERVES: Riverside County.

ALCOHOLICS ANONYMOUS/VICTOR VLY
18888 Outer Highway 18, Ste 107
Apple Valley, CA 92307
(760) 242-9292
(760) 242-4855 FAX

24-hr info on AA meetings and referrals. FUNDING: Nonprofit. OFC HRS: M-F 9am-4pm, 24-hr phone srv. Spanish spoken. SERVES: Victor Valley and Barstow.

AMERICAN COUNCIL ON ALCOHOLISM
1000 E. Indian School Rd.
Phoenix, AZ 85014
(800) 527-5344
(602) 264-7403 FAX

Referrals for the treatment of alcoholism and guidance for alcoholics and others. FUNDING: Donations, grants, members, nonprofit. OFC HRS: M-F 10am-6pm. SERVES: U.S.A.

AURORA LAS ENCINAS HOSPITAL
2900 E. Del Mar Blvd.
Pasadena, CA 91107
(800) 792-2345
(626) 792-2919 FAX

Las Encinas Hospital is a 118-bed licensed psychiatric hospital providing quality patient care in the following areas: chemical dependency, medical detox, intensive outpatient, dual-diagnosis, LGBT, adult partial prgm, adult psychiatric inpatient, 38-bed residential treatment prgm, partial prgm and free community-based support groups. FUNDING: Pvt for profit. OFC HRS: 24 hrs, 7 days. ADM REQ: Call for free assessment 24 hrs a day. Accepts indemnity insurance, managed care, self-pay contracts, Medi-Cal, and Medicare. SERVES: U.S.A.

AXIS RESIDENTIAL TREATMENT
75450 Fairway Dr.
Indian Wells, CA 92210
(760) 636-5427
(760) 346-8032
www.axishouse.net

Axis Residential Treatment offers highly effective individual substance abuse treatment and recovery support. Our goal is to empower clients with the tools and knowledge necessary to bring about permanent recovery and productive lives. Call (760) 409-1287. ADM REQ: Ages 18 yrs+. SERVES: So Calif.

B.R.I.D.G.E.S., INC.
Adminstrative Office

1977 N. Garey Ave., Ste 6
Pomona, CA 91767
(909) 623-6651
(909) 623-0455 FAX

L.A. County Dept of Mental Health contract provider focusing on serving individuals with mental illness. Residential and outpatient prgms; 5 social rehabilitation facilities (6-14 beds each) with stay up to 18 months. Residential prgms offered in San Fernando Valley and San Gabriel Valley. Outpatient prgm in SFV offers individual and group specialized mental health counseling, substance abuse support, case mgmt, medication and psychiatry. Wellness & Recovery Ctr in El Monte provides mental health counseling, recreational and vocational support, peer support, medication, and other srvs. FUNDING: Nonprofit. OFC HRS: M-F 8am-4:30pm. Spanish spoken. ADM REQ: Intake (626) 350-5304. Residential prgms house clients ages 18-59 yrs with mental illness and co-occurring disorders; outpatient srvs for up to age 21 yrs. Accepts Medi-Cal, SSI. Limited beds may be available without any funding. SERVES: Los Angeles & San Bernardino Counties.

BABY STEP INN
See "So Calif Alcohol & Drug Prgm"

BEAUTY FOR ASHES WOMEN'S CENTER
Aftercare Program
9791 Arrow Route
Rancho Cucamonga, CA 91730
(909) 477-2781

BFA provides training, education, support and spiritual guidance for life following treatment and/or incarceration. 12-Step prgms, personal development courses, and job training. Volunteer opportunities available. Located at R.C. Family Resource Center. FUNDING: Nonprofit. Spanish spoken. ADM REQ: Adult women ages 18 yrs+, in crisis. SERVES: L.A., Riverside & San Bernardino Counties.

BEHAVIORAL SYSTEMS SOUTHWEST
118 Avenida Victoria
San Clemente, CA 92672
(949) 492-3574
(949) 492-6798 FAX

Residential treatment prgms for offenders released from federal and state prison. Outpatient counseling for individuals convicted of drunk driving. FUNDING: Federal Bureau of Prisons, Calif Dept of Corrections, nonprofit. OFC HRS: M-F 8am-4:30pm. ADM REQ: Approved by fed, state or county for placement. SERVES: So. Calif.

BETTY FORD CENTER
39000 Bob Hope Dr.
Rancho Mirage, CA 92270
(800) 434-7365
(760) 773-4100
(760) 773-4126 FAX

Residential chemical dependency treatment. Inpatient residential day treatment & outpatient prgms for adults. Family & children's prgms, five-day intensive prgm for relapse prevention & co-dependency. Free assessment. FUNDING: Nonprofit. OFC HRS: 24 hrs, 7 days. Spanish spoken. ADM REQ: Alcohol or drug dependent, ages 18 yrs+. Accepts insurance, self-pay (financial assist available). SERVES: U.S.A.

BILINGUAL FAMILY COUNSELING
317 West F Street
Ontario, CA 91762
(909) 986-7111
(909) 986-0941 FAX

County-funded center offers outpatient drug/alcohol and child abuse treatment. Prgms for adults, adolescents & children (including play therapy). Prevention prgms include school & community presentations and parent edu. Also crisis intervention, OTP Jag prgrm, individual, family & group counseling, referrals for suicide intervention and post-intervention srvs. FUNDING: Ofc of Alcohol/Drug Prgms, Human Srvs System, nonprofit. OFC HRS: M-Th 9am-8pm. Spanish spoken. Accepts Medi-Cal for drug/alcohol treatment, pvt fees. SERVES: San Bernardino County.

CALIF ALCOHOLIC BEV CONTROL
3737 Main St., Ste 900
Riverside, CA 92501
(951) 782-4400
(951) 781-0531 FAX

OFC HRS: M-F 8am-5pm. Closed the 1st three F of each month. Spanish spoken. SERVES: Calif.

CALIF DEPT ALCOHOL & DRUG PRGMS
Resource Center
1700 K Street, 1st Fl.
Sacramento, CA 95814
(800) 879-2772
(916) 327-3728
(916) 323-1270 FAX

Clearinghouse and library for info regarding alcohol & drug abuse issues. Info & treatment referral, DUI prgms, etc. Also info on licensing & certification of alcohol & drug prgms. Also call (800) 662-4357. TTY (916) 445-1942. FUNDING: State. OFC HRS: M-F 8am-4:30pm. Spanish spoken. SERVES: Calif.

CALIF DEPT HEALTH SRVS
Prevention Srvs Division
1616 Capitol Ave., Ste 616
Sacramento, CA 95814
(916) 449-5900
(916) 449-5909 FAX

Drug assist, HIV/AIDS srvs. Mailing address: P.O. Box 997426, Sacramento, CA 95899-7426. FUNDING: Govt. OFC HRS: M-F 8am-5pm. Spanish spoken. Free srvs. SERVES: Calif.

CALIF POISON CONTROL SYSTEM
UC San Francisco School of Pharmacy
P.O. Box 1262
3333 California St., Ste 420
San Francisco, CA 94143-1262
(800) 222-1222
(415) 502-8600
(415) 502-8620 FAX

Immediate treatment advice and info in case of exposure to poisonous, hazardous or toxic substances. Info is available to both health professionals & the public. Public outreach & edu provided. Health edu (pamphlets, stickers, prgms) (800) 582-3387. TTY (800) 972-3323. Emerg 24-hr hotline for Calif (800) 876-4766. FUNDING: Nonprofit. OFC HRS: 24 hrs, 7 days. Interpreter srv in over 100 languages. SERVES: Calif.

CALIF RECOVERY CLINICS

710 S. Rimpau Ave., Ste 102
Corona, CA 92879
(951) 549-8888
(951) 549-8808 FAX

Outpatient drug & alcohol treatment prgm. Full srvs for mental health and chemical dependency. Edu, parenting, and anger mgmt. State ID: 330061AN. FUNDING: County, nonprofit. OFC HRS: M-F 8am-9pm. Spanish spoken. Sliding fee scale, accepts pvt pay, insurance, Medi-Cal. SERVES: Corona, Norco, surrounding communities of Western Riverside County.

CALIF SMOKERS' HELPLINE

University Calif San Diego
9500 Gilman Dr., Dept. 0905
La Jolla, CA 92093-0905
(800) 662-8887
(858) 300-1099 FAX

Materials and/or telephone counseling to help people stop using tobacco. Specialized srvs for teens & pregnant women. Cantonese & Mandarin (800) 838-8917; Korean (800) 556-5564; Spanish (800) 45NO-FUME; Vietnamese (800) 778-8440; TDD (800) 933-4TDD; tobacco chewers (800) 844-CHEW. FUNDING: Govt, Calif Dept of Health Srvs, Prop 99. OFC HRS: M-F 7am-9pm; Sat 9am-1pm. 24-hr voicemail. Free srvs. SERVES: Calif.

CASA DE SAN BERNARDINO, INC.

735 North D Street
San Bernardino, CA 92401
(909) 381-5507
(909) 888-5938 FAX

Outpatient drug & alcohol treatment prgm. Info & referral. PC-1000 drug diversion. State ID: 360013AN. FUNDING: Nonprofit. OFC HRS: M-Th 8am-5pm. Spanish spoken. ADM REQ: Ages 14-21 yrs. SERVES: San Bernardino County.

CASA LAS PALMAS RECOVERY HOME

Riverside Co. Dept of Mental Health
83-844 Hopi Ave.
Indio, CA 92201
(760) 347-9442
(760) 342-8022 FAX

90-day, 7-bed social model recovery home for men and women. Open AA & NA meetings for people from the community, study meetings, support groups and individual guidance. State ID: 330037AN. FUNDING: Riverside Co. Dept of Mental Health. OFC HRS: M-F 8am-5pm. Spanish spoken. ADM REQ: Any resident of Riverside County who wishes to stop drug and alcohol abuse. Sliding fee scale. No one turned away for lack of funds. SERVES: Riverside County.

CATHOLIC CHARITIES/COUNSELING

Caritas Counseling Srvs
1441 North D Street, Ste 4
San Bernardino, CA 92405
(909) 763-4970
(909) 763-4977 FAX

Professional counseling without regard to race, creed, sex, or age. Marriage, family, child counseling for a wide range of issues such as child abuse, anger mgmt, relationships, parent edu. Counseling provided days, eve & Sat in various locations. FUNDING: Nonprofit. OFC HRS: M-F 10am-4:30pm. Spanish spoken. Sliding fee scale. Some free srvs. SERVES: San Bernardino & Riverside Counties.

CEDAR HOUSE REHAB CENTER

P.O. Box 657
18612 Santa Ana Ave.
Bloomington, CA 92316
(909) 421-7120
(800) 246-4357
(909) 421-7128 FAX

Outpatient prgms available on a sliding fee scale. Inpatient prgms available for a fee of $100 per day. Offers family groups, aftercare, referral, sober living houses. Prgms for women with children and those with co-occurring disorders. 1st, 2nd and multiple offender DUI prgms. Prop 36, SASCA. State ID: 360002DN. Outpatient state ID: 360002CN. FUNDING: County, United Way, nonprofit. OFC HRS: M-F 8am-6pm. Spanish spoken. ADM REQ: Ages 18 yrs+. SERVES: So. Calif.

CEDARS-SINAI PSYCH/MENTAL HLTH

Dept of Psychiatry & Mental Health
8730 Alden Dr., Plaza Level
Los Angeles, CA 90048
(800) 233-2771
(310) 423-0428 FAX

Adult & geriatric inpatient and partial hospitalization & day treatment. Adult, geriatric, adol, child, infant and family outpatient mental health srvs. Dual-diagnosis, IOP srvs, psych and chemical dep srvs. Day treatment & intensive outpatient chemical dependency treatment. For TDD, call (310) 423-2655. FUNDING: Nonprofit. OFC HRS: 24-hr for emerg. Accepts Medi-Cal, Medicare, insurance. SERVES: U.S.A.

CELEBRATE RECOVERY

Canyon Lake Community Church
30515 Railroad Canyon Rd.
Canyon Lake, CA 92586
(951) 244-1877
(951) 244-4397 FAX

Christ-centered, 12-Step recovery prgm. Support groups for all types of problems and addictions, including: food, sex or relationship addictions, co-dependency and chemical dependency. Meets Th at 6pm for dinner, 7pm for worship & meeting. Child care available. FUNDING: Nonprofit. OFC HRS: M-Th 8am-4:30pm. SERVES: Riverside County.

CELEBRATE RECOVERY

Mosaic Inland Church
5540 Schaefer Ave.
Chino, CA 91710
(909) 628-1571

Christ-centered, 12-Step recovery prgm. Support groups for all types of problems & addictions, including: food, sex or relationship addictions, co-dependency and chemical dependency. Meets F at 6pm-10pm. Contact: Jim or Terry Moon. FUNDING: Nonprofit. OFC HRS: M-F 8:30am-4pm. Spanish spoken. SERVES: San Bernardino County.

CELEBRATE RECOVERY

Centerpoint Church
P.O. Box 787
170 West F Street
Colton, CA 92324
(909) 825-3670

Christ-centered, 12-Step recovery prgm. Support groups for all types of problems & addictions, including: food, sex or relationship addictions, co-dependency and chemical dependency. Meets Th at 6:30pm in children's ministries building. FUNDING: Nonprofit. OFC HRS: Tu-F 9am-5pm. SERVES: San Bernardino County.

CELEBRATE RECOVERY

Crossroads Christian Church
2331 Kellogg Ave.
Corona, CA 92881
(951) 737-4664
(951) 278-3176 FAX

Christ-centered 12-Step recovery prgm. Support groups for all types of problems & addictions, including: food, sex or relationship addictions, co-dependency and chemical dependency. Meets F at 7pm in the fellowship hall. Light dinner and fellowship at 6:30pm. Open share, workbook, and other recovery groups also available. FUNDING: Nonprofit. OFC HRS: M-Th 8am-4:30pm; F 8am-3pm. SERVES: Riverside County.

CELEBRATE RECOVERY

8348 3rd Street
Downey, CA 90241
(562) 923-1261
(562) 861-1614 FAX

Christ-centered and biblically based support group for all hurts, habits (addictions) and hang-ups (co-dependency, anger, etc). Separate men's and women's open share groups and 12-Step study groups. Meets F in the fellowship hall from 6pm-9pm. FUNDING: Nonprofit. Spanish spoken. SERVES: L.A. & San Bernardino Counties.

CELEBRATE RECOVERY

Southwest Community Church
77701 Fred Waring Dr.
Indian Wells, CA 92210
(760) 200-2000
(760) 360-4139 FAX

Turning Point: Christ-centered 12-Step recovery prgm. Big event every 8 weeks. Small groups meet often. Contact Pastor Dave Jenkins, ext. 2283. Additional recovery prgrms available. FUNDING: Nonprofit. OFC HRS: M-Th 9am-5pm. SERVES: Riverside County.

CELEBRATE RECOVERY

Cathedral of Praise
1100 E. Holt Blvd.
Pomona, CA 91767
(626) 806-1890
(909) 987-1636 FAX

Christ-centered, 12-Step recovery prgm. Support groups for all types of problems & addictions, including: food, sex or relationship addictions, co-dependency and chemical dependency. OFC HRS: M-W, F, Sat 10am-8pm. Free srvs. SERVES: San Gabriel Valley & San Bernardino Co.

CELEBRATE RECOVERY

Sunrise Church
2759 N. Ayala Dr.
Rialto, CA 92377
(909) 875-5566
(909) 820-6281 FAX

Christ-centered, 12-Step recovery prgm. Support groups for all types of problems & addictions, including: food, sex or relationship addictions, co-dependency and chemical dependency. Professional counseling referrals available. Meets Tu from 7pm-9pm in room 260 and Fri at 7pm in chapel (room 170). FUNDING: Nonprofit. OFC HRS: M-F 8am-5pm. Spanish spoken. SERVES: San Bernardino County.

CELEBRATE RECOVERY
Bethel Christian Center
2425 Van Buren Blvd.
Riverside, CA 92503
(951) 359-1123
(951) 359-3372 FAX

Christ-centered, 12-Step recovery prgm. Support groups for all types of problems & addictions, including: food, sex, or relationship addictions, co-dependency and chemical dependency. Meets F at 7pm. Contact: Jerry or Julia Thromson. FUNDING: Nonprofit. OFC HRS: M-F 9am-5pm. SERVES: Riverside & nearby.

CELEBRATE RECOVERY
Pathway Christian Church
6755 Victoria Ave.
Riverside, CA 92506
(951) 781-8465
(951) 781-8896 FAX

Christ-centered, 12-Step recovery prgm. Support groups for all types of problems & addictions, including: food, sex or relationship addictions, co-dependency and chemical dependency. Meets F at 6pm for dinner; 7pm for large group; 8pm for small group, 8pm one-time newcomers 101 meeting; 9pm Holy Grounds Cafe fellowship (dessert served). Call for more information regarding 12-Step groups for men & women. FUNDING: Nonprofit. OFC HRS: M-F 9am-5pm. ADM REQ: $3 for dinner. SERVES: Riverside County.

CELEBRATE RECOVERY
Riverside Community Church
4850 Jurupa Ave.
Riverside, CA 92504
(951) 686-1886
(951) 684-7313 FAX

Christ-centered, 12-Step recovery prgm. Support groups for all types of problems & addictions, including: food, sex or relationship addictions, co-dependency and chemical dependency. Meets Th at 6pm for dinner; 7pm worship; 8pm gender-specific share groups; 9pm coffee and dessert accountability fellowship. Call for more info regarding 12-Step groups. Contact: Carlos Davila. FUNDING: Nonprofit. OFC HRS: T-Th 9am-4pm; F 9am-12noon. SERVES: Riverside County.

CELEBRATE RECOVERY
Northpoint Christian Fellowship
2055 Elks Dr.
San Bernardino, CA 92405
(909) 882-2564
(909) 882-8708 FAX

Christ-centered, 12-Step recovery prgm. Meets Tu from 6:30pm-9pm. FUNDING: Nonprofit. OFC HRS: M-Th 8:30am-4:30pm. SERVES: San Bernardino County.

CELEBRATE RECOVERY
Judson Baptist Church
1406 E. Pacific St.
San Bernardino, CA 92404
(909) 889-0781
(909) 889-0783 FAX

Christ-centered, 12-Step recovery prgm. Support groups for all types of problems & addic-

tions. Life recovery worship service Sun 9am, 12-Step study groups for women Sun 11am, and Tu 6:30pm. For men, Tu and Th 6:30pm. FUNDING: Nonprofit. SERVES: San Bernardino City.

CELEBRATE RECOVERY
Cornerstone Community Church
34570 Monte Vista Dr.
Wildomar, CA 92595
(951) 674-8661
(951) 674-9603 FAX

Christ-centered, 12-Step recovery prgm. Support groups for all types of problems & addictions, including: food, sex or relationship addictions, co-dependency and chemical dependency. Meets F at 6pm for dinner; 7pm worship and msg; 8pm open share groups. Childcare for ages birth-12yrs. Celebrate Recovery for teens meets Th 6:30pm-8:30pm in youth chapel. Contact: Pastor Bill Aanestad. FUNDING: Nonprofit. OFC HRS: M-Th 8am-5pm. SERVES: Riverside County.

CELEBRATE WHOLENESS
Campus Hill Church
11057 Hill Dr.
Loma Linda, CA 92354
(909) 796-0222
(909) 796-1992 FAX

Christ-centered, 12-Step recovery prgm. Support groups for all types of problems & addictions, including: food, sex or relationship addictions, co-dependency and chemical dependency. Meets F at 7pm in Linda Hall. Contact: Pastor Larry. FUNDING: Nonprofit. OFC HRS: M-Th 8am-5pm; F 8am-12noon. SERVES: San Bernardino County.

CENTER FOR CRIMINALITY & ADDICTION RESEARCH, TRAINING
UCSD School of Medicine
5060 Shoreham Pl., Mail Code 0930, Ste 200
San Diego, CA 92122
(858) 334-4600
(858) 334-4601 FAX

University of Calif, San Diego School of Medicine facilitates a variety of science-based edu, training & networking events annually addressing substance abuse prevention, treatment & publishing-related materials. The Criminal Justice Institute provides those involved in substance abuse treatment with the most up-to-date knowledge & skills. The purpose is to enhance the knowledge, skills, & attitudes of those engaged (or preparing to be) in the delivery of treatment & recovery srvs, or for those performing health & social srvs to patients & clients who may be troubled by alcohol & other drug use. FUNDING: Nonprofit, grants. SERVES: Calif.

CENTER FOR HEALTH PROMOTION
Loma Linda University Evans Hall, Rm. 111
24785 Stewart St.
Loma Linda, CA 92350
(909) 558-4594
(909) 558-0433 FAX

Wide range of srvs offered from community clinics. Clearview alcohol & drug prgm, stress mgmt, weight mgmt, smoking cessation, health eval and extensive individual risk eval. Prgms staffed by univ medical staff and students. FUNDING: Nonprofit. OFC HRS: M-Th 8am-12noon, 1pm-5pm; F 8am-12noon. ADM

REQ: Open to anyone. Srv fees vary. SERVES: So. Calif.

CENTER FOR SUBSTANCE ABUSE PREV
Drug-Free Workplace Helpline
1 Choke Cherry Rd.
Rockville, MD 20857
(800) 967-5752
(301) 443-3031 FAX

Confidential tech assist & guidance for employers, labor unions, and community organizations in workplace prevention matters. Helps develop and implement drug-free workplace prgms including drug testing, EAP, training & edu and policy dev. FUNDING: Govt. OFC HRS: M-F 9am-5:30pm, EST. Free srvs. SERVES: U.S.A.

CHAPMAN HOUSE, INC.
3894 4th Street
Riverside, CA 92501
(714) 288-9779
(714) 288-6130 FAX

Specializes in drug/alcohol detox. Treatment of chemical dependency, dual diagnosis, chronic pain. 30, 60, and 90 day prgms. Hlps those in need of alternative sentencing. CARF accredited. FUNDING: Nonprofit. OFC HRS: Counselor available 24 hrs, 7 days. SERVES: Riverside County.

CHAPMAN HOUSE, INC.
3293 Locust St.
Riverside, CA 92501
(714) 288-9779
(714) 288-6130 FAX

See location above for more information.

CHINO COMMUNITY SERVICES
Youth & Family Counseling Srvs
13201 Central Ave.
Chino, CA 91710
(909) 591-9822
(909) 628-4093 FAX

Counseling for individuals, families and groups. Info & referral, prevention and edu for alcohol and drug abuse. Also call (909) 628-1010 (emerg). FUNDING: County, city, govt. OFC HRS: M-Th 8am-8pm; F 8am-6pm. Spanish spoken. ADM REQ: Phone assessment with counselor. Free to residents of Chino, $26 per session for non-residents. SERVES: Western San Bernardino County.

CHRISTIAN FAMILY COUNSELING
6117 Brockton Ave., Ste 100
Riverside, CA 92506
(951) 682-7138
(877) 777-0755
(951) 686-2271 FAX

Marriage, individual, family, teen, adol, drug & alcohol counseling. FUNDING: Donations, nonprofit. OFC HRS: M-F 9am-8pm, Sat 10am-5pm. $45 per session. SERVES: Riverside, San Bernardino Counties.

CHRISTOPHER WAHL YOUTH CENTER
12401 Slauson Ave., Ste G
Whittier, CA 90606
(562) 693-2247
(562) 954-7264 FAX

Offers free HIV testing and prevention edu. Houses various support groups and 12-Step prgms including Celebrate Recovery. FUNDING: Nonprofit. OFC HRS: M-F 9am-5pm. Free srvs. SERVES: L.A. County, San Bernardino County.

COCAINE ANONYMOUS
National Referral Line
(800) 347-8998

Info for prgms in your area. OFC HRS: 24 hrs; 7 days SERVES: U.S.A.

COCAINE ANONYMOUS
Mailing Address
3243 Arlington Ave., Ste 246
Riverside, CA 92506-3244
(951) 359-3895

12-Step meetings for addicts to share their experience, strength and hope to recover from their addiction. See website for meetings, (www.ca.org). High Desert (760)255-1093. CA World Srvs (310)559-5833. FUNDING: Donations, nonprofit. ADM REQ: Desire to stop using mind-altering substances. SERVES: Riverside & San Bernardino Counties.

COCAINE ANONYMOUS WORLD SRVS
P.O. Box 2000
3740 Overland Ave., Ste C
Los Angeles, CA 90034
(310) 559-5833
(310) 559-2554 FAX

12-Step, anonymous, self-help fellowship of men and women who share their common problem and help others to recover from their addiction. Call (800) 347-8998 for internatl referrals to local CA meetings. FUNDING: Contributions, nonprofit. OFC HRS: M-F 9am-5pm. SERVES: Internatl.

COMMUNITY ANTI-DRUG COALITIONS OF AMERICA (CADCA)
625 Slaters Lane, Ste 300
Alexandria, VA 22314
(703) 706-0560
(703) 706-0565 FAX

Home of the Natl Community Anti-Drug Coalition Institute and the Drug-Free Kids Campaign. Premier natl membership organization representing more than 5,000 community anti-drug coalitions nationwide, providing training & technical assist, info & support. Not a direct srv provider. For more info, write to the address above or visit (www.cadca.org) or (www.drug-freekids.org). FUNDING: Grants, contracts, donations. SERVES: U.S.A.

COMMUNITY SETTLEMENT ASSOCIATION
Drinking Driver Program
4366 Bermuda Ave.
Riverside, CA 92507
(951) 782-2336
(951) 686-6267
(951) 782-2337 FAX

1st offender: 16 weeks; 2nd offender: 52 weeks (one yr); 18-month prgm. FUNDING: Nonprofit. OFC HRS: M-F 8am-5pm. DUI prgm hrs: Tu-Sat 9:30am-6:30pm; Sat 9am-12noon. Spanish spoken. ADM REQ: Ages 18 yrs+. Sliding fee scale. SERVES: Riverside & nearby.

CRYSTAL METH ANONYMOUS
4470 W. Sunset Blvd., PMB 555, Ste 107
Los Angeles, CA 90027
(213) 488-4455

Fellowship of individuals who have had problems with crystal meth. Meetings held regularly to share and offer each other support in overcoming addiction. Based on 12-Step tradition. Call for meeting locations and times or visit (www.crystalmeth.org). FUNDING: Nonprofit. SERVES: U.S.A.

CSAT HOTLINE
(800) 729-6686

CSAT (Center for Substance Abuse Treatment) answers questions about drug abuse & AIDS as it relates to IV drug users. Referrals to support groups & drug treatment prgms. TDD (800)487-4889, Spanish (877)767-8432. FUNDING: Govt. OFC HRS: 24 hrs, 7 days. Spanish spoken. SERVES: U.S.A.

CSP WORKPLACE HELPLINE
See "Center for Substance Abuse Prev"

DALTON & ASSOCIATES
16200 Bear Valley Rd., Ste 111
Victorville, CA 92392
(760) 241-1777
(760) 245-2253 FAX

Licensed DUI 1st offender, 2nd offender, and multiple offender prgms. FUNDING: Nonprofit. OFC HRS: M-F 9am-9pm; Sat 8am-11:30am. Spanish spoken. ADM REQ: Ages 18 yrs+. SERVES: San Bernardino County.

DAVID & MARGARET YOUTH & FAMILY SRVS
1350 3rd Street
La Verne, CA 91750
(909) 596-5921
(909) 596-7583 FAX

Residential treatment prgm and specialized non-public school for girls ages 11-18 yrs. Shelter care for children ages 11-18 yrs. Foster family agency and adoption srvs serving children ages birth-18 yrs. Learning enhancement ctr for youth and adults with LD, ADHD, ADD. Community based edu prgms including self-injury, alcohol and drug intervention, anger mgmt courses. Social srvs, probation and mental health agency referrals. Serves children and families. Provides transitional housing for youth ages 18-25 yrs who are at-risk of homelessness. Provides mentoring prgm for foster youth and pvt counseling on a sliding scale basis. FUNDING: State, county, donations, nonprofit. OFC HRS: M-F 8:30am-5pm. Spanish spoken. Accepts insurance, Medicare, Medi-Cal. Sliding fee scale. Set fee to public. SERVES: So. Calif.

DELANCEY STREET FOUNDATION
600 Embarcadero
San Francisco, CA 94107
(415) 512-5104
(415) 512-5141 FAX

Rehab prgm provides assist to ex-felons, substance abusers, gang members, perpetrators, and victims of abuse to assist them with skills to rebuild their lives. Literacy, homeless issues, anger mgmt, edu & voc mentoring. Does not accept people with mental disorders, people on medication or with disabilities, arsonists, or sex offenders. FUNDING: Nonprofit, donations. OFC HRS: 24/7. ADM REQ: Ages 18 yrs+. Free srvs. SERVES: Calif.

DESERT REHABILITATION SERVICES
See "Hacienda Valdez"

DISABLED AMERICAN VETERANS
National Headquarters
3725 Alexandria Pike
Newport, KY 41076
(877) 426-2838

(859) 441-7300

Helps with benefits assist from the Dept. of Veterans Affairs, provides a network of volunteers who offer rides to and from VA medical facilities for veterans, grassroots advocacy & srvs. Also offers special prgms for homeless vets and those suffering from substance abuse issues. Visit (www.dav.org) for more info and to find a chapter near you. Free srvs. SERVES: U.S.A.

DOUBLE CHECK RETREAT
P.O. Box 639
47552 Florida Ave.
Hemet, CA 92544
(951) 927-2567

Social model 12-Step residential alcohol abuse recovery prgm for men capable of working an eight-hour day. Client pays their own way by working at outside locations. Must have a positive attitude and be willing to work toward their own recovery. FUNDING: Nonprofit. OFC HRS: 24 hrs, 7 days. ADM REQ: Men ages 25 yrs+. SERVES: Riverside County.

DRUG & ALC TREATMENT REFERRAL
Mental Health/Drug/Alcohol Abuse Hotline
(866) 716-3460

Referrals & help to those in crisis. Executive rehab, prescription addiction prgm, Christian-based prgm, teen & family rehab, intervention partners, gay & lesbian prgm, west & east coast adult rehabs, residential treatment, teen outpatient, 12-Step rehab. FUNDING: Nonprofit. OFC HRS: 24 hrs, 7 days. Spanish spoken. SERVES: U.S.A.

DRUG & ALCOHOL ABUSE INFO/REF
National Inst on Drug & Alcohol Abuse
1 Choke Cherry Rd.
Rockville, MD 20857
(800) 729-6686

24-hr referral to alcohol & drug prev & treatment prgms & srvs. FUNDING: Grants, contracts. Spanish spoken. Free srvs. SERVES: U.S.A.

DRUG ABUSE PROGRAMS
See "Riverside Co. Dept./Mental Health"

DRUG ABUSE PROGRAMS/RIV CO.
See "Riverside Co. Office/Education"

DRUG ENDANGERED CHILDREN PRGM
P.O. Box 1267
Riverside, CA 92502
(877) 955-6384

Multi-agency approach by Child Protective Services, District Attorney, Sheriff's Department, and other public health agencies to assist and protect drug-endangered children whose lives are jeopardized by families who have been involved with drug manufacturing, sales, or use. Srvs include: comprehensive medical screening, drug screening, mental and dental care, background checks and home-eval, removal from toxic chemical exposure and drug environments. Call the METH hotline at (877) 955-METH if you supect the manufacturing of methamphetamines. FUNDING: Govt. Spanish spoken. ADM REQ: Children who have been endangered due to familial involvement with drugs. Free srvs. SERVES: Riverside Co.

DRUG STRATEGIES
www.bubblemonkey.com
1150 Conneticut Ave., NW
Washington, DC 20036
(202) 289-9070

Internet site aimed at teens who want to learn more about the dangers of drugs and alcohol but are afraid to ask. For Spanish, visit (www.changobomba.com). FUNDING: Calif. Endowment grant. SERVES: Internatl.

ETTIE LEE YOUTH & FAMILY SERVICES

P.O. Box 339
5146 N. Maine Ave.
Baldwin Park, CA 91706-0339
(626) 960-4861
(626) 337-2621 FAX

Family-style homes for severely emotionally disturbed young men ages 8-18 yrs. 24-hr care by trained staff. Individual & group therapy, gang intervention srvs, independent living skills training, case mgmt, family counseling, therapeutic recreation, 12-Step prgms, substance abuse treatment & on-site school. Licensed treatment foster family agency for boys & girls ages birth-18 yrs. Mental health therapy, case mgmt & family counseling. FUNDING: Nonprofit. OFC HRS: M-F 8am-5pm. Spanish spoken. ADM REQ: County referral for group home & foster care. SERVES: So. Calif.

FAMILIES ANONYMOUS

P.O. Box 3475
Culver City, CA 90231-3475
(800) 736-9805
(310) 815-8010
(310) 815-9682 FAX

12-Step internatl fellowship of support groups for parents, family and friends affected by someone with drug, alcohol or behavior problems. Call for referral to local meetings. FUNDING: Donations, sale of literature, nonprofit. OFC HRS: M-F 10am-4pm. Spanish referrals. ADM REQ: Ages 15 yrs+. Free srvs. SERVES: U.S.A. & internatl.

FAMILY SERVICES OF THE DESERT

81-711 Highway 111, Ste 101
Indio, CA 92201
(760) 347-2398
(800) 536-4357
(760) 347-6468 FAX

Family, individual and group counseling. Locations in Indio, Desert Hot Springs and Blythe. FUNDING: United Way, donations, client fees, nonprofit. OFC HRS: M-F 9am-5pm. Eve & weekend by appt. Spanish spoken. SERVES: Coachella Valley.

FOUNDATION FOR RECOVERY, INC.

4750 W. Sahara Ave., Ste 10
Las Vegas, NV 89102
(702) 257-8199
(702) 257-8299 FAX

Maintains a study center and archival library of both historical and modern material related to addiction & recovery. Provides meeting space to the recovering community. Visit (www.therooms.org). Also a recovery museum and bookstore. Scholarships available for addiction treatment and studies. FUNDING: Nonprofit. OFC HRS: M-F 11am-8pm; Sat 12noon-8pm; Sun 12noon-6pm. ADM REQ: Open to students, academics, professionals and the general public. SERVES: So. Calif & Nevada.

FREE INDEED CHRISTIAN FELLOWSHIP

430 South D Street
Perris, CA 92570
(951) 657-2449

(951) 657-2229 FAX

A variety of prgms and activities offered. The ranch helps addicts to find sobriety with the aid of worship. Other prgms include: Soul Patrol Outreach, discipleship, homeless shelter, food ministries, motorcycle ministries, etc. Call Patrick Smith for appt. Men's ranch (951) 943-5159. FUNDING: Nonprofit. OFC HRS: M-F 9am-5pm. SERVES: Perris & Riverside areas.

FRIDAY NIGHT LIVE/ADMIN

Calif Friday Night Live Partnership
P.O. Box 5091
2637 W. Burrel Ave.
Visalia, CA 93278
(559) 733-6496
(559) 737-4231 FAX

This is the admin office that provides tech assist & training for the Friday Night Live prgms in Calif. Most chapters are in public schools but some are affiliated with community groups or faith-based prgms. Also directly responsible for "Teenwork" and "Calif Youth Council." FUNDING: State, govt. OFC HRS: M-F 8am-5pm. Spanish spoken. SERVES: Calif.

FRIDAY NIGHT LIVE/RIVERSIDE CO.

3525 Presley Ave.
Riverside, CA 92507
(951) 782-5004
(951) 682-3576 FAX

Community-based prgms to prevent or reduce alcohol, tobacco and other drug use among youth. FNL is for high school students and Club Live (CL) for junior high students, FNL Kids for grades 4-5. Youth join a chapter at school or community ctr & plan drug-free, fun activities. Prevention prgm has community srv projects, assemblies, etc. FUNDING: Grants, govt, nonprofit. OFC HRS: M-F 8am-5pm. SERVES: Riverside County.

FRIDAY NIGHT LIVE/SAN BERNARDINO CO.

351 N. Mountain View Ave., Rm. 305
San Bernardino, CA 92415-0010
(800) 387-6623
(909) 387-6348 FAX

Friday Night Live/Club Live is a peer prgm designed to prevent alcohol, tobacco and other drug use among teenagers. FUNDING: Govt. OFC HRS: M-F 8am-5pm. Spanish spoken. SERVES: San Bernardino County.

FRIENDSHIP HOUSE ASSN/AMER INDIANS

Friendship House Amer Indian Lodge
56 Julian Ave.
San Francisco, CA 94103
(415) 865-0964
(415) 865-5428 FAX

Residential drug & alcohol treatment prgm. AA meetings, parenting classes. CARF accredited. State ID: 380004BN. FUNDING: Nonprofit. OFC HRS: M-F 9am-4pm. ADM REQ: Ages 18 yrs+, min stay 90 days. SERVES: U.S.A.

GAM-ANON INTERNATL

P.O. Box 157
Whitestone, NY 11357
(718) 352-1671
(718) 746-2571 FAX

12-Step self-help prgm for those affected by the gambling problem of a loved one. Meetings & local hotline numbers listed online at

(www.gam-anon.org) for all of U.S.A. Spanish & French literature available. FUNDING: Member contributions. Spanish meetings available in L.A. area. SERVES: U.S.A. & internatl.

GOT RECOVERY, INC.

Sober Living Homes
3475 Mulberry St.
Riverside, CA 92501
(951) 328-8778
(951) 328-8787 FAX

Faith-based homes for men and women. Info and referral srvs. No min stay. FUNDING: Nonprofit. OFC HRS: M-Sat 8am-5pm; 24-hr voicemail. ADM REQ: Ages 18 yrs+. Clean and sober 7 days. SERVES: Riverside.

HACIENDA CHRISTIAN LIFE CAMPUS

God's Helping Hand
1040 Tepee Lane
Perris, CA 92570
(951) 657-3041
(951) 657-0426 FAX

Christian residential substance abuse prgm. Men's discipleship prgm for drug addicts, alcoholics & homeless men coming out of prison. Vocational training, anger mgmt, domestic violence counseling. FUNDING: Nonprofit. OFC HRS: M-F 9am-5pm. ADM REQ: One year prgm. Phone for intake interview. Cannot have been convicted with sex crime or arson. Cannot be on any psych medication. Non-smoking facility. Free srvs. SERVES: Riverside County.

HACIENDA VALDEZ

The Ranch Recovery Centers, Inc.
12890 Quinta Way
Desert Hot Springs, CA 92240

Residential drug & alcohol treatment prgm. Sober living home, AA meetings, detox prgm, parenting classes, dual-diagnosis, counseling. State ID: 330003BN. For Men's Treatment Services, call (800) 955-2924. For Women's Treatment Services, call (800) 446-2959. FUNDING: Nonprofit. OFC HRS: 24 hrs, 7 days. ADM REQ: Women and men ages 18 yrs+, min stay 60 days. SERVES: Riverside County.

HIGH DESERT CENTER

See "High Desert Child/Adol/Fam Srvs"

HIGH DESERT CHILD/ADOL/FAM SRVS

High Desert Center
16248 Victor St.
Victorville 92395
(760) 243-7151
(760) 952-1432 FAX

Alcohol & drug prevention and treatment. Outpatient treatment for ages 12 yrs+. Group classes: anger mgmt, parenting, gang avoidance, shoplifting, smoking cessation. Delayed entry of judgement classes as scheduled. Wait varies. State ID: 360030AN. FUNDING: County, nonprofit. OFC HRS: M-Th 9am-6pm. Spanish spoken. Accepts Medi-Cal. No charge for prevention srvs. Outpatient srvs on a sliding fee scale. SERVES: Victor Valley.

HOUSE OF HOPE/SOROPTIMIST

628 S. 8th Street
Banning, CA 92220
(951) 849-9491
(951) 849-8262 FAX

5-bed residential drug & alcohol treatment prgm. AA meetings, parenting classes, domestic violence prev edu, re-entry prgm. State ID:

330016BN. FUNDING: County, nonprofit. OFC HRS: M-Sun 8am-7pm. Spanish spoken. ADM REQ: Women ages 18 yrs+. Accepts pvt pay. SERVES: Riverside County.

HOUSE OF HOPE/SOROPTIMIST

13525 Cielo Azul Way
Desert Hot Springs, CA 92240
(760) 329-4673
(760) 329-7311 FAX

Residential drug & alcohol treatment prgm. So-ber living home, AA meetings, parenting classes. FUNDING: Nonprofit. OFC HRS: 24 hrs, 7 days. Spanish spoken. ADM REQ: Adult women ages 18 yrs+, min stay 90 days. SERVES: Riverside County.

I AM NEW LIFE RANCH

38400 San Ignacio Rd.
Hemet, CA 92544
(951) 767-2575
(951) 767-0951 FAX

Faith-based residential drug & alcohol treat-ment prgm, 12-Step, group meetings, treatment planning, exit planning, anger mgmt, counsel-ing, parenting, family sessions. Sober living, transitional housing, and outpatient prgms also available. State ID: 330024AN. FUNDING: Nonprofit. OFC HRS: 24-hr srvs. ADM REQ: Men ages 18 yrs+, min stay 90 days for residen-tial. SERVES: Riverside County.

IDEAL CARE & HEALTH SRVS, INC.

1920-A N. Garey Ave.
Pomona, CA 91767
(909) 865-0191
(909) 865-0193 FAX

Offers outpatient substance abuse treatment for men, women, and children ages 10-21 yrs. Srvs include: intake, assessment, diagnosis, eval, individual & group counseling, HIV/AIDS edu and preventon, UA testing, behavior modi-fication and more. Admission and assessment available by appt. FUNDING: Nonprofit. OFC HRS: M-F 10am-7pm. Accepts Medi-Cal. Slid-ing fee scale. SERVES: Pomona Valley, L.A. County, Riverside County, San Bernardino County.

IMPACT DRUG/ALCOHOL TREATMNT CTR

1680 N. Fair Oaks Ave.
Pasadena, CA 91103
(626) 798-0884
(626) 798-6970 FAX

Recovery home for substance abuse clients. Outpatient aftercare prgm for clients who have been through residential prgm. Four to six month residential treatment ctr based on 12-Step prgm. Co-ed prgm with 130 beds. Of-fers 30, 60, 90, 120 day prgms. NA meetings, parenting classes, prevention & edu, day treat-ment, info & referral. Residential State ID: 190091AN. FUNDING: Nonprofit. OFC HRS: M-F 8am-4:30pm. Spanish spoken at outpa-tient srvs. ADM REQ: Ages 18 yrs+. Phone re-ferral needed. Sliding fee scale. SERVES: So. Calif.

INLAND BEHAV & HEALTH SERVICES

Westside Counseling Ctr
1963 North E Street
San Bernardino, CA 92405
(909) 881-6146
(909) 881-0111 FAX

Comprehensive health care, substance abuse, mental health and homeless support srvs. Of-fers crisis intervention, primary prevention edu, PC-1000 classes, anger mgmt, parenting STEP classes. Perinatal prgm for expectant and parenting mothers who are addicted to drugs with both pre- and post-natal srvs. Provides transportation as well as child care. State ID: 360015AN. FUNDING: Govt, contracts, grants, nonprofit. OFC HRS: M-Th 8am-6pm; F 8am-5pm. Spanish spoken. ADM REQ: Ages 13 yrs+, referrals & walk in. Accepts Medicare, Medi-Cal. SERVES: San Bernardino County.

INLAND VLY DRUG/ALCOHOL RECOVERY

Administration/Residential
916 N. Mountain Ave., Ste A
Upland, CA 91786
(909) 932-1069
(909) 932-1087 FAX

Residential substance abuse treatment for sin-gle or parenting adults. Outpatient and court-re-ferred DUI, anger mgmt srvs, domestic violence batterer's treatment, parent project classes. Sub-acute detox prgm also available. State ID: 360001BN. FUNDING: CalWORKs, CPS, PSN, SASCA, county, resident fees, nonprofit. OFC HRS: M-F 8am-5pm; 24-hr facility. Spanish spoken. Accepts most insurance and pvt pay. Sliding fee scale. SERVES: L.A., Riverside & San Bernardino Counties.

INLAND VLY DRUG/ALCOHOL RECOVERY

Adolescent Srvs
934 N. Mountain Ave.
Upland, CA 91786
(909) 949-4667
(909) 931-3774 FAX

Outpatient drug and alcohol prgm, anger mgmt, truancy, shoplifting, family component srvs. Also offers domestic violence assist, anger mgmt, parenting edu, and smoking cessation classes for adults. Outpatient counseling srvs for adults, couples, and families. FUNDING: Nonprofit, Calif Dept of Probation. OFC HRS: M-F 8am-5pm; 24-hr facility. SERVES: L.A., Riverside & San Bernardino Counties.

INSIGHT COUNSELING

23232 Peralta Dr., Ste 211
Laguna Hills, CA 92653
(949) 707-5100
(949) 488-2418 FAX

Comprehensive individual, family, couples and group therapy. Edu classes in anger mgmt and parenting. Therapists specialize in: drug/alco-hol treatment; interventions; eating disorders; anxiety; panic attacks; depression; teen, family and couples issues. FUNDING: Nonprofit. OFC HRS: M-Th 9am-9pm; F 7am-9pm; Sat 9am-1pm. Spanish spoken. Accessible and af-fordable srvs. SERVES: Orange, Riverside & San Bernardino Counties.

KAISER PERMANENTE/CHEMICAL DEP

Chemical Dependency Recovery
17046 Marygold Ave.
Fontana, CA 92335
(909) 427-5128
(909) 427-6268 FAX

20-bed, inpatient chemical dependency recovery unit treats adult patients undergoing minor chemical dependency withdrawal. A team of physicians, trained chemical depend-ency nurses, and counselors provide edu and medical eval to the patient. The outpatient srvs provide a medically based treatment prgm which includes: day treatment, individual, group, family counseling & medical eval. FUNDING: Nonprofit. OFC HRS: 24 hrs, 7 days for phone only. Triage/visit: 8am-6pm.. Sat, Sun 8am-3pm. Spanish spoken. ADM REQ: Ages, 18 yrs+, KP Health Plan. Adolescents referred out. SERVES: San Bernardino County.

LA VISTA ALCOHOL/DRUG RECOVERY CTR

P.O. Box 1411
2220 Girard St.
San Jacinto, CA 92583
(877) 316-9477
(951) 925-8450
(951) 658-6686 FAX

6-bed residential drug & alcohol treatment prgm, AA meetings, non-medical detox prgm, parenting classes, info & referral, prevention & edu, counseling, NA meetings. 3-4 month wait list. State ID: 330002BN. FUNDING: County, nonprofit. OFC HRS: 24 hrs, 7 days. Spanish spoken. ADM REQ: Women ages 18 yrs+, sug-gested stay is 90 days. SERVES: Riverside County.

LA VISTA WOMEN'S RECOVERY HOME & WHOLENESS CENTER

P.O. Box 1411
2220 Girard St.
San Jacinto, CA 92583
(951) 925-8450
(951) 658-6686 FAX

30-bed residential, social model, non-medical detox, recovery & perinatal 90-day prgm. Perinatal srvs with separate house for pregnant women. Mother's House, a separate recovery home for senior women includes: social, non-medical detox srvs; 24-hr live-in recovery srvs; AA meetings; self-help peer group rap sessions and recreational events. Alcoholism edu, info & referral. Senior & environmental pre-vention prgms free to community. State ID: 330002AN. FUNDING: Fees, donations, United Way, nonprofit. OFC HRS: M-F 8am-5pm. 24-hr srvs. Spanish spoken. ADM REQ: Fe-males ages 18 yrs+, meets ADA requirements. SERVES: So. Calif.

LOMA LINDA UNIV/MARRIAGE/FAMILY

Marriage & Family Therapy Clinic
1686 Barton Rd.
Redlands, CA 92373
(909) 558-4934
(909) 558-0334 FAX

Individual, group, marriage, family, child & adol counseling. Srvs for child abuse prevention, grief counseling, domestic violence, chemical addiction and other issues. FUNDING: Non-profit. OFC HRS: Sun 9am-5pm; M-Th 9am-8pm; F 9am-2:30pm. Spanish spoken. Sliding fee scale starts at $25 per session. Medi-Cal not accepted. Will not bill insurance. SERVES: San Bernardino, Riverside Counties.

LOMA LINDA UNIV BEHAV MED CTR

(See Display Ad on Page 101)
Chemical Dependency
1710 Barton Rd.
Redlands, CA 92373
(800)752-5999
(909) 558-9224
(909)558-9201 FAX

Specializes in the care of individuals addicted to chronic pain prescription medication. Our multidisciplinary treatment team provides holistic care on multiple levels. FUNDING: Private, nonprofit. OFC HRS: M-F 9am-6pm. ADM REQ: Ages 18 yrs+. Accepts Medicare, pvt insurance, pvt pay. SERVES: Inland Empire.

LORD OF LIFE LUTHERAN CHURCH
P.O. Box 53
13600 Nason St.
Moreno Valley, CA 92556
(951) 924-4887
(951) 247-1938 FAX

Al-Anon meetings. Call for days & times. FUNDING: Nonprofit. OFC HRS: M, T, Th 8:30am - 5pm; F, 8:30am-12:30pm. Korean spoken. SERVES: Moreno Valley, Nuevo, Lake View, Perris, Loma Linda, Beaumont, Redlands.

M.A.D.D.

See "Mothers Against Drunk Driving"

MATRIX INSTITUTE ON ADDICTIONS
1849 Sawtelle Blvd., Ste 100
Los Angeles, CA 90025
(310) 478-8305
(310) 478-8639 FAX

Evidence-based adult and adolescent outpatient treatment for chemical dependence and co-occurring disorders. Free evalutation and referrals. Treatment is structured, intensive and cognitive-behaviorally based. Day and evening groups and individual sessions available. Clinics located in Los Angeles and San Bernardino Counties. FUNDING: Insurance, private pay, nonprofit. County funding for adolescents. OFC HRS: M-F 9am-9pm. SERVES: L.A. and San Bernardino Counties.

MATRIX INSTITUTE ON ADDICTIONS
11777 Sebastian Way, Ste 102 A-B
Rancho Cucamonga, CA 91730
(909) 989-9724
(909) 989-0249 FAX

Intensive outpatient substance abuse/co-occurring treatment offered to adults and adolescents. FUNDING: County, Prop 36, parole, DCS, CalWORKs, drug court, nonprofit, private/county (adolescent) prgm. OFC HRS: M-F 5am-9pm. Translator provided for other languages. Accepts Medi-Cal, insurance, pvt pay, county funding for low-income adolescents. SERVES: Los Angeles, San Bernardino Counties.

MAVERICK HOUSE FOUNDATION INC.
216 S. Citrus St., Ste 225
West Covina, CA 91791
(626) 841-8259
(626) 339-7051 FAX

Transitional living prgm provides low-cost sober living for men, women and women with children. Must work 12-Step prgm. Public transportation accessible. FUNDING: Nonprofit. OFC HRS: M-Sun 8am-8pm. Spanish & Japanese spoken. ADM REQ: Adults ages 18 yrs+. Accepts SSI, SDI, CalWORKS and self-pay. SERVES: L.A. & San Bernardino Counties.

MENTAL HEALTH SYSTEMS, INC.
Central Vly Regional Recovery Ctr
1076 Santo Antonio Dr., Ste B
Colton, CA 92324
(909) 433-9824
(909) 433-9830 FAX

Outpatient drug and alcohol treatment prgm, NA meetings, anger mgmt, parenting classes, dual-diagnosis. Substance abuse classes in English & Spanish. Call for appt. State ID: 360033HN. FUNDING: Nonprofit. OFC HRS: M-F 8am-9pm; Sat 8am-5pm. Spanish spoken. Sliding fee scale. SERVES: San Bernardino County.

MENTAL HEALTH SYSTEMS, INC.
Redlands Center for Change
802 W. Colton Ave., Ste C
Redlands, CA 92374
(909) 335-2989
(909) 335-1701 FAX

Court-supervised, comprehensive outpatient substance abuse treatment prgm for non-violent defendants. Voluntary prgm with drug testing, individual and group counseling, and regular attendance at 12-Step meetings. 18-month prgm. State ID: 360033DN. FUNDING: Nonprofit. OFC HRS: M-F 10am-7pm. ADM REQ: Court-ordered males and females ages 18 yrs+. SERVES: Redlands, Yucaipa & nearby.

MENTAL HEALTH SYSTEMS, INC.
Pride Program
1874 Business Center Dr., Ste B
San Bernardino, CA 92408
(909) 386-0437
(909) 386-0529 FAX

Intensive court-ordered outpatient drug & alcohol treatment prgm. Info & referral, prevention & edu, HIV testing, counseling. State ID: 360033AN. FUNDING: Nonprofit. OFC HRS: M-Th 9:30am-7pm; F 7am-3:30pm. ADM REQ: Ages 18 yrs+. Must be court-referred. Min stay 18 mos. SERVES: San Bernardino County.

Drug/Alcohol/Tobacco/Addictions

METH RESOURCES
www.methresources.gov
(916) 324-5523
Visit website to find various resources and prgms in the fight against meth. FUNDING: Govt. SERVES: U.S.A.

MICHAEL'S HOUSE
The Treatment Center for Men
430 S. Cahuilla Rd.
Palm Springs, CA 92262
(760) 320-5486
(877) 345-8494
(760) 778-6020 FAX
24-bed intensive residential treatment center for chemically dependent men, some with a dual-diagnosis. CARF accredited. State ID: 330014AN. FUNDING: Client fees, insurance. OFC HRS: M-F 8am-5pm; 24-hr srvs. ADM REQ: Men ages 18 yrs+, min stay 60 days. Set fees. SERVES: U.S.A.

MORONGO BASIN COUNSELING & RECOVERY SERVICES
55475 Santa Fe Trail
Yucca Valley, CA 92284
(760) 365-3022
(760) 365-3513 FAX
Services in mental health, substance abuse recovery & treatment. Individual & group therapy for children & adults. School counseling available. Specialized prgms for DUI court referrals, Welfare-to-Work transition prgms. Inpatient & outpatient drug & alcohol counseling prgm. FUNDING: Nonprofit. OFC HRS: M-F 8am-5pm. Crisis walk-in clinic 24 hrs, 7 days. Spanish spoken. ADM REQ: Ages 18 yrs+. Children with legal guardian/parent. SERVES: Morongo Basin, San Bernardino County.

MOTHERS AGAINST DRUNK DRIVERS
77-760 Country Club #I
Palm Desert, CA 92211
(760) 772-6237
(760) 772-0710 FAX
Awareness of drunk driving issues and underage drinking through presentations, literature, media campaigns & youth prgms. Offers statistics, publishes a quarterly newsletter, support groups for survivors and victims families. FUNDING: Nonprofit. OFC HRS: M-F 8am-4pm. Victim srvs 24 hrs. SERVES: Riverside County.

MOTHERS AGAINST DRUNK DRIVING
California State Office
4629 Whitney Ave., Ste 7
Sacramento, CA 95821
(916) 481-6233
(800) 426-6233
(916) 485-9623 FAX
MADD is a volunteer-based natl nonprofit organization. Membership is free and open to all who claim solidarity with the MADD mission to stop drunk driving. Supports the victims of this violent crime and prevents underage drinking. Members & volunteers work collectively to enact mission through edu, public awareness, legislative action & victim advocacy. FUNDING: Donations, nonprofit. OFC HRS: M-F 9am-5pm. Spanish spoken. Free srvs. SERVES: Calif.

MOTHERS AGAINST DRUNK DRIVING
242 Airport Dr., Ste 200
San Bernardino, CA 92408
(909) 888-6233
(909) 885-1503 FAX
MADD is a natl organization that helps victims of drunk or drugged drivers and promotes legislation that will help victims of traffic crashes related to alcohol and drugs. Provides victim support srvs & advocacy, active in building public awareness of substance abuse & its cost to society. 24-hr grief counselors at (877) MADD-HELP. FUNDING: Nonprofit. OFC HRS: M, W, F 8:30am-4pm. SERVES: San Bernardino County.

NAADAC (ASSN FOR ADDICTION PROF)
1001 N. Fairfax St., Ste 101
Alexandria, VA 22314
(800) 548-0497
(800) 377-1136 FAX
NAADAC is the largest natl organization for addiction-focused health care professionals. Dev workshops, conferences & publications that include Addiction Professional Magazine, NAADAC newsletter, natl edu directory. Insurance-approved edu provider prgm, natl certification and advocacy efforts. Committed to increasing general awareness of alcohol & drug disorders and enhancing care of individuals through advocacy, edu and prevention prgms. CAADAC continuing edu provider. Call for more info. FUNDING: Member dues, revenue prgms, nonprofit. OFC HRS: M-F 9am-5pm, EST. SERVES: U.S.A.

NAR-ANON/FAMILY/HEADQUARTERS
22527 Crenshaw Blvd., Ste 200-B
Torrance, CA 90505
(310) 534-8188
(800) 477-6291
World srv office serves families and friends of drug addicts. Info & referral to self-help groups in local communities (12-Step support group for family and friends of drug abusers, similar to Al-Anon). Call for list of weekly meeting locations. 24-hr answering machine, calls returned. Addtl Southern CA info at (888)297-9560. Addtl helplines (714)647-7725 and (858)492-8720. FUNDING: Nonprofit. OFC HRS: M-Th 9am-5pm. Spanish spoken. SERVES: Internatl.

NARCONON INTERNATIONAL
Drug Prev, Edu & Rehab Srvs
4652 Hollywood Blvd.
Los Angeles, CA 90027
(323) 962-2404
(323) 962-6872 FAX
The aim of this prgm is to help the drug abuser become drug free. Prevention and edu to youth and adults. Parent center provides edu info, videos & booklets. FUNDING: Nonprofit. OFC HRS: M-F 9am-6pm. Spanish, Italian, French, Filipino & Armenian spoken SERVES: Internatl.

NARCONON SAN DIEGO COUNTY
35025 Highway 79
Warner Springs, CA 92086
(760) 782-0471
(800) 871-4350
(760) 782-0695 FAX
42-bed residential alcohol & drug treatment prgm. State ID: 370087AN. FUNDING: Nonprofit. OFC HRS: 24 hrs, 7 days. Spanish spoken. ADM REQ: Ages 18 yrs+. Min stay is 3 months. SERVES: U.S.A.

NARCONON SOUTHERN CALIF
1810 W. Ocean Front
Newport Beach, CA 92663
(949) 675-8988
(800) 405-8409
(949) 675-8991 FAX
32-bed residential facility located in Newport. One-time flat-fee for the prgm, regardless of how long the individual needs the srv. State ID: 300077AN. FUNDING: Nonprofit. OFC HRS: 24 hrs, 7 days. Spanish spoken. ADM REQ: Ages 18 yrs+, min stay 90 days. SERVES: U.S.A.

NARCOTIC EDU FNDN OF AMERICA
28245 Crocker Ave., Ste 230
Santa Clarita, CA 91355-1201
(661) 775-6960
(877) 775-6272
(661) 775-1648 FAX
Conducts an edu prgm revealing the dangers that result from the illicit and abusive use of narcotics and dangerous drugs so that youth and adults will be protected from both mental and physical drug dependency and harm. Prints and distributes an array of drug edu warning materials. Single copies of our various drug edu warning materials are free. A stamped, self-addressed envelope is appreciated. FUNDING: Donations, nonprofit. OFC HRS: Tu-Th 10am-5pm. SERVES: U.S.A.

NARCOTICS ANONYMOUS
So Calif Regional Serv Office, Inc.
1937 S. Myrtle Ave.
Monrovia, CA 91016
(626) 359-0084
(626) 305-0354 FAX
12-Step prgm referral to mutual NA groups. Regional helpline (800) TODAYNA. Spanish regional helpline (888) NAAHORA. FUNDING: Nonprofit. OFC HRS: Tu-F 2pm-7pm; Sat 9am-4pm. SERVES: So. Calif.

NARCOTICS ANONYMOUS
Eastern Inland Empire Area
1937 S. Myrtle Ave.
Monrovia, CA 91016
(626) 359-0084
(626) 305-0354 FAX
12-Step, self-help prgm for those recovering from the disease of addiction. Referral to associated self-help meetings in eastern Inland Empire area. Helpline 24 hrs: (800) 397-2333 or (909) 370-3568 Spanish info on request. For Spanish, call (888) NA-AHORA. FUNDING: Nonprofit. OFC HRS: Tu, Th 2pm-7pm; W 2pm-8pm; F 2pm-6pm; Sat 9am-3pm. Spanish spoken. Free srvs. SERVES: San Bernardino, Highland, Loma Linda, Colton, Rialto, Bloomington, Fontana, Riverside, Moreno Vly, Perris, Rubidoux, Muscoy, Corona & Norco.

NARCOTICS ANONYMOUS
Inland Empire West Region
P.O. Box 9413
Ontario, CA 91762
(909) 622-4274
Self-help prgm with various meetings throughout the area. Helpline 24 hrs. FUNDING: Nonprofit. Spanish available upon request. Free srvs. SERVES: Pomona, Upland, Ontario, Chino, Claremont, Montclair, Rancho, La Verne, Chino Hills.

NARCOTICS ANONYMOUS
World Service Office
P.O. Box 9999

Van Nuys, CA 91409-9999
(818) 773-9999
(818) 700-0700 FAX

Internatl community organization of recovering addicts who meet regularly to help each other recover from the disease of addiction. FUNDING: Literature sales, nonprofit. OFC HRS: M-F 9am-5pm. Spanish, German & French spoken. Free srvs. Some publications available for a fee. SERVES: U.S.A. & internatl.

NATL ASSN FOR SHOPLIFTING PREVENTION
380 N. Broadway, Ste 306
Jericho, NY 11753
(800) 848-9595
(516) 932-0165
(516) 932-9393 FAX

Adult & juvenile home study & class prgms, self-help groups, info & referral to counseling for individuals with shoplifting problems. FUNDING: Client fees, nonprofit. OFC HRS: M-F 9am-5pm, EST. Spanish spoken. Some set fees, sliding fee scale. SERVES: U.S.A.

NATL ASSN/CHILDREN/ALCOHOLICS
11426 Rockville Pike, Ste 301
Rockville, MD 20852
(888) 554-2627
(301) 468-0985
(301) 468-0987 FAX

NACOA advocates for children & families affected by alcoholism & other drug dependencies. Edu materials, videos, publications & training. Info provided upon request. FUNDING: Grants, membership, nonprofit. OFC HRS: M-F 8:30am-5pm, EST. Free srvs. SERVES: U.S.A.

NATL CENTER FOR SUBSTANCE ABUSE
Treatment Referral Srvs
P.O. Box 2345
Rockville, MD 20847
(800) 662-4357
(301) 468-6433 FAX

Info & referral to support groups and/or treatment for all types of drug and alcohol abuse. Free 24-hr hotline. FUNDING: Govt. Spanish spoken.

NATL CLEARINGHOUSE/ALCOHOL/DRUG
U.S. Department of Health Srvs
P.O. Box 2345
Rockville, MD 20847
(800) 729-6686
(301) 468-6433 FAX

Natl substance abuse treatment center provides more than 10,000 printed items for drug & alcohol prevention & drug-free workplace. Also some workplace videotapes (employer & employee versions) and info on govt prgms. Also conducts database searches on alcohol & drug related topics. Catalog lists hundreds of free publications for consumers & educators. Prgms include: Girl Power and Race Against Drugs Reality Check. For TDD, call (800) 487-4889. No referrals to treatment, only prevention prgms & materials. FUNDING: Govt. OFC HRS: 24 hrs, 7 days. Spanish spoken. Free srvs. SERVES: U.S.A.

NATL COUNCIL ON ALCOHOL/DRUG DEP
Hopeline
244 E. 58th Street, 4th Fl.
New York, NY 10022
(800) 622-2255

(212) 269-7797
(212) 269-7510 FAX

Referrals to offices throughout the U.S. Recorded message asks for the zip code and then provides the phone number for the location which serves that area. Written material on adol or adult drug and alcohol addiction issues. FUNDING: Nonprofit. OFC HRS: 24 hrs, 7 days. SERVES: U.S.A.

NATL COUNCIL ON ALCOHOL/DRUG DEP
Santa Ana DDP
1631 N. Bristol St., Ste 300
Santa Ana, CA 92706
(714) 835-4252
(714) 560-1680 FAX

Info & referral, prevention & edu. DUI 1st offender & 2nd offender (18-month) prgms. Maintains an alcoholism and drug addiction info center for Asian community. Counsels individuals and family members seeking assist for alcoholism & other drug abuse problems. Counseling to the point of referral is free. DUI prgms include first offender level 1 (3-month), level II varies from 6-12 mos. FUNDING: United Way, fees, donations, nonprofit. OFC HRS: M-F 9am-5pm; Sat 9am-12noon. Spanish, Korean, Japanese, Vietnamese & Chinese spoken. ADM REQ: Ages 18 yrs+. Fees vary. SERVES: So. Calif.

NATL CRIMINAL JUSTICE REFERENCE
P.O. Box 6000
Rockville, MD 20849-6000
(800) 851-3420
(301) 519-5212 FAX

Six basic functions of this srv: (1) National Victims Resource Center Library, database srv and free publications; (2) Juvenile Justice Clearinghouse; info on gang prevention and intervention. Printed material explains the Juvenile Justice System; (3) Bureau of Justice Assist (grants, training & tech assist, etc.); (4) Bureau of Justice Statistics (criminal statistics nationwide); (5) National Institute of Justice (research on criminal behavior); and (6) Office of National Drug Control Policy. Additional Info and ordering online at (www.ncjrs.gov). TDD (877) 712-9279. FUNDING: Govt. OFC HRS: M-F 10am-6pm, EST. Free publications, though shipping and handling applies. Rates found online. SERVES: U.S.A.

NATL FAMILY PARTNERSHIP (NFP)
Informed Families Edu Center
2490 Coral Way, Ste 501
Miami, FL 33145
(305) 856-4886
(800) 705-8997
(305) 856-4815 FAX

Natl resource for drug prevention for parents, state & local partners. Advocates for drug awareness & prevention. Info, materials, tech assist, and networking opportunities. Annual Red Ribbon celebration campaign. FUNDING: Donations, nonprofit. OFC HRS: M-F 9am-5:30pm, EST. Spanish spoken. SERVES: U.S.A.

NATL INHALANT PREVENTION COALITION
2904 Kerbey Ln.
Austin, TX 78703
(800) 269-4237
(512) 480-8953

(512) 477-3932 FAX

Referrals & info regarding inhalant abuse. Provides awareness, edu, training & technical assist to state agencies, schools, businesses, media, law enforcement, poison control centers, etc. Visit (www.inhalants.org). FUNDING: Private, nonprofit, donations, govt. SERVES: U.S.A.

NATL NETWORK FOR YOUTH
P.O. Box 66492
Washington, DC 20036
(202) 783-7949
(202) 783-7955 FAX

Dedicated to ensuring that young people can be safe and lead healthy, productive lives. Network informs on public policy, educates the public and strengthens the field of youth work. Members provide safety, shelter, counseling, social, health, edu and job related srvs. Promotes positive dev of youth through community srv, peer edu, alcohol and drug free clubs, drama groups, etc. Emphasizes youth and adults working together. Networks with regional, state, community-based agencies and individuals. FUNDING: Members, fndn, donations, nonprofit, govt. OFC HRS: M-F 9am-5pm, EST. Spanish spoken. Free srvs. SERVES: U.S.A.

NATL SUBSTANCE ABUSE PROFESSIONALS NETWORK
1481 Ford St., Ste 202
Redlands, CA 92373
(800) 879-6428
(909) 307-3246 FAX

Network organization set up to resolve DOT or non-DOT (Dept of Transportation) compliance issues when an employee tests positive for drugs and/or alcohol. Coordinates all aspects of compliance prgm processes, determines need for edu and/or treatment. FUNDING: Nonprofit. OFC HRS: M-F 6:30am-5pm. Spanish spoken. SERVES: So. Calif.

NAVAL HOSPITAL CAMP PENDLETON
Substance Abuse Rehab Program
P.O. Box 555191
Bldg. H-49 (Code 03A)
Camp Pendleton, CA 92055-5191
(760) 725-0063
(760) 725-1544 FAX

Outpatient & residential drug & alcohol treatment prgm. AA meetings, co-dependency, gambling, sexual addictions, smoking & nicotine srvs, info & referral, dual-diagnosis (including PTSD), counseling. Patient srvs center (760) 725-4357. FUNDING: Fed, govt. OFC HRS: M-F 6am-5pm. Spanish spoken. ADM REQ: Ages 18 yrs+, min stay 21 days, max stay 42 days, active military, retired or family of military. SERVES: U.S.A. & internatl.

NCADD/NATL CNCL ALC/DRUG DEP
See "Natl Council on Alcohol/Drug Dep"

NEW HOUSE INC.
2075 N. Arrowhead Ave.
San Bernardino, CA 92401
(909) 881-0390
(909) 881-0391 FAX

Residential drug & alcohol treatment for adults with up to 2 children. AA/NA meetings, parenting groups, multi-family group, couples counseling. Anger mgmt, price parenting. FUNDING: Mental Health Systems, county, pvt pay. OFC HRS: M-F 8am-5pm, 24-hr srvs.

Spanish spoken. ADM REQ: Ages 18 yrs+, min stay 3 mos. SERVES: San Bernardino County.

NEW WINE CHURCH RETREAT, INC.
10970 Kendall Rd.
Lucerne Valley, CA 92356
(760) 248-7315

Residential alcohol and drug prgm, counseling & support groups for men only, ages 18 yrs+. FUNDING: Nonprofit. OFC HRS: 24 hrs, 7 days. ADM REQ: Desire to use love & the word of God to heal themselves. SERVES: San Bernardino County.

NICOTINE ANONYMOUS/SO CALIF
(800) 642-0666

24-hr message refers caller to mutual self-help groups for smokers. Based on 12-Step prgm. FUNDING: Nonprofit. SERVES: So. Calif.

NICOTINE ANONYMOUS/WORLD SRVS
419 Main St., PMB 370
Huntington Beach, CA 92648
(415) 750-0328
(714) 969-4493 FAX

12-Step fellowship of men & women recovering from all forms of nicotine addiction. FUNDING: Nonprofit. OFC HRS: 24-hr voicemail. Literature in Spanish, French, Portuguese, Swedish & Dutch. SERVES: U.S.A.

OAK GROVE CENTER
Formerly Oak Grove Institute
24275 Jefferson Ave.
Murrieta, CA 92562
(951) 677-5599
(951) 698-0461 FAX

Residential treatment for children and adol, ages 8-18 yrs experiencing social, emotional and behavioral disorders, neurological problems, chronic medical problems with concurrent behavioral difficulties, school problems, family dysfunction and secondary alcohol or substance abuse. Partial hospitalization & day treatment. Non-public school on grounds. Also offers an autism center for children with mild to severe autism. FUNDING: Dept of Children's Srvs, school districts, Regional Ctr, nonprofit. OFC HRS: M-F 8am-5pm. ADM REQ: Clinically appropriate for residential or day treatment & funding available. SERVES: So. Calif.

OBSESSIVE COMPULSIVE ANONYMOUS
P.O. Box 215
New Hyde Park, NY 11040
(516) 739-0662

12-Step fellowship of men & women suffering from obsessive compulsive disorders. Call for meeting times and locations. FUNDING: Nonprofit. Free srvs. SERVES: Internatl.

OUR HOUSE
See "Riverside Recovery Resources"

OVERCOMER'S OUTREACH
12828 Acheson Dr.
Whittier, CA 90601
(800) 310-3001
(562) 698-9000
(562) 698-2211 FAX

Referrals and worldwide Christian 12-Step recovery support groups dealing with addictive or compulsive behaviors for all of the family. FUNDING: Nonprofit. OFC HRS: M-F 9am-4pm. SERVES: U.S.A. & internatl.

PACIFIC CLINICS
Administration
800 S. Santa Anita Ave.
Arcadia, CA 91006
(626) 254-5000
(877) 722-2737

Outpatient mental health srvs to seriously ill children, youth, adults and seniors regardless of ability to pay. Prgms include: day treatment for children & adol, homeless mentally ill outreach, geriatric outreach and Asian-Pacific srvs. Adult clubhouse drop-in prgms at some sites. Multilingual prgms. APA-accredited intern prgm. Most referrals are through county health care agencies. For child & adol srvs, call (626) 441-4221. Also outpatient & residential alcohol & drug treatment prgm at various sites. Locations in L.A., Orange, Riverside, San Bernardino and Ventura countries. State ID: 190254EN. FUNDING: County, state, United Way, donations, nonprofit. OFC HRS: M-F 8am-5pm. Multiple languages spoken. Accepts Medi-Cal SERVES: L.A., Orange & Riverside Counties.

PANORAMA RECOVERY RANCH
P.O. Box 335
65675 Sullivan Rd.
Joshua Tree, CA 92252
(760) 366-9100
(760) 366-3663 FAX

30-bed facility for men and women. 90-day social model residential recovery home. 12-Step alcohol and drug recovery prgm. Anger mgmt, parenting, domestic violence, life skills, relapse prevention, job skills, resume, communications, AA & NA meetings, aftercare, referrals. State ID: 360006AN. FUNDING: County MHS, patient fees, nonprofit. OFC HRS: M-F 7:30am-5pm. Spanish spoken. ADM REQ: Ages 18 yrs+ and problems of alcohol or drugs. Sliding fee scale. SERVES: San Bernardino County.

PATH OF LIFE FAMILY SHELTER
2530 3rd Street
Riverside, CA 92507
(951) 275-8755
(951) 275-8775 FAX

60-day emerg shelter for families. Case mgmt srvs include: info & referral, employment dev, housing placement, mental health, residential srvs, social srvs (re-entrance into society), counseling. Also provides several shelters for single men and women. For those shelters, call intake at (951) 683-4101 or (951) 275-8750. FUNDING: Nonprofit. Spanish spoken. ADM REQ: Must commit to alcohol/drug prgm. SERVES: Riverside County.

PATH OF LIFE MINISTRIES
Men's Recovery Home
P.O. Box 1445
Riverside, CA 92501
(951) 786-9048
(951) 786-9049 FAX

Christian residential prgm addressing the needs of dysfunction, addiction and incarceration by means of a holistic approach to rebuilding lives. Goal is to help individuals identify the root cause of their problem, train in life values, both practically and spiritually and to give necessary tools to obtain and maintain gainful employment. Homeless food prgm and three homeless centers. FUNDING: Donations, nonprofit. OFC HRS: M-F 9am-6pm. Spanish spoken. ADM REQ: One year prgm. SERVES: Riverside County.

PEACE IN THE VALLEY
17487 Arrow Blvd.
Fontana, CA 92335
(909) 355-2008

Christian residential atmosphere. Currently offering classes in PC-1000 drug diversion. Admission procedure consists of an interview with Rehab Director, personal eval, final decision by prgm admin Virginia Valenzuela. FUNDING: Nonprofit. OFC HRS: M-F 8am-3:30pm. ADM REQ: Must schedule appt. SERVES: Inland Empire.

PERRIS VALLEY RECOVERY PRGMS, INC.
236 E. 3rd Street, Ste B
Perris, CA 92570
(951) 657-2960
(951) 940-4600 FAX

Outpatient adol & adult substance abuse treatment, therapeutic, individual, and family counseling. substance abuse edu, anger mgmt, PC-1000, info & referral srvs, parenting edu, psychotherapy, Employee Assist Srvs. FUNDING: Nonprofit. OFC HRS: M-W 8:30am-5pm; Th 10:30am-6pm; F 9am-3pm. Accepts Medi-Cal. Sliding fee scale. SERVES: Riverside County and surrounding areas.

POINT OF GRACE CHRISTIAN FELLOWSHIP
9774 Hawthorne Dr., Ste 901
Rancho Cucamonga, CA 91730
(909) 944-9909
(909) 944-7789 FAX

Community closet, food pantry, learning center, behavioral support groups such as Celebrate Recovery & divorce care ministries (based on demand), anger mgmt for kids & teens, Steps to Hope. FUNDING: Nonprofit, donations. OFC HRS: Tu-Th 12noon-4pm. SERVES: San Bernardino County.

POISON INFORMATION
See "Calif Poison Control System"

POMONA COMMUNITY CRISIS CTR
Drug Diversion & Outpatient Group
240 Monterey Ave.
Pomona, CA 91767
(909) 623-1588
(909) 629-2470 FAX

PC-1000 drug diversion prgm for 1st time court-ordered, drug-related arrests. Classes for 20 weeks. Outpatient drug free group counseling, domestic violence classes, weekly individual & group counseling for six months-one year. State ID: 190281AN. FUNDING: L.A. County, donations, nonprofit. OFC HRS: M-Th 9am-6pm; F 8:30am-12:30pm; Sat 8am-12noon. Spanish spoken. ADM REQ: Ages 18 yrs+. Course: $30 to enroll, $25 per class. Fees are broken into easy weekly payments. Free counseling for GR and CalWORKs recipients. SERVES: L.A. & San Bernardino Counties.

PROJECT CUDDLE, INC.
2973 Harbor Blvd., Ste 326
Costa Mesa, CA 92626
(888) 628-3353
(714) 432-9681
(714) 433-6815 FAX

24-hr, toll-free hotline for pregnant women or women contemplating abandoning their children. Support & edu for those caring for drug-exposed babies and children. Training for birth parents and caregivers. Speakers and lectures for teens on drugs during pregnancy. FUNDING: Donations, grants, nonprofit. OFC HRS: M-F 9am-4pm. Spanish spoken. Free srvs. SERVES: U.S.A.

PROVISIONAL EDUCATIONAL SRVS
P.O. Box 7100
2450 Blake St.
San Bernardino, CA 92407
(909) 887-7002
(909) 887-8942 FAX

High school diploma & GED prep classes, Earn & Learn prgm, Upward Bound prgm, summer youth prgms & child care facility. FUNDING: Grants, donations, nonprofit. OFC HRS: M-F 8am-4:30pm. Spanish spoken. SERVES: San Bernardino County.

R.A.P. COMMUNITY RECOVERY SRVS
17205 Arrow Blvd.
Fontana, CA 92335
(909) 350-0278
(909) 356-9390
(909) 356-0120 FAX

DUI, petty theft, and anger mgmt for youth. State ID: 360051AN. FUNDING: Nonprofit. OFC HRS: M-F 8am-4:30pm. Spanish spoken. ADM REQ: Ages 10 yrs+. Sliding fee scale. SERVES: San Bernardino County.

RANCHO COMMUNITY CHURCH
31300 Rancho Community Way
Temecula, CA 92592
(951) 303-6789
(951) 303-6066 FAX

Celebrate Recovery meets Th at 6:30pm, including large group worship, lesson time and small groups. Several support groups available. Groups include addiction recovery, grief, chronic pain, divorce/separation relief, and family of those with Alzheimer's. Call for dates and times. Groups open to the public and anyone is welcome at any time during the year. FUNDING: Nonprofit. OFC HRS: M-F 9am-4pm. Spanish spoken. SERVES: Riverside County.

RANCHO PHOENIX
P.O. Box 3868
Hemet, CA 92546
(951) 929-1968
(951) 925-5172 FAX

Residential treatment for dual-diagnosis adults ages 18-65 yrs. Clients attend group therapy every day. FUNDING: County, donations, nonprofit. OFC HRS: 24-hr srvs. Spanish spoken. SERVES: Riverside County.

REACH OUT WEST END
1126 W. Foothill Blvd., Ste 150
Upland, CA 91786-3768
(909) 982-8641
(909) 982-8642 FAX

Science-based drug abuse prevention edu for public schools. Mentoring for at-risk middle school students for pregnancy and drug abuse prevention. PC-1000 drug diversion edu prgm for court-ordered clients. Smoking cessation, parenting classes. FUNDING: County, grants, donations, nonprofit. OFC HRS: M-F 9am-4pm. Spanish spoken. SERVES: West end San Bernardino County.

RIM FAMILY SRVS, INC.
P.O. Box 578
28545 Highway 18
Skyforest, CA 92385
(909) 336-1800
(909) 336-0990 FAX

Individual, group and family counseling, trauma recovery for victims of crime, domestic violence, etc. Community edu prgm. Info & referral; prevention & edu; outpatient counseling; DUI 1st offender & multiple (18-month) prgms; outpatient drug & alcohol treatment prgm. PC-1000, Strengthening Family prgm, mobile resource center, aftercare prgm. State ID: 360036AN. FUNDING: Nonprofit. OFC HRS: M-Th 8am-6pm; F 8am-5pm; Sat 8am-2pm. Spanish spoken. Interpreter as needed. ADM REQ: Counseling for all ages. DUI for ages 16 yrs+. Accepts Medi-Cal for drug/alcohol, sliding fee scale. SERVES: San Bernardino County.

RIVERSIDE CO. DEPT/MENTAL HEALTH
Substance Abuse Prgm/Blythe
1297 W. Hobson Way
Blythe, CA 92225-1423
(760) 921-5000
(760) 921-5002 FAX

Info & referral, prevention & edu, outpatient counseling, co-occurring, community drop-in ctr. Prgms for youth, men, women, transgendered. State ID: 330023FN. FUNDING: Nonprofit. OFC HRS: M-Th 8am-5:30pm. Spanish spoken. ADM REQ: Must be a county resident. Sliding fee scale for substance abuse. Medi-cal for mental health. SERVES: Riverside County.

RIVERSIDE CO. DEPT/MENTAL HEALTH
Substance Abuse Prgm/Corona
623 N. Main St., Ste D-11
Corona, CA 92880
(951) 737-2962
(951) 737-2783 FAX

County sponsored counseling srvs for alcohol & drug abusers and their families: group counseling; referral to 24-hr residential prgms; medical eval; alcohol prevention srvs; prenatal women's group referral. State ID: 330023DN. FUNDING: Nonprofit. OFC HRS: M-Th 8am-5pm. Spanish spoken. Accepts Medi-Cal, sliding fee scale. SERVES: Riverside County.

RIVERSIDE CO. DEPT/MENTAL HEALTH
Drinking Driver Program/Indio
45596 Fargo St., Ste 6
Indio, CA 92201
(760) 863-8471
(760) 342-4469 FAX

DUI prgm. FUNDING: Federal, county, state. OFC HRS: M-Th 7:30am-5pm. Spanish spoken. SERVES: Desert areas.

RIVERSIDE CO. DEPT/MENTAL HEALTH
Substance Abuse Prgm/Indio
83-912 Avenue 45, Ste 9
Indio, CA 92201
(760) 347-0754
(760) 347-8507 FAX

Srvs to substance abusers and their families. Outpatient treatment, edu, counseling & referral, prevention edu, detox. Wait varies. Adol prgm. State ID: 330023EN. FUNDING: Nonprofit. OFC HRS: M-Th 8am-6pm. Spanish spoken. ADM REQ: Riverside County residents.

Accepts Medi-Cal, sliding fee scale. SERVES: Coachella Valley.

RIVERSIDE CO. DEPT/MENTAL HEALTH
Substance Abuse Treatment
1827 Atlanta Ave., Ste D-1
Riverside, CA 92507
(951) 955-2105
(951) 955-8060 FAX

Srvs provided to substance abusers and their families. Outpatient counseling, referral to residential treatment and detox, prevention edu, pregnant addicts and women's prgms. Outpatient day prgm for men, women, youth, transgendered and parolees. Non-medical detox, co-occurring srvs. HIV certified counselor, pre-test and post-test counseling, HIV tests. Lectures on AIDS edu and prevention. For detox, call (951) 955-2100. State ID: 330023CN. FUNDING: Nonprofit. OFC HRS: M-Th 8am-6pm. Spanish spoken. ADM REQ: Ages 13 yrs+ and Medi-Cal eligible. Call for more info. Accepts Medi-Cal, sliding fee scale. SERVES: Riverside County.

RIVERSIDE CO. DEPT/MENTAL HEALTH
Administrative Office
P.O. Box 7549
4095 County Circle Dr.
Riverside, CA 92513
(951) 358-4500
(951) 358-4513 FAX

Overall planning, implementation, direction, coordination and eval of the Dept of Mental Health prgms in Riverside County. Treatment for adults: residential, outpatient, day care, socialization ctrs, crisis srvs, case mgmt, continuing care, etc. Children's prgms: outpatient, case mgmt, foster home placement, etc. Also main admin office for drug abuse and alcohol control prgms. No actual srvs available at this location. FUNDING: Govt. Spanish spoken. Accepts Medi-Cal. SERVES: Riverside County.

RIVERSIDE CO. DEPT/MENTAL HEALTH
Substance Abuse Prgm/Temecula
41002 County Center Dr., Ste 320
Temecula, CA 92591
(951) 600-6360
(951) 600-6365 FAX

Outpatient assessment and referral. Outpatient treatment for substance abuse. For 24-hr detox hotline, call (800) 499-3008. FUNDING: County. OFC HRS: M-Th 8am-6pm. Interpreters available. Sliding fee scale. SERVES: Temecula, Lake Elsinore.

RIVERSIDE CO. DRUG COURT
Desert Drug Court
68-615 Perez Rd., Ste 2A
Cathedral City, CA 92234
(760) 770-2241
(760) 770-2240 FAX

Outpatient drug & alcohol treatment prgm. Licensed prgm. FUNDING: County. OFC HRS: M-Th 8am-5pm. Spanish spoken. ADM REQ: Ages 18 yrs+, referred by court. SERVES: Riverside County.

RIVERSIDE CO. LATINO COMMISSION
Casa Cecilia Recovery Home
83-385 Rosa Ave.
Thermal, CA 92274
(760) 398-2008
(760) 398-2008 FAX

6-bed residential drug & alcohol treatment prgm. AA meetings, NA meetings, info & referral, women's groups. State ID: 330037BN. FUNDING: Nonprofit. Spanish spoken. ADM REQ: Females ages 18 yrs+, min stay is three months. SERVES: Riverside County.

RIVERSIDE CO. OFFICE/EDUCATION
Admin Office/Substance Abuse Prgm
3525 Presley Ave.
Riverside, CA 92507
(951) 782-2400
(951) 683-4904 FAX

This is the admin office for the clinics. No direct srvs at this location. Outpatient drug & alcohol treatment prgm; info & referral; prevention & edu; DUI prgm; dual-diagnosis; counseling. For 24-hr detox hotline, call (800) 499-3008. FUNDING: County, govt, nonprofit. OFC HRS: M-Th 8am-5pm. Spanish spoken. ADM REQ: Ages 12 yrs+. SERVES: Riverside County.

RIVERSIDE CO. PUBLIC HEALTH DEPT
Perinatal Substance Abuse Prgm
P.O. Box 7600
Riverside, CA 92513-7600
(951) 358-5039
(951) 358-5386 FAX

Referrals provided to drug/alcohol & smoking cessation prgms. Provides training & technical support to OB/Family Practice Physicians who participate in the perinatal SART prgm. FUNDING: Nonprofit. Spanish spoken. Free srvs. SERVES: Riverside County.

RIVERSIDE CO. SUBSTANCE ABUSE
P.O. Box 830
650 N. State St. 92543
Hemet, CA 92546
(951) 791-3350
(951) 791-3353 FAX

Clinic provides assessment and referral for substance abuse. Outpatient treatment available. State ID: 330023BN. For detox hotline, call (800) 499-3008. FUNDING: County. OFC HRS: M-F 8am-6pm. Spanish spoken. ASL available. Sliding fee scale. SERVES: Riverside County.

RIVERSIDE RECOVERY RESOURCES
Alcohol & Drug Dep/1st Step House
40329 Stetson Ave.
Hemet, CA 92544
(951) 658-4466
(951) 765-2757 FAX

4-bed residential detox, primary and re-entry prgms for alcohol & drug abuse. State ID: 330009DN. Srvs include: counseling, coping skills, prevention edu, re-socialization, recreation, AA groups, etc. Also have 18-bed, 60-day residential facility. FUNDING: Nonprofit. OFC HRS: 24 hrs. ADM REQ: Ages 18 yrs+. Pvt pay, sliding fee scale. 2 county-funded beds. SERVES: Riverside County.

RIVERSIDE RECOVERY RESOURCES
Our House
41052 Acacia Ave.
Hemet, CA 92544
(951) 766-7969
(951) 765-5692 FAX

Residential drug & alcohol treatment & edu prgm for women & children, AA meetings, parenting classes. State ID: 330009IN. FUNDING: Nonprofit. OFC HRS: 24 hrs, 7 days. ADM

REQ: Ages 18 yrs+, women with and without children. SERVES: Riverside County.

RIVERSIDE RECOVERY RESOURCES
Admin Office
600 3rd Street, Ste C
Lake Elsinore, CA 92530
(951) 674-5354

Alcohol & drug abuse recovery prgms, parenting classes, DUI prgm, counseling & speaker's bureau. 38-bed residential facility for women with children in Hemet. 18-bed residential men's center & sober living in Hemet. Outpatient centers in Riverside, Lake Elsinore & Perris. Adol outpatient facilities in Lake Elsinore & Perris. State ID: 330009ON. FUNDING: Nonprofit. OFC HRS: M-F 9am-7pm; Sat 6am-12noon. Spanish spoken in Perris office. Accepts pvt pay. Sliding fee scale. SERVES: Riverside, Lake Elsinore, Temecula, Moreno Valley, Perris, Hemet, San Jacinto & nearby.

RIVERSIDE RECOVERY RESOURCES
Omega & Beta Programs
2055 N. Perris Blvd., Ste G-5, G-6
Perris, CA 92571
(951) 940-6061
(951) 940-1691 FAX

Outpatient drug & alcohol treatment prgm. Licensed prgm for adults and adols. FUNDING: Nonprofit. OFC HRS: M-F 9am-5pm. Spanish spoken. ADM REQ: Ages 18 yrs+. Ages 14-17 yrs for adol prgm. SERVES: Riverside County.

RIVERSIDE RECOVERY RESOURCES
Alpha Program
3757 Elizabeth St.
Riverside, CA 92506
(951) 788-0411
(951) 788-4803 FAX

DUI 1st & 2nd offender (18-month). Outpatient & residential drug & alcohol treatment. AA meetings. State ID: 330006QN. FUNDING: Nonprofit. OFC HRS: M-Th 9am-7pm; F 9am-4pm; Sat 8am-12noon. Accepts pvt pay, sliding fee scale. SERVES: Riverside County.

RIVERSIDE/SAN BERN INDIAN HEALTH CLINIC
P.O. Box 1098
66-735 Martinez Rd.
Thermal, CA 92274
(760) 397-4476
(800) 717-4476
(760) 397-0066 FAX

Free clinic for Native American families residing in Riverside or San Bernardino Counties. Mental health, substance abuse, nutrition, dental, general medicine. State ID: 330057DN. FUNDING: Federal, govt, nonprofit. OFC HRS: M-Th 8am-5pm; F 8am-2pm. Spanish spoken. ADM REQ: Proof of Indian heritage, linkage, proof of residency. SERVES: Riverside & San Bernardino Counties.

RIVERSIDE/SAN BRDO CO. INDIAN HLTH
Morongo Indian Health Clinic
11555 1/2 Potrero Rd.
Banning, CA 92220
(800) 732-8805
(951) 849-4761
(951) 849-5612 FAX

Outpatient alcohol & drug treatment prgm, AA meetings, parenting classes, counseling. Comprehensive health care: medical, dental, vision, mental health (individual & family counseling),

pharmacy, lab, nursing, family planning, AIDS testing, WIC prgm, transportation. Serves all ages. FUNDING: Govt. OFC HRS: M, W, Th 8am-5pm; Tu 8am-7pm; F 8am-2pm. ADM REQ: Must have appt. Accepts Medi-Cal. Free srvs to qualified Indians. SERVES: Riverside & San Bernardino Counties.

ROLLING START, INC.
570 W. 4th Street, Ste 107
San Bernardino, CA 92401
(909) 884-2129
(909) 386-7446 FAX

Independent living skills training, attendant referral, housing referral, info & referral, advocacy, deaf srvs, helpline, peer counseling for seniors and disabled. ADA tech assist, free workshops. Assistive technology, computer classes. For TDD, call (909) 884-7396. FUNDING: Govt, county, city. OFC HRS: M-F 8am-5pm. ASL available. ADM REQ: Ages 18 yrs+, county resident with disability. Free srvs except helpline. SERVES: San Bernardino County.

S.A.F.E./SUBSTANCE ABUSE/ED
Center for Drug Free Communities
14252 Culver Dr., Ste A-261
Irvine, CA 92604
(714) 505-4692
(714) 505-4887 FAX

S.A.F.E. (Substance Abuse For Educators) offers levels I & II of training for professionals & the community supporting the dev and implementation of successful drug & alcohol prevention & intervention prgms. Conducts PAL Camps (Peer Assistance Leadership). Focus is on conflict resolution, ATOD prevention. Call to arrange workshop. FUNDING: Nonprofit. OFC HRS: M-F 8am-6pm. Spanish spoken. SERVES: So. Calif.

SAFE HARBOR
Olive Branch Church
7702 El Cerrito Rd.
Corona, CA 92881-4295
(951) 279-4477
(951) 520-9797 FAX

Christ-centered, 12-Step recovery prgm. Support groups for all types of problems & addictions including: food, sex or relationship addictions, co-dependency and chemical dependency. Safe Harbor meets W at 7pm. Call for location. FUNDING: Nonprofit. OFC HRS: M-F 9am-5pm. SERVES: Riverside County.

SAFETY & EMERG EDUCATOR'S COUNCIL
3707 5th Avenue, Ste 706
San Diego, CA 92103
(619) 692-2011
(619) 298-9977 FAX

Joint employer/employee prgm to initiate tobacco control policies in the workplace. Health edu course includes: CPR, first aid, AIDS, TB, earthquake preparedness. FUNDING: Nonprofit. OFC HRS: M-F 8am-5:30pm. ADM REQ: No age limits. Fixed fees. SERVES: Calif.

SALVATION ARMY/ADULT REHAB
P.O. Box 278
24201 Orange Ave.
Perris, CA 92572-0278
(951) 940-5790
(951) 943-2248 FAX

Christian adult residential rehab center for male substance abusers. FUNDING: Donations, nonprofit. SERVES: Riverside County.

SALVATION ARMY/ADULT REHAB

363 S. Doolittle Rd.
San Bernardino, CA 92408
(909) 889-9605
(909) 889-0378 FAX

Christian-based,122-bed facility for men using work therapy. Six to twelve month social model prgm for men. Church srvs, prayer and Bible study. Also have AA meetings. FUNDING: Donations, nonprofit. OFC HRS: M-F 7:30am-4pm. ADM REQ: Ages 18-62 yrs with ID card & are able to work 8 hrs per day. Free srvs. SERVES: Riverside, San Bernardino Counties.

SALVATION ARMY/VICTORY PLACE

11301 Wilshire Blvd., Bldg. 212, 2nd Fl.
Los Angeles, CA 90073
(310) 478-3711
(310) 268-3669 FAX

100-bed shelter & medical care for veterans with an alcohol and/or drug addiction. Accepts single men and women ages 18 yrs+. Max stay is 90 days. State ID: 190023DN. FUNDING: Donations, nonprofit. OFC HRS: M-F 8am-4pm. SERVES: So. Calif.

SAMHSA

Substance Abuse & Mental Hlth Srvs Admin
P.O. Box 2345
1 Choke Cherry Rd.
Rockville, MD 20857
(240) 276-2000
(240) 276-2010 FAX

Established to provide info on prevention, diagnosis & treatment srvs for substance abuse and mental illness. Clearinghouse for prevention & treatment info (800) 729-6686. For mental health info, call (877)SAMHSA7. FUNDING: Govt. OFC HRS: M-F 8am-5pm, EST. Spanish spoken. SERVES: U.S.A.

SAN BERNARDINO CO. ALCOHOL/DRUG

Needles Center for Change
300 H Street
Needles, CA 92363
(760) 326-4590
(888) 743-1478
(760) 326-3154 FAX

Alcohol & drug outpatient prgm, info & referral, outpatient counseling, DUI 1st offender & 2nd offender (18-month) prgms, individual and group therapy, PC-1000, drug court. Walk in or call. State ID: 360033IN. FUNDING: Nonprofit. OFC HRS: M-Th 8am-12noon, 1pm-6pm. ADM REQ: Ages 18 yrs+. SERVES: San Bernardino County.

SAN BERNARDINO CO. ALCOHOL/DRUG

Admin Alcohol & Drug Srvs
850 E. Foothill Blvd.
Rialto, CA 92376
(909) 421-4601
(909) 421-9466 FAX

Referrals to residential treatment prgms and referrals to more than 30 contract agencies in outlying areas of San Bernardino Co. Outpatient alcohol & drug treatment, primarily group treatment, individual, marital and family provided on a limited basis as needed. Follow-up by medical director. Anti-abuse treatment, dual-diagnosis, DUI. Testing upon entry. 24 hrs abuse referral srv, (888) 743-1478. For treatment sites anywhere in the USA, www.findtreatment.samhsa gov. FUNDING: Govt. OFC HRS: M-F 8am-5pm. Spanish spoken. ADM REQ: Depends on provider. SERVES: San Bernardino metro area.

SAN BERNARDINO CO. ALCOHOL/DRUG

850 E. Foothill Blvd.
Rialto, CA 92376
(909) 421-9465
(909) 421-9457 FAX

Outpatient, non-residential, co-occurring disorders services. FUNDING: Govt. OFC HRS: M-F 8am-5pm. Spanish spoken. ADM REQ: Women only ages 18 yrs+ either with children or pregnant. Self referrals, by Medi-Cal, CPS, drug corps, CalWORKS. SERVES: Central Valley.

SAN BERNARDINO CO. PUBLIC HEALTH

Administrative Office
385 Arrowhead Ave.
San Bernardino, CA 92415-0120
(909) 387-7020
(909) 387-6228 FAX

Administers branch offices at various locations throughout San Bernardino Co. including: Barstow, Big Bear, Chino, Fontana, Joshua Tree, Needles, Ontario, Redlands, San Bernardino, Trona, Victorville & Twin Peaks. Edu, alcohol & drug prevention, animal control, birth & death certificates, Calif Children's Srvs, epidemiology, family planning, high-risk infant prgm, immunizations, nutrition, WIC, public health nursing, school health, senior health, VD control, TB, HIV/AIDS control. TDD (909) 397-6354. OFC HRS: M-F 8am-5pm; clinic hrs may vary. SERVES: San Bernardino County.

SAN BERNARDINO CO. PUBLIC HEALTH

Health Promotion & Education Srvs
351 N. Mountain View Ave., 2nd Fl
San Bernardino, CA 92415-0010
(800) 782-4264
(909) 387-6280
(909) 387-0102 FAX

Health promotion & edu srvs. For TDD, call (909) 387-6359. OFC HRS: M-F 8am-5pm. Spanish spoken. SERVES: San Bernardino County.

SEEKING PEACEFUL SOLUTIONS, INC.

8724 S. Vermont Ave.
Los Angeles, CA 90047
(323) 753-1314
(323) 753-6619 FAX

Conflict and dispute resolution srvs that assist in the reduction and prevention of violence among youth, adolescents, adults and communities at large. These srvs provided in partnership with schools, law enforcement, businesses, communities and within families. FUNDING: Nonprofit. OFC HRS: M-F 8:30am-7pm; Sat 9am-3:30pm; Sun by appt only. Spanish spoken. SERVES: L.A., Orange, Riverside & San Bernardino Counties.

SERENITY ALANO CLUB

3964 N. Sierra Way
San Bernardino, CA 92405
(909) 881-0170

Sober & clean atmosphere for recovering alcoholics & drug addicts. Meeting place for AA & NA. Walk in. OFC HRS: M-Sun 11am-end of last meeting

SERENITY OUTREACH

5511 Riverside Dr.
Chino, CA 91710
(909) 464-0400
(949) 464-0433 FAX

Outpatient treatment alternative to adults and adolescents who are in need of chemical dependency services. Will provide solutions to chemical dependency through individual & group counseling sessions for: domestic violence, anger mgmt, self-esteem, life skills, parenting skills, drug edu as well as mentoring and peer support. Will provide a discreet, drug-free environment that will allow our clients and their families to deal with the real issues related to their substance abuse misuse. FUNDING: Nonprofit. OFC HRS: M-F 10am-8pm; Sat 10am-1pm. ADM REQ: All ages. SERVES: Inland Empire.

SET FREE CHRISTIAN FELLOWSHIP

16947 D Street
Victorville, CA 92392
(760) 241-9428

Faith-based adult recovery ranch. Crisis intervention including: drug, alcohol addiction, homelessness, poor work ethic, lack of discipline & direction. FUNDING: Nonprofit. OFC HRS: 24 hrs, 7 days. Spanish spoken. ADM REQ: 60-day prgm, must not have outside commitments. Free srvs. SERVES: So. Calif.

SEXAHOLICS ANONYMOUS (S.A.)

Central Office
P.O. Box 3565
Brentwood, TN 37024-3565
(615) 370-6062
(866) 424-8777
(615) 370-0882 FAX

12-Step recovery prgm for those who want to stop sexually self-destructive thinking and behavior. This prgm is also available to sexaholics in correctional institutions (literature srv; sponsor-by-mail srvs where inmates are linked with members outside who can help them work the 12-Step prgm; support for starting SA meetings at the prisons; connection srv that helps parolees find the nearest SA contact). FUNDING: Nonprofit. OFC HRS: M-F 9am-5pm. SERVES: U.S.A.

SINGLE PARENTS OF POWER EMLAC HEALTH SRVS

P.O. Box 452602
1620 Centinela Ave, Ste 202
Inglewood, CA 90302
(310) 753-7860

Counseling services include: mental health, sexual abuse, anger mgmt, parenting, alcohol and drug abuse. Advocacy and counseling for victims of violent crimes and post-traumatic counseling for veterans. FUNDING: Nonprofit. OFC HRS: M-F 9am-9pm; Sat 10am-3pm. Spanish, Swahili spoken. Free counseling for victims of domestic violence. All other srvs on a sliding fee scale. SERVES: L.A. & San Bernardino Counties.

SMOKENDERS

P.O. Box 316
Kensington, MD 20895
(800) 828-4357
(301) 563-6192 FAX

Self-study prgms including: workbook, telephone support and CDs that teach how to quit smoking. FUNDING: Nonprofit. Fee $125 plus shipping cost. SERVES: U.S.A.

SO CALIF ALCOHOL & DRUG PRGM

Angel Step Inn
11500 Paramount Blvd.
Downey, CA 90241
(323) 780-7235 FAX

30-bed emerg shelter for women ages 18 yrs+ and their children (up to age 17 yrs) with co-occuring domestic violence & substance abuse issues. Max 45-day prgm. Also serves pregnant women. 24-hr hotline (323) 780-4357. Address above is for admin only, call for specific prgm site. FUNDING: Donation, nonprofit, state, county, United Way, SCADP, OC Health Care Agency. Spanish spoken. SERVES: L.A., Ventura, Orange, San Bernardino & Riverside Counties.

SOBOBA INDIAN HEALTH CLINIC

Substance Abuse Prgm
607 Donna Way
San Jacinto, CA 92583
(800) 851-5816
(951) 487-9634 FAX

Outpatient drug & alcohol treatment prgm, info & referral, prevention & edu, dual-diagnosis. State ID: 330057BN. FUNDING: Nonprofit. OFC HRS: M, Tu, Th 8am-5pm; W 8am-7pm; F 8am-2pm. ADM REQ: Proof of residency, proof of Indian heritage. SERVES: Riverside County.

SOCIAL SCIENCE SRVS-CEDAR HOUSE

See "Cedar House Rehab Center"

SOROPTIMIST HOUSE OF HOPE

See "House of Hope/Soroptimist"

SOS (SECULAR ORGANIZATION FOR SOBRIETY)

S.O.S. National Clearinghouse
4773 Hollywood Blvd.
Hollywood, CA 90027
(323) 666-4295
(323) 666-4271 FAX

S.O.S. is an alternative recovery method for alcoholics or drug addicts uncomfortable with spiritual content of the 12-Step prgms. Goal is to promote sobriety. More than 2,000 groups nationwide. Write to above address for a list of local groups. FUNDING: Nonprofit. SERVES: U.S.A.

STUDENT ASSISTANCE PROGRAM

Corona-Norco USD Pupil Srvs
2820 Clark Ave.
Norco, CA 92860-1903
(951) 736-5106
(951) 736-8202 FAX

Edu, prevention, intervention, support and referral srvs by trained school and community personnel for students in the Corona/Norco area. Prgms include: after school activities & clubs; parenting edu workshops; student conflict resolution and mediation; Healthy Families/Medi-Cal application assist; school-aged parenting and infant care; peer assist, drug insight and general support groups; community prevention and edu efforts through U.N.I.T.Y. coalition. FUNDING: SDFSC & TUPE, general fund, donations, AB1113. OFC HRS: M-F 8am-4:30pm. Spanish spoken. ADM REQ: Must live in Corona or Norco school district area or your group must serve this area. Free srvs.

SERVES: Corona & Norco school district boundaries.

SUN RAY ADDICTIONS

Counseling and Education
960 N. State St., Ste B
Hemet, CA 92543
(951) 652-3560
(951) 929-2780 FAX

Adult/Adolescent Outpatient drug and alcohol treatment/education programs, Anger Mgmt, & Gambling programs, Alcohol/Drug urine screen, hair, DOT breath, analysis (testing). State/County Certified. FUNDING: Riverside County Mental Health Substance Abuse Program. OFC HRS: M, Tu, Th, F 9am-8pm; W 9am-4:30pm. ADM REQ: Open to public: Outpatient treatment and edu programs, urine and hair alcohol drug screens, court-mandated PC-1000 program. Prop 36 adult and adol programs. State ID: 330045AP. Accepts Medi-Cal and SASCA. Sliding fee scale for counseling and assessment appts up to $85 per session. SERVES: Riverside County.

TEEN CHALLENGE INTERNATIONAL

Orange County Headquarters
P.O. Box 236
418 S. Main St.
Santa Ana, CA 92702
(714) 835-8822
(714) 835-8825 FAX

Free 1-year adult residential drug & alcohol rehab. Christian discipleship prgm. Learning center, computer lab, homework help M-F 2pm-5pm for jr. high & elem students, M-F 6pm-8pm for high school students. Call Frank Jimenez at (714) 836-7140. Gang & drug intervention & prevention prgm for teens Tu 7pm and for adolescents Sat 10am-12pm. TC New Creation Choir Outreach Prgm available for songs, testimonies & presentations in local churches. Anti-gang & drug presentations in local schools. Speakers for civil groups. FUNDING: Nonprofit. OFC HRS: M-F 8:30am-5pm. ADM REQ: Sign-up & interviews required. Free srvs. SERVES: U.S.A.

TEEN CHALLENGE INTERNATL/SO CALIF

5445 Chicago Ave.
Riverside, CA 92507
(951) 682-8990
(951) 682-3754 FAX

One-year residential drug and alcohol treatment prgm for men ages 18 yrs+, Christian structure. Wait: 1-2 weeks. Eight sites in So Calif. FUNDING: Nonprofit. OFC HRS: M-F 8:30am-5pm. ADM REQ: Sincere desire to change lifestyle. Free srvs. SERVES: So. Calif.

TEEN SAVERS

Chapman House, Inc.
4675 MacArthur Blvd., Ste 930
Newport Beach, CA 92660
(714) 288-9779
(714) 288-6130 FAX

Intervention, transportation, residential treatment, day treatment and outpatient care for children ages 9-17 yrs with substance abuse, behavioral and/or emotional problems. State licensed and CARF-accredited. FUNDING: Private. OFC HRS: 24 hrs, 7 days. Spanish & Armenian spoken. ADM REQ: Ages 9-17 yrs. Pvt pay and insurance accepted. No Medi-Cal. Reduced rates for probation clients, indigent cli-

ents and other clients referred by governing agencies. SERVES: Orange, Riverside, L.A. & San Diego Counties.

THE GOODEN CENTER

Formerly Bishop Gooden Home
191 N. El Molino Ave.
Pasadena, CA 91101
(626) 356-0078
(800) 931-9884
(626) 795-2844 FAX

Licensed and CARF accredited drug and alcohol treatment prgm for men offering residential day treatment and IOP levels of care. Sober living also available. FUNDING: Donations, grants, client fees, nonprofit. OFC HRS: M-F 8am-7pm. ADM REQ: Men ages 18 yrs+. Must interview and be sober. Financial assist available. Insurance friendly. 3 partial scholarships available for those in need. SERVES: So. Calif.

THE GROVE COMMUNITY CHURCH

19900 Grove Community Dr.
Riverside, CA 92508
(951) 571-9090
(951) 571-9091 FAX

Celebrate Recovery, a faith-based 12-Step support group dealing with anger mgmt, chemical dependency, co-dependency, eating disorders and sexual addictions, meets M at 7pm. Recovery worship service F at 7pm. Pre-marital, individual & family counseling and various support groups available. FUNDING: Nonprofit. OFC HRS: M-F 8am-5pm. Sat sessions by appt. Must call to register for counseling. Fees vary. $40 before 5pm, $50 after 5pm. No one turned away due to lack of funds. SERVES: Riverside.

THE JACQUELINE SIDMAN HEALTH FNDN

4199 Campus Dr., Ste 550
Irvine, CA 92612
(949) 251-9550
(949) 509-6599 FAX

An effective, drug-free treatment for the recovery of behavioral and physical health from addiction through the use of the subconscious mind. FUNDING: Nonprofit. OFC HRS: M-Sun 11:30am-6:30pm. SERVES: Calif.

THE OTHER BAR NATIONAL HOTLINE

(800) 222-0767

24-hr hotline for confidential counseling and referral assist for judges, lawyers, law students and other legal professionals affected by alcohol and drug abuse. Also offers support group meetings throughout Calif. FUNDING: Nonprofit, State Bar, donations. Free srvs. SERVES: Calif.

THE RECOVERY CENTER

Inland Vly Drug/Alcohol Recovery Srvs
934 N. Mountain Ave., Ste A & B
Upland, CA 91786
(909) 949-4667
(909) 931-3774 FAX

Outpatient substance abuse classes, domestic violence classes, anger mgmt, seminars & workshops, 12-Step meeting rooms, job skills prgm, parenting classes, aftercare, youth prgm, adult probation prgm. FUNDING: County, client fees, nonprofit, pvt health insurance. OFC HRS: M-F 9am-9pm; Sat 9am-12noon. Spanish spoken. Payment based on sliding fee scale. SERVES: San Bernardino County.

THE SOLUTIONS ALCOHOL/DRUG RECOVERY

The Solutions Foundation, Inc.
3210 W. Jefferson Blvd.
Los Angeles, CA 90018
(323) 731-4981
(323) 731-4958 FAX

Collaborates with individuals, communities and agencies to break down barriers based on illiteracy, substance abuse, unemployment, crime and homelessness. Assists the recovering addict in rebuilding their lives & creating responsible environments through partnerships that positively impact their lives, their families and communities. FUNDING: Nonprofit. OFC HRS: M-F 8am-8pm, Sat 8am-4pm. SERVES: L.A., Ventura, Orange, Riverside & San Bernardino Counties.

THE TRINITY HOUSE

133 Highland Ave., Ste A2
National City, CA 91950
(619) 477-7158
(619) 330-4749 FAX

Faith-based human srvs organization. Safe, clean, healthy transitional living environment for women, with or without children. Academic edu, employment, training and career guidance srvs. FUNDING: Nonprofit. OFC HRS: M-F 8am-5pm. Spanish spoken. SERVES: Calif.

THE WAY

Ministry of the Way, Inc.
P.O. Box 5912
Buena Park, CA 90620
(714) 906-9097

Christ-centered home open to women who have made a commitment to do what is necessary to change their lives. Contact Helen Reid, Coalition member. FUNDING: Nonprofit. OFC HRS: M-Sat 9am-5pm. ADM REQ: Ages 18 yrs+. Fee $540 per month. SERVES: So. Calif.

TRINITY EVANGELICAL CHURCH

Pathways Support Group Ministries
1551 Reservoir Rd.
Redlands, CA 92373
(909) 335-7333
(909) 798-7096 FAX

Offers a variety of support groups including: divorce care groups for adults and children ages 5-12 yrs, grief share group, group for caregivers, struggling relationships. Also offers "Every Man's Challenge" prgm for men who battle sexual compulsivity and special prgms for women who have gone through an abortion, struggle with sexual matters, or have been sexually abused. Child care available by arrangement for children 12 and under. FUNDING: Nonprofit. OFC HRS: M-F 8am-5pm. ADM REQ: Some classes require pre-registration, call ahead. SERVES: San Bernardino County.

VALLEY IMPROVEMENT PROGRAMS, INC.

210 West B Street
Ontario, CA 91762
(909) 983-3665
(909) 467-3646 FAX

DUI 1st & 2nd offender (18-month) prgms. PC-1000. State ID: 360049CP. FUNDING: Nonprofit. OFC HRS: M-Th 9am-8pm. Spanish spoken. ADM REQ: Ages 18 yrs+. Payment plans available. SERVES: San Bernardino County.

VALLEY IMPROVEMENT PROGRAMS, INC.

8540 Archibald Ave., Bldg. 18, Ste A
Rancho Cucamonga, CA 91730
(909) 987-4036
(909) 481-5368 FAX

DUI 1st & multiple offender prgms. State ID: 360049AP. FUNDING: Nonprofit. OFC HRS: M-Th 9am-5pm; F 9am-1pm. Classes held M-Th evenings, some mornings, and Sat. ADM REQ: Ages 18 yrs+. SERVES: San Bernardino County.

VALLEY IMPROVEMENT PROGRAMS, INC.

1589 W. 9th Street, Ste E
Upland, CA 91786
(909) 985-2785
(909) 982-5597 FAX

Court-ordered DUI, 1st and 2nd offender, PC-1000 drug diversion, substance abuse referral. State ID: 360019BP. FUNDING: Fees, nonprofit. OFC HRS: M-Th 8:30am-8:30pm; F 9am-1pm. ADM REQ: Ages 18 yrs+. Free referrals. SERVES: San Bernardino County.

VALLEY-WIDE COUNSELING SRVS

A Program of MFI Recovery Center
1604 S. Santa Fe Ave., Ste 403
San Jacinto, CA 92583
(951) 654-2026
(951) 654-9277 FAX

Adol chemical dependency srvs. Also offers anger mgmt, parenting edu and mental health counseling. Specialized prgms for high risk children and youth. OFC HRS: M-Th 8am-9pm; F 8am-5pm. Spanish spoken. Accepts pvt insurance and Medi-Cal. Fees based on ability to pay.

VARP, INC.

Metcalf Recovery Ranch
9826 18th Avenue
Blythe, CA 92225
(760) 922-8625
(760) 922-6717 FAX

State-certified peer group, AA/NA oriented social model recovery prgms, offering srvs to men only, with 60-day primary care and 6-9 months aftercare. State ID: 330020AN. FUNDING: United Way, donations, fees, nonprofit. OFC HRS: M-F 8am-5pm; treatment 24 hrs. Spanish spoken. Sliding fee scale. SERVES: San Bernardino, Riverside Counties.

VARP, INC.

Gibson House for Men
1100 North D Street
San Bernardino, CA 92410
(909) 884-0840
(909) 381-6845 FAX

State-certified peer group; AA/NA oriented social model recovery prgms offering srvs to men. 40-bed residential facility has 60-day primary with 6-9 months aftercare. State ID: 360004BN. FUNDING: Donations, fees, nonprofit. OFC HRS: M-F 8am-5pm, treatment 24 hrs. Spanish spoken. ADM REQ: Ages 18 yrs+, minimum stay 60-90 days. Sliding fee scale. SERVES: San Bernardino, Riverside Counties.

VARP, INC.

Harris House
907 W. Rialto Ave.
San Bernardino, CA 92410
(909) 885-8804
(909) 381-6845 FAX

State-certified peer group; AA/NA-oriented social model recovery prgms, offering srvs for men only. Affiliated with Veteran's Hospital. 30-day prgm with 6-9 month aftercare. State ID: 360004AN. FUNDING: Nonprofit. OFC HRS: 8am-5pm. Spanish spoken. ADM REQ: Referral by any Veteran's Hospital. Men ages 18 yrs+, min stay 30 days. SERVES: San Bernardino, Riverside Counties.

VARP, INC.

Rialto House
921 Rialto Ave.
San Bernardino, CA 92410
(909) 381-3774
(909) 381-6845 FAX

Residential drug & alcohol treatment prgm, AA meetings. State ID: 360004HN. FUNDING: Nonprofit. OFC HRS: 24-hr srvs. ADM REQ: Men ages 18 yrs+, min stay 60 days. SERVES: San Bernardino County.

VARP, INC.

Stoddard House II
1087 N. Stoddard St.
San Bernardino, CA 92410
(909) 381-3774
(909) 381-6845 FAX

Residential drug & alcohol treatment prgm, AA meetings. State ID: 360004GN. FUNDING: Nonprofit. OFC HRS: 24-hr srvs. ADM REQ: Men ages 18 yrs+, min stay 60 days. SERVES: San Bernardino County.

VARP, INC.

1135 North D Street
San Bernardino, CA 92410
(909) 381-3774
(909) 381-6845 FAX

Residential drug & alcohol treatment prgm, AA meetings. State ID: 36004DN. FUNDING: Nonprofit. OFC HRS: 24-hr srvs. ADM REQ: Men ages 18 yrs+, min stay 60 days. SERVES: San Bernardino County.

VICTORY OUTREACH/HELENDALE

Men's & Women's Homes
73 Lords Rd.
Helendale, CA 92342
(760) 245-0042
(760) 245-0042 FAX

Faith-based program believing in Jesus Christ. Men's and women's residential drug prevention and rehab prgm. Drug-free detox phase. FUNDING: Nonprofit. Spanish spoken. ADM REQ: Ages 18 yrs+. Must refer those linked to Megan's Law to another program. SERVES: San Bernardino County.

VICTORY OUTREACH/INLAND ADMIN

Administration Office
P.O. Box 5712
990 W. Mill St.
San Bernardino, CA 92410-2636
(909) 884-1921
(909) 383-9077 FAX

Christian prgm with two residential drug & alcohol recovery homes. Only spiritual methods are used in recovery without the assist of medication. Focus is to help the drug addict, gang member and/or alcoholic. Sponsors 350 homes internationally. FUNDING: Donations, nonprofit. OFC HRS: M-Th 9am-4pm. F 9am-3pm. Spanish spoken. SERVES: Inland Empire.

VICTORY OUTREACH/INTERNATL

Admin Office
P.O. Box 3760
250 W. Arrow Hwy.
San Dimas, CA 91773
(909) 599-4437
(909) 599-6244 FAX

Men and women are given spiritual guidance and are encouraged to stay involved with various church-related activities until they are able to completely re-enter mainstream society. Victory Outreach sponsors 328 prgms in the U.S. and other countries including: prison and jail ministry (counseling and after-release placement), drug and assist prgms. Sponsors several 24-hr residential prgms. FUNDING: Donations, nonprofit. OFC HRS: M-F 9am-5pm. SERVES: U.S.A.

VICTORY OUTREACH/RIVERSIDE

Men's Program
4680 Park Ave.
Riverside, CA 92507
(951) 784-6313

Christian residential prgm for men in need of lifestyle change (min 9 months). Call for phone interview. No smoking, no drinking. No contact with the outside community for the first 30 days. Bible study and prayer are the main activities. FUNDING: Donations, nonprofit. OFC HRS: Vary. Spanish spoken. ADM REQ: Males ages 18 yrs+ with no major medical problems (no medication allowed). No one turned away for lack of funds. SERVES: Riverside County.

VICTORY OUTREACH/SANTA ANA

Men's & Women's Homes
1628 E. 4th Street
Santa Ana, CA 92702-0981
(714) 245-2580
(714) 245-7158 FAX

Free Christian residential drug prevention & rehab prgm. Detox phase with no drugs; requires one-yr commitment. For the men's home, call Alfonso at (714) 586-0551. For the women's home, call Alice at (714) 650-1630. Number above goes to the church admin office. FUNDING: Nonprofit. OFC HRS: Tu-F 9am-3pm. Spanish spoken. SERVES: So. Calif.

VILLAGE COUNSELING

Breaking Free
73302 Highway 111
Palm Desert, CA 92260
(760) 773-0669
(760) 773-0569 FAX

Outpatient drug & alcohol treatment prgm, parenting classes, marriage & family counseling, adol and individual counseling, anger mgmt, trauma & abuse counseling, life transitions, etc. State ID: 330052AP. FUNDING: Nonprofit. OFC HRS: Tu-F 9am-5pm. ADM REQ: Open to all ages SERVES: Riverside County.

VINEYARD ANAHEIM

Recovery Solutions
5340 E. La Palma Ave.
Anaheim, CA 92807
(714) 777-4777
(714) 777-5423 FAX

Christ-centered 12-Step prgm. Speaker's meeting in rm. 205 on M from 7pm-9pm, includes 15 minutes of worship and a weekly message on some aspect of Christ-centered recovery or one of the 12 steps. Small groups are held following the speaker's meeting. Current groups: anger mgmt, CEA-HOW, chemical/alcohol dependency, co-dependency, Peace with the Plate, SA, S-Anon. Free child care. FUNDING: Nonprofit. OFC HRS: M-Th 8:30am-5pm. SERVES: So. Calif.

WESTCARE FOUNDATION, INC.

Admin Office
900 Grier Dr.
Las Vegas, NV 89119
(702) 385-2090
(702) 658-0480 FAX

Various srvs offered for the edu, prevention and treatment of alcohol/drug abuse. Counseling, referrals, runaway youth emerg shelter, civil protective custody, detox, residential and day treatment. HIV/AIDS case mgmt. FUNDING: Donations, grants, contracts, nonprofit. OFC HRS: M-F 8am-5pm. Spanish spoken. Sliding fee scale. SERVES: Calif.

WISR MINISTRIES, INC.

13800 Heacock St., Ste C242
Moreno Valley, CA 92553
(951) 897-5560
(951) 653-9084 FAX

WISR is an outpatient facility that specializes in spiritual recovery. Individual and group counseling for substance abuse, anger mgmt, domestic violence, sexual assault, parenting, intervention, prevention for teens. FUNDING: Nonprofit, donations. OFC HRS: W, F 12noon-8pm; Sat 10am-6pm. More hours likely to be added. Spanish spoken. ADM REQ: No one will be discriminated against based on disability, religion, sexual orientation, race or ability to pay. Counseling fee based on sliding scale. Accepts Drug Medi-Cal and Medi-Cal. SERVES: Riverside, Moreno Valley, Perris.

WOMEN FOR SOBRIETY

New Life Prgm
P.O. Box 618
Quakertown, PA 18951-0618
(215) 536-8026
(215) 538-9026 FAX

New Life Prgm is a self-help prgm that focuses on the special needs of women alcoholics. Send a self-addressed, stamped envelope to the address above or call or visit (www.womenforsobriety.org). FUNDING: Donations, nonprofit. OFC HRS: M-F 9am-4:30pm, EST. ADM REQ: Sincere desire to stop drinking. Donations requested. SERVES: U.S.A.

WWW.DUIFOUNDATION.ORG

Website dedicated to educating people on the dangers of drinking and driving by providing all necessary info required to help prevent future incidents. FUNDING: Nonprofit. SERVES: U.S.A.

YWCA LIVING FREE

40-8172 Magnolia Ave.
Riverside, CA 92504
(951) 530-8127
(951) 688-5270 FAX

12-Step recovery home for women with children. In-house NA and AA meetings available, outside meetings required. Call for interview. FUNDING: Nonprofit. OFC HRS: 7 days per week until 8pm. ADM REQ: Must be employed or attending school, and have completed an alcohol/drug treatment prgm. Sliding fee scale. SERVES: Riverside County and surrounding areas.

YWCA/RIVERSIDE CO.

Born Free Women's Residential Prgm
8172 Magnolia Ave.
Riverside, CA 92504
(951) 530-8280
(951) 688-5270 FAX

24-hr residential treatment prgm for chemically dependent women. Srvs include: transportation to medical/legal appts, 12-Step prgms, parenting classes, one-on-one counseling, group sessions, NA/AA meetings, in-home nurse to discuss child birthing issues, budgeting and meal prep classes, exit plans. FUNDING: Donations, nonprofit. OFC HRS: 24 hrs, 7 days. Spanish spoken. ADM REQ: Ages 18 yrs+, pregnant, and addicted to a substance. This is not a detox facility. Sliding fee scale, no one turned away due to the inability to pay. SERVES: Los Angeles County, Orange County, Riverside County, San Bernadino County.

ACADEMY FOR EATING DISORDERS

111 Deer Lake Rd., Ste 100
Deerfield, IL 60015
(847) 498-4274
(847) 480-9282 FAX

Promotes effective treatment of eating disorders, develops prevention initiatives, stimulates research, sponsors internatl conferences & regional workshops. FUNDING: Nonprofit. OFC HRS: M-F 9am-5pm, CST. ADM REQ: Edu professional. SERVES: Internatl.

ALLIANCE/EATING DISORDERS AWARENESS

1016 Forum Place, Ste 10
West Palm Beach, FL 33401
(866) 662-1235
(561) 841-0900
(561) 653-0043 FAX

Works to prevent eating disorders and promote positive body image. Offers info & referral, advocacy, training, support and mentoring srvs. FUNDING: Nonprofit. Free srvs. SERVES: U.S.A.

AMERICAN ANOREXIA BULIMIA ASSN

See "Natl Eating Disorders Assn"

AMERICAN DIETETIC HOTLINE

See "Consumer Nutrition Info Line"

ANAD NATL OFFICE

See "Natl Assn of Anorexia Nervosa"

BINGE EATING DISORDER ASSN

637 Emerson Place
Severna Park, MD 21146
(443) 597-0066
(410) 741-3037 FAX

Provides individuals who suffer from binge eating disorder with the resources they need to begin recovery. Focuses on prevention, diagnosis, and treatment referrals. FUNDING: Nonprofit. SERVES: U.S.A.

CELEBRATE RECOVERY

Canyon Lake Community Church
30515 Railroad Canyon Rd.
Canyon Lake, CA 92586
(951) 244-1877
(951) 244-4397 FAX

Christ-centered 12-Step recovery prgm. Support groups for all types of problems and addictions, including: food, sex or relationship dependency. Meets Th at 6pm for dinner, 7pm for worship & meeting. Child care available. FUNDING: Nonprofit. OFC HRS: M-Th 8am-4:30pm. SERVES: Riverside County.

CELEBRATE RECOVERY

Mosaic Inland Church
5540 Schaefer Ave.
Chino, CA 91710
(909) 628-1571

Christ-centered 12-Step recovery prgm. Support groups for all types of problems & addictions, including: food, sex or relationship and chemical dependency. Meets F at 6pm-10pm. Contact: Jim or Terry Moon. FUNDING: Nonprofit. OFC HRS: M-F 8:30am-4pm. Spanish spoken. SERVES: San Bernardino County.

CELEBRATE RECOVERY

Centerpoint Church
P.O. Box 787
170 West F Street
Colton, CA 92324
(909) 825-3670

Christ-centered, 12-Step recovery prgm. Support groups for all types of problems & addictions, including: food, sex or relationship addictions, co-dependency and chemical dependency. Meets Th at 6:30pm in children's Ministries building. FUNDING: Nonprofit. OFC HRS: Tu-F 9am-5pm. SERVES: San Bernardino County.

CELEBRATE RECOVERY

Crossroads Christian Church
2331 Kellogg Ave.
Corona, CA 92881
(951) 737-4664
(951) 278-3176 FAX

Christ-centered, 12-Step recovery prgm. Support groups for all types of problems & addictions, including: food, sex or relationship addictions, co-dependency and chemical dependency. Meets F at 7pm in the fellowship hall. Light dinner and fellowship at 6:30pm. Open share, workbook, and other recovery groups also available. See website for more info. FUNDING: Nonprofit. OFC HRS: M-Th 8am-4:30pm; F 8am-3pm. SERVES: Riverside County.

CELEBRATE RECOVERY

Cathedral of Praise
1100 E. Holt Blvd.
Pomona, CA 91767
(626) 806-1890
(909) 987-1636 FAX

Christ-centered, 12-Step recovery prgm. Support groups for all types of problems & addictions, including: food, sex or relationship addictions, co-dependency and chemical dependency. OFC HRS: M-W, F, Sat 10am-8pm. Free srvs. SERVES: San Gabriel Valley & San Bernardino Co.

CELEBRATE RECOVERY

Sunrise Church
2759 N. Ayala Dr.
Rialto, CA 92377
(909) 875-5566
(909) 820-6281 FAX

Christ-centered, 12-Step recovery prgm. Support groups for all types of problems & addictions, including: food, sex or relationship addictions, co-dependency and chemical dependency. Professional counseling referrals available. Meets Tu from 7pm-9pm in room 260 and F at 7pm in chapel (room 170). FUNDING: Nonprofit. OFC HRS: M-F 8am-5pm. Spanish spoken. SERVES: San Bernardino County.

CELEBRATE RECOVERY

Pathway Christian Church
6755 Victoria Ave.
Riverside, CA 92506
(951) 781-8465
(951) 781-8896 FAX

Christ-centered, 12-Step recovery prgm. Support groups for all types of problems & addic-

tions, including: food, sex or relationship addictions, co-dependency and chemical dependency. Meets F at 6pm for dinner; 7pm large group; 8pm small group; 8pm one-time newcomers 101 meeting; 9pm Holy Grounds Cafe fellowship (dessert served). Call for more information regarding 12-Step groups for men & women. FUNDING: Nonprofit. OFC HRS: M-F 9am-5pm. ADM REQ: $3 for dinner. SERVES: Riverside County.

CELEBRATE RECOVERY

Riverside Community Church
4850 Jurupa Ave.
Riverside, CA 92504
(951) 686-1886
(951) 684-7313 FAX

Christ-centered, 12-Step recovery prgm. Support groups for all types of problems & addictions, including: food, sex or relationship addictions, co-dependency and chemical dependency. Meets Th. 6pm dinner; 7pm worship; 8pm gender-specific share groups; 9pm coffee and dessert accountability fellowship. Call for more info regarding 12-Step groups. Contact: Carlos Davila. FUNDING: Nonprofit. OFC HRS: Tu-Th 9am-4pm; F 9am-12noon. SERVES: Riverside County.

CELEBRATE RECOVERY

Cornerstone Community Church
34570 Monte Vista Dr.
Wildomar, CA 92595
(951) 674-8661
(951) 674-9603 FAX

Christ-centered, 12-Step recovery prgm. Support groups for all types of problems & addictions, including: food, sex or relationship addictions, co-dependency and chemical dependency. Meets F at 6pm dinner; 7pm worship and msg; 8pm open share groups. Childcare for ages birth-12yrs. Celebrate Recovery for teens meets Th 6:30pm-8:30pm in youth chapel. Contact: Pastor Bill Aanestad. FUNDING: Nonprofit. OFC HRS: M-Th 8am-5pm. SERVES: Riverside County.

CELEBRATE WHOLENESS

Campus Hill Church
11057 Hill Dr.
Loma Linda, CA 92354
(909) 796-0222
(909) 796-1992 FAX

Christ-centered, 12-Step recovery prgm. Support groups for all types of problems & addictions, including: food, sex or relationship addictions, co-dependency and chemical dependency. Meets F at 7pm in Linda Hall. Contact: Pastor Larry. FUNDING: Nonprofit. OFC HRS: M-Th 8am-5pm; F 8am-12noon. SERVES: San Bernardino County.

CENTER FOR HEALTH PROMOTION

Loma Linda University Evans Hall, Rm. 111
24785 Stewart St.
Loma Linda, CA 92354
(909) 558-4594
(909) 558-0433 FAX

Preventive medicine, weight mgmt, smoking cessation, executive health & wellness counseling. Prgms staffed by univ medical professionals. Several weight control prgms: Optifast for people 50+ lbs overweight, uses food supplements & behavioral change; Lean Choices focuses on real causes of obesity: lifestyles, exercise, interpersonal relationships, nutrition, & goal setting. Team approach for treatment. Also low cholesterol cooking, fitness testing & stress mgmt. FUNDING: Nonprofit. OFC HRS: M-Th 8am-5pm; F 8am-12noon. Open to anyone. Fees vary. SERVES: So. Calif.

COMPULSIVE EATERS ANONYMOUS

World Service Office
5500 E. Atherton St., Ste 227-B
Long Beach, CA 90815
(562) 342-9344
(562) 342-9344 FAX

12-Step fellowship of men & women who wish to recover from compulsive eating & food addiction. Visit (www.ceahow.org); includes chat room & dozens of meetings in Calif. To fax, call the office first. FUNDING: Nonprofit. OFC HRS: M-F 9am-1pm. No dues or fees. SERVES: U.S.A.

CONSUMER NUTRITION INFO LINE

The American Dietetic Association
120 S. Riverside Plaza, Ste 2000
Chicago, IL 60606-6995
(800) 877-1600
(312) 899-4873 FAX

Recorded messages are available with a touchtone phone. Referrals are given to registered dietitians for nutrition guidance and consultation. FUNDING: Nonprofit. OFC HRS: M-F 8am-5pm, CST. SERVES: U.S.A.

EATING DISORDER FOUNDATION OF O.C.

23232 Peralta Dr., Ste 211
Laguna Hills, CA 92653
(800) 342-8793
(949) 285-9827
(949) 488-2418 FAX

Dedicated to the awareness and prevention of eating disorders by providing edu to local schools, businesses, and youth organizations. Community outreach, edu, teacher in-service training, consultations, eating disorder assessments, counseling, fitness and nutrition referrals, support groups, group presentations for youth sports, individual assessments for athletes and coaches. FUNDING: Nonprofit. OFC HRS: M-Th 8am-9pm; F 8am-7pm; Sat 9am-2pm. Spanish spoken. SERVES: Orange, Riverside & San Bernardino Counties.

EATING DISORDER REFERRAL & INFO CTR

2923 Sandy Pointe, Ste 6
Del Mar, CA 92014
(858) 792-7463
(858) 220-7417 FAX

Visit (www.edreferral.org) for info & referrals on all types of eating disorders. OFC HRS: M-F 8am-5pm. Language line available. Free srvs. SERVES: U.S.A.

EATING DISORDERS ANONYMOUS (EDA)

P.O. Box 55876
Phoenix, AZ 85078
(218) 339-2500

Info and support groups for persons with eating disorders. Referral to groups throughout U.S.A. Visit (www.eatingdisordersanonymous.org). FUNDING: Nonprofit. OFC HRS: M-F 8am-5pm. SERVES: U.S.A.

EATING DISORDERS COALITION

Research, Policy and Action
720 7th Street NW, Ste 300
Washington, DC 20001
(202) 543-9570

Advocates for federal recognition of eating disorders as a public health priority. Also offers memorial quilt for those who have died from eating disorders. FUNDING: Nonprofit. OFC HRS: M-F 8am-5pm, EST. SERVES: U.S.A.

FOOD ADDICTS ANONYMOUS

4623 Forest Hill Blvd., Ste 109-4
West Palm Beach, FL 33415
(561) 967-3871
(561) 967-9815 FAX

12-Step prgm to give guidance & support to people suffering from food addiction. Currently 13 groups in Calif. FUNDING: Nonprofit. OFC HRS: M-F 9am-3pm, EST. No dues or fees. SERVES: U.S.A.

FOOD ADDICTS IN RECOVERY ANONYMOUS

400 W. Cummings Park, Ste 1700
Woburn, MA 01801
(781) 932-6300

12-Step fellowship of men and women who are constantly obsessed with food. Visit website to view a current list of meetings (www.foodaddicts.org). FUNDING: Nonprofit. ADM REQ: All ages welcome. SERVES: U.S.A.

HARRIS EATING DISORDERS CENTER

Formerly Harvard Eating Disorders Center
Massachusetts General Hospital
2 Longfellow Place, Ste 200
Boston, MA 02114
(617) 726-8470

Professional training, educator conferences, research, prevention prgms & community outreach dedicated to eating disorders. FUNDING: Nonprofit. OFC HRS: M-F 8am-5pm, EST. SERVES: U.S.A.

INSIGHT COUNSELING

23232 Peralta Dr., Ste 211
Laguna Hills, CA 92653
(949) 707-5100
(949) 488-2418 FAX

Comprehensive individual, family, couples and group therapy. Edu classes in anger mgmt and parenting. Therapists specialize in: drug/alcohol treatment; interventions; eating disorders; anxiety; panic attacks; depression; teen, family and couples issues. FUNDING: Nonprofit. OFC HRS: M-Th 9am-9pm; F 7am-9pm; Sat 9am-1pm. Spanish spoken. Accessible and affordable srvs. SERVES: Orange, Riverside & San Bernardino Counties.

INTERNATL ASSN EATING DISORDER PROFESSIONALS

P.O. Box 1295
Pekin, IL 61555-1295
(800) 800-8126
(800) 800-8126 FAX

IAEDP offers certification for professionals providing therapy for eating disorders, conferences, and referrals to eating disorder. Visit (www.iaedp.com) for referral to specialist. FUNDING: Nonprofit. OFC HRS: M-F 9am-4:30pm, CST. SERVES: U.S.A.

KAISER PERMANENTE

Psychiatry

5225 Canyon Crest Dr., Bldg. 100, Ste 103
Riverside, CA 92507
(951) 248-4000
(951) 248-4021 FAX

Individual & group prgm for eating disorders. FUNDING: Nonprofit. OFC HRS: M,Tu,Th 7am-9pm; W 7am-7pm; F 7am-5pm. Spanish spoken. SERVES: Riverside County.

NATL ASSN FOR MALES WITH EATING DISORDERS

118 Palm Dr., Ste 11
Naples, FL 34112
(877) 780-0080

This is the only org exclusively dedicated to providing support to males with eating disorders. Also seeks to educate the public on this issue. Visit (www.namedinc.org). FUNDING: Nonprofit. SERVES: U.S.A.

NATL ASSN OF ANOREXIA NERVOSA & ASSOCIATED DISORDERS

P.O. Box 640
Naperville, IL 60566
(630) 577-1330
(847) 831-3765 FAX

Working to prevent and alleviate the problems of eating disorders. Referral to therapists, self-help prgms & groups, hotline counseling, extensive edu & prevention prgms. Early detection packets for schools and other groups, advocacy campaigns to protect potential victims of eating disorders. Call or write. FUNDING: Nonprofit. OFC HRS: M-F 9am-5pm, CST. Spanish spoken. Free srvs. SERVES: U.S.A.

NATL DAIRY COUNCIL

40 Inland Marketing Srvs, Customer Srvs
10255 W. Higgens Rd., Ste 900
Rosemont, IL 60018-5616
(847) 803-2000
(847) 803-2077 FAX

Develops and provides edu materials on nutrition. Ask for catalog and price list of printed materials: brochures, posters, videos, etc. Referrals to Dairy Councils throughout the U.S. (Calif is served by the natl office). FUNDING: Nonprofit. OFC HRS: M-F 8am-5pm, CST. SERVES: U.S.A.

NATL EATING DISORDERS ASSN

603 Stewart St., Ste 803
Seattle, WA 98101-1264
(206) 382-3587
(206) 829-8501 FAX

Promotes public awareness and understanding of eating disorders and promotes access to quality treatment. Support for families through edu & research. Database of more than 700 treatment providers. Also distributes curricula to school districts. Helpline for eating disorders info/referrals (800) 931-2237. FUNDING: Nonprofit. OFC HRS: M-F 8am-5pm. Free srvs. SERVES: U.S.A.

NEW HOPE/MORENO VALLEY

12818 Heacock St., Ste C-6
Moreno Valley, CA 92553
(951) 247-6542
(951) 247-9819 FAX

Christian counseling center. Serves as a training facility for those in the counseling profession. Psychological testing, child abuse counseling, crisis eval, parenting issues, school problems, teenage issues such as suicide, runaway, depression, eating disorders and substance abuse, bereavement counseling, adult abuse issues, pain mgmt and a host of other adult counseling needs. FUNDING: Donations, fees, nonprofit. OFC HRS: By appt. ADM REQ: Low income. Accepts insurance in most cases, Victim-Witness Program, Recovery Assistance Foundation. Sliding scale basis upon request. SERVES: So. Calif.

O-ANON GENERAL SERVICE OFFICE
Region 2 Office
4733 Torrance Blvd., PMB 335
Torrance, CA 90503

Comfort, help and friendship to families and friends of compulsive overeaters. Call for meeting times and locations. Phone message hrs: M-Sun 8am-9pm. World srv (505) 891-2664. FUNDING: Nonprofit. OFC HRS: Open evenings after 6pm. Accepts voluntary contributions. SERVES: U.S.A.

OLIVE BRANCH COUNSELING CTR, INC.
9033 Baseline Rd., Ste H
Rancho Cucamonga, CA 91730
(909) 989-9030
(909) 466-4594 FAX

Counseling services for individuals, families, couples & groups including: anger mgmt, eating disorders, grief recovery, domestic violence, sexual abuse, victims of crime. Pre-marital, divorce recovery, parenting classes. Court-certified for anger mgmt, domestic violence (DV), parenting & co-parenting classes. Certified visitation. All programs available for high-risk youth and adults. Locations in Claremont, Riverside, and Rancho Cucamonga. FUNDING: Nonprofit. OFC HRS: M-F 9am-8pm; Sat 9am-5pm. Spanish spoken. Accepts insurance, sliding fee scale. SERVES: San Bernardino County.

OLIVE BRANCH COUNSELING CTR, INC.
4041 Brockton Ave.
Riverside, CA 92501
(951) 369-8534
(951) 369-1145 FAX

Counseling services for individuals, families, couples & groups including: anger mgmt, eating disorders, grief recovery, domestic violence, sexual abuse, victims of crime. Pre-marital, divorce recovery, parenting classes. Court-certified for anger mgmt, domestic violence (DV), parenting & co-parenting classes. Certified visitation. All programs available for high-risk youth and adults. Locations in Claremont, Riverside, and Rancho Cucamonga. FUNDING: Nonprofit. OFC HRS: M-F 9am-5pm; Sat 8:30am-5pm. Evening counseling available by appt. Spanish spoken. Accepts insurance, sliding fee scale. SERVES: Riverside.

OVERCOMERS IN CHRIST
P.O. Box 34460
Omaha, NE 68134
(402) 573-0966
(402) 573-0960 FAX

Biblically based, Christ-centered resources for those with life controlling problems. Network with others to establish OIC support groups. Online (www.overcomersinchrist.org). FUNDING: Nonprofit. OFC HRS: M-F 9am-12noon, CST. SERVES: U.S.A & internatl.

OVEREATERS ANONYMOUS/HDQR
World Service Office
P.O. Box 44020

6075 Zenith Court N.E.
Rio Rancho, NM 87124
(505) 891-2664
(505) 891-4320 FAX

Referral to Overeaters Anonymous (OA) meetings throughout U.S. Info & literature for compulsive overeaters. 12-Step prgm deals with food and compulsive overeating. FUNDING: Donation, nonprofit. OFC HRS: M-F 8am-4:30pm, MST. No fees or dues. SERVES: Internatl.

OVEREATERS ANONYMOUS/I.E.
Inland Empire Intergroup
P.O. Box 56021
Riverside, CA 92517
(951) 715-2080
(951) 681-9713 FAX

Self-help group patterned after AA. Call for meeting locations, dates & times Goal is to stop compulsive eating. FUNDING: Contributions, nonprofit. OFC HRS: M-F 9am-5pm. Free srvs. No dues, fees or weigh-ins. SERVES: Inland Empire.

RANCHO COMMUNITY CHURCH
31300 Rancho Community Way
Temecula, CA 92592
(951) 303-6789
(951) 303-6066 FAX

Celebrate Recovery meets Th at 6:30pm, including large group worship, lesson time and small groups. Several support groups available. Groups include addiction recovery, grief, chronic pain, divorce/separation relief, and family of those with Alzheimer's. Call for dates and times. Groups open to the public and anyone is welcome at any time during the year. FUNDING: Nonprofit. OFC HRS: M-F 9am-4pm. Spanish spoken. SERVES: Riverside County.

SAFE HARBOR
Olive Branch Church
7702 El Cerrito Rd.
Corona, CA 92881-4295
(951) 279-4477
(951) 520-9797 FAX

Christ-centered 12-Step recovery prgm. Support groups for all types of problems & addictions including: food, sex or relationship addictions, co-dependency and chemical dependency. Safe Harbor meets W at 7pm. Call for location. FUNDING: Nonprofit. OFC HRS: M-F 9am-5pm. SERVES: Riverside County.

SCREENING FOR MENTAL HEALTH, INC.
One Washington St., Ste 304
Wellesley Hills, MA 02481-1706
(781) 239-0071
(781) 431-7447 FAX

Coordinates nationwide mental health screening prgms: Natl Depression Screening Day, Natl Alcohol Screening Day and Natl Eating Disorders Screening Prgm, Signs of Suicide Prgm. Crisis line: (800) 273-8255. FUNDING: Nonprofit. OFC HRS: M-F 9am-6pm, EST. Spanish spoken. SERVES: U.S.A, Canada, Bermuda & Virgin Islands.

SUSAN B. KREVOY EATING DISORDERS PRGM
Wright Institute Los Angeles
9911 W. Pico Blvd., Ste 720
Los Angeles, CA 90035
(310) 277-2682
(310) 277-8903 FAX

Low fee individualized outpatient prgm. Individual, group & family therapy. Nutritional counseling to differentiate between physical & psychological hunger; art therapy, yoga, meditation. Cognitive behavior groups on topics such as self-esteem, body image & communication skills. Free comprehensive assessment. Case mgr will devise a three or four evening/week prgm structured to meet the patient's needs. When the patient is ready to leave the prgm, an aftercare group provides continued support for adolescents and adults. FUNDING: Nonprofit. OFC HRS: M-F 8am-5pm. Accepts most insurance, sliding fee scale. SERVES: So. Calif.

THE ELISA PROJECT
3102 Oak Lawn Ave., Ste 520
Dallas, TX 75219
(214) 369-5222
(866) 837-1999
(214) 987-4518 FAX

Promotes the recognition of eating disorder warning signs & increases community awareness. Distributes a list of therapists for srvs nationwide, treatment centers and informative materials. Bi-annual newsletter and support groups. Annual symposium & community dinner on the prevention & treatment of eating disorders. FUNDING: Nonprofit. OFC HRS: M-F 9am-4pm, CST. SERVES: U.S.A.

THE GROVE COMMUNITY CHURCH
19900 Grove Community Dr.
Riverside, CA 92508
(951) 571-9090
(951) 571-9091 FAX

Celebrate Recovery, a faith-based 12-Step support group dealing with anger mgmt, chemical dependency, co-dependency, eating disorders and sexual addictions; meets M at 7pm. Recovery Worship Service F at 7pm. Pre-marital, individual & family counseling and various support groups available. FUNDING: Nonprofit. OFC HRS: M-F 8am-5pm. Sat sessions by appt. Must call to register for counseling. Fees vary. $40 before 5pm, $50 after 5pm. No one turned away due to lack of funds. SERVES: Riverside.

THE JACQUELINE SIDMAN HEALTH FNDN
4199 Campus Dr., Ste 550
Irvine, CA 92612
(949) 251-9550
(949) 509-6599 FAX

An effective drug-free treatment for the recovery of behavioral and physical health, from addiction through the use of the subconscious mind. FUNDING: Nonprofit. OFC HRS: M-Sun 11:30am-6:30pm. SERVES: Calif.

TOPS (TAKE OFF POUNDS SENSIBLY)
Headquarters
4575 S. 5th Street
Milwaukee, WI 53207
(800) 932-8677
(414) 482-4620

Non-commercial weight control organization. Weekly support groups. Call for local chapter. FUNDING: Nonprofit. OFC HRS: M-F 8am-4:30pm, CST. Annual membership fee of $24. SERVES: U.S.A.

UCLA NEUROPSYCHIATRIC HOSPITAL
150 UCLA Medical Plaza
Los Angeles, CA 90095

(800) 825-9989
(310) 825-9111
(310) 267-0376 FAX

Comprehensive inpatient & outpatient srvs for a wide variety of psychiatric, emotional and dev disorders. Prgms in geriatric, adult, child & adol psychiatry. Spanish-speaking psychosocial clinic. Individual prgms target: eating disorders, depression, obsessive compulsive disorder, schizophrenia & seizure disorders, anxiety. Matrix UCLA Alcoholism and Addiction Medicine Srv: (310) 206-7518. FUNDING: Nonprofit. OFC HRS: M-F 8am-5pm. Multilingual staff. Accepts insurance, Medicare, Medi-Cal. SERVES: So. Calif.

ACTS/ADVENTIST COMM TEAM SRVS

See "Adventist Comm Team Srvs"

ADVENTIST COMM TEAM SRVS (ACTS)

P.O. Box 477
24914 Barton Rd.
Loma Linda, CA 92354
(909) 796-8357
(909) 799-5653 FAX

Primary goal is to assist disadvantaged people, without regard to race or creed, in living as independently as possible. Info & referral, food for homeless, case mgmt, ACTS transit provides transportation srv to medical appts, markets, beauty parlor for a fee. Must be registered with ACTS. Also offer Meals on Wheels. FUNDING: Donations, nonprofit. OFC HRS: M-Th 8am-1pm; F 8am-12noon. ADM REQ: Appt needed. SERVES: Loma Linda.

AFDC

Commonly referred to as Welfare, now known as TANF or CalWORKS. Prgms are administered by county social srvs depts; listings are shown under the county name.

AIDS ASSISTANCE PROGRAM

P.O. Box 4182
1276 N. Palm Cyn., Ste 108
Palm Springs, CA 92262
(760) 325-8481
(760) 325-1893 FAX

Food vouchers to low income people who are HIV+ or who are living with AIDS. Bilingual website (www.aidsassistance.org). FUNDING: Nonprofit. OFC HRS: M-F 8am-3pm. Spanish by arrangement. ADM REQ: Must live in the area one year, proof of income, valid ID, application. Must meet income level. No cost to client. SERVES: Desert communities.

AMERICAN RED CROSS/29 PALMS

Marine Corps Air Ground Combat Ctr
P.O. Box 6043
Bldg. 1551 (Village Center)
Twentynine Palms, CA 92278
(760) 830-6685
(760) 825-8822 FAX

Armed forces emerg srvs. FUNDING: CFC, donors, nonprofit. OFC HRS: M-F 7:30am-4pm. SERVES: 29 Palms Marine Base.

AMERICAN RED CROSS/FT. IRWIN

P.O. Box 10047
Bldg. 565
Fort Irwin, CA 92310
(760) 380-3697

Emerg assist to families in disasters, maintains communication between military families in an emerg, emerg leave, etc. First aid classes, including CPR, youth srvs. Call to confirm srvs. FUNDING: Nonprofit. OFC HRS: W 8am-3pm. SERVES: Ft. Irwin.

AMERICAN RED CROSS/ONTARIO

Inland Valley West Chapter
9140 Haven Ave., Ste 115
Rancho Cucamonga, CA 91730
(909) 481-2835
(800) 951-5600
(909) 481-4629 FAX

Disaster assist & srv to military families, food assist for low income families 2 W a month, senior food voucher prgm (must submit application), health & safety edu prgms, including first aid & CPR. FUNDING: United Way, donations, nonprofit. OFC HRS: M-F 8am-5pm. Free srvs except for health & safety classes. SERVES: Ontario, Upland, Rancho Cucamonga, Alta Loma, Chino, Chino Hills, Montclair, Mt. Baldy, Lytle Creek & Fontana.

AMERICAN RED CROSS/SAN BRDO

Inland Empire Chapter
P.O. Box 183
202 W. Rialto Ave.
San Bernardino, CA 92408
(909) 888-1481
(866) 330-9911
(909) 888-1485 FAX

Military emerg communication, disaster emerg srvs (edu, preparedness & assist). Health srvs: training in CPR, first aid, HIV/AIDS edu, new training for automated ext defibrillator (heart attacks), pet first aid and babysitting training prgms. Nurse's assistant training, home health aide training, and state competency eval for nurse assistants. FUNDING: Contributions, United Way, grants, nonprofit. OFC HRS: M-F 8am-5pm. SERVES: San Bernardino, Redlands, East Valley & mountain region.

ARLINGTON SDA COMMUNITY SRVS

8778 Magnolia Ave.
Riverside, CA 92503-4413
(951) 688-6632
(951) 688-7070 FAX

Food baskets and clothing to needy families who live in the 92503 zip. Srvs offered on a first come, first served basis every Tu from 8am-10:30am. No rent or utility asst. Call during week from 8am-12pm for more info.

ARLINGTON TEMPORARY ASSISTANCE

9000 Arlington, Ste 112
Riverside, CA 92503
(951) 689-5620

Emerg food and clothing with support designed to go beyond the usual physical and monetary needs of those who come for food and clothing. Call for info. OFC HRS: M, W, F 11am-4pm; Tu-Th 10am-1pm. Spanish spoken. ADM REQ: Driver's license, Social Security card for all family members, proof of low income and utility bill. Proof of residence. SERVES: Riverside, Mira Loma, Woodcrest.

ASSIST LEAGUE/FOOTHILL COMMUNITIES

P.O. Box 927
Upland, CA 91785
(909) 987-2813
(909) 484-0504 FAX

Three main areas of srv: (1) Operation School Bell is a prgm that provides clothing for needy children grades K-6 when referrals are made through the school districts; (2) Dental prgm is co-sponsored with San Antonio Community Hospital for children in grades K-8 whose parents are not on welfare, do not have insurance and are low income. Referrals are made through the school district and (3) A-LUV prgm provides teddy bears to fire and police staff to give to victims of accidents, crimes, or trauma who need this special srv. Also ASK (Assault Survivor Kit) provides clothing, hygiene kits, and A-Luv Bear for assault victims through San Antonio Emerg Hospital. FUNDING: Donations, nonprofit. OFC HRS: Vary, this is a volunteer-staffed prgm. ADM REQ: Call first. Varies with prgm. SERVES: Upland, Montclair, Rancho Cucamonga, Alta Loma, Ontario, Fontana, Etiwanda.

ASSIST LEAGUE/HEMACINTO

180 N. Girard St.
Hemet, CA 92544
(951) 652-8307
(951) 927-6703 FAX

Operation School Bell prgm provides clothing to needy elem school children recommended by teachers in Hemet & San Jacinto school dists. Over 1,000 children clothed each year. Also food baskets at Thanksgiving, Christmas and Easter to families recommended by 23 schools. Usually helps 75+ families. Select scholarships offered to some eligible, returning women. Help for teen mothers. HAL BEARS prgm; teddy bears provided to all law enforcement agencies for distribution to children in traumatic situations. Operates a thrift shop at the above location. FUNDING: Donations, thrift shop, nonprofit. OFC HRS: Thrift Store: M-F 9am-1pm, Sat 10am-2pm. Some Spanish spoken. ADM REQ: Must be referred by school nurse/teacher/etc. and live in the school districts of Hemet or San Jacinto. SERVES: Hemet & San Jacinto USDs.

ASSIST LEAGUE/PALM SPRINGS/DESERT

P.O. Box 3056
Rancho Mirage, CA 92270-2849
(760) 321-1990

Operation School Bell (clothing for needy elementary schoolchildren). Tutoring, bears for traumatized children, assault survivor prgm, senior srvs. Thrift store at 68-355 Ramon Rd, Cathedral City, 92234; (760)321-1990. FUNDING: Nonprofit. OFC HRS: M-Tu and Th-Sat 10am-4pm. Closed during summer (May 31-October 1). Spanish spoken. SERVES: Palm Springs, Desert area.

ASSIST LEAGUE/REDLANDS

506 W. Colton Ave.
Redlands, CA 92374-3054
(909) 792-2675
(909) 798-0436 FAX

Operation School Bell (clothing for needy children in Redlands School District). Dental center for children in grades K-12 (must be referred by family srvs). Assault survivor kit and stuffed animals for traumatized children provided through the police dept. FUNDING: Nonprofit. OFC HRS: M-F 9am-3pm; Sat 10am-1pm. Spanish spoken. SERVES: Redlands & nearby.

ASSIST LEAGUE/RIVERSIDE

3707 Sunnyside Dr.
Riverside, CA 92506
(951) 682-3445
(951) 684-1703 FAX

Programs providing brand-new clothing for referred, needy, elementary school children, SAT help, camp sponsorships for child burn victims, holiday essentials for a family, teaching scholarship, 2-day job seeking workshop for students, waiting room activity kits for children ages 3-10 yrs, teddy bears for child victims, help for community needs, snacks for homeless children, volunteer help for developmentally delayed children, SafeHouse for at-risk teens. Thrift Store, 3707 Sunnyside Dr., Riverside, 92506; (951)682-3445. FUNDING: Donations, nonprofit. OFC HRS: Thrift Store: Tu, 10am-6pm; W-Sat 10am-2pm. SERVES: Riverside metro.

ASSIST LEAGUE/SAN BERNARDINO
Children's Dental Center
580 W. 6th Street
San Bernardino, CA 92410
(909) 885-2045

Dental care provided to low-income children. Also Operation School Bell provides clothing to needy children. FUNDING: Nonprofit. OFC HRS: M-F 8:30am-4pm. ADM REQ: Must attend SBUSD and meet income guidelines. SERVES: San Bernardino County.

ASSIST LEAGUE/TEMECULA VALLEY
28720 Via Montezuma
Temecula, CA 92590
(951) 694-8018
(951) 694-8298 FAX

Alternatives to Domestic Violence, Operation School Bell (clothing for needy children in four local school districts), Heart & Hand, Assists teens, Kids on the Block puppet program, Operation Bookworm (for School Bell kids), Project Smile, college scholarships. FUNDING: Nonprofit. OFC HRS: M, W-F 10am-4pm; Tu 2pm-7pm; Sat 11am-2pm. Donate during business hrs. Spanish spoken. ADM REQ: Must be enrolled in local school dist. Must have referral from school personnel. Free srvs. SERVES: Temecula Valley.

ASSIST LEAGUE/VICTOR VALLEY
P.O. Box 39
Apple Valley, CA 92307
(760) 961-2468
(760) 961-2118 FAX

Operation School Bell provides clothing for needy children. I'm in Charge prgm teaches kids safety skills, Operation Hug provides bears for traumatized children, Kids on the Block puppet prgm, Project R.E.A.D., assault survivor kits. Common Cents Thrift Shop: 22021 Hwy 18, Suite A, Apple Valley, 92307, (760)961-1377. FUNDING: Nonprofit. OFC HRS: Vary. Office open infrequently. Call number provided for more info or to leave message. Thrift Store: Tu-Sat 10am-2pm. SERVES: San Bernardino County.

BEAUMONT PRESBYTERIAN CHURCH
702 Euclid Ave.
Beaumont, CA 92223
(951) 845-1506

Carol's Kitchen on site to serve lunch W 11:30am-1pm. No photo ID required. FUNDING: Nonprofit. OFC HRS: M-F 9am-12noon; Sun 8:30am-11am. ADM REQ: No photo ID required. No one turned away due to lack of funds. SERVES: Riverside County.

BETA CENTER HUNGER PROGRAM
See "Pomona/Inland Vly Council/Church"

BETHEL CHRISTIAN FELLOWSHIP
9134 Mango Ave., Ste C

Fontana, CA 92335
(909) 823-1198
(909) 823-1587 FAX

Food for Living food distribution outreach services for families in need, 3rd Sat of the month. OFC HRS: 10:30am-12noon. FUNDING: Nonprofit. T-F 9am-4pm SERVES: Fontana.

BIRTH CHOICE
277 S. Rancho Santa Fe Rd., Ste S
San Marcos, CA 92069-2343
(760) 744-1313

Counseling, supportive services, info and referrals to medical professionals. Financial aid prgms, post-abortion counseling and adoption srvs. FUNDING: Nonprofit. OFC HRS: M 9am-6pm; Tu-Th 9am-8pm; F 8am-12noon; Sat 10am-12noon. Spanish spoken. Free srvs. SERVES: San Marcos.

BREAST CANCER SOLUTIONS
3843 S. Bristol St., Ste 152
Santa Ana, CA 92704
(866) 960-9222
(866) 781-6068 FAX

Offers financial assist to meet the every day needs of people undergoing breast cancer treatment. Offers rental, utility, food, medical, and car payment assist. Visit (www.breastcancersolutions.org) for more info. FUNDING: Nonprofit. Spanish spoken. ADM REQ: Receiving breast cancer treatment. Free srvs. SERVES: Southern Calif.

CA ASSOCIATION OF FOOD BANKS
1624 Franklin St., Ste 722
Oakland, CA 94612
(510) 272-4435
(510) 272-9171 FAX

Network of food banks that distribute food to community-based agencies which in turn distribute to individuals & families in need. Works to develop & advocate food sharing resources & public policy. No direct srvs to the public. FUNDING: Nonprofit. SERVES: Calif.

CALIMESA SEVENTH DAY ADVENTIST CHURCH
391 Myrtlewood Dr.
Calimesa, CA 92320
(909) 795-9741
(909) 795-8205 FAX

Food and clothes provided to individuals & families residing in the Calimesa area. Recipients can return once a month. All srvs upon availability. Twice a year blood drive, member services, Thanksgiving food baskets. FUNDING: Nonprofit. PRGM HRS: M-Th 9am-2pm. Volunteers meet M 8am. ADM REQ: Must have ID. SERVES: Calimesa.

CALVARY PRESBYTERIAN CHURCH
4495 Magnolia Ave.
Riverside, CA 92501-4198
(951) 686-0761
(951) 686-1488 FAX

Hot meal served Sun evenings from 5:30pm-6pm. Clean used clothes, live music, and information for additional help also provided. Special meals during Thanksgiving and Christmas. Walk in. Nearly monthly dental van prior to hot meal. Contact Pam Shoulders to volunteer, (951) 351-4403. OFC HRS: M-Th 9am-5pm; F 9am-1pm. Free srvs. SERVES: Riverside County.

CALWORKS
CalWORKs prgm is the Calif Welfare-to-Work prgm with the goal of getting people off TANF and welfare prgms and into a self-sufficient lifestyle. The prgm requires adults who receive public assist to participate in work activities. Single parents may be required to account for 32 hrs of work activity per week and persons from two parent homes up to 35. Prgm includes: 1) appraisal & job search; 2) assessment & Welfare-to-Work plan; 3) Welfare-to-Work activities; 4) re-appraisal; 5) community srvs. Participants are provided with support srvs such as child care to remove barriers to success in the prgm. Access these srvs through the local county social srvs agency. FUNDING: Fed, state, county govt. See "Employment/Job Training" chapter of this directory.

CALWORKS
See "Riverside Co. Public Social Srvs"

CALWORKS
See "San Bernardino Co. Human Srvs Sy"

CASA BLANCA HOME OF NEIGHBORLY SRV
7680 Casa Blanca St.
Riverside, CA 92504
(951) 688-3043
(951) 688-3286 FAX

Senior prgms, Head Start prgm & emerg assist. Walk in. FUNDING: United Way, Riverside Co. Depts of Mental Health, Probation & Office of Ed, nonprofit. OFC HRS: Tu-F 8:30am-5pm. Spanish spoken. ADM REQ: Primarily for residents of the Casa Blanca community. Free srvs. SERVES: Riverside.

CATHEDRAL OF PRAISE CHURCH
P.O. Box 736
1521 S. Riverside Ave
Rialto, CA 92376
(909) 874-8676
() 90-9874 FAX

Food and clothing distribution to needy families and individuals on 1st and 3rd Sat from 8:30am-11am. Can return each week. FUNDING: Nonprofit. OFC HRS: M-F 9am-4pm. Spanish spoken. ADM REQ: Low income, photo ID. SERVES: Riverside, Rubidoux.

CATHOLIC CHARITIES USA
66 Canal Center Plaza, Ste 600
Alexandria, VA 22314
(703) 549-1390
(703) 549-1656 FAX

The nation's largest pvt network of people helping people. Independent social srv agencies and thousands of concerned volunteers work to reduce poverty, support families & build communities in the U.S. FUNDING: Nonprofit. OFC HRS: M-F 9am-5pm. SERVES: U.S.A.

CATHOLIC CHARITIES/COMMUNITY SRVS
Inland Valleys Regional Center
23623 Sunnymead Blvd., Ste E
Moreno Valley, CA 92553
(951) 924-9964
(951) 924-9997 FAX

Emerg srvs for low income. Assists with food, utility, rental assist & motel vouchers (when funding is available). Info & referral, immigration & citizenship prgm, HIV/AIDS housing assist. Counseling (909) 763-4970 or (951) 801-5282. FUNDING: Nonprofit. OFC

HRS: M-Th 8:30am-4:30pm. By appt only. Spanish spoken. Most srvs free. SERVES: Moreno Valley, Riverside, Perris, Hemet, San Jacinto, Sun City, Corona, Lake Elsinore, Banning, Beaumont, Cherry Valley.

CATHOLIC CHARITIES/COMMUNITY SRVS
West End Regional Center
9375 Archibald Ave., Ste 302
Rancho Cucamonga, CA 91730
(909) 481-7196
(909) 481-6305 FAX

Food baskets, assist with rental & mortgage payments, utility payments, pre-arranged motel accommodations, info & referral, transportation, medical referrals, clothing & furniture assist, tax prep & holiday baskets. Call for appt. FUNDING: Nonprofit. OFC HRS: M-F 8:30am-4:30pm. Spanish spoken. SERVES: Fontana, Etiwanda, Ontario, Montclair, Upland, Alta Loma, Rancho Cucamonga, Chino, Chino Hills.

CATHOLIC CHARITIES/COMMUNITY SRVS
Administration
1450 North D Street
San Bernardino, CA 92405
(909) 388-1239
(909) 384-1130 FAX

Psychological counseling for individuals & family, case mgmt, emerg food, diapers, clothing, furniture (when available), utility assist, holiday baskets, transportation, advocacy, HIV/AIDS srvs, info & referrals. Emerg housing for needy transients with pre-arranged motel accommodations (as funds allow). Refugee & immigration srvs, parolee reintegration. FUNDING: Donations, nonprofit. OFC HRS: M-F 8:30am-4:30pm. Spanish, Chinese, Filipino, Vietnamese, Russian spoken. Sliding fee scale. SERVES: San Bernardino & Riverside Counties.

CATHOLIC CHARITIES/COMMUNITY SRVS
San Bernardino Regional Center
1800 Western Ave., Ste 107
San Bernardino, CA 92411
(909) 880-3625
(909) 880-9847 FAX

Food baskets, assists with rental & mortgage payment, utility payments, transportation, info & referral, medical referrals, clothing, furniture assist (as funds are available). FUNDING: Nonprofit. OFC HRS: M-F 8:30am-4:30pm. Spanish spoken. SERVES: San Bernardino County except Morongo Basin & the west side.

CENTRAL COUNTY UNITED WAY
See "United Way/..."

CHARITY CARS
750 Miami Springs Dr.
Longwood, FL 32779
(800) 242-7489

Donated vehicles are provided to disadvantaged families who are working but cannot afford to purchase. Case workers or social srv agencies who would like to refer a client, please send info to (info@800charitycars.org) and someone will contact you. FUNDING: Donations, nonprofit. OFC HRS: Operators 24 hrs, 7 days. ADM REQ: Families, please do not contact Charity Cars directly. Contact must come from referring agency. Pre-screening process. Free srvs. SERVES: U.S.A.

CHILDREN'S FUND
County Government Center
825 E. Hospitality Lane, 2nd Fl.
San Bernardino, CA 92415-0132
(909) 387-4949
(909) 383-9758 FAX

Provides for the needs of children (ages birth-18 yrs) who are at-risk because of abuse, poverty, neglect. Accessed through case mgrs of any of the 19 Children's Network agencies in the county. Other resources must be explored before requesting assist from Children's Fund, as its mission is to provide for those things that "fall through the cracks." FUNDING: Nonprofit. OFC HRS: M-F 8am-5pm. SERVES: San Bernardino County.

CHILDREN'S HUNGER FUND
12820 Pierce St.
Pacoima, CA 91331
(818) 899-5122
(800) 708-7589
(818) 899-9552 FAX

Distributes food, clothing, medicine, and toys to local non-profit agencies and churches to provide to their clients in need. No direct food services at this location. FUNDING: Donations, nonprofit, foundations. OFC HRS: M-F 8am-5pm; Sat 9am-11am. Spanish spoken. ADM REQ: Agencies must fill out an application and complete training. Free services. SERVES: S. Calif.

CHINO NEIGHBORHOOD HOUSE
13130 W. 6th Street
Chino, CA 91710
(909) 628-5608

Emerg assist of non-perishable food items and clothing to low income families residing in Chino Unified School District, Chino Hills. FUNDING: United Way, City of Chino, donations, grants and govt funds (FEMA, CDBG). OFC HRS: M, W, F, Sat 9am-1pm. Spanish spoken. ADM REQ: Income at or below poverty level. Free srvs. SERVES: Chino, Chino Hills

COACHELLA VALLEY RESCUE MISSION
Family Shelter
P.O. Box 10660
47518 Van Buren St.
Indio, CA 92202
(760) 347-3512
(760) 347-8073 FAX

Food, clothing, showers, shelter, spiritual support and referrals to those in need. Public meals 2 times a day, 7 days. 3 meals for residents. Provide groceries for 25-100 families each week. Family shelter for women and children and men's shelter. New Life program. FUNDING: Donations. OFC HRS: 24 hrs. SERVES: Coachella Valley.

COMMUNITY ACTION PARTNERSHIP
Weatherization Prgms/Utility Assist
2038 Iowa Ave., Ste B102
Riverside, CA 92507
(951) 955-6418
(951) 955-6506 FAX

Home weatherization for low income families only. For utility assist prgm, call (951) 955-6448. OFC HRS: M-F 8am-5pm. Spanish spoken. ADM REQ: Must meet guidelines to qualify for assist. SERVES: Riverside County.

COMMUNITY ACTION PARTNERSHIP
Home Energy Assist Prgm (HEAP)
696 S. Tippecanoe Ave.
San Bernardino, CA 92415-0610
(909) 723-1620
(909) 723-1509 FAX

HEAP provides an annual credit toward gas or electric bills to qualifying clients. Energy edu workshops teach clients how to apply energy-saving means to reduce utility costs. For non-emerg utility credit, you may request application by phone. For emerg, call to set up appt at (909)723-1680 or (909)723-1681. OFC HRS: M-F 8am-5pm. Emerg utility assist: Call for appt, M-F 8am-4:30pm. Spanish spoken. ADM REQ: Gas & electric bills, CA photo ID or driver's license with current address, SS card for all residents, verification of income for prior 30 days for all household members, rental agreement/mortgage statement. Courtesy calls to the utility companies verifying HEAP credits. Payments come from Sacramento. SERVES: San Bernardino County.

COMMUNITY ACTION PARTNERSHIP
Family Development Prgm
696 S. Tippecanoe Ave.
San Bernardino, CA 92415-0610
(909) 723-1500
(909) 723-1509 FAX

Holistic case mgmt to homeless families. Transitional housing, rent security deposit prgm, food & motel vouchers, gas vouchers, bus tickets, clothing, rental assist, budgeting, counseling and info & referral. Summer camp, Christmas celebration. OFC HRS: M-Th 7:30am-5:30pm; F 8am-5pm. ADM REQ: Low income. SERVES: San Bernardino County.

COMMUNITY ACTION PARTNERSHIP
696 S. Tippecanoe Ave.
San Bernardino, CA 92415-0610
(909) 723-1500
(909) 723-1509 FAX

CAPSBC has been developing and implementing programs that address the most crucial needs of low-income residents in SB County. Designated as the "Community Action Agency" for the county by the State of Calif and is one of the 1,000 Community Action Agencies nationwide dedicated to assisting individuals and families to become self-reliant and stable. FUNDING: Private nonprofit. OFC HRS: M-F 8am-5pm. Spanish spoken. ADM REQ: An applicant organization must complete an application and receive final approval from the CAP Board of Directors. SERVES: San Bernardino County.

COMMUNITY ASSISTANCE PRGM (CAP)
8440 Nuevo St
Fontana, CA 92335
(909) 803-1059
(909) 770-8256 FAX

Referrals for low-cost or free srvs for Fontana residents. Community srvs, counseling, day care, education, finances, disabilities prgrms, domestic violence and sexual assault, family srvs, food distribution, health srvs, housing/rental, legal, senior prgrms, shelter/transitional housing, suicide prevention, youth prgrms. Networking meeting held 3rd Th of each month 9am-11am at Water of Life Community Church. Visit (www.FontanaCAP.org). FUNDING: Nonprofit. OFC HRS: M-F 9am-1:30pm SERVES: Fontana.

COMMUNITY FOOD PANTRY

Faith Lutheran Church
6336 Hallee Rd.
Joshua Tree, CA 92252
(760) 364-3957
(760) 366-8146 FAX

Emerg food distributed W 9am-11am to the needy. FUNDING: Nonprofit. ADM REQ: Must have ID and proof of income and residency. SERVES: Joshua Tree.

COMMUNITY OUTREACH MINISTRY

23905 Clinton Keith Rd., Ste 114, 116
Wildomar, CA 92595
(951) 698-7650
(951) 698-1649 FAX

Emerg srvs to youth, adults & the elderly. Referral srvs for food, clothing, shelters, utilities, insurance, counseling. Work force dev, holiday toys, food baskets, angel tree Christmas party, mentoring & summer camp for disadvantaged youth. FUNDING: Nonprofit. OFC HRS: M-F 8am-5pm. ADM REQ: Must call for appt. SERVES: Riverside County.

COMMUNITY OUTREACH PROGRAM

c/o Corona Public Library
650 S. Main St.
Corona, CA 92882
(951) 736-2381
(951) 736-2499 FAX

Assists in completing paperwork for Medi-Cal, CalWORKs, social security, interpretation, work applications. Referral for emerg assist. OFC HRS: M-Tu 10am-9pm; W-Th 10pm-6pm; Sat 10am-5pm. Spanish spoken. Free srvs. SERVES: Corona & Norco.

COMMUNITY PANTRY

135 N. San Jacinto St.
Hemet, CA 92543-4443
(951) 929-1101

Food assist not to exceed four times per year, per family. Clients are screened for previous use. FEMA for motel & housing (as funds are available). Walk in or call. FUNDING: Nonprofit. OFC HRS: M-F 9am-10am. Spanish spoken. ADM REQ: Photo ID needed. SSN for each family member. Must arrive no later than 9am for assist. Free srvs. SERVES: Hemet, Homeland, Idyllwild, Lakeview, Nuevo, Romoland, San Jacinto, Winchester.

COMMUNITY SERVICES DEPARTMENT

See "Community Action Partnership"

COMMUNITY SETTLEMENT ASSOCIATION

4366 Bermuda Ave.
Riverside, CA 92507
(951) 686-6266
(951) 782-2337 FAX

Social & recreational activities for seniors. Drinking Driving Prgm (listed separately) and referrals for treatment of alcoholism. Free food for all ages in 92507 zip code only, M, W, F 10:30am-11am. Walk in or call. Senior nights once a month for 55+. Summer camp. FUNDING: Nonprofit. OFC HRS: M-Fr 8am-5pm. Spanish spoken. ADM REQ: After school & summer prgms for grades 1-7. Food prgm recipients must have photo ID, proof of residency, proof of income. Accepts donations. SERVES: Riverside metro.

COMPASSION NETWORK, THE

520 N. Parker, Ste B
Orange, CA 92868
(714) 924-0223

Food, clothing & basic needs for low-income persons. FUNDING: Nonprofit. OFC HRS: M-Th 10am-4pm. ADM REQ: Must call for appt. SERVES: L.A., Orange & Riverside Counties.

CORONA NORCO SETTLEMENT HOUSE

507 S. Vicentia Ave.
Corona, CA 92882
(951) 737-3504
(951) 737-3201 FAX

Emerg food, basic sustenance, clothing, rent (once a year), mortgage, utility assist, info & referrals to appropriate agencies. All srvs subject to availability & eligibility. Walk in or call. FUNDING: Nonprofit. OFC HRS: M-F 10am-5:30pm. Thrift store: M-F 10am-5pm; Sat 9am-2:30pm. Food pantry prgm: M-F 4pm-5:30pm. ADM REQ: Proof of income. Free srvs. Visit food pantry once a month. SERVES: Corona-Norco USD area.

CRISIS MINISTRY

Emergency Assistance
P.O. Box 727
20700 Standing Rock Rd.
Apple Valley, CA 92307
(760) 247-6494
(760) 247-1836 FAX

Food pantry M-Th 10am-1:30pm. Free clothing, emerg assist as funds allow. FUNDING: Nonprofit. OFC HRS: M-F 9am-4:30pm. ADM REQ: Must have photo ID. SERVES: High desert area.

CROSSLIGHT FAMILY MINISTRIES

9720 Wilson Ave.
Rancho Cucamonga, CA 91737
(909) 980-6939
(909) 980-8126 FAX

Food distribution on F. Also showers before 9am. Walk-in basis. 1456 N. Grove Ave., Ontario. FUNDING: Nonprofit. OFC HRS: M-Th 9am-4pm. SERVES: Ontario.

DELMANN HEIGHTS COMM CENTER

2969 Flores St.
San Bernardino, CA 92407
(909) 384-5417
(909) 880-0809 FAX

Prgms include: senior nutrition, quilting, ESL, piano lessons, county health nurse and food distribution (USDA commodities). Open recreation. Free summer lunch for ages 1-18 yrs. Teen prgm, swimming pool (June-August) and Head Start preschool. OFC HRS: M-F 9am-6pm. Spanish spoken. SERVES: San Bernardino County.

DESERT HOT SPRINGS FAMILY RESOURCE CTR

14201 Palm Dr., Ste 108
Desert Hot Springs, CA 92240
(760) 288-3313
(760) 288-2854 FAX

Classes offered on parenting skills, family planning, adult edu. Healthy Children Connection, Healthy Families, Medi-Cal enrollment (through Catholic Charities), immunization info, utility assist clinic provided with Community Action Partnership, WIC info, job search, GED classes, veteran support group, individual, family, &

group counseling. Referrals to emerg srvs. FUNDING: Nonprofit. OFC HRS: M-F 8am-5pm. Spanish spoken. ADM REQ: Must call first, except for job search srvs. SERVES: Bermuda Dunes, Cathedral City, Coachella, Desert Hot Springs, Indio, Indio Hills, North Palm Springs, Palm Springs, Rancho Mirage.

DESERT MANNA/EMERGENCY HOUSING

209 North 1st Avenue
Barstow, CA 92311
(760) 256-7797
(760) 256-4043 FAX

Shelter accommodations for homeless individuals and families. Hot meals Th-Sun 5pm-6pm; hot lunches 11am-1pm daily, food pantry by referral, USDA commodities 1st & 3rd Th, showers M-F 9am-12noon, bread and produce as available. Emergency clothing with referral. Enter from 2nd Ave. door. For shelter, call (760)255-9025. FUNDING: Churches, donations, United Way, county, state, nonprofit. OFC HRS M-F 9am-4pm; shelter 24 hrs. SERVES: San Bernardino County.

DESERT S.O.S.

1733 N. Palm Canyon Dr., Ste A
Palm Springs, CA 92262
(760) 327-4394
(760) 327-4516 FAX

Provides srvs for the homeless in western Coachella Valley. Nightengale Manor provides 45 clients with 60-day housing, meals, and case mgmt. Desert Horizon provides 32 people with transitional housing; clients pay 30% of their income (HUD guidelines) towards rent. Also offers an overnight shleter that feeds and houses 25 people (or 40 during cold weather season). FUNDING: Nonprofit, JFS, Coachella Valley Association of Governments. ADM REQ: Must be homeless; background check required for overnight shelter. Free srvs. SERVES: Western Coachella Valley.

DESERT SANCTUARY/HALEY HOUSE

P.O. Box 1781
703 E. Main St.
Barstow, CA 92312
(760) 256-3441
(760) 256-3733
(760) 256-4002 FAX

16-bed shelter for battered women & their children up to 6 mos. Also outreach for community & area victims in need of srvs not inclusive of shelter. Outreach srvs include: rent/utility assist, anger mgmt, therapy, sexual assault srvs, court-ordered supervised visitation, legal aid, housing stabilization. 24-hr hotline: (800) 982-2221. FUNDING: Nonprofit. OFC HRS: Hotline 24 hrs. Outreach M-F 9am-5pm. German & Spanish spoken. ADM REQ: Women in abusive surroundings. Free srvs. SERVES: So. Calif.

ECHOES OF FAITH CHRISTIAN CTR

Operation Fresh Start
5376 Phillips Blvd.
Ontario, CA 91761
(909) 627-0927
(909) 464-9882 FAX

Food distribution for needy families 2nd Sat of each month 9am-11:30am. No financial assist available. FUNDING: Church, donations. OFC HRS: M-Th 8:30am-4:30pm. Spanish spoken.

ADM REQ: Photo ID. Free srvs. SERVES: Ontario, Pomona & Upland.

EMMANUEL TEMPLE CHURCH

Emergency Assistance
P.O. Box 1237
17288 Stoddard Wells Rd.
Victorville, CA 92394
(760) 245-4973
(760) 245-8922
(760) 245-1453 FAX

Food and clothing provided F 10am-11:30am. FUNDING: Nonprofit. OFC HRS: M-Th 10am-3pm; F 10am-2pm. SERVES: Victorville.

FAMILY SERVICE AGENCY/SAN BRDO

Crest Forest Family Srvs
23406 Crest Forest Dr.
Crestline, CA 92325
(909) 338-4689

Emerg food distribution, utility payment assist, USDA commodities. FUNDING: United Way, fees, nonprofit. OFC HRS: F 9am-5pm. Spanish spoken. ADM REQ: Low income, must show proof of residency. Medi-Cal and sliding fee scale for counseling. SERVES: San Bernardino County.

FAMILY SERVICE ASSN/REDLANDS

612 Lawton St.
Redlands, CA 92374
(909) 793-2673
(909) 793-7324 FAX

Srvs provided to low income and homeless families. Case mgmt, food, clothing, utility and rental assist, cold weather motel vouchers, screening for dental & vision, prescription assist, and edu prgms. Home Again Project is a long-term comprehensive prgm helping homeless families into permanent housing and employment. Client srv M-W, F 9am-12noon, 1:30pm-7pm. Surplus food available on walk-in basis, all other srvs require appt. FUNDING: Donations, United Way, grants, nonprofit. OFC HRS: M-W 8am-7pm; Th 8am-12noon; F 8am-4:30pm. Spanish spoken. ADM REQ: Low or no income. Free srvs. SERVES: Redlands, East Valley area.

FAMILY SERVICE ASSN/WEST RIVERSIDE

Mead Valley Comm/Senior & Disabled Srvs
21091 Rider St.
Perris, CA 92570
(951) 657-0686
(951) 657-9208 FAX

Home-delivered meals, wellness center, advisory board meetings, senior meetings, AA & NA meetings, kinship meeting, summer school prgms, computers, Bingo, commodity food distribution, crafts, business network, congregate meals, THRIVE forums, food bank, postmaster's community srv. FUNDING: Nonprofit. OFC HRS: M-F 9am-5pm. Spanish spoken. ADM REQ: Depends on srvs. SERVES: Western Riverside County.

FAMILY SERVICE ASSOCIATION OF REDLANDS

Home Again Project
612 Lawton St.
Redlands, CA 92374
(909) 792-2673
(909) 793-7324 FAX

Comprehensive homeless assist prgm focusing on permanent housing. Daytime prgm only (not a 24-hr shelter) offering child care, case mgmt,

meals daily, etc. FUNDING: Fndns, United Way, govt, nonprofit. OFC HRS: M-Th 9am-7pm; F 9am-4:30pm. Spanish spoken. ADM REQ: Must be screened by Family Service Assn. Must have children under the age of 18 yrs and a continuing source of income. Also accepts the disabled and those receiving SSI. Free srvs. SERVES: San Bernardino County.

FELLOWSHIP BAPTIST CHURCH

3624 Arlington Ave.
Riverside, CA 92506
(951) 684-8071
(951) 684-7290 FAX

Food pantry (dry goods) Tu-Th 8:30am-12:30pm, call first FUNDING: Nonprofit. OFC HRS: Tu-Th 8am-1pm. ADM REQ: Must have ID. SERVES: Riverside County.

FINANCIAL CRISIS

See also Chapter headings for "Homeless...," "Emergency," & "Housing/Low Income..."

FIND (FOOD IN NEED OF DISTRIBUTION)

Food Bank
P.O. Box 10080
83775 Citrus Ave.
Indio, CA 92201
(760) 775-3663
(760) 775-0252 FAX

Food bank available to nonprofit community agencies who help those in need. FUNDING: Nonprofit, donations. OFC HRS: M-F 8am-4pm. Spanish spoken. ADM REQ: Open to approved nonprofit organizations. Accepts non-perishable food donations. SERVES: Eastern Riverside County.

FIRST CALL FOR HELP

Volunteer Center of Victor Valley
P.O. Box 1992
16692 Mojave Dr.
Victorville, CA 92393
(760) 243-9646
(760) 243-4762 FAX

Info & referral for people seeking srvs or info on community agencies. Interaction with individuals in crisis situations in order to reduce tension and stress, allowing that person to utilize available resources more effectively. FUNDING: Donations, grants, nonprofit. OFC HRS: M-Th 9am-2:45pm. Spanish spoken. SERVES: San Bernardino County.

FIRST CONGREGATIONAL CHURCH

3504 Mission Inn Ave.
Riverside, CA 92501
(951) 684-2494
(951) 778-0309 FAX

Congregate dinner every W at 5:30pm. Also clothing and medical clinic twice per month. FUNDING: Nonprofit. ADM REQ: Homeless or low income. Free srvs. SERVES: Riverside County.

FISH/LOWER COACHELLA VALLEY

Food Bank
P.O. Box 458
52555 Oasis Palm
Coachella, CA 92236
(760) 398-1600
(760) 398-1625 FAX

Food for the needy. Walk in. No shelter, housing, rental or transportation assist. Govt food distributed once a month; call for info. FUNDING: Grants, donations, nonprofit. OFC HRS:

M-F 10am-12noon. Summer hrs: M-F 9am-11pm. Spanish available on request. ADM REQ: Must have ID. Free srvs. SERVES: Greater Indio area, La Quinta, Palm Desert, Riverside County.

FOOD NOW

11555 Palm Dr.
Desert Hot Springs, CA 92240
(760) 329-4100
(760) 329-3388 FAX

Emerg food for anyone in need. FUNDING: Nonprofit. OFC HRS: Tu-Th 9am-11am and by appt. SERVES: Riverside County.

FOOD STAMPS

See "Riverside Co. Public Social Srvs" & "San Bernardino Co. Human Srvs Sy"

FOUNTAIN OF LIFE TEMPLE

Church of God in Christ
1518 E. Williams
Banning, CA 92220
(951) 849-1517

Food distribution 1st & 3rd Tu of each month from 9am-12noon & 4th W. FUNDING: Nonprofit. ADM REQ: Low income, seniors, disabled. SERVES: Banning, Beaumont, Cabazon.

FRAZEE COMMUNITY CENTER

1140 W. Mill St.
San Bernardino, CA 92412
(909) 889-4424
(909) 889-6865 FAX

Emerg srvs, hot meals, food boxes for families as available, homeless shelters. Transitional shelter and thrift store. Walk in or call. FUNDING: Govt grants, United Way, donations, nonprofit. OFC HRS: M-F 7:30am-3:30pm. Some Spanish spoken. ADM REQ: Low income. Free srvs. SERVES: San Bernardino.

G.A.P. FOOD BANK

God Always Provides Food Bank
8768 Helms St., Ste A
Rancho Cucamonga, CA 91730
(909) 945-1020
(909) 945-5001

Emerg food boxes Th 4pm-6pm. Parking lot and food line open at 3pm. Helps about 450 families per week. Donate Th between 9am and 6pm. M-F Spanish spoken. ADM REQ: New applicants must have Calif ID/driver's license. SERVES: Alta Loma.

GAIN/CALWORKS PROGRAMS

These prgms are administered by the San Bernardino County Human Srvs System and can be found in "Employment Placement/Job Training." Look for CalWORKs or WIA prgms for some of these srvs.

GENESIS SHELTER

See "Lutheran Social Srvs/Shelter Prgm"

GOD'S HELPING HAND

13958 Old Highway 215
Moreno Valley, CA 92553
(951) 653-2529
(951) 657-0426 FAX

Sponsors four thrift stores and seven food banks. Provides needy families with clothing and food by appt (immediate in extreme cases). Admin ofc: 1040 Teepee Lane, Perris, CA 92570, phone (951) 657-3041. FUNDING: Nonprofit. OFC HRS: M-F 9am-4:30pm. Sat

9am-2pm. ADM REQ: Must have photo ID, proof of income & residence. SERVES: Riverside Metro, Moreno Valley, Banning, Beaumont, Hemet, Perris, Sun City, Nuevo & adjacent areas.

GOD'S HELPING HAND
631 W. 4th Street
Perris, CA 92570
(951) 943-9445

Food bank at this location. Food served upon availability. FUNDING: Nonprofit. Food donations accepted. SERVES: Perris, Lake Elsinore.

GOD'S HELPING HAND
26701 McCall Blvd.
Sun City, CA 92587
(951) 679-4667

Food bank at this location. 1st and 3rd W, 10am-12noon. FUNDING: Nonprofit. ADM REQ: Must call for appt and have ID. SERVES: Sun City area.

GOLDEN SHARE FOODS
Rialto Christian Center
234 W. Merrill Ave.
Rialto, CA 92376
(909) 873-5380

Buy groceries for less. Call to verify location and date of sign-up and grocery pick-up. FUNDING: Nonprofit. Accepts cash and money orders. SERVES: Rialto.

H.E.L.P. INC.
53 S. 6th Street
Banning, CA 92220
(951) 922-2305
(951) 922-1183 FAX

Hope, Empathy, Love and Prayer (H.E.L.P.). Food, referrals, clothing, any emerg srvs within our means. Walk in. Also a thrift store. FUNDING: Donations, USDA, FEMA, nonprofit. OFC HRS: M-Th 9am-3pm; F 9am-12noon. Spanish spoken upon request. Free srvs. SERVES: San Gorgonio Pass Area (Banning, Beaumont, Cherry Valley, Calimesa), and transients.

HELPING HANDS MINISTRY OF MOUNT ZION
224 W. California St.
Ontario, CA 91762
(909) 983-2411
(909) 983-6244 FAX

Food distribution held each Th 9am-12noon. All needy persons welcome. SERVES: Ontario.

HELPING OUR PEOPLE IN ELSINORE
29885 2nd Street, Ste R
Elsinore, CA 92532
(951) 245-7510
(951) 245-7405 FAX

Food distributed 2nd Sat of each month. Must have box or container. In event of rain, distribution will be delayed one week, unless otherwise noted. FUNDING: Nonprofit. OFC HRS: Tu-Th 9am-12noon. SERVES: Elsinore.

HELPLINE INFO & REFERRAL
See "Volunteer Center/Riverside Co."

HERMANDAD MEXICANA NACIONAL
611 W. Civic Center Dr.
Santa Ana, CA 92701
(714) 541-0250

Citizenship and immigration paperwork for a low fee. USDA surplus foods on the 3rd Th of each month. FUNDING: Nonprofit. OFC HRS: M-F 10am-7pm. Spanish spoken. ADM REQ: Must be resident. SERVES: Riverside County.

HERNANDEZ COMMUNITY CENTER
222 N. Lugo Ave.
San Bernardino, CA 92408
(909) 384-5420
(909) 384-5160 FAX

Food distribution 3rd Tu 8am-11am. Program subject to change without notification. Call to confirm. OFC HRS: M-Th 9am-8pm ADM REQ: Must live in the code area: 92401, 92408, 92409, 92410 east of Sierra Way. Must show proof of residency and income. SERVES: San Bernardino County.

HOLY FAMILY CATHOLIC CHURCH
9974 I Avenue
Hesperia, CA 92345
(760) 244-9180
(760) 244-1959 FAX

Emerg food provided 2nd, 3rd, 4th W 10am-12noon. In need of volunteers, and any donation is greatly appreciated. Contact Eva Aguilera for more info (760) 244-0316. FUNDING: Nonprofit. Spanish spoken. ADM REQ: Call to confirm. SERVES: Hesperia.

HOME ENERGY ASSIST PRGM (HEAP)
Community Srvs & Dev
P.O. Box 1947
Sacramento, CA 95812-1947
(916) 576-7109
(866) 675-6623
(916) 263-1406 FAX

Prgm to offset the cost of energy for Calif low income households. HEAP provides a payment, once every calendar year in the form of either a direct payment to a utility company, a dual-party warrant made payable to the applicant and a utility company, or a single-party warrant if utilities are included in the rent or the applicant is submetered. Federal law requires states to give priority to households with low incomes & high energy costs; takes into consideration households with children under age 6 yrs, disabled persons and other individuals. TDD/TTY (800) 725-2922. OFC HRS: M-F 8am-5pm. ADM REQ: Total gross monthly income does not exceed income guidelines and a high proportion of the household income pays for home energy; primarily meets immediate home energy needs. SERVES: Calif.

HOME OF NEIGHBORLY SERVICE
839 N. Mt. Vernon Ave.
San Bernardino, CA 92411
(909) 885-3491
(909) 884-0181 FAX

After school enrichment prgm for children in first grade and up. Recreation, youth skill building, counseling groups, gang intervention & prevention, homework assist/tutoring for youth, Boy & Girl Scouts, nutrition classes for adults, ESL for adults, children's clothes closet, Narcotics Anonymous meetings, parenting support groups, sewing for adults, boxing, hip hop dancing, aerobics & emerg food srv, resource & referrals. OFC HRS: M-Th 8am-5:30pm; F 8am-5pm. Spanish spoken. Free srvs & referrals. SERVES: San Bernardino County.

HOPE LUTHERAN CHURCH
29141 Vallejo Ave.
Temecula, CA 92592
(951) 676-6262
(951) 694-3451 FAX

Small sack of food given to those in need. One paper sack of non-perishable, donated items. Eligible 4 times a year. FUNDING: Nonprofit. OFC HRS: M-Th 10am-3pm for food. ADM REQ: Must sign guestbook. SERVES: Temecula area.

INLAND TEMPORARY HOMES
P.O. Box 239
Loma Linda, CA 92354-0239
(909) 796-6381
(909) 796-6885 FAX

30-90 day emerg shelter for homeless families with children. Highly structured & directive prgm designed to place families in permanent housing. Support srvs include: job skills assessment, individual counseling, food and clothing assist & savings plan dev. Parenting classes, anger mgmt, stress mgmt, computer basics. Wait: 15-20 wks. Check in every W once on list. FUNDING: Donations, grants, nonprofit. OFC HRS: M-Th 9am-4pm; F 9am-1pm. Spanish spoken. ADM REQ: Photo ID, Social Security number for all persons seeking shelter. Families with at least one child ages 17 yrs or younger. SERVES: San Bernardino County.

JAMES L. BRULTE SENIOR CTR
11200 Baseline Rd.
Rancho Cucamonga, CA 91730
(909) 477-2782
(909) 477-2787 FAX

Crafts, Bingo, commodity food distribution, info & referral, HICAP, blood pressure checks 2nd Tu, health edu, legal counseling, senior transportation and nutrition prgm. FUNDING: City. OFC HRS: M-F 8am-10pm; Sat 8am-6pm; Sun 9am-5pm. ADM REQ: Must fill out application and pay a $25 annual fee for transportation services for. $12 fee for gym. Rancho Cucamonga residents only. SERVES: West End San Bernardino County, primarily Rancho Cucamonga.

JORDAN OUTREACH MINISTRIES INTERNATL
P.O. Box 818
50930 Calhoun St.
Coachella, CA 92236
(760) 398-3352
(760) 398-6352 FAX

Emerg food, clothing, and other items provided to low income families. Clothes F 6pm. FUNDING: Nonprofit. OFC HRS: M 9am-4pm; Tu-Th 9am-7pm; F 9am-3pm. Spanish spoken. Free srvs. SERVES: Thermal.

JOSHUA TREE COMMUNITY CENTER
P.O. Box 1245
6171 Sunburst Ave.
Joshua Tree, CA 92252
(760) 366-8415
(760) 366-1227 FAX

USDA surplus food 9am-11am, 3rd M of each month. Senior lunch M-F 11:30am (donation $3). Several recreational activities and classes for youths & adults. OFC HRS: M-F 9am-5pm. SERVES: Joshua Tree.

L'TANYA JAMES MINISTRIES
P.O. Box 900065
Palmdale, CA 93590
(661) 265-9784

Distributes clothing, warm meals, groceries, job information and referrals to other help agencies. FUNDING: Nonprofit. Free srvs. SERVES: Lancaster & Palmdale.

LA QUINTA SENIOR CENTER
F.I.N.D. Prgm
78450 Avenida La Fonda
La Quinta, CA 92253
(760) 564-0096
(760) 564-5004 FAX

Bakery goods F at 10:30am. M-F 8am-5pm ADM REQ: Must be resident of La Quinta. Must sign up. Available to adults and seniors.

LIVING WATERS
Food Pantry
21811 Ottawa Rd
Apple Valley, CA 92307
(760) 247-6488
(760) 247-4715 FAX

Food given to those in need; must first attend the worship srv. Distribution: F 2pm-4pm. FUNDING: Nonprofit. OFC HRS: M-F vary. ASL available. ADM REQ: Must have ID. SERVES: Calif.

LUTHERAN SOCIAL SRVS/SHELTER PRGM
Genesis Transitional Housing Prgm
3772 Taft Ave.
Riverside, CA 92503
(951) 689-7847
(951) 687-7299 FAX

Eight 1-bedroom apts for homeless women with children. Average stay is ninety days-two yrs as the transition is made from homelessness to permanent housing, employment & self-sufficiency. Emerg food assist, counseling, legal advocacy, substance abuse prgm, anger mgmt, info & referral. Food pantry M-Th 11am-3pm. FUNDING: Govt grants, United Way, donations, churches, nonprofit. OFC HRS: M-Th 9am-5pm; F 9am-4pm. ADM REQ: Homeless women. Must have two forms of ID for food pantry. Eligible every 30 days. SERVES: Riverside & San Bernardino Counties.

MARCH A.F.B./FAMILY SUPPORT
1261 Graeber St., Bldg. 2313, Rm. 1A
March Air Base, CA 92518-1775
(951) 655-5350
(951) 655-4719 FAX

Info & referral. Assessment and referral assist to families in crisis, support during family separation, relocation assist, skill workshops as needed on family issues and job search skills. FUNDING: Govt. OFC HRS: M-F 7:30am-4pm (some weekends). ADM REQ: Military staff or family member. SERVES: March Air Reserve area.

MARINE CORPS AIR GROUND COMBAT CTR
Navy/Marine Relief Core Society
P.O. Box 6041
Building 1551, MCAGCC
Twentynine Palms, CA 92278-0018
(760) 830-6323
(760) 830-7189 FAX

Emerg assist with food & other basic needs, including budget counseling, layettes, and visiting nurse srvs. FUNDING: Nonprofit, govt. OFC HRS: M-F 8am-4pm. ADM REQ: Military. SERVES: 29 Palms.

MARTHA'S VILLAGE & KITCHEN, INC.
83791 Date Ave.

Indio, CA 92201-4737
(760) 347-4741
(760) 347-9551 FAX

Hot meals M-Sun 11am-12:30pm, canned food baskets offered to families M-F 8am-10am, 1pm-4pm, 3rd W of month 10am-12noon for singles. Store distributes clothing to families by request. Medical referrals & prescription vouchers for those with no other access to medical care. Showers M-F 8am-10:45am & seasonal shelter. Offers computer, ESL & EED classes. FUNDING: Donations, nonprofit. OFC HRS: M-F 8am-5pm. SERVES: Coachella Vly area.

MARY'S MERCY CENTER
P.O. Box 7563
641 Roberds Ave.
San Bernardino, CA 92411
(909) 889-2558
(909) 386-7704 FAX

Hot meal kitchen open M-Th 11:30am-1:30pm. Also open Sat and Sun (except 1st Sun of the month). Emerg food (beans, rice, tomato sauce, bread) every W 1:30pm-3pm (except 1st W of the month). Clothes available M 9am-11am for women & children; Th 1:30pm-2:30pm for men. Free showers for women M 8am-12noon & W 8am-11pm; men Tu, Th 8am-10:30am. FUNDING: Donations, nonprofit. OFC HRS: M-Th 9am-4pm. Spanish spoken. SERVES: San Bernardino County.

MASTER'S TABLE FOOD MINISTRY
3510 Fairmont
Riverside, CA 92501
(951) 686-5233

Food distribution 2nd and 4th W at 2:30pm. Food bags for those in the 92501 zipcode.. No rental or utility assist. FUNDING: Nonprofit. ADM REQ: Must have current CA ID/Driver's License. SERVES: Riverside County.

MENIFEE VALLEY COMMUNITY CUPBOARD
P.O. Box 2253
26808 Cherry Hills Blvd.
Sun City, CA 92586
(951) 301-4414

Food provided to low income families, individuals, & seniors. Recipients can return once a month. Home delivery for seniors & physically challenged upon request. Donations welcome. Phone or walk in. Thrift store at 26944 Cherry Hills Blvd., (951)672-3078. FUNDING: Nonprofit. Prgm hrs: M-F 10am-2pm. Ofc Hrs: 8am-4:30pm. ADM REQ: Low income, seniors, must have photo ID, proof of income, proof of residency. Free srvs. SERVES: Zip code areas: 92584, 92585, 92586, portions of 92857; Quail Valley, Cottonwood Canyon.

MERCY AIRLIFT
P.O. Box 90452
Los Angeles, CA 90009
(800) 637-2945
(714) 518-5980
(714) 518-5982 FAX

Disaster and humanitarian relief providing immediate transportation of food, medical supplies, medicines, and medica & relief personnel to disaster sites. Transports patients for medical srvs they are otherwise unable to reach. Emerg response (562) 209-2912. FUNDING: Nonprofit. SERVES: Internat.

MERCY HOUSE
905 E. Holt Ave., Ste 7
Ontario, CA 91761
(909) 391-2630
(909) 391-2803 FAX

Emerg intake center. Hygiene supplies, motel and food vouchers when available. Support resources and a phone for anyone to use. FUNDING: Nonprofit, county. OFC HRS: M-F 9am-1pm. Spanish spoken. SERVES: Riverside County.

MODEST NEEDS FOUNDATION
115 E. 30th Street, 1st Fl.
New York, NY 10016
(212) 463-7042

Visit (www.modestneeds.org) to learn more about the prgm and to apply for grant assist. Self-sufficiency grants, back-to-work grants, independent living grants, nonprofit grants. FUNDING: Nonprofit. OFC HRS: M-F 9am-5pm, EST. Donations welcome. SERVES: U.S.A.

MONTCLAIR HUMAN SRVS DIVISION
5111 Benito St.
Montclair, CA 91763
(909) 625-9460
(909) 399-9751 FAX

Senior activities and meals M-F 11:30am-1pm ($1.75 donation for ages 60 yrs+). USDA surplus food 3rd Th of each month to Montclair residents. Call (909)625-9483 or (909)625-9462 for info. Low-cost medical and immunization clinic. Weight room and racquet ball courts. After-school prgms and recreation activities. Also offers free parenting and nutrition classes. See website (www.ci.montclair.ca.us/) for more info on all srvs. FUNDING: DAAS, CDD, First 5, State after-school Edu & Safety Prgms, grants, Healthy Start Planning Grant. OFC HRS: Rec Office: M-Th 7:30am-6pm. Rec Facility: M-F 7:30-9:30pm; Sat 8am-5pm. Spanish spoken. ADM REQ: Proof of income/uninsured for clinic srvs. SERVES: San Bernardino County.

MORENO VALLEY COMMUNITY ASSIST
24594 Sunnymead Blvd., Ste W
Moreno Valley, CA 92553
(951) 485-7792
(951) 485-7792 FAX

Food, clothing and utility assist (Feb & March) to people in need. OFC HRS: Tu,Th 10am-1pm. ADM REQ: Must prove residence and need. Income verification, ID & SS card required. SERVES: Moreno Valley area.

MOSES HOUSE MINISTRIES
P.O. Box 2033
15180 Anacapa Rd.
Victorville, CA 92393
(866) 606-6737
(760) 955-1895
(760) 955-1303 FAX

Private Christian family homes offer pregnant young women and teens housing during their pregnancy. Case mgmt, assists with family reunification, edu, employment, parenting, or placing their babies for adoption. Transportation srvs available. Emerg assist prgm for pregnant or parenting moms with children ages birth-5 yrs offers bottles, formula, and other necessary supplies. Research ctr for single moms. FUNDING: Nonprofit, United Way, donations. OFC HRS: M-F 9am-4pm. SERVES: San Bernardino County.

MOUNTAIN VIEW COMMUNITY CHURCH
8833 Palmetto Ave.
Fontana, CA 92335
(909) 357-9377
(909) 357-0445 FAX

Food pantry for those in need, W 10am-12noon. FUNDING: Nonprofit. OFC HRS: M-F 8am-4pm; Sun 8am-12noon. ADM REQ: Must have ID. SERVES: Fontana, Rialto, Bloomington.

NEW HOPE MINISTRIES
Fellowship in the Pass Church
650 Oak Valley Pkwy.
Beaumont, CA 92223
(951) 845-2693
(951) 769-0114 FAX

Five-day supply of perishable and non-perishable food to families, single men and women. Clients can use this srv every month. Clothing is given to people in need. Serves approx 500 people monthly. Must be a resident of the Banning, Cherry Valley, Cabazon or Beaumont area. Walk in. FUNDING: Nonprofit. OFC HRS: Prgm: M-F 9am-12noon. Office: M-F 8am-4:30pm. ADM REQ: Must have ID. Free srvs. SERVES: Banning, Cherry Valley or Beaumont area.

NEW HOPE VILLAGE, INC.
SHP/Transitional Housing for the Homeless
203 W. Fredricks St., Ste 3
Barstow, CA 92311
(760) 256-3656
(760) 255-3314 FAX

Five-apartment complex. Transitional housing for the homeless individuals & families. May stay in prgm for up to two yrs. Intensive life skills edu, budgeting, time mgmt, employment, edu, health, safety, nutrition, goals, community & fundraising events. FUNDING: Grants, United Way, donations. OFC HRS: M-F 8am-4pm. ADM REQ: Must be in prgm to receive srvs. Must be motivated to become self-sufficient. SERVES: High desert area.

NORTH TOWN COMMUNITY CENTER
10071 Freon Blvd.
Rancho Cucamonga, CA 91730
(909) 941-7465

Food distribution held every 1st M of the month from 9am-11am. M-F 8am-5pm. Spanish spoken. ADM REQ: Must bring proof of residency, income and I.D. SERVES: Rancho Cucamonga.

NORTHTOWN HOUSING DEVELOPMENT
Northtown Housing College Scholarship
8599 Haven Ave., Ste 205
Rancho Cucamonga, CA 91730
(909) 980-0465

Community center offers free summer lunch prgm, ESL classes, GED, govt food commodities, after school recreation & tutoring, immunizations, summer day camp, holiday toy giveaway, info & referrals, job skills workshops, affordable housing. FUNDING: Nonprofit. OFC HRS: M-F 8am-5pm. Spanish spoken. SERVES: Rancho Cucamonga & nearby.

ONTARIO CHRISTIAN CENTER
1336 N. Baker Ave.
Ontario, CA 91764

(909) 983-5269
(909) 983-5852 FAX

Food referral for needy families. Food bank every F 5pm. FUNDING: Donations, nonprofit. OFC HRS: M 8am-4:30pm, Tu-F 8am-5pm. Some Spanish spoken. ADM REQ: Low income, resident, ID required. SERVES: Inland Empire.

OPERATION PROVIDER
P.O. Box 26
26517 Pine Ave.
Twin Peaks, CA 92391
(909) 337-8585
(909) 336-4021 FAX

Emerg food Tu, F 12noon-2pm, clothing, info & referral, limited utility assist, motel vouchers, baby food, holiday baskets. FUNDING: Donations, nonprofit. OFC HRS: Tu-F 12noon-2pm. ADM REQ: Proof of income & residency. SERVES: San Bernardino Mountains.

OUR LADY OF GUADALUPE
Emergency Food Pantry
P.O. Box 218
65-100 Dale Killer Rd.
Mecca, CA 92254
(760) 396-2717
(760) 396-0047 FAX

Emerg food bags on the last Sat of each month. Bread on F 12noon-4pm. FUNDING: Nonprofit. Spanish spoken. SERVES: Mecca.

OUR LADY OF HOPE FOOD PANTRY
Formerly St. Anne's Emergency Outreach
P.O. Box 3860
6885 Del Rosa Ave.
San Bernardino, CA 92404
(909) 884-6375
(909) 884-8976 FAX

Food pantry, emerg food boxes, clothing, baby food (M-W 9am-11am, closed 1st week of each month). USDA surplus food 3rd F and Christmas baskets. For USDA food boxes must show proof of address, as only give out to zip code 92404 on the 3rd F in rm. B-2. Food Pantry (909)884-5400. FUNDING: Parish donations. OFC HRS: Tu, Th, F 9am-5pm; Sat, Sun 9am-2pm. Spanish spoken. ADM REQ: Proof of income, photo ID. SERVES: East San Bernardino from Waterman East including City of Highland, North to 48th St and South to 3rd Ave.

OUR LADY OF MT. CARMEL CHURCH
10079 8th Street
Rancho Cucamonga, CA 91730
(909) 987-2717

Food pantry Tu 3pm-4:30pm. Also referral srvs. FUNDING: Nonprofit. OFC HRS: M-F 9am-5pm, Sat 8:30am-3pm. Spanish spoken. ADM REQ: Fill out application. SERVES: Rancho Cucamonga, Fontana and Ontario.

OUR LADY OF PERPETUAL HELP
Charities Program
5250 Central Ave.
Riverside, CA 92504
(951) 689-8921
(951) 689-3619 FAX

Emerg food available M-F 9am-11:30am. No geographic restrictions. OFC HRS: M-F 9am-5pm. Spanish spoken. ADM REQ: Must have picture ID and SS #'s for the entire household. SERVES: Riverside County.

OUR LADY OF PERPETUAL HELP/MEALS
See "Martha's Village & Kitchen, Inc."

OUR LADY OF THE DESERT CATHOLIC FOOD PANTRY
18386 Corwin Rd.
Apple Valley, CA 92307
(760) 242-4427
(760) 242-1195 FAX

Food pantry W & Th 9am-11:30am. People may access this srv once every other month. FUNDING: Nonprofit. OFC HRS: M-F 8am-2:30pm ADM REQ: All family members must have ID. SERVES: Apple Valley.

PERRIS VALLEY FAMILY RESOURCE CENTER
371 Wilkerson Ave., Ste L
Perris, CA 92570
(951) 443-1158
(951) 940-1964 FAX

Comprehensive srvs to families and children. Parents & teen classes, counseling, training workshops, food referrals, rental assist, ESL, anger mgmt, Healthy Families Applications, college enrollment information. FUNDING: Govt. OFC HRS: M-Th 8am-5pm. Spanish spoken. SERVES: Perris Valley area, Moreno Valley, Lake Elsinore, Hemet and surrounding areas.

POINT OF GRACE CHRISTIAN FELLOWSHIP
9774 Hawthorne Dr., Ste 901
Rancho Cucamonga, CA 91730
(909) 944-9909
(909) 944-7789 FAX

Community closet, food pantry, learning center, behavioral support groups such as Celebrate Recovery divorce care ministry based on demand, anger mgmt for kids & teens, Steps to Hope. FUNDING: Nonprofit, donations. OFC HRS: Tu-Th 12noon-4pm. SERVES: San Bernardino County.

POMONA/INLAND VLY COUNCIL/CHURCH
See also "West End Hunger..."

POMONA/INLAND VLY COUNCIL/CHURCH
Beta Center Hunger Program
1095 W. Grand Ave.
Pomona, CA 91766
(909) 622-7278
(909) 622-6138 FAX

Emerg food for those meeting income guidelines. Five-day supply of food given to family members with two forms of ID; address and income verification required. Also classes in nutrition & low-cost recipes. Advocacy and referrals. Clients can also receive USDA commodities once every 30 days. Walk in. FUNDING: FEMA, donations, nonprofit. OFC HRS: M-F 9am-11am, 1:30pm-3pm. Spanish spoken. ADM REQ: Income eligibility (federal poverty guideline), proof of address, ID for each household member. Also for those who are homeless. Free srvs. SERVES: Pomona, Diamond Bar, Claremont, Montclair, Chino & Walnut.

PRECIOUS BLOOD
157 W. Nicolet St.
Banning, CA 92220
(951) 849-2434
(951) 849-8698 FAX

Food provided to families & individuals every W from 10am-12noon. Recipients can return once a month for assist. Diapers & baby food when available. FUNDING: Nonprofit. OFC HRS: M-F 8am-4pm. Spanish spoken. ADM REQ: Low income, must have photo ID. SERVES: Riverside County.

QUEEN OF ANGELS CHURCH
4824 Jones Ave.
Riverside, CA 92505
(951) 689-3674
(951) 687-6146 FAX

Food assist to needy individuals & families. Can return every week. FUNDING: Nonprofit. PRGM HRS: Th 9am-11am. Spanish, German, Tagalog spoken. ADM REQ: Photo ID, proof of residency, low income. SERVES: Zip code areas: 92503, 92505.

R.E.A.C.H.
St. Catherine's Catholic Community
339 N. Sycamore Ave.
Rialto, CA 92376
(909) 875-1360
(909) 874-4052
(909) 875-2822 FAX

R.E.A.C.H. (Rialto Ecumenical And Community Hospitality) is a food outreach prgm. FUNDING: Donations. OFC HRS: Tu-F 8:30am-12:30pm, 1:30pm-6:30pm. Spanish spoken. ADM REQ: Must provide proof of Rialto residency, ID. SERVES: Rialto.

RANCHO CUCAMONGA RESOURCE CENTER
9791 Arrow Route
Rancho Cucamonga, CA 91730
(909) 477-2781
(909) 919-2625 FAX

Resource center provides access to various srvs provided to the community. Prgms include: emerg needs (food and clothing), domestic abuse prevention workshops and counseling, ESL classes, parenting classes, youth socialization prgms, room rentals, info & referral srvs. FUNDING: Govt, city, donations. OFC HRS: M-F 8am-10pm. Spanish spoken. ADM REQ: Residents, however no one will be turned away. SERVES: Riverside, San Bernardino Counties.

REBUILDING MOUNTAIN HEARTS & LIVES
P.O. Box 4644
27315 N. Bay Rd.
Blue Jay, CA 92317
(909) 337-9922
(909) 337-6130 FAX

General info & referral srvs provided to the low income Rim community. FUNDING: Nonprofit, First 5 prgm grants. OFC HRS: M-F 9am-4pm. ADM REQ: Must show proof of address. Children need either birth certificate or document with DOB. SERVES: Crestline to Green Valley Lake.

RIVERSIDE CITY MISSION
3878 6th Street
Riverside, CA 92501
(951) 341-5055
(951) 341-5058 FAX

Clothing, hygiene items & community food pantry from 10am-1pm. Call Th 9am-11am to order food box. Send self-addressed, stamped envelope for application. Tu at Yahweh House of Worship, 6200 Pegasus Dr. Suite 3 in Riverside; W, Living Way Christian Fellowship 12125

Day St. Suite U-101 in Moreno Valley; Th at Power of the Word Fellowship Church, 6240 Morton Ave. in Riverside. Bible studies in the evening at Yahweh and Living Way. Regular church services on Sun. FUNDING: Nonprofit. OFC HRS: M-F 8am-3pm. ADM REQ: Must have ID. Proof of rent and income. Birth certificates for children under age 18 yrs. SERVES: Aruba & Moreno Valleys, Riverside County.

RIVERSIDE CO. PUBLIC HEALTH DEPT
Nutrition Services Branch
P.O. Box 7600
4065 County Circle Dr., Ste 207
Riverside, CA 92513-7600
(951) 358-7200
(951) 358-5472 FAX

A supplemental food & nutrition prgm for pregnant or breastfeeding women, women who just had a baby & children under 5 yrs of age. WIC offers special checks for healthy foods, nutrition & health edu, breastfeeding support & referrals to health care & other srvs. Breastfeeding info call (888) 451-2499. FUNDING: Federal. OFC HRS: M-F 7:30am-5pm. Eve & Sat by appt. Spanish, Vietnamese spoken. Srvs are income-based; working families may be eligible. SERVES: Riverside County.

RIVERSIDE CO. PUBLIC SOCIAL SRVS
Income Maintenance/Medi-Cal
P.O. Box 7500
63 S. 4th Street
Banning, CA 92220
(951) 922-7000
(951) 922-7005 FAX

Financial assist (TANF, CalWORKs, General Relief), nutritional (food stamps), and medical assist (Medi-Cal). Walk in or call. FUNDING: Govt. OFC HRS: M-Th 7am-5:30pm; F 8am-5pm. Spanish, Hmong spoken. SERVES: Banning, Beaumont, Calimesa, Cabazon & Pass area.

RIVERSIDE CO. PUBLIC SOCIAL SRVS
Income Maintenance/Medi-Cal
1225 W. Hobson Way
Blythe, CA 92225
(760) 921-5700
(760) 921-7715 FAX

Financial assist (TANF, General Relief, etc.), nutritional (food stamps), and medical assist (Medi-Cal). Walk in or call. FUNDING: Govt. OFC HRS: M-Th 7am-5:30pm; F 8am-5pm. Spanish spoken. ADM REQ: Varies per prgm. SERVES: Blythe & nearby.

RIVERSIDE CO. PUBLIC SOCIAL SRVS
Income Maintenance/Medi-Cal
68-615A Perez Rd., Ste 9
Cathedral City, CA 92234
(760) 770-2300
(760) 770-2324 FAX

Financial assist (TANF, CalWORKs, General Relief, etc.), nutritional (food stamps), and medical assist (Medi-Cal), limited home repair and emerg loans for SSI/SSD recipients. Walk in or call. FUNDING: Govt. OFC HRS: M-Th 7am-5:30pm; F 8am-5pm. Spanish spoken. SERVES: Palm Springs, Cathedral City areas.

RIVERSIDE CO. PUBLIC SOCIAL SRVS
68-615-A Perez Rd., Ste 9, 5
Cathedral City, CA 92234
(760) 773-2300
(760) 773-6720 FAX

CalWORKs, food stamps, General Relief. GAIN: (760)773-6800. FUNDING: Govt. OFC HRS: M-F 9am-6pm. GAIN: M-Th 7:30am-5:30pm. Spanish spoken. ADM REQ: Low income. SERVES: Riverside County.

RIVERSIDE CO. PUBLIC SOCIAL SRVS
Temp Assist/Medi-Cal/Food Stamps
541 N. San Jacinto St.
Hemet, CA 92543
(951) 791-3000
(951) 791-3050 FAX

Financial assist (CalWORKs, General Relief, etc.), nutritional (Food Stamps), and medical assist (Medi-Cal). FUNDING: Govt. OFC HRS: M-Th 7am-5:30pm; F 8am-5pm. Spanish spoken. SERVES: Mid-County.

RIVERSIDE CO. PUBLIC SOCIAL SRVS
Income Maintenance/CalWORKs
44-199 Monroe St., Ste D
Indio, CA 92201
(760) 863-2700
(760) 863-2864 FAX

Financial assist (CalWORKs, General Relief, etc.), nutritional (food stamps), and medical assist (Medi-Cal). Walk in or call. FUNDING: Govt. OFC HRS: M-Th 7am-5:30pm; F 8am-5pm. Spanish spoken. SERVES: Coachella Valley, Indio, Palm Desert, Thermal, Mecca.

RIVERSIDE CO. PUBLIC SOCIAL SRVS
CalWorks/Medi-Cal/Food Stamps
1400 Minthorn St.
Lake Elsinore, CA 92530
(951) 245-3100
(951) 674-5948 FAX

Financial assist (CalWORKs, GAIN, General Relief, etc.), nutritional (food stamps), and medical assist (Medi-Cal). FUNDING: Govt. OFC HRS: M-Th 7am-5:30pm; F 8am-5pm. ADM REQ: Varies with prgm. SERVES: Mid-Riverside County.

RIVERSIDE CO. PUBLIC SOCIAL SRVS
Income Maintenance/Medi-Cal
3178 Hamner Ave.
Norco, CA 92860
(951) 272-5550
(951) 272-5482 FAX

Financial assist (TANF, CalWORKs, General Relief, etc.), nutritional (food stamps), and medical assist (Medi-Cal). Walk in or call. FUNDING: Govt. OFC HRS: M-Th 7am-5:30pm; F 8am-5pm. Spanish spoken. ADM REQ: Varies with prgm. SERVES: Norco.

RIVERSIDE CO. PUBLIC SOCIAL SRVS
Temporary Assistance Medical Div
2055 N. Perris Blvd., Ste B
Perris, CA 92571
(951) 940-6600
(951) 940-6610 FAX

Financial assist (CalWORKs, TANF, General Relief, etc.), nutritional (food stamps), and medical assist (Medi-Cal). Walk in to apply, appts for continuing. FUNDING: Govt. OFC HRS: M-Th 7am-5:30pm; F 8am-5pm. Spanish spoken. SERVES: Riverside County.

RIVERSIDE CO. PUBLIC SOCIAL SRVS
County Administrative Offices
4060 County Circle Dr.
Riverside, CA 92503
(951) 358-3000

(951) 358-3036 FAX

CalWORKs offers financial assist to families with children who are deprived of support due to incapacity, unemployment or continued absence of one or more parents. Food Stamps prgm offers an increased food purchase power for low income families. Medical assist prgm (Medi-Cal). General Relief Prgm: assist to indigent individuals & families in temporary need of housing, food or transportation. This is a loan prgm and recipients are to repay benefits. In Home Supportive Srvs (IHSS) provides household and personal care to allow elderly and disabled persons to remain in their own homes. For adult abuse, call (800) 491-7123. FUNDING: County, state, fed, govt. OFC HRS: M-Th 7:30am-5:30pm. Spanish spoken. Interpreters available in local offices by appointment. ADM REQ: Varies with prgm & srvs. SERVES: Riverside County.

RIVERSIDE CO. PUBLIC SOCIAL SRVS
Assistance Programs
11060 Magnolia Ave.
Riverside, CA 92505
(951) 358-3400

Financial assist (CalWORKs, TANF, General Relief, etc.), nutritional (food stamps), and medical assist (Medi-Cal). Walk in or call. FUNDING: Govt. OFC HRS: M-Th 7am-5:30pm; F 8am-5pm. Spanish, Vietnamese spoken. ASL available. SERVES: Riverside County.

RIVERSIDE CO. PUBLIC SOCIAL SRVS
Income Maintenance/Medi-Cal
43264 Business Park Dr., Ste B1
Temecula, CA 92590
(951) 600-6500
(951) 600-6502 FAX

Financial assist (CalWORKs, TANF, General Relief, etc.), nutritional (food stamps), and medical assist (Medi-Cal). Walk in or call. FUNDING: Govt. OFC HRS: M-Th 7am-5:30pm; F 8am-5pm. Spanish spoken. ADM REQ: Varies with prgm. SERVES: Mid-County.

ROY'S DESERT RESOURCE CENTER
19531 McLane St.
Palm Springs, CA 92262
(760) 676-5200

Homeless shelter for families and single adults. Srvs include: case mgmt, meals, showers, laundry, and social srvs assist. Pick-up points throughout the city of Palm Springs. Also accepts clients who have their own means of transportation. FUNDING: Nonprofit. ADM REQ: Must be homeless, drug free, physically able to take care of themselves. Does not accept those convicted of a violent felony or sexual offense. Free srvs. SERVES: Coachella Valley.

SACRED HEART CHURCH
9935 Mission Blvd.
Riverside, CA 92509
(951) 685-5058
(951) 685-1056 FAX

Food distribution to low income families, individuals & seniors 1st & 3rd Tu of each month. FUNDING: Nonprofit. OFC HRS: M-F 8am-4pm. Spanish spoken. ADM REQ: Photo ID and proof of income. SERVES: Zip code area 91752, 92509.

SALVATION ARMY/CATHEDRAL CITY
Family Services

30-400 Landu Blvd.
Cathedral City, CA 92234
(760) 324-2275
(760) 321-4813 FAX

Emerg food, shelter, info and referral. Emerg food bag with four-day supply every third W (max six times per yr). Crisis relief, utility asst through Edison rental asst. Info and resources for families in the Western Coachella Valley. School uniform assist (limited), pre-marital, marital, family, drug, and spiritual guidance, summer camp. After school prgm: computer classes (based on availability), reading lab, math lab classes at no cost to student. Thanksgiving and Christmas food baskets and toys. OFC HRS: M-W 9am-5:30pm. Spanish spoken. SERVES: Palm Springs, Cathedral City, Desert Hot Springs, Rancho Mirage and Thousand Palms.

SALVATION ARMY/FAMILY SRVS
Family Srvs
14068 Graham St.
Moreno Valley, CA 92553-8816
(951) 656-1822
(951) 653-2852 FAX

Info and referral for emerg srvs including: food, clothing, Christmas help, and disaster relief as funds are available. After school tutoring. Youth programs. FUNDING: Nonprofit. OFC HRS: Food Assistance: M, Tu 8:30am-12:30pm. Spanish spoken. ADM REQ: Must have photo I.D. for all adult family members, medical card or copy of birth certificate for children and proof of income and residence. SERVES: Parris, Moreno Valley.

SALVATION ARMY/FAMILY SRVS
Social Srvs
3695 1st Street
Riverside, CA 92501-2501
(951) 784-4490
(951) 784-0790 FAX

Info and referral on emerg srvs including: food & utility assist as funds permit. FUNDING: Nonprofit. OFC HRS: M-F 9am-4pm. SERVES: Riverside & nearby.

SALVATION ARMY/HEMET
1779 E. Florida Ave., Ste D-2
Hemet, CA 92543
(951) 766-2020
(951) 925-5796 FAX

Emerg food. Senior food prgm once a month for ages 60 yrs+ who are residents of Hemet. FUNDING: Nonprofit. OFC HRS: M-F 9am-11:30am. ADM REQ: Call for more information. SERVES: Hemet & nearby.

SALVATION ARMY/ONTARIO
P.O. Box 408
1412 S. Euclid Ave.
Ontario, CA 91762
(909) 986-6748
(909) 986-9979 FAX

Emerg short-term assist to resident families and transients including food and lodging assist. Case mgmt is also provided. Salvation Army Ontario Corps serves Western San Bernardino County. This regional office will provide referrals for needed srvs at various srv locations. Also provides youth prgms and women's srvs. Shelter when funding avail, disaster relief, summer camp, scouting activities for children, and an after school prgm. FUND-

ING: FEMA, United Way, donations. OFC HRS: M-F 8:30am-4:30pm. Spanish spoken. ADM REQ: Photo ID, proof of income, address verification. SERVES: Ontario, Fontana, Upland, Rialto, Chino, Chino Hills & Rancho Cucamonga.

SALVATION ARMY/REDLANDS CORPS
P.O. Box 26
838 N. Alta St.
Redlands, CA 92374
(909) 792-6868
(909) 335-3140 FAX

Emerg food. Dinner daily M-F 5pm. Food pantry, emerg materials assist, emerg gas, peer counseling, crisis counseling, referrals for morning showering, utility, rehab assist in San Bernardino. USDA commodities 4th F 10am-12noon, 1:30pm-4pm. Worship srvs. Walk in. FUNDING: Donations, FEMA, United Way. OFC HRS: M, Tu, Th, F 1:15pm-4pm. ADM REQ: Low income. Free srvs. SERVES: Redlands, Loma Linda, Mentone, Bryn Mawr.

SALVATION ARMY/RIVERSIDE CORPS
3695 1st Street
Riverside, CA 92501
(951) 784-3571
(951) 784-0790 FAX

Disaster relief and summer camp. Referral for adult rehab for substance abuse and teenage parent prgm through Booth Memorial Center. FUNDING: United Way, donations, nonprofit. OFC HRS: M-F 8:30am-4pm. ADM REQ: Anyone in need, referral from Social Srvs or food bank. SERVES: Riverside Metro, Corona, Norco, Rubidoux, March AFB.

SALVATION ARMY/VICTORVILLE CORPS
14585 La Paz Dr.
Victorville 92395
(760) 245-2545
(760) 245-1130 FAX

Emerg food prgm (Tu, Th 9am-12noon), emerg temporary shelter (when funds are available), info & referral. Utilities and rent when funds are available. Walk in. FUNDING: Donations, United Way. Phone Hrs: M-F 9am-12noon. ADM REQ: Photo ID, proof of income. SS card or medical card for everyone. Free srvs. SERVES: Victorville, Apple Valley, Hesperia, Lucerne Valley, Adelanto, Oro Grande, Barstow, Big Bear.

SALVATION ARMY/YUCCA VLY SRVS
56659 Twentynine Palms Hwy., Ste E
Yucca Valley, CA 92284
(760) 228-0114

Comprehensive emerg assist on a case by case basis. Food bank on W, utility asst by appt. Certified emerg disaster responders. Other resources as available. Inquiries welcome. FUNDING: United Way, county, donations, nonprofit. OFC HRS: Tu-Th 10am-3pm. SERVES: Morongo Basin.

SAMARITAN'S HELPING HAND
15527 8th Street
Victorville, CA 92393
(760) 243-5933
(760) 243-9570 FAX

M, Tu 10am-12noon for food pantry and clothing vouchers. Motel vouchers, emergency prescriptions, day bus passes, ID assistance, Greyhound tickets as funds are available, utility and rental assist by appt only. Info & referrals for srvs not provided. Walk in or call. FUNDING: Donations, United Way, FEMA, nonprofit. OFC HRS: M, Tu 10am-12noon; W, Th by appt. ADM REQ: Must have proof of income, residency, photo ID for all adults in the home & SS card for all residents (adults and children). Free srvs. SERVES: High Desert.

SAN BERNARDINO CITY MISSION
P.O. Box 3489
719 North D Street
San Bernardino, CA 92413
(909) 889-2700
(909) 649-0014 FAX

Clothing, household items, food box, nutrition classes, hygiene items, drop-in ctr, info & referral, community food pantry. Various speakers, holiday celebrations. For food box, call Th 9am-2pm, delivered to home on 4th Sat. FUNDING: Nonprofit. OFC HRS: Tu-Th 9am-2pm. Other hrs by appt. ADM REQ: Must have both photo ID and SS card to receive food boxes. For children under 18, birth certificate and SS. Preassigned; must fill out prequalification form. SERVES: San Bernardino County.

SAN BERNARDINO CO. BEHAV HEALTH
268 W. Hospitality Lane, Ste 400
San Bernardino, CA 92415
(909) 382-3133
(909) 382-3106 FAX

Behavioral health srvs for depression, bipolar disorder, schizophrenia within the low income community when funds are available. FUNDING: County. OFC HRS: M-F 8am-5pm, closed alt F. Spanish spoken. Accepts Medi-Cal, Medicare. No insurance. SERVES: San Bernardino County.

SAN BERNARDINO CO. HUMAN SRVS SY
Transitional Assistance
7977 Sierra Ave.
Fontana, CA 92335
(909) 356-3160
(909) 356-3221
(909) 356-3169 FAX

Transitional assist prgms include financial assist (CalWORKs, General Relief, etc.), nutritional (food stamps), and medical assist (Medi-Cal). Subsidized child care (CalWORKs & alternative payment). FUNDING: Govt. OFC HRS: M-F 8:30am-4:30pm. Spanish spoken. SERVES: Fontana for all prgms. Child care srvs provided for all San Bernardino County.

SAN BERNARDINO CO. HUMAN SRVS SY
Medi-Cal/TAD/CalWORKs/Food Stamps
1300 Bailey Ave.
Needles, CA 92363
(760) 326-9261
(760) 326-9270 FAX

Income maintenance prgms include: TANF, General Relief, food stamps, Medi-Cal, CalWORKs, child abuse hotline (800) 827-8724, adoption srvs (909) 891-3300. FUNDING: Govt. OFC HRS: M-F 8:30am-4:30pm. Spanish spoken. ADM REQ: Low income. SERVES: San Bernardino County.

SAN BERNARDINO CO. HUMAN SRVS SY
Medi-Cal
1627 E. Holt Blvd.
Ontario, CA 91761
(909) 933-6330
(909) 933-6450 FAX

Income maintenance prgms. Medical assist (Medi-Cal). FUNDING: Govt. OFC HRS: M-F 9am-4pm. Spanish spoken. SERVES: San Bernardino County.

SAN BERNARDINO CO. HUMAN SRVS SY
Income Maintenance/Transitional Assist
2050 N. Massachusetts
San Bernardino, CA 92415
(909) 475-2074
(909) 475-2231 FAX

Income maintenance prgms include financial assist (CalWORKs, TANF, General Relief, etc.), nutritional (food stamps), and medical assist (Medi-Cal). FUNDING: Govt. OFC HRS: M-F 8:30am-4:30pm. Spanish spoken. SERVES: Specific areas in San Bernardino.

SAN BERNARDINO CO. PUBLIC HEALTH
Reproductive Health Centers
800 E. Lugonia Ave., Ste F
Redlands, CA 92374
(800) 722-4777
(909) 793-6399

Reproductive health exams for men & women. STD testing & treatment, HIV testing & referral to care. Edu srvs, pregnancy testing, counseling, lab testing, young adult clinics. FUNDING: Govt. OFC HRS: M-F 8am-5pm. Spanish spoken. ADM REQ: Must have appt. Accepts Medi-Cal, F-PACT, sliding fee scale. No one denied srvs due to lack of funds. SERVES: San Bernardino County.

SAN BERNARDINO CO. PUBLIC SOC SRVS
See "San Bernardino Co. Human Srvs Sy"

SECOND HARVEST FOOD BANK
2950-B Jefferson St.
Riverside, CA 92504
(951) 359-4757
(951) 359-8314 FAX

Food bank for nonprofit agencies. The agencies who help needy families can submit an application and those who are approved may receive food for distribution to needy and pay only a shared maintenance fee of 18 cents per pound to help maintain the food bank. This bank serves 860 different agencies but has no direct srvs for needy families. FUNDING: United Way, grants, donations. OFC HRS: M-F 8am-3:30pm. Spanish spoken. ADM REQ: Agencies who have been approved (churches and other nonprofit groups) SERVES: Riverside, San Bernardino Counties.

SEVENTH DAY ADVENTIST COMM SRVS
P.O. Box 52439
4491 Kansas Ave.
Riverside, CA 92517
(951) 682-9810
(951) 682-4861 FAX

Emerg clothing, food. Food is available 1st M of each month except holidays, then it will be the following M. FUNDING: Nonprofit. OFC HRS: M-Th 9am-4pm; F 9am-12noon. ADM REQ: Must have valid ID, low income, must show proof of 92507 zip code residency. SERVES: Riverside County.

SO CALIF INDIAN CENTER, INC.
Corporate Office
10175 Slater Ave., Ste 150
Fountain Valley, CA 92708-4702
(714) 962-6673
(714) 962-6343 FAX

Edu, cultural, economic & recreational prgms for American Indians. Indian Child & Family Srvs (counseling, parenting, foster parents, etc.), WIA (employment assist & voc training), edu tutoring for Indian students in grades K-12. Emerg shelter, food, clothing, referral srvs. FUNDING: United Way, govt, nonprofit. OFC HRS: M-F 8am-5pm. ADM REQ: American-Indian verification. SERVES: So. Calif.

SOCIAL SERVICES
See "Riverside Co. Public Social Srvs"

SOCIAL SERVICES
See "San Bernardino Co. Human Srvs Sy"

SOUTH ASIAN HELPLINE & REFERRAL AGENCY (SAHARA)
17100 S. Pioneer Blvd., Ste 260
Artesia, CA 90701
(562) 402-4132
(562) 402-6093 FAX

Serves the South Asian community by providing them with info, referrals, skills dev and other culturally sensitive support srvs including mental health, health care, legal assist, transitional living ctrs, client advocacy, case mgmt, financial assist, job training and placement, community edu prgms, and senior srvs. FUNDING: Nonprofit. OFC HRS: M-F 8am-5pm. Hindi, Gujarati, Bengali, Urdu, Nepali, Tamil & Telugu spoken. Free srvs. SERVES: Southern California.

SOUTHLAND FARMERS' MARKET ASSN
P.O. Box 858
638 Trophy Trail
Topanga, CA 90290
(310) 455-0181
(310) 455-0824 FAX

Certified Farmers' Markets offers farm fresh fruit, vegetables, nuts & eggs grown by Calif family farmers. Food stamps and WIC are accepted at some member markets. Visit (www.sfma.net). FUNDING: Nonprofit. HRS: M-F 9am-5pm. SERVES: So. Calif.

ST. ANN'S CATHOLIC OUTREACH
P.O. Box 190
218 D Street
Needles, CA 92363
(760) 326-2721
(760) 326-3068 FAX

Emerg food assist, helps complete papers for immigration, youth prgms, Hispanic ministry. Call St. Vincent de Paul srv (760) 326-4420 for more info on prgms, food pantry & thrift store. FUNDING: Nonprofit. OFC HRS: M-F 8:30am-1:30pm. Spanish spoken. ASL available. SERVES: Needles & nearby.

ST. CATHERINE OF SIENA CHURCH
339 N. Sycamore Ave.
Rialto, CA 92376
(909) 875-1360
(909) 875-2822 FAX

Emerg food W 9am-12noon. OFC HRS: M, F 9am-2pm. SERVES: Rialto.

ST. CHRISTOPHER'S CHURCH
25075 Cottonwood Ave.
Moreno Valley, CA 92553
(951) 924-1968
(951) 247-6477 FAX

Parish members donate food which is given to needy families M 1pm-3pm. Spanish spoken. ADM REQ: Photo I.D., Social Security card, school records for children in house and proof of residency. SERVES: Moreno Valley.

ST. ELIZABETH CHURCH

Food Program
66700 Pierson Blvd.
Desert Hot Springs, CA 92240
(760) 329-8794
(760) 329-6760 FAX

Food supplements twice monthly Tu 9am-10:45am. FUNDING: Nonprofit. OFC HRS: M-F 8:30am-3:30pm. Summer Hrs: M-F 8:30am-12noon. ADM REQ: Must show proof of residency in Desert Hot Springs, valid Calif I.D. or Driver's license and Social Security card for each member in the family. SERVES: Desert Hot Springs only.

ST. GEORGE CATHOLIC CHURCH

505 N. Palm Ave.
Ontario, CA 91762
(909) 983-2637

Food srvs W 8am-10am. Jubilee House distribution of groceries for first 25 people. FUNDING: Nonprofit. OFC HRS: M, W 1pm-7pm; T, Th, F 9am-4:30pm. Closed daily 12noon-1pm. ADM REQ: ID required for proof of residency. SERVES: Ontario residents.

ST. JOAN OF ARC

The Lord's Table
15512 6th Street
Victorville, CA 92395
(760) 241-2043
(760) 245-7077 FAX

Lunches M-F 11am-12noon. 3rd F of each month have govt food for Victorville residents (ID required). FUNDING: Nonprofit. OFC HRS: M-F 8am-1pm. Spanish spoken. ADM REQ: Low income. SERVES: Victor Valley area.

ST. MARTHA'S THRIFT STORE

38444 Sky Canyon Dr., Ste 170/190
Murrieta, CA 92563
(951) 677-6347
(951) 696-7413 FAX

Food pantry W, Th 8:30am-10am. Sign up at office 190, 8:30am-10am. FUNDING: Nonprofit. OFC HRS: M-W, F 9am-3pm; Th 9am-5pm; Sat 10am-2pm. ADM REQ: Must call first. SERVES: Murrieta.

ST. MEL'S FOOD PANTRY

4140 Corona Ave.
Norco, CA 92860
(951) 737-7144
(951) 735-8332 FAX

2-3 day food supply provided to families, individuals & seniors. Diapers & formula when available, Th 10am-1pm. FUNDING: Nonprofit. OFC HRS: M-F 9am-4:30pm. Spanish spoken. ADM REQ: Must have ID and utility bill. Must bring immunization records for children. Must register. SERVES: Zip code areas: 91752, 92860, 92880.

ST. THERESA'S CHURCH

Food Pantry
2800 E. Ramon Rd.
Palm Springs, CA 92264
(760) 323-2669
(760) 322-8581 FAX

Emerg food M 7:45am. ADM REQ: Must show ID and proof of residency in Palm Springs. SERVES: Palm Springs.

SURVIVE FOOD BANK

See "Second Harvest Food Bank"

SWEET RELIEF MUSICIANS FUND

4952 Warner Ave., Ste 242
Huntington Beach, CA 92649
(714) 846-3030
(714) 846-3636 FAX

Provides financial assist to all types of career musicians who are struggling to make ends meet while facing illness, disability or age-related problems. For more info, please visit (www.sweetrelief.org). FUNDING: Nonprofit. OFC HRS: M-Th 8:30am-5:30pm; F 8:30am-5pm. ADM REQ: Must meet eligibility requirements. Free srvs. SERVES: U.S.A.

TANF

Temporary Assistance/Needy Families
See "San Bernardino Co. Human Srvs Sy" and "Riverside Co. Public Social Srvs"

TEMECULA VLY SENIOR SERVICE CTR

Rancho-Temecula Valley Senior Srvs
41538 Eastman Dr.
Murrieta, CA 92562
(951) 600-9557

Senior Service Center with various food programs. Emerg food daily. Senior Brown Bag, senior SHARE, USDA commodities, bread. Paralegal srvs every three months, Social Security monthly, immunizations by Dept of Health when available. Walk in or call. FUNDING: United Way. OFC HRS: M-Th 8am-11pm; F 7:30am-11:30am. Spanish spoken. ADM REQ: Low income. SERVES: Temecula & nearby.

THE CHURCH FOR WHOSOEVER

Emergency Assistance Prgm
18628 Seneca Rd.
Apple Valley, CA 92307
(760) 242-3191
(760) 946-9199 FAX

Basic food items 1st & 3rd Sun after the 10:45am service. FUNDING: Nonprofit. OFC HRS: Tu-F 10am-3pm. Spanish spoken. SERVES: Victor Valley area.

THE CLOSET

The Flipside
10912 Jersey Blvd.
Rancho Cucamonga, CA 91730
(909) 466-7789

Clothing distributed to families in need. Walk in 2nd Sat each month from 1pm-2:30pm. FUNDING: Nonprofit. OFC HRS: Tu-F 9:30am-4:30pm. SERVES: Ranch Cucamonga.

THE SALVATION ARMY

"Salvation Army/..."

THE WELL IN THE DESERT

555 Commercial Rd., Ste 10
Palm Springs, CA 92262
(760) 327-8577
(760) 327-8559 FAX

Congregate meal prgm M-F 11am-1pm. Also grocery distribution (no case mgmt), Sat 7am-10am at 181 N. Indian Canyon, Palm Springs. FUNDING: Pvt nonprofit. OFC HRS: M-F 9am-3pm. ADM REQ: Sign guestbook, case mgmt and social srvs must have photo ID. Free srvs. SERVES: Cathedral City, Desert Hot Springs, Palm Springs, Thousand Palms.

TWENTYNINE PALMS COMMUNITY FOOD PANTRY

Immanuel Prince of Peace Lutheran Church
P.O. Box 782
6450 Stardune Rd
Twentynine Palms, CA 92277
(760) 361-3663

Bag of groceries, enough for 5 or 6 meals depending on size of family. Eligible once a month. OFC HRS: M-F 9:30am-11:30am; 2nd and 4th W 5pm-6:30pm. 2nd and 4th Sat 9:30am-11:30am. Closed 3rd M of the month. ADM REQ: Must have photo ID, SS Card for all residents and current utility bill for proof of residence in 92277 area code. SERVES: Wonder Valley, Marine Corps Base,

UNITED WAY OF THE DESERT

1027 S. Palm Canyon Dr.
Palm Springs, CA 92264
(760) 323-2731
(760) 778-1421 FAX

Volunteer organization addresses the human and health needs of the residents of the Coachella Valley by mobilizing comm resources, assessing comm needs and providing support to 25 member agencies. Srvs range from youth, family, and senior care to medical care and shelter for the homeless. Money is raised to support these agencies and provide the most needed human and health care srvs. Request a complete list of their member agencies. FUNDING: Contributions from employee groups and individuals. OFC HRS: M-F 8:30am-5pm. SERVES: Coachella Valley.

UNITED WAY/ARROWHEAD

P.O. Box 796
646 North D Street
San Bernardino, CA 92402
(909) 884-9441
(909) 885-4096 FAX

Volunteer organization with a goal of "people helping people." Fundraising and involvement in community problem solving are important roles for this agency. Supports 38 local agencies offering many various health and human srv prgms. Call for more info and a list of the agencies and prgms. FUNDING: Donations, nonprofit. OFC HRS: M-F 8am-5pm. SERVES: San Bernardino & nearby.

UNITED WAY/CENTRAL COUNTY

418 E. Florida Ave.
Hemet, CA 92543
(951) 929-9691
(951) 652-0064 FAX

Assists community agencies in developing, fundraising, maintaining srvs and evaluating prgms for people. FUNDING: Donations, nonprofit. OFC HRS: M-F 8:30am-5pm. SERVES: Mid-county region.

UNITED WAY/CORONA/NORCO

815 W. 6th Street, Ste 160
Corona, CA 92882
(951) 736-0620
(951) 736-0304 FAX

Volunteer organization helping people help people. Sponsors 21 agencies offering health and social srvs for individuals and families in Corona and Norco. Call to confirm hours and to obtain a list of the United Way agencies. Ofc at 3954 Old Hamner Rd., Norco. FUNDING: Contributions from employee groups and individuals. OFC HRS: M-F vary. Spanish spoken. SERVES: Corona, Norco & nearby.

UNITED WAY/DESERT COMMUNITIES

16192 Siskiyou Rd., Ste 4
Apple Valley, CA 92307-1316
(760) 242-5370
(760) 242-5375 FAX

Organization that helps people help themselves by providing funding and assist for local prgms for the needy. Funding to 27 different agencies from child care and youth activities to substance abuse and emerg food and shelter. Call for a list of agencies and srvs. FUNDING: Contributions from employee groups and individuals. OFC HRS: M-F 8am-5pm. SERVES: Victor Valley, High Desert area.

UNITED WAY/INLAND VALLEYS

Southwest Co. Regional Office
5109 Jefferson Ave., Ste 225-A
Murrieta, CA 92562
(951) 697-4700
(951) 656-8210 FAX

Partners with donors to support many nonprofit health & human srv agencies. Prgms include: srvs for battered women, child care, youth, low-cost counseling, medical srvs, senior prgms, homeless srvs, emerg assist, volunteer srvs, etc. FUNDING: Donations, grants, nonprofit. OFC HRS: Vary. SERVES: Inland Valley.

UNITED WAY/INLAND VALLEYS

6215 River Crest Dr., Ste B
Riverside, CA 92507
(951) 697-4700
(951) 656-8210 FAX

Local volunteer-driven organization with the purpose of addressing identified local health and human care needs, by raising funds through a community-wide campaign and then allocating or distributing the funds to local service providers and/or community initiatives. FUNDING: Nonprofit. OFC HRS: M-F 8am-5pm. Chinese, Spanish & Tagalog spoken. SERVES: Major portion of Western Riverside County & Riverside Metro.

UNITED WAY/MOJAVE VALLEY

P.O. Box 362
210 E. Williams 92311
Barstow, CA 92312
(760) 256-8789
(760) 256-8789 FAX

Nonprofit organization providing a partnership for all facets of the community to come together and offer needed health and social srvs in the local area. Call for a list of member agencies and info on local social srvs. FUNDING: Contributions from employee groups and individuals. OFC HRS: Vary. SERVES: Mojave Valley area.

VALLEY RESTART CENTER

200 E. Menlo Ave.
Hemet, CA 92543
(951) 766-7476
(951) 925-0566 FAX

Shelter for homeless. No drop-ins or mail services. Showers 4pm-5pm daily. Evening meals daily at 6pm, case mgmt srvs, laundry facilities, job info & referrals, housing referrals. Meeting space provided for AA/NA meetings on Th, shelter access 24 hrs. Interviews and intake M-F 9am-1:30pm. Emergency interviews upon request. Rental assist when funds available. No utility asst. No underage, unaccompanied

youth. Not for those needing medical treatment. Same criteria for showers as for residency. Eligible for food box once every 3 months. FUNDING: Nonprofit. OFC HRS: M-F 9am-5pm. ADM REQ: CA picture ID, no warrants, not on parole, not on Megan's List, no history of violent charges, no repeats recipients. Free srvs. SERVES: Hemet, San Jacinto Valley.

VCF COMMUNITY SERVICES

17421 Van Buren Blvd.
Riverside, CA 92504
(951) 789-8514
(951) 780-5433
(951) 780-1981 FAX

Assists all people in need with sack lunches, hygiene packages for homeless, emerg food box (for monthly food srvs, must be involved in Change Your Life Prgm), clothing, housing & utility assist, job search and counseling regarding employment, resume assist, outreach prgms. Mailing address: 16445 Porter Ave., Riverside, CA 92505. FUNDING: Church, donations, nonprofit. OFC HRS: Tu-F 9am-4pm. SERVES: Riverside County

VERONICA'S HOME OF MERCY

1495 W. Victoria St.
San Bernardino, CA 92411
(909) 888-9064
(909) 888-7390 FAX

Long-term, faith-based residential home (room for up to 20 women) for adult pregnant women & children or women with small children, as an alternative to domestic violence, addictions, abortion and/or homelessness. Women must be involved with the prgm and be willing to continue their education. Not an emergency shelter. Transitional living. FUNDING: Nonprofit. OFC HRS: M-F 8am-4pm. Spanish spoken. ADM REQ: Must be ages 18 yrs+ or emancipated by court. SERVES: So. Calif.

VICTOR VALLEY RESCUE MISSION

16611 Tracy St., Ste C
Victorville, CA 92395
(760) 955-5958
(760) 955-5958 FAX

Clothing and household items distributed once per week. Food boxes available for delivery or pick-up. Call for more info. FUNDING: Nonprofit. OFC HRS: M-F 9am-5pm. ADM REQ: Must fill out client form, proof of residency, I.D. or SS card. SERVES: San Bernardino County.

VICTOR VLY COMMUNITY SRVS COUNCIL

P.O. Box 1992
16692 Mojave Dr.
Victorville, CA 92393
(760) 243-9646
(760) 243-4762 FAX

Volunteer organization provides umbrella oversight to start-up organizations pending confirmation of nonprofit and charitable status. Encourages prgm formulation to serve unmet needs. Operates Volunteer Ctr of Victor Valley, including placing court referrals for community srv. "First Call for Help" a 24-hr info & referral srv. FUNDING: United Way, fees, donations, nonprofit. OFC HRS: M-Th 9am-2:45pm. Some Spanish spoken. SERVES: High Desert areas.

VINEYARD OF THE NEW WINE

Circle of Care
P.O. Box 218
Temecula, CA 92593

(951) 973-3582

Food distribution W at 4pm at Margarita Park. Call for other location addresses and more info. FUNDING: Nonprofit. OFC HRS: M-F 9am-5pm. ADM REQ: Low income, homeless. SERVES: Temecula.

VOLUNTEER CENTER/RIVERSIDE CO.

2-1-1 Helpline, Inform Riverside County
2060 University Ave., Ste 212
Riverside, CA 92507
(951) 686-4402
(951) 686-4357
(951) 686-7417 FAX

Helpline is a free, confidential crisis/suicide intervention service, 24/7. Countywide human srv info & referral line for agencies & individuals during ofc hrs. Medi-Cal provider referrals. Maintains computerized human srv database and publishes directory of human service agencies for the county of Riverside. Bilingual info. Speakers available to educate about assessment process and community resources. 24-hr line, dial 2-1-1. OFC HRS: M-F 8am-5pm. 24-hr srvs. Free srvs. SERVES: Riverside County.

WAY STATION/YUCCA VALLEY

P.O. Box 613
61722 Commercial St.
Joshua Tree, CA 92252
(760) 366-8088
(760) 366-7344 FAX

Counseling, info & referral, emerg food, diapers, clothing, holiday baskets and hot meals. For emerg, call (760) 366-2278 (24 hrs). OFC HRS: M-F 8am-1pm. SERVES: San Bernardino County.

WELFARE

See "San Bernardino Co. Human Srvs Sy"

WEST END HUNGER PROGRAM/SOVA

Inland Valley Council of Churches
904 E. California St.
Ontario, CA 91762
(909) 391-4882
(909) 391-1364 FAX

5 days of food provided every 30 days for each member of a family, as well as USDA commodities. Rental & utility assist. Motel vouchers when funding is available. FUNDING: Various. OFC HRS: M-F 9am-11:30am, 1:30pm-3:30pm. ADM REQ: Must have proof of address, proof of income, and ID for each person in the household. SERVES: West End of San Bernardino County.

WESTERN EAGLE FOUNDATION

Food Bank Program
40940 County Center Dr.
Temecula, CA 92591
(951) 695-7206
(951) 695-7207 FAX

Food bank for nonprofit agencies. Agency pays only a weekly membership fee of $75 and receives canned goods, breads, meats, milk, staples and other available foods adequate for the number of needy families served by their agency. Organization must complete application form and show proof of nonprofit status. Food available once a week. Also offer box of food for needy. FUNDING: Donations, nonprofit. OFC HRS: M-F 9am-4pm; Sat 9am-3pm. Spanish spoken. Food box $25. SERVES: So. Calif.

WIC/WOMEN, INFANT AND CHILDREN

See "San Bernardino Co. Public Health" WIC program

WONDER VALLEY FIRE STATION

80526 Amboy Rd.
Twentynine Palms, CA 92277
(760) 367-3761
(760) 367-5639 FAX

Food distribution 3rd M each month, 10:30am-11:30am. OFC HRS: M-F 7am-3pm. ADM REQ: Low income resident. SERVES: Wonder Valley only.

1736 FAMILY CRISIS CENTER
Admin Office
2116 Arlington Ave., Ste 200
Los Angeles, CA 90018
(323) 737-3900
(323) 737-3993 FAX

This location is one of the 21 Family Source Centers in L.A. County providing the One e-App system for financial assist, case mgmt, and high-risk youth/young adult employment and edu srvs. 24-hr srvs provided to runaway and homeless adols, including: counseling, food, clothing, advocacy and other basic needs. 2-week emerg youth shelter for adols ages 10-17 yrs who need short-term, crisis-oriented shelter. Also operates four shelters for battered women and their children (ages birth-17 yrs) for 1-24 months offering a comprehensive survival and job dev prgm to promote long-term safety, survival & success. 24-hr hotlines in South Bay (310) 379-3620, (310) 370-5902; Long Beach (562) 388-7652; South L.A. (213) 222-1237, (213) 745-6434. May call collect if needed. 24-hr drop-in center at 1736 Monterey Blvd., Hermosa Beach. FUNDING: Donations, grants, govt, CDBG, nonprofit. OFC HRS: M-F 8:30am-5pm. Spanish spoken. Free srvs. SERVES: So. Calif, Southwest L.A.

ABILITY COUNTS, INC.
775 Trademark Cir., Ste 101
Corona, CA 92879
(951) 734-6595
(951) 734-5574 FAX

Job training & opportunities for dev disabled. Open entry & exit prgm. FUNDING: Nonprofit. OFC HRS: M-F 8am-4:30pm. ADM REQ: Ages 18 yrs+, developmentally disabled, can deal with own personal needs, active interest and motivation to work 8-hr days, eligible for Regional Center or State Dept of Rehab srvs. Exceptions on indiv basis. SERVES: Riverside & Orange Counties.

ADECCO
5483 Philadelphia, Ste B
Chino, CA 91710
(909) 464-0810
(909) 464-0838 FAX

Temporary and permanent employment positions available to qualified people. No fee to applicant. Free placement and training. FUNDING: Fees billed to companies using srvs. OFC HRS: M-F 7:30am-5:30pm. Spanish spoken. SERVES: Chino, Montclair, Ontario & Rancho Cucamonga & nearby.

ADECCO
268 W. Hospitality Lane, Ste 107
San Bernardino, CA 92408
(909) 381-2251
(909) 889-9892 FAX

Clerical, office automation, accounting, legal, technical and light industrial. No cost to a temp employee. Light industrial and clerical staffing out of this office. OFC HRS: M-F 7:30am-5:30pm by appt. Spanish spoken. SERVES: Inland Empire.

AGRICULTURAL LABOR RELATIONS BOARD
915 Capitol Mall, 3rd Fl.
Sacramento, CA 95814
(916) 653-3699
(800) 449-3699
(916) 653-8750 FAX

Protects the rights of the agricultural worker. Works to prevent unfair labor practices. FUNDING: Govt. OFC HRS: M-F 8am-5pm. Spanish spoken. SERVES: Calif.

ARC/RIVERSIDE
Ray Strebe Resource Ctr
702 E. 11th Street
Beaumont, CA 92223-1909
(951) 845-3385
(951) 769-1706 FAX

Dedicating to improving the welfare of those with developmental disabilities and their families. Expert training in self-help skills, activities of daily living, vocational skills, community awareness, and social interaction skills. Also advocacy and info. FUNDING: Inland Regional Center, Depts of Rehab. OFC HRS: M-F 8am-4:30pm. Spanish spoken. ADM REQ: Ages 18 yrs+, primary diagnosis of mental retardation, free from behavioral and medical conditions posing hazard to self, others, and/or association property, able to tolerate 6-hr prgm day. Referred by Inland Regional Center. Free srvs if approved by Dept of Rehab. SERVES: Moreno Valley, Beaumont, Banning, Redlands, Hemet, Cinta Cino, Yucaipa.

ARC/RIVERSIDE
Administrative Office
8138 Mar Vista Court
Riverside, CA 92504
(951) 688-5141
(951) 688-7207 FAX

Work centers, prgms & srvs for adults with dev disability. Packaging and assembly for moderate and mild mental retardation. Day activity centers for severe mental retardation. Also advocacy and info. Minimal wait if openings; if no openings, may be placed on waiting list. FUNDING: Inland Regional Center, Depts of Rehab & Dev Srvs. OFC HRS: M-F 8am-5pm. Spanish spoken. ADM REQ: Adults with mental retardation assessed as appropriate for prgms. Free srvs. SERVES: West Riverside County, including Corona, Norco, Moreno Valley, Beaumont, Banning, San Jacinto, Hemet, Calimesa, Yucaipa.

ARC/SAN BERNARDINO
796 E. 6th Street
San Bernardino, CA 92410
(909) 884-6484
(909) 885-3111 FAX

Work, training, and activities for dev disabled adults ages 18 yrs+. Receive referrals through Inland Regional Center. OFC HRS: M-F 9am-3:30pm. Spanish spoken, ASL available. SERVES: San Bernardino area.

ARMY NATIONAL GUARD
2501 Fairmount Blvd.
Riverside, CA 92501
(951) 684-1713

Recruiting young men and women, prior and no prior srv for part-time state military units and jobs. FUNDING: Govt. OFC HRS: M-F 7am-5:30pm. ADM REQ: Healthy, physically fit, ages 17-34 yrs, high school diploma, or GED. SERVES: Riverside Metro, Moreno Valley area.

ASIAN AMERICAN ECONOMIC DEVELOP
216 W. Garvey Ave., Ste E
Monterey Park, CA 91754
(626) 572-7021
(626) 572-6533 FAX

Business workshops, business consulting, internships for students. Srvs open to anyone. FUNDING: Donations, grants, nonprofit. OFC HRS: M-F 9am-5pm. Free srvs. SERVES: So. Calif.

BANNING HIGH ADULT EDUCATION
Banning Unified School District
541 N. Alessandro Rd.
Banning, CA 92220
(951) 922-2740
(951) 922-9499 FAX

ABE deals with English, math, science, history and geography needs to get diploma. GED prep for high school equivalency diploma tests. ESL is open to non-English speaking students ages 18 yrs+, however, they try to acccommodate everyone. Open enrollment. Some individual tutoring. Concurrent adult education. OFC HRS: M-F 7:30am-4:30pm. SERVES: Riverside County.

BARSTOW COMMUNITY COLLEGE
2700 Barstow Rd.
Barstow, CA 92311
(760) 252-2411
(760) 252-1875 FAX

Institution of higher edu offers counseling, testing, vocational edu & rehab srvs, financial aid, veteran srvs, servicemen's opportunity college srvs, extended opportunity prgms, disabled student prgm, scholarship awards, etc. TTY (760) 252-6759. FUNDING: Govt. OFC HRS: M-F 8am-5pm. Foreign languages available upon request. SERVES: Barstow & nearby.

BOYS & GIRLS CLUB/SAN BERNARDINO
1180 W. 9th Street
San Bernardino, CA 92411
(909) 888-6751
(909) 888-1474 FAX

Youth and family srvs agency. Youth dev, counseling, day camp, homework & tutorial srvs, before & after school child care, parent edu, employment srvs, physical and social recreation, community srvs, youth drug & alcohol counseling, ESL classes, GED. FUNDING: Donations, fundraising, United Way, nonprofit. OFC HRS: M-F 7am-7pm; Sat 8:30am-2:30pm. Spanish spoken. Annual membership $7. SERVES: San Bernardino metro area.

CALIF BOARD/BARBERS/COSMETOLOGY
Dept of Consumer Affairs
P.O. Box 944226
2420 Del Paso Rd., Ste 100
Sacramento, CA 94244-2260
(800) 952-5210
(916) 575-7281 FAX

Licenses cosmetologists, barbers, estheticians, manicurists, electrologists, cosmetology & barber instructors & establishments. FUNDING: Govt. OFC HRS: M-F 8am-5pm. Phone hrs: M-F 8am-4:50pm. SERVES: Calif.

CALIF BOARD/MEDICAL ASSISTANT
Dept of Consumer Affairs
2005 Evergreen St., Ste 1200
Sacramento, CA 95815
(916) 263-8382
(916) 263-2944 FAX

FUNDING: Govt. OFC HRS: M-F 8am-5pm. Spanish spoken. SERVES: Calif.

CALIF BOARD/VOC NURSE/PSYCH TECH
Dept of Consumer Affairs
2535 Capitol Oaks Dr., Ste 205
Sacramento, CA 95833
(916) 263-7800
(916) 263-7855 FAX

Administers exam licenses & enforces rules of practice for licensed vocational nurses and psychiatric technicians. FUNDING: Govt. OFC HRS: M-F 8am-5pm. SERVES: Calif.

CALIF CONSERVATION CORPS
Pomona Service District
3530 W. Pomona Blvd.
Pomona, CA 91768
(909) 594-4206
(909) 598-2633 FAX

Work ethic prgm with a dual mission: the employment and dev of young people and the enhancement of natural resources. Disaster and emerg response included. One-year prgm. Wait: 1 mo. Call for appt. Recruitment (909) 708-8488. FUNDING: Govt. OFC HRS: M-F 8am-4:30pm. ADM REQ: Ages 18-25 yrs and Calif resident. Not on parole/probation. SERVES: Calif.

CALIF DEPT FAIR EMPLOY/HOUSING
Los Angeles District Office
1055 W. 7th Street, Ste 1400
Los Angeles, CA 90017
(800) 884-1684
(213) 439-6799
(213) 439-6715 FAX

Civil rights agency for Calif. Will accept, investigate and conciliate complaints in the areas of employment & housing discrimination. Complaints must be filed within one yr of offense. Does not accept files over one yr. TTY (800) 700-2320. FUNDING: Govt. OFC HRS: M-F 8am-5pm. Spanish spoken. Free srvs. SERVES: Calif.

CALIF DEPT INDUSTRIAL RELATIONS
Division of Labor Standards
320 W. 4th Street, Ste 450
Los Angeles, CA 90013
(213) 620-6330
(213) 897-4059 FAX

Wages, hours, work comp, labor disputes, etc. Info available in Spanish & Korean. Work comp (213)576-7389. FUNDING: Govt. OFC HRS: M-F 8am-5pm. Closed first 3 F of the month. Chinese, Korean & Spanish spoken. SERVES: Calif.

CALIF DEPT REHAB/ADMIN
State Headquarters
721 Capitol Mall
Sacramento, CA 95814
(916) 558-5300

Works in partnership with consumers and other stakeholders to provide srvs and advocacy resulting in employment, independent living and equality for individuals with disabilities. TTY (916) 558-5302. OFC HRS: M-F 8am-5pm. Closed first three F of the month. Live in California. Citizenship or valid work permit. Free srvs. SERVES: Calif.

CALIF DEPT REHAB/BARSTOW
See "Calif Dept Rehab/Victorville"

CALIF DEPT REHAB/BLYTHE
Blythe Branch
1277 W. Hobson Way
Blythe, CA 92225
(760) 922-2118
(760) 922-8678 FAX

Assists people with all types of disabilities to retain employment and live independently. Srvs include: vocational rehab (training, edu, transportation, job placement), assistive technology, deaf & hearing srvs, blind srvs, and tech assist. FUNDING: State, govt. OFC HRS: M-F 8am-5pm. Spanish spoken. ADM REQ: Eligible disability. SERVES: Blythe.

CALIF DEPT REHAB/HEMET
See "Calif Dept Rehab/Temecula"

CALIF DEPT REHAB/JOSHUA TREE
Copper Mountain College
6162 Rotary Way
Joshua Tree, CA 92252
(760) 366-2681
(760) 365-4569 FAX

Assists people with all types of disabilities to retain employment and live independently. Srvs include: vocational rehab (training, edu, job placement, transportation), assistive technology, deaf & hearing srvs, blind srvs and tech assist. FUNDING: State, govt. OFC HRS: M-F 8am-5pm. ADM REQ: Eligible disability. SERVES: High Desert.

CALIF DEPT REHAB/PALM DESERT
73-720 Fred Waring Dr., Ste 102
Palm Desert, CA 92260
(760) 674-0262
(760) 674-0268 FAX

Assists people with all types of disabilities to retain employment and live independently. Srvs include: vocational rehab (training, edu, transportation, job placement), assistive technology, deaf & hearing srvs, blind srvs, tech assist, college, orthotic and prosthetic devices. Wait: varies. TTY (760) 674-0266. FUNDING: State, federal. OFC HRS: M-F 8am-5pm. Spanish spoken. ASL available. ADM REQ: Eligible disability. Free srvs. SERVES: Coachella Valley.

CALIF DEPT REHAB/RIVERSIDE
Inland Empire District Office
3130 Chicago Ave.
Riverside, CA 92507-3445
(951) 782-6650
(951) 782-6676 FAX

Assists people with all types of disabilities to retain employment and live independently. Srvs include: vocational rehab (training, edu, transportation, job placement), assistive technology, deaf & hearing srvs, blind srvs, and tech assist. For TTY, call (951) 682-0143, (951) 320-2061 or (951) 782-4277. FUNDING: State, federal. OFC HRS: M-F 8am-5pm. Spanish spoken, ASL available. ADM REQ: Eligible disability. SERVES: Riverside, San Bernardino, Imperial Counties.

CALIF DEPT REHAB/SAN BERNARDINO
San Bernardino District Office
464 W. 4th. Street, Ste 152
San Bernardino, CA 92401-1419
(909) 383-4401
(909) 383-6880 FAX

Assists people with all types of disabilities to retain employment and live independently. Srvs include: vocational rehab (training, edu, job placement), assistive technology, deaf & hearing srvs, blind srvs, and tech assist. For TTY, call (909)885-0028. FUNDING: State, govt. OFC HRS: M-F 8am-5pm. Spanish spoken. ASL available. ADM REQ: Eligible disability. SERVES: East San Bernardino County.

CALIF DEPT REHAB/TEMECULA
27555 Ynez Rd., Ste 310
Temecula, CA 92591-4678
(951) 693-4451
(951) 693-4462 FAX

Assists people with all types of disabilities to retain employment and live independently. Srvs include: vocational rehab (training, edu, transportation, job placement), assistive technology, deaf & hearing srvs, blind srvs, & tech assist. TTY (951) 693-4468. FUNDING: State, govt. OFC HRS: M-F 8am-5pm. Spanish spoken. ASL available. ADM REQ: Eligible disability. SERVES: Riverside County.

CALIF DEPT REHAB/UPLAND
3585 E. Inland Empire Blvd., Bldg. 4
Ontario, CA 91764
(909) 948-6050

Assists people with all types of disabilities to retain employment and live independently. Srvs include: vocational rehab (training, edu, job placement), assistive technology, deaf & hearing srvs, blind srvs, and tech assist. Call first. FUNDING: State, govt. OFC HRS: M-F 8am-5pm. Spanish spoken. ADM REQ: Eligible disability. Majority of srvs are free. SERVES: Western San Bernardino County.

CALIF DEPT REHAB/VICTORVILLE
15415 W. Sand St., 2nd Fl.
Victorville, CA 92392
(760) 243-6024
(760) 243-0522 FAX

Assists people with all types of disabilities to retain employment and live independently. Srvs include: vocational rehab (training, edu, job placement), assistive technology, deaf & hearing srvs, blind srvs, and tech assist. For TTY, call (760) 245-4127. FUNDING: State, govt. OFC HRS: M-F 8am-5pm. Spanish spoken, ASL available. ADM REQ: Eligible disability. SERVES: Victorville, Southern San Bernardino.

CALIF DEPT TRANSPORTATION
Civil Rights Business Enterprise Prgm
1823 14th Street
Sacramento, CA 95811
(916) 324-1700
(916) 324-1949 FAX

Certifies disadvantaged business enterprises, minority businesses and women business enterprises. Purpose is to increase the level of participation of these groups in all of the state and federal contracting activities. TTY 711. OFC HRS: M-F 8am-5pm. SERVES: Calif.

CALIF FAMILY LIFE CENTER

Empower Youth Program
930 N. State St.
Hemet, CA 92543
(951) 765-0917
(951) 652-8287 FAX

Work readiness skills, technology skills, work experience & career exploration, leadership dev, edu srvs for youth. FUNDING: Nonprofit. OFC HRS: M-Th 7:30am-8pm; F 7:30am-7pm. ADM REQ: Ages 16-21 yrs, from low income families. Must meet eligibility criteria. SERVES: Hemet, San Jacinto, Banning, Beaumont, Quail Valley.

CALIF INDIAN MANPOWER CONSORTIUM

21250 Box Springs Rd., Ste 204
Moreno Valley, CA 92557
(800) 499-2462
(951) 784-9962
(951) 784-9945 FAX

Employment training program for Native American Indians, Alaskans or Hawaiians. Wait depends on eligibility, ASA certified. FUNDING: Dept of Labor, fed govt. OFC HRS: M-F 8am-5pm. SERVES: Riverside & San Bernardino Counties.

CALIF INDUSTRIAL RELATIONS DEPT

Worker's Comp Benefits
464 W. 4th Street, 2nd Fl., Ste 239
San Bernardino, CA 92401
(909) 383-4522
(800) 736-7401

OFC HRS: M-F 8am-5pm. Spanish spoken. SERVES: San Bernardino, Riverside Counties.

CALIF INDUSTRIAL RELATIONS DEPT

Labor Standards Enforcement
464 W. 4th Street, Rm. 348
San Bernardino, CA 92401
(909) 383-4334
(909) 889-8120
(909) 383-6397 FAX

Info on wage claims, minimum wage, hours, working conditions. OFC HRS: M-F 8am-5pm. SERVES: San Bernardino & Riverside Counties.

CALIF INDUSTRIAL RELATIONS DEPT.

3737 Main St., Ste 300
Riverside, CA 92501-3337
(951) 782-4269
(800) 736-7401

Info & assist to injured workers & employers. Also distributes pamphlets, workers' comp forms and will mediate disputes between injured workers and insurance carriers. Workshops held 1st Tu of each month at 1:30pm. For the info/assistance unit, call (951) 782-4347. FUNDING: State. OFC HRS: M-F 8am-5pm. Spanish spoken. SERVES: Riverside County.

CALIF OFC OF SMALL BUSINESS

Small Business Certification/Resources
707 3rd Street, 2nd Fl.
West Sacramento, CA 95605
(800) 559-5529
(916) 375-4400
(916) 375-4613 FAX

Issues the small business certification necessary to obtain a 5% preference in source selection for state contracts and issues the Disabled Veteran Business Enterprise (DVBE) certification. Provides assist to small businesses and DVBEs applying for certification. TTY/TDD (916) 322-7535. FUNDING: Govt. OFC HRS: M-F 8am-5pm. SERVES: Calif.

CALIF UNEMPLOYMENT INS APPEALS

P.O. Box 3100
9655 Arrow Rte., Bldg. 19
Rancho Cucamonga, CA 91729-3100
(909) 987-2212
(909) 481-5779 FAX

Unemployment insurance appeals. OFC HRS: M-F 8am-4:45pm. SERVES: L.A., San Bernardino & Riverside Counties.

CALJOBS

Experience Unlimited
2450 E. Lincoln Ave.
Anaheim, CA 92801
(714) 518-2323
(714) 518-2394 FAX

Internet-based job opening and resume listing system that increases the public's access to employment srvs. Provided by Calif EDD, Job Service Div Prgm serves both employers who want to fill job openings and individuals seeking employment. Visit (www.caljobs.ca.gov). Call (800) 758-0398 for questions, M-F 8am-5pm. FUNDING: State. OFC HRS: M-F 8am-4:30pm ADM REQ: Business attire SERVES: Calif.

CALWORKS

CalWORKs prgm is the Calif Welfare-to-Work prgm with the goal of getting people off TANF and welfare prgms and into a self-sufficient lifestyle. The prgm requires adults who receive public assist to participate in work activities. Single parents may be required to account for 32 hrs of work activity per week and persons from two parent homes up to 35. Prgm includes: 1) appraisal & job search; 2) assessment & Welfare-to-Work plan; 3) Welfare-to-Work activities; 4) re-appraisal; 5) community srvs. Participants are provided with support srvs such as child care to remove barriers to success in the prgm. Access these srvs through the local county social srvs agency. FUNDING: Fed, state, county govt.

CASA COLINA RETURN TO WORK SRV

Vocational Evaluation Facility
P.O. Box 6001
255 E. Bonita Ave.
Pomona, CA 91769
(909) 596-7733
(866) 724-4127
(909) 596-7845 FAX

Vocational eval, work hardening and clerical training for disabled adults. Call for locations. FUNDING: Nonprofit. OFC HRS: M-F 9am-5pm.

CENTER FOR EMPLOYMENT TRAINING

1430 Cooley Ct.
San Bernardino, CA 92408
(909) 478-3818
(909) 478-9506 FAX

Training in automated, machine tool operator, CNC machine setup operator, light gauge welding, field maintenance, welding fabrication, accounting clerk ESL, GED. FUNDING: Nonprofit. OFC HRS: M-F 8am-5pm. Spanish spoken. Financial assist to those who qualify. SERVES: Riverside & San Bernardino Counties.

CENTER FOR EMPLOYMENT TRAINING

Vocational Skill Training/Injured Worker

27941 Jefferson Ave., Ste A
Temecula, CA 92590
(951) 699-8180
(951) 699-3851 FAX

Training school offers shipping & receiving, forklift certification, accounting & payroll clerk, computer clerk, Medical and admin assist, GED, ESL offered concurrent with training. TRA, ITA, Rehab, financial aid funds available. FUNDING: Nonprofit. OFC HRS: M-F 8am-5pm. Spanish spoken. SERVES: Temecula & nearby.

CENTER FOR LIVING AND LEARNING

14549 Archwood St., Ste 221
Van Nuys, CA 91405
(818) 781-1073
(888) 266-1919
(818) 781-9754 FAX

Helps to prepare clients for the job search process and improve chances of landing an interview, obtaining employment, and retaining the job. Clients have access to resources such as computers, telephones, and fax machines. Course supervisors provide individual assistance with career counseling, resume writing, computer courses and referrals to other agencies as needed. FUNDING: Nonprofit. OFC HRS: M-Th 9am-4pm; F 9am-2pm. Spanish spoken. All services free. SERVES: L.A. and San Bernardino Counties.

CHAFFEY COLLEGE/EOPS

5885 Haven Ave.
Rancho Cucamonga, CA 91737
(909) 652-6349
(909) 652-6342 FAX

EOPS offers support services to economically disadvantaged students who have experienced limited success in high school and/or college. Endeavors to ensure student retention and success through academic support and financial assistance CARE is a special EOPS prgm for single parents (all ages) receiving govt financial assist & helps with child care, cafeteria food vouchers, books and supplies, etc. Also offers prgm for youth ages 16-21 yrs emancipating from foster care or seeking to live independent of their guardians. FUNDING: Govt. OFC HRS: M-W 8am-4:30pm; Th 8am-6:30pm; F 8am-2pm. Spanish, Vietnamese spoken. ADM REQ: Call or see website for eligibility req. SERVES: San Bernardino County.

CHINO COMMUNITY ADULT SCHOOL

See "Chino Valley Adult School"

CHINO VALLEY ADULT SCHOOL

Chino Valley Unified School District
12970 3rd Street
Rancho Cucamonga, CA 91701
(909) 627-9613
(909) 548-6016 FAX

ESL, citizenship, GED prep, GED testing center, high school diploma. Walk in or call. FUNDING: State, federal, nonprofit. OFC HRS: M-F 7:30am-9pm. Spanish, Portuguese spoken. SERVES: San Bernardino County.

CLAREMONT ADULT SCHOOL

170 W. San Jose Ave. 3rd Fl.
Claremont, CA 91711
(909) 398-0609
(909) 398-0690 FAX

ESL, HS diploma, literacy, parent edu enrichment, vocational, older adult and community srvs classes. Located near bus route. FUNDING: State, local, govt. OFC HRS: M-Th 8am-3pm, F 8:30am-12pm. Spanish spoken. ADM REQ: Ages 18 yrs+. SERVES: Claremont, Pomona, Montclair, San Dimas, La Verne & Upland.

COACHELLA VALLEY ADULT SCHOOL
Coachella Valley Adult School/GED Ctr
1099 Orchard Ave.
Coachella, CA 92236
(760) 398-6302
(760) 398-0436 FAX

ESL and ABE with open enrollment. High school diploma, GED prep and testing, computer skills classes, citizenship, business financial management, notary public, local center for employment training. OFC HRS: M-Th 8am-9pm; F 8am-5pm. Spanish spoken. ADM REQ: Ages 18 yrs+. Accepts pvt pay. SERVES: Coachella.

COLLEGE OF THE DESERT/EOPS
43-500 Monterey Ave.
Palm Desert, CA 92260-9399
(760) 773-2539
(760) 346-8041
(760) 776-0147 FAX

EOPS offers various counseling, financial aid for books, transfer fee waiver, laptops and graphing calculators on loan, priority registration, long-term edu planning, tutoring, student ID card, assistance with health fee. CARE is a special EOPS prgm for single parents (all ages) receiving govt financial assist to help them go to college and obtain skills for meaningful employment. Helps with child care, gas cards & many other srvs. Also offer prgm for youth ages 16-21 yrs emancipating from foster care or seeking to live independent of their guardians. EOPS and CARE srvs subject to change. FUNDING: Govt. OFC HRS: M-Th 9am-5pm; F 9am-12noon. Spanish spoken. ADM REQ: Must be full-time COD student. Apply online or in person. Inquire about requirements. SERVES: Riverside County.

COMMUNITY ACTION EAP
1481 Ford St., Ste 201
Redlands, CA 92373
(800) 777-9376
(909) 307-3246 FAX

Implementation and admin of Employee Assist Prgm srvs. Healthcare professionals helping employers help their employees through confidential assist with issues affecting their professional and personal lives. FUNDING: Nonprofit. Employer-sponsored. OFC HRS: 24 hrs, 7 days. SERVES: So. Calif.

COMMUNITY ACTION PARTNERSHIP
Emergency Assistance Prgms
2038 Iowa Ave., Ste B-102
Riverside, CA 92507
(951) 955-4900
(800) 511-1110
(951) 955-6506 FAX

Several emerg assist prgms offered. Prgms for dev skills in small business. Training & technical assist in planning, grantsmanship, program & fiscal mgmt, needs assessments, resource mobilization, prgm dev and eval. Sponsors activities and community forums. Wait: varies.

Call first. FUNDING: Fed, state, pvt. OFC HRS: M-F 8am-5pm. Spanish upon request. ADM REQ: Low income resident. SERVES: Riverside County.

COMMUNITY OUTREACH PROGRAM
c/o Corona Public Library
650 S. Main St.
Corona, CA 92882
(951) 736-2381
(951) 736-2499 FAX

Assists in completing paperwork for Medi-Cal, CalWORKs, social security, interpretation, work applications. Referral for emerg assist. OFC HRS: M-Tu 10am-9pm; W-Th 10am-6pm; Sat 10am-5pm. Spanish spoken. Free srvs. SERVES: Corona & Norco.

COPPER MOUNTAIN COLLEGE/EOPS
6162 Rotary Way
Joshua Tree, CA 92252
(760) 366-3791
(760) 366-5257 FAX

EOPS & CARE are state-funded prgms assisting the academically & economically disadvantaged student. EOPS srvs include, but are not limited to, academic counseling, book assist, tutoring, parking permits. CARE provides grants, food cards, parenting info, gas cards. All srvs upon availability or state funding. TDD (760) 366-3241. FUNDING: Govt. OFC HRS: M-Th 8:15am-5pm; F 8:15am-3pm. Spanish spoken. ADM REQ: Must be full-time student, less than 70 degree-applicable units, BOG waiver A or B, and academically disadvantaged. CARE students must be EOPS eligible, ages 18 yrs+, have at least one child under the age of 14 yrs, and currently on CalWORKs/TANF & receiving cash aid. SERVES: Calif.

CORONA-NORCO ADULT SCHOOL
Corona-Norco Unified School District
300 Buena Vista Ave.
Corona, CA 92882-1937
(951) 736-3325
(951) 736-7159 FAX

Classes in literacy, ESL, ABE, GED, high school diploma. Short-term training in computers, medical and office occupations. Open year-round, open enrollment. Bilingual staff. Day & eve classes. OFC HRS: M-Th 9am-8pm; F 8am-1pm. Spanish spoken. Fees for some classes.

CRAFTON HILLS COLLEGE/EOPS
11711 Sand Canyon Rd.
Yucaipa, CA 92399-1799
(909) 389-3239
(909) 794-2161
(909) 389-3621 FAX

EOPS offers info & referral, counseling, edu grants, financial aid for books, transportation assist, mentoring, student work prgm, emerg no- interest loans, transfer fee waiver. CARE is a special EOPS prgm for single parents (all ages) receiving govt financial assist & helps with child care, gas cards & many other srvs. Also offer prgm for youth ages 16-21 yrs emancipating from foster care or seeking to live independent of their guardians. OFC HRS: M-Th 8am-6pm; F 8am-1pm. Spanish spoken. ADM REQ: CA resident, qualify for BOGW A/B, enrolled in 12 units unless in disabled student prgm, have less than 70 degree-applicable units & be edu disadvantaged. CARE head of

household, single parent receiving TANF/CalWORKs with a Welfare-to-Work plan & have a child under 14 yrs of age. SERVES: San Bernardino County.

D.A.R.T.
See "Desert Area Resources/..."

DEPT OF REHABILITATION
See "Calif Dept Rehab/..."

DEPT. OF WORKFORCE DEV
658 E. Brier Dr, Ste 100
San Bernardino, CA 92410-4108
(909) 382-0440
(909) 382-0427 FAX

Job listing srv for local businesses via web-based job match system. Candidates for employment are screened based on employer specs. Srvs open to public, 17 locations throughout San Bernardino County. Also call Job Employment Srv at (909) 386-7884. FUNDING: Fed, state, county. OFC HRS: M-F 8:30am-5pm. Employment srvs are free. SERVES: San Bernardino County.

DESERT AREA RESOURCES/TRAINING
Inform/Employ/Supported Living
201 E. Ridgecrest Blvd.
Ridgecrest, CA 93555
(760) 375-9787
(760) 375-1288 FAX

Multi-srv agency serving special needs individuals. Prgms include: INFORM, a centrally located resource lab with info & resources open to anyone. Community Employment Srvs offers a variety of ways to increase vocational skills through on-the-job training, pre-vocational training skills, and supported job placement. CREST (Crafts, Recreation, Exercise & Socialization Together) provides recreation and social opportunities for persons living in the Indian Wells Valley, ages 7 yrs+. Supported living provides adults with disabilities an opportunity to live in their own homes, via srvs & support for agencies, families and friends. DART also provides early childhood srvs from ages birth-3 yrs in in-home and group settings. Preschool for ages 3-5 yrs. FUNDING: Nonprofit. OFC HRS: M-F 7:30am-4:30pm. Spanish spoken. SERVES: Ridgecrest, Trona & Rand, Inyo & Kern Counties.

DESERT HOT SPRINGS FAMILY RESOURCE CTR
14201 Palm Dr., Ste 108
Desert Hot Springs, CA 92240
(760) 288-3313
(760) 288-2854 FAX

Classes offered on parenting skills, family planning, adult edu. Healthy Children Connection, Healthy Families, Medi-Cal enrollment (through Catholic Charities), immunization info, utility assist clinic provided with Community Action Partnership, WIC info, job search, GED classes, veteran support group, individual, family, & group counseling. Referrals to emerg srvs. FUNDING: Nonprofit. OFC HRS: M-F 8am-5pm. Spanish spoken. ADM REQ: Must call first, except for job search srvs. SERVES: Bermuda Dunes, Cathedral City, Coachella, Desert Hot Springs, Indio, Indio Hills, North Palm Springs, Palm Springs, Rancho Mirage.

DISABILITY INSURANCE
See "Employment Dev Dept/..."

EDUCATIONAL OPTIONS CENTER
Riverside USD Adult & Alt Edu
6401 Lincoln Ave.
Riverside, CA 92506
(951) 276-7670
(951) 276-7685 FAX

Home health aid, CNA, medical asst, ofc occupations (including computers), medical billing and coding, medical terminology and anatomy, computer classes, ESL, high school diploma and GED. FUNDING: Nonprofit. OFC HRS: M-Th 8am-4:30pm; F 7:30am-4pm. Summer hrs: M-F 7:30am-4pm. Spanish spoken. SERVES: Riverside County.

EMPLOYMENT & BUSINESS RESOURCE CTR
WDD/WIA
15555 Main St., Ste G-4
Hesperia, CA 92345
(760) 949-8526
(760) 949-8541 FAX

Several agencies are co-located in one place in order to serve each individual's employment or job training needs. Agencies may include reps from WIA, Social Srvs, Dept of Rehab, EDD, community college counselors, etc. Clients who come to the One-Stop Center should find answers to a wide range of employment-related questions. Also business assist. FUNDING: San Bernardino Co, govt. OFC HRS: M-F 7am-5pm. Spanish spoken. SERVES: High Desert & Victor Valley.

EMPLOYMENT DEV DEPT/DISABILITY
P.O. Box 469
Long Beach, CA 90801
(800) 480-3287

Disability insurance coverage for workers who become ill, injured or pregnant. This is coverage for non-job related matters (Workers' Comp covers job related). Wait: 7 days. TTY (800) 563-2441. Spanish (866) 658-8846. See website for additional language lines (www.edd.ca.gov). FUNDING: Employee payroll deduction. OFC HRS: M-F 8am-5pm. Spanish spoken. Call for eligibility criteria. Free srvs. SERVES: Riverside County.

EMPLOYMENT DEV DEPT/DISABILITY
Disability Insurance
P.O. Box 781
371 W. 3rd Street
San Bernardino, CA 92402-0781
(800) 480-3287

Disability insurance coverage for workers who become ill, injured or pregnant. This is coverage for off-the-job injuries (Workers' Comp covers job-related). Wait: 7 days. Spanish (866) 658-8846. See website for additional language lines (www.edd.ca.gov). FUNDING: Earnings, contributions. OFC HRS: M-F 8am-5pm. Spanish spoken. Free srvs. SERVES: San Bernardino County.

EMPLOYMENT DEV DEPT/JOB SRVS
Blythe Job Service
1277 W. Hobson Way
Blythe, CA 92225
(760) 922-3172
(760) 922-4052 FAX

State-sponsored employment srv. Job placement, unemployment insurance benefits, recruitment and placement of veterans including disabled veterans. Walk in. FUNDING: Govt.

OFC HRS: M-F 8am-5pm. Spanish spoken. Free srvs. SERVES: Riverside.

EMPLOYMENT DEV DEPT/JOB SRVS
Corona Job Service
237 W. River Rd.
Corona, CA 92880
(951) 340-4036
(951) 734-5783 FAX

State-sponsored employment srv. Job search assist, recruitment and placement of veterans including disabled veterans. Walk in. FUNDING: State, govt. OFC HRS: M-F 8am-5pm. Spanish spoken. Free srvs. SERVES: Riverside County.

EMPLOYMENT DEV DEPT/JOB SRVS
Hemet Job Service
1025 N. State St.
Hemet, CA 92543
(951) 791-3500

County-sponsored employment srv. Job training, unemployment insurance benefits, referral and placement of veterans including disabled veterans. Walk in. Computers, printers, training. FUNDING: county, govt. OFC HRS: M-Th 7:30am-5:30pm. Spanish spoken. Free srvs. SERVES: Riverside County.

EMPLOYMENT DEV DEPT/JOB SRVS
Indio Job Service
44-199 Monroe St., Ste B
Indio, CA 92203
(760) 863-2600

State-sponsored employment srv. Job placement, unemployment insurance benefits, recruitment and placement of veterans including disabled veterans. Walk in. FUNDING: State, govt. OFC HRS: M-Th 7:30am-5:30pm. Spanish spoken. Free srvs. SERVES: Riverside County.

EMPLOYMENT DEV DEPT/JOB SRVS
Workforce Development Center
30135 Technology Dr.
Murrieta, CA 92563
(951) 304-5900
(951) 304-5785 FAX

State-sponsored employment srv. Job placement, recruitment and placement of veterans including disabled veterans. Walk in. Partnered together with EDD employment srvs. See website (www.rivcojobs) for list of srvs. FUNDING: State, govt. OFC HRS: M-F 8am-5pm. Spanish spoken. Free srvs. SERVES: Southwest Riverside County.

EMPLOYMENT DEV DEPT/JOB SRVS
Rancho Employment Resource Center
9650 9th Street, Ste A
Rancho Cucamonga, CA 91730
(909) 948-6606
(909) 941-6500
(909) 941-1676 FAX

EDD offers employment srvs to employers & job seekers. Srvs include: employer recruitment, workshops & access to computers, fax machines & the Internet. EDD provides priority srvs to veterans & personalized assist to persons with disabilities & youth ages 15-21 yrs with employment barriers. FUNDING: State. OFC HRS: M-F 8am-5pm. Spanish spoken. Free srvs. SERVES: San Bernardino County.

EMPLOYMENT DEV DEPT/JOB SRVS
Riverside Job Service

1325 Spruce St
Riverside, CA 92507
(951) 955-2200

State-sponsored employment srv. EDD provides CalJobs, an Internet-based srv designed to match job seekers & employers. Other co-located agencies providing training and job placement include WIA, Dept of Rehab, Veteran Srvs, ROP, and CalWORKs. FUNDING: State, govt. OFC HRS: Call for office hours. Spanish spoken. Free srvs. SERVES: Riverside County.

EMPLOYMENT DEV DEPT/JOB SRVS
Victorville Job Service
P.O. Box 1379
15419 Cholame Rd.
Victorville, CA 92393
(760) 241-1682
(800) 300-5616
(760) 241-2468 FAX

State-sponsored employment srv. Job placement, unemployment insurance benefits, recruitment and placement of veterans including disabled veterans. Walk in. OFC HRS: M-F 8am-5pm. Spanish spoken. Free srvs. SERVES: Victorville, Hesperia, Apple Valley, Lucerne Valley, Adelanto, Barstow, Yermo, Daggett, Baker, Needles & Phelan.

EMPOWERTECH COMPUTER ACCESS CTR
Empowering & Educating People with Disabilities
6234 W. 87th Street
Los Angeles, CA 90045
(310) 338-1597
(310) 338-9318 FAX

Provides children and adults who have physical and dev disabilities with edu and training to lead independent and productive lives utilizing assistive technology. Open Access prgm available free of charge every W. FUNDING: Donations, nonprofit. OFC HRS: M-F 9am-5pm. Spanish & French spoken. SERVES: L.A., Orange & Riverside Counties.

EQUAL RIGHTS ADVOCATES
180 Howard St., Ste 300
San Francisco, CA 94103
(415) 621-0672
(800) 839-4372
(415) 621-6744 FAX

Advice and counseling line provides legal advice and info on rights, options and remedies in sex discrimination, employment & sexual harassment issues. Focus is to reduce sex discrimination in employment & edu. Welcomes calls from people in Welfare-to-Work job placements with questions or issues about discrimination. FUNDING: Donations, grants, nonprofit. OFC HRS: M-F 9am-5:30pm. Spanish spoken. SERVES: U.S.A.

ROP/FONTANA HIGH SCHOOL
9453 Citrus Ave.
Fontana, CA 92335
(909) 357-5500
(909) 357-5629 FAX

Career & technical edu courses, career guidance & job placement assist. FUNDING: Govt. OFC HRS: Tu-F 8:30am-12:30pm. Spanish spoken. ADM REQ: high school students, adults. SERVES: Fontana area.

FONTANA REHAB WORKSHOP

Industrial Support Systems
P.O. Box 848
8333 Almeria Ave.
Fontana, CA 92335
(909) 428-3833
(800) 755-4755
(909) 428-3835 FAX

Vocational training & eval, job dev and placement, supported employment srvs, consulting. Wait depends on needed paperwork from other agencies. FUNDING: Fed, state, pvt, industry, nonprofit. OFC HRS: M-F 7:30am-4:15pm. Spanish spoken. ADM REQ: Medically documented disabling condition, ages 16 yrs+, set for third party sponsorship. SERVES: Inland Empire.

G.A.I.N. PROGRAMS

San Bernardino Co. Human Srvs System

See "Jobs and Employment Services"

GAIN/CALWORKS PROGRAMS

See "Riverside Co. Public Social Srvs"

GED HOTLINE

(800) 626-9433

Obtain info regarding testing sites, testing prep, GED transcripts, etc. See website (www.gedtest.org) for more info. FUNDING: Private for profit. Spanish spoken. SERVES: U.S.A.

GOODWILL INDUSTRIES/INLAND CO.

Vocational Services
14580 7th Street, Ste Q-1
Victorville, CA 92394
(760) 951-5572
(760) 951-5350
(760) 951-5679 FAX

Supported employment for the dev or physically challenged adult. Includes job placement assist, employment prep srvs, career resource center. OFC HRS: M-Th 9am-5pm; F 9am-12noon. Spanish spoken. ADM REQ: Referral from Dept of Rehab. SERVES: San Bernardino County.

GOODWILL INDUSTRIES/SAN BRDO

8120 Palm Lane
San Bernardino, CA 92410
(909) 885-3831
(909) 386-6251 FAX

Vocation eval, skill training, job placement, and supported employment for people with disabilities and other major barriers to employment. Wait: 1-2 weeks. FUNDING: Retail sales, fees, nonprofit. OFC HRS: M-F 7:30am-4:30pm. Spanish spoken. ADM REQ: Ready to pursue vocational prgm leading to competitive employment. Free to those who qualify. SERVES: San Bernardino County.

GOODWILL INDUSTRIES/SO CALIF

Corporate Office
342 N. San Fernando Rd.
Los Angeles, CA 90031
(323) 223-1211
(323) 343-9927 FAX

Srvs to physically, mentally and emotionally disabled and other disadvantages such as illiteracy, homelessness, former gang affiliation, etc. Job training & placement prgms, career counseling, WIA, training in food srvs, janitorial, & retail. Metro North Work Source Ctr, Career Evaluation Ctr. Vintage Fashion show for busi-

ness, club or groups (323) 223-1211, ext 2329. FUNDING: Self-funded, VR, WIA, VA, nonprofit. OFC HRS: M-F 8am-5pm. Spanish spoken. ADM REQ: Ages 18 yrs+, barrier to employment. Youth prgm available. Free srvs. SERVES: L.A. & San Bernardino Counties.

HANDS ON INLAND EMPIRE

9624 Hermosa Ave.
Rancho Cucamonga, CA 91730
(909) 980-2857
(909) 980-2957 FAX

Brings individuals, families, teams and corporate groups together to strengthen communities through meaningful volunteer action within San Bernardino & Riverside Counties and the Pomona Valley. FUNDING: Nonprofit. OFC HRS: M-F 8am-5pm. Spanish spoken. Free srvs. SERVES: San Bernardino, Riverside and Pomona Valley.

HART COMMUNITY HOMES

208 N. Lemon
Fullerton, CA 92832
(714) 526-2729
(714) 526-2653 FAX

Residential treatment for foster care youth ages 13-18 yrs. Treatment model is tailored to meet individual needs. Prgm focuses on emancipation and has a vocational center providing a life skills workforce dev prgm. Also offers Monkey Business Cafe which provides paid work experience in a cafe setting for foster care youth in and emancipating out of the foster care system. Visit (www.hartcommunityhomes.org). FUNDING: Nonprofit. OFC HRS: M-F 9am-5pm. Cafe open M-F 7am-3pm. Spanish, Korean spoken. ADM REQ: Abused and abandoned boys ages 13-18 yrs. SERVES: L.A., Orange & San Bernardino Counties.

HEMET ADULT SCHOOL

26866 San Jacinto St.
Hemet, CA 92544
(951) 765-5190
(951) 925-7478 FAX

High school diploma, GED, ESL. Walk in. Spanish class available. FUNDING: ADA. OFC HRS: M-Th 1pm-7pm. ADM REQ: Transcripts for high school diploma students. $10 registration fee. $20 per semester for computer classes; all other classes are free. SERVES: Hemet.

INSTITUTE OF MULTISENSORY LEARNING

c/o Community College Foundation
1901 Royal Oaks Dr.
Sacramento, CA 95815
(916) 418-5100
(800) 400-5881
(916) 418-5150 FAX

Computer and multimedia training for edu groups, govt agencies or pvt companies. Courses include basic computing skills, Internet search skills, webpage creation, mutimedia authoring, digital image manipulation, and others. The Institute has a mobile Multisensory Learning Lab (a renovated RV with $250,000 worth of multimedia hardware & software); wireless laptop network (30 multimedia laptop network). Customized courses are available. FUNDING: Nonprofit. OFC HRS: M-F 8am-5pm. SERVES: Calif

JEFFERSON TRANSITIONAL PROGRAMS

3839 Brockton Ave.
Riverside, CA 92501

(951) 686-5484
(951) 686-6630 FAX

Vocational & supportive living prgms for mentally ill and dually diagnosed individuals. Supported housing prgm for men & women, life mgmt skills, one-to-one sessions, house meetings. FUNDING: Nonprofit. OFC HRS: M-F 8am-4pm. ADM REQ: Ability to meet prgm goals & objectives. SERVES: Riverside County.

JOB ACCOMMODATION NETWORK

West Virginia University
P.O. Box 6080
Morgantown, WV 26506-6080
(800) 526-7234
(304) 293-5407 FAX

Ideas for accommodating disabled persons in the workplace & info on availability of accommodation aids & procedures. Answers questions about Americans With Disabilities Act, etc. TTY (877) 781-9403. FUNDING: Govt, nonprofit. OFC HRS: 9am-6pm, EST. Recording accepts messages after hours. Spanish spoken. Free srvs. SERVES: U.S.A.

JOB CORPS INFORMATION HOTLINE

Job Corps Admissions for Women
405 14th Street, Ste 401
Oakland, CA 94612
(510) 832-2549
(510) 832-4352 FAX

Voc & edu training for young women ages 16-24 yrs from low income families. Dormitory facilities, food, health care, etc. are all free for those involved in the prgm. Women, call number above. Men, call (800) 733-5627. Chinese (415) 981-7835. FUNDING: Govt, nonprofit. OFC HRS: M-F 8am-5pm. Spanish & Chinese spoken. Free srvs. SERVES: U.S.A.

JOB OPPORTUNITIES FOR THE BLIND

Natl Federation of the Blind
200 E. Wells St.
Baltimore, MD 21230
(410) 659-9314
(410) 685-5653 FAX

Organization of blind people working together to improve opportunities for the blind and the understanding of blindness by the general public. Special prgms and srvs include: job opportunities for the blind (free job search prgm & training for job-ready blind clients); internatl Braille and technology center; newsline talking newspaper; as well as info and literature on all aspects of blindness including aids, appliances, and special items for the blind. FUNDING: Donations, govt. OFC HRS: M-F 8am-5pm, EST. Spanish spoken. SERVES: U.S.A.

JOBS AND EMPLOY SRVS/ONE-STOP

See "One-Stop Center"

JOBS AND EMPLOYMENT SERVICES

Fontana ESP
16730 Arrow Blvd.
Fontana, CA 92335
(909) 854-4000
(909) 854-4002 FAX

ESP is a special employment prgm for individuals receiving public assist. The prgm offers edu, skills assessment, job search assist, training, child care, transportation assist, etc., all intended to assist the individual getting off public assist prgm. FUNDING: Govt. OFC HRS: M-F

8:30am-4:30pm. Spanish spoken. SERVES: Fontana.

JOBS AND EMPLOYMENT SERVICES
Workforce Dev Dept/Business Resource Ctr
15555 Main St., Ste G-4
Hesperia, CA 92345
(760) 949-8526
(760) 949-8541 FAX

Several agencies are co-located in one place to serve each individual's employment or job training needs. Representation from WIA, Social Srvs, Dept of Rehab, Employment Dev, Community colleges, ROP, etc. Full srvs for people starting businesses also. FUNDING: Govt. OFC HRS: M-F 8am-4:30pm. Spanish spoken. ASL available. Free srvs. SERVES: Hesperia.

JOBS AND EMPLOYMENT SERVICES
ESP Program
1300 Bailey Ave.
Needles, CA 92363
(760) 326-9289
(760) 326-9281 FAX

Special employment prgm for individuals receiving public assist. The prgm offers edu, training, skills assessment, job search assist, child care, transportation assist. Intended to assist the individual getting off the public assist prgm. FUNDING: Govt. OFC HRS: M-F 8am-5pm, closed alt F. Spanish spoken. SERVES: Needles area.

JOBS AND EMPLOYMENT SERVICES
Transition Assistance Service
1637 E. Holt Blvd.
Ontario, CA 91761
(909) 458-9700
(909) 933-6482 FAX

ESP is a special prgm for individuals receiving public assist. The prgm offers edu, training, skills assessment, job search assist, child care, transportation assist, etc. all intended to assist the individual to get off public assist prgm. FUNDING: Govt. OFC HRS: M-F 8:30am-4:30pm. Spanish spoken. Free srvs. SERVES: San Bernardino County.

JOBS AND EMPLOYMENT SERVICES
Welfare to Work
10825 Arrow Route, 2nd Fl.
Rancho Cucamonga, CA 91730
(909) 945-0901
(909) 945-0875 FAX

A special employment prgm for individuals receiving public assist. The prgm offers edu, training, skills assessment, job search assist, child care, transportation assist, etc., all intended to assist the individual to get off public assist prgm. FUNDING: Govt. OFC HRS: M-F 8:30am-4:30pm. SERVES: Western San Bernardino County.

JOBS AND EMPLOYMENT SERVICES
ESP
56357 Pima Trail
Yucca Valley, CA 92284-3607
(760) 228-5301
(760) 228-5342 FAX

CalWORKs prgm for individuals receiving welfare. Also job search skills and transitions into job market. FUNDING: CalWORKs. OFC HRS: M-F 8:30am-4:30pm. ADM REQ: Barriers to employment. Employment srvs are free. SERVES: Yucca Valley.

JTPA
See "Workforce Investment" or "WIA."

JTPA/JOBS AND EMPLOYMENT SRVS
See "Jobs and Employment Services"

JURUPA ADULT EDUCATION
Jurupa Unified School District
4041 Pacific Ave.
Riverside, CA 92509
(951) 222-7739
(951) 788-8689 FAX

Opportunity for many to complete their high school edu or prep for the GED test, review & upgrade skills needed for new or better employment. All levels of ESL are provided. Fee-based enrichment classes are offered on a demand basis. FUNDING: ADA, grants, nonprofit. OFC HRS: M-Th 8am-7:30pm; F 8am-4pm. Spanish spoken. ADM REQ: Call for info on basic computer skill classes. SERVES: Jurupa, Mira Loma, Glen Avon, Pedley, Rubidoux.

MARCH A.F.B./FAMILY SUPPORT
1261 Graeber St., Bldg. 2313, Rm. 1A
March Air Base, CA 92518-1775
(951) 655-5350
(951) 655-4719 FAX

Info & referral. Assessment and referral assist to families in crisis, support during family separation, relocation assist, skill workshops as needed on family issues and job search skills. FUNDING: Govt. OFC HRS: M-F 7:30am-4pm (some weekends). ADM REQ: Military staff or family member. SERVES: March Air Reserve area.

MARINE CORP AIR GROUND COMBAT CTR
Career Resource Management Ctr
Bldg. 1438, POB 788105
Twentynine Palms, CA 92278-8150
(760) 830-7225
(760) 830-5955 FAX

Employment and transition counseling and assist. Monthly workshops include: skills assessment, career testing, resume prep, job interviewing, job search, completing fed applications and other special events. Career fair twice a year and quarterly recruitment days. Extensive computer lab with automated job search and career planning prgms that assist with job search worldwide. OFC HRS: M-F 7:30am-4:30pm. ADM REQ: Military ID. Free srvs. SERVES: San Bernardino County.

MODERN TECHNOLOGY SCHOOL
16560 Harbor Blvd., Ste K
Fountain Valley, CA 92708
(714) 418-9100
(714) 418-9109 FAX

X-Ray tech, ultrasound, medical assistant training. OFC HRS: M-F 8am-5pm. Financial aid if qualified. SERVES: Orange & Riverside Counties.

MT. SAN JACINTO COLLEGE/EOPS
1499 N. State Street
San Jacinto, CA 92583
(951) 487-3295
(951) 654-4812 FAX

EOPS offers info & referral, counseling, edu grants, financial aid for books, transportation assist, mentoring, student work prgm, emerg no-interest loans, transfer fee waiver. CARE is a special EOPS prgm for single parents receiv-

ing govt financial assist & helps with child care, gas cards & many other srvs. Also prgm for youth ages 16-21 yrs emancipating from foster care or seeking to live independent of their guardians. Wait: approx. 3-4 wks. See website (www.msjc.edu) for more info. FUNDING: Govt. OFC HRS: M-Th 8am-5pm; F 8am-12noon. Spanish spoken. SERVES: Riverside County.

MT. SAN JACINTO COMMUNITY COLLEGE
Counseling Department
1499 N. State St.
San Jacinto, CA 92583
(951) 487-3255
(951) 487-9240 FAX

Edu, vocational, career counseling. Open admission. Walk-in counseling W only. FUNDING: State & fed. OFC HRS: M & Th 8am-7pm; Tu & W 8am-5pm; F 8am-12noon. Spanish spoken. ADM REQ: Ages 18 yrs+, grades K-12 by petition. SERVES: San Jacinto, Hemet, Sage, Beaumont, Banning, Redlands, Moreno Vly, Perris, Riverside.

NATL INDIAN COUNCIL ON AGING, INC.
5997 Brockton Ave., Ste C
Riverside, CA 92506
(951) 369-8581
(951) 369-8565 FAX

Senior employment prgm. Title 5 prgms. E-fax (501)423-4429. FUNDING: Grants, govt, nonprofit. OFC HRS: M-F 8am-5pm. ADM REQ: Meet federal poverty guidelines, ages 55 yrs+. Free srvs. SERVES: Riverside, San Bernardino, San Diego, Imperial Counties.

NORTHTOWN HOUSING DEVELOPMENT
Northtown Housing College Scholarship
8599 Haven Ave., Ste 205
Rancho Cucamonga, CA 91730
(909) 980-0465

Community center offers free summer lunch prgm, ESL classes, GED, govt food commodities, after school recreation & tutoring, immunizations, summer day camp, holiday toy giveaway, info & referrals, job skills workshops, affordable housing. FUNDING: Nonprofit. OFC HRS: M-F 8am-5pm. Spanish spoken. SERVES: Rancho Cucamonga & nearby.

ONE-STOP CENTER
See "Workforce Development Center"

ONE-STOP CENTER/SAN BERNARDINO
Employment & Training Agency
600 N. Arrowhead Ave., Ste 300
San Bernardino, CA 92401-1148
(909) 888-7881
(909) 889-7833 FAX

State-sponsored employment srv. Several agencies are co-located in one place in order to serve each individual's employment or job training needs. These agencies may include representation from WIA, Social Srvs, Calif Dept of Rehab, EDD, community college counselors, etc. Clients who come to the One-Stop Center should find answers to a wide range of employment related questions. Also offers limited summer srvs for youth. TDD (800)735-2922. FUNDING: State, govt. OFC HRS: M-Th 7:30am-5:30pm; F 7:30am-4:30pm. Spanish spoken. ADM REQ: Open to all job seekers. Free srvs. SERVES: San Bernardino County.

ONE-STOP KIOSK/JOB BOARD
County Administrative Center

1325 Spruce St.
Riverside, CA 92507
(951) 955-3100
(951) 955-3310 FAX

One-Stop kiosk with limited job listings & training info. FUNDING: Govt. OFC HRS: M-Th 7:30am-5:30pm. Spanish spoken. ADM REQ: Open to all job seekers. Free srvs. SERVES: Riverside County.

ONE-STOP KIOSK/JOB BOARD

San Bernardino Valley College
701 S. Mount Vernon Ave.
San Bernardino, CA 92410
(909) 888-6511
(909) 885-6699 FAX

Career Center job listings, resume writing, interview prep, career exploration, transfer assist. FUNDING: Govt. OFC HRS: M-Th 8am-7pm; F 8am-4:30pm. Summer Hrs: M-Th 8am-6pm. Spanish spoken. ADM REQ: Open to all job seekers. Free srvs. SERVES: San Bernardino County.

OPARC/ADULT DEVELOPMENT CTR

Passport Senior Srvs
8333 Rochester Ave., Ste 112
Rancho Cucamonga, CA 91730
(909) 948-5592
(909) 980-4682 FAX

Community life training for dev disabled adults. VTDD machines at each site for the hearing impaired. FUNDING: Pvt donations. OFC HRS: M-F 8am-5pm. Spanish spoken. ADM REQ: Dev disability. SERVES: Pomona Valley & Inland Empire.

PALO VERDE COMMUNITY COLLEGE/EOPS

1 College Dr.
Blythe, CA 92225
(760) 921-5402
(760) 921-3608 FAX

EOPS offers info & referral, counseling, edu grants, financial aid for books, transportation assist, mentoring, student work prgm, emerg no-interest loans, transfer fee waiver. CARE is a special EOPS prgm for single parents receiving govt financial assist and helps with children, gas cards and many other srvs. Also prgm for youth ages 16-21 yrs emancipating from foster care or seeking to live independent of their guardians. FUNDING: Govt. OFC HRS: M-F 8am-5pm. Spanish spoken. ADM REQ: Must be full-time student, less than 70 units of college credit, low income and below average score on either English or math placement tests. CARE students must qualify for EOPS and also be receiving govt aid. SERVES: Riverside County.

PATH OF LIFE FAMILY SHELTER

2530 3rd Street
Riverside, CA 92507
(951) 275-8755
(951) 275-8775 FAX

60-day emerg shelter for families. Case mgmt srvs include: info & referral, employment dev, housing placement, mental health, residential srvs, social srvs (re-entrance into society), counseling. Also provides several shelters for single men and women. For those shelters, call intake at (951) 683-4101 or (951) 275-8750. FUNDING: Nonprofit. 4pm-8pm Spanish spoken. ADM REQ: Must commit to alcohol/drug prgm. SERVES: Riverside County.

PEACE CORPS

See "U.S. Peace Corps"

PERRIS UNION HIGH SCHOOL DISTRICT

155 E. 4th Street
Perris, CA 92570-2124
(951) 943-6369
(951) 943-4159 FAX

Grades 7-12 and adult edu. Prgm serves students with special edu needs, vocational training, college prep and honors advanced placement prgms. Complete pupil personnel srvs are provided. Call for info. FUNDING: State, other public funds. OFC HRS: M-Th 8am-4:30pm; F 8am-3:30pm. Spanish, French spoken. SERVES: Perris, Nuevo, Menifee, Romoland.

PIC JOB TRAINING

See "San Bernardino Co. Pvt Ind Council"

PIC JOB TRAINING

See "Riverside Co. Economic Dev Agency"

PLANET YOUTH

400 W. Graham Ave.
Lake Elsinore, CA 92530
(951) 471-8415
(951) 245-7627 FAX

Work readiness skills, career exploration, leadership dev, job training & placement in entry level positions, internships, edu srvs for youth. FUNDING: Nonprofit. OFC HRS: M-F 8am-5pm. ADM REQ: Ages 14-21 yrs from low income families. Must meet eligibility criteria. SERVES: Lake Elsinore, Wildomar, Lakeland Village, Murrieta, Temecula.

POMONA VALLEY WORKSHOP

4650 Brooks St.
Montclair, CA 91763
(909) 624-3555
(909) 624-5675 FAX

Senior work activity, voc edu, supported employment & adult socialization provided to persons with dev disabilities. OFC HRS: M-F 7:30am-4pm. Fixed fees. SERVES: Eastern L.A. County, western San Bernardino County.

PROVISIONAL EDUCATIONAL SRVS

P.O. Box 7100
2450 Blake St.
San Bernardino, CA 92407
(909) 887-7002
(909) 887-8942 FAX

High school diploma & GED prep classes, Earn & Learn prgm, Upward Bound prgm, summer youth prgms & child care facility. FUNDING: Grants, donations, nonprofit. OFC HRS: M-F 8am-4:30pm. Spanish spoken. SERVES: San Bernardino County.

R.O.P. PROGRAMS

See "ROP/..."

REDLANDS ADULT SCHOOL

Redlands Unified School District
820 W. Stuart Ave.
Redlands, CA 92374
(909) 748-6930
(909) 307-5324 FAX

Vocational prgms include: vocational nursing, nursing assistant, clerical skills, word processing, home health aid acute care, pharmacy technician. OFC HRS: M, Tu 9am-8pm; W, Th 9am-5pm; F 9am-4:30pm. Summer: M-F 9am-4:30pm. SERVES: Redlands.

REDLANDS EMPLOYMENT RESOURCE CTR

One-Stop Career Ctr
814 W. Colton Ave.
Redlands, CA 92374
(909) 798-1795
(909) 798-6857 FAX

Several agencies are co-located in one place in order to serve each individual's employment or job training needs. The agencies may include representation from WIA, Social Srvs, Calif Dept of Rehab, EDD, community college counselors, etc. Clients who come to the One-Stop Center should find answers to a wide range of employment related questions. OFC HRS: M-F 8am-5pm. Spanish spoken. SERVES: San Bernardino County.

RIALTO ADULT SCHOOL

Alternative Education Center
182 E. Walnut Ave.
Rialto, CA 92376
(909) 879-6010
(909) 421-7533 FAX

ESL, GED (no testing), diploma classes (computer assisted instruction) and vocational classes (word processing & health occupations). Open enrollment. Students must be either ages 18 yrs+, exempt from high school attendance, or referred by high school counselor for concurrent enrollment. Enroll: 750. OFC HRS: M-Th 7am-6pm. Spanish spoken. SERVES: Rialto.

RIVERSIDE CO. ECONOMIC DEV AGENCY

Workforce Development Center
1325 Spruce St.
Riverside, CA 92507
(951) 955-3100
(951) 955-3131 FAX

Assists residents with job search & career development srvs. A variety of prgms & srvs available. Locations in Hemet, Temecula, Indio, Riverside. Wait: none. Walk in or by appt. TTY (951) 955-8087. Disability prgm navigator TTY (951) 955-9050, or voicemail (951) 955-3092. FUNDING: Federal. OFC HRS: M-F 8am-5pm. Spanish spoken. ADM REQ: No requirements for use of career resource areas & workshops. Staff assisted srvs require verification of income, right to work and worker dislocation. Free srvs. SERVES: Riverside County.

RIVERSIDE CO. HUMAN RESOURCES DEPT

General Information
P.O. Box 1569
4080 Lemon St., Rm. 102
Riverside, CA 92501
(951) 955-3500
(951) 955-3523 FAX

OFC HRS: M-F 8am-5pm. SERVES: Riverside County.

RIVERSIDE CO. MENTAL HEALTH

Jefferson Wellness Center
1827 Atlanta Ave., Ste D-3
Riverside, CA 92507
(951) 955-8000
(951) 955-8010 FAX

Develops life skills including: socialization, job skills, time mgmt, specialized skills (computer classes, math, woodwork), health-related skills, food prep, independent living and various other skills. FUNDING: County. OFC HRS: M-Th 9am-6pm. Spanish spoken. ADM REQ: Diagnosed as mentally disabled. SERVES: West

Riverside County from Corona to Moreno Valley.

RIVERSIDE CO. OFFICE ON AGING
6296 Rivercrest Dr., Ste K
Riverside, CA 92507-0738
(951) 867-3800
(800) 510-2020
(951) 867-3830 FAX

Office administers & implements planning, advocacy, prgm dev and coordination of senior srvs which include elder abuse edu & advocacy, info & assist, peer counseling, RSVP of the Coachella Valley, senior employment (for ages 55 yrs+) and nutrition srvs. Contracts for personal care and homemaker srvs, respite, adult day care, legal srvs, ombudsman, info & assist, outreach, congregate and home-delivered meals, phone reassurance, community edu and transportation. Senior HelpLink will make referrals to public and pvt agencies for srvs to seniors in Riverside County. TTY (951) 697-4699. FUNDING: Fed, state, county, pvt resources. OFC HRS: M-F 7:30am-5:30pm. Spanish spoken. ADM REQ: Ages 60 yrs+. Case mgmt for seniors and those with disabilities; can be under ages 60 yrs. SERVES: Riverside County.

RIVERSIDE CO. OFFICE/EDUCATION
Job Lines
P.O. Box 868
3939 13th Street
Riverside, CA 92502
(951) 826-3000
(951) 826-6199 FAX

Listing of classified & certified mgmt positions throughout Riverside County Edu System. FUNDING: Govt. OFC HRS: M-F 7:30am-5pm. Jobline open 24 hrs. ADM REQ: All applications must be completed online. SERVES: Riverside County.

RIVERSIDE CO. PUBLIC SOCIAL SRVS
68-615-A Perez Rd., Ste 9, 5
Cathedral City, CA 92234
(760) 773-2300
(760) 773-6720 FAX

CalWORKs, food stamps, General Relief. GAIN (760)773-6800. FUNDING: Govt. OFC HRS: M-F 9am-6pm. GAIN: M-Th 7:30am-5:30pm. Spanish spoken. ADM REQ: Low income. SERVES: Riverside County.

RIVERSIDE CO. PUBLIC SOCIAL SRVS
GAIN Program
541 N. San Jacinto St.
Hemet, CA 92543
(951) 791-3200
(951) 791-3110 FAX

GAIN Prgm is the Greater Avenues of Independence Prgm for individuals who are receiving public assist. Edu and training to recipients who volunteer or who are mandated to participate in this prgm. Other srvs include: skills assessment, job search assist, child care, transportation assist, etc. connected with securing or retaining employment. Walk in or call. OFC HRS: M-Th 7:30am-5:30pm; F 8am-5pm. Spanish spoken. ADM REQ: Public assist recipient. SERVES: Mid County.

RIVERSIDE CO. PUBLIC SOCIAL SRVS
GAIN Program
1400 Minthorn St.
Lake Elsinore, CA 92530

(951) 245-3150
(951) 674-0569 FAX

Edu, training, and job placement for CalWORKs, TANF, welfare clients only. Srvs may include child care, transportation, books, etc. OFC HRS: M-Th 7:30-5:30pm; F 8am-5pm. Spanish spoken. SERVES: Lake Elsinore, Canyon Lake, Temecula, Perris, Murrieta.

RIVERSIDE CO. PUBLIC SOCIAL SRVS
County Administrative Offices
4060 County Circle Dr.
Riverside, CA 92503
(951) 358-3000
(951) 358-3036 FAX

CalWORKs offers financial assist to families with children who are deprived of support due to incapacity, unemployment or continued absence of one or more parents. Food stamps prgm offers an increased food purchase power for low income families. Medical assist prgm (Medi-Cal). General Relief Prgm: assist to indigent individuals & families in temporary need of housing, food or transportation. (This is a loan prgm and recipients are to repay benefits). In Home Supportive Srvs (IHSS) provides household and personal care to allow elderly and disabled to remain in their own home. For adult abuse, call (800) 491-7123. FUNDING: County, state, fed, govt. OFC HRS: M-Th 7:30am-5:30pm. Spanish spoken. Interpreters available in local offices by appointment. ADM REQ: Varies with prgm & srvs. SERVES: Riverside County.

RIVERSIDE CO. PUBLIC SOCIAL SRVS
GAIN Program
1020 Iowa Ave., Ste A
Riverside, CA 92507
(951) 955-3300
(951) 955-9800 FAX

GAIN (Greater Avenues for Independence Prgm) for individuals who are receiving public assist. Edu and training to recipients who volunteer or who are mandated to participate in this prgm. Other srvs include: skills assessment, job search assist, child care, transportation assist, etc., connected with securing or retaining employment. Walk in or call. OFC HRS: M-Th 7:30am-5:30pm; F 8am-5pm. Spanish spoken. ADM REQ: Public assist recipient. SERVES: Riverside County.

RIVERSIDE COMMUNITY COLLEGE/EOPS
4800 Magnolia Ave.
Riverside, CA 92506-1293
(951) 222-8045
(951) 222-8046 FAX

EOPS offers info & referral, counseling, edu grants, financial aid for books, transportation assist, mentoring, student work prgm. CARE is a special EOPS prgm for single parents (all ages) receiving govt financial assist & helps with child care, gas cards & many other srvs. Also offer prgm for youth ages 16-21 yrs emancipating from foster care or seeking to live independent of their guardians. FUNDING: Govt. OFC HRS: M-W, F 8am-4pm; Th 8am-5:45pm. Summer hrs: M-W 8am-4pm; Th 8am-4:50pm. Spanish, Vietnamese spoken. ADM REQ: Must be full-time student, less than 70 units of college credit, low income & below average score on either English or math placement tests. CARE students must qualify for EOPS and also

be receiving govt aid. SERVES: Riverside County.

RIVERSIDE WORKFORCE DEV CENTER
See "Workforce Development Center"

ROP/BALDY VIEW
8265 Aspen Ave., Ste 100
Rancho Cucamonga, CA 91730
(909) 980-6498
(909) 980-8364 FAX

Guidance and instructional prgms for students to enter or re-enter the job market, change careers, or seek advancement. On-the-job internships and job placement assist. Offers certificates of competency in different employment areas. FUNDING: State. OFC HRS: M-F 7:30am-4:30pm. ADM REQ: Ages 16 yrs+ and interested in career training. Set registration and materials fees. SERVES: Chaffey Joint UHSD, Chino Valley USD, Claremont USD & Upland USD.

ROP/COLTON-REDLANDS-YUCAIPA
P.O. Box 8640
1214 Indiana Ct.
Redlands, CA 92375-8640
(909) 793-3115
(909) 793-6901 FAX

Career edu in over 40 high-demand occupations for high school and adult students. Skills assessment and job search assist available. Specialized equipment, curriculum and structural modifications and tutoring may be provided for those students with special needs. Wait: classes year-round. Walk in. TDD (909) 793-7871. FUNDING: State, govt. OFC HRS: M-F 7:30am-4:30pm. ADM REQ: Ages 16 yrs+ and interested in career training. SERVES: Colton, Redlands & Yucaipa.

ROP/RIVERSIDE COUNTY
Riverside Co. Office of Education
P.O. Box 868
144 N. Mountain View Ave.
Riverside, CA 92508
(951) 826-6797
(951) 826-6440 FAX

Guidance and instructional prgms for students to enter or re-enter the job market, change careers, or seek advancement. Career guidance, on-the-job internships and job placement assist. Certificates of competency in different employment areas. Vocational & occupational training in over 40 skills in preparation for entry level jobs. FUNDING: State, govt. OFC HRS: M-F 8am-5pm. Spanish spoken. ADM REQ: Ages 16 yrs+ and interested in career training. Courses are free except for some materials fees. SERVES: Riverside County.

ROP/SAN BRNDO CO. SUPT OF SCHOOLS
Regional Occupational Prgm
144 N. Mt. View Ave.
San Bernardino, CA 92408
(909) 252-4550
(909) 252-4565 FAX

Guidance and instructional prgms for students to enter or re-enter the job market, change careers, or seek advancement. Career guidance, on-the-job internships and job placement assist. Certificates of competency in different employment areas. Walk in. FUNDING: State. OFC HRS: M-F 7:30am-4:30pm. Spanish spoken. ADM REQ: Ages 16 yrs+ and interested in career training. Free srvs, except for some materials fees. SERVES: San Bernardino County.

ROP/VICTORVILLE

16350 Mojave Dr., Bldg. 2
Victorville 92395
(760) 955-3201
(760) 245-4634 FAX

Hands-on job training, career guidance and job placement assist. Classes include: law enforcement, word processing, banking, child care, graphic arts, healthcare. FUNDING: Govt. OFC HRS: M-F 7am-4pm. ADM REQ: Ages 16 yrs+. Free srvs. SERVES: Victorville, Hesperia, Adelanto, Apple Valley, High Desert area.

RUBIDOUX COMMUNITY RESOURCE CTR

5473 Mission Blvd.
Riverside, CA 92509
(951) 328-1575
(951) 683-2613 FAX

Child Abuse Prevention Ctr provides parenting classes, recruitment for in-home supportive srvs every other month. Classes in nutrition, adult edu, ESL, and job training for youth. Healthy Kids Club, counseling referrals. FUNDING: Nonprofit. OFC HRS: M-F 8am-5pm. ADM REQ: Must sign up for classes. Free srvs. SERVES: Glen Avon, Mira Loma, Riverside, Rubidoux, Sunnyslope.

S.C.O.R.E./SMALL BUSINESS ADMIN

Service Corps of Retired Exec
1700 E. Florida Ave.
Hemet, CA 92544-4679

Info & assist in starting up a new business & dealing with specific areas in the operation of on-going business. Regular workshops, also members of SCORE will meet with people in or starting business & offer specific individual assist. Phone number no longer in service. E-mail (score503@netzero.net) for an appt. OFC HRS: Varies by location. By appt. only. French, Polish and Spanish spoken. Counseling is free. SERVES: Riverside County.

S.C.O.R.E./SMALL BUSINESS ADMIN

Service Corps of Retired Exec
200 W. Santa Ana Blvd., 7th Fl.
Santa Ana, CA 92701-4134
(714) 550-7369
(714) 550-0191 FAX

Info & assist in starting up a new business and dealing with specific areas in the operation of on-going business. Regular workshops, members of SCORE will meet with people in or starting business and offer specific individual assist. Admin office operates 10 locations throughout O.C. OFC HRS: M-F 9am-1:30pm. Counseling is free. SERVES: Orange, Riverside & San Bernardino Counties.

SALVATION ARMY/ADULT REHAB

363 S. Doolittle Rd.
San Bernardino, CA 92408
(909) 889-9605
(909) 889-0378 FAX

Christian-based,122-bed facility for men using work therapy. Six to twelve month social model prgm for men. Church srvs, prayer and Bible study. Also have AA meetings. FUNDING: Donations, nonprofit. OFC HRS: M-F 7:30am-4pm. ADM REQ: Ages 18-62 yrs with ID card & who are able to work 8 hrs per day. Free srvs. SERVES: Riverside, San Bernardino Counties.

SAN BERNARDINO ADULT SCHOOL

1200 North E Street
San Bernardino, CA 92405
(909) 388-6000
(909) 381-2887 FAX

ENROLL: 11,000. Provides instruction for high school diploma (GED), testing, vocational classes, nursing prgms, ESL, computer classes, etc. FUNDING: State, fed, grants. OFC HRS: M-Th 7:45am-7pm; F 7:30am-3:30pm. Summer hrs: 7:45am-3:30pm. Spanish spoken. ADM REQ: Ages 16.5 yrs+. SERVES: San Bernardino.

SAN BERNARDINO CO. AGING/ADULT

Senior Info & Assist
8572 Sierra Ave.
Fontana, CA 92335
(909) 829-8515
(909) 829-0313 FAX

Info & referral for legal, transportation, home repair, senior employment, ombudsman prgm, meals, home health care, emerg response, Med Alert and outreach srvs. Offices located throughout the county. FUNDING: Older American Act, Title 3. OFC HRS: M-F 5am-5pm. ADM REQ: Ages 60 yrs+ or disabled. Free srvs. SERVES: Fontana, Bloomington.

SAN BERNARDINO CO. AGING/ADULT

Senior Info & Assist
1300 Bailey
Needles, CA 92363
(760) 326-9224
(760) 326-9340 FAX

Info & referral, eval & follow up, outreach, comprehensive assessment. IHSS (760) 326-9328, APS (877) 565-2020 & CPS (800) 827-8724. OFC HRS: M-F 8am-5pm.

SAN BERNARDINO CO. AGING/ADULT

Senior Info & Assist
P.O. Box 75
111 W. Lugonia Ave.
Redlands, CA 92374
(909) 793-7707
(909) 793-4129 FAX

Info & referral, eval & follow-up, outreach, comprehensive assessment. Walk in or call. FUNDING: Govt. OFC HRS: M-F 8am-5pm. Spanish spoken. ADM REQ: Ages 60 yrs+. Free srvs. SERVES: Redlands, Loma Linda, Mentone, Yucaipa.

SAN BERNARDINO CO. HUMAN SRVS SY

G.A.I.N. Programs

See "Jobs and Employment Services"

SAN BERNARDINO CO. HUMAN SRVS SY

HSS Administration
385 N. Arrowhead Ave., 5th Fl.
San Bernardino, CA 92415-0515
(909) 357-4717
(909) 387-5430 FAX

HSS is composed of the following depts: Aging & Adult Srvs, Behavioral Health, Children's Srvs, Community Srvs, Preschool Srvs, Public Health, Transitional Assist, and Veterans Affairs. OFC HRS: M-F 7:30am-5pm. SERVES: San Bernardino County.

SAN BERNARDINO CO. PVT IND COUNCIL

Workforce Development
215 North D Street, Ste 301
San Bernardino, CA 92415-0041
(909) 387-9835

(909) 387-9880 FAX

OFC HRS: M-F 8am-5pm. Spanish spoken. SERVES: San Bernardino County.

SAN BERNARDINO VLY COLLEGE/EOPS

701 S. Mt. Vernon Ave.
San Bernardino, CA 92410-2798
(909) 384-4412
(909) 888-6511
(909) 888-3071 FAX

EOPS offers info & referral, counseling, edu grants, financial aid for books, transportation assist, mentoring, student work prgm, emerg no interest loans, transfer fee waiver. CARE is a special EOPS prgm for single parents (all ages) receiving govt financial assist & helps with child care, gas cards & many other srvs. Also offer prgm for youth ages 16-21 yrs emancipating from foster care or seeking to live independent of their guardians. FUNDING: Govt. OFC HRS: M-F 8am-5pm. Spanish spoken. ADM REQ: Must be full-time student, less than 70 units of college credit, low income & below average score on either English or math placement tests. CARE students must qualify for EOPS and also be receiving govt aid. SERVES: San Bernardino County.

SENIOR COMMUNITY SERVICE EMPLOYMENT PROGRAM SCSEP

686 E. Mill St.
San Bernardino, CA 92415
(909) 891-3913
(909) 891-3919 FAX

Part-time community srv employment, on-the-job training, job search assist, job referrals, edu assist, referrals to other supportive srvs. Wait: depends upon available openings in area. FUNDING: Title V of Older Americans Act, Dept of Labor. OFC HRS: M-Th 7:30am-5pm; F 8am-5pm. Spanish spoken upon request. Otherwise, must allow time for an interpreter to be set up. ADM REQ: Ages 55 yrs+ and meet low income criteria and not employed. Free srvs. SERVES: San Bernardino County.

SO CALIF INDIAN CENTER, INC.

Corporate Office
10175 Slater Ave., Ste 150
Fountain Valley, CA 92708-4702
(714) 962-6673
(714) 962-6343 FAX

Edu, cultural, economic & recreational prgms for American Indians. Indian Child & Family Srvs (counseling, parenting, foster parents, etc.), WIA (employment assist & voc training), edu tutoring for Indian students in grades K-12. Emerg shelter, food, clothing, referral srvs. FUNDING: United Way, govt, nonprofit. OFC HRS: M-F 8am-5pm. ADM REQ: American-Indian verification. SERVES: So. Calif.

SOUTH ASIAN HELPLINE & REFERRAL AGENCY (SAHARA)

17100 S. Pioneer Blvd., Ste 260
Artesia, CA 90701
(562) 402-4132
(562) 402-6093 FAX

Serves the South Asian community by providing them with info, referrals, skills dev and other culturally sensitive support srvs including mental health, health care, legal assist, transitional living ctrs, client advocacy, case mgmt, financial assist, job training and placement, community edu prgms, and senior srvs. FUNDING: Nonprofit. OFC HRS: M-F 8am-5pm. Hindi, Gujarati, Bengali, Urdu, Nepali, Tamil & Telugu spoken. Free srvs. SERVES: Southern California.

THE TRINITY HOUSE

133 Highland Ave., Ste A2
National City, CA 91950
(619) 477-7158
(619) 330-4749 FAX

Faith-based human srvs organization. Safe, clean, healthy transitional living environment for women, with or without children. Academic edu, employment, training and career guidance srvs. FUNDING: Nonprofit. OFC HRS: M-F 8am-5pm. Spanish spoken. SERVES: Calif.

U.S. DEPT OF LABOR/OSHA

Occupational Safety and Health Admin
200 Constitution Ave., NW
Washington, DC 20210
(877) 889-5657
(800) 321-6742
(410) 865-2068 FAX

OSHA's mission is to save lives, prevent injuries and protect the health of America's workers. Since 1970, OSHA has been partnering with state govts to protect more than 100 million working men and women and their six and a half million employers who are covered by the Occupational Safety and Health Act. The regional number for Calif is (415)625-2547. FUNDING: Govt. OFC HRS: M-F 8am-5pm, EST. SERVES: U.S.A.

U.S. PEACE CORPS

Regional Recruitment Office
2361 Rosecrans Ave., Ste 155
El Segundo, CA 90245
(800) 424-8580
(310) 356-1125 FAX

Volunteers work in a developing nation for 27 mos. Must be 18 yrs of age. Volunteers need a Bachelor's degree or 3-5 yrs experience in a skill or trade, be a U.S. citizen, no dependents under age 18 yrs. Living allowance, travel expenses and medical are covered. Year-round openings in a variety of work projects: edu, agriculture, environmental resources, business & health. Visit (www.peacecorps.gov). FUNDING: Govt. OFC HRS: M-F 8:30am-5pm. SERVES: U.S.A.

U.S. SMALL BUSINESS ADMINISTRATION

Santa Ana District Office
200 W. Santa Ana Blvd., Ste 700
Santa Ana, CA 92701-4134
(714) 550-7420
(714) 550-0191 FAX

Counseling & training on starting and managing small businesses through a monthly mgmt training calendar with the Service Corps of Retired Executives (SCORE) and Small Business Dev Center partners. Financial assist prgms, & assist with govt contracting srvs & contracting certification prgms. TTY (704) 344-6640. OFC HRS: M-F 8am-4:30pm. SCORE: M-F 9am-2pm. Korean & Spanish spoken. SERVES: Orange, Riverside & San Bernardino Counties.

UNEMPLOYMENT INSURANCE CLAIMS

P.O. Box 1379
15419 Cholame St.
Victorville, CA 92393
(800) 300-5616
(760) 241-1629
(760) 241-2468 FAX

Claims must be filed in person at the office closest to the claimant. Must bring social security card & driver's license. Employment srvs. Spanish (800) 326-8937, Chinese (800) 547-3506, Vietnamese (800) 547-2058. FUNDING: Govt. OFC HRS: M-F 8am-5pm. Vietnamese, Korean, Spanish, Cantonese spoken. ADM REQ: Unemployed. SERVES: San Bernardino County.

VALLEY RESOURCE CENTER

EXCEED Program
79-733 Country Club Dr., Ste 2
Bermuda Dunes, CA 92203
(760) 345-3830
(800) 689-7552
(760) 345-7634 FAX

Vocational, living skills and job placement for dev disabled. Srvs provided on an individual basis. FUNDING: State & fed rehab, regional ctrs, pvt funds, donations, grants, contracts. OFC HRS: M-F 8am-5pm. Spanish spoken. ADM REQ: Ages 18 yrs+, able to take care of personal needs. SERVES: Desert communities.

VALLEY RESOURCE CENTER

Sheltering Wings Corp
721 E. Hobson Way
Blythe, CA 92225
(760) 922-3139
(760) 922-6630 FAX

Day prgm, vocational and job placement for dev disabled. Thrift store open M-F 9am-5pm. FUNDING: Dept of Rehab, pvt funds, contracts, nonprofit. OFC HRS: M-F 8am-3pm. Spanish spoken. ADM REQ: Ages 18 yrs+, able to take care of personal needs. SERVES: Desert communities.

VALLEY RESOURCE CENTER

EXCEED Program
1285 N. Santa Fe
Hemet, CA 92543
(951) 766-8659
(800) 647-3451
(951) 929-9758 FAX

Vocational, living skills, training and job placement for dev disabled. Wait for funding to be authorized. Call first. FUNDING: Dept of Rehab, Regional Center, pvt funds, contracts, nonprofit. OFC HRS: M-F 8am-5pm. Spanish spoken. ASL available. ADM REQ: Ages 18 yrs+, able to take care of personal needs. SERVES: Riverside & San Bernardino Counties.

VALLEY RESOURCE CENTER

EXCEED Program
P.O. Box 1773
2050 Trumble Rd.
Perris, CA 92572
(951) 657-0609
(800) 423-1227
(951) 657-2277 FAX

Vocational, living skills and job placement for dev disabled. Wait for funding to be authorized. Fee scale as funding source. FUNDING: Regional Ctr/Dept of Rehab, pvt funds, contracts. OFC HRS: M-F 8am-5pm. Spanish spoken. ADM REQ: Ages 18 yrs+, able to take care of personal needs. SERVES: Riverside & San Bernardino Counties.

VCF COMMUNITY SERVICES

17421 Van Buren Blvd.
Riverside, CA 92504
(951) 789-8514
(951) 780-5433
(951) 780-1981 FAX

Assists all people in need with sack lunches, hygiene packages for homeless, emerg food box (for monthly food srvs, must be involved in Change Your Life Prgm), clothing, housing & utility assist, job search and counseling regarding employment, resume assist, outreach prgms. Mailing address: 16445 Porter Ave., Riverside, CA 92505. FUNDING: Church, donations, nonprofit. OFC HRS: Tu-F 9am-4pm. SERVES: Riverside County.

VICTOR VLY COMM COLLEGE/EOPS

18422 Bear Valley Rd
Victorville, CA 92392-5849
(760) 245-4271
(760) 951-9225 FAX

EOPS offers info & referral, counseling, edu grants, financial aid for books, transportation assist, mentoring, student work prgm, emerg no-interest loans, transfer fee waiver. CARE is a special EOPS prgm for single parents (all ages) receiving govt financial assist & helps with child care, gas cards & many other srvs. Prgm for youth ages 16-21 yrs emancipating from foster care or seeking to live independent of their guardians. FUNDING: Govt. OFC HRS: M-F 8:30am-5pm. Spanish spoken. ADM REQ: Must be full-time student, less than 70 units of college credit, low income & below average score on either English or math placement tests. CARE students must qualify for EOPS and also be receiving govt aid. SERVES: San Bernardino County.

VIP, INC.

Formerly J.O.B., Inc.
17292 Eucalyptus St.
Hesperia, CA 92345
(760) 948-1312
(760) 948-0993 FAX

Sheltered workshop for dev disabled adults. FUNDING: Dept of Rehab, donations, grants, contracts, nonprofit. OFC HRS: M-F 7:30am-4pm. Spanish spoken. ADM REQ: Certifiable disability. SERVES: Victor Valley area.

WESTVIEW SERVICES, INC.

Westview Vocational Srvs
11728 Magnolia, Ste D
Riverside, CA 92503
(951) 343-8730
(951) 343-8732 FAX

Supported employment prgm for disabled. Job training, placement, self-advocacy, behavior mgmt, vocational assessments. FUNDING: Regional Center, Dept of Rehab, nonprofit. OFC HRS: M-F 8am-4:30pm. Spanish spoken, ASL available. ADM REQ: Referral by Regl Ctr or Dept of Rehab. No cost to applicants. SERVES: Inland Empire.

WIA

See "One-Stop Center/San Bernardino"

WOMEN IN TECHNOLOGY INTERNATL

11500 Olympic Blvd., Ste 400
Los Angeles, CA 90064
(818) 788-9484
(818) 788-9410 FAX

Organization dedicated to serving women pursuing careers in technology and related industries. FUNDING: Nonprofit. OFC HRS: M-F 9am-5pm. SERVES: U.S.A.

WORKFORCE DEVELOPMENT CENTER
44-199 Monroe St., Ste B
Indio, CA 92201
(760) 863-2500

Employment & job training info, limited job listings. TTY (760) 863-2555. FUNDING: Govt. OFC HRS: M-F 8am-5pm. Spanish spoken. ADM REQ: Open to all job seekers. Free srvs. SERVES: Riverside County.

WWW.HELPMYRESUME.ORG
P.O. Box 7663
Goodyear, AZ 85338

Volunteers offer free re-writes of resumes and cover letters for the unemployed. Also offers a prgm that helps purchase work attire for low-income families and gives scholarships for individuals to go back to school. FUNDING: Nonprofit. ADM REQ: Proof of unemployment. Free srvs. SERVES: U.S.A.

WWW.NURSETOWN.COM
1232 Shasta Ave.
San Jose, CA 95126
(877) 282-2416
(408) 292-2628 FAX

Website for employers and job seekers in the field of nursing. SERVES: U.S.A. & Canada.

YUCAIPA ADULT SCHOOL
35948 Susan St.
Yucaipa, CA 92399
(909) 790-8580
(909) 790-8584 FAX

Comprehensive adult edu srvs for immigrants, older adults: amnesty, vocational, literacy and high school diploma (includes GED prep and testing), srvs for disabled, parent edu, homemaking and community srv. Walk in or call. FUNDING: SDE Adult Revenue, federal. OFC HRS: M-Th 8am-6pm; F 8am-12noon. Some Spanish spoken. SERVES: Yucaipa, Calimesa.

AGRICULTURAL LABOR RELATIONS BOARD
915 Capitol Mall, 3rd Fl.
Sacramento, CA 95814
(916) 653-3699
(800) 449-3699
(916) 653-8750 FAX

Protects the rights of the agricultural worker. Works to prevent unfair labor practices. FUNDING: Govt. OFC HRS: M-F 8am-5pm. Spanish spoken. SERVES: Calif.

ASIAN AMERICAN ECONOMIC DEVELOP
216 W. Garvey Ave., Ste E
Monterey Park, CA 91754
(626) 572-7021
(626) 572-6533 FAX

Business workshops, business consulting, internships for students. Srvs open to anyone. FUNDING: Donations, grants, nonprofit. OFC HRS: M-F 9am-5pm. Free srvs. SERVES: So. Calif.

BLACK INFANT HEALTH PRGM
Riverside Co. Health Srvs
4065 County Circle Dr., Ste 211
Riverside, CA 92503
(951) 210-1392
(800) 794-4814

Case mgmt & referral for pregnant African American women. FUNDING: State, govt. OFC HRS: M-F 8am-5pm. Free srvs. SERVES: Riverside County.

BLACK RESOURCE CENTER
Co. of L.A. Public Library/Central L.A.
150 E. El Segundo Blvd.
Los Angeles, CA 90061
(310) 538-3350
(310) 327-0824 FAX

Phone reference, research, info & referral. Emphasis on social, historical & cultural info by and about African Americans. Walk in or call. HRS: M-Th 10am-8pm; F 10am-6pm; Sat 10am-5pm. SERVES: So. Calif.

CALIF RURAL LEGAL ASSISTANCE
Coachella Office
P.O. Box 35
1460 6th Street
Coachella, CA 92236
(760) 398-7261
(760) 398-1050 FAX

Legal srvs to migrant farm workers in the areas of labor and housing. OFC HRS: M-F 9am-5:30pm. Spanish spoken. ADM REQ: Low income, employed in agriculture. Free srvs. SERVES: Riverside, San Bernardino & Imperial Counties.

CESAR E. CHAVEZ FOUNDATION
634 S. Spring St., Ste 400
Los Angeles, CA 90014
(213) 362-0260
(213) 362-2065 FAX

Srvs include: learning tools for grades K-12, youth action prgm, sustainable communities prgm, civic engagement, culture, arts, nonviolence. FUNDING: Nonprofit. OFC HRS: M-F 8am-5pm. Spanish spoken. SERVES: Calif.

CHICANO RESOURCE CENTER
Co. of L.A. Public Library/East L.A.

4837 E. 3rd Street
Los Angeles, CA 90022
(323) 263-5087
(323) 264-5465 FAX

Special library collection of documents on Chicano & Mexican history & culture. Books, journals, films, video, records, CDs and clipping file of articles. FUNDING: Nonprofit. HRS: M-Th 10am-9pm; F 9am-5pm; Sat 10am-5pm; Sun 1pm-5pm. Spanish spoken. SERVES: So. Calif.

CHINESE AMERICAN MUSEUM
425 N. Los Angeles St.
Los Angeles, CA 90012
(213) 485-8567
(213) 485-8238 FAX

Promotes Chinese American history and culture. FUNDING: Donations, fndns. OFC HRS: Tu-Sun 10am-3pm. Suggested donation $3. Seniors ages 60 yrs+ and students with ID $2. SERVES: So. Calif.

CHINESE CONSULATE GENERAL
443 Shatto Place
Los Angeles, CA 90020
(213) 807-8088
(213) 807-8091 FAX

Promotes cultural awareness commerce. For the passport/visa office, call (213) 807-8006. FUNDING: Fndns. OFC HRS: M-F 9am-12noon, 1:30pm-5pm. Passport and Visa hrs: M-F 9am-3pm. SERVES: So. Calif, Arizona, Hawaii, New Mexico, American Pacific Islands.

CHINESE HISTORICAL SOCIETY OF SO CALIF
(Mailing Address)
415 Bernard St.
Los Angeles, CA 90012
(323) 222-0856

Conducts pvt & public tours of Chinatown, self-guided tour maps available. Photographs, artifacts and transcripts on display. Bookstore stocks Chinese American history. FUNDING: Donations, fndns. OFC HRS: W-F 11am-3pm. Tours are $5 for adults & $3 for children. SERVES: So. Calif.

COLTON NEIGHBORHOOD SRVS DEPT
670 Colton Ave.
Colton, CA 92324
(909) 370-6153
(909) 777-3351 FAX

City office offers 3 different types of srvs: child care, recreation prgm & community center activities, family srvs including a senior nutrition prgm. Info & referral for child care, health care, housing and other human srv prgms and assist with translations, interpretation, completion of forms, senior health screening and income tax assist for residents of the Colton area. OFC HRS: M-F 8am-8pm. Spanish spoken. Free srvs. Donation requested for senior nutrition prgm. SERVES: San Bernardino County.

CONSEJO DE LATINOS UNIDOS
Counsel of United Latinos
820 S. Indiana St.
Los Angeles, CA 90023
(800) 474-7576

Edu and assist provided in the areas of healthcare, immigration and police protection. FUNDING: Nonprofit. Spanish spoken. SERVES: Calif.

FIESTA EDUCATIVA, INC.
161 S. Avenue 24, Ste 201
Los Angeles, CA 90031
(323) 221-6696
(323) 221-6699 FAX

Info, edu seminars, training & referral srvs to Latino families with disabled children. "Fiesta Familiar" in-home training held in L.A., Orange County, Imperial Valley, San Jose, Sacramento & San Diego Counties. FUNDING: Nonprofit. OFC HRS: M-F 8am-5pm. Spanish spoken. Free srvs. SERVES: Calif.

HANMI FAMILY COUNSELING CENTER
Formerly Korean American Counseling Ctr
12362 Beach Blvd., Ste 1
Stanton, CA 90680
(714) 892-9910
(714) 892-9927 FAX

Serves the Korean American community. Counseling, referrals, community edu, support groups for gamblers, parenting edu, alternative high school on site. FUNDING: Private for profit. OFC HRS: M-F 9am-5pm. Korean spoken. Sliding fee scale. SERVES: U.S.A.

IMMIGRATION EXPRESS
18830 Norwalk Blvd.
Artesia, CA 90701
(800) 985-1234
(562) 924-1981
(562) 860-1689 FAX

Immigration and non-immigration srvs provided. Also assists with citizenship, adoption, wills/estate, green card, paperwork, translation, etc. FUNDING: Nonprofit. OFC HRS: M-F 9am-6pm. SERVES: U.S.A.

INDIAN CHILD & FAMILY SERVICES
P.O. Box 2269
29377 Rancho California Rd., Ste 200
Temecula, CA 92591
(800) 969-4237
(951) 676-8832
(951) 676-3950 FAX

Counseling referrals for abused children, foster placements, adoptive placements. Tribal Kinship Model used to intervene in the cycle of child abuse. CASA prgm. Spirit Prgm is a prevention/intervention parenting prgm. FUNDING: Bureau of Indian Affairs. OFC HRS: M-F 8am-5pm. ADM REQ: Must be enrolled or eligible for federally recognized tribe. No fees. SERVES: Riverside, San Diego, San Bernardino Counties.

INSTITUTE FOR BLACK PARENTING
Adoption, Foster Care, Family Preservation
3120 Chicago Ave., Ste 130
Riverside, CA 92507
(951) 274-2800
(877) 367-8858
(951) 782-9768 FAX

Adoption and foster care agency specializing in recruiting African-American families for special needs children. Culturally sensitive, personalized free srvs, streamlined application, edu training process. Open to all ethnic groups. FUNDING: Nonprofit. OFC HRS: M-F 8am-5pm. ADM REQ: Foster children ages birth-17 yrs, adults ages 21 yrs+. SERVES: So. Calif.

JAPAN BUSINESS ASSN/SO CALIF
1411 W. 190th Street, Ste 270
Gardena, CA 90248
(310) 515-9522
(310) 515-9722 FAX

Promotes mutual understanding, business and good will between the people of So. Calif and Japan. FUNDING: Nonprofit. OFC HRS: M-F 9am-5pm. SERVES: So. Calif.

NAACP
See "Natl Assn/Advance/Colored People"

NATL ALLIANCE FOR HISPANIC HEALTH
Su Familia (Family Health Helpline)
1501 16th Street, NW
Washington, DC 20036
(866) 783-2645
(202) 797-4353 FAX

Bilingual health helpline and website. Callers are referred to health care providers in their area. For prenatal info, call La Linea Nacional Prenatal Hispana (800) 504-7081. For hospice info, call (877) 658-8896. Visit (www.hispanichealth.org). FUNDING: Grants, donations. OFC HRS: M-F 9am-6pm, EST. Spanish spoken. SERVES: U.S.A.

NATL ASSN FOR HISPANIC ELDERLY
234 E. Colorado Blvd., Ste 300
Pasadena, CA 91101
(626) 564-1988
(626) 564-2659 FAX

Info on srvs for low income Hispanic seniors ages 55 yrs+. FUNDING: Nonprofit. OFC HRS: M-F 9am-5pm. Spanish spoken. SERVES: U.S.A.

NATL ASSN/ADVANCE/COLORED PEOPLE
NAACP/San Bernardino Branch
1505 W. Highland Ave., Ste 11
San Bernardino, CA 92411
(909) 887-7411
(909) 945-9660 FAX

Free info and perhaps legal assist. Walk in or call for appt. FUNDING: Members, nonprofit. OFC HRS: M-F 9am-5pm. ADM REQ: Belief in equal rights for all. SERVES: San Bernardino, Highland & Redlands area.

NATL BLACK UNITED FUND, INC.
40 Clinton St., 5th Fl.
Newark, NJ 07102
(973) 643-5122
(800) 223-0866
(973) 648-8350 FAX

Info regarding donations & prgms. Coordinates community srv prgms through family resource centers. OFC HRS: M-F 9:30am-6pm, EST. SERVES: U.S.A.

NATL INSTITUTE FOR JEWISH HOSPICE
732 University St.
North Woodmere, NY 11581
(800) 446-4448

Nationwide helpline. Serves terminally ill patients, families, professional health caregivers and volunteers. Offers counseling and referral srv for Jewish hospice care and support, database with natl references. Variety of publications on issues of the terminally ill, their families

and caregivers. NIJH gives accreditation to hospices across the country. FUNDING: Donation, nonprofit. OFC HRS: 24 hrs, 7 days. Free referrals, counseling. SERVES: U.S.A.

NATL LATINO ALLIANCE FOR THE ELIMINATION OF DOMESTIC VIOLENCE
P.O. Box 7886
Albuquerque, NM 87194
(505) 224-9080
(505) 224-9079 FAX

Provides culturally sensitive training, tech assist, resources, community edu, and outreach srvs to Latino communities regarding domestic violence. FUNDING: Nonprofit. SERVES: U.S.A.

NIKKEI HELPLINE
231 E. 3rd Street, Ste G-106
Los Angeles, CA 90013
(213) 473-3030
(800) 645-5341
(213) 473-3031 FAX

Helpline, info & referrals. Trained volunteers listen to all types of problems; some referrals are made for counseling in L.A. Co. only. FUNDING: Nonprofit. OFC HRS: M-F 9:30am-5:30pm. Japanese & Korean spoken. SERVES: So. Calif.

NORTHERN CALIF TRANSLATORS ASSN
P.O. Box 14015
Berkeley, CA 94712-5015
(510) 845-8712

NCTA is an assn of interpreters and translators. Provides guidance to those entering the field. Translator & interpreter referral srv at (www.ncta.org). OFC HRS: 24-hr line. ADM REQ: Must apply for membership. Fees: individual $50 per yr; corporate $75 per yr. SERVES: U.S.A. & internatl.

OFFICE/MINORITY HEALTH RESOURCE
P.O. Box 37337
Washington, DC 20013-7337
(800) 444-6472
(240) 453-2883 FAX

Responds to consumer and professional inquiries on minority health-related topics. Free database searches, resource list, fact sheet, publications, etc. Referrals to other resources, tech assist. TDD (301) 230-7199. FUNDING: Govt. OFC HRS: M-F 9am-5pm, EST. Spanish and Korean spoken. Free srvs. SERVES: U.S.A.

POLISH AMERICAN CONGRESS/SO CAL
3919 Myrtle Ave.
Long Beach, CA 90807
(562) 426-9830
(562) 426-5485 FAX

Cultural, social & networking organization for Polish Americans. An umbrella group of 40 various social, cultural, sports, political, veterans and religious Polish American organizations, as well as encouraging investments in Poland. "Voice of Polonia" offers info, edu & cultural events: folk dances, history, language classes, newspaper, etc. FUNDING: Donations, dues, nonprofit. ADM REQ: Polish origin, descent or marriage. SERVES: U.S.A. & Internatl.

SO CALIF INDIAN CENTER, INC.
Corporate Office
10175 Slater Ave., Ste 150
Fountain Valley, CA 92708-4702
(714) 962-6673

(714) 962-6343 FAX

Edu, cultural, economic & recreational prgms for American Indians. Indian Child & Family Srvs (counseling, parenting, foster parents, etc.), WIA (employment assist & voc training), edu tutoring for Indian students in grades K-12. Emerg shelter, food, clothing, referral srvs. FUNDING: United Way, govt, nonprofit. OFC HRS: M-F 8am-5pm. ADM REQ: American-Indian verification. SERVES: So. Calif.

SOUTH ASIAN HELPLINE & REFERRAL AGENCY (SAHARA)
17100 S. Pioneer Blvd., Ste 260
Artesia, CA 90701
(562) 402-4132
(562) 402-6093 FAX

Serves the South Asian community by providing them with info, referrals, skills dev and other culturally sensitive support srvs including mental health, health care, legal assist, transitional living ctrs, client advocacy, case mgmt, financial assist, job training and placement, community edu prgms, and senior srvs. FUNDING: Nonprofit. OFC HRS: M-F 8am-5pm. Hindi, Gujarati, Bengali, Urdu, Nepali, Tamil & Telugu spoken. Free srvs. SERVES: Southern California.

SURVIVORS OF TORTURE INTERNATL
P.O. Box 151240
San Diego, CA 92175-1240
(619) 278-2400
(619) 294-9405 FAX

Case mgmt srvs & referrals for psych, medical, & social srvs for survivors of torture and their families. For emerg, call (619) 278-2403; intake (619) 278-2404. Info provided for So. Calif, assist primarily for San Diego. FUNDING: Nonprofit. OFC HRS: M-F 8am-5pm. Chaldean, Kurdish, Arabic, Cambodian, Farsi, French & Spanish spoken. Interpretation for all languages available. Free srvs. Insurance utilized where applicable. Referrals to Medi-Cal providers. Accepts workers' compensation. SERVES: So. Calif.

TAIPEI ECONOMIC & CULTURAL OFFICE
Information Division Los Angeles
6300 Wilshire Blvd., Ste 1510
Los Angeles, CA 90048-5204
(323) 782-8765
(323) 782-8761 FAX

Up-to-date info about Taiwan. Works with local and natl media networks, think tanks, and the academic community. OFC HRS: M-F 9am-5:30pm. SERVES: So. Calif, Arizona, New Mexico, Hawaii.

U.S. DEPT OF INTERIOR/SO. CALIF AGENCY
Bureau of Indian Affairs
1451 Research Park Dr., Ste 100
Riverside, CA 92507-2154
(951) 276-6624
(951) 276-6641 FAX

Srvs for Indian tribes and their tribal members living on the srv area reservations only. Srvs include: real property, natural resources, housing, welfare assist, social srvs, tribal operation, tribal documents. Info & referral for other federally recognized tribal members. FUNDING: Govt. OFC HRS: M-F 8am-4:30pm. SERVES: So. Calif.

UN LIBRO, MIL MUNDOS
One Book, a Thousand Worlds
Riverside County Public Library
(951) 233-6160

Reading prgm aimed at Latino students to improve literacy skills by offering books that focus on life matters they can relate to. Prgm runs weekly at select branch libraries and features book clubs and discussion groups focusing on Latino authors. Contact Arlene Cano, literacy coordinator. FUNDING: County. Spanish spoken. Free srvs. SERVES: Libraries in Coachella, Mecca, Home Gardens, Lake Elsinore and Glen Avon.

FAMILY PLANNING/PREGNANCY/CHILD BIRTH

ABORTION RECOVERY INTERNATL NTWK

5319 University Dr., Ste 252
Irvine, CA 92612
(949) 679-9276
(866) 469-7326
(949) 551-9771 FAX

Srvs provided to those touched by the abortion experience. Support and guidance for those mourning the loss of a terminated pregnancy. Helps wounded women, men and their families find peace and victory from their past. Also provides edu opportunities to increase abortion awareness. Public speaking for schools, universities, companies or groups. 24-hr hotline to assist those in crisis, (800) 395-4357. FUNDING: Nonprofit. OFC HRS: M-F 8am-5pm. SERVES: So. Calif.

ACCESS FOR INFANTS/MOTHERS (AIM)

Calif Major Risk Medical Ins. Board
P.O. Box 15559
Sacramento, CA 95852-0559
(800) 433-2611
(888) 889-9238 FAX

Maternity, delivery and infant care srvs for mid-income women between 200-300% of the Federal Poverty Level. Low-cost prenatal health insurance to uninsured pregnant women who are not receiving health care through Medi-Cal. The cost is 2% of her family's gross income. The policy pays 100% of the medical costs during the pregnancy, plus post-partum care for 60 days and the medical cost for the infant during the first two years of life. Insurance renewal after infant's 2nd year is $100 or $50 with proof of immunization. For payments: P.O. Box 15207, Sacramento, CA 95851. FUNDING: State. OFC HRS: M-F 8am-8pm; Sat 8am-5pm. Spanish spoken. ADM REQ: Calif resident; expectant mother must be no more than 30 weeks pregnant. SERVES: Calif.

ALTERNATE AVENUES

Women's Resource Center
9675 Monte Vista, Unit G
Montclair, CA 91763
(909) 621-4800

Fully licensed medical clinic offering free services to couples facing an unplanned pregnancy. Pregnancy tests, ultrasound (when needed), Medi-Cal, WIC along with other resources. FUNDING: Nonprofit. OFC HRS: Tu 12pm-5pm; Th 2pm-7pm; F, Sat 8am-1pm. Spanish, Tagalog spoken. SERVES: Inland Empire.

AMERICAN PREGNANCY ASSOCIATION

1431 Greenway Dr., Ste 440
Irving, TX 75038
(972) 815-2337
(972) 550-0140
(972) 550-0800 FAX

Natl organization provides edu, counseling & referrals to local resources. Referrals to maternity homes, pregnancy centers, medical care, adoption srvs, Medicare and other govt related srvs. Not a clinic. FUNDING: Nonprofit. OFC HRS: M-F 7am-10pm. 24-hr hotline. Some Spanish spoken. Free referrals. SERVES: U.S.A.

AMERICAN PREGNANCY HELPLINE

(866) 942-6466

24-hr hotline available 7 days a week to answer any questions about pregnancy, family planning, and adoption. Also offers info website about pregnancy, visit (www.thehelpline.org) for more info. FUNDING: Nonprofit. OFC HRS: 24 hrs, 7 days. Free srvs. SERVES: U.S.A.

ASPO/LAMAZE

See "Lamaze International"

BABY SAFE

Safely Surrendered Baby Prgm
(877) 222-9723

Safe haven hotline for nearest locations which allow parents to safely surrender their babies at any hospital or fire station without fear of legal prosecution. Call the hotline for more info. OFC HRS: 24 hrs, 7 days. Over 140 languages spoken. SERVES: U.S.A.

BETHANY CHRISTIAN SRVS/NATL

Headquarters
P.O. Box 294
901 Eastern Ave., NE
Grand Rapids, MI 49501-0294
(800) 238-4269
(616) 224-7595
(616) 224-7611 FAX

Domestic & internatl adoption (traditional, private or open adoption), foster home placement, pregnancy counseling, assist during pregnancy, special needs children's fund, refugee resettlement, child & family counseling. More than 75 offices in U.S. 800# open 7 days a wk. FUNDING: Fees, donations, churches, nonprofit. OFC HRS: M-F 8:30am-5pm. SERVES: U.S.A.

BETHANY CHRISTIAN SRVS/SO CAL

14125 Telephone Rd., Ste 12
Chino, CA 91710
(877) 465-0057
(909) 465-0057
(909) 628-8294 FAX

Pregnancy counseling, pre-adoptive foster care, adoption srvs. FUNDING: Church, donations, fees, nonprofit. OFC HRS: M-F 9am-5pm. ADM REQ: Adoptive couples must be Christian. Sliding fee scale for adoptive parents. Free pregnancy counseling & srvs for birth parents. SERVES: So. Calif.

BIRTH CHOICE OF TEMECULA

27488 Enterprise Circle West, Bldg. 4
Temecula, CA 92590
(951) 699-9808
(951) 699-7268 FAX

Pregnancy counseling and testing. Right to Life perspective. Maternity and baby clothes available. Walk in or call for appt. 24-hr hotline (800) 848-LOVE (5683). Volunteering opportunities available. FUNDING: Nonprofit. OFC HRS: M, W 10am-4pm; Tu, Th 10am-3pm. Spanish speaker available on Tu. ADM REQ: Pregnant or suspected pregnancy. Free srvs. SERVES: Lake Elsinore, Perris, Hemet, Menifee, Temecula, Fallbrook, Murrieta, Wildomar.

BIRTH CONTROL INFO FOR STATE

Calif Office of Family Planning

(800) 942-1054

Referrals to family planning and birth control srvs throughout Calif. Female cancer testing. Low-cost testing and counseling for HIV. Spanish available upon request. OFC HRS: 24 hrs, 7 days. SERVES: Calif.

BIRTH CONTROL INFO LINE

San Bernardino Co. Public Health
(800) 722-4777
(909) 389-3340 FAX

One-stop family planning health srvs for men and women ages 21 yrs and under. Call for the clinic nearest you. FUNDING: Govt. OFC HRS: M-F 8am-5pm. Spanish spoken. Free srvs. SERVES: Riverside & San Bernardino Counties.

BREAST FEEDING ADVOCACY

See "La Leche League"

CALIF CHILDREN & FAMILIES COMM

2389 Gateway Oaks Dr., Ste 260
Sacramento, CA 95833
(916) 263-1050
(916) 263-1360 FAX

Early childhood dev srvs, school readiness, health care, child care, parent edu, intervention prgms for families at risk. FUNDING: Nonprofit. OFC HRS: M-F 8am-5pm. ADM REQ: Ages birth-5 yrs. SERVES: Calif.

CALIF OFC OF FAMILY PLANNING

Info/Referral Srv
1615 Capitol Ave.
Sacramento, CA 95899
(800) 942-1054

Recorded info & referral to local birth control, F-PACT and family planning srvs for all of Calif. Referrals are targeted by ZIP code. FUNDING: Govt. OFC HRS: 24 hrs, 7 days. Spanish and Vietnamese spoken. SERVES: Calif.

CHILD BIRTH

Website provides links to various topics related to child birth. Visit (www.childbirth.org).

CHILDREN'S HEALTH ACCESS PRGMS

Medi-Cal/Healthy Families Info Line
P.O. Box 138005
Sacramento, CA 95813-8005
(888) 747-1222
(866) 848-4974 FAX

Free and low-cost medical care for children and pregnant women. Eligibility is determined by children's ages and family income. Available to citizens and qualified immigrants. If the family does not qualify for this prgm, there are other options. Call (800) 880-5305 for application status. Call (866) 848-9166 if already enrolled. FUNDING: State, fed govt. OFC HRS: M-F 8am-8pm; Sat 8am-5pm. Cambodian, Farsi, Russian, Spanish, Chinese and Vietnamese spoken. ADM REQ: Must submit application. $5-$15 per child based on provider and county. SERVES: Calif.

CLINICAS DE SALUD DEL PUEBLO, INC.

Mecca Health Clinic
91275 66th Avenue, Ste 500
Mecca, CA 92254
(760) 396-1249
(760) 396-1253 FAX

Outpatient center offers immunizations, pregnancy testing, counseling, birth control, physical exams, general medical, well-baby, pediactric, health edu, TB testing, AIDS testing, STD, dental, optical (van comes occasionally). Serves all ages. FUNDING: BPHC site, donations, nonprofit. OFC HRS: M-Th 8am-6:30pm; F 8am-6pm; Sat 8am-12pm. Spanish spoken. ADM REQ: Low income. Accepts insurance, Medi-Cal, Medicare, sliding fee scale. SERVES: Mecca & nearby.

COMMUNITY HEALTH SYSTEMS, INC.

I.E. Community Health Center
18601 Valley Blvd.
Bloomington, CA 92316
(909) 877-0510
(909) 877-1818
(909) 877-5468 FAX

Primary health care for all ages. OB/GYN, prenatal, dental srvs, optometry, referrals, pediatrician, internal medicine. No-cost dental screenings offered to clients, must provide proof of income or unemployment. FUNDING: Donations, nonprofit. OFC HRS: M-F 8am-5:30pm. Spanish spoken. ADM REQ: Low income. Accepts insurance, Medicare, Medi-Cal, sliding fee scale, I.E.H.P., Molina. SERVES: San Bernardino County.

COMMUNITY HEALTH SYSTEMS, INC.

Eastside Health Ctr
1970 University Ave.
Riverside, CA 92507
(951) 224-8220
(951) 328-9574 FAX

Primary health care for all ages. Prenatal, HIV testing, AIDS/STD screenings, teen clinic, family planning, immunizations, counseling. Enrollment assist for Medi-Cal, Healthy Families, Healthy Kids. FUNDING: BPHC site, donations, nonprofit. OFC HRS: M-F 8am-5:30pm. Spanish spoken. ADM REQ: Low income. Accepts insurance, Medicare, Medi-Cal, sliding fee scale. SERVES: Riverside County.

COMMUNITY HEALTH SYSTEMS, INC.

Arlanza Family Health Ctr
8856 Arlington Ave.
Riverside, CA 92503
(951) 353-2702
(951) 353-2976 FAX

Primary care for all ages. Family planning, HIV/AIDS, STD testing, Teenage Edu to Avoid Motherhood (T.E.A.M.), Child Health and Disability prgm. Also dental clinic. FUNDING: Nonprofit. OFC HRS: M-F 8am-5:30pm. Accepts Medi-Cal, Medicare, insurance, sliding fee scale. SERVES: Riverside County.

CRISIS PREGNANCY CENTER

44750 San Pablo Ave.
Palm Desert, CA 92255
(760) 568-2200
(888) 956-4357

Pregnancy tests, ultrasound. Referrals for basic needs. Call or walk in. Volunteer opportunities. FUNDING: Nonprofit, donations. OFC HRS: M-Th 12noon-4:30pm; F 11am-3pm. Spanish spoken. Free and confidential. SERVES: Riverside County.

CTIS PREGNANCY RISK INFO LINE

Dept of Pediatrics, UCSD Med Ctr
9500 Gilman Dr., Ste 0828
La Jolla, CA 92093-0828
(800) 532-3749
(619) 270-0278 FAX

The infoline is a statewide telephone srv operated by Calif Teratogen Info Srv & Clinical Research Prgm. Call with questions regarding concerns about the effects of medications, environmental exposures, or illness on pregnancy. The call is free and confidential. Info is based on current scientific data. Satellite offices: UCLA OB/GYN, Institute of Fetal & Maternal Health at Children's Hospital in L.A. and Medical Genetics, Dept of Pediatrics, Stanford Univ School of Medicine. FUNDING: Govt, nonprofit. OFC HRS: M-F 9am-5pm. Spanish and Tagalog spoken. Free srvs. SERVES: Calif.

FAMILY PACT

State of Calif D.H.S.
P.O. Box 997413
1615 Capitol Ave., MS 8400
Sacramento, CA 95899-7413
(916) 650-0414
(916) 650-0454 FAX

Calif Family PACT Prgm provides clinical srvs for family planning & reproductive health at no cost to eligible uninsured residents, filling a critical gap in healthcare for the indigent low income & working poor. Visit (http://www.familypact.org) for enrollment forms and to locate a clinic. FUNDING: Govt. OFC HRS: M-F 8am-5pm. ADM REQ: Women & men are eligible if they reside in Calif, are at-risk of pregnancy or causing pregnancy, have a gross family income at or below 200% of the Federal Poverty Level, and have no other source of healthcare coverage for family planning srvs. SERVES: Calif.

FAMILY PLANNING ASSOCIATES (CALIF INFO/REF)

See "Calif Ofc of Family Planning"

FAMILY PLANNING ASSOCIATES MED GRP

(See Display Ad on Page 147)
5050 San Bernardino St.
Montclair, CA 91763
(909) 626-2463
(909) 624-6297 FAX

Presumptive eligbility screening. Early pregnancy testing, The Morning-After pill, birth control, gynecological exam, info on methods, STD testing. Surgical and nonsurgical abortion, first trimester dilation/curettage, general or local anesthesia, second trimester dilation and extraction. Sterilization by tubal cauterization. Gardasil and IUDs. Patients are given complete info about what to expect when they leave the facility. FUNDING: Private for profit. OFC HRS: M-F 8am-4:30pm; Sat 8am-12noon. Spanish, Korean, Armenian, Russian, Chinese, Tagalog, Vietnamese, Hmong spoken. Accepts Medi-Cal Insurance/HMO, pvt pay, Family Pact. SERVES: Calif.

FAMILY PLANNING ASSOCIATES MED GRP

(See Display Ad on Page 147)
3893 Mission Inn Ave.
Riverside, CA 92501
(951) 683-1486
(951) 683-0977 FAX

Presumptive eligbility screening. Early pregnancy testing, The Morning-After pill, birth control, gynecological exam, info on methods, STD testing. Surgical and nonsurgical abortion, first trimester dilation/curettage, general or local anesthesia, second trimester dilation and extraction. Sterilization by tubal cauterization. Gardasil and IUDs. Patients are given complete info about what to expect when they leave the facility. FUNDING: Private for profit. OFC HRS: M-F 8am-4:30pm; Sat 8am-12noon. Spanish, Korean, Armenian, Russian, Chinese, Tagalog, Vietnamese, Hmong spoken. Accepts Medi-Cal Insurance/HMO, pvt pay, Family Pact. SERVES: Calif.

FAMILY PLANNING ASSOCIATES MED GRP

(See Display Ad on Page 147)
165 W. Hospitality Lane, Ste 1
San Bernardino, CA 92408
(909) 885-0282
(909) 889-7367 FAX

Presumptive eligibility screening. Early pregnancy testing, The Morning-After pill, birth control, gynecological exam, info on methods, STD testing. Surgical and nonsurgical abortion, first trimester dilation/curettage, general or local anesthesia, second trimester dilation and extraction. Sterilization by tubal cauterization. Gardasil and IUDs. Patients are given complete info about what to expect when they leave the facility. FUNDING: Private for profit. OFC HRS: M-F 8am-4:30pm; Sat 8am-12noon. Spanish, Korean, Armenian, Russian, Chinese, Tagalog, Vietnamese, Hmong spoken. Accepts Medi-Cal Insurance/HMO, pvt pay, Family Pact. SERVES: Calif.

GARDEN OF ANGELS

Safe Arms - Safe Haven for Newborns
P.O. Box 1776
Yucaipa, CA 92399
(909) 797-8599
(909) 797-9766 FAX

Works to prevent the abandonment of newborn babies. Advocacy, helpline, edu materials. Mothers are encouraged to leave infants with any hospital emerg room or fire station employee legally and confidentially. FUNDING: Nonprofit. OFC HRS: M-F 8am-4pm. SERVES: Calif.

HEALTHY FAMILY CLINIC

JFK Memorial Fndn
73-555 San Gorgonio Way
Palm Desert, CA 92260
(760) 776-1600
(760) 776-4500 FAX

Medical srvs for children of all ages. Nutrition srvs, parenting edu, public health care application assist. FUNDING: Nonprofit. OFC HRS: M-F 8am-5pm. ADM REQ: Call for appt. Accepts Medi-Cal, CHDP, Healthy Families, Healthy Kids. SERVES: Palm Desert.

HEARTLINE MINISTRIES

See "Pregnancy Counseling Center"

HEARTLINE PREGNANCY COUNSELING CTR

Heartline Ministries
6881 Brockton Ave.
Riverside, CA 92506
(951) 682-2400
(951) 682-6881
(951) 682-0251 FAX

Counsels pregnant women from a pro-life perspective. Free pregnancy testing, referrals for financial, medical and legal assist. Adoption info provided upon request. Free clothing & baby furniture. Also offers post-abortion counseling. Call first before sending a fax. FUNDING: Donations. OFC HRS: By appt, 24-hr hotline. ADM REQ: Must have appt. Free srvs. SERVES: Riverside Metro.

LA LECHE LEAGUE

Info & support for women who wish to breast-feed, 24-hr phone help, monthly meetings, lending library with books on breast-feeding, childbirth, family & nutrition. Visit website for phone list & web addresses in So. Calif & Nevada (www.lalecheleaguescnv.org). TDD (847) 592-7570. FUNDING: Nonprofit. OFC HRS: M-F 9am-9pm. SERVES: Mid County.

LA LECHE LEAGUE INTERNATL

P.O. Box 4079
957 N. Plum Grove Rd.
Schaumburg, IL 60168-4079
(800) 525-3243
(847) 519-7730
(847) 969-0460 FAX

Worldwide organization provides support to pregnant & breast-feeding women. Edu materials, free catalog & referrals to local leaders. Call for monthly meeting info. FUNDING: Donations, members, nonprofit. OFC HRS: M-F 9am-5pm, CST. Spanish spoken. SERVES: Internatl.

LAMAZE INTERNATIONAL

Lamaze Childbirth Education
2025 M Street NW, Ste 800
Washington, DC 20036-3309
(800) 368-4404
(202) 367-1128
(202) 367-2128 FAX

Info on Lamaze classes nationwide and on becoming a certified Lamaze educator. FUNDING: Donors, members, nonprofit. OFC HRS: M-F 9am-5pm, EST. Spanish spoken. SERVES: U.S.A.

LDS FAMILY SERVICES

Unwed Pregnancy Options Counseling
791 N. Pepper Ave.
Colton, CA 92324
(909) 824-0480
(909) 824-0487 FAX

No pressure, confidential counseling to unwed parents & their families. A safe, comfortable place provided to discuss various options. Licensed adoption srvs. Individual, marital, and family counseling. Community outreach to interested agencies and organizations. FUNDING: Nonprofit. OFC HRS: M-F 8am-5pm. Spanish & German spoken. Free counseling srvs. SERVES: So. Calif.

LDS FAMILY SERVICES

Adoption Service
13042 Burbank Blvd.
Van Nuys, CA 91401-5409
(818) 781-5511
(800) 537-2229
(818) 781-5595 FAX

Free pregnancy planning and adoption counseling for birth parents, regardless of denomination. Adoptive parents must be LDS members. Satellite clinics in Menifee, Murrieta, Palm Desert, Yucca Valley, Hesperia, Victorville, Corona, Ridgecrest, Arcadia and Ventura. FUNDING: Nonprofit. OFC HRS: M-F

8am-5pm. Spanish spoken. SERVES: So. Calif.

LIBERTY GODPARENT HOME

P.O. Box 4199
124 Liberty Mountain Dr.
Lynchburg, VA 24502
(888) 760-5433
(434) 845-3466
(434) 845-1751 FAX

Christian, residential maternity home offers housing, edu, medical care & counseling for single, pregnant young women who either parent their child or place their child up for adoption. Also network with over 1,300 referrals in U.S.A. & Canada. Srvs for women ages 10-21 yrs. Client must intake by the 24th week of pregnancy. 24-hr helpline. FUNDING: Thomas Road Baptist Church, Lynchburg, Virginia, other churches, donations, nonprofit. OFC HRS: M-F 8am-4:30pm. ADM REQ: Arrangements must be made for medical portion of prgm through admissions coordinator. Free srvs. SERVES: U.S.A. & Canada.

LIFE CENTER PREGNANCY COUNSELING

1106 E. 17th Street, Ste C
Santa Ana, CA 92701
(714) 835-5433
(714) 835-0476 FAX

24-hr hotline, counseling, free pregnancy testing, medical, financial, legal & housing referrals. Pro-life perspective. So. Calif. offices: L.A. Co.: (562) 691-9395 or (818) 895-2500; Orange Co.: (714) 835-5433; Riverside Co.: (951) 682-2400 or (951) 784-2422; San Bernardino Co.: (909) 825-6656 or (909) 985-0205. FUNDING: Donations, nonprofit. OFC HRS: M-Th 10am-4pm. Free srvs. SERVES: So. Calif.

LIFE CHOICE OF HEMET

475 W. Stetson PMB-T225
Hemet, CA 92543
(951) 652-3111

Counseling, adoption asst, abortion referral, phone referrals and resources, baby formula and diapers (limited). May add more srvs at later date. FUNDING: Donations, nonprofit. SERVES: Riverside County.

MARCH OF DIMES BIRTH DEFECTS FNDN

Greater Los Angeles Division
3699 Wilshire Blvd., Ste 520
Los Angeles, CA 90010-2719
(213) 637-5050
(213) 637-5055 FAX

Goal is to improve the health of babies by preventing birth defects, premature births and infant mortality. Supports campaign for healthier babies, prgms of research, community srvs, edu and advocacy. Provides grants, Comenzando Bien, (a Spanish-speaking prgm), info & referral srvs, speaker's bureau, visiting professorship in nursing, work site prgms including the Babies and You prgm. FUNDING: Nonprofit. OFC HRS: M-F 9am-5pm. Spanish spoken. SERVES: L.A., Ventura, Santa Barbara, Riverside, San Bernardino, San Luis Obispo, Mono, Inyo & Kern Counties.

MARCH OF DIMES BIRTH DEFECTS FNDN

Inland Empire Division
3600 Lime St., Ste 524
Riverside, CA 92501
(951) 341-0903

(951) 276-4755 FAX

Goal is to improve the health of babies by preventing birth defects, premature births and infant mortality. Supports campaign for healthier babies, prgms of research, community srvs, edu and advocacy. Provides grants, Comenzando Bien, a Spanish-speaking prgm, info & referral srvs, speaker's bureau, visiting professorship in nursing including the Babies and You prgm. FUNDING: Nonprofit. OFC HRS: M-F 9am-5pm. Spanish spoken. SERVES: Riverside & San Bernardino Counties.

MATERNITY INFORMATION

San Antonio Community Hospital
999 San Bernardino Rd.
Upland, CA 91786
(909) 980-2229
(909) 985-7659 FAX

Info on maternity srvs at San Antonio plus info & schedules for maternity edu prgms including lamaze, infant CPR, maternity exercise and other prenatal classes. OFC HRS: M-F 8am-4:30pm. Spanish spoken. SERVES: Rancho Cucamonga, Upland, Ontario, Montclair, Chino, Fontana, Pomona and Claremont.

MEDICAL BOARD OF CALIFORNIA

Licensed Midwife Prgm
2005 Evergreen St., Ste 1200
Sacramento, CA 95815
(916) 263-2382
(916) 263-2944 FAX

Midwifery constitutes the furthuring or undertaking by any licensed midwife to assist a woman in childbirth. Does not include assisting childbirth by artificial, forcible or mechanical means. FUNDING: Govt. SERVES: Calif.

MOSES HOUSE MINISTRIES

P.O. Box 2033
15180 Anacapa Rd.
Victorville, CA 92393
(866) 606-6737
(760) 955-1895
(760) 955-1303 FAX

Private Christian family homes offer pregnant young women and teens housing during their pregnancy. Case mgmt, assists with family reunification, edu, employment, parenting, or placing their babies for adoption. Transportation srvs available. Emerg assist prgm for prenant or parenting moms with children ages birth-5 yrs offers bottles, formula, and other necessary supplies. Research ctr for single moms. FUNDING: Nonprofit, United Way, donations. OFC HRS: M-F 9am-4pm. SERVES: San Bernardino County.

NATL ALLIANCE FOR HISPANIC HEALTH

Su Familia (Family Health Helpline)
1501 16th Street, NW
Washington, DC 20036
(866) 783-2645
(202) 797-4353 FAX

Bilingual health helpline and website. Callers are referred to health care providers in their area. For prenatal info, call La Linea Nacional Prenatal Hispana (800) 504-7081. For hospice info, call (877) 658-8896. Visit (www.hispanichealth.org). FUNDING: Grants, donations. OFC HRS: M-F 9am-6pm, EST. Spanish spoken. SERVES: U.S.A.

NATL LIFE CENTER

Pregnancy Srvs
686 N. Broad St.
Woodbury, NJ 08096
(800) 848-5683
(856) 848-1819
(856) 848-2380 FAX

24-hr hotline with live response every day. Refers callers to local agencies based on identified needs. Pregnancy tests, clothing, housing, medical referral, adoption info. Serves women in a crisis pregnancy. Phone counseling & post-abortion support groups, maternity & infant clothing. FUNDING: Donations, nonprofit. OFC HRS: 10am-6pm, EST. ADM REQ: Suspect pregnancy. Free & confidential srvs. SERVES: U.S.A.

PECHANGA INDIAN HEALTH CLINIC

12784 Pechanga Rd.
Temecula, CA 92592
(951) 676-6810
(951) 676-0744 FAX

Comprehensive health care, mental health (individual and family counseling), nutrition, pharmacy, lab, nursing, AIDS testing, family planning, patient transportation srvs. FUNDING: Fed, state, county. OFC HRS: M-Th 8am-5pm; F 8am-2pm. ADM REQ: Eligible American Indian dependents only. Must have appt. Accepts Medi-Cal for eligible patients only. Sliding fee scale. Free srvs to qualified Indians.

PERRIS VALLEY FAMILY RESOURCE CENTER

371 Wilkerson Ave., Ste L
Perris, CA 92570
(951) 443-1158
(951) 940-1964 FAX

Comprehensive srvs to families and children. Parents & teen classes, counseling, training workshops, food referrals, rental assist, ESL, anger mgmt, Healthy Families Applications, college enrollment information. FUNDING: Govt. OFC HRS: M-Th 8am-5pm. Spanish spoken. SERVES: Perris Valley area, Moreno Valley, Lake Elsinore, Hemet and surrounding areas.

PLANNED PARENTHOOD

(800) 230-7526

Planned Parenthood offers access to edu and srvs needed to make responsible choices about parenthood and reproductive health. Family planning srvs include: WIC prgms, edu srvs, birth control and emerg contraception. Info is provided for prenatal care, adoption and abortion. PPOSBC ensures that quality comprehensive health care and edu is available to all at low to no cost. Qualified medical staff trained to answer questions and offer referrals. Visit (www.PPOSBC.org). FUNDING: Family PACT, donations, nonprofit. OFC HRS: Vary by center. Spanish spoken.

PLANNED PARENTHOOD/INDIO CENTER

71777 San Jacinto Dr., Ste 202
Rancho Mirage, CA 92270
(760) 674-0040
(760) 674-3440 FAX

Outpatient health care clinic for ages 14 yrs+. Immunizations, pregnancy testing, counseling, birth control, physical exams, AIDS testing & treatment, STD. FUNDING: Nonprofit. OFC

HRS: M, W 8am-5pm; Tu, Th 10:30am-7:30pm; Sat 8:30am-5pm. Closed last W of each month 8am-12noon. Spanish spoken. Accepts Medi-cal, sliding fee scale. SERVES: Riverside County.

PLANNED PARENTHOOD/MORENO VLY

12900 Frederick St., Ste C
Moreno Valley, CA 92553
(951) 601-2322

Reproductive health care. Birth control including: pills, Norplant, IUD, condoms, foam, morning-after, etc. Pregnancy testing and counseling, HIV/STD testing, post-menopause hormone replacement therapy & mammograms. FUNDING: Nonprofit. OFC HRS: M, W, F 8am-5pm; Tu, Th 10:30am-7:30pm; Sat 8:30am-5pm. Closed last W of each month 8am-12noon. Spanish spoken. Accepts Medi-Cal, Military, sliding fee scale. SERVES: Moreno Valley area.

PLANNED PARENTHOOD/RIVERSIDE

3772 Tibbetts St., Ste A
Riverside, CA 92506
(888) 743-7526
(951) 682-7904 FAX

Birth control, pap smear, gynecology exams, breast exams, morning-after pill, pregnancy testing, option counseling, pregnancy termination, diagnosis and treatment of STDs for men and women, sterilization for men and women, HIV testing, counseling. Health educator offers presentations to community groups on issues relating to reproductive health care. Wait varies. FUNDING: State (Office of Family Planning), donations. Surgical Srvs Hrs: M-F 8am-7:30pm, Sat 8:30am-5pm. Spanish spoken. Accepts Medi-Cal, sliding fee scale. Annual exams $0-66 (based on income). Donations requested. SERVES: Riverside, San Diego Counties.

PLANNED PARENTHOOD/SAN BRDO

San Bernardino Medical Center
1873 Commercenter West
San Bernardino, CA 92408
(909) 890-5511
(909) 890-4599 FAX

Planned Parenthood provides affordable health care to women, men and teens. Experienced and caring medical staff gives each client honest informational and personal attention. Srvs include: pregnancy testing and counseling, post-menopause hormone replacement therapy and mammograms. Health srvs are confidential FUNDING: Nonprofit. OFC HRS: M 7:30am-5:30pm; Tu 7:30am-6pm; W 7:30am-7pm; Th 7:30am-5pm; F 6:30am-4:30pm; Sat, 7:30am-4:30pm. Accepts insurance, Medicare, Medi-Cal, sliding fee scale.

PLANNED PARENTHOOD/UPLAND

918 W. Foothill Blvd., Ste A
Upland, CA 91786-0531
(909) 890-5511
(909) 985-0351 FAX

Upland's Planned Parenthood outpatient center offers: pregnancy testing, counseling, birth control, health edu, option counseling, medical referrals, immunizations, emerg contraception, AIDS testing and counseling, STD screening. FUNDING: Nonprofit. Phone Hrs: M, W 8am-6:30pm; Tu, Th, F 8am-5pm; Sat, Sun

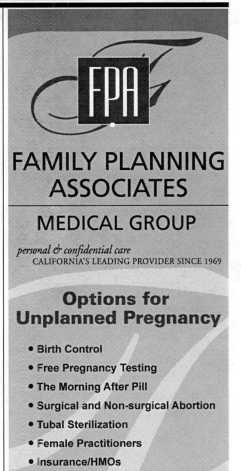

9am-5pm. Spanish spoken. ADM REQ: Ages 16 yrs+. Free clinic. Accepts Medi-Cal, sliding fee scale.

POMONA VALLEY HOSPITAL MED CTR

Women's & Children's Srvs
1798 N. Garey Ave.
Pomona, CA 91767
(909) 620-6663
(909) 629-0890 FAX

Childbirth classes, Baby Express, CPR, Boot Camp for Dads, Safe Sitter prgm, community resources, & physician referrals. Srvs include: labor, delivery, recovery suites, perinatal diagnostic/treatment ctr, lactation consultation and maternal/neonatal transport from other hospitals. FUNDING: Nonprofit. OFC HRS: M-F 9am-4:30pm. But hours vary depending on dpt. Spanish spoken. SERVES: Inland, San Gabriel Valleys.

POSTPARTUM SUPPORT INTERNATL

706 S.W. 54th Avenue
Portland, OR 97219
(503) 894-9453
(503) 894-9452 FAX

Promotes awareness, prev & treatment of mental health issues related to childbearing. Provides resources to local social support networks and support groups, info on diagnosis & treatment of postpartum mood & anxiety disorders, postpartum chat rooms & edu. Professional memberships available. Visit (www.postpartum.net). Helpline: (800) 944-4773. FUNDING: Nonprofit. OFC HRS: M-F 9am-3pm. Free srvs. SERVES: Internatl.

PREGNANCY COUNSELING CENTER

P.O. Box 164
8780 19th Street
Alta Loma, CA 91701
(909) 948-6702
(909) 481-8867 FAX

24-hr hotline (909) 985-0205. Free pregnancy testing, counsel from a pro-life perspective, medical, financial, legal, and housing referrals. Free maternity clothes, baby clothes, furniture. Adoption referrals, speakers. FUNDING: Nonprofit. OFC HRS: M, W, Sat 11am-1:30pm. Spanish spoken. SERVES: San Bernardino County.

PREGNANCY COUNSELING CENTER

Upland Center
P.O. Box 9000-164
Rancho Cucamonga, CA 91701
(909) 985-0205
(909) 481-8867 FAX

24-hr hotline, free pregnancy testing, counseling, medical, financial, legal and housing referrals. Free maternity clothes, baby clothes and furniture. Adoption referrals and speakers. Pro-life perspective. Located at 121 East F Street, Ontario. Walk in or call. FUNDING: Donations, nonprofit. OFC HRS: M, W, Sat 11am-1:30pm. Some Spanish spoken. Free srvs. SERVES: Pomona Valley, Ontario, Chino, Claremont, Upland, Rancho Cucamonga.

RESOLVE

The National Infertility Assn
1760 Old Meadow Rd., Ste 500
Mc Lean, VA 22102
(703) 556-7172
(703) 506-3266 FAX

Edu, advocacy and support for people with infertility problems and/or who are interested professionals through natl magazine, fact sheets, helpline, physician referral system and member-to-member contact. FUNDING: Member dues, donations, nonprofit. OFC HRS: M-F 9am-5:30pm, EST. Annual dues $55. SERVES: U.S.A.

RIDGECREST COMMUNITY HEALTH CENTER

1133 N. Chelsea St.
Ridgecrest, CA 93555
(760) 446-7978
(760) 446-2850 FAX

Primary health care for all ages. OB/GYN, prenatal, AIDS/STD. FUNDING: BPHC site, donations, nonprofit. OFC HRS: M-F 8am-5pm. Spanish spoken. ADM REQ: Low income. Accepts insurance, Medi-Cal & Medicare. SERVES: Kern County.

RIVERSIDE CO. PUBLIC HEALTH DEPT

Banning Family Health Center
3055 W. Ramsey St.
Banning, CA 92220
(951) 849-6794
(951) 849-0060 FAX

Family planning, CHDP, prenatal care, medical care, physical exams, immunization for adults and children, pap smears, pregnancy testing, screening for STDs and TB, HIV/AIDS testing & counseling. OFC HRS: M-F 7:30am-5pm. Spanish spoken. Accepts Medi-Cal, MISP/MIA, PPOs. Medical srv for any Calif resident, fees based on ability to pay. SERVES: Riverside County.

RIVERSIDE CO. PUBLIC HEALTH DEPT

Corona Health/Family Care Center
505 S. Buena Vista Ave., Ste 101
Corona, CA 92882-1901
(951) 272-5445
(951) 272-5489 FAX

Primary care srvs, family planning, pregnancy testing, STD testing, diagnosis and treatment, OB/GYN, family planning, pediatric, treatment of non-emerg medical problems. Wait: Varies. For an appt, call (800) 720-9553. FUNDING: Govt. OFC HRS: M-F 7:30am-5pm. Spanish spoken. Accepts Medi-Cal/MIA, ability to pay, insurance, pvt pay. Fee scale based on family size, income, & srv provided. SERVES: Corona, Norco.

RIVERSIDE CO. PUBLIC HEALTH DEPT

Hemet Health/Family Care Center
880 N. State St.
Hemet, CA 92543
(951) 766-2450
(951) 766-2479 FAX

Family srvs include: treatment of non-emerg medical problems, nutrition info & counseling, STD testing with diagnosis and treatment, family planning srvs, public health nursing assist to families in maintaining good health and promoting wellness in the home. Srvs for children include: immunizations, preventive health, family planning edu for teens, assist to pregnant teens, referral for medical care and rehab for physically disabled up to age 21 yrs. Srvs for women include: pregnancy testing, breast cancer screening, pap smears, WIC supplemental food & prenatal care. FUNDING: Nonprofit. OFC HRS: M-F 7:30am-5pm. Spanish spoken.

ADM REQ: Low income. Accepts insurance, Medicare, Medi-Cal. SERVES: Riverside County.

RIVERSIDE CO. PUBLIC HEALTH DEPT

Indio Family Health Center
47-923 Oasis St.
Indio, CA 92201
(760) 863-8283
(760) 863-8366 FAX

Primary care srvs for various medical conditions. Preventive medical srvs includes: WIC, child health, disability prevention, prenatal care, women's health, HIV testing & counseling, immunizations, family planning, STD testing & treatment. Preventive medical srvs available to all county residents. FUNDING: BPHC site, donations, county, nonprofit. OFC HRS: M-F 7:30am-5pm. Spanish spoken. ADM REQ: Low income. Accepts Medi-Cal, Medicare, pvt insurance, Managed Care. Fees based on ability to pay. SERVES: Riverside County.

RIVERSIDE CO. PUBLIC HEALTH DEPT

Lake Elsinore Health/Family Care Ctr
2499 E. Lakeshore Dr.
Lake Elsinore, CA 92530
(951) 471-4200
(951) 471-4205 FAX

Primary care, family planning, comprehensive perinatal care, cancer screening, STDs, immunizations, TB clinic & skin tests, pregnancy testing & counseling, teen clinic, well-child care, nutrition, WIC, public health nursing, AFLP. FUNDING: BPHC site, donations, nonprofit. Clinic hrs: M-F 7:30am-5pm. Spanish spoken. ADM REQ: Low income. Accepts insurance, Medicare, Medi-Cal, sliding fee scale. SERVES: Riverside Co.

RIVERSIDE CO. PUBLIC HEALTH DEPT

Palm Springs Health/Family Care Ctr
1515 N. Sunrise Way
Palm Springs, CA 92262
(760) 778-2210
(760) 778-2214 FAX

HIV/STD testing, diagnosis and treatment, well-child care, prenatal care, women's health care, family planning, teen clinic, primary care treatment of non-emerg medical problems. For an appt, call (800) 720-9553. FUNDING: BPHC site, donations, nonprofit. OFC HRS: M-F 7:30am-5pm. Children's Clinic Sat 8am-5pm. Spanish spoken. ADM REQ: Low income. Accepts Medi-Cal, insurance. Fees based on family size, income, & srvs provided. SERVES: Riverside County.

RIVERSIDE CO. PUBLIC HEALTH DEPT

Perris Health/Family Care Center
308 E. San Jacinto Ave.
Perris, CA 92570
(951) 940-6700
(951) 940-6726 FAX

Srvs for the whole family include treatment of non-emerg medical problems, nutrition info and counseling, STD testing with diagnosis and treatment, family planning srvs, public health nursing assist to families in maintaining good health and promoting wellness in the home. Srvs for children include: immunizations, preventive health, family planning edu for teens, assist to pregnant teens, referral for medical care. Srvs for women include: pregnancy testing, breast cancer screening and pap smears,

breastfeeding women, infants, children. Wait: Varies. For an appt, call (800) 720-9553. FUNDING: BPHC site, donations, nonprofit. OFC HRS: M-F 7:30am-5pm. Spanish spoken. ADM REQ: Low income. Accepts insurance, Medicare, Medi-Cal. Sliding fee scale based on family size, income, srvs provided. SERVES: Riverside County.

RIVERSIDE CO. PUBLIC HEALTH DEPT
Family Planning Prgm
7140 Indiana Ave.
Riverside, CA 92504
(951) 358-6000

Basic contraceptive srvs including: birth control, emerg contraception, pregnancy testing and counseling. Special teen srvs at Jurupa, Corona, Hemet, Indio, Elsinore, Palm Springs, Riverside Neighborhood Health Ctr. Visit (www.birthcontrol4u.com) for more info. Website also lists San Bernardino Co. srvs. OFC HRS: M-F 7:30am-5pm. Spanish spoken. SERVES: Riverside & San Bernardino Counties.

RIVERSIDE CO. PUBLIC HEALTH DEPT
Nutrition Services
P.O. Box 7600
4065 County Circle Dr., Ste 207
Riverside, CA 92503
(951) 358-5311
(951) 358-5472 FAX

Food & nutrition info, edu, consultation srvs. Professional & paraprofessional edu & WIC Prgm srvs. Breastfeeding info (888) 451-2499. WIC appts outside the county, call (800) 455-4942. Riverside Co., call (951) 358-7200. OFC HRS: M-F 7:30am-5pm. Spanish spoken. SERVES: Riverside County.

RIVERSIDE CO. PUBLIC HEALTH DEPT
Riverside Neighborhood Family Health Ctr
7140 Indiana Ave.
Riverside, CA 92504
(951) 358-6000
(951) 358-6044 FAX

Well-child exams, adult physicals, teen clinic, prenatal care, family planning, treatment of non-emerg medical problems. Wait: Varies. FUNDING: BPHC site, donations, nonprofit. OFC HRS: M-F 7:35am-5pm. OB/GYN, HIV/STD testing: M 8am-5pm; Tu 1pm-5pm; Th 8am-12noon. Spanish spoken. ADM REQ: Medi-Cal/MIA, sliding fee scale. Accepts Medi-Cal, Medicare, pvt pay. Sliding fee scale based on family size, income & srvs provided. SERVES: Riverside County.

RIVERSIDE CO. PUBLIC HEALTH DEPT
Jurupa Family Care Center
9415 Mission Blvd., Ste R
Riverside, CA 92509
(951) 360-8795
(951) 360-8798 FAX

Primary care limited to uncomplicated medical conditions. Preventative medical srvs, well-child, immunizations, prenatal care, WIC, CHDP. Also family planning, STD screening. For an appt, call (800) 720-9553. OFC HRS: M-F 7:30am-5pm. Spanish spoken. ADM REQ: Srvs open to all county residents. Call for appt. Accepts Medi-Cal, Medicare, some pvt insurance, sliding fee scale. SERVES: Riverside County.

RIVERSIDE CO. PUBLIC HEALTH DEPT
Rubidoux Family Care Center
5256 Mission Blvd.
Riverside, CA 92509
(951) 955-0840
(951) 955-5317 FAX

Primary care, perinatal care, immunizations, cancer screening, STD tests, TB tests, well-child care, nutrition. FUNDING: County. OFC HRS: M-F 7:30am-5pm. Spanish spoken. Accepts Medi-Cal, Medicare, insurance, sliding fee scale. SERVES: Riverside County.

RIVERSIDE LIFE SRVS
3727 McCray St.
Riverside, CA 92506
(951) 784-2422
(951) 276-2907 FAX

Pregnancy testing & counseling from pro-life perspective, pre-abortion & post-abortion counseling, adoption referrals, medical & legal aid referrals, free maternity clothes, formula, baby items. 24-hr message line (951) 784-2725. FUNDING: Nonprofit. OFC HRS: M-Th 10am-4pm. Spanish spoken. SERVES: Riverside County.

RIVERSIDE/SAN BRDO CO. INDIAN HLTH
Morongo Indian Health Clinic
11555 1/2 Potrero Rd.
Banning, CA 92220
(800) 732-8805
(951) 849-4761
(951) 849-5612 FAX

Outpatient alcohol & drug treatment prgm, AA meetings, parenting classes counseling. Comprehensive health care: medical, dental, vision, mental health (indiv & family counseling), pharmacy, lab, nursing, family planning, AIDS testing, WIC prgm, transportation. Serves all ages. FUNDING: Govt. OFC HRS: M, W, Th 8am-5pm; Tu 8am-7pm; F 8am-2pm. ADM REQ: Must have appt. Accepts Medi-Cal. Free srvs to qualified Indians. SERVES: Riverside & San Bernardino Counties.

ROSE OF SHARON LIFE CENTER
14725 7th Street, Ste 600
Victorville, CA 92392
(760) 243-5006
(760) 243-5015 FAX

Free confidential pregnancy test. Counseling, referrals & alternatives to abortions. FUNDING: Nonprofit. OFC HRS: M-F 9:30am-3:30pm. Spanish spoken. Free srvs. SERVES: Victor Valley.

SAN BERNARDINO CO. PUBLIC HEALTH
Reproductive Health Centers
303 E. Mountain View
Barstow, CA 92311
(800) 722-4777
(760) 256-4715
(760) 256-4909 FAX

Reproductive health exams for men & women. STD testing & treatment, HIV testing & referral to care. Edu srvs, pregnancy testing, counseling, lab testing, young adult clinics. FUNDING: Dept Public Health. OFC HRS: Tu-Th 9am-4pm. ADM REQ: Must have appt. Accepts Medi-Cal. Fees based on srvs provided. SERVES: Barstow.

SAN BERNARDINO CO. PUBLIC HEALTH
Reproductive Health Centers

P.O. Box 2835
477 Summit Blvd.
Big Bear Lake, CA 92315
(800) 722-4777
(909) 866-0177

Reproductive health exams for men & women. STD testing & treatment, HIV testing & referral to care. Edu srvs, pregnancy testing, counseling, lab testing, young adult clinic. FUNDING: Calif Office of Family Planning, govt. OFC HRS: F 9am-4pm. Spanish spoken. ADM REQ: Must have appt. Accepts Medi-Cal, F-PACT, sliding fee scale, no one turned away for lack of funds. SERVES: San Bernardino Mtns.

SAN BERNARDINO CO. PUBLIC HEALTH
Reproductive Health Centers
16453 Bear Valley Rd.
Hesperia, CA 92345
(800) 722-4777
(760) 956-4465
(760) 956-4450 FAX

Reproductive health exams for men & women. STD testing & treatment, HIV testing & referral to care. Edu srvs, pregnancy testing, counseling, lab testing, young adult clinics. For HIV testing, call (909) 383-3060 W 9am-3pm. FUNDING: Dept Public Health. OFC HRS: M-F 9am-4pm. Spanish spoken. ADM REQ: Must have appt. Accepts Medi-Cal. Sliding fee scale. No one denied srvs due to lack of funds. SERVES: Victor Valley area.

SAN BERNARDINO CO. PUBLIC HEALTH
Reproductive Health Centers
P.O. Box 1066
1406 Bailey Ave., Ste D
Needles, CA 92363
(800) 722-4777
(760) 326-9230
(760) 326-9235 FAX

Reproductive health exams for men & women. STD testing & treatment, HIV testing & referral to care. Edu srvs, pregnancy testing, counseling, lab testing, young adult clinics. FUNDING: Dept Public Health. OFC HRS: Tu-Th 7am-4:30pm. Accepts Medi-Cal, insurance. Fees based on srv. SERVES: Amboy, Big River, Essex, Needles, Havasu Landing, Parkers Dam.

SAN BERNARDINO CO. PUBLIC HEALTH
Reproductive Health Centers
1647 E. Holt Blvd.
Ontario, CA 91764
(800) 722-4777
(909) 458-9716
(909) 458-9729 FAX

Reproductive health exams for men & women. STD testing & treatment, HIV testing & referral to care. Edu srvs, pregnancy testing, counseling, lab testing, young adult clinics. For HIV testing, call (909) 383-3060 F 8am-3:30pm. FUNDING: Dept Public Health. OFC HRS: M-F 8am-5pm. Spanish spoken. ADM REQ: Must have appt. Sliding fee scale. No one denied srvs due to lack of funds. SERVES: Ontario.

SAN BERNARDINO CO. PUBLIC HEALTH
Reproductive Health Centers
800 E. Lugonia Ave., Ste F
Redlands, CA 92374
(800) 722-4777
(909) 793-6399

Reproductive health exams for men & women. STD testing & treatment, HIV testing & referral to care. Edu srvs, pregnancy testing, counseling, lab testing, young adult clinics. FUNDING: Govt. OFC HRS: M-F 8am-5pm. Spanish spoken. ADM REQ: Must have appt. Accepts Medi-Cal, F-PACT, sliding fee scale. No one denied srvs due to lack of funds. SERVES: San Bernardino County.

SAN BERNARDINO CO. PUBLIC HEALTH

Administrative Office
385 Arrowhead Ave.
San Bernardino, CA 92415-0120
(909) 387-7020
(909) 387-6228 FAX

Administers branch offices at various locations throughout San Bernardino Co. including: Barstow, Big Bear, Chino, Fontana, Joshua Tree, Needles, Ontario, Redlands, San Bernardino, Trona, Victorville & Twin Peaks. Edu, alcohol & drug prevention, animal control, birth & death certificates, Calif Children's Srvs, epidemiology, family planning, high-risk infant prgm, immunizations, nutrition, WIC, public health nursing, school health, senior health, VD control, TB, HIV/AIDS control. TDD (909) 397-6354. OFC HRS: M-F 8am-5pm; clinic hrs may vary. SERVES: San Bernardino County.

SAN BERNARDINO CO. PUBLIC HEALTH

Reproductive Health Centers
799 E. Rialto Ave.
San Bernardino, CA 92415-0011
(800) 722-4777
(909) 885-9962
(909) 387-3340 FAX

Birth control, male & female exams, pregnancy testing, counseling, referrals, verification, HIV & Sexually Transmitted Infection (STI) testing and counseling, male sterilization. Srvs are confidential and low-cost. Call individual clinic to schedule appt. Weekly young adult clinics on a walk-in basis at Fontana, Ontario, Redlands, San Bernardino and Hesperia sites. FUNDING: Calif Office of Family Planning. OFC HRS: M-F 8am-5pm. Spanish spoken. Accepts Medi-Cal, managed care plans, pvt pay through sliding fee scale. SERVES: San Bernardino County.

SEXUALITY INFO & EDU COUNCIL OF THE U.S.

90 John St., Ste 402
New York, NY 10038
(212) 819-9770
(212) 819-9776 FAX

Provides edu and info about sexuality and sexual & reproductive health. Also provides advocacy. Visit (www.familiesaretalking.org). FUNDING: Nonprofit, govt. SERVES: U.S.A.

SOBOBA INDIAN HEALTH CLINIC

607 Donna Way
San Jacinto, CA 92583
(800) 851-5816
(951) 654-0803
(951) 487-9634 FAX

Comprehensive health care: medical, dental, vision, mental health (individual & family counseling), pharmacy, lab, AIDS testing, nursing, family planning, well-baby, pediatric, health edu, transportation srvs. FUNDING: Fed, state, county. OFC HRS: M, Tu, Th 8am-5pm; W 8am-7pm; F 8am-2pm. ADM REQ: American Indian. Accepts Medi-Cal. Free to qualified Indians. SERVES: Riverside County.

UCI WOMEN'S HEALTHCARE CENTER

Dept of Obstetrics & Gynecology
200 S. Manchester Ave., Ste 600
Orange, CA 92868
(714) 456-7002
(888) 456-7002
(714) 456-8383 FAX

Experts in women's health care. Full range of consultative & treatment srvs. Low & high-risk obstetrics, prenatal diagnosis & treatment, fetal eval & antepartum testing and menopause, complex gynecologic surgery, screening, treatment of gynecologic cancers, reproductive disorders & infertility. FUNDING: Govt. OFC HRS: M-F 8am-5pm.

WIC/WOMEN, INFANT AND CHILDREN

See "San Bernardino Co. Public Health"

YWCA/RIVERSIDE CO.

Born Free Women's Residential
8172 Magnolia Ave.
Riverside, CA 92504
(951) 530-8280
(951) 688-5270 FAX

24-hr residential treatment prgm for chemically dependent women. Srvs include: transportation to medical/legal appts, 12-Step prgms, parenting classes, one-on-one counseling, group sessions, NA/AA meetings, in-home nurse to discuss child birthing issues, budgeting and meal prep classes, exit plans. FUNDING: Donations, nonprofit. OFC HRS: 24 hrs, 7 days. Spanish spoken. ADM REQ: Ages 18 yrs+, pregnant, and addicted to a substance. This is not a detox facility. Sliding fee scale, no one turned away due to the inability to pay. SERVES: Los Angeles County, Orange County, Riverside County, San Bernadino County.

A NOTE ABOUT THIS CHAPTER

Additional resources will be listed in the "Emergency Assistance" and "Homeless" chapters in this directory. Many local churches and adult edu prgms offer instruction on budgeting.

1736 FAMILY CRISIS CENTER

Admin Office
2116 Arlington Ave., Ste 200
Los Angeles, CA 90018
(323) 737-3900
(323) 737-3993 FAX

This location is one of the 21 Family Source Centers in L.A. County providing the One e-App system for financial assist, case mgmt, and high-risk youth/young adult employment and edu srvs. 24-hr srvs provided to runaway and homeless adols, including: counseling, food, clothing, advocacy and other basic needs. 2-week emerg youth shelter for adols ages 10-17 yrs who need short-term, crisis-oriented shelter. Also operates four shelters for battered women and their children (ages birth-17 yrs) for 1-24 months offering a comprehensive survival and job dev prgm to promote long-term safety, survival & success. 24-hr hotlines in South Bay (310) 379-3620, (310) 370-5902; Long Beach (562) 388-7652; South L.A. (213) 222-1237, (213) 745-6434. May call collect if needed. 24-hr drop-in center at 1736 Monterey Blvd., Hermosa Beach. FUNDING: Donations, grants, govt, CDBG, nonprofit. OFC HRS: M-F 8:30am-5pm. Spanish spoken. Free srvs. SERVES: So. Calif, Southwest L.A.

AFDC

Commonly referred to as Welfare, now known as TANF or CalWORKs. Prgms are administered by county social srvs depts; listings are shown under the county name.

ALTURA CREDIT UNION

P.O. Box 60039
2847 Campus Pkwy.
PO Box in City of Industry, CA 91716
Riverside, CA 92506
(951) 684-6414

Free checking, loans, home banking, investment info, credit cards, low-cost wire transfer abroad, one time new member fee $12, $100 min balance/checking to start. Will reduce over time. FUNDING: Nonprofit. OFC HRS: M-F 8am-6pm; Sat 9am-2pm. Spanish spoken. ADM REQ: Live, work, worship, or study in Riverside Co, San Diego Co, parts of San Bernardino, or parts of Orange County.

ARROWHEAD CREDIT UNION

Pacific Marine CU
170 N. Yucca Ave.
Barstow, CA 92311
(800) 743-7228
(760) 243-1782 FAX

Free checking, loans, home banking, investment info, credit cards, low-cost wire transfer abroad. FUNDING: Nonprofit. OFC HRS: M-F 9am-6pm; Sat 9am-2pm. Spanish spoken. New member fee $5. SERVES: Inland Empire.

ARROWHEAD CREDIT UNION

Pacific Marine CU
170 N. Yucca Ave., Ste A
Barstow, CA 92311
(800) 743-7228
(760) 256-8352 FAX

Checking, loans, home banking, investment info, credit cards, low-cost wire transfer abroad. FUNDING: Nonprofit. OFC HRS: M-F 8am-6pm; Sat 9am-2pm. Spanish spoken. new member fee $5. SERVES: San Bernardino County.

ARROWHEAD CREDIT UNION

42171 L Big Bear Blvd.
Big Bear Lake, CA 92315
(909) 866-5781

Free checking, loans, home banking, investment info, credit cards, low-cost wire transfer abroad. FUNDING: Nonprofit OFC HRS: M-Th 9am-5:30pm; F 9am-6pm; Sat 9am-2pm. Spanish spoken. New member fee $5. SERVES: San Bernardino County.

ARROWHEAD CREDIT UNION

12099 Central Ave.
Chino, CA 91710
(909) 383-7300
(800) 743-7228

Free checking, loans, home banking, investment info, credit cards, low-cost wire transfer abroad. FUNDING: Nonprofit. OFC HRS: M-F 8am-6pm; Sat 9am-2pm. Spanish spoken. New member fee $5. SERVES: San Bernardino County.

ARROWHEAD CREDIT UNION

Altura CU
390 McKinley, Ste 100
Corona, CA 92879
(888) 883-7228

Free checking, loans, home banking, investment info, credit cards, low-cost wire transfer abroad. FUNDING: Nonprofit. OFC HRS: M-F 12noon-7pm; Sat 9am-2pm. New member fee $5. SERVES: Apple Valley.

ARROWHEAD CREDIT UNION

23971 Lake Dr.
Crestline, CA 92325
(800) 743-7228
(909) 383-7300

Free checking, loans, home banking, investment info, credit cards, low-cost wire transfer abroad. FUNDING: Nonprofit. OFC HRS: M-F 9am-6pm; Sat 9am-2pm. Spanish spoken. New member fee $5. SERVES: San Bernardino County.

ARROWHEAD CREDIT UNION

16014 Foothill Blvd.
Fontana, CA 92335
(800) 743-7228
(909) 383-7300

Free checking, loans, home banking, investment info, credit cards, low-cost wire transfer abroad. FUNDING: Nonprofit. OFC HRS: M-F 8am-6pm; Sat 9am-2pm. Spanish spoken. New member fee $5. SERVES: San Bernardino County.

ARROWHEAD CREDIT UNION

Fontana Summit
9389 Cherry Ave.
Fontana, CA 92335
(909) 822-1810

Free checking, loans, home banking, investment info, credit cards, low-cost wire transfer abroad. FUNDING: Nonprofit. OFC HRS: M-F 12noon-7pm; Sat 9am-2pm. SERVES: Fontana.

ARROWHEAD CREDIT UNION

7285 Boulder Ave.
Highland, CA 92346
(909) 863-9003
(800) 743-7228

Free checking, loans, home banking, investment info, credit cards, low-cost wire transfer abroad. Safe deposit boxes available. FUNDING: Nonprofit. OFC HRS: M-F 8am-6pm; Sat 9am-2pm. Spanish spoken. New member fee $5. SERVES: San Bernardino County.

ARROWHEAD CREDIT UNION

California Coast CU
24716 Madison Ave.
Murrieta, CA 92562
(877) 495-1600

Free checking, loans, home banking, investment info, credit cards, low-cost wire transfer abroad. FUNDING: Nonprofit. OFC HRS: M-F 9am-7pm; Sat 9am-2pm. New member fee $5 SERVES: Wildomar.

ARROWHEAD CREDIT UNION

9267 Haven Ave., Ste 101
Rancho Cucamonga, CA 91730-5449
(909) 987-7300
(800) 743-7228

Free checking, loans, home banking, investment info, credit cards, low-cost wire transfer abroad. FUNDING: Nonprofit. OFC HRS: M-F 9am-6pm; Sat 9am-2pm. Spanish spoken. New member fee $5. SERVES: San Bernardino County.

ARROWHEAD CREDIT UNION

1580 Industrial Park Ave.
Redlands, CA 92373
(800) 743-7228
(909) 383-7300

Free checking, loans, home banking, investment info, credit cards, low-cost wire transfer abroad. FUNDING: Nonprofit. OFC HRS: M-F 9am-6pm; Sat 9am-2pm. Spanish spoken. New member fee $5. SERVES: San Bernardino County.

ARROWHEAD CREDIT UNION

592 W. Foothill Blvd.
Rialto, CA 92376
(909) 383-7300
(800) 743-7228

Free checking, loans, home banking, investment info, credit cards, low-cost wire transfer abroad. FUNDING: Nonprofit. OFC HRS: M-F 9am-6pm; Sat 9am-2pm. Spanish spoken. New member fee $5. SERVES: San Bernardino County.

ARROWHEAD CREDIT UNION

11150 Magnolia Ave, Ste D
Riverside, CA 92505
(800) 743-7228
(909) 383-7300

Free checking, loans, home banking, investment info, credit cards, low-cost wire transfer abroad. FUNDING: Nonprofit. OFC HRS: M-F

9am-6pm; Sat 9am-2pm. Spanish spoken. New member fee $5. SERVES: Riverside County.

ARROWHEAD CREDIT UNION
421 N. Sierra Way
San Bernardino, CA 92402
(800) 743-7228
(909) 383-7300

Free checking, loans, home banking, investment info, credit cards, low-cost wire transfer abroad. Safe deposit boxes available. FUNDING: Nonprofit. OFC HRS: M-F 9am-6pm; Sat 9am-2pm. Spanish spoken. New member fee $5. SERVES: San Bernardino County.

ARROWHEAD CREDIT UNION
2500 N. Del Rosa Ave.
San Bernardino, CA 92405
(800) 743-7228
(909) 383-7300

Free checking, loans, home banking, investment info, credit cards, low-cost wire transfer abroad. FUNDING: Nonprofit. OFC HRS: M-F 9am-6pm; Sat 9am-2pm. Spanish spoken. New member fee $5. SERVES: San Bernardino County.

ARROWHEAD CREDIT UNION
P.O. Box 735
San Bernardino, CA 92402
(800) 743-7228
(909) 383-7300

Checking, loans, home banking, investment info, credit cards, low-cost wire transfer abroad. FUNDING: Nonprofit. OFC HRS: M-F 8am-6pm; Sat 9am-2pm. new member fee $5. SERVES: Apple Valley.

ARROWHEAD CREDIT UNION
Alta Vista CU
295 S. Tippecanoe Ave.
San Bernardino, CA 92408
(800) 743-7228

Free checking, loans, home banking, investment info, credit cards, low-cost wire transfer abroad. Safe deposit boxes available. FUNDING: Nonprofit. OFC HRS: M-Tu 12noon-5pm; Th 12noon-5pm; F 12noon-6pm; Sat 10am-2pm. New member fee $5. SERVES: Hesperia.

ARROWHEAD CREDIT UNION
Altura CU
480 N. State, Ste E
San Jacinto, CA 92581
(888) 883-7228

Free checking, loans, home banking, investment info, credit cards, low-cost wire transfer abroad. FUNDING: Nonprofit. OFC HRS: M-F 8am-6pm; Sat 9am-2pm. new member fee $5. SERVES: Apple Valley.

ARROWHEAD CREDIT UNION
Inside Yucaipa Valley Shopping Ctr
33598 Yucaipa Blvd., Ste 1
Yucaipa, CA 92399
(800) 743-7228
(909) 383-7300

Free checking, loans, home banking, investment info, credit cards, low-cost wire transfer abroad. FUNDING: Nonprofit. OFC HRS: M-F 9am-6pm; Sat 9am-2pm. Spanish spoken. New member fee $5.

BREAST CANCER ANGELS
6889 Andrew Way
Cypress, CA 90630
(562) 795-0100
(714) 898-8966 FAX

Provides financial, emotional and spiritual assist to women and their families as they are going through breast cancer treatment. Visit (www.breastcancerangels.org). FUNDING: Nonprofit. SERVES: Southern Calif.

BREAST CANCER SOLUTIONS
3843 S. Bristol St., Ste 152
Santa Ana, CA 92704
(866) 960-9222
(866) 781-6068 FAX

Offers financial assist to meet the everyday needs of people undergoing breast cancer treatment. Offers rental, utility, food, medical, and car payment assist. Visit (www.breastcancersolutions.org) for more info. FUNDING: Nonprofit. Spanish spoken. ADM REQ: Receiving breast cancer treatment. Free srvs. SERVES: So Calif.

BUSINESS, TRANSPORT/HOUSING AGENCY
Loan Guarantee/Small Business Prgms
980 9th Street, Ste 2450
Sacramento, CA 95814-2719
(916) 323-5400
(916) 323-5440 FAX

The Small Business Loan Guarantee Program helps small businesses including agricultural or ag-related businesses secure market-rate conventional financing which the businesses may not otherwise be able to obtain. Under the program, repayment guarantees are issued to lenders for making the loans. Guarantees are negotiated and made by 11 Financial Development Corporations located throughout the state. Guarantee terms are negotiated and depending on loan type (term vs line of credit) may be limited to 90% of the defaulted loan balance, equaling no more than $500,000 and running no longer than seven consecutive years. Contact: Karen Kawada FUNDING: Govt. OFC HRS: M-F 8am-5pm. SERVES: Calif.

CALWORKS
See "Riverside Co. Public Social Srvs"

CALWORKS
See "San Bernardino Co. Human Srvs Sy"

CATHOLIC CHARITIES/COMMUNITY SRVS
Inland Valleys Regional Center
23623 Sunnymead Blvd., Ste E
Moreno Valley, CA 92553
(951) 924-9964
(951) 924-9997 FAX

Emerg srvs for low income. Assists with food, utility, rental assist & motel vouchers (when funding is available). Info & referral, immigration & citizenship prgm, HIV/AIDS housing assist. Counseling (909)763-4970 or (951)801-5282. FUNDING: Nonprofit. OFC HRS: M-Th 8:30am-4:30pm. By appt only. Spanish spoken. Most srvs free. SERVES: Moreno Valley, Riverside, Perris, Hemet, San Jacinto, Sun City, Corona, Lake Elsinore, Banning, Beaumont, Cherry Valley.

CATHOLIC CHARITIES/COMMUNITY SRVS
West End Regional Center
9375 Archibald Ave., Ste 302
Rancho Cucamonga, CA 91730
(909) 481-7196
(909) 481-6305 FAX

Food baskets, assist with rental & mortgage payments, utility payments, pre-arranged motel accommodations, info & referral, transportation, medical referrals, clothing & furniture assist, tax prep & holiday baskets. Call for appt. FUNDING: Nonprofit. OFC HRS: M-F 8:30am-4:30pm. Spanish spoken. SERVES: Fontana, Etiwanda, Ontario, Montclair, Upland, Alta Loma, Rancho Cucamonga, Chino, Chino Hills.

CATHOLIC CHARITIES/COMMUNITY SRVS
San Bernardino Regional Center
1800 Western Ave., Ste 107
San Bernardino, CA 92411
(909) 880-3625
(909) 880-9847 FAX

Food baskets, assists with rental & mortgage payment, utility payments, transportation, info & referral, medical referrals, clothing, furniture assist (as funds are available). FUNDING: Nonprofit. OFC HRS: M-F 8:30am-4:30pm. Spanish spoken. SERVES: San Bernardino County except Morongo Basin & the west side.

CHARITY CARS
750 Miami Springs Dr.
Longwood, FL 32779
(800) 242-7489

Donated vehicles are provided to disadvantaged families who are working but cannot afford to purchase. Case workers or social srv agencies who would like to refer a client, please send info to (info@800charitycars.org) and someone will contact you. FUNDING: Donations, nonprofit. OFC HRS: Operators 24 hrs, 7 days. ADM REQ: Families, please do not contact Charity Cars directly. Contact must come from referring agency. Pre-screening process. Free srvs. SERVES: U.S.A.

COMMUNITY ACTION PARTNERSHIP
Home Energy Assist Prgm (HEAP)
696 S. Tippecanoe Ave.
San Bernardino, CA 92415-0610
(909) 723-1620
(909) 723-1509 FAX

HEAP provides an annual credit toward gas or electric bills to qualifying clients. Energy edu workshops teach clients how to apply energy-saving means to reduce utility costs. For non-emerg utility credit you may request application by phone. For emerg, call to set up appt at (909)723-1680 or (909)723-1681. OFC HRS: M-F 8am-5pm. Emerg utility assist: Call for appt, M-F 8am-4:30pm. Spanish spoken. ADM REQ: Gas & electric bills, CA photo ID or driver's license with current address, SS card for all residents, verification of income for prior 30 days for all household members, rental agreement/mortgage statement. Courtesy calls to the utility companies verifying HEAP credits. Payments come from Sacramento. SERVES: San Bernardino County.

COMMUNITY ACTION PARTNERSHIP
Energy Conservation Program
696 S. Tippecanoe Ave.
San Bernardino, CA 92415-0610
(909) 723-1621
(909) 723-1500
(909) 723-1509 FAX

Main objective is to help conserve energy by reducing the consumption of natural resources. Aims to make homes more comfortable and healthful, lower cost of utilities, provide energy edu, and process HEAP applications. Includes weatherization srvs, HEAP, CARE, and lead reduction srvs. OFC HRS: M-F 8am-5pm. ADM REQ: Homeowner or renter in San Bernardino County and income eligible. SERVES: San Bernardino County.

COMMUNITY ACTION PARTNERSHIP
Family Development Prgm
696 S. Tippecanoe Ave.
San Bernardino, CA 92415-0610
(909) 723-1500
(909) 723-1509 FAX

Holistic case mgmt to homeless families. Transitional housing, rent security deposit prgm, food & motel vouchers, gas vouchers, bus tickets, clothing, rental assist, budgeting, counseling and info & referral. Summer camp, Christmas celebration. OFC HRS: M-Th 7:30am-5:30pm; F 8am-5pm. ADM REQ: Low income. SERVES: San Bernardino County.

COMMUNITY HEALTH RESOURCE CENTER
One-Stop Center/San Bernardino
600 N. Arrowhead Ave., Ste 300
San Bernardino, CA 92401
(909) 888-7881
(909) 889-7833 FAX

Offers phone access to health and wellness info & referral, financial literacy info, legal aid and consumer counseling by the Legal Aid Society of San Bernardino, homeownership resource info. For TDD, call (800) 735-2922. FUNDING: Govt. OFC HRS: M-F 8am-5pm. SERVES: San Bernardino Co.

COMMUNITY SERVICES DEPARTMENT
See "Community Action Partnership"

CONGENITAL HEART INFO NETWORK
101 N. Washington St., Ste 1A
Margate City, NJ 08402
(609) 822-1572
(609) 822-1574 FAX

Offers info & resources for people with congenital heart defects. Also sponsors several support groups. Spencer's Fund prgm provides financial assist including meals, utility assist, and travel expenses to families with a child who is hospitalized for a long period of time. FUNDING: Nonprofit. Free srvs. Memberships available at several donation levels. SERVES: U.S.A.

CONSUMER CREDIT COUNSELING SRVS
Main Office
P.O. Box 11330
1920 Old Tustin Ave.
Santa Ana, CA 92711
(800) 213-2227
(714) 245-1680 FAX

CCCS provides free budget & credit counseling and edu classes to adults experiencing financial difficulty with debt or credit. Debt mgmt prgm works with creditors for lower regular monthly payments and a viable alternative to bankruptcy. Counseling srvs via Internet, phone or in person. Also offers branches located in Anaheim, Brea and Costa Mesa. FUNDING: Donations, HUD grants, nonprofit. OFC HRS: M-Th 8am-8pm; F 8am-5pm; Sat 9am-1pm. Spanish spoken. Free counseling, debt mgmt prgm fee ranges from $0-$35 monthly, plus one time $50 setup fee. SERVES: So. Calif.

CREDIT COUNSELING
See "Consumer Credit Counseling Srvs"

DEBT COUNSELING
See "Consumer Credit Counseling Srvs"

DEBTORS ANONYMOUS/SO CALIF
P.O. Box 2862
Winnetka, CA 91396
(781) 453-2743
(800) 421-2383
(781) 453-2745 FAX

Daily meetings throughout So. Calif, also literature for compulsive spenders and debtors. Monthly workshops. FUNDING: Donations, nonprofit. Free srvs. SERVES: So. Calif.

FAITH'S HOPE FOUNDATION
2271 W. Malvern Ave., Ste 332
Fullerton, CA 92833
(714) 871-4673

Assistance is provided to families experiencing financial hardship due to hospitalization of a loved one. Services provided to families facing homelessness and/or poverty. Volunteer opportunities available. Bilingual encouraged. Visit (www.faithshopefoundation.org) or e-mail (fhf@faithshopefoundation.org). FUNDING: Nonprofit, donations, fundraisers. OFC HRS: M-F 9am-5pm. ADM REQ: Must submit application. Parent or child in recent or current hospital stay. SERVES: Nationwide.

FAMILY SERVICE ASSN/REDLANDS
612 Lawton St.
Redlands, CA 92374
(909) 793-2673
(909) 793-7324 FAX

Srvs provided to low income and homeless families. Case mgmt, food, clothing, utility and rental assist, cold weather motel vouchers, screening for dental & vision, prescription assist, and edu prgms. Home Again Project is a long-term comprehensive prgm helping homeless families into permanent housing and employment. Client srv M-W, F 9am-12noon, 1:30pm-7pm. Surplus food avail on walk-in basis, all other srvs require appt. FUNDING: Donations, United Way, grants, nonprofit. OFC HRS: M-W 8am-7pm; Th 8am-12noon; F 8am-4:30pm. Spanish spoken. ADM REQ: Low or no income. Free srvs. SERVES: Redlands, East Valley area.

FEDERAL RES BANK
Consumer Complaints
P.O. Box 1200
Minneapolis, MN 55480
(888) 851-1920
(877) 766-8533
(877) 888-2520 FAX

Contact with complaints about state-chartered banks that are members of the Federal Reserve System. Also answers questions about consumer laws and regulations affecting loans and deposit accounts. FUNDING: Govt. OFC HRS: M-F 8am-6pm, CST. SERVES: United States.

FINANCIAL CRISIS
See also chapter headings for "Homeless...," & "Emergency Assist/..."

FINANCIAL FRAUD ENFORCE TASK FORCE
(202) 514-2000

One-stop resource website for reporting illegal financial activities. Consumers are able to access a list of govt agencies and report their claims 24 hrs, 7 days. FUNDING: Govt. SERVES: U.S.A.

FIRST FINANCIAL CREDIT UNION
8750 Central Ave.
Montclair, CA 91763
(800) 537-8491
(990) 949-7609 FAX

Free checking, loans, home banking, investment info, credit cards, low-cost wire transfer abroad. FUNDING: Nonprofit. OFC HRS: M & F 9am-6pm; Tu-Th 9am-5pm; Sat 9am-1pm. Spanish spoken. New member fee $10 for educator. SERVES: San Bernardino County.

FIRST FINANCIAL CREDIT UNION
41789 Nicole Lane, Ste 3
Temecula, CA 92591
(800) 537-8491
(951) 296-6026 FAX

Free checking, loans, home banking, investment info, credit cards, low-cost wire transfer abroad. FUNDING: Nonprofit. OFC HRS: M, F 9am-6pm; Tu-Th 9am-5pm; Sat 9am-1pm. Spanish spoken. New member fee $10 for educator, $30 for non-educator. SERVES: Riverside County.

FLOWERS HERITAGE FOUNDATION
Bridge the Gap Program
200 Webster St., Ste 200
Oakland, CA 94607
(510) 587-2668
(510) 587-2794 FAX

Prgm helps people with HIV/AIDS who have low incomes afford their medications. Also offers health edu, advocacy, and community grants for nonprofit agencies. FUNDING: Nonprofit. Free srvs SERVES: Calif.

FREE ANNUAL CREDIT REPORT SRVS
Federal Trade Commission
P.O. Box 105283
Atlanta, GA 30348-5283

The only authorized source for consumers to access their credit reports online. The Fair Credit Reporting Act (FCRA) requires each of the nationwide consumer reporting companies (Equifax, Experian, Trans Union) to provide U.S. consumers with a free copy of their credit report once every 12 months. The FACT Act promotes the accuracy and privacy of information in the files of the nation's consumer reporting companies. The FTC, the nation's consumer protection agency, enforces the FACT Act with respect to consumer reporting companies. You may order your reports from each of the three nationwide consumer reporting companies at the same time. Visit (www.annualcreditreport.com). ADM REQ: Provide your name, address, SS #, and date of birth. SERVES: U.S.A.

HOME ENERGY ASSIST PRGM (HEAP)
Community Srvs & Dev
P.O. Box 1947
Sacramento, CA 95812-1947
(916) 576-7109
(866) 675-6623
(916) 263-1406 FAX

Prgm to offset the cost of energy for Calif low income households. HEAP provides a payment, once every calendar year in the form of either a direct payment to a utility company, a dual-party warrant made payable to the applicant and a utility company, or a single-party warrant if utilities are included in the rent or the applicant is submetered. Federal law requires states to give priority to households with low incomes & high energy costs; takes into consideration households with children under age 6 yrs, disabled persons and other individuals. TDD/TTY (800) 725-2922. OFC HRS: M-F 8am-5pm. ADM REQ: Total gross monthly income does not exceed income guidelines and a high proportion of the household income pays for home energy; primarily meets immediate home energy needs. SERVES: Calif.

INLAND EMPIRE CREDIT UNION
435 W. Mission Blvd., Ste 100
Pomona, CA 91766
(909) 865-2655
(909) 622-7184 FAX

Free checking, loans, three branch locations, investment info, credit cards, low-cost wire transfer abroad. 24-hr audio teller: (909) 623-7733 FUNDING: Nonprofit. OFC HRS: M,W,F 9am-6pm; Tu,Th 9am-5pm; Sat 9am-1pm. Spanish spoken. ADM REQ: Live, work, worship, or go to school in Ontario, Pomona, Chino, Chino Hills, San Dimas, La Verne, Diamond Bar, Claremont or San Bernardino. New member $25 min savings deposit. SERVES: Ontario, Pomona, Chino Hills, San Bernardino.

INLAND EMPIRE SMALL BUSINESS DEV
Coachella Valley SBDC
500 S. Palm Canyon Dr., Ste 222
Palm Springs, CA 92264
(760) 864-1311
(760) 864-1319 FAX

Business consulting and low-cost seminars to small businesses. Consulting minimal to free charge. FUNDING: Federal grants. OFC HRS: M-F 8am-5pm; call first. Closed 12noon-1pm for lunch. SERVES: Coachella Valley area.

INLAND EMPIRE SMALL BUSINESS DEV
Main Office
1650 Spruce St., Ste 500
Riverside, CA 92507
(909) 888-9011

Business consulting and low-cost seminars to small businesses. Consulting minimal to free charge. FUNDING: Federal grants. OFC HRS: M-F 8am-5pm. SERVES: Riverside, San Bernardino Counties.

INLAND EMPIRE SMALL BUSINESS DEV
High Desert SBDC
15490 Civic Dr., Ste 102
Victorville, CA 92392
(760) 951-1592
(760) 951-8929 FAX

Business consulting and low-cost seminars to small businesses. Consulting minimal to free charge. FUNDING: Federal grants. OFC HRS: M-F 8am-5pm. SERVES: Northern Inland Empire.

INLAND EMPIRE UNITED WAY
Chamber of Commerce
7945 Vineyard Ave., Ste D5
Rancho Cucamonga, CA 91730
(909) 888-9011

Mission is to engage a caring community to respond to human need by: helping disadvantaged kids succeed in school, providing easy access to health and social srvs, developing op-

portunities for volunteers to create positive change, strengthening financial stability opportunities for low-income familes and individuals. FUNDING: Nonprofit. OFC HRS: M-F 8am-5pm. Free srvs. SERVES: Pomona Valley, Redlands/Yucaipa, Palo Verde Valley, Western San Bernardino County.

INTERNAL REVENUE SERVICE (IRS)
Taxpayer Edu
P.O. Box 30210
24000 Avila Rd., Ste 3401
Laguna Niguel, CA 92677
(949) 389-4002
(949) 389-5023 FAX

IRS and the Franchise Tax Board co-sponsor two prgms to assist taxpayers with prep of their state and federal income tax returns. VITA (Volunteer Income Tax Assist) and TCE (Tax Counseling for the Elderly) volunteers offer free tax prep assist Feb 1-April 15 at many community locations. OFC HRS: Tu, Th, F 8:30am-4:30pm; closed from 1pm-2pm. SERVES: So. Calif, except L.A. County.

IRS HELPLINES
Internal Revenue Services
(800) 829-1040

Free tax assist for all taxpayers. During filing season (Jan 1-April 15) assist 24 hrs a day. Automated info on the status of a refund or for recorded tax info, call TeleTax (above number) 24 hrs all yr. For IRS publications or tax forms (800) 829-3676. TDD (800) 829-4059. FUNDING: Govt. OFC HRS: M-F 7am-10pm. Spanish spoken. SERVES: U.S.A.

KINECTA FEDERAL CREDIT UNION
11563 Foothill Blvd., Ste 101
Rancho Cucamonga, CA 91730
(800) 854-9846

Free checking, loans, home banking, investment info, credit cards, low-cost wire transfer abroad. Mailing Address: P.O. Box 10003, Manhattan Beach, CA, 90266. 24-hr phone: (800)854-9846. FUNDING: Nonprofit. OFC HRS: M-F 7am-7pm; Sat 9am-5pm. Language line available. New member fee $5-$15. SERVES: San Bernardino County.

LIFE SERVICES, INC.
1111 N. Brand Blvd., Ste K
Glendale, CA 91202
(818) 547-0585
(818) 547-1093 FAX

Complete personalized care encompassing medical, financial, social, spiritual, and psych needs for seniors ages 60 yrs+. Srvs include: life care planning, personalized care, professional conservatorship (a guardian), trust mgmt, estate admin and referrals. FUNDING: Client fees, nonprofit. OFC HRS: M-F 9am-4:30pm; 24-hr srvs. Chinese and Spanish spoken. ADM REQ: Ages 60 yrs+. Sliding fee scale. SERVES: L.A. & adjoining counties.

MARCH A.F.B./FAMILY SUPPORT
1261 Graeber St., Bldg. 2313, Rm. 1A
March Air Base, CA 92518-1775
(951) 655-5350
(951) 655-4719 FAX

Info & referral. Assessment and referral assist to families in crisis, support during family separation, relocation assist, skill workshops as needed on family issues and job search skills. FUNDING: Govt. OFC HRS: M-F 7:30am-4pm

(some weekends). ADM REQ: Military staff or family member. SERVES: March Air Reserve area.

MORENO VALLEY COMMUNITY ASSIST
24594 Sunnymead Blvd., Ste W
Moreno Valley, CA 92553
(951) 485-7792
(951) 485-7792 FAX

Food, clothing and utility assist (Feb & March) to people in need. OFC HRS: Tu,Th 10am-1pm. ADM REQ: Must prove residence and need. Income verification, ID & SS card required. SERVES: Moreno Valley area.

NATIONAL FNDN FOR CREDIT COUNSELING
2000 M Street NW, Ste 505
Washington, DC 20036
(800) 388-2227
(202) 677-4300

Visit (www.NFCC.org) for tips on foreclosure prevention, pre-purchase counseling, homebuyer education, seminars, down payment assist prgms, homeless counseling and more. To speak to a Spanish-speaking counselor, call (800) 682-9832. FUNDING: Nonprofit. SERVES: Nationwide.

NATIONAL GUARD FAMILY PROGRAM
1411 Jefferson Davis Hwy.
Arlington, VA 22202
(703) 607-5411

Offers financial, emotional, and supportive assist to the families of National Guard members. Special prgms to help those who are dealing the deployment of a loved one. Visit (www.jointservicessupport.org). FUNDING: Govt. SERVES: U.S.A.

OPERATION PROVIDER
P.O. Box 26
26517 Pine Ave.
Twin Peaks, CA 92391
(909) 337-8585
(909) 336-4021 FAX

Emerg food Tu, F 12noon-2pm, clothing, info & referral, limited utility assist, motel vouchers, baby food, holiday baskets. FUNDING: Donations, nonprofit. OFC HRS: Tu-F 12noon-2pm. ADM REQ: Proof of income & residency. SERVES: San Bernardino Mountains.

PACIFIC MARINE CREDIT UNION
170 N. Yucca Ave.
Barstow, CA 92311
(800) 736-4500
(760) 256-6572 FAX

Free checking, loans, home banking, investment info, credit cards, low-cost wire transfer abroad. FUNDING: Nonprofit. OFC HRS: M-Th 9am-5pm; F 9am-6pm; Sat 9am-4pm. Spanish spoken. No new member fee. SERVES: San Bernardino County.

PACIFIC MARINE CREDIT UNION
Camp Pendleton Branch
MCX Complex
Camp Pendleton, CA 92055
(800) 736-4500
(760) 385-0142 FAX

Free checking, loans, home banking, investment info, credit cards, low-cost wire transfer abroad. FUNDING: Nonprofit. OFC HRS: M-Th 9am-5pm; F 9am-6pm; Sat 9am-4pm. No new member fee. SERVES: San Diego, Riverside, San Bernardino Counties.

PACIFIC MARINE CREDIT UNION

Bldg. 1515, MCAGCC
Twentynine Palms, CA 92278
(800) 736-4500
(760) 830-7597 FAX

Free checking, loans, home banking, investment info, credit cards, low-cost wire transfer abroad. FUNDING: Nonprofit OFC HRS: M-F 9am-5pm. Spanish spoken. No new member fee. SERVES: San Bernardino County.

PACIFIC MARINE CREDIT UNION

550 Hacienda Dr., Ste 102
Vista 92081
(800) 736-4500
(760) 758-1145 FAX

Free checking, loans, home banking, investment info, credit cards, low-cost wire transfer abroad. FUNDING: Nonprofit. OFC HRS: M-Th 9am-5pm; F 9am-6pm; Sat 9am-4pm. Spanish spoken. No new member fee. SERVES: San Bernardino County.

PACIFIC TRUST BANK

5030 Arlington Ave.
Riverside, CA 92504
(951) 352-5980
(877) 441-5020
(951) 352-0107 FAX

Free checking, loans, home banking, investment info, credit cards, low-cost wire transfer abroad. FUNDING: Nonprofit. OFC HRS: M-Th 9am-5pm; F 9am-6pm; Sat 9am-2pm. Call center hrs: M-Th 8:30am-6pm; F 8:30am-7pm; Sat 9am-4pm. Spanish spoken. No new member fee. SERVES: Riverside County.

PACIFIC TRUST BANK

27425 Ynez Rd.
Temecula, CA 92591
(951) 699-9091
(877) 441-2265
(951) 699-1985 FAX

Free checking, loans, home banking, investment info, credit cards, low-cost wire transfer abroad. Call center hrs: M-F 8:30am-6pm; Sat 9am-4pm. FUNDING: Nonprofit. OFC HRS: M-Th 9am-5pm; F 9am-6pm; Sat 9am-2pm. Spanish spoken. No new member fee. SERVES: Riverside County.

PARTNERSHIP FOR PRESCRIPTION ASSIST

(877) 777-7815

Free or low-cost prescription srv for uninsured, underinsured or those with limited income. Call or visit (www.RXHelpforCA.org). SERVES: Calif.

RIVERSIDE CITY PUBLIC UTILITIES

3460 Orange St.
Riverside, CA 92501
(951) 782-0330

Sharing Households Assist Riverside's Energy (SHARE) fund is a bill assist prgm for qualified low income residential electric & water customers. Utility bills and deposits are paid up to $175 on a one-time basis in a 12 month period. FUNDING: Voluntary contributions and state-mandated electric public benefits charge. OFC HRS: M-F 7am-7pm. Sat 8am-5pm. Foreign languages available upon request. ADM REQ: Must meet income requirements to qualify. SERVES: City of Riverside.

RIVERSIDE CO. CHILD SUPPORT SRVS

260 N. Broadway
Blythe, CA 92225
(866) 901-3212
(760) 921-5608 FAX

Establishes child and medical support orders, paternity orders, locates parents, enforces support orders. Walk in welcome. Send payments to P.O. Box 989067, West Sacramento, CA 95798. FUNDING: Federal, county OFC HRS: M-F 7:30am-5pm. ADM REQ: Application for srvs. Free srvs. SERVES: Riverside County.

RIVERSIDE CO. CHILD SUPPORT SRVS

47-950 Arabia St.
Indio, CA 92201
(866) 901-3212
(760) 863-7016 FAX

Establishes child and medical support orders, paternity orders, locates parents, enforces support orders. Walk in. FUNDING: Federal, county. OFC HRS: M-F 7:30am-5pm. Spanish spoken. ADM REQ: Application for srvs. Free srvs. SERVES: Riverside County.

RIVERSIDE CO. CHILD SUPPORT SRVS

2041 Iowa Ave.
Riverside, CA 92507
(866) 901-3212
(951) 955-4224 FAX

Establishes and/or enforces child and medical support orders, paternity orders, locates noncustodial parents. FUNDING: Federal, county. OFC HRS: M-F 7:30am-5pm. Spanish spoken. ADM REQ: Application for srvs. Free srvs. SERVES: Riverside County.

RIVERSIDE CO. CHILD SUPPORT SRVS

1370 S. State St., Ste A
San Jacinto, CA 92583
(866) 901-3212
(951) 791-2054 FAX

Establishes child and medical support orders, paternity orders, locates parents, enforces support orders. Walk in or call. FUNDING: Federal, county. OFC HRS: M-F 7:30am-5:30pm. Spanish spoken. ADM REQ: Application for srvs. Free srvs. SERVES: Riverside County.

RIVERSIDE CO. PUBLIC SOCIAL SRVS

Income Maintenance/Medi-Cal
P.O. Box 7500
63 S. 4th Street
Banning, CA 92220
(951) 922-7000
(951) 922-7005 FAX

Financial (TANF, CalWORKs, General Relief), nutritional (food stamps), and medical assist (Medi-Cal). Walk in or call. FUNDING: Govt. OFC HRS: M-Th 7am-5:30pm; F 8am-5pm. Spanish, Hmong spoken. SERVES: Banning, Beaumont, Calimesa, Cabazon & Fass area.

RIVERSIDE CO. PUBLIC SOCIAL SRVS

Income Maintenance/Medi-Cal
1225 W. Hobson Way
Blythe, CA 92225
(760) 921-5700
(760) 921-7715 FAX

Financial (TANF, General Relief, etc.), nutritional (food stamps), and medical assist (Medi-Cal). Walk in or call. FUNDING: Govt. OFC HRS: M-Th 7am-5:30pm; F 8am-5pm. Spanish spoken. ADM REQ: Varies per prgm. SERVES: Blythe & nearby.

RIVERSIDE CO. PUBLIC SOCIAL SRVS

Income Maintenance/Medi-Cal
68-615A Perez Rd., Ste 9
Cathedral City, CA 92234
(760) 770-2300
(760) 770-2324 FAX

Financial (TANF, CalWORKS, General Relief, etc.), nutritional (food stamps), and medical assist (Medi-Cal), limited home repair and emerg loans for SSI/SSD recipients. Walk in or call. FUNDING: Govt. OFC HRS: M-Th 7am-5:30pm; F 8am-5pm. Spanish spoken. SERVES: Palm Springs, Cathedral City areas.

RIVERSIDE CO. PUBLIC SOCIAL SRVS

Temp Assist/Medi-Cal/Food Stamps
541 N. San Jacinto St.
Hemet, CA 92543
(951) 791-3000
(951) 791-3050 FAX

Financial (CalWORKs, General Relief, etc.), nutritional (Food Stamps), and medical assist (Medi-Cal). FUNDING: Govt. OFC HRS: M-Th 7am-5:30pm; F 8am-5pm. Spanish spoken. SERVES: Mid-County.

RIVERSIDE CO. PUBLIC SOCIAL SRVS

Income Maintenance/CalWORKs
44-199 Monroe St., Ste D
Indio, CA 92201
(760) 863-2700
(760) 863-2864 FAX

Financial (CalWORKs, General Relief, etc.), nutritional (food stamps), and medical assist (Medi-Cal). Walk in or call. FUNDING: Govt. OFC HRS: M-Th 7am-5:30pm; F 8am-5pm. Spanish spoken. SERVES: Coachella Valley, Indio, Palm Desert, Thermal, Mecca.

RIVERSIDE CO. PUBLIC SOCIAL SRVS

CalWorks/Medi-Cal/Food Stamps
1400 Minthorn St.
Lake Elsinore, CA 92530
(951) 245-3100
(951) 674-5948 FAX

Financial (CalWORKs, GAIN, General Relief, etc.), nutritional (food stamps), and medical assist (Medi-Cal). FUNDING: Govt. OFC HRS: M-Th 7am-5:30pm; F 8am-5pm. ADM REQ: Varies with prgm. SERVES: Mid-Riverside County.

RIVERSIDE CO. PUBLIC SOCIAL SRVS

Income Maintenance/Medi-Cal
3178 Hamner Ave.
Norco, CA 92860
(951) 272-5550
(951) 272-5482 FAX

Financial (TANF, CalWORKs, General Relief, etc.), nutritional (food stamps), and medical assist (Medi-Cal). Walk in or call. FUNDING: Govt. OFC HRS: M-Th 7am-5:30pm; F 8am-5pm. Spanish spoken. ADM REQ: Varies with prgm. SERVES: Norco.

RIVERSIDE CO. PUBLIC SOCIAL SRVS

Temporary Assistance Medical Div
2055 N. Perris Blvd., Ste B
Perris, CA 92571
(951) 940-6600
(951) 940-6610 FAX

Financial (CalWORKs, TANF, General Relief, etc.), nutritional (food stamps), and medical assist (Medi-Cal). Walk in to apply, appts for continuing. FUNDING: Govt. OFC HRS: M-Th

7am-5:30pm; F 8am-5pm. Spanish spoken. SERVES: Riverside County.

RIVERSIDE CO. PUBLIC SOCIAL SRVS
Assistance Programs
11060 Magnolia Ave.
Riverside, CA 92505
(951) 358-3400

Financial (CalWORKs, TANF, General Relief, etc.), nutritional (food stamps), and medical assist (Medi-Cal). Walk in or call. FUNDING: Govt. OFC HRS: M-Th 7am-5:30pm; F 8am-5pm. Spanish, Vietnamese spoken. ASL available. SERVES: Riverside County.

RIVERSIDE CO. PUBLIC SOCIAL SRVS
Income Maintenance/Medi-Cal
43264 Business Park Dr., Ste B1
Temecula, CA 92590
(951) 600-6500
(951) 600-6502 FAX

Financial (CalWORKs, TANF, General Relief, etc.), nutritional (food stamps), and medical assist (Medi-Cal). Walk in or call. FUNDING: Govt. OFC HRS: M-Th 7am-5:30pm; F 8am-5pm. Spanish spoken. ADM REQ: Varies with prgm. SERVES: Mid-County.

SALVATION ARMY/REDLANDS CORPS
P.O. Box 26
838 N. Alta St.
Redlands, CA 92374
(909) 792-6868
(909) 335-3140 FAX

Emerg food. Dinner daily M-F 5pm. Food pantry, emerg materials assist, emerg gas, peer counseling, crisis counseling, referrals for morning showering, utility, rehab assist. in San Bernardino. USDA commodities 4th F 10am-12noon, 1:30pm-4pm. Worship srvs. Walk in. FUNDING: Donations, FEMA, United Way. OFC HRS: M, Tu, Th, F 1:15pm-4pm. ADM REQ: Low income. Free srvs. SERVES: Redlands, Loma Linda, Mentone, Bryn Mawr.

SALVATION ARMY/VICTORVILLE CORPS
14585 La Paz Dr.
Victorville 92395
(760) 245-2545
(760) 245-1130 FAX

Emerg food prgm (Tu, Th, 9am-12noon), emerg temporary shelter (when funds are available), info & referral. Utilities and rent when funds are available. Walk in. FUNDING: Donations, United Way. Phone Hrs: M-F 9am-12noon. ADM REQ: Photo ID, proof of income. SS card or medical card for everyone. Free srvs. SERVES: Victorville, Apple Valley, Hesperia, Lucerne Valley, Adelanto, Oro Grande, Barstow, Big Bear.

SALVATION ARMY/YUCCA VLY SRVS
56659 Twentynine Palms Hwy., Ste E
Yucca Valley, CA 92284
(760) 228-0114

Comprehensive emerg assist on a case-by-case basis. Food bank on W, utility asst by appt. Certified emerg disaster responders. Other resources as available. Inquiries welcome. FUNDING: United Way, county, donations, nonprofit. OFC HRS: Tu-Th 10am-3pm. SERVES: Morongo Basin.

SAN BERNARDINO CO. CHILD SUPPORT
Dept of Child Support Services
10417 Mountain View Ave.

Loma Linda, CA 92354
(866) 901-3212
(909) 478-6922 FAX

24-hr info on child support srvs. Represents the interest of the minor children by: (1) determining who the parents are; (2) locating a child's parents for the purpose of establishing child support and/or paternity; (3) establishing and enforcing a child support order; (4) collecting child and spousal support payments. FUNDING: County, state, federal. OFC HRS: M-F 8am-5pm. Spanish spoken. ADM REQ: Demonstrates need for child support srvs. Free srvs. SERVES: San Bernardino County.

SAN BERNARDINO CO. CHILD SUPPORT
Desert Region
15400 Civic Dr.
Victorville, CA 92392
(866) 901-3212
(909) 478-6922 FAX

Establishes paternity & court-ordered child support. Collects child, medical & spousal support payments, also modifies orders. FUNDING: Govt. OFC HRS: M-F 8am-5pm. Spanish spoken. SERVES: San Bernardino County.

SAN BERNARDINO CO. HUMAN SRVS SY
Transitional Assistance
7977 Sierra Ave.
Fontana, CA 92335
(909) 356-3160
(909) 356-3221
(909) 356-3169 FAX

Transitional assist prgms include financial (CalWORKs, General Relief, etc.), nutritional (food stamps), and medical assist (Medi-Cal). Subsidized child care (CalWORKs & alternative payment). FUNDING: Govt. OFC HRS: M-F 8:30am-4:30pm. Spanish spoken. SERVES: Fontana. Child care srvs provided for all San Bernardino County.

SAN BERNARDINO CO. HUMAN SRVS SY
Medi-Cal/TAD/CalWORKs/Food Stamps
1300 Bailey Ave.
Needles, CA 92363
(760) 326-9261
(760) 326-9270 FAX

Income maintenance prgms include: TANF, General Relief, food stamps, Medi-Cal, CalWORKs, child abuse hotline (800) 827-8724, adoption srvs (909) 891-3300. FUNDING: Govt. OFC HRS: M-F 8:30am-4:30pm. Spanish spoken. ADM REQ: Low income. SERVES: San Bernardino County.

SAN BERNARDINO CO. HUMAN SRVS SY
Medi-Cal
1627 E. Holt Blvd.
Ontario, CA 91761
(909) 933-6330
(909) 933-6450 FAX

Income maintenance prgms. Medical assist (Medi-Cal). FUNDING: Govt. OFC HRS: M-F 9am-4pm. Spanish spoken. SERVES: San Bernardino County.

SAN BERNARDINO CO. HUMAN SRVS SY
Income Maintenance/Transitional Assist
2050 N. Massachusetts
San Bernardino, CA 92415
(909) 475-2074
(909) 475-2231 FAX

Income maintenance prgms include financial (CalWORKs, TANF, General Relief, etc.), nutritional (food stamps), and medical assist (Medi-Cal). FUNDING: Govt. OFC HRS: M-F 8:30am-4:30pm. Spanish spoken. SERVES: Specific areas in San Bernardino.

SAN BERNARDINO CO. PUBLIC HEALTH
Administrative Office
385 Arrowhead Ave.
San Bernardino, CA 92415-0120
(909) 387-7020
(909) 387-6228 FAX

Administers branch offices at various locations throughout San Bernardino Co. including: Barstow, Big Bear, Chino, Fontana, Joshua Tree, Needles, Ontario, Redlands, San Bernardino, Trona, Victorville & Twin Peaks. Edu, alcohol & drug prevention, animal control, birth & death certificates, Calif Children's Srvs, epidemiology, family planning, high-risk infant prgm, immunizations, nutrition, WIC, public health nursing, school health, senior health, VD control, TB, HIV/AIDS control. TDD (909) 397-6354. OFC HRS: M-F 8am-5pm; clinic hrs may vary. SERVES: San Bernardino County.

SO CALIF EDISON/LOW INCOME PRGM
Low Income Programs Dept
12701 Schabarum Ave.
Rosemead, CA 91770
(800) 736-4777
(626) 302-8313 FAX

Low income customers should call about energy efficiency srvs to needy customers; efficient lighting, evaporative coolers & weatherization. Qualifying customers may also be eligible for a 15% discount on electricity rates. OFC HRS: M-F 8am-5pm. Spanish spoken. SERVES: L.A., Orange, Riverside & San Bernardino Counties.

SPRINGBOARD CONSUMER CREDIT MGMT
1555 W. Florida Ave.
Hemet, CA 92543
(800) 947-3752
(951) 781-0114

Free & low-cost budget & credit counseling, edu classes, debt mgmt prgm. Housing pre-purchase, housing delinquency counseling. Counseling via internet, phone, in person. FUNDING: Nonprofit OFC HRS: M-F 5am-9pm; Sat 6am-3pm; Sun 9am-5pm. Spanish spoken. SERVES: Riverside County.

SPRINGBOARD CONSUMER CREDIT MGMT
Headquarters
28570 Marguerite Pkwy., Ste 210
Mission Viejo, CA 92692
(877) 947-3752
(951) 781-0114
(951) 781-8027 FAX

Assists consumers in money mgmt and debt liquidation plans with their creditors. Certified counselors. HUD-approved housing counseling agency can help with foreclosure prevention. Approved for tax debt repayment. First time homebuyers and edu prgms. FUNDING: Nonprofit. OFC HRS: M-F 5am-9pm; Sat 8am-3pm; Sun 9am-5pm. Spanish spoken. Free confidential counseling in person, over the Internet or by phone 24 hrs. SERVES: So. Calif.

SPRINGBOARD CONSUMER CREDIT MGMT

1001 S. Palm Canyon Dr., Ste 103
Palm Springs, CA 92262
(800) 947-3752
(951) 781-0114

Free & low-cost budget edu classes, debt mgmt prgm, housing pre-purchase, housing delinquency counseling. Counseling via Internet, phone, in person. FUNDING: Nonprofit. OFC HRS: M-F 5am-9pm; Sat 6am-3pm; Sun 9am-5pm. Spanish spoken. SERVES: Riverside County.

SPRINGBOARD CONSUMER CREDIT MGT

1814 Commercenter West, Ste B
San Bernardino, CA 92408
(877) 947-3752

Free & low-cost budget edu classes, debt mgmt prgm, housing pre-purchase, housing delinquency counseling. Counseling via Internet, phone, in person. FUNDING: Nonprofit. OFC HRS: M-F 5am-9pm; Sat 6am-3pm; Sun 9am-5pm. Spanish spoken. SERVES: San Bernardino County.

SUMMIT PAYEE SRVS, INC.

1361 North E Street
San Bernardino, CA 92405
(909) 884-5299
(951) 263-9527
(909) 885-2859 FAX

Approved representative payee srvs through the Social Security Administration. FUNDING: Nonprofit. OFC HRS: M-F 9am-4pm. ADM REQ: Inability to manage financial resources. SERVES: Inland Empire. Srvs also available in limited areas throughout So Calif.

SWEET RELIEF MUSICIANS FUND

4952 Warner Ave., Ste 242
Huntington Beach, CA 92649
(714) 846-3030
(714) 846-3636 FAX

Provides financial assist to all types of career musicians who are struggling to make ends meet while facing illness, disability or age-related problems. For more info, please visit (www.sweetrelief.org). FUNDING: Nonprofit. OFC HRS: M-Th 8:30am-5:30pm; F 8:30am-5pm. ADM REQ: Must meet eligibility requirements. Free srvs. SERVES: U.S.A.

TANF

Temporary Assistance/Needy Families

See "San Bernardino Co. Human Srvs Sy" and "Riverside Co. Public Social Srvs"

THE GOLDEN 1 CREDIT UNION

2254 S. Euclid Ave.
Ontario, CA 91762
(877) 465-3361

Free checking, loans, home banking, investment info, credit cards, low-cost wire transfer abroad. TDD (916)363-7407. FUNDING: Nonprofit. OFC HRS: M-Th 9am-5:30pm; F 9am-6pm; Sat 10am-2pm. Spanish spoken. New member fee $2. Min of $101 in savings account. SERVES: San Bernardino County.

THE U.S. UNINSURED HELPLINE

(800) 234-1317

Hotline available 24 hrs, 7 days to assist the uninsured with navigating free and low-cost health insurance options. FUNDING: Nonprofit. OFC HRS: 24 hrs, 7 days. Spanish spoken. Free srvs. SERVES: U.S.A.

TRINITY COMM OUTREACH CORP

29175 Ironwood Ave.
Moreno Valley, CA 92555
(951) 601-0253
(951) 601-0412 FAX

Parenting classes to teach democratic parenting techniques. Practical discipline method, guidelines for building self-esteem and better family communication. Must attend all sessions to obtain a certificate of completion. Also small group financial study. A 12-week in-depth study of all that scripture teaches about money. Topics include: debt, spending, earning, saving, investing, giving and teaching children how to handle money. FUNDING: Client fees, nonprofit. OFC HRS: Tu-F 9am-4pm. Registration fee is $30 per individual or $40 per married couple which covers the cost of the study manuals and workbooks. SERVES: Riverside County.

UNIVERSITY OF CALIF COOP EXT

21150 Box Springs Rd., Ste 202
Moreno Valley, CA 92557-8718
(951) 683-6491
(951) 788-2615 FAX

Informal edu branch of Univ of Calif. Disseminates research findings to the general public via meetings, media, conferences, workshops, demonstrations, field days, newsletters & manuals. Workshops on nutrition, food safety, money mgmt, agriculture & urban horticulture. The Master Gardener Prgm provides info about gardening and landscaping. Workshops periodically. Answer gardening questions by phone M-F 9am-12noon. FUNDING: Govt. OFC HRS: M-F 9am-5pm. Closed 12noon-1pm for lunch. Spanish spoken. SERVES: Riverside County.

UNIVERSITY OF CALIF COOP EXT

777 E. Rialto Ave.
San Bernardino, CA 92415
(909) 387-2171
(909) 387-3306 FAX

Education: agricultural production, dairy, master food preservation and master gardeners assist, consumer edu, family budgeting and finances, Univ of Calif publications (free catalog), Family Nutrition info and 4-H youth prgm (ages 5-19). Master Gardeners Prgm hours vary, call (909) 387-2182 or email mgsanber@ucdavis.edu. FUNDING: County, state, federal, nonprofit. OFC HRS: Vary. Spanish spoken. ADM REQ: County resident. SERVES: San Bernardino County.

USA FEDERAL CREDIT UNION

Lake Elsinore Marketplace
29261 Central Ave., Ste C
Lake Elsinore, CA 92532
(888) 842-6328

Free checking, loans, home banking, investment info, credit cards, low-cost wire transfer abroad. FUNDING: Nonprofit. OFC HRS: M-F 10am-6pm; Sat 9am-3pm. Membership fee $5. Must have $5 in savings account at all times. SERVES: Lake Elsinore.

USA FEDERAL CREDIT UNION

Madison Marketplace
25359 Madison Ave., Ste 105
Murrieta, CA 92562
(888) 842-6328
(858) 831-8192 FAX

Free checking, loans, home banking, investment info, credit cards, low-cost wire transfer abroad. FUNDING: Nonprofit. OFC HRS: M-F 10am-6pm; Sat 9am-3pm. Spanish spoken. New member fee $5. Must have $5 in savings account at all times. SERVES: Riverside County.

USA FEDERAL CREDIT UNION

Bel Villaggio Center
41273 Margarita Rd., Ste 101
Temecula, CA 92591
(888) 842-6328
(858) 831-8192 FAX

Free checking, loans, home banking, investment info, credit cards, low-cost wire transfer abroad. FUNDING: Nonprofit. OFC HRS: M-F 10am-6pm; Sat 9am-3pm. Spanish spoken. New member fee $5. Must have $5 in savings account at all times. SERVES: Riverside County.

VISTERRA CREDIT UNION

Corona Branch
650 S. Lincoln Ave., Ste 101
Corona, CA 92882
(800) 755-2347
(951) 656-5121 FAX

Free checking, loans, home banking, investment info, credit cards, low-cost wire transfer abroad. FUNDING: Nonprofit. OFC HRS: M-Th 9am-5pm; F 9am-6pm; Sat 9am-2pm. ADM REQ: Live, work or attend school in Riverside County, or immediate family or household member of current Visterra CU member. New member fee $5. SERVES: Riverside County.

VISTERRA CREDIT UNION

P.O. Box 9500
23540 Cactus Ave.
Moreno Valley, CA 92553
(951) 656-4411
(800) 755-2347
(951) 656-5121 FAX

Free checking, loans, home banking, investment info, credit cards, low-cost wire transfer abroad. FUNDING: Nonprofit. Lobby HRS: M-Th 9am-5pm; F 9am-6pm; Sat 9am-2pm. Drive-up M-Th 8am-6pm; F 8am-7pm; Sat 8am-2pm. ADM REQ: Live, work or attend school in Riverside County, or immediate family or household member of current Visterra CU member. New member fee $5. SERVES: Riverside County.

VISTERRA CREDIT UNION

25040 Hancock Ave.
Murrieta, CA 92562
(951) 656-4411
(800) 755-2347
(951) 656-5121 FAX

Free checking, loans, home banking, investment info, credit cards, low-cost wire transfer abroad. FUNDING: Nonprofit. OFC HRS: M-Th 9am-5pm; F 9am-6pm; Sat 9am-2pm. ADM REQ: Live, work or attend school in Riverside County, or immediate family or household member of current Visterra CU member. New member fee $5. SERVES: Murrieta.

WELFARE

See "San Bernardino Co. Human Srvs Sy"

WESCOM CREDIT UNION

Inside Albertson's

3255 Grand Ave.
Chino Hills, CA 91709
(888) 493-7266

Free checking, loans, home banking, investment info, credit cards, low-cost wire transfer abroad. TTY (888)937-2661. Apply online (www.wescom.org). FUNDING: Nonprofit. OFC HRS: M-F 9am-6pm; Sat 9am-4pm. Language line available. $100 min deposit. SERVES: San Bernardino County.

WESCOM CREDIT UNION

4330 E. Mills Circle
Ontario, CA 91764
(888) 493-7266

Free checking, loans, home banking, investment info, credit cards, low-cost wire transfer abroad. TTY (888)937-2661. Apply online (www.wescom.org). FUNDING: Nonprofit. OFC HRS: M-F 9am-6pm; Sat 9am-4pm. Language line available. $100 min deposit. SERVES: San Bernardino County.

WESCOM CREDIT UNION

3825 Tyler St.
Riverside, CA 92503
(888) 493-7266

Free checking, loans, home banking, investment info, credit cards, low-cost wire transfer abroad. FUNDING: Nonprofit. OFC HRS: M-F 9am-6pm; Sat 9am-4pm. Language line available. $100 min deposit. SERVES: Riverside County.

WWW.CALMEDICARE.ORG

Medicare info
5380 Elvas Ave.
Sacramento, CA 95819
(800) 434-0222
(916) 231-5114 FAX

Visit website or call for info on prescription drugs, Medicare coverage, counseling, fraud, low income help. FUNDING: Calif Healthcare Fndn, nonprofit. OFC HRS: M-F 8am-4pm. SERVES: Calif.

WWW.HUD.GOV/FORECLOSURE/

Visit this site to find info regarding foreclosure. Talk to a housing counselor in your state, find resources, and tips. SERVES: Nationwide.

WWW.WECONNECT.NET

A website designed to assist working families with resources and programs designed to help with financial stability. FUNDING: Nonprofit. SERVES: Calif.

AARP/PHARMACY SERVICE

Walgreens Health Initiatives
P.O. Box 2301
Muscle Shoals, AL 35662
(877) 422-7719
(800) 530-5014 FAX

Prescriptions and non-prescriptions at lower cost by mail. Srv not limited to AARP members. Allow 7 days for delivery. TTY (800) 925-0178. FUNDING: Nonprofit. OFC HRS: 24 hrs, 7 days. Pharmacist hrs: M-F 8am-4:30pm, EST. Spanish spoken. Accepts Medi-Cal. SERVES: U.S.A.

ACCESS FOR INFANTS/MOTHERS (AIM)

Calif Major Risk Medical Ins. Board
P.O. Box 15559
Sacramento, CA 95852-0559
(800) 433-2611
(888) 889-9238 FAX

Maternity, delivery and infant care srvs for mid-income women between 200-300% of the Federal Poverty Level. Low-cost prenatal health insurance to uninsured pregnant women who are not receiving health care through Medi-Cal. The cost is 2% of her family's gross income. The policy pays 100% of the medical costs during the pregnancy, plus post-partum care for 60 days and the medical cost for the infant during the first two years of life. Insurance renewal after infant's 2nd year is $100 or $50 with proof of immunization. For payments: P.O. Box 15207, Sacramento, CA 95851. FUNDING: State. OFC HRS: M-F 8am-8pm; Sat 8am-5pm. Spanish spoken. ADM REQ: Calif resident; expectant mother must be no more than 30 weeks pregnant. SERVES: Calif.

AEROBICS/FITNESS ASSN OF AMER

15250 Ventura Blvd., Ste 200
Sherman Oaks, CA 91403
(877) 968-7263
(818) 990-5468 FAX

Professional organization that promotes safety and excellence in exercise instruction. World's largest fitness educator offering certifications in aerobics, personal training, step, kickboxing, emerg response, Fitness Practitioner (AFP) and the Wave Workout. OFC HRS: M-F 6:30am-6:30pm; Sat 9am-1pm. Spanish spoken. SERVES: Internatl.

ALISA ANN RUCH BURN FOUNDATION

Administrative Office
2501 W. Burbank Blvd., Ste 201
Burbank, CA 91505
(800) 242-2876
(818) 848-0223
(818) 848-0296 FAX

Free brochures & info on burn prevention & care. Assist to burn survivors of all ages including counseling, summer camp, back-to-school, back-to-work, resourcing assist for medical care & therapeutic aids. Support groups meet monthly at various sites. FUNDING: Donations, nonprofit. OFC HRS: M-F 9am-3pm. Free srvs. SERVES: Calif.

ALIVE AND WELL

AIDS Alternatives
11684 Ventura Blvd.
Studio City, CA 91604
(818) 780-1875
(877) 922-5483
(818) 780-7093 FAX

Support, edu, and advocacy network. Free monthly events, distributes free info packets upon request. Also provides referrals and resources. Please e-mail (info@aliveandwell.org) or visit website (www.aliveandwell.org). FUNDING: Nonprofit, donations. Spanish and Italian spoken. SERVES: U.S.A.

ALLERGY & ASTHMA NETWORK

Mothers of Asthmatics
8201 Greensboro Dr, Ste 300
Mc Lean, VA 22102
(800) 878-4403
(703) 573-7794 FAX

Worldwide health edu assn dedicated to assisting and educating families with asthma and allergies. Monthly newsletter, quarterly magazine, and other resources. Donation-based membership (any dollar amount) includes publications. FUNDING: Subsidy, donations, selling of resource materials, nonprofit. OFC HRS: M-Th 8am-5pm; F 9am-12noon, EST. Spanish spoken. SERVES: U.S.A. & internatl.

ALS ASSOCIATION/NATIONAL

National Office (Lou Gehrig's Disease)
27001 Agoura Rd., Ste 250
Calabasas Hills, CA 91301-5104
(818) 880-9007
(818) 880-9006 FAX

Info, resource and referral srv for ALS patients & families. Public awareness and research support to find the cause and cure of ALS (Lou Gehrig's Disease). Support groups, patient srvs prgms. Patient hotline: (800) 782-4747. FUNDING: Donations, nonprofit. OFC HRS: M-F 7:30am-4pm. Free srvs. SERVES: U.S.A.

ALZHEIMER'S DISEASE EDU & REFERRAL

Natl Institute on Aging
P.O. Box 8250
Silver Spring, MD 20907-8250
(800) 438-4380
(301) 495-3334 FAX

Info, publications & referrals on Alzheimer's disease. Online order form for publications. After hrs recording accepts phone number and address for publications. TTY (800) 222-4225. Visit (www.alzheimers.org). FUNDING: Govt. OFC HRS: M-F 8:30am-5pm, EST. Spanish spoken. SERVES: U.S.A.

ALZHEIMER'S DISEASE RES/TREATMT CTR

UCI Institute for Memory Impairments
1100 Gottschalk Medical Plaza
Irvine, CA 92697
(949) 824-2382
(949) 824-3049 FAX

Specialized multidisciplinary assessment & treatment srvs for individuals with dementia or memory problems. Family conferences, ongoing support groups, and referral to other community resources as needed. Participation in ongoing univ research, including clinical drug trials and behavior studies. Testing available. The center is one of 11 state-designated ARCCs and operates at the UCI College of Medicine in Irvine. FUNDING: Nonprofit. OFC HRS: M-F 8:30am-5pm. Spanish & Vietnamese spoken. Accepts Medicare, Medi-Cal supplemental insurance and pvt payment. SERVES: So. Calif.

AMERICAN ACAD OF FAM PHYSICIANS

P.O. Box 11210
11400 Tomahawk Creek Pkwy.
Shawnee Mission, KS 66207-1210
(800) 274-2237
(913) 906-6000
(913) 906-6075 FAX

Medical assn of physicians and medical students. FUNDING: Nonprofit. OFC HRS: M-F 9am-5pm. SERVES: U.S.A.

AMERICAN ACAD OF PEDIATRICS

141 Northwest Point Blvd.
Elk Grove Village, IL 60007-1098
(847) 434-4000
(847) 434-8000 FAX

Organization of 55,000 primary care pediatricians, pediatric medical sub-specialists, and pediatric surgical specialists dedicated to the health, safety and well-being of infants, children, adolescents and young adults. FUNDING: Nonprofit.

AMERICAN ASSN OF KIDNEY PATIENTS

3505 E. Frontage Rd., Ste 315
Tampa, FL 33607-1796
(800) 749-2257
(813) 636-8100
(813) 636-8122 FAX

Helps fellow kidney patients & their families deal with the physical, social & emotional impacts of kidney disease. Advocates for rights of kidney patients, publishes bi-monthly magazine (Renalife), monitors legislative issues, and supports chapters located across the country. FUNDING: Donations, grants, nonprofit. OFC HRS: M-F 8:30am-4:30pm, EST. SERVES: U.S.A.

AMERICAN BOARD/MED SPECIALTIES

222 N. La Salle St., Ste 1500
Chicago, IL 60601
(312) 436-2600
(847) 491-9091
(847) 328-3596 FAX

Represents 24 approved medical certification boards in the U.S. & verifies board certification of physicians for consumers only. FUNDING: Member boards. OFC HRS: M-F 8:30am-5pm, CST. SERVES: U.S.A.

AMERICAN BRAIN TUMOR ASSN

2720 River Rd.
Des Plaines, IL 60018
(847) 827-9910
(800) 886-2282
(847) 827-9918 FAX

Publications on brain tumors, treatment & coping for all ages. Nationwide listings of support groups and physicians who offer investigative treatments, free social work consultations & resource info. Connections & Bridges (pen-pal prgms), mentorship prgm for new brain tumor support group leaders. Funding for brain tumor research across the U.S. & Canada. FUNDING: Nonprofit. OFC HRS: M-F 9am-5pm, CST. Free srvs to patients and their families. SERVES: U.S.A. & internatl.

AMERICAN CANCER SOCIETY

Desert Palms Unit
73-161 Fred Waring Dr., Ste 100
Palm Desert, CA 92260
(760) 568-2691
(800) 227-2345
(760) 341-8783 FAX

Info, guidance, volunteer visitor prgm, support groups, transportation to treatment, medical equipment loans, edu prgms, including smoking cessation, nutrition, breast self-exam and others. FUNDING: Nonprofit. OFC HRS: M-F 9am-5pm. Spanish spoken. ADM REQ: Cancer patients, family members & community. Free srvs. SERVES: Coachella Valley, Blythe & Morongo Basin.

AMERICAN CANCER SOCIETY

Inland Empire Unit
6355 Riverside Ave., Ste A
Riverside, CA 92506
(951) 683-6415
(951) 682-6804 FAX

Info, guidance & edu on prevention and early detection of cancer, transportation assist, wheelchair and hospital beds loaned for home use as available. Support and encouragement by volunteers. Wait: depends on srv. FUNDING: Nonprofit. OFC HRS: M-F 9am-5pm. Spanish spoken. ADM REQ: Cancer patients and family members. Free srvs. SERVES: Riverside, San Bernardino Counties.

AMERICAN CHRONIC PAIN ASSN (ACPA)

Internatl Office
P.O. Box 850
Rocklin, CA 95677
(916) 632-0922
(800) 533-3231
(916) 632-3208 FAX

Support groups, teaches coping skills to maximize life. FUNDING: Donations, grants, nonprofit. OFC HRS: M-F 9am-5pm. 24-hr answering machine. Free srvs, membership fees. SERVES: U.S.A.

AMERICAN COLL/ALLERGY/IMMUN

Allergy & Asthma Resource
85 W. Algonquin Rd., Ste 550
Arlington Heights, IL 60005-4425
(800) 842-7777
(847) 427-1200
(847) 427-1294 FAX

Will send info on allergies and immunology nationally. SERVES: U.S.A.

AMERICAN COUNCIL FOR HEADACHE EDU

American Headache Society
19 Mantua Rd.
Mount Royal, NJ 08061
(856) 423-0043
(856) 423-0082 FAX

Partnership dedicated to raising public awareness of headaches as a valid, biologically based illness as well as increasing treatment & mgmt methods. Info, edu, & support. FUNDING: Nonprofit. SERVES: U.S.A.

AMERICAN DIABETES ASSOCIATION

National Office
1701 N. Beauregard St.
Alexandria, VA 22311
(800) 342-2383

(703) 549-6995 FAX

Free info packet provides literature, info on health edu and refers to local affiliates for support group assist. FUNDING: Nonprofit. OFC HRS: M-F 8:30am-8pm, EST. Spanish spoken. SERVES: U.S.A.

AMERICAN DIABETES ASSOCIATION

5060 Shoreham Place., Ste 100
San Diego, CA 92102-1022
(619) 234-9897
(858) 824-9424 FAX

Literature, physician referral, support group referral, patient, public and professional edu, Camp Conrad/Chinnock (summer camp for insulin dependent children), diet and nutritional info. Diabetes info available, call (888) 342-2383. OFC HRS: M-F 8:30am-5pm. SERVES: Riverside, Palm Desert, Palm Springs, Rancho Mirage, Indian Wells, & San Bernardino County.

AMERICAN DIETETIC HOTLINE

See "Consumer Nutrition Info Line"

AMERICAN HEART ASSOCIATION

Los Angeles County Division
816 S. Figueroa St.
Los Angeles, CA 90017
(213) 291-7000
(800) 439-2911
(213) 291-7001 FAX

Prgms & info about heart disease prevention and stroke, rehab, treatment and comm resources. Professional edu prgm. Funds cardiovascular & stroke research, comm prgms. FUNDING: Donations, nonprofit. OFC HRS: M-F 8:30am-5pm. SERVES: Calif, Nevada and Utah.

AMERICAN HEART ASSOCIATION

Palm Desert Division
P.O. Box 1639
74-020 Alessandro, Ste A
Palm Desert, CA 92260
(760) 346-8109
(760) 773-0766 FAX

School site, healthcare site, and community site prgms, speaker's bureau. FUNDING: Nonprofit. OFC HRS: M-F 9am-5pm. SERVES: Coachella Valley.

AMERICAN HEART ASSOCIATION

Inland Empire Division
1700 Iowa Ave., Ste 240
Riverside, CA 92507
(310) 424-4160
(951) 684-3162 FAX

School site prgms, heart health info, speaker's bureau, health fair info. Limited free literature. FUNDING: Donations, nonprofit. OFC HRS: M-F 8:30am-5pm. Spanish spoken. SERVES: Riverside, San Bernardino Counties.

AMERICAN HOLISTIC HEALTH ASSN

P.O. Box 17400
Anaheim, CA 92817-7400
(714) 779-6152

AHHA encourages participation in creating personal wellness. Provides lists of self-help resources that promote a holistic approach, considering the whole person and wellness-oriented lifestyles. No on-site srvs. Call or mail request. All materials are free. FUNDING: Donations, nonprofit. OFC HRS: Vary. Volunteer staff. SERVES: U.S.A.

AMERICAN INST/CANCER RESEARCH

1759 R Street, NW
Washington, DC 20009
(800) 843-8114
(202) 328-7226 FAX

Fosters research on diet, nutrition and cancer, & educates the public on the results. Free edu materials, quarterly newsletter, nutrition hotline, cancer resource for newly diagnosed patients, pen pals support network, memorial donations, gift annuities and estate planning. Call to request info. FUNDING: Donations, grants, nonprofit. OFC HRS: M-F 8:30am-6pm. Free srvs. SERVES: U.S.A.

AMERICAN KIDNEY FUND (AKF)

6110 Executive Blvd., Ste 1010
Rockville, MD 20852
(800) 638-8299
(301) 881-3052
(301) 881-0898 FAX

Directs financial aid to needy dialysis patients, transplant recipients and kidney donors to help cover the cost of treatment-specific expenses. Grants to assist patients in affording medication, transportation, emerg transient dialysis, special diet needs. Fund also supports public and prof edu, kidney donor dev & research. Publishes many brochures about kidney disease and its treatment, including selections in Spanish. FUNDING: Donations, grants, nonprofit. OFC HRS: M-Th 9am-5pm; F 9am-3pm, EST. Spanish spoken. ADM REQ: Must have chronic renal failure. Free srvs. SERVES: U.S.A.

AMERICAN LEPROSY MISSIONS

1 Alm Way
Greenville, SC 29601
(800) 543-3135
(864) 271-7040
(864) 271-7062 FAX

Raises funds to treat & cure people affected by leprosy around the world. FUNDING: Donations, grants, govt, nonprofit. OFC HRS: M-Th 8am-5pm; F 8am-12noon. SERVES: U.S.A. & internatl.

AMERICAN LIVER FNDN/SAN DIEGO

2515 Camino del Rio South, Ste 122
San Diego, CA 92108
(619) 291-5483
(619) 295-7181 FAX

Edu prgms about liver disease & Hepatitis. Monthly support groups for patients & families. FUNDING: Nonprofit. OFC HRS: M-F 8am-5pm. Materials in Spanish, Chinese, Vietnamese. No fees. SERVES: San Diego, Riverside & Imperial Counties.

AMERICAN LIVER FOUNDATION

75 Maiden Lane, Ste 603
New York, NY 10038
(800) 465-4837
(212) 668-1000
(212) 483-8179 FAX

Makes physician and support group referrals and offers info, including fact sheets. Single copies of liver disease info are available at no cost. Also (888) 443-7872. FUNDING: Donations, member dues, nonprofit. OFC HRS: M-F 9am-5pm. SERVES: U.S.A.

AMERICAN LUNG ASSN/INLAND CO.

441 MacKay Dr.

San Bernardino, CA 92408
(909) 884-5864
(800) 586-4872
(909) 884-6249 FAX

Edu prgms for schools, smoking cessation prgms for businesses and general public (Freedom From Smoking Prgm, 8-session smoking cessation clinic). Better Breathers Club support group for patients with lung disease. Also asthma summer camp for ages 8-14 yrs. Also give referrals to local cessation clinics. FUNDING: Community health charities, Christmas Seals, donations, nonprofit. OFC HRS: M-F 8:30am-4:30pm. Spanish spoken. Free srvs. SERVES: Riverside, San Bernardino, Inyo & Mono Counties.

AMERICAN PAIN FOUNDATION
201 N. Charles St., Ste 710
Baltimore, MD 21201-4111
(888) 615-7246
(410) 385-1832 FAX

Info clearinghouse for pain mgmt. Advocacy, research & support. FUNDING: Nonprofit. SERVES: U.S.A.

AMERICAN PARKINSON DISEASE ASSN
10850 Wilshire Blvd., Ste 230
Los Angeles, CA 90024
(800) 908-2732
(310) 474-0292 FAX

Info, support and medical referrals to patients, families and caregivers in U.S. FUNDING: Donations, nonprofit. OFC HRS: M-F 9am-5pm. Spanish spoken. Free srvs. SERVES: U.S.A.

AMERICAN PARKINSON DISEASE ASSN
135 Parkinson Ave., Ste 4B
Staten Island, NY 10305-1425
(800) 223-2732
(718) 981-8001
(718) 981-4399 FAX

Info & referrals to patients and families for support groups and treatment centers. Supports research to discover cause & cure of Parkinson's. FUNDING: Donations, nonprofit. OFC HRS: M-F 8:30am-4:30pm, EST. Spanish and Italian spoken. Free info packet is available. SERVES: U.S.A.

AMERICAN PARKINSON DISEASE ASSN
Info & Referral Ctr
25 N. Winfield Rd.
Winfield, IL 60190
(877) 223-3801
(630) 933-4380 FAX

Info & support to young people diagnosed with Parkinson's Disease. For more info, visit (www.apdaparkinson.org). FUNDING: Nonprofit. OFC HRS: M-F 9am-5pm, CST. Free srvs. SERVES: U.S.A.

AMERICAN SLEEP APNEA ASSN
6856 Eastern Ave., NW, Ste 203
Washington, DC 20012
(202) 293-3650
(202) 293-3656 FAX

Find resources and support group contacts at (www.sleepapnea.org). FUNDING: Nonprofit. OFC HRS: M-F 9am-5pm, EST. SERVES: U.S.A.

AMERICAN SOC/DERM SURGERY
American Society/Dermatologic Surgery
P.O. Box 4014
Schaumburg, IL 60168

(847) 330-0230
(866) 503-7546
(847) 240-1859 FAX

Info about surgical treatment for skin conditions and procedures as well as referrals to dermatologic surgeons in local areas. Some common questions are about laser surgery, liposuction, varicose veins, laser resurfacing, chemical peel treatment, hair loss, acne scarring, etc. Address above is for mailing only. Physical address: 930 E. Woodfield Rd., Schaumburg, IL 60173. Additional office: 1445 New York Ave., N.W., Ste. 800., Washington, D.C. 20005. FUNDING: Membership, donations, nonprofit. OFC HRS: M-F 8:30am-5pm, CST. SERVES: U.S.A.

AMERICAN SOC/PLASTIC SURGEONS (ASPS)
Referral Srvs
444 E. Algonquin Rd.
Arlington Heights, IL 60005
(888) 475-2784
(847) 228-9131 FAX

Assists members of the public in their search for qualified plastic surgeons in their area. Callers are mailed three active members who practice in the geographic area specified and are certified by the American Board of Plastic Surgery. After hours and interactive phone message system gives callers the option of leaving specific info to receive referrals automatically. Referral srvs also available at (www.plasticsurgery.org). FUNDING: Nonprofit. OFC HRS: M-F 8:30am-4:30pm, CST. SERVES: U.S.A.

AMERICAN STROKE ASSN/HEART ASSN
Division of American Heart Assn
7272 Greenville Ave.
Dallas, TX 75231
(888) 478-7653
(214) 706-5231 FAX

Wide array of prgms, products & srvs, from patient edu & info to scientific statements with cutting-edge info for health care professionals. Info on stroke risk factors and warning signs. Life after a stroke resources, referrals and access to support groups. Stroke Connection magazine is a bi-monthly publication for stroke survivors, caregivers & health care professionals. Warmline is a srv for families who have experienced stroke. FUNDING: Nonprofit OFC HRS: 24 hrs, 7 days. Interpreter srv available. Free srvs. SERVES: U.S.A.

AMERICAN TINNITUS ASSN
P.O. Box 5
522 S.W 5th Avenue
Portland, OR 97204
(800) 634-8978
(503) 248-9985
(503) 248-0024 FAX

Provides support, advocacy and referrals to people with Tinnitus. Also raises money for research. FUNDING: Nonprofit. OFC HRS: M-F 8:30am-4:30pm. SERVES: U.S.A.

AMERICAN TRAUMA SOCIETY (ATS)
7611 S. Osborne Rd., Ste 202
Upper Marlboro, MD 20772
(800) 556-7890
(301) 574-4300
(301) 574-4301 FAX

Trauma prevention info to health professionals and the public as well as improving trauma care.

Goal is to prevent trauma and improve trauma care. FUNDING: Dues, donations, grants, nonprofit. OFC HRS: M-F 8:30am-4:30pm, EST. Turkish spoken. SERVES: U.S.A.

APLASTIC ANEMIA & MDS INTNL FNDN
100 Park Ave., Ste 108
Rockville, MD 20850
(800) 747-2820
(301) 279-7202
(301) 279-7205 FAX

The Aplastic Anemia & MDS Intnl Fndn (AA & MDSIF) was founded in 1983 to help patients and families around the world with aplastic anemia, myelodysplastic syndromes and PNH. Distributes edu materials, provides emotional support, funds medical research, maintains a voluntary registry and hosts annual internatl conferences, all free of charge. FUNDING: Donations, nonprofit. OFC HRS: M-F 9am-5pm, EST. Spanish spoken. SERVES: Internatl.

ARTHRITIS FNDN/COACHELLA VLY
73-710 Fred Waring Dr., Ste 104
Palm Desert, CA 92260
(760) 773-3076
(760) 773-0858 FAX

Physician referral, exercise classes, monthly lecture series, support groups. Also distributes brochures on all kinds of arthritis. FUNDING: Donations, city grants, nonprofit, events. OFC HRS: M-Th 8:30am-5pm; F 8:30am-4:30pm. Free srvs. SERVES: Desert communities.

ARTHRITIS FNDN/INFO LINE
National Headquarters
P.O. Box 7669
Atlanta, GA 30357
(800) 283-7800
(404) 872-7100
(404) 872-0457 FAX

Current info, printed info on arthritis & referrals to local Arthritis Fndn offices. FUNDING: Nonprofit. OFC HRS: M-F 9am-6pm, EST. 24-hr recorded message. Spanish spoken. SERVES: U.S.A.

ARTHRITIS FNDN/INLAND EMPIRE
P.O. Box 53490
Irvine, CA 92619
(949) 585-0201
(949) 585-0202 FAX

Pamphlets, brochures, edu prgms, exercise classes, support groups, arthritis self-help courses, aquatics prgms offered on over 100 forms of arthritis. FUNDING: Donations, fundraising, nonprofit. OFC HRS: M-Th 8:30am-5pm; F 8:30am-4:30pm. Spanish spoken. SERVES: Riverside & San Bernardino Counties.

ASTHMA & ALLERGY FNDN OF AMER
Southern California Chapter
5900 Wilshire Blvd., Ste 710
Los Angeles, CA 90036
(800) 624-0044
(323) 937-7859
(323) 937-7815 FAX

AAFA provides the following prgms & srvs: summer asthma camp, children's athletic prgms, community & professional edu prgms, physician referrals and certified pollen counts. FUNDING: Donations, grants, nonprofit. OFC HRS: M-F 9am-5pm. Spanish and Tagalog spoken. Free srvs. SERVES: So. Calif.

ASTHMA INFO & REFERRAL LINE
555 E. Wells St., Ste 1100
Milwaukee, WI 53202-3823
(800) 822-2762
(414) 272-6071

Free info packet on asthma and allergies and a referral to specialists practicing in your ZIP code area. Srv of the American Academy of Allergy & Immunology. FUNDING: Nonprofit. OFC HRS: 24 hrs. Spanish spoken. SERVES: U.S.A.

ATTENTION DEFICIT DISORDER ASSN
P.O. Box 7557
Wilmington, DE 19803
(800) 939-1019

Offers info, advocacy, resources, and networking to adults with AD/HD and to the professionals who work with them. Also produces "Focus," the quarterly publication of the organization and an annual national conference. Individual, family, and professional memberships available. FUNDING: Nonprofit. OFC HRS: M-F 8:30am-5pm, EST. SERVES: U.S.A.

AUA FOUNDATION
Formerly Amer Fndn/Urological Disease
1000 Corporate Blvd.
Linthicum, MD 21090
(860) 746-4282
(410) 689-3700
(410) 689-3800 FAX

Call to request printed material about urological diseases. FUNDING: Donations, grants, nonprofit. OFC HRS: M-F 8:30am-5pm, EST. SERVES: U.S.A.

BATTEN DISEASE SUPP/RESEARCH ASSN
166 Humphries Dr.
Reynoldsburg, OH 43068
(800) 448-4570
(740) 927-4298

Batten disease is a life-shortening genetic disease that kills cells, one by one. The four different types are: infantile, late infantile, juvenile and adult. Phone counseling, quarterly newsletter, support groups, literature and referrals to other organizations worldwide, including 16 chapters. FUNDING: Donations, grants, nonprofit. OFC HRS: M-F 8am-5pm. SERVES: U.S.A.

BECKSTRAND CANCER FOUNDATION
P.O. Box 15451
20341 Birch St., Ste 310
Newport Beach, CA 92660
(949) 955-0099
(949) 955-0070 FAX

Assists needy cancer patients and their families through direct aid and support prgms. Weekly youth support prgm (JST 4 KDZ) for ages 6-18 yrs who have a family member with cancer, includes free bereavement counseling. FUNDING: Donations, nonprofit. OFC HRS: M-F 9am-5pm. ADM REQ: Submit application of request for patient assist. SERVES: So. Calif.

BETTER HEARING INSTITUTE (BHI)
1444 I Street, NW, Ste 700
Washington, DC 20005
(800) 327-9355
(202) 449-1100
(202) 216-9646 FAX

Edu organization providing natl public info prgms on hearing loss and available medical, surgical, hearing aid and rehab assist for millions with uncorrected hearing problems. Series of television and print media public service messages include many celebrities who overcame hearing loss. "Hearing HelpLine" provides info on hearing loss and hearing to callers from anywhere in the U.S. and Canada. FUNDING: Nonprofit. OFC HRS: 24 hrs. Free srvs. SERVES: U.S.A.

BIO SCRIP
Formerly Intravenous Therapy Service
320 S. Flower St.
Burbank, CA 91502
(800) 584-0265
(800) 584-0635 FAX

Home care, home infusion, skilled nursing. FUNDING: Nonprofit. OFC HRS: M-F 8:30am-6pm, 24-hr srvs. Spanish, German, Farsi, Russian, Armenian, Greek and Japanese spoken. Accepts insurance for nursing, Medicare, Medi-Cal for pharmacy only. SERVES: So. Calif.

BIRTH CHOICE
277 S. Rancho Santa Fe Rd., Ste S
San Marcos, CA 92069-2343
(760) 744-1313

Counseling, supportive services, info and referrals to medical professionals. Financial aid prgms, post-abortion counseling and adoption srvs. FUNDING: Nonprofit. OFC HRS: M 9am-6pm; Tu-Th 9am-8pm; F 8am-12noon; Sat 10am-12noon. Spanish spoken. Free srvs. SERVES: San Marcos.

BLACK INFANT HEALTH PRGM
Riverside Co. Health Srvs
4065 County Circle Dr., Ste 211
Riverside, CA 92503
(951) 210-1392
(800) 794-4814

Case mgmt & referral for pregnant African-American women. FUNDING: State, govt. OFC HRS: M-F 8am-5pm. Free srvs. SERVES: Riverside County.

BREAST CANCER ANGELS
6889 Andrew Way
Cypress, CA 90630
(562) 795-0100
(714) 898-8966 FAX

Provides financial, emotional and spiritual assist to women and their families as they are going through breast cancer treatment. Visit (www.breastcancerangels.org). FUNDING: Nonprofit. SERVES: Southern Calif.

BREAST CANCER NET OF STRENGTH
Formerly Y-Me Natl Breast Cancer Org
Southland California Affiliate
1901 E. 4th Street, Ste 300
Santa Ana, CA 92705-3918
(714) 361-2106
(714) 361-2120 FAX

Breast cancer edu, support group info. Increases awareness & ensures, through info, empowerment & peer support, that no one faces breast cancer alone. 24-hr hotline available in 150 languages, call (800) 221-2141. For Spanish hotline, call (800) 986-9605. Spanish spoken. SERVES: So. Calif.

BREAST CANCER SOLUTIONS
3843 S. Bristol St., Ste 152
Santa Ana, CA 92704
(866) 960-9222
(866) 781-6068 FAX

Offers financial assist to meet the everyday needs of people undergoing breast cancer treatment. Offers rental, utility, food, medical, and car payment assist. Visit (www.breastcancersolutions.org) for more info. FUNDING: Nonprofit. Spanish spoken. ADM REQ: Receiving breast cancer treatment. Free srvs. SERVES: Southern Calif.

BUDDHIST TZU CHI FREE CLINIC
1000 S. Garfield Ave.
Alhambra, CA 91801
(626) 281-3383
(626) 281-5303 FAX

Clinic provides one-stop medical srvs, including treatment, medicine, lab srvs, X-rays, alternative and dental care to residents who have no other access to medical care. FUNDING: Nonprofit, donations, grants. OFC HRS: Tu-Sat 9am-11:30am, 1pm-5pm. Spanish, Vietnamese & Chinese spoken. ADM REQ: Under 200% of federal poverty guideline & no other health insurance. All ages welcome. Free srvs. SERVES: Southern Calif.

CALIF ACUPUNCTURE BOARD
Dept of Consumer Affairs
P.O. Box 942521
444 N. 3rd Street, Ste 260
Sacramento, CA 95814
(916) 445-3021
(916) 445-3015 FAX

Licenses acupuncturists & enforces laws relating to the practice of acupuncture. FUNDING: Govt. OFC HRS: M-F 8am-5pm. SERVES: Calif.

CALIF BOARD/MEDICAL ASSISTANT
Dept of Consumer Affairs
2005 Evergreen St., Ste 1200
Sacramento, CA 95815
(916) 263-8382
(916) 263-2944 FAX

FUNDING: Govt. OFC HRS: M-F 8am-5pm. Spanish spoken. SERVES: Calif.

CALIF BOARD/MEDICAL LICENSING
Central Complaint Unit
2005 Evergreen St., Ste 1200
Sacramento, CA 95815
(800) 633-2322
(916) 263-2382
(916) 263-2444 FAX

State office licenses & regulates physicians, surgeons and some allied health professions. Central Complaint Unit accepts complaints against physicians & surgeons, physician assists, podiatrists, registered dispensing opticians, medical assistants & midwives. Complaints must be in writing, request forms through (800) number. For info about a physician's license, call (916) 263-2382; TDD (916) 263-2687. FUNDING: Govt. OFC HRS: M-F 8am-5pm. SERVES: Calif.

CALIF BOARD/PHARMACY
1625 N. Market Blvd., Ste N219
Sacramento, CA 95834
(916) 574-7900
(916) 574-8618 FAX

Sets minimum requirements for license & registration of pharmacists, pharmacy interns & pharmacy technicians; inspects & licenses pharmacies, drug wholesalers, clinics & other specialized facilities regularly for compliance with rules & regulations regarding the sale, storage, transportation & dispensing of prescription drugs & products; investigates consumer complaints & other violations of pharmacy law. FUNDING: Govt. OFC HRS: M-F 8am-5pm. SERVES: Calif.

CALIF BOARD/PHYSICAL THERAPY

Dept of Consumer Affairs
2005 Evergreen St., Ste 1350
Sacramento, CA 95815
(916) 561-8200
(916) 263-2560 FAX

Regulates the profession of physical therapy. FUNDING: Govt. OFC HRS: M-F 8am-5pm. SERVES: Calif.

CALIF BOARD/PODIATRIC MEDICINE

Dept of Consumer Affairs
2005 Evergreen St., Ste 1300
Sacramento, CA 95815
(916) 263-2647
(916) 263-2651 FAX

Consumer protection through the proper use of the licensing and enforcement authorities that are assigned to it by the state legislature. License verifications: (916) 263-2382; consumer complaints: (800) 633-2322. FUNDING: Govt. HRS: M-F 8am-5pm. Spanish spoken. SERVES: Calif.

CALIF BOARD/REGISTERED NURSING

P.O. Box 944210
1625 N. Market Blvd., Ste N217
Sacramento, CA 95834-1924
(916) 322-3350
(916) 327-4402 FAX

Licenses registered nurses and certifies nurse midwives, public health nurses, nurse anesthetists, psychiatric mental health nurses, nurse practitioners, clinical nurse specialists and continuing edu providers. Accepts consumer complaints about nurses. Callers must have permanent RD license # to verify license: (800) 838-6828. TDD: (916) 322-1700. FUNDING: Govt. OFC HRS: M-F 8am-5pm. SERVES: Calif.

CALIF BOARD/RESPIRATORY CARE

Depart of Consumer Affairs
444 N. 3rd Street, Ste 270
Sacramento, CA 95811
(916) 323-9983
(866) 375-0386
(916) 323-9999 FAX

Examines, licenses and regulates respiratory care practitioners. Also investigates complaints. FUNDING: Govt. OFC HRS: M-F 8am-5pm. SERVES: Calif.

CALIF BOARD/VOC NURSE/PSYCH TECH

Dept of Consumer Affairs
2535 Capitol Oaks Dr., Ste 205
Sacramento, CA 95833
(916) 263-7800
(916) 263-7855 FAX

Administers exam licenses & enforces rules for practice for licensed vocational nurses and psychiatric technicians. FUNDING: Govt. OFC HRS: M-F 8am-5pm. SERVES: Calif.

CALIF CHILDREN'S SERVICES (CCS)

Riverside Co. Dept of Health
10769 Hole Ave., Ste 220
Riverside, CA 92505
(951) 358-5401
(951) 358-5198 FAX

State-sponsored specialized medical & rehab care for disabled children whose families are unable to provide such srvs. Referrals based on medical, residential & financial criteria. Provides case mgmt & reimbursement for care. PT & OT to children with neuromuscular or musculoskeletal conditions. FUNDING: State, county. OFC HRS: M-Th 8am-5pm. ADM REQ: Ages birth-21 yrs. SERVES: Riverside County.

CALIF DEPT HEALTH SRVS

Licensing & Certification/Hosp/Clinics
2000 Evergreen St., Ste 200
Sacramento, CA 95815
(800) 554-0354
(916) 263-5800
(916) 263-5840 FAX

Licensing for hospitals, clinics. Gives listings of nursing homes. For CNA licensing, call (916) 327-2445 (same building). OFC HRS: M-F 8am-5pm. SERVES: Calif.

CALIF DEPT HEALTH SRVS

State Health Srvs Programs Info
P.O. Box 942732
714-744 P Street
Sacramento, CA 94234-7320
(916) 445-4171
(916) 657-0240 FAX

Assist with locating state health srv prgms. Call for local agency. OFC HRS: M-F 8am-5pm. Spanish spoken.

CALIF DEPT HLTH SRVS/FOOD/DRUG

So Calif Regl Office - Food & Drug
1449 W. Temple St., Rm. 224
Los Angeles, CA 90026
(800) 495-3232
(213) 580-5720
(213) 580-5750 FAX

Licenses and registers manufacturers & distributors of foods, drugs, medical devices; inspects cosmetics and hazardous home products; investigates health frauds; monitors processed foods for pesticides, chemical contaminants & microbiological problems. Takes complaints about Calif-produced food, bottled water, tableware, health fraud (non-doctors), cosmetics, medical devices, drugs and hazardous household products. Offices in Santa Ana, Long Beach & Ontario. FUNDING: Govt. OFC HRS: M-F 8am-5pm. Spanish spoken. SERVES: So. Calif.

CALIF DIABETES & PREGNANCY PRGM

See "Sweet Success"

CALIF HOSPICE ASSN (CHAPCA)

3841 N. Freeway Blvd., Ste 225
Sacramento, CA 95834
(916) 925-3770
(888) 252-1010
(916) 925-3780 FAX

Represents hospice & palliative care providers, residential facilities for the elderly and healthcare professionals. Advocates for those facing life-threatening illness, promotes availability and access to quality care. Also provides info & referral srvs to people interested in hospice. FUNDING: Nonprofit. OFC HRS: M-F 8am-5pm. SERVES: Calif & Nevada.

CALIF MAJOR RISK MED INSURANCE

P.O. Box 2769
Sacramento, CA 95812
(916) 324-4695
(916) 324-4878 FAX

Alternative insurance prgm for individuals who are uninsurable, have pre-existing conditions which companies refuse to insure, or have insurance options only with excessively high premiums. Max payment of $75,000 per yr, $750,000 over life. Limited to 36 months of coverage, after which guaranteed issuance in the post-MRMIP graduate product plans will be available. Applications must be mailed. FUNDING: Prop 99 Tobacco Tax Fund, govt. Phone hrs: M-F 8:30am-7pm. Spanish & Tagalog spoken. Translator srvs available. SERVES: Calif.

CALIF MEDICAL ASSOCIATION

1201 J Street, Ste 200
Sacramento, CA 95814-2906
(800) 786-4262
(415) 882-5116 FAX

Professional assn representing 34,000 Calif physicians. Promotes the science and art of medicine, the care and well-being of patients, the protection of the public health, and the betterment of the medical profession. FUNDING: Nonprofit. OFC HRS: M-F 9am-5pm. SERVES: Calif.

CALIF MEDICAL REVIEW, INC. (CMRI)

See "Lumetra (Formerly CMRI)"

CALIF POISON CONTROL SYSTEM

UC San Francisco School of Pharmacy
P.O. Box 1262
3333 California St., Ste 420
San Francisco, CA 94143-1262
(800) 222-1222
(415) 502-8600
(415) 502-8620 FAX

Immediate treatment advice and info in case of exposure to poisonous, hazardous or toxic substances. Info is available to both health professionals & the public. Public outreach & edu provided. Health edu (pamphlets, stickers, prgms) (800) 582-3387. TTY (800) 972-3323. Emerg 24-hr hotline for Calif (800) 876-4766. FUNDING: Nonprofit. OFC HRS: 24 hrs, 7 days. Interpreter srv in over 100 languages. SERVES: Calif.

CALIF SMOKERS' HELPLINE

University Calif San Diego
9500 Gilman Dr., Dept. 0905
La Jolla, CA 92093-0905
(800) 662-8887
(858) 300-1099 FAX

Materials and/or telephone counseling to help people stop using tobacco. Specialized srvs for teens & pregnant women. Cantonese & Mandarin (800) 838-8917; Korean (800) 556-5564; Spanish (800) 45NO-FUME; Vietnamese (800) 778-8440; TDD (800) 933-4TDD; tobacco chewers (800) 844-CHEW. FUNDING: Govt, Calif Dept of Health Srvs, Prop 99. OFC HRS: M-F 7am-9pm; Sat 9am-1pm. 24-hr voicemail. Free srvs. SERVES: Calif.

CALIFORNIAKIDS HEALTH INSURANCE

See "Children's Health Access Prgms"

CALMA

Calif Advocates for Long-Term Care and Medi-Cal Assist

17130 Van Buren Blvd., Ste 181
Riverside, CA 92504
(877) 225-6202

Serves older adults and persons with disabilities at risk throughout Calif. Mission is to promote adult empowerment, prevent abuse and advocate for the rights and dignity of those experiencing health and aging issues. Dedicated to serving the needs of vulnerable adults. FUNDING: Nonprofit. Free srvs. SERVES: Calif.

CANCER CARE
www.cancercare.org
275 7th Avenue, 22nd Fl.
New York, NY 10001
(800) 813-4673
(212) 712-8400
(212) 712-8495 FAX

Counseling, edu & referral info for cancer patients. Direct financial assist for some patient costs. Over 70 telephone edu prgms per year. Info on treatment and other cancer-related issues can be found at (www.cancercare.org). FUNDING: Nonprofit. OFC HRS: M-Th 9am-7pm; F 9am-5pm, EST. Spanish spoken. Free srvs. SERVES: U.S.A.

CANCER CARE CENTER
Pomona Valley Hospital Medical Center
1910 Royalty Dr.
Pomona, CA 91767
(909) 865-9555
(909) 865-9697 FAX

Free standing outpatient cancer care ctr designed to anticipate and meet the needs of cancer patients & their families. Clinical srvs include full medical oncology and radiation oncology srvs. Cancer prgms include a variety of support groups, a cancer volunteer prgm, screenings, early detection and edu prgms. The Robert & Beverly Lewis Family Cancer Care Center serves as the hub for all cancer srvs and prgms, and is fully integrated with the Pomona Valley Hospital Medical Center's inpatient care srvs. FUNDING: Donations, grants, client fees, nonprofit. OFC HRS: M-F 7:30am-5pm. French, Arabic, Vietnamese, Spanish, Middle Eastern Indian, Chinese & Tagalog available upon request. ADM REQ: Varies depending on prgm. Accepts Medi-Cal, Medicare, set fees. Some srvs are free. SERVES: Pomona Valley & Inland Empire.

CANCER CONTROL SOCIETY
Alternative Therapies
2043 N. Berendo St.
Los Angeles, CA 90027
(323) 663-7801
(323) 663-7757 FAX

Hotline for people seeking info on alternative therapies for cancer, AIDS, arthritis, diabetes, heart disease and MS. Cancer clinic tours, cancer book house, info packet with names of recovered cancer patients and doctors around the world who treat in a natural and non-toxic way. Annual 3-day conference every Labor Day weekend. Info packets for the public & professionals sent with a $10 donation. FUNDING: Memorials, donations, nonprofit. OFC HRS: Office visits by appt only. SERVES: U.S.A.

CANCER FEDERATION
P.O. Box 1298
711 W. Ramsey St.

Banning, CA 92220
(951) 849-4325
(951) 849-0156 FAX

Info & counseling provided for cancer patients, their families & friends. Edu materials & meetings available. Also publishes magazines. FUNDING: Nonprofit. OFC HRS: Vary. Spanish spoken. SERVES: U.S.A.

CANCER LEGAL RESOURCE CENTER
919 Albany St.
Los Angeles, CA 90015
(866) 843-2572
(213) 736-1455
(213) 736-1428 FAX

Info and edu outreach on cancer-related legal issues to people with cancer, their families, friends, employers and those who provide srvs to them. Includes: cancer in the workplace, insurance coverage, navigating managed care/HMOs, estate planning, govt benefits, and advanced directives. TDD (213) 736-8310. FUNDING: Donations, grants, nonprofit. OFC HRS: M-F 9am-5pm. Free srvs. SERVES: U.S.A.

CANCER PREVENTION COALITION
P.O. Box 6851
Malibu, CA 90264
(310) 457-5176
(888) 377-8877
(877) 885-4657 FAX

Public health and cancer prev edu. Learn to create an environment safe from cancer-causing products. Outreach, public edu, advocacy. Free cancer awareness and prev seminars. FUNDING: Nonprofit. SERVES: U.S.A.

CANCER RECOVERY FNDN OF AMERICA
P.O. Box 238
Hershey, PA 17033
(800) 238-6479
(717) 545-7600
(717) 545-7602 FAX

An edu and self-help support group for cancer patients and their families. Emphasis on integration of body, mind and spirit for total wellness. Conducts a variety of seminars and support groups, resource materials available. Also children's project which provides emerg funding, camp scholarships & gift bags to children currently undergoing treatment. FUNDING: Donations, seminar fees, nonprofit. OFC HRS: M-F 9am-5pm, EST. Spanish and German spoken. ADM REQ: Cancer patient or support person. SERVES: U.S.A.

CANCER RESEARCH INSTITUTE
One Exchange Plaza
55 Broadway, Ste 1802
New York, NY 10006
(800) 992-2623
(212) 688-7515
(212) 832-9376 FAX

Fundraising prgm accepts contributions and memorials from the public and distributes them to research institutes nationally. OFC HRS: M-F 9am-5pm, EST. SERVES: U.S.A.

CANCER SOCIETY
See "American Cancer Society"

CELIAC DISEASE FOUNDATION
13251 Ventura Blvd., Ste 1
Studio City, CA 91604-1838
(818) 990-2354

(818) 990-2379 FAX

Nationwide srvs & support to persons with Celiac disease and dermatitis herpetiformis and their families. Distributes info about the disease and the gluten-free diet. Seeks to increase awareness among health care professionals, food and drug manufacturers, the food srv industry, the media and the public. Conducts edu prgms. Offers children's srvs and medical referrals. FUNDING: Nonprofit. OFC HRS: M-F 10am-6pm. Spanish spoken. SERVES: U.S.A.

CELIAC SPRUE ASSN CSA/USA
Orange County Chapter #14
P.O. Box 6643
Santa Ana, CA 92706-0643
(714) 750-9543

Natl support organization that focuses on research & edu relating to Celiac disease. Support groups for people with Celiac disease and/or dermatitis herpetiformas. Quarterly meetings, reference materials & extensive listing of gluten-free products. FUNDING: Nonprofit. Fee $15/year. SERVES: Orange & L.A. Counties, parts of Ventura & Riverside Counties.

CENTER FOR HEALTH PROMOTION
Loma Linda University Evans Hall, Rm. 111
24785 Stewart St.
Loma Linda, CA 92350
(909) 558-4594
(909) 558-0433 FAX

Wide range of srvs offered from community clinics. Clearview alcohol & drug prgm, stress mgmt, weight mgmt, smoking cessation, health eval and extensive individual risk eval. Prgms staffed by univ medical staff and students. FUNDING: Nonprofit. OFC HRS: M-Th 8am-12noon, 1pm-5pm; F 8am-12noon. ADM REQ: Open to anyone. Srv fees vary. SERVES: So. Calif.

CHARGE SYNDROME FOUNDATION, INC.
141 Middle Neck Rd.
Sands Point, NY 11050
(516) 684-4720
(800) 442-7604
(516) 883-9060 FAX

Provides support to individuals with CHARGE Syndrome and their families. Gathers, develops, maintains and distributes info about CHARGE Syndrome. Promotes awareness and research regarding its identification, cause and mgmt. Additional office at 2004 Parkade Blvd., Columbia, MO 65202, (573) 499-4694. FUNDING: Nonprofit. OFC HRS: Vary, EST. Free srvs. SERVES: U.S.A.

CHEMO ANGELS
P.O. Box 1971
Julian, CA 92036

Prgm matches people undergoing chemo or radiation treatment with "angel" volunteers who provide support during the process. Volunteers maintain weekly contact with their patient throughout the entire treatment process. Visit (www.chemoangels.net) for more info. FUNDING: Nonprofit. Free srvs. SERVES: U.S.A.

CHILDREN'S BURN FOUNDATION
5000 Van Nuys Blvd., Ste 450
Sherman Oaks, CA 91403
(818) 907-2822
(800) 949-8898
(818) 501-4005 FAX

Advocates for children who have been burned by abuse or neglect. Educates children, families, caregivers & emerg providers in burn prevention & treatment. Provides financial resources to severely burned children. FUNDING: Donations. OFC HRS: M-F 8am-5pm. SERVES: U.S.A.

CHILDREN'S HEALTH ACCESS PRGMS
Kaiser Permanente Cares for Kids
(800) 255-5053

Low-cost health insurance for uninsured children whose families do not qualify for Medi-Cal or Healthy Families. This prgm covers children who are enrolled in public schools within Kaiser Permanente Calif srv area. Prgm will also cover siblings of children eligible for this prgm. FUNDING: Nonprofit. Eligibility and cost are based on family size and income. SERVES: Calif.

CHILDREN'S HEALTH ACCESS PRGMS
Medi-Cal/Healthy Families Info Line
P.O. Box 138005
Sacramento, CA 95813-8005
(888) 747-1222
(866) 848-4974 FAX

Free and low-cost medical care for children and pregnant women. Eligibility is determined by children's ages and family income. Available to citizens and qualified immigrants. If the family does not qualify for this prgm, there are other options. Call (800) 880-5305 for application status. Call (866) 848-9166 if already enrolled. FUNDING: State, fed govt. OFC HRS: M-F 8am-8pm; Sat 8am-5pm. Cambodian, Farsi, Russian, Spanish, Chinese and Vietnamese spoken. ADM REQ: Must submit application. $5-$15 per child based on provider and county. SERVES: Calif.

CHILDREN'S TUMOR FOUNDATION
Calif Regional Office
8939 S. Sepulveda Blvd., Ste 516
Los Angeles, CA 90045
(310) 216-9570
(800) 323-7938
(310) 216-7789 FAX

Dedicated to finding the treatment & cure of Neurofibromatosis. Refers individuals to genetic counseling, medical diagnosis and care; connects them with local support groups, supplies, edu brochures; provides professional and public edu, public awareness, health professional edu packets, speakers, resources & referrals. FUNDING: Dues, donations, nonprofit. OFC HRS: M-F 9am-5pm. SERVES: Calif.

CHRISTIAN HERITAGE CARE CTRS
Skilled Nursing Facility
275 Garnet Way
Upland, CA 91786
(909) 949-4887
(909) 949-8476 FAX

Specializes in orthopedic care & rehab. Specific care srvs: skilled nursing, wound care, PT, OT, speech therapy, strengthening, mobility, & flexibility, ADL enhancing therapies, post-hospital care, pain mgmt, infection control, stroke & surgery recovery, injury rehab. FUNDING: Nonprofit. OFC HRS: M-F 8am-7pm. Spanish spoken. Accepts Medi-Cal, Medicare, SSI. SERVES: San Bernardino County.

CHRISTOPHER REEVE FNDN
Formerly American Paralysis Association
2113 Seville Ave.

Newport Beach, CA 92661
(949) 673-8474
(800) 225-0292
(949) 723-4818 FAX

Raises funds for research to develop a cure for paralysis. Grants given to improve the quality of life for people with disabilities. Info & referral. FUNDING: Donors, nonprofit. OFC HRS: M-F 9am-5pm. SERVES: Western U.S.A.

CHRISTOPHER REEVE FNDN
Resource Center
636 Morris Turnpike, Ste 3A
Short Hills, NJ 07078
(800) 225-0292
(973) 467-2870
(973) 467-9845 FAX

Natl clearinghouse for info, referral and edu materials on paralysis. Also call (800) 225-0292. FUNDING: Nonprofit. OFC HRS: M-F 9am-5pm, EST. SERVES: U.S.A.

CHRONIC FATIGUE IMMUNE DYSFUNCTION SYNDROME ASSN OF AMERICA (CFIDS)
P.O. Box 220398
Charlotte, NC 28222-0398
(704) 365-2343
(704) 365-9755 FAX

Edu info & referral srvs to persons with inquiries on CFIDS. Supports research & publishes journal. FUNDING: Nonprofit. OFC HRS: M-Th 9am-5pm; F 9am-1pm, EST. Free srvs. SERVES: U.S.A.

CITY OF HOPE
Duarte Campus
1500 E. Duarte Rd.
Duarte, CA 91010
(626) 256-4673

Contact the community srvs dept for more info on the various support and edu srvs offered to patients, their families, local community and health care professionals. Also visit (www.cityofhope.org). OFC HRS: M-F 8am-5pm. SERVES: U.S.A.

CITY OF HOPE NATL MEDICAL CTR
New Patient Srvs
1500 E. Duarte Rd.
Duarte, CA 91010-3000
(800) 826-4673
(626) 256-4673

212-bed center focuses on treatment and clinical research efforts for cancer. Treatment and clinical research prgms for other diseases include: diabetes, HIV/AIDS, sickle-cell disease and hemophilia. Basic research conducted at the Beckman Research Institute concentrates on broader areas of genetics, gene therapy, immunology and neuroscience. Referrals M-F 8am-5pm. FUNDING: Nonprofit. Spanish spoken. Accepts pvt insurance, Medicare, Medi-Cal. SERVES: U.S.A.

CLINICAS DE SALUD DEL PUEBLO, INC
Blythe Family Health Center
321 W. Hobson Way, Ste C
Blythe, CA 92225
(760) 922-4981
(760) 922-4442 FAX

Primary health care for all ages. AIDS/STD, pediatrics. FUNDING: BPHC site, donations, nonprofit. OFC HRS: M-F 8am-5pm. Spanish spoken. ADM REQ: Low income. Accepts in-

surance, Medicare, Medi-Cal, sliding fee scale. SERVES: Blythe & nearby.

COMMUNITY HEALTH CHARITIES
2115 W. Crescent Ave., Ste 260
Anaheim, CA 92801-3836
(714) 502-9153
(714) 502-9177 FAX

Raises funds for 40 nonprofit agencies through payroll deduction fundraising campaigns. Member agencies include the Leukemia Society, Cystic Fibrosis Fndn & Alzheimer's Assn. FUNDING: Fundraising, nonprofit. OFC HRS: M-F 9am-6pm. SERVES: Orange County & Inland Empire.

COMMUNITY HEALTH RESOURCE CENTER
One-Stop Center/San Bernardino
600 N. Arrowhead Ave., Ste 300
San Bernardino, CA 92401
(909) 888-7881
(909) 889-7833 FAX

Offers phone access to health and wellness info & referral, financial literacy info, legal aid and consumer counseling by the Legal Aid Society of San Bernardino, homeownership resource info. For TDD, call (800) 735-2922. FUNDING: Govt. OFC HRS: M-F 8am-5pm. SERVES: San Bernardino Co.

COMMUNITY HEALTH SYSTEMS, INC.
I.E. Community Health Center
18601 Valley Blvd.
Bloomington, CA 92316
(909) 877-0510
(909) 877-1818
(909) 877-5468 FAX

Primary health care for all ages. OB/GYN, prenatal, dental srvs, optometry, referrals, pediatrician, internal medicine. No cost dental screenings offered to clients, must provide proof of income or unemployment. FUNDING: Donations, nonprofit. OFC HRS: M-F 8am-5:30pm. Spanish spoken. ADM REQ: Low income. Accepts insurance, Medicare, Medi-Cal, sliding fee scale, I.E.H.P., Molina. SERVES: San Bernardino County.

COMMUNITY HEALTH SYSTEMS, INC.
Eastside Health Ctr
1970 University Ave.
Riverside, CA 92507
(951) 224-8220
(951) 328-9574 FAX

Primary health care for all ages. Prenatal, HIV testing, AIDS/STD screenings, teen clinic, family planning, immunizations, counseling. Enrollment assist for Medi-Cal, Healthy Families, Healthy Kids. FUNDING: BPHC site, donations, nonprofit. OFC HRS: M-F 8am-5:30pm. Spanish spoken. ADM REQ: Low income. Accepts insurance, Medicare, Medi-Cal, sliding fee scale. SERVES: Riverside County.

COMMUNITY HEALTH SYSTEMS, INC.
Arlanza Family Health Ctr
8856 Arlington Ave.
Riverside, CA 92503
(951) 353-2702
(951) 353-2976 FAX

Primary care for all ages. Family planning, HIV/AIDS, STD testing, Teenage Edu to Avoid Motherhood (T.E.A.M.), Child Health and Disability Prgm (CHDP). Also dental clinic. FUNDING: Nonprofit. OFC HRS: M-F 8am-5:30pm.

Accepts Medi-Cal, Medicare, insurance, sliding fee scale. SERVES: Riverside County.

COMMUNITY HOME HEALTH
1805 Medical Center Dr.
San Bernardino, CA 92411
(909) 887-6333
(877) 966-3066
(909) 806-1059 FAX

Skilled health care to homebound patients, RN, home health aide, PT, OT, speech pathology, medical social srvs, mental health, perinatal & pediatric care. JCAHO accredited. FUNDING: Nonprofit. OFC HRS: M-F 8am-4:30pm. Spanish spoken. ADM REQ: Physician order, medical necessity, homebound. Accepts Medi-Cal, Medicare, HMO, pvt pay, insurance. SERVES: East San Bernardino County.

CONGENITAL HEART INFO NETWORK
101 N. Washington St., Ste 1A
Margate City, NJ 08402
(609) 822-1572
(609) 822-1574 FAX

Offers info & resources for people with congenital heart defects. Also sponsors several support groups. Spencer's Fund prgm provides financial assist including meals, utility assist, and travel expenses to families with a child who is hospitalized for a long period of time. FUNDING: Nonprofit. Free srvs. Memberships available at several donation levels. SERVES: U.S.A.

CONSUMER NUTRITION INFO LINE
The American Dietetic Association
120 S. Riverside Plaza, Ste 2000
Chicago, IL 60606-6995
(800) 877-1600
(312) 899-4873 FAX

Recorded messages are available with a touchtone phone. Referrals are given to registered dietitians for nutrition guidance and consultation. FUNDING: Nonprofit. OFC HRS: M-F 8am-5pm, CST. SERVES: U.S.A.

COOLEY'S ANEMIA FOUNDATION
330 7th Avenue, Ste 900
New York, NY 10001
(800) 522-7222
(212) 279-5999 FAX

Focus is advancing treatment & cure of Cooley's Anemia (known as Thalassemia), an inherited blood disorder found in over 60 countries that affects children of the Mediterranean, Asian-Indian, Southeast Asian and Chinese ancestry. If untreated, it is fatal. Conducts natl prgms that provide medical research, patient srvs, awareness and edu. Chapters throughout U.S.A. Also sponsors the Thalassemia Action Group (TAG), a support group for patients and their families. Provides info about the disease, brochures (available in a variety of languages), newsletters, and other info. FUNDING: Donation, grants, nonprofit. OFC HRS: M-F 9am-5pm. Free srvs. SERVES: U.S.A.

CORNELIA DE LANGE SYNDROME FNDN
302 W. Main St., Ste 100
Avon, CT 06001
(800) 223-8355
(860) 676-8166
(860) 676-8337 FAX

Info, support, & materials for families, friends & professionals about CDLS (birth defect causing slow mental and physical dev in children). The condition is thought to have a genetic origin. Some publications available in Spanish. After hours answering machine takes your contact information to request printed info. FUNDING: Private, donations. OFC HRS: M-F 9am-5pm, EST. SERVES: U.S.A.

CROHN'S & COLITIS FNDN OF AMER
National Headquarters
386 Park Ave., South, 17th Fl.
New York, NY 10016-8804
(800) 932-2423
(212) 779-4098 FAX

Edu materials on Crohn's disease and ulcerative colitis. Refers to local support groups and provides names of physician members. Visit (www.ccfa.org). FUNDING: Donations, members, nonprofit. OFC HRS: M-F 9am-5pm, EST. Spanish spoken. SERVES: U.S.A.

CROHN'S & COLITIS FNDN/GREATER L.A.
1640 S. Sepulveda Blvd., Ste 214
Los Angeles, CA 90025
(310) 478-4500
(866) 831-9157
(310) 478-4546 FAX

Educational and support services for people suffering from Crohn's Disease and Ulcerative Colitis. Support groups serving L.A. & Orange Counties, Camp Oasis Youth Club, '20s-'30s group, hospital visitation prgm, parent network, etc. Call the information resource ctr at (888) MY-GUT PAIN. Call for meeting times and locations. Visit the website (www.ccfa.org/chapters/losangeles). FUNDING: Donations, nonprofit. OFC HRS: M-F 9am-5pm. Free srvs. SERVES: L.A., Ventura, Orange, San Bernardino, San Luis Obispo, Santa Barbara and Kern Counties.

CTIS PREGNANCY RISK INFO LINE
Dept of Pediatrics, UCSD Med Ctr
9500 Gilman Dr., Ste 0828
La Jolla, CA 92093-0828
(800) 532-3749
(619) 270-0278 FAX

The infoline is a statewide telephone srv operated by Calif Teratogen Info Srv & Clinical Research Prgm. Call with questions regarding concerns about the effects of medications, environmental exposures, or illness while pregnant. The call is free and confidential. Info is based on current scientific data. Satellite offices: UCLA OB/GYN, Institute of Fetal & Maternal Health at Children's Hospital in L.A. and Medical Genetics, Dept of Pediatrics, Stanford Univ School of Medicine. FUNDING: Govt, nonprofit. OFC HRS: M-F 9am-5pm. Spanish and Tagalog spoken. Free srvs. SERVES: Calif.

CYSTIC FIBROSIS FOUNDATION
2150 Towne Centre Pl., Ste 120
Anaheim, CA 92806
(714) 938-1393
(800) 232-8731
(714) 938-1462 FAX

Focus is to raise money to cure and control cystic fibrosis and to fund care facilities specializing in cystic fibrosis care and treatment. FUNDING: Fundraising efforts. OFC HRS: M-F 8:30am-5:30pm. Spanish spoken. SERVES: So. Calif.

CYSTIC FIBROSIS FOUNDATION
National Headquarters
6931 Arlington Rd.
Bethesda, MD 20814
(800) 344-4823
(301) 951-4422
(301) 951-6378 FAX

Answers questions about cystic fibrosis and provides free literature. Provides referrals to local cystic fibrosis care centers throughout the U.S. FUNDING: Donations, grants, nonprofit. OFC HRS: M-F 8:30am-5:30pm, EST. Free srvs. SERVES: U.S.A.

CYSTIC FIBROSIS FOUNDATION
San Diego and Imperial Counties Chapter
10455 Sorento Valley Rd., Ste 103
San Diego, CA 92121
(858) 452-2873
(858) 452-2872 FAX

Supports Cystic Fibrosis care, teaching & resource center at UCSD Medical Center. Info & referral srvs. Supports professional edu prgms & raises money for research. FUNDING: Nonprofit, donations. OFC HRS: M-F 8:30am-5:30pm. Free srvs. SERVES: So. Calif.

DES ACTION USA
P.O. Box 7296
Jupiter, FL 33468
(800) 337-9288

Medical and legal info & referrals for those exposed in-utero and during pregnancy to the hormone drug DES. Not a primary care agency. Physical address: 187 Via Catalunha, Jupiter, FL 33458. FUNDING: Donations, nonprofit. OFC HRS: M-F 9am-2pm, CST. Spanish spoken. SERVES: U.S.A.

DESERT AIDS PROJECT
P.O. Box 2890
1695 N. Sunrise Way
Palm Springs, CA 92263-2890
(760) 323-2118
(866) 331-3344
(760) 323-9865 FAX

HIV health center (outpatient specialty clinic), support groups for HIV positive, caregivers, partners or family. Anonymous testing for HIV & syphilis. Counseling, in-home care, pro bono legal clinic, prevention & edu, case mgmt, "friend-to-friend" & admin volunteer prgm, substance abuse srvs, transportation, food, child care. ADAP enrollment site. Satellite ofc: (760) 342-4197. TDD (760) 969-1796. FUNDING: Nonprofit. OFC HRS: M-F 8am-5pm. Spanish spoken. ADM REQ: HIV positive. Free srvs or sliding fee scale. SERVES: Eastern Riverside Co & upper desert of San Bernardino County.

DESERT AREA RESOURCES/TRAINING
Early Intervention
201 E. Ridgecrest Blvd.
Ridgecrest, CA 93555
(760) 375-8494
(760) 375-1288 FAX

Promotes the physical, emotional, social and cognitive dev of children from ages birth-3 yrs, who are dev delayed, high-risk and premature. Encourages active involvement of parents in their child's prgm and provides support srvs to the families. FUNDING: Nonprofit. OFC HRS: M-F 7:30am-4:30pm. Spanish spoken. SERVES: Ridgecrest & nearby.

DESERT HOSPITAL MEDICAL DIRECTORY
1150 N. Indian Canyon Dr.
Palm Springs, CA 92262
(760) 323-6511
(760) 323-6580 FAX

Desert Hospital Cancer Center Physician directory is a free computerized physician referral srv staffed by registered nurses who can help make your choice much easier & more informed. Call (888) 765-6274 or visit (http://desertmedctr.com).

DESERT SIERRA PARTNERSHIP

Inland Agency
1737 Atlanta, Ste H-5
Riverside, CA 92507
(951) 241-8723
(800) 511-2300
(951) 684-7980 FAX

Breast & cervical cancer early detection prgm for low-income women ages 40 yrs+, not covered by insurance or health plan, unable to pay insurance co-payment or deductible, unable to pay medical share of cost or have limited or restricted coverage. Referrals to health care providers, community outreach & edu, resource library, workshops. For counseling support, call (951) 697-7605. For info call (800) 824-0088. FUNDING: Nonprofit. OFC HRS: M-F 8am-5pm. Spanish, Cantonese, Korean, Mandarin, Vietnamese spoken. ADM REQ: Low income. Free srvs for those who qualify. SERVES: Riverside, San Bernardino, Inyo Counties.

DIABETES ASSOCIATION

See "American Diabetes Association"

DIABETES INFO CLEARINGHOUSE

See "Natl Diabetes Info Clearinghouse"

DIABETES/PREGNANCY PRGM/CAL

See "Sweet Success"

DIABETIC HELP LINE/SUPPORT GRP

St. Jude Medical Center
101 E. Valencia Mesa Dr.
Fullerton, CA 92835
(714) 992-3037

St. Jude Medical Center maintains a special helpline located in its Diabetes Metabolic Unit. Calls will be answered by nurse specialists who understand special problems of diabetes. Also offers support group. FUNDING: Nonprofit. OFC HRS: 24 hrs, 7 days. SERVES: So. Calif.

DIETETICS ASSOCIATION

See "Consumer Nutrition Info Line"

DIGESTIVE DISEASE INFO

See "Natl Digestive Disease Info"

DOLPHINS MOBILE HEALTH VAN OUTREACH

811 W. Chanslorway
Blythe, CA 92225
(760) 922-1349
(760) 921-8399 FAX

Referral srvs to pregnant and parenting teens, nutrition, immunizations, hearing, vision, physical activity, and injury prevention to preschool children. Also dental treatment srvs. Assist with completing Healthy Families applications. FUNDING: First 5. OFC HRS: M-F 8am-5pm. Spanish spoken. ADM REQ: Ages birth-5 yrs, and pregnant women. Free srvs. SERVES: Blythe.

DYSTONIA MEDICAL RESEARCH FNDN

One E. Wacker Dr., Ste 2810
Chicago, IL 60601-1905
(800) 377-3978
(312) 755-0198

(312) 803-0138 FAX

Supports medical research for dystonia; builds awareness to medical and lay communities; distributes info about dystonia and assists in starting support groups throughout North America. FUNDING: Donations, nonprofit. OFC HRS: M-F 8:30am-4:30pm, CST. Spanish spoken. Free srvs. SERVES: Internatl.

EAR FOUNDATION (THE)

P.O. Box 330867
415 4th Avenue, South
Nashville, TN 37201
(615) 248-8828
(866) 385-6524
(615) 248-4797 FAX

Committed to the goal of better hearing and balance through public and professional edu prgms, support srvs and applied research. Includes Meniere's Network, Young Ear's Program & senior EARs. Provides disease and other literature, including newsletters. FUNDING: Donations, grants, nonprofit. OFC HRS: M-F 8am-4:30pm, CST; leave message after hours. SERVES: U.S.A.

EISENHOWER MEDICAL CENTER

Diabetes Program
39000 Bob Hope Dr., Ste P-100B
Rancho Mirage, CA 92270
(760) 773-1403
(760) 773-1880 FAX

Specialized diet prgms include: nutrition counseling for persons with diabetes mellitus, diabetes self-mgmt training & edu. Free monthly support groups for adults, teens and insulin pump users. FUNDING: Pvt, nonprofit. OFC HRS: M-F 8am-4:30pm. Spanish spoken. ADM REQ: Referral from physician. Accepts insurance, pvt pay. SERVES: Riverside & San Bernardino Counties.

ELSINORE HEALTH CENTER

See "Riverside Co. Public Health Dept"

ENDOMETRIOSIS ASSOCIATION

8585 N. 76th Place
Milwaukee, WI 53223
(800) 992-3636
(414) 355-2200
(414) 355-6065 FAX

Self-help prgm for women with endometriosis and others interested in exchanging info. Mutual support and help, educating the public and medical community about the disease and promoting research. Recorded message invites callers to leave their name and address; info is mailed to the caller. Contact for info about support groups in Calif. Brochures in 29 languages. FUNDING: Member dues, grants, donations, nonprofit. OFC HRS: M-F 8:30am-5pm. SERVES: U.S.A.

EPILEPSY FNDN OF AMERICA

National Office
8301 Professional Pl.
Landover, MD 20785-7223
(800) 332-1000
(301) 459-3700
(301) 577-4941 FAX

Represents people with epilepsy. Devoted to helping create a better world for people with epilepsy. Provides info on local and natl levels for everything from technical info to finding another person to talk to. Answers questions and dis-

cusses caller's concerns about seizure disorders and treatments. Prof library (800) 332-4050. FUNDING: Donation, grants, govt, nonprofit. OFC HRS: M-Th 9am-5pm; F 9am-3pm, EST. Spanish spoken. Free srvs. SERVES: U.S.A.

EPILEPSY FNDN OF GREATER L.A.

5777 W. Century Blvd., Ste 820
Los Angeles, CA 90045
(800) 564-0445
(310) 670-2870
(310) 670-6124 FAX

Info & referral, self-help groups, edu outreach, residential and family camps, parent phone network, conferences, medical ID bracelets and necklaces, seizure first aid training, advocacy, literature and written edu guides. Srvs for persons with seizure disorders, their family members and the community. FUNDING: Donations, grants, nonprofit. OFC HRS: M-F 9am-4:30pm. Spanish spoken. Free srvs. SERVES: So. Calif.

EPILEPSY FNDN OF SAN DIEGO

Camp Quest
2055 El Cajon Blvd.
San Diego, CA 92104-1092
(619) 296-0161
(619) 296-0802 FAX

A medically supervised summer camp for children with seizure disorders. Camp Quest is held for one week in July at a mountain camp. Agency provides individual, family & group counseling, employment prgms, info & referral, advocacy, epilepsy edu. FUNDING: Donations, United Way, nonprofit. OFC HRS: M-F 9am-5pm. ADM REQ: Camp for children ages 8-12 yrs. Application deadline is June 1st. SERVES: Calif.

EYECARE AMERICA

Seniors EyeCare Prgm
P.O. Box 429098
655 Beach St.
San Francisco, CA 94142-9098
(877) 887-6327
(415) 561-8567 FAX

Provides a comprehensive medical eye exam and up to one year of care for anything diagnosed at exam time at no out-of-pocket cost. Uninsured are seen at no charge for physician's services. FUNDING: Knights Templar Eye Fndn Inc., state ophthalmological societies, nonprofit. OFC HRS: 24 hrs, 7 days. Spanish spoken. ADM REQ: Ages 65 yrs+, a citizen or legal resident who has not seen an ophthalmologist in 3 yrs or more. Medicare and insurance are billed and accepted as payment in full. SERVES: U.S.A.

FACIAL PLASTIC SURGERY INFO

310 S. Henry St.
Alexandria, VA 22314
(800) 332-3223
(703) 299-9291
(703) 299-8898 FAX

Free brochures on different types of facial plastic surgery and a list of surgeons by region. OFC HRS: M-F 9am-5pm, answering srv after hours. SERVES: U.S.A.

FAMILY CARE CENTER

See "Riverside Co. Public Health Dept"

FAMILY SOLUTIONS
Central Cluster
214 West E Street
Ontario, CA 91762
(909) 418-6923
(909) 459-2932 FAX

Works to improve the health & well-being of children & their families. Mental health & case mgmt, parenting classes, medical srvs. Crisis intervention, diagnostic assessment, individual family, group counseling. Alt location: 1501-A S. Bon View Ave. in Ontario, (909) 673-1794. FUNDING: Nonprofit. OFC HRS: M-F 7:30am-4:30pm. SERVES: Zip code areas 91761, 91762, 91764.

FIRST CALL FOR HELP
Volunteer Center of Victor Valley
P.O. Box 1992
16692 Mojave Dr.
Victorville, CA 92393
(760) 243-9646
(760) 243-4762 FAX

Info & referral for people seeking srvs or info on community agencies. Interaction with individuals in crisis situations in order to reduce tension and stress, allowing that person to utilize available resources more effectively. FUNDING: Donations, grants, nonprofit. OFC HRS: M-Th 9am-2:45pm. Spanish spoken. SERVES: San Bernardino County.

FLOWERS HERITAGE FOUNDATION
Bridge the Gap Program
200 Webster St., Ste 200
Oakland, CA 94607
(510) 587-2668
(510) 587-2794 FAX

Prgm helps people with HIV/AIDS who have low incomes to afford their medications. Also offers health edu, advocacy, and community grants for nonprofit agencies. FUNDING: Nonprofit. Free srvs SERVES: Calif.

FONTANA FAMILY HEALTH CENTER
Arrowhead Regl Med Ctr - Family Practice
16854 Ivy St.
Fontana, CA 92335
(909) 422-8029
(909) 580-1000
(909) 428-0709 FAX

Comprehensive health care for all family members. OB, pediatrics, adult care. FUNDING: Govt. OFC HRS: M-F 9am-5pm. Spanish spoken. ADM REQ: Wait 6-8 wks for new patients. Accepts Medi-Cal, Medicare, Molina, pvt pay. SERVES: Western San Bernardino County.

FOUNDATION FIGHTING BLINDNESS
11435 Cronhill Dr.
Owings Mills, MD 21117-2220
(800) 683-5555
(410) 568-0150
(410) 363-2393 FAX

Funds research to discover the causes, treatments, preventive methods, and cures for retinitis pigmentosa, macular degeneration, Usher Syndrome, Stargardt disease and the entire spectrum of retinal degenerative diseases. Offers info & referral for affected individuals and their families as well as doctors and eye care professionals. Provides comprehensive info kits. Newsletter presents articles on coping, research updates and Foundation News and is published three times per yr. Natl

conferences are held annually. TDD (800) 683-5551. FUNDING: Donations, nonprofit. OFC HRS: M-F 8:30am-5pm. SERVES: U.S.A.

FRAGILE X ASSN OF SO CALIF
P.O. Box 6924
Burbank, CA 91510-6924
(818) 754-4227
(310) 276-9251 FAX

Parent group offering info & referral, peer support groups. Monthly meetings and other edu activities. FUNDING: Donations, nonprofit. OFC HRS: 24-hr answering machine. Spanish spoken. Free srvs. SERVES: So. Calif.

FRESH START SURGICAL GIFTS
2011 Palomar Airport Rd., Ste 206
Carlsad, CA 92011
(760) 944-7774
(888) 551-1003
(760) 944-1729 FAX

Reconstructive surgery for children suffering from physical deformities caused by birth defects, accidents, abuse or disease. Medical professionals donate skills to provide needed surgery not covered by insurance, state or subsidized prgms. OFC HRS: M-F 9am-5pm. Spanish spoken. ADM REQ: Ages 1-21 yrs. Call for screening & wait list. Free srvs. SERVES: U.S.A & internatl.

GAY & LESBIAN MEDICAL ASSOCIATION
1326 18th Street NW, Ste 22
Washington, DC 20036
(202) 600-8037
(202) 478-1500 FAX

Mission is to ensure equality in health care for lesbian, gay, bisexual and transgender individuals and health care providers. Provides an online directory of LGBT-friendly medical, dental, and mental health professionals. Also publishes various fact sheets on important health topics for the LGBT population. Visit (www.glma.org) for more info. FUNDING: Nonprofit. Memberships available, free srvs. SERVES: U.S.A.

GENETIC & RARE DISEASES INFO CTR
31 Center Dr., MSC 2152
9000 Rockville Pike
Bethesda, MD 20892
(301) 402-0911
(301) 402-2218 FAX

Info about 6,000+ genetic & rare diseases. TTY (888) 205-3223; internatl number (301) 519-3194. FUNDING: Govt. OFC HRS: M-F 12noon-6pm, EST. Spanish spoken. SERVES: U.S.A.

GENETIC ALLIANCE
Connections to Natl Support Groups/Srvs
4301 Connecticut Ave., NW, Ste 404
Washington, DC 20008-2369
(202) 966-5557
(202) 966-8553 FAX

Resources through toll-free infoline (800) 336-GENE. FUNDING: Donations, grants, govt, nonprofit. OFC HRS: M-F 9am-6pm, EST. Free srvs. SERVES: U.S.A.

GENETICALLY HANDICAPPED PERSONS
Calif Dept of Health Srvs
P.O. Box 997413
MS 8105
Sacramento, CA 95899-7413
(800) 639-0597

(916) 327-1112 FAX

Helps pay medical cost of enrolled persons with hemophilia, sickle-cell, cystic fibrosis, Huntington's disease, PKU, etc. FUNDING: State, nonprofit. OFC HRS: M-F 8am-5pm. Spanish spoken. ADM REQ: Resident of state, medical eligibility restricted to specific inherited diseases. Accepts Medi-Cal. Enrollment fees based on sliding fee scale. SERVES: Calif.

GLAUCOMA FOUNDATION
80 Maiden Lane, Ste 700
New York, NY 10038
(212) 285-0080
(212) 651-1888 FAX

Research & support to find new treatments & cures for glaucoma. FUNDING: Nonprofit. OFC HRS: M-F 9am-5pm, EST. SERVES: U.S.A.

HAEMOSTASIS & THROMBOSIS
Orthopaedic Hospital, L.A.
2400 S. Flower St., 4th Fl.
Los Angeles, CA 90007
(213) 742-6509
(212) 742-1000
(213) 742-1355 FAX

Comp treatment and care for haemostosis & thrombosis patients who have hemophilia, sickle cell, thrombon disorders and hereditary disorders of coagulation, and their families. FUNDING: Nonprofit. OFC HRS: M-F 8am-4pm. Spanish spoken. Accepts Medi-Cal. SERVES: U.S.A.

HANSEN'S DISEASE
See "American Leprosy Missions"

HEADACHE FOUNDATION
See "Natl Headache Foundation"

HEALING ODYSSEY
23591 El Toro Rd., Ste 214
Lake Forest, CA 92630
(949) 951-3930
(949) 951-8095 FAX

Three-day retreat and follow-up support prgm for female cancer survivors. Camp facility in the Malibu mountains four times per year for women with all forms of cancer. Also year-round workshops for couples. FUNDING: Donations, nonprofit. OFC HRS: M-F 9am-5pm. Spanish spoken. Fee for 3 day retreat is $125, with partial or full scholarships when available. SERVES: So. Calif.

HEALTH INFO LINE/RIVERSIDE CO.
Riverside Co. Dept of Health
4065 County Circle Dr.
Riverside, CA 92503
(951) 358-5000
(951) 358-4529 FAX

A comprehensive health info and referral line to help the public access the county health system. For TDD, call (951) 358-5124. OFC HRS: M-Th 7:30am-5pm. Spanish spoken. SERVES: Riverside County.

HEALTH INSURANCE PLAN/CALIF
See "Managed Risk Medical/Insurance Board"

HEALTH RESOURCES & SRVS ADMIN (HRSA)
P.O. Box 2910
Merrifield, VA 22116
(888) 275-4772
(703) 442-9051
(703) 821-2098 FAX

Info on health care srvs for low income, uninsured individuals & those with special care needs. Publications, referrals and resources. TTY/TDD (877) 489-4772. FUNDING: Govt. OFC HRS: M-F 8:30am-5pm, EST. Spanish spoken. SERVES: U.S.A.

HEALTHY FAMILIES

See "Children's Health Access Prgms"

HEALTHY FAMILY CLINIC

JFK Memorial Fndn
73-555 San Gorgonio Way
Palm Desert, CA 92260
(760) 776-1600
(760) 776-4500 FAX

Medical srvs for children of all ages. Nutrition srvs, parenting edu, public health care application assist. FUNDING: Nonprofit. OFC HRS: M-F 8am-5pm. ADM REQ: Call for appt. Accepts Medi-Cal, CHDP, Healthy Families, Healthy Kids. SERVES: Palm Desert.

HEART ASSOCIATION

See "American Heart Association"

HEART TOUCH PROJECT

3400 Airport Ave., Ste 42
Santa Monica, CA 90405
(310) 391-2558
(310) 391-2168 FAX

Compassionate & healing touch therapy provided by professional therapists & volunteers to persons with AIDS, non-ambulatory persons, senior citizens, persons receiving hospice care, infants & children. FUNDING: Nonprofit. OFC HRS: M-F 10am-6pm. ADM REQ: Must have approval of primary health provider to ensure that the massage is allowed for the patient's condition. Accepts donations. Free srvs. SERVES: So. Calif.

HEMOPHILIA FNDN OF SO CALIF

6720 Melrose Ave., Ste 102
Hollywood, CA 90038
(800) 371-4123
(323) 525-0440
(323) 525-0445 FAX

Info & referral srvs related to hemophilia, HIV/ AIDS and hepatitis C, summer camp, youth Medic-Alert sponsorships, scholarships, resource library, info seminars, family retreats, holiday parties, and counseling referrals. FUNDING: Donations, grants, nonprofit. OFC HRS: M-F 10am-5pm. Spanish spoken. ADM REQ: All ages with hemophilia & other bleeding disorders, & their families. Free srvs. SERVES: So. Calif.

HEMOPHILIA TREATMENT CENTER

See "Haemostasis & Thrombosis"

HI-DESERT MEDICAL CENTER

6601 White Feather Rd.
Joshua Tree, CA 92252
(760) 366-3711
(760) 366-6136 FAX

24-hr emerg srvs, acute care hospital, skilled nursing facility, community edu, home health srvs and outpatient srvs. Walk in or call. FUNDING: District hospital. OFC HRS: 24 hrs. Accepts Medi-Cal. SERVES: Morongo Basin.

HICAP

Health Insurance Counseling/Advocacy Prgm
1737 Atlanta, Ste H-5
Riverside, CA 92507
(800) 434-0222

(951) 697-6560
(951) 694-7980 FAX

Counseling & advocacy in Medicare-related issues, health insurance, HMOs, Medicare billing & LTC. Community edu to groups at no cost. FUNDING: Calif Dept of Aging. OFC HRS: M-F 8am-4pm. Spanish spoken. ADM REQ: Ages 60 yrs+ or Medicare beneficiary. Accepts donations. Free srvs. SERVES: Riverside, Inyo, Mono, San Bernardino Counties.

HILL-BURTON FREE MED CARE PRGM

Health Resources & Srvs
5600 Fishers Ln., Ste 10C-16
Rockville, MD 20857
(301) 443-5656
(800) 638-0742
(301) 443-0619 FAX

Info on hospitals and other health facilities participating in the Hill-Burton Hospital Free Care Prgm. A srv of the Health Resources & Srvs Admin, U.S. Dept of Health & Human Srvs. Accepts name and phone number and calls are returned during next business day. FUNDING: Nonprofit. OFC HRS: M-F 8:30am-5pm, EST. Spanish spoken. SERVES: U.S.A.

HISTIOCYTOSIS ASSOCIATION

332 N. Broadway, Ste 101
Pitman, NJ 08071
(856) 589-6606
(800) 548-2758
(856) 589-6614 FAX

Patient and family support, quarterly newsletter, info & referral, brochures. Primary purpose is to fund medical research. Info available on Langerhans cell histiocytosis, hemophagocytic lymphohistiocytosis, diabetes insipidus. FUNDING: Donations, nonprofit. OFC HRS: M-F 9am-4:30pm, EST; voicemail after hrs. Free srvs. SERVES: U.S.A.

HOUSE EAR INSTITUTE

House Ear Clinic
2100 W. 3rd Street
Los Angeles, CA 90057
(213) 483-4431
(800) 388-8612
(213) 483-8789 FAX

Research, edu, and clinical srvs for deaf and hard-of-hearing children & their families. Srvs include: outpatient infant screenings, diagnostic testing, auditory rehab with referrals to edu prgms and therapy, pre- and post- evaluations for Cochlear Implant srvs. Also camp for families and children with parent workshops and fun activities for children. TDD (213) 484-2642; for L.A. appts, call (213) 483-5706; for Orange County appts, call (714) 516-9570; for the Care Children's Center, call (213) 353-7005. FUNDING: Nonprofit, donations. OFC HRS: M-F 8:30am-5pm. ADM REQ: Must pre-register for family camp. SERVES: U.S.A.

HUMAN GROWTH FOUNDATION

National Office
997 Glen Cove Ave., Ste 5
Glen Head, NY 11545
(800) 451-6434
(516) 671-4041
(516) 671-4055 FAX

Edu materials & mutual support. Supports research & promotes public awareness of physical & emotional problems of growth abnormalities and adult growth hormone defi-

ciency. Free edu material for families. FUNDING: Donations, grants, nonprofit. OFC HRS: M-F 9am-5pm, EST. SERVES: U.S.A.

HUNTINGTON DISEASE SOCIETY

Greater L.A. Chapter
9903 Santa Monica Blvd., Ste 106
Beverly Hills, CA 90212
(888) 443-7252
(800) 986-9868

Referral to support groups, helpline, edu, info & referral. Leave message; calls returned in 24 hrs. FUNDING: Nonprofit. SERVES: So. Calif.

HUNTINGTON'S DISEASE SOCIETY/NATL

505 8th Avenue, Ste 902
New York, NY 10018
(800) 345-4372
(212) 242-1968
(212) 239-3430 FAX

Identifies HD families; offers edu to family; general public & medical professionals operating a patient srvs prgm, coordination with various community srvs to assist families in meeting the social, economic & emotional problems resulting from Huntington's Disease. Referral srvs for genetic counseling & other needs, materials & reprints. FUNDING: Donations, nonprofit. OFC HRS: M-F 9am-5pm, EST, 24-hr helpline. SERVES: U.S.A.

IBS COMMUNITY HEALTH CARE CLINIC

1963 North E Street
San Bernardino, CA 92405-3919
(909) 381-6146
(909) 381-0111 FAX

Outpatient medical, dental, mental health, substance abuse clinic. Immunizations, pregnancy testing, counseling, birth control, physical exams, general medical, well-baby, pediatric, health edu, TB testing, AIDS testing & treatment, STDs. Serves all ages. FUNDING: Nonprofit, fed govt. OFC HRS: M-Th 8am-6pm; F 8am-5pm. Spanish, Vietnamese spoken. Accepts Medi-Cal, Medicare, sliding fee scale. SERVES: San Bernardino County.

IMPOTENCE/URINARY INCONTINENCE

(800) 843-4315

Free printed materials for prospective patients regarding causes and treatments for impotence. FUNDING: Nonprofit. OFC HRS: M-Th 8am-4pm, CST. Spanish spoken. Language line available. SERVES: U.S.A.

INLAND AGENCY

1737 Atlanta, Ste H-5
Riverside, CA 92507
(951) 241-8723
(951) 683-7980 FAX

Challenges of Youth. Adelanto Community Toolbox. HICAP (Health Insurance Counseling and Advocacy Prgm), Desert Sierra Breast Cancer Partnership. Part of a state and nationwide prgm for Medicare beneficiaries. FUNDING: Fed, state, county, fndn, donations, nonprofit. OFC HRS: M-F 8am-5pm. Spanish spoken. Free srvs. SERVES: Riverside, San Bernardino, Inyo, Mono Counties.

INLAND BEHAV & HEALTH SERVICES

See "IBS Community Health Care Clinic"

INLAND COUNTIES HEALTH SYSTEMS

See "Inland Agency"

INLAND EMPIRE HEALTH PLAN
(See Display Ad on Page 171)
303 E. Vanderbilt Way
San Bernardino, CA 92408
(800)440-4347
(866)294-4347

We provide affordable health care to low-income families. Please contact us to see if your child qualifies for Medi-Cal or Healthy Families prgm. Coverage includes doctor and hospital visits, vision, prescriptions and immunizations. FUNDING: Nonprofit. SERVES: Riverside and San Bernardino Counties.

JUVENILE DIABETES RESEARCH FNDN
26 Broadway, 14th Fl.
New York, NY 10004
(800) 533-2873
(212) 785-9500
(212) 785-9595 FAX

Primary objective is to support and fund research into the cause, treatment and prev of diabetes, and, ultimately through research, find a cure. Also serves the needs of those with diabetes and their families by providing prgms of edu & info. Strives to inform the general public on the seriousness of diabetes. Provides brochures, fact sheets, referrals. FUNDING: Donations, nonprofit. OFC HRS: M-F 9am-5pm, EST. Spanish spoken. SERVES: U.S.A.

JUVENILE DIABETES RESEARCH FNDN
Inland Empire Chapter
2023 Chicago Ave., Ste B-13
Riverside, CA 92507
(951) 784-4156
(951) 784-4628 FAX

Primary objective is to support and fund research, treatment and prev of diabetes. Also serves the needs of those with diabetes and their families by providing prgms of edu & info. Strives to alert the general public to the seriousness of diabetes. Provides brochures, fact sheets, referrals. FUNDING: Nonprofit. OFC HRS: M-F 9am-5pm. SERVES: Inland Empire.

KAISER PERMANENTE/CARES FOR KIDS
See "Children's Health Access Prgms"

KIDNEY & UROLOGIC DISEASES FNDN
See "Natl Kidney/Urologic Diseases Info"

KIDNEY FOUNDATION
See "Natl Kidney Fndn of So Calif"

KRISTIE'S PLACE
1747 S. Claudina Way
Anaheim, CA 92805
(714) 408-9781
(714) 956-1475 FAX

A place for children with life-threatening illnesses to come with their families for their So. Calif wish trip or for a short compassion stay. Wishland's Kid's Club and family support prgms bring joy and hope to all. FUNDING: Nonprofit. OFC HRS: M-F 8:30am-4pm; Sat 8:30am-10am. Spanish spoken. SERVES: L.A., Orange & San Bernardino Counties.

LAW ENFORCEMENT CANCER SUPPORT FNDN
26421 Crown Valley Pkwy., Ste 100
Mission Viejo, CA 92691
(888) 456-5327

Supports individuals in the law enforcement community going through cancer treatment. In-

dividuals are matched with volunteer mentors throughout the duration of their journey. Also provides cancer edu and advocates for early detection and prevention. FUNDING: Nonprofit.

LEAD POISONING
See "Natl Lead Info Center/U.S. EPA"

LEUKEMIA & LYMPHOMA SOCIETY, THE
Orange County/Inland Empire Chapter
2020 E. 1st Street, Ste 120
Santa Ana, CA 92705
(888) 535-9300
(714) 481-5600
(714) 481-5677 FAX

Serves patients and families affected with leukemia, lymphoma, myeloma and Hodgkin's disease. Research, public & prof edu, financial aid, info regarding community srvs, family support groups, one-on-one support & financial aid. Written material available in English and Spanish. Walk in or call. FUNDING: Fundraising, nonprofit. OFC HRS: M-F 9am-5pm. Spanish spoken. Free srvs. SERVES: Orange, Riverside & San Bernardino Counties.

LIFELINE SYSTEMS, INC.
111 Lawrence St.
Framingham, MA 01702-8156
(800) 380-3111
(800) 448-0107 FAX

Partnership project of state, community and pvt hospitals and health care affiliates using a communication device located in the home. Allows at-risk elders or disabled residents to electronically call for medical assist when a health crisis occurs and they are unable to use the phone. Local providers are identified by ZIP code to calling parties. OFC HRS: M-F 8am-8pm, EST. SERVES: U.S.A.

LIVING BANK, THE
P.O. Box 6725
Houston, TX 77265-6725
(800) 528-2971
(713) 961-9431
(713) 961-0979 FAX

Centralized nationwide registry open to anyone who wishes to donate organs and/or tissues for transplantation or research at time of death. For individuals wishing to donate their whole bodies for anatomical research and study, request info on how to pre-register with the nearest medical school. Edu literature and speakers for the public about organ donation and transplantation. FUNDING: Donations, grants, nonprofit. OFC HRS: M-Th 8am-5pm; F 9am-12noon, CST; emerg calls accepted 24 hrs. Spanish spoken. Free srvs. SERVES: U.S.A.

LOCKS OF LOVE
234 Southern Blvd.
West Palm Beach, FL 33405
(561) 833-7332
(561) 833-7962 FAX

Accepts donated hair to provide hairpieces to low-income children ages birth-18 yrs, who have lost their hair due to a medical condition. FUNDING: Donations, nonprofit. OFC HRS: M-F 8:30am-5pm, EST. Spanish spoken. Each case reviewed for financial circumstance. SERVES: U.S.A. & Canada.

LOMA LINDA CTR/HEALTH PROMOTION
See "Center for Health Promotion"

LOMA LINDA OUTPATIENT SURGERY CTR
11370 Anderson St.
Loma Linda, CA 92354
(909) 558-2867
(909) 558-2166 FAX

Outpatient and surgery center for all ages. Obstetrics, urology, general surgery. Spanish spoken. Accepts Medi-Cal, Medicare, pvt insurance.

LOU GEHRIG'S DISEASE
See "ALS Association/National"

LUMETRA (FORMERLY CMRI)
Medicare's Quality Improvement Organization
1 Sansome St., Ste 600
San Francisco, CA 94104
(800) 841-1602
(415) 677-2000
(415) 677-2193 FAX

Works to improve the quality of srvs provided to Medi-Care beneficiaries. Mail in complaints or call the helpline. Medicare beneficiaries, HMO enrollees & their representatives can contact Lumetra for immediate review of hospital discharge notices, health plan termination notices, review of clinical quality of care concerns, info & referral regarding Medicare & health improvement, & to obtain written materials & community edu on health care consumer & Medicare patient rights. Works with health care providers & community-based organizations to identify opportunities to improve the health status of the Medicare population. TDD (800) 881-5980. OFC HRS: M-F 9am-5pm. Appeals open M-Sun 9am-5pm. Translation srv available. SERVES: Calif.

LUNG ASSOCIATION
See "American Lung Assn/Inland Co."

LUNG LINE INFORMATION SERVICE
1400 Jackson St.
Denver, CO 80206
(877) 225-5654
(303) 398-1076
(303) 270-2103 FAX

Registered nurses answer questions about lung diseases, asthma, emphysema, chronic bronchitis, allergies, juvenile rheumatoid arthritis, smoking and other respiratory and immune system conditions and treatment prgms. This is a srv of the National Jewish Medical and Research Center. "Lung Facts" (800) 552-LUNG is available for health care consumers and health care professionals. 24-hr srv with recorded health messages on lung disease and allergies. OFC HRS: M-F 8am-4:30pm, MST. SERVES: U.S.A.

LUPUS FOUNDATION OF AMERICA, INC.
National Headquarters
2000 L Street, NW, Ste 710
Washington, DC 20036
(202) 349-1155
(202) 349-1156 FAX

Dedicated to providing comprehensive prgms and srvs to advance the understanding of the cause and the treatment of lupus. LFA prgms include: research, public awareness, info, patient & professional edu, patient & family support and advocacy. Infoline (800) 558-0121. Spanish (800) 558-0231. FUNDING: Donations, CFC, grants, nonprofit. OFC HRS: M-F

8am-5pm, EST. Spanish spoken. SERVES: U.S.A.

LUPUS FOUNDATION OF SO. CALIF
4699 Murphy Canyon Road, Ste 104
San Diego, CA 92123
(858) 278-2788
(858) 278-2782 FAX

Conducts seminars, provides lending library for patients and their families on issues of Lupus. Facilitates support groups. Supports research to treat & cure lupus. FUNDING: Nonprofit. OFC HRS: M-F 10:30am-4:30pm; 24-hr ans machine. ADM REQ: All ages served. Fixed fee schedule, $20 annual membership. SERVES: Orange, Riverside, San Diego and Imperial Counties, City of Ojai.

LUPUS INTERNATIONAL
Support Center & Lupus Library
17985 Sky Park Cir., Ste J
Irvine, CA 92614
(949) 833-2121
(888) 532-2322
(949) 833-1183 FAX

Edu materials, newsletters, etc. Quarterly symposium with panel of doctors providing up-to-date info on lupus (attendance ranges from 150-300 people). Rap session monthly. Call for time and location of support groups. Visit website for local helpline numbers (www.lupusinternational.com). FUNDING: Nonprofit. OFC HRS: M-F 9am-5pm. Spanish spoken. Fees: $25 per yr individual membership. Free general meetings & support groups. SERVES: So. Calif.

LUPUS SUPPORT NETWORK
P.O. Box 127

2026 N. Riverside Ave.
Rialto, CA 92377
(909) 874-9257
(909) 874-5312 FAX

Organization for lupus, fibromyalgia, arthritis, thyroid, diabetes and other autoimmune disorders. Partners with natl organizations to help patients and their families find srvs to help them live the highest quality of life. These srvs include, but are not limited to support groups, self-help courses, edu, doctors, food, clothing and housing, when able. FUNDING: Nonprofit. OFC HRS: M-Sat 10am-5pm. SERVES: So. Calif.

LYMPHOMA RESEARCH FNDN
8800 Venice Blvd., Ste 207
Los Angeles, CA 90034
(310) 204-7040
(800) 500-9976
(310) 204-7043 FAX

Funds medical research to find a cure for lymphoma and improve treatments. Provides support & info for lymphoma patients and their families regarding diagnosis treatment, clinical trials, support srvs, literature. Also provides info through a quarterly newsletter. Serves patients with a patient support system. Supports lymphoma-specific edu for both patients and health care professionals. Promotes advocacy. FUNDING: Private, nonprofit. OFC HRS: M-F 9am-5pm. Spanish spoken. SERVES: U.S.A.

MAMMOGRAPHY/LOW COST
See American Cancer Society for local screening test referrals.

MANAGED RISK MEDICAL INSURANCE BOARD (MRMIP)
P.O. Box 2769
Sacramento, CA 95812-2769
(916) 324-4695
(916) 324-4878 FAX

Health care insurance for Californians who are unable to get health insurance from a regular insurance carrier. TDD/TTY (800) 735-2929. OFC HRS: M-F 8:30am-4:30pm. Spanish spoken. Fees based on age, health plan selection and county of residence. SERVES: Calif.

MARCH OF DIMES BIRTH DEFECTS FNDN
Greater Los Angeles Division
3699 Wilshire Blvd., Ste 520
Los Angeles, CA 90010-2719
(213) 637-5050
(213) 637-5055 FAX

Goal is to improve the health of babies by preventing birth defects, premature births and infant mortality. Supports campaign for healthier babies, prgms of research, community srvs, edu and advocacy. Provides grants, Comenzando Bien, a Spanish-speaking prgm, info & referral srvs, speaker's bureau, visiting professorship in nursing, work site prgms including the Babies and You prgm. FUNDING: Nonprofit. OFC HRS: M-F 9am-5pm. Spanish spoken. SERVES: L.A., Ventura, Santa Barbara, Riverside, San Bernardino, San Luis Obispo, Mono, Inyo & Kern Counties.

MARCH OF DIMES BIRTH DEFECTS FNDN
Inland Empire Division
3600 Lime St., Ste 524
Riverside, CA 92501
(951) 341-0903

(951) 276-4755 FAX

Goal is to improve the health of babies by preventing birth defects, premature births and infant mortality. Supports campaign for healthier babies, prgms of research, community srvs, edu and advocacy. Provides grants, Comenzando Bien, a Spanish-speaking prgm, info & referral srvs, speaker's bureau, visiting professorship in nursing, work site prgms including the Babies and You prgm. FUNDING: Nonprofit. OFC HRS: M-F 9am-5pm. Spanish spoken. SERVES: Riverside & San Bernardino Counties.

MARTHA'S VILLAGE & KITCHEN, INC.
83791 Date Ave.
Indio, CA 92201-4737
(760) 347-4741
(760) 347-9551 FAX

Hot meals M-Sun 11am-12:30pm, canned food baskets offered to families M-F 8am-10am & 1pm-4pm, 3rd W of month 10am-12noon for singles. Store distributes clothing to families by request. Medical referrals & prescription vouchers for those with no other access to medical care. Showers M-F 8am-10:45am & seasonal shelter. Offers computer, ESL & EED classes. FUNDING: Donations, nonprofit. OFC HRS: M-F 8am-5pm. SERVES: Coachella Vly area.

MCNEAL NUTRITIONAL
7050 Camp Hill Rd.
Fort Washington, PA 19034
(800) 522-8243
(215) 273-4070 FAX

Answer consumer questions regarding lactose intolerance. OFC HRS: M-F 9am-5pm, EST. SERVES: U.S.A.

MEDI-CAL FIELD OFFICE
Dept of Health Services
464 W. 4th Street, Ste 354
San Bernardino, CA 92401
(909) 383-4192
(909) 383-6929 FAX

Reviews requests to provide health srvs to Medi-Cal beneficiaries. Reviews patient records on-site at acute hospitals, reviews patients and patient records at intermediate care facilities for the dev disabled, skilled nursing homes. Call for info. FUNDING: State. OFC HRS: M-F 8am-5pm. Spanish spoken. Free srvs. SERVES: San Bernardino, Riverside, Orange, Mono, Inyo Counties.

MEDICAL BOARD OF CALIFORNIA
Licensed Midwife Prgm
2005 Evergreen St., Ste 1200
Sacramento, CA 95815
(916) 263-2382
(916) 263-2944 FAX

Midwifery constitutes the furthuring or undertaking by any licensed midwife to assist a woman in childbirth. Does not include assisting childbirth by artificial, forcible or mechanical means. FUNDING: Govt. SERVES: Calif.

MEDICAL SOCIETY
See "San Bernardino Co. Medical Society"

MEDICALLY INDIGENT SERVICES
See "Riverside Co. Public Health Dept"

MEDICARE & MEDICAID INFO SRVS
Customer Relations Branch
75 Hawthorne St., Ste 408
San Francisco, CA 94105-3901

(415) 744-3602
(415) 744-3771 FAX

Info on Medicare-related questions. Call (800) Medicare or visit (www.medicare.gov). FUNDING: Govt. OFC HRS: M-F 8am-4:30pm. SERVES: Calif, Nevada, Arizona & Hawaii.

MEDICARE TELEPHONE HOTLINE
U.S. Dept of Health & Human Srvs
(800) 633-4227

General Medicare info & reporting of Medicare fraud. Srv of the Health Care Financing Admin, U.S. Dept of Health & Human Srvs. FUNDING: Govt. Hotline Hrs: M-F 8am-8pm, EST. Spanish spoken. SERVES: U.S.A.

MEN'S HEALTH NETWORK
P.O. Box 75972
Washington, DC 20013
(202) 543-6461
(202) 543-2727 FAX

Info & edu organization that maintains an on-going network of health care providers & srvs dealing with men's health issues. FUNDING: Nonprofit. OFC HRS: 24-hr recording. Spanish spoken. SERVES: U.S.A.

MENIERE'S DISEASE NETWORK
See "Ear Foundation (The)"

MERCYCARE, INC.
993-C S. Santa Fe, Ste 149
Vista, CA 92083
(888) 776-3729
(800) 498-7077 FAX

Dedicated to assisting accident injury patients in obtaining medical funding and accident-related assist. FUNDING: Nonprofit. OFC HRS: M-F 8:30am-5pm. Spanish spoken. Free or low-cost medical srvs to those who qualify. SERVES: U.S.A.

MICHELLE'S PLACE
Women's Breast Cancer Resource Center
27645 Jefferson Ave., Ste 117
Temecula, CA 92590
(866) 304-1280
(951) 699-5455
(951) 699-3631 FAX

Education resources, community awarenes and support services for women with breast cancer. Support groups in English and Spanish. Volunteers welcome. FUNDING: Nonprofit. OFC HRS: M-F 9am-3:30pm; W evening by appt. Spanish spoken. SERVES: Riverside County.

MOJAVE VALLEY VOLUNTEER HOSPICE
Elder Haven
P.O. Box 504
516 E. Williams St.
Barstow, CA 92312-0504
(760) 256-5706
(760) 256-5197 FAX

Volunteer-driven organization with a coordinated prgm of supportive srvs for terminally ill patients and their families. Senior day care prgm. FUNDING: United Way, donations, nonprofit. OFC HRS: M, Tu, Th, F 9am-1pm. Spanish spoken. ADM REQ: Srvs ordered by M.D. Member should be mobile with assistance of a cane/walker or wheelchair and usually continent. Free srvs. SERVES: Barstow, Newberry, Daggett, Helendale.

MONTCLAIR COMMUNITY CENTER
City of Montclair

5111 Benito St.
Montclair, CA 91763
(909) 399-3173
(909) 625-9464
(909) 399-9751 FAX

Immunization, physicals, blood pressure screening, blood work twice a month. Women's clinic & other non-emerg med srvs. Senior info & referral, outreach, income tax prep assist. Senior nutrition prgm M-F 11:30am for ages 60 yrs+. Suggested donation: $1.75. Eggs and produce sold at reduced prices. Social & recreational activites for children and adults, excursions, after school prgm & edu classes. OFC HRS: Vary with prgm. Spanish spoken. SERVES: San Bernardino County.

MORONGO BASIN ADULT HEALTH SRVS
P.O. Box 106
57121 Sunnyslope Dr.
Yucca Valley, CA 92284
(760) 365-9661
(760) 994-1337 FAX

Prgms include a senior center and pool to help keep people in their own homes by helping them stay healthy and fit. For applications and payment info, visit (www.mbahs.org). FUNDING: Client fees, grants, insurance, donations, nonprofit. OFC HRS: M-F 8am-4pm; F 8am-2pm. SERVES: Morongo Basin.

MORONGO BASIN COUNSELING & RECOVERY
55475 Santa Fe Trial
Yucca Valley, CA 92284
(760) 365-3022
(760) 248-3389 FAX

Outpatient mental health srvs. Behavioral health screening, medication assist & support srvs. Counseling, group therapy, vocational srvs. FUNDING: County. OFC HRS: M-F 8am-5pm. Spanish spoken. ADM REQ: Children under age 18 yrs. SERVES: San Bernardino County.

MULTIPLE SCLEROSIS CLINIC/LLU
Loma Linda Univ Medical Center
Neurology Clinic
11370 Anderson St., Ste 2400
Loma Linda, CA 92354
(909) 558-2880
(888) 558-8705
(909) 558-2237 FAX

Diagnosis, eval, medical advice, clinical follow up and info. FUNDING: Donations, nonprofit. OFC HRS: M-Th 8am-5pm; F 8am-2pm; MS Clinic on Tu afternoon. Spanish spoken. ADM REQ: Diagnosed or suspected multiple sclerosis. Accepts pvt insurance. SERVES: U.S.A.

MULTIPLE SCLEROSIS SOCIETY
See "Natl Multiple Sclerosis Society"

MYASTHENIA GRAVIS FNDN/CALIF
5675 Telegraph Rd., Ste 230
Los Angeles, CA 90040-1570
(323) 887-0056
(323) 887-4915 FAX

Referral, info & support groups for patients with Myasthenia Gravis, an incurable auto-immune disease. Drug bank prgm for patients to obtain medications at tolerable cost, info packets, peer counseling, and support groups. Offers a MG clinic in Long Beach which can treat Myasthenics on an outpatient basis. Also clinic at UC Irvine & for Veterans at Long Beach Veteran's Hospital. FUNDING: Grants, donors, nonprofit. OFC HRS: M-F 8:30am-4:30pm. Spanish & Tagalog spoken. ADM REQ: MG patient. Free srvs available at clinics. Must qualify for free medication. SERVES: Calif. & Las Vegas.

MYASTHENIA GRAVIS FNDN/NATL
National Office
355 Lexington Ave., 15th Fl.
New York, NY 10017
(877) 596-1491
(212) 370-9047 FAX

Promotes medical research, patient care & srvs, professional and public edu related to Myasthenia Gravis. FUNDING: Donors, grants, nonprofit. OFC HRS: M-F 8am-4:30pm, CST. Accepts pvt pay. SERVES: U.S.A.

NATL ALLIANCE FOR HISPANIC HEALTH
Su Familia (Family Health Helpline)
1501 16th Street, NW
Washington, DC 20036
(866) 783-2645
(202) 797-4353 FAX

Bilingual health helpline and website. Callers are referred to health care providers in their area. For prenatal info, call La Linea Nacional Prenatal Hispana (800) 504-7081. For hospice info, call (877) 658-8896. Visit (www.hispanichealth.org). FUNDING: Grants, donations. OFC HRS: M-F 9am-6pm, EST. Spanish spoken. SERVES: U.S.A.

NATL ASSN FOR CONTINENCE
P.O. Box 1019
Charleston, SC 29402-1019
(843) 377-0900
(843) 377-0905 FAX

Public edu & advocacy in an effort to improve the quality of life for incontinence sufferers. Pamphlets, books. Toll-free health edu line: 1-800-BLADDER. FUNDING: Private, nonprofit. OFC HRS: M-F 9am-5pm, EST. SERVES: U.S.A.

NATL BREAST CANCER COALITION
1101 17th Street, NW, Ste 1300
Washington, DC 20036
(800) 622-2838
(202) 296-7477
(202) 265-6854 FAX

Srvs include: edu, referral, screening, support srvs, advocacy and financial assist. Visit (www.stopbreastcancer.org). FUNDING: Nonprofit. OFC HRS: M-F 9am-5pm, EST. SERVES: U.S.A.

NATL CHILDHOOD CANCER FNDN
440 E. Huntington Dr., Ste 400
Arcadia, CA 91066-6012
(800) 458-6223

Organization dedicated to childhood cancer research. Patients, families and health professionals can locate info and assist by visiting (www.curesearch.org). FUNDING: Nonprofit. OFC HRS: M-F 8:30am-5pm. SERVES: U.S.A.

NATL CTR FOR CHRONIC DISEASE PREV AND HEALTH PROMOTION
4770 Buford Hwy. N.E., K-40
Atlanta, GA 30341-3717
(800) 232-4636

Gathers info on chronic disease prevention & health promotion. Provides info & referrals to related resources. Extensive collection of info

available for use by appt. For TTY, call (888) 232-6348 FUNDING: Govt. OFC HRS: M-F 8am-5pm, EST. SERVES: U.S.A.

NATL CTR FOR COMP/ALTERNATIVE MED
Complementary & Alternative Medicine Info
9000 Rockville Pike
Bethesda, MD 20892
(888) 644-6226
(301) 519-3153
(866) 464-3616 FAX

Info specialists answer questions about complementary or alternative medicine (CAM) and therapies. Does not provide medical referrals, advice or recommendations for specific therapies. TTY (866) 464-3615. FUNDING: Govt. OFC HRS: M-F 8:30am-5pm, EST. Spanish spoken. Free srvs. SERVES: U.S.A.

NATL DIABETES INFO CLEARINGHOUSE
1 Information Way
Bethesda, MD 20892-3560
(800) 860-8747
(703) 738-4929 FAX

NDIC is an info & referral srv of the Natl Institute of Diabetes & Digestive & Kidney Diseases, one of the Natl Institutes of Health. The clearinghouse responds to written inquires, develops and distributes publications about diabetes and provides referrals to diabetes organizations. The NDIC maintains a database of patient and professional edu materials, from which literature searches are generated. For TTY, call (866) 569-1162 FUNDING: Govt. OFC HRS: M-F 8:30am-5pm, EST. SERVES: U.S.A.

NATL DIGESTIVE DISEASE INFO
Information Clearinghouse
2 Information Way
Bethesda, MD 20892-3570
(866) 569-1162
(800) 891-5389
(703) 738-4929 FAX

Info & referral srv of the National Institute of Diabetes and Digestive and Kidney Diseases, one of the National Institutes of Health. A central info resource on the prevention and mgmt of digestive diseases, the clearinghouse responds to written inquires, develops & distributes publications about digestive diseases & provides referrals to organizations, including support groups. Maintains a database of patient and professional edu materials from which literature searches are generated. OFC HRS: M-F 8:30am-5pm, EST. Spanish spoken. SERVES: U.S.A.

NATL FIBROMYALGIA ASSN
2121 S. Towne Centre Place, Ste 300
Anaheim, CA 92806
(714) 921-0150
(714) 921-6920 FAX

Dedicated to fibromyalgia, a chronic pain disorder. Develops and executes prgms dedicated to improving the quality of life. Efforts include patient edu and assistance, healthcare, provider edu, awareness outreach, advocacy and the facilitation of research. Visit (www.fmaware.org). FUNDING: Nonprofit. OFC HRS: M-F 8:30am-5pm SERVES: U.S.A.

NATL HEADACHE FOUNDATION
820 N. Orleans, Ste 217
Chicago, IL 60610-3132
(888) 643-5552

(312) 274-2650
(312) 640-9049 FAX

Dedicated to serving headache sufferers, their families and the healthcare practitioners who treat them. Promotes research into headache causes and treatments. Educates the public that headaches are a legitimate biological disease and sufferers should receive understanding and continuity of care. FUNDING: Dues, grants, donations, nonprofit. OFC HRS: M-F 9am-5pm, CST. $25 for printed info, $20 per yr for online info. SERVES: U.S.A.

NATL HEALTH FEDERATION
P.O. Box 688
1230 Huntington Dr., Ste 4
Monrovia, CA 91017
(626) 357-2181
(626) 303-0642 FAX

Consumer edu and health rights organization working to protect the consumer's right to buy and use vitamins, minerals, amino acids, enzymes and herbs; the manufacturer's right to produce the above supplements; and the freedom for health food stores to provide the supplements consumers choose. Publishes newsletters, articles and sponsors events on natural health subjects. Quarterly magazine for members. FUNDING: Dues, donations, nonprofit. OFC HRS: M-F 9am-5pm. Spanish spoken. Natl annual fees $36, Internatl fees $48-$81. SERVES: U.S.A & internatl.

NATL HEALTH INFORMATION CENTER
P.O. Box 1133
Washington, DC 20013-1133
(800) 336-4797
(301) 984-4256 FAX

The NHIC is a health info referral srv which links consumers and health professionals who have health questions with organizations best able to provide answers. The center maintains an online directory of more than 1,100 health-related organizations that can provide health info. They include federal & state agencies, voluntary assns, self-help and support groups, trade associations, and professional societies. Prints directories and resource guides on a variety of health topics. FUNDING: Fed. OFC HRS: M-F 9am-5:30pm, EST. Spanish spoken. Free srvs. SERVES: U.S.A.

NATL HEART, LUNG & BLOOD INSTITUTE
Health Information Center
P.O. Box 30105
Bethesda, MD 20824-0105
(301) 592-8573
(240) 629-3246 FAX

Info & materials on risk factors for cardiovascular disease. TTY (240) 629-3255. FUNDING: Govt. OFC HRS: M-F 8:30am-5pm, EST. SERVES: U.S.A.

NATL HIV/AIDS CLINICIANS CONSULT CTR
Univ San Francisco/SF General Hospital
P.O. Box 1365
1001 Potrero Ave., Bldg. 20, Ward 22
San Francisco, CA 94143-1365
(415) 206-8700
(415) 476-3454 FAX

Natl HIV telephone consultation srv warmline. Clinical & drug info through individualized case consultation. Natl Clinician's Post-Exposure Prophylaxis Hotline (888) 448-4911, PEPline offers advice for health care providers managing occupational exposures to HIV and hepatitis B/C. 24-hr hotline (888) 448-8765, for perinatal HIV+ pregnant women. Visit (www.ucsf.edu/ hivcntr). FUNDING: Govt. OFC HRS: Warmline M-F 8am-8pm, EST, 24-hr voicemail. PEPline & perinatal line 24 hrs, 7 days. Free srvs for health care providers only. SERVES: U.S.A.

NATL HYDROCEPHALUS FOUNDATION
12413 Centralia Rd.
Lakewood, CA 90715-1653
(888) 857-3434
(562) 924-6666

Offers brochures, help guides, a reference library, videos & CDs on Hydrocephalus. Several support groups and assist in starting new ones. Publishes quarterly newsletter: Life~Line. Visit (http://www.nhfonline.org) for more info. FUNDING: Nonprofit. Free srvs.

NATL IMMUNIZATION INFO HOTLINE
1600 Clifton Rd. N.E.
Mailstop E-05
Atlanta, GA 30333
(800) 232-4636
(919) 361-8425 FAX

Support, edu materials and referrals about vaccine-preventable diseases, including Hepatitis B. Spanish (800) 232-0233. TTY (800) 243-7889. FUNDING: Nonprofit. OFC HRS: M-F 8am-11pm, EST. Spanish spoken. Free srvs. SERVES: U.S.A.

NATL INST ALLERGY/INFECTIOUS DISEASES
Office of Communications/Public Liason
6610 Rockledge Dr., MSC 6612
Bethesda, MD 20892-6612
(301) 496-5717
(866) 284-4107
(301) 402-3573 FAX

Info on HIV/AIDS, allergy & asthma, autoimmune disorders & other infectious diseases (hepatitis, Lyme disease, malaria, TB, bacterial, fungal, viral, parasitic & immunologic diseases). Various publications distributed. TDD (800) 877-8339. FUNDING: Govt. OFC HRS: M-F 8:30am-5pm, EST. Free srvs. SERVES: U.S.A.

NATL INST DEAFNESS/COMM DISORDERS (NIDCD)
31 Center Dr., MSC 2320
Bethesda, MD 20892-2320
(800) 241-1044
(301) 770-8977 FAX

Collects & disseminates info on hearing, balance, smell, taste, voice, speech & language. Maintains a database of references to brochures, books, articles, factsheets, organizations, etc. TTY (800) 241-1055. FUNDING: Govt. OFC HRS: M-F 8:30am-5pm, EST. SERVES: U.S.A.

NATL INST OF ENVIRONMTL HLTH SCI
Comm/Pub Liaison Mail Drop K3-16
P.O. Box 12233
111 T.W. Alexander Dr.
Research Triangle Pk, NC 27709
(919) 541-3345
(919) 541-4395 FAX

Part of the Natl Institutes of Health, conducts basic biomedical research on environmental agents such as air pollutants, heavy metal, pesticides and their effect on human health. Info offered on many health issues: lead & mercury poisoning, air pollutants, lung disease, etc. New brochures aimed at teenagers, free by writing or visiting (www.niehs.nih.gov). Some topics are "Environmental Diseases A-Z," "Ozone Alerts" and "Making it in a Tough Environment." FUNDING: Fed, govt. OFC HRS: M-F 8:30am-5pm, EST. SERVES: U.S.A.

NATL INSTITUTE ON AGING
See "Alzheimer's Disease Ed & Referral"

NATL INSTITUTES OF HEALTH
Clinical Trials
9000 Rockville Pike
Bethesda, MD 20892
(301) 496-4000

Maintains website giving info on current clinical trials for those wanting to participate in various research studies. Includes purpose of trial, eligibility & contact info. Visit (www.clinicaltrials.gov). FUNDING: U.S. Dept of Health & Human Srvs. OFC HRS: M-F 9am-4pm, EST. SERVES: U.S.A.

NATL KIDNEY FNDN HOTLINE
30 E. 33rd Street
New York, NY 10016
(800) 622-9010
(212) 689-9261 FAX

Dedicated to preventing kidney & urinary tract diseases, improving the health & well being of individuals & families affected by these diseases, & increasing the availability of all organs for transplantation. FUNDING: Nonprofit. OFC HRS: M-F 8:30am-5:30pm, EST. Spanish spoken. Free srvs. SERVES: U.S.A.

NATL KIDNEY FNDN OF SO CALIF
Southern Calif Regional Office
15490 Ventura Blvd., Ste 210
Sherman Oaks, CA 91403
(800) 747-5527
(818) 783-8153
(818) 783-8160 FAX

Info on kidney and urinary tract diseases and referrals to local dialysis centers. Some financial assist for people with kidney disease. Supports camp prgms for children and adults with kidney failure. Prgms for people living with kidney disease. Promotes organ donor awareness. Provides edu materials regarding kidney disorders. Funds research into causes and treatment of kidney disease. Fall symposium for health care professionals. Walk in or call. FUNDING: Donations, nonprofit. OFC HRS: M-F 9am-5pm. Spanish spoken. Free srvs. SERVES: So. Calif.

NATL KIDNEY/UROLOGIC DISEASES INFO
3 Information Way
Bethesda, MD 20892-3580
(800) 891-5390
(301) 654-4415
(703) 738-4929 FAX

NKUDIC is an info & referral srv of the National Institute of Diabetes and Digestive and Kidney Diseases, one of the Natl Institutes of Health. The clearinghouse responds to written inquires, develops and distributes publications about kidney and urologic diseases, and provides referrals to kidney and urologic organizations. Maintains a database of patient and professional edu materials from which literature searches are generated. FUNDING: Govt. OFC HRS: M-F 8:30am-5pm, EST. SERVES: U.S.A.

NATL LEAD INFO CENTER/U.S. EPA
ABUI Goodwill
422 S. Clinton Ave.
Rochester, NY 14620
(800) 424-5323
(585) 232-3111 FAX

Clearinghouse is staffed by trained info specialists who can provide in-depth tech info on a range of lead-related issues. Offered in English & Spanish. Serves professional audiences such as govt officials, industry reps and abatement staff, community-based organizations, media & the general public. Also has a database of lead edu materials, a speaker's referral srv and posters. FUNDING: EPA, HUD, CDC, govt. OFC HRS: M-F 8:30am-6pm, EST. SERVES: U.S.A.

NATL LYMPHEDEMA NETWORK
Latham Square
116 New Montgomery St., Ste 235
San Francisco, CA 94105
(800) 541-3259
(415) 908-3681
(415) 908-3813 FAX

Disseminates info on primary and secondary lymphedema via an extensive newsletter, edu website, edu materials and conferences. Refer to lymphedema specialists, support groups, penpals, netpals, and more. FUNDING: Donations, nonprofit. OFC HRS: M-F 9am-5pm. Dutch spoken. SERVES: U.S.A.

NATL MARROW DONOR PROGRAM
3001 Broadway St. NE, Ste 100
Minneapolis, MN 55413
(800) 627-7692
(612) 627-5877 FAX

Facilitates unrelated donor stem cell transplants for patients with life-threatening blood diseases who do not have matching donors in their families. Provides a single point of access for all sources of blood stem cells used in transplantation: marrow, peripheral blood and umbilical cord blood. The registry is able to search its database and provide physicians with info on multiple stem cell sources for life-saving transplants. Free of charge for both potential donors and patients. Written materials in English, Spanish and Chinese. FUNDING: Nonprofit. OFC HRS: M-F 8am-6pm, CST. Access to interpreters in over 141 languages. SERVES: U.S.A.

NATL MULTIPLE SCLEROSIS SOCIETY
Headquarters
733 3rd Ave., 3rd Fl.
New York, NY 10017
(212) 463-7787
(800) 344-4867
(212) 986-7981 FAX

Publications regarding MS and living with MS. Info & referrals. OFC HRS: M-F 9am-5pm, EST. Free srvs. SERVES: U.S.A.

NATL MULTIPLE SCLEROSIS SOCIETY
Coachella Valley Branch
73710 Fred Waring Dr., Ste 103
Palm Desert, CA 92260
(760) 776-5740
(760) 776-5742 FAX

Current info and research data on MS. Referral to support groups, srvs, health professionals and other community resources. Call for schedule of prgms appropriate for individuals, family members or friends. Materials available in Spanish. FUNDING: Nonprofit. OFC HRS: M-F 9am-5pm. SERVES: Coachella Valley, Morongo Basin and Palo Verde Valley.

NATL MULTIPLE SCLEROSIS SOCIETY
Inland Empire Field Office
869 E. Foothill Blvd., Ste I
Upland, CA 91786
(800) 752-1773
(909) 949-1363

General info & research data on multiple sclerosis. Referral to support groups and srvs. FUNDING: Donations, grants, nonprofit. OFC HRS: M-F 9am-5pm. Spanish spoken. SERVES: Riverside & San Bernardino Counties.

NATL ORG DISORDERS/CORPUS CALLOSUM
18032-C Lemon Dr.
Yorba Linda, CA 92886
(714) 747-0063
(714) 693-0202 FAX

Natl org for fisorders of the corpus callosum. Strives to enhance the quality of life and promote opportunities for individuals with disorders of the corpus callosum and raise the profile, understanding and acceptance of these disorders through research, edu, advocacy and networking. FUNDING: Nonprofit. OFC HRS: Vary on a part-time basis. SERVES: U.S.A.

NATL ORG RARE DISORDERS (NORD)
P.O. Box 1968
55 Kenosia Ave.
Danbury, CT 06813-1968
(203) 744-0100
(203) 798-2291 FAX

Clearinghouse for info on rare "orphan" diseases. Reports in lay language on specific diseases. Info includes symptoms, causes, affected populations, standard and experimental therapies, resources and networking. For TDD srv, call (203) 797-9590. FUNDING: Donations, nonprofit. OFC HRS: M-F 9am-5pm, EST. First disease report is free; additional reports $7.50. Memberships available $30 per yr. SERVES: Internatl.

NATL PARKINSON FNDN/O.C. CHAPTER
Hoag Hospital
P.O. Box 2207
One Hoag Dr.
Newport Beach, CA 92658
(949) 764-6998
(949) 548-4624 FAX

Patient srvs & outreach prgm for those needing edu material, support group & chapter info, physician & social srv referral. Leave your name, phone number or address for info. Mailing address: 351 Old Newport Blvd., Ste. 114, Newport Beach, CA 92663. FUNDING: Nonprofit. Free srvs. SERVES: Orange, Riverside, South L.A. & North San Diego Counties.

NATL PARKINSON FOUNDATION HDQR
National Headquarters
1501 NW 9th Avenue
Miami, FL 33136
(800) 327-4545
(305) 243-6073 FAX

PT, OT, speech, and neuropsychological therapies. Conducts research to find the cause and cure for Parkinson's disease and allied neurological disorders. Provides edu to medical practitioners on how to detect early warning signs;

educates patients, caregivers, and the general public; and provides diagnostic and therapeutic srvs with a goal of improving the quality of life for both patient and caregiver. Nurses answer questions about the disease including general info and research info. Also physican referrals and printed materials available at no charge. Helpline: (800) 473-4636 FUNDING: Donations, grants, nonprofit. OFC HRS: M-F 9am-5pm, EST. Spanish spoken. SERVES: U.S.A.

NATL PATIENT TRAVEL CENTER
4620 Haygood Rd., Ste 1
Virginia Beach, VA 23455
(800) 296-1217
(800) 550-1767 FAX

Assists patients with finding charitable medical air transportation resources. OFC HRS: M-F 9am-5pm, EST. After hours helpline available. SERVES: U.S.A.

NATL PSORIASIS FOUNDATION
6600 S.W. 92nd Avenue, Ste 300
Portland, OR 97223-7195
(800) 723-9166
(503) 244-7404
(503) 245-0626 FAX

Edu and advocacy to improve the lives of people who have psoriasis and psoriatic arthritis supporting research to cure the millions of people with these chronic skin diseases. FUNDING: Nonprofit. OFC HRS: M-F 8am-5pm. SERVES: U.S.A.

NATL REYE'S SYNDROME FNDN
P.O. Box 829
426 N. Lewis St.
Bryan, OH 43506
(800) 233-7393
(419) 636-9897 FAX

Awareness materials provided to the public & med community. Guidance & counseling to victms of Reye's Syndrome. Leave message after hrs. Materials in Spanish. FUNDING: Donations, nonprofit. OFC HRS: M-F 8am-5pm, EST. SERVES: U.S.A. & internatl.

NATL SPASMODIC TORTICOLLIS ASSN
9920 Talbert Ave.
Fountain Valley, CA 92708
(800) 487-8385
(714) 378-9837
(714) 378-7830 FAX

Also known as cervical dystonia. Resources and info for physicians who treat this debilitating neurological movement disorder. Also offers support group contacts. FUNDING: Nonprofit. OFC HRS: M-F 8am-5pm. SERVES: U.S.A.

NATL SPINAL CORD INJURY ASSN
Natl Office Resource Center
1 Church St., Ste 600
Rockville, MD 20850
(800) 962-9629
(866) 387-2196 FAX

Info, data, local resources & referrals to persons with SCI. Health care staff. Various fact sheets provide valuable info to individuals with SCI. Local chapters offer seven rehab centers, visitation and peer counseling to those with SCI. FUNDING: Donations, grants, nonprofit. OFC HRS: M-F 8:30am-5pm, EST. Spanish spoken. SERVES: U.S.A.

NATL STROKE ASSN
9707 E. Easter Lane, Bldg. B
Centennial, CO 80112
(800) 787-6537
(303) 649-9299
(303) 649-1328 FAX

Organization dedicated to educating stroke survivors, families, health care professionals and the general public about strokes. Referrals are also made to resources in communities throughout the U.S. Newsletter, stroke journal, and national clearinghouse for info & referrals. Promotes research & disseminates findings. Offers stroke survivor and caregiver srvs. Provides guidance in developing stroke clubs and stroke support groups. Offers screening and other prevention prgms. Operates Stroke Center Network prgm to help professionals provide the best srvs to stroke patients. FUNDING: Grants, donations, nonprofit. OFC HRS: M-F 8am-4:30pm. SERVES: U.S.A.

NATL WOMEN'S HEALTH RESOURCE CTR (NWHRC)
157 Broad St., Ste 106
Red Bank, NJ 07701
(877) 986-9472
(732) 530-3425
(732) 530-3347 FAX

Natl clearinghouse for women's health info and bimonthly newsletter. FUNDING: Grants, donations, nonprofit. OFC HRS: M-F 9am-5pm. SERVES: U.S.A.

NEIGHBORHOOD HEALTHCARE
41715 Winchester Rd., Ste 106, 204
Temecula, CA 92591
(951) 694-9449
(951) 719-1414

Srvs include: physicals, immunizations, pediatrics, OB/GYN, family planning, primary care, HIV/STD testing, treatment, acute, chronic & preventative care, lab srvs. FUNDING: Nonprofit. OFC HRS: M, W-F 7am-4:30pm; Tu 7am-7:30pm. Spanish spoken. ADM REQ: Low-to-moderate income. Accepts Medi-Cal, Medicare, Molina, MISP, exclusive care (Healthy Families), CHDP, IHEP, sliding fee scale starting at $30. SERVES: Southwest Riverside County.

NEUROFIBROMATOSIS FOUNDATION
See "Children's Tumor Foundation"

NEUROFIBROMATOSIS, INC
P.O. Box 66884
Chicago, IL 60666
(800) 942-6825
(630) 627-1117 FAX

Info & referral to medical & other srvs. Peer counseling, printed materials (including NF-1, NF-2), newsletters. Supports, promotes and funds research. Summer camp for youth. Natl physician referrals. FUNDING: Donations, nonprofit. OFC HRS: 24 hrs, 7 days. SERVES: U.S.A. & Internatl.

NUTRITION HOTLINE
See "Consumer Nutrition Info Line "

OBSESSIVE-COMPULSIVE FNDN, INC.
P.O. Box 961029
112 Water St., Ste 501
Boston, MA 02129
(617) 973-5801

Internatl organization composed of people with obsessive-compulsive disorder (OCD) and related disorders, their families, friends, professionals and others. Individual membership is $45 per yr and includes bi-monthly newsletter with latest research, resources and recovery, conferences, research awards, related support groups, etc. FUNDING: Nonprofit. OFC HRS: M-F 9am-5pm, EST. Spanish spoken. ADM REQ: Membership. SERVES: U.S.A. & internatl.

OFFICE ON SMOKING & HEALTH

Centers for Disease Control & Prevention
1600 Clifton Rd
Atlanta, GA 30333
(800) 232-4636
(770) 488-5705
(770) 488-5939 FAX

Info on smoking cessation, environmental tobacco smoke & passive smoking, pregnancy & infants, professional & tech info, & publications upon request. Distributes annual Surgeon General's Report on Smoking & Health, and coordinates natl public info & edu prgms. TTY (888) 232-6348. FUNDING: Govt. OFC HRS: M-F 8am-5pm, EST. SERVES: U.S.A.

OFFICE/MINORITY HEALTH RESOURCE

P.O. Box 37337
Washington, DC 20013-7337
(800) 444-6472
(240) 453-2883 FAX

Responds to consumer and professional inquiries on minority health-related topics. Free database searches, resource list, fact sheet, publications, etc. Referrals to other resources, tech assist. TDD (301) 230-7199. FUNDING: Govt. OFC HRS: M-F 9am-5pm, EST. Spanish and Korean spoken. Free srvs. SERVES: U.S.A.

ONELEGACY

1701 Orange Tree Lane
Redlands, CA 92374
(909) 801-3701
(800) 786-4077
(909) 801-3707 FAX

Organ and tissue bank works with hospitals and coroners' offices in Riverside, San Bernardino and Kern Counties to supply donor tissue for cornea transplants and many other life enhancing transplant surgeries. Encourages public awareness about organ donations, donor cards, and cooperates with other eye banks and tissue banks in the distribution of tissues worldwide. FUNDING: Donations, nonprofit. OFC HRS: M-F 8am-5pm. Free srvs.

ORTHOPAEDIC HOSPITAL L.A.

See "Haemostasis & Thrombosis"

PACIFIC AIDS EDU & TRAINING CTR

50 Beale St., Ste 1300
San Francisco, CA 94105-0661
(415) 597-8198
(415) 897-9213 FAX

AIDS/HIV training, edu & info srvs provided to health care providers. Various locations in Calif. OFC HRS: M-F 8am-5pm. SERVES: U.S.A.

PARKINSON'S CENTER

Eisenhower Medical Center
39000 Bob Hope Dr., Ste 202
Rancho Mirage, CA 92270
(760) 340-3911

(760) 773-4200 FAX

Info & referral to resources, edu on disease, diagnostic and therapeutic srvs to improve the quality of life for both patients and their caregivers. Free info, pamphlets, doctor referrals. FUNDING: Donations, nonprofit. OFC HRS: M-F 8:30am-5pm. Closed on F during summer. SERVES: U.S.A.

PARKINSON'S DISEASE

See "American Parkinson Disease Assn"

PARKINSON'S EDUCATIONAL PRGM

Parkinson's Disease Fndn
1359 Broadway, Ste 1509
New York, NY 10018
(800) 457-6676
(212) 923-4778 FAX

Natl info center. FUNDING: Nonprofit. OFC HRS: M-F 9am-5pm, EST. Spanish spoken. SERVES: U.S.A.

PECHANGA INDIAN HEALTH CLINIC

12784 Pechanga Rd.
Temecula, CA 92592
(951) 676-6810
(951) 676-0744 FAX

Comprehensive health care, mental health (individual and family counseling), nutrition, pharmacy, lab, nursing, AIDS testing, family planning, patient transportation srvs. FUNDING: Fed, state, county. OFC HRS: M-Th 8am-5pm; F 8am-2pm. ADM REQ: Eligible American Indian dependents only. Must have appt. Accepts Medi-Cal for eligible patients only. Sliding fee scale. Free srvs to qualified Indians.

PEDIATRIC CANCER RESEARCH FNDN

9272 Jeronimo Rd., Ste A-107A
Irvine, CA 92618
(949) 859-6312
(949) 859-6323 FAX

Supports pediatric cancer research. No direct srvs. FUNDING: Donations, grants, nonprofit. OFC HRS: M-F 8:30am-5pm. SERVES: USA.

PHYSICIAN REFERRAL SERVICE

Eisenhower Medical Center
39000 Bob Hope Dr., Ste K103
Rancho Mirage, CA 92270
(760) 340-3911
(760) 773-1335 FAX

Free telephone referral srv designed to help individuals find a physician or contact any of the Eisenhower Medical Center's health care prgms. OFC HRS: M-F 9am-4:30pm. SERVES: Coachella Valley.

PHYSICIAN REFERRAL SERVICE

Loma Linda University Medical Center
245 E. Redlands Blvd.
San Bernardino, CA 92407
(877) 558-6248
(909) 558-0012 FAX

Physician referral srv provides individuals in the community with referrals to Loma Linda University Medical Center faculty physicians. OFC HRS: M-Th 7am-8pm; F 7am-5pm. Spanish spoken. Free srvs. SERVES: San Bernardino County.

PLASTIC SURGERY INFO

See "American Soc/Plastic Surgeons"

POISON INFORMATION

See "Calif Poison Control System"

POMONA VALLEY HOSPITAL MED CTR

Family Education & Resource Ctr
1770 N. Orange Grove Ave.
Pomona, CA 91767
(909) 865-9858
(909) 865-9782
(909) 629-0890 FAX

Free referrals to support groups, physicians and community resources. Offers ongoing classes & support prgms. FUNDING: Nonprofit. OFC HRS: M-F 8:30am-5pm; Sat 8:30am-1pm. Spanish spoken. SERVES: Inland & San Gabriel Valleys.

PREVENTIVE HEALTH FOR ADULTS

Formerly "Preventive Health Care/Aging Prgm"

For a complete list of the senior centers and sites go to the "Senior/Multiple Services" chapter of this directory. Contact a local senior center for a free health assessment for seniors ages 50 yrs+. Also preventive health prgms including: blood pressure screening, flu shots, health education, wellness check, cholesterol test, etc.

PROJECT INFORM

1375 Mission St.
San Francisco, CA 94103
(415) 558-8669
(415) 558-0684 FAX

Fights for an HIV and HCV cure by advancing national research agenda to generate optimal treatments; helps secure expanded access to quality health care for low-income individuals. Provides free, reliable info on living with HIV disease through its natl HIV treatment and care benefits hotline: (866) HIV-INFO, M-F 10am-4pm. FUNDING: Nonprofit. OFC HRS: M-F 9am-5pm. Spanish spoken. SERVES: Internatl.

PROSTATE & SKIN CANCER SCREENING

Contact your local American Cancer Society for prgms & dates and referrals for screening, (800) 227-2345 or visit (www.cancer.org).

RIDGECREST COMMUNITY HEALTH CENTER

1133 N. Chelsea St.
Ridgecrest, CA 93555
(760) 446-7978
(760) 446-2850 FAX

Primary health care for all ages. OB/GYN, prenatal, AIDS/STD. FUNDING: BPHC site, donations, nonprofit. OFC HRS: M-F 8am-5pm. Spanish spoken. ADM REQ: Low income. Accepts insurance, Medi-Cal & Medicare. SERVES: Kern County.

RIDGECREST REGIONAL HOSPITAL

Home Health Agency
1081 N. China Lake Blvd.
Ridgecrest, CA 93555
(760) 499-3615
(760) 499-3614 FAX

Skilled nursing, intermittent care, IV therapy, PT, OT, & speech therapy, CHHA and social srvs. 24-hr on-call RN. Wait: 1-3 days. Hospital main #(760) 446-3551. State ID: 120000194. FUNDING: Nonprofit. OFC HRS: M-F 8am-4:30pm. ADM REQ: Physician-ordered srv. Accepts Medi-Cal, Medicare. SERVES: Trona, Ridgecrest, Inyokern.

RIVERSIDE CO. COMM HEALTH AGENCY

Dept Of Public Health/Nursing
4065 County Circle Dr., Ste 305
Riverside, CA 92503
(951) 358-5438
(951) 358-4762 FAX

In-home srvs include assessment, guidance, counseling, teaching, intervention, referral & family case mgmt in the following categories: child health, senior health, perinatal, postpartum, family planning, parenting edu, high-risk pregnancy, high-risk infant, grief/loss, child abuse prevention, adult/elder abuse, communicable disease, tuberculosis, infant death, drug-exposed infant, birth/newborn screening follow-up, homeless, domestic violence, teen parenting. Group parenting edu classes are provided in many locations. TDD (951) 358-5124. OFC HRS: M-F 8am-5pm. SERVES: Riverside County.

RIVERSIDE CO. MEDICAL ASSN

3993 Jurupa Ave.
Riverside, CA 92506-2257
(951) 686-3342
(951) 686-1692 FAX

Physician referral, assist patient with quality assurance, ethics and treatment, etc. Directory of physician members. FUNDING: Members, nonprofit. OFC HRS: M-F 8am-5pm. Spanish spoken. ADM REQ: Physician. SERVES: Riverside County.

RIVERSIDE CO. PUBLIC HEALTH DEPT

Banning Family Health Center
3055 W. Ramsey St.
Banning, CA 92220
(951) 849-6794
(951) 849-0060 FAX

Family planning, CHDP, prenatal care, medical care, physical exams, immunization for adults and children, pap smears, pregnancy testing, screening for STDs and TB, HIV/AIDS testing & counseling. OFC HRS: M-F 7:30am-5pm. Spanish spoken. Accepts Medi-Cal, MISP/MIA, PPOs. Medical srv for any Calif resident, fees based on ability to pay. SERVES: Riverside County.

RIVERSIDE CO. PUBLIC HEALTH DEPT

Corona Health/Family Care Center
505 S. Buena Vista Ave., Ste 101
Corona, CA 92882-1901
(951) 272-5445
(951) 272-5489 FAX

Primary care srvs, family planning, pregnancy testing, STD testing, diagnosis and treatment, OB/GYN, family planning, pediatric, treatment of non-emerg medical problems. Wait: Varies. For an appt, call (800) 720-9553. FUNDING: Govt. OFC HRS: M-F 7:30am-5pm. Spanish spoken. Accepts Medi-Cal/MIA, ability to pay, insurance, pvt pay. Fee scale based on family size, income, & srv provided. SERVES: Corona, Norco.

RIVERSIDE CO. PUBLIC HEALTH DEPT

Hemet Health/Family Care Center
880 N. State St.
Hemet, CA 92543
(951) 766-2450
(951) 766-2479 FAX

Family srvs include: treatment of non-emerg medical problems, nutrition info & counseling, STD testing with diagnosis and treatment, family planning srvs, public health nursing assist to families in maintaining good health and promoting wellness in the home. Srvs for children include: immunizations, preventive health, family planning edu for teens, assist to pregnant teens, referral for medical care and rehab for physically disabled up to age 21 yrs. Srvs for women include: pregnancy testing, breast cancer screening, pap smears, WIC supplemental food & prenatal care. FUNDING: Nonprofit. OFC HRS: M-F 7:30am-5pm. Spanish spoken. ADM REQ: Low income. Accepts insurance, Medicare, Medi-Cal. SERVES: Riverside County.

RIVERSIDE CO. PUBLIC HEALTH DEPT

Indio Family Health Center
47-923 Oasis St.
Indio, CA 92201
(760) 863-8283
(760) 863-8366 FAX

Primary care srvs for various medical conditions. Preventive medical srvs include: WIC, child health, disability prevention, prenatal care, women's health, HIV testing & counseling, immunizations, family planning, STD testing & treatment. Preventive medical srvs available to all county residents. FUNDING: BPHC site, donations, county, nonprofit. OFC HRS: M-F 7:30-5pm. Spanish spoken. ADM REQ: Low income. Accepts Medi-Cal, Medicare, pvt insurance, managed care. Fees based on ability to pay. SERVES: Riverside County.

RIVERSIDE CO. PUBLIC HEALTH DEPT

Lake Elsinore Health/Family Care Ctr
2499 E. Lakeshore Dr.
Lake Elsinore, CA 92530
(951) 471-4200
(951) 471-4205 FAX

Primary care, family planning, comprehensive perinatal care, cancer screening, STDs, immunizations, TB clinic & skin tests, pregnancy testing & counseling, teen clinic, well-child care, nutrition, WIC, public health nursing, AFLP. FUNDING: BPHC site, donations nonprofit. Clinic hrs: M-F 7:30am-5pm. Spanish spoken. ADM REQ: Low income. Accepts insurance, Medicare, Medi-Cal, sliding fee scale. SERVES: Riverside Co.

RIVERSIDE CO. PUBLIC HEALTH DEPT

Medical Indigent Services
26520 Cactus Ave.
Moreno Valley, CA 92555
(951) 486-5375
(951) 486-5415 FAX

Health care financial assist prgm primarily oriented to emerg life-threatening situational relief. Limited scope of non-emerg srvs available through the Public Health Centers and Riverside Medical Center. Wait: Varies, allow two hrs minimum for processing as a walk in. Must check in by 11am. Walk in or call. FUNDING: Govt. OFC HRS: M-F 7:30am-4pm. Spanish spoken. ADM REQ: County resident, ages 21-64 yrs not eligible for other assist including Medi-Cal. Accepts sliding fee scale, may be free. SERVES: Riverside County.

RIVERSIDE CO. PUBLIC HEALTH DEPT

Palm Springs Health/Family Care Ctr
1515 N. Sunrise Way
Palm Springs, CA 92262
(760) 778-2210
(760) 778-2214 FAX

HIV/STD testing, diagnosis and treatment, well-child care, prenatal care, women's health care, family planning, teen clinic, primary care treatment of non-emerg medical problems. For an appt, call (800) 720-9553. FUNDING: BPHC site, donations, nonprofit. OFC HRS: M-F 7:30am-5pm. Children's Clinic Sat 8am-5pm. Spanish spoken. ADM REQ: Low income. Accepts Medi-Cal, insurance. Fees based on family size, income, & srvs provided. SERVES: Riverside County.

RIVERSIDE CO. PUBLIC HEALTH DEPT

Perris Health/Family Care Center
308 E. San Jacinto Ave.
Perris, CA 92570
(951) 940-6700
(951) 940-6726 FAX

Srvs for the whole family include treatment of non-emerg medical problems, nutrition info and counseling, STD testing with diagnosis and treatment, family planning srvs, public health nursing assist to families in maintaining good health and promoting wellness in the home. Srvs for children include: immunizations, preventive health, family planning edu for teens, assist to pregnant teens, referral for medical care. Srvs for women include: pregnancy testing, breast cancer screening and pap smears, breastfeeding women, infants, children. Wait: Varies. For an appt, call (800) 720-9553. FUNDING: BPHC site, donations, nonprofit. OFC HRS: M-F 7:30am-5pm. Spanish spoken. ADM REQ: Low income. Accepts insurance, Medicare, Medi-Cal. Sliding fee scale based on family size, income, srvs provided. SERVES: Riverside County.

RIVERSIDE CO. PUBLIC HEALTH DEPT

Public Health Laboratory
P.O. Box 7600
4065 County Circle Dr.
Riverside, CA 92503
(951) 358-5070
(951) 358-5015 FAX

Infectious disease testing. OFC HRS: M-F 8am-5pm. SERVES: Riverside County.

RIVERSIDE CO. PUBLIC HEALTH DEPT

HIV/AIDS Program
P.O. Box 7600
6370 Magnolia Ave.
Riverside, CA 92503
(800) 243-7275
(909) 358-5307
(951) 358-5407 FAX

Edu, testing srvs, HIV primary care, and surveillance activities. Outreach activities are targeted at high-risk individuals: men who have sex with men, women of childbearing age, IV drug users and other drug abusers, sex workers, and youth. HIV primary care is available at Riverside Neighborhood Health Center. Edu sessions provided to community groups, schools, jails, and others upon request. Classes ordered by the courts are provided on scheduled dates at sites throughout the county. OFC HRS: M-F 8am-5pm. Spanish spoken. Free testing srvs. SERVES: Riverside County.

RIVERSIDE CO. PUBLIC HEALTH DEPT

Child Health & Disability Prev CHDP
P.O. Box 7600
10769 Holve Ave., Ste 210
Riverside, CA 92513-7600
(800) 346-6520

(951) 358-5481
(951) 358-5002 FAX

Well-child check-ups to children under age 21 yrs. Physical exam, dental assessment, nutritional assessment, vision & hearing screening, blood & urine testing, TB testing, immunizations, and health edu referrals for diagnosis & treatment. Children up to age 19 yrs who do not qualify for Medi-Cal may qualify for CHDP srvs depending on family size and income. Srvs offered at all county clinics and 120 CHDP providers. FUNDING: Govt. OFC HRS: M-Th 8am-5:30pm. ADM REQ: Children who have Medi-Cal and are not enrolled in a Medi-Cal managed care prgm. Free srvs. SERVES: Riverside County.

RIVERSIDE CO. PUBLIC HEALTH DEPT
Riverside Neighborhood Family Health Ctr
7140 Indiana Ave.
Riverside, CA 92504
(951) 358-6000
(951) 358-6044 FAX

Well-child exams, adult physicals, teen clinic, prenatal care, family planning, treatment of non-emerg medical problems. Wait: Varies. FUNDING: BPHC site, donations, nonprofit. OFC HRS: M-F 7:35am-5pm. OB/GYN, HIV/STD testing: M 8am-5pm; Tu 1pm-5pm; Th 8am-12noon. Spanish spoken. ADM REQ: Medi-Cal/MIA, sliding fee scale. Accepts Medi-Cal, Medicare, pvt pay. Sliding fee scale based on family size, income & srvs provided. SERVES: Riverside County.

RIVERSIDE CO. PUBLIC HEALTH DEPT
Community Health Agency
4065 County Circle Dr.
Riverside, CA 92503
(951) 358-5000
(951) 358-4529 FAX

Agency includes: Riverside County Dept of Public Health (Riverside Co. Dept of Health), including 13 public clinics as well as various other prgms intended to improve health and quality of life; Riverside Co. Dept of Environmental Health, which includes animal control and environmental resources. TDD (951) 358-5124. OFC HRS: M-F 8am-5pm. Spanish spoken. SERVES: Riverside County.

RIVERSIDE CO. PUBLIC HEALTH DEPT
Nutrition Services Branch
P.O. Box 7600
4065 County Circle Dr., Ste 207
Riverside, CA 92513-7600
(951) 358-7200
(951) 358-5472 FAX

A supplemental food & nutrition prgm for pregnant or breastfeeding women, women who just had a baby & children under 5 yrs of age. WIC offers special checks for healthy foods, nutrition & health edu, breastfeeding support & referrals to health care & other srvs. Breastfeeding info call (888) 451-2499. FUNDING: Federal. OFC HRS: M-F 7:30am-5pm. Eve & Sat by appt. Spanish, Vietnamese spoken. Srvs are income-based; working families may be eligible. SERVES: Riverside County.

RIVERSIDE CO. PUBLIC HEALTH DEPT
Jurupa Family Care Center
9415 Mission Blvd., Ste R
Riverside, CA 92509
(951) 360-8795

(951) 360-8798 FAX

Primary care limited to uncomplicated medical conditions. Preventative medical srvs, well-child, immunizations, prenatal care, WIC, CHDP. Also family planning, STD screening. For an appt, call (800) 720-9553. OFC HRS: M-F 7:30am-5pm. Spanish spoken. ADM REQ: Srvs open to all county residents. Call for appt. Accepts Medi-Cal, Medicare, some pvt insurance, sliding fee scale. SERVES: Riverside County.

RIVERSIDE CO. PUBLIC HEALTH DEPT
Childhood Lead Poisoning Prev Prgm
P.O. Box 7600
10769 Holve, Ste 210
Riverside, CA 92503
(800) 346-6520
(951) 358-5481
(951) 358-5002 FAX

Community and school edu & presentations regarding the dangers of lead poisoning, sources of lead, importance of lead testing and case mgmt of lead-poisoned children. FUNDING: Govt. OFC HRS: M-Th 8am-5pm. ADM REQ: Directed to families with children ages birth-6 yrs and children diagnosed with lead poisoning. Free srvs. SERVES: Riverside County.

RIVERSIDE CO. PUBLIC HEALTH DEPT
Rubidoux Family Care Center
5256 Mission Blvd.
Riverside, CA 92509
(951) 955-0840
(951) 955-5317 FAX

Primary care, perinatal care, immunizations, cancer screening, STD tests, TB tests, well-child care, nutrition. FUNDING: County. OFC HRS: M-F 7:30am-5pm. Spanish spoken. Accepts Medi-Cal, Medicare, insurance, sliding fee scale. SERVES: Riverside County.

RIVERSIDE CO. PUBLIC SOCIAL SRVS
Income Maintenance/Medi-Cal
P.O. Box 7500
63 S. 4th Street
Banning, CA 92220
(951) 922-7000
(951) 922-7005 FAX

Financial (TANF, CalWORKs, General Relief), nutritional (food stamps), and medical assist (Medi-Cal). Walk in or call. FUNDING: Govt. OFC HRS: M-Th 7am-5:30pm; F 8am-5pm. Spanish, Hmong spoken. SERVES: Banning, Beaumont, Calimesa, Cabazon & Pass area.

RIVERSIDE CO. PUBLIC SOCIAL SRVS
Income Maintenance/Medi-Cal
1225 W. Hobson Way
Blythe, CA 92225
(760) 921-5700
(760) 921-7715 FAX

Financial (TANF, General Relief, etc.), nutritional (food stamps), and medical assist (Medi-Cal). Walk in or call. FUNDING: Govt. OFC HRS: M-Th 7am-5:30pm; F 8am-5pm. Spanish spoken. ADM REQ: Varies per prgm. SERVES: Blythe & nearby.

RIVERSIDE CO. PUBLIC SOCIAL SRVS
Income Maintenance/Medi-Cal
68-615A Perez Rd., Ste 9
Cathedral City, CA 92234
(760) 770-2300
(760) 770-2324 FAX

Financial (TANF, CalWORKS, General Relief, etc.), nutritional (food stamps), and medical assist (Medi-Cal), limited home repair and emerg loans for SSI/SSD recipients. Walk in or call. FUNDING: Govt. OFC HRS: M-Th 7am-5:30pm. F 8am-5pm. Spanish spoken. SERVES: Palm Springs, Cathedral City areas.

RIVERSIDE CO. PUBLIC SOCIAL SRVS
Temp Assist/Medi-Cal/Food Stamps
541 N. San Jacinto St.
Hemet, CA 92543
(951) 791-3000
(951) 791-3050 FAX

Financial (CalWORKs, General Relief, etc.), nutritional (Food Stamps), and medical assist (Medi-Cal). FUNDING: Govt. OFC HRS: M-Th 7am-5:30pm; F 8am-5pm. Spanish spoken. SERVES: Mid-County.

RIVERSIDE CO. PUBLIC SOCIAL SRVS
Income Maintenance/CalWORKs
44-199 Monroe St., Ste D
Indio, CA 92201
(760) 863-2700
(760) 863-2864 FAX

Financial (CalWORKs, General Relief, etc.), nutritional (food stamps), and medical assist (Medi-Cal). Walk in or call. FUNDING: Govt. OFC HRS: M-Th 7am-5:30pm; F 8am-5pm. Spanish spoken. SERVES: Coachella Valley, Indio, Palm Desert, Thermal, Mecca.

RIVERSIDE CO. PUBLIC SOCIAL SRVS
CalWorks/Medi-Cal/Food Stamps
1400 Minthorn St.
Lake Elsinore, CA 92530
(951) 245-3100
(951) 674-5948 FAX

Financial (CalWORKs, GAIN, General Relief, etc.), nutritional (food stamps), and medical assist (Medi-Cal). FUNDING: Govt. OFC HRS: M-Th 7am-5:30pm; F 8am-5pm. ADM REQ: Varies with prgm. SERVES: Mid-Riverside County.

RIVERSIDE CO. PUBLIC SOCIAL SRVS
Income Maintenance/Medi-Cal
3178 Hamner Ave.
Norco, CA 92860
(951) 272-5550
(951) 272-5482 FAX

Financial (TANF, CalWORKs, General Relief, etc.), nutritional (food stamps), and medical assist (Medi-Cal). Walk in or call. FUNDING: Govt. OFC HRS: M-Th 7am-5:30pm; F 8am-5pm. Spanish spoken. ADM REQ: Varies with prgm. SERVES: Norco.

RIVERSIDE CO. PUBLIC SOCIAL SRVS
Temporary Assistance Medical Div
2055 N. Perris Blvd., Ste B
Perris, CA 92571
(951) 940-6600
(951) 940-6610 FAX

Financial (CalWORKs, TANF, General Relief, etc.), nutritional (food stamps), and medical assist (Medi-Cal). Walk in to apply, appts for continuing. FUNDING: Govt. OFC HRS: M-Th 7am-5:30pm; F 8am-5pm. Spanish spoken. SERVES: Riverside County.

RIVERSIDE CO. PUBLIC SOCIAL SRVS
Assistance Programs
11060 Magnolia Ave.
Riverside, CA 92505

(951) 358-3400

Financial (CalWORKs, TANF, General Relief, etc.), nutritional (food stamps), and medical assist (Medi-Cal). Walk in or call. FUNDING: Govt. OFC HRS: M-Th 7am-5:30pm; F 8am-5pm. Spanish, Vietnamese spoken. ASL available. SERVES: Riverside County.

RIVERSIDE CO. PUBLIC SOCIAL SRVS

Income Maintenance/Medi-Cal
43264 Business Park Dr., Ste B1
Temecula, CA 92590
(951) 600-6500
(951) 600-6502 FAX

Financial (CalWORKs, TANF, General Relief, etc.), nutritional (food stamps), and medical assist (Medi-Cal). Walk in or call. FUNDING: Govt. OFC HRS: M-Th 7am-5:30pm; F 8am-5pm. Spanish spoken. ADM REQ: Varies with prgm. SERVES: Mid-County.

RIVERSIDE/SAN BERN INDIAN HLTH CLINIC

P.O. Box 1098
66-735 Martinez Rd.
Thermal, CA 92274
(760) 397-4476
(800) 717-4476
(760) 397-0066 FAX

Free clinic for Native American families residing in Riverside or San Bernardino Counties. Mental health, substance abuse, nutrition, dental, general medicine. State ID: 330057DN. FUNDING: Federal, govt, nonprofit. OFC HRS: M-Th 8am-5pm; F 8am-2pm. Spanish spoken. ADM REQ: Proof of Indian heritage, linkage, proof of residency. SERVES: Riverside & San Bernardino Counties.

RIVERSIDE/SAN BRDO CO. INDIAN HLTH

Morongo Indian Health Clinic
11555 1/2 Potrero Rd.
Banning, CA 92220
(800) 732-8805
(951) 849-4761
(951) 849-5612 FAX

Outpatient alcohol & drug treatment prgm, AA meetings, parenting classes, counseling. Comprehensive health care: medical, dental, vision, mental health (indiv & family counseling), pharmacy, lab, nursing, family planning, AIDS testing, WIC prgm, transportation. Serves all ages. FUNDING: Govt. OFC HRS: M, W, Th 8am-5pm; Tu 8am-7pm; F 8am-2pm. ADM REQ: Must have appt. Accepts Medi-Cal. Free srvs to qualified Indians. SERVES: Riverside & San Bernardino Counties.

SAC HEALTH SYSTEM

1455 E. 3rd Street
San Bernardino, CA 92408
(909) 382-7100
(909) 382-7101 FAX

Health care at low cost to all ages. Srvs include: physical exams, pap smears, diagnosis & treatment of disease, preventive srvs, health edu, referrals to specialists, and case mgmt. Complete physical exams, preventive health srvs and immunizations (i.e. CHDP care) are free for children and youth (ages birth-19 yrs) who are from families of limited income and have no health insurance. Additional clinics located at SAC-Arrowhead Community Center: 1293 North D Street in San Bernardino, (909) 381-1663 and 488 South K Street, Ste. B in

Frazee, (909) 383-8092. OFC HRS: M-Th 7:30am-5pm; F 7:30am-12noon. Spanish spoken. Accepts Medi-Cal. Sliding fee based on family size and income. SERVES: San Bernardino County.

SAFETY & EMERG EDUCATOR'S COUNCIL

3707 5th Avenue, Ste 706
San Diego, CA 92103
(619) 692-2011
(619) 298-9977 FAX

Joint employer/employee prgm to initiate tobacco control policies in the workplace. Health edu course includes: CPR, first aid, AIDS, TB, earthquake preparedness. FUNDING: Nonprofit. OFC HRS: M-F 8am-5:30pm. ADM REQ: No age limits. Fixed fees. SERVES: Calif.

SAN BERNARDINO CO. BEHAV HEALTH

268 W. Hospitality Lane, Ste 400
San Bernardino, CA 92415
(909) 382-3133
(909) 382-3106 FAX

Behavioral health srvs for depression, bipolar disorder, schizophrenia within the low income, community when funds are available. FUNDING: County. OFC HRS: M-F 8am-5pm, closed alt F. Spanish spoken. Accepts Medi-Cal, Medicare. No insurance. SERVES: San Bernardino County.

SAN BERNARDINO CO. HUMAN SRVS SY

Transitional Assistance
7977 Sierra Ave.
Fontana, CA 92335
(909) 356-3160
(909) 356-3221
(909) 356-3169 FAX

Transitional prgms include financial assist (CalWORKs, General Relief etc.), nutritional (food stamps), and medical assist (Medi-Cal). Subsidized child care (CalWORKs & alternative payment). FUNDING: Govt. OFC HRS: M-F 8:30am-4:30pm. Spanish spoken. SERVES: Fontana. Child care srvs provided for all San Bernardino County.

SAN BERNARDINO CO. HUMAN SRVS SY

Medi-Cal
1627 E. Holt Blvd.
Ontario, CA 91761
(909) 933-6330
(909) 933-6450 FAX

Income maintenance prgms. Medical assist (Medi-Cal). FUNDING: Govt. OFC HRS: M-F 9am-4pm. Spanish spoken. SERVES: San Bernardino County.

SAN BERNARDINO CO. HUMAN SRVS SY

HSS Administration
385 N. Arrowhead Ave., 5th Fl.
San Bernardino, CA 92415-0515
(909) 357-4717
(909) 387-5430 FAX

HSS is composed of the following depts: Aging & Adult Srvs, Behavioral Health, Children's Srvs, Community Srvs, Preschool Srvs, Public Health, Transitional Assist, and Veterans Affairs. OFC HRS: M-F 7:30am-5pm. SERVES: San Bernardino County.

SAN BERNARDINO CO. HUMAN SRVS SY

Medi-Cal Information
2050 N. Massachusetts
San Bernardino, CA 92415
(909) 475-2074

(909) 475-2231 FAX

Medi-Cal prgm provides comprehensive medical care to all public assist recipients and to certain other eligible persons such as aged, blind, and disabled individuals, and to children who do not have sufficient funds to meet the cost of medical care. Automated line. For operator, call (909) 475-2006. FUNDING: County, state, fed, govt. OFC HRS: M-F 9am-4pm. Spanish spoken. SERVES: San Bernardino County.

SAN BERNARDINO CO. HUMAN SRVS SY

Income Maintenance/Transitional Assist
2050 N. Massachusetts
San Bernardino, CA 92415
(909) 475-2074
(909) 475-2231 FAX

Income maintenance prgms include financial (CalWORKs, TANF, General Relief, etc.), nutritional (food stamps), and medical assist (Medi-Cal). FUNDING: Govt. OFC HRS: M-F 8:30am-4:30pm. Spanish spoken. SERVES: Specific areas in San Bernardino.

SAN BERNARDINO CO. MEDICAL SOCIETY

3993 Jurupa Ave.
Riverside, CA 92506
(951) 787-7700
(951) 787-8795 FAX

Free health edu info to the residents of San Bernardino County, including a physician speaker's bureau of over 200 current health topics. Medical museum. Up-to-date legislative and edu info on health and medical policy issues from the Calif Medical Assn and American Medical Assn also available. FUNDING: Pvt, nonprofit. OFC HRS: M-F 8:30am-5pm. SERVES: San Bernardino County.

SAN BERNARDINO CO. PUBLIC HEALTH

Westside Park Elem School
18270 Casaba Rd., Rm. 304
Adelanto, CA 92301
(760) 246-4118
(760) 246-5446 FAX

Primary health care for ages birth-11 yrs. FUNDING: County. OFC HRS: M-F 8am-4pm. Spanish spoken. ADM REQ: Low income. Accepts CHDP. SERVES: Westside Elem only.

SAN BERNARDINO CO. PUBLIC HEALTH

Reproductive Health Centers
303 E. Mountain View
Barstow, CA 92311
(800) 722-4777
(760) 256-4715
(760) 256-4909 FAX

Reproductive health exams for men & women. STD testing & treatment, HIV testing & referral to care. Edu srvs, pregnancy testing, counseling, lab testing, young adult clinics. FUNDING: Dept Public Health. OFC HRS: Tu-Th 9am-4pm. ADM REQ: Must have appt. Accepts Medi-Cal. Fees based on srvs provided. SERVES: Barstow.

SAN BERNARDINO CO. PUBLIC HEALTH

Reproductive Health Centers
P.O. Box 2835
477 Summit Blvd.
Big Bear Lake, CA 92315
(800) 722-4777
(909) 866-0177

Reproductive health exams for men & women. STD testing & treatment, HIV testing & referral to care. Edu srvs, pregnancy testing, counseling, lab testing, young adult clinic. FUNDING: Calif Office of Family Planning, govt. OFC HRS: F 9am-4pm. Spanish spoken. ADM REQ: Must have appt. Accepts Medi-Cal, F-PACT, sliding fee scale, no one turned away for lack of funds. SERVES: San Bernardino Mtns.

SAN BERNARDINO CO. PUBLIC HEALTH
Reproductive Health Centers
16453 Bear Valley Rd.
Hesperia, CA 92345
(800) 722-4777
(760) 956-4465
(760) 956-4450 FAX

Reproductive health exams for men & women. STD testing & treatment, HIV testing & referral to care. Edu srvs, pregnancy testing, counseling, lab testing, young adult clinics. For HIV testing, call (909) 383-3060 W 9am-3pm. FUNDING: Dept Public Health. OFC HRS: M-F 9am-4pm. Spanish spoken. ADM REQ: Must have appt. Accepts Medi-Cal. Sliding fee scale. No one denied srvs due to lack of funds. SERVES: Victor Valley area.

SAN BERNARDINO CO. PUBLIC HEALTH
Reproductive Health Centers
P.O. Box 1066
1406 Bailey Ave., Ste D
Needles, CA 92363
(800) 722-4777
(760) 326-9230
(760) 326-9235 FAX

Reproductive health exams for men & women. STD testing & treatment, HIV testing & referral to care. Edu srvs, pregnancy testing, counseling, lab testing, young adult clinics. FUNDING: Dept Public Health. OFC HRS: Tu-Th 7am-4:30pm. Accepts Medi-Cal, insurance. Fees based on srv. SERVES: Amboy, Big River, Essex, Needles, Havasu Landing, Parkers Dam.

SAN BERNARDINO CO. PUBLIC HEALTH
Reproductive Health Centers
1647 E. Holt Blvd.
Ontario, CA 91764
(800) 722-4777
(909) 458-9716
(909) 458-9729 FAX

Reproductive health exams for men & women. STD testing & treatment, HIV testing & referral to care. Edu srvs, pregnancy testing, counseling, lab testing, young adult clinics. For HIV testing, call (909) 383-3060 F 8am-3:30pm. FUNDING: Dept Public Health. OFC HRS: M-F 8am-5pm. Spanish spoken. ADM REQ: Must have appt. Sliding fee scale. No one denied srvs due to lack of funds. SERVES: Ontario.

SAN BERNARDINO CO. PUBLIC HEALTH
Reproductive Health Centers
800 E. Lugonia Ave., Ste F
Redlands, CA 92374
(800) 722-4777
(909) 793-6399

Reproductive health exams for men & women. STD testing & treatment, HIV testing & referral to care. Edu srvs, pregnancy testing, counseling, lab testing, young adult clinics. FUNDING: Govt. OFC HRS: M-F 8am-5pm. Spanish spoken. ADM REQ: Must have appt. Accepts Medi-Cal, F-PACT, sliding fee scale. No one

denied srvs due to lack of funds. SERVES: San Bernardino County.

SAN BERNARDINO CO. PUBLIC HEALTH
Public Health Nursing Field Services
120 Carousel Mall, 2nd St., Ste 120
San Bernardino, CA 92415-0010
(909) 388-0400
(909) 387-3887 FAX

Public health nurses (PHNs) provide health screening, case mgmt, health edu, home environmental assessments and counseling to individuals and/or families in various settings such as home, offices and homeless shelters. Referrals are made by individuals, hospitals, other agencies. FUNDING: Govt. OFC HRS: M-F 8am-5pm. Spanish spoken. Free srvs. SERVES: San Bernardino County.

SAN BERNARDINO CO. PUBLIC HEALTH
Administrative Office
385 Arrowhead Ave.
San Bernardino, CA 92415-0120
(909) 387-7020
(909) 387-6228 FAX

Administers branch offices at various locations throughout San Bernardino Co. including: Barstow, Big Bear, Chino, Fontana, Joshua Tree, Needles, Ontario, Redlands, San Bernardino, Trona, Victorville & Twin Peaks. Edu, alcohol & drug prevention, animal control, birth & death certificates, Calif Children's Srvs, epidemiology, family planning, high-risk infant prgm, immunizations, nutrition, WIC, public health nursing, school health, senior health, VD control, TB, HIV/AIDS control. TDD (909) 397-6354. OFC HRS: M-F 8am-5pm; clinic hrs may vary. SERVES: San Bernardino County.

SAN BERNARDINO CO. PUBLIC HEALTH
California Children's Srvs
150 Carousel Mall
San Bernardino, CA 92415
(909) 387-8400
(909) 387-8401 FAX

Assists families with payment of medical bills for children ages birth-21 yrs, who have serious injury, disability or illness. Also provides PT & OT. FUNDING: Govt. OFC HRS: M-F 8am-5pm. Spanish spoken. ADM REQ: Must meet medical, financial, and residential criteria. SERVES: San Bernardino County.

SAN BERNARDINO CO. PUBLIC HEALTH
Child & Adolescent Prgm
120 Carousel Mall, 2nd St., Ste 120
San Bernardino, CA 92415-0010
(800) 722-3777
(909) 388-0401 FAX

Well-child physical exams & immunizations for ages birth-18 yrs. Testing, urine, blood lead level, TB, hearing and vision, plus counseling by RN, some dental referrals. Call for appt. FUNDING: Fed, state, county, nonprofit. OFC HRS: M-F 8am-5pm. Spanish spoken. Free srvs, depending on income level; CHDP accepted. SERVES: San Bernardino County.

SAN BERNARDINO CO. PUBLIC HEALTH
Immunization Services
351 N. Mountain View Ave.
San Bernardino, CA 92415
(800) 722-4794
(909) 387-6521
(909) 387-6676 FAX

Immunizations to all persons ages 6 weeks+. Includes DTaP, polio, measles, mumps, hib meningitis, hepatitis b, varicella, and rubella. Travelers immunizations for yellow fever, typhoid fever, hepatitis a & b, etc. Senior citizens can receive low-cost flu shot. Srvs are provided at clinics throughout the county. FUNDING: State, county, fees. OFC HRS: M-F 9am-11:30am, 1pm-4pm. Spanish spoken. ADM REQ: Open to anyone. Verification of parenthood. Fee $10 per person for pediatric immunizations (no child turned away for lack of funds). $15-70 for travelers. Administrative fees $15 per person per visit. SERVES: San Bernardino County.

SAN BERNARDINO CO. PUBLIC HEALTH
Health Nursing
120 Carousel Mall
San Bernardino, CA 92415-0048
(800) 722-3777
(909) 388-0401 FAX

Services include: physical, psychosocial and environmental assessments with focus on capacity to meet own needs and needs of the child. Info & referral and dev of support systems. Call first and referral will be sent out. FUNDING: County. OFC HRS: M-F 8am-5pm. Spanish spoken. ADM REQ: High-risk for child abuse. SERVES: San Bernardino County.

SAN BERNARDINO CO. PUBLIC HEALTH
AIDS Program
799 E. Rialto Ave.
San Bernardino, CA 92415
(909) 755-6560
(909) 383-3212 FAX

HIV clinic provides medical exam, eval & treatment, psychological eval & counseling, nutrition assessment & counseling, prevention edu & behavior change support, medication adherance edu support, case mgmt & benefits. Counseling for persons with HIV, referral for substance abuse counseling, dental care & other srvs, edu & prevention prgms for any community group requesting srvs. Clinic hrs: M, W 8am-11:30am; Tu 5pm-6:30pm; Th 8am-11:30am, 1pm-4pm. Walk-ins taken M, W, Th 8am-9am. Other locations in Ontario & Victorville. ADAP enrollment site. FUNDING: State, federal. OFC HRS: M-F 8am-4:30pm; Tu until 6:30pm. Spanish spoken. Accepts Medi-Cal. SERVES: San Bernardino County.

SAN BERNARDINO CO. PUBLIC HEALTH
Maternal Health Program
505 N. Arrowhead Ave., 3rd Fl.
San Bernardino, CA 92415-0048
(800) 227-3034
(909) 388-5755 FAX

AFLP prgm provides case mgmt to pregnant and parenting teens. Srv coordination for pregnant and parenting teens and their families. Also counseling and info for families who have had an infant die from SIDS. Prenatal mgmt care to low income residents of San Bernardino Co. Call for prenatal referrals. FUNDING: Govt. OFC HRS: M-F 8am-5pm. Spanish spoken. Accepts Medi-Cal, pvt pay.

SAN BERNARDINO CO. PUBLIC HEALTH
Health Promotion & Education Srvs
351 N. Mountain View Ave., 2nd Fl.
San Bernardino, CA 92415-0010
(800) 782-4264
(909) 387-6280

(909) 387-0102 FAX

Health promotion & edu srvs. For TDD, call (909) 387-6359. FAX (909) 387-6430. OFC HRS: M-F 8am-5pm. Spanish spoken. SERVES: San Bernardino County.

SAN BERNARDINO CO. PUBLIC HEALTH

Reproductive Health Centers
799 E. Rialto Ave.
San Bernardino, CA 92415-0011
(800) 722-4777
(909) 885-9962
(909) 387-3340 FAX

Birth control, male & female exams, pregnancy testing, counseling, referrals, verification, HIV & sexually transmitted infection (STI) testing and counseling, male sterilization. Srvs are confidential and low-cost. Call individual clinic to schedule appt. Weekly young adult clinics (YAC) on a walk-in basis at Fontana, Ontario, Redlands, San Bernardino and Hesperia sites. FUNDING: Calif Office of Family Planning. OFC HRS: M-F 8am-5pm. Spanish spoken. Accepts Medi-Cal, managed care plans, pvt pay through sliding fee scale. SERVES: San Bernardino County.

SCLERODERMA FNDN

300 Rosewood Dr., Ste 105
Danvers, MA 01923
(800) 722-4673
(978) 463-5843
(978) 463-5809 FAX

Provides edu and emotional support to persons with scleroderma and their families. Stimulates and supports research designed to identify a cause and cure for scleroderma and improve methods of treatment. Enhances awareness of the disease. Call to receive info about membership, newsletters, and other edu materials, physician referrals, chapters, and support groups. FUNDING: Donations, nonprofit. OFC HRS: M-F 8:30am-5pm, EST. Limited Spanish spoken. SERVES: Internatl.

SCLERODERMA FNDN/SO CALIF

11704 Wilshire Blvd., Ste 250
Los Angeles, CA 90025
(310) 477-8225
(800) 722-4673
(310) 477-8774 FAX

Support srvs for patients & loved ones, public awareness, newsletter, funding for research, support groups, patient & physician edu. FUNDING: Members, donors, nonprofit. OFC HRS: M-F 9am-5pm. Spanish spoken. Free srvs. SERVES: So. Calif.

SENIORS EYECARE PROGRAM

See "EyeCare America"

SICKLE CELL DISEASE ASSN OF AMER

231 E. Baltimore St., Ste 800
Baltimore, MD 21202
(800) 421-8453
(410) 528-1555
(410) 528-1495 FAX

Referrals for genetic counseling, support groups and other srvs related to sickle-cell conditions. Free info package and edu materials price list on request. 69 local chapters in USA. FUNDING: Donations, grants, nonprofit. OFC HRS: M-F 8:30am-5pm, EST. SERVES: U.S.A.

SICKLE CELL ORGANIZATION/INLAND CO.

Administrative Office

2060 University Ave., Ste 206
Riverside, CA 92507
(800) 992-6722
(909) 684-0420
(951) 684-0340 FAX

Testing, edu & counseling and newborn screening srv. Wait: none. Walk in or call. FUNDING: State of Calif. OFC HRS: M-F 8am-5pm. Spanish spoken. Free srvs. SERVES: So. Calif.

SIDS INFORMATION CLEARINGHOUSE

National SIDS Resource Center
Georgetown University
2115 Wisconsin Ave., NW, Ste 601
Washington, DC 20007-2292
(866) 866-7437
(202) 687-7466
(202) 784-9777 FAX

NSIDRC produces and provides professional & consumer edu materials; makes referrals to natl, state, and local organizations; publishes the "Information Exchange" newsletter, and maintains an in-house bibliographical database of public awareness and medical research materials. Resource center staff provides resources, referrals and technical assist to health care professionals, counselors, legal professionals & emerg medical personnel. Also assists parents, families, and the general public in acquiring info on SIDS and related topics. FUNDING: Nonprofit. OFC HRS: M-F 8:30am-5pm, EST. SERVES: U.S.A.

SIMON FOUNDATION FOR CONTINENCE

P.O. Box 815
Wilmette, IL 60091
(800) 237-4666
(847) 864-3913
(847) 864-9758 FAX

Info on incontinence, including a quarterly newsletter, books and video tapes. Free packets are mailed upon request. FUNDING: Nonprofit. OFC HRS: 24 hrs. SERVES: U.S.A.

SOBOBA INDIAN HEALTH CLINIC

607 Donna Way
San Jacinto, CA 92583
(800) 851-5816
(951) 654-0803
(951) 487-9634 FAX

Comprehensive health care: medical, dental, vision, mental health (individual & family counseling), pharmacy, lab, AIDS testing, nursing, family planning, well-baby, pediatric, health edu, transportation srvs. FUNDING: Fed, state, county. OFC HRS: M, Tu, Th 8am-5pm; W 8am-7pm; F 8am-2pm. ADM REC: American Indian. Accepts Medi-Cal. Free to qualified Indians. SERVES: Riverside County.

SOUTH COAST COMMUNITY SRVS

San Bernardino Co. Srvs Office
2930 Inland Empire Blvd., Ste 120
Ontario, CA 92764
(909) 980-6700

Provides life-essential srvs to troubled children, youth and families. Offers 4 group homes for abused, neglected and abandoned children ages 10-18 yrs and 2 group homes for young adults ages 18-25 yrs in need of short-term assist. Wraparound prgm offers family intervention srvs. Children's intensive srvs prgm provides outpatient counseling for individuals, children, teens and their families. Eval, assessment, testing, therapy, medication support, cri-

sis intervention, case mgmt. Offers mental health clinics in Redlands (909) 792-0747 & Yucaipa (909) 790-0210. FUNDING: Nonprofit. Accepts Medi-Cal and pvt pay; sliding fee scale available. SERVES: San Bernardino County.

SPANISH ASSEMBLY OF GOD/HLTH PRG

Healthy Families Program
P.O. Box 298
Cathedral City, CA 92235
(760) 324-1471
(760) 324-1471 FAX

State-sponsored insurance prgm for children from low income families. OFC HRS: Tu-F 8am-3:30pm, by appt only. Spanish spoken.

SPINA BIFIDA ASSN OF AMERICA

Greater San Diego Chapter
P.O. Box 232272
San Diego, CA 92193-2272
(619) 491-9018
(619) 275-3361 FAX

Focus on education support & advocacy for those living with Spina Bifida. Info, printed materials, resource center. Monthly support group meetings for kids & adults, social activities, outreach. Natl Office (800) 621-3141. E-mail (sbaofgsd@hotmail.com). FUNDING: Donations, grants, nonprofit. Spanish spoken. SERVES: U.S.A.

SPINA BIFIDA ASSN OF AMERICA

Research/Support/Awareness
4590 MacArthur Blvd., NW, Ste 250
Washington, DC 20007-4226
(202) 944-3285
(800) 621-3141
(202) 944-3295 FAX

Fosters and promotes the rights and well-being of persons with spina bifida, promotes research into the causes, treatment, and prevention of spina bifida and promotes public awareness. Toll-free info & referral srv, bi-monthly newsletter offers insights to members and serves as a liaison to other organizations sharing similar goals. Also a professional advisory council on edu, medicine, legislation. 60 chapters nationwide. Free info packets. Annual natl conference. FUNDING: Donations, grants, govt, client fees, nonprofit. OFC HRS: M-F 9am-5pm, EST. Free srvs. SERVES: U.S.A.

SPINAL CORD INJURY NETWORK INTL

3911 Princeton Dr.
Santa Rosa, CA 95405-7013
(800) 548-2673
(707) 577-8796
(707) 577-0605 FAX

Member of the Natl Network of Libraries of Medicine. Dedicated to providing high quality info srvs. The library maintains a collection of 500 volumes, 50 journals, and numerous publications worldwide about spinal cord injury and/or diseases. A lending prgm of over 200 info videotapes. Contact SCINI for registration info. Various topics include exercise, health issues, sports, and travel. FUNDING: Donations, grants. OFC HRS: M-Th 9am-4pm. SERVES: U.S.A.

SPONDYLITIS ASSN OF AMERICA

P.O. Box 5872
Sherman Oaks, CA 91413
(800) 777-8189
(818) 892-1616
(818) 981-9826 FAX

Natl membership organization focusing attention solely on a family of arthritic conditions that primarily affect the spine. Includes: ankylosing, spondylitis, reactive arthritis/Reiter's Syndrome, psoriatic arthritis, inflammatory bowel disease (IBD), undifferentiated spondyloarthritis and juvenile spondyloarthritis. Printed info & videos available. Bi-monthly newsletter for members. FUNDING: Dues, donations, nonprofit. OFC HRS: M-F 8am-5pm. SERVES: U.S.A.

STARLIGHT CHILDREN'S FOUNDATION
5757 Wilshire Blvd., Ste M-100
Los Angeles, CA 90036
(310) 479-1212
(800) 315-1212
(310) 479-1235 FAX

When a child or teenager has a serious medical condition, everyone in the famliy is affected. The Starlight Fndn has dedicated itself to helping seriously ill children and their families cope with pain, fear and isolation through entertainment, edu, and family activities. Starlight's prgms have been proven to distract children from their pain, help them better understand and manage their illness. Connect families facing similar challenges so that no one feels alone. Outpatient, hospital-based and web offerings. To learn more, visit (www.starlight.org). FUNDING: Nonprofit. OFC HRS: M-F 8am-5pm. Accepts donations. SERVES: U.S.A., Canada, Australia, U.K. & Japan.

STROKE ASSOCIATION OF SO CALIF
2125 Arizona Ave., Ste 205
Santa Monica, CA 90404
(310) 575-1699
(310) 575-1696 FAX

Support groups for stroke survivors and caregivers, phone helpline, home & hospital visitations, info & referral, literature available. Volunteers needed. FUNDING: Donations, nonprofit. OFC HRS: M-F 9am-5pm. Free srvs. SERVES: So. Calif.

STURGE-WEBER FOUNDATION, THE
P.O. Box 418
Mount Freedom, NJ 07970-0418
(800) 627-5482
(973) 895-4445
(973) 895-4846 FAX

List of publications, support groups and referrals for individuals with Sturge-Weber Syndrome (SWS), Port-Wine Stains & Klippel Trenaunay (KT), their family, friends & professionals. After hrs voicemail (calls are returned). FUNDING: Donations, grants, nonprofit. OFC HRS: M-F 8am-3pm, EST. Spanish can be arranged. SERVES: Internatl.

SUSAN G. KOMEN BREAST CANCER FNDN
Orange County Affiliate
3191-A Airport Loop Dr.
Costa Mesa, CA 92626
(714) 957-9157
(800) 462-9273
(714) 957-9155 FAX

Natl organization working to eradicate breast cancer as a life-threatening disease through edu, research, screening and treatment. FUNDING: Grants, nonprofit. OFC HRS: M-F 8:30am-5:30pm. SERVES: U.S.A.

SWEET SUCCESS
Calif Diabetes/Pregnancy Prgm
P.O. Box 2000
MVP, Ste 179
Loma Linda, CA 92354
(909) 558-3996
(909) 558-3935 FAX

Referral srv for outpatient-based comprehensive diabetes and pregnancy edu prgm, designed to improve pregnancy outcome for women with overt diabetes before conception & women who develop gestational diabetes. Support team works with physicians, community prgms and other srv providers to secure quality, cost-effective prenatal srvs. The prgm exists throughout Calif. State office: (916) 657-1498. After hours voicemail; calls are returned. FUNDING: Nonprofit. OFC HRS: M-F 9am-3pm. SERVES: Calif.

TEEN IMPACT
Children's Hospital of Los Angeles Center for Cancer & Blood Diseases
4650 Sunset Blvd., MS #99
Los Angeles, CA 90027
(323) 361-4660
(323) 361-7128 FAX

Psycho-social support for teens, pre-teens, and young adults undergoing post-treatment for cancer and for their families. Self-referred or recommended by medical staff. Srvs include: twice-monthly support groups, 3-day retreats, adventure therapy getaways, social events, referral srvs & mentoring prgm. Can attend from any hospital. Call for days and times. FUNDING: Nonprofit. Spanish spoken. Free srvs. SERVES: Calif.

TEMECULA FAMILY HEALTH CENTER
See " Neighborhood Healthcare"

THE CALIFORNIA ENDOWMENT
1000 N. Alameda St.
Los Angeles, CA 90012
(800) 449-4149
(213) 928-8800
(213) 928-8801 FAX

Works to improve access to affordable, quality health care for underserved individuals & communities & to promote fundamental improvements in the health status of the people of Calif. OFC HRS: M-F 8am-5pm. SERVES: Greater L.A. County, Riverside, San Bernardino, Ventura Counties.

THE FACIAL PAIN ASSN
Trigeminal Neuralgia Assn
408 W. University Ave., Ste 602
Gainesville, FL 32601
(800) 923-3608
(352) 384-3600
(352) 384-3606 FAX

Info, support & encouragement to those afflicted, their families and friends. Natl group with support groups in O.C., (949) 472-1272. FUNDING: Nonprofit. OFC HRS: M-F 9am-5pm EST SERVES: U.S.A.

THE JOHN HENRY FOUNDATION
403 N. Susan St.
Santa Ana, CA 92703
(714) 554-8906
(714) 554-8770 FAX

Provides a safe, welcoming and clinically supervised long-term, residential community for adults with schizophrenia spectrum disorders. JHF provides a home, medical and psychiatric care, a therapeutic community, family support & edu, recreational activities, and a supported work prgm to promote stabilization and healing for the individual and their family. FUNDING: Nonprofit. OFC HRS: 24 hrs, 7 days. SERVES: Southern Calif.

THE U.S. UNINSURED HELPLINE
(800) 234-1317

Hotline available 24 hrs, 7 days to assist the uninsured with navigating free and low-cost health insurance options. FUNDING: Nonprofit. OFC HRS: 24 hrs, 7 days. Spanish spoken. Free srvs. SERVES: U.S.A.

TOURETTE SYNDROME ASSOCIATION
National Office
42-40 Bell Blvd., Ste 205
Bayside, NY 11361-2820
(718) 224-2999
(718) 279-9596 FAX

Natl voluntary health organization dedicated to identifying the cause, finding the cure and controlling the effects of TS. Research, professional and public edu and individual and family srvs. Support group meetings at locations throughout the U.S. FUNDING: Donations, nonprofit. OFC HRS: M-F 9am-5pm, EST. SERVES: U.S.A.

TUBEROUS SCLEROSIS ALLIANCE
801 Roeder Rd., Ste 750
Silver Spring, MD 20910
(800) 225-6872
(301) 562-9890
(301) 562-9870 FAX

Goal is to find a cure for tuberous sclerosis & improve the lives of those affected. Activities include: research, edu, info & support. Free literature to families & professionals. FUNDING: Donations, members, nonprofit. OFC HRS: M-F 8:30am-5pm, EST. SERVES: U.S.A.

TUBEROUS SCLEROSIS ASSOCIATION
See "Tuberous Sclerosis Alliance"

UCI WOMEN'S HEALTHCARE CENTER
Dept of Obstetrics & Gynecology
200 S. Manchester Ave., Ste 600
Orange, CA 92868
(714) 456-7002
(888) 456-7002
(714) 456-8383 FAX

Experts in women's health care. Full-range of consultative & treatment srvs. Low & high-risk obstetrics, prenatal diagnosis & treatment, fetal eval & antepartum testing, menopause, complex gynecologic surgery; screening, treatment of gynecologic cancers, reproductive disorders & infertility. FUNDING: Govt. OFC HRS: M-F 8am-5pm.

UNITED CANCER RESEARCH SOCIETY
3545 20th Street
Highland, CA 92346
(800) 222-1533
(800) 888-2747 FAX

Referral srv for cancer patients. FUNDING: Nonprofit. HRS: M-F 8am-5pm

UNITED CEREBRAL PALSY ASSN
Dennis James Center
35325 Date Palm Dr., Ste 136
Cathedral City, CA 92234
(760) 321-8184

(760) 321-8284 FAX

Info & referral, family resource center, in-home respite care, recreation & camping prgms, parent support groups. "Skillbuilders" after school prgm for ages 8-18 yrs. "Little Bridges" recreation prgm for ages 3-6 yrs. FUNDING: Nonprofit. OFC HRS: M-F 8:30am-4:30pm. Spanish spoken. Srvs paid through Inland Regional Center. SERVES: San Bernardino, Riverside Counties.

UNITED MITOCHONDRIAL DISEASE FNDN

8085 Saltsburg Rd., Ste 201
Pittsburgh, PA 15239-1925
(412) 793-8077
(888) 317-8633
(412) 793-6477 FAX

Promotes research & edu for diagnosis, treatment and research of mitochondrial disorders. Provides support to affected individuals & families. Nationwide chapters & support groups, members receive newsletters, support info, networking benefits and internatl symposiums. FUNDING: Donations, grants, dues, nonprofit. OFC HRS: M-F 8am-5pm, EST. Some Spanish spoken. SERVES: U.S.A.

USC NORRIS COMP CANCER CTR

1441 Eastlake Ave.
Los Angeles, CA 90033
(800) 872-2273
(323) 865-3000
(323) 865-0033 FAX

60-bed hospital dedicated to treating cancer patients. Outpatient srvs. Bone marrow transplant unit, surgical unit, radiation oncology dept. Expert specialists in treating cancers of the genitourinary system, central nervous system, female reproductive system, breast, lung and gastrointestinal tract as well as melanoma, leukemia, lymphomas and AIDS-related cancers. No emerg room. FUNDING: Nonprofit. Spanish spoken. ADM REQ: Call for appt. M-F 8am-5pm. Accepts Medicare, insurance and most PPOs. SERVES: Internatl.

V.A. HEALTH ADMIN CLINIC

41-865 Boardwalk, Ste 103
Palm Desert, CA 92211
(760) 341-5570
(760) 341-5622 FAX

General medicine, immunizations, HIV/AIDS testing, lab srvs. FUNDING: Govt. OFC HRS: M-Th 8am-5pm; F 8am-2:30pm. Spanish spoken. ADM REQ: Veteran. SERVES: Riverside County.

V.A. HEALTH ADMIN CLINIC

28125 Bradley Rd., Ste 130
Sun City, CA 92586
(951) 672-1931
(951) 672-1935 FAX

Outpatient community clinic. Internal medicine only. FUNDING: Govt. OFC HRS: M-Th 8am-5pm; F 8am-2:30pm. Spanish spoken. ADM REQ: Veteran. SERVES: Riverside County.

V.A. HEALTH ADMIN CLINIC

1238 E. Arrow Hwy., Ste 100
Upland, CA 91786
(909) 946-5348
(909) 946-6598 FAX

General medicine, immunizations, HIV/AIDS testing, mental health, drug/alcohol treatment.

FUNDING: Govt. OFC HRS: M-Th 8am-5pm; F 8am-2:30pm. Spanish spoken. SERVES: San Bernardino County.

V.A. HEALTH ADMIN CLINIC

12138 Industrial Blvd., Ste 120
Victorville, CA 92392
(760) 951-2599
(760) 951-5819 FAX

General medicine, immunizations. FUNDING: Govt. OFC HRS: M-Th 8am-5pm; F 8am-2:30pm. Spanish spoken. ADM REQ: Veteran. SERVES: San Bernardino County.

V.A. HEALTH ADMINISTRATION

Admin Ofc/Desert Pacific Network
5901 E. 7th Street
Long Beach, CA 90822
(562) 826-8000
(888) 769-8387
(562) 826-5987 FAX

Administrative office. No direct srvs. FUNDING: Govt. OFC HRS: M-F 8am-5pm. SERVES: San Diego, Long Beach, Los Angeles, Loma Linda.

V.A. MEDICAL CENTER/LOMA LINDA

Jerry L. Pettis Memorial V.A. Med Ctr
11201 Benton St.
Loma Linda, CA 92357
(909) 825-7084
(800) 741-8387
(909) 422-3106 FAX

200+ bed hospital. 24-hr emerg room with doctor on duty. General medical and some specialty srvs, surgical, rehab, psychiatric, primary outpatient care, STD testing & treatment, HIV treatments & therapies, extended and long-term care and homeless prgms. FUNDING: Federal. OFC HRS: M-F 8am-4:30pm. 24-hr srvs. Spanish, Vietnamese spoken. ADM REQ: Military srv veterans. Fees vary with eligibility. SERVES: San Bernardino, Riverside Counties.

VALLEY ORTHOPAEDIC CLINIC

352 E. 1st Street
Calexico, CA 92231
(760) 357-3931
(760) 357-1280 FAX

Outpatient orthopaedic surgery clinic. Also offers optical srvs. Serves all ages. Free clinic. FUNDING: Nonprofit. OFC HRS: M-F 9am-5pm. Spanish spoken.

VISITING HOME NURSES INC.

8273 White Oak Ave., Ste 110
Rancho Cucamonga, CA 91730
(909) 484-7881
(909) 484-7880 FAX

Home care, home infusion, nursing assist, skilled nursing, PT, OT, and speech therapy, CHHA. FUNDING: Nonprofit. OFC HRS: M-F 8:30am-5:30pm. Spanish & Tagalog spoken. ADM REQ: Srvs ordered by M.D. Accepts Medicare, insurance. SERVES: San Bernardino County

VITILIGO SUPPORT INTERNATL

P.O. Box 4008
Valley Village, CA 91617-0008
(818) 752-9002

Offers vitiligo edu, research and awareness for those whose lives have been affected by the disease. Also sponsors support groups and advocacy. FUNDING: Nonprofit, donations. Free srvs. SERVES: U.S.A.

WIGS FOR KIDS

24231 Center Ridge Rd., Ste 26
Westlake, OH 44145
(440) 333-4433
(440) 835-1084 FAX

Accepts donated hair to provide hairpieces to low-income children who have lost their hair due to a medical condition. FUNDING: Donations, nonprofit. ADM REQ: Children under 18 yrs of age. SERVES: Calif.

WOMEN'S CANCER NETWORK

www.wcn.org
230 W. Monroe, Ste 2528
Chicago, IL 60606
(800) 444-4441
(312) 578-1439
(312) 578-9769 FAX

Interactive website designed to educate the community on gynecologic cancers. Learn more about treatment options and clinical trials and understand the disease. Contact WCN for copies of brochures. FUNDING: Nonprofit, donations, fndns. SERVES: U.S.A.

WORLD RESEARCH FOUNDATION

41 Bell Rock Plaza
Sedona, AZ 86351-8804
(928) 284-3300
(928) 284-3530 FAX

Info on alternative & conventional therapies for major diseases. Library has research on all major diseases plus worldwide info on any health problem from A-Z, library searches on most health concerns. Publishes a quarterly newsletter for min donation of $20 annually. Walk in or call. FUNDING: Donors, nonprofit. HRS: M, W, F 10am-5pm. Accepts donations. Fee for health searches. SERVES: Internatl.

WWW.HEALTHFINDER.GOV

U.S. Dept of Health & Human Srvs
P.O. Box 113
Washington, DC 20012

Website that offers a comprehensive encyclopedia of over 1,600 entries regarding conditions & diseases, tools to check your personal health, and ways to locate a doctor or health center. FUNDING: Govt. Spanish Free srvs. SERVES: U.S.A.

WWW.OEFOIF.VA.GOV

Resource website by the Dept. of Veterans Affairs for newly returning service members (OEF/OIF). Topics include health care eligibility, life insurance benefits, edu/training, and prgms that specialize in the treatment of PTSD. If you are an OEF/OIF veteran, and have not been contacted by VA about your health care benefits, call (866) 606-8216.

WWW.TRANSPLANTLIVING.ORG

(888) 894-6361

Information and resources for pre- and post-transplant patients. State listing for support groups. Use website to contact through email. FUNDING: Nonprofit. Spanish spoken. SERVES: U.S.A.

WWW.YOUNGSURVIVAL.ORG

Young Survival Coalition
61 Broadway, Ste 2235
New York, NY 10006
(877) 972-1011
(646) 257-3000
(646) 257-3030 FAX

Advocacy and support resources. Network for breast cancer survivors and their families. Telephone networking sessions and one-to-one peer support. FUNDING: Nonprofit. SERVES: U.S.A.

Y-ME NATIONAL BREAST CANCER ORGN
135 S. La Salle St., Ste 2000
Chicago, IL 60603
(312) 986-8338
(312) 294-8597 FAX

Support and info for anyone touched by breast cancer. 24-hr Y-ME Natl Breast Cancer Hotline (800) 221-2141; Spanish (800) 986-9505. Staffed entirely by breast cancer survivors who are trained peer counselors. Visit (www.y-me.org). FUNDING: Donations, nonprofit. OFC HRS: M-F 9am-5pm, CST Hotline 24 hrs. Spanish spoken. Interpreters in 150 languages. SERVES: U.S.A.

1736 FAMILY CRISIS CENTER
Homeless Resources & Prgms
2116 Arlington Ave., Ste 200
Los Angeles, CA 90018
(323) 737-3900
(323) 737-3993 FAX

Outpatient counseling and case mgmt for adults, families and children. Battered women's support groups, community edu, outreach. Also shelter, counseling, food, clothing, advocacy and other 24-hr srvs free of charge to battered women and their children and to runaway and homeless adols. Operates five shelters: four for battered women and their children (ages birth-17 yrs) for 1-24 months offering a comprehensive survival and job dev prgm to promote long-term safety, survival, and success; one emerg shelter for runaways (two-week crisis-oriented shelter). 24-hr hotlines in South Bay (310) 379-3620, (310) 370-5902; Long Beach (562) 388-7652; South L.A. (213) 222-1237, (213) 745-6434. 24-hr drop-in center at 1736 Monterey Blvd., Hermosa Beach. May call collect if needed. FUNDING: Grants, donations, govt, nonprofit. OFC HRS: M-F 8:30am-5pm. Spanish spoken. ADM REQ: Vary by prgm. Free srvs. SERVES: So. Calif.

ABODE COMMUNITIES
701 E. 3rd Street, Ste 400
Los Angeles, CA 90013
(213) 629-2702
(213) 225-2805 FAX

Low-income housing throughout greater Los Angeles County. Mission is to open new doors in people's lives through creative and responsible design, dev and operation of service-enhanced affordable housing. Child care centers, community centers and computer labs are built into each facility. Provides an enriching resident services prgm. Abode encourages participation and leadership, and enhances children's academic achievement and self-esteem. Also helps adults to become confident and educated contributors to society. FUNDING: Nonprofit. OFC HRS: M-F 8:30am-6pm. Spanish spoken. SERVES: L.A., Orange and Riverside Counties.

ADVENTIST COMM TEAM SRVS (ACTS)
P.O. Box 477
24914 Barton Rd.
Loma Linda, CA 92354
(909) 796-8357
(909) 799-5653 FAX

Primary goal is to assist disadvantaged people, without regard to race or creed, in living as independently as possible. Info & referral, food for homeless, case mgmt, ACTS transit provides transportation srv to medical appts, markets, beauty parlor for a fee. Must be registered with ACTS. Also offers Meals on Wheels. FUNDING: Donations, nonprofit. OFC HRS: M-Th 8am-1pm; F 8am-12noon. ADM REQ: Appt needed. SERVES: Loma Linda.

AFDC
Commonly referred to as Welfare, now known as TANF or CalWORKs. Prgms are administered by county social srvs depts; listings are shown under the county name.

AMEILA'S LIGHT TRANSITIONAL HOUSE
Lutheran Social Srvs
23310 Meyer Dr.
March Air Force Base, CA 92518
(951) 656-6020
(951) 656-6644 FAX

Thirty 1-bedroom apts for homeless women. Transition is made from homelessness to permanent housing, employment & self-sufficiency. FUNDING: Nonprofit, govt grants, United Way, donations, churches. OFC HRS: M-Th 9am-5pm; F 9am-4pm. SERVES: Riverside & San Bernardino Counties.

B.R.I.D.G.E.S., INC.
Adminstrative Office
1977 N. Garey Ave., Ste 6
Pomona, CA 91767
(909) 623-6651
(909) 623-0455 FAX

L.A. County Dept of Mental Health contract provider focusing on serving individuals with mental illness. Residential and outpatient prgms; 5 social rehabilitation facilities (6-14 beds each) with stay up to 18 months. Residential prgms offered in San Fernando Valley and San Gabriel Valley. Outpatient prgm in SFV offers individual and group specialized mental health counseling, substance abuse support, case mgmt, medication and psychiatry. Wellness & Recovery Ctr in El Monte provides mental health counseling, recreational and vocational support, peer support, medication, and other srvs. Intake (626) 350-5304. FUNDING: Nonprofit. OFC HRS: M-F 8am-4:30pm. Spanish spoken. ADM REQ: Residential prgms house clients ages 18-59 yrs with mental illness and co-occurring disorders; outpatient prgms accept those up to age 21 yrs. Accepts Medi-Cal, SSI. Limited beds may be available without any funding. SERVES: Los Angeles & San Bernardino Counties.

BETHEL CHRISTIAN FELLOWSHIP
9134 Mango Ave., Ste C
Fontana, CA 92335
(909) 823-1198
(909) 823-1587 FAX

Food for Living food distribution outreach services for families in need 3rd Sat of the month 10:30am-12noon. FUNDING: Nonprofit. OFC HRS: Tu-F 9am-4pm. SERVES: Fontana.

CALIF HOUSING LAW PROJECT
1107 9th Street, Ste 801
Sacramento, CA 95814
(916) 446-9241
(916) 442-7966 FAX

Partnership of agencies concerned with assist, shelter, transitional & long-term housing issues that affect hungry & homeless people. Advocacy, public policy support, resources, networking & tech assist. No direct srvs for clients. FUNDING: Nonprofit. SERVES: Calif.

CALVARY PRESBYTERIAN CHURCH
4495 Magnolia Ave.
Riverside, CA 92501-4198
(951) 686-0761
(951) 686-1488 FAX

Hot meal served Sun evenings from 5:30pm-6pm. Clean used clothes, live music, and information for additional help also provided. Special meals during Thanksgiving and Christmas. Walk in. Dental van prior to hot meal as available. Contact Pam Shoulders to volunteer at (951) 351-4403. OFC HRS: M-Th 9am-5pm; F 9am-1pm. Free srvs. SERVES: Riverside County.

CATHOLIC CHARITIES/COMMUNITY SRVS
See "Desert Manna/Emergency Housing"

CATHOLIC CHARITIES/COMMUNITY SRVS
Inland Valleys Regional Center
23623 Sunnymead Blvd., Ste E
Moreno Valley, CA 92553
(951) 924-9964
(951) 924-9997 FAX

Emerg srvs for low income. Assists with food, utility, rental assist & motel vouchers (when funding is available). Info & referral, immigration & citizenship prgm, HIV/AIDS housing assist. Counseling (909) 763-4970 or (951) 801-5282. FUNDING: Nonprofit. OFC HRS: M-Th 8:30am-4:30pm, by appt only. Spanish spoken. Most srvs free. SERVES: Moreno Valley, Riverside, Perris, Hemet, San Jacinto, Sun City, Corona, Lake Elsinore, Banning, Beaumont, Cherry Valley.

CATHOLIC CHARITIES/COMMUNITY SRVS
Administration
1450 North D Street
San Bernardino, CA 92405
(909) 388-1239
(909) 384-1130 FAX

Psychological counseling for individuals & family, case mgmt, emerg food, diapers, clothing, furniture (when available), utility assist, holiday baskets, transportation, advocacy, HIV/AIDS srvs, info & referrals. Emerg housing for needy transients with pre-arranged motel accommodations (as funds allow). Refugee & immigration srvs, parolee reintegration. FUNDING: Donations, nonprofit. OFC HRS: M-F 8:30am-4:30pm. Spanish, Chinese, Filipino, Vietnamese, Russian spoken. Sliding fee scale. SERVES: San Bernardino & Riverside Counties.

CENTRAL CITY LUTHERAN MISSION
1354 North G Street
San Bernardino, CA 92405
(909) 381-6921
(909) 884-5104 FAX

Transitional housing for homeless persons with HIV. Edu & prevention, info & referral, outreach srvs. FUNDING: Nonprofit. OFC HRS: M-F 9am-5pm. Spanish spoken. Free srvs. SERVES: San Bernardino County.

CIRCLE OF HOPE FAMILY SHELTER
420 W. Harrison St.
Corona, CA 92880
(951) 278-2215
(951) 278-2236 FAX

Homeless srvs for single women, males with children & married couples. 90-day emerg shelter prgm for women, no overnight srvs for single men. Showers, breakfast, and dinner available for overnight. Sack lunches for children. FUND-

ING: Donations, nonprofit. OFC HRS: 24 hrs, 7 days, 365 days a year. ADM REQ: Must have ID, no felony convictions within the last 3 yrs. Mental health clearance upon request. SERVES: Riverside County.

COACHELLA VALLEY RESCUE MISSION
Family Shelter
P.O. Box 10660
47518 Van Buren St.
Indio, CA 92202
(760) 347-3512
(760) 347-8073 FAX

Food, clothing, showers, shelter, spiritual support and referrals to those in need. Public meals 2 times a day, 7 days. 3 meals for residents. Provide groceries for 25-100 families each week. Family shelter for women and children and men's shelter. New Life program. FUNDING: Donations. OFC HRS: 24 hrs. SERVES: Coachella Valley.

COMMUNITY ACTION PARTNERSHIP
Family Development Prgm
696 S. Tippecanoe Ave.
San Bernardino, CA 92415-0610
(909) 723-1500
(909) 723-1509 FAX

Holistic case mgmt to homeless families. Transitional housing, rent security deposit prgm, food & motel vouchers, gas vouchers, bus tickets, clothing, rental assist, budgeting, counseling and info & referral. Summer camp, Christmas celebration. OFC HRS: M-Th 7:30am-5:30pm; F 8am-5pm. ADM REQ: Low income. SERVES: San Bernardino County.

COMMUNITY SERVICES DEPARTMENT
See "Community Action Partnership"

CORONA NORCO SETTLEMENT HOUSE
507 S. Vicentia Ave.
Corona, CA 92882
(951) 737-3504
(951) 737-3201 FAX

Emerg food, basic sustenance, clothing, rent (once a year-call in), mortgage, utility assist, info & referrals to appropriate agencies. All srvs subject to availability & eligibility. Walk in or call. FUNDING: Nonprofit. OFC HRS: M-F 10am-5:30pm. Thrift store: M-F 10am-5pm; Sat 9am-2:30pm. Food pantry prgm: M-F 4pm-5:30pm. ADM REQ: Proof of income. Free srvs. Visit food pantry once a month. SERVES: Corona-Norco USD area.

DESERT MANNA/EMERGENCY HOUSING
209 N. 1st Avenue
Barstow, CA 92311
(760) 256-7797
(760) 256-4043 FAX

Shelter accommodations for homeless individuals and families. Hot meals Th-Sun 5pm-6pm; hot lunches 11am-1pm daily, food pantry by referral, USDA commodities 1st & 3rd Th, showers M-F 9am-12noon, bread and produce as available. Emerg clothing with referral. Enter from 2nd Ave. door. For shelter, call (760)255-9025. FUNDING: Churches, donations, United Way, county, state, nonprofit. OFC HRS M-F 9am-4pm; shelter 24 hrs. SERVES: San Bernardino County.

DESERT S.O.S.
1733 N. Palm Canyon Dr., Ste A
Palm Springs, CA 92262

(760) 327-4394
(760) 327-4516 FAX

Provides srvs for the homeless in western Coachella Valley. Nightengale Manor provides 45 clients with 60-day housing, meals, and case mgmt. Desert Horizon provides 32 people with transitional housing; clients pay 30% of their income (HUD guidelines) towards rent. Also offers an overnight shleter that feeds and houses 25 people (or 40 during cold weather season). FUNDING: Nonprofit, JFS, Coachella Valley Association of Governments. ADM REQ: Must be homeless; background check required for overnight shelter. Free srvs. SERVES: Western Coachella Valley.

ESSENCE OF LIGHT
744 W. 111th Street
Los Angeles, CA 90044
(323) 779-2727
(323) 779-2727 FAX

Emerg, transitional housing for homeless women with or without children. Case mgmt, referrals to community srvs. Will consider older children. FUNDING: Nonprofit. OFC HRS: M-F 9am-7pm. SERVES: L.A. & San Bernardino Counties.

FAMILY SERVICE ASSOCIATION OF REDLANDS
Home Again Project
612 Lawton St.
Redlands, CA 92374
(909) 792-2673
(909) 793-7324 FAX

Comprehensive homeless assist prgm focusing on permanent housing. Daytime prgm only (not a 24-hr shelter) offering child care, case mgmt, meals daily, etc. FUNDING: Fndns, United Way, govt, nonprofit. OFC HRS: M-Th 9am-7pm; F 9am-4:30pm. Spanish spoken. ADM REQ: Must be screened by Family Service Assn. Must have children under the age of 18 and a continuing source of income. Also accepts the disabled and those receiving SSI. Free srvs. SERVES: San Bernardino County.

FOOTHILL FAMILY SHELTER
1501 W. 9th Street, Ste D
Upland, CA 91786
(909) 920-5568
(909) 946-1860 FAX

120-day transitional housing for families who are homeless with children. Emerg shelter not available. FUNDING: Donors, nonprofit. OFC HRS: Tu-F 9am-5pm. Closed 12noon-1pm for lunch. ADM REQ: Families with children. No fees. SERVES: So. Calif.

FOOTHILL FAMILY SHELTER HOMELESS COURT
(909) 608-2865

Assist to homeless or low-income clients who have outstanding San Bernardino misdemeanor tickets, warrants, or high fines. Court held 4th F of each month. FUNDING: Nonprofit. OFC HRS: Tu-F 9am-5pm. Closed 12noon-1pm for lunch. ADM REQ: Must call a month in advance to pre-register. Must have driver's license and citation number if possible, as well as name, DOB, and phone number. SERVES: San Bernardino County.

FRAZEE COMMUNITY CENTER
1140 W. Mill St.
San Bernardino, CA 92412

(909) 889-4424
(909) 889-6865 FAX

Emerg srvs, hot meals, food boxes for families as available, homeless shelters. Transitional shelter and thrift store. Walk in or call. FUNDING: Govt grants, United Way, donations, nonprofit. OFC HRS: M-F 7:30am-3:30pm. Some Spanish spoken. ADM REQ: Low income. Free srvs. SERVES: San Bernardino.

FREE INDEED CHRISTIAN FELLOWSHIP
430 South D Street
Perris, CA 92570
(951) 657-2449
(951) 657-2229 FAX

A variety of prgms and activities offered. The Ranch helps addicts find sobriety with the aid of worship. Other prgms include: Soul Patrol Outreach, discipleship, homeless shelter, food ministries, motorcycle ministries, etc. Call Patrick Smith for appt. Men's ranch (951) 943-5159. FUNDING: Nonprofit. OFC HRS: M-F 9am-5pm. SERVES: Perris & Riverside areas.

GENESIS SHELTER
See "Lutheran Social Srvs/Shelter Prgm"

H.E.L.P. INC.
53 S. 6th Street
Banning, CA 92220
(951) 922-2305
(951) 922-1183 FAX

Hope, Empathy, Love and Prayer (H.E.L.P.). Food, referrals, clothing, any emerg srvs within means. Walk in. Also a thrift store. FUNDING: Donations, USDA, FEMA, nonprofit. OFC HRS: M-Th 9am-3pm; F 9am-12noon. Spanish upon request. Free srvs. SERVES: San Gorgonio Pass Area (Banning, Beaumont, Cherry Valley, Calimesa), and transients.

HARMONY SOUP KITCHEN
P.O. Box 2067
219 S. Main St.
Blythe, CA 92225
(760) 921-4508

Meals provided to the homeless or low income. All are welcome. FUNDING: Nonprofit. OFC HRS: M-F 10:30am-12:30pm. SERVES: Blythe.

HIGH DESERT HOMELESS SERVICES
14049 Amargosa Rd.
Victorville, CA 92392
(760) 245-5991
(760) 245-7513 FAX

55-bed shelter providing 1-90 day emerg and transitional housing. Srvs to in-house residents only. Breakfast, lunch and dinner served, shower available daily 7:30pm-10pm. Laundry available for shelter residents only. Clothing, personal items, etc. Placement referral for drug/alcohol. Dental care provided in exchange for volunteer work. FUNDING: United Way, pvt, nonprofit. Free srvs. SERVES: Barstow to San Bernardino.

HOMEAID AMERICA
Natl Office
20201 S.W. Birch St., Ste 255
Newport Beach, CA 92660
(949) 258-0850
(949) 258-0840 FAX

22 chapters in USA. Works with the building industry and local care providers to build & renovate shelters for homeless providers. Dev

transitional housing prgms, including job skills training & counseling for self-sufficiency. Also call (800) 3-HOMEAID. No direct srvs. FUNDING: Donations, grants, nonprofit. OFC HRS: M-F 8:30am-5pm. ADM REQ: Shelter prgm provider. SERVES: So. Calif.

HOMEAID/INLAND EMPIRE
3891 11th Street
Riverside, CA 92501
(951) 686-0628

Works with nonprofit agencies to build or renovate shelters for the homeless. No direct srvs to homeless individuals. FUNDING: Donations, grants, nonprofit. OFC HRS: M-F 8:30am-5pm. SERVES: Inland Empire.

HOMELESS VETERANS STAND DOWNS
Calif Dept of Veterans Affairs

Stand Downs are 1-3 day events providing free srvs to homeless veterans such as food, shelter, clothing, health screenings, benefits counseling, and info & referral srvs. Events are held throughout the year at locations throughout Calif. Visit (www.cdva.ca.gov/Resources/StandDown.aspx) to find the schedule of upcoming events and contact information for your area. SERVES: Calif.

INLAND BEHAV & HEALTH SERVICES
Westside Counseling Ctr
1963 North E Street
San Bernardino, CA 92405
(909) 881-6146
(909) 881-0111 FAX

Comprehensive health care, substance abuse, mental health and homeless support srvs. Offers crisis intervention, primary prevention edu, PC-1000 classes, anger mgmt, parenting STEP classes. Perinatal prgm for expectant and parenting mothers who are addicted to drugs with both pre- and post-natal srvs. Provides transportation as well as child care. State ID: 360015AN. FUNDING: Govt, contracts, grants, nonprofit. OFC HRS: M-Th 8am-6pm; F 8am-5pm. Spanish spoken. ADM REQ: Ages 13 yrs+, referrals & walk in. Accepts Medicare, Medi-Cal. SERVES: San Bernardino County.

INLAND TEMPORARY HOMES
P.O. Box 239
Loma Linda, CA 92354-0239
(909) 796-6381
(909) 796-6885 FAX

Thirty-90 day emerg shelter for homeless families with children. Highly structured & directive prgm designed to place families in permanent housing. Support srvs include: job skills assessment, individual counseling, food and clothing assist & savings plan dev. Parenting classes, anger mgmt, stress mgmt, computer basics. Wait: 15-20 wks. Check in every W once on list. FUNDING: Donations, grants, nonprofit. OFC HRS: M-Th 9am-4pm; F 9am-1pm. Spanish spoken. ADM REQ: Photo ID, Social Security number for all persons seeking shelter. Families with at least one child ages 17 yrs or younger. SERVES: San Bernardino County.

LUTHERAN SOCIAL SRVS/SHELTER PRGM
Genesis Transitional Housing Prgm
3772 Taft Ave.
Riverside, CA 92503
(951) 689-7847
(951) 687-7299 FAX

Eight 1-bedroom apts for homeless women with children. Average stay is ninety days-two yrs as the transition is made from homelessness to permanent housing, employment & self-sufficiency. Emerg food assist, counseling, legal advocacy, substance abuse prgm, anger mgmt, info & referral. Food pantry M-Th 11am-3pm; eligible every 30 days. FUNDING: Govt grants, United Way, donations, churches, nonprofit. OFC HRS: M-Th 9am-5pm; F 9am-4pm. ADM REQ: Homeless women. Must have two forms of ID for food pantry. SERVES: Riverside & San Bernardino Counties.

MARTHA'S VILLAGE & KITCHEN, INC.
83791 Date Ave.
Indio, CA 92201-4737
(760) 347-4741
(760) 347-9551 FAX

Hot meals M-Sun 11am-12:30pm; canned food baskets offered to families M-F 8am-10am, 1pm-4pm; 3rd W of month 10am-12noon for singles. Store distributes clothing to families by request. Medical referrals & prescription vouchers for those with no other access to medical care. Showers M-F 8am-10:45am & seasonal shelter. Offers computer, ESL & GED classes. FUNDING: Donations, nonprofit. OFC HRS: M-F 8am-5pm. SERVES: Coachella Vly area.

MARY'S MERCY CENTER
P.O. Box 7563
641 Roberds Ave.
San Bernardino, CA 92411
(909) 889-2558
(909) 386-7704 FAX

Hot meal kitchen open M-Th 11:30am-1:30pm. Also open Sat and Sun (except 1st Sun of the month). Emerg food (beans, rice, tomato sauce, bread) every W 1:30-3pm (except 1st W of the month). Clothes available M 9am-11am for women & children; Th 1:30pm-2:30pm for men. Free showers for women M 8am-12noon & W 8am-11pm; men Tu,Th 8am-10:30am. FUNDING: Donations, nonprofit. OFC HRS: M-Th 9am-4pm. Spanish spoken. SERVES: San Bernardino County.

MERCY HOUSE
Assisi House Transitional Shelter
Ontario, CA 91764
(909) 460-6768
(909) 460-6769 FAX

Transitional shelter for 8 single men, 8 single women, 6 mothers and their children. Planning for success, wellness, and learning prgms. Available 6-24 mos. FUNDING: Nonprofit, county. Spanish spoken. ADM REQ: homeless, drug and alcohol free, employed, readily employable, or going to school, other criteria may vary by prgm. SERVES: Riverside County.

MERCY HOUSE TRANSITIONAL LIVING
P.O. Box 1905
730 Garfield St.
Santa Ana, CA 92702
(714) 836-7188
(714) 836-7901 FAX

Operates 3 transitional living centers in Santa Ana: Joseph House serves single, employable men; Regina House serves single, employable mothers and their children, ages 10 yrs and under; Emmanuel House serves single adults living with HIV or AIDS; Guadalupe House and Assisi House in Ontario offer supportive hous-

ing for single mothers, single men and single women. Also offers Trinity House for men, case mgmt, life skills classes, job dev, & referrals. All prgms require sobriety. Also offers rental assist and cold weather shelters (Fullerton and Santa Ana) during winter months. FUNDING: Grants, donations, nonprofit. Spanish spoken. ADM REQ: Homeless, drug and alcohol free, employed, readily employable or going to school. Other criteria vary by program. SERVES: Southern California.

NEW DIRECTIONS, INC.
11303 Wilshire Blvd., Bldg. 116
Los Angeles, CA 90073
(310) 914-5966
(310) 914-4045
(310) 914-5495 FAX

NDI has five residential treatment facilities on the westside of L.A. Serves men and women veterans who are homeless and suffering from the co-occurring disorders of substance abuse and mental illness. Specific facilities include those for veterans involved with OIF/OEF and female dependents of veterans. Also offers a non-residential facility in Pacoima. FUNDING: Grants, donations, nonprofit. Spanish spoken. SERVES: L.A., Orange, San Bernardino and Riverside Counties.

NEW HOPE VILLAGE, INC.
SHP/Transitional Housing for the Homeless
203 W. Fredricks St., Ste 3
Barstow, CA 92311
(760) 256-3656
(760) 255-3314 FAX

Five-apartment complex. Transitional housing for the homeless individuals & families. May stay in prgm for up to two yrs. Intensive life skills edu, budgeting, time mgmt, employment, edu, health, safety, nutrition, goals, community & fundraising events. FUNDING: Grants, United Way, donations. OFC HRS: M-F 8am-4pm. ADM REQ: Must be in prgm to receive srvs. Must be motivated to become self-sufficient. SERVES: High desert area.

NEW LIFE BEGINNINGS
835 E. 6th Street
Long Beach, CA 90802
(562) 590-1538
(562) 590-4920 FAX

Long-term homeless shelter for pregnant women, with or without children. FUNDING: Nonprofit. OFC HRS: M-F 9am-4pm. ADM REQ: Pregnant women ages 18 yrs+. SERVES: U.S.A.

OPERATION GRACE
1595 E. Art Townsend Dr.
San Bernardino, CA 92408
(909) 382-8540
(909) 382-8542 FAX

Assists homeless, single women without children and very low-income persons find housing for up to six months. Info & referral to other housing prgms for low income. Life skills classes & food ministry Tu 10am-1pm. FUNDING: Nonprofit. OFC HRS: M-F 9am-5pm. ADM REQ: Homeless or low income. SERVES: San Bernardino County.

OUR LADY OF PERPETUAL HELP/MEALS
See "Martha's Village & Kitchen, Inc."

PACIFIC CLINICS

Administration
800 S. Santa Anita Ave.
Arcadia, CA 91006
(626) 254-5000
(877) 722-2737

Outpatient mental health srvs to seriously ill children, youth, adults and seniors regardless of ability to pay. Prgms include: day treatment for children & adols, homeless mentally ill outreach, geriatric outreach and Asian-Pacific srvs. Adult clubhouse drop-in prgms at some sites. Multilingual prgms. APA-accredited intern prgm. Most referrals are through county health care agencies. For child & adol srvs, call (626) 441-4221. Also outpatient & residential alcohol & drug treatment prgm at various sites. Locations in L.A., Orange, Riverside, San Bernardino and Ventura countries. State ID: 190254EN. FUNDING: County, state, United Way, donations, nonprofit. OFC HRS: M-F 8am-5pm. Multiple languages spoken. Accepts Medi-Cal SERVES: L.A., Orange & Riverside Counties.

PACIFIC LIFELINE

Transitional Shelter for Women/Children
P.O. Box 1424
Upland, CA 91784-1424
(909) 931-2624
(909) 931-2631 FAX

Transitional shelter for women with children. Counseling, graduate prgm, children's prgm, women's prgm for residents of the shelter. FUNDING: Nonprofit. ADM REQ: Must be referred. At least one child under age 11 for boys age 12 for girls. No more than 5 children. Clean & sober 9 mos. Referral applications are available. No pregnant women. Legal citizen. Willing to work within 60 days of entering the program. English-speaking preferred, but not mandatory. SERVES: San Bernardino County.

PATH OF LIFE FAMILY SHELTER

2530 3rd Street
Riverside, CA 92507
(951) 275-8755
(951) 275-8775 FAX

60-day emerg shelter for families. Case mgmt srvs include: info & referral, employment dev, housing placement, mental health, residential srvs, social srvs (re-entrance into society), counseling. Also provides several shelters for single men and women. For those shelters, call intake at (951) 683-4101 or (951) 275-8750. FUNDING: Nonprofit. OFC HRS: M-F 4pm-8pm Spanish spoken. ADM REQ: Must commit to alcohol/drug prgm. SERVES: Riverside County.

PATH OF LIFE MINISTRIES

Men's Recovery Home
P.O. Box 1445
Riverside, CA 92501
(951) 786-9048
(951) 786-9049 FAX

Christian residential prgm addressing the needs of dysfunction, addiction and incarceration by means of a holistic approach to rebuilding lives. Goal is to help individuals identify the root cause of their problem, train in life values, both practically and spiritually and to give necessary tools to obtain and maintain gainful employment. Homeless food prgm and three homeless centers. FUNDING: Donations, non-

profit. OFC HRS: M-F 9am-6pm. Spanish spoken. ADM REQ: One year prgm. SERVES: Riverside County.

PHILIP ALLRED CHILD DEV CTR

San Bernardino City USD
303 South K Street
San Bernardino, CA 92410
(909) 388-6307
(909) 885-4068 FAX

Srvs to children ages birth-5 yrs whose parents are receiving public assist, or are below 75% of the state median income, adjusted for family size, homeless families, and children in need of protective srvs. Walk in or call for info. FUNDING: Govt. OFC HRS: M-F 7am-5:30pm. Spanish spoken. ADM REQ: Parents need to be working or going to school to be qualified. Sliding fee scale. SERVES: San Bernardino City USD.

POMONA/INLAND VLY COUNCIL/CHURCH

Shelter Program
1753 N. Park Ave.
Pomona, CA 91768
(909) 622-3806
(909) 622-0484 FAX

Shelter up to a maximum of 90 days to homeless people wishing to locate to this area. Daily case mgmt providing supportive srvs for homeless clients aimed at enabling clients to re-enter into a stable environment and lifestyle. Cannot house single men. Wait list if space is unavailable. Call first. FUNDING: Donations, grants, nonprofit. OFC HRS: M-Th 8am-5pm; F 8am-12noon. Spanish spoken. ADM REQ: Must be homeless. Free srvs. SERVES: Pomona, Diamond Bar, Walnut, Montclair, Upland, La Verne, Ontario, Chino & nearby.

RIVERSIDE CITY MISSION

3878 6th Street
Riverside, CA 92501
(951) 341-5055
(951) 341-5058 FAX

Clothing, hygiene items & community food pantry from 10am-1pm. Call Th 9am-11am to order food box. Send self-addressed, stamped envelope for application. Tu at Yahweh House of Worship, 6200 Pegasus Dr. Suite 3 in Riverside; W, Living Way Christian Fellowship 12125 Day St. Suite U-101 in Moreno Valley; Th at Power of the Word Fellowship Church, 6240 Morton Ave. in Riverside. Bible studies in the evening at Yahweh and Living Way. Regular church services on Sun. FUNDING: Nonprofit. OFC HRS: M-F 8am-3pm. ADM REQ: Must have ID. Proof of rent and income. Birth certificates for children under age 18 yrs. SERVES: Aruba & Moreno Valleys, Riverside County.

RIVERSIDE CO. DEPT/MENTAL HEALTH

Administrative Office
P.O. Box 7549
4095 County Circle Dr.
Riverside, CA 92513
(951) 358-4500
(951) 358-4513 FAX

Overall planning, implementation, direction, coordination and eval of the Dept of Mental Health prgms in Riverside County. Treatment for adults: residential, outpatient, day care, socialization ctrs, crisis srvs, case mgmt, continuing care, etc. Children's prgms: outpatient, case

mgmt, foster home placement, etc. Also main admin office for drug abuse and alcohol control prgms. No actual srvs available at this location. FUNDING: Govt. Spanish spoken. Accepts Medi-Cal SERVES: Riverside County.

RIVERSIDE CO. PUBLIC SOCIAL SRVS

Income Maintenance/Medi-Cal
P.O. Box 7500
63 S. 4th Street
Banning, CA 92220
(951) 922-7000
(951) 922-7005 FAX

Financial (TANF, CalWORKS, General Relief), nutritional (food stamps), and medical assist (Medi-Cal). Walk in or call. FUNDING: Govt. OFC HRS: M-Th 7am-5:30pm; F 8am-5pm. Spanish, Hmong spoken. SERVES: Banning, Beaumont, Calimesa, Cabazon & Pass area.

RIVERSIDE CO. PUBLIC SOCIAL SRVS

Income Maintenance/Medi-Cal
1225 W. Hobson Way
Blythe, CA 92225
(760) 921-5700
(760) 921-7715 FAX

Financial (TANF, General Relief, etc.), nutritional (food stamps), and medical assist (Medi-Cal). Walk in or call. FUNDING: Govt. OFC HRS: M-Th 7am-5:30pm; F 8am-5pm. Spanish spoken. ADM REQ: Varies per prgm. SERVES: Blythe & nearby.

RIVERSIDE CO. PUBLIC SOCIAL SRVS

Income Maintenance/Medi-Cal
68-615A Perez Rd., Ste 9
Cathedral City, CA 92234
(760) 770-2300
(760) 770-2324 FAX

Financial (TANF, CalWORKS, General Relief, etc.), nutritional (food stamps), and medical assist (Medi-Cal), limited home repair and emerg loans for SSI/SSD recipients. Walk in or call. FUNDING: Govt. OFC HRS: M-Th 7am-5:30pm; F 8am-5pm. Spanish spoken. SERVES: Palm Springs, Cathedral City areas.

RIVERSIDE CO. PUBLIC SOCIAL SRVS

Temp Assist/Medi-Cal/Food Stamps
541 N. San Jacinto St.
Hemet, CA 92543
(951) 791-3000
(951) 791-3050 FAX

Financial (CalWORKS, General Relief, etc.), nutritional (Food Stamps), and medical assist (Medi-Cal). FUNDING: Govt. OFC HRS: M-Th 7am-5:30pm; F 8am-5pm. Spanish spoken. SERVES: Mid-County.

RIVERSIDE CO. PUBLIC SOCIAL SRVS

Income Maintenance/CalWORKs
44-199 Monroe St., Ste D
Indio, CA 92201
(760) 863-2700
(760) 863-2864 FAX

Financial (CalWORKs, General Relief, etc.), nutritional (food stamps), and medical assist (Medi-Cal). Walk in or call. FUNDING: Govt. OFC HRS: M-Th 7am-5:30pm; F 8am-5pm. Spanish spoken. SERVES: Coachella Valley, Indio, Palm Desert, Thermal, Mecca.

RIVERSIDE CO. PUBLIC SOCIAL SRVS

CalWorks/Medi-Cal/Food Stamps
1400 Minthorn St.
Lake Elsinore, CA 92530

(951) 245-3100
(951) 674-5948 FAX

Financial (CalWORKs, GAIN, General Relief, etc.), nutritional (food stamps), and medical assist (Medi-Cal). FUNDING: Govt. OFC HRS: M-Th 7am-5:30pm; F 8am-5pm. ADM REQ: Varies with prgm. SERVES: Mid-Riverside County.

RIVERSIDE CO. PUBLIC SOCIAL SRVS

Income Maintenance/Medi-Cal
3178 Hamner Ave.
Norco, CA 92860
(951) 272-5550
(951) 272-5482 FAX

Financial (TANF, CalWORKs, General Relief, etc.), nutritional (food stamps), and medical assist (Medi-Cal). Walk in or call. FUNDING: Govt. OFC HRS: M-Th 7am-5:30pm; F 8am-5pm. Spanish spoken. ADM REQ: Varies with prgm. SERVES: Norco.

RIVERSIDE CO. PUBLIC SOCIAL SRVS

Temporary Assistance Medical Div
2055 N. Perris Blvd., Ste B
Perris, CA 92571
(951) 940-6600
(951) 940-6610 FAX

Financial (CalWORKs, TANF, General Relief, etc.), nutritional (food stamps), and medical assist (Medi-Cal). Walk in to apply, appts for continuing. FUNDING: Govt. OFC HRS: M-Th 7am-5:30pm; F 8am-5pm. Spanish spoken. SERVES: Riverside County.

RIVERSIDE CO. PUBLIC SOCIAL SRVS

County Administrative Offices
4060 County Circle Dr.
Riverside, CA 92503
(951) 358-3000
(951) 358-3036 FAX

CalWORKs offers financial assist to families with children who are deprived of support due to incapacity, unemployment or continued absence of one or more parents. Food stamps prgm offers an increased food purchase power for low-income families. Medical assist prgm (Medi-Cal). General Relief Prgm: assist to indigent individuals & families in temporary need of housing, food or transportation. This is a loan prgm and recipients are to repay benefits. In Home Supportive Srvs (IHSS) provides household and personal care to allow elderly and disabled to remain in their own home. For adult abuse, call (800) 491-7123. FUNDING: County, state, fed, govt. OFC HRS: M-Th 7:30am-5:30pm. Spanish spoken. Interpreters available in local offices by appointment. ADM REQ: Varies with prgm & srvs. SERVES: Riverside County.

RIVERSIDE CO. PUBLIC SOCIAL SRVS

Assistance Programs
11060 Magnolia Ave.
Riverside, CA 92505
(951) 358-3400

Financial (CalWORKs, TANF, General Relief, etc.), nutritional (food stamps), and medical assist (Medi-Cal). Walk in or call. FUNDING: Govt. OFC HRS: M-Th 7am-5:30pm; F 8am-5pm. Spanish, Vietnamese spoken. ASL available. SERVES: Riverside County.

RIVERSIDE CO. PUBLIC SOCIAL SRVS

Income Maintenance/Medi-Cal
43264 Business Park Dr., Ste B1

Temecula, CA 92590
(951) 600-6500
(951) 600-6502 FAX

Financial (CalWORKs, TANF, General Relief, etc.), nutritional (food stamps), and medical assist (Medi-Cal). Walk in or call. FUNDING: Govt. OFC HRS: M-Th 7am-5:30pm; F 8am-5pm. Spanish spoken. ADM REQ: Varies with prgm. SERVES: Mid-County.

ROY'S DESERT RESOURCE CENTER

19531 McLane St.
Palm Springs, CA 92262
(760) 676-5200

Homeless shelter for families and single adults. Srvs include, case mgmt meals, showers, laundry, and social srvs assist. Pick up points throughout the city of Palm Springs. Also accepts clients who have their own means of transportation. FUNDING: Nonprofit. ADM REQ: Must be homeless, drug free, physically able to take care of themselves, and have not been convicted of a violent felony or sexual offense. Free srvs. SERVES: Coachella Valley.

SALVATION ARMY/CATHEDRAL CITY

Family Services
30-400 Landu Blvd.
Cathedral City, CA 92234
(760) 324-2275
(760) 321-4813 FAX

Emerg food, shelter, info and referral. Emerg food bag with four-day supply every third W (max six times per yr). Crisis relief, utility asst through Edison. Rental assist, info and resources for families in the Western Coachella Valley. School uniform assist (limited), premarital, marital, family, drug, and spiritual guidance, summer camp. After school prgm: computer classes (based on availability), reading lab, math lab classes at no cost to student. Thanksgiving and Christmas food baskets and toys. OFC HRS: M-W 9am-5:30pm. Spanish spoken. SERVES: Palm Springs, Cathedral City, Desert Hot Springs, Rancho Mirage and Thousand Palms.

SALVATION ARMY/FAMILY SRVS

Family Srvs
14068 Graham St.
Moreno Valley, CA 92553-8316
(951) 656-1822
(951) 653-2852 FAX

Info and referral for emerg srvs including: food, clothing, Christmas help, and disaster relief as funds are available. After school tutoring. Youth programs. FUNDING: Nonprofit. OFC HRS: Food assistance: M, Tu, 9:30am-12:30pm. Spanish spoken. ADM REQ: Must have photo I.D. for all adult family members, medical card or copy of birth certificate for children and proof of income and residence. SERVES: Perris, Moreno Valley.

SALVATION ARMY/FAMILY SRVS

Social Srvs
3695 1st Street
Riverside, CA 92501-2501
(951) 784-4490
(951) 784-0790 FAX

Info and referral on emerg srvs including: food & utility assist as funds permit. FUNDING: Nonprofit. OFC HRS: M-F 9am-4pm. SERVES: Riverside & nearby.

SALVATION ARMY/HOSPITALITY HOUSE

925 W. 10th Street
San Bernardino, CA 92410
(909) 888-1336
(909) 888-4196 FAX

Food baskets 2nd and 4th Tu of every month at 1pm. Info & referral, tutoring prgm, shelter. Dinner is served for homeless at this site every day but Sat at 6pm until food runs out. Food baskets 2nd and 4th Tu of every month at 1pm, 730 W. Spruce St. For shelter call (909) 888-4880; opens at 3:30pm. Spanish spoken. SERVES: San Bernardino County.

SALVATION ARMY/REDLANDS CORPS

P.O. Box 26
838 N. Alta St.
Redlands, CA 92374
(909) 792-6868
(909) 335-3140 FAX

Emerg food. Dinner daily M-F 5pm. Food pantry, emerg materials assist, emerg gas, peer counseling, crisis counseling, referrals for morning showering, utility, rehab assist. in San Bernardino. USDA commodities 4th F 10am-12noon, 1:30pm-4pm. Worship srvs. Walk in. FUNDING: Donations, FEMA, United Way. OFC HRS: M, Tu, Th, F 1:15pm-4pm. ADM REQ: Low income. Free srvs. SERVES: Redlands, Loma Linda, Mentone, Bryn Mawr.

SALVATION ARMY/RIVERSIDE CORPS

3695 1st Street
Riverside, CA 92501
(951) 784-3571
(951) 784-0790 FAX

Disaster relief and summer camp. Referral to adult rehab for substance abuse and to teenage parent prgm through Booth Memorial Center. FUNDING: United Way, donations, nonprofit. OFC HRS: M-F 8:30am-4pm. ADM REQ: Anyone in need, referral from Social Srvs or food bank. SERVES: Riverside Metro, Corona, Norco, Rubidoux, March AFB.

SALVATION ARMY/VICTORVILLE CORPS

14585 La Paz Dr.
Victorville 92395
(760) 245-2545
(760) 245-1130 FAX

Emerg food prgm (Tu, Th, 9am-12noon), emerg temporary shelter (when funds are available), info & referral. Utilities and rent when funds are available. Walk in. FUNDING: Donations, United Way. Phone hrs: M-F 9am-12noon. ADM REQ: Photo ID, proof of income. SS card or medical card for everyone. Free srvs. SERVES: Victorville, Apple Valley, Hesperia, Lucerne Valley, Adelanto, Oro Grande, Barstow, Big Bear.

SALVATION ARMY/YUCCA VLY SRVS

56659 Twentynine Palms Hwy., Ste E
Yucca Valley, CA 92284
(760) 228-0114

Comprehensive emerg assist on a case-by-case basis. Food bank on W, utility asst by appt. Certified emerg disaster responders. Other resources as available. Inquiries welcome. FUNDING: United Way, county, donations, nonprofit. OFC HRS: Tu-Th 10am-3pm. SERVES: Morongo Basin.

SAN BERNARDINO CITY MISSION

P.O. Box 3489

---

719 North D Street
San Bernardino, CA 92413
(909) 889-2700
(909) 649-0014 FAX

Clothing, household items, food box, nutrition classes, hygiene items, drop-in ctr, info & referral, community food pantry. Various speakers, holiday celebrations. For food box, call Th. 9am-2pm, delivered to home on 4th Sat. Preassigned; must fill out pre-qualification form. FUNDING: Nonprofit. OFC HRS: Tu-Th 9am-2pm. Other hrs by appt. ADM REQ: Must have both photo ID and SS card to receive food boxes. For children under age 18 yrs, birth certificate and SS. SERVES: San Bernardino County.

SAN BERNARDINO CITY U.S.D.

School Link Services
1535 W. Highland Ave.
San Bernardino, CA 92411
(909) 880-6701
(909) 880-6702 FAX

Homeless liason, HIV & health srvs, family resource center. FUNDING: Donations. OFC HRS: M-F 8am-4:30pm. Spanish spoken. SERVES: San Bernardino USD.

SAN BERNARDINO CO. BEHAV HEALTH

Mentally Ill Homeless Program
237 W. Mill St.
San Bernardino, CA 92408
(909) 388-4133
(909) 388-4190 FAX

Shelter provided to the mentally ill homeless adults in San Bernardino County. Clients must have a major mental diagnosis. Prgm utilizes intensive case mgmt and assists clients in obtaining SSI, temporary housing and employment. Walk-in clients and call referrals are accepted. Limited availability for 30 days. FUNDING: Govt. OFC HRS: M-F 8am-5pm. Spanish spoken. Free srvs. SERVES: San Bernardino County.

SAN BERNARDINO CO. HUMAN SRVS SY

Transitional Assistance
7977 Sierra Ave.
Fontana, CA 92335
(909) 356-3160
(909) 356-3221
(909) 356-3169 FAX

Transitional assist prgms include financial (CalWORKs, General Relief, etc.), nutritional (food stamps), and medical assist (Medi-Cal). Subsidized child care (CalWORKs & alternative payment). FUNDING: Govt. OFC HRS: M-F 8:30am-4:30pm. Spanish spoken. SERVES: Fontana for all prgms. Child care srvs provided for all San Bernardino County.

SAN BERNARDINO CO. HUMAN SRVS SY

Medi-Cal
1627 E. Holt Blvd.
Ontario, CA 91761
(909) 933-6330
(909) 933-6450 FAX

Income maintenance prgms. Medical assist (Medi-Cal). FUNDING: Govt. OFC HRS: M-F 9am-4pm. Spanish spoken. SERVES: San Bernardino County.

SAN BERNARDINO CO. HUMAN SRVS SY

Income Maintenance/Transitional Assist
2050 N. Massachusetts
San Bernardino, CA 92415

(909) 475-2074
(909) 475-2231 FAX

Income maintenance prgms include financial (CalWORKs, TANF, General Relief, etc.), nutritional (food stamps), and medical assist (Medi-Cal). FUNDING: Govt. OFC HRS: M-F 8:30am-4:30pm. Spanish spoken. SERVES: Specific areas in San Bernardino.

SEVENTH DAY ADVENTIST COMM SRVS

P.O. Box 52439
4491 Kansas Ave.
Riverside, CA 92517
(951) 682-9810
(951) 682-4861 FAX

Emerg clothing, food. Food is available 1st M of each month except holidays, then it will be the following M. FUNDING: Nonprofit. OFC HRS: M-Th 9am-4pm; F 9am-12noon. ADM REQ: Must have valid ID, low income, must show proof of 92507 zip code residency. SERVES: Riverside County.

SHEEPFOLD, THE

P.O. Box 4487
Orange, CA 92863
(877) 743-3736
(714) 237-1444
(714) 237-1440 FAX

Shelter for homeless and abused women with children. Christian atmosphere, daily Bible studies. FUNDING: Donations, nonprofit. OFC HRS: M-F 9am-4pm. ADM REQ: Must attend church on Sunday. SERVES: Orange & Riverside Counties.

SHELTER FOR THE HOMELESS

American Family Housing Prgms
15161 Jackson St.
Midway City, CA 92655-1432
(714) 897-3221
(714) 893-6858 FAX

330 units of emergency, transitional and permanent housing. Counseling and case mgmt. Financial, personal, and communication information. FUNDING: Govt agencies, donations, nonprofit. OFC HRS: M-F 8am-5pm. Spanish spoken. ADM REQ: Ages 18 yrs+. Drug free, willing to abide by rules; 14-30 days to get a job, determined at intake. SERVES: So. Calif.

ST. CHRISTOPHER'S CHURCH

25075 Cottonwood Ave.
Moreno Valley, CA 92553
(951) 924-1968
(951) 247-6477 FAX

Parish members donate food which is given to needy families M only 1pm-3pm. Spanish spoken. ADM REQ: Photo I.D., Social Security card, school records for children in-house and proof of residency. SERVES: Moreno Valley.

ST. ELIZABETH CHURCH

Food Program
66700 Pierson Blvd.
Desert Hot Springs, CA 92240
(760) 329-8794
(760) 329-6760 FAX

Food supplements twice monthly Tu 9am-10:45am. FUNDING: Nonprofit. OFC HRS: M-F 8:30am-3:30pm. Summer hrs: M-F 8:30am-12noon. ADM REQ: Must show proof of residency in Desert Hot Springs, valid Calif I.D. or driver's license and Social Security card

for each member in the family. SERVES: Desert Hot Springs only.

TANF

Temporary Assistance/Needy Families

See "San Bernardino Co. Human Srvs Sy" and "Riverside Co. Public Social Srvs"

THE TRINITY HOUSE

133 Highland Ave., Ste A2
National City, CA 91950
(619) 477-7158
(619) 330-4749 FAX

Faith-based human srvs organization. Safe, clean, healthy transitional living environment for women, with or without children. Academic edu, employment, training and career guidance srvs. FUNDING: Nonprofit. OFC HRS: M-F 8am-5pm. Spanish spoken. SERVES: Calif.

V.A. MEDICAL CENTER/LOMA LINDA

Jerry L. Pettis Memorial V.A. Med Ctr
11201 Benton St.
Loma Linda, CA 92357
(909) 825-7084
(800) 741-8387
(909) 422-3106 FAX

200+ bed hospital. 24-hr emerg room with doctor on duty. General medical and some specialty srvs, surgical, rehab, psychiatric, primary outpatient care, STD testing & treatment, HIV treatments & therapies, extended and long-term care and homeless prgms. FUNDING: Federal. OFC HRS: M-F 8am-4:30pm. 24-hr srvs. Spanish, Vietnamese spoken. ADM REQ: Military srv veterans. Fees vary with eligibility. SERVES: San Bernardino, Riverside Counties.

VALLEY OASIS ACCESS CENTER

Formerly Homeless Solution Access Center
45134 N. Sierra Hwy., Bldg. B
Lancaster, CA 93534
(661) 942-2758

Case mgmt, mail & phone srvs, emerg housing referrals, transportation, food referrals, domestic violence issues, mental health srvs, & job assist. Tarzana treatment referrals and showers available. Also call hotline, (800) 282-4808. Walk-in hrs: M, Tu, Th, F 9am-1pm. Schedule appts on M-F 8am-5pm. Spanish spoken. ADM REQ: Ages 18 yrs+ & facing eviction within seven days. Referrals within the U.S.A. SERVES: Calif.

VALLEY RESTART CENTER

200 E. Menlo Ave.
Hemet, CA 92543
(951) 766-7476
(951) 925-0566 FAX

Shelter for homeless. No drop-ins or mail services. Showers 4pm-5pm daily. For residents: Evening meals daily at 6pm, case mgmt srvs, laundry facilities, job info & referrals, housing referrals. Meeting space provided for AA/NA meetings on Th, shelter access 24 hrs. Interviews and intake M-F 9-1:30pm. Emergency interviews upon request. Rental assist when funds available. No utility asst. No underage, unaccompanied youth. Not for those needing medical treatment. Same criteria for showers as for residency. Eligible for food box once every 3 months. FUNDING: Nonprofit. OFC HRS: M-F 9am-5pm. ADM REQ: CA picture ID, no warrants, not on parole, not on Megan's List, no history of violent charges, no repeats recipients.

Free srvs. SERVES: Hemet, San Jacinto Valley.

VCF COMMUNITY SERVICES

17421 Van Buren Blvd.
Riverside, CA 92504
(951) 789-8514
(951) 780-5433
(951) 780-1981 FAX

Assists all people in need with sack lunches, hygiene packages for homeless, emerg food box (for monthly food srvs, must be involved in Change Your Life Prgm), clothing, housing & utility assist, job search and counseling regarding employment, resume assist, outreach prgms. Mailing address: 16445 Porter Ave. Riverside, CA 92505. FUNDING: Church, donations, nonprofit. OFC HRS: Tu-F 9am-4pm. SERVES: Riverside County.

VERONICA'S HOME OF MERCY

1495 W. Victoria St.
San Bernardino, CA 92411
(909) 888-9064
(909) 888-7390 FAX

Long-term, faith-based residential home (room for up to 20 women) for adult pregnant women & children or women with small children, as an alternative to domestic violence, addictions, abortion and/or homelessness. Women must be involved with the prgm and be willing to continue their education. Not an emergency shelter. Transitional living. FUNDING: Nonprofit. OFC HRS: M-F 8am-4pm. Spanish spoken. ADM REQ: Must be ages 18 yrs+ or emancipated by court. SERVES: So. Calif.

VICTOR VALLEY RESCUE MISSION

16611 Tracy St., Ste C
Victorville, CA 92395
(760) 955-5958
(760) 955-5958 FAX

Clothing and household items distributed once per week. Food boxes available for delivery or pick-up. Call for more info. FUNDING: Nonprofit. OFC HRS: M-F 9am-5pm. ADM REQ: Must fill out client form, proof of residency, I.D. or SS card. SERVES: San Bernardino County.

WAY STATION/YUCCA VALLEY

P.O. Box 613
61722 Commercial St.
Joshua Tree, CA 92252
(760) 366-8088
(760) 366-7344 FAX

Counseling, info & referral, emerg food, diapers, clothing, holiday baskets and hot meals. For emerg, call (760) 366-2278 (24 hrs). OFC HRS: M-F 8am-1pm. SERVES: San Bernardino County.

WELFARE

See "San Bernardino Co. Human Srvs Sy"

YWCA/RIVERSIDE CO.

Born Free Women's Residential Prgm
8172 Magnolia Ave.
Riverside, CA 92504
(951) 530-8280
(951) 688-5270 FAX

24-hr residential treatment prgm for chemically dependent women. Srvs include: transportation to medical/legal appts, 12-Step prgms, parenting classes, one-on-one counseling, group sessions, NA/AA meetings, in-home nurse to discuss child birthing issues, budgeting and meal prep classes, exit plans. FUNDING: Donations, nonprofit. OFC HRS: 24 hrs, 7 days. Spanish spoken. ADM REQ: Ages 18 yrs+, pregnant, and addicted to a substance. This is not a detox facility. Sliding fee scale, no one turned away due to the inability to pay. SERVES: Los Angeles County, Orange County, Riverside County San Bernadino County.

HOSPITALS (MEDICAL & PSYCHIATRIC)

AMBULANCE/EMERGENCY DIAL 911

AMERICAN HOSP ASSN/RESOURCE

155 N. Wacker Dr.
Chicago, IL 60606-3421
(312) 422-3000
(312) 422-4796 FAX

Answers questions about hospitals in the U.S., including hospitals with special units for AIDS, number of hospital beds, address for a specific hospital and other questions about hospitals. FUNDING: Nonprofit. OFC HRS: M-F 7:30am-5:30pm, CST. General info & referral srvs are free. SERVES: U.S.A.

BALLARD REHABILITATION HOSPITAL

1760 W. 16th Street
San Bernardino, CA 92411
(909) 473-1200
(909) 473-1276 FAX

Comprehensive physical rehab srvs for adults and pediatric patients diagnosed with brain injury, spinal cord injuries, multiple trauma, amputation, stroke, neurological disorders or orthopedic injuries. Complete inpatient and outpatient medical rehab prgms & srvs. Specialty areas include: indoor therapeutic pool, transitional living suites, mobility court, outpatient workers' comp, pain mgmt prgm & orthopedic srvs. Offers OT, PT, speech and language pathology, therapeutic recreation, respiratory therapy, rehab nursing, neuropsychology case mgmt, pharmacy, rehab nursing and physician, dietary, lab, radiology, social srvs, case mgmt & community re-entry. Forms in English and Spanish. FUNDING: Nonprofit. OFC HRS: M-F 8am-5pm. Spanish, Tagalog, Thai, German, Polish, Russian, Slovac, French spoken. Accepts pvt insurance HMO, PPO, Medicare, Medi-Cal. SERVES: So. Calif.

BEAR VALLEY COMMUNITY HOSPITAL

P.O. Box 1649
41870 Garstin Dr.
Big Bear Lake, CA 92315
(909) 878-8268
(909) 878-8282 FAX

9-bed acute care hospital, 21-bed skilled nursing facility, PT. 24-hr emerg room with physician on duty. FUNDING: Nonprofit. OFC HRS: 24 hrs. Interpreters available for Spanish, German, Tagalog. Accepts Medicare, insurance, pvt pay. SERVES: Big Bear Valley.

CALIF DEPT HEALTH SRVS

Licensing & Certification/Hosp/Clinics
2000 Evergreen St., Ste 200
Sacramento, CA 95815
(800) 554-0354
(916) 263-5800
(916) 263-5840 FAX

Licensing for hospitals & clinics. Gives listings of nursing homes. For CNA licensing, call (916) 327-2445 (same building). OFC HRS: M-F 8am-5pm. SERVES: Calif.

CHILDREN'S HOSP L.A.

4650 Sunset Blvd.
Los Angeles, CA 90027
(323) 660-2450
(323) 663-1645 FAX

314-bed hospital treats children ages birth-18 yrs. Srvs include: hematology, oncology, cystic fibrosis, AIDS prgm, intensive neonatal unit, Regional Level I Pediatric Trauma Center, 24-hr emerg room. FUNDING: Nonprofit. Spanish spoken. Accepts pvt insurance, Medi-Cal. SERVES: So. Calif.

CHINO VALLEY MEDICAL CENTER

5451 Walnut Ave.
Chino, CA 91710
(909) 464-8600
(909) 464-8882 FAX

126-bed general acute care hospital srvs include: obstetrics, outpatient surgery, orthopedics, pain mgmt. Paramedic base station. Emerg dept., doctor at facility 24 hrs. FUNDING: Private for profit. Spanish spoken. Accepts pvt insurance, Medicare, Medi-Cal. SERVES: San Bernardino County.

CITY OF HOPE NATL MEDICAL CTR

New Patient Srvs
1500 E. Duarte Rd.
Duarte, CA 91010-3000
(800) 826-4673
(626) 256-4673

212-bed center focuses on treatment and clinical research efforts for cancer. Treatment and clinical research prgms for other diseases include: diabetes, HIV/AIDS, sickle-cell disease and hemophilia. Basic research conducted at the Beckman Research Institute concentrates on broader areas of genetics, gene therapy, immunology and neuroscience. Referrals M-F 8am-5pm. FUNDING: Nonprofit. Spanish spoken. Accepts pvt insurance, Medicare, Medi-Cal. SERVES: U.S.A.

COLORADO RIVER MEDICAL CENTER

1401 Bailey Ave.
Needles, CA 92363
(760) 326-4531
(760) 326-4532 FAX

25-bed hospital, critical inpatient & two outpatient physical rehab offices. Doctor at the facility 24 hrs. Alt fax (760) 326-7275. FUNDING: Private for profit. Japanese and Spanish spoken. Accepts insurance, Medicare, Medi-Cal. SERVES: San Bernardino County.

DESERT VALLEY HOSPITAL

16850 Bear Valley Rd.
Victorville 92395
(760) 241-8000
(760) 241-8220 FAX

83-bed hospital. Obstetrics, cardiology, oncology, specialized surgery, nephrology, orthopedics. 24-hr emerg room, cancer center, intensive care. FUNDING: Private for profit. OFC HRS: 24-hr srvs. Spanish spoken. Accepts insurance, Medicare, Medi-Cal. SERVES: High Desert including: Apple Valley, Adelanto, Barstow, Victorville, Silver Lakes, Hesperia, Big Bear and nearby.

EISENHOWER MEDICAL CENTER

39000 Bob Hope Dr.
Rancho Mirage, CA 92270
(760) 340-3911
(760) 773-1425 FAX

Special centers include: Betty Ford Center for substance abuse treatment & Barbara Sinatra Children's Center for victims of child abuse. Also cardiac, orthopedic and cancer care, general practice, general surgery, birthing center, MRI facility, outpatient care ctr including minor surgery, adult day care center for people with Alzheimer's disease, Parkinson's disease and other medical conditions. 24-hr emerg dept, four immediate care centers. Dell E. Webb and Eisenhower Health Ctr near Sun City & Palm Desert. Arthritis edu prgm, cardiovascular fitness ctr, diabetes prgm, home care srvs, home medical equipment, hospice srvs, rehab facility, physical therapy pool and nutrition counseling. Also offers support groups for bereavement, cancer, breast cancer, diabetes, families of hospice patients, prostate cancer and families of Alzheimer's and Parkinson's disease patients. FUNDING: Nonprofit. OFC HRS: 24-hr srvs. Many languages spoken. Accepts Medi-Cal, Medicare, pvt insurance. SERVES: Calif.

EL CENTRO REGIONAL MEDICAL CENTER

1415 Ross Ave.
El Centro, CA 92243
(760) 339-7100
(760) 339-7363 FAX

165-bed general acute care hospital, 24-hr emerg room, OB, pediatric, ICU, CCU. FUNDING: Nonprofit. OFC HRS: 24 hrs, 7 days. Spanish spoken. Accepts insurance, Medicare, Medi-Cal. SERVES: Imperial County.

HI-DESERT MEDICAL CENTER

6601 White Feather Rd.
Joshua Tree, CA 92252
(760) 366-3711
(760) 366-6136 FAX

24-hr emerg srvs, acute care hospital, skilled nursing facility, community edu, home health srvs and outpatient srvs. Walk in or call. FUNDING: District hospital. OFC HRS: 24 hrs. Accepts Medi-Cal. SERVES: Morongo Basin.

HILL-BURTON FREE MED CARE PRGM

Health Resources & Srvs
5600 Fishers Ln., Ste 10C-16
Rockville, MD 20857
(301) 443-5656
(800) 638-0742
(301) 443-0619 FAX

Info on hospitals and other health facilities participating in the Hill-Burton Hospital Free Care Prgm. A srv of the Health Resources & Srvs Admin, U.S. Dept of Health & Human Srvs. Accepts name and phone number and calls are returned during next business day. FUNDING: Nonprofit. OFC HRS: M-F 8:30am-5pm, EST. Spanish spoken. SERVES: U.S.A.

KAISER PERMANENTE/MEDICAL CTR

9961 Sierra Ave.
Fontana, CA 92335
(909) 427-5000
(909) 427-7359 FAX

444-bed acute care hosp for Kaiser members. Prgms & srvs for: allergy, anesthesiology, cardiology, critical care ctr, emerg medicine, chemical dependence srvs, dermatology, ear-nose-throat, gastroenterology, newborn intensive care unit, neurosurgery, neurology, nuclear medicine, obstetrics, ophthalmology, orthopedics, optometry, pathology, pediatrics, physical medicine (biofeedback, PT, OT, speech pathology), preventive medicine, psychiatry, radiology, respiratory therapy, surgery and urology. TTY (909) 427-5549. FUNDING: Private for profit. Many languages spoken. Accepts Kaiser insurance, Medi-Cal, Medicare. SERVES: San Bernardino & Riverside Counties.

KAISER PERMANENTE/MEDICAL CTR
10800 Magnolia Ave.
Riverside, CA 92505
(951) 353-2000
(951) 353-4611 FAX

215-bed general acute care hospital for Kaiser members. Obstetrics, cardiology, oncology, specialized surgery, nephrology, orthopedics, chemical dependency prgm (family recovery srvs), inpatient psychiatry srvs, and partial hospitalization prgm. Doctor at facility 24 hrs. FUNDING: HMO. Language line available. Accepts Kaiser insurance. SERVES: Riverside County.

LOMA LINDA UNIV MEDICAL CTR
11234 Anderson St.
Loma Linda, CA 92354
(909) 558-4006
(909) 588-4000
(909) 558-0149 FAX

The only state-designated, 797-bed, level 1 Regional Trauma Center for the four Inland Counties of Riverside, San Bernardino, Inyo & Mono. Up to 35 percent of the Medical Center's patients served in nine ICUs: surgical & trauma, neurosurgical, cardio-thoracic, pediatric cardio-thoracic, respiratory, coronary, medical, neonatal, and pediatric. Hosts various bereavement groups. Spanish speaking srvs (909) 558-4367. SAFE KIDS prgm at (909) 558-4704. Facilities include: acute rehab, total care birthing center, computerized tomography, MRI, lithotripsy, and hospital-based proton accelerator for the treatment of cancer, and a children's hospital. Also HIV/AIDS treatments & therapies. Wait: varies. Many languages spoken. Accepts Medi-Cal, Medicare, pvt insurance. SERVES: Riverside, San Bernardino, Inyo, Mono Counties.

LOMA LINDA UNIV MEDICAL CTR
East Campus
25333 Barton Rd.
Loma Linda, CA 92354
(909) 558-6000
(909) 796-0167
(909) 558-6669 FAX

120-bed acute care hospital, ICU, 24-hr emerg room srvs, medical and surgical units, intensive care, outpatient srvs. No maternity. FUNDING: Pvt, nonprofit. OFC HRS: 24-hr srvs. Chinese, Spanish & Tagalog spoken. Accepts Medi-Cal, Medicare, insurance. SERVES: San Bernardino County.

MENIFEE VALLEY MEDICAL CENTER
28400 McCall Blvd.
Sun City, CA 92586
(951) 679-8888
(951) 672-7050 FAX

84-bed acute care hospital, I.C.U., 24-hr emerg room, 24-hr pharmacy, inpatient and outpatient surgery, special rehab unit, cancer center, CCU. Walk in or call. Free comm edu, health fair. FUNDING: Nonprofit. Spanish spoken, ASL available. Accepts Medi-Cal, Medicare, insurance. SERVES: Riverside County.

MILESTONES RESIDENTIAL FACILITY
82485 Miles Ave.
Indio, CA 92201-4249
(760) 347-4347
(760) 342-7829 FAX

Residential mental health srvs for adults ages 18-59 yrs. Substance abuse treatment, counseling. FUNDING: Govt. OFC HRS: 24-hr srvs. Spanish spoken. ADM REQ: Ages 18 yrs+. SERVES: Riverside County.

NORRIS COMPREHENSIVE CANCER CTR
See "USC Norris Comp Cancer Ctr"

ORTHOPAEDIC HOSPITAL L.A.
2400 S. Flower
Los Angeles, CA 90007
(213) 742-1000
(800) 339-6784
(213) 742-1137 FAX

100 outpatient clinics for children with wide range of problems: spina bifida, scoliosis, cerebral palsy, bone tumor, arthritis, osteogenesis imperfecta, and muscle disease. For adult orthopaedic physician referrals, call (213) 742-6509. For the children's clinic, call (213) 742-1300. Provides orthopaedic care for children under age 18 yrs, regardless of ability to pay. FUNDING: Nonprofit. OFC HRS: M-F 8am-5pm Spanish spoken. Accepts Medi-Cal for children's clinic. SERVES: Western U.S.A.

REDLANDS COMMUNITY HOSPITAL
(See Display Ad on Page 194)
350 Terracina Blvd.
Redlands, CA 92373
Home Health: (909)335-5647
Hospice: (909) 335-5643
Referrals/Authorization: (909) 335-5520
www.redlandshospital.org

Redlands Community Hospital Home Health and Hospice Services are Medicare certified, state licensed and Joint Commission accredited. Our Home Health and Hospice Services offer: Rehabilitiation, Skilled Nursing, Diabetic Management, Wound Care Heart Failure Management, and much more Our Hospice Services has Specialized Staff (Nursing, Hospice Chaplain, Home Health Aic and Volunteers), Social Worker Support.

ROBERT E. BUSH NAVAL HOSPITAL
P.O. Box 788250
Bldg 1145, MCAGCC
Twentynine Palms, CA 92278
(760) 830-2190
(760) 830-2182 FAX

29-bed hospital & outpatient prgm for active duty members, their dependents, retirees and other eligible people. FUNDING: Nonprofit, govt. OFC HRS: 24 hrs. Japanese, Spanish, Tagalog spoken. ADM REQ: Military. SERVES: 29 Palms.

SAN BERNARDINO CO. HUMAN SRVS SY
Medi-Cal Information
2050 N. Massachusetts
San Bernardino, CA 92415
(909) 475-2074
(909) 475-2231 FAX

Medi-Cal prgm provides comprehensive medical care to all public assist recipients and to certain other eligible persons such as aged, blind, and disabled individuals, and to children who do not have sufficient funds to meet the cost of medical care. Automated line. For operator, call (909) 475-2006. FUNDING: County, state, fed, govt. OFC HRS: M-F 9am-4pm. Spanish spoken. SERVES: San Bernardino County.

SAN BERNARDINO CO. MENTAL HEALTH
Arrowhead Regional Med Center
400 N. Pepper Ave.
Colton, CA 92324
(909) 580-1000
(909) 580-2809 FAX

Mental health unit of the county hospital. 5150s are taken to this unit. Assessment and eval for severe cases. Inpatient srvs. FUNDING: County. Spanish, Vietnamese, Chinese, Tagalog spoken. Accepts Medicare, Medi-Cal. SERVES: San Bernardino County.

SAN GORGONIO MEMORIAL HOSPITAL
600 N. Highland Springs Ave.
Banning, CA 92220
(951) 845-1121
(951) 845-2836 FAX

77-bed acute care hospital, 24-hr emerg room, psychiatric units, maternity ward, ICU, CCU, skilled nursing. FUNDING: Nonprofit. OFC HRS: 24-hr srvs. Spanish spoken. Accepts Medi-Cal, Medicare, pvt pay & most HMOs, PPOs. SERVES: Banning, Beaumont, Cabazon, Cherry Valley.

SHANDIN HILLS BEHAV THERAPY CTR
4164 N. 4th Avenue
San Bernardino, CA 92407
(909) 886-6786
(909) 886-2953 FAX

47-bed psychiatric institute providing residential care for those with mental disease. Six to 9 month prgm. Discharge planning goal is lower level care. FUNDING: County of San Bernardino. OFC HRS: 24-hr srvs. Some Spanish spoken. ADM REQ: Referral by San Bernardino County Mental Health. Accepts Medi-Cal. SERVES: San Bernardino County.

SHRINERS HOSPITALS FOR CHILDREN/L.A.
3160 Geneva St.
Los Angeles, CA 90020-1199
(213) 388-3151
(213) 387-7528 FAX

60-bed pediatric hospital, inpatient & outpatient srvs limited to orthopedics, orthotics, reconstructive burn care & prosthetics. Wait: 30 days. Visiting hrs: 10am-7pm. For applications, call (888) 489-KIDS (5437). To reach one of the 22 Shriners Hospitals in North America call, (800) 237-5055. FUNDING: Shriners, nonprofit. OFC HRS: M-F 8:30am-5pm. Spanish, Tagalog, French, Burmese, Chinese and Korean spoken. ADM REQ: Medical need, child must be ages 18 yrs or younger & have a medical condition treated by Shriners hospitals. No payment accepted, no billing dept. Free srvs. SERVES: So. Calif, So. Nevada, Arizona, New Mexico, Northern Mexico (children do not need to be legal US citizens to receive treatment).

ST. BERNARDINE MEDICAL CENTER
2101 N. Waterman Ave.
San Bernardino, CA 92404-4836
(909) 883-8711

433-bed acute care facility. Emerg srvs, OB, pediatrics, open heart surgery, cancer center. FUNDING: Nonprofit. OFC HRS: 24-hr srvs. Various languages spoken. Accepts insurance, Medicare, Medi-Cal. SERVES: San Bernardino County.

ST. JUDE CHILDREN'S RESEARCH HOSP

12365 Lewis St., Ste 101
Garden Grove, CA 92840
(800) 227-6737
(714) 663-7200
(714) 663-7222 FAX

Unique institution dedicated to research & treatment for children with cancer, pediatric AIDS and other catastrophic childhood diseases. FUNDING: Fundraisers, donations, nonprofit. OFC HRS: M-F 8am-4:30pm. Spanish spoken. Accepts Medi-Cal, no one turned away for lack of funds. Free srvs to terminally ill children ages 18 yrs or under. SERVES: So. Calif.

ST. MARY MEDICAL CENTER

P.O. Box 7025
18300 Highway 18
Apple Valley, CA 92307
(760) 242-2311
(888) 767-6202
(760) 946-8812 FAX

Acute medical facility co-ministered and designed by the Sisters of St. Joseph of Orange and the Brothers of St. John of God who believe that modern technology and human love form an excellent combination for healing the acutely ill. Free support groups, community edu classes. FUNDING: Nonprofit. OFC HRS: 24-hr srvs. Spanish spoken. Language line available. ADM REQ: Patient in need of acute skilled nursing. Accepts Medi-Cal, Medicare, HMO, pvt pay. SERVES: High desert & nearby.

THE JOHN HENRY FOUNDATION

403 N. Susan St.
Santa Ana, CA 92703
(714) 554-8906
(714) 554-8770 FAX

Provides a safe, welcoming and clinically supervised long-term, residential community for adults with schizophrenia spectrum disorders. JHF provides a home, medical and psychiatric care, a therapeutic community, family support & edu, recreational activities, and a supported work prgm to promote stabilization and healing for the individual and their family. FUNDING: Nonprofit. OFC HRS: 24 hrs, 7 days. SERVES: Southern Calif.

UCI MEDICAL CTR

101 The City Dr., South
Orange, CA 92868-3298
(714) 456-7890
(714) 456-8741 FAX

462-bed acute care med & surgical facility. Offers neurosurgery, cardiovascular surgery, bone marrow, kidney and liver transplant center, Level 3 infant special care unit, licensed burn center, NCI designated clinical cancer center, Level 1 trauma center, neurology, orthopedics, ophthalmology and optometry, speech pathology and audiology, obstetrics, pediatrics, and extensive outpatient srvs including primary care, psychiatric inpatient and outpatient srvs, in-house rehab unit. FUNDING: Private, nonprofit, county, state, fed health insurance prgms. Many languages spoken. Accepts most managed care plans including CalOptima, Medi-Cal and Medicare. SERVES: So. Calif.

UCLA MEDICAL CENTER

Ronald Reagan Medical Center
757 Westwood Plaza
Los Angeles, CA 90095
(310) 825-9111
(310) 206-5552 FAX

733-bed acute care hospital with a trauma ctr, obstetrics, pediatrics, ICU, CCU, MRI, PET scanning, cancer ctr, ophthamology, neonatal, all types of surgery including transplants (heart, liver, etc.), extensive outpatient srvs. Physican referral (800) UCLA-MD1, M-F 8am-5pm. 24-hr emerg room with doctor on duty. FUNDING: Nonprofit. Multilingual staff. Fees vary by doctor. SERVES: So. Calif.

UCLA NEUROPSYCHIATRIC HOSPITAL

150 UCLA Medical Plaza
Los Angeles, CA 90095
(800) 825-9989
(310) 825-9111
(310) 267-0376 FAX

Comprehensive inpatient & outpatient srvs for a wide variety of psychiatric, emotional and dev disorders. Prgms in geriatric, adult, child & adol psychiatry. Spanish-speaking psychosocial clinic. Individual prgms target: eating disorders, depression, obsessive compulsive disorder, schizophrenia & seizure disorders, anxiety. Matrix UCLA Alcoholism and Addiction Medicine Srv: (310) 206-7518. FUNDING: Nonprofit. OFC HRS: M-F 8am-5pm. Multilingual staff. Accepts insurance, Medicare, Medi-Cal. SERVES: So. Calif.

USC NORRIS COMP CANCER CTR

1441 Eastlake Ave.
Los Angeles, CA 90033
(800) 872-2273
(323) 865-3000
(323) 865-0033 FAX

60-bed hospital dedicated to treating cancer patients. Outpatient srvs. Bone marrow transplant unit, surgical unit, radiation oncology dept. Expert specialists in treating cancers of the genitourinary system, central nervous system, female reproductive system, breast, lung and gastrointestinal tract as well as melanoma, leukemia, lymphomas and AIDS-related cancers. No emerg room. FUNDING: Nonprofit. Spanish spoken. ADM REQ: Call for appt. M-F 8am-5pm. Accepts Medicare, insurance and most PPOs. SERVES: Internatl.

V.A. MEDICAL CENTER/LOMA LINDA

Jerry L. Pettis Memorial V.A. Med Ctr
11201 Benton St.
Loma Linda, CA 92357
(909) 825-7084
(800) 741-8387
(909) 422-3106 FAX

200+ bed hospital. 24-hr emerg room with doctor on duty. General medical and some specialty srvs, surgical, rehab, psychiatric, primary outpatient care, STD testing & treatment, HIV treatments & therapies, extended and long-term care and homeless prgms. FUNDING: Federal. OFC HRS: M-F 8am-4:30pm. 24-hr srvs. Spanish, Vietnamese spoken. ADM REQ: Military srv veterans. Fees vary with eligibility. SERVES: San Bernardino, Riverside Counties.

VICTOR VLY COMMUNITY HOSPITAL

15248 11th Street
Victorville, CA 92392
(760) 245-8691
(760) 843-6015 FAX

120-bed acute care hospital, including 24-hr emerg room and urgent care ICU-CCU, oncology, outpatient surgery, CT scan and OB, pediatrics, NICU, cardiovascular I.C.U., social srvs and discharge planning srvs. FUNDING: Nonprofit. OFC HRS: 24-hr srvs. Spanish spoken. Accepts pvt insurance, Medicare, Medi-Cal. SERVES: Inland Empire.

1 (800) GAMBLER

Compulsive Gambling Institute
27620 Landau Blvd., Ste 1
Cathedral City, CA 92234
(800) 426-2537

Assist provided to compulsive gamblers and their families, 24 hrs a day, 7 days a week. Visit (www.gamblingaddiction.cc) or (www.problemgambling.ca.gov). FUNDING: Nonprofit. SERVES: Calif.

1-800-RELAPSE

U.S. Department of Health Srvs
(800) 729-6686

Info and referral to substance abuse prgms. 24-hr hotline. Natl Substance Abuse Treatment Center. TDD (800) 487-4889. Spanish (877) 767-8432. FUNDING: Govt. Free srvs. SERVES: U.S.A.

24-HR HOTLINES

1736 Family Crisis Center
2116 Arlington Ave., Ste 200
Los Angeles, CA 90018
(323) 737-3900
(213) 745-6923 FAX

24-hr counseling and referrals to resources for battered women and children, youth and adults. Additional hotlines (310) 379-3620, (310) 370-5902, (562) 388-7652. FUNDING: Donations, grants, govt, nonprofit. Spanish spoken.

A.V. DOMESTIC VIOLENCE COUNCIL

Valley Oasis Shelter
P.O. Box 2980
Lancaster, CA 93539
(800) 282-4808
(661) 945-5509
(661) 940-3422 FAX

24-hr domestic violence hotline, outreach, emerg shelter and transitional housing. FUNDING: Private nonprofit. OFC HRS: 24 hrs, 7 days. Armenian and Spanish spoken. Free srvs. SERVES: So. Calif.

ADULT ABUSE REPORTING

Riverside Co. Public Social Srvs
(800) 491-7123
(951) 413-5815 FAX

To report any actual or suspected abuse, neglect or exploitation of elders or dependent adults, call the number shown above. FUNDING: County. Spanish spoken. Free srvs. SERVES: Riverside County.

AIDS CLINICAL TRIAL INFO SRV

See "AIDS Info"

AIDS INFO

P.O. Box 6303
Rockville, MD 20849-6303
(800) 448-0440
(301) 318-2818 FAX

Current info on federally & privately sponsored clinical trials for adults and children at all stages of HIV infection. Provides contacts for open clinical trials, printouts, custom database searches, press releases and relevant pamphlets and booklets via mail, fax, etc. Phone reference srvs for people with HIV, their families and health care providers. Offers treatment info. TTY/TDD (888) 480-3739. Web chat 12noon-4pm, EST (www.aidsinfo.nih.gov). FUNDING: Govt. OFC HRS: M-F 12noon-5pm, EST. Spanish reference specialist. Free srvs. SERVES: U.S.A.

AIDS/HIV NIGHTLINE

P.O. Box 191350
San Francisco, CA 94119
(800) 273-2437
(415) 984-1921 FAX

Evening phone line offering emotional support, info & referrals to persons with concerns about AIDS/HIV. Phone lines are open during the evening hours when other agencies are closed. Toll-free Spanish line in Calif only: (800) 303-7432, line open M-F 6pm-10pm. 24-hr crisis line: (415) 781-0500. FUNDING: Nonprofit, donations, private, city. OFC HRS: M-Sun 5pm-5am. SERVES: U.S.A.

ALCOHOL 24-HR HELPLINE

1316 South Coast Hwy.
Laguna Beach, CA 92651
(800) 334-0394
(800) 252-6465
(949) 376-6862 FAX

Info, referrals & crisis interventions. FUNDING: Nonprofit. OFC HRS: 24 hrs, 7 days. SERVES: U.S.A.

ALCOHOL ABUSE 24-HR HELPLINE

8889 Corporate Square Ct.
Jacksonville, FL 32216
(954) 972-7014

Helpline & treatment prgm. FUNDING: Private for profit. OFC HRS: 24 hrs, 7 days. Spanish spoken. SERVES: U.S.A.

ALCOHOL AND DRUG HELPLINE

7309 South 180 West
Midvale, UT 84047
(800) 821-4357
(801) 567-1490 FAX

General info, AA groups & treatment prgm referrals for any drug and/or alcohol issue. FUNDING: Private for profit. OFC HRS: 24 hrs, 7 days.

ALCOHOLICS ANONYMOUS/I.E.

Inland Empire Central Office
897 Via Lata, Ste AA
Colton, CA 92324
(909) 825-4700
(909) 825-7370 FAX

Helps anyone with an alcohol problem who wants to stop drinking by putting them in touch with sober members of AA or directing them to AA meetings. Primary purpose is to stay sober and help other alcoholics achieve sobriety. FUNDING: Self-supported by AA members. OFC HRS: M-F 9am-5pm; Sat 9am-1pm. Spanish spoken upon request. ADM REQ: Desire to stop drinking. Free srvs. SERVES: Riverside Metro, Corona, Norco, Banning, Beaumont, Moreno Valley, Hemet, Perris, Lake Elsinore, Temecula, San Bernardino Metro, Ontario, Upland, Pomona Valley and mountain areas.

ALZHEIMER'S FOUNDATION OF AMERICA

322 8th Avenue, 7th Fl.
New York, NY 10001
(866) 232-8484

Toll-free hotline to help answer questions regarding Alzheimer's and related illnesses. Will direct caller to local resources. FUNDING: Nonprofit. OFC HRS: M-F 9am-5pm, EST. SERVES: U.S.A.

AMC CANCER RESEARCH CENTER

Cancer Info & Counseling Line
1600 Pierce St.
Denver, CO 80214
(800) 321-1557
(303) 239-3400 FAX

Counseling, emotional support & resources, medical info. FUNDING: Nonprofit. OFC HRS: M-F 8:30am-5pm, MST. Spanish spoken by request. Free srvs. SERVES: U.S.A.

AMERICAN LIVER FNDN/SAN DIEGO

2515 Camino del Rio South, Ste 122
San Diego, CA 92108
(619) 291-5483
(619) 295-7181 FAX

Edu prgms about liver disease & hepatitis. Monthly support groups for patients & families. FUNDING: Nonprofit. OFC HRS: M-F 8am-5pm. Materials in Spanish, Chinese, Vietnamese. No fees. SERVES: San Diego County, Riverside & Imperial Counties.

AMERICAN LIVER FOUNDATION

75 Maiden Lane, Ste 603
New York, NY 10038
(800) 405-4837
(212) 668-1000
(212) 483-8179 FAX

Natl info & referral srvs for liver diseases. Hotline open from 6am-4pm, CST. FUNDING: Nonprofit. OFC HRS: M-F 9am-5pm, EST. SERVES: U.S.A.

AMERICAN PARKINSON DISEASE ASSN

10850 Wilshire Blvd., Ste 230
Los Angeles, CA 90024
(800) 908-2732
(310) 474-0292 FAX

Info, support and medical referrals to patients, families and caregivers in U.S. FUNDING: Donations, nonprofit. OFC HRS: M-F 9am-5pm. Spanish spoken. Free srvs. SERVES: U.S.A.

AMERICAN PREGNANCY ASSOCIATION

1431 Greenway Dr., Ste 440
Irving, TX 75038
(972) 815-2337
(972) 550-0140
(972) 550-0800 FAX

Natl organization provides edu, counseling & referrals to local resources. Referrals to maternity homes, pregnancy centers, medical care, adoption srvs, Medicare and other govt related srvs. Not a clinic. FUNDING: Nonprofit. OFC HRS: M-F 7am-10pm. 24-hr hotline. Some Spanish spoken. Free referrals. SERVES: U.S.A.

AMERICAN PREGNANCY HELPLINE

(866) 942-6466

24-hr hotline available 7 days a week to answer any questions about pregnancy, family planning, and adoption. Also offers info website about pregnancy, visit (www.thehelpline.org) for more info. FUNDING: Nonprofit. OFC HRS: 24 hrs, 7 days. Free srvs. SERVES: U.S.A.

AMERICAN SOCIAL HEALTH ASSN

P.O. Box 13827
Durham, NC 27709
(919) 361-8400
(919) 361-8425 FAX

Operates the CDC National STD and AIDS Hotline, 24 hrs, 7 days: (800) 342-2437, or (800) 227-8922. Spanish (800) 344-7432; TDD (800) 243-7889; Herpes hotline (919) 361-8488; HPV hotline (877) 478-5868. FUNDING: Nonprofit, donations, grants. OFC HRS: M-F 8am-5pm. Free srvs. SERVES: U.S.A.

ANONYMOUS CRIME HOTLINE-WE TIP

P.O. Box 1296
Rancho Cucamonga, CA 91730
(800) 782-7463
(909) 987-2477 FAX

For the general public to report criminal activities in their community, school, workplace or home. FUNDING: Nonprofit. OFC HRS: 24 hrs, 7 days. Spanish spoken. SERVES: U.S.A.

ARSON HOTLINE-WE TIP

(800) 472-7766
(909) 948-0144 FAX

24-hr hotline for anonymous arson reports. FUNDING: Nonprofit. Spanish spoken. SERVES: U.S.A.

ASTHMA INFO & REFERRAL LINE

555 E. Wells St., Ste 1100
Milwaukee, WI 53202-3823
(800) 822-2762
(414) 272-6071

Free info packet on asthma and allergies and a referral to specialists practicing in your ZIP code area. Srv of the American Academy of Allergy & Immunology. FUNDING: Nonprofit. OFC HRS: 24 hrs. Spanish spoken. SERVES: U.S.A.

BABY SAFE

Safely Surrendered Baby Prgm
(877) 222-9723

Safe haven hotline for nearest locations which allow parents to safely surrender their babies at any hospital or fire station without fear of legal prosecution. Call the hotline for more info. OFC HRS: 24 hrs, 7 days. Over 140 languages spoken. SERVES: U.S.A.

BEAR HAWK EDUCATION SERVICES

100 S. Sunrise Way, PMB 292
Palm Springs, CA 92262
(760) 329-4457
(800) 367-2437
(760) 329-7803 FAX

HIV & outreach srvs to high-risk populations. Pre- and post-HIV testing srvs, edu, referral srvs, hotline info, mental health & shelter facilities. Srvs provided at 65861 Pearson St., Ste C, Desert Hot Springs. FUNDING: Nonprofit. OFC HRS: M 9am-5pm; Tu-Th 9am-3pm. SERVES: Blythe to Banning.

BIRTH CONTROL INFO FOR STATE

Calif Office of Family Planning
(800) 942-1054

Referrals to family planning and birth control srvs throughout Calif. Female cancer testing. Low-cost testing and counseling for HIV. Spanish spoken. OFC HRS: 24 hrs, 7 days. SERVES: Calif.

BIRTH CONTROL INFO LINE

San Bernardino Co. Public Health
(800) 722-4777
(909) 389-3340 FAX

One-stop family planning health srvs for men and women ages 21 yrs and under. Call for the clinic nearest you. FUNDING: Govt. OFC HRS: M-F 8am-5pm. Spanish spoken. Free srvs. SERVES: Riverside & San Bernardino Counties.

BOYS TOWN NATL HOTLINE

See "Girls & Boys Town Natl Hotline"

C.P.A.F. SHELTER & HOTLINE

See "Domestic Violence/Sexual Assault"

CALIF COUNCIL OF THE BLIND

1510 J Street, Ste 125
Sacramento, CA 95814
(800) 221-6359
(916) 441-2100
(916) 441-2188 FAX

Membership organization. Toll-free # is for Calif residents only. FUNDING: Nonprofit. OFC HRS: M-F 8am-5pm. Hotline M-F 10am-4pm. Recording after hours. Free srvs. SERVES: Calif.

CALIF COUNCIL ON PROBLEM GAMBLING

800 S. Harbor Blvd., Ste 225
Anaheim, CA 92805
(714) 765-5804
(800) 522-4700
(714) 765-5807 FAX

Offers 24-hr problem gambling helpline. Needs assessment & referral to GA, outpatient or inpatient therapy as appropriate throughout Calif. Calif certified gambling counselor training, speakers bureau, books, pamphlets and general problem gambling literature. FUNDING: Nonprofit. SERVES: Calif.

CALIF HIGHWAY INFORMATION

CalTrans
1120 N Street
Sacramento, CA 94273
(800) 427-7623

24-hr recorded message about highway conditions, wind advisories, storm conditions and other factors that will impede travel plans. Provides info about roads & freeways throughout the state. Visit (www.dot.ca.gov) for local office addresses. FUNDING: Govt. SERVES: So. Calif.

CALIF OFC OF EMERGENCY SRVS

Safety Info and Referral Line
4671 Liberty Ave., Ste 283
Los Alamitos, CA 90720
(800) 550-5234

TTY (800) 550-5281. Spanish spoken. SERVES: U.S.A.

CALIF OFC OF FAMILY PLANNING

Info/Referral Srv
1615 Capitol Ave.
Sacramento, CA 95899
(800) 942-1054

Recorded info & referral to local birth control, F-PACT and family planning srvs for all of Calif. Referrals are targeted by ZIP code. FUNDING: Govt. OFC HRS: 24 hrs, 7 days. Spanish and Vietnamese spoken. SERVES: Calif.

CALIF POISON CONTROL SYSTEM

UC San Francisco School of Pharmacy
P.O. Box 1262
3333 California St., Ste 420
San Francisco, CA 94143-1262
(800) 222-1222
(415) 502-8600
(415) 502-8620 FAX

Immediate treatment advice and info in case of exposure to poisonous, hazardous or toxic substances. Info is available to both health professionals & the public. Public outreach & edu provided. Health edu (pamphlets, stickers, prgms) (800) 582-3387. TTY (800) 972-3323. Emerg 24-hr hotline for Calif (800) 876-4766. FUNDING: Nonprofit. OFC HRS: 24 hrs, 7 days. Interpreter srv in over 100 languages. SERVES: Calif.

CALIF YOUTH CRISIS LINE

Calif Coalition for Youth
P.O. Box 161448
Sacramento, CA 95816
(800) 843-5200
(916) 340-0505
(916) 340-0510 FAX

Statewide, 24-hr crisis intervention counseling for youth ages 12-24 yrs & their families on a wide range of mental health, drug & alcohol, peer, family and relationship issues. Youth-to-parent message srv, phone connections to srv providers & families, info & referrals. Rides provided to youth who cannot afford transportation home. FUNDING: Nonprofit, donations. OFC HRS: 24 hrs, 7 days. Spanish spoken. Translation srvs available. Free srvs. SERVES: Calif.

CANCER HELPLINE

Support and Outreach
Auburn, CA 95603
(800) 748-6722

Volunteer-run hotline for survivors, friends and professionals. Support and info srvs to help persons find solutions to cancer issues. Problem solvers who offer support to the newly diagnosed. After hours leave a msg with a phone number and the call will be returned. FUNDING: Nonprofit. SERVES: U.S.A.

CANCER LEGAL RESOURCE CENTER

919 Albany St.
Los Angeles, CA 90015
(866) 843-2572
(213) 736-1455
(213) 736-1428 FAX

Info and edu outreach on cancer-related legal issues to people with cancer, their families, friends, employers and those who provide srvs to them. Includes: cancer in the workplace, insurance coverage, navigating managed care/HMOs, estate planning, govt benefits, and advanced directives. TDD (213) 736-8310. FUNDING: Donations, grants, nonprofit. OFC HRS: M-F 9am-5pm. Free srvs. SERVES: U.S.A.

CDC NATL AIDS HOTLINE

English or Spanish
(800) 232-4636
(888) 282-7681 FAX

24-hr hotline offering AIDS & STD info, nationwide referrals and free literature for anyone in the U.S. TTY (888) 232-6348. Free srvs. SERVES: U.S.A.

CHADD/NATL

Children/Adults with Attention Deficit Disorder

8181 Professional Place, Ste 150
Hyattsville, MD 20785
(800) 233-4050
(301) 306-7090 FAX

Info & referral. Membership and annual conference. FUNDING: Nonprofit. OFC HRS: M-F 9am-5pm. Spanish spoken. SERVES: U.S.A.

CHILD ABUSE HOTLINE/HIGH DESERT
Women's Center High Desert, Inc.
P.O. Box 309
134 S. China Lake Blvd., Ste A
Ridgecrest, CA 93555
(760) 375-7100
(760) 371-3449 FAX

24-hr hotline for info & referral. OFC HRS: 24 hrs, 7 days. Spanish spoken. Free srvs. SERVES: East Kern County.

CHILD ABUSE REPORTING HOTLINE
Riverside Co. Public Social Srvs
(800) 442-4918
(951) 413-5122 FAX

Report actual or suspected physical or sexual child abuse, neglect, or exploitation 24 hrs, 7 days. SERVES: Riverside County.

CHILD ABUSE REPORTING HOTLINE
Human Social Srvs
412 W. Hospitality Lane
San Bernardino, CA 92415-0029
(800) 827-8724
(909) 384-9233
(909) 891-3545 FAX

Report actual or suspected physical or sexual child abuse, neglect or exploitation. FUNDING: Nonprofit. OFC HRS: 24 hrs. Spanish spoken. Free srvs. SERVES: San Bernardino County.

CHILD FIND OF AMERICA, INC
P.O. Box 277
New Paltz, NY 12561
(800) 426-5678
(800) 292-9688
(845) 255-5706 FAX

Register & search for abducted children, photo dissemination of missing children. Mediation to return parentally abducted children & mediation to prevent parental child abduction. FUNDING: Nonprofit. OFC HRS: M-F 9am-5pm, EST. SERVES: So. Calif.

CHILDHELP USA/HOTLINE
National Child Abuse Hotline
15757 N. 78th Street, Ste B
Scottsdale, AZ 85260
(800) 422-4453
(480) 922-8212
(480) 922-7061 FAX

Professional hotline counselors available 24 hrs, 7 days to respond to crisis calls regarding child abuse & related issues. Crisis intervention & contact for mandated reporters, concerned citizens or worried friends & family. Info & referral. Visit (www.childhelpusa.org). FUNDING: Nonprofit. Communication available in 140 different languages. Free srvs. SERVES: U.S.A. & Canada.

CHILDREN OF THE NIGHT
14530 Sylvan St.
Van Nuys, CA 91411
(800) 551-1300
(818) 908-4474
(818) 908-1468 FAX

Assist for children forced into prostitution. Natl 24-hr hotline; shelter home & school receives child prostitutes 24 hrs a day from every state. Structured prgm, includes transportation. FUNDING: Nonprofit, donations, grants. Spanish spoken. ADM REQ: Ages 11-17 yrs involved in prostitution. Free srvs. SERVES: U.S.A.

CHILDREN'S CRANIOFACIAL ASSN
13140 Coit Rd., Ste 517
Dallas, TX 75240
(800) 535-3643

Callers will hear recorded info regarding resources and publications. Leave a phone number and msg for a return call. FUNDING: Nonprofit. OFC HRS: M-F 8:30am-4:30pm, CST. 24-hr answering srv. SERVES: U.S.A.

CHRONIC FATIGUE IMMUNE DYSFUNCTION SYNDROME ASSN OF AMERICA (CFIDS)
P.O. Box 220398
Charlotte, NC 28222-0398
(704) 365-2343
(704) 365-9755 FAX

Edu info & referral srvs to persons with inquiries on CFIDS. Supports research & publishes journal. FUNDING: Nonprofit. OFC HRS: M-Th 9am-5pm; F 9am-1pm, EST. Free srvs. SERVES: U.S.A.

CITIZENSHIP & IMMIGRATION SRVS
Forms Request Line
(800) 870-3676

24-hr request hotline for INS forms. OFC HRS: 24 hrs, 7 days. Spanish spoken. SERVES: U.S.A.

COLTON NEIGHBORHOOD SRVS DEPT
Gonzales Center
670 Colton Ave.
Colton, CA 92324
(909) 370-6153
(909) 777-3351 FAX

Recreation prgm and community center activities. Senior nutrition prgm. Info & referral for child care, health care, housing and other human srv prgms and assist with translations, interpretation and completion of forms. Senior health screenings and income tax assist for residents of the Colton area. FUNDING: Govt. OFC HRS: M-Th 7am-6pm. Spanish spoken. SERVES: San Bernardino County.

COMMUNITY ASSISTANCE PRGM (CAP)
8440 Nuevo St
Fontana, CA 92335
(909) 803-1059
(909) 770-8256 FAX

Fontana residents provided with referrals to low-cost or free srvs. Community srvs, counseling, day care, education, finances, disabilities prgms, domestic violence and sexual assault, family srvs, food distribution, health srvs, housing/rental, legal, senior prgms, shelter/transitional housing, suicide prevention, youth prgms. Networking meeting held 3rd Th of each month 9am-11am at Water of Life Community Church. Visit (www.FontanaCAP.org). FUNDING: Nonprofit. OFC HRS: M-F 9am-1:30pm SERVES: Fontana.

COMMUNITY HELPLINE
A Division of Helpline Youth Counseling, Inc.
P.O. Box 2503
Palos Verdes Peninsula, CA 90274
(310) 793-1415

(877) 541-2525
(310) 802-6164 FAX

Confidential listening, crisis intervention, info & referral toll-free hotline. Assist with loneliness, relationships, family violence, depression, grieving & losses, alcohol & drug abuse, anxiety, teen issues and suicide. Volunteering opportunities available. FUNDING: Nonprofit. OFC HRS: Daily 7am-10pm. Free srvs. SERVES: Calif.

COVENANT HOUSE NINELINE
461 8th Avenue
New York, NY 10001
(800) 999-9999
(212) 727-4000
(212) 989-9098 FAX

24-hr natl crisis intervention hotline for runaways, homeless, troubled youth & their families. Refers caller to help in his or her own community. Conference call capability & message relays to runaway youth. TDD/TYY hotline (800) 999-9915. FUNDING: Donations, nonprofit. OFC HRS: 24 hrs, 7 days. Spanish spoken. ADM REQ: Ages 18-21 yrs. Free srvs. SERVES: U.S.A.

CRISIS HOTLINE
First Call for Help
(760) 240-8255

Info & referral helpline 7 days a week, for all crisis, such as suicide prevention etc, assists residents, including children, neighbors, parents and relatives to recognize, report and deal with child abuse, referrals and info for all crisis situations. Located in Victorville area. FUNDING: Nonprofit. SERVES: High Desert.

CSAT HOTLINE
(800) 729-6686

CSAT (Center for Substance Abuse Treatment) answers questions about drug abuse & AIDS as it relates to IV drug users. Referrals to support groups & drug treatment prgms. TDD (800)487-4889. Spanish (877)767-8432. FUNDING: Govt. OFC HRS: 24 hrs, 7 days. Spanish spoken. SERVES: U.S.A.

D.O.V.E.S. OF BIG BEAR VALLEY
Domestic Violence Edu Srvs
P.O. Box 3646
Big Bear Lake, CA 92315
(800) 851-7601
(909) 866-8580 FAX

24-hr hotline, 2nd step recovery prgm for battered women and children, women's support groups, community outreach, restraining order assist, info & referral, and an emerg shelter prgm. Outreach (909) 866-1546. For the Blue Jay/Lake Arrowhead area, call (909) 337-5300. Accepts donations. Free srvs. SERVES: So. Calif.

DEPT OF VETERANS AFFAIRS EDUCATION
GI Bill Helpline
(888) 442-4551

Recording gives info about VA edu & training, GI bill assist. Visit (www.va.gov). SERVES: U.S.A.

DES ACTION USA
P.O. Box 7296
Jupiter, FL 33468
(800) 337-9288

Medical and legal info & referrals for those exposed in-utero and during pregnancy to the hormone drug DES. Not a primary care agency. Physical address: 187 Via Catalunha, Jupiter, FL 33458. FUNDING: Donations, nonprofit. OFC HRS: M-F 9am-2pm, CST. Spanish spoken. SERVES: U.S.A.

DESERT SANCTUARY/HALEY HOUSE

P.O. Box 1781
Barstow, CA 92312
(760) 256-3441
(760) 256-4002 FAX

Shelter for battered women and their children. Referrals, restraining order assist. Outreach ctr (760) 256-3733. OFC HRS: 24 hrs, 7 days. Spanish spoken. Free srvs. SERVES: So. Calif.

DOMESTIC ABUSE HELPLINE

P.O. Box 252
Harmony, ME 04942
(888) 743-5754

24-hr helpline for victims of domestic violence, specializing in male victim domestic abuse. Refers callers to resources in their area and if applicable, "male friendly" facilities. FUNDING: Nonprofit. Free srvs. SERVES: U.S.A.

DOMESTIC VIOLENCE HELPLINE

Multilingual Info & Srvs
(800) 978-3600
(800) 799-7233

Helpline system is a single point of entry system that links callers directly to the domestic violence shelter nearest to them based on their language needs. 24-hr, toll-free helpline provides a safe way out to all victims of domestic violence in all areas. M-Th 8am-6pm for literature & referral to county-funded shelters. FUNDING: Nonprofit. OFC HRS: 24 hrs, 7 days. Multiple languages spoken. Free srvs. SERVES: U.S.A.

DOMESTIC VIOLENCE HOTLINE

Option House
(909) 381-3471
(909) 889-7312 FAX

Operates a shelter for abused women. The hotline staff counsel and try to assist any abused person. OFC HRS: 24 hrs, 7 days. Spanish spoken. SERVES: San Bernardino & nearby.

DOMESTIC VIOLENCE/SEXUAL ASSAULT

Ctr for the Pacific Asian Family (CPAF)
543 N. Fairfax Ave., Ste 108
Los Angeles, CA 90036
(800) 339-3940
(323) 653-7913 FAX

24-hr hotline for women & children who are survivors of domestic violence, sexual assault, & child abuse. Crisis intervention, confidential emerg shelter, transitional shelter, counseling, info & referral. FUNDING: Nonprofit. OFC HRS: M-F 9am-5pm. Hotline 24 hrs, 7 days. API languages. Free srvs. SERVES: Calif.

DRUG & ALC TREATMENT REFERRAL

Mental Health/Drug/Alcohol Abuse Hotline
(866) 716-3460

Referrals & help to those in crisis. Executive rehab, prescription addiction prgm, Christian-based prgm, teen & family rehab, intervention partners, gay & lesbian prgm, west coast adult rehab, east coast adult rehab, residential treatment, teen outpatient, 12-Step rehab. FUNDING: Nonprofit. OFC HRS: 24 hrs, 7 days. Spanish spoken. SERVES: U.S.A.

DRUG & ALCOHOL ABUSE INFO/REF

National Inst on Drug & Alcohol Abuse
1 Choke Cherry Rd.
Rockville, MD 20857
(800) 729-6686

24-hr referral to alcohol & drug prev & treatment prgms & srvs. FUNDING: Grants, contracts. Spanish spoken. Free srvs. SERVES: U.S.A.

EAST L.A. HOTLINE/SHELTER

Chicana Service Action Center
3601 E. 1st Street
Los Angeles, CA 90063
(800) 548-2722
(323) 268-5669 FAX

24-hr hotline and shelter for women and children. The shelter is described separately under "Free Spirit Shelter," which can be found in the Battered Persons/Victim/Adult Abuse chapter. FUNDING: Nonprofit. Spanish spoken. ADM REQ: Domestic violence, homeless. Free srvs. SERVES: So. Calif.

EQUIFAX CREDIT INFO

P.O. Box 740241
Atlanta, GA 30374
(800) 685-1111

Recorded info on how to obtain credit file or score. OFC HRS: Daily 8am-3am, EST. Spanish spoken. SERVES: Calif.

ESCORT/MIGRANT EDUCATION

National Migrant Education Hotline
State University College, Bugbee Hall 304
Oneonta, NY 13820-4051
(800) 451-8058
(607) 436-3606 FAX

24-hr hotline for migrant farm workers and their families to access edu, health and other supportive srvs. The hotline number is intended for use by migrant families. FUNDING: U.S Office of Migrant Edu, govt. OFC HRS: M-F 8am-4:30pm, EST. Spanish spoken. Free referral srvs to migrant families. SERVES: U.S.A.

FAMILY PLANNING (CALIF INFO/REF)

See "Calif Ofc of Family Planning"

FAMILY SERVICE AGENCY/FONTANA

7993 N. Sierra Ave., Ste F
Crestline, CA 92325
(909) 822-3533
(909) 822-3050 FAX

Child counseling for all subjects except drug and alcohol abuse. Call for info M-F 8am-1pm, 2pm-8pm. FUNDING: Nonprofit. OFC HRS: M, W 12pm-8pm; Tu 12pm-9pm; Th 9am-9pm; Sat 8:30am-2pm. SERVES: San Bernardino County.

FEDERAL IDENTIFICATION THEFT HOTLINE

Federal Trade Commission
600 Pennsylvania Ave., NW
Washington, DC 20580
(877) 438-4338

Website of info and resources regarding identity theft. Visit (www.ftc.gov/idtheft). Spanish spoken. SERVES: Calif.

FEDERAL INFORMATION CENTER

U.S. General Srvs Administration
1800 F Street, NW
Washington, DC 20405
(800) 333-4636

Toll-free phone line to call for basic info about govt offices and referral for the appropriate federal office to contact in your area. FUNDING: Govt. OFC HRS: 24-hr srvs. Spanish spoken. SERVES: U.S.A.

FIND THE CHILDREN

(888) 477-6721
(310) 314-3169 FAX

Assists families and law enforcement in locating missing children through natl and local media exposure; includes referrals. OFC HRS: M-F 9am-5pm. SERVES: U.S.A.

FIRST CALL FOR HELP

Volunteer Center of Victor Valley
P.O. Box 1992
16692 Mojave Dr.
Victorville, CA 92393
(760) 243-9646
(760) 243-4762 FAX

Info & referral for people seeking srvs or info on community agencies. Interaction with individuals in crisis situations in order to reduce tension and stress, allowing that person to utilize available resources more effectively. FUNDING: Donations, grants, nonprofit. OFC HRS: M-Th 9am-2:45pm. Spanish spoken. SERVES: San Bernardino County.

GAM-ANON HOTLINE

(818) 377-5144

Callers will hear a recorded message giving phone numbers of individuals to call to find meetings in your area. FUNDING: Nonprofit. SERVES: So. Calif.

GAMBLERS ANONYMOUS

Palm Springs, CA 92262
(760) 325-2808

Support line will direct callers to support srvs in their area. SERVES: Coachella Valley.

GAMBLING HELPLINE

P.O. Box 944255
Sacramento, CA 94244
(888) 277-3115

Callers can speak to phone counselors regarding problems with gambling. FUNDING: State. SERVES: Calif.

GAY & LESBIAN NATIONAL HOTLINE

2261 Market St., PMB #296
San Francisco, CA 94114
(888) 843-4564
(415) 355-0003
(415) 522-5498 FAX

Free and confidential peer counseling and local resources for the gay & lesbian community. Maintains a database with info on social & support groups, HIV/AIDS, organizations, student groups, etc. National GLBT Youth Talkline (800) 246-7743. FUNDING: Nonprofit. OFC HRS: M-F 1pm-9pm; Sat 9am-2pm. SERVES: U.S.A.

GAY MEN'S DOMESTIC VIOLENCE PROJECT

955 Massachusetts Ave., PMB 131
Cambridge, MA 02139
(617) 354-6056
(617) 354-6072 FAX

Provides crisis intervention, support, and resources to gay victims and survivors of domestic violence. 24-hr hotline: (800) 832-1901. FUNDING: Nonprofit. SERVES: U.S.A.

GED INFO
Calif State Edu Dept
1430 N Street
Sacramento, CA 95814-5901
(916) 445-9438
(916) 319-0800

Automated info regarding GED testing sites. Visit (www.cde.ca.gov). Call (866) 370-4740 for records. TTY/TDD (916) 445-4556. SERVES: U.S.A.

GIRLS & BOYS TOWN NATL HOTLINE
14100 Crawford St.
Boys Town, NE 68010
(800) 448-3000
(402) 498-1348 FAX

Toll-free crisis and resource referral srvs for children and parents. Highly trained telephone counselors to help deal with any problem. Hotline serves USA & Canada. TDD (800) 448-1833. FUNDING: Nonprofit. OFC HRS: 24 hrs, 7 days. Spanish spoken. SERVES: U.S.A.

HEALTH INFO CLEARINGHOUSE
National Health Info Ctr
P.O. Box 1133
Washington, DC 20013-1133
(301) 565-4167
(800) 336-4797
(301) 984-4256 FAX

Info & referral to appropriate organization for health professionals and consumers. For a list of toll-free numbers, visit (www.health.gov/nhic). FUNDING: Govt. OFC HRS: M-F 9am-5:30pm, EST. Spanish spoken. SERVES: U.S.A.

HELPLINE CRISIS HOTLINE
See "Volunteer Center/Riverside Co."

HEMET VALLEY MENTAL HEALTH CTR
(951) 652-2811

Emerg psychiatric srvs, referrals srvs. FUNDING: Nonprofit. Spanish spoken. SERVES: Riverside County.

HEPATITIS FOUNDATION INTERNATIONAL
504 Blick Dr.
Silver Spring, MD 20904
(800) 891-0707
(301) 622-4200
(301) 622-4702 FAX

Education materials, liver wellness training prgms, support group referrals, news updates on viral hepatitis, and nurses' advisory council on. FUNDING: Nonprofit. OFC HRS: M-F 9am-5pm, EST. Fee for training. SERVES: U.S.A.

HIGH DESERT DOMESTIC VIOLENCE PRGM
15075 7th St. 92395
(760) 949-4357
(760) 843-0701

Self-Esteem House, 90-day shelter for battered women & their children, hotline, emerg food, clothing, counseling & support groups, local resource referrals. OFC HRS: 24 hrs, 7 days. Spanish spoken. Free srvs. SERVES: San Bernardino County.

HIGHWAY REPORTS
See "Calif Highway Information"

HOTLINE OF SOUTHERN CALIFORNIA
P.O. Box 32

Los Alamitos, CA 90720
(562) 596-5548
(714) 894-4242
(562) 594-7417 FAX

General listening phone srv. Crisis intervention, info, referrals. Referrals for food, shelter, rent, and utility payments to needy people in area served. New Hope Crisis Line (714) 639-4673, Suicide Prev (310) 391-1253. FUNDING: United way, donations, grants, nonprofit. OFC HRS: Daily 8am-12midnight. Free srvs. SERVES: So. Calif.

HOUSE OF RUTH/CLAREMONT
P.O. Box 459
Claremont, CA 91711
(909) 623-4364
(909) 629-9581 FAX

Advocates for and assist to battered women and their children. Srvs include: 24-hr hotline (909) 988-5559, 30-day emerg safe shelter, individual counseling, support groups for women, children and teens, transitional living shelter, career, edu & housing assist, TRO clinics, community outreach, edu, and teen dating violence prgm. FUNDING: United Way, CDBG, donations, nonprofit. OFC HRS: M-F 9am-5pm. Shelter 24 hrs, 7 days. Spanish spoken. ADM REQ: Women abused by intimate partner. Free srvs. SERVES: L.A., San Bernardino & Riverside Counties.

HOUSING & URBAN DEV
451 7th Street, SW
Washington, DC 20410
(800) 669-9777

Info on HUD prgms. Fair housing rights & responsibilities. Housing discrimination hotline. OFC HRS: M-F 9am-5pm, EST. Spanish spoken. SERVES: Calif.

INSPECTOR GENERAL'S HOTLINE
See "U.S. Dept of Health & Human Srvs"

INTERNATL DYSLEXIA ASSN
40 York Rd., 4th Fl.
Baltimore, MD 21204
(800) 222-3123
(410) 296-0232
(410) 321-5069 FAX

FUNDING: Nonprofit. OFC HRS: M-F 8:30am-4:30pm, EST. SERVES: U.S.A.

JUVENILE DIABETES RESEARCH FNDN
26 Broadway, 14th Fl.
New York, NY 10004
(800) 533-2873
(212) 785-9500
(212) 785-9595 FAX

Primary objective is to support and fund research into the cause, treatment and prev of diabetes, and, ultimately through research, find a cure. Also serves the needs of those with diabetes and their families by providing prgms of edu & info. Strives to inform the general public on the seriousness of diabetes. Provides brochures, fact sheets, referrals. FUNDING: Donations, nonprofit. OFC HRS: M-F 9am-5pm, EST. Spanish spoken. SERVES: U.S.A.

JUVENILE DIABETES RESEARCH FNDN
Inland Empire Chapter
2023 Chicago Ave., Ste B-13
Riverside, CA 92507
(951) 784-4156
(951) 784-4628 FAX

Primary objective is to support and fund research, treatment and prev of diabetes. Also serves the needs of those with diabetes and their families by providing prgms of edu & info. Strives to alert the general public to the seriousness of diabetes. Provides brochures, fact sheets, referrals. FUNDING: Nonprofit. OFC HRS: M-F 9am-5pm. SERVES: Inland Empire.

KIDSPEACE
KidsPeace Helpline
4085 Independence Dr.
Schnecksville, PA 18078
(800) 257-3223
(610) 799-8900 FAX

Hotline provides counseling, info & referral srvs to children & parents in crisis. Also mental health & behavioral health srvs, children's psychiatric hospital, residential, foster care, juvenile justice & outpatient. FUNDING: Nonprofit. OFC HRS: 24 hrs, 7 days. Free helpline. SERVES: U.S.A.

L.A. CO. INFO/OPERATOR
320 W. Temple St., Hall of Records
Los Angeles, CA 90012
(213) 974-1234
(562) 803-1757 FAX

Info & referral for L.A. County-operated prgms or srvs such as health and social srvs. Also helps with emerg referrals/assist. FUNDING: County. OFC HRS: 24 hrs, 7 days. Spanish spoken. Language line available. SERVES: L.A. County.

LAWYER REFERRAL SERVICE
Western San Bernardino Co. Bar Assn
10630 Town Center Dr., Ste 119
Rancho Cucamonga, CA 91730
(909) 483-0548
(909) 483-0553 FAX

Referrals to local attorneys on a variety of legal matters. Low-cost initial consultation fee of $35 with fee waived on workers' compensation, bankruptcy and personal injury cases. FUNDING: Nonprofit. OFC HRS: M-F 9am-5pm. Spanish spoken. SERVES: Rancho Cucamonga, Upland, Ontario, Fontana, Montclair, Pomona, Bloomington, Claremont, Rialto.

LIGHTHOUSE INTERNATIONAL
Info & Resource Service
111 E. 59th Street
New York, NY 10022-1202
(800) 829-0500
(212) 821-9705 FAX

Free literature on eye diseases, resource lists, etc. A guide to reading options, intro to assistive computer tech, financial aid resource list for persons with impaired vision. Referrals to low vision srvs, rehab agencies, support groups, state agencies and advocacy groups. TDD (212) 821-9713. FUNDING: Donations, nonprofit. OFC HRS: M-F 9am-8pm, EST. Spanish & Chinese spoken. SERVES: Internatl.

MEDICARE TELEPHONE HOTLINE
U.S. Dept of Health & Human Srvs
(800) 633-4227

General Medicare info & reporting of Medicare fraud. Srv of the Health Care Financing Admin, U.S. Dept of Health & Human Srvs. FUNDING: Govt. Hotline M-F 8am-8pm, EST. Spanish spoken. SERVES: U.S.A.

MEDICARE/MEDICAID COMPLAINTS

Inspector General's Ofc
330 Independence Ave., SW
Washington, DC 20201
(800) 447-8477
(800) 223-8164 FAX

Hotline to report fraud of health and human srvs. Also call (800) 633-4227 for insurance info. OFC HRS: M-F 8am-5:30pm, EST. Spanish and Vietnamese spoken. SERVES: U.S.A.

MULTIPLE SCLEROSIS FOUNDATION

6350 N. Andrews Ave.
Fort Lauderdale, FL 33309-2130
(800) 441-7055
(800) 225-6495
(954) 938-8708 FAX

Info and referrals for homecare. Also has a free quarterly magazine. Visit (www.msfocus.org). FUNDING: Nonprofit. OFC HRS: M-F 8:30am-4:30pm. Spanish spoken. Free srvs. SERVES: U.S.A.

NAR-ANON/FAMILY/HEADQUARTERS

22527 Crenshaw Blvd., Ste 200-B
Torrance, CA 90505
(310) 534-8188
(800) 477-6291

World srv office serves families and friends of drug addicts. Info & referral to self-help groups in local communities (12-Step support group for family and friends of drug abusers, similar to Al-Anon). Call for list of weekly meeting locations. 24-hr answering machine, calls returned. Addtl Southern CA info at (888)297-9560. Addtl helplines (714)647-7725 and (858)492-8720. FUNDING: Nonprofit. OFC HRS: M-Th 9am-5pm. Spanish spoken. SERVES: Internatl.

NARCONON INTERNATIONAL

Drug Prev, Edu & Rehab Srvs
4652 Hollywood Blvd.
Los Angeles, CA 90027
(323) 962-2404
(323) 962-6872 FAX

The aim of this prgm is to help the drug abuser become drug free. Prevention and edu to youth and adults. Parent center provides edu info, videos & booklets. FUNDING: Nonprofit. OFC HRS: M-F 9am-6pm. Spanish, Italian, French, Filipino & Armenian spoken SERVES: Internatl.

NARCOTICS ANONYMOUS

(909) 622-4274

24-hr hotline and info & referral, listing of meetings for most areas of Inland Empire. FUNDING: Nonprofit. Spanish spoken. Free srvs. SERVES: Inland Empire.

NARCOTICS ANONYMOUS

(760) 346-5800

24-hr hotline for the desert communities in Riverside County. Info on meeting schedules, and caller can speak to a recovered addict. FUNDING: Nonprofit. SERVES: Morongo Basin, Blythe, Coachella Valley.

NATL ASYLEE INFO & REFERRAL LINE

Catholic Legal Immigration Network, Inc.
415 Michigan Ave., NE, Rm. 150
Washington, DC 20017
(800) 354-0365
(202) 635-2649 FAX

Refers asylees to more than 500 local providers of resettlement srvs such as English language classes, employment training, placement assist, financial resources, and health care. FUNDING: Nonprofit, Office of Refugee Resettlement. Over 18 different languages spoken. ADM REQ: Must be an asylee to call. Free srvs. SERVES: U.S.A.

NATL BRAIN TUMOR FOUNDATION

22 Battery St., Ste 612
San Francisco, CA 94111-5520
(800) 934-2873
(415) 834-9970
(415) 834-9980 FAX

Raises funds for research to treat and cure brain tumors and provides info, edu and support to patients, family members and friends. Publishes brochures and quarterly newsletter. Some Spanish publications available. FUNDING: Nonprofit. OFC HRS: M-F 9am-5pm. SERVES: U.S.A.

NATL CENTER FOR STUTTERING

(800) 221-2483

Info & referral. OFC HRS: M-F 10am-5pm, EST. SERVES: U.S.A.

NATL CENTER FOR SUBSTANCE ABUSE

Treatment Referral Srvs
P.O. Box 2345
Rockville, MD 20847
(800) 662-4357
(301) 468-6433 FAX

Info & referral to support groups and/or treatment for all types of drug and alcohol abuse. Free 24-hr hotline. FUNDING: Govt. Spanish spoken.

NATL CNCL ON CHILD ABUSE/FAM VIOL

Family Violence Helpline
1025 Connecticut Ave., NW, Ste 1000
Washington, DC 20036
(202) 429-6695
(202) 521-3479 FAX

24-hr counseling, info & referral srv on domestic & family violence issues. FUNDING: Nonprofit. SERVES: U.S.A.

NATL DOMESTIC VIOLENCE HOTLINE

P.O. Box 161810
Austin, TX 78716-3074
(800) 799-7233
(512) 453-8541 FAX

Info & referral for victims of domestic violence and those who assist victims. Also provides crisis intervention, resource materials, bilingual advocates and a nationwide database of resources. TDD/TTY (800) 787-3224, e-mail (deafhelp@ndvh.org). FUNDING: Grants, fed, nonprofit. OFC HRS: M-F 8:30am-5:30pm, CST. 24-hr hotline. Spanish spoken. Over 170 other languages available. Free srvs. SERVES: U.S.A.

NATL HUMAN TRAFFICKING RESOURCE CTR

U.S. Admin of Children & Families
370 L'Enfant Promenade, S.W.
Washington, DC 20447
(888) 373-7888

24-hr hotline number for reporting potential victims of human trafficking within the U.S. Also answers questions from community members and distributes info. OFC HRS: 24 hrs, 7 days. Free srvs. SERVES: U.S.A.

NATL IMMUNIZATION INFO HOTLINE

1600 Clifton Rd. N.E.
Mailstop E-05
Atlanta, GA 30333
(800) 232-4636
(919) 361-8425 FAX

Support, edu materials and referrals about vaccine-preventable diseases, including hepatitis b. Spanish (800) 232-0233. TTY (800) 243-7889. FUNDING: Nonprofit. OFC HRS: M-F 8am-11pm, EST. Spanish spoken. Free srvs. SERVES: U.S.A.

NATL INST OF CHILD HEALTH & HUMAN DEV

Info and Resource Center
P.O. Box 3006
Rockville, MD 20847
(800) 370-2943
(866) 760-5947
(301) 984-1473 FAX

Info on SIDS. TTY (888) 320-6942. FUNDING: Nonprofit. OFC HRS: M-F 8:30am-5pm, EST. Spanish spoken. SERVES: U.S.A.

NATL KIDNEY FNDN HOTLINE

30 E. 33rd Street
New York, NY 10016
(800) 622-9010
(212) 689-9261 FAX

Dedicated to preventing kidney & urinary tract diseases, improving the health & well being of individuals & families affected by these diseases, & increasing the availability of all organs for transplantation. FUNDING: Nonprofit. OFC HRS: M-F 8:30am-5:30pm, EST. Spanish spoken. Free srvs. SERVES: U.S.A.

NATL LEAD INFO CENTER/U.S. EPA

ABUI Goodwill
422 S. Clinton Ave.
Rochester, NY 14620
(800) 424-5323
(585) 232-3111 FAX

Clearinghouse is staffed by trained info specialists who can provide in-depth tech info on a range of lead-related issues. Offered in English & Spanish. Serves professional audiences such as govt officials, industry reps and abatement staff, community-based organizations, media & the general public. Also has a database of lead edu materials, a speaker's referral srv and posters. FUNDING: EPA, HUD, CDC, govt. OFC HRS: M-F 8:30am-6pm, EST. SERVES: U.S.A.

NATL ORGANIZATION/VICTIM ASSISTANCE

(NOVA)
510 King St., Ste 424
Alexandria, VA 22314
(800) 879-6682
(703) 535-6682
(703) 535-5500 FAX

Crisis counseling, advocacy, and referral srvs to crime victims and their families. Also crisis response team. Refers victims & survivors to nearby srvs. FUNDING: Nonprofit. OFC HRS: M-F 9am-6pm, EST. SERVES: U.S.A.

NATL OSTEOPOROSIS FNDN

1232 22nd Street, NW
Washington, DC 20037
(800) 223-9994

Info srv line for professionals and the community. Leave name and mailing address to receive specific requested info. Visit (www.nof.org). OFC HRS: M-F 8:30am-5pm, EST. SERVES: U.S.A.

NATL RUNAWAY SWITCHBOARD

3080 N. Lincoln Ave.
Chicago, IL 60657
(800) 786-2929
(773) 929-5150 FAX

24-hr hotline for runaway and homeless youth and their families, crisis intervention, info & referral, message delivery and conferencing srvs. Free bus rides home for runaways through the Home Free prgm. FUNDING: Nonprofit. Language line available. SERVES: U.S.A.

NATL SEXUAL ASSAULT HOTLINE

RAINN
2000 L Street NW
Washington, DC 20036
(800) 656-4673
(202) 544-3556 FAX

Emerg 24-hr confidential hotline will connect caller to nearest srvs. FUNDING: Nonprofit. OFC HRS: 24 hrs. SERVES: U.S.A.

NATL SUICIDE PREVENTION LIFELINE

Natl Hopeline Network
1250 24th Street, NW
Washington, DC 20037
(800) 784-2433

Info lifeline regarding depression and suicide. Callers will be automatically connected to a crisis center. Also visit (www.hopeline.com). FUNDING: Nonprofit, grants, donations. Spanish spoken. SERVES: U.S.A.

NATL TEEN DATING ABUSE HELPLINE

www.loveisrespect.org
P.O. Box 16180
Austin, TX 78716
(866) 331-9474

Phone or Internet info & referral for teen victims of domestic violence and those who assist victims. Provides crisis intervention, resource materials, bilingual advocates and a nationwide database of resources. Chat online from 4pm-2am, CST. TTY (800) 331-8453. FUNDING: Grants, fed, nonprofit. OFC HRS: M-F 8:30am-5:30pm, CST. Hotline 24 hrs. Spanish spoken. Over 170 other languages available. SERVES: U.S.A.

NATL WOMEN'S HEALTH INFO CENTER

(800) 994-9662

TDD (888) 220-5446. Visit (www.womenshealth.gov). OFC HRS: M-F 9am-6pm. Spanish spoken. SERVES: U.S.A.

NEUROFIBROMATOSIS, INC

P.O. Box 66884
Chicago, IL 60666
(800) 942-6825
(630) 627-1117 FAX

Info & referral to medical & other srvs. Peer counseling, printed materials (including NF-1, NF-2), newsletters. Supports, promotes and funds research. Summer camp for youth. Natl physician referrals. FUNDING: Donations, nonprofit. OFC HRS: 24 hrs, 7 days. SERVES: U.S.A. & internatl.

NEW HOPE CRISIS COUNSELING

Crystal Cathedral
12141 Lewis St.
Garden Grove, CA 92840
(714) 639-4673
(714) 971-4327 FAX

24-hr phone counseling and online counseling in a pvt chat room for all types of problems: crisis intervention, suicide prev, info & referral. Srvs provided by trained & caring volunteers. To learn about training classes & the benefits of volunteering, e-mail (quinnw@crystalcathedral.org) or call (714) 971-4123. Hotline (714) NEW-HOPE. Teenline: M-F 4pm-10pm, (714) 639-TEEN. Visit (www.newhopenow.org). FUNDING: Church, donations, nonprofit. OFC HRS: M-F 9am-5pm. Crisis helplines 24 hrs, 7 days. Spanish spoken. Free srvs. SERVES: U.S.A.

OMBUDSMAN PROGRAM

See "San Bernardino Co. Ombudsman"

OPTION HOUSE/DV INTERV & PREV

Domestic Violence Interv & Prev Agency
P.O. Box 970
San Bernardino, CA 92401
(909) 381-3471
(909) 889-7312 FAX

Confidential emerg & temporary shelter, 24-hr crisis intervention hotline. One-on-one advocacy, emotional support, resource & referrals to female victims of domestic violence & their children. Six-week in-house prgm for residents in shelter, 18-month transitional housing, legal assist for TROs, child custody, court & mediation accompaniment, women's support groups for non-shelter victims (English & Spanish), teen relationship, violence prevention workshops, children's prgm, speakers bureau, community edu, training & workshops. For Tri-City DV Prevention Outreach Ctr, Courthouse Family Violence Outreach Srvs & Teen Dating Violence Prevention Srvs, call (909) 884-4802. FUNDING: Donations, grants, nonprofit. OFC HRS: M-F 8am-5pm. Spanish spoken. ADM REQ: Women, children & teens who are victims of domestic violence. SERVES: San Bernardino & nearby.

PARKINSON'S EDUCATIONAL PRGM

Parkinson's Disease Fndn
1359 Broadway, Ste 1509
New York, NY 10018
(800) 457-6676
(212) 923-4778 FAX

Natl info center. FUNDING: Nonprofit. OFC HRS: M-F 9am-5pm, EST. Spanish spoken. SERVES: U.S.A.

PHYSICIAN REFERRAL SERVICE

Eisenhower Medical Center
39000 Bob Hope Dr., Ste K103
Rancho Mirage, CA 92270
(760) 340-3911
(760) 773-1335 FAX

Free telephone referral srv designed to help individuals find a physician or contact any of the Eisenhower Medical Center's health care prgms. OFC HRS: M-F 9am-4:30pm. SERVES: Coachella Valley.

PHYSICIAN REFERRAL SERVICE

Loma Linda University Medical Center
245 E. Redlands Blvd.
San Bernardino, CA 92407
(877) 558-6248
(909) 558-0012 FAX

Physician referral srv provides individuals in the community with referrals to Loma Linda University Medical Center faculty physicians. OFC HRS: M-Th 7am-8pm; F 7am-5pm. Spanish spoken. Free srvs. SERVES: San Bernardino County.

PROJECT INFORM

1375 Mission St.
San Francisco, CA 94103
(415) 558-8669
(415) 558-0684 FAX

Fights for an HIV and HCV cure by advancing national research agenda to generate optimal treatments; helps secure expanded access to quality health care for low-income individuals. Provides free, reliable info on living with HIV disease through its natl HIV treatment and care benefits hotline: (866) HIV-INFO, M-F 10am-4pm. FUNDING: Nonprofit. OFC HRS: M-F 9am-5pm. Spanish spoken. SERVES: Internatl.

RAPE CRISIS CENTER/RIVERSIDE AREA

1845 Chicago Ave., Ste A
Riverside, CA 92507
(951) 686-7273

24-hr crisis line. Advocacy, accompany to hospitals, law enforcement & court. Personal counseling, support group, info & referral, and community edu prgms include: assault awareness & prevention, child abuse prevention, teen abuse prevention, Hispanic and senior outreach. FUNDING: Nonprofit. OFC HRS: M-F 8am-5pm. Spanish spoken. Free srvs. SERVES: Western Riverside County.

RAPE CRISIS HOTLINE

(760) 568-9071

Rape crisis hotline and crisis prgm for rape survivors, their families, and friends, adults molested as children. OFC HRS: 24 hrs, 7 days. Spanish spoken. SERVES: Coachella Valley, Morongo Basin.

RIVERSIDE CO. BAR ASSOCIATION

Lawyer Referral Service
4129 Main St., Ste 100
Riverside, CA 92501
(951) 682-7520
(760) 568-5555
(951) 682-0106 FAX

Refers callers to lawyers specializing in different areas of law, including administrative law, criminal law, employment law, and family law. FUNDING: Nonprofit, donations. OFC HRS: M-F 8:30am-12noon, 1pm-4:30pm. Spanish spoken. Private pay accepted for referral fee. SERVES: Riverside Co.

RIVERSIDE CO. CRISIS/REFERRAL

See "Volunteer Center/Riverside Co."

RIVERSIDE CO. INFO SRVS

Information Line for County Services
(951) 955-1000

Phone numbers and/or addresses provided for all Riverside County-operated prgms. FUNDING: Govt. OFC HRS: M-F 8am-5pm. Spanish spoken. Free srvs. SERVES: Riverside County.

RIVERSIDE CO. SHERIFF'S DEPT

Non-Emergency/Crime Reporting Hotline
7477 Mission Blvd.
Riverside, CA 92509
(800) 950-2444
(951) 776-1099
(951) 955-2630 FAX

West county (909) 776-1099. East county (760) 836-3215. Both locations have TDD available.

S. COACHELLA VLY COMM SRVS DIST

91-260 Avenue 66, Ste 116

Mecca, CA 92254
(760) 396-1014
(760) 369-1517
(760) 396-1924 FAX

Hard to get rid of refuge removal srvs, supplemental law enforcement srvs, grafitti removal hotline (888) 472-3488. FUNDING: Govt. OFC HRS: M-F 8am-5pm. Spanish spoken. SERVES: Mecca, Thermal.

SAFE SITTER
8604 Allisonville Rd., Ste 248
Indianapolis, IN 46250
(800) 255-4089

Refers callers to babysitters who have been extensively trained in first aid/CPR, and behavior mgmt techniques. Visit (www.safesitter.org) for more info. OFC HRS: M-F 8am-4pm, CST. SERVES: U.S.A.

SAMHSA CTR FOR SUBSTANCE ABUSE PREV
Workplace Helpline
(800) 967-5752

Info & referrals to businesses wanting to start a drug-free workplace prgm. Visit (www.drugfreeworkplace.org). FUNDING: State. OFC HRS: M-F 9am-5pm, EST. SERVES: U.S.A.

SAN BERNARDINO CO. INFO SRVS
670 E. Gilbert St.
San Bernardino, CA 92415
(909) 388-5500
(909) 358-5555 FAX

Information line for phone numbers and/or addresses to all San Bernardino County-operated prgms. FUNDING: Govt. OFC HRS: M-F 8am-5pm. Spanish spoken. SERVES: San Bernardino County.

SAN BERNARDINO CO. OMBUDSMAN
686 E. Mill St.
San Bernardino, CA 92415-0640
(909) 891-3928
(866) 229-0284
(909) 891-3957 FAX

Investigates complaints, problems of long-term care facilities for the elderly and dev disabled adults in licensed facilities. FUNDING: Federal, state. OFC HRS: M-F 8am-5pm. Free srvs. SERVES: San Bernardino County.

SENIOR INFO & ASSISTANCE
Barstow/Northern Desert
536 E. Virginia Way
Barstow, CA 92311
(760) 256-5544
(760) 256-1605 FAX

Info & referral, eval, follow-up, outreach, comprehensive assessment. OFC HRS: M-F 8am-5pm. Free srvs. SERVES: San Bernardino County.

SENIOR INFO & ASSISTANCE
San Brdo Co/Aging & Adult Services
8572 Sierra Ave.
Fontana, CA 92335
(909) 829-8515
(909) 829-0313 FAX

Info & referrals for senior citizens to resources, evaluation, follow-up, outreach, and comprehensive assessment. Goal is to assist the senior in locating needed srvs. OFC HRS: M-F 8am-5pm. Spanish spoken. SERVES: San Bernardino County.

SENIOR INFO & ASSISTANCE
12202 1st Street
Yucaipa, CA 92399
(909) 797-1177
(909) 797-7597 FAX

Info & referral, eval & follow-up, outreach, comprehensive assessment. FUNDING: Nonprofit. OFC HRS: M-F 9am-4pm. Free srvs. SERVES: Yucaipa, Oak Glen.

SEXUAL ASSAULT SRVS/SAN BRDO
444 N. Arrowhead Ave., Ste 101-104
San Bernardino, CA 92401-1221
(909) 885-8884
(909) 383-8478 FAX

Support for victims of sexual assault and significant others. Individual and group counseling, hospital & court accompaniment, community edu prgms and self-defense. Rape crisis ctr has support groups for adolescents, adults molested as children, etc., 24-hr crisis line (800) 656-4673. Coachella Valley (760) 568-9071; Morongo Basin (760) 369-3353. FUNDING: United Way, Ofc of Emergency Services, nonprofit. OFC HRS: M-Th 8am-5pm, F 8am-2pm. Spanish spoken. ADM REQ: Victims of sexual assault. Free srvs. SERVES: San Bernardino County.

SMALL BUSINESS ADMINISTRATION
409 3rd Street, NW
Washington, DC 20416
(800) 827-5722

Info on starting a business, obtaining business loans, grants, tax questions, disaster assist. FUNDING: Govt. OFC HRS: M-F 9am-5pm, EST. Spanish spoken. SERVES: U.S.A.

SO CALIF ALCOHOL & DRUG PRGM
Angel Step Inn
11500 Paramount Blvd.
Downey, CA 90241
(323) 780-4357
(323) 780-7235 FAX

30-bed emerg shelter for women ages 18 yrs+ and their children (up to age 17 yrs) with co-occuring domestic violence & substance abuse issues. Max 45-day prgm. Also serves pregnant women. Address above is for admin only, call for specific prgm site. FUNDING: Donation, nonprofit, state, county, United Way, SCADP, OC Health Care Agency. Spanish spoken. SERVES: L.A., Ventura, Orange, San Bernardino & Riverside Counties.

SOCIAL SECURITY BENEFITS INFO
(800) 772-1213

Answers questions on benefits, missing checks, referral for senior assist (shelter, etc.), supplemental benefits and Medicare. Phone is answered M-F 7am-7pm with a recorded message after hours. FUNDING: Govt. OFC HRS: M-F 9am-7pm. Spanish spoken. SERVES: U.S.A.

SOUTH ASIAN HELPLINE & REFERRAL AGENCY (SAHARA)
17100 S. Pioneer Blvd., Ste 260
Artesia, CA 90701
(562) 402-4132
(562) 402-6093 FAX

Serves the South Asian community by providing them with info, referrals, skills dev and other culturally sensitive support srvs including mental health, health care, legal assist, transitional living ctrs, client advocacy, case mgmt, financial assist, job training and placement, community edu prgms, and senior srvs. FUNDING: Nonprofit. OFC HRS: M-F 8am-5pm. Hindi, Gujarati, Bengali, Urdu, Nepali, Tamil & Telugu spoken. Free srvs. SERVES: Southern California.

SUICIDE HOTLINES
Additional nonprofit hotlines for all types of crises, including suicide: Hotline of So. Calif (562) 596-5548 or (714) 894-4242; Calif Youth Crisis Line (800) 843-5200; Covenant House Nineline (800) 999-9999. SERVES: So. Calif.

SUICIDE PREVENTION CENTER
(877) 727-4747
(310) 398-5690 FAX

24-hr crisis hotline. AAS Certified. Crisis counseling & referrals to resources. Also Survivors After Suicide bereavement support groups to help cope with loss. Prevention speakers for schools & other community outreach. Toll-free for L.A. & Orange Counties only. FUNDING: Govt, United Way, donations, nonprofit. OFC HRS: 24 hrs, 7 days. Free srvs. SERVES: So. Calif.

SUICIDE PREVENTION LIFELINE
Veteran's Assistance
(800) 273-8255

Toll-free, 24-hr crisis hotline to assist veterans. TTY (800) 799-4889. FUNDING: Substance Abuse & Mental Hlth Srvs (HHS). OFC HRS: 24 hrs, 7 days. SERVES: U.S.A.

SUN CITY CONCERN, INC
Kay Ceniceros Community Center
29995 Evans Rd.
Sun City, CA 92586
(951) 679-2374
(951) 301-1923 FAX

Free info and referral srvs for seniors. Telephone reassurance prgm, gatekeeper prgm, Friendly Visitor prgm. Bus trips, Bingo. Volunteer opportunities. FUNDING: S.C. United Fund, nonprofit. OFC HRS: M-F 8am-12noon, 1pm-4pm. ADM REQ: Ages 55 yrs+. SERVES: Riverside County.

TEEN CRISIS LINE
Casa Youth Shelter
10911 Reagan St.
Los Alamitos, CA 90720
(800) 914-2272
(562) 594-9185 FAX

Srvs for youth in crisis ages 12-17 yrs. Help for pregnant youth and runaways. OFC HRS: 24 hrs, 7 days. Spanish spoken. SERVES: So. Calif.

TEEN LINE
P.O. Box 48750
Los Angeles, CA 90048
(310) 855-4673
(310) 423-0456 FAX

Teen-to-teen 24-hr hotline (800) 852-8336. Referrals given to community agencies as needed. FUNDING: Nonprofit. OFC HRS: M-F 6pm-10pm. SERVES: Calif.

THE FRIENDSHIP LINE
Center for Elderly Suicide Prevention
3626 Geary Blvd.
San Francisco, CA 94118
(415) 752-3778

Free and supportive telephone counseling for seniors who are bereaved, depressed, isolated, or abused. Also offers srvs for their caregivers and advocates; grief support groups available in the San Francisco area. FUNDING: Nonprofit. OFC HRS: 24 hrs, 7 days. Free srvs. SERVES: Calif.

THE LIGHTHOUSE, INC.

See "Lighthouse International"

THE OTHER BAR NATIONAL HOTLINE

(800) 222-0767

24-hr hotline for confidential counseling and referral assist for judges, lawyers, law students and other legal professionals affected by alcohol and drug abuse. Also offers support group meetings throughout Calif. FUNDING: Nonprofit, State Bar, donations. Free srvs. SERVES: Calif.

THE TREVOR PROJECT

Trevor Helpline
8704 Santa Monica Blvd., Ste 200
West Hollywood, CA 90069
(866) 488-7386
(310) 271-8845
(310) 271-8846 FAX

24-hr toll-free helpline for gay and questioning teens. Counseling for youth ages 25 yrs or younger. Visit (www.thetrevorproject.org) for resources, suicide warning signs, events, etc. Ages 25 yrs and younger call, (800) 246-7743; for ages 25 yrs+ call, (888) 843-4564. FUNDING: Nonprofit. SERVES: U.S.A.

THE U.S. UNINSURED HELPLINE

(800) 234-1317

Hotline available 24 hrs, 7 days to assist the uninsured with navigating free and low-cost health insurance options. FUNDING: Nonprofit. OFC HRS: 24 hrs, 7 days. Spanish spoken. Free srvs. SERVES: U.S.A.

TOLL-FREE NUMBER INFORMATION

(800) 555-1212

TRANS UNION CREDIT INFO

P.O. Box 1000
2 Baldwin Place
Crum Lynne, PA 19022
(800) 888-4213

Info on requesting credit reports & credit scores. OFC HRS: M-F 8am-8pm, EST. SERVES: U.S.A.

U.S. CONSUMER PRODUCT SAFETY HOTLINE

(800) 638-2772

Messages including referral numbers for product recall, reporting hazardous products, product related injury or death, and safety issues with child protection as a primary goal. Several publications and fact sheets available: Super Sitter, Toy Safety, Playground Safety, Poison Lookout Checklist. For TTY, call (301) 595-7054. OFC HRS: M-F 8am-4:30pm, EST. Spanish spoken. SERVES: U.S.A.

U.S. CTR FOR DISEASE CONTROL/ PREVENTION

Public Response Hotline
1600 Clifton Rd.
Atlanta, GA 30333
(888) 246-2675

For Spanish line, call (888) 246-2857. TTY (866) 874-2646. FUNDING: Govt. OFC HRS:

M-F 8am-5pm; Sat, Sun 7am-5pm. SERVES: U.S.A.

U.S. CUSTOMS DRUG SMUGGLING

(800) 232-5378
(866) 247-2878

Report drug smuggling. Spanish spoken.

U.S. DEPT OF HEALTH & HUMAN SRVS

Inspector General's Hotline
P.O. Box 1133
Washington, DC 20013-1133
(800) 447-8477
(800) 223-8164 FAX

Accepts calls and letters regarding fraud, waste, abuse or mis-management of prgms or operation, Medicaid & Medicare fraud associated with home health care, nursing homes, durable medical equipment, suppliers, etc. TTY (800) 337-4950. Toll-free fax (maximum 10 pages). The hotline is set up only to take in info. FUNDING: Govt. OFC HRS: M-F 8am-5:30pm, EST. Spanish spoken. SERVES: U.S.A.

U.S. FEDERAL TRADE COMMMISSION

Nationwide Do Not Call Registry
CRC-240
Washington, DC 20580
(888) 382-1222

The Natl Do Not Call Registry gives you a choice about whether to receive telemarketing calls at home. Most telemarketers should not call your number once it has been on the registry for three months. You can register your home or mobile phone and will be effective for five yrs. Also takes complaints against violating telemarketers. Register via website (www.donotcall.gov) or phone. FUNDING: Fed govt. OFC HRS: 24-hr recording. Spanish spoken. Registration is free. SERVES: U.S.A.

U.S. IMMIGRATION/CUSTOMS ENFORCE

Homeland Security/Ofc of Investigations
501 W. Ocean Blvd., Ste 7200
Long Beach, CA 90802
(562) 980-3170
(562) 590-7352 FAX

Investigative & law enforcement arm of the Dept of Homeland Security dealing with commodities, weapons, narcotics & human smuggling and trafficking, benefit and trade fraud, child pornography & money laundering. On-call 24 hrs. FUNDING: Govt. OFC HRS: M-F 8:30am-5pm. SERVES: U.S.A.

UNEMPLOYMENT COMPENSATION

Benefits and Info line
(800) 494-4944

Spanish spoken. SERVES: Calif.

UNEMPLOYMENT COMPENSATION

Weekly Claims System
(800) 978-7887

Spanish spoken. SERVES: Calif.

UNITED WAY/INLAND EMPIRE

Information & Referral Dial 2-1-1
1235 Indiana Court, Ste 104
Redlands, CA 92375
(888) 435-7565

Info & referral srvs to assist in identifying srvs based on individual needs. OFC HRS: M-F 8:30am-5pm. SERVES: East Valley.

VA HEALTH CARE BENEFITS

(877) 222-8387

Info & referrals for VA healthcare benefits. Also enrollment assist. FUNDING: Govt. OFC HRS: M-F 6am-7pm, CST. ADM REQ: Veteran. SERVES: U.S.A.

VA LIFE INSURANCE HELPLINE

(800) 669-8477

Info on life insurance, death benefits, dividends, cash value, etc. SERVES: U.S.A.

VEHICLE SAFETY HOTLINE

U.S. Dept of Transportation
1200 New Jersey Ave., SE West Building, Ste 38
Washington, DC 20590
(888) 327-4236
(202) 484-0231 FAX

Toll-free safety hotline is designed to help identify safety problems in motor vehicles, tires, and automotive equipment such as child safety seats. Representatives are available to provide you with info on motor vehicle safety recalls or other safety literature. For TTY, call (800) 424-9153. FUNDING: Govt. OFC HRS: M-F 8am-10pm, EST. Spanish spoken. SERVES: U.S.A.

VOLUNTEER CENTER/RIVERSIDE CO.

2-1-1 Helpline, Inform Riverside County
P.O. Box 5376
2060 University Ave., Ste 212
Riverside, CA 92517-5376
(951) 686-4402
(951) 686-4357
(951) 686-7417 FAX

Helpline is a free, confidential crisis/suicide intervention service, 24/7. Countywide human srv info & referral line for agencies & individuals during ofc hrs. Medi-Cal provider referrals. Maintains computerized human srv database and publishes directory of human service agencies for the county of Riverside. Bilingual info. Speakers available to educate about assessment process and community resources. 24-hr line, dial 2-1-1. OFC HRS: M-F 8am-5pm. 24 hr srvs. Free srvs. SERVES: Riverside County.

WE CAN HELP

(760) 375-7100

Hotline to report child abuse or to assist stressed parents. Sponsored by the High Desert Child Abuse Prevention Council. FUNDING: Nonprofit. Free srvs. SERVES: San Bernardino County.

WE TIP CRIME HOTLINE

P.O. Box 1296
Rancho Cucamonga, CA 91729
(800) 782-7463
(909) 987-2477 FAX

Takes info from anonymous informants about all major crimes (drug traffic, arson, murder, rape, fraud, etc.) and passes it to law enforcement agencies. Callers remain anonymous. Calls taken 24 hrs a day. Additional phone numbers: (800) 78-CRIME, (800) 47-ARSON, (800) 87-FRAUD, (800) 47-DRUGS. Visit (www.wetip.com). See actual photos of criminals wanted in every state. See photos of missing and kidnapped children throughout the nation. Info can be provided on crime or criminals on WeTip-encrypted e-mail at (wetiphome@wetip.com). Possible reward of up to $1,000 upon conviction. SEEK prgm: Support Enforcement Enriching Kids, new prgm for O.C. available through any of the toll-free numbers. This prgm invites the callers to turn in parents not paying their child support. FUNDING: Nonprofit. OFC HRS: 24 hrs, 7 days. Spanish spoken. Free srvs. SERVES: U.S.A.

WOMEN'S HEALTH AMERICA
Pre-Menstrual Syndrome & Menopause
1289 Deming Way
Madison, WI 53717
(800) 558-7046
(888) 898-7412 FAX

Instruction to physicians & women on PMS, perimenopause, pre-menopause & menopause, how to manage symptoms. Info packets available. Hotline (800) 222-4767. Physician-ordered testing at hormone levels using saliva testing & rate of bone loss. Also natural hormone replacement therapy prescriptions on a mail order basis throughout the U.S. Visit (www.womenshealth.com). OFC HRS: 24 hrs, 7 days. SERVES: U.S.A.

WOUNDED WARRIOR RESOURCE CTR
U.S. Dept. of Defense
(800) 342-9647

Website and 24-hr hotline which provides wounded service members, their families and caregivers with info they need on military facilities, health care srvs, and benefits. To speak with a specialist, call the number above or send an e-mail to (wwrc@militaryonesource.com). V i s i t (www.woundedwarriorresourcecenter.com). Free srvs. SERVES: U.S.A.

WWW.BEFRIENDERS.ORG

Offers anonymous, non-immediate, supportive email srvs for those having thoughts of suicide. This is not an emergency service. Trained volunteers answer emails on a daily basis and all go by the pseudonym "Jo." Email (jo@samaritans.org). Website also offers a directory of emotional distress centers throughout the U.S.A. and internatl. FUNDING: Nonprofit. OFC HRS: 24 Hrs, 7 Days. Free srvs. SERVES: Internatl.

YWCA/WINGS SHELTER
For Battered Women
P.O. Box 1464
West Covina, CA 91793
(626) 338-3123
(626) 338-5419 FAX

24-hr helpline (626) 967-0658, with crisis intervention & referrals. 45-day shelter prgm for women and their children who are victims of domestic violence. Legal referrals, restraining order clinic, support groups, community edu, substance abuse counseling. Accompaniment to court, DPSS, and medical srvs. FUNDING: State, county, United Way, CSBC, donations, nonprofit. OFC HRS: M-F 8am-5pm; 24-hr shelter. Spanish & Mandarin spoken. ADM REQ: Battered women & their children. Free srvs. SERVES: Calif, will shelter women from outside the area.

HOUSING/ASSISTANCE/TENANT RIGHTS

CALIF APARTMENT LAW INFO FOUNDATION

621 S. Westmoreland Ave.
Los Angeles, CA 90005
(213) 251-9665
(213) 380-4571 FAX

Info bank covering landlord-tenant law in Calif. Also contests state and local laws which violate rights of citizens. Visit (www.califweb.org). FUNDING: Nonprofit. SERVES: Calif.

CALIF DEPT FAIR EMPLOY/HOUSING

Los Angeles District Office
1055 W. Seven Street, Ste 1400
Los Angeles, CA 90017
(800) 884-1684
(213) 439-6799
(213) 439-6715 FAX

Civil rights agency for the State of Calif. Will accept, investigate and conciliate complaints in the areas of employment & housing discrimination. Complaints must be filed within one yr of offense. Does not accept files over one yr. TTY (800) 700-2320. FUNDING: Govt. OFC HRS: M-F 8am-5pm. Spanish spoken. Free srvs. SERVES: Calif.

CALIF DEPT VETERANS AFFAIRS

CAL-VET Home Loans
1770 Iowa Ave., Ste 260
Riverside, CA 92507
(951) 774-0102
(800) 700-2127
(951) 774-0111 FAX

Cal-Vet home loans for eligible veterans. This is a Calif state agency. Walk in or call for brochures & info packets. FUNDING: Govt. OFC HRS: M-F 8am-5pm. Spanish spoken. SERVES: Calif.

CALIF FRANCHISE TAX BOARD

See "Homeowner/Renter Assistance"

CALIF HOUSING FINANCE AGENCY

CALHFA
100 Corporate Pointe, Ste 250
Culver City, CA 90230
(310) 342-1250
(310) 342-1226 FAX

Support for renters and first-time homebuyers. Income-specified prgms for affordable housing. FUNDING: State. OFC HRS: M-F 8am-5pm. SERVES: Calif.

CALIF HOUSING/COMMUNITY DEV

Mobile Home Registration/Titling
P.O. Box 2111
1800 3rd Street
Sacramento, CA 95812-2111
(800) 952-8356

Handles mobile home registration and titling for homeowners, dealers, and manufacturers. OFC HRS: M-F 8am-5pm. SERVES: Calif.

CATHEDRAL CITY/OFC OF HOUSING ASSIST

68-700 Avenue Lalo Guerrero
Cathedral City, CA 92234
(760) 770-0376
(760) 202-1470 FAX

Grants of up to $1,000 per fiscal year for home repairs to eligible low to moderate income homeowners, plus yearly assist with payment of assessment fees. Walk in or call. Wait: 1-30 days. FUNDING: City Redevelopment Agency. OFC HRS: Tu, W 7:30am-4pm; Th 9am-3pm. Spanish, Portuguese, Dutch spoken. ADM REQ: Resident homeowners with low, very low or moderate income. Free srvs to qualified homeowners. SERVES: Cathedral City.

CATHOLIC CHARITIES/COMMUNITY SRVS

West End Regional Center
9375 Archibald Ave., Ste 302
Rancho Cucamonga, CA 91730
(909) 481-7196
(909) 481-6305 FAX

Food baskets, assist with rental & mortgage payments, utility payments, pre-arranged motel accommodations, info & referral, transportation, medical referrals, clothing & furniture assist, tax prep & holiday baskets. Call for appt. FUNDING: Nonprofit. OFC HRS: M-F 8:30am-4:30pm. Spanish spoken. SERVES: Fontana, Etiwanda, Ontario, Montclair, Upland, Alta Loma, Rancho Cucamonga, Chino, Chino Hills.

CATHOLIC CHARITIES/COMMUNITY SRVS

San Bernardino Regional Center
1800 Western Ave., Ste 107
San Bernardino, CA 92411
(909) 880-3625
(909) 880-9847 FAX

Food baskets, assists with rental & mortgage payment, utility payments, transportation, info & referral, medical referrals, clothing, furniture assist (as funds are available). FUNDING: Nonprofit. OFC HRS: M-F 8:30am-4:30pm. Spanish spoken. SERVES: San Bernardino County except Morongo Basin & the west side.

CITIZENS OF INGLEWOOD TENANT ASSN

6824 La Tijera Blvd.
Los Angeles, CA 90045
(310) 677-7294

Housing & legal srvs. Also consumer affairs info. FUNDING: Nonprofit. OFC HRS: M-F 8am-7pm. ADM REQ: Must call for appt. SERVES: Calif.

COACHELLA VALLEY HOUSING COALITION

45-701 Monroe St., Ste G
Indio, CA 92201
(760) 347-3157
(800) 689-4663
(760) 342-6466 FAX

Developer of affordable housing to low- and very-low income people. Also child care, community dev, self-help. Equal housing opportunity. Walk in or call. Wait: Varies. FUNDING: State, fed, city, county, nonprofit. OFC HRS: M-F 8:30am-5pm. Spanish spoken. ADM REQ: Must meet federal low income guidelines. Free srvs. SERVES: Riverside County.

COMMUNITY ACTION PARTNERSHIP

Weatherization Prgms/Utility Assist
2038 Iowa Ave., Ste B102
Riverside, CA 92507
(951) 955-6418
(951) 955-6506 FAX

Home weatherization for low-income families only. For utility assist prgm, call (951) 955-6448. OFC HRS: M-F 8am-5pm. Spanish spoken. ADM REQ: Must meet guidelines to qualify for assist. SERVES: Riverside County.

COMMUNITY ACTION PARTNERSHIP

Energy Conservation Program
696 S. Tippecanoe Ave.
San Bernardino, CA 92415-0610
(909) 723-1621
(909) 723-1500
(909) 723-1509 FAX

Main objective is to help conserve energy by reducing the consumption of natural resources. Aims to make homes more comfortable and healthful, lower cost of utilities, provide energy edu, and process HEAP applications. Includes weatherization srvs, HEAP, CARE, and lead reduction srvs. OFC HRS: M-F 8am-5pm. ADM REQ: Homeowner or renter in San Bernardino County and income eligible. SERVES: San Bernardino County.

COMMUNITY DEV & HOUSING

Economic Development Agency
385 N. Arrowhead Ave., 3rd Fl.
San Bernardino, CA 92415
(909) 388-0800
(909) 388-0844 FAX

Administers a wide range of public srvs and housing prgms. FUNDING: HUD and Comm Dev Block Grant (CDBG). OFC HRS: M-Th 7:30am-5:30pm; F 7:30am-4:30pm. SERVES: San Bernardino County.

COMMUNITY HEALTH RESOURCE CENTER

One-Stop Center/San Bernardino
600 N. Arrowhead Ave., Ste 300
San Bernardino, CA 92401
(909) 888-7881
(909) 889-7833 FAX

Offers phone access to health and wellness info & referral, financial literacy info, legal aid and consumer counseling by the Legal Aid Society of San Bernardino, homeownership resource info. For TDD, call (800) 735-2922. FUNDING: Govt. OFC HRS: M-F 8am-5pm. SERVES: San Bernardino Co.

COMMUNITY SERVICES DEPARTMENT

See "Community Action Partnership"

CONSUMER HOME MORTGAGE INFO

State of Calif website (http://yourhome.ca.gov) provides info and links regarding home mortgage and foreclosure resources in Calif. Site also available in Spanish. SERVES: Calif.

CORONA ECONOMIC DEVELOPMENT

400 S. Vincentia Ave., Ste 310
Corona, CA 92882
(951) 736-2297

Housing and economic dev srvs for Corona residents and businesses. Low-interest loans & home improvement grants for income qualified home owners, senior citizens, and mobile home owners. Administers Federal Community Dev Block Grant Prgm (CDBG) for revitalization, housing, street & public facility improvements, public srvs prgms. Wait: varies (application required). For home improvement/housing assist, call (951) 817-5715. FUNDING: Redev and CDBG. OFC HRS: M-Th 7:30am-5:30pm. SERVES: Corona city limits.

DEPT OF FAIR EMPLOYMENT/HOUSING

See "Calif Dept Fair Employ/Housing"

DESERT MANNA/EMERGENCY HOUSING

209 N. 1st Avenue
Barstow, CA 92311
(760) 256-7797
(760) 256-4043 FAX

Shelter accommodations for homeless individuals and families. Hot meals Th-Sun 5pm-6pm; hot lunches 11am-1pm daily, food pantry by referral, USDA commodities 1st Th & 3rd Th, showers. M-F 9am-12noon, bread and produce as available. Emergency clothing with referral. Enter from 2nd Ave. door. For shelter, call (760)255-9025. FUNDING: Churches, donations, United Way, county, state, nonprofit. OFC HRS M-F 9am-4pm; shelter 24 hrs. SERVES: San Bernardino County.

FAIR HOUSING COUNCIL/RIVERSIDE CO.

East County Office
P.O. Box 1871
655 N. Palm Canyon Dr., Ste 202
Palm Springs, CA 92263
(760) 864-1540
(800) 655-1812
(760) 322-9068 FAX

Accepts discrimination complaints and offers info regarding landlord/tenant issues. Accepts, investigates and mediates disputes. Walk in or call. FUNDING: Nonprofit. OFC HRS: M-F 9am-5pm. Free srvs. SERVES: Riverside County.

FAIR HOUSING COUNCIL/RIVERSIDE CO.

West County Office
3933 Mission Inn Ave.
Riverside, CA 92501
(951) 682-6581
(800) 655-1812
(951) 682-0262 FAX

Accepts discrimination complaints and offers info regarding landlord and tenant issues. Accepts, investigates and mediates disputes. Walk in or call. FUNDING: Nonprofit. OFC HRS: M-F 8am-5pm. Spanish spoken. Free srvs. SERVES: Riverside County.

FAMILY SERVICE ASSN/REDLANDS

612 Lawton St.
Redlands, CA 92374
(909) 793-2673
(909) 793-7324 FAX

Srvs provided to low-income and homeless families. Case mgmt, food, clothing, utility and rental assist, cold weather motel vouchers, screening for dental & vision, prescription assist, and edu prgms. Home Again Project is a long-term comprehensive prgm helping homeless families into permanent housing and employment. Client srv M-W, F 9am-12noon, 1:30pm-7pm. Surplus food available on walk-in basis, all other srvs require appt. FUNDING: Donations, United Way, grants, nonprofit. OFC HRS: M-W 8am-7pm; Th 8am-12noon; F 8am-4:30pm. Spanish spoken. ADM REQ: Low or no income. Free srvs. SERVES: Redlands, East Valley area.

GOLDEN STATE MOBILE HOME OWNERS

P.O. Box 876
11021 Magnolia Blvd.
Garden Grove, CA 92842
(714) 826-4071

(800) 888-1727
(714) 826-2401 FAX

Info for mobile home owners regarding civil code protection. FUNDING: Nonprofit. OFC HRS: M-F 9am-4pm. Membership dues $20 yr. SERVES: Calif.

HOME IMPROVEMENT PROGRAM

Economic Dev Agency/Riverside Co.
3403 10th Street, Ste 500
Riverside, CA 92502
(951) 351-0700
(800) 655-4228
(951) 955-6686 FAX

Prgm designed to improve residential neighborhoods by assisting the low and moderate income seniors and disabled persons with rehab financing. Currently two prgms available: deferred loans and low interest loan prgm. 60-day escrow. TDD (951)351-9844. FUNDING: CDBG, federal (HUD), govt. OFC HRS: M-Th 8am-5pm. Spanish spoken. ADM REQ: Income within HUD guidelines. Application is free. SERVES: Riverside County, except Riverside City, Corona, Palm Springs, Moreno Valley.

HOMEOWNER/RENTER ASSISTANCE

Calif Franchise Tax Board
(800) 868-4171
(916) 845-0484 FAX

Assists homeowners and renters ages 62 yrs+, blind or disabled, with low income. Eligible recipients receive annual refund. TDD (800) 822-6268. FUNDING: Govt. OFC HRS: M-F 8am-5pm. Spanish spoken. Free srvs. SERVES: Calif.

HOMEOWNERSHIP PRESERVATION FNDN

3033 Excelsior Blvd., Ste 500
Minneapolis, MN 55416
(888) 995-4673
(612) 230-4020

Info regarding housing foreclosure, debt solutions, money mgmt, and homeownership. Counseling staff available by phone or submit online request. FUNDING: Nonprofit. OFC HRS: 24 hrs, 7 days. Spanish spoken. Free srvs. SERVES: Nationwide.

HUD USER CLEARINGHOUSE

P.O. Box 23268
Washington, DC 20026-3263
(800) 245-2691
(202) 708-9981 FAX

Computer-based info srv designed to disseminate the printed reports of research sponsored by the Dept of Housing & Urban Dev. Reports include housing safety, home mortgage prgm, housing for the elderly and disabled, or other HUD prgms. This office does not make referrals to local housing resources. OFC HRS: M-F 8:30am-5:15pm, EST.

INLAND FAIR HOUSING & MEDIATION

222 E. Main St., Ste 211
Barstow, CA 92311
(760) 256-7779

Landlord/tenant, fair housing, alternative dispute resolution, outreach, FHA counseling, foreclosure counseling. FUNDING: CDBG. OFC HRS: M-Th 8am-5pm. Spanish spoken. Free srvs. SERVES: San Bernardino Co.

INLAND FAIR HOUSING & MEDIATION

45110 Oasis St.
Indio, CA 92201

(760) 775-3151

Lanlord/tenant, fair housing, senior srvs, foreclosure counseling. FUNDING: CDBG. OFC HRS: M-Th 8am-5pm. Spanish spoken. Free srvs. SERVES: Riverside Co.

INLAND FAIR HOUSING & MEDIATION

Main Office
10681 Foothill Blvd., Ste 101
Rancho Cucamonga, CA 91730
(909) 984-2254
(909) 460-0274 FAX

Landlord/tenant, fair housing, senior srvs, foreclosure counseling, alternative dispute resolution, outreach. FUNDING: CDBG. OFC HRS: M-Th 8am-5pm. Spanish spoken. Free srvs. SERVES: San Bernardino Co.

INLAND FAIR HOUSING & MEDIATION

560 N. Arrowhead Ave., Ste 7A
San Bernardino, CA 92401
(909) 388-3763
(909) 889-5034 FAX

Fair housing, housing mediation, senior srv, FHA default & foreclosure counseling. Walk in or call. FUNDING: CDBG. OFC HRS: M-Th 8am-5pm. Spanish spoken. Free srvs. SERVES: San Bernardino County.

INLAND FAIR HOUSING & MEDIATION

14201 Kentwood Blvd., Ste 3
Victorville, CA 92392
(760) 243-2412
(760) 243-3312 FAX

Fair housing and landlord/tenant mediation. FUNDING: CDBG. OFC HRS: M-Th 8am-5pm. Spanish spoken. SERVES: Victorville.

JANET GOESKE CENTER

5257 Sierra St.
Riverside, CA 92504
(951) 351-8800
(951) 351-9731 FAX

Nutrition, phone assist, info & referral, Ombudsman (other than nursing homes). Housing info, health eval, stroke and arthritis support groups. Line dancing, exercise, fitness and srvs for the disabled seniors, food sharing, estate planning and bridge tournaments. Walk in or call. FUNDING: City of Riverside. OFC HRS: M-F 7am-9pm; Sat 7:30am-4:30pm; Sun 1pm-5pm. ADM REQ: Ages 50 yrs+. Free srvs.

MOBILE HOME OMBUDSMAN

Dept of Housing & Community Dev
P.O. Box 31
1800 3rd Street
Sacramento, CA 95812-0031
(800) 952-5275
(916) 445-4782
(916) 327-4712 FAX

Processes complaints regarding mobile home park health & safety issues as they relate to operation & maintenance. Complaints regarding licensed manufactured home sales activity of manufacturers, dealers & salespersons as related to advertising, contracts, escrow, fraud or misrepresentation, illegal sales, non-receipt of title, unlicensed activity or warranty. Also info on mobile home residency law. FUNDING: Govt. OFC HRS: M-F 7:30am-2:30pm. SERVES: Calif.

NATIONAL FNDN FOR CREDIT COUNSELING

2000 M Street NW, Ste 505

Washington, DC 20036
(800) 388-2227
(202) 677-4300

Visit (www.NFCC.org) for tips on foreclosure prevention, pre-purchase counseling, homebuyer education, seminars, down payment assist prgms, homeless counseling and more. To speak to a Spanish-speaking counselor, call (800) 682-9826. FUNDING: Nonprofit. SERVES: Nationwide.

NEEDLES HOUSING AUTHORITY

817 3rd. St.
Needles, CA 92363
(760) 326-5740
(760) 326-2741 FAX

Public housing prgm for low income people. The Housing Authority owns about 52 rental units and they also have Section 8 prgms. FUNDING: Federal. OFC HRS: Tu-Th 10am-3pm. ADM REQ: Low income. SERVES: Needles area.

NEIGHBORHOOD HOUSING SRVS

Inland Empire Office
1390 North D Street
San Bernardino, CA 92405
(909) 884-6891
(909) 884-6893 FAX

Home ownership edu and counseling. First and second mortgages for low to moderate income families; down payment assist for first time home buyers. FUNDING: Grants, fees, nonprofit. OFC HRS: M-F 8:30am-5:30pm. ADM REQ: Low to moderate income family. SERVES: Riverside, San Bernardino Counties.

NEIGHBORWORKS AMERICA

1325 G Street, NW, Ste 800
Washington, DC 20005-3100
(202) 220-2300
(202) 376-2600 FAX

Visit (www.nw.org) to find local and natl housing resources for residents and communities. FUNDING: Nonprofit. SERVES: Nationwide.

NORTHTOWN HOUSING DEVELOPMENT

Northtown Housing College Scholarship
8599 Haven Ave., Ste 205
Rancho Cucamonga, CA 91730
(909) 980-0465

Community center offers free summer lunch prgm, ESL classes, GED, govt food commodities, after school recreation & tutoring, immunizations, summer day camp, holiday toy giveaway, info & referrals, job skills workshops, affordable housing. FUNDING: Nonprofit. OFC HRS: M-F 8am-5pm. Spanish spoken. SERVES: Rancho Cucamonga & nearby.

ONTARIO HOUSING AGENCY

Housing Department
208 W. Emporia
Ontario, CA 91762
(909) 395-2006
(909) 395-2288 FAX

Emerg grants for very low income households who have health or safety-related conditions. Exterior beautification prgm. FUNDING: HUD. OFC HRS: M-Th 7:30am-5:30pm; F 8am-5pm. Spanish spoken. ADM REQ: Low income home owners and rental property owners with low to moderate income tenants. SERVES: Ontario.

OPERATION GRACE

1595 E. Art Townsend Dr.

San Bernardino, CA 92408
(909) 382-8540
(909) 382-8542 FAX

Assists homeless, single women without children and very low income persons find housing for up to six months. Info & referral to other housing prgms for low income. Life skills classes & food ministry Tu 10am-1pm. FUNDING: Nonprofit. OFC HRS: M-F 9am-5pm. ADM REQ: Homeless or low income. SERVES: San Bernardino County.

PALM SPRINGS REDEVELOP AGENCY

City of Palm Springs
P.O. Box 2743
3200 E. Tahquitz Canyon Way
Palm Springs, CA 92263-2743
(760) 323-8264
(760) 322-8325 FAX

Owner-occupied home repair grants to very low income Palm Springs homeowners. FUNDING: CDBG. OFC HRS: M-F 8am-5pm. ADM REQ: Must meet income guidelines. Free srvs. SERVES: Palm Springs.

REBUILDING TOGETHER SO CALIF COUNCIL

P.O. Box 51088
Irvine, CA 92619
(714) 657-8174

Rehabilitates homes for low income persons, the elderly & disabled, or anyone who is unable to do it themselves. Volunteer opportunities available. FUNDING: Nonprofit, donations. OFC HRS: M-F 9am-5pm. SERVES: So. Calif.

RIVERSIDE HOUSING DEVELOP CORP

First Time Home Buyer/Rehab/Rentals
4250 Brockton Ave.
Riverside, CA 92501
(951) 341-6511
(951) 341-6514 FAX

First-time home buyer prgm offers a silent second trust deed with no monthly payments until end of loan. Buyers must purchase a home in an approved area and the prgm offers a loan for most of the down payment and a portion of closing costs. Agency also purchases homes that are a blight to the neighborhood and completely rehabilitates the home and sells it to a buyer who wants to live in that neighborhood. Rehab prgm for homeowners offers low-cost grants and loans up to $40,000 to repair homes. Rental units for lower income families also available. FUNDING: City grants. OFC HRS: M-F 8am-5pm. Spanish spoken. ADM REQ: Low to moderate income families. Free srvs. SERVES: Riverside County.

SALVATION ARMY/REDLANDS CORPS

P.O. Box 26
838 N. Alta St.
Redlands, CA 92374
(909) 792-6868
(909) 335-3140 FAX

Emerg food. Dinner daily M-F 5pm. Food pantry, emerg materials assist, emerg gas, peer counseling, crisis counseling, referrals for morning showering, utility, rehab assist in San Bernardino. USDA commodities 4th F 10am-12noon, 1:30pm-4pm. Worship srvs. Walk in. FUNDING: Donations, FEMA, United Way. OFC HRS: M, Tu, Th, F 1:15pm-4pm. ADM REQ: Low income. Free srvs. SERVES: Redlands, Loma Linda, Mentone, Bryn Mawr.

SALVATION ARMY/YUCCA VLY SRVS

56659 Twentynine Palms Hwy., Ste E
Yucca Valley, CA 92284
(760) 228-0114

Comprehensive emerg assist on a case-by-case basis. Food bank on W, utility asst by appt. Certified emerg disaster responders. Other resources as available. Inquiries welcome. FUNDING: United Way, county, donations, nonprofit. OFC HRS: Tu-Th 10am-3pm. SERVES: Morongo Basin.

SAN BERNARDINO CO. HOUSING AUTH

Housing Assistance-Section 8
672 S. Waterman
San Bernardino, CA 92405
(909) 890-9533
(909) 381-3052 FAX

Currently the application list is closed for Section 8 housing vhoice voucher prgm. Applications for Public Housing is ongoing. To request an application, contact the office(s) that handles the area(s) where you wish to reside. A list of offices can be found at (www.hacsb.com), or call (909) 890-0644 or you may write to HACSB, 715 E. Brier Dr, San Bernardino, CA 92408-2841 to receive a list of those offices. FUNDING: Fed govt. OFC HRS: M-F 9am-4pm, closed alt F. Spanish spoken.

SIMPSON CENTER

305 E. Devonshire Ave.
Hemet, CA 92543
(951) 765-2390
(951) 765-2398 FAX

Senior nutrition, info & referral srvs, tax assist, blood pressure testing, blood bank, homeowners and renters assist, senior activities, phone assurance, outreach. Walk in or call. FUNDING: Taxes, general fund, income from room rentals, nonprofit. OFC HRS: M-Th 8am-4:30pm. Spanish spoken. Most free srvs. SERVES: Hemet, San Jacinto.

SO CALIF ASSN NONPROFIT HOUSING

3345 Wilshire Blvd., Ste 1005
Los Angeles, CA 90010-1821
(213) 480-1249
(213) 480-1788 FAX

SCANPH is a membership group that supports and assists nonprofit housing dev corporations in carrying out their objectives. Bi-monthly newsletter, training workshops, brown bag forums on housing, legislative advocacy. Monitors local, state & federal legislatures as they relate to affordable housing. FUNDING: City, county, fndn, corporate, dues, workshop income, grants, contracts, nonprofit. OFC HRS: M-F 9am-5pm. SERVES: So. Calif.

SO CALIF ASSN OF GOVERNMENTS

818 W. 7th Street, 12th Fl.
Los Angeles, CA 90017
(213) 236-1800
(213) 236-1825 FAX

Regional planning; economic and growth forecasting; housing assessment & air quality planning; transportation planning for all local govt agencies in the six county regions of So Calif. Catalog of publications & reports. Walk in or call. Satellite ofc in Riverside County. FUNDING: Govt. OFC HRS: M-Th 8am-5pm; F 8am-4pm. Spanish, Japanese, Chinese & Korean spoken. SERVES: Imperial, L.A., Orange, Riverside, San Bernardino & Ventura Counties.

UPLAND CITY HOUSING AUTHORITY

1200 N. Campus Ave.
Upland, CA 91786
(909) 982-2649
(909) 982-0237 FAX

Public housing & rental assist Section 8 for low income. Walk in. FUNDING: Federal. OFC HRS: M-Th 7am-4:30pm. Spanish spoken. ADM REQ: Low income. Fee scale 30% of monthly income. SERVES: Upland, Montclair, Rancho Cucamonga, Ontario, Chino.

VCF COMMUNITY SERVICES

17421 Van Buren Blvd.
Riverside, CA 92504
(951) 789-8514
(951) 780-5433
(951) 780-1981 FAX

Assists all people in need with sack lunches, hygiene packages for homeless, emerg food box (for monthly food srvs, must be involved in Change Your Life Prgm), clothing, housing & utility assist, job search and counseling regarding employment, resume assist, outreach prgms. Mailing address: 16445 Porter Ave., Riverside, CA 92505. FUNDING: Church, donations, nonprofit. OFC HRS: Tu-F 9am-4pm. SERVES: Riverside County.

HOUSING/LOW INCOME/HUD

ABILITY AWARENESS
1440 E. 1st St., Ste 107
Santa Ana, CA 92701
(714) 277-4330
(714) 277-3743 FAX

Natl organization dedicated to enhancing the quality of life for people with disabilities through housing, employment, edu, media and volunteer opportunities. Ability House, developed in partnership with Habitat for Humanity affiliates, is an accessible home built for low income families to which one or more members have a health condition or disability. A unique aspect of this prgm is the outreach to volunteers with disabilities during all phases of construction. FUNDING: Nonprofit. OFC HRS: M-F 8:30am-5:30pm. SERVES: U.S.A.

ABODE COMMUNITIES
701 E. 3rd Street, Ste 400
Los Angeles, CA 90013
(213) 629-2702
(213) 225-2805 FAX

Low-income housing throughout greater Los Angeles County. Mission is to open new doors in people's lives through creative and responsible design, dev and operation of service-enhanced affordable housing. Child care centers, community centers and computer labs are built into each facility. Provides an enriching resident services prgm. Encourages participation and leadership in communities, and enhances children's academic achievement and self-esteem. Also helps adults to become confident and educated contributors to society. FUNDING: Nonprofit. OFC HRS: M-F 8:30am-6pm. Spanish spoken. SERVES: L.A., Orange and Riverside Counties.

ADOBE VILLAS APTS
Professional Property Management, LLC
73747 Raymond Way
Twentynine Palms, CA 92277-1676
(760) 367-2966
(760) 367-0516 FAX

Affordable rental housing for families, Section 8. Wait is 6 mos-1 yr. OFC HRS: M-F 9am-1pm, by appt. ADM REQ: Low income. SERVES: San Bernardino County.

ARROWHEAD VISTA
Sk Mgmt Company
15910 Ventura Blvd., Ste 1400
Encino, CA 91436
(323) 930-2300
(323) 935-3605 FAX

Affordable Section 8 rental housing for families. Section 236 for the disabled. No waiting list. For TDD, call (800) 464-4418. OFC HRS: M-F 8am-5pm. ADM REQ: Low income. SERVES: San Bernardino County.

ASCOT PARK APARTMENTS
Coastline Real Estate Advisors Inc.
1422 E. 9th Street
San Bernardino, CA 92410
(909) 884-5575
(909) 888-4242 FAX

Rental housing for families, Section 8. OFC HRS: M-F 9am-5pm; Sat, Sun 11am-4pm.

Spanish spoken. ADM REQ: Low income. SERVES: San Bernardino County.

BARKER MANAGEMENT, INC.
1101 E. Orangewood Ave., Ste 200
Anaheim, CA 92805
(714) 533-3450
(714) 533-8608 FAX

Affordable rental units for families & seniors. A property mgmt agent of the Community Redevelopment Agency of L.A. Call for availability. OFC HRS: M-F 9am-5pm. ADM REQ: Must meet income and/or age requirements. SERVES: So. Calif.

CASA MARIA APTS
Professional Property Management, LLC
46425 Tyler St.
Coachella, CA 92236-2008
(760) 398-0011
(760) 398-4222 FAX

Section 8 rental housing for families. Section 236 for the disabled. Wait: 6 mos-1 yr. OFC HRS: M-F 8am-5pm. Spanish spoken. ADM REQ: Low income or disabled. SERVES: Riverside County.

CO-ABODE
1223 Wilshire Blvd., Ste 102
Santa Monica, CA 90403

Nationwide, web-based shared housing and support group for single mothers and their children. Guest memberships are free, as is access to the extensive resource directory with links to housing, parenting and other info. Visit (www.co-abode.com). FUNDING: Nonprofit, membership fees. OFC HRS: 24 hrs, 7 days. SERVES: U.S.A.

COACHELLA COMMUNITY HOMES
Hyder & Co.
84720 Avenue 52
Coachella, CA 92236-2466
(760) 398-6411
(760) 398-1252 FAX

Rental housing for families, Section 8. OFC HRS: M-F 8am-5pm. Spanish spoken. ADM REQ: Low income. SERVES: Riverside County.

COMMUNITY DEV & HOUSING
Economic Development Agency
385 N. Arrowhead Ave., 3rd Fl.
San Bernardino, CA 92415
(909) 388-0800
(909) 388-0844 FAX

Administers a wide range of public srvs and housing prgms. FUNDING: HUD and Comm Dev Block Grant (CDBG). OFC HRS: M-Th 7:30am-5:30pm; F 7:30am-4:30pm. SERVES: San Bernardino County.

CORONA COMMUNITY TOWERS
SK Mgmt Company
910 S. Belle Ave.
Corona, CA 91720
(323) 930-2300
(323) 935-3605 FAX

Affordable rental housing for seniors, Section 202. No waiting list. OFC HRS: M-F 8am-5pm. ADM REQ: Low income. SERVES: Riverside County.

FAMILY SELF-SUFFICIENCY
See "Riverside Co. Housing Authority"

FNDN FOR AFFORDABLE HOUSING
30950 Rancho Viejo Rd., Ste 100
San Juan Capistrano, CA 92675
(949) 443-9101
(949) 443-9133 FAX

Developer, owner and manager of over 80 tax-advantaged affordable housing units for senior citizens and families of low or moderate income. Most properties located in So. Calif. Additional srvs offered at some locations. FUNDING: Nonprofit. OFC HRS: M-F 9am-5pm. 24-hr voicemail. Spanish spoken. SERVES: U.S.A.

H.U.D. (HUD)
See "U.S. Dept of Housing/Urban Dev"

HABITAT FOR HUMANITY/HEMET
328 N. State St., Ste D
Hemet, CA 92543
(951) 658-0235
(951) 658-3295 FAX

Christian-based organization that builds houses for low income families living in poverty conditions who qualify for a Habitat Mortgage with a no-interest loan payable over a span of 20-25 yrs. Selected families must put in 500 hrs of "sweat equity" and make a down payment. Work is completed with volunteers, donated materials and monetary donations. FUNDING: Nonprofit, donations. OFC HRS: M-F 9am-4pm. ADM REQ: Low income. SERVES: San Jacinto Valley.

HABITAT FOR HUMANITY/PALM DESERT
P.O. Box 11738
Palm Desert, CA 92255
(760) 770-3723
(760) 770-3821 FAX

Christian-based organization that builds houses for low income families living in poverty conditions who qualify for a Habitat Mortgage with a no-interest loan payable over a span of 20-25 yrs. Selected families must put in 500 hrs of "sweat equity" and make a down payment. Work is completed with volunteers, donated materials and monetary donations. FUNDING: Donations, nonprofit. OFC HRS: M-F 9am-5pm. ADM REQ: Low income. SERVES: Coachella Valley.

HABITAT FOR HUMANITY/RIVERSIDE
2180 Iowa Ave.
Riverside, CA 92507
(951) 787-6754
(951) 787-6750 FAX

Christian-based organization that builds houses for low income families living in poverty conditions who qualify for a Habitat Mortgage with a no interest loan payable over a span of 20-25 yrs. Selected families must put in 500 hrs of "sweat equity" and make a down payment. Work is completed with volunteers, donated materials and monetary donations. Habitat Store is open M-Sat 8:30am-4:30pm. FUNDING: Nonprofit. OFC HRS: M-Sat 8am-4:30pm. SERVES: Moreno Valley, Riverside, Jurupa, Corona, Belltown, Norco and Glen Avon.

HABITAT FOR HUMANITY/SAN GORGONIO

P.O. Box 269
Banning, CA 92220
(951) 922-3944
(951) 922-3934 FAX

Christian-based organization that builds houses for low income families living in poverty conditions who qualify for a Habitat Mortgage with a no-interest loan payable over a span of 20-25 yrs. Selected families must put in 500 hrs of "sweat equity" and make a down payment. Work is completed with volunteers, donated materials and monetary donations. FUNDING: Nonprofit. OFC HRS: M-F 9am-12noon. ADM REQ: Low income. SERVES: Banning, Beaumont, Cabazon, Calimesa, Cherry Valley.

HEMET ESTATES

1101 E. Menlo Ave.
Hemet, CA 92543-1830
(951) 925-5222
(951) 765-5575 FAX

Affordable rental housing for families, Section 8. Wait: 6 mos-1 yr. OFC HRS: M-F 8am-5pm. ADM REQ: Low income. SERVES: Riverside County.

HOMEOWNERSHIP PRESERVATION FNDN

3033 Excelsior Blvd., Ste 500
Minneapolis, MN 55416
(888) 995-4673
(612) 230-4020

Info regarding housing foreclosure, debt solutions, money mgmt, and homeownership. Counseling staff available by phone or submit online request. FUNDING: Nonprofit. OFC HRS: 24 hrs, 7 days. Spanish spoken. Free srvs. SERVES: Nationwide.

HOUSING & URBAN DEV

451 7th Street, SW
Washington, DC 20410
(800) 669-9777

Info on HUD prgms. Fair housing rights & responsibilities. Housing discrimination hotline. OFC HRS: M-F 9am-5pm, EST. Spanish spoken. SERVES: Calif.

HOUSING CALIFORNIA

900 J Street, 2nd Fl.
Sacramento, CA 95814
(916) 447-0503
(916) 447-1900 FAX

Promotes & advocates for decent, safe, and affordable housing for all of Calif. FUNDING: Nonprofit, donations. OFC HRS: M-F 8am-5pm. SERVES: Calif.

JACKSON TERRACE APARTMENTS

Arm Mgmt Group
46211 Jackson St.
Indio, CA 92201
(760) 347-1718
() 76-0342 FAX

Rental housing for families, Section 8. OFC HRS: M-F 8am-5pm. Spanish spoken. ADM REQ: Low income. SERVES: Riverside County.

JAMBOREE HOUSING CORPORATION

17701 Cowan Ave., Ste 200
Irvine, CA 92614
(949) 263-8676
(949) 263-0647 FAX

Builds, preserves and maintains affordable rental & home ownership for low-income families and seniors. Helping Educate, Activate, and Respond Together (HEART) assists residents in maintaining self-sufficiency. On-site srvs may include: health & safety classes, computer learning centers with Internet access, after school tutoring, budgeting & parenting classes, home buying seminars, and referrals to local agencies. Senior resident srvs include transportation to appts & off-site events, also daily living assist. FUNDING: Nonprofit, govt, grants, donations. OFC HRS: M-F 7:30am-5pm. ADM REQ: Vary per location. SERVES: So. Calif.

LAKEVIEW APARTMENTS

CBR Property Management LLC
32211 Riverside Dr.
Lake Elsinore, CA 92530-7834
(951) 674-6004
(951) 674-6075 FAX

Rental housing for families, Section 8. Wait: 6 mos-1 yr. OFC HRS: M-F 9am-5pm. Spanish spoken. ADM REQ: Low income. SERVES: Riverside County.

LILLY HILL APTS

Interstate Realty Mgmt Co.
1001 Lilly Hill Dr.
Needles, CA 92363
(760) 326-2433
(760) 326-4046 FAX

Rental housing for families, Section 8. OFC HRS: M-F 8am-5pm. ADM REQ: Low income. SERVES: San Bernardino County.

MARYGOLD GARDENS APARTMENTS

Development, LLC (GMD)
17225 Marygold Ave.
Fontana, CA 92335-6799
(909) 822-8046

Affordable rental housing for families, Section 8. Waiting list 1-2 yrs. OFC HRS: M-F 8am-5pm. Spanish, Armenian, French, Arabic, Tongan, Filipino spoken. ADM REQ: Low income. SERVES: San Bernardino County.

NATIONAL FNDN FOR CREDIT COUNSELING

2000 M Street NW, Ste 505
Washington, DC 20036
(800) 388-2227
(202) 677-4300

Visit (www.NFCC.org) for tips or foreclosure prevention, pre-purchase counseling, homebuyer education, seminars, down payment assist prgms, homeless counseling and more. To speak to a Spanish-speaking counselor, call (800) 682-9832. FUNDING: Nonprofit. SERVES: Nationwide

NATL COMMUNITY RENAISSANCE

9065 Haven Ave., Ste 100
Rancho Cucamonga, CA 91730
(909) 483-2444
(909) 483-2448 FAX

Affordable housing prgm for single-parent families, seniors and the disabled. OFC HRS: M-F 9am-5pm. Spanish spoken. ADM REQ: Must meet income guidelines. SERVES: So. Calif.

NEIGHBORWORKS AMERICA

1325 G Street, NW, Ste 800
Washington, DC 20005-3100
(202) 220-2300
(202) 376-2600 FAX

Visit (www.nw.org) to find local and natl housing resources for residents and communities. FUNDING: Nonprofit. SERVES: Nationwide.

RANCHO & MILL APTS

Beacon Prop Mgmt
2170 N. Rancho Ave.
Colton, CA 92324-1037
(909) 889-8417
(909) 889-3077 FAX

Rental housing for families, Section 8. Wait: 6 mos-1 yr. OFC HRS: M-F 8am-5pm. ADM REQ: Low income. SERVES: San Bernardino County.

RIVER RANCH MOBILE HOME PARK

Jamboree Housing Corp. Project
15940 Stoddard Wells Rd.
Victorville, CA 92392
(760) 245-9831
(760) 245-6205 FAX

136 mobile home spaces for purchased/owned mobile homes for low-income seniors ages 55 yrs+. No rentals. Low monthly space fees from $140-$285 per month. Some assist to access local senior prgms. Contact Barbi Brooks for more info. FUNDING: State HCD MPROP. SERVES: San Bernardino County.

RIVERSIDE CO. HOUSING AUTHORITY

P.O. Box 1747
44-199 Monroe St., Ste B
Indio, CA 92202
(760) 863-2828
(800) 609-5708
(760) 863-2838 FAX

Rental assist for low-income households. Public housing & Section 8. No emerg assist available. Tenants pay no more than 30% of income for rent. There is a waiting list. Walk in. TDD (760) 863-2830. FUNDING: Federal, state, local. OFC HRS: M-Th 7:30am-5:30pm. Spanish spoken. ADM REQ: Income levels below 50% of median. SERVES: Riverside County.

RIVERSIDE CO. HOUSING AUTHORITY

Housing Assistance Information
5555 Arlington Ave.
Riverside, CA 92504
(951) 351-0700
(800) 655-4228
(951) 354-6324 FAX

Housing prgms include: Section 8 tenant-based assist which provides rental assist to low & moderate income seniors and disabled. Tenants pay between 30% and 40 % of their adjusted income; a housing vhoice voucher is given to eligible participants. Affordable housing prgm allows families to live in selected HUD housing units. The Planning & Dev Dept is responsible for formulation, processing & implementation of new construction projects and maintenance of all the existing housing units. Also have a senior home repair prgm. Application is free. FUNDING: Govt. OFC HRS: M-Th 8am-5pm. Spanish spoken. SERVES: Riverside County.

RIVERSIDE CO. HOUSING AUTHORITY

Family Self-Sufficiency Program
5555 Arlington Ave.
Riverside, CA 92504
(951) 343-5442
(951) 354-6324 FAX

Assists families receiving federal rental assist move to economic independence so they are free of any govt assist. TDD (951) 351-9844. OFC HRS: M-Th 7:30am-5:30pm. Spanish spoken. SERVES: Riverside County.

RODEO DRIVE APTS
Barker Mgmt
14200 Rodeo Dr.
Victorville, CA 92392-4424
(760) 245-2922

Affordable rental housing for families, Section 8. 99 locations. Waiting list 6 mos-2 yrs, call for info. OFC HRS: M-F 8am-5pm. ADM REQ: Low income. SERVES: San Bernardino County.

SAN BERNARDINO CO. HOUSING AUTH
Rental Office
421 S. 7th Street
Barstow, CA 92311
(760) 256-8814
(760) 256-8873 FAX

Rental office only. 231 units. TTY (760) 951-7872. OFC HRS: M-F 9am-4pm; closed alt F. ADM REQ: Low income. SERVES: Adelanto, Apple Valley, Barstow, Hesperia, & Victorville.

SAN BERNARDINO CO. HOUSING AUTH
Rental and Scattered Site Office
13088 Monte Vista Ave.
Chino, CA 91710
(909) 628-3413
(909) 628-2204 FAX

Subsidized and affordable housing. Rents units in the Chino Housing Project and scattered sites in San Bernardino County. One of several scattered site offices in the county. TTY (909) 388-9279. OFC HRS: M-F 9am-4pm, closed alt F. Spanish spoken. SERVES: Chino, Ontario, Montclair, & Rancho Cucamonga.

SAN BERNARDINO CO. HOUSING AUTH
Rental Office
772 Pine St.
Colton, CA 92324
(909) 824-8277
(909) 824-8121 FAX

Strictly a rental office. TTY (909) 388-9279. OFC HRS: M-F 9am-4pm, closed alt F. Spanish spoken. SERVES: Colton, Bloomington, Rialto, & Fontana.

SAN BERNARDINO CO. HOUSING AUTH
424 N. Lemon Ave.
Ontario, CA 91764
(909) 983-1318
(909) 381-3052 FAX

Housing choice voucher prgm. Assist for very low income families, seniors, & the disabled. TTY (909) 391-5058. FUNDING: County. OFC HRS: M-Th 7:30am-5:30pm; alt F 7:30am-4:30pm. ADM REQ: Low income, poverty level. SERVES: Fontana, Rialto, Pomona Valley, Unicorp Areas, West Side San Bernardino County.

SAN BERNARDINO CO. HOUSING AUTH
Public Housing
131 E. Lugonia Ave.
Redlands, CA 92374
(909) 798-3332
(909) 798-6762 FAX

Assist with low income housing. Waiting List. TTY (909) 388-9279. OFC HRS: M-F 9am-4pm, closed alt F. Spanish spoken. SERVES: Redlands, Yucaipa, Yucca Valley, 29 Palms, Joshua Tree, Highland, San Bernardino.

SAN BERNARDINO CO. HOUSING AUTH
Administrative Office
715 E. Brier Dr.
San Bernardino, CA 92408-2841
(909) 890-0644
(909) 890-4618 FAX

Administers two rental assist prgms for low-income families, seniors, and disabled. Public housing prgm comprised of 2,500+ units owned or managed by Housing Authority, and scattered throughout 23 cities in San Bernardino Co. Housing choice voucher prgm provides rental subsidy to very low income individuals by providing subsidy payments directly to the owners on behalf of participant, who is required to pay at least 30% of their income toward rent. TTY (909) 388-9279. FUNDING: HUD. OFC HRS: M-Th 7:30am-5:30pm; alt F 7:30am-4:30pm. ADM REQ: Gross yearly income within HUD guidelines. SERVES: San Bernardino County, except the cities of Needles and Upland.

SAN BERNARDINO CO. HOUSING AUTH
Rental Office
1738 W. 9th Street
San Bernardino, CA 92411
(909) 885-6915
(909) 388-2546 FAX

Property for public housing. TTY (909) 388-9279. OFC HRS: M-F 9am-4pm;closed alt F. Spanish spoken.

SAN BERNARDINO CO. HOUSING AUTH
Housing Assistance-Section 8
672 S. Waterman
San Bernardino, CA 92405
(909) 890-9533
(909) 381-3052 FAX

Currently the application list is closed for Section 8 housing choice voucher prgm. Applications for public housing is ongoing. To request an application, contact the office(s) that handles the area(s) where you wish to reside. A list of offices can be found at (www.hacsb.com), or call (909) 890-0644 or you may write to HACSB, 715 E. Brier Dr., San Bernardino, CA 92408-2841 to receive a list of those offices. FUNDING: Fed govt. OFC HRS: M-F 9am-4pm, closed alt F. Spanish spoken.

SAN BERNARDINO CO. HOUSING AUTH
Rental Office Waterman Gardens
425 Crestview
San Bernardino, CA 92410
(909) 885-1593
(909) 388-2218 FAX

Office handles the rental of approx 300 units. OFC HRS: M-F 9am-4pm; closed alt F.

SAN BERNARDINO CO. HOUSING AUTH
15465 Seneca Rd.
Victorville, CA 92392
(760) 243-1043
(760) 243-2123 FAX

Housing choice voucher prgm. Assist for very low income families, seniors & the disabled. TTY (760) 951-7872. FUNDING: County. OFC HRS: M-Th 7:30am-5:30pm; alt F 7:30am-4:30pm. ADM REQ: Low income, poverty level. SERVES: High Desert, Mid Desert, Mountains

SAN BERNARDINO VILLAGE GREEN APTS
2122 W. Chestnut St.

San Bernardino, CA 92410
(909) 888-3001
(909) 381-3171 FAX

Affordable rental housing for families, Section 8. OFC HRS: M-F 8am-5pm (winter); 9am-6pm (summer). ADM REQ: Low income. SERVES: San Bernardino County.

SEMINOLE GARDEN APARTMENTS
Preservation Partners Mgmt Group, Inc.
2607 S. Linden Way
Palm Springs, CA 92264-5610
(760) 328-5913

Sixty, two-and-three bdrm units for low income individuals and families. Apply on site. Possible wait list. Resident prgms on site. FUNDING: Govt., Section 8, HUD, tax credit. OFC HRS: M-F 9am-5pm. Spanish spoken. ADM REQ: Meet income eligibility, credit history/criminal background check requirements. Move-in cost: security deposit plus 1st months rent. Riverside County.

SILBY GARDENS
Hyder & Co.
200 N. 9th Street
Blythe, CA 92225
(760) 922-4035 FAX

Rental housing for families, Section 8. Wait: 6 mos-1 yr. OFC HRS: M-F 1pm-5pm. ADM REQ: Low income. SERVES: Riverside County.

SK MANAGEMENT COMPANY
Resident Relations/Social Service Dept
15910 Ventura Blvd., Ste 1400
Encino, CA 91436
(323) 930-2300
(323) 935-3605 FAX

Affordable housing. Section 8 & Section 236 rental property units for low income individuals, families, seniors & disabled persons offering social srvs and community prgms. TDD (800) 464-4418. OFC HRS: M-F 9am-5pm. SERVES: L.A., Riverside, San Bernardino, Butte, Fresno & Kern Counties.

SUN WEST VILLAS
Hyder & Co.
7017 Mohawk Trail
Yucca Valley, CA 92284
(760) 365-0563 FAX

Affordable rental housing for families, Section 8. Wait is 4 yrs. OFC HRS: M-F 8am-5pm. Spanish spoken. ADM REQ: Low income. SERVES: San Bernardino County.

SUNRISE APTS
Hyder & Co.
481 N. Eucalyptus Ave.
Blythe, CA 92225
(760) 591-9737

Rental housing for families, Section 8. Wait: 6 mos-2 yrs. OFC HRS: M-F 8am-5pm. Spanish spoken. ADM REQ: Low income. SERVES: Riverside County.

U.S. DEPT OF HOUSING/URBAN DEV
34 Civic Center Plaza, Rm. 7015, Ste 101
Santa Ana, CA 92701-4003
(888) 827-5605
(714) 796-5577
(714) 796-1285 FAX

Affordable rental housing for low-income individuals and families. TTY (714) 796-5517. FUNDING: Govt. OFC HRS: M-F 8am-8pm,

EST. SERVES: Orange, Riverside & San Bernardino Counties.

U.S. DEPT OF HOUSING/URBAN DEV

451 7th Street, SW
Washington, DC 20410
(202) 597-1112

Natl website can help you locate a HUD office near you. Also info regarding family unification vouchers, home ownership, senior housing, Welfare-to-Work, Section 8, mgmt assessment, assist for people with disabilities, American Indian housing, etc. Visit (www.hud.gov). TTY (202)708-1455. FUNDING: Govt. SERVES: U.S.A.

U.S. FAIR HOUSING/EQUAL OPPORT

See "U.S. Dept of Housing/Urban Dev"

VICTORIA HEIGHTS APTS

JAE Properties
7650 Lincoln Ave.
Riverside, CA 92504-0000
(951) 687-2070
(951) 359-7014 FAX

Rental housing for families, Section 8. Wait: 6 mos-1 yr. FUNDING: HUD. OFC HRS: M-F 8am-4pm. Spanish spoken. ADM REQ: Low income. SERVES: Riverside County.

VILLA MIRAGE II

C.R.I. Inc
34-160 Rebecca Way
Rancho Mirage, CA 92270
(760) 328-6005
(760) 328-8896 FAX

Rental housing for families, Section 8. OFC HRS: M-F 9am-5pm. Spanish spoken. ADM REQ: Low income. SERVES: Riverside County.

VIRGINIA TERRACE APTS

PMG Properties
615 E. Virginia Way
Barstow, CA 92311
(760)256-0341
(760) 255-3070 FAX

Affordable rental housing for families, Section 8. Wait is 6 mos-5 yrs. OFC HRS: M-Th 9am-5pm. ADM REQ: Low income. SERVES: San Bernardino County.

VISTA PARK CHINO

Aimco Properties
5819 Riverside Dr.
Chino, CA 91710
(909) 591-4212
(909) 627-3322 FAX

Affordable rental housing for families, Section 8. Wait is 1.5 yrs. OFC HRS: M-F 8am-5pm. ADM REQ: Low income. SERVES: San Bernardino County.

VOLUNTEER CENTER/RIVERSIDE CO.

Shared Housing/Riverside
2060 University Ave., Ste 201
Riverside, CA 92507
(951) 686-4402
(951) 781-2737 FAX

Shared housing is a give and take arrangement between participants offering alternatives to persons unable to afford or maintain safe and suitable housing, especially the elderly who often live alone. Alternative for single parents, displaced homemakers and young adults over age 18 yrs. Satellite office in Hemet (951) 652-3591. Wait: varies. Walk in. FUNDING:

City, United Way. OFC HRS: M-Th 8am-5pm. Spanish spoken, language line available. Free srvs. SERVES: Western Riverside County.

WESTVIEW TERRACE

Winn Residential
287 Westward
Banning, CA 92220-4934
(951) 849-4333
(951) 849-9793 FAX

Affordable rental housing for families, Section 8. Wait is 12-18 months OFC HRS: M-F 8am-5pm. Spanish spoken. ADM REQ: Low income. SERVES: Riverside County.

WOODHAVEN MANOR

National Community Renaissance of CA Corp.
6230 Haven Ave.
Rancho Cucamonga, CA 91701-3828
(909) 980-3106
(909) 944-5524 FAX

Affordable rental housing for families, Section 8. Wait is 1.5 yrs. OFC HRS: M-F 8am-5pm. Spanish spoken. ADM REQ: Low income. SERVES: San Bernardino County.

WWW.HUD.GOV/FORECLOSURE/

Visit this site to find info regarding foreclosure. Talk to a housing counselor in your state, find resources, and tips. SERVES: Nationwide.

CALIF RURAL LEGAL ASSISTANCE

Coachella Office
P.O. Box 35
1460 6th Street
Coachella, CA 92236
(760) 398-7261
(760) 398-1050 FAX

Legal srvs to migrant farm workers in the areas of labor and housing. OFC HRS: M-F 9am-5:30pm. Spanish spoken. ADM REQ: Low income, employed in agriculture. Free srvs. SERVES: Riverside, San Bernardino & Imperial Counties.

CATHOLIC CHARITIES/COMMUNITY SRVS

Inland Valleys Regional Center
23623 Sunnymead Blvd., Ste E
Moreno Valley, CA 92553
(951) 924-9964
(951) 924-9997 FAX

Emerg srvs for low income. Assists with food, utility, rental assist & motel vouchers (when funding is available). Info & referral, immigration & citizenship prgm, HIV/AIDS housing assist. Counseling (909)763-4970 or (951)801-5282. FUNDING: Nonprofit. OFC HRS: M-Th 8:30am-4:30pm, by appt only. Spanish spoken. Most srvs free. SERVES: Moreno Valley, Riverside, Perris, Hemet, San Jacinto, Sun City, Corona, Lake Elsinore, Banning, Beaumont, Cherry Valley.

CATHOLIC CHARITIES/IMMIGRATION SRVS

Immigration and Refugee Services
1450 North D Street
San Bernardino, CA 92405
(909) 388-1243
(909) 383-0448 FAX

Assist with prep of applications for residency and low-cost document prep. Srvs include: family unity, Visa petition, work authority, lottery Visa advice, and referrals. Naturalization srvs include: help completing forms, taking pictures, follow up & inquiry with INS for pending application. Staff is BIA-accredited. FUNDING: Donors, govt, churches, United Way, nonprofit. OFC HRS: M-F 8am-4pm. Spanish, Chinese, Vietnamese spoken. ADM REQ: Consultation. SERVES: Riverside & San Bernardino Counties.

CHINESE CONSULATE GENERAL

443 Shatto Place
Los Angeles, CA 90020
(213) 807-8088
(213) 807-8091 FAX

Promotes cultural awareness commerce. For the passport/visa office, call (213) 807-8006. FUNDING: Fndns. OFC HRS: M-F 9am-12noon, 1:30pm-5pm. Passport and Visa hrs: M-F 9am-3pm. SERVES: So. Calif, Arizona, Hawaii, New Mexico, American Pacific Islands.

COALITION TO ABOLISH SLAVERY/ TRAFFICKING (CAST)

5042 Wilshire Blvd., Ste 586
Los Angeles, CA 90036
(213) 365-1906
(213) 365-5257 FAX

Multi-ethnic, multilingual human rights organization dedicated exclusively to serving survivors of trafficking. CAST has become a pioneering leader in the U.S. anti-trafficking movement. Comprehensive social srvs & legal assist is provided to trafficking survivors & promotes policy advocacy at the state & national levels. The shelter prgm has become a model prgm for victim srvs around the country. FUNDING: Nonprofit. OFC HRS: M-F 8:30am-5pm. Korean, Mandarin, Russian, Spanish & Tagalog spoken. SERVES: U.S.A.

CONSEJO DE LATINOS UNIDOS

Counsel of United Latinos
820 S. Indiana St.
Los Angeles, CA 90023
(800) 474-7576

Edu and assist provided in the areas of healthcare, immigration and police protection. FUNDING: Nonprofit. Spanish spoken. SERVES: Calif.

ESCORT/MIGRANT EDUCATION

National Migrant Education Hotline
State University College, Bugbee Hall 304
Oneonta, NY 13820-4051
(800) 451-8058
(607) 436-3606 FAX

24-hr hotline for migrant farm workers and their families to access edu, health and other supportive srvs. The hotline number is intended for use by migrant families. FUNDING: U.S Office of Migrant Edu, govt. OFC HRS: M-F 8am-4:30pm, EST. Spanish spoken. Free referral srvs to migrant families. SERVES: U.S.A.

FEDERAL CITIZEN INFORMATION CENTER

Pueblo, CO 81009
(888) 878-3256

Consumer info website (www.pueblo.gsa.gov), find links to govt srvs, recall lists, immigration srvs, social security, income tax, federal employment. Free srvs. SERVES: U.S.A.

FONTANA ADULT SCHOOL

10755 Oleander Ave.
Fontana, CA 92337
(909) 357-5490
(909) 357-5556 FAX

ESL and citizenship open enrollment. High school diploma prgm, GED prep & testing. Adult literacy. OFC HRS: M-Th 1pm-9pm; F 11am-4pm; Sat 8am-2pm. SERVES: Fontana.

HERMANDAD MEXICANA NACIONAL

Administrative Office
611 W. Civic Center Dr.
Santa Ana, CA 92701
(714) 541-0250
(714) 541-2460 FAX

Serves the immigrant and ethnic minority communities in areas of edu, legal issues, immigration & citizenship. Walk-in or call for info. FUNDING: Nonprofit. OFC HRS: M-F 9:30am-6pm; Sat 9am-1pm. Spanish spoken. SERVES: So. Calif.

HERMANDAD MEXICANA NACIONAL

611 W. Civic Center Dr.
Santa Ana, CA 92701
(714) 541-0250

Citizenship and immigration paperwork for a low fee. USDA surplus foods on the 3rd Th of each month. FUNDING: Nonprofit. OFC HRS: M-F 10am-7pm. Spanish spoken. ADM REQ: Must be resident. SERVES: Riverside County.

IMMIGRATION & NATURALIZATION SVC

See "U.S. Immigration/Naturalization"

IMMIGRATION EXPRESS

18830 Norwalk Blvd.
Artesia, CA 90701
(800) 985-1234
(562) 924-1981
(562) 860-1689 FAX

Immigration and non-immigration srvs provided. Also assists with citizenship, adoption, wills/estate, green card, paperwork, translation, etc. FUNDING: Nonprofit. OFC HRS: M-F 9am-5pm. SERVES: U.S.A.

MEXICAN AMER LEGAL DEFENSE & EDU

634 S. Spring St., 11th Fl.
Los Angeles, CA 90014
(213) 629-2512
(213) 629-0266 FAX

Advocates for civil rights of latinos in U.S.A. Litigation, advocacy, community outreach & edu to secure the rights of all latinos in employment, edu, immigration, political access and public resource equity. Offers major scholarships to students pursuing graduate degrees in law. FUNDING: Nonprofit. OFC HRS: M-F 8am-5pm. Spanish spoken. SERVES: U.S.A.

NATL ASYLEE INFO & REFERRAL LINE

Catholic Legal Immigration Network, Inc.
415 Michigan Ave., NE, Rm. 150
Washington, DC 20017
(800) 354-0365
(202) 635-2649 FAX

Refers asylees to more than 500 local providers of resettlement srvs such as English language classes, employment training, placement assist, financial resources, and health care. FUNDING: Nonprofit, Office of Refugee Resettlement. Over 18 different languages spoken. ADM REQ: Must be an asylee to call. Free srvs. SERVES: U.S.A.

PASSPORT AGENCY

Federal Building
11000 Wilshire Blvd., Ste 1000
Los Angeles, CA 90024-3615
(877) 487-2778
(877) 854-7771 FAX

Message tape invites the caller to respond "yes, I would" to more than a dozen questions regarding passports. Passport processing by mail takes 3 weeks. Info on how to get a passport, where to apply, how to amend or extend your passport, report a lost or stolen passport, emerg passports, directions to passport offices. Application can be mailed to you and you can then apply by mail. Documentation will be required when applying for a passport. FUNDING: Govt. OFC HRS: M-F 7am-3pm, by appt. Spanish spoken.

REFUGEE PROGRAMS BUREAU

Calif Dept of Social Srvs
P.O. Box 944243
MS 8-9-646

Sacramento, CA 94244-2430
(916) 654-4356
(916) 654-7187 FAX

Provides statewide admin to Refugee Resettlement Prgm (RRP) and the Cuban/Haitian Entrant Prgm. Responsible for coordinating the delivery of benefits and srvs to refugee and entrant populations. FUNDING: Govt. OFC HRS: M-F 8am-5pm. SERVES: Calif.

SALVATION ARMY/MISSING PERSONS
P.O. Box 22646
Long Beach, CA 90801-5646
(800) 698-7728
(562) 491-8520 FAX

Reunification of families; internatl missing persons bureau for family members only throughout 90 countries. This agency will not search for: individuals seeking friends; debt collection for child support; runaway minors under age 18 yrs; adopted children seeking their natural parent or parent seeking formerly placed children for adoption; children born out of wedlock seeking their natural parent; genealogical searches; cases involving custody disputes or parental kidnappings; persons missing less than 6 mos. Non-refundable $25 registration fee. Physical address: 180 E. Ocean Blvd., 11th Fl., Long Beach, CA 90802. FUNDING: Nonprofit. OFC HRS: M-F 8:30am-12noon, 1pm-4pm. Spanish spoken. SERVES: Internatl.

SAN BERNARDINO CO. LIB/LITERACY
Lake Arrowhead Mt. Literacy Prgm
P.O. Box 1043
27235 Hwy. 189
Blue Jay, CA 92317
(909) 337-5420
(909) 337-2287 FAX

One-to-one tutoring by trained volunteers. Literacy staff interviews, matches learners & tutors. Provides families for literacy portion. Small group classes. Computer classes, 13 levels from beginning to advanced, includes: Excel, Word, Powerpoint. Citizenship classes & GED. OFC HRS: M, Tu 12noon-8pm; W-F 10am-6pm. Free tutoring & materials. SERVES: Crestline, Lake Arrowhead, Running Springs.

ST. ANN'S CATHOLIC OUTREACH
P.O. Box 190
218 D Street
Needles, CA 92363
(760) 326-2721
(760) 326-3068 FAX

Emerg food assist, helps complete papers for immigration, youth prgms, Hispanic ministry. Call St. Vincent de Paul srv, for more info on prgms, food pantry & thrift store at (760) 326-4420. FUNDING: Nonprofit. OFC HRS: M-F 8:30am-1:30pm. Spanish spoken. ASL available. SERVES: Needles & nearby.

SURVIVORS OF TORTURE INTERNATL
P.O. Box 151240
San Diego, CA 92175-1240
(619) 278-2400
(619) 294-9405 FAX

Case mgmt srvs & referrals for psych, medical, & social srvs for survivors of torture and their families. For emerg, call (619) 278-2403; intake (619) 278-2404. Info provided for So. Calif, assist primarily for San Diego. FUNDING: Nonprofit. OFC HRS: M-F 8am-5pm. Chaldean, Kurdish, Arabic, Cambodian, Fars, French & Spanish spoken. Interpretation for all languages available. Free srvs. Insurance utilized where applicable. Referrals to Medi-Cal providers. Accepts workers' compensation. SERVES: So. Calif.

U.S. IMMIGRATION/NATURALIZATION
L.A. District
300 N. Los Angeles St., Rm 1001
Los Angeles, CA 90012
(800) 375-5283

OFC HRS: M-W, F 6am-3pm; Th 6am-12noon. SERVES: L.A., Orange, Riverside, San Bernardino, Santa Barbara, San Luis Obispo & Ventura Counties.

U.S. IMMIGRATION/NATURALIZATION
San Bernardino
655 W. Rialto Ave.
San Bernardino, CA 92410
(800) 375-5283

ADM REQ: Must call for appt. SERVES: San Bernardino County.

U.S. PASSPORT OFFICE
See "Passport Agency"

YUCAIPA ADULT SCHOOL
35948 Susan St.
Yucaipa, CA 92399
(909) 790-8580
(909) 790-8584 FAX

Comprehensive adult edu srvs for immigrants, older adults: amnesty, vocational, literacy and high school diploma (includes GED prep and testing), srvs for disabled, parent edu, homemaking and community srv. Walk in or call. FUNDING: SDE adult revenue, federal. OFC HRS: M-Th 8am-6pm; F 8am-12noon. Some Spanish spoken. SERVES: Yucaipa, Calimesa.

LEGAL ASSISTANCE

A BETTER WAY

See "Victor Vly Domestic Violence, Inc."

ABA CENTER/CHILDREN & LAW

740 15th Street, NW, 9th Fl.
Washington, DC 20005-1019
(202) 662-1720
(800) 285-2221
(202) 662-1755 FAX

Info, tech assist, consulting & training on legal issues related to child welfare & protection, publications on issues. Sponsored by the American Bar Assn. Voicemail after hours. FUNDING: Nonprofit. OFC HRS: M-F 9am-5pm, EST. SERVES: U.S.A.

ACLU/SOUTHERN CALIFORNIA

See "American Civil Liberties Union"

AMERICAN CIVIL LIBERTIES UNION

Southern California
1313 W. 8th Street
Los Angeles, CA 90017
(213) 977-9500
(213) 977-5297 FAX

Considers issues regarding constitutional rights. Because of severely limited resources, only a few of the thousands of complaints & issues brought to attention can be pursued. Cases not taken are referred to an appropriate agency. No live intake is conducted. Write to: Legal Intake, 1616 Beverly Blvd, Los Angeles, CA 90026, or use the intake form on website (www.aclu-sc.org/legalhelp). Volunteer pre-screeners will return the call. Intake sent via e-mail must include a mailing address; all replies are via U.S. mail. FUNDING: Donations, grants, nonprofit. OFC HRS: M-F 9am-5pm. Spanish spoken. Free srvs. SERVES: Kern, L.A., Orange, Riverside, San Bernardino, San Luis Obispo, Santa Barbara & Ventura Counties.

BAZELON CENTER/MENTAL HLTH LAW

1101 15th Street, NW, Ste 1212
Washington, DC 20005
(202) 467-5730
(202) 223-0409 FAX

Supports the legal rights of mentally disabled people through litigation & policy reform. Also offers advocacy manuals & consumer publications. Does not provide individual legal representation. For TDD, call (202) 223-0409. FUNDING: Donations, grants, nonprofit. OFC HRS: M-F 9am-5pm, EST. SERVES: U.S.A.

CALIF ADVOCATES/NURSING HOME REF

650 Harrison St., 2nd Fl.
San Francisco, CA 94107
(800) 474-1116
(415) 974-5171
(415) 777-2904 FAX

Referrals to attorneys who specialize in elder law issues, including financial abuse, neglect & estate planning for long-term care. Provides statewide consumer info on Medi-Cal eligibility, pre-placement counseling & quality info on all nursing homes in Calif. FUNDING: Nonprofit. OFC HRS: M-F 9am-12noon, 1pm-5pm. ADM REQ: Call for appt, all ages served. Fees vary. Initial consultation is free. SERVES: Calif.

CALIF APARTMENT LAW INFO FOUNDATION

621 S. Westmoreland Ave.
Los Angeles, CA 90005
(213) 251-9665
(213) 380-4571 FAX

Info bank covering landlord-tenant law in Calif. Also contests state and local laws which violate rights of citizens. Visit (www.califweb.org). FUNDING: Nonprofit. SERVES: Calif.

CALIF BOARD/VICTIM COMPENSATION

Government Claims Board
P.O. Box 3035
Sacramento, CA 95812-3035
(800) 777-9229
(916) 327-2933 FAX

If you are a victim of a crime of violence which occurred in Calif (or were a Calif resident victimized outside of the state) and you cooperated with the police investigation of the crime, you may apply to the state for compensation for qualifying unreimbursed expenses. Local victim witness center can help file. Hearing impaired, call California Relay Service (800) 735-2929 FUNDING: Govt. OFC HRS: M-F 8am-5pm. Spanish spoken. $25 filing fee and a surcharge paid by state agencies on approved claims. SERVES: Calif.

CALIF DEPT FAIR EMPLOY/HOUSING

Los Angeles District Office
1055 W. Seven Street, Ste 1400
Los Angeles, CA 90017
(800) 884-1684
(213) 439-6799
(213) 439-6715 FAX

Civil rights agency for Calif. Will accept, investigate and conciliate complaints in the areas of employment & housing discrimination. Complaints must be filed within one yr of offense. Does not accept files over one yr. TTY (800) 700-2320. FUNDING: Govt. OFC HRS: M-F 8am-5pm. Spanish spoken. Free srvs. SERVES: Calif.

CALIF RURAL LEGAL ASSISTANCE

Coachella Office
P.O. Box 35
1460 6th Street
Coachella, CA 92236
(760) 398-7261
(760) 398-1050 FAX

Legal srvs to migrant farm workers in the areas of labor and housing. OFC HRS: M-F 9am-5:30pm. Spanish spoken. ADM REQ: Low income, employed in agriculture. Free srvs. SERVES: Riverside, San Bernardino & Imperial Counties.

CALIF STATE ATTORNEY GENERAL

Public Inquiry Unit
P.O. Box 944255
Attn: Public Inquiry Unit
Sacramento, CA 94244-2550
(800) 952-5225
(916) 322-3360
(916) 323-5341 FAX

Responds to written and phone inquiries and complaints concerning violations of the law; info & referrals; assists law enforcement agencies

in the investigation of consumer and business fraud, charity fraud and diversion of funds. FUNDING: Govt. OFC HRS: M-F 8am-5pm. Spanish spoken. SERVES: Calif.

CALIF STATE BAR ASSN

1149 S. Hill St.
Los Angeles, CA 90015-2299
(213) 765-1000
(213) 765-1168 FAX

Maintains professional standards for attorneys and accepts written complaints. FUNDING: Nonprofit. OFC HRS: M-F 8:45am-5pm. SERVES: Calif.

CALIFORNIANS FOR DISABILITY RIGHTS

Chapter #34
5567 Peacock Lane
Riverside, CA 92505
(909) 343-1327

Volunteer advocacy organization with a goal of influencing legislation that impacts the physically disabled, including getting legislation passed to improve lifestyle. Monthly meetings. President: Leslie Robinson. FUNDING: Membership dues, donations. OFC HRS: Vary. SERVES: San Bernardino, Riverside Counties.

CANCER LEGAL RESOURCE CENTER

919 Albany St.
Los Angeles, CA 90015
(866) 843-2572
(213) 736-1455
(213) 736-1428 FAX

Info and edu outreach on cancer-related legal issues to people with cancer, their families, friends, employers and those who provide srvs to them. Includes: cancer in the workplace, insurance coverage, navigating managed care/HMOs, estate planning, govt benefits, and advanced directives. TDD (213) 736-8310. FUNDING: Donations, grants, nonprofit. OFC HRS: M-F 9am-5pm. Free srvs. SERVES: U.S.A.

CASA

See "Court Appointed Special Adv"

CENTER FOR ENFORCEMENT/FAM SUP

Enforcement For Family Support
5855 Green Valley Cir., Ste 315
Culver City, CA 90230
(310) 417-4141
(310) 417-5060 FAX

Assists in collection of past due child and spousal support. Cases accepted for collection of support on a 1/3 contingency basis. Client pays a $35 set-up fee if case is accepted and cost (usually less than $100). OFC HRS: M-F 9am-6pm. SERVES: Calif.

CITIZENS OF INGLEWOOD TENANT ASSN

6824 La Tijera Blvd.
Los Angeles, CA 90045
(310) 677-7294

Housing & legal srvs. Also consumer affairs info. FUNDING: Nonprofit. OFC HRS: M-F 8am-7pm. ADM REQ: Must call for appt. SERVES: Calif.

COALITION TO ABOLISH SLAVERY/ TRAFFICKING (CAST)

5042 Wilshire Blvd., Ste 586
Los Angeles, CA 90036

(213) 365-1906
(213) 365-5257 FAX

Multi-ethnic, multilingual human rights organization dedicated exclusively to serving survivors of trafficking. CAST has become a pioneering leader in the U.S. anti-trafficking movement. Comprehensive social srvs & legal assist is provided to trafficking survivors & promotes policy advocacy at the state & national levels. The shelter prgm has become a model prgm for victim srvs around the country. FUNDING: Nonprofit. OFC HRS: M-F 8:30am-5pm. Korean, Mandarin, Russian, Spanish & Tagalog spoken. SERVES: U.S.A.

COMMUNITY HEALTH RESOURCE CENTER
One-Stop Center/San Bernardino
600 N. Arrowhead Ave., Ste 300
San Bernardino, CA 92401
(909) 888-7881
(909) 889-7833 FAX

Offers phone access to health and wellness info & referral, financial literacy info, legal aid and consumer counseling by the Legal Aid Society of San Bernardino, homeownership resource info. For TDD, call (800) 735-2922. FUNDING: Govt. OFC HRS: M-F 8am-5pm. SERVES: San Bernardino Co.

COUNCIL/SIZE/WEIGHT DISCRIMINATION
P.O. Box 305
Mount Marion, NY 12456
(845) 679-1209
(845) 679-1206 FAX

Advocates for plus-size people and provides edu and info on fairness in employment, medical treatment and media image. FUNDING: Nonprofit. OFC HRS: M-F 9am-5pm. SERVES: U.S.A. & internatl.

COURT APPOINTED SPECIAL ADV
Indio Center
P.O. Box 3008
44-199 Monroe St.
Indio, CA 92202-3008
(760) 863-7539
(760) 863-7431 FAX

Consists of trained community volunteers appointed by the Juvenile Court of Riverside County to act as advocates for dependent, abused or neglected children. Represents the child's needs, provides second point of view during the dependency process. Supportive & positive adult model for the abused or neglected child. The volunteer has weekly contact with the child. Walk in or call to apply. For Spanish, call (760) 863-7424. FUNDING: Nonprofit. OFC HRS: M-F 8:30am-4:30pm. Spanish spoken. Free srvs. SERVES: Riverside County.

COURT APPOINTED SPECIAL ADV
Southwest Justice Center
30755-D Auld Rd., Ste 1226
Murrieta, CA 92563
(951) 304-5220
(951) 304-5210 FAX

Consists of trained community volunteers appointed by the Juvenile Court of Riverside County to act as advocates for dependent, abused or neglected children. Represents the child's needs, provides second point of view during the dependency process. Supportive and positive adult model for the abused or neglected child. The volunteer has weekly contact with the child. Walk in or call to apply. FUND-

ING: Nonprofit. OFC HRS: M-F 8:30am-4:30pm. Spanish spoken. Free srvs. SERVES: Riverside County.

COURT APPOINTED SPECIAL ADV
437 N. Riverside Ave, Ste 10
Rialto, CA 92376
(909) 881-6760
(909) 881-6764 FAX

Recruits, screens and trains community volunteers to act as advocates for dependent, abused or neglected children. Volunteers represent the child's needs, provide a second point of view during the dependency process. Supportive and positive adult model for the abused or neglected child. The volunteer has regular contact with the child. Call to apply. FUNDING: Nonprofit. OFC HRS: M-F 8am-5pm. Spanish spoken. Free srvs. SERVES: San Bernardino County.

COURT APPOINTED SPECIAL ADV
Riverside Office
9991 County Farm Rd.
Riverside, CA 92503
(951) 358-4305
(951) 358-4302 FAX

Consists of trained community volunteers appointed by the Juvenile Court of Riverside County to act as advocates for dependent, abused or neglected children. Represents the child's needs, provides second point of view during the dependency process. Supportive and positive adult model for the abused or neglected child. The volunteer has weekly contact with the child. Walk in or call to apply. For Spanish, call (951) 358-4343. FUNDING: Nonprofit. OFC HRS: M-F 8:30am-4:30pm. Free srvs. SERVES: Riverside County.

COURT APPOINTED SPECIAL ADV/NATL
National CASA Assn
100 W. Harrison St., North Tower, Ste 500
Seattle, WA 98119
(800) 628-3233
(206) 270-0078 FAX

Supports a nationwide network of CASA prgms that train & support community volunteers to act as advocates for dependent, abused or neglected children. Represents the child's needs, provides a second point of view during the dependency process. Supportive and positive adult model for the abused or neglected child. FUNDING: Nonprofit. OFC HRS: M-F 8am-5pm. Spanish spoken. Free srvs. SERVES: U.S.A.

DESERT SANCTUARY/HALEY HOUSE
P.O. Box 1781
703 E. Main St.
Barstow, CA 92312
(760) 256-3441
(760) 256-3733
(760) 256-4002 FAX

16-bed shelter for battered women & their children up to 6 mos. Also outreach for community & area victims in need of srvs not inclusive of shelter. Outreach srvs include: rent/utility assist, anger mgmt, therapy, sexual assault srvs, court-ordered supervised visitation, legal aid, housing stabilization. 24-hr hotline: (800) 982-2221. FUNDING: Nonprofit. OFC HRS: Hotline 24 hrs. Outreach M-F 9am-5pm. German & Spanish spoken. ADM REQ: Women in

abusive surroundings. Free srvs. SERVES: So. Calif.

DEV DISABILITIES AREA BOARD #12
650 E. Hospitality Ln., Ste 280
San Bernardino, CA 92408
(909) 890-1259
(909) 890-1635 FAX

Advocates for people with dev disabilities, conducts public info prgms, encourages the dev of needed srvs and reviews the policies and practices of publicly funded agencies serving people with dev disabilities. FUNDING: Govt. OFC HRS: M-F 8am-5pm. ADM REQ: Must have a dev disability (mental retardation, cerebral palsy, epilepsy, autism). Free srvs. SERVES: Riverside, San Bernardino, Inyo, Mono Counties.

DISABILITY RIGHTS ADVOCATES
2001 Center St., 4th Fl.
Berkeley, CA 94704-1204
(510) 665-8644
(510) 665-8716 FAX

Legal representation & advocacy of people with disabilities whose civil rights have been violated. TTY (510) 665-8716. FUNDING: Nonprofit. OFC HRS: M-F 9am-5:30pm. Spanish spoken. SERVES: U.S.A.

DISABILITY RIGHTS CALIFORNIA
Formerly Protection and Advocacy, Inc.
3580 Wilshire Blvd., Ste 902
Los Angeles, CA 90010-2512
(213) 427-8747
(800) 776-5746
(213) 427-8767 FAX

Legal assist to people with physical, dev & psychiatric disabilities. Srvs include: info & referral to other sources of assist; peer and self-advocacy training; representation in admin and judicial proceedings; investigations of abuse, neglect & legislative advocacy. For TTY/TDD, call (800) 776-5746. FUNDING: Fed, nonprofit. OFC HRS: M-F 9am-5pm. Intake M-F 9am-3pm. Vietnamese, Chinese, Spanish & Korean spoken. ADM REQ: Must go through an intake process. Free srvs. SERVES: So. Calif.

DISABILITY RIGHTS EDU/DEFENSE FUND
3075 Adeline St., Ste 210
Berkeley, CA 94703
(510) 644-2555
(800) 348-4232
(510) 841-8645 FAX

Info, advocacy, training and referral srvs for people with disabilities & parents of children with disabilities on a full range of disability civil rights laws. Wait: 1-2 wks for special edu tech assist. FUNDING: Donations, grants, nonprofit. OFC HRS: M-F 9am-5pm. Spanish, Mandarin & Cantonese spoken. Most srvs are free, copy costs for some info. SERVES: U.S.A. for some trainings & Calif for parent trainings.

DISTRICT ATTORNEY
See "San Bernardino Co. Dist Attorney"

DISTRICT ATTORNEY
See "Riverside Co. Dist Attorney"

DON A. TURNER LAW LIBRARY
See "Law Library for San Bernardino Co."

EQUAL RIGHTS ADVOCATES
180 Howard St., Ste 300
San Francisco, CA 94103
(415) 621-0672

(800) 839-4372
(415) 621-6744 FAX

Advice and counseling line provides legal advice and info on rights, options and remedies in sex discrimination, employment & sexual harassment issues. Focus is to reduce sex discrimination in employment & edu. Welcomes calls from people in Welfare-to-Work job placements with questions or issues about discrimination. FUNDING: Donations, grants, nonprofit. OFC HRS: M-F 9am-5:30pm. Spanish spoken. SERVES: U.S.A.

FAIR HOUSING COUNCIL/RIVERSIDE CO.

East County Office
P.O. Box 1871
655 N. Palm Canyon Dr., Ste 202
Palm Springs, CA 92263
(760) 864-1540
(800) 655-1812
(760) 322-9068 FAX

Accepts discrimination complaints and offers info regarding landlord/tenant issues. Accepts, investigates and mediates disputes. Walk in or call. FUNDING: Nonprofit. OFC HRS: M-F 9am-5pm. Free srvs. SERVES: Riverside County.

FAIR HOUSING COUNCIL/RIVERSIDE CO.

West County Office
3933 Mission Inn Ave.
Riverside, CA 92501
(951) 682-6581
(800) 655-1812
(951) 682-0262 FAX

Accepts discrimination complaints and offers info regarding landlord and tenant issues. Accepts, investigates and mediates disputes. Walk in or call. FUNDING: Nonprofit. OFC HRS: M-F 8am-5pm. Spanish spoken. Free srvs. SERVES: Riverside County.

FEDERAL PUBLIC DEFENDER

3801 University Ave., Ste 150
Riverside, CA 92502
(951) 276-6346
(951) 276-6368 FAX

OFC HRS: M-F 8am-5pm. SERVES: Riverside County.

FONTANA VICTIM SERVICES CENTER

San Bernardino District Attorney
17830 Arrow Blvd.
Fontana, CA 92335
(909) 356-6406

Short-term emerg assist, counseling referrals, special srvs to victims of sexual assault, crime prevention & info. Also srvs for witnesses, child, elderly and domestic violence victims. FUNDING: State. OFC HRS: M-F 8am-5pm. Spanish spoken. SERVES: San Bernardino County.

FOOTHILL FAMILY SHELTER HOMELESS COURT

(909) 608-2865

Assist to homeless or low-income clients who have outstanding San Bernardino misdemeanor tickets, warrants, or high fines. Court held 4th F of each month. FUNDING: Nonprofit. OFC HRS: Tu-F 9am-5pm. Closed 12noon-1pm for lunch. ADM REQ: Must call a month in advance to pre-register. Must have driver's license and citation number if possible, as well as name, DOB, and phone number. SERVES: San Bernardino County.

FOUNDATION FOR MEXICAN AMERICAN SRVS

P.O. Box 702
Moreno Valley, CA 92556
(951) 485-3394
(951) 485-6804 FAX

Represents families at IEP, IFSP, & IPP meetings. Special edu, regional center & fair hearings. In-home supportive srvs. Suspension & expulsion hearings. Parent workshops & training. FUNDING: Nonprofit. OFC HRS: Vary by appt. Spanish spoken. SERVES: So. Calif.

HERMANDAD MEXICANA NACIONAL

Administrative Office
611 W. Civic Center Dr.
Santa Ana, CA 92701
(714) 541-0250
(714) 541-2460 FAX

Serves the immigrant and ethnic minority communities in areas of edu, legal issues, immigration & citizenship. Walk in or call for info. FUNDING: Nonprofit. OFC HRS: M-F 9:30am-6pm; Sat 9am-1pm. Spanish spoken. SERVES: So. Calif.

HERMANDAD MEXICANA NACIONAL

611 W. Civic Center Dr.
Santa Ana, CA 92701
(714) 541-0250

Citizenship and immigration paperwork for a low fee. USDA surplus foods on the 3rd Th of each month. FUNDING: Nonprofit. OFC HRS: M-F 10am-7pm. Spanish spoken. ADM REQ: Must be resident. SERVES: Riverside County.

INLAND COUNTIES LEGAL SRVS/INDIO

82632C U.S. Highway 111
Indio, CA 92201
(800) 226-4257
(760) 342-1591
(760) 342-9400 FAX

ICLS provides legal assist to people in Riverside and San Bernardino Counties who cannot afford a lawyer. Assists low income people in certain areas of civil (non-criminal) law. Consultation & advice, prep of documents, court papers, & representation in court or before administrative hearings in family law, housing and citizenship. FUNDING: Fed, state, county. OFC HRS: M-F 8:30am-5pm. Spanish spoken. Free srvs to eligible low income and needy seniors ages 60 yrs+.

INLAND COUNTIES LEGAL SRVS/R.C.

10601 Civic Center Dr., Ste 260
Rancho Cucamonga, CA 91730
(909) 980-0982
(800) 977-4257
(909) 980-4871 FAX

ICLS provides legal assist to residents of Riverside & San Bernardino Counties who cannot afford a lawyer. Assists low income people in certain areas of civil (non-criminal) law. Provide consultation and advice, prep of documents and court papers, and representation in court or before administrative hearings in the following areas: family law, housing, consumer law, public benefits, and elder law. Consultations and/or appts available in person or by phone. FUNDING: Fed, state, county. OFC HRS: M-F 8:30am-5pm. Spanish spoken. Free srvs to eligible low income and needy seniors ages 60 yrs+. SERVES: Riverside, San Bernardino Counties.

INLAND COUNTIES LEGAL SRVS/RIV

1040 Iowa Ave., Ste 109
Riverside, CA 92507
(951) 368-2555
(888) 245-4257
(951) 368-2550 FAX

ICLS provides legal assist to people in Riverside County who cannot afford a lawyer. Assists low income people in certain areas of civil (non-criminal) law. Consultation and advice, prep of documents and court papers and representation in court or before administrative hearings in family law & housing. FUNDING: Fed, state, county, govt. OFC HRS: M-F 8:30am-5pm. Spanish spoken. ADM REQ: Demonstrate need. Free srvs to eligible low income and needy seniors ages 60 yrs+. SERVES: Riverside County.

INLAND COUNTIES LEGAL SRVS/SAN BRD

715 N. Arrowhead Ave., Ste 113
San Bernardino, CA 92401
(909) 884-8615
(800) 677-4257
(909) 884-8281 FAX

ICLS provides legal assist to people in Riverside and San Bernardino Counties who cannot afford a lawyer. Assists low-income people in certain areas of civil (non-criminal) law. Provide consultation and advice, prep of documents and court papers, and representation in court or before administrative hearings in the following areas: family law, housing and consumer law. Outreach prgm available for seniors ages 60 yrs+. FUNDING: Federal, state, county. OFC HRS: M-F 8:30am-5pm. Spanish spoken. Free srvs to eligible low income and needy seniors ages 60 yrs+. SERVES: Greater San Bernardino area, and Eastern San Bernardino County desert areas & West Valley area.

INLAND COUNTIES LEGAL SRVS/V VLY

14196 Amargosa Rd., Ste K
Victorville, CA 92392
(760) 241-7073
(888) 805-6455

ICLS provides legal assist to people in Riverside and San Bernardino Counties who cannot afford a lawyer. Assists low income people in certain areas of civil (non-criminal) law. Provide consultation and advice, prep of documents and court papers, and representation in court or before administrative hearings in the following areas: family law and housing. FUNDING: Fed, state, county, govt. OFC HRS: M-F 8:30am-5pm. Spanish spoken. Free srvs to eligible low income and needy seniors ages 60 yrs+.

INLAND EMPIRE LATINO LAWYERS ASSOC

Ceasr Chavez Community Center
2060 University Ave., Ste 113
Riverside, CA 92507
(951) 369-3009
(951) 369-6211 FAX

One-on-one consultation with attorneys, prep of court documents. Assists low-income families on such issues as minor custody, divorces, civil summons, restraining orders, etc. FUNDING: United Way, state, donations, nonprofit. OFC HRS: M, Tu, Th, F 10am-5pm. Spanish spoken. Srvs free to low income persons. SERVES: Riverside, San Bernardino Counties.

INLAND FAIR HOUSING & MEDIATION
222 E. Main St., Ste 211
Barstow, CA 92311
(760) 256-7779

Landlord/tenant, fair housing, alternative dispute resolution, outreach, FHA counseling, foreclosure counseling. FUNDING: CDBG. OFC HRS: M-Th 8am-5pm. Spanish spoken. Free srvs. SERVES: San Bernardino Co.

INLAND FAIR HOUSING & MEDIATION
Main Office
10681 Foothill Blvd., Ste 101
Rancho Cucamonga, CA 91730
(909) 984-2254
(909) 460-0274 FAX

Landlord/tenant, fair housing, senior srvs, foreclosure counseling, alternative dispute resolution, outreach. FUNDING: CDBG. OFC HRS: M-Th 8am-5pm. Spanish spoken. Free srvs. SERVES: San Bernardino Co.

INLAND FAIR HOUSING & MEDIATION
560 N. Arrowhead Ave., Ste 7A
San Bernardino, CA 92401
(909) 888-3763
(909) 889-5034 FAX

Fair housing, housing mediation, senior srv, FHA default & foreclosure counseling. Walk in or call. FUNDING: CDBG. OFC HRS: M-Th 8am-5pm. Spanish spoken. Free srvs. SERVES: San Bernardino County.

INLAND FAIR HOUSING & MEDIATION
14201 Kentwood Blvd., Ste 3
Victorville, CA 92392
(760) 243-2412
(760) 243-3312 FAX

Fair housing and landlord/tenant mediation. FUNDING: CDBG. OFC HRS: M-Th 8am-5pm. Spanish spoken. SERVES: Victorville.

JUVENILE JUSTICE CLEARINGHOUSE
Natl Criminal Justice Reference Srvs
P.O. Box 6000
Rockville, MD 20849-6000
(800) 851-3420
(301) 519-5212 FAX

A link between the Office of Juvenile Justice and Delinquency Prev (OJJDP) and the community at-large interested in juvenile justice, delinquency prev and missing and exploited children. The clearinghouse offers publications, references and referrals through an 800 number, conference support and attendance, online resources and other outreach activities. TDD (877) 712-9279 or (301) 712-9279. FUNDING: Govt. SERVES: U.S.A. & internatl.

LAW LIBRARY FOR SAN BERNARDINO CO.
Rancho Cucamonga Branch
8401 N. Haven Ave.
Rancho Cucamonga, CA 91730
(909) 944-5106

Materials for library use only; librarian cannot interpret, define or discuss the law with patrons. FUNDING: Nonprofit. HRS: M-F 8:30am-1:15pm, 2pm-5pm. SERVES: Rancho Cucamonga.

LAW LIBRARY FOR SAN BERNARDINO CO.
San Bernardino Branch
402 North D Street
San Bernardino, CA 92401
(909) 885-3020
(909) 885-1869 FAX

Research library, reference only. Govt depository with Calif state law, taxation law, regional reporters, federal law and aw review collections. HRS: M-Th 8:30am-7pm; F 8:30am-5pm; Sat 9am-3pm. Spanish spoken. SERVES: San Bernardino County.

LAW OFFICES OF THE PUBLIC DEFENDER
Juvenile Division
9991 County Farm Rd., Rm. 118
Riverside, CA 92503
(951) 358-4134
(951) 358-4287 FAX

OFC HRS: M-F 8am-5pm. SERVES: Riverside County.

LAWYER REFERRAL SERVICE
See "San Bernardino Co. Bar Assn"

LAWYER REFERRAL SERVICE
Western San Bernardino Co. Bar Assn
10630 Town Center Dr., Ste 119
Rancho Cucamonga, CA 91730
(909) 483-0548
(909) 483-0553 FAX

Referrals to local attorneys on a variety of legal matters. Low-cost initial consultation fee of $35 with fee waived on workers' compensation, bankruptcy and personal injury cases. FUNDING: Nonprofit. OFC HRS: M-F 9am-5pm. Spanish spoken. SERVES: Rancho Cucamonga, Upland, Ontario, Fontana, Montclair, Pomona, Bloomington, Claremont, Rialto.

LEGAL PROTECTION FOR WOMEN
5300 E. Beverly Blvd., Ste D
Los Angeles, CA 90022
(323) 721-9882
(323) 721-7731 FAX

Paralegal srvs, including prep of family law forms for divorce, legal separation, nullity, TRO, civil harassment order, modification of child custody, support of visitation, alimony, name change, wage assignment for unpaid support, paternity and step-parent adoption. FUNDING: Nonprofit. OFC HRS: Tu-F 9am-5pm; Sat 10am-2pm, by appt only. Spanish spoken. Sliding fee scale, $20-$550 depending on action. SERVES: Calif.

MCGEORGE SCHOOL OF LAW
See "Natl Criminal Justice Reference"

MEDIATION RESOURCES
Successor to Claremont Dispute Res Ctr
415 W. Foothill Blvd.
Claremont, CA 91711
(909) 621-0092
(909) 621-0096 FAX

Mediation concerning divorce, consumer/merchant, neighbor/neighbor, employer/employee, auto accident, business, landlord/tenant, and others. Arbitration is available, call for fee rate. FUNDING: Nonprofit. OFC HRS: M-F 9am-5pm. Spanish spoken. Low fee for srvs. Free info & referral. SERVES: So. Calif.

MEXICAN AMER LEGAL DEFENSE & EDU
634 S. Spring St., 11th Fl.
Los Angeles, CA 90014
(213) 629-2512
(213) 629-0266 FAX

Advocates for civil rights of Latinos in U.S.A. Litigation, advocacy, community outreach & edu to secure the rights of all Latinos in employment, edu, immigration, political access and

public resource equity. Offers major scholarships to students pursuing graduate degrees in law. FUNDING: Nonprofit. OFC HRS: M-F 8am-5pm. Spanish spoken. SERVES: U.S.A.

NATL ASSN/ADVANCE/COLORED PEOPLE
NAACP/San Bernardino Branch
1505 W. Highland Ave., Ste 11
San Bernardino, CA 92411
(909) 887-7411
(909) 945-9660 FAX

Free info, and perhaps legal assist. Walk in or call for appt. FUNDING: Members, nonprofit. OFC HRS: M-F 9am-5pm. ADM REQ: Belief in equal rights for all. SERVES: San Bernardino, Highland & Redlands area.

NATL CENTER FOR VICTIMS OF CRIME
2000 M Street, NW, Ste 480
Washington, DC 20036
(800) 394-2255
(202) 467-8700
(202) 467-8701 FAX

A nationwide helpline offering info and referral for victims of crime. Assist with accessing victim compensation, developing personalized safety plans, legal referrals, and accessing social srvs. TTY (800) 211-7996. FUNDING: Nonprofit. OFC HRS: M-F 10am-6pm, EST. Hotline: M-F 8:30am-8:30pm, EST. Serves victims in any language through the language line. Spanish, French, & Japanese speakers on staff. Free srvs. SERVES: U.S.A.

NATL CRIMINAL JUSTICE REFERENCE
P.O. Box 6000
Rockville, MD 20849-6000
(800) 851-3420
(301) 519-5212 FAX

Six basic functions of this srv: (1) National Victims Resource Center Library, database srv and free publications; (2) Juvenile Justice Clearinghouse. Info on gang prevention and intervention. Printed material explains the Juvenile Justice System; (3) Bureau of Justice Assist (grants, training & tech assist, etc.); (4) Bureau of Justice Statistics (criminal statistics nationwide); (5) National Institute of Justice (research on criminal behavior); and (6) Office of National Drug Control Policy. Additional Info and ordering online at (www.ncjrs.gov). TDD (877) 712-9279. FUNDING: Govt. OFC HRS: M-F 10am-6pm, EST. Free publications, though shipping and handling applies. Rates found online. SERVES: U.S.A.

NATL HEALTH LAW PRGM
2639 S. La Cienega Blvd.
Los Angeles, CA 90034-2675
(310) 204-6010
(310) 204-0891 FAX

Legal info, training and tech assist to advocates for low income persons on matters of access to health care. No direct srvs. Prgm for lawyers & advocates of the poor. OFC HRS: M-F 9am-5pm. SERVES: U.S.A.

NATL LEGAL STUDIES INSTITUTE & LEGAL CTR
13800 Heacock, Ste D141
Moreno Valley, CA 92553
(951) 653-4240
(951) 653-4245 FAX

Low-cost prep of legal documents. Workshops, seminars, attorney referrals. Does not give legal advice. FUNDING: Private nonprofit, donations. OFC HRS: M-F 9am-5pm; Sat 10am-1pm. Spanish spoken. SERVES: Inland Empire.

NATL ORGANIZATION/VICTIM ASSISTANCE (NOVA)
510 King St., Ste 424
Alexandria, VA 22314
(800) 879-6682
(703) 535-6682
(703) 535-5500 FAX

Crisis counseling, advocacy, and referral srvs to crime victims and their families. Also crisis response team. Refers victims & survivors to nearby srvs. FUNDING: Nonprofit. OFC HRS: M-F 9am-6pm, EST. SERVES: U.S.A.

NATL SENIOR CITIZENS LAW CENTER
1444 I Street, NW, Ste 1100
Washington, DC 20005
(202) 289-6976
(202) 289-7224 FAX

Support center advocates through litigation, legislative and agency representation. Assists attorneys and paralegals in field prgm. FUNDING: Nonprofit. SERVES: U.S.A.

POLICE WATCH
Police Misconduct Lawyer Referral Srvs
611 S. Catalina St., Ste 409
Los Angeles, CA 90005
(213) 387-3325
(213) 387-9085 FAX

Civil rights advocates against police misconduct. Offers consultation & assist to anyone in filing claims for damages or citizens' complaints of misconduct against a law enforcement officer. Panel of attorneys takes referrals on a contingency basis. FUNDING: Nonprofit. OFC HRS: M-F 1pm-9pm. Some Spanish spoken. SERVES: So. Calif.

PUBLIC DEFENDER
See "Riverside Co. Public Defender"

PUBLIC DEFENDER
See "San Bernardino Co. Public Defndr"

RIVERSIDE CO. BAR ASSOCIATION
Public Service Law Corporation
4129 Main St., Ste 100
Riverside, CA 92501
(951) 682-1015
(951) 682-0106 FAX

Free legal srvs to low income clients. Srvs provided by private lawyers who donate their time. Assist provided in certain areas of civil law (criminal cases or fee-generating cases are not accepted). Srvs primarily in family law, guardianship, landlord and tenant, housing, consumer, general civil. FUNDING: LSC (federal), state bar, donations, nonprofit. OFC HRS: M-F 8:30am-5pm. Some attorneys speak different languages. SERVES: Riverside County.

RIVERSIDE CO. BAR ASSOCIATION
Lawyer Referral Service
4129 Main St., Ste 100
Riverside, CA 92501
(951) 682-7520
(760) 568-5555
(951) 682-0106 FAX

Refers callers to lawyers specializing in different areas of law including administrative law, criminal law, employment law, and family law. FUNDING: Nonprofit, donations. OFC HRS: M-F 8:30am-12noon, 1pm-4:30pm. Spanish

spoken. Private pay accepted for referral fee. SERVES: Riverside Co.

RIVERSIDE CO. CHILD SUPPORT SRVS
260 N. Broadway
Blythe, CA 92225
(866) 901-3212
(760) 921-5608 FAX

Establishes child and medical support orders, paternity orders, locates parents, enforces support orders. Walk-ins welcome. Send payments to P.O. Box 989067 West Sacramento, CA 95798. FUNDING: Federal, county. OFC HRS: M-F 7:30am-5pm. ADM REQ: application for srvs Free srvs. SERVES: Riverside County.

RIVERSIDE CO. CHILD SUPPORT SRVS
47-950 Arabia St.
Indio, CA 92201
(866) 901-3212
(760) 863-7016 FAX

Establishes child and medical support orders, paternity orders, locates parents, enforces support orders. Walk in. For payment inquiries, call (866) 901-3212. FUNDING: Federal, county. OFC HRS: M-F 7:30am-5pm. Spanish spoken. ADM REQ: Application for srvs. Free srvs. SERVES: Riverside County.

RIVERSIDE CO. CHILD SUPPORT SRVS
2041 Iowa Ave.
Riverside, CA 92507
(866) 901-3212
(951) 955-4224 FAX

Establishes and/or enforces child and medical support orders, paternity orders, locates non-custodial parents. For payment inquiries, call (866) 901-3212. FUNDING: Federal, county. OFC HRS: M-F 7:30am-5pm. Spanish spoken. ADM REQ: Application for srvs. Free srvs. SERVES: Riverside County.

RIVERSIDE CO. CHILD SUPPORT SRVS
1370 S. State St., Ste A
San Jacinto, CA 92583
(866) 901-3212
(951) 791-2054 FAX

Establishes child and medical support orders, paternity orders, locates parents, enforces support orders. Walk in or call. For payment inquiries, call (866)901-3212. FUNDING: Federal, county. OFC HRS: M-F 7:30am-5:30pm. Spanish spoken. ADM REQ: Application for srvs. Free srvs. SERVES: Riverside County.

RIVERSIDE CO. DIST ATTORNEY
Criminal Division
135 N. Alessandro, Rm. 210
Banning, CA 92220
(951) 922-7130
(951) 922-7135 FAX

OFC HRS: M-F 8am-5pm. SERVES: Riverside County.

RIVERSIDE CO. DIST ATTORNEY
82-675 Hwy. 111, 4th Fl.
Indio, CA 92201
(760) 863-8216
(760) 863-8215 FAX

Works with every component of the criminal justice system and the entire community to protect the innocent, to convict and appropriately punish the guilty and protect the rights of victims. OFC HRS M-F 8am-5pm. Spanish spoken. SERVES: Eastern Riverside County.

RIVERSIDE CO. DIST ATTORNEY
Main Office
3960 Orange St.
Riverside, CA 92501
(951) 955-5400
(951) 955-5518 FAX

OFC HRS: M-F 8am-5pm. SERVES: Riverside County.

RIVERSIDE CO. DIST ATTORNEY
Juvenile Court
9991 County Farm Rd.
Riverside, CA 92503
(951) 358-4140
(951) 358-4497 FAX

OFC HRS: M-F 8am-5pm. Spanish spoken. SERVES: Riverside County.

RIVERSIDE CO. LAW LIBRARY
Desert Branch
46-200 Oasis St.
Indio, CA 92201-5933
(760) 863-8316
(760) 342-2581 FAX

Reference assist, inter-library loans, computers, conference rooms, photocopy machines. Walk in. FUNDING: Civil court fees, nonprofit. HRS: M-F 8am-5pm. Fax $10 plus $.50 a page, copies $.15 a page. SERVES: Indio.

RIVERSIDE CO. LAW LIBRARY
Victor Miceli Law Library
3989 Lemon St.
Riverside, CA 92501-4203
(951) 955-6390
(951) 955-6394 FAX

Reference assist, inter-library loans, photocopy machines. Walk in. FUNDING: Civil court fees, nonprofit. HRS: M-Th 8am-7pm; F 8am-5pm; Sat 9am-1pm. Fax $10 plus $.50 per page. Photocopies $.25 per page. SERVES: Riverside County.

RIVERSIDE CO. PUBLIC DEFENDER
155 E. Hayes St., Ste 203
Banning, CA 92220-5506
(951) 922-7230
(951) 922-7235 FAX

Attorneys to assist in the defense of persons accused of a crime who are financially unable to provide their own attorney. Public defenders are appointed by a court judge. OFC HRS: M-F 8am-5pm.

RIVERSIDE CO. PUBLIC DEFENDER
230 N. Broadway Ave.
Blythe, CA 92225
(760) 921-7800
(760) 921-7805 FAX

Attorneys to assist in the defense of persons accused of a crime and are financially unable to provide their own attorney. Public defenders are appointed by a court judge. OFC HRS: M-F 8am-5pm. SERVES: Blythe area.

RIVERSIDE CO. PUBLIC DEFENDER
82-675 Highway 11, Rm. 314
Indio, CA 92201
(760) 863-8231
(760) 863-8908 FAX

Attorneys to assist in the defense of persons accused of a crime who are financially unable to provide their own attorney. Public defenders are appointed by a court judge. OFC HRS: M-F 8am-5pm. SERVES: Eastern Riverside County.

RIVERSIDE CO. PUBLIC DEFENDER
Southwest Justice Center
30755 Auld Rd., Ste 2233
Murrieta, CA 92563-2506
(951) 303-5600
(951) 304-5605 FAX

Attorneys to assist in the defense of persons accused of a crime who are financially unable to provide their own attorney. Public defenders are appointed by a court judge. OFC HRS: M-F 8am-5pm. SERVES: Southwest Riverside County.

RIVERSIDE CO. PUBLIC DEFENDER
4200 Orange St.
Riverside, CA 92501
(951) 955-6000
(951) 955-6025 FAX

Assists all indigents charged with criminal offenses who need an attorney, but cannot afford one. Represents persons subject to Child Protective Srvs investigation or probate conservatorship. Public defenders are appointed by a court judge. OFC HRS: M-F 8am-5pm. SERVES: Central Riverside County.

RIVERSIDE CO. PUBLIC GUARDIAN
Public Guardian & Public Conservators
P.O. Box 1405
3190 Chicago
Riverside, CA 92501
(951) 341-6440
(951) 341-6403 FAX

Public guardians, when appointed by the court, act as a guardian for persons legally incapable of administering their affairs and assets. Conservators investigate referrals for probate & LPS. FUNDING: Govt. OFC HRS: M-F 8am-5pm. Spanish spoken. ADM REQ: Must meet legal requirements. SERVES: Riverside County.

RIVERSIDE CO. SUPERIOR COURT
Banning Court
135 N. Alessandro Rd.
Banning, CA 92220
(951) 922-7145
(951) 922-7160 FAX

Civil & small claims courts, criminal division call number above. Traffic division (951) 922-7140. FUNDING: Govt. OFC HRS: M-F 7:30am-4pm. Spanish spoken. SERVES: Riverside County.

RIVERSIDE CO. SUPERIOR COURT
265 N. Broadway
Blythe, CA 92225
(760) 921-7981
(760) 921-7941 FAX

Civil matters. Criminal division (760) 921-7828. FUNDING: Govt. OFC HRS: M-F 7:30am-4pm. Spanish spoken. SERVES: Riverside County.

RIVERSIDE CO. SUPERIOR COURT
Hemet Court
880 N. State St.
Hemet, CA 92543
(951) 766-2321
(951) 766-2317 FAX

Civil & small claims courts. Family law (951) 766-2525. FUNDING: Govt. OFC HRS: M-F 7:30am-4pm. Spanish spoken. SERVES: Riverside County.

RIVERSIDE CO. SUPERIOR COURT
Larson Justice Center
46-200 Oasis St.

Indio, CA 92201
(760) 863-8208
(760) 863-7965 FAX

Civil matters. Criminal division (760) 863-8206. Family law (760) 863-8209. Juvenile division (760) 863-8992. Traffic division (760) 775-0300. FUNDING: Govt. OFC HRS: M-F 7:30am-4pm. Spanish spoken. SERVES: Riverside County.

RIVERSIDE CO. SUPERIOR COURT
Southwest Justice Center
30755-D Auld Rd., Ste 1226
Murrieta, CA 92563
(951) 304-5000

Criminal, family law, & juvenile divisions. FUNDING: Govt. OFC HRS: M-F 7:30am-4pm. Spanish spoken. SERVES: Riverside County.

RIVERSIDE CO. SUPERIOR COURT
Juvenile Court
9991 County Farm Rd.
Riverside, CA 92503
(951) 358-4137
(951) 358-4124 FAX

FUNDING: Govt. OFC HRS: M-F 8am-4pm. Spanish spoken. SERVES: Western Riverside County. All other juvenile matters heard at the Indio Branch.

RIVERSIDE CO. SUPERIOR COURT
Riverside Historical Court
P.O. Box 431
4100 Main St.
Riverside, CA 92501
(951) 955-4600

FUNDING: Govt. OFC HRS: M-F 7:30am-4pm. Spanish spoken. SERVES: Riverside County.

RIVERSIDE CO. SUPERIOR COURT
Hall of Justice/Criminal Division
P.O. Box 431
4100 Main St.
Riverside, CA 92501
(951) 955-4600

Traffic division (951) 341-3876. FUNDING: Govt. OFC HRS: M-F 7:30am-4pm. Spanish spoken. SERVES: Riverside County.

RIVERSIDE CO. SUPERIOR COURT
41002 County Center Dr., Ste 100
Temecula, CA 92591
(951) 600-6400

Civil, small claims, and traffic. FUNDING: Govt. OFC HRS: M-F 7:30am-4pm. Spanish spoken.

RIVERSIDE SUPERIOR COURT
Family Law Assistance Center
4175 Main St.
Riverside, CA 92501
(951) 955-4600

Legal counseling on family law, workshops on form prep for divorce, child support, custody, property & potential domestic violence. OFC HRS: M-F 7:30am-4pm Spanish spoken SERVES: Calif.

SAN BERNARDINO CO. BAR ASSN
Lawyer Referral Service
555 N. Arrowhead Ave.
San Bernardino, CA 92401
(909) 885-1986
(909) 889-0400 FAX

Professional assn for attorneys. If you need a lawyer and do not know one, the number listed above is the best overall referral source for San

Bernardino County. Edu pamphlets, speaker's bureau, client relations activities, and a wide range of special prgms. FUNDING: Membership dues. OFC HRS: M-Th 9am-4pm; F 9am-12noon. Spanish spoken. ADM REQ: Call first. Fee $35. SERVES: San Bernardino County.

SAN BERNARDINO CO. BEHAV HEALTH
Patient's Rights Office
850 E. Foothill Blvd.
Rialto, CA 92376
(800) 440-2391

This office protects the patient, consumer and human rights of all recipients of psychiatric srvs. Consultation and training are available to providers of psychiatric srvs. Advocates investigate complaints concerning behavioral health srvs, monitor mental health facilities, provide training and edu regarding mental health law, and ensure that recipients of mental health srvs are notified of their rights. FUNDING: Govt. OFC HRS: M-F 8am-5pm. Spanish SERVES: San Bernardino County.

SAN BERNARDINO CO. CHILD SUPPORT
Dept of Child Support Services
10417 Mountain View Ave.
Loma Linda, CA 92354
(866) 901-3212
(909) 478-6922 FAX

24-hr info on child support srvs. Represents the interest of the minor children by: (1) determining who the parents are; (2) locating a child's parents for the purpose of establishing child support and/or paternity; (3) establishing and enforcing a child support order; (4) collecting child and spousal support payments. FUNDING: County, state, federal. OFC HRS: M-F 8am-5pm. Spanish spoken. ADM REQ: Demonstrates need for child support srvs. Free srvs. SERVES: San Bernardino County.

SAN BERNARDINO CO. CHILD SUPPORT
Desert Region
15400 Civic Dr.
Victorville, CA 92392
(866) 901-3212
(909) 478-6922 FAX

Establishes paternity & court-ordered child support. Collects child, medical & spousal support payments, also modifies orders. FUNDING: Govt. OFC HRS: M-F 8am-5pm. Spanish spoken. SERVES: San Bernardino County.

SAN BERNARDINO CO. DIST ATTORNEY
Barstow Branch Office
235 E. Mountain View Ave.
Baker, CA 92309
(760) 256-4810
(760) 256-4869 FAX

Represents the citizens of the county in the prosecution of all criminal matters. Walk in or call. OFC HRS: M-F 8am-5pm. Spanish spoken. SERVES: San Bernardino County.

SAN BERNARDINO CO. DIST ATTORNEY
Chino Division Office
13260 Central Ave.
Chino, CA 91710
(909) 465-5255
(909) 465-5253 FAX

OFC HRS: M-F 8am-5pm.

SAN BERNARDINO CO. DIST ATTORNEY
Fontana Office

17830 Arrow Blvd.
Fontana, CA 92335
(909) 355-5935
(909) 356-6779 FAX

Represents the citizens of the county in the prosecution of criminal matters. Also victim-witness srvs. Walk in or call. OFC HRS: M-F 8am-5pm. Spanish spoken. Free srvs. SERVES: Fontana, Rialto, Bloomington, Lytle Creek.

SAN BERNARDINO CO. DIST ATTORNEY
Child Support Division
10417 Mountain View Ave.
Loma Linda, CA 92354
(866) 901-3212
(909) 478-7475 FAX

OFC HRS: M-F 8am-5pm. Spanish spoken. SERVES: San Bernardino County.

SAN BERNARDINO CO. DIST ATTORNEY
Rancho Cucamonga Division Office
8303 N. Haven Ave., 4th Fl.
Rancho Cucamonga, CA 91730
(909) 989-0056
(909) 945-4035 FAX

Represents the citizens of the county in the prosecution of criminal matters. Walk in or call. OFC HRS: M-F 8am-5pm. Spanish spoken. Free srvs. SERVES: San Bernardino County.

SAN BERNARDINO CO. DIST ATTORNEY
316 N. Mountain View Ave.
San Bernardino, CA 92415-0004
(909) 387-8309
(909) 387-6313 FAX

Represents the citizens of the county in the prosecution of criminal and family support matters. Refer to separate listings for Victim-Witness Assist Prgm which provides counseling and assist for victims and witnesses of crimes. Walk in or call. OFC HRS: M-F 8am-5pm. Spanish spoken. Free srvs. SERVES: San Bernardino County.

SAN BERNARDINO CO. DIST ATTORNEY
Victorville Office
14455 Civic Dr.
Victorville, CA 92392
(760) 243-8600
(760) 243-8767 FAX

Represents the citizens of the county in the prosecution of criminal matters. Walk in or call. OFC HRS: M-F 8am-5pm. Spanish spoken. Free srvs. SERVES: San Bernardino County.

SAN BERNARDINO CO. LAW LIBRARY
See "Law Library for San Bernardino Co."

SAN BERNARDINO CO. PUBLIC ADMIN
175 S. Lena Rd.
San Bernardino, CA 92415
(909) 387-2481
(909) 387-2335 FAX

Administers estates of persons who died in San Bernardino Co. where no executor or administrator was appointed. OFC HRS: M-F 8am-5pm. SERVES: San Bernardino County.

SAN BERNARDINO CO. PUBLIC DEFNDR
Branch Office
235 E. Mountain View Ave.
Barstow, CA 92311
(760) 256-4722
(760) 256-4825 FAX

Attorneys assist in the defense of persons accused of a crime who are financially unable to provide their own attorney. Public defenders are appointed by a court judge. OFC HRS: M-F 8am-5pm.

SAN BERNARDINO CO. PUBLIC DEFNDR
Branch Office
13260 Central Ave.
Chino, CA 91710
(909) 465-5212
(909) 465-5338 FAX

Attorneys assist in the defense of persons accused of a crime who are financially unable to provide their own attorney. Public defenders are appointed by a court judge. OFC HRS: M-F 8am-5pm. Spanish spoken. SERVES: Chino & Chino Hills.

SAN BERNARDINO CO. PUBLIC DEFNDR
Branch Office
17830 Arrow Blvd.
Fontana, CA 92335
(909) 356-6420
(909) 356-6419 FAX

Attorneys to assist in the defense of persons accused of a crime who are financially unable to provide their own attorney. Public Defenders are appointed by a court judge. OFC HRS: M-F 8am-5pm. Spanish spoken.

SAN BERNARDINO CO. PUBLIC DEFNDR
Branch Office
6527 White Feather Rd.
Joshua Tree, CA 92252
(760) 366-5789
(760) 366-4135 FAX

Attorneys assist in the defense of persons accused of a crime who are financially unable to provide their own attorney. Public defenders are appointed by a court judge. OFC HRS: M-F 8am-5pm.

SAN BERNARDINO CO. PUBLIC DEFNDR
Branch Office
1111 Bailey Ave.
Needles, CA 92363
(760) 326-9242
(760) 326-9318 FAX

Attorneys assist in the defense of persons accused of a crime who are financially unable to provide their own attorney. Public defenders are appointed by a court judge. OFC HRS: M-F 8am-5pm.

SAN BERNARDINO CO. PUBLIC DEFNDR
Branch Office
8303 N. Haven Ave.
Rancho Cucamonga, CA 91730
(909) 948-4669
(909) 945-4295 FAX

Attorneys assist in the defense of persons accused of a crime who are financially unable to provide their own attorney. Public defenders are appointed by a court judge. OFC HRS: M-F 8am-5pm.

SAN BERNARDINO CO. PUBLIC DEFNDR
Central Office
364 N. Mountain View Ave.
San Bernardino, CA 92415-0005
(909) 387-8373
(909) 387-4414 FAX

Attorneys assist in the defense of persons accused of a crime who are financially unable to provide their own attorney. Public defenders

are appointed by a court judge. OFC HRS: M-F 8am-5pm.

SAN BERNARDINO CO. PUBLIC DEFNDR
Branch Office
14455 Civic Drive, Ste 600
Victorville, CA 92392
(760) 241-0413
(760) 243-8766 FAX

Attorneys assist in the defense of persons accused of a crime who are financially unable to provide their own attorney. Public defenders are appointed by a court judge. OFC HRS: M-F 8am-5pm. Spanish spoken.

SAN BERNARDINO CO. PUBLIC DEFNDR
Juevenile Branch Office
14344 Cajon St., Ste 203
Victorville, CA 92392
(760) 261-5322
(760) 245-5114 FAX

Attorneys assist in the defense of persons accused of a crime who are financially unable to provide their own attorney. Public defenders are appointed by a court judge. OFC HRS: M-F 8am-5pm.

SAN BERNARDINO CO. SUPERIOR CRT
Barstow Division Office
235 E. Mountain View Ave.
Barstow, CA 92311
(760) 256-4758
(760) 256-4711 FAX

Municipal court handles traffic offenses, felony preliminary hearings, misdemeanor cases, small claims, and civil cases. Civil/small claims, (760) 256-4817. FUNDING: Govt. OFC HRS: M-F 7:30am-4pm. Spanish spoken. SERVES: San Bernardino County.

SAN BERNARDINO CO. SUPERIOR CRT
Big Bear Courthouse
P.O. Box 2806
477 Summit Blvd.
Big Bear Lake, CA 92315
(909) 866-0150
(909) 866-0160 FAX

Traffic matters. FUNDING: Govt. OFC HRS: M-F 8am-4pm. SERVES: Big Bear.

SAN BERNARDINO CO. SUPERIOR CRT
Chino Division
13260 Central Ave.
Chino, CA 91710
(909) 356-5337
(909) 465-5221 FAX

Handles traffic offenses, felony preliminary hearings, misdemeanor cases, small claims, and civil unlawful detainer cases. FUNDING: Govt. OFC HRS: M-F 8am-4pm. Spanish spoken. SERVES: San Bernardino County.

SAN BERNARDINO CO. SUPERIOR CRT
Mental Health Counselors
400 N. Pepper Ave.
Colton, CA 92324
(909) 580-1812
(909) 580-2165 FAX

70-bed psychiatric hospital. Screening eval & consultations for involuntary psychiatric hospitalization. Edu presentation to promote community awareness of mental health laws and resources. FUNDING: Govt. OFC HRS: 24 hrs. Spanish spoken. SERVES: San Bernardino County.

SAN BERNARDINO CO. SUPERIOR CRT
Fontana District
17780 Arrow Blvd.
Fontana, CA 92335
(909) 350-9322
(909) 829-4149 FAX

Handles traffic, felony preliminary hearings, misdemeanor cases, small claims and unlawful detainer cases up to $25,000. FUNDING: Govt. OFC HRS: M-F 7:30am-4pm. Spanish spoken. SERVES: San Bernardino County.

SAN BERNARDINO CO. SUPERIOR CRT
Division Office
6527 White Feather Rd.
Joshua Tree, CA 92252
(760) 366-5770
(760) 366-5770
(760) 366-4156 FAX

Handles traffic and parking offenses, felony preliminary hearings, misdemeanor cases, small claims, and civil cases up to $25,000. Traffic (760) 366-5775. FUNDING: Govt. OFC HRS: M-F 7:30am-4pm. SERVES: San Bernardino County.

SAN BERNARDINO CO. SUPERIOR CRT
1111 Bailey Ave.
Needles, CA 92363
(760) 326-9245
(760) 326-9254 FAX

Traffic matters. FUNDING: Govt. OFC HRS: M-F 8am-4pm. SERVES: San Bernardino County.

SAN BERNARDINO CO. SUPERIOR CRT
Juvenile Traffic Division
8303 Haven Ave.
Rancho Cucamonga, CA 91730
(909) 285-3558
(909) 285-3529 FAX

FUNDING: Govt. OFC HRS: M-F 8am-4pm. Spanish spoken. SERVES: San Bernardino County.

SAN BERNARDINO CO. SUPERIOR CRT
Family Law Filings
351 N. Arrowhead Ave., 1st Fl.
San Bernardino, CA 92415-0210
(909) 387-3922
(909) 387-4428 FAX

FUNDING: Govt. OFC HRS: M-F 8am-4pm. Spanish spoken. SERVES: Majority of San Bernardino County (contact office for exact service area).

SAN BERNARDINO CO. SUPERIOR CRT
Court Investigator
351 N. Arrowhead Ave., Rm. 200
San Bernardino, CA 92415-0240
(909) 384-1888

FUNDING: Govt. OFC HRS: M-F 8am-5pm. SERVES: San Bernardino County.

SAN BERNARDINO CO. SUPERIOR CRT
Administrative Office
351 N. Arrowhead Ave., 2nd Fl.
San Bernardino, CA 92415
(909) 387-0207

Handles traffic and parking offenses, felony preliminary hearings, misdemeanor cases, small claims and civil cases up to $25,000. Call (909) 387-3922 for small claims & civil cases. FUNDING: Govt. OFC HRS: M-F 7:30am-4pm. Spanish spoken. SERVES: San Bernardino County.

SAN BERNARDINO CO. SUPERIOR CRT
Victorville District
14455 Civic Dr., Ste 100 & 200
Victorville, CA 92392
(760) 245-6215
(760) 243-8790 FAX

Handles traffic offenses, felony preliminary hearings, misdemeanor cases, small claims, civil cases, family law, child support, probate. FUNDING: Govt. OFC HRS: M-F 8am-4pm. Spanish interpreters for court hearings. SERVES: Victor Valley area.

SEXUAL ASSAULT SRVS/YUCAIPA
Yucaipa Outreach/Domestic Viol Prgm
34282 Yucaipa Blvd.
Yucaipa, CA 92399
(909) 790-9374
(909) 790-3111 FAX

Srvs to survivors of domestic violence. Individual & group counseling, community edu, referrals, court accompaniment & 24-hr hotline (800) 656-4673. FUNDING: Members, donations, nonprofit. OFC HRS: M-F 8am-5pm. Spanish spoken. Free srvs. SERVES: Inland Empire.

SMALL CLAIMS ADVISORY PRGM
13800 Heacock St., Bldg. D
Moreno Valley, CA 92553
(951) 683-3700
(951) 683-1749 FAX

Visit websites (www.courts.co.riverside.ca.us/kiosk) also (www.courtinfo.ca.gov). Attempts to return all small claim litigants. You may fax or e-mail small claims questions. OFC HRS: M-F 8:30am-5pm. Spanish spoken. SERVES: Riverside County.

SOUTH ASIAN HELPLINE & REFERRAL AGENCY (SAHARA)
17100 S. Pioneer Blvd., Ste 260
Artesia, CA 90701
(562) 402-4132
(562) 402-6093 FAX

Serves the South Asian community by providing them with info, referrals, skills dev and other culturally sensitive support srvs including mental health, health care, legal assist, transitional living ctrs, client advocacy, case mgmt, financial assist, job training and placement, community edu prgms, and senior srvs. FUNDING: Nonprofit. OFC HRS: M-F 8am-5pm. Hindi, Gujarati, Bengali, Urdu, Nepali, Tamil & Telugu spoken. Free srvs. SERVES: Southern California.

U.S. ATTORNEY'S OFFICE
U.S. Courthouse/Criminal Division
312 N. Spring St., Ste 1200
Los Angeles, CA 90012
(213) 894-2434
(213) 894-0141 FAX

Prosecutes federal offenses and represents U.S. govt. OFC HRS: M-F 8:30am-5pm. SERVES: L.A., Orange, Ventura, Riverside, San Bernardino, Santa Barbara & San Luis Obispo Counties.

U.S. ATTORNEY'S OFFICE
U.S. Courthouse/Branch Office
411 W. 4th Street, Ste 8000
Santa Ana, CA 92701
(714) 338-3500
(714) 338-3523 FAX

OFC HRS: M-F 8:30am-5pm. SERVES: Orange & Riverside Counties.

U.S. BANKRUPTCY COURT
3420 12th Street, Ste 125
Riverside, CA 92501-3819
(951) 774-1000

OFC HRS: M-F 9am-4pm. SERVES: San Bernardino & Riverside Counties.

UNITED LAW CENTERS/WOMENS LAW CTR
950 W. 17th Street, Ste D
Santa Ana, CA 92706-3573
(714) 667-1038
(714) 667-2388 FAX

Legal srvs for men & women for about half the cost of traditional lawyers. Flat rate fees and payment plans. Family law, divorce, custody, domestic violence, TRO, paternity, child support, criminal law, and immigration. FUNDING: Grants, nonprofit. OFC HRS: M-F 8am-5pm. Spanish, Vietnamese spoken. Sliding fee scale according to income. Free adoption srv to birth mothers includes free medical care. Free consultation. SERVES: Court srvs in L.A., Orange & Riverside Counties.

VICTIM SERVICES CENTER
Dist Attorney at Colton Police Dept.
650 N. La Cadena Dr.
Colton, CA 92324
(909) 370-5164
(909) 370-5158 FAX

Short-term emerg assist, counseling referrals, special srvs to victims of sexual assault, crime prevention & info. Also srvs for witnesses, child, elderly and domestic violence victims. FUNDING: State. OFC HRS: M-F 8am-5pm. Spanish spoken. SERVES: San Bernardino County.

VICTIM SERVICES CENTER
Ontario Police Dept
2500 S. Archibald Ave.
Ontario, CA 91761
(909) 395-2713

Short-term emerg assist, counseling referrals, special srvs to victims of sexual assault, crime prevention & info. Also srvs for witnesses, child, elderly and domestic violence victims. FUNDING: State. OFC HRS: M-F 8am-5pm. Spanish spoken. SERVES: San Bernardino County.

VICTIM SERVICES CENTER
San Bernardino Police Dept
710 North D Street
San Bernardino, CA 92401
(909) 388-4900

Short-term emerg assist, counseling referrals, special srvs to victims of sexual assault, crime prevention & info. Also srvs for witnesses, child, elderly and domestic violence victims. FUNDING: State. OFC HRS: M-F 8am-5pm. Spanish spoken. SERVES: San Bernardino County.

VICTIM-WITNESS ASSISTANCE
San Bernardino Co. District Attorney
235 E. Mountain View
Barstow, CA 92311
(760) 256-4810
(760) 256-4869 FAX

Apply for Victim of Violent Crimes Funds (via State Board of Control), crisis counseling, crime victims counseling, brochures, and referrals to providers and court support witnesses and victims. Explains criminal justice system, gives feedback on what is happening with court. Walk in or call. FUNDING: State and county district attorney's office. OFC HRS: M-F 8am-5pm. ADM REQ: Victim or witness of crime. Free srvs. SERVES: Barstow, Daggett, Hinkley, Lenwood, Baker, Needles and surrounding area.

VICTIM-WITNESS ASSISTANCE

Riverside Co. District Attorney
82-675 Hwy. 111, 4th Fl.
Indio, CA 92201
(760) 863-8216
(760) 863-8987 FAX

Crisis intervention, emerg assist, info & referral, court support & assist in filing for victim of crime compensation. FUNDING: State. OFC HRS: M-F 8am-5pm. Spanish spoken. Free srvs. SERVES: Riverside County.

VICTIM-WITNESS ASSISTANCE

San Bernardino Co. District Attorney
P.O. Box 6602
6527 White Feather Rd.
Joshua Tree, CA 92252
(760) 366-4120
(760) 366-4126 FAX

Apply for Victim of Violent Crimes Funds (via State Board of Control), crisis & crime victims counseling, brochures, referrals to providers and court support witnesses and victims. Explains criminal justice system, gives feedback on what is happening with court. Also assists after sentencing with regard to release date, etc. Works with victim upon contact. Walk in or call. FUNDING: State and county district attorney's office. OFC HRS: M-F 8am-5pm. ADM REQ: Victim or witness of crime. Free srvs. SERVES: Morongo Basin.

VICTIM-WITNESS ASSISTANCE

Riverside Co. District Attorney
30123 Technology Dr., Ste 130
Murrieta, CA 92563
(951) 304-5500
(951) 677-9326 FAX

Info, guidance and support to victims of crime. Assist victims with the application for the Victims of Crime prgm. FUNDING: Govt. OFC HRS: M-F 8am-5pm. Spanish spoken. SERVES: Southwest Riverside County.

VICTIM-WITNESS ASSISTANCE

San Bernardino Co. District Attorney
8303 Haven Ave., 4th Fl.
Rancho Cucamonga, CA 91730
(909) 945-4241
(909) 945-4035 FAX

Prgm assists victims of violent crimes with reimbursement process for medical bills, loss of wages, psychological fees and funeral and burial expenses not covered by insurance. Assists in criminal justice process including trial process. Referral to comm agencies for counseling. FUNDING: State. OFC HRS: M-F 8am-5pm. Spanish spoken. ADM REQ: Cooperation with investigation and prosecution. Free srvs. SERVES: West San Bernardino County.

VICTIM-WITNESS ASSISTANCE

Riverside Co. District Attorney
3960 Orange St.
Riverside, CA 92501
(951) 955-5400
(951) 955-5682 FAX

Direct and referral assist provided to victims of violent crimes and their families. Srvs include: emerg assist, crisis intervention, crime victim compensation, orientation to criminal justice system, court info, accompaniment, and restraining order assist. Walk in or call. FUNDING: State grants. OFC HRS: M-F 7am-5pm. SERVES: Riverside County.

VICTIM-WITNESS ASSISTANCE

Bureau of Victim Srvs/Dist Attorney
303 W. 3rd Street, 5th Fl.
San Bernardino, CA 92415
(909) 382-7671
(909) 382-7676 FAX

Prgm is designed to assist victims by providing emerg assist for short-term needs, referral to community agencies for counseling, special srvs to victims of sexual assault and domestic violence, elder orientation to criminal system, and for victims of violent crimes, assist in applying for financial compensation from state Victim Compensation Prgm. Call for info. FUNDING: State. OFC HRS: M-F 8am-5pm. Some Spanish spoken. Free srvs. SERVES: San Bernardino County.

VICTIM-WITNESS ASSISTANCE

Victorville Victim Srvs Center
15371 Civic Dr., 2nd Fl.
Victorville, CA 92392
(760) 552-6944
(760) 552-6941 FAX

Prgm is designed to assist victims and witnesses by providing emerg assist for short-term needs, referrals to community agencies for counseling, special srvs to victims of sexual assault and domestic violence & elder abuse, orientation to criminal system. Assists victims of violent crimes in applying for financial compensation from state Victim Compensation Prgm. FUNDING: State. OFC HRS: M-F 8am-5pm. Some Spanish spoken. Free srvs. SERVES: San Bernardino County.

VICTIMS OF CRIME PROGRAM

See "Calif Board/Victim Compensation"

VICTIMS OF CRIME RESOURCE CTR

Univ of Pacific/McGeorge School of Law
3200 5th Avenue
Sacramento, CA 95817
(800) 842-8467
(916) 739-7395 FAX

Info & referral srvs to crime victims in Calif. Referrals to counselors or legal assist who provide info concerning crime victims' rights in the justice system. State funds available for certain crime-related expenses and civil lawsuits. FUNDING: State Office of Criminal Justice Planning, nonprofit. OFC HRS: M-F 8am-6pm. Spanish spoken. Free srvs. SERVES: Calif.

VICTOR VLY DOMESTIC VIOLENCE, INC.

A Better Way/Outreach Office
P.O. Box 2825
14114 Hesperia Rd.
Victorville, CA 92393
(760) 955-8010
(760) 955-8248 FAX

18-bed shelter for abused women and their children. Outreach, TRO assist, children's prgms, parenting classes, When Love Hurts prgm, peer support groups, anger mgmt, health, nutrition, basic budgeting. Max stay is 90 days. Counseling, transitional housing. 24-hr hotline

(760) 955-8723. FUNDING: Donations, non-profit. OFC HRS: M-F 8am-4pm. Some Spanish spoken. ADM REQ: Victim of domestic violence. SERVES: High Desert.

WOMEN'S LAW CENTER

See "United Law Centers/..."

WORTHWHILE REFERRAL SOURCES

13547 Ventura Blvd., Ste 374
Sherman Oaks, CA 91423
(818) 995-6646
(818) 995-4515 FAX

Referrals to a variety of srvs including legal, medical, psychological and many others. Also networking meetings, business consulting, workshops & seminars. FUNDING: Members, ad fees. OFC HRS: M-F 9am-5pm. SERVES: L.A., Ventura, Orange, Riverside & San Bernardino Counties.

BANNING PUBLIC LIBRARY

21 W. Nicolet St.
Banning, CA 92220
(951) 849-3192
(951) 849-6355 FAX

Special district library. Large print books, audios, videos, music CDs, copier, typewriters, Computer: Apple IIE, IBM, Internet search. Books in Spanish; a few in French and German. Lots of historical material for the area including old photos, etc. Literacy prgm, ESL classes. HRS: M-Th 9am-7pm; F, Sat 9am-5pm. Spanish spoken.

BANNING PUBLIC LIBRARY

Cabazon Branch Library
50171 Ramona Ave.
Cabazon, CA 92230
(951) 849-4082

Large print books, typewriter, computer, Internet, videos, books in Spanish. HRS: M-Th 1:30pm-5pm. Spanish spoken. SERVES: Cabazon.

BEAUMONT LIBRARY DISTRICT

125 E. 8th Street
Beaumont, CA 92223
(951) 845-1357
(951) 845-6217 FAX

Independent special district library provides srvs for people in a 60 sq. mile radius of Beaumont, but is open to anyone. Large print books, copier, videos, Preschool story hour, family literacy prgm, small collection of Spanish books. HRS: M, W, F, Sat 10am-6pm; Tu, Th 10am-8pm; Sun 1pm-6pm. SERVES: Beaumont, Banning, Cherry Valley area.

BLACK RESOURCE CENTER

Co. of L.A. Public Library/Central L.A.
150 E. El Segundo Blvd.
Los Angeles, CA 90061
(310) 538-3350
(310) 327-0824 FAX

Phone reference, research, info & referral. Emphasis on social, historical & cultural info by and about African Americans. Walk in or call. HRS: M-Th 10am-8pm; F 10am-6pm; Sat 10am-5pm. SERVES: So. Calif.

CHICANO RESOURCE CENTER

Co. of L.A. Public Library/East L.A.
4837 E. 3rd Street
Los Angeles, CA 90022
(323) 263-5087
(323) 264-5465 FAX

Special library collection of documents on Chicano & Mexican history & culture. Books, journals, films, video, records, CDs and clipping file of articles. FUNDING: Nonprofit. HRS: M-Th 10am-9pm; F 9am-5pm; Sat 10am-5pm; Sun 1pm-5pm. Spanish spoken. SERVES: So. Calif.

CITY OF RIVERSIDE PUBLIC LIBRARY

City of Riverside Central Library
P.O. Box 468
3581 Mission Inn Ave.
Riverside, CA 92501
(951) 826-5201
(951) 826-5213
(951) 826-5407 FAX

Large print books, copier, typewriter, computer, videos, CDs, DVDs, Internet. Books in Asian languages, European languages, large collection in Spanish. Meeting room. Online database. Depository for state and federal documents. Preschool story hour. Excellent collections on African-Americans and sheet music. Local history collection. For TTY, call (909) 826-5410. Adult literacy (909) 688-9302. HRS: M-W 11am-7pm; Th 11am-9pm; F, Sat 10am-6pm; Sun 12noon-5pm. Spanish spoken. SERVES: Riverside County

CITY OF RIVERSIDE PUBLIC LIBRARY

Arlington Branch Library
9556 Magnolia Ave.
Riverside, CA 92503
(951) 689-6612
(951) 689-6612 FAX

Large print books, copier, videos, computers, Internet access, CDs. Books in Spanish, special Native American collection. Call for info on children's prgms. HRS: M-Th 11am-7pm; F-Sun 10am-6pm. Spanish spoken. SERVES: Riverside County.

CITY OF RIVERSIDE PUBLIC LIBRARY

Casa Blanca Branch Library
2985 Madison St.
Riverside, CA 92504
(951) 826-2120
(951) 826-2196 FAX

Large print books, copier, videos, large collection of books in Spanish for adults and children, also Spanish records, cassettes and magazines. Good collection of Mexican-American history and culture. Preschool story hour. Call to confirm hours. HRS: M-Th 11am-7pm; F, Sat 10am-6pm. SERVES: Riverside County.

CITY OF RIVERSIDE PUBLIC LIBRARY

La Sierra Branch Library
4600 La Sierra Ave.
Riverside, CA 92505
(951) 688-7740
(951) 352-7578 FAX

Large print books, copier, videos, CDs. Preschool story hour. Meeting room. Literacy program headquarters (909) 688-9302. Internet available to the public. HRS: M-Th 11am-7pm; F, Sat 10am-6pm; Sun 12noon-5pm. SERVES: Riverside.

CITY OF RIVERSIDE PUBLIC LIBRARY

Marcy Branch Library
6927 Magnolia Ave.
Riverside, CA 92506
(951) 826-2078

Large print books, copier, books in Spanish for adults and children. HRS: M-Sa: 10am-6pm. SERVES: Riverside County.

CITY OF RIVERSIDE PUBLIC LIBRARY

Eastside Library Connection/Nichols Cybrary Connection
4033-C Chicago Ave.
Riverside, CA 92507
(951) 684-8347
(951) 684-8347 FAX

Info learning center for children, ages 10-14 yrs, and their families. Free computer training, Internet, info, literacy, homework assist, literacy

& special presentations for adults. FUNDING: Riverside Public Library, grants, nonprofit. HRS: M-Th 11am-7pm; F, Sat 10am-6pm. SERVES: Riverside County.

COLTON PUBLIC LIBRARY

656 N. 9th Street
Colton, CA 92324
(909) 370-5083
(909) 422-0873 FAX

Sponsored by the City of Colton. Large print books, copier, CDs, DVDs, computers, Internet, books in Spanish, meeting room, story hour; literacy prgm (909) 370-5170. HRS: M, F, Sat 10am-6pm; W 12pm-8pm. SERVES: Colton.

COLTON PUBLIC LIBRARY

Peter Luque Branch Library
294 East O Street
Colton, CA 92324
(909) 370-5182
(909) 422-0124 FAX

Large print books, copier, videos, books in Spanish, Cambodian, periodical in Spanish. Preschool story hour, literacy prgm. Computers, Internet, DVDs, CDs. HRS: Tu, Th 9am-5pm. Spanish spoken. SERVES: Colton.

CORONA PUBLIC LIBRARY

650 S. Main Street
Corona, CA 92882
(951) 736-2381
(951) 736-2386
(951) 736-2499 FAX

Sponsored by the City of Corona. Large print books, copier, videos, CDs, meeting rooms, books in Spanish. Story hour for infants-elem school children. Typewriters, computers and Internet access. Adult and family literacy prgm. Great Heritage Room and excellent source of info on the care and treatment of rare books. Passport srvs in the Heritage Room, M-Th 12noon-8pm; F, Sat 10am-4pm (by appt only). HRS: M, Tu 12noon-9pm; W, Th 10am-6pm; Sat 10am-5pm. SERVES: Corona.

DON A. TURNER LAW LIBRARY

See "Law Library for San Bernardino Co."

FIRST BAPTIST CHURCH OF YUCAIPA

34784 Yucaipa Blvd.
Yucaipa, CA 92399
(909) 790-1971
(909) 797-5062 FAX

Church has a library media center with books and tapes for all ages. Public is welcome. HRS: M-Th 8am-5pm; F 8am-12noon. SERVES: Yucaipa.

FOUNDATION FOR RECOVERY, INC.

4750 W. Sahara Ave., Ste 10
Las Vegas, NV 89102
(702) 257-8199
(702) 257-8299 FAX

Maintains a study center and archival library of both historical and modern material related to addiction & recovery. Provides meeting space to the recovering community. Visit (www.therooms.org). Also a recovery museum and book store. Scholarships available for addiction treatment and studies. FUNDING: Nonprofit. OFC HRS: M-F 11am-8pm; Sat 12noon-8pm; Sun 12noon-6pm. ADM REQ:

Open to students, academics, professionals and the general public. SERVES: So. Calif & Nevada.

HEMET PUBLIC LIBRARY
300 E. Latham Ave.
Hemet, CA 92543
(951) 765-2440
(951) 765-2446 FAX

Large print books, videos, copier. Small collection of books in Spanish. Preschool story hour. Calif and local history collection. Depository for Braille Institute, literacy prgm. TDD (951) 765-2447. HRS: W, Th 9am-7pm; F, Sat 9am-6pm. SERVES: Hemet.

L.A. FAMILY HISTORY LIBRARY
Formerly L.A. Family Regional History Ctr
10741 Santa Monica Blvd.
Los Angeles, CA 90025
(310) 474-9990

Helps people find ancestors (genealogy). Center is on the LDS Temple grounds in the basement of the visitor ctr, open to the public. Large genealogical library with books, computers, microfilm and microfiche, consultants and classes. Non-circulating library. FUNDING: Nonprofit. HRS: M, F, Sat 9am-5pm; Tu-Th 9am-9pm. Spanish, German, Norwegian, French, Jewish and Polish spoken. Free srvs except copy machines, computer disks, etc. SERVES: So. Calif.

LAW LIBRARY FOR SAN BERNARDINO CO.
Rancho Cucamonga Branch
8401 N. Haven Ave.
Rancho Cucamonga, CA 91730
(909) 944-5106

Materials for library use only; librarian cannot interpret, define or discuss the law with patrons. FUNDING: Nonprofit. HRS: M-F 8:30am-1:15pm, 2pm-5pm. SERVES: Rancho Cucamonga.

LAW LIBRARY FOR SAN BERNARDINO CO.
San Bernardino Branch
402 North D Street
San Bernardino, CA 92401
(909) 885-3020
(909) 885-1869 FAX

Research library, reference only. Govt depository with Calif state law, taxation law, regional reporters, federal law and law review collections. HRS: M-Th 8:30am-7pm; F 8:30am-5pm; Sat 9am-3pm. Spanish spoken. SERVES: San Bernardino County.

LAW LIBRARY FOR SAN BERNARDINO CO.
High Desert Branch
15455 Seneca Rd.
Victorville, CA 92392
(760) 243-2044

Research library. Materials must be used at the library. Librarian cannot interpret, define or discuss the law with patrons. FUNDING: Nonprofit. HRS: M-F 9am-1:30pm, 2pm-5pm. Spanish spoken. SERVES: Victorville, Hesperia, Barstow.

MURRIETA PUBLIC LIBRARY
Eight Town Square
24700 Adams Ave.
Murrieta, CA 92562
(951) 304-2665

Internet, large print books, video tapes, cassette tapes, biography books, periodicals, DVDs, books on CD, summer reading prgm, preschool story time (call for times & dates). Inter-library loan prgm. FUNDING: City, govt. HRS: M, Tu 12noon-8pm; W, Th 10am-6pm; Sat 10am-5pm. SERVES: Western Riverside County.

NATL LIBRARY SRVS FOR THE BLIND & PHYSICALLY HANDICAPPED
1291 Taylor St., NW
Washington, DC 20542
(888) 657-7323
(202) 707-5100
(202) 707-0712 FAX

Network of regional and subregional libraries. Provides free library srvs to the blind or visually impaired. Recorded or Braille books & magazines, specially designed phonographs & cassette players on loan. TDD (202) 707-0744. FUNDING: Govt. HRS: M-F 8am-4:30pm, EST. Free srvs. SERVES: U.S.A.

NATL REFERENCE/BIOETHICS LIT
Georgetown Univ. Kennedy Inst of Ethics
P.O. Box 571212
Washington, DC 20057-1212
(202) 687-3885
(888) 246-3849
(202) 687-8089 FAX

Reference assist, conducts free bioethics searches, and publishes material on bioethical and medical ethics topics. FUNDING: Nonprofit. HRS: M-F 9am-5pm; Sat 12noon-5pm. SERVES: Internatl.

NATL REHABILITATION INFO CENTER
8201 Corporate Dr., Ste 600
Landover, MD 20785
(800) 346-2742
(301) 459-5900
(301) 459-4263 FAX

Library and info center on disability and rehab. Quick reference and referral; REHABDATA searches bibliographic database of more than 70,000 documents, both federally funded and commercially produced. Doc delivery provides photocopies of docs in their collection. TTY (301) 459-5984. Visit (www.NARIC.com). FUNDING: Natl Inst on Disability, rehab research, nonprofit. HRS: M-F 9am-5pm, EST. Small charge for REHABDATA searches. SERVES: U.S.A.

NATL TECHNICAL INFO SERVICE
5301 Shawnee Rd.
Alexandria, VA 22161-0001
(703) 605-6050
(800) 553-6847
(703) 605-6900 FAX

Federal govt central source for the sale of scientific, technical, engineering and related business info produced by or for the U.S. govt and complimentary material from internatl sources. Nearly 3 million products available from NTIS in a variety of formats including: microfiche, paper, diskette, audiovisual, CD-ROM and online. TDD (703) 487-4639. FUNDING: Self-sustaining, govt. HRS: M-F 8am-6pm, EST. SERVES: Internatl.

ONTARIO CITY LIBRARY
Main Library
215 East C Street
Ontario, CA 91764-4111
(909) 395-2004
(909) 395-2043 FAX

Sponsored by the city of Ontario. Large print books, copier, videos, CDs, cassettes, books on tape. Meeting room. Books in Spanish, Vietnamese, Chinese & Korean. Preschool story hour. Good reference collection. Model colony history room (call for specific hours). Govt depository. Typewriters, computers & Internet access. HRS: M-Th 10am-9pm; F, Sat 10am-6pm; Sun 1pm-4pm. SERVES: Ontario.

ONTARIO CITY LIBRARY
Colony High Branch
3850 E. Riverside Dr.
Ontario, CA 91761-2603
(909) 395-2014
(909) 930-0836 FAX

Branch of the Ontario City Library. Internet, copier, videos, DVDs, CDs, books on tape, cassettes, books in Spanish. Preschool story hour. Toddler & after school story hour. HRS: M-W 12noon-8pm; Th-Sat 10am-6pm.

PALM SPRINGS PUBLIC LIBRARY
Library Center
300 S. Sunrise Way
Palm Springs, CA 92262
(760) 322-7323
(760) 320-9834 FAX

Sponsored by the City of Palm Springs. Large print books, copier, videos, CDs. Books in Spanish. Preschool story hour. Good business, art & Calif Collection. Literacy prgm. Distance learning prgm. HRS: Tu 10am-7pm; W-Sat 10am-5pm. SERVES: Palm Springs.

PALO VERDE VALLEY LIBRARY DISTRICT
125 W. Chanslorway
Blythe, CA 92225
(760) 922-5371
(760) 922-5371 FAX

Independent district library serves primarily residents of Palo Verde Valley but open to the public. Large print books, copier, typewriter, videos, books in Spanish, plus 3 magazines in Spanish. Preschool story hour. Special local history and picture collection of Blythe area since the advent of the camera. Internet access. HRS: M-F 10am-6pm; Sat 10am-4pm. SERVES: Blythe.

RANCHO CUCAMONGA PUBLIC LIBRARY
7368 Archibald Ave.
Rancho Cucamonga, CA 91730
(909) 477-2720
(909) 477-2721 FAX

Internet & computer srvs, large print books, videotapes, CDs, DVDs, books in Spanish, storytime, literacy prgm. Children's bookmobile. Will deliver to homebound. FUNDING: City. HRS: M-Th 10am-9pm; F 12noon-6pm; Sat 10am-5pm; Sun 1pm-5pm. SERVES: Rancho Cucamonga.

RANCHO CUCAMONGA PUBLIC LIBRARY
Paul A. Biane Library
12505 Cultural Center Dr.
Rancho Cucamonga, CA 91739
(909) 477-2720

Internet & computer srvs, large print books, videotapes, CDs, DVDs, books in Spanish, storytime, literacy prgm. Children's bookmobile. FUNDING: City. HRS: M-Th 10am-9pm; F, Sat 10am-6pm. SERVES: Rancho Cucamonga.

RANCHO MIRAGE PUBLIC LIBRARY
71-100 Hwy. 111
Rancho Mirage, CA 92270

(760) 341-7323
(760) 341-5213 FAX

Full srv library with large print books, video tapes, CDs, DVDs, audio books, print and electronic resources. Internet, storytimes, electronic homework center and summer reading prgms. Located in the Rancho Las Palmas Shopping Ctr. HRS: M, Tu, Th-Sat 9am-6pm; W 9am-8pm. Spanish, French spoken. SERVES: Rancho Mirage.

RANCHO SANTA ANA BOTANIC GARDEN LIBRARY

1500 N. College Ave.
Claremont, CA 91711
(909) 625-8767
(909) 626-7670 FAX

Private library for researchers interested in botany and horticulture. Copier, online reference to Honnold at Claremont College, books on drought tolerant plants, ethnobotany of Calif Indians. Living collection of drought resistant plants (Calif native plants). Public garden open daily 8am-5pm. FUNDING: Nonprofit. HRS: M-F 9am-4pm. Daily admission fee $8 adults, $6 students with valid ID, $6 seniors ages 65 yrs+. Free to members. SERVES: Claremont.

REDLANDS CITY LIBRARY

A. K. Smiley Public Library
125 W. Vine St.
Redlands, CA 92373
(909) 798-7565
(909) 798-7566 FAX

Sponsored by the city of Redlands and also known as the Smiley Library. Large print books, videos, CDs, computers, Internet. Preschool story hour. One wing houses the heritage room collection including books, documents and photos on local and California history. Lincoln shrine collection with books, photos, memorabilia on Lincoln and the Civil War (open Tu-Sun 1pm-5pm). Literacy prgm for ages 18 yrs+. FUNDING: Govt. HRS: M, Tu 11am-9pm; W, Th 10am-6pm; F, Sat 10am-5pm; Sun 1pm-5pm. Spanish spoken. SERVES: Redlands.

RICHARD NIXON LIBRARY/BIRTHPLACE

18001 Yorba Linda Blvd.
Yorba Linda, CA 92886-3949
(714) 993-5075
(714) 528-0544 FAX

High-tech interactive presidential museum that chronicles the life and times of former President Richard Nixon and his 4 decade political career. HRS: M-Sat 10am-5pm; Sun 11am-5pm. SERVES: U.S.A.

RIVERSIDE CO. LAW LIBRARY

Desert Branch
46-200 Oasis St.
Indio, CA 92201-5933
(760) 863-8316
(760) 342-2581 FAX

Reference assist, inter-library loans, computers, conference rooms, photocopy machines. Walk in. FUNDING: Civil court fees, nonprofit. HRS: M-F 8am-5pm. Fax $10 plus $.50 a page, copies $.15 a page. SERVES: Indio.

RIVERSIDE CO. LAW LIBRARY

Victor Miceli Law Library
3989 Lemon St.
Riverside, CA 92501-4203
(951) 955-6390
(951) 955-6394 FAX

Reference assist, inter-library loans, photocopy machines. Walk in. FUNDING: Civil court fees, nonprofit. HRS: M-Th 8am-7pm; F 8am-5pm; Sat 9am-1pm. Fax $10 plus $.50 per page. Photocopies $.25 per page. SERVES: Riverside County.

RIVERSIDE CO. LIBRARY SYSTEM

Anza Library
57430 Mitchell Rd.
Anza, CA 92539
(951) 763-4216
(951) 763-0657 FAX

Computers, Internet access, books in Spanish, large print books, storytime (summer only), CDs, books on tape. FUNDING: County. HRS: Tu, W 3pm-7pm; Th, Sat 10am-2pm. Hrs vary. Spanish spoken. SERVES: Riverside County.

RIVERSIDE CO. LIBRARY SYSTEM

Calimesa Library
974 Calimesa Blvd.
Calimesa, CA 92320
(909) 795-9807
(909) 795-3198 FAX

Large print books, computers, Internet, books in Spanish, CDs, DVDs, video tapes, audio tapes, preschool story time. FUNDING: County. HRS: Tu, Th, F 10am-6pm; W 12noon-8pm; Sat 9am-5pm. Russian spoken. SERVES: Riverside County.

RIVERSIDE CO. LIBRARY SYSTEM

Canyon Lake Library
31516 Railroad Canyon Rd.
Canyon Lake, CA 92587
(951) 244-9181
(951) 244-7382 FAX

Large print books, video tapes, copier. Books in Spanish. FUNDING: County. HRS: M 10am-7pm; W, F 10am-6pm; Sat 10am-3pm. SERVES: Canyon Lake.

RIVERSIDE CO. LIBRARY SYSTEM

Cathedral City Library
33520 Date Palm Dr.
Cathedral City, CA 92234
(760) 328-4262
(760) 770-9828 FAX

Copier, preschool story hour, bilingual storytime, computers, large print books, CDs, DVDs, videos, books on tape, literacy prgm, Spanish language collection. Free Internet access. Temp closed due to fire damage. Visit temp site: 68-727 E. Palm Canyon Dr., Cathedral City, CA 92234. FUNDING: County. HRS: M, Tu, Th, Sat 10am-6pm; W 12noon-8pm; Sun 1pm-5pm. Spanish spoken. SERVES: Riverside County.

RIVERSIDE CO. LIBRARY SYSTEM

Coachella Library
1538 7th Street
Coachella, CA 92236
(760) 398-5148
(760) 398-1068 FAX

Videos, books & magazines in Spanish, French, Italian, Korean, Japanese, Thai. Computers, Internet access, large print books, storytime, CDs, DVDs, books on tape. FUNDING: County. HRS: M, Tu, Th 10am-6pm; W 12pm-8pm; Sat 10am-5pm. Spanish spoken. SERVES: Riverside County.

RIVERSIDE CO. LIBRARY SYSTEM

Home Gardens Library

3785 Neece St.
Corona, CA 92879
(951) 279-2148
(951) 789-2812 FAX

Large print books, video tapes, copier. Books in Spanish. FUNDING: County. HRS: M, Tu 12noon-8pm; W, Th 10am-6pm; F, Sat 10am-5pm; Sun 1pm-5pm. SERVES: Corona.

RIVERSIDE CO. LIBRARY SYSTEM

Lake Tamarisk Library
P.O. Box 260
43-880 Tamarisk Dr.
Desert Center, CA 92239
(760) 227-3273
(760) 227-0043 FAX

Large print books, video tapes, copier. Books in Spanish. FUNDING: County. HRS: Tu, Th 10am-6pm; Sat 10am-2pm. SERVES: Metropolitan Water District.

RIVERSIDE CO. LIBRARY SYSTEM

Desert Hot Springs Library
11691 West Dr.
Desert Hot Springs, CA 92240
(760) 329-5926
(760) 329-3593 FAX

Computers, Internet access, books in Spanish, large print books, storytime, CDs, DVDs, videos, books on tape. FUNDING: County. HRS: M-W 10am-6pm; Th 12noon-8pm; Sat 9am-3pm. SERVES: Riverside County.

RIVERSIDE CO. LIBRARY SYSTEM

Valle Vista Library
25757 Fairview Ave.
Hemet, CA 92544
(951) 927-2611
(951) 927-7902 FAX

Large print books, copier, videos, CDs, DVDs, books on tape, Internet access, books in Spanish, preschool story hour. Summer reading prgm for ages 2-16 yrs. FUNDING: County. HRS: M, W 10am-7pm; Tu, Th 10am-6pm; F 10am-5pm; Sat 10am-2pm. SERVES: Riverside County.

RIVERSIDE CO. LIBRARY SYSTEM

Idyllwild Library
P.O. Box 68
54185 Pinecrest Ave.
Idyllwild, CA 92549-0068
(951) 659-2300
(951) 659-2453 FAX

Large print books, copier, videos, computers, Internet access, books on tape, CDs, DVDs, phone books, preschool story hour, local history collection. Complete bound copies of Idyllwild Town Crier. FUNDING: County. HRS: M, W, F 10am-6pm; Sat 10am-4pm. Spanish spoken. SERVES: Riverside County.

RIVERSIDE CO. LIBRARY SYSTEM

Coachella Valley Bookmobile
Indio, CA 92201
(760) 347-2385

Spanish and children's books. Call for location and time schedule. FUNDING: County. Spanish spoken. SERVES: Indio.

RIVERSIDE CO. LIBRARY SYSTEM

Indio Branch Library/Literacy Office
200 Civic Center Mall
Indio, CA 92201
(760) 347-2383
(760) 347-3159 FAX

Large print books, copier, computer, Internet access, microfilm, typewriter, videos, CDs, books in Spanish for adults and children, preschool story hour, meeting room. Good source for reference. This library is also the location for the Coachella Valley literacy office, (760) 342-2580. FUNDING: County. HRS: M 12noon-8pm; Tu-Th, Sat 10am-6pm. SERVES: Cathedral City, Coachella, Desert Hot Springs, Indio, La Quinta, Lake Tamarisk, Mecca, Palm Dessert, Palms, Thousand Palms.

RIVERSIDE CO. LIBRARY SYSTEM
La Quinta Library
78-275 Calle Tampico
La Quinta, CA 92253
(760) 564-4767
(760) 771-0237 FAX

Large print books, books in Spanish, copier, videos, CDs, DVDs, computers, Internet, preschool story hour. Grandparents and Books prgm, summer reading prgm, Friends of the Library. FUNDING: County. HRS: M-Th 10am-7pm; F, Sat 10am-6pm; Sun 12noon-4pm. SERVES: La Quinta.

RIVERSIDE CO. LIBRARY SYSTEM
Lake Elsinore Library
600 W. Graham
Lake Elsinore, CA 92530
(951) 674-4517
(951) 245-7715 FAX

Large print books, videos, books on tape and CD. Books in Spanish, preschool story hour. Comprehensive local history collection. FUNDING: County. HRS: M, Th, F 10am-6pm; Tu, W 1pm-8pm; Sat 10am-3pm. Some Spanish spoken. SERVES: Lake Elsinore.

RIVERSIDE CO. LIBRARY SYSTEM
Mecca Library
91-260 Avenue 66
Mecca, CA 92254
(760) 396-2363
(760) 396-1503 FAX

Large print books. Books in Spanish. Computers, Internet access, storytime, CDs, DVDs, books on tape. FUNDING: County. HRS: M-Th, Sat 10am-6pm. Spanish spoken. SERVES: Riverside County.

RIVERSIDE CO. LIBRARY SYSTEM
Sun City Library
26982 Cherry Hills
Menifee, CA 92586
(951) 679-3534
(951) 672-8293 FAX

Large print book, copier, videos, CDs, DVDs, computers, Internet, books in Spanish. FUNDING: County. HRS: M, W, F 10am-6pm; Tu, Thu 11am-7pm; Sat 9am-3pm; Sun 12noon-4pm. SERVES: Riverside County.

RIVERSIDE CO. LIBRARY SYSTEM
Norco Library
3954 Old Hamner Rd.
Norco, CA 92860-1270
(951) 735-5329
(951) 735-0263 FAX

Large print books, copier, videos, CDs. Books in Spanish. Meeting room. Collection on horses and other domestic animals. FUNDING: County. HRS: M-Th 10am-8pm; Sat 10am-4pm. SERVES: Norco.

RIVERSIDE CO. LIBRARY SYSTEM
Nuview Library
P.O. Box 769
29990 Lakeview Ave.
Nuevo, CA 92567-0769
(951) 928-0769
(951) 928-3360 FAX

Large print books, copier, videos. Literacy books in Spanish. Audio books. Local history collection on Lakeview, Nuevo, Perris. FUNDING: County. HRS: Tu 3pm-7pm; W, F 10am-6pm. SERVES: Nuevo, Lakeview, Perris.

RIVERSIDE CO. LIBRARY SYSTEM
Palm Desert Library
73-300 Fred Waring Dr.
Palm Desert, CA 92260
(760) 346-6552
(760) 341-7862 FAX

Large print books, copier, videos, books on tape, computers, Internet, DVDs, CDs, adult book group, preschool story hour. Books in Spanish. Golf collection. FUNDING: County. HRS: M-Th 10am-8pm; F, Sat 10am-5pm; Sun 1pm-5pm. Spanish spoken. SERVES: Riverside County.

RIVERSIDE CO. LIBRARY SYSTEM
Perris Library
163 E. San Jacinto Ave.
Perris, CA 92570
(951) 657-2358
(951) 657-9849 FAX

Copiers, typewriter, Internet access, large print books, Spanish books, teen-tech center, children's prgms. FUNDING: County. HRS: M, Th-Sat 10am-6pm; Tu, W 12noon-8pm; Sun 1pm-5pm. SERVES: Riverside County.

RIVERSIDE CO. LIBRARY SYSTEM
Highgrove Library
530 W. Center St.
Riverside, CA 92507
(951) 682-1507
(951) 321-4107 FAX

Large print books, copier, books in Spanish, computer, Internet, videos, DVDs, audio books. Good collection of current fiction. FUNDING: County. SERVES: Riverside County.

RIVERSIDE CO. LIBRARY SYSTEM
Rubidoux Library
5840 Mission Blvd.
Riverside, CA 92509
(951) 682-5485
(951) 682-8641 FAX

Large print books, copier, videos, DVDs, CDs. Books in Spanish. Preschool story time. Literacy prgm. Career planning collection. Personal computers with Internet access. Computer lab. FUNDING: County. HRS: M-W, Sat 10am-6pm; Th 12pm-8pm. Spanish spoken. SERVES: West Riverside, Rubidoux, Mira Loma, Jurupa & Belltown.

RIVERSIDE CO. LIBRARY SYSTEM
Glen Avon Library
9244 Galena
Riverside, CA 92509
(951) 685-8121
(951) 685-7158 FAX

Large print books, video tapes, copier. Books in Spanish. FUNDING: County. HRS: M, Th 10am-6pm; Tu, W 10am-8pm; F, Sat 10am-4pm; Sun 1pm-5pm. SERVES: Riverside City.

RIVERSIDE CO. LIBRARY SYSTEM
Woodcrest Library
16625 Krameria
Riverside, CA 92504
(951) 789-7324
(951) 789-7321 FAX

Large print books, video tapes, copier. Books in Spanish. FUNDING: County. OFC HRS: M-W 10am-7pm; Th, Sat 10am-4pm; F 12pm-5pm. SERVES: Riverside City.

RIVERSIDE CO. LIBRARY SYSTEM
San Jacinto Library
500 Idyllwild Dr.
San Jacinto, CA 92583
(951) 654-8635
(951) 487-8069 FAX

Large print books, copier, videos, computers, Internet access, DVDs, books on tape, books in Spanish. Preschool story hour. Extensive local history collection for Hemet Valley. FUNDING: County. HRS: M, F 7:30am-6pm; Tu-Th 7:30am-7pm; Sat 9am-1pm. Spanish spoken. SERVES: Riverside County.

RIVERSIDE CO. LIBRARY SYSTEM
Grace Mellman Community Library
41000 County Center Dr.
Temecula, CA 92591
(951) 296-3893
(951) 296-0229 FAX

Free Internet access, CDs, DVDs and audiobooks. ESL and literacy classes. Story time hour, Spanish materials, summer reading program, crafts, movies and a community room. Prgms for adults, teens and children. FUNDING: County. HRS: M 12noon-7pm; Tu, W 10am-6pm; Th 10am-5pm; F 10am-4pm; Sat 10am-2pm. SERVES: Temecula.

RIVERSIDE CO. LIBRARY SYSTEM
Temecula Public Library
30600 Pauba Rd.
Temecula, CA 92592
(951) 693-8900
(951) 693-8997 FAX

Internet access, large print books, CDs, DVDs, preschool story times, toddler storytime, family prgms, bilingual storytime, local history, adult literacy prgms, community rooms, study rooms, digital microform reader/printer, language collections, technology homework ctr, e-books, and online databases. FUNDING: County. HRS: M-Th 10am-9pm; F 10am-6pm; Sat 10am-5pm; Sun 1pm-5pm. SERVES: Inland Empire.

RIVERSIDE CO. LIBRARY SYSTEM
Art Samson Community Library
31189 Robert Rd.
Thousand Palms, CA 92276
(760) 343-1556
(760) 343-0957 FAX

Large print books, video tapes, audio tapes, books in Spanish, Homework help center, story & crafts hour. Computer, Internet, CDs, DVDs. FUNDING: County. HRS: M, Tu, Th 10am-6pm; W 10am-8pm; Sat 10am-4pm. SERVES: Thousand Palms, Tri-Palm, Ivy Ranch, Sky Valley.

RIVERSIDE CO. LIBRARY SYSTEM
Mission Trail Library
34303 Mission Trail

Wildomar, CA 92595
(951) 471-3855
(951) 471-0188 FAX

Large print books, video tapes, copier. Books in Spanish. FUNDING: County. HRS: M 12noon-8pm; Tu-F 10am-6pm; Sat 10am-3pm. SERVES: Wildomar.

RURAL INFORMATION CENTER

National Agricultural Library
10301 Baltimore Ave., Rm. 132
Beltsville, MD 20705-2351
(800) 633-7701
(301) 504-5181 FAX

Located at the Natl Agricultural Library (NAL), RIC provides info & referral srvs about U.S. rural prgms & issues to local, state & fed govt officials, community organizations, libraries, businesses and rural area citizens. One of the 4 natl libraries in the U.S. with more than 3 million volumes and subscriptions to over 27,000 periodicals from all over the world. Customized info to specific inquiries. FUNDING: Govt. HRS: M-F 8:30am-4:30pm, EST. Free srvs. SERVES: U.S.A.

SAN BERNARDINO CO. LAW LIBRARY

See "Law Library for San Bernardino Co."

SAN BERNARDINO CO. LAW LIBRARY

402 North D Street
San Bernardino, CA 92401
(909) 885-3020
(909) 381-0957 FAX

HRS: M-Th 8:30am-7pm; F 8:30am-5pm; Sat 9am-3pm. SERVES: San Bernardino County.

SAN BERNARDINO CO. LIBRARY

Adelanto Branch
P.O. Box 37
11497 Bartlett Ave.
Adelanto, CA 92301
(760) 246-5661
(760) 246-4157 FAX

Large print books, computers, copier, books in Spanish. HRS: M 12noon-8pm; Tu, Th 12noon-6pm; W, F 10am-6pm; Sat 10am-5pm. Spanish spoken. SERVES: Adelanto.

SAN BERNARDINO CO. LIBRARY

Apple Valley Branch
14901 Dale Evans Pkwy.
Apple Valley, CA 92307
(760) 247-2022
(760) 247-9729 FAX

Large print books, copier, videos, cassettes, CDs, DVDs, computers, Internet, mobile unit, books in Spanish, preschool activities & story hour. Literacy prgm. HRS: M 10am-8pm; Tu 12noon-8pm; W-F 10am-6pm; Sat 9am-5pm. Spanish spoken. SERVES: Apple Valley.

SAN BERNARDINO CO. LIBRARY

Barstow Branch
304 E. Buena Vista St.
Barstow, CA 92311
(760) 256-4850
(760) 256-4852 FAX

Large print books, typewriter, videos, CDs, DVDs, magazines, books in Spanish, preschool story hour. Good collection of topographical maps of area, literacy prgm. Monthly children's prgms. HRS: M, W 12noon-8pm; Tu, Th, F 10am-6pm; Sat 9am-5pm. SERVES: Barstow.

SAN BERNARDINO CO. LIBRARY

Big Bear Lake Branch

P.O. Box 1809
41930 Garstin Dr.
Big Bear Lake, CA 92315
(909) 866-5571
(909) 866-4382 FAX

Internet access, large print books, books on tape, copier, typewriter, videos, CDs, preschool story hour, literacy prgm, meeting room. Books in Spanish. LITE Center. Good collection on natural history and North American Indians. HRS: M, Tu 12noon-8pm; W-F 10am-6pm; Sat 9am-5pm. SERVES: Big Bear Lake.

SAN BERNARDINO CO. LIBRARY

Bloomington Branch
10145 Orchard St.
Bloomington, CA 92316
(909) 877-1453
(909) 820-0533 FAX

Large print books, books on tape, videos, cassettes, CDs, DVDs, computers, Internet, summer reading prgm, typewriter, copier, books in English and Spanish. HRS: M, Tu 12noon-8pm; W 12noon-6pm; Th, F 11am-6pm; Sat 11am-5pm. SERVES: Bloomington.

SAN BERNARDINO CO. LIBRARY

Lake Arrowhead Branch
P.O. Box 766
27235 Hwy. 189
Blue Jay, CA 92317
(909) 337-3118
(909) 337-2287 FAX

Books on tape, large print books, depository for Braille books, copier, Internet, computer, videos, CDs, books in Spanish, literacy prgm. Good local history collection. Summer reading prgm, adult book club, storytime, medical references. HRS: M, Tu 12noon-8pm; W-F 10am-6pm; Sat 9am-5pm. SERVES: Blue Jay.

SAN BERNARDINO CO. LIBRARY

Chino Branch Library
13180 Central Ave.
Chino, CA 91710
(909) 465-5280
(909) 465-5240 FAX

Large print books, copier, computers, Internet, videos, CDs, books & magazines in Spanish. Meeting room, literacy prgm, storytimes for children. HRS: M-Th 10am-8pm; F 10am-6pm; Sat 9am-5pm. SERVES: Chino.

SAN BERNARDINO CO. LIBRARY

Chino Hills Branch
14020 City Center Dr.
Chino Hills, CA 91709
(909) 590-5380
(909) 591-5267 FAX

Six Internet computers, large print books, video tapes, CDs, DVDs, books in Spanish, summer reading time, story time, literacy prgm. HRS: M-Th 10am-8pm; F 10am-6pm; Sat 9am-5pm; Sun 1pm-5pm. Spanish, Tagalog spoken. SERVES: Chino Hills.

SAN BERNARDINO CO. LIBRARY

Crestline Branch
P.O. Box 1087
23555 Knapps Cutoff
Crestline, CA 92325
(909) 338-3294
(909) 338-0964 FAX

Internet, computers, books on cassette, large print books, copier, videos. Preschool story hour, literacy prgm. Books in Spanish. HRS: M, Th 12noon-8pm; Tu 10am-6pm; W 11am-6pm; F 10am-5pm; Sat 10am-2pm. SERVES: Crestline.

SAN BERNARDINO CO. LIBRARY

Fontana Lewis Library & Tech Ctr
8437 Sierra Ave.
Fontana, CA 92335
(909) 574-4500

Large print books, typewriter, videos, cassettes, CDs, books in Spanish, French, German. Preschool story hour, literacy prgm, magazines & newspapers. Adopt-a-Book prgm. Computer available to public for $6.50. HRS: M-Th, Sat 10am-9pm; F 10am-6pm; Sun 12noon-5pm. SERVES: Fontana.

SAN BERNARDINO CO. LIBRARY

Kaiser Branch
11155 Almond Ave.
Fontana, CA 92337
(909) 357-5900
(909) 428-8494 FAX

Large print books, books on tape, copier, computer, CDs, homework center, Internet, juvenile videos, books in Spanish, preschool story hour. HRS: M-Th 3pm-8pm; Sat 9am-5pm. Spanish spoken. SERVES: Fontana.

SAN BERNARDINO CO. LIBRARY

Summit Branch
15551 Summit Ave.
Fontana, CA 92336
(909) 357-5950

Large print books, books on tape, copier, computer, CDs, homework center, Internet, books in Spanish, preschool story hour. Summer reading program. OFC HRS: M-Th 3pm-8pm; Sat 9am-5pm. SERVES: Fontana.

SAN BERNARDINO CO. LIBRARY

Grand Terrace Branch
22795-A Barton Rd.
Grand Terrace, CA 92313
(909) 783-0147
(909) 783-1913 FAX

Copier, Internet, word processing, videos, DVDs, CD-ROMs, reference materials, music CDs, e-books, online reference & library assist. Computer intro classes every Tu 10am-11:30am; bookgroup 3rd Th at 7pm. Grandparents and Books (call for schedule). Storytime W 11am. Active volunteer prgm for ages 12 yrs+. HRS: M, Th 10pm-8pm; Tu, F 10am-6pm; W 12noon-8pm; Sat 9am-5pm; Sun 1pm-5pm. SERVES: Grand Terrace & nearby.

SAN BERNARDINO CO. LIBRARY

Hesperia Branch
9565 7th Avenue
Hesperia, CA 92345
(760) 244-4898
(760) 244-1530 FAX

Large print books, copier, typewriter, videos, computer, Internet, DVDs, CDs, books in Spanish, German, Russian. Meeting room. Depository for Braille Institute. HRS: M-Th 10am-8pm; F 10am-6pm; Sat 9am-5pm; Sun 1pm-5pm. Spanish spoken. SERVES: Victor Valley, including Oak Hills, Phelan, Baldy Mesa, Pinon Hills.

SAN BERNARDINO CO. LIBRARY

Highland Branch
7863 Central Ave.

Highland, CA 92346
(909) 425-4700

Large print books, copier, typewriter, videos, CDs, DVDs. Books in Spanish, literacy prgm. Internet access, computer lab, environmental prgms & resource materials. HRS: M-W 10am-8pm; Th, F 10am-6pm; Sat 9am-5pm. SERVES: Highland.

SAN BERNARDINO CO. LIBRARY
Joshua Tree Branch
6465 Park Blvd.
Joshua Tree, CA 92252
(760) 366-8615
(760) 366-8615 FAX

Large print books, Internet, computers, copier, videos, literacy prgm, preschool story hour. HRS: M-F 10am-6pm; Sat 10am-2pm. SERVES: Joshua Tree.

SAN BERNARDINO CO. LIBRARY
Loma Linda Branch
25581 Barton Rd.
Loma Linda, CA 92354
(909) 796-8621
(909) 796-4221 FAX

Computers, DVDs, CDs, videos, story hour, Internet, copier. Books in Spanish, Chinese. Good collection of vegetarian cookbooks. African American collection. HRS: M, Tu 12noon-8pm; W, Th 10am-8pm; F 10am-6pm; Sun 1pm-5pm. SERVES: Loma Linda.

SAN BERNARDINO CO. LIBRARY
Lucerne Valley Branch
P.O. Box 408
33103 Old Woman Springs Rd.
Lucerne Valley, CA 92356
(760) 248-7521
(760) 248-1131 FAX

Books on cassette, large print books, copier, Internet, computer, DVDs, videos. Desert adult reading, literacy prgm. Preschool story hour. Also have children's prgms. HRS: M-F 10am-6pm; Sat 9am-5pm. SERVES: Lucerne Valley.

SAN BERNARDINO CO. LIBRARY
Mentone Branch
1331 Opal Ave.
Mentone, CA 92359
(909) 794-0327

Large print books, computers, Internet, copier, videos, Children's story & craft hour. Summer reading prgm for children & young adults. HRS: M, Tu 12noon-8pm; W-F 10am-6pm; Sat 9am-5pm. Spanish spoken. SERVES: Mentone.

SAN BERNARDINO CO. LIBRARY
Montclair Branch
9955 Fremont Ave.
Montclair, CA 91763
(909) 624-4671
(909) 621-1261 FAX

Large print books, videos, CDs, Internet, computers. Books in Spanish, Vietnamese. Preschool story hour. Meeting room. San Bernardino Co. Hall of Records has a satellite branch at this library; birth certificates, marriage licenses & death abstracts are issued and marriages are performed here as well. Call (909) 624-7247 for these srvs. HRS: M-W 10pm-8pm; Th, F 10am-6pm; Sat 9am-5pm. Spanish spoken. SERVES: Montclair.

SAN BERNARDINO CO. LIBRARY
Needles Branch
1111 Bailey Ave.
Needles, CA 92363
(760) 326-9255
(760) 326-9238 FAX

Large print books, copier, videos, storytime, DVDs, CDs, summer reading prgm, computers, Internet access, books in Spanish. Local history collection with lots of photos, microfilm to 1889, maps. Laubach literacy prgm. HRS: M, Tu 10am-6pm; W 10am-4pm; Th-Sat 10am-5pm. SERVES: Needles.

SAN BERNARDINO CO. LIBRARY
Phelan Memorial Library
9292 Sheep Creek Rd.
Phelan, CA 92371
(760) 868-0583

Large print books, books on tape, copier, computer, CDs, homework center, Internet, books in Spanish, preschool story hour. Volunteer training workshops. Summer reading programs. OFC HRS: M, Tu 12noon-8pm; W-F 10am-6pm; Sat 9am-5pm. SERVES: Phelan.

SAN BERNARDINO CO. LIBRARY
Rialto Branch
251 W. 1st Street
Rialto, CA 92376
(909) 875-0144
(909) 875-2801 FAX

Large print books, computers, Internet, copier, videos, CDs, DVDs, books on tape, books in Spanish. Tutor prgm for elementary students. Preschool story hour. Calif Literacy Campaign. HRS: M-W 10am-8pm; Th, F 10am-6pm; Sat 9am-5pm. Spanish spoken. SERVES: Rialto.

SAN BERNARDINO CO. LIBRARY
Carter Branch
2630 N. Linden Ave.
Rialto, CA 92377
(909) 854-4100

Large print books, books on tape, copier, computer, CDs, homework center, Internet, books in Spanish, preschool story hour. Summer reading program for children and teens. OFC HRS: M-Th 3pm-8pm; Sat 9am-5pm; closed F, Sun. SERVES: Rialto.

SAN BERNARDINO CO. LIBRARY
Running Springs Branch
P.O. Box 248
2677 Whispering Pines Dr.
Running Springs, CA 92382
(909) 867-3604

Large print books, Internet, computers, books on tape, magazines, CDs, DVDs, videos, copier, school-aged prgms and preschool story hour in the summer, literacy prgm. HRS: M, Tu 12noon-8pm; W- F 10am-6pm; Sat 10am-2pm. French and Spanish spoken. SERVES: Running Springs.

SAN BERNARDINO CO. LIBRARY
Administrative Office
104 W. 4th Street
San Bernardino, CA 92415
(909) 387-5720
(909) 387-5728
(909) 387-5724 FAX

Admin office for the county-sponsored libraries. Contact the branch library directly for info about srvs, hrs, etc. Books, audio cassettes, CDs, vid-

eos, photocopy machines, literacy prgm, computers for public use, Internet srvs, books by mail, homework assist. FUNDING: County. HRS: M-F 8am-5pm. Spanish spoken. SERVES: San Bernardino County.

SAN BERNARDINO CO. LIBRARY
Trona Branch
82805 Mountain View
Trona, CA 93562
(760) 372-5847
(760) 372-5847 FAX

Large print books, computers, Internet, copier, videos, books in Spanish. Children's storytime. HRS: M 10am-8pm; Tu-F 10am-6pm. SERVES: Trona.

SAN BERNARDINO CO. LIBRARY
Twentynine Palms Branch
6078 Adobe Rd.
Twentynine Palms, CA 92277
(760) 367-9519
(760) 361-0703 FAX

Large print books, Internet, computer, videos, CDs, preschool story hour, books on tape. Local history, desert section, adult literacy prgm. HRS: M, Tu 12noon-8pm; W-F 10am-6pm; Sat 9am-5pm. SERVES: Twentynine Palms.

SAN BERNARDINO CO. LIBRARY
Victorville Branch
15011 Circle Dr.
Victorville, CA 92392
(760) 245-4222
(760) 245-2273 FAX

Large print books, computers, Internet, typewriter, preschool story hour, CDs, DVDs, books on tape, videos, magazines. Books in Spanish, German, French, Chinese. Literacy prgm. HRS: M-Th 9am-8pm; F 9am-6pm. SERVES: Victorville.

SAN BERNARDINO CO. LIBRARY
Wrightwood Branch Library
P.O. Box 1962
6011 Pine St.
Wrightwood, CA 92397
(760) 249-4577
(760) 249-3263 FAX

Books on cassette, large print books, Internet, copier, literacy prgm, preschool story hour. FUNDING: Friends of the Library. HRS: M, W 12noon-7pm; Tu, Th, F 10am-6pm; Sat 10am-2pm. SERVES: Wrightwood, Phelan, Pinon Hills.

SAN BERNARDINO CO. LIBRARY
Yucaipa Branch
12040 5th Street
Yucaipa, CA 92399
(909) 790-3146
(909) 790-3151 FAX

Books on cassette. large print books, Internet, copier, computer, videos, CDs. Books in Spanish, literacy prgm, microfilm printer, preschool story hour. HRS: M-Th 10am-8pm; F 10am-6pm; Sat 9am-5pm. SERVES: San Bernardino County.

SAN BERNARDINO CO. LIBRARY
Yucca Valley Branch Library
57098 Twentynine Palms Hwy.
Yucca Valley, CA 92284
(760) 228-5455
(760) 228-5459 FAX

Books on tape, large print books, typewriter, Internet, copier, computer, videos, CDs. Meeting room, lteracy prgm, LITE Center. Located in the Yucca Valley Community Center. HRS: M, W, F 10am-6pm; Tu, Th 12noon-8pm; Sat 9am-5pm. SERVES: San Bernardino County.

SAN BERNARDINO PUBLIC LIBRARY
Feldheym Central Library
555 W. 6th Street
San Bernardino, CA 92410
(909) 381-8201
(909) 381-8229 FAX

Sponsored by the city of San Bernardino. Large print books, books on tape, copiers, typewriter, Internet, computers, DVDs. Some books in Spanish, a few other languages. Preschool story hour. 200,000 volumes. Meeting rooms. California history room. Literacy prgm headquarters. For details, call (909) 341-8240. HRS: M-W 10am-8pm; Th-Sat 10am-6pm. SERVES: San Bernardino County.

SAN BERNARDINO PUBLIC LIBRARY
Howard M. Rowe Branch Library
108 E. Marshall Blvd.
San Bernardino, CA 92404
(909) 883-3411
(909) 882-4941 FAX

Books on cassette, large print books, Internet, copier, DVDs, videos. Preschool story hour. Good children's books collection. HRS: M, Tu 3pm-8pm; W,Th 10am-3pm. Spanish spoken. SERVES: San Bernardino County.

SAN BERNARDINO PUBLIC LIBRARY
Paul Villasenor Branch Library
525 N. Mt. Vernon Ave.
San Bernardino, CA 92411
(909) 383-5156
(909) 381-1766 FAX

Copiers, videos, meeting room, Internet. Excellent Spanish book and magazine collection. Art gallery. HRS: M, Tu 3pm-8pm; W, Th 10am-3pm. SERVES: San Bernardino County.

SAN BERNARDINO PUBLIC LIBRARY
Dorothy Inghram Branch Library
1505 W. Highland Ave.
San Bernardino, CA 92411
(909) 887-4494
(909) 887-6594 FAX

Typewriter, computer, Internet, copier, videos, DVDs. Excellent black studies collection, books in Spanish. HRS: M, Tu 3pm-8pm; W, Th 10am-3pm. SERVES: San Bernardino County.

SO CALIF COLLEGE OF OPTOMETRY/LIB
M. B. Ketchum Memorial Library
2575 Yorba Linda Blvd.
Fullerton, CA 92831-1699
(714) 449-7440
(714) 879-0481 FAX

Library materials focus on issues regarding vision. HRS: M-Th 7:30am-11pm; F 7:30am-5pm; Sat 9am-5pm; Sun 11am-11pm. ADM REQ: Library is open to anyone but check-out privileges are limited to faculty, students, health care professionals. SERVES: So. Calif

SO CALIF GENEALOGICAL SOCIETY LIBR
417 Irving Dr.
Burbank, CA 91504-2408
(818) 843-7247
(818) 843-7262 FAX

Library has 30,000+ volumes related to genealogical research. Open to the public. Genealogy reference library only. HRS: Tu 10am-9pm; W-F 10am-4pm; 1st & 2nd Sun and 3rd & 4th Sat 10am-4pm. SERVES: U.S.A.

UNIV OF CALIF-RIVERSIDE LIBRARY
UC Riverside, Bldg. 053
P.O. Box 5900
Riverside, CA 92517
(951) 827-1012
(951) 787-3285 FAX

Primarily an academic library used by students and faculty with secondary users being the community. Assist with access to or line catalog & reference srvs. HRS: M-Th 8am-7pm; F 8am-5pm; Sat, Sun 10am-5pm. Fee for library card valid for one year. SERVES: Riverside County.

UNIV OF CALIF-RIVERSIDE LIBRARY
Water Resources Center Archives
P.O. Box 5900
Riverside, CA 92521
(951) 827-2934
(951) 827-6378 FAX

Water resource info for the public & professional. Info about legal issues as well as ground water, pollution, drinking water, waste water, coasts, estuaries & precipitation. Visit (http://wrca.library.ucr.edu/). FUNDING: Univ Calif Division of Agriculture & Natural Resources. SERVES: Calif.

UNIVERSITY OF LA VERNE/LAW LIBRARY
Law Library
320 East D Street
Ontario, CA 91764
(909) 460-2070
(909) 460-2083 FAX

An academic law library. Copier, govt deposit: state, fed (partial collection). FUNDING: Nonprofit. HRS: M-Th 8am-11pm; F 8am-9pm; Sat 9am-9pm; Sun 12noon-9pm. SERVES: U.S.A.

UNIVERSITY OF REDLANDS LIBRARY
George and Verda Armacost Library
1129 E. Colton Ave.
Redlands, CA 92374
(909) 335-4021
(909) 335-3403 FAX

Sponsored by the University of Redlands. CDs. Study Carrels. Farquhar Collection on American South West & MacNair Collection (China, Japan, Korea). Also depository for govt publications and maps. Call for hours. OFC HRS: M-Th 8am-12midnight; F 8am-9pm; Sat 10am-9pm; Sun 1pm-12midnight. French & Spanish spoken. ADM REQ: Primarily for students of the univ but available to the public with a fee for a visitors card. SERVES: Redlands.

UPLAND PUBLIC LIBRARY
450 N. Euclid Ave.
Upland, CA 91786
(909) 931-4200
(909) 931-4209 FAX

Sponsored by the city of Upland. Books on cassette, large print books, copier, videos, CDs, DVDs, Internet. Books in Spanish & Chinese. Meeting room, preschool story time, literacy prgm. Good local history collection and Calif collection. Excellent reference srv. HRS: M, Tu 10am-8pm; W, Th 10am-7pm; Sat 10am-4pm; Sun 1pm-5pm. SERVES: Upland & nearby.

VICTOR VALLEY COLLEGE LIBRARY
18422 Bear Valley Rd.
Victorville, CA 92392
(760) 245-4271
(760) 245-4373 FAX

Community college library is open for students and the community. Law library, local history, INFOTRAC, newsbank, periodicals, searching, visual tek machine for partially sighted. Books on cassette, typewriter, copier, videos, microfiche/film reader. OFC HRS: M-Th 8am-9pm; F 8am-4pm; Sat 10am-3pm. ADM REQ: Student library card requires proof of current registration. Community member library card requires a social security number, current Calif driver's license and a $12 annual fee. SERVES: Victorville.

WORLD RESEARCH FOUNDATION
41 Bell Rock Plaza
Sedona, AZ 86351-8804
(928) 284-3300
(928) 284-3530 FAX

Info on alternative & conventional therapies for major diseases. Library has research on all major diseases plus worldwide info on any health problem from A-Z, library searches on most health concerns. Publishes a quarterly newsletter for min donation of $20 annually. Walk in or call. FUNDING: Donors, nonprofit. HRS: M, W, F 10am-5pm. Accepts donations. Fee for health searches. SERVES: Internatl.

LITERACY/ESL PROGRAMS

APPLE VALLEY USD STATE PRESCHOOL PRGM

Preschool Family Resource Center
121951 Mesquite Rd.
Apple Valley, CA 92308
(760) 247-2052
(760) 247-5681 FAX

State preschool prgm for children ages 3-4 yrs. Free to eligible families. Offers family resource center that supports cognitive and language dev which will prepare the children for successful opportunities. FUNDING: State. OFC HRS: M-F 8am- 4pm. Spanish spoken. SERVES: High Desert.

BANNING HIGH ADULT EDUCATION

Banning Unified School District
541 N. Alessandro Rd.
Banning, CA 92220
(951) 922-2740
(951) 922-9499 FAX

ABE deals with English, math, science, history and geography needs to get diploma. GED prep for high school equivalency diploma tests. ESL is open to non-English speaking students ages 18 yrs+, however, they try to acccommodate everyone. Open enrollment. Some individual tutoring. Concurrent adult education. OFC HRS: M-F 7:30am-4:30pm. SERVES: Riverside County.

BANNING PUBLIC LIBRARY

Literacy Program
21 W. Nicolet St.
Banning, CA 92220
(951) 769-0361

One-to-one tutoring in reading and writing to English-speaking adults. Laubach materials are used. Tutoring provided year round. ESL classes for non-English speaking persons ages 18 yrs+. Spanish spoken. SERVES: Riverside County.

BARSTOW LITERACY COALITION

304 E. Buena Vista St.
Barstow, CA 92311
(760) 256-4847
(760) 256-4852 FAX

Dedicated to helping adults ages 18 yrs+, who want to improve reading, writing, basic math & English. Volunteers tutor one-on-one or in small groups. FUNDING: United Way, govt, donations, nonprofit. HRS: Call M-W 12noon-8pm; Tu, Th, F 10am-6pm; Sat 9am-5pm. Spanish spoken. Free srvs. SERVES: Barstow, Needles, Trona, Lucerne Valley & nearby.

CENTER FOR EMPLOYMENT TRAINING

1430 Cooley Ct.
San Bernardino, CA 92408
(909) 478-3818
(909) 478-9506 FAX

Training in automated, machine tool operator, CNC machine setup operator, light gauge welding, field maintenance, welding fabrication, accounting clerk ESL, GED. FUNDING: Nonprofit. OFC HRS: M-F 8am-5pm. Spanish spoken. Financial assist to those who qualify. SERVES: Riverside & San Bernardino Counties.

CENTER FOR EMPLOYMENT TRAINING

Vocational Skill Training/Injured Worker

27941 Jefferson Ave, Ste A
Temecula, CA 92590
(951) 699-8180
(951) 699-3851 FAX

Training school offers shipping & receiving, forklift certification, accounting & payroll clerk, computer clerk, Medical and admin assist, GED, ESL offered concurrent with training. TRA, ITA, Rehab, financial aid funds available. FUNDING: Nonprofit. OFC HRS: M-F 8am-5pm. Spanish spoken. SERVES: Temecula & nearby.

CHAFFEY ADULT SCHOOL

557 W. 5th Street
Ontario, CA 91762
(909) 983-7102

High school diploma classes, GED, some vocational courses. FUNDING: Govt. OFC HRS: M-F 8:30am-4pm. Spanish spoken. ADM REQ: Ages 18 yrs+. Various payment options. SERVES: Ontario.

CHINO COMMUNITY ADULT SCHOOL

See "Chino Valley Adult School"

CHINO VALLEY ADULT SCHOOL

Chino Valley Unified School District
12970 3rd Street
Rancho Cucamonga, CA 91701
(909) 627-9613
(909) 548-6016 FAX

ESL, citizenship, GED prep, GED testing center, high school diploma. Walk in or call. FUNDING: State, federal, nonprofit. OFC HRS: M-F 7:30am-9pm. Spanish, Portuguese spoken. SERVES: San Bernardino County.

CITY LIBRARY LITERACY CENTER

San Bernardino Public Library

See "San Bernardino Co. Lib/Literacy"

CITY OF RIVERSIDE PUBLIC LIBRARY

Eastside Library Connection/Nichols Cybrary Connection
4033-C Chicago Ave.
Riverside, CA 92507
(951) 684-8347
(951) 684-8347 FAX

Info learning center for children ages 10-14 yrs, and their families. Free computer training, Internet, info literacy, homework assist, literacy & special presentations for adults. FUNDING: Riverside Public Library, grants, nonprofit. HRS: M-Th 11am-7pm; F, Sat 10am-6pm. SERVES: Riverside County.

CLAREMONT ADULT SCHOOL

170 W. San Jose Ave., 3rd Fl.
Claremont, CA 91711
(909) 398-0609
(909) 398-0690 FAX

ESL, HS diploma, literacy, parent edu enrichment, vocational, older adult and community srvs classes. Located near bus route. FUNDING: State, local, govt. OFC HRS: M-Th 8am-3pm; F 8:30am-12pm. Spanish spoken. ADM REQ: Ages 18 yrs+. SERVES: Claremont, Pomona, Montclair, San Dimas, La Verne & Upland.

COACHELLA VALLEY ADULT SCHOOL

Coachella Valley Adult School/GED Ctr

1099 Orchard Ave.
Coachella, CA 92236
(760) 398-6302
(760) 398-0436 FAX

ESL and ABE with open enrollment. High school diploma, GED prep and testing, computer skills classes, citizenship, business financial management, notary public, local center for employment training. OFC HRS: M-Th 8am-9pm; F 8am-5pm. Spanish spoken. ADM REQ: Ages 18 yrs+. Accepts pvt pay. SERVES: Coachella.

COLLEGE OF THE DESERT

43-500 Monterey Ave.
Palm Desert, CA 92260
(760) 346-8041
(760) 776-0136 FAX

Two-year community college with an enrollment of more than 8,000 students each semester. Associate degrees and certificate prgms offered in more than 70 areas of study. Students may attend classes at the college's main campus in Palm Desert, at the Eastern Valley Center in Indio, or at the Western Valley Ctr in Palm Springs. Committed to meeting the edu needs of students in academic transfer, vocational and occupational studies. High school completion prgms and classes in community edu. Library maintains 45,000 volumes accessible to students, residents and the community. OFC HRS: M, Th 9am-4pm; Tu, W 9am-6pm; F 9am-1pm. Spanish spoken. Calif residents classes cost $20 per unit. SERVES: Riverside County.

COLTON PUBLIC LIBRARY

Advance To Literacy
656 N. 9th Street
Colton, CA 92324
(909) 370-5170
(909) 422-0873 FAX

Adult literacy prgm for ages 16 yrs+. Teaches reading and writing 3-4 hrs each week. English language learning intensive prgm. Also offers family literacy prgm and homework assist center. FUNDING: Grants, donations, nonprofit. OFC HRS: M, F, Sat 10am-6pm; W 12pm-8pm. Free srvs. SERVES: Colton area.

CORONA-NORCO ADULT SCHOOL

Corona-Norco Unified School District
300 Buena Vista Ave.
Corona, CA 92882-1937
(951) 736-3325
(951) 736-7159 FAX

Classes in literacy, ESL, ABE, GED, high school diploma. Short-term training in computers, medical and office occupations. Open enrollment. Bilingual staff. Day & eve classes. OFC HRS: M-Th 9am-8pm; F 8am-1pm. Spanish spoken. Fees for some classes.

DESERT HIGHLAND EVEN START

Palm Springs Unified School Dist
980 E. Tahquitz Canyon Way
Palm Springs, CA 92262
(760) 416-6000
(760) 416-8278 FAX

Adult edu, ESL, adult literacy. Phone number above is for the district contact. To reach the site directly, call (760) 416-8279. FUNDING: Federal. OFC HRS: M-F 7:30am-4:30pm. Spanish spoken. ADM REQ: Adults with children ages birth-8 yrs. Low literacy, low income. Free srvs. SERVES: Palm Springs.

EDUCATIONAL OPTIONS CENTER

Riverside USD Adult & Alt Edu
6401 Lincoln Ave.
Riverside, CA 92506
(951) 276-7670
(951) 276-7685 FAX

Home health aid, CNA, medical assist, ofc occupations (including computers), medical billing and coding, medical terminology and anatomy, computer classes, ESL, high school diploma and GED. FUNDING: Nonprofit. OFC HRS: M-Th 8am-4:30pm; F 7:30am-4pm. Summer hrs: M-F 7:30am-4pm. Spanish spoken. SERVES: Riverside County.

ENGLISH AS A SECOND LANGUAGE

See listings in this chapter showing "ESL" classes or prgms.

FONTANA ADULT SCHOOL

10755 Oleander Ave.
Fontana, CA 92337
(909) 357-5490
(909) 357-5556 FAX

ESL and citizenship open enrollment prgms. High school diploma prgm, GED prep & testing. Adult literacy. OFC HRS: M-Th 1pm-9pm; F 11am-4pm; Sat 8am-2pm. SERVES: Fontana.

HADASSAH SOUTHERN CALIFORNIA

Administrative Office
9463 Gregory Way
Beverly Hills, CA 90212
(310) 234-8300
(310) 248-4944 FAX

Five area resource ctrs in L.A. & Orange Counties. Offers local programming to advocate for all women's health issues, promotes literacy and edu, encourages social action and volunteerism, and ensures Jewish growth and continuity. Long Beach & Orange County (714) 545-7162; Metro L.A. (310) 276-0036; Valley (818) 343-9316; San Diego (858) 547-9200; Desert (760) 327-7059. OFC HRS: M-Th 8:30am-4:30pm; F 8:30am-3pm. SERVES: L.A. Co.

HEMET ADULT SCHOOL

26866 San Jacinto St.
Hemet, CA 92544
(951) 765-5190
(951) 925-7478 FAX

High school diploma, GED, ESL. Walk in. Spanish class available. FUNDING: ADA. OFC HRS: M-Th 1am-7pm. ADM REQ: Transcripts for high school diploma students. $10 registration fee. $20 per semester for computer classes; all other classes are free. SERVES: Hemet.

HEMET PUBLIC LIBRARY

Adult Literacy Services
315 E. Latham Ave.
Hemet, CA 92543
(951) 765-3856
(951) 765-3857 FAX

One-on-one and small group tutoring for English-speaking adults in reading, writing, spelling, and math (grades K-7). Address above is the physical location, call for mailing address.

OFC HRS: M-Th 8am-5pm. Free srvs. SERVES: Riverside County

HOME OF NEIGHBORLY SERVICE

839 N. Mt. Vernon Ave.
San Bernardino, CA 92411
(909) 885-3491
(909) 884-0181 FAX

After school enrichment prgm for children in grades 1 and up. Recreation, youth skill building, counseling groups, gang intervention & prevention, homework assis/tutoring for youth, Boy & Girl Scouts, nutrition classes for adults, ESL for adults, children's clothes closet, Narcotics Anonymous meetings, parenting support groups, sewing for adults, boxing, hip hop dancing, aerobics & emerg food srv, resource & referrals. OFC HRS: M-Th 8am-5:30pm; F 8am-5pm. Spanish spoken. Free srvs & referrals. SERVES: San Bernardino County.

INSTITUTE/STUDY OF ADULT LITERACY

Penn State University
405 Keller Bldg.
University Park, PA 16802
(814) 863-3777
(814) 863-6108 FAX

Research & dev, prgm eval, staff training, consulting in workforce edu, family, adult & adol literacy. FUNDING: Grants. OFC HRS: M-F 8am-5pm, EST. SERVES: U.S.A.

INTERNATL DYSLEXIA ASSN

Formerly Orton Dyslexia Society
40 York Rd., 4th Fl.
Baltimore, MD 21204
(410) 296-0232
(800) 222-3123
(410) 321-5069 FAX

Clearinghouse with 47 branches providing info on testing, tutoring and effective teaching methods used to aid people with dyslexia. Call to confirm address. FUNDING: Nonprofit. OFC HRS: M-F 8:30am-4:30pm, EST. SERVES: U.S.A.

INTERNATL DYSLEXIA ASSN

Inland Empire Branch
P.O. Box 308
5225 Canyon Crest Dr., Ste 71
Riverside, CA 92507-630
(951) 686-9837

Dyslexia teaching strategies, prgms, articles, and fact sheets. FUNDING: Nonprofit. OFC HRS: Tu, Th 6pm-8pm; Sat 10am-1pm. ADM REQ: Ages 16 yrs+. Free srvs. SERVES: Inland Empire.

JURUPA ADULT EDUCATION

Jurupa Unified School District
4041 Pacific Ave.
Riverside, CA 92509
(951) 222-7739
(951) 788-8689 FAX

Opportunity for many to complete their high school edu or prep for the GED test, review & upgrade skills needed for new or better employment. All levels of ESL are provided. Fee-based enrichment classes are offered on a demand basis. FUNDING: ADA, grants, nonprofit. OFC HRS: M-Th 8am-7:30pm; F 8am-4pm. Spanish spoken. ADM REQ: Call for info on basic computer skill classes. SERVES: Jurupa, Mira Loma, Glen Avon, Pedley, Rubidoux.

LAUBACH LANGUAGE DEVELOPMENT CLASSES

Church of the Valley
P.O. Box 727
20700 Standing Rock Rd.
Apple Valley, CA 92307
(760) 247-6494
(760) 247-1836 FAX

Literacy classes, ESL. Laubach language development. Classes held at various times and locations by a tutor. OFC HRS: W 9am-12noon. Free classes. SERVES: Victor Valley, Barstow & Lucerne Valley.

LITERACY NETWORK OF GREATER L.A.

6505 Wilshire Blvd., Ste 200
Los Angeles, CA 90048
(323) 761-8888
(800) 707-7323
(323) 761-8575 FAX

Prgm links volunteers, learners & teaching materials with 200 literacy prgms operating at more than 1,100 locations in So. Calif. FUNDING: Nonprofit. OFC HRS: M-F 9am-5pm. Free srvs. SERVES: So. Calif.

MICROREAD/LITERACY PROGRAM

San Bernardino Public Library

See "San Bernardino Co. Lib/Literacy"

MORENO VALLEY ADULT SCHOOL

Moreno Valley Unified School District
13350 Indian St.
Moreno Valley, CA 92553
(951) 571-4790
(951) 571-4795 FAX

ESL, ABE, literacy, high school diploma, ESL civics, GED prep & testing. Most classes are open enrollment. OFC HRS: M-Th 8:30am-3:30pm, 5pm-7:30pm; F 8:30am-3:15pm. No fees for classes. SERVES: Riverside County.

MORENO VALLEY CITY LIBRARY

Moreno Valley Library/Literacy
25480 Alessandro Blvd.
Moreno Valley, CA 92553
(951) 413-3880
(951) 247-8346 FAX

Blueprint for literacy prgm teaches adults to read. Contact Laura (951) 242-6366. OFC HRS: M-Th 9am-8pm; Sat 9am-6pm. SERVES: Moreno Valley.

MORONGO BASIN COALITION/ADULT LIT

San Bernardino Co. Library Literacy
6078 Adobe Rd.
Twentynine Palms, CA 92277
(760) 367-1146
(760) 361-0703 FAX

One-to-one tutoring by trained volunteers. Literacy special interview, matches learners with tutors. Families for Literacy prgm. Also call (760) 228-5461 for Yucca Valley site. FUNDING: Nonprofit. ADM REQ: Adults 18 yrs+, not registered in a formal edu prgm. Call to schedule an appt. Free tutoring & materials. SERVES: Morongo Basin.

NATL INST FOR LITERACY HOTLINE

c/o Literacy Directory
1775 I Street, NW, Ste 730
Washington, DC 20006-2401
(800) 228-8813
(202) 233-2050 FAX

Referrals to local and natl prgms for adult edu students, volunteers and srv providers. Visit (http://www.literacydirectory.org). FUNDING: Private, nonprofit. OFC HRS: M-F 9am-6pm, EST. Spanish spoken. Free referrals. SERVES: U.S.A.

NORTHTOWN HOUSING DEVELOPMENT

Northtown Housing College Scholarship
8599 Haven Ave., Ste 205
Rancho Cucamonga, CA 91730
(909) 980-0465

Community center offers free summer lunch prgm, ESL classes, GED, govt food commodities, after school recreation & tutoring, immunizations, summer day camp, holiday toy giveaway, info & referrals, job skills workshops, affordable housing. FUNDING: Nonprofit. OFC HRS: M-F 8am-5pm. Spanish spoken. SERVES: Rancho Cucamonga & nearby.

ORTON DYSLEXIA SOCIETY

See "Internatl Dyslexia Assn"

PALM SPRINGS PUBLIC LIBRARY

Library Center
300 S. Sunrise Way
Palm Springs, CA 92262
(760) 322-7323
(760) 320-9834 FAX

Sponsored by the city of Palm Springs. Large print books, copier, videos, CDs. Books in Spanish. Preschool story hour. Good business, art & Calif Collection. Literacy prgm. Distance learning prgm. HRS: Tu 10am-7pm; W-Sat 10am-5pm. SERVES: Palm Springs.

PALM SPRINGS UNIFIED SCHOOL DIST

Palm Springs Adult School
2248 Ramon Rd.
Palm Springs, CA 92262
(760) 778-0494
(760) 778-0497 FAX

ESL, family literacy courses, GED prep & testing, high school diploma prgm, computer & business courses all with open enrollment, medical back ofc assist, medical front ofc insurance billing prgm, medical terminology required for med assist prgm, community enrichment. OFC HRS: M-Th 9am-7pm; F 9am-1pm. Spanish spoken. ADM REQ: Ages 18 yrs. SERVES: Palm Springs, Thousand Palms, Desert Hot Springs, Cathedral City, Rancho Mirage.

PALO VERDE COMMUNITY COLLEGE

1 College Dr.
Blythe, CA 92225
(760) 922-6168
(760) 921-3608 FAX

ESL classes. Evening and daytime classes. Walk in or call. OFC HRS: M-Th 8am-6:30pm; F 8am-4:30pm. Spanish spoken. Fees: $20 per unit, fees may be waived for low income people. SERVES: Eastern Riverside & San Bernardino Counties, includes Blythe, Needles.

PAPA DIDOS IDEALS FOUNDATION

1392 Spectrum Dr.
Irvine, CA 92618
(949) 500-3030

Promotes literacy, primarily to underpriviliged and at-risk youth. Writes and donates their own books to the cause. Visit (www.papadidos.com) for more info. FUNDING: Nonprofit. OFC HRS: M-F 9am-9pm; Sat, Sun 10am-7pm. Spanish, Mandarin, Japanese, Cantonese, Vietnamese

spoken. SERVES: L.A., Orange, and Riverside Counties.

PERRIS VALLEY FAMILY RESOURCE CENTER

371 Wilkerson Ave., Ste L
Perris, CA 92570
(951) 443-1158
(951) 940-1964 FAX

Comprehensive srvs to families and children. Parents & teen classes, counseling, training workshops, food referrals, rental assist, ESL, anger mgmt, Healthy Families applications, college enrollment information. FUNDING: Govt. OFC HRS: M-Th 8am-5pm. Spanish spoken. SERVES: Perris Valley area, Moreno Valley, Lake Elsinore, Hemet and surrounding areas.

PRO LITERACY WORLDWIDE

Formerly Literacy Volunteers of America
1320 Jamesville Ave.
Syracuse, NY 13210
(888) 528-2224
(315) 422-6369 FAX

Help with establishment of local adult literacy prgms. Currently working in 50 states and D.C., 1,200 affiliate prgms. Provides accreditation, advocacy & tech assist to prgms. FUNDING: Nonprofit. OFC HRS: M-F 9am-5pm, EST. Spanish & Hebrew spoken. Free srvs to students. SERVES: U.S.A. & Internatl.

RANCHO CUCAMONGA PUBLIC LIBRARY

West End Literacy League
7368 Archibald Ave.
Rancho Cucamonga, CA 91730
(909) 477-2720
(909) 477-2721 FAX

Adult literacy srvs to English-speaking adults who want to improve basic reading and writing skills. Adult learners are matched with trained volunteer tutors for free one-to-one tutoring. Instruction is based on the learner's needs and goals. Families for literacy srvs are available to adults who are enrolled in the literacy prgm and who have preschool children. Back to Basics improves reading and writing skills of children ages 7-12 yrs. OFC HRS: M-Th 10am-9pm; F 12pm-6pm; Sat 10am-5pm; Sun 1pm-5pm. Free srvs. SERVES: Alta Loma, Etiwanda, Ontario, Rancho Cucamonga, Upland.

RANCHO CUCAMONGA RESOURCE CENTER

9791 Arrow Route
Rancho Cucamonga, CA 91730
(909) 477-2781
(909) 919-2625 FAX

Resource center provides access to various srvs provided to the community. Prgms include: emerg needs (food and clothing), domestic abuse prevention workshops and counseling, ESL classes, parenting classes, youth socialization prgms, room rentals, info & referral srvs. FUNDING: Govt, city, donations. OFC HRS: M-F 8am-10pm. Spanish spoken. ADM REQ: Residents, however no one will be turned away. SERVES: Riverside, San Bernardino Counties.

RANDALL PEPPER SCHOOL

Even Start Project
16613 Randall Ave.
Fontana, CA 92335
(909) 357-5730
(909) 357-5736 FAX

Family literacy, ESL, math, computers, citizenship, GED & parenting. FUNDING: Nonprofit. OFC HRS: M-F 7:30am-4pm. Spanish spoken. SERVES: North Fontana & South Fontana

REDLANDS ADULT SCHOOL

Redlands Unified School District
820 W. Stuart Ave.
Redlands, CA 92374
(909) 748-6930
(909) 307-5324 FAX

Vocational prgms include: vocational nursing, nursing assistant, clerical skills, word processing, home health aid acute care, pharmacy technician. OFC HRS: M, Tu 9am-8pm; W, Th 9am-5pm; F 9am-4:30pm. Summer: M-F 9am-4:30pm. SERVES: Redlands.

REDLANDS CITY LIBRARY

A. K. Smiley Public Library
125 W. Vine St.
Redlands, CA 92373
(909) 798-7565
(909) 798-7566 FAX

Sponsored by the city of Redlands and also known as the Smiley Library. Large print books, videos, CDs, computers, Internet. Preschool story hour. One wing houses the heritage room collection including books, documents and photos on local and California history. Lincoln shrine collection with books, photos, memorabilia on Lincoln and the Civil War (open Tu-Sun 1pm-5pm). Literacy prgm for ages 18 yrs+. FUNDING: Govt. HRS: M, Tu 11am-9pm; W, Th 10am-6pm; F, Sat 10am-5pm; Sun 1pm-5pm. Spanish spoken. SERVES: Redlands.

RIALTO ADULT SCHOOL

Alternative Education Center
182 E. Walnut Ave.
Rialto, CA 92376
(909) 879-6010
(909) 421-7533 FAX

ESL, GED (no testing), diploma classes (computer assisted instruction) and vocational classes (word processing & health occupations). Open enrollment. Students must be either ages 18 yrs+, exempt from high school attendance, or referred by high school counselor for concurrent enrollment. Enroll: 750. OFC HRS: M-Th 7am-6pm. Spanish spoken. SERVES: Rialto.

RIVERSIDE ADULT SCHOOL

Education Services; Riverside U.S.D.
6735 Magnolia Ave.
Riverside, CA 92506
(951) 788-7185
(951) 369-4966 FAX

Open enrollment for ESL, ABE, high school diploma, and GED for adults ages 18 yrs+. Special computer-oriented literacy prgm. Older adult prgm. Eve classes on M-Th 6pm-9:10pm. Authorized GED test. Call for dates & times. OFC HRS: M-F 8am-4:30pm; Tu-Th 5:30am-8:30pm. Spanish spoken. SERVES: Riverside.

RIVERSIDE CO. LIBRARY LITERACY PRGM

Perris Library
163 E. San Jacinto
Perris, CA 92570
(951) 657-0796
(951) 657-9849 FAX

One-to-one literacy help for adults who read and write below 8th grade level. Tutor training is also available. FUNDING: County. HRS: M, Th, Sat 10am-6pm; Tu, W 12noon-8pm; Sun 1pm-5pm. ADM REQ: English speaking, ages 16 yrs+ and out of school. Srvs are confidential & free. SERVES: Anza, Canyon Lake, Idyllwild, Lake Elsinore, Nuview, Perris, San Jacinto, Sun City, Temecula and Valle Vista, Wildomar.

RIVERSIDE CO. LIBRARY LITERACY PRGM
5840 Mission Blvd.
Riverside, CA 92509
(951) 685-6901
(951) 685-3856 FAX

Adult literacy prgm offers one-on-one reading and writing tutoring for English-speaking, and advanced ESL adults ages 16 yrs+. ESL classes offered in the fall and spring semesters. FUNDING: County, Calif State Library, Calif Dept of Edu. HRS: M-F 8am-5pm. SERVES: Indio, Lake Tamarisk, Mecca, Thousand Palms, Palm Desert, Cathedral City, Coachella, Desert Hot Springs, La Quinta.

RIVERSIDE CO. LIBRARY LITERACY PRGM
Glen Avon Library/Program Headquarters
9244 Galena
Riverside, CA 92509
(951) 685-6901
(951) 685-3856 FAX

Adult literacy prgm offers one-on-one reading and writing tutoring for English-speaking adults, ages 16 yrs+ & ESL. The "Families For Literacy" component offers encouragement to adult students, who are parents of pre-school children, to read aloud at home and attend family storytime. FUNDING: County. HRS: M, W 9am-6pm; Tu, F 9am-2pm. Free srvs. SERVES: Highgrove, Rubidoux, Norco, Jurupa, Calimesa, Woodcrest, Glen Avon, Mira Loma.

RIVERSIDE CO. LIBRARY SYSTEM
Cathedral City Library
33520 Date Palm Dr.
Cathedral City, CA 92234
(760) 328-4262
(760) 770-9828 FAX

Copier, preschool story hour, bilingual storytime, computers, large print books, CDs, DVDs, videos, books on tape, literacy prgm, Spanish language collection. Free Internet access. Temp closed due to fire damage. Visit temp site: 68-727 E. Palm Canyon Dr., Cathedral City, CA 92234. FUNDING: County. HRS: M, Tu, Th, Sat 10am-6pm; W 12noon-8pm; Sun 1pm-5pm. Spanish spoken. SERVES: Riverside County.

RIVERSIDE CO. LIBRARY SYSTEM
Paloma Valley Library
31375 Bradley Rd.
Menifee, CA 92584
(951) 301-3682

Adult literacy classes. FUNDING: County. HRS: M-W 12noon-7pm; Th 12noon-5pm; Sat 10am-2pm. SERVES: Menifee.

RIVERSIDE CO. LITERACY NETWORK
6215 River Crest Dr., Ste B
Riverside, CA 92507
(951) 697-4700
(951) 656-8210 FAX

Network for providers of literacy. Call for info. FUNDING: United Way, community collaboration. OFC HRS: M-F 8am-5pm. SERVES: Riverside County.

RIVERSIDE COMMUNITY COLLEGE
ESL and Literacy Programs
4800 Magnolia Ave.
Riverside, CA 92506
(951) 222-8000
(951) 222-8863 FAX

ESL & basic reading classes offered. OFC HRS: M-F 7am-4pm.

RUBIDOUX COMMUNITY RESOURCE CTR
5473 Mission Blvd.
Riverside, CA 92509
(951) 328-1575
(951) 683-2613 FAX

Child abuse prevention ctr provides parenting classes, recruitment for in-home supportive srvs every other month. Classes in nutrition, adult edu, ESL, and job training for youth. healthy kids club, counseling referrals. FUNDING: Nonprofit. OFC HRS: M-F 8am-5pm. ADM REQ: Must sign up for classes. Free srvs. SERVES: Glen Avon, Mira Loma, Riverside, Rubidoux, Sunnyslope.

SAN BERNARDINO CO. LIB/LITERACY
Big Bear Vly Read-to-Learn Program
P.O. Box 1809
41930 Garstin Dr.
Big Bear Lake, CA 92315
(909) 866-4512
(909) 866-4382 FAX

One-on-one tutoring by trained volunteers. Literacy staff interviews and matches learners and tutors. Families for Literacy prgm, English improvement prgm, computer classes. Contact Marta. FUNDING: Nonprofit grants. OFC HRS: Vary. ADM REQ: Ages 18 yrs+. Free tutoring & materials. SERVES: Big Bear Valley.

SAN BERNARDINO CO. LIB/LITERACY
Lake Arrowhead Mt. Literacy Prgm
P.O. Box 1043
27235 Hwy. 189
Blue Jay, CA 92317
(909) 337-5420
(909) 337-2287 FAX

One-to-one tutoring by trained volunteers. Literacy staff interviews, matches learners & tutors. Provides Families for Literacy portion. Small group classes. Computer classes, 13 levels from beginning to advanced, includes: Excel, Word, Powerpoint. Citizenship classes & GED. OFC HRS: M, Tu 12noon-8pm; W-F 10am-6pm. Free tutoring & materials. SERVES: Crestline, Lake Arrowhead, Running Springs.

SAN BERNARDINO CO. LIB/LITERACY
Chino Literacy Campaign
13180 Central Ave.
Chino, CA 91710
(909) 465-5239
(909) 465-5240 FAX

One-on-one tutoring by trained volunteers using the LVA method. Literacy staff interviews, matches learners & tutors. Families for Literacy Prgm. Free tutoring & materials. SERVES: San Bernardino County.

SAN BERNARDINO CO. LIB/LITERACY
Highland Literacy Campaign
27167 E. Base Line
Highland, CA 92346
(909) 862-6469
(909) 864-0816 FAX

One-on-one tutoring by trained volunteers using the LVA method. Literacy staff interviews, matches learners & tutors. Families for Literacy Prgm. OFC HRS: M-W 10am-8pm; Th, F 10am-6pm; Sat 9am-5pm. Spanish spoken. ADM REQ: Ages 18 yrs+ or out of school. Free tutoring & materials. SERVES: San Bernardino County.

SAN BERNARDINO CO. LIB/LITERACY
Administration
104 W. 4th Street
San Bernardino, CA 92415
(909) 574-4561

30 library literacy prgms offer free, confidential, one-on-one tutoring, by trained volunteers, to adults who wish to improve their reading, writing, spelling and math skills. Tutor training schedules are available from your branch library literacy specialist or by calling the literacy hotline # above. OFC HRS: M-F 8am-5pm. SERVES: San Bernardino County.

SAN BERNARDINO CO. LIB/LITERACY
Yucaipa Literacy Coalition
12040 5th Street
Yucaipa, CA 92399
(909) 790-3147
(909) 790-3151 FAX

One-on-one adult tutoring by trained volunteers. Literacy staff interviews, matches learners & tutors. English improvement, Families for Literacy. OFC HRS: Tu 10am-3pm; Th 10am-5pm. ADM REQ: Call for appt. Free tutoring & materials. SERVES: Yucaipa, Mentone, Loma Linda, Redlands, Calimesa.

SAN BERNARDINO PUBLIC LIB/LITERACY
California Literacy Campaign
555 W. 6th Street
San Bernardino, CA 92410
(909) 381-8205
(909) 384-9882 FAX

Volunteers are trained to work with English speaking adults who need to improve basic reading and writing skills. Also assist adults with life skills & computer literacy. Also have after school homework assist & literacy, Families for Literacy, ESL, citizenship classes. OFC HRS: M, Tu 10am-7:30pm; W, Th 10am-5pm. Spanish spoken. ADM REQ: Ages 16 yrs+. SERVES: San Bernardino County.

SO CALIF LIBRARY LITERACY NETWORK
Corona Public Library/Adult Literacy
650 S. Main Street
Corona, CA 92882
(951) 279-3789
(951) 279-3790 FAX

Computer lab, one-to-one tutoring, some ESL, Spanish classes. FUNDING: Nonprofit. OFC HRS: M-Th 10am-9pm; F, Sun 1pm-5pm; Sat 10am-5pm. Free srvs. SERVES: Corona.

TEMECULA VALLEY USD
First 5 Family Literacy Program
41951 Moraga Rd., Rm. 50
Temecula, CA 92591
(951) 695-7153
(951) 695-7173 FAX

Offers a free preschool and four-component family literacy prgms. Adult edu, early childhood edu, parenting edu, parent & child edu. At least one adult parent needs to be involved. FUNDING: Govt. OFC HRS: M-F 8am-12:30pm.

Spanish spoken. Free srvs. SERVES: Temecula Valley USD.

THE 'I AM' FOUNDATION

7825 Fay Ave., Ste 200
La Jolla, CA 92037
(619) 297-7010

Gifts books and music to children and adults world-wide to build their self-esteem and promote literacy. Also works with children in private & public schools and hospitals within the U.S. FUNDING: Nonprofit. Free srvs. Donations accepted. SERVES: Internatl.

TWIN PALMS ADULT EDUCATION

Palo Verde Unified School Dist
190 N. 5th Street
Blythe, CA 92225
(760) 922-4884
(760) 922-1177 FAX

Individualized instruction for adults, ABE, GED and learning lab. Open entry, open exit. OFC HRS: M, W 5pm-8pm. $50 refundable deposit for books and materials. SERVES: Palo Verde Valley & nearby.

UN LIBRO, MIL MUNDOS

One Book, a Thousand Worlds
Riverside County Public Library
(951) 233-6160

Reading prgm aimed at Latino students to improve literacy skills by offering books that focus on life matters they can relate to. Prgm runs weekly at select branch libraries and features book clubs and discussion groups focusing on Latino authors. Contact Arlene Cano, literacy coordinator. FUNDING: County. Spanish spoken. Free srvs. SERVES: Libraries in Coachella, Mecca, Home Gardens, Lake Elsinore and Glen Avon.

UPLAND PUBLIC LIBRARY

Carnegie Literacy Center
450 N. Euclid Ave.
Upland, CA 91786
(909) 931-4212
(909) 931-4226 FAX

Adult literacy srvs to English-speaking adults who want to improve basic reading and writing skills. Adult learners are matched with trained volunteer tutors for one-to-one tutoring. Instruction is based on the learner's needs and goals. Families for Literary Srvs are available to adults who are enrolled in the literacy prgm and who have preschool children. OFC HRS: M-Th 8am-6pm. ADM REQ: Ages 16 yrs+. Free srvs. SERVES: San Bernardino County.

WORLD LITERACY CRUSADE INTERNATL

3209 N. Alameda, Ste B
Compton, CA 90222
(310) 537-2273
(310) 537-2139 FAX

Tutoring individuals to improve their ability to read & communicate. Courses on learning how to learn, how to use a dictionary & communicating is fun. Also classes in parenting, drug edu, art, pro survival life skills & anger mgmt. Some low-income families may apply for sponsorships. All tutoring & classes in English. FUNDING: Grants, donations, govt, client fees, nonprofit. OFC HRS: M-F 9:30am-8:30pm; Sat 11:30am-2:30pm. Some Spanish spoken. Sliding fee scale. Tutor fee applies. SERVES: U.S.A.

YUCAIPA ADULT SCHOOL

35948 Susan St.
Yucaipa, CA 92399
(909) 790-8580
(909) 790-8584 FAX

Comprehensive adult edu srvs for immigrants, older adults: amnesty, vocational, literacy and high school diploma (includes GED prep and testing), srvs for disabled, parent edu, homemaking and community srv. Walk in or call. FUNDING: SDE adult revenue, federal. OFC HRS: M-Th 8am-6pm; F 8am-12noon. Some Spanish spoken. SERVES: Yucaipa, Calimesa.

AMERICAN COUNCIL OF THE BLIND

2200 Wilson Blvd., Ste 650
Arlington, VA 22201
(800) 424-8666
(202) 467-5081
(703) 465-5085 FAX

Membership group for blind and visually impaired persons. Info on blindness, referrals to clinics, rehabs, research centers & local chapters. Publishes resource lists & monthly magazine. Hotline M-F 2pm-5pm, EST. FUNDING: Donations, nonprofit. OFC HRS: M-F 9am-5pm, EST. Free srvs. SERVES: U.S.A.

AUDIO VISION READING FOR THE BLIND

Audio Vision Radio Reading
35242 Yucaipa Blvd., Ste C
Yucaipa, CA 92399
(909) 797-4336
(909) 797-3516 FAX

Radio reading srvs for the blind. 24 hrs, 7 days. FUNDING: Donation, grants, nonprofit. OFC HRS: M-F 8am-2pm; Sat-Sun 8am-12noon. ADM REQ: Blindness or disability preventing reading or understanding print. Sign up for radio. Free srvs. SERVES: So. Calif.

BEACH CITIES BRAILLE GUILD, INC.

P.O. Box 712
Huntington Beach, CA 92648
(714) 969-7992
(714) 960-1815 FAX

Volunteer transcription into Braille. Jumbo Braille for the touch-impaired blind. Counseling resources for blind or visually impaired. FUNDING: Donations, nonprofit. OFC HRS: M-F 9am-5pm. Fees for cost of materials only. Free counseling. SERVES: U.S.A.

BLIND CHILDREN'S CENTER

4120 Marathon St.
Los Angeles, CA 90029
(323) 664-2153
(800) 222-3567
(323) 665-3828 FAX

Diversified srvs which meet special needs of visually impaired or multi-handicapped blind children, ages birth-5yrs and their families. Infant and preschool prgms, extended day care M-F, family support & training, publications, info & referral. Call first. FUNDING: Nonprofit. OFC HRS: M-F 8am-4pm. Spanish spoken. Free srvs. SERVES: Internatl.

BLINDED VETERANS ASSN OF SO CALIF

11000 Wilshire Blvd., Rm. 5212
Los Angeles, CA 90024
(310) 235-6125
(310) 235-6110 FAX

Support & referral to blind veterans & their families. Leave name and phone number on voicemail for a return call. FUNDING: Govt, donation, nonprofit. OFC HRS: M-F 8am-3pm. Spanish spoken. Free srvs. SERVES: So. Calif.

BLINDED VETERANS ASSOCIATION

477 H Street, NW
Washington, DC 20001-2694
(800) 669-7079
(202) 371-8880
(202) 371-8258 FAX

Seeks out blind veterans, offers srv-enhancing employment opportunities, assists in procuring benefits offered by public and pvt agencies, edu info & scholarships. Membership not required. FUNDING: Donations, grants, nonprofit. OFC HRS: M-F 8am-4:30pm, EST. Spanish spoken. Free srvs. SERVES: U.S.A.

BRAILLE INSTITUTE

Desert Center
70-251 Ramon Rd.
Rancho Mirage, CA 92270
(760) 321-1111
(760) 321-9715 FAX

Library srvs. visual aids consultation, counseling, as well as classes for training for independence in the areas of orientation, mobility, sensory awareness, independent living skills, home mgmt, etc. FUNDING: Donations, grants, nonprofit. OFC HRS: M-F 8:30am-5pm. ADM REQ: Blind or visually impaired. No certificate needed. Free srvs. SERVES: Riverside & San Bernardino Counties.

CALIF BOARD OF OPTOMETRY

2420 Del Paso Rd., Ste 255
Sacramento, CA 95834
(866) 585-2666
(916) 575-7170
(916) 575-7292 FAX

Administers exams & issues licenses for practice of optometry, branch offices; registers optometric corporations and fictitious name permits. Enforces regulations for the protection of the consumer patient. Contact this state office if you wish to complain about an optometrist. FUNDING: Govt. OFC HRS: M-F 8am-5pm. SERVES: Calif.

CALIF BOARD/DISPENSING OPTICIANS

Dept of Consumer Affairs
2005 Evergreen St., Ste 1200
Sacramento, CA 95815
(916) 263-2382
(800) 633-2322
(916) 263-2944 FAX

Prgm ensures compliance with the law by Registered Dispensing Opticians (RDO), Spectacle Lens Dispensers (SLD) and Contact Lens Dispensers (CLD). TTY (916) 263-0935. FUNDING: Govt. OFC HRS: M-F 8am-5pm. SERVES: Calif.

CALIF BOARD/GUIDE DOGS FOR BLIND

Dept of Consumer Affairs
1625 N. Market Blvd., Ste S-202
Sacramento, CA 95834
(916) 574-7825
(866) 512-9103
(916) 324-9340 FAX

State agency regulates schools & instructors that provide guide dogs for the blind. No dogs are provided directly through this office. FUNDING: Govt. OFC HRS: M-F 9am-5pm. SERVES: Calif.

CALIF COUNCIL OF THE BLIND

Executive Office
1510 J Street, Ste 125
Sacramento, CA 95814
(800) 221-6359
(916) 441-2100
(916) 441-2188 FAX

Info & referral to legally blind, visually impaired, those experiencing loss of vision and parents/caregivers. Low-cost loans for adaptive equip & referrals. 32 chapters & 8 statewide affiliates in Calif. "California Connection" weekly news line. Advocacy for the blind community, financial scholarships for blind Calif residents going to a Calif vocational or academic institution. Crisis loan fund for members only. After 4pm, call this number to hear recorded news updated weekly. FUNDING: Nonprofit. OFC HRS: M-F 10am-4pm. ADM REQ: Calif residents who are blind or who are interested in blindness issues. Member dues vary per chapter. SERVES: Calif.

CALIF DEAF/BLIND SRVS

2001 Junipero Serra Blvd., 7th Fl.
Daly City, CA 94014
(800) 822-7884
(415) 405-7560
(415) 405-7562 FAX

Srvs available to personnel from public & pvt schools & public agencies, family members & care providers of individuals who are deaf-blind. Voice/TTY (415) 239-8089, ext. 23. FUNDING: U.S. Dept of Ed Special Edu Prgms. ADM REQ: Ages birth-21 yrs. SERVES: Calif.

CALIF-HAWAII ELKS MAJOR PROJECT, INC.

5450 E. Lamona Ave.
Fresno, CA 93727-2224
(559) 255-4531
(559) 456-2659 FAX

Vision screening for children in preschool-3rd grade in pvt or parochial preschools, primary and day care centers. Referrals for speech therapy, OT & PT. FUNDING: Donations, nonprofit. OFC HRS: M-F 8am-4:30pm. ADM REQ: Preschool through 3rd grade for vision screening, ages birth-18 yrs for therapy srvs. Free srvs. SERVES: Calif & Hawaii.

CALIF-HAWAII ELKS VISION SCREENING

P.O. Box 704
Sun City, CA 92586
(951) 672-0667
(951) 672-0667 FAX

Not a child care prgm, but provides free vision screening for preschool up to 3rd grade in private or parochial preschools, primary schools, day care centers and nursery schools. FUNDING: Dues, nonprofit. OFC HRS: M-F 8am-4:30pm. ADM REQ: Call for times. Cannot duplicate srvs. Free srvs. SERVES: Riverside, Corona, Norco, Lake Elsinore, Perris, San Jacinto, Hemet, Temecula.

CENTER FOR THE PARTIALLY SIGHTED

6101 W. Centinela Ave., Ste 150
Culver City, CA 90230
(310) 988-1970
(310) 988-1980 FAX

Low-vision srvs for the partially sighted and/or legally blind. Training with prescribed visual devices, psych counseling, diabetes edu & support group, HIV & vision loss prgm, pediatric vision assessments, orientation & mobility instruction, independent living skills classes & independent living aids, home safety assessments. Technology assessments including intro to specific devices for work or school such as computer software, telescopic lenses.

Transportation for appts in L.A. area. Wait: 1-3 weeks. FUNDING: Corp, grants, donors, state, fees, nonprofit. OFC HRS: M-F 8:30am-5pm, by appt. Spanish spoken. ASL available. Other languages available upon request. ADM REQ: Visually impaired, including legally blind. Accepts Medicare & Medi-Cal to cover portion of exams. Sliding fee scale. SERVES: U.S.A.

COMMUNITY HEALTH SYSTEMS, INC.

I.E. Community Health Center
18601 Valley Blvd.
Bloomington, CA 92316
(909) 877-0510
(909) 877-1818
(909) 877-5468 FAX

Primary health care for all ages. OB/GYN, prenatal, dental srvs, optometry, referrals, pediatrician, internal medicine. No-cost dental screenings offered to clients, must provide proof of income or unemployment. FUNDING: Donations, nonprofit. OFC HRS: M-F 8am-5:30pm. Spanish spoken. ADM REQ: Low income. Accepts insurance, Medicare, Medi-Cal, sliding fee scale, I.E.H.P., Molina. SERVES: San Bernardino County.

DOHENY EYE INSTITUTE

Univ of So Calif Health Sciences
1450 San Pablo St.
Los Angeles, CA 90033
(323) 442-7100
(323) 342-7127 FAX

Umbrella organization for six fully integrated entities which encompass patient care, edu, consultations and research missions. Doheny Eye Medical Group provides tertiary and quaternary eye care. Patients are usually referred by their doctor, but may also self-refer for second opinion. Satellite facilities in: Orange, Arcadia, Pasadena, Riverside. Doheny USC Eyeglasses and Contact Lens Srv provides basic vision exams & eye care. Full-srv optical shop. Surgical facilities including the Doheny Ambulatory Surgery Ctr and the USC Laser Vision Center. Most languages available upon request. For eye medical group appts (323) 442-6335. Refractive surgery appts (323) 342-6377. FUNDING: Private fees, nonprofit. OFC HRS: M-F 8:30am-5pm. Spanish, Chinese, Korean, Hindi, Tagalog and Portuguese spoken. Accepts Medi-Cal, almost all types of insurance. SERVES: U.S.A. & internatl.

ESTELLE DOHENY EYE FOUNDATION

See "Doheny Eye Institute"

EYE CARE CLINIC

So Calif College of Optometry
2575 Yorba Linda Blvd.
Fullerton, CA 92831
(714) 449-7444
(714) 992-7811 FAX

Complete vision care including vision exams, ophthalmic materials (eye glasses), contact lens eval & fitting, vision therapy, pediatric vision care, low vision & vision enhancement, ocular disease eval & treatment and eval for computer-related vision problems. Also srvs for dyslexia. Call for appt. FUNDING: Patient fees, nonprofit. OFC HRS: M-Tu 9am-6pm; W 11am-8pm; Th 10am-7pm; F-Sat 8am-5pm. Spanish spoken. Accepts Medi-Cal. SERVES: So. Calif.

EYE FOUNDATION

See "Doheny Eye Institute"

EYECARE AMERICA

Seniors EyeCare Prgm
P.O. Box 429098
655 Beach St.
San Francisco, CA 94142-9098
(877) 887-6327
(415) 561-8567 FAX

Provides a comprehensive medical eye exam and up to one year of care for anything diagnosed at exam time at no out-of-pocket cost. Uninsured are seen at no charge for physician's services. FUNDING: Knights Templar Eye Fndn Inc., state ophthalmological societies, nonprofit. OFC HRS: 24 hrs, 7 days. Spanish spoken. ADM REQ: Ages 65 yrs+, a citizen or legal resident who has not seen an ophthalmologist in 3 yrs or more. Medicare and insurance are billed and accepted as payment in full. SERVES: U.S.A.

FAMILY SERVICE ASSN/REDLANDS

612 Lawton St.
Redlands, CA 92374
(909) 793-2673
(909) 793-7324 FAX

Srvs provided to low-income and homeless families. Case mgmt, food, clothing, utility and rental assist, cold weather motel vouchers, screening for dental & vision, prescription assist, and edu prgms. Home Again Project is a long-term comprehensive prgm helping homeless families into permanent housing and employment. Client srv M-W, F 9am-12noon, 1:30pm-7pm. Surplus food available on walk-in basis, all other srvs require appt. FUNDING: Donations, United Way, grants, nonprofit. OFC HRS: M-W 8am-7pm; Th 8am-12noon; F 8am-4:30pm. Spanish spoken. ADM REQ: Low or no income. Free srvs. SERVES: Redlands, East Valley area.

FOUNDATION FIGHTING BLINDNESS

Southern California
11900 W. Olympic Blvd., Ste 560
Los Angeles, CA 90064
(310) 207-2089
(310) 207-2039 FAX

Info on retinal degenerative diseases including RP & macular degeneration. FUNDING: Nonprofit. OFC HRS: M-F 9am-5pm. SERVES: So. Calif.

FOUNDATION FIGHTING BLINDNESS

11435 Cronhill Dr.
Owings Mills, MD 21117-2220
(800) 683-5551
(410) 568-0150
(410) 363-2393 FAX

Info & referral srvs for affected individuals & their families as well as for doctors & eye care professionals. The fndn also provides comprehensive info kits on retinitis pigmentosa, macular degeneration, and Usher syndrome. Newsletter, InFocus, and e-newsletter, InSight, present articles on coping, research updates, and fndn news. Local TDD (410) 363-7139. FUNDING: Donations, grants, nonprofit. OFC HRS: M-F 9am-4pm, EST. SERVES: U.S.A.

GUIDE DOG FOUNDATION FOR BLIND

371 E. Jericho Turnpike
Smithtown, NY 11787-2976

(800) 548-4337
(631) 930-9000
(631) 930-9009 FAX

Increased mobility through the use of guide dogs. The blind applicant and guide dog train together as a team for 25 days at campus at no cost to the recipient. Transportation provided to and from the fndn within North America. Emerg calls 24 hrs. FUNDING: Nonprofit. OFC HRS: M-F 8am-5pm, EST. ADM REQ: Applicants must be legally blind. Free srvs. SERVES: U.S.A.

GUIDE DOGS FOR THE BLIND

350 Los Ranchitos Rd.
San Rafael, CA 94903
(800) 295-4050
(415) 499-4035 FAX

Provides highly trained guide dogs & training in their use to qualified blind men and women. More than 8,000 people have received guide dogs & in-residence training. FUNDING: Donors, nonprofit. OFC HRS: M-F 8am-5pm. Free srvs. SERVES: U.S.A. & Canada.

GUIDE DOGS OF AMERICA

An Internatl Guiding Eyes Prgm
13445 Glenoaks Blvd.
Sylmar, CA 91342
(818) 362-5834
(800) 459-4843
(818) 362-6870 FAX

Guide dog prgm includes training guide dogs and providing instruction to legally blind people in the use of a guide dog (28-day training in residence). In-home training prgm. FUNDING: Donations, nonprofit. OFC HRS: M-F 8:30am-12noon, 12:45pm-4:30pm. ADM REQ: Must be ages 16 yrs+, physically and mentally able to complete training. Free srvs. SERVES: U.S.A. & Canada.

GUIDE DOGS OF THE DESERT

P.O. Box 1692
Palm Springs, CA 92263
(760) 329-6257
(760) 329-2866 FAX

Trains guide dogs for the blind and multi-handicapped blind and instructs them in their use during a 28-day in-residence training class at facility. Wait: 4 months. FUNDING: Donations, nonprofit. OFC HRS: M-F 8:30am-5pm. ADM REQ: Legally blind ages 16 yrs+. Free srvs. SERVES: U.S.A., Canada & Mexico.

INLAND EMPIRE LIGHTHOUSE FOR THE BLIND

San Brndo Vly Lighthouse For The Blind
762 N. Sierra Way
San Bernardino, CA 92410
(909) 884-3121
(909) 884-2964 FAX

Teaches independent daily living skills and provides recreational and social prgms to the legally and totally blind. Classes Tu-Th 10am-2pm. Health screening 4th Tu 9:30-11:30am, appt required. FUNDING: Donations, nonprofit. OFC HRS: M-F 8am-5pm. Spanish spoken. ADM REQ: Must be legally blind with certificate signed by a doctor. Free srvs. SERVES: Inland Empire.

INSTITUTE FOR FAMILIES

4650 Sunset Blvd., MS 111
Los Angeles, CA 90027
(323) 361-4649

(323) 665-7869 FAX

Counseling for families of children who have visual impairments and other anomolies. Referrals for visually impaired children. FUNDING: Grants, donors, nonprofit. OFC HRS: M-F 8am-4pm. Spanish spoken. ADM REQ: Visually impaired child. Free srvs. SERVES: So. Calif.

LIGHTHOUSE INTERNATIONAL

Info & Resource Service
111 E. 59th Street
New York, NY 10022-1202
(800) 829-0500
(212) 821-9705 FAX

Free literature on eye diseases, resource lists, etc. A guide to reading options, intro to assistive computer tech, financial aid resource list for persons with impaired vision. Referrals to low vision srvs, rehab agencies, support groups, state agencies and advocacy groups. TDD (212) 821-9713. FUNDING: Donations, nonprofit. OFC HRS: M-F 9am-8pm, EST. Spanish & Chinese spoken. SERVES: Internatl.

LOUISIANA CENTER FOR THE BLIND

101 S. Trenton St.
Ruston, LA 71270
(800) 234-4166
(318) 251-2891
(318) 251-0109 FAX

Residential rehab for adults who are legally blind. Adult orientation to blindness and adjustment training, employment assist, training in computer literacy and adaptive technology, summer training and employment project for teens, summer buddy prgm for blind children, special seminars, outreach and referral srvs, internships & training for rehab professionals. Prgm for persons ages 55 yrs+ who are losing their vision. FUNDING: Nonprofit. OFC HRS: M-F 8am-5pm, CST. SERVES: U.S.A.

MEDI-CAL OPTICAL SURGERY

Pacific Eye Institute
555 N. 13th Avenue
Upland, CA 91786
(909) 982-8846
(562) 377-0389
(909) 949-3967 FAX

Outpatient eye surgery center serves ages 20 yrs+. OFC HRS: M-F 8am-5pm. Spanish spoken. Accepts Medi-Cal, Medicare.

MEDI-CAL OPTOMETRIST

Brian Van Dusen, O.D.
3559 W. Ramsey, Ste D-6
Banning, CA 92220
(951) 849-2020
(951) 849-4869 FAX

OFC HRS: M-F 8:30am-5:30pm. Spanish spoken.

MEDI-CAL OPTOMETRIST

Dr. Port
836 E. Hobson Way
Blythe, CA 92225
(760) 922-3951
(760) 922-5202 FAX

OFC HRS: M-Th 8am-5:30pm; F 8am-3pm. Spanish spoken.

MEDI-CAL OPTOMETRIST

Canyon Lake Optometry
31740 Railroad Canyon Rd., Ste 4
Canyon Lake, CA 92587

(951) 244-4444
(951) 244-1414 FAX

OFC HRS: M 9am-4pm; Tu, Th 9am-5pm; W 9am-4:30pm; F 7:30am-3pm; Sat 8am-1pm. Spanish spoken. Accepts Medi-Cal, Medicare.

MEDI-CAL OPTOMETRIST

Chino Optometry Center
11640 Central Ave.
Chino, CA 91710
(909) 627-7363
(909) 627-9854 FAX

OFC HRS: M, W, Th 10am-7pm; Tu 10am-8pm; F 9am-6pm; Sat 9am-5pm. Spanish spoken. Accepts Medicare.

MEDI-CAL OPTOMETRIST

Daniel A. Paul
12530 10th Street
Chino, CA 91710
(909) 627-7518
(909) 591-1380 FAX

OFC HRS: M, W, F 8am-5pm; Tu 9am-5pm; Th 10am-7pm. Spanish spoken. Accepts Medi-Cal & VSP.

MEDI-CAL OPTOMETRIST

Optometric Group
190 West H Street, Ste 105
Colton, CA 92324
(909) 825-9044
(909) 825-7392 FAX

OFC HRS: M-F 9am-5pm. Spanish spoken.

MEDI-CAL OPTOMETRIST

Corona Vision Center
734 N. Main St.
Corona, CA 92880
(951) 737-2020
(951) 737-2072 FAX

OFC HRS: M-F 10am-6pm; W 10am-8pm; Sat 10am-2pm. Spanish, Farsi spoken. Accepts Medi-Cal, Medicare.

MEDI-CAL OPTOMETRIST

Family Vision Care
8275 Sierra Ave., Ste 103
Fontana, CA 92335
(909) 822-1115
(909) 822-6346 FAX

OFC HRS: M-F 8am-5pm; Sat 8am-12pm. Spanish spoken.

MEDI-CAL OPTOMETRIST

Lawrence E Young O.D.
10004 Sierra Ave.
Fontana, CA 92335
(909) 822-8002
(909) 822-3985 FAX

OFC HRS: M-F 8am-5pm; Sat 8am-3pm. Spanish spoken.

MEDI-CAL OPTOMETRIST

Dr. Duncan & Dr. Kragness
9268 Sierra Ave.
Fontana, CA 92335
(909) 350-2020
(909) 350-2341 FAX

OFC HRS: M-F 9am-5pm. Spanish spoken. Accepts Medi-Cal, Medicare.

MEDI-CAL OPTOMETRIST

Hemet Optometric Ctr/S. Simpson, OD
41705 State Hwy. 74
Hemet, CA 92544
(951) 652-1420
(951) 766-4933 FAX

OFC HRS: M 8am-5:30pm; Tu-Th 8:30am-5pm; F 8am-5pm; Sat 8am-12noon. Spanish spoken. Accepts Medi-Cal, Medicare.

MEDI-CAL OPTOMETRIST

Buri Optometric, Markus Buri
731 E. Florida Ave.
Hemet, CA 92543
(951) 766-8587
(951) 929-2020 FAX

OFC HRS: M-F 8am-5:30pm, Sat by appt. Spanish spoken. Accepts Medi-Cal, Medicare.

MEDI-CAL OPTOMETRIST

Charles Richards, O.D.
17151 Main St., Ste C
Hesperia, CA 92345
(760) 244-4904
(760) 244-7804 FAX

OFC HRS: M-F 9am-5:30pm, alt Sat 9am-1pm. Spanish spoken. Accepts Medi-Cal, Medicare.

MEDI-CAL OPTOMETRIST

Dr. Mark Gillispie
82-227 Hwy. 111
Indio, CA 92201
(760) 347-6636
(760) 342-5987 FAX

OFC HRS: M-F 9am-7pm; Sat 9am-6pm. Spanish spoken.

MEDI-CAL OPTOMETRIST

Mission Optometric Eye Care Center
32245 Mission Trail, Ste D-4
Lake Elsinore, CA 92530
(951) 674-1561
(951) 674-5300 FAX

OFC HRS: M-F 9am-5pm; Sat 8am-4pm. Spanish spoken. Accepts Medi-Cal.

MEDI-CAL OPTOMETRIST

Affordable Family Vision Center
Rosali Quintanar, OD
10258 Central Ave.
Montclair, CA 91763
(909) 624-3024
(909) 482-4596 FAX

OFC HRS: M-Th 9am-5pm; Sat 8:30am-3:30pm. Spanish spoken.

MEDI-CAL OPTOMETRIST

William Dorrance, O.D.
24250 Postal Ave., Ste 100
Moreno Valley, CA 92553
(951) 242-2020
(951) 488-0910 FAX

OFC HRS: M, Tu, Th 8am-5pm; F 8am-3:30pm. Spanish spoken.

MEDI-CAL OPTOMETRIST

Golden Triangle Optometrics
25460 Medical Center Dr., Ste 103
Murrieta, CA 92562
(951) 698-4575
(951) 698-5499 FAX

OFC HRS: M 8:30am-5:30pm; Tu, W 10am-7pm; Th, F 8:30am-5:30pm. Spanish spoken. Accepts Medi-Cal, Medicare.

MEDI-CAL OPTOMETRIST

Dr. Richard Kraus
1548 N. Palm Canyon Dr.
Palm Springs, CA 92262
(760) 320-4441
(760) 320-5305 FAX

OFC HRS: M-F 8am-4:30pm. Spanish spoken.

MEDI-CAL OPTOMETRIST
Perris Valley Vision Center
136 W. Nuevo Rd., Ste E & F
Perris, CA 92571
(951) 943-4949
(951) 943-1067 FAX

OFC HRS: M 9am-7:30pm; Tu-F 8am-5pm; Sat 9am-3pm. Spanish spoken.

MEDI-CAL OPTOMETRIST
Dr. Keller
9596 Baseline Rd.
Rancho Cucamonga, CA 91701
(909) 989-1791
(909) 989-0782 FAX

OFC HRS: M,Tu 9am-6pm; W-F 8am-5pm; Sat 8am-12noon. Spanish spoken. Accepts Medi-Cal, Medicare.

MEDI-CAL OPTOMETRIST
Dr. Blaurock
42-390 Bob Hope Dr.
Rancho Mirage, CA 92270
(760) 340-4524
(760) 340-4796 FAX

OFC HRS: M-F 8am-5pm.

MEDI-CAL OPTOMETRIST
Orange Plaza St.
568 Orange St.
Redlands, CA 92374
(909) 335-0300
(909) 335-0303 FAX

OFC HRS: M-Th 9am-6pm; F 9am-5pm; Sat 9am-1pm. Spanish spoken.

MEDI-CAL OPTOMETRIST
Rialto Optometric Center
1850 N. Riverside Ave., Ste 100
Rialto, CA 92376
(909) 421-3030
(909) 421-3059 FAX

OFC HRS: M-F 8:30am-5pm. Spanish spoken.

MEDI-CAL OPTOMETRIST
Dr. Freestone
1850 N. Riverside Ave., Ste 220
Rialto, CA 92377
(909) 875-1144
(909) 875-0640 FAX

OFC HRS: M 10:30am-5:30pm; Tu-F 8:30am-5pm; Sat 8am-12pm. Spanish spoken. Accepts Medi-Cal, Medicare.

MEDI-CAL OPTOMETRIST
Vision Lab
4212 Market St.
Riverside, CA 92501
(951) 684-9700
(951) 684-4515 FAX

OFC HRS: M 10am-7pm; W 9:30am-6:30pm; Tu ,Th, F 9am-5pm; Sat 9am-2pm. Spanish spoken.

MEDI-CAL OPTOMETRIST
Riverside Family Vision Ctr/Dr. G. Fishburn
5225 Canyon Crest Dr., Ste 201
Riverside, CA 92507
(951) 788-2020
(951) 684-2020 FAX

OFC HRS: M-W, F 9am-6pm; Th 9am-7pm; Sat 9am-2pm. Spanish spoken.

MEDI-CAL OPTOMETRIST
Dr. Ragsdale
6690 Alessandra Blvd., Ste B
Riverside, CA 92506

(951) 780-5151
(951) 780-6847 FAX

OFC HRS: M, W 10am-7pm; Tu,Th, F 10am-5pm. Accepts Medi-Cal, Medicare.

MEDI-CAL OPTOMETRIST
Janet Kohtz, O.D.
5300 Arlington Ave., Ste C
Riverside, CA 92504
(951) 689-9180
(951) 359-6300 FAX

OFC HRS: Tu-F 9am-5:30pm; Sat 8am-12:30pm. Spanish spoken. Accepts Medi-Cal, Medicare.

MEDI-CAL OPTOMETRIST
Family Vision Center
19530 Van Buren Blvd., Ste G-8
Riverside, CA 92508
(951) 656-0500
(951) 697-0101 FAX

OFC HRS: Tu, Th 10am-7pm; W 10am-4pm; F 8am-5pm; Sat 9am-3pm. Spanish spoken. Accepts Medi-Cal, Medicare.

MEDI-CAL OPTOMETRIST
Inland Empire Optometry
1900 N. Waterman Ave.
San Bernardino, CA 92404-4833
(909) 888-4000
(909) 886-4000 FAX

OFC HRS: M-F 8am-6pm. Spanish, Mandarin Chinese spoken. SERVES: Inland Empire.

MEDI-CAL OPTOMETRIST
Inland Vision Center Optometry
424 E. Hospitality Lane, Ste B-6
San Bernardino, CA 92408
(909) 884-1838
(909) 884-0865 FAX

OFC HRS: M-F 9am-5:30pm; Sat 9am-1pm. Spanish, Punjabi spoken. Accepts Medi-Cal, Medicare.

MEDI-CAL OPTOMETRIST
Mark Huang, O.D.
168 South E Street
San Bernardino, CA 92401
(909) 885-0184
(714) 884-4859
(909) 383-8924 FAX

OFC HRS: M-F 9am-5pm; Sat 9am-3pm. Spanish spoken. Accepts Medi-Cal, Medicare.

MEDI-CAL OPTOMETRIST
Bartlett & Kascius, O.D.
965 South E Street
San Bernardino, CA 92408
(909) 889-5669
(909) 885-0428 FAX

OFC HRS: M-W, F 10am-6pm; Th 10am-8pm.

MEDI-CAL OPTOMETRIST
Dr. Markus Buri
41257 Margarita Rd., Ste B-103
Temecula, CA 92591
(951) 587-2333

OFC HRS: M, W, F 9am-pm; Tu, Th 10am-7pm; Sat 9am-2pm. Spanish spoken. Accepts Medi-Cal, Medicare.

NATL ASSN/PARENTS OF CHILDREN WITH VISUAL IMPAIRMENTS
P.O. Box 317
Watertown, MA 02471
(800) 562-6265
(617) 972-7441

(617) 972-7444 FAX

Members receive help immediately after child is diagnosed. Connections to families who have children with similar conditions, practical suggestions, info & referral, advocacy, research info, related publications etc. 24-hr recording asks for an address to have info mailed or callers may leave a phone number for a return call. FUNDING: Donations, grants, nonprofit. OFC HRS: M-F 9am-5pm, EST. Spanish spoken. SERVES: U.S.A.

NATL EYE CARE PROJECT
See "EyeCare America"

NATL RETINITIS PIGMENTOSA FNDN
See "Foundation Fighting Blindness"

ONELEGACY
1701 Orange Tree Lane
Redlands, CA 92374
(909) 801-3701
(800) 786-4077
(909) 801-3707 FAX

Organ and tissue bank works with hospitals and coroners' offices in Riverside, San Bernardino and Kern Counties to supply donor tissue for cornea transplants and many other life enhancing transplant surgeries. Encourages public awareness about organ donations, donor cards, and cooperates with other eye banks and tissue banks in the distribution of tissues worldwide. FUNDING: Donations, nonprofit. OFC HRS: M-F 8am-5pm. Free srvs.

OPTOMETRY BOARD
See "Calif Board of Optometry"

PREVENT BLINDNESS AMERICA
211 W. Wacker Dr., Ste 1700
Chicago, IL 60606
(800) 331-2020
(312) 363-6052 FAX

Eye health and safety organization dedicated to fighting blindness and preserving sight. Serves millions of people each year through public & community prgms, patient srvs & research. FUNDING: Donations, nonprofit. OFC HRS: M-F 8:30am-5pm, CST. Free srvs except quantity brochure orders. SERVES: U.S.A.

RECORDING FOR THE BLIND & DYSLEXIC
Inland Empire/Orange County
1844 W. 11th Street, Ste C
Upland, CA 91786
(909) 949-4316
(909) 981-8457 FAX

Natl volunteer srv organization records academic texts for loan to persons having a visual, physical, or perpetual print-reading disability. Srvs for individual and institutional members after registration. Individual borrowers, $65 one-time registration fee. $35 annually (1st yr, total $100). Works with schools to provide recorded texts for students with print-reading disabilities. FUNDING: Donations, grants, nonprofit. OFC HRS: M, Tu 8am-9pm; W, Th 8am-5pm; F 8am-3pm; Sat 8am-12noon. ADM REQ: Volunteers ages 18-90 yrs. SERVES: Inland Empire and Orange County.

RESEARCH TO PREVENT BLINDNESS
Public Information
645 Madison Ave., 21st Fl.
New York, NY 10022
(800) 621-0026
(212) 752-4333

(212) 688-6231 FAX

Supports eye research and provides related info about eye disease and preventing blindness. FUNDING: Bequests, donations, nonprofit. OFC HRS: M-F 9am-5pm, EST. SERVES: U.S.A.

RETINITIS PIGMENTOSA INTERNATL

P.O. Box 900
Woodland Hills, CA 91365
(800) 344-4877
(818) 992-0500
(818) 992-3265 FAX

Natl info & referral. Special prgms include: Eyes of Christmas (Dec), Vision Awards (June) and Theatre Vision (description of motion pictures for the blind). Hotline (800) FIGHT-RP. Info & consultation for the vision impaired. FUNDING: Donations, grants, nonprofit. OFC HRS: M-F 9am-6pm. SERVES: U.S.A.

SENIORS EYECARE PROGRAM

See "EyeCare America"

THE LIGHTHOUSE, INC.

See "Lighthouse International"

PARENTING RESOURCES/EDUCATION

ACCESS FOR INFANTS/MOTHERS (AIM)

Calif Major Risk Medical Ins. Board
P.O. Box 15559
Sacramento, CA 95852-0559
(800) 433-2611
(888) 889-9238 FAX

Maternity, delivery and infant care srvs for mid-income women between 200-300% of the federal poverty level. Low-cost prenatal health insurance to uninsured pregnant women who are not receiving health care through Medi-Cal. The cost is 2% of her family's gross income. The policy pays 100% of the medical costs during the pregnancy, plus post-partum care for 60 days and the medical cost for the infant during the first two years of life. Insurance renewal after infant's 2nd year is $100 or $50 with proof of immunization. For payments: P.O. Box 15207, Sacramento, CA 95851. FUNDING: State. OFC HRS: M-F 8am-8pm; Sat 8am-5pm. Spanish spoken. ADM REQ: Calif resident; expectant mother must be no more than 30 weeks pregnant. SERVES: Calif.

ACTION PARENT & TEEN SUPPORT

11372 Ventura Blvd., Ste 200
Studio City, CA 91604
(818) 763-9556
(800) 367-8336
(818) 763-9568 FAX

Weekly support groups for parents and teens. Support to families dealing with low self-esteem, drug/alcohol abuse, depression, runaways, teen pregnancy and other family-related issues. Low-cost drug testing, crisis intervention. FUNDING: Donations, nonprofit. OFC HRS: M-Th 12noon-9pm; F 9am-3:30pm. Spanish spoken. Accepts pvt insurance; individual & family therapy on a sliding fee scale. SERVES: So. Calif.

ALTERNATE AVENUES

Women's Resource Center
9675 Monte Vista, Unit G
Montclair, CA 91763
(909) 621-4800

Fully licensed medical clinic offering free services to couples facing an unplanned pregnancy. Pregnancy tests, ultrasound (when needed), Medi-Cal, WIC along with other resources. FUNDING: Nonprofit. OFC HRS: Tu 12pm-5pm; Th 2pm-7pm; F, Sat 8am-1pm. Spanish, Tagalog spoken. SERVES: Inland Empire.

ALTERNATIVE SENTENCING

Indio Probation Department
47-940 Arabia St.
Indio, CA 92201
(760) 863-8420
(760) 863-8916 FAX

Domestic violence, sexual deviance, anger mgmt, parenting, child batterer classes, community srv provider, referrals for home monitoring. Administers court-ordered vehicle ignition interlock prgm. FUNDING: Nonprofit. OFC HRS: M-Th 8am-4pm, Fri 8am-3pm. Spanish spoken. ADM REQ: Assigned by court, probation, parole or DPSS depts. Fees vary by service, money order only accepted. SERVES: Coachella Valley.

APU COMMUNITY COUNSELING CENTER

Formerly Child and Family Dev Center
P.O. Box 7000
918 E. Alosta Ave.
Azusa, CA 91702
(626) 815-5421
(626) 633-0651 FAX

Community-based counseling facility featuring a therapeutic staff that provides quality counseling and consulting srvs in a variety of locations throughout the east San Gabriel Valley. The clinicians at the CCC provide a broad range of cutting-edge treatment srvs for individuals, couples, and families including support for life transition dilemmas, crisis-related issues, and disorders of depression and anxiety. Counseling and edu srvs are provided by licensed professionals, interns, and trainees, depending on the need. Also offers the Pediatrics Neurodevelopment Institute (PNI) which works with a spectrum of disorders including mental retardation. Testing, treatment, and eval available. Affliated with Azusa Pacific Univ Dept of Graduate Psychology, APA approved. OFC HRS: M-Th 9am-9pm; F 9am-6pm; Sat 10am-2pm. Low cost srvs, sliding fee scale, insurance reimbursement. SERVES: L.A., Orange, San Bernardino and Riverside Counties.

BABY CARE AND NUTRITION

Beech-Nut Nutrition Corp
13023 Tesson Ferry Rd., Ste 105
Saint Louis, MO 63128
(800) 233-2468

Info & referrals about Beech-Nut products and infant feeding, as well as general baby care. Spanish (800) 232-4867. FUNDING: Nonprofit. OFC HRS: M-F 8am-5pm, CST. Spanish spoken. Free srvs. SERVES: U.S.A.

BIG BROTHERS/SISTERS/GTR L.A. & I.E.

Administration Office
800 S. Figueroa, Ste 620
Los Angeles, CA 90017
(213) 481-3611
(800) 207-7567
(213) 481-1148 FAX

Prgm matches boys ages 7-18 yrs, and girls ages 6-16 yrs from single parent homes with volunteer Big Brothers and Big Sisters. Provides positive role models, friendship, companionship and guidance on a one-to-one basis. Each volunteer is trained to provide ongoing support to ensure that each mentoring relationship thrives. Also has an additional office at 5601 W. Slauson Ave., Ste. 130, Culver City 90230; (310) 338-0055. FUNDING: Nonprofit. OFC HRS: M-F 9am-5:30pm. Spanish spoken. Free srvs. SERVES: L.A. Co. & Inland Empire.

BIRTH CHOICE

277 S. Rancho Santa Fe Rd., Ste S
San Marcos, CA 92069-2343
(760) 744-1313

Counseling, supportive services, info and referrals to medical professionals. Financial aid prgms, post-abortion counseling and adoption srvs. FUNDING: Nonprofit. OFC HRS: M 9am-6pm; Tu-Th 9am-8pm; F 8am-12noon; Sat 10am-12noon. Spanish spoken. Free srvs. SERVES: San Marcos.

BIRTH CHOICE OF TEMECULA

27488 Enterprise Cir., West, Bldg. 4
Temecula, CA 92590
(951) 699-9808
(951) 699-7268 FAX

Pregnancy counseling and testing. Right to Life perspective. Maternity and baby clothes available. Walk in or call for appt. 24-hr hotline (800) 848-LOVE (5683). Volunteering opportunies available. FUNDING: Nonprofit. OFC HRS: M, W 10am-4pm; Tu, Th 10am-3pm. Spanish speaker on Tu. ADM REQ: Pregnant or suspected pregnancy. Free srvs. SERVES: Lake Elsinore, Perris, Hemet, Menifee, Temecula, Fallbrook, Murietta, Wildomar.

BIRTH DEFECT RESEARCH FOR CHILDREN

976 Lake Baldwin Ln., Ste 104
Orlando, FL 32814
(407) 895-0802

Free info for families of children with birth defects. Referral to local support groups. Visit (www.birthdefects.org). FUNDING: Nonprofit. OFC HRS: M-F 9am-5pm, EST. Birth defect info free to parents & expectant parents. Memberships available. SERVES: U.S.A.

BLINDNESS SUPPORT SERVICES

Children's Division
3696 Beatty Dr., Ste A
Riverside, CA 92506
(951) 341-9244
(951) 341-6335 FAX

Prgms for blind or visually impaired children. Provider training for licensed preschool and family day care. FUNDING: First 5, nonprofit. OFC HRS: M-F 8am-5pm. Spanish spoken. ADM REQ: Children ages birth-5 yrs. SERVES: Riverside County.

BOOT CAMP FOR NEW DADS

Medical Ofc. Bldg. 2, 5th Fl., Conference Rm.
6650 Alton Pkwy.
Irvine, CA 92618
(949) 754-9067
(949) 754-9087 FAX

Designed for new fathers to help ensure every child an opportunity for a caring and capable father, beginning at birth. Workshops in English and Spanish, video-based orientation prgm. Veteran fathers help fathers-to-be gain knowledge and skills to increase their confidence to nurture and participate in the care of their babies. FUNDING: Nonprofit. OFC HRS: M-F 8am-5pm. SERVES: U.S.A.

CALIF ASSN/SCHOOL PSYCHOLOGISTS

1020 12th Street, Ste 200
Sacramento, CA 95814
(916) 444-1595
(916) 444-1597 FAX

Statewide membership organization for school psychologists in Calif. Provides professional dev, acts as a liaison with state boards & commissions. The goal is to ensure schools are responsive to psych needs of students. Fact sheets are available online to members and non-members. OFC HRS: M-F 8:30am-5pm. SERVES: Calif.

CALIF CHILDREN & FAMILIES COMM
2389 Gateway Oaks Dr., Ste 260
Sacramento, CA 95833
(916) 263-1050
(916) 263-1360 FAX

Early childhood dev srvs, school readiness, health care, child care, parent edu, intervention prgms for families at risk. FUNDING: Nonprofit. OFC HRS: M-F 8am-5pm. ADM REQ: Ages birth-5 yrs. SERVES: Calif.

CALIFORNIA KIDS
Information Line
5200 Lankershim Blvd., Ste 3360
North Hollywood, CA 91601
(818) 755-9700
(818) 755-9443 FAX

Child insurance prgm infoline for children ages 2-18 yrs. OFC HRS: M-Th 9am-5pm; F 9am-3pm. Spanish spoken. Plan cost & co-pay depends on income. SERVES: Calif.

CANYON ACRES CHILDREN & FAMILY SRVS
1845 W. Orangewood Ave., Ste 300
Orange, CA 92868
(714) 383-9401
(714) 383-9300 FAX

Serves children & families through a comprehensive list of community prgms. The mental health clinic includes individual, family, & group therapy, psych medication support, and parent edu classes. The therapeutic afterschool prgm contains an array of structured group activities and a therapeutic horse riding prgm for children that have been identified as needing additional support for a mental health issue. The Creating Family Connections prgm works to find family or kin for dependent youth and engage them in the child's life. Foster care and adoption srvs prgm helps find kids forever families. FUNDING: AFDC-FC, EPSDT, County of Orange Health Care Agency, donations. OFC HRS: M-F 7am-5pm. Sat appts also available. Spanish spoken. Accepts Medi-Cal. Pvt insurance and cash pay for select srvs. SERVES: Orange Co (all prgms). Select prgms in L.A., Riverside, San Bernardino, & San Diego Counties.

CENTER FOR FAMILY LIVING
1128 E. 6th Street, Ste 8
Corona, CA 92879
(951) 734-8831
(951) 734-8518 FAX

Multi-disciplinary group (MFTs) offering srvs to children, adolescents and adults. Specialties include: family, marital, court-ordered, co-parenting counseling, PTSD (Post Traumatic Stress Syndrome), children's behavior problems, depression, anxiety, personal growth. FUNDING: Client fees. OFC HRS: M-F 8:30am-5:30pm; Sat 9am-3pm. Spanish spoken. ADM REQ: Call for appt. Accepts insurance, sliding fee scale. SERVES: Riverside County.

CENTER FOR HEALING CHILDHOOD TRAUMA
101 S. Olive Ave.
Rialto, CA 92376
(909) 875-5288
(909) 875-0608 FAX

Counseling for children, adolescents and adult victims of sexual abuse. Also family resource ctr offering a wide range of parenting curricula.

Parents United certified providers. Also has an office in O.C. at 1420 E. Chapman Ave., Orange 92866, (949) 348-1717. FUNDING: Nonprofit. OFC HRS: M-Th 9am-7pm; F 10am-5pm. Spanish spoken. Accepts pvt pay. Victims of Crime. SERVES: Orange, Riverside & San Bernardino Counties.

CENTER FOR THE IMPROVEMENT OF CHILD CARING
6260 Laurel Canyon Blvd., Ste 304
North Hollywood, CA 91606
(818) 980-0903
(800) 325-2242
(818) 753-1054 FAX

Trains instructors to run a variety of parenting prgms, including prgms for black and latino parents. Conducts one-day parent training seminars with local schools and agencies. Provides guidelines for effective parenting campaigns. Online bookstore of parenting and child dev materials and a free newsletter, Effective Parenting. FUNDING: Fees, corp, foundation, govt grants, nonprofit. OFC HRS: M-F 8am-5pm. Spanish spoken. Fees or contract for instructor and for parenting seminars & training SERVES: U.S.A., emphasis So. Calif.

CHILDHELP USA/HOTLINE
National Child Abuse Hotline
15757 N. 78th Street, Ste B
Scottsdale, AZ 85260
(800) 422-4453
(480) 922-8212
(480) 922-7061 FAX

Professional hotline counselors available 24 hrs, 7 days to respond to crisis calls regarding child abuse & related issues. Crisis intervention & contact for mandated reporters, concerned citizens or worried friends & family. Info & referral. Visit (www.childhelpusa.org). FUNDING: Nonprofit. Communication available in 140 different languages. Free srvs. SERVES: U.S.A. & Canada.

CHILDREN'S HEALTH ACCESS PRGMS
Kaiser Permanente Cares for Kids
(800) 255-5053

Low-cost health insurance for uninsured children whose families do not qualify for Medi-Cal or Healthy Families. This prgm covers children who are enrolled in public schools within Kaiser Permanente Calif srv area. Prgm will also cover siblings of children eligible for this prgm. FUNDING: Nonprofit. Eligibility and cost are based on family size and income. SERVES: Calif.

CHILDREN'S HEALTH ACCESS PRGMS
Medi-Cal/Healthy Families Info Line
P.O. Box 138005
Sacramento, CA 95813-8005
(888) 747-1222
(866) 848-4974 FAX

Free and low-cost medical care for children and pregnant women. Eligibility is determined by children's ages and family income. Available to citizens and qualified immigrants. If the family does not qualify for this prgm, there are other options. Call (800) 880-5305 for application status. Call (866) 848-9166 if already enrolled. FUNDING: State, fed govt. OFC HRS: M-F 8am-8pm; Sat 8am-5pm. Cambodian, Farsi, Russian, Spanish, Chinese and Vietnamese spoken. ADM REQ: Must submit application.

$5-$15 per child based on provider and county. SERVES: Calif.

CHINO COMMUNITY SERVICES
Human Services Division
13201 Central Ave.
Chino, CA 91710
(909) 591-9822
(909) 628-4093 FAX

Counseling srvs for children & adults. Community & school-based prevention & edu. Drug prevention, family treatment, teen and adult parenting classes, domestic violence, anger mgmt, community outreach, senior srvs, disabled srvs info & referral, PC-1000. For emergencies, call (909) 628-1010. FUNDING: State, county, school, city, govt. OFC HRS: M-Th 8am-8pm; F 8am-6pm. Spanish spoken. Free srvs or a fee of $26. SERVES: Western San Bernardino County.

CHINO VALLEY TYKES PROGRAM
13220 Central Ave.
Chino, CA 91710
(909) 590-5562
(909) 590-1803 FAX

School readiness prgm for ages birth-5 yrs. Also, parenting classes, edu workshops, case mgmt srvs. FUNDING: County, city. OFC HRS: M-F 9am-5pm; 1st Sat each month 9am-1pm. Spanish spoken. SERVES: Chino.

CLAREMONT ADULT SCHOOL
170 W. San Jose Ave., 3rd Fl.
Claremont, CA 91711
(909) 398-0609
(909) 398-0690 FAX

ESL, HS diploma, literacy, parent edu enrichment, vocational, older adult and community srvs classes. Located near bus route. FUNDING: State, local, govt. OFC HRS: M-Th 8am-3pm; F 8:30am-12pm. Spanish spoken. ADM REQ: Ages 18 yrs+. SERVES: Claremont, Pomona, Montclair, San Dimas, La Verne & Upland.

CLINICAS DE SALUD DEL PUEBLO, INC.
Mecca Health Clinic
91275 66th Avenue, Ste 500
Mecca, CA 92254
(760) 396-1249
(760) 396-1253 FAX

Outpatient center offers immunizations, pregnancy testing, counseling, birth control, physical exams, general medical, well-baby, pediatric, health edu, TB testing, AIDS testing, STD, dental, optical (van comes occasionally). Serves all ages. FUNDING: BPHC site, donations, nonprofit. OFC HRS: M-Th 8am-6:30pm; F 8am-6pm; Sat 8am-12pm. Spanish spoken. ADM REQ: Low income. Accepts insurance, Medi-Cal, Medicare, sliding fee scale. SERVES: Mecca & nearby.

CO-ABODE
1223 Wilshire Blvd., Ste 102
Santa Monica, CA 90403

Nationwide, web-based shared housing and support group for single mothers and their children. Guest memberships are free, as is access to the extensive resource directory with links to housing, parenting and other info. Visit (www.co-abode.com). FUNDING: Nonprofit, membership fees. OFC HRS: 24 hrs, 7 days. SERVES: U.S.A.

Parenting Resources/Education

COACHELLA VALLEY USD
School Readiness Program Center
83800 Airport Blvd.
Thermal, CA 92274
(760) 399-8129
(760) 399-4421 FAX

Medical, dental, vision, mental health counseling & special needs assessments & treatment. OFC HRS: M-F 8am-4pm. ADM REQ: Low income families with children ages birth-5 yrs. SERVES: East Valley Riverside County.

COLTON EARLY CHILDHOOD EDUCATION
Community Srvs
660 Colton Ave.
Colton, CA 92324
(909) 370-6171
(909) 370-6173 FAX

Program for grades K-6. Four elementary school sites in the city of Colton, two preschool sites, state preschool for ages 3-5 yrs. Curriculum-based, no-cost psychological srvs, NSACA accreditation, parenting classes. Capacity varies by site. FUNDING: State, city of Colton, parent fees, GAIN, CDBG. OFC HRS: M-Th 6:30am-5:30pm; prgm hrs: M-F 7am-6pm. Spanish spoken. ADM REQ: State income requirements. Sliding fee scale. Parents may qualify for subsidized srvs. SERVES: Colton & nearby.

CROSSROADS CHURCH
S.M.U.R.F.
31805 Temecula Pkwy., Ste 389
Temecula, CA 92592
(951) 541-8574
(951) 541-0886 FAX

Address listed above is for mailing only. Single Moms United in Rewarding Fellowship meets Sun at 5pm. Support group for single mothers & their children. Free child care and a Sun night meal. Meets at 28753 Via Montezuma in Temecula. Subject to change. FUNDING: Nonprofit, donations. OFC HRS: By appointment. ADM REQ: Single mothers & their children. SERVES: Southwest County.

DESERT HOT SPRINGS FAMILY RESOURCE CTR
14201 Palm Dr., Ste 108
Desert Hot Springs, CA 92240
(760) 288-3313
(760) 288-2854 FAX

Classes offered on parenting skills, family planning, adult edu. Healthy children connection, Healthy Families, Medi-Cal enrollment (through Catholic Charities), immunization info, utility assist clinic provided with Community Action Partnership, WIC info, job search, GED classes, veteran support group, individual, family, & group counseling. Referrals to emerg srvs. FUNDING: Nonprofit. OFC HRS: M-F 8am-5pm. Spanish spoken. ADM REQ: Must call first, except for job search srvs. SERVES: Bermuda Dunes, Cathedral City, Coachella, Desert Hot Springs, Indio, Indio Hills, North Palm Springs, Palm Springs, Rancho Mirage.

DOLPHINS MOBILE HEALTH VAN OUTREACH
811 W. Chanslorway
Blythe, CA 92225
(760) 922-1349
(760) 921-8399 FAX

Referral srvs to pregnant and parenting teens, nutrition, immunizations, hearing, vision, physical activity, and injury prevention to preschool children. Also dental treatment srvs. Assist with completing Healthy Families applications. FUNDING: First 5. OFC HRS: M-F 8am-5pm. Spanish spoken. ADM REQ: Ages birth-5 yrs, and pregnant women. Free srvs. SERVES: Blythe.

EARLY START FAMILY RESOURCE NTWK
P.O. Box 6127
1425 S. Waterman Ave.
San Bernardino, CA 92412-6127
(800) 890-4794
(909) 890-4709 FAX

Resource center for families with children ages birth-36 months, born medically at-risk or having dev delays or disabilities. Parent support groups, newsletters, resource library. Call for location. FUNDING: Donations, govt, nonprofit. OFC HRS: M-F 8am-5pm. Spanish spoken, ASL available. ADM REQ: Call for appt. SERVES: Inland Empire.

EATING DISORDER FOUNDATION OF O.C.
23232 Peralta Dr., Ste 211
Laguna Hills, CA 92653
(800) 342-8793
(949) 285-9827
(949) 488-2418 FAX

Dedicated to the awareness and prevention of eating disorders by providing edu to local schools, businesses, and youth organizations. Community outreach, edu, teacher in-service training, consultations, eating disorder assessments, counseling, fitness and nutrition referrals, support groups, group presentations for youth sports, individual assessments for athletes and coaches. FUNDING: Nonprofit. OFC HRS: M-Th 8am-9pm; F 8am-7pm; Sat 9am-2pm. Spanish spoken. SERVES: Orange, Riverside & San Bernardino Counties.

EMMANUEL UNIQUE OUTREACH PARTNERS
P.O. Box 1861
Corona, CA 92878
(951) 279-0031
(760) 955-0007 FAX

Various prgms offered including: homework assist, literacy, enrichment for students, senior visits, summer food srvs, personal training, nonprofit creation. FUNDING: Nonprofit. OFC HRS: M-F 8am-5pm. SERVES: Riverside County.

EMPOWERTECH COMPUTER ACCESS CTR
Empowering & Educating People with Disabilities
6234 W. 87th Street
Los Angeles, CA 90045
(310) 338-1597
(310) 338-9318 FAX

Provides children and adults who have physical and dev disabilities with edu and training to lead independent and productive lives utilizing assistive technology. Open Access prgm available free of charge every W 3:30pm-6:30pm. FUNDING: Donations, nonprofit. OFC HRS: M-F 9am-5pm. Spanish & French spoken. SERVES: L.A., Orange & Riverside Counties.

EXCEPTIONALLY EXCITED KIDS (EEK)
P.O. Box 185
San Jacinto, CA 92581

(951) 375-6906
(951) 491-5598

Mission is to provide latest in exercise science to those with special needs through play, fitness, games, nutrition, etc. Online support, education and resources for special needs children and adults ages 2-25 yrs. Down Syndrome, autism, cerebral palsy, etc. Visit (www.eekandfriends.com/) FUNDING: Nonprofit. SERVES: Inland Empire.

FAMILY SERVICE AGENCY/SAN BRDO
Crest Forest Family Srvs
P.O. Box 4484
23406 Crest Forest Dr.
Crestline, CA 92325
(909) 338-4689
(909) 338-8230 FAX

Counseling and mental health treatment for child sexual abuse, dysfunctional families. Anger diversion classes, court-ordered batterer's intervention prgm, high-risk youth prgms, limited utility asst. 24-hr suicide and crisis hotline (800) 832-9119. Food bank available F 9am-12noon, 1pm-5:30pm; call ahead to get more info. FUNDING: United Way, client fees, nonprofit. OFC HRS: M-Th 8:30am-6pm. ADM REQ: Varies per prgm. Ages 5 yrs+. Accepts Medi-Cal, sliding fee scale. SERVES: San Bernardino County.

FAMILY SERVICE AGENCY/SAN BRDO
Outpatient Mental Health Srvs
1669 North E Street
San Bernardino, CA 92405
(909) 886-6737
(909) 881-3871 FAX

Info & referral, counseling & mental health treatment for child sexual abuse, domestic violence intervention counseling, dysfunctional families, parenting classes, anger diversion classes, high-risk youth prgms. S.N.A.A.P. (narcotics/alcohol abuse prgm for teens). State ID: 360044AN. FUNDING: United Way, client fees, nonprofit. OFC HRS: M-Th 9am-9pm. Spanish spoken. ADM REQ: Varies per prgm. Ages birth-21 yrs. Accepts Medi-Cal for youth only, sliding fee scale. SERVES: San Bernardino County.

FAMILY SERVICE ASSN/CORONA
Alternatives to Domestic Violence
Outreach Office
515 S. Corona Mall
Corona, CA 92879
(951) 737-8410
(951) 737-3517 FAX

Counseling for individuals, marriages & familes. Anger mgmt, edu, child abuse prevention & treatment. Employee assist prgm, mental health advocacy, social mentorship & family life edu. Anonymous shelter, advocacy for domestic violence. 24-hr crisis line (800) 339-SAFE or (951)683-0829. Riverside (951) 320-1370. Hemet (951)929-3079. OFC HRS: M-F 9am-5pm. Spanish spoken. ADM REQ: Victim of domestic violence. Sliding fee scale for therapeutic srvs and anger mgmt. SERVES: West Riverside County.

FAMILY SERVICE ASSN/WEST RIVERSIDE
JND/Family Counseling
21250 Box Springs Rd., Ste 106
Moreno Valley, CA 92557
(951) 686-3706

(951) 686-7267 FAX

Full-srv marriage, family, child, individual & group counseling. Parenting groups. Call for times & locations. FUNDING: Nonprofit. OFC HRS: M-F 8am-5pm Spanish spoken. Sliding fee scale $30-$120. Some srvs free for those who qualify. SERVES: Western Riverside County.

FAMILY SERVICE ASSN/WEST RIVERSIDE

La Sierra Clinic
11290 Pierce St.
Riverside, CA 92505
(951) 509-8733
(951) 509-8479 FAX

Individual, family counseling, anger mgmt classes. OFC HRS: M-Th 1pm-9pm. Sliding fee scale. SERVES: Riverside County.

FAMILY SERVICES

Parent Center
24300 Las Brisas Rd., North
Murrieta, CA 92562
(951) 304-1623
(951) 304-1627 FAX

Edu & personal support srvs to parents & educators. Classes & workshops: Parent Project, Parent & Me, child health & safety. Support groups including: Al-Anon, Families & Friends of Murder Victims, Special Ed Parent Advisory Council, Mommy & Me. For parenting center, call (951) 304-1624. For Head Start, State Preschool, call (915) 304-1625. FUNDING: Nonprofit. OFC HRS: M-Th 9am-1pm, 2pm-4:30pm, F 9am-1pm, 2pm-4pm. Prgm hrs vary. Spanish spoken. SERVES: Southwest Riverside County.

FAMILY SERVICES OF THE DESERT

81-711 Highway 111, Ste 101
Indio, CA 92201
(760) 347-2398
(800) 536-4357
(760) 347-6468 FAX

Family, individual and group counseling. Locations in Indio, Desert Hot Springs and Blythe. FUNDING: United Way, donations, client fees, nonprofit. OFC HRS: M-F 9am-5pm. Eve & weekend by appt. Spanish spoken. SERVES: Coachella Valley.

FAMILY SOLUTIONS

Central Cluster
214 West E Street
Ontario, CA 91762
(909) 418-6923
(909) 459-2932 FAX

Works to improve the health & well-being of children & their families. Mental health & case mgmt, parenting classes, medical srvs. Crisis intervention, diagnostic assessment, individual family, group counseling. Alt location: 1501-A S. Bon View Ave. in Ontario, (909) 673-1794. FUNDING: Nonprofit. OFC HRS: M-F 7:30am-4:30pm. SERVES: Zip code areas 91761, 91762, 91764.

FATHERS NETWORK

16120 N.E. 8th Street
Bellevue, WA 98008-3937
(425) 653-4286
(425) 747-1069 FAX

Website devoted to fathers of children with special health care needs and/or dev disabilities. Printed materials available in Spanish & other languages when possible. Visit (www.fathersnetwork.org). FUNDING: Office of Children with Special Health Care Needs, Washington State Dept of Health, fndns, donations. SERVES: U.S.A.

FEMA FOR KIDS

Resources for parents and teachers to teach disaster prep to kids. Visit (www.fema.gov/kids). FUNDING: Govt. SERVES: U.S.A.

FIESTA EDUCATIVA, INC.

161 S. Avenue 24, Ste 201
Los Angeles, CA 90031
(323) 221-6696
(323) 221-6699 FAX

Info, edu seminars, training & referral srvs to Latino families with disabled children. "Fiesta Familiar" in-home training held in L.A., Orange County, Imperial Valley, San Jose, Sacramento & San Diego Counties. FUNDING: Nonprofit. OFC HRS: M-F 8am-5pm. Spanish spoken. Free srvs. SERVES: Calif.

FIRST 5 CALIFORNIA

2389 Gateway Oaks Dr., Ste 260
Sacramento, CA 95833
(916) 263-1050
(916) 263-1360 FAX

FUNDING: State. OFC HRS: M-F 8am-5pm. Spanish spoken. SERVES: Calif.

GRANDPARENT INFORMATION CENTER

AARP
9750 3rd Avenue, N.E., Ste 450
Seattle, WA 98115
(866) 227-7457
(206) 517-9350 FAX

Info & referral, resources and policy efforts regarding grandparents raising grandchildren. Booklets available in Spanish or English. Free newsletter. FUNDING: Nonprofit. OFC HRS: M-F 9am-5pm, EST. SERVES: U.S.A.

GRANDPARENTS RAISING GRANDCHILDREN

Riverside Co. Office on Aging
1075 N. State St.
Hemet, CA 92543
(800) 303-0001

This warmline was established to assist grandparents with issues they face when raising grandchildren. Child care srvs (as funds are available) and case management available. Also call (951) 791-3575. FUNDING: County. OFC HRS: M-Th 8am-5pm. SERVES: Riverside County.

H.E.A.R.T., INC. FOUNDATION

Heart For The Children
P.O. Box 1922
Temecula, CA 92593-1922
(951) 506-4488
(760) 723-1116 FAX

Underwrites therapy, counseling funding and child care tuition for abused children and families in crisis. Assist is usually provided on a short-term basis (three months) and is given to families who have no other financial resources available to them. Additional counseling may be available depending on case evaluation, waiting list, and available funds.Tax exempt ID#: 33-00787074. FUNDING: Nonprofit. SERVES: Southwest Riverside County.

HANMI FAMILY COUNSELING CENTER

Formerly Korean American Counseling Ctr

12362 Beach Blvd., Ste 1
Stanton, CA 90680
(714) 892-9910
(714) 892-9927 FAX

Serves the Korean American community. Counseling, referrals, community edu, support groups for gamblers, parenting edu, alternative high school on site. OFC HRS: M-F 9am-5pm. Korean spoken. Sliding fee scale. SERVES: U.S.A.

HEALTHY FAMILY CLINIC

JFK Memorial Fndn
73-555 San Gorgonio Way
Palm Desert, CA 92260
(760) 776-1600
(760) 776-4500 FAX

Medical srvs for children of all ages. Nutrition srvs, parenting edu, public health care application assist. FUNDING: Nonprofit. OFC HRS: M-F 8am-5pm. ADM REQ: Call for appt. Accepts Medi-Cal, CHDP, Healthy Families, Healthy Kids. SERVES: Palm Desert.

HOUSE EAR INSTITUTE

House Ear Clinic
2100 W. 3rd Street
Los Angeles, CA 90057
(213) 483-4431
(800) 388-8612
(213) 483-8789 FAX

Research, edu, and clinical srvs for deaf and hard-of-hearing children & their families. Srvs include: outpatient infant screenings, diagnostic testing, auditory rehab with referrals to edu prgms and therapy, pre- and post- evaluations for Cochlear Implant srvs. Also camp for families and children with parent workshops and fun activities for children. TDD (213) 484-2642; For L.A. appts, call (213) 483-5706; For Orange County appts, call (714) 516-9570; For the Care Children's Center, call (213) 353-7005. TDD (213) 483-2226. FUNDING: Nonprofit, donations. OFC HRS: M-F 8:30am-5pm. ADM REQ: Must pre-register for family camp. SERVES: U.S.A.

IMPACT

34130 Gannon Terrace
Fremont, CA 94555
(877) 322-7299

Volunteer group of professionals and parents working for quality prgms, and advocacy for students who are deaf and/or hard-of-hearing. Visit (www.deafkids.org). Also support for parents. FUNDING: Nonprofit. Spanish spoken. SERVES: Calif.

INCREDABLES SPECIAL NEEDS PROGRAM

Rancho Cucamonga Civic Center
10500 Civic Center Dr.
Rancho Cucamonga, CA 91730
(909) 477-2782
(909) 477-2848 FAX

Recreational programs offered to residents and non-residents with special needs. Sports, singing, dancing, cooking, etc. Call for more info. Volunteers welcome. FUNDING: City. OFC HRS: M-Th 7am-6pm. ADM REQ: Ages 5-22 yrs, no one turned away. Fees for some activities. SERVES: Rancho Cucamonga.

INFANT DEVELOPMENT ASSN OF CALIF

P.O. Box 186550
3210 24th Street
Sacramento, CA 95818-9550

(916) 453-8801
(916) 453-0627 FAX

Advocates for children, ages birth-3 yrs, with disabilities & those at-risk for dev disabilities & their families. Workshops, training, public forums, etc. Chapters in Alameda, Yolo/Sacramento, San Diego/Imperial, L.A. areas. Visit (www.idaofcal.org). FUNDING: Nonprofit. SERVES: Calif.

INFANT FAMILY SERVICES
5855 E. Naples Plaza, Ste 103
Long Beach, CA 90803

In-home early intervention prgm serving children ages birth-3 yrs with special needs or who are at-risk for dev delays. Support srvs to child & families during transition to center and/or school prgms. Assists families in accessing community resources, home visitation, parent-child play groups, OT consultation, speech & language consultation, infant massage instruction, lending library, newsletter. OFC HRS: M-F 8:30am-5pm. ADM REQ: Referral from regional center. SERVES: L.A., Orange & San Bernardino Counties.

INLAND BEHAV & HEALTH SERVICES
Westside Counseling Ctr
1963 North E Street
San Bernardino, CA 92405
(909) 881-6146
(909) 881-0111 FAX

Comprehensive health care, substance abuse, mental health and homeless support srvs. Offers crisis intervention, primary prevention edu, PC-1000 classes, anger mgmt, parenting STEP classes. Perinatal prgm for expectant and parenting mothers who are addicted to drugs with both pre- and post-natal srvs. Provides transportation as well as child care. State ID: 360015AN. FUNDING: Govt, contracts, grants, nonprofit. OFC HRS: M-Th 8am-6pm; F 8am-5pm. Spanish spoken. ADM REQ: Ages 13 yrs+, referrals & walk in. Accepts Medicare, Medi-Cal. SERVES: San Bernardino County.

INLAND EMPIRE UNITED WAY
Chamber of Commerce
7945 Vineyard Ave., Ste D5
Rancho Cucamonga, CA 91730
(909) 888-9011

Mission is to engage a caring community to respond to human need by: helping disadvantaged kids succeed in school, providing easy access to health and social srvs, developing opportunities for volunteers to create positive change, strengthening financial stability opportunities for low-income familes and individuals. FUNDING: Nonprofit. OFC HRS: M-F 8am-5pm. Free srvs. SERVES: Pomona Valley, Redlands/Yucaipa, Palo Verde Valley, Western San Bernardino County.

INLAND HOSPICE ADULT PRGM
A Volunteer Prgm
233 W. Harrison Ave.
Claremont, CA 91711
(909) 399-3289
(909) 626-4369 FAX

Volunteers & staff tend to the physical, emotional & spiritual needs of the terminally ill, the frail & elderly & their families. Adult bereavement groups offered at various locations, open to those who are experiencing the loss of a loved one. The Common Threads Project is a bereavement support for children & youth ages 6-17 yrs & their families. Call to register. FUNDING: United Way, fundraisers, nonprofit. OFC HRS: M-F 9am-5pm. ADM REQ: Must register for Common Threads. Free srvs. SERVES: East L.A. & West San Bernardino.

INSIGHT COUNSELING
23232 Peralta Dr., Ste 211
Laguna Hills, CA 92653
(949) 707-5100
(949) 488-2418 FAX

Comprehensive individual, family, couples and group therapy. Edu classes in anger mgmt and parenting. Therapists specialize in: drug/alcohol treatment, interventions, eating disorders, anxiety, panic attacks, depression, teen, family and couples issues. FUNDING: Nonprofit. OFC HRS: M-Th 9am-9pm; F 7am-9pm; Sat 9am-1pm. Spanish spoken. Accessible and affordable srvs. SERVES: Orange, Riverside & San Bernardino Counties.

INSTITUTE FOR BLACK PARENTING
Adoption, Foster Care, Family Preservation
3120 Chicago Ave., Ste 130
Riverside, CA 92507
(951) 274-2800
(877) 367-8858
(951) 782-9768 FAX

Adoption and foster care agency specializing in recruiting African-American families for special needs children. Culturally sensitive, personalized free srvs, streamlined application, edu training process. Open to all ethnic groups. FUNDING: Nonprofit. OFC HRS: M-F 8am-5pm. ADM REQ: Foster children ages birth-17 yrs, adults ages 21 yrs+. SERVES: So. Calif.

INTERNATIONAL CHILD ABUSE NETWORK
P.O. Box 155
7657 Winnetka Ave.
Canoga Park, CA 91306-2677
(888) 224-4226
(818) 716-0658 FAX

Online-facilitated chat rooms for child abuse and domestic violence survivors. Visit (www.yesican.org). FUNDING: Nonprofit. OFC HRS: M-F 8am-5pm. SERVES: Internatl.

INTERNATL SOUNDEX REUNION REGISTER
P.O. Box 371179
Las Vegas, NV 89137
(888) 886-4777
(775) 882-7755

Register providing a matching system for any adult searching for a reunion with next of kin by birth. Serves birth family members separated from their families due to circumstances out of their control. OFC HRS: M-Th 9am-3:30pm. ADM REQ: Ages 18 yrs+. Free srvs. SERVES: U.S.A.

JEWELS FOR KIDS
560 Greenbrier Rd., Ste 210
Oceanside, CA 92054
(888) 770-7456
(760) 730-5437
(760) 730-5438 FAX

Accepts donations of unwanted jewelry in return for a free appraisal and 501(c)(3) tax credit. Items are re-designed and re-created, and auctioned at a yearly children's benefit concert. All proceeds go to support children's charities. Main goal is to work for the reunification of families. Four supervised visitation rooms available. Secure mailing address: 1835A South Centre City Pkwy., #323, Escondido, CA 92025. FUNDING: Nonprofit. OFC HRS: Varies daily. SERVES: U.S.A.

JUVENILE DIABETES RESEARCH FNDN
26 Broadway, 14th Fl.
New York, NY 10004
(800) 533-2873
(212) 785-9500
(212) 785-9595 FAX

Primary objective is to support and fund research into the cause, treatment and prev of diabetes, and, ultimately through research, find a cure. Also serves the needs of those with diabetes and their families by providing prgms of edu & info. Strives to inform the general public on the seriousness of diabetes. Provides brochures, fact sheets, referrals. FUNDING: Donations, nonprofit. OFC HRS: M-F 9am-5pm, EST. Spanish spoken. SERVES: U.S.A.

JUVENILE DIABETES RESEARCH FNDN
Inland Empire Chapter
2023 Chicago Ave., Ste B-13
Riverside, CA 92507
(951) 784-4156
(951) 784-4628 FAX

Primary objective is to support and fund research, treatment and prev of diabetes. Also serves the needs of those with diabetes and their families by providing prgms of edu & info. Strives to alert the general public to the seriousness of diabetes. Provides brochures, fact sheets, referrals. FUNDING: Nonprofit. OFC HRS: M-F 9am-5pm. SERVES: Inland Empire.

KIDS WISH NETWORK
4060 Louis Ave.
Holiday, FL 34691
(727) 937-3600
(888) 918-9004

Established to provide wishes to children suffering from life-threatening medical illness. Nationally recognized charitable organization. Visit (www.kidswishnetwork.com). FUNDING: Nonprofit. ADM REQ: Ages 3-18 yrs. SERVES: U.S.A.

KIDSNCARE/CHILD DEV SRVS
San Bernardino Co. Supt of Schools
1111 E. Mill St., Ste 100
San Bernardino, CA 92408
(909) 384-1492
(800) 722-1091
(909) 384-8030 FAX

Resource & referral for child care centers & licensed family child care home settings and Livescan (fingerprint) site. Assists in starting a child care prgm. Child care food prgm (CCFP) for family child care providers. Alternative payment prgm (APP) to assist low-income families with child care costs. (APP also serves other counties where parents are employed). Walk in or call. FUNDING: Donations, grants, state, nonprofit. OFC HRS: M-F 8am-4:30pm. Spanish spoken. Free srvs. SERVES: Riverside & San Bernardino Counties (except the west end).

KIDSNCARE/CHILD DEV SRVS
San Bernardino Co. Supt of Schools
14397 Amargosa Rd.

Victorville, CA 92392
(760) 245-0770
(760) 245-1072 FAX

Resource & referral for child care centers and licensed family child care home settings and Livescan (fingerprint) site. Assists in starting a child care prgm. Child care food prgm (CCFP) for family child care providers. Alternative payment prgm (APP) to assist low income families with child care costs. (APP also serves other counties where parents are employed). Walk in or call. FUNDING: Donations, grants, state, nonprofit. OFC HRS: M-F 7:30am-4:30pm. Spanish spoken. Free srvs. SERVES: High Desert area.

KIDSPEACE

KidsPeace Helpline
4085 Independence Dr.
Schnecksville, PA 18078
(800) 257-3223
(610) 799-8900 FAX

Hotline provides counseling, info & referral srvs to children & parents in crisis. Also mental health & behavioral health srvs, children's psychiatric hospital, residential, foster care, juvenile justice & outpatient. FUNDING: Nonprofit. OFC HRS: 24 hrs, 7 days. Free helpline. SERVES: U.S.A.

KINSHIP CENTER

Seedling Project
1504 Brookhollow Dr., Ste 117
Santa Ana, CA 92705
(714) 432-8584
(714) 432-8588 FAX

Early intervention srvs to help decrease children's dev delays. Provides dev & behavioral screenings for children in their homes, in-home support, psychological testing, occupational therapy eval. FUNDING: Nonprofit. OFC HRS: M-F 8am-5pm. Spanish spoken. ADM REQ: Ages birth-6 yrs and have Orange Co. Medi-Cal. SERVES: Orange, Riverside & San Bernardino Counties.

KRISTIE'S PLACE

1747 S. Claudina Way
Anaheim, CA 92805
(714) 408-9781
(714) 956-1475 FAX

A place for children with life-threatening illnesses to come with their families for their So. Calif wish trip or for a short compassion stay. Wishland's Kid's Club and family support prgms bring joy and hope to all. FUNDING: Nonprofit. OFC HRS: M-F 8:30am-4pm; Sat 8:30am-10am. Spanish spoken. SERVES: L.A., Orange & San Bernardino Counties.

LA LECHE LEAGUE

Info & support for women who wish to breast-feed, 24-hr phone help, monthly meetings, lending library with books on breast-feeding, childbirth, family & nutrition. Visit website for phone list & web addresses in So. Calif & Nevada (www.lalecheleaguescnv.org). TDD (847) 592-7570. FUNDING: Nonprofit. OFC HRS: M-F 9am-9pm. SERVES: Mid County.

LA LECHE LEAGUE INTERNATL

P.O. Box 4079
957 N. Plum Grove Rd.
Schaumburg, IL 60168-4079
(800) 525-3243
(847) 519-7730

(847) 969-0460 FAX

Worldwide organization provides support to pregnant & breast-feeding women. Edu materials, free catalog & referrals to local leaders. Call for monthly meeting info. FUNDING: Donations, members, nonprofit. OFC HRS: M-F 9am-5pm, CST. Spanish spoken. SERVES: Internatl.

LAURA'S HOUSE

Emergency Shelter
999 Corporate Dr., Ste 225
Ladera Ranch, CA 92694
(949) 361-3775
(949) 361-3548 FAX

Emergency shelter prgm for battered women with or without children; pregnant women accepted. Emergency shelter provides case mgmt, counseling and legal advocacy. Counseling & resource center for men, women & child victims of domestic violence. 24-hr hotline (866) 498-1511. Counseling hrs: M-F 9am-5pm, eve by appt. Shelter: 24 hrs, 7 days. Spanish & Farsi spoken. Language line available. Sliding fee scale. No one turned away for lack of funds. SERVES: So Calif. Able to refer out of area if needed

MATERNITY INFORMATION

San Antonio Community Hospital
999 San Bernardino Rd.
Upland, CA 91786
(909) 980-2229
(909) 985-7659 FAX

Info on maternity srvs at San Antonio plus info & schedules for maternity edu prgms including lamaze, infant CPR, maternity exercise and other prenatal classes. OFC HRS: M-F 8am-4:30pm. Spanish spoken. SERVES: Rancho Cucamonga, Upland, Ontario, Montclair, Chino, Fontana, Pomona and Claremont.

MEAD VALLEY COMMUNITY COMPLEX

Family Service Assn/Riverside
21091 Rider St.
Perris, CA 92570
(951) 657-0686
(951) 657-9208 FAX

Prgms for youth, families, and seniors. Health screening, dental & medical srvs, independent studies, counseling, parenting classes, Bingo, senior lunch and home-delivered meals, utility assist, commodities, etc. FUNDING: Nonprofit. OFC HRS: M-F 8am-5pm. Spanish spoken. Most prgms are free. SERVES: Mead Valley, Perris.

METH RESOURCES

www.methresources.gov
(916) 324-5523

Visit (www.methresources.gov) to find various resources and prgms in the fight against meth. FUNDING: Govt. SERVES U.S.A.

MISSING CHILDREN INTERNATL, INC.

1905 E. 17th Street, Ste 110
Santa Ana, CA 92705-8628
(714) 542-8083
(800) 339-4357
(714) 210-1163 FAX

State-by-state search for missing persons. 24-hr hotline: (714) 323-6730. FUNDING: Nonprofit. OFC HRS: M-F 8am-5pm. SERVES: U.S.A. & internatl.

MONTCLAIR HUMAN SRVS DIVISION

5111 Benito St.
Montclair, CA 91763
(909) 625-9460
(909) 399-9751 FAX

Senior activities and meals M-F 11:30am-1pm ($1.75 donation for ages 60 yrs+). USDA surplus food 3rd Th of each month to Montclair residents. Call (909)625-9483 or (909)625-9462 for info. Low-cost medical and immunization clinic. Weight room and racquet ball courts. After-school prgms and recreation activities. Also offers free parenting and nutrition classes. See website for more info on all srvs. FUNDING: DAAS, CDD, First 5, state after school edu & safety prgms, grants, Healthy Start Planning Grant. OFC HRS: M-Th 7:30am-6pm. Rec Facility: M-F 7:30am-9:30pm; Sat 8am-5pm. Spanish spoken. ADM REQ: Proof of income/uninsured for clinic srvs. SERVES: San Bernardino County.

MOURNING STAR

Bereavement Support for Children
6235 River Crest Dr.
Riverside, CA 92507
(951) 413-1317

Bereavement support for children and teens who have experienced the death of a loved one. Prgm provided by the Visiting Nurses Assn. Also parent group. FUNDING: Nonprofit, grants. ADM REQ: Call for appt. Free srvs. SERVES: Riverside County.

MT. SAN JACINTO CHILDREN'S SRVS

950 Ramona Blvd., Ste 2
San Jacinto, CA 92582
(951) 487-2674
(951) 487-2679 FAX

Info & referral srvs, intake assessments, psychiatric evaluations & treatment, case mgmt. In-home behavioral srvs, 5150 evaluations, transportation srvs, individual therapy, group therapy & family therapy to seriously disturbed children & adolescents. FUNDING: County. OFC HRS: M-Th 8am-5pm. Spanish spoken. ADM REQ: Ages birth-18 yrs. Must meet county criteria. Accepts Medi-Cal and Healthy Families. In a crisis, help is available. SERVES: Riverside County.

NAMI-LOS ANGELES

Natl Alliance on Mental Illness
824 Moraga Dr.
Los Angeles, CA 90049
(310) 889-7200

NAMI is a natl organization that provides families of mentally ill persons with edu support and resources. Click the "Find Support" tab on the website for srvs in your area (www.nami.org). FUNDING: Nonprofit. OFC HRS: M-F 8am-6pm. Spanish spoken. SERVES: U.S.A.

NARCONON INTERNATIONAL

Drug Prev, Edu & Rehab Srvs
4652 Hollywood Blvd.
Los Angeles, CA 90027
(323) 962-2404
(323) 962-6872 FAX

The aim of this prgm is to help the drug abuser become drug free. Prevention and edu to youth and adults. Parent center provides edu info, videos & booklets. FUNDING: Nonprofit. OFC HRS: M-F 9am-6pm. Spanish, Italian, French,

Filipino & Armenian spoken. SERVES: Internatl.

NATL CHILDHOOD CANCER FNDN

440 E. Huntington Dr., Ste 400
Arcadia, CA 91066-6012
(800) 458-6223

Organization dedicated to childhood cancer research. Patients, families and health professionals can locate info and assist by visiting (www.curesearch.org). FUNDING: Nonprofit. OFC HRS: M-F 8:30am-5pm. SERVES: U.S.A.

NATL PARENTING INSTITUTE

P.O. Box 1252
Temecula, CA 92593
(951) 694-8910
(951) 694-8910 FAX

Contracts with agencies (schools, PTAs, churches, businesses, govt) to provide parenting edu courses, seminars, workshops, keynotes for conferences, staff dev. Three DPSS approved courses (2 on-site and 1 home study). Covers ages birth-9 yrs, pre-teen, teen, First 5. FUNDING: Donations, grants, govt, client fees, nonprofit. OFC HRS: Call for hours. Courses in Spanish and English. Fees vary. SERVES: U.S.A.

NEW HOPE/MORENO VALLEY

12818 Heacock St., Ste C-6
Moreno Valley, CA 92553
(951) 247-6542
(951) 247-9819 FAX

Christian counseling center. Serves as a training facility for those in the counseling profession. Psychological testing, child abuse counseling, crisis eval, parenting issues, school problems, teenage issues such as suicide, runaway, depression, eating disorders and substance abuse, bereavement counseling, adult abuse issues, pain mgmt and a host of other adult counseling needs. FUNDING: Donations, fees, nonprofit. OFC HRS: By appt. ADM REQ: Low income. Accepts insurance in most cases, Victim-Witness Program, Recovery Assistance Foundation. Sliding scale basis upon request. SERVES: So. Calif.

OPEN DOORS SUPPORT GROUPS

Riverside Co. Dept. of Mental Health
9707 Magnolia Ave.
Riverside, CA 92503
(951) 358-6858

Support groups for parents/caregivers who are raising a child with mental health, emotional or behavioral challenges. Meets 4th Th of the month at 6pm. Call for more details. Free srvs. Child care available for $2 per child, per hour. Call ahead for these srvs. SERVES: Riverside Co.

PARENTS ANONYMOUS, INC.

675 W. Foothill Blvd., Ste 220
Claremont, CA 91711
(909) 621-6184
(909) 625-6304 FAX

Child abuse prev organization. Free weekly ongoing community-based support groups. FUNDING: Donations, govt, nonprofit. OFC HRS: M-F 8am-5pm. Spanish spoken. SERVES: U.S.A.

PARENTS WITHOUT PARTNERS (ADMIN)

Internatl Headquarters
1650 S. Dixie Hwy., Ste 510

Boca Raton, FL 33432
(800) 637-7974
(561) 391-8833
(561) 395-8557 FAX

PWP serves single parents, of any age, who are divorced, widowed, never married or separated, whether or not they have child custody. Request literature by mail. FUNDING: Membership dues, nonprofit. OFC HRS: M-F 8:30am-5pm, EST. SERVES: U.S.A.

PARTNERSHIP FOR PRESCRIPTION ASSIST

(877) 777-7815

Free or low-cost prescription srv for the uninsured, underinsured or those with limited income. Call or visit (www.RXHelpforCA.org). SERVES: Calif.

POMONA VALLEY HOSPITAL MED CTR

Women's & Children's Srvs
1798 N. Garey Ave.
Pomona, CA 91767
(909) 620-6663
(909) 629-0890 FAX

Childbirth classes, Baby Express, CPR, Boot Camp for Dads, Safe Sitter prgm, community resources, & physician referrals. Srvs include: labor, delivery, recovery suites, perinatal diagnostic/treatment ctr, lactation consultation and maternal/neonatal transport from other hospitals. FUNDING: Nonprofit. OFC HRS: M-F 9am-4:30pm. But hours vary depending on dept. Spanish spoken. SERVES: Inland, San Gabriel Valleys.

POMONA VALLEY HOSPITAL MED CTR

Family Education & Resource Ctr
1770 N. Orange Grove Ave.
Pomona, CA 91767
(909) 865-9858
(909) 865-9782
(909) 629-0890 FAX

Free referrals to support groups, physicians and community resources. Offers ongoing classes & support prgms. FUNDING: Nonprofit. OFC HRS: M-F 8:30am-5pm; Sat 8:30am-1pm. Spanish spoken. SERVES: Inland & San Gabriel Valleys.

POSTPARTUM SUPPORT INTERNATL

706 S.W. 54th Avenue
Portland, OR 97219
(503) 894-9453
(503) 894-9452 FAX

Promotes awareness, prev & treatment of mental health issues related to childbearing. Provides resources to local social support networks and support groups, info on diagnosis & treatment of postpartum mood & anxiety disorders, postpartum chat rooms & edu. Professional memberships available. Visit (www.postpartum.net). Helpline: (800) 944-4773. FUNDING: Nonprofit. OFC HRS: M-F 9am-3pm. Free srvs. SERVES: Internatl.

PROJECT CUIDAR

Cal State San Bernardino
5500 University Pkwy.
San Bernardino, CA 92407
(909) 537-5945
(909) 537-7759 FAX

Promotes healthy parent-child relationships and optimal child dev through culturally and developmentally appropriate early intervention srvs for children ages birth-5 yrs and their par-

ents. Srvs include: parent edu, child enrichment groups, & provider training and are offered in both English & Spanish. Groups meeet at various locations within the community. Free child care for ages birth-12 yrs. Spanish spoken. ADM REQ: No new parents accepted after the second week of classes. Free srvs. SERVES: San Bernardino County.

R.A.P. COMMUNITY RECOVERY SRVS

17205 Arrow Blvd.
Fontana, CA 92335
(909) 350-0278
(909) 356-9390
(909) 356-0120 FAX

DUI, petty theft, and anger mgmt for youth. State ID: 360051AN. FUNDING: Nonprofit. OFC HRS: M-F 8am-4:30pm. Spanish spoken. ADM REQ: Ages 10 yrs+. Sliding fee scale. SERVES: San Bernardino County.

RANCHO CUCAMONGA RESOURCE CENTER

9791 Arrow Route
Rancho Cucamonga, CA 91730
(909) 477-2781
(909) 919-2625 FAX

Resource center provides access to various srvs provided to the community. Prgms include: emerg needs (food and clothing), domestic abuse prevention workshops and counseling, ESL classes, parenting classes, youth socialization prgms, room rentals, info & referral srvs. FUNDING: Govt, city, donations. OFC HRS: M-F 8am-10pm. Spanish spoken. ADM REQ: Residents, however no one will be turned away. SERVES: Riverside, San Bernardino Counties.

REDLANDS ADULT SCHOOL

Redlands USD
P.O. Box 3008
10568 California St.
Redlands, CA 92373-1508
(909) 748-6930
(909) 307-5324 FAX

Parent edu classes and parent participation preschool. Call for waiting list availability. OFC HRS: M-Th 9am-8pm; F 9am-4:30pm. Summer Hrs: M-F 9am-4:30pm. Closed at 12noon 1st F each month. Spanish spoken. SERVES: Redlands.

RITA PROJECT, INC.

Mailing Address
2046 Hillhurst Ave.
Los Angeles, CA 90027
(866) 775-7482

Rita (Sanskrit for truth) is a global movement to stop suicide and celebrate life. Devoted to using the arts to help survivors of suicide connect with the power of creation, and in doing so, foster transformation. Prgms offered through Rita Studios, Rita Workshops & Rita Exhibitions. Assist with healing, suicide prev, edu and public awareness on the importance of the arts to mental health. Visit (www.ritaproject.org). Rita Studios are held weekly at the Bergamot Cafe, 2525 Michigan Ave., #A-3, Santa Monica, CA 90404. Please call to register. FUNDING: Nonprofit. OFC HRS: 24 hrs. ADM REQ: Ages 18 yrs+. SERVES: So. Calif.

RIVERSIDE CO. CHILD SUPPORT SRVS

260 N. Broadway
Blythe, CA 92225
(866) 901-3212

(760) 921-5608 FAX

Establishes child and medical support orders, paternity orders, locates parents, enforces support orders. Walk in welcome. Send payments to P.O. Box 989067, West Sacramento, CA 95798 FUNDING: Federal, county. OFC HRS: M-F 7:30am-5pm. ADM REQ: Application for srvs. Free srvs. SERVES: Riverside County.

RIVERSIDE CO. CHILD SUPPORT SRVS

47-950 Arabia St.
Indio, CA 92201
(866) 901-3212
(760) 863-7016 FAX

Establishes child and medical support orders, paternity orders, locates parents, enforces support orders. Walk in. For payment inquiries, call (866)901-3212. FUNDING: Federal, county. OFC HRS: M-F 7:30am-5pm. Spanish spoken. ADM REQ: Application for srvs. Free srvs. SERVES: Riverside County.

RIVERSIDE CO. CHILD SUPPORT SRVS

2041 Iowa Ave.
Riverside, CA 92507
(866) 901-3212
(951) 955-4224 FAX

Establishes and/or enforces child and medical support orders, paternity orders, locates noncustodial parents. For payment inquiries, call (866) 901-3212. FUNDING: Federal, county. OFC HRS: M-F 7:30am-5pm. Spanish spoken. ADM REQ: Application for srvs. Free srvs. SERVES: Riverside County.

RIVERSIDE CO. CHILD SUPPORT SRVS

1370 S. State St., Ste A
San Jacinto, CA 92583
(866) 901-3212
(951) 791-2054 FAX

Establishes child and medical support orders, paternity orders, locates parents, enforces support orders. Walk in or call. For payment inquiries, call (866)901-3212. FUNDING: Federal, county. OFC HRS: M-F 7:30am-5:30pm. Spanish spoken. ADM REQ: Application for srvs. Free srvs. SERVES: Riverside County.

RIVERSIDE CO. COMM HEALTH AGENCY

Dept Of Public Health/Nursing
4065 County Circle Dr., Ste 305
Riverside, CA 92503
(951) 358-5438
(951) 358-4762 FAX

In-home srvs include assessment, guidance, counseling, teaching, intervention, referral & family case mgmt in the following categories: child health, senior health, perinatal, postpartum, family planning, parenting edu, high-risk pregnancy, high-risk infant, grief/loss, child abuse prevention, adult/elder abuse, communicable disease, tuberculosis, infant death, drug-exposed infant, birth/newborn screening follow-up, homeless, domestic violence, teen parenting. Group parenting edu classes are provided in many locations. TDD (951) 358-5124. OFC HRS: M-F 8am-5pm. SERVES: Riverside County.

RIVERSIDE CO. DEPT OF PUBLIC HEALTH

4065 County Circle Dr.
Riverside, CA 92503
(951) 358-4977

Programs include: childhood asthma prgm, tobacco control project, smoking cessation.

FUNDING: County. OFC HRS: M-F 8am-5pm. Spanish spoken for some classes. ADM REQ: Must call for pre-registration. Not all programs are county-wide, call for more info. SERVES: Desert Area Riverside County.

RIVERSIDE CO. DEPT/MENTAL HEALTH

Open Doors Parent Group/Phone Support
4020 Jefferson St.
Riverside, CA 92504
(951) 358-3622

Community support group open to families & caregivers who are experiencing difficulties raising children with mental health, emotional and/or behavioral challenges. The meeting objective is to provide families an opportunity to meet, speak and join with other families who are experiencing similar challenges in order to share support, info, resources & solutions that will empower one another. Helpline for community info (800) 464-1123. 24-hr suicide helpline (909) 686-4357. FUNDING: Riverside Co. Dept/Mental Health Children's Srvs. OFC HRS: M-Th 8am-6pm. SERVES: Riverside County.

RIVERSIDE CO. MENTAL HEALTH

Hemet Mental Health Clinic
650 N. State St.
Hemet, CA 92543
(951) 791-3300
(909) 791-3333 FAX

Family advocate prgm provides info & support to families of the mentally ill. Outpatient medication clinic for the mentally ill. Homeless department. Substance abuse department. FUNDING: Govt. OFC HRS: M-Th 8am-5:30pm. Spanish, Tagalog spoken. ADM REQ: Severely mentally ill. Accepts Medi-Cal, Medicare, indigent prgms. SERVES: Hemet, San Jacinto, Idyllwild, Anza, Winchester.

RIVERSIDE CO. MENTAL HEALTH

Children's Services Parent Support
9707 Magnolia Ave.
Riverside, CA 92503
(951) 358-6858
(951) 687-3478 FAX

Parent support srvs provide liaison and referral for respite care, parent support networking and social mentorship for clients of the dept. Also access to donated goods and srvs fund, minority outreach activities, dev of info resources for parents plus staff edu trainings. FUNDING: Govt. OFC HRS: M-F 8am-5pm. SERVES: Riverside County.

RIVERSIDE CO. OFFICE/EDUCATION

Children's Srvs Unit
2300 Market St.
Riverside, CA 92501
(800) 442-4927
(951) 826-6626
(951) 826-4478 FAX

Child care resource & referral, subsidized child care, parenting edu, brochures, early childhood conferences & trainings, toy loan prgm. FUNDING: State Dept of Edu, govt. OFC HRS: M-F 8am-5pm. Spanish spoken. ADM REQ: Income eligibility for child care, none for other srvs. Free srvs except sliding fee scale for child care based on state median income level. SERVES: Riverside County.

RIVERSIDE CO. PUBLIC HEALTH DEPT

Child Health & Disability Prev (CHDP)
P.O. Box 7600

10769 Holve Ave., Ste 210
Riverside, CA 92513-7600
(800) 346-6520
(951) 358-5481
(951) 358-5002 FAX

Well-child check-ups to children under age 21 yrs. Physical exam, dental assessment, nutritional assessment, vision & hearing screening, blood & urine testing, TB testing, immunizations, and health edu referrals for diagnosis & treatment. Children up to age 19 yrs who do not qualify for Medi-Cal may qualify for CHDP srvs depending on family size and income. Srvs offered at all county clinics and 120 CHDP providers. FUNDING: Govt. OFC HRS: M-Th 8am-5:30pm. ADM REQ: Children who have Medi-Cal and are not enrolled in a Medi-Cal managed care prgm. Free srvs. SERVES: Riverside County.

RIVERSIDE CO. PUBLIC HEALTH DEPT

Childhood Lead Poisoning Prev Prgm
P.O. Box 7600
10769 Holve, Ste 210
Riverside, CA 92503
(800) 346-6520
(951) 358-5481
(951) 358-5002 FAX

Community and school edu & presentations regarding the dangers of lead poisoning, sources of lead, importance of lead testing and case mgmt of lead-poisoned children. FUNDING: Govt. OFC HRS: M-Th 8am-5pm. ADM REQ: Directed to families with children ages birth-6 yrs and children diagnosed with lead poisoning. Free srvs. SERVES: Riverside County.

RIVERSIDE CO. PUBLIC SOCIAL SRVS

Children's Protective Srvs
1225 W. Hobson Way
Blythe, CA 92225
(760) 921-5800
(760) 921-7715 FAX

24-hr emerg response, protective srvs for children in danger of abuse, exploitation, neglect, etc. Call to report incidents or suspicions of child abuse or neglect. Full range of srvs from emerg shelter to investigation. 24-hr hotline (800) 442-4918. Walk in or call. FUNDING: State, county, fed. OFC HRS: M-Th 7am-5:30pm; F 8am-5pm. Spanish spoken. SERVES: Desert area.

RIVERSIDE CO. PUBLIC SOCIAL SRVS

Children's Protective Srvs
547 N. San Jacinto Ave.
Hemet, CA 92543
(951) 791-3200
(800) 442-4918
(951) 791-3210 FAX

24-hr emerg response, protective srvs for children in danger of abuse, exploitation, neglect, etc. Call to report incidents or suspicions of child abuse or neglect. Full range of srvs from emerg shelter to investigation. Walk in or call. FUNDING: County, state, fed. OFC HRS: M-F 8am-5pm. Spanish spoken. SERVES: Riverside County.

RIVERSIDE CO. PUBLIC SOCIAL SRVS

Child Protective Srvs
48113 Jackson St.
Indio, CA 92201
(760) 863-7210
(800) 442-4918

(760) 863-7225 FAX

24-hr emerg response, protective srvs for children in danger of abuse, exploitation, neglect, etc. Call to report incidents or suspicions of child abuse or neglect. Full range of srvs from emerg shelter to investigation. Walk in or call. FUNDING: County, state, fed. OFC HRS: M-F 8am-5pm. Spanish spoken. SERVES: Coachella Valley.

RIVERSIDE CO. PUBLIC SOCIAL SRVS

Children's Srvs/Child Protection
23119 Cottonwood Ave., Bldg. A, 2nd Fl.
Moreno Valley, CA 92553
(951) 413-5000
(951) 413-5016 FAX

Children's prgm provides preventive and protective srvs to victims of child abuse and their families, emerg response, investigation, out-of-home placement, info & referral, sex abuse treatment, and case mgmt (voluntary or juvenile court related) to link families with counseling, parent edu, drug treatment, testing, child care and respite care. 24-hr hotline for reporting child abuse (800) 442-4918. OFC HRS: M-F 8am-5pm. Spanish spoken. SERVES: Mid-county area.

RUBIDOUX COMMUNITY RESOURCE CTR

5473 Mission Blvd.
Riverside, CA 92509
(951) 328-1575
(951) 683-2613 FAX

Child abuse prevention ctr provides parenting classes, recruitment for in-home supportive srvs every other month. Classes in nutrition, adult edu, ESL, and job training for youth. Healthy Kids Club, counseling referrals. FUNDING: Nonprofit. OFC HRS: M-F 8am-5pm. ADM REQ: Must sign up for classes. Free srvs. SERVES: Glen Avon, Mira Loma, Riverside, Rubidoux, Sunnyslope.

SAFE KIDS INLAND EMPIRE COALITION

Loma Linda Univ Children's Hospital
11234 Anderson St.
Loma Linda, CA 92354
(909) 558-8118

Goal is to protect children ages birth-14 yrs from accidental injuries. Prgms include injury prevention prgms, child passenger safety events, legislative advocacy and professional networking. Also offers drowning prevention network that meets the 4th W of each month from 9am-10am at various sites in the community. Email (kelly.donaldson@cityofrc.us) for more info about the drowning prevention network and (kpatrick@llu.edu) for general info. SERVES: Inland Empire.

SAN BERNARDINO CO. CHILD ABUSE REPORTING

Dept of Children's Srvs
170 N. Yucca Ave., 2nd Fl., Ste D
Barstow, CA 92311
(800) 827-8724
(760) 255-5400
(760) 255-1501 FAX

24-hr emerg response, protective srvs for children in danger of abuse, exploitation, neglect, etc. Call to report incidents or suspicions of child abuse or neglect. Full range of emerg srvs including shelter and investigations. OFC HRS: M-F 8am-5pm. Spanish spoken. SERVES: San Bernardino County.

SAN BERNARDINO CO. CHILD SUPPORT

Dept of Child Support Services
10417 Mountain View Ave.
Loma Linda, CA 92354
(866) 901-3212
(909) 478-6922 FAX

24-hr info on child support srvs. Represents the interest of the minor children by: (1) determining who the parents are; (2) locating a child's parents for the purpose of establishing child support and/or paternity; (3) establishing and enforcing a child support order; (4) collecting child and spousal support payments. FUNDING: County, state, federal. OFC HRS: M-F 8am-5pm. Spanish spoken. ADM REQ: Demonstrates need for child support srvs. Free srvs. SERVES: San Bernardino County.

SAN BERNARDINO CO. CHILD SUPPORT

Desert Region
15400 Civic Dr.
Victorville, CA 92392
(866) 901-3212
(909) 478-6922 FAX

Establishes paternity & court-ordered child support. Collects child, medical & spousal support payments, also modifies orders. FUNDING: Govt. OFC HRS: M-F 8am-5pm. Spanish spoken. SERVES: San Bernardino County.

SAN BERNARDINO CO. CHILDREN'S SRVS

See "San Bernardino Co. Human Srvs Sy"

SAN BERNARDINO CO. HUMAN SRVS SY

Children's Srvs/Child Protective Srvs
1300 Bailey Ave.
Needles, CA 92363
(760) 326-9293
(800) 827-8724
(760) 326-9340 FAX

24-hr emerg response, protective srvs for children in danger of abuse, exploitation, neglect, etc. Call to report incidents or suspicions of child abuse or neglect. Full range of emerg srvs including shelter and investigations. SERVES: Needles.

SAN BERNARDINO CO. HUMAN SRVS SY

Children's Srvs/Child Protective Srvs
P.O. Box 1088
9638 7th Street
Rancho Cucamonga, CA 91730
(909) 945-3762
(909) 945-3784
(909) 945-3785 FAX

24-hr emerg response, protective srvs for children in danger of abuse, exploitation, neglect etc. Call to report incidents or suspicions of child abuse or neglect. Full range of emerg srvs, including shelter and investigations. OFC HRS: M-F 8am-5pm. Hindi, Spanish & Vietnamese spoken. SERVES: West San Bernardino County.

SAN BERNARDINO CO. HUMAN SRVS SY

Children's Srvs/Child Protective Srvs
1504 Gifford
San Bernardino, CA 92415
(909) 386-1100
(909) 386-1913 FAX

Child protection after hours (909) 384-9233. Hotline within Calif (800) 827-8724. OFC HRS: M-F 8am-5pm. Spanish spoken. SERVES: San Bernardino County.

SAN BERNARDINO CO. HUMAN SRVS SY

Children's Srvs/Child Protective Srvs
15400 Civic Dr., Ste 250
Victorville, CA 92392
(760) 243-5227
(800) 827-8724
(760) 843-4932 FAX

24-hr emerg response, protective srvs for children in danger of abuse, exploitation, neglect, etc. Call to report incidents or suspicions of child abuse or neglect. Full range of emerg srvs, including shelter and investigations. OFC HRS: M-F 8am-5pm. Spanish spoken. SERVES: Victorville & nearby.

SAN BERNARDINO CO. HUMAN SRVS SY

Children's Srvs/Child Protective Srvs
56311 Pima Trail
Yucca Valley, CA 92284
(760) 228-5300
(800) 827-8724
(760) 228-5321 FAX

24-hr emerg response, protective srvs for children in danger of abuse, exploitation, neglect, etc. Call to report incidents or suspicions of child abuse or neglect. Full range of emerg srvs, including shelter and investigations. OFC HRS: M-F 8am-5pm. Spanish spoken. SERVES: Morongo Basin.

SAN BERNARDINO CO. PUBLIC HEALTH

Health Nursing
120 Carousel Mall
San Bernardino, CA 92415-0048
(800) 722-3777
(909) 388-0401 FAX

Services include: physical, psychosocial and environmental assessments with focus on capacity to meet own needs and needs of the child. Info & referral and dev of support systems. Call first and referral will be sent out. FUNDING: County. OFC HRS: M-F 8am-5pm. Spanish spoken. ADM REQ: High risk for child abuse. SERVES: San Bernardino County.

SAN BERNARDINO CO/FIRST 5

Kelly Torres Resource Center
330 North D Street
San Bernardino, CA 92401
(909) 386-7706
(909) 386-7703 FAX

Parent edu, resource ctr, child dev & child health srvs. FUNDING: Govt. OFC HRS: M-F 8:30am-4:30pm. Spanish, Vietnamese, Tagalog, Chinese spoken. SERVES: San Bernardino County.

SIERRA CLUB/SAN GORGONIO

4079 Mission Inn Ave.
Riverside, CA 92501-3204
(951) 684-6203
(951) 684-6172 FAX

24-hr hotline for all upcoming activities for youth and adults. SERVES: Riverside, San Bernardino Counties.

SILVER LAKES COMMUNITY CHURCH

P.O. Box 1073
14766 Smithson Rd.
Helendale, CA 92342
(760) 952-1485
(760) 955-3797 FAX

Variety of srvs including: edu, resources, Bible classes, Christian counseling. FUNDING: Donations, Born Again Treasures (thrift store).

OFC HRS: Tu-Th 9am-4pm. No fees. SERVES: High Desert.

SINGLE PARENT SUPPORT GRP

Covina Valley Chapter
P.O. Box 1166
Covina, CA 91722
(626) 294-3211

Group and individual activities for parents who are divorced, widowed, single or separated. To become a member, call Trina at (626)332-9350. Many activities available. Dances held 2nd F at Elk Lodge in West Covina. FUNDING: Nonprofit. SERVES: San Gabriel Valley.

SINGLE PARENTS OF POWER

Emlac Health Srvs
P.O. Box 452602
1620 Centinela Ave, Ste 202
Inglewood, CA 90302
(310) 753-7860

Counseling services include: mental health, sexual abuse, anger mgmt, parenting, alcohol and drug abuse. Advocacy and counseling for victims of violent crimes and post-traumatic counseling for veterans. FUNDING: Nonprofit. OFC HRS: M-F 9am-9pm; Sat 10am-3pm. Spanish, Swahili spoken. Free counseling for victims of domestic violence. All other srvs on a sliding fee scale. SERVES: L.A. & San Bernardino Counties.

SO CALIF INDIAN CENTER, INC.

Corporate Office
10175 Slater Ave., Ste 150
Fountain Valley, CA 92708-4702
(714) 962-6673
(714) 962-6343 FAX

Edu, cultural, economic & recreational prgms for American Indians. Indian Child & Family Srvs (counseling, parenting, foster parents, etc.), WIA (employment assist & voc training), edu tutoring for Indian students in grades K-12. Emerg shelter, food, clothing, referral srvs. FUNDING: United Way, govt, nonprofit. OFC HRS: M-F 8am-5pm. ADM REQ: American-Indian verification. SERVES: So. Calif.

STARLIGHT CHILDREN'S FOUNDATION

5757 Wilshire Blvd., Ste M-100
Los Angeles, CA 90036
(310) 479-1212
(800) 315-1212
(310) 479-1235 FAX

When a child or teenager has a serious medical condition, everyone in the famliy is affected. The Starlight Fndn has dedicated itself to helping seriously ill children and their families cope with pain, fear and isolation through entertainment, edu, and family activities. Starlight's prgms have been proven to distract children from their pain, help them better understand and manage their illness. Connect families facing similar challenges so that no one feels alone. Outpatient, hospital-based and web offerings. To learn more, visit (www.starlight.org). FUNDING: Nonprofit. OFC HRS: M-F 8am-5pm. Accepts donations. SERVES: U.S.A., Canada, Australia, UK & Japan.

STOMP OUT BULLYING

www.stompoutbullying.org
(877) 602-8559

Anti-bullying and cyberbullying prgm for kids and teens. Website provides info and prevention techniques regarding bullying. FUNDING: Nonprofit. SERVES: U.S.A.

TALK ABOUT CURING AUTISM (TACA)

3070 Bristol Ave., Ste 340
Costa Mesa, CA 92626
(949) 640-4401
(949) 640-4424 FAX

Info and connection to improve the quality of life of people with autism and their families. For families who have just received the autism diagnosis, TACA aims to speed up the cycle time that gets them from the diagnosis to the appropriate info that will lead to effective treatment and support. TACA builds the autism community by connecting people with each other & the professionals who can help them. FUNDING: Nonprofit. OFC HRS: M-F 9am-5pm. SERVES: So. Calif.

TALK IT OVER WITH MAMA

250 S. Grand Ave., Ste 402
Los Angeles, CA 90012
(323) 525-1393
(313) 932-8202 FAX

An online resource for parental advice and guidance in solving every day problems. Advice provided by seniors ages 60 yrs+, who share their experience and wit earned through raising children and grandchildren. Also, if you need advice from Papa, indicate that in the request. Visit (www.talkitoverwithmama.com). Spanish, Vietnamese spoken. SERVES: L.A. & Riverside Counties.

TEAM OF ADVOCATES FOR SPECIAL KIDS (TASK)

100 W. Cerritos Ave.
Anaheim, CA 92805
(714) 533-8275
(866) 828-8275
(714) 533-2533 FAX

Parent training and info center serving families of children with disabilities. Support, legal rights info, phone advocacy, workshops and referral srvs. Conducts eval & tech explorations with reports for ages 12 mos+. Workshops on adapted toys, adaptive hardware and specialized software. Phone assist advocacy. Minimal cost for workshops, seminars, in-office IEP consulting, IEP attendance & tech consultation. Also offices in San Diego & L.A. FUNDING: Donations, fed, fndn, nonprofit. OFC HRS: M-F 8am-4pm. Spanish & Vietnamese spoken. SERVES: So. Calif.

TEXT4BABY

Natl Healthy Mothers, Healthy Babies Coalition

Mobile health prgm provides pregnant women and new moms with the health information they need to give their babies a great start. Topics include: birth defects prevention, immunization, nutrition, safe sleep, prenatal care, and infant care srvs. To register, text 'baby' (or 'bebe' for Spanish) to 511411. Visit (www.text4baby.org) for more info. FUNDING: Nonprofit. Free srvs. SERVES: U.S.A.

THE UNFORGETTABLES FOUNDATION

7197 Brockton Ave., Ste 5
Riverside, CA 92506
(951) 680-9996
(951) 680-9981 FAX

Burial assist prgm for families who have lost a child ages 18 yrs or younger. Also CPR training.

FUNDING: Nonprofit. OFC HRS: M-F 8am-5pm. Spanish spoken. ADM REQ: Low income. SERVES: Riverside, San Bernardino Counties.

TRANS YOUTH FAMILY ALLIES

P.O. Box 1471
Holland, MI 49422
(888) 462-8932

Partners with educators, srv providers, and communities to develop supportive environments in which gender may be expressed and respected. Edu prgms, online forums, speaker's bureau, and support for parents of trans children. FUNDING: Nonprofit. SERVES: U.S.A.

TRINITY COMM OUTREACH CORP

29175 Ironwood Ave.
Moreno Valley, CA 92555
(951) 601-0253
(951) 601-0412 FAX

Parenting classes to teach democratic parenting techniques. Practical discipline method, guidelines for building self-esteem and better family communication. Must attend all sessions to obtain a certificate of completion. Also small group financial study. A 12-week in-depth study of all that scripture teaches about money. Topics include: debt, spending, earning, saving, investing, giving and teaching children how to handle money. FUNDING: Client fees, nonprofit. OFC HRS: Tu-F 9am-4pm. Registration fee is $30 per individual or $40 per married couple which covers the cost of the study manuals and workbooks. SERVES: Riverside County.

TRUSTLINE

Calif Child Care Resource/Referral Network
111 New Montgomery St., 7th Fl.
San Francisco, CA 94105
(800) 822-8490
(415) 882-0234
(415) 882-6233 FAX

Conducts background checks on child care providers exempt from licensing, babysitters and nannies. FUNDING: Govt, nonprofit. OFC HRS: M-F 9am-5pm. Spanish spoken. SERVES: Calif.

UCLA PARENT TRAINING PRGM

Friendship Prgm
300 UCLA Medical Plaza
Los Angeles, CA 90095-6967
(310) 825-0142
(310) 267-0378 FAX

Teaches parents easy, effective techniques to increase cooperation and reduce conflict in the home and at school. Small classes or individual sessions. Also 12-week social skills training for youth in grades 1-6 who have difficulty making & keeping friends. FUNDING: Govt. OFC HRS: M-F 9am-5pm. Accepts insurance, regional center funding. Some free research studies. SERVES: So. Calif.

UNO MAS! DOWN SYNDROME ONLINE

Mailing Address
40485 Murrieta Hot Springs Rd., Ste 207
Murrieta, CA 92563

Online sharing and support for parents of children born with Down Syndrome: activities, bulletin & message board, share stories, etc. Visit (www.unomas21.com). Donations accepted to maintain the site. SERVES: Riverside County.

URBAN EDUCATIONAL PARTNERSHIP

1055 W. 7th Street, Ste 200
Los Angeles, CA 90017
(213) 622-5237
(213) 629-5288 FAX

Edu opportunities for students in high-needs schools. Partners with teachers, principals, parents, edu & community leaders by providing training & dev in restructuring schools to create more effective teaching & learning. Separate prgm for children ages birth-5 yrs. Offers parent edu, assist, workshops, and support groups. FUNDING: Nonprofit. OFC HRS: M-F 8:30am-5pm. Free srvs. SERVES: U.S.A.

VICTOR VLY DOMESTIC VIOLENCE, INC.

A Better Way/Outreach Office
P.O. Box 2825
14114 Hesperia Rd.
Victorville, CA 92393
(760) 955-8010
(760) 955-8248 FAX

18-bed shelter for abused women and their children. Outreach, TRO assist, children's prgms, parenting classes, When Love Hurts prgm, peer support groups, anger mgmt, health, nutrition, basic budgeting. Max stay is 90 days. Counseling, transitional housing. 24-hr hotline (760) 955-8723. FUNDING: Donations, nonprofit. OFC HRS: M-F 8am-4pm. Some Spanish spoken. ADM REQ: Victim of domestic violence. SERVES: High Desert.

VOLUNTEERS OF AMERICA/SOUTHWEST CC

Family Resource Center
304 N. Pepper Ave.
Rialto, CA 92376
(909) 562-0901

Provides free srvs to families with children ages birth-5 yrs. Child care, preschool, parenting edu and resources, info & referral. FUNDING: Nonprofit. OFC HRS: M-F 8am-4pm. Free srvs. SERVES: Riverside County.

WEB WISE KIDS

P.O. Box 27203
Santa Ana, CA 92799
(866) 932-9473
(714) 435-0523 FAX

Internet safety prgms provide to edu in the use of computers, e-mail, chat rooms. For kids, parents, teachers, law enforcement, caregivers, etc. Visit (www.webwisekids.org). FUNDING: Nonprofit. OFC HRS: M-F 9am-5pm. German spoken. SERVES: U.S.A.

WOMEN HELPING WOMEN SRVS

543 N. Fairfax Ave.
Los Angeles, CA 90036
(323) 651-2930
(323) 651-5348 FAX

Callers receive emotional support and practical info on any issue. Support groups dealing with issues such as divorce, single parenting, domestic violence, self-esteem, individual counseling, case mgmt and volunteering. Talkline counselor training, specialized srvs for residents of CIPA3, including case mgmt, counseling, workshops & resources. Also offers edu scholarships. Talkline: (877)655-3807. FUNDING: Natl Council of Jewish Women, fndn, donations, nonprofit. Talkline hrs: M, Tu, Th 10am-12:30pm; W 6pm-8pm. 24-hr voicemail, calls returned. For srvs at this physical location,

must have an appt. Spanish, Hebrew & French spoken. Free srvs or on low sliding fee scale. SERVES: So. Calif.

WWW.AGING-PARENTS-AND-ELDER-CARE .COM

950 Tower Lane, 6th Fl.
San Mateo, CA 94404

Helpful website for caregivers. Free referral srv, newsletter. SERVES: U.S.A.

WWW.GIRLSHEALTH.GOV

Website created by the Natl Women's Health Info Center to help young girls learn about health and various other topics that concern and motivate them. ADM REQ: Girls ages 10-16 yrs. SERVES: U.S.A.

WWW.GRANDPARENTING.ORG

108 Farnham Rd.
Ojai, CA 93023

Website dedicated to help grandparents raising grandchildren. Info, edu, research, networking. FUNDING: Nonprofit. SERVES: U.S.A.

WWW.GRANDPARENTS.COM

589 8th Avenue, 6th Fl.
New York, NY 10018
(646) 839-8800

Info website to assist grandparents with kid-friendly activities, advice for new grandparents, long-distant grandparenting, etc. SERVES: U.S.A.

WWW.INCRISIS.NET

Online Behavioral Screening & Reports
965 NE Wiest Way, No. 2
Bend, OR 97701

Online mental health screening software that generates reports with analysis and treatment suggestions for teens who may have mental or addictive disorders. Reports are used to share with professionals in seeking help for troubled youth. Free public srv for parents, caregivers, educators, and youth professionals. Contact agency via website. FUNDING: Nonprofit, Mentor Research Institute. SERVES: U.S.A.

WWW.NCTEQUALITY.ORG

1325 Massachusetts Ave., NW, Ste 700
Washington, DC 20005
(202) 903-0112
(202) 393-2241 FAX

Social justice organization for transgender equality. FUNDING: Nonprofit. SERVES: U.S.A.

WWW.TALKINGWITHKIDS.ORG

(800) 244-5344

A natl initiative website in partnership with Children Now & the Kaiser Family Fndn to encourage parents to talk to their children earlier and more often about drugs, alcohol, violence, HIV/AIDS & sex. Guide booklets can be downloaded from the site (English & Spanish), also publishes a quarterly e-mail newsletter. FUNDING: Nonprofit. SERVES: U.S.A.

YOUTH CHANGE

Problem Kid-Problem Solver
275 N. 3rd Street
Woodburn, OR 97071-4705
(800) 545-5736
(503) 982-7910 FAX

Online info & resources for solving troubled youth problems & offering motivational materials, workshops. Toll-free number & online

helpline for professional youth workers. Internet info & materials available for general public. Continuing edu workshops conducted for teachers & youth professionals around the country. Visit (www.youthchg.com). OFC HRS: 24 hrs. Some free resources. Fees for materials and workshops. SERVES: U.S.A.

YWCA/RIVERSIDE

8172 Magnolia Ave.
Riverside, CA 92504
(951) 687-9922
(951) 688-5270 FAX

Program offers parenting skills classes which meet or exceed current California state guidelines governing parenting classes. The YWCA also offers numerous support groups for parents, and anger mgmt. Also women's sobriety, TOPS, & AA meetings. Twinges in the Hinges prgm for arthritis patients. Also offers teen pregnancy prevention classes. Sober living house. FUNDING: Nonprofit, class fees, donations, United Way. OFC HRS: M-F 8am-8pm; Sat 9am-1pm. Spanish spoken. Fees for classes. Y members $10 off. SERVES: Riverside County.

ZERO TO THREE

Natl Ctr for Infants, Toddlers, & Families
1255 23rd Street, Ste 350
Washington, DC 20037
(202) 638-1144
(202) 638-0851 FAX

Informs, trains and supports professionals, policymakers and parents in their efforts to improve the lives of infants and toddlers. Special prgms for military families and low-income communities. FUNDING: Nonprofit. SERVES: U.S.A.

ABORTION RECOVERY INTERNATL NTWK
5319 University Dr., Ste 252
Irvine, CA 92612
(949) 679-9276
(866) 469-7326
(949) 551-9771 FAX

Srvs provided to those touched by the abortion experience. Support and guidance for those mourning the loss of a terminated pregnancy. Helps wounded women, men and their families find peace and victory from their past. Also provides edu opportunities to increase abortion awareness. Public speaking for schools, universities, companies or groups. 24-hr hotline to assist those in crisis (800) 395-4357. FUNDING: Nonprofit. OFC HRS: M-F 8am-5pm. SERVES: So. Calif.

ACCESS FOR INFANTS/MOTHERS (AIM)
Calif Major Risk Medical Ins. Board
P.O. Box 15559
Sacramento, CA 95852-0559
(800) 433-2611
(888) 889-9238 FAX

Maternity, delivery and infant care srvs for mid-income women between 200-300% of the federal poverty level. Low-cost prenatal health insurance to uninsured pregnant women who are not receiving health care through Medi-Cal. The cost is 2% of her family's gross income. The policy pays 100% of the medical costs during the pregnancy, plus post-partum care for 60 days and the medical cost for the infant during the first two years of life. Insurance renewal after infant's 2nd year is $100 or $50 with proof of immunization. For payments: P.O. Box 15207, Sacramento, CA 95851. FUNDING: State. OFC HRS: M-F 8am-8pm; Sat 8am-5pm. Spanish spoken. ADM REQ: Calif resident; expectant mother must be no more than 30 weeks pregnant. SERVES: Calif.

ALTERNATE AVENUES
Women's Resource Center
9675 Monte Vista, Unit G
Montclair, CA 91763
(909) 621-4800

Fully licensed medical clinic offering free services to couples facing an unplanned pregnancy. Pregnancy tests, ultrasound (when needed), Medi-Cal, WIC along with other resources. FUNDING: Nonprofit. OFC HRS: Tu 12pm-5pm; Th 2pm-7pm; F, Sat 8am-1pm. Spanish, Tagalog spoken. SERVES: Inland Empire.

AMERICAN PREGNANCY ASSOCIATION
1431 Greenway Dr., Ste 440
Irving, TX 75038
(972) 815-2337
(972) 550-0140
(972) 550-0800 FAX

Natl organization provides edu, counseling & referrals to local resources. Referrals to maternity homes, pregnancy centers, medical care, adoption srvs, Medicare and other govt related srvs. Not a clinic. FUNDING: Nonprofit. OFC HRS: M-F 7am-10pm. 24-hr hotline. Some Spanish spoken. Free referrals. SERVES: U.S.A.

AMERICAN PREGNANCY HELPLINE
(866) 942-6466

24-hr hotline available 7 days a week to answer any questions about pregnancy, family planning, and adoption. Also offers info website about pregnancy, visit (www.thehelpline.org) for more info. FUNDING: Nonprofit. OFC HRS: 24 hrs, 7 days. Free srvs. SERVES: U.S.A.

BABY SAFE
Safely Surrendered Baby Prgm
(877) 222-9723

Safe haven hotline for nearest locations which allow parents to safely surrender their babies at any hospital or fire station without fear of legal prosecution. Call the hotline for more info. OFC HRS: 24 hrs, 7 days. Over 140 languages spoken. SERVES: U.S.A.

BETHANY CHRISTIAN SRVS/SO CAL
14125 Telephone Rd., Ste 12
Chino, CA 91710
(877) 465-0057
(909) 465-0057
(909) 628-8294 FAX

Pregnancy counseling, pre-adoptive foster care, adoption srvs. FUNDING: Church, donations, fees, nonprofit. OFC HRS: M-F 9am-5pm. ADM REQ: Adoptive couples must be Christian. Sliding fee scale for adoptive parents. Free pregnancy counseling & srvs for birth parents. SERVES: So. Calif.

BIRTH CHOICE
277 S. Rancho Santa Fe Rd., Ste S
San Marcos, CA 92069-2343
(760) 744-1313

Counseling, supportive services, info and referrals to medical professionals. Financial aid prgms, post-abortion counseling and adoption srvs. FUNDING: Nonprofit. OFC HRS: M 9am-6pm; Tu-Th 9am-8pm; F 8am-12noon; Sat 10am-12noon. Spanish spoken. Free srvs. SERVES: San Marcos.

BIRTH CONTROL INFO FOR STATE
Calif Office of Family Planning
(800) 942-1054

Referrals to family planning and birth control srvs throughout Calif. Female cancer testing. Low-cost testing and counseling for HIV. Spanish-speaking referral available. OFC HRS: 24 hrs, 7 days. SERVES: Calif.

BIRTH CONTROL INFO LINE
San Bernardino Co. Public Health
(800) 722-4777
(909) 389-3340 FAX

One-stop family planning health srvs for men and women ages 21 yrs and under. Call for the clinic nearest you. FUNDING: Govt. OFC HRS: M-F 8am-5pm. Spanish spoken. Free srvs. SERVES: Riverside & San Bernardino Counties.

BLACK INFANT HEALTH PRGM
Riverside Co. Health Srvs
4065 County Circle Dr., Ste 211
Riverside, CA 92503
(951) 210-1392
(800) 794-4814

Case mgmt & referral for pregnant African-American women. FUNDING: State, govt. OFC HRS: M-F 8am-5pm. Free srvs. SERVES: Riverside County.

CAL-SAFE/APPLE VALLEY
Apple Valley Unified School District
11837 Navajo Rd.
Apple Valley, CA 92308
(760) 247-7206
(760) 247-2018 FAX

Public edu for pregnant and parenting teens. Info on nutrition, child dev, prenatal and child birth classes, career edu. Free child care for children (ages birth-5 yrs) of teen parents. FUNDING: Govt. OFC HRS: Vary. ADM REQ: Pregnant or parenting students in grades 7-12. Free srvs. SERVES: Apple Valley U.S.D.

CAL-SAFE/BIG BEAR LAKE
Bear Valley Unified School District
Chautauqua High School
P.O. Box 1529
42271 Moonridge Rd.
Big Bear Lake, CA 92315
(909) 866-4631
(909) 866-2040 FAX

Public edu for pregnant & parenting teens. Info on nutrition, child dev, prenatal & child birth classes, career edu. Free child care for children (ages birth-5 yrs) of teen parents. FUNDING: Govt. OFC HRS: Vary. ADM REQ: Pregnant or parenting students in grades 7-12. Free srvs. SERVES: Bear Valley U.S.D.

CAL-SAFE/CHINO
Chino Valley Unified School District
5130 Riverside Dr.
Chino, CA 91710
(909) 628-1201

Public edu for pregnant & parenting teens. Info on nutrition, child dev, prenatal & child birth classes, career edu. Free child care for children (ages birth-5 yrs) of teen parents. FUNDING: Govt. OFC HRS: Vary. ADM REQ: Pregnant or parenting students in grades 7-12. Free srvs. SERVES: Chino Valley U.S.D.

CAL-SAFE/CORONA-NORCO UNIFIED SCHOOL DISTRICT
Centennial High School
1820 Rimpau Ave.
Corona, CA 92881
(951) 739-5670
(951) 739-5693 FAX

Public edu for pregnant & parenting teens. Info on nutrition, child dev, prenatal & child birth classes, career edu. Free child care for children (ages birth-5 yrs) of teen parents. FUNDING: Govt. OFC HRS: M-F 8am-4:30pm. ADM REQ: Pregnant or parenting students in grades 7-12. Free srvs. SERVES: Corona-Norco U.S.D.

CAL-SAFE/FONTANA
Fontana Unified School District
P.O. Box 5090
9600 Citrus Ave.
Fontana, CA 92335
(909) 357-5000
(909) 357-5632 FAX

Public edu for pregnant & parenting teens. Info on nutrition, child dev, prenatal & child birth classes, career edu. Free child care for children (ages birth-5 yrs) of teen parents. FUNDING: Govt. OFC HRS: M-F 7:30am-4:30pm. Spanish spoken. ADM REQ: Pregnant or parenting students in grades 7-12. Free srvs. SERVES: Fontana U.S.D.

CAL-SAFE/HESPERIA
Hesperia Unified School District
16633 Lemon St.
Hesperia, CA 92345
(760) 948-3999
(760) 948-0508 FAX

Public edu for pregnant & parenting teens. Info on nutrition, child dev, prenatal & child birth classes, career edu. Free child care for children (ages birth-5 yrs) of teen parents. FUNDING: Govt. OFC HRS: Vary. ADM REQ: Pregnant or parenting students in grades 7-12. Free srvs. SERVES: Hesperia U.S.D.

CAL-SAFE/REDLANDS
Orangewood High School
P.O. Box 3008
515 Texas St.
Redlands, CA 92373
(909) 307-5380
(909) 307-5384 FAX

Public edu for pregnant & parenting teens. Info on nutrition, child dev, prenatal & child birth classes, career edu. Free child care for children (ages birth-5 yrs) of teen parents. FUNDING: Govt. OFC HRS: M-F 7:30am-4pm. ADM REQ: Pregnant or parenting students in grades 9-12. Free srvs. SERVES: Redlands U.S.D.

CAL-SAFE/RIVERSIDE CO.
Riverside Co. Office of Education
P.O. Box 868
3939 13th Street
Riverside, CA 92502
(951) 826-6464

Public edu for pregnant & parenting teens. Info on nutrition, child dev, prenatal & child birth classes, career edu. Free child care for children (ages birth-5 yrs) of teen parents. FUNDING: Govt. OFC HRS: Vary. ADM REQ: Pregnant or parenting students in grades 7-12. Free srvs. SERVES: Riverside County.

CAL-SAFE/UPLAND UNIFIED SCHOOL DISTRICT
Hillside High School
1558 W. 9th Street
Upland, CA 91786
(909) 985-1864
(909) 949-7862 FAX

Public edu for pregnant & parenting teens. Info on nutrition, child dev, prenatal & child birth classes, career edu. Free child care for children (ages birth-5 yrs) of teen parents. FUNDING: Govt. OFC HRS: Vary. ADM REQ: Pregnant or parenting students in grades 7-12. Free srvs. SERVES: Upland U.S.D.

CAL-SAFE/YUCAIPA
Yucaipa-Calimesa Joint Unified School Dist
Green Valley High School
12797 3rd Street
Yucaipa, CA 92399
(909) 790-8550

Public edu for pregnant & parenting teens. Info on nutrition, child dev, prenatal & child birth classes, career edu. Free child care for children (ages birth-5 yrs) of teen parents. FUNDING: Govt. OFC HRS: Vary. ADM REQ: Pregnant or parenting students in grades 7-12. Free srvs. SERVES: Yucaipa-Calimesa J.U.H.S.D.

CALIF YOUTH CRISIS LINE
Calif Coalition for Youth
P.O. Box 161448
Sacramento, CA 95816
(800) 843-5200
(916) 340-0505
(916) 340-0510 FAX

Statewide, 24-hr crisis intervention counseling for youth ages 12-24 yrs & their families on a wide range of mental health, drug & alcohol, peer, family and relationship issues. Youth-to-parent message srv, phone connections to srv providers & families, info & referrals. Rides provided to youth who cannot afford transportation home. FUNDING: Nonprofit, donations. OFC HRS: 24 hrs, 7 days. Spanish spoken. Translation srvs available. Free srvs. SERVES: Calif.

CHILD BIRTH
Website provides links to various topics related to child birth. Visit (www.childbirth.org).

CHILDREN'S HEALTH ACCESS PRGMS
Medi-Cal/Healthy Families Info Line
P.O. Box 138005
Sacramento, CA 95813-8005
(888) 747-1222
(866) 848-4974 FAX

Free and low-cost medical care for children and pregnant women. Eligibility is determined by children's ages and family income. Available to citizens and qualified immigrants. If the family does not qualify for this prgm, there are other options. Call (800) 880-5305 for application status. Call (866) 848-9166 if already enrolled. FUNDING: State, fed govt. OFC HRS: M-F 8am-8pm; Sat 8am-5pm. Cambodian, Farsi, Russian, Spanish, Chinese and Vietnamese spoken. ADM REQ: Must submit application. $5-$15 per child based on provider and county. SERVES: Calif.

CHINO COMMUNITY SERVICES
Human Services Division
13201 Central Ave.
Chino, CA 91710
(909) 591-9822
(909) 628-4093 FAX

Counseling srvs for children & adults. Community & school-based prevention & edu. Drug prevention, family treatment, teen and adult parenting classes, domestic violence, anger mgmt, community outreach, senior srvs, disabled srvs info & referral, PC-1000. For emergencies, call (909) 628-1010. FUNDING: State, county, school, city, govt. OFC HRS: M-Th 8am-8pm; F 8am-6pm. Spanish spoken. Free srvs or a fee of $26. SERVES: Western San Bernardino County.

COMMUNITY HEALTH SYSTEMS, INC.
Arlanza Family Health Ctr
8856 Arlington Ave.
Riverside, CA 92503
(951) 353-2702
(951) 353-2976 FAX

Primary care for all ages. Family planning, HIV/AIDS, STD testing, Teenage Edu to Avoid Motherhood (T.E.A.M.), Child Health and Disability prgm. Also dental clinic. FUNDING: Nonprofit. OFC HRS: M-F 8am-5:30pm. Accepts Medi-Cal, Medicare, insurance, sliding fee scale. SERVES: Riverside County.

COVENANT HOUSE NINELINE
461 8th Avenue
New York, NY 10001
(800) 999-9999
(212) 727-4000
(212) 989-9098 FAX

24-hr natl crisis intervention hotline for runaways, homeless, troubled youth & their families. Refers caller to help in his or her own community. Conference call capability & message relays to runaway youth. TDD/TYY hotline (800) 999-9915. FUNDING: Donations, nonprofit. OFC HRS: 24 hrs, 7 days. Spanish spoken. ADM REQ: Ages 18-21 yrs. Free srvs. SERVES: U.S.A.

CRISIS PREGNANCY CENTER
44750 San Pablo Ave.
Palm Desert, CA 92255
(760) 568-2200
(888) 956-4357

Pregnancy tests, ultrasound. Referrals for basic needs. Call or walk in. Volunteer opportunities. FUNDING: Nonprofit, donations. OFC HRS: M-Th 12noon-4:30pm; F 11am-3pm. Spanish spoken. Free and confidential. SERVES: Riverside County.

CTIS PREGNANCY RISK INFO LINE
Dept of Pediatrics, UCSD Med Ctr
9500 Gilman Dr., Ste 0828
La Jolla, CA 92093-0828
(800) 532-3749
(619) 270-0278 FAX

The infoline is a statewide telephone srv operated by Calif Teratogen Info Srv & Clinical Research Prgm. Call with questions regarding concerns about the effects of medications, environmental exposures, or illness on pregnancy. The call is free and confidential. Info is based on current scientific data. Satellite offices: UCLA OB/GYN, Institute of Fetal & Maternal Health at Children's Hospital in L.A. and Medical Genetics, Dept of Pediatrics, Stanford Univ School of Medicine. FUNDING: Govt, nonprofit. OFC HRS: M-F 9am-5pm. Spanish and Tagalog spoken. Free srvs. SERVES: Calif.

DOLPHINS MOBILE HEALTH VAN OUTREACH
811 W. Chanslor Way
Blythe, CA 92225
(760) 922-1349
(760) 921-8399 FAX

Referral srvs to pregnant and parenting teens, nutrition, immunizations, hearing, vision, physical activity, and injury prevention to preschool children. Also dental treatment srvs. Assist with completing Healthy Families applications. FUNDING: First 5. OFC HRS: M-F 8am-5pm. Spanish spoken. ADM REQ: Ages birth-5 yrs, and pregnant women. Free srvs. SERVES: Blythe.

FIRST FIVE/RIALTO
Formerly Cal-Safe/Rialto
260 S. Willow
Rialto, CA 92376
(909) 421-4201
(909) 421-7602 FAX

Public edu for pregnant & parenting teens. Info on nutrition, child dev, prenatal & child birth classes, career edu. Free child care for children (ages birth-5 yrs) of teen parents. Support srvs enabling teens to sucessfully graduate high school. FUNDING: Govt. OFC HRS: M-F 6:45am-3:30pm. ADM REQ: Pregnant or parenting students in grades 7-12. Free srvs. SERVES: Rialto U.S.D.

GARDEN OF ANGELS

Safe Arms - Safe Haven for Newborns
P.O. Box 1776
Yucaipa, CA 92399
(909) 797-8599
(909) 797-9766 FAX

Works to prevent the abandonment of newborn babies. Advocacy, helpline, edu materials. Mothers are encouraged to leave newborn with any hospital emerg room or fire station employee legally and confidentially. FUNDING: Nonprofit. OFC HRS: M-F 8am-4pm. SERVES: Calif.

HEARTLINE PREGNANCY COUNSELING CTR

Heartline Ministries
6881 Brockton Ave.
Riverside, CA 92506
(951) 682-2400
(951) 682-6881
(951) 682-0251 FAX

Counsels pregnant women from a pro-life perspective. Free pregnancy testing, referrals for financial, medical and legal assist. Adoption info provided upon request. Free clothing & baby furniture. Also offers post-abortion counseling. Call first before sending a fax. FUNDING: Donations. OFC HRS: By appt, 24-hr hotline. ADM REQ: Must have appt. Free srvs. SERVES: Riverside Metro.

HOLY FAMILY SERVICES

Inland Empire
1441 North D Street, Ste 201
San Bernardino, CA 92405-4738
(909) 885-4882
(800) 464-2367
(909) 888-7065 FAX

HFS is an accredited California state-licensed, non-denominational, adoption and foster care agency. Srvs are provided to birth parents and prospective adoptive parents, adult adoptees (adopted through HFS), and those who wish to become temporary, short-term foster parents. Provides birth parent counseling to those working with other adoption providers and conducts home studies for prospective adoptive parents involved in international and other state adoptions. FUNDING: Donations, adoption fees, United Way, fndns, guilds, nonprofit. OFC HRS: M-Th 8:30am-5:30pm; F 8:30am-1pm, by appt after hours; 24-hr pager for birth parents who require immediate help. Spanish spoken. Birth parents receive free srvs. Adoptive parents srvs on a sliding fee scale. SERVES: L.A., Orange, Riverside, San Bernardino & Ventura Counties.

KNOTTS FAMILY AGENCY

1505 W. Highland Ave., Ste 19
San Bernardino, CA 92411
(909) 880-0600
(909) 473-1918 FAX

Residential care facility providing long-term srvs for pregnant & parenting teens & their infants/toddlers. Srvs to troubled adol girls whose lives are complicated by pregnancy or single parenthood. Also srvs to non-pregnant, abused, neglected or abandoned girls ages 12-17 yrs. Adol girls in juvenile probation or DPSS. Foster care agency, parenting prgm for parents with children ages birth-5 yrs. FUNDING: Private, nonprofit. OFC HRS: 24 hrs, 7 days. SERVES: Riverside, San Bernardino Counties.

LDS FAMILY SERVICES

Unwed Pregnancy Options Counseling
791 N. Pepper Ave.
Colton, CA 92324
(909) 824-0480
(909) 824-0487 FAX

No pressure, confidential counseling to unwed parents & their families. A safe, comfortable place provided to discuss various options. Licensed adoption srvs. Individual, marital, and family counseling. Community outreach to interested agencies and organizations. FUNDING: Nonprofit. OFC HRS: M-F 8am-5pm. Spanish & German spoken. Free counseling srvs. SERVES: So. Calif.

LDS FAMILY SERVICES

Adoption Service
13042 Burbank Blvd.
Van Nuys, CA 91401-5409
(818) 781-5511
(800) 537-2229
(818) 781-5595 FAX

Free pregnancy planning and adoption counseling for birth parents, regardless of denomination. Adoptive parents must be LDS members. Satellite clinics in Menifee, Murrieta, Palm Desert, Yucca Valley, Hesperia, Victorville, Corona, Ridgecrest, Arcadia and Ventura. FUNDING: Nonprofit. OFC HRS: M-F 8am-5pm. Spanish spoken. SERVES: So. Calif.

LIBERTY GODPARENT HOME

P.O. Box 4199
124 Liberty Mountain Dr.
Lynchburg, VA 24502
(888) 760-5433
(434) 845-3466
(434) 845-1751 FAX

Christian, residential maternity home offers housing, edu, medical care & counseling for single, pregnant young women who either parent their child or place their child up for adoption. Also network with over 1,300 referrals in U.S.A. & Canada. Srvs for women ages 10-21 yrs. Client must intake by the 24th week of pregnancy. 24-hr helpline. FUNDING: Thomas Road Baptist Church, Lynchburg, Virginia, other churches, donations, nonprofit. OFC HRS: M-F 8am-4:30pm. ADM REQ: Arrangements must be made for medical portion of prgm through admissions coordinator. Free srvs. SERVES: U.S.A. & Canada.

LIFE CENTER PREGNANCY COUNSELING

1106 E. 17th Street, Ste C
Santa Ana, CA 92701
(714) 835-5433
(714) 835-0476 FAX

24-hr hotline, counseling, free pregnancy testing, medical, financial, legal & housing referrals. Pro-life perspective. So. Calif. offices: L.A. Co. (562) 691-9395, (818) 895-2500; Orange Co. (714) 835-5433; Riverside Co. (951) 682-2400, (951) 784-2422; San Bernardino Co. (909) 825-6656, (909) 985-0205. FUNDING:

Donations, nonprofit. OFC HRS: M-Th 10am-4pm. Free srvs. SERVES: So. Calif.

LIFE CHOICE OF HEMET

475 W. Stetson PMB-T225
Hemet, CA 92543
(951) 652-3111

Counseling, adoption assist, abortion referral, phone referrals and resources, baby formula and diapers (limited). May add more srvs at later date. FUNDING: Donations, nonprofit. SERVES: Riverside County.

LINCOLN INFANT CENTER

Riverside Co. Office of Edu
4341 Victoria Ave.
Riverside, CA 92507
(951) 684-3082
(951) 788-1182 FAX

Cal-SAFE prgm on site at Lincoln Continuation High School. Public edu for pregnant & parenting teens. Info on nutrition, child dev, prenatal & child birth classes, career edu. FUNDING: State. OFC HRS: Vary. Free child care for children ages birth-5 yrs of teen parents. SERVES: Riverside.

MARCH OF DIMES BIRTH DEFECTS FNDN

Greater Los Angeles Division
3699 Wilshire Blvd., Ste 520
Los Angeles, CA 90010-2719
(213) 637-5050
(213) 637-5055 FAX

Goal is to improve the health of babies by preventing birth defects, premature births and infant mortality. Supports campaign for healthier babies, prgms of research, community srvs, edu and advocacy. Provides grants, Comenzando Bien, a Spanish-speaking prgm, info & referral srvs, speaker's bureau, visiting professorship in nursing, work site prgms including the Babies and You prgm. FUNDING: Nonprofit. OFC HRS: M-F 9am-5pm. Spanish spoken. SERVES: L.A., Ventura, Santa Barbara, Riverside, San Bernardino, San Luis Obispo, Mono, Inyo & Kern Counties.

MARCH OF DIMES BIRTH DEFECTS FNDN

Inland Empire Division
3600 Lime St., Ste 524
Riverside, CA 92501
(951) 341-0903
(951) 276-4755 FAX

Goal is to improve the health of babies by preventing birth defects, premature births and infant mortality. Supports campaign for healthier babies, prgms of research, community srvs, edu and advocacy. Provides grants, Comenzando Bien, a Spanish-speaking prgm, info & referral srvs, speaker's bureau, visiting professorship in nursing, work site prgms including the Babies and You prgm. FUNDING: Nonprofit. OFC HRS: M-F 9am-5pm. Spanish spoken. SERVES: Riverside & San Bernardino Counties.

MARY'S SHELTER

Pregnant Teens, Teen Moms & Babies
P.O. Box 10433
Santa Ana, CA 92711-0433
(714) 730-0930
(714) 730-3487 FAX

Comprehensive residential prgm for pregnant minors and teen moms with babies, both pvt placement and wards of the court. Individual, group & family counseling, social srvs, childbirth, adoption & parent edu, on-site school. FUNDING: Nonprofit, donations, fndn grants, govt subsidies. OFC HRS: M-F 9am-5pm, 24-hr srvs. Spanish spoken. ADM REQ: Ages 12-17 yrs, pregnant teen or teen mom with infant. Accepts Medi-Cal, sliding fee scale. SERVES: So. Calif.

MOSES HOUSE MINISTRIES
P.O. Box 2033
15180 Anacapa Rd.
Victorville, CA 92393
(866) 606-6737
(760) 955-1895
(760) 955-1303 FAX

Private, Christian family homes offer pregnant young women and teens secure housing during their pregnancy. Case mgmt, assists with family reunification, edu, employment, parenting, or placing their babies for adoption. Transportation srvs available. Emerg assist prgm for pregnant or parenting moms with children ages birth-5 yrs offers bottles, formula, and other necessary supplies. Resource ctr for single moms. FUNDING: Nonprofit, United Way, donations. OFC HRS: M-F 9am-4pm. SERVES: San Bernardino County.

NATL LIFE CENTER
Pregnancy Srvs
686 N. Broad St.
Woodbury, NJ 08096
(800) 848-5683
(856) 848-1819
(856) 848-2380 FAX

24-hr hotline with live response every day. Refers callers to local agencies based on identified needs. Pregnancy tests, clothing, housing, medical referral, adoption info. Serves women in a crisis pregnancy. Phone counseling & person-to-person post-abortion support groups, maternity & infant clothing. FUNDING: Donations, nonprofit. OFC HRS: 10am-6pm, EST. ADM REQ: Suspect pregnancy. Free & confidential srvs. SERVES: U.S.A.

PLANNED PARENTHOOD
(800) 230-7526

Planned Parenthood offers access to edu and srvs needed to make responsible choices about parenthood and reproductive health. Family planning srvs include: WIC prgms, edu srvs, birth control and emerg contraception. Info is provided for prenatal care, adoption and abortion. PPOSBC ensures that quality comprehensive health care and edu is available to all at low to no cost. Qualified medical staff trained to answer questions and offer referrals. Visit (www.PPOSBC.org). FUNDING: Family PACT, donations, nonprofit. OFC HRS: Vary by center. Spanish spoken.

PLANNED PARENTHOOD/INDIO CENTER
71777 San Jacinto Dr., Ste 202
Rancho Mirage, CA 92270
(760) 674-0040
(760) 674-3440 FAX

Outpatient health care clinic for ages 14 yrs+. Immunizations, pregnancy testing, counseling, birth control, physical exams, AIDS testing & treatment, STD. FUNDING: Nonprofit. OFC HRS: M, W 8am-5pm; Tu, Th 10:30am-7:30pm; Sat 8:30am-5pm. Closed last W of each month 8am-12noon. Spanish spoken. Accepts

Medi-Cal, sliding fee scale. SERVES: Riverside County.

PLANNED PARENTHOOD/MORENO VLY
12900 Frederick St., Ste C
Moreno Valley, CA 92553
(951) 601-2322

Reproductive health care. Birth control including: pills, Norplant, IUD, condoms, foam, morning-after pill, etc. Pregnancy testing and counseling, HIV/STD testing, post-menopause hormone replacement therapy & mammograms. FUNDING: Nonprofit. OFC HRS: M, W, F 8am-5pm; Tu, Th 10:30am-7:30pm; Sat 8:30am-5pm. Closed last W of each month 8am-12noon. Spanish spoken. Accepts Medi-Cal, V.A. insurance, sliding fee scale. SERVES: Moreno Valley area.

PLANNED PARENTHOOD/SAN BRDO
San Bernardino Medical Center
1873 Commercenter West
San Bernardino, CA 92408
(909) 890-5511
(909) 890-4599 FAX

Planned Parenthood provides affordable health care to women, men and teens. Experienced and caring medical staff gives each client honest, informational and personal attention. Srvs include: pregnancy testing and counseling, post-menopause hormone replacement therapy and mammograms. Health srvs are confidential FUNDING: Nonprofit. OFC HRS: M 7:30am-5:30pm; Tu 7:30am-6pm; W 7:30am-7pm; Th 7:30am-5pm; F 6:30am-4:30pm; Sat, 7:30am-4:30pm. Accepts insurance, Medicare, Medi-Cal, sliding fee scale.

PLANNED PARENTHOOD/UPLAND
918 W. Foothill Blvd., Ste A
Upland, CA 91786-0531
(909) 890-5511
(909) 985-0351 FAX

Upland's Planned Parenthood outpatient center offers: pregnancy testing, counseling, birth control, health edu, option counseling, medical referrals, immunizations, emerg contraception, AIDS testing and counseling, STI screening. FUNDING: Nonprofit. Phone Hrs: M, W 8am-6:30pm; Tu, Th, F 8am-5pm; Sat, Sun 9am-5pm. Spanish spoken. ADM REQ: Ages 16 yrs+. Accepts Medi-Cal, sliding fee scale.

PREGNANCY COUNSELING CENTER
Upland Center
P.O. Box 9000-164
Rancho Cucamonga, CA 91701
(909) 985-0205
(909) 481-8867 FAX

24-hr hotline, free pregnancy testing, counseling, medical, financial, legal and housing referrals. Free maternity clothes, baby clothes and furniture. Adoption referrals and speakers. Pro-life perspective. Located at 121 East F Street, Ontario. Walk in or call. FUNDING: Donations, nonprofit. OFC HRS: M, W, Sat 11am-1:30pm. Some Spanish spoken. Free srvs. SERVES: Pomona Valley, Ontario, Chino, Claremont, Upland, Rancho Cucamonga.

PREGNANCY HELPLINE
See "Liberty Godparent Home"

PROJECT CUDDLE, INC.
2973 Harbor Blvd., Ste 326

Costa Mesa, CA 92626
(888) 628-3353
(714) 432-9681
(714) 433-6815 FAX

24-hr, toll-free hotline for pregnant women or women contemplating abandoning their children. Support & edu for those caring for drug-exposed babies and children. Training for birth parents and caregivers. Speakers and lectures for teens on drugs during pregnancy. FUNDING: Donations, grants, nonprofit. OFC HRS: M-F 9am-4pm. Spanish spoken. Free srvs. SERVES: U.S.A.

PROJECT CUIDAR
Cal State San Bernardino
5500 University Pkwy.
San Bernardino, CA 92407
(909) 537-5945
(909) 537-7759 FAX

Promotes healthy parent-child relationships and optimal child dev through culturally and developmentally appropriate early intervention srvs for children ages birth-5 yrs and their parents. Srvs include: parent edu, child enrichment groups, & provider training and are offered in both English & Spanish. Groups meeet at various locations within the community. Free child care for ages birth-12 yrs. Spanish spoken. ADM REQ: No new parents accepted after the second week of classes. Free srvs. SERVES: San Bernardino County.

RIVERSIDE CO. OFFICE/EDUCATION
Student Prgms & Srvs
P.O. Box 868
3939 13th Street
Riverside, CA 92502
(951) 826-6436
(951) 826-6906 FAX

Counseling, mentoring and outreach component. 24 hrs of parent edu provided to males and females. Emphasis is on male responsibility; health, birth, finances, incarceration, child abuse, foster youth srvs, tutoring, communication, discipline, employment prep. FUNDING: Nonprofit. OFC HRS: M-F 8am-5pm. Spanish spoken. Free srvs. SERVES: Riverside County.

RIVERSIDE CO. PUBLIC HEALTH DEPT
Hemet Health/Family Care Center
880 N. State St.
Hemet, CA 92543
(951) 766-2450
(951) 766-2479 FAX

Family srvs include: treatment of non-emerg medical problems, nutrition info & counseling, STD testing with diagnosis and treatment, family planning srvs, public health nursing assist to families in maintaining good health and promoting wellness in the home. Srvs for children include: immunizations, preventive health, family planning edu for teens, assist to pregnant teens, referral for medical care and rehab for physically disabled up to age 21 yrs. Srvs for women include: pregnancy testing, breast cancer screening, pap smears, WIC supplemental food & prenatal care. FUNDING: Nonprofit. OFC HRS: M-F 7:30am-5pm. Spanish spoken. ADM REQ: Low income. Accepts insurance, Medicare, Medi-Cal. SERVES: Riverside County.

RIVERSIDE CO. PUBLIC HEALTH DEPT
Perris Health/Family Care Center

308 E. San Jacinto Ave.
Perris, CA 92570
(951) 940-6700
(951) 940-6726 FAX

Srvs for the whole family include treatment of non-emerg medical problems, nutrition info and counseling, STD testing with diagnosis and treatment, family planning srvs, public health nursing assist to families in maintaining good health and promoting wellness in the home. Srvs for children include: immunizations, preventive health, family planning edu for teens, assist to pregnant teens, referral for medical care. Srvs for women include: pregnancy testing, breast cancer screening and pap smears. Wait: Varies. For an appt, call (800) 720-9553. FUNDING: BPHC site, donations, nonprofit. OFC HRS: M-F 7:30am-5pm. Spanish spoken. ADM REQ: Low income. Accepts insurance, Medicare, Medi-Cal. Sliding fee scale based on family size, income, srvs provided. SERVES: Riverside County.

RIVERSIDE CO. PUBLIC HEALTH DEPT
Family Planning Prgm
7140 Indiana Ave.
Riverside, CA 92504
(951) 358-6000

Basic contraceptive srvs including: birth control, emerg contraception, pregnancy testing and counseling. Special teen srvs at Jurupa, Corona, Hemet, Indio, Elsinore, Palm Springs, Riverside Neighborhood Health Ctr. Visit (www.birthcontrol4u.com) for more info. Website also lists San Bernardino Co. srvs. OFC HRS: M-F 7:30am-5pm. Spanish spoken. SERVES: Riverside & San Bernardino Counties.

RIVERSIDE CO. PUBLIC HEALTH DEPT
Nutrition Services Branch
P.O. Box 7600
4065 County Circle Dr., Ste 207
Riverside, CA 92513-7600
(951) 358-7200
(951) 358-5472 FAX

A supplemental food & nutrition prgm for pregnant or breastfeeding women, women who just had a baby & children under 5 yrs of age. WIC offers special checks for healthy foods, nutrition & health edu, breastfeeding support & referrals to health care & other srvs. For breastfeeding info, call (888) 451-2499. FUNDING: Federal. OFC HRS: M-F 7:30am-5pm. Eve & Sat by appt. Spanish, Vietnamese spoken. Srvs are income-based; working families may be eligible. SERVES: Riverside County.

RIVERSIDE CO. PUBLIC SOCIAL SRVS
Adoption Services
10769 Hole Ave., Ste 200
Riverside, CA 92505
(951) 358-3645
(951) 358-3555
(951) 358-6061 FAX

Social workers assist parents who are considering adoption as a plan for their child. Home studies completed on families wishing to adopt a child through this agency. FUNDING: Federal, state, county. OFC HRS: M-F 8am-5pm. Spanish spoken. SERVES: Riverside County.

RIVERSIDE LIFE SRVS
3727 McCray St.
Riverside, CA 92506

(951) 784-2422
(951) 276-2907 FAX

Pregnancy testing & counseling from pro-life perspective, pre-abortion & post-abortion counseling, adoption referrals, medical & legal aid referrals, free maternity clothes, formula, baby items. 24-hr message line (951) 784-2725. FUNDING: Nonprofit. OFC HRS: M-Th 10am-4pm. Spanish spoken. SERVES: Riverside County.

SAN BERNARDINO CO. HUMAN SRVS SY
Dept Children's Srvs/Adoption Srvs
412 W. Hospitality Lane, 2nd Fl.
San Bernardino, CA 92415
(909) 891-3300
(909) 891-3399 FAX

Public agency providing relinquishment adoption srvs to children, birthparents and potential adoptive parents. Pregnancy counseling provided at no charge to any person who asks to discuss the alternatives in a non-pressured, relaxed manner. Counseling srvs are also available to birthfathers. Birthparents may select and meet adoptive parents and participate in "open adoptions." When it is not possible or practical for children to live with their birth parents, permanent families interested in adopting are educated about the adoption process and the adopted child. All adoptive families participate in the home study process prior to being considered for placement of an adoptive child or siblings. Child abuse hotline (800) 827-8724. FUNDING: County, state, federal. OFC HRS: M-F 8am-5pm. Spanish spoken. SERVES: San Bernardino County.

SAN BERNARDINO CO. PUBLIC HEALTH
Reproductive Health Centers
303 E. Mountain View
Barstow, CA 92311
(800) 722-4777
(760) 256-4715
(760) 256-4909 FAX

Reproductive health exams for men & women. STD testing & treatment, HIV testing & referral to care. Edu srvs, pregnancy testing, counseling, lab testing, young adult clinics. FUNDING: Dept Public Health. OFC HRS: Tu-Th 9am-4pm. ADM REQ: Must have appt. Accepts Medi-Cal. Fees based on srvs provided. SERVES: Barstow.

SAN BERNARDINO CO. PUBLIC HEALTH
Reproductive Health Centers
P.O. Box 2835
477 Summit Blvd.
Big Bear Lake, CA 92315
(800) 722-4777
(909) 866-0177

Reproductive health exams for men & women. STD testing & treatment, HIV testing & referral to care. Edu srvs, pregnancy testing, counseling, lab testing, young adult clinic. FUNDING: Calif Office of Family Planning, govt. OFC HRS: F 9am-4pm. Spanish spoken. ADM REQ: Must have appt. Accepts Medi-Cal, F-PACT, sliding fee scale, no one turned away for lack of funds. SERVES: San Bernardino Mtns.

SAN BERNARDINO CO. PUBLIC HEALTH
Reproductive Health Centers
16453 Bear Valley Rd.
Hesperia, CA 92345
(800) 722-4777

(760) 956-4465
(760) 956-4450 FAX

Reproductive health exams for men & women. STD testing & treatment, HIV testing & referral to care. Edu srvs, pregnancy testing, counseling, lab testing, young adult clinics. For HIV testing, call (909) 383-3060 on W 9am-3pm. FUNDING: Dept Public Health. OFC HRS: M-F 9am-4pm. Spanish spoken. ADM REQ: Must have appt. Accepts Medi-Cal. Sliding fee scale. No one denied srvs due to lack of funds. SERVES: Victor Valley area.

SAN BERNARDINO CO. PUBLIC HEALTH
Reproductive Health Centers
P.O. Box 1066
1406 Bailey Ave., Ste D
Needles, CA 92363
(800) 722-4777
(760) 326-9230
(760) 326-9235 FAX

Reproductive health exams for men & women. STD testing & treatment, HIV testing & referral to care. Edu srvs, pregnancy testing, counseling, lab testing, young adult clinics. FUNDING: Dept Public Health. OFC HRS: Tu-Th 7am-4:30pm. Accepts Medi-Cal, insurance. Fees based on srv. SERVES: Amboy, Big River, Essex, Needles, Havasu Landing, Parkers Dam.

SAN BERNARDINO CO. PUBLIC HEALTH
Reproductive Health Centers
1647 E. Holt Blvd.
Ontario, CA 91764
(800) 722-4777
(909) 458-9716
(909) 458-9729 FAX

Reproductive health exams for men & women. STD testing & treatment, HIV testing & referral to care. Edu srvs, pregnancy testing, counseling, lab testing, young adult clinics. For HIV testing, call (909) 383-3060 on F 8am-3:30pm. FUNDING: Dept Public Health. OFC HRS: M-F 8am-5pm. Spanish spoken. ADM REQ: Must have appt. Sliding fee scale. No one denied srvs due to lack of funds. SERVES: Ontario.

SAN BERNARDINO CO. PUBLIC HEALTH
Reproductive Health Centers
800 E. Lugonia Ave., Ste F
Redlands, CA 92374
(800) 722-4777
(909) 793-6399

Reproductive health exams for men & women. STD testing & treatment, HIV testing & referral to care. Edu srvs, pregnancy testing, counseling, lab testing, young adult clinics. FUNDING: Govt. OFC HRS: M-F 8am-5pm. Spanish spoken. ADM REQ: Must have appt. Accepts Medi-Cal, F-PACT, sliding fee scale. No one denied srvs due to lack of funds. SERVES: San Bernardino County.

SAN BERNARDINO CO. PUBLIC HEALTH
Maternal Health Program
505 N. Arrowhead Ave., 3rd Fl.
San Bernardino, CA 92415-0048
(800) 227-3034
(909) 388-5755 FAX

AFLP prgm provides case mgmt to pregnant and parenting teens. Srv coordination for pregnant and parenting teens and their families. Also counseling and info for families who have had an infant die from SIDS. Prenatal mgmt care to low income residents of San Bernardino Co. Call for prenatal referrals. FUNDING: Govt. OFC HRS: M-F 8am-5pm. Spanish spoken. Accepts Medi-Cal, pvt pay.

SAN BERNARDINO CO. PUBLIC HEALTH

Reproductive Health Centers
799 E. Rialto Ave.
San Bernardino, CA 92415-0011
(800) 722-4777
(909) 885-9962
(909) 387-3340 FAX

Birth control, male & female exams, pregnancy testing, counseling, referrals, verification, HIV & sexually transmitted infection (STI) testing and counseling, male sterilization. Srvs are confidential and low-cost. Call individual clinic to schedule appt. Weekly young adult clinics (YAC) on a walk-in basis at Fontana, Ontario, Redlands, San Bernardino and Hesperia sites. FUNDING: Calif Office of Family Planning. OFC HRS: M-F 8am-5pm. Spanish spoken. Accepts Medi-Cal, managed care plans, pvt pay through sliding fee scale. SERVES: San Bernardino County.

ST. ANNE'S

155 N. Occidental Blvd.
Los Angeles, CA 90026-4641
(213) 381-2931
(213) 381-7804 FAX

Residential care prgm provides a safe haven for teenagers, ages 13-18 yrs, and their babies where they can grow to be caring and nurturing parents. Transitional housing prgm for single mothers available for up to 24 months. Residents receive edu and vocational srvs, medical care, psychiatric counseling, social srvs, parenting training, substance abuse counseling, life skills dev, info & referral srvs. Family-based srvs prgm offers in-home care to at-risk young women and their families. FUNDING: Donation, grants, govt, nonprofit. OFC HRS: M-F 9am-6pm; 24-hr facility. Spanish spoken. SERVES: Calif.

TEXT4BABY

Natl Healthy Mothers, Healthy Babies Coalition

Mobile health prgm provides pregnant women and new moms with the health information they need to give their babies a great start. Topics include: birth defects prevention, immunization, nutrition, safe sleep, prenatal care, and infant care srvs. To register, text 'baby' (or 'bebe' for Spanish) to 511411. Visit (www.text4baby.org) for more info. FUNDING: Nonprofit. Free srvs. SERVES: U.S.A.

TLC TEEN MOMS & DADS

So Calif Youth For Christ
P.O. Box 7125
3435 San Anseline Ave., Bldg. 3, Ste 2
Long Beach, CA 90808
(562) 429-1782
(562) 425-7934 FAX

Support for pregnant and parenting teens. Lamaze, support groups, mentors, babysitting during support groups, relationship building. For O.C., call (714) 776-1700; Inland & San Gabriel, (626) 331-0066. FUNDING: Nonprofit. OFC HRS: M-F 9am-4:30pm. Spanish, some Chinese spoken. SERVES: L.A., Orange & San Bernardino Counties.

VERONICA'S HOME OF MERCY

1495 W. Victoria St.
San Bernardino, CA 92411
(909) 888-9064
(909) 888-7390 FAX

Long-term, faith-based residential home (room for up to 20 women) for adult pregnant women & children or women with small children, as an alternative to domestic violence, addictions, abortion and/or homelessness. Women must be involved with the prgm and be willing to continue their education. Not an emergency shelter. Transitional living. FUNDING: Nonprofit. OFC HRS: M-F 8am-4pm. Spanish spoken. ADM REQ: Must be ages 18 yrs+ or emancipated by court. SERVES: So. Calif.

WIC/WOMEN, INFANT AND CHILDREN

See "San Bernardino Co. Public Health"

A NOTE ABOUT THIS CHAPTER

Most hospitals, large churches, adult edu prgms, health assns, and counseling offices offer a wide variety of self-help and support groups for anyone in the community. Some of the groups include: bereavement, divorce recovery, drug & alcohol addictions, emotional health, physical or mental illness, suicide prevention, suicide survivors, diet control, etc. If the support group you wish is not shown in this chapter, call your local hospitals, larger churches, and hotlines for more resources.

A GIFT FROM WITHIN

16 Cobb Hill Rd.
Camden, ME 04843
(207) 236-8858
(207) 236-2818 FAX

Website dedicated to those who suffer from post-traumatic stress disorder (PTSD), those at-risk for PTSD, and those who care for people affected by PTSD. No direct srvs. Website provides educational material and resources. Visit (www.giftfromwithin.org). FUNDING: Nonprofit, donations. SERVES: U.S.A.

ABRAHAM LOW SELF-HELP SYSTEMS

Formerly Recovery, Inc.
105 W. Adams St., Ste 2940
Chicago, IL 60603
(866) 221-0302
(312) 726-4446 FAX

An internatl organization with self-help mental heath groups helping people with symptoms such as anxiety, depression, panic, phobias and fears learn common sense methods of handling their symptoms. Encourages cooperation with the professional. Voluntary contributions at meetings. FUNDING: Nonprofit. SERVES: U.S.A.

ACTION PARENT & TEEN SUPPORT

11372 Ventura Blvd., Ste 200
Studio City, CA 91604
(818) 763-9556
(800) 367-8336
(818) 763-9568 FAX

Weekly support groups for parents and teens. Support to families dealing with low self-esteem, drug/alcohol abuse, depression, runaways, teen pregnancy and other family-related issues. Low-cost drug testing, crisis intervention. FUNDING: Donations, nonprofit. OFC HRS: M-Th 12noon-9pm; F 9am-3:30pm. Spanish spoken. Accepts pvt insurance; individual & family therapy on a sliding fee scale. SERVES: So. Calif.

ADULT CHILDREN OF ALCOHOLICS (ACA)

ACA World Service Organization, Inc.
P.O. Box 3216
Torrance, CA 90510
(310) 534-1815

Self-help, 12-Step prgm of recovery for individuals who grew up in an alcoholic or dysfunctional household. Send self-addressed, stamped, business-sized envelope to the above address for info. Write for meeting times & places. FUNDING: Donations, nonprofit. OFC HRS: Volunteer staffed, no physical office location. Spanish & Chinese spoken. Suggested donation $5. SERVES: U.S.A. & Internatl.

ADULTS MOLESTED AS CHILDREN

Barbara Sinatra Childrens Center
39000 Bob Hope Dr.
Rancho Mirage, CA 92270
(760) 340-2336
(760) 340-1851 FAX

Counseling group for adults molested as children (AMAC) meets W from 4pm-5pm at the Children's Center. FUNDING: Nonprofit. OFC HRS: M-F 8am-5pm. SERVES: Rancho Mirage & nearby.

AL-ANON FAMILY GROUPS HEADQUARTERS

1600 Corporate Landing Pkwy.
Virginia Beach, VA 23454-5617
(888) 425-2666
(757) 563-1600
(757) 563-1655 FAX

Support & community groups for relatives & friends of those with drinking problems. Also provides printed materials specifically aimed at helping families deal with problems of alcoholism. Referrals to local meetings & chapters throughout the U.S.A. & Canada. Alateen support prgm for younger family members. Meeting info in English, Spanish & French. Visit (www.al-anon.alateen.org). FUNDING: Member donations, sale of literature, nonprofit. OFC HRS: M-F 8am-7pm, EST.

AL-ANON FAMILY GROUPS, INC.

Inland Empire Ctr
1016 E. Cooley Dr., Ste C2
Colton, CA 92324
(909) 824-1516
(909) 824-1515 FAX

More than 200 Al-Anon group meetings throughout Riverside & San Bernardino Counties every week. Above phone number will refer you to the meeting location in your area and provide a list of times, days etc. Al-Anon is a self-help group for family or friends of problem drinkers. Groups for adults as well as teens (Alateen for ages 13-19 yrs) and children (Pre-Alateen for ages 8-12 yrs). FUNDING: Nonprofit. OFC HRS: M-F 12noon-4pm; Sat 9am-1pm. Spanish spoken. ADM REQ: Family member or friend who is a problem drinker. No fees. Donations accepted. SERVES: Inland Empire.

ALATEEN

Al-Anon Family Group, Inc.
1600 Corporate Landing Pkwy.
Virginia Beach, VA 23454-5617
(757) 563-1600
(888) 425-2666
(757) 563-1655 FAX

Meeting resource for young people whose lives have been affected by someone else's drinking. Based on 12-Step prgm. Referrals to local meetings and chapters throughout the U.S. and Canada. Includes Alateen support prgm for younger family members. Meeting info in English, Spanish & French. FUNDING: Member donations, sale of literature, nonprofit. OFC HRS: M-F 8am-6pm, EST. SERVES: U.S.A.

ALCOHOLICS ANONYMOUS/ADMIN

Southern Calif Central Office
P.O. Box 70159
4311 Wilshire Blvd., Ste 104
Los Angeles, CA 90010
(323) 936-4343
(323) 936-8729 FAX

24-hr self-help info for alcoholics. Will help anyone who wants to stop drinking. This is an original 12-Step self-help group. AA meeting info. Spanish (323) 735-2089. FUNDING: Nonprofit. OFC HRS: M-F 8am-7:30pm; Sat, Sun, holidays 9am-4:30pm. Spanish & Russian spoken. Free srvs. SERVES: So. Calif.

ALCOHOLICS ANONYMOUS/DESERT

Central Office of the Desert
35-325 Date Palm Dr., Ste 134
Cathedral City, CA 92234
(760) 324-4880
(760) 324-4851 FAX

Help for the alcoholic who still suffers from the disease of alcoholism. Referral to meetings. For east valley, call (760) 568-4004. FUNDING: Nonprofit. OFC HRS: M-F 9am-8pm; Sat, Sun 10am-2pm. Free srvs except for printed material. SERVES: Desert communities to Blythe.

ALCOHOLICS ANONYMOUS/I.E.

Inland Empire Central Office
897 Via Lata, Ste AA
Colton, CA 92324
(909) 825-4700
(909) 825-7370 FAX

Helps anyone with an alcohol problem who wants to stop drinking by putting them in touch with sober members of AA or directing them to AA meetings. Primary purpose is to stay sober and help other alcoholics achieve sobriety. FUNDING: Self-supported by AA members. OFC HRS: M-F 9am-5pm; Sat 9am-1pm. Spanish upon request. ADM REQ: Desire to stop drinking. Free srvs. SERVES: Riverside Metro, Corona, Norco, Banning, Beaumont, Moreno Valley, Hemet, Perris, Lake Elsinore, Temecula, San Bernardino Metro, Ontario, Upland, Pomona Valley and mountain areas.

ALCOHOLICS ANONYMOUS/VICTOR VLY

18888 Outer Highway 18, Ste 107
Apple Valley, CA 92307
(760) 242-9292
(760) 242-4855 FAX

24-hr info on AA meetings and referrals. FUNDING: Nonprofit. OFC HRS: M-F 9am-4pm, 24-hr phone srv. Spanish spoken. SERVES: Victor Valley and Barstow.

ALISA ANN RUCH BURN FOUNDATION

Administrative Office
2501 W. Burbank Blvd., Ste 201
Burbank, CA 91505
(800) 242-2876
(818) 848-0223
(818) 848-0296 FAX

Free brochures & info on burn prevention & care. Assist to burn survivors of all ages including counseling, summer camp, back-to-school, back-to-work, resourcing assist for medical care & therapeutic aids. Support groups meet monthly at various sites. FUNDING: Donations,

Self-Help/Support Groups

nonprofit. OFC HRS: M-F 9am-3pm. Free srvs. SERVES: Calif.

ALIVE AND WELL
AIDS Alternatives
11684 Ventura Blvd.
Studio City, CA 91604
(818) 780-1875
(877) 922-5483
(818) 780-7093 FAX

Support, edu, and advocacy network. Free monthly events, distributes free info packets upon request. Also provides referrals and resources. Please e-mail (info@aliveandwell.org) or visit website (www.aliveandwell.org). FUNDING: Nonprofit, donations. Spanish and Italian spoken. SERVES: U.S.A.

ALLIANCE FOR DONATION & TRANSPLANTATION AWARENESS & SUPPORT (ADTAS)
P.O. Box 8503
Riverside, CA 92515
(951) 689-2822
(909) 795-7411

Awareness and support group meets at the Blood Bank of San Bernardino & Riverside Counties: 384 W. Orange Show Rd., San Bernardino, CA 92408. Meets 1st Th at 6pm and 3rd M at 6pm. Visit (www.freewebs.com/adtas.) SERVES: Riverside, San Bernardino Counties

ALLIANCE ON MENTAL ILLNESS
See "NAMI..."

ALS ASSOCIATION/NATIONAL
National Office (Lou Gehrig's Disease)
27001 Agoura Rd., Ste 250
Calabasas Hills, CA 91301-5104
(818) 880-9007
(818) 880-9006 FAX

Info, resource and referral srv for ALS patients & families. Public awareness and research support to find the cause and cure of ALS (Lou Gehrig's Disease). Support groups, patient srvs prgms. Patient hotline (800) 782-4747. FUNDING: Donations, nonprofit. OFC HRS: M-F 7:30am-4pm. Free srvs. SERVES: U.S.A.

ALWAYS IN MY HEART SUPPORT GROUP
Loma Linda Univ Medical Center
11234 Anderson St.
Loma Linda, CA 92354
(909) 558-7261

Support groups for parents who have suffered a miscarriage, stillbirth, or infant death. Meets 2nd M from 7pm-8:30pm, in room 129A (South Entrance) at Loma Linda Univ Rehab Institute, 11406 Loma Linda Dr. Also 4th Tu 9:30-11am at Mt. View Plaza Suite 10 (south end), 11255 Mountain View Ave., Loma Linda. For questions or more info, call Cheri Moreno. No childcare available. Welcome to attend one or both meetings. SERVES: San Bernardino County.

ALZHEIMER'S ASSN/COACHELLA VALLEY
69730 Highway 111, Ste 202
Rancho Mirage, CA 92270
(760) 328-6767
(760) 328-2747 FAX

Info about Alzheimer's disease and related disorders. Referral to day care, diagnostic centers, support groups, legal srvs, case mgmt, home health agencies, physicians, nursing homes, etc. Literature, edu prgms. Edu events through-

out the community for lay & professional people. Helpline (800) 272-3900. FUNDING: Nonprofit, donations. OFC HRS: M-F 8:30am-5pm. Spanish spoken. SERVES: Riverside County.

ALZHEIMER'S ASSN/NATIONAL
Natl Info & Referral Services
225 N. Michigan Ave., 17th Fl.
Chicago, IL 60601-7633
(800) 272-3900
(312) 335-8700
(866) 699-1246 FAX

Works to eliminate Alzheimer's disease through the advancement of research & enhanced care & support for individuals, families & caregivers. Refers callers to their local chapters. Also provides literature on Alzheimer's disease. TDD (312) 335-5886. FUNDING: Nonprofit. OFC HRS: M-F 8:30am-5pm, CST. AT&T translators available. SERVES: U.S.A.

ALZHEIMER'S SUPP GRP/CALIMESA
D.A.S.H. Inc.
P.O. Box 8370
306 W. Colton Ave.
Redlands, CA 92374
(909) 798-1667
(909) 335-0238 FAX

Support group for caregivers of dependent older adults, sponsored by DASH. Meets the 2nd & 4th W of every month from 6pm-7pm at 306 W. Colton Ave. in Redlands. Contact Larry. SERVES: San Bernardino & Riverside Counties.

ALZHEIMER'S SUPP GRP/CORONA
Corona Senior Center
921 S. Belle Ave.
Corona, CA 92882
(951) 736-2363
(951) 279-3683 FAX

Support group for Alzheimer's caregivers. Monthly meeting held on 2nd Th of each month from 7pm-8:30pm. Contact Leona. ADM REQ: All are welcome. SERVES: Corona.

ALZHEIMER'S SUPP GRP/RIVERSIDE
Care Connex Us
4130 Adams St., Ste B
Riverside, CA 92504
(951) 509-2500
(951) 509-2578 FAX

Support group for Alzheimer's caregivers. Call or see website (www.careconnexxus.com) for meeting times and locations. SERVES: Riverside County.

ALZHEIMER'S SUPP GRP/TEMECULA
Care Connexx US
29995 Evans Rd.
Sun City, CA 92586
(951) 672-9536
(951) 672-0486 FAX

Support group for Alzheimer's caregivers and persons with related disorders. Meetings 1st Tu, 10am-11:30am in Temecula & 2nd & 4th W 9:30am-11am in Sun City; 4th Th 5:30pm-6:30pm in Riverside. Respite care available during meeting with prior reservation. See website for more info (www.careconnexxus.com). SERVES: Sun City, Temecula, Riverside

AMERICAN ASSN OF SUICIDOLOGY
5221 Wisconsin Ave., NW
Washington, DC 20015

(202) 237-2280
(202) 237-2282 FAX

Website with info and resources for those concerned with suicide, survivors of, and those in crisis. Visit (www.suicidology.org). No direct srvs. FUNDING: Nonprofit. SERVES: U.S.A.

AMERICAN CHRONIC PAIN ASSN (ACPA)
Internatl Office
P.O. Box 850
Rocklin, CA 95677
(916) 632-0922
(800) 533-3231
(916) 632-3208 FAX

Support groups teach coping skills to maximize life. FUNDING: Donations, grants, nonprofit. OFC HRS: M-F 9am-5pm. 24-hr answering machine. Free srvs, membership fees. SERVES: U.S.A.

AMERICAN DIABETES ASSOCIATION
National Office
1701 N. Beauregard St.
Alexandria, VA 22311
(800) 342-2383
(703) 549-6995 FAX

Free info packet provides literature, info on health edu and refers to local affiliates for support group assist. FUNDING: Nonprofit. OFC HRS: M-F 8:30am-8pm, EST. Spanish spoken. SERVES: U.S.A.

AMERICAN DIABETES ASSOCIATION
1701 N. Beauregard St.
Alexandria, VA 22311
(800) 342-2383
(703) 549-6995 FAX

Natl call center for persons seeking diabetes info, support or prgms. Online camp directory listing American Diabetes Assn affiliated camps for diabetic children and teens. Visit (www.diabetes.org). FUNDING: Nonprofit. OFC HRS: M-F 8:30am-8pm, EST. After hrs: 24-hr recording. Spanish spoken. SERVES: U.S.A.

AMERICAN FNDN FOR SUICIDE PREV
120 Wall St., 22nd Fl.
New York, NY 10005
(888) 333-2377
(212) 363-3500
(212) 363-6237 FAX

Works to prevent suicide through research, edu, training and support. Srvs include: literature, conferences and a directory of support groups nationwide. FUNDING: Nonprofit. OFC HRS: M-F 9am-5pm, EST. Free srvs. SERVES: U.S.A.

AMERICAN HOLISTIC HEALTH ASSN
P.O. Box 17400
Anaheim, CA 92817-7400
(714) 779-6152

AHHA encourages participation in creating personal wellness. Provides lists of self-help resources that promote a holistic approach, considering the whole person and wellness-oriented lifestyles. No on-site srvs. Call or mail request. All materials are free. FUNDING: Donations, nonprofit. OFC HRS: Vary. Volunteer staff. SERVES: U.S.A.

AMERICAN INST/CANCER RESEARCH
1759 R Street, NW
Washington, DC 20009
(800) 843-8114
(202) 328-7226 FAX

Fosters research on diet, nutrition and cancer, & educates the public on the results. Free edu materials, quarterly newsletter, nutrition hotline, cancer resource for newly diagnosed patients, pen pals support network, memorial donations, gift annuities and estate planning. Call to request info. FUNDING: Donations, grants, nonprofit. OFC HRS: M-F 8:30am-6pm. Free srvs. SERVES: U.S.A.

AMERICAN LIVER FNDN/SAN DIEGO

2515 Camino del Rio South, Ste 122
San Diego, CA 92108
(619) 291-5483
(619) 295-7181 FAX

Edu prgms about liver disease & hepatitis. Monthly support groups for patients & families. FUNDING: Nonprofit. OFC HRS: M-F 8am-5pm. Materials in Spanish, Chinese, Vietnamese. No fees. SERVES: San Diego County, Riverside & Imperial Counties.

AMERICAN LIVER FOUNDATION

75 Maiden Lane, Ste 603
New York, NY 10038
(800) 465-4837
(212) 668-1000
(212) 483-8179 FAX

Makes physician and support group referrals and offers info, including fact sheets. Single copies of liver disease info are available at no cost. Also (888) 443-7872. FUNDING: Donations, member dues, nonprofit. OFC HRS: M-F 9am-5pm. SERVES: U.S.A.

AMERICAN LUNG ASSN/INLAND CO.

441 MacKay Dr.
San Bernardino, CA 92408
(909) 884-5864
(800) 586-4872
(909) 884-6249 FAX

Edu prgms for schools, smoking cessation prgms for businesses and general public (Freedom from Smoking Prgm, 8-session smoking cessation clinic). Better Breathers Club support group for patients with lung disease. Also asthma summer camp for ages 8-14 yrs. Gives referrals to local cessation clinics. FUNDING: Community Health Charities, Christmas Seals, donations, nonprofit. OFC HRS: M-F 8:30am-4:30pm. Spanish spoken. Free srvs. SERVES: Riverside, San Bernardino, Inyo & Mono Counties.

AMERICAN SLEEP APNEA ASSN

6856 Eastern Ave., NW, Ste 203
Washington, DC 20012
(202) 293-3650
(202) 293-3656 FAX

Find resources and support group contacts at (www.sleepapnea.org). FUNDING: Nonprofit. OFC HRS: M-F 9am-5pm, EST. SERVES: U.S.A.

AMERICAN STROKE ASSN/HEART ASSN

Division of American Heart Assn
7272 Greenville Ave.
Dallas, TX 75231
(888) 478-7653
(214) 706-5231 FAX

Wide array of prgms, products & srvs, from patient edu & info to scientific statements with cutting-edge info for health care professionals. Info on stroke risk factors and warning signs. Life after a stroke resources, referrals and access to support groups. Stroke Connection magazine is a bi-monthly publication for stroke survivors, caregivers & health care professionals. Warmline is a srv for families who have experienced stroke. FUNDING: Nonprofit. OFC HRS: 24 hrs, 7 days. Interpreter srv available. Free srvs. SERVES: U.S.A.

AMPUTEE CONNECTION/REDLANDS

Redlands Community Hospital
350 Terracina Blvd.
Redlands, CA 92373
(951) 735-7963
(909) 423-0562

Support group for amputees meets 3rd Sun 2pm-4pm at Weisser Pavilion (follow signs). Pot luck snacks.

ANAD NATL OFFICE

See "Natl Assn of Anorexia Nervosa..."

ARTHRITIS FNDN/COACHELLA VLY

73-710 Fred Waring Dr., Ste 104
Palm Desert, CA 92260
(760) 773-3076
(760) 773-0858 FAX

Physician referral, exercise classes, monthly lecture series, support groups. Also distributes brochures on all kinds of arthritis. FUNDING: Donations, city grants, nonprofit, events. OFC HRS: M-Th 8:30am-5pm; F 8:30am-4:30pm. Free srvs. SERVES: Desert communities.

BATTEN DISEASE SUPP/RESEARCH ASSN

166 Humphries Dr.
Reynoldsburg, OH 43068
(800) 448-4570
(740) 927-4298

Batten disease is a life-shortening genetic disease that kills cells, one by one. The four different types are: infantile, late infantile, juvenile and adult. Phone counseling, quarterly newsletter, support groups, literature and referrals to other organizations worldwide, including 16 chapters. FUNDING: Donations, grants, nonprofit. OFC HRS: M-F 8am-5pm. SERVES: U.S.A.

BEREAVEMENT SUPP GRP/MORONGO

Hospice of Morongo Basin
61675 Twentynine Palms Hwy.
Joshua Tree, CA 92252
(760) 366-1308
(760) 366-1935 FAX

Bereavement support group. Meetings 1st & 3rd Th 1:30pm-3:30pm or 5pm-7pm. SERVES: Morongo Basin.

BOOT CAMP FOR NEW DADS

Medical Ofc. Bldg. 2, 5th Fl., Conference Rm.
6650 Alton Pkwy
Irvine, CA 92618
(949) 754-9067
(949) 754-9087 FAX

Designed for new fathers to help ensure every child has an opportunity for a caring and capable father, beginning at birth. Workshops in English and Spanish, video-based orientation prgm. Veteran fathers help fathers-to-be gain knowledge and skills to increase their confidence to nurture and participate in the care of their babies. FUNDING: Nonprofit. OFC HRS: M-F 8am-5pm. SERVES: U.S.A.

BREAST CANCER NET OF STRENGTH

Formerly Y-Me Natl Breast Cancer Org
Southern California Affiliate
1901 E. 4th Street, Ste 300
Santa Ana, CA 92705-3918
(714) 361-2106
(714) 361-2120 FAX

Breast cancer edu, support group info. Increases awareness & ensures, through info, empowerment & peer support, that no one faces breast cancer alone. 24-hr hotline available in 150 languages, call (800) 221-2141. For Spanish hotline, call (800) 986-9605. Spanish spoken. SERVES: So. Calif.

BREAST CANCER SUPPORT GROUP

Pomona Valley Medical Center
1910 Royalty Dr.
Pomona, CA 91767
(909) 865-9555
(909) 865-9691
(909) 865-9697 FAX

Members share concerns, support each other and address issues related to breast cancer. Meets in the professional library at the Robert and Beverly Lewis Family Cancer Care Center at the address above. Meetings are held the 2nd M of each month at 7pm. FUNDING: Nonprofit, donations, grants. OFC HRS: M-F 7:30am-5pm. Free srvs. SERVES: Pomona Valley and Inland Empire.

BREAST CANCER SUPPORT GROUP

Kaiser Permanente Park Sierra Medical Offices
10800 Magnolia Ave.
Riverside, CA 92505
(951) 353-4755

Support group meets the 2nd Tu each month from 2pm-4pm. Contact Elvira Pan, LCSW, for room info. SERVES: Riverside County.

BREAST FEEDING SUPPORT GROUPS

See "La Leche League..."

CAMP GOOD GRIEF

Loma Linda Univ Children's Hospital
11234 Anderson St., Rm. 2816
Loma Linda, CA 92354
(909) 558-4073
(800) 825-5437

Three-day camp for children and teens who have had a sibling or parent die. Also have special victims prgm sponsored by the San Bernardino Co. Dist Atty's office. Held at various locations. FUNDING: Loma Linda Univ Children's Hospital Fndn. ADM REQ: Must make reservation and fill out application. Ages 10-16 yrs. Free srvs. SERVES: So. Calif.

CANCER PREVENTION COALITION

P.O. Box 6851
Malibu, CA 90264
(310) 457-5176
(888) 377-8877
(877) 885-4657 FAX

Public health and cancer prev edu. Learn to create an environment safe from cancer-causing products. Outreach, public edu, advocacy. Free cancer awareness and prev seminars. FUNDING: Nonprofit. SERVES: U.S.A.

CANCER SUPPORT GROUP

Kaiser Permanente Park
Sierra Medical Offices
10800 Magnolia Ave.
Riverside, CA 92505
(951) 353-4755

Support group meets 4th Tu 2pm-4pm. Contact Elvira Pan, LCSW, for room info. SERVES: Riverside County.

CANCER SUPPORT GROUPS

Also contact your local hospitals.

CANCER411

1316 W. Alameda Ave
Burbank, CA 91506
(818) 842-1504

Resources and info about cancer. Visit website (www.cancer411.org). FUNDING: Nonprofit. SERVES: U.S.A.

CANDLELIGHTERS CHILDHOOD CANCER FNDN

P.O. Box 1663
11155 Mountian View Ave., Ste 105
Loma Linda, CA 92354
(909) 558-3419
(909) 558-3420 FAX

Assistance provided to families who have or have had a child with cancer. Volunteer opportunities available. FUNDING: Nonprofit. SERVES: Loma Linda.

CAREGIVER SUPPORT GROUP

P.O. Box 6001
255 E. Bonita Ave., Bldg. 5
Pomona, CA 91769-6001
(909) 596-7733
(909) 593-7541 FAX

Free support group for families and caregivers caring for individuals recovering from stroke, dementia, brain injury, etc. Group meets every Tu 6pm-7pm in the transitional living center. Also have group for survivors of TBI; meets Tu 11am-12noon. FUNDING: Nonprofit. SERVES: L.A. & San Bernardino Counties.

CAREGIVER SUPPORT GROUP

Kaiser Permanente Park Sierra Medical Offices
10800 Magnolia Ave.
Riverside, CA 92505
(951) 353-4755

Group meets every other W each month 10:30am-11:30am. Contact Elvira Pan, LCSW for more info. SERVES: Riverside County.

CELEBRATE RECOVERY

Canyon Lake Community Church
30515 Railroad Canyon Rd.
Canyon Lake, CA 92586
(951) 244-1877
(951) 244-4397 FAX

Christ-centered, 12-Step recovery prgm. Support groups for all types of problems and addictions, including: food, sex or relationship addictions, co-dependency and chemical dependency. Meets Th at 6pm for dinner, 7pm for worship & meeting. Child care available. FUNDING: Nonprofit. OFC HRS: M-Th 8am-4:30pm. SERVES: Riverside County.

CELEBRATE RECOVERY

Mosaic Inland Church
5540 Schaefer Ave.
Chino, CA 91710
(909) 628-1571

Christ-centered, 12-Step recovery prgm. Support groups for all types of problems & addictions, including: food, sex or relationship addictions, co-dependency and chemical dependency. Meets F at 6pm-10pm. Contact: Jim or Terry Moon. FUNDING: Nonprofit. OFC

HRS: M-F 8:30am-4pm. Spanish spoken. SERVES: San Bernardino County.

CELEBRATE RECOVERY

Centerpoint Church
P.O. Box 787
170 West F Street
Colton, CA 92324
(909) 825-3670

Christ-centered, 12-Step recovery prgm. Support groups for all types of problems & addictions, including: food, sex or relationship addictions, co-dependency and chemical dependency. Meets Th at 6:30pm in children's ministries building. FUNDING: Nonprofit. OFC HRS: Tu-F 9am-5pm. SERVES: San Bernardino County.

CELEBRATE RECOVERY

Crossroads Christian Church
2331 Kellogg Ave.
Corona, CA 92881
(951) 737-4664
(951) 278-3176 FAX

Christ-centered, 12-Step recovery prgm. Support groups for all types of problems & addictions, including: food, sex or relationship addictions, co-dependency and chemical dependency. Meets F at 7pm in the fellowship hall. Light dinner and fellowship at 6:30pm. Open share, workbook, and other recovery groups also available. See website for more info. FUNDING: Nonprofit. OFC HRS: M-Th 8am-4:30pm; F 8am-3pm. SERVES: Riverside County.

CELEBRATE RECOVERY

8348 3rd Street
Downey, CA 90241
(562) 923-1261
(562) 861-1614 FAX

Christ-centered and biblically based support group for all hurts, habits (addictions) and hang-ups (co-dependency, anger, etc). Separate men's and women's open share groups and 12-Step study groups. Meets F in the fellowship hall from 6pm-9pm. FUNDING: Nonprofit. Spanish spoken. SERVES: L.A. & San Bernardino Counties.

CELEBRATE RECOVERY

Southwest Community Church
77701 Fred Waring Dr.
Indian Wells, CA 92210
(760) 200-2000
(760) 360-4139 FAX

Turning Point is a Christ-centered 12-Step recovery prgm. Big event every 8 weeks. Small groups meet often. Contact Pastor Dave Jenkins, ext. 2283. Additional recovery prgrms available. FUNDING: Nonprofit. OFC HRS: M-Th 9am-5pm. SERVES: Riverside County.

CELEBRATE RECOVERY

Cathedral of Praise
1100 E. Holt Blvd.
Pomona, CA 91767
(626) 806-1890
(909) 987-1636 FAX

Christ-centered, 12-Step recovery prgm. Support groups for all types of problems & addictions, including: food, sex or relationship addictions, co-dependency and chemical dependency. OFC HRS: M-W, F, Sat 10am-8pm. Free srvs. SERVES: San Gabriel Valley & San Bernardino Co.

CELEBRATE RECOVERY

Sunrise Church
2759 N. Ayala Dr.
Rialto, CA 92377
(909) 875-5566
(909) 820-6281 FAX

Christ-centered, 12-Step recovery prgm. Support groups for all types of problems & addictions, including: food, sex or relationship addictions, co-dependency and chemical dependency. Professional counseling referrals available. Meets Tu from 7pm-9pm in room 260 and F at 7pm in chapel (room 170). FUNDING: Nonprofit. OFC HRS: M-F 8am-5pm. Spanish spoken. SERVES: San Bernardino County.

CELEBRATE RECOVERY

Bethel Christian Center
2425 Van Buren Blvd.
Riverside, CA 92503
(951) 359-1123
(951) 359-3372 FAX

Christ-centered, 12-Step recovery prgm. Support groups for all types of problems & addictions, including: food, sex, or relationship addictions, co-dependency and chemical dependency. Meets F at 7pm. Contact: Jerry or Julia Thromson. FUNDING: Nonprofit. OFC HRS: M-F 9am-5pm. SERVES: Riverside & nearby.

CELEBRATE RECOVERY

Pathway Christian Church
6755 Victoria Ave.
Riverside, CA 92506
(951) 781-8465
(951) 781-8896 FAX

Christ-centered, 12-Step recovery prgm. Support groups for all types of problems & addictions, including: food, sex or relationship addictions, co-dependency and chemical dependency. Meets F at 6pm for dinner. 7pm large group; 8pm small group; 8pm one-time newcomers 101 meeting; 9pm Holy Grounds Cafe fellowship (dessert served). Call for more information regarding 12-Step groups for men & women. FUNDING: Nonprofit. OFC HRS: M-F 9am-5pm. ADM REQ: $3 for dinner. SERVES: Riverside County.

CELEBRATE RECOVERY

Riverside Community Church
4850 Jurupa Ave.
Riverside, CA 92504
(951) 686-1886
(951) 684-7313 FAX

Christ-centered, 12-Step recovery prgm. Support groups for all types of problems & addictions, including: food, sex or relationship addictions, co-dependency and chemical dependency. Meets Th. 6pm dinner; 7pm worship; 8pm gender-specific share groups; 9pm coffee and dessert accountability fellowship. Call for more info regarding 12-Step groups. Contact: Carlos Davila. FUNDING: Nonprofit. OFC HRS: T-Th 9am-4pm; F 9am-12noon. SERVES: Riverside County.

CELEBRATE RECOVERY

Northpoint Christian Fellowship
2055 Elks Dr.
San Bernardino, CA 92405
(909) 882-2564
(909) 882-8708 FAX

Christ-centered, 12-Step recovery prgm. Meets Tu from 6:30pm-9pm. FUNDING: Nonprofit. OFC HRS: M-Th 8:30am-4:30pm. SERVES: San Bernardino County.

CELEBRATE RECOVERY
Judson Baptist Church
1406 E. Pacific St.
San Bernardino, CA 92404
(909) 889-0781
(909) 889-0783 FAX

Christ-centered, 12-Step recovery prgm. Support groups for all types of problems & addictions. Life recovery worship service Sun 9am, 12-Step study groups for women Sun 11am, and Tu 6:30pm. For men, Tu and Th 6:30pm. FUNDING: Nonprofit. SERVES: San Bernardino City.

CELEBRATE RECOVERY
Cornerstone Community Church
34570 Monte Vista Dr.
Wildomar, CA 92595
(951) 674-8661
(951) 674-9603 FAX

Christ-centered, 12-Step recovery prgm. Support groups for all types of problems & addictions, including: food, sex or relationship addictions, co-dependency and chemical dependency. Meets F at 6pm dinner; 7pm worship and msg; 8pm open share groups. Childcare for ages birth-12yrs. Celebrate Recovery for teens meets Th 6:30pm-8:30pm in youth chapel. Contact: Pastor Bill Aanestad. FUNDING: Nonprofit. OFC HRS: M-Th 8am-5pm. SERVES: Riverside County.

CELEBRATE WHOLENESS
Campus Hill Church
11057 Hill Dr.
Loma Linda, CA 92354
(909) 796-0222
(909) 796-1992 FAX

Christ-centered, 12-Step recovery prgm. Support groups for all types of problems & addictions, including: food, sex or relationship addictions, co-dependency and chemical dependency. Meets F at 7pm in Linda Hall. Contact: Pastor Larry. FUNDING: Nonprofit. OFC HRS: M-Th 8am-5pm; F 8am-12noon. SERVES: San Bernardino County.

CHINO COMMUNITY SERVICES
Counseling Srvs
13201 Central Ave.
Chino, CA 91710
(909) 591-9822
(909) 628-4093 FAX

Low-cost outpatient family and individual counseling. Community outreach for residents of Chino. Domestic violence prgms. FUNDING: State, county, school, city, nonprofit. OFC HRS: M-Th 8am-8pm; F 8am-6pm. Spanish spoken. Free srvs for juveniles & low-income residents of Chino. School-based counseling free. Outpatient family treatment $26 per visit. SERVES: Western San Bernardino County.

CHRONIC FATIGUE IMMUNE DYSFUNCTION SYNDROME ASSN OF AMERICA (CFIDS)
P.O. Box 220398
Charlotte, NC 28222-0398
(704) 365-2343
(704) 365-9755 FAX

Edu info & referral srvs to persons with inquiries on CFIDS. Supports research & publishes journal. FUNDING: Nonprofit. OFC HRS: M-Th 9am-5pm; F 9am-1pm, EST. Free srvs. SERVES: U.S.A.

CITY OF HOPE
Duarte Campus
1500 E. Duarte Rd.
Duarte, CA 91010
(626) 256-4673

Contact the community srvs dept for more info on the various support and edu srvs offered to patients, their families, local community and health care professionals. Also visit (www.cityofhope.org). OFC HRS: M-F 8am-5pm. SERVES: U.S.A.

CLEANSLATE, INC.
Gang Recovery Group & Tattoo Removal
12401 Slauson Ave., Ste G
Whittier, CA 90606
(562) 945-9111

CleanSlate is a gang violence recovery, rage resolution and tattoo removal prgm that helps to erase the visible signs of gang involvement while working with gang members to reconnect with their emotions. Individual counselors give one-on-one support. Gang recovery group every F 7:30pm-9pm at the So. Calif. Counseling Ctr. 5615 W. Pico Blvd., L.A. 90019. No appt needed for F groups. Tattoo removal prgm is at different locations one Sat a month. Address above is mailing address only. Visit (www.cleanslatela.org) for tattoo removal dates. FUNDING: Nonprofit. Spanish spoken. Groups $5 donation. SERVES: So. Calif.

CLUTTERERS ANONYMOUS (CLA)
World Service Office
P.O. Box 91413
Los Angeles, CA 90009-1413
(310) 281-6064

Meetings & literature for individuals who want to eliminate clutter and bring order into their lives. 12-Step-based groups. Phone number has recorded meeting info and will receive messages. Nightly meeting number (712)432-3900, code: 727176#. FUNDING: Self-sustaining through donations. SERVES: U.S.A.

CO-ABODE
1223 Wilshire Blvd., Ste 102
Santa Monica, CA 90403

Nationwide, web-based shared housing and support group for single mothers and their children. Guest memberships are free, as is access to the extensive resource directory with links to housing, parenting and other info. Visit (www.co-abode.com). FUNDING: Nonprofit, membership fees. OFC HRS: 24 hrs, 7 days. SERVES: U.S.A.

CO-ANON FAMILY GROUPS WORLD SRVS
P.O. Box 12722
Tucson, AZ 85732-2722
(800) 898-9985
(520) 513-5028

Support group for friends and relatives of cocaine addicts. Based on the 12-Steps and 12-Traditions of AA. Visit (www.co-anon.org) for meeting sites. FUNDING: Nonprofit. OFC HRS: Leave a message and a volunteer will return your call. No fees. SERVES: Meetings in La Crescenta, Montrose & Fontana; includes L.A. & San Bernardino.

COCAINE ANONYMOUS
National Referral Line
(800) 347-8998

Info for prgms in your area. OFC HRS: 24 hrs; 7days SERVES: U.S.A.

COCAINE ANONYMOUS
Mailing Address
3243 Arlington Ave., Ste 246
Riverside, CA 92506-3244
(951) 359-3895

12-Step meetings for addicts to share their experience, strength and hope to recover from their addiction. High Desert (760) 255-1093. CA World Srvs (310)559-5833. FUNDING: Donations, nonprofit. ADM REQ: Desire to stop using mind-altering substances. SERVES: Riverside & San Bernardino Counties.

COCAINE ANONYMOUS WORLD SRVS
P.O. Box 2000
3740 Overland Ave., Ste C
Los Angeles, CA 90034
(310) 559-5833
(310) 559-2554 FAX

12-Step, anonymous, self-help fellowship of men and women who share their common problem and help others to recover from their addiction. Call (800) 347-8998 for internatl referrals to local CA meetings. FUNDING: Contributions, nonprofit. OFC HRS: M-F 9am-5pm. SERVES: Internatl.

COMMUNITY BAPTIST CHURCH
Support Groups
9090 19th Street
Rancho Cucamonga, CA 91701
(909) 945-5001
(909) 948-3174 FAX

Visit (www.cbconline.org) for current support group info. Meetings vary, including: Al-Anon, AA groups, O.A. (Overeaters Anonymous) group. FUNDING: Nonprofit. SERVES: Rancho Cucamonga.

COMPASSIONATE FRIENDS/MORONGO
Hospice of Morongo Basin
61675 29 Palms Hwy.
Joshua Tree, CA 92252
(877) 969-0010
(760) 250-7295

Self-help support group for bereaved parents. Meets 2nd W 4:30pm-6pm. Visit website (www.thecompassionatefriends.com). FUNDING: Nonprofit. OFC HRS: M-F 9am-4:30pm. Free srvs. SERVES: Morongo Basin.

COMPASSIONATE FRIENDS/NATL
The Compassionate Friends, Inc.
P.O. Box 3626
Oak Brook, IL 60522-3696
(877) 969-0010
(630) 990-0246 FAX

Natl self-help organization will refer you to over 550 local chapters in U.S.A. Provides support and understanding to families who have experienced the death of a child, grandchild or siblings of any age, from any cause. The goal is positive resolution of grief. Brochures, videos, newsletters and helpful materials are available. All inquiries can be sent to above address. FUNDING: Donations, nonprofit. OFC HRS: M-F 9am-4pm, CST. 24-hr voicemail. Free group srvs. SERVES: U.S.A.

CONCERNED UNITED BIRTHPARENTS (CUB)

P.O. Box 341442
Los Angeles, CA 90034
(800) 822-2777
(858) 712-3317 FAX

Support, search & edu for those affected by the separation of family by adoption, divorce, family feud, etc. Free support meetings & search workshops. Meets 4th Sat of the month at Mesa Vista Hospital, Day Wing, 7850 Vista Hill Ave., San Diego, CA. FUNDING: Donations, nonprofit. New member fee $40. SERVES: Orange, Riverside & San Bernardino Counties, referral to other areas.

CONGENITAL HEART INFO NETWORK

101 N. Washington St., Ste 1A
Margate City, NJ 08402
(609) 822-1572
(609) 822-1574 FAX

Offers info & resources for people with congenital heart defects. Also sponsors several support groups. Spencer's Fund prgm provides financial assist including meals, utility assist, and travel expenses to families with a child who is hospitalized for a long period of time. FUNDING: Nonprofit. Free srvs. Memberships available at several donation levels. SERVES: U.S.A.

COSA NATL SERVICE ORGANIZATION

Co-Dependents of Sex Addicts
P.O. Box 14537
Minneapolis, MN 55414
(763) 537-6904

Recovery prgm for friends & family members whose lives have been affected by another person's compulsive sexual behavior. Based on the 12-Steps and 12-Traditions of AA. Call for local meeting times and locations. FUNDING: Nonprofit, member donations. No fees for membership. SERVES: U.S.A.

CRIME VICTIMS UNITED OF CALIF

11400 Atwood Rd.
Auburn, CA 95603
(530) 885-9544
(530) 885-4608 FAX

Political action committee. Works to enhance public safety using edu & political action. Endorses political candidates who share in this mission. FUNDING: Nonprofit. OFC HRS: M-F 9am-5pm. SERVES: Calif.

CROHN'S & COLITIS FNDN/GREATER L.A.

1640 S. Sepulveda Blvd., Ste 214
Los Angeles, CA 90025
(310) 478-4500
(866) 831-9157
(310) 478-4546 FAX

Educational and support services for people suffering from Crohn's Disease and ulcerative colitis. Support groups serving L.A. & Orange Counties, Camp Oasis Youth Club, '20s-'30s group, hospital visitation prgm, parent network, etc. Call the information resource ctr at (888) MY-GUT PAIN. Call for meeting times and locations. Visit (www.ccfa.org/chapters/losangeles). FUNDING: Donations, nonprofit. OFC HRS: M-F 9am-5pm. Free srvs. SERVES: L.A., Ventura, Orange, San Bernardino, San Luis Obispo, Santa Barbara and Kern Counties.

CROHN'S & COLITIS SUPPORT GROUP

Foundation of America
386 Park Avenue South
New York, NY 10016
(800) 932-2423
(714) 547-8500

Info & referral for people with Crohn's, colitis and I.B.D. (Inflammatory Bowel Disease). Meets 3rd M 6:30pm-8:30pm. In L.A. Co., call (310) 478-4500. Visit (www.ccfa.org). FUNDING: Nonprofit. OFC HRS: M-F 9am-5pm. SERVES: U.S.A.

CROSSROADS CHRISTIAN CHURCH

2331 Kellogg Ave.
Corona, CA 92881
(951) 737-4664
(951) 278-3176 FAX

Church provides various support groups including: Celebrate Recovery and grief recovery. FUNDING: Nonprofit. OFC HRS: M-Th 8am-4:30pm; F 8am-3pm. SERVES: Corona.

CROSSROADS CHURCH

S.M.U.R.F.
31805 Temecula Pkwy., Ste 389
Temecula, CA 92592
(951) 541-8574
(951) 541-0886 FAX

Address listed above is for mailing only. Single Moms United in Rewarding Fellowship meets Sun at 5pm. Support group for single mothers & their children. Free child care and a Sun night meal. Meets at 28753 Via Montezuma in Temecula. Subject to change. FUNDING: Nonprofit, donations. OFC HRS: By appointment. ADM REQ: Single mothers & their children. SERVES: Southwest County.

CRYSTAL METH ANONYMOUS

4470 W. Sunset Blvd., PMB 555, Ste 107
Los Angeles, CA 90027
(213) 488-4455

Fellowship of individuals who have had problems with crystal meth. Meetings held regularly to share and offer each other support in overcoming addiction. Based on 12-Step tradition. Call for meeting locations and times or visit (www.crystalmeth.org). FUNDING: Nonprofit. SERVES: U.S.A.

CYSTIC FIBROSIS FOUNDATION

2150 Towne Centre Pl., Ste 120
Anaheim, CA 92806
(714) 938-1393
(800) 232-8731
(714) 938-1462 FAX

Info & referral to support groups throughout So. Calif for patients, families and siblings. Ask Gary Green for assist to nearest group. Also offers a location at 153 E. Whittier Blvd., Ste. A, La Habra, CA 90631 OFC HRS: M-F 8:30am-5:30pm. SERVES: So. Calif.

DEBTORS ANONYMOUS/SO CALIF

P.O. Box 2862
Winnetka, CA 91396
(781) 453-2743
(800) 421-2383
(781) 453-2745 FAX

Daily meetings throughout So. Calif, also literature for compulsive spenders and debtors. Monthly workshops. FUNDING: Donations, nonprofit. Free srvs. SERVES: So. Calif.

DEPRESSED ANONYMOUS

P.O. Box 17414
Louisville, KY 40217
(502) 569-1989

Resources for depressed individuals of all ages, printed info, support groups, referrals, advocacy, education. Website contains info on books and support groups. Visit (www.depressedanon.com). FUNDING: Nonprofit. SERVES: U.S.A.

DEPRESSION & BIPOLAR SUPPORT ALLIANCE

16280 Whispering Spur
Riverside, CA 92504
(714) 744-8718
(714) 750-3519
(714) 744-8715 FAX

Support group for persons diagnosed with depression or bipolar disorder and those who support them. Group meets Sat 10am-12noon, at 4095 County Circle Dr., Riverside, CA 92503. Can provide group info for nearby areas. Also call Leroy at (951) 686-5047. Contact address for mailing only, c/o Jo Ann Martin. FUNDING: Nonprofit. ADM REQ: Ages 17 yrs+ Free srvs. SERVES: Riverside County.

DEPRESSIONRECOVERYGROUPS.COM

Website that hosts several depression support groups each day for depression. Users only need a microphone and computer to participate. Facilitated by Dr. Vincent Caimano, Ph.D. Donations accepted, no one turned away for lack of funds. SERVES: U.S.A.

DESERT AIDS PROJECT

P.O. Box 2890
1695 N. Sunrise Way
Palm Springs, CA 92263-2890
(760) 323-2118
(866) 331-3344
(760) 323-9865 FAX

HIV health center (outpatient specialty clinic). Support groups for HIV positive persobns, and their caregivers, partners or family. Anonymous testing for HIV & syphilis. Counseling, in-home care, pro bono legal clinic, prevention & edu, case mgmt, "friend-to-friend" & admin volunteer prgm, substance abuse srvs, transportation, food, child care. ADAP enrollment site. Satellite ofc (760) 342-4197. TDD (760) 969-1796. FUNDING: Nonprofit. OFC HRS: M-F 8am-5pm. Spanish spoken. ADM REQ: HIV positive. Free srvs or sliding fee scale. SERVES: Eastern Riverside Co & upper desert of San Bernardino County.

DIABETES SUPPORT GROUPS

Loma Linda University Diabetes Center
11285 Mt. View Ave., Ste 40
Loma Linda, CA 92354
(909) 558-3022
(909) 558-3023 FAX

Meets 1st Tu 6pm on the corner of Mountain View Ave. and Barton Rd. at the Spanish Seventh Day Adventist Church at N side of the Plaza. OFC HRS: M-Th 8am-5pm; F 8am-12noon. Spanish spoken. ADM REQ: Must register for meeting. SERVES: Greater San Bernardino, Riverside Counties.

DIABETIC HELP LINE/SUPPORT GRP

St. Jude Medical Center
101 E. Valencia Mesa Dr.
Fullerton, CA 92835
(714) 992-3037

St. Jude Medical Center maintains a special helpline located in its diabetes metabolic unit.

Calls will be answered by nurse specialists who understand special problems of diabetes. Also offers support group. FUNDING: Nonprofit. OFC HRS: 24 hrs, 7 days. SERVES: So. Calif.

DIVORCE CARE SUPPORT GROUP

Chino Valley Community Church
14601 Peyton Dr.
Chino Hills, CA 91709
(909) 606-4848

13-week support series for those who are separated or divorced. New subject each week. Can join at any time. Meets Th 7pm-9pm. No meetings in August, resuming in Sept. Call to confirm. Contact Ed or Kay Caragher (909)606-1475. Workbook fee $13. SERVES: Chino Hills.

DIVORCE CARE SUPPORT GROUP

Centerpoint Church
170 West F Street
Colton, CA 92324
(909) 825-3670

Weekly support series on W for those who are separated or divorced. Call church office for more info. Also Celebrate Recovery Th and grief share programs. Call for more info. SERVES: Colton.

DIVORCE CARE SUPPORT GROUP

First Baptist Church
9280 Maple Ave.
Hesperia, CA 92345
(760) 244-4109

Weekly support series for those who are separated or divorced. Meets Tu 6:30pm-8pm. Call for more info. OFC HRS: M-Th 8am-3pm; F 8am-12pm. SERVES: Hesperia.

DIVORCE CARE SUPPORT GROUP

Rancho Community Church
31300 Rancho Community Way
Temecula, CA 92592
(951) 303-6789

Weekly support series for those who are separated or divorced. Divorce Care for Kids as well. Contact church office for more information. SERVES: Temecula.

DUAL RECOVERY ANONYMOUS

World Service Central Office
P.O. Box 8107
Prairie Village, KS 66208
(877) 883-2332
(913) 991-2703

12-Step fellowship of men & women who meet to support each other in a common recovery from two no-fault illnesses: an emotional or psychiatric illness and chemical dependency. Meetings in Northern, Central & So. Calif. FUNDING: Nonprofit. OFC HRS: M-F 9am-5pm, CST. 24-hr recorded info. SERVES: U.S.A.

DYSLEXIA AWARE/RESOURCE CTR

928 Carpinteria St., Ste 2
Santa Barbara, CA 93103
(805) 963-7339
(805) 963-6581 FAX

Info on dyslexia, ADD, Tourette's Syndrome: videotapes, audiotapes, workshops, referrals for testing can be requested. Info available in Spanish. FUNDING: Donations, grants, nonprofit. OFC HRS: M-F 9am-5pm. Spanish-speaker on W only. Free srvs. Requests donations. SERVES: U.S.A.

EASTER SEALS/SO CALIF

Stroke Support Group
241 E. 9th Street
San Bernardino, CA 92410
(800) 922-7325
(909) 888-4125
(909) 884-5741 FAX

Meets weekly and offers relaxed environment where stroke patients can share their experiences. Doctors and other medical professionals are encouraged to get involved in these groups. Call for more details. OFC HRS: M-F 8:30am-4:30pm. SERVES: San Bernardino & Riverside Counties.

EATING DISORDERS ANONYMOUS (EDA)

P.O. Box 55876
Phoenix, AZ 85078
(218) 339-2500

Info and support groups for persons with eating disorders. Referral to groups throughout U.S.A. Visit (www.eatingdisordersanonymous.org). FUNDING: Nonprofit. OFC HRS: M-F 8am-5pm. SERVES: U.S.A.

EMOTIONS ANONYMOUS

(909) 873-2273

Support group fellowship of men and women. 12-Step prgm to become emotionally healthy. Everyone welcome. Call for times and locations. FUNDING: Nonprofit. SERVES: Rialto, Fontana, Riverside, Hemet.

EMOTIONS ANONYMOUS

(323) 589-3768

12-Step support groups. Call for contact numbers, meeting dates and times. San Fernando Valley/West L.A. (818) 377-4341; Long Beach/Southeast L.A. (562) 928-0646; SB/Riverside (909) 873-2273; Orange Co (714) 739-5449 or (714) 903-7999. FUNDING: Nonprofit. OFC HRS: 24-hr srvs. No fees. SERVES: So. Calif.

EPILEPSY FNDN OF GREATER L.A.

5777 W. Century Blvd., Ste 820
Los Angeles, CA 90045
(800) 564-0445
(310) 670-2870
(310) 670-6124 FAX

Info & referral, self-help groups, edu outreach, residential and family camps, parent phone network, conferences, medical ID bracelets and necklaces, seizure first aid training, advocacy, literature and written edu guides. Srvs for persons with seizure disorders, their family members and the community. FUNDING: Donations, grants, nonprofit. OFC HRS: M-F 9am-4:30pm. Spanish spoken. Free srvs. SERVES: So. Calif.

EXCEPTIONALLY EXCITED KIDS (EEK)

P.O. Box 185
San Jacinto, CA 92581
(951) 375-6906
(951) 491-5598

Mission is to provide latest in exercise science to those with special needs through play, fitness, games, nutrition, etc. Online support, education and resources for special needs children and adults ages 2-25 yrs. Down Syndrome, autism, cerebral palsy, etc. Visit (www.eekandfriends.com.) FUNDING: Nonprofit. SERVES: Inland Empire.

EXECUTIVE WOMEN INTERNATL

515 South 700 East, Ste 2A

Salt Lake City, UT 84102
(801) 355-2800
(877) 439-4669
(801) 355-2852 FAX

Professional assn for support & professional dev for women. Scholarships given. FUNDING: Nonprofit. OFC HRS: M-F 8am-5pm. SERVES: U.S.A.

FAMILY AND FRIENDS OF MURDER VICTIMS

26396 Beckman Court
Murrieta, CA 92562
(951) 757-4419

Support group meets 3rd W each month at 7pm at Avaxat Elem School. To arrange for child care, please call 24 hrs in advance (951) 304-1623; $1 per child. SERVES: Riverside County.

FAMILY AND FRIENDS OF MURDER VICTIMS

P.O. Box 11222
San Bernardino, CA 92423-1222
(909) 387-6384
(909) 798-6273 FAX

Info, support & friendship to those who have experienced the murder of a loved one, as well as those who are victims of attempted murder. So. Calif. chapters in Riverside & San Bernardino Counties. Call for meeting times. FUNDING: Nonprofit, donations. Spanish spoken. Free srvs. SERVES: Calif.

FAMILY AND FRIENDS OF MURDER VICTIMS

Bilingual Meeting
Upland, CA 91786
(909) 215-7063

Support group for those who have lost a loved one through homicide. Meets 2nd Th each month 7pm-9pm. St. Anthony's Catholic Church in Upland CA . Spanish spoken. SERVES: Riverside County.

FAMILY CAREGIVER ALLIANCE

Natl Center
180 Montgomery St., Ste 1100
San Francisco, CA 94104
(800) 445-8106
(415) 434-3388
(415) 434-3508 FAX

Website lists resources and online support groups for families and friends who have become caregivers. Up-to-date info, fact sheets, newsletter, publications. Visit (www.caregiver.org). FUNDING: Nonprofit. SERVES: U.S.A.

FAMILY SERVICE ASSN/WEST RIVERSIDE

JND/Family Counseling
21250 Box Springs Rd., Ste 106
Moreno Valley, CA 92557
(951) 686-3706
(951) 686-7267 FAX

Full-srv marriage, family, child, individual & group counseling. Parenting groups. Call for times & locations. FUNDING: Nonprofit. OFC HRS: M-F 8am-5pm Spanish spoken. Sliding fee scale $30-$120. Some srvs free for those who qualify. SERVES: Western Riverside County.

FEDERAL IDENTIFICATION THEFT HOTLINE

Federal Trade Commission
600 Pennsylvania Ave., NW

Washington, DC 20580
(877) 438-4338

Website of info and resources regarding identity theft. Visit (www.ftc.gov/idtheft). Spanish spoken. SERVES: Calif.

FIRST CANDLE/SIDS ALLIANCE

National Headquarters
1314 Bedford Ave., Ste 210
Baltimore, MD 21208
(800) 221-7437
(410) 653-8226
(410) 653-8709 FAX

SIDS (Sudden Infant Death Syndrome) group provides emotional support to families. Educates the public and financially supports research. Will send a free packet of info on SIDS and assist families in finding local resources and support groups. After hrs emerg referrals to on-call counselors. For Orange County, contact the "Guild for Infant Survival" at (714) 973-8417 or (800) 247-4370. FUNDING: Nonprofit. OFC HRS: M-F 9am-5pm, EST. Spanish spoken. Free srvs. SERVES: U.S.A.

FOOD ADDICTS IN RECOVERY ANONYMOUS

400 W. Cummings Park, Ste 1700
Woburn, MA 01801
(781) 932-6300

12-Step fellowship of men and women who are constantly obsessed with food. Visit website to view a current list of meetings (www.foodaddicts.org). FUNDING: Nonprofit. ADM REQ: All ages welcome. SERVES: U.S.A.

FOOTHILL FAMILY SHELTER HOMELESS COURT

(909) 608-2865

Assist to homeless or low-income clients who have outstanding San Bernardino misdemeanor tickets, warrants, or high fines. Court held fourth F of each month. FUNDING: Nonprofit. OFC HRS: Tu-F 9am-5pm. Closed 12noon-1pm for lunch. ADM REQ: Must call a month in advance to pre-register. Must have driver's license and citation number if possible, as well as name, DOB, and phone number. SERVES: San Bernardino County.

FRAGILE X ASSN OF SO CALIF

P.O. Box 6924
Burbank, CA 91510-6924
(818) 754-4227
(310) 276-9251 FAX

Parent group offering info & referral, peer support groups. Monthly meetings and other edu activities. FUNDING: Donations, nonprofit. OFC HRS: 24-hr answering machine. Spanish spoken. Free srvs. SERVES: So. Calif.

FREE INDEED CHRISTIAN FELLOWSHIP

430 South D Street
Perris, CA 92570
(951) 657-2449
(951) 657-2229 FAX

A variety of prgms and activities offered. The Ranch helps addicts find sobriety with the aid of worship. Other prgms include: Soul Patrol Outreach, discipleship, homeless shelter, food ministries, motorcycle ministries, etc. Call Patrick Smith for appt. Men's ranch (951) 943-5159. FUNDING: Nonprofit. OFC HRS: M-F 9am-5pm. SERVES: Perris & Riverside areas.

FREEDOM FROM FEAR

Anxiety & Depression Resource Org
308 Seaview Ave.
Staten Island, NY 10305
(718) 351-1717
(718) 980-5022 FAX

Agency seeks to impact the lives of those affected by anxiety, depression and related disorders through advocacy, edu, research, and community support. Also offers a free anxiety and depression screening prgm. Visit (www.freedomfromfear.org) for more info. FUNDING: Nonprofit. Free srvs. SERVES: U.S.A.

GAY & LESBIAN NATIONAL HOTLINE

2261 Market St., PMB #296
San Francisco, CA 94114
(888) 843-4564
(415) 355-0003
(415) 522-5498 FAX

Free and confidential peer counseling and local resources for the gay & lesbian community. Maintains a database with info on social & support groups, HIV/AIDS, organizations, student groups, etc. National GLBT Youth Talkline (800) 246-7743. FUNDING: Nonprofit. OFC HRS: M-F 1pm-9pm; Sat 9am-2pm. SERVES: U.S.A.

GENETIC ALLIANCE

Connections to Natl Support Groups/Srvs
4301 Connecticut Ave., NW, Ste 404
Washington, DC 20008-2369
(202) 966-5557
(202) 966-8553 FAX

Resources through toll-free infoline (800) 336-GENE. FUNDING: Donations, grants, govt, nonprofit. OFC HRS: M-F 9am-6pm, EST. Free srvs. SERVES: U.S.A.

GET ON THE BUS

5411 Camelia Ave.
North Hollywood, CA 91601
(818) 980-7714
(818) 980-7702 FAX

Transportation, counseling and support srvs for children visiting their mothers and/or fathers incarcerated in the Calif prison system. For Northern Calif, call (925) 335-9314; for Central Calif, call (805) 544-2357, ext. 32. FUNDING: Nonprofit. OFC HRS: M-F 9am-5pm. ADM REQ: Must sign up. Free srvs. SERVES: Calif.

GILDA'S CLUB DESERT CITIES

67-625 E. Palm Canyon Dr., Ste 7-A
Cathedral City, CA 92234
(760) 770-5678
(760) 770-5667 FAX

Support for persons with cancer, their families & friends. Networking, lectures, workshops and social events. Also youth prgm. FUNDING: Nonprofit. OFC HRS: M-W 9am-5pm; Th 9am-7:30pm; 2nd Sat 10am-2pm. Spanish spoken. ADM REQ: Call for new member meeting. Free srvs SERVES: Cathedral City.

GRIEF RECOVERY GROUP

Loma Linda University Med Center
11406 Loma Linda Dr., Ste 129 A
Loma Linda, CA 92354
(909) 558-7261
(909) 558-4000

Bereavement support group for parents who have lost a baby. Various bereavement support programs available. Call or see website for info. Visit (www.lomalindahealth.org). SERVES: San Bernardino County.

GRIEF RECOVERY SUPPORT GROUP

Immanuel Baptist Church
28355 E. Baseline
Highland, CA 92346
(909) 425-1777

Group meets every W at 5:45pm. Call for more info. ADM REQ: Please do not bring children. SERVES: Highland.

GRIEF SHARE

Victory Christian Church
P.O. Box 5060
34-500 Bob Hope Dr.
Palm Springs, CA 92263
(760) 328-3313

Designed to support those who are suffering the loss of a loved one through death or for those dealing with long-term illness. Coping skills and sharing are offered in a caring environment. Meets W at 7pm. Call for dates. FUNDING: Nonprofit. OFC HRS: M-F 10am-5pm. Free srvs. SERVES: Coachella Valley.

GRIEF SHARE RECOVERY GROUP

Southwest Community Church
77-701 Fred Waring Dr., Rm. 209
Indian Wells, CA 92210
(760) 772-8462
(760) 902-2678

Support for those who have experienced the death of a loved one. Meets Tu 6:30pm-8:30pm. No child care available. Contact facilitator Ealeene Reynolds at (760) 772-7053. ADM REQ: Must call first. SERVES: Riverside County.

HADASSAH SOUTHERN CALIFORNIA

Administrative Office
9463 Gregory Way
Beverly Hills, CA 90212
(310) 234-8300
(310) 248-4944 FAX

Five area resource ctrs in L.A. & Orange Counties. Offers local programming to advocate for all women's health issues, promotes literacy and edu, encourages social action and volunteerism, and ensures Jewish growth and continuity. Long Beach & Orange County (714) 545-7162; Metro L.A. (310) 276-0036; Valley (818) 343-9316; San Diego (858) 547-9200; Desert (760) 327-7059. OFC HRS: M-Th 8:30am-4:30pm; F 8:30am-3pm. SERVES: L.A. Co.

HEALING ODYSSEY

23591 El Toro Rd., Ste 214
Lake Forest, CA 92630
(949) 951-3930
(949) 951-8095 FAX

Three-day retreat and follow-up support prgm for female cancer survivors. Camp facility in the Malibu mountains four times per year for women with all forms of cancer. Also year-round workshops for couples. FUNDING: Donations, nonprofit. OFC HRS: M-F 9am-5pm. Spanish spoken. Fee for 3 day retreat is $125, with partial or full scholarships when available. SERVES: So. Calif.

HEARING LOSS SUPPORT GROUP

Tri-Palms Club House

32700 Desert Moon Dr.
Thousand Palms, CA 92276-3713
(760) 343-3828

Meets last F each month at 1pm, October-March at the Tri-Palms Country Club clubhouse. Call for more information. SERVES: Coachella Valley.

HEP C CONNECTION
1325 S. Colorado Blvd., Bldg. B, Ste 302
Denver, CO 80222
(303) 860-0800
(303) 860-7481 FAX

Support system for hepatitis c patients and their families or partners. Info, referral to local support groups, newsletter. Helpline is available by calling (800) 522-HEPC. Spanish-speaking counselors available. FUNDING: Nonprofit. OFC HRS: M-F 7am-5pm, MST. Spanish spoken. SERVES: U.S.A.

HEPATITIS C SUPPORT GROUP
Coachella Valley
45480 Portola Ave.
Palm Desert, CA 92260
(760) 200-2766

Support, edu, awareness & advocacy for quality medical care for all persons with liver disease. Meets 2nd M 11am at Portola Community Ctr in Palm Desert. FUNDING: Nonprofit. SERVES: Desert Hot Springs, Morongo, Indio, La Quinta, Palm Springs, Cathedral City, Rancho Mirage.

HEPATITIS FOUNDATION INTERNATIONAL
504 Blick Dr.
Silver Spring, MD 20904
(800) 891-0707
(301) 622-4200
(301) 622-4702 FAX

Education materials, liver wellness training prgms, support group referrals, news updates on viral hepatitis, and nurses' advisory council. FUNDING: Nonprofit. OFC HRS: M-F 9am-5pm, EST. Fee for training. SERVES: U.S.A.

HERPES RESOURCE CENTER
CDC National STI Hotline
P.O. Box 13827
Research Triangle Park, NC 27709
(800) 227-8922
(919) 361-8488
(919) 361-8425 FAX

ASHA (American Social Health Assn) provides a network of over 90 herpes (HELP) and HPV support groups throughout the U.S. Write to request a complete list of groups or call (919) 361-8400. Visit (www.ashastd.org) or call hotline (919) 361-4848 for info & counseling about any aspect of the herpes simplex virus. 24-hr hotline for STDs/AIDS (800) 342-2437. FUNDING: Nonprofit. Hotline hrs: M-F 9am-6pm, EST. Free srvs. SERVES: U.S.A.

HIGH DESERT DOMESTIC VIOLENCE PRGM
15075 7th Street
Victorville 92395
(760) 843-0701
(866) 770-7867
(760) 843-9551 FAX

Domestic violence counseling Tu 2pm-2:30pm and 2pm-3:30 pm; Th 1:30pm-3pm. Spanish-speaking support group F 1:30pm-3pm. Parenting class (in Spanish) W 3pm-5pm. TRO

clinic W 8:30am-2:30pm and by appt M, Tu, Th, F. Anger mgmt F 3pm-4:30pm. Court-ordered supervised visitation 1st and 3rd Sat by appt. Also provides a 24-hr staffed shelter and 24-hr hotline (760) 949-4357. OFC HRS: M-F 8am-5pm. Spanish spoken. SERVES: High Desert.

HUNTINGTON DISEASE SOCIETY
Greater L.A. Chapter
9903 Santa Monica Blvd., Ste 106
Beverly Hills, CA 90212
(888) 443-7252
(800) 986-9868

Referral to support groups, helpline, edu, info & referral. Leave message; calls returned in 24 hrs. FUNDING: Nonprofit. SERVES: So. Calif.

I CAN COPE
6355 Riverside Ave.
Riverside, CA 92506
(951) 683-6415
(951) 300-1200
(951) 682-6804 FAX

Sponsored by American Cancer Society as a unique course designed to help patients and families cope with cancer. Call for course info dates. FUNDING: Nonprofit. OFC HRS: M-F 9am-5pm. Spanish spoken. SERVES: Riverside & San Bernardino Counties.

I CAN COPE EDUCATION SERIES
Kaiser Permanente Park
Sierra Medical Offices
10800 Magnolia Ave.
Riverside, CA 92505
(915) 353-4755

Cancer education and support classes 1st and 3rd Tu of every other month, 1:30pm-4pm. Contact Elvira Pan, LCSW, for more info. SERVES: Riverside County.

INLAND AIDS PROJECT
3767 Elizabeth St.
Riverside, CA 92506
(951) 224-8314
(951) 683-2965 FAX

Case mgmt for HIV-infected persons, counseling, support groups, emerg food and shelter, utility assist, relapse prevention counseling, edu outreach, advocacy and medical referrals. Counseling available for significant others. FUNDING: Nonprofit. OFC HRS: M-F 8:30am-5pm. ADM REQ: HIV+. SERVES: Riverside County.

INLAND HOSPICE ADULT PRGM
A Volunteer Prgm
233 W. Harrison Ave.
Claremont, CA 91711
(909) 399-3289
(909) 626-4369 FAX

Volunteers & staff tend to the physical, emotional & spiritual needs of the terminally ill, frail & elderly & their families. Adult bereavement groups offered at various locations, open to those who are experiencing the loss of a loved one. The Common Threads Project provides bereavement support for children & youth ages 6-17 yrs & their families. Call to register. FUNDING: United Way, fundraisers, nonprofit. OFC HRS: M-F 9am-5pm. ADM REQ: Must register for Common Threads. Free srvs. SERVES: East L.A. & West San Bernardino.

JEFFEREY OWENS COMMUNITY CENTER
Mailing Address
5198 Arlington Ave., Ste 922
Riverside, CA 92504

Promotes the health and well-being of youth and adults by providing support, edu, and advocacy regarding sexual orientation and gender identity. For more information on how to get involved, email (jocc-info@jocc.org). Visit (www.jocc.org). FUNDING: Nonprofit. SERVES: Riverside and San Bernardino Counties.

KAIROS PRISON MINISTRY & KAIROS OUTSIDE
Palm Desert, CA 92211
(760) 772-0330

Support for women with incarcerated loved ones. Contact Audrey for more info. Kairos Inside Prison Ministry is a faith-based outreach program for incarcerated men and women throughout the world. 3 open and running locations in the area. Contact Harry for more info. SERVES: Riverside County, Coachella Valley.

KIDSAID
2 Kids 4 Kids by Kids
P.O. Box 3272
Ann Arbor, MI 48106-3272

Website with resources for kids dealing with grief or loss. E-mail support groups, bookstore. A safe place for kids to share experiences with other kids. Visit (www.kidsaid.com). FUNDING: Nonprofit, donations. SERVES: U.S.A.

KRISTIE'S PLACE
1747 S. Claudina Way
Anaheim, CA 92805
(714) 408-9781
(714) 956-1475 FAX

A place for children with life-threatening illnesses to come with their families for their So. Calif wish trip or for a short compassion stay. Wishland's Kid's Club and family support prgms bring joy and hope to all. FUNDING: Nonprofit. OFC HRS: M-F 8:30am-4pm; Sat 8:30am-10am. Spanish spoken. SERVES: L.A., Orange & San Bernardino Counties.

LA LECHE LEAGUE
Info & support for women who wish to breast-feed, 24-hr phone help, monthly meetings, lending library with books on breast-feeding, childbirth, family & nutrition. Visit website for phone list & web addresses in So. Calif & Nevada (www.lalecheleaguescnv.org). TDD (847) 592-7570. FUNDING: Nonprofit. OFC HRS: M-F 9am-9pm. SERVES: Mid County.

LA LECHE LEAGUE INTERNATL
P.O. Box 4079
957 N. Plum Grove Rd.
Schaumburg, IL 60168-4079
(800) 525-3243
(847) 519-7730
(847) 969-0460 FAX

Worldwide organization provides support to pregnant & breast-feeding women. Edu materials, free catalog & referrals to local leaders. Call for monthly meeting info. FUNDING: Donations, members, nonprofit. OFC HRS: M-F 9am-5pm, CST. Spanish spoken. SERVES: Internatl.

LEAGUE OF WOMEN VOTERS/CLAREMONT
P.O. Box 1532

Claremont, CA 91711-8532
(909) 624-9457
(909) 624-9839 FAX

Promotes political responsibility by active & informed participation in govt, voter registration, addresses for political leaders, candidate info, issues info. Visit (www.claremont.ca.lwvnet.org or www.smartvoter.org). FUNDING: Nonprofit. OFC HRS:Tu-F 9am-12noon. SERVES: Parts of San Gabriel & Pomona Valley & West San Bernardino County.

LEUKEMIA SUPPORT GROUP
Kaiser Permanente/Park Sierra Medical Ofc
10800 Magnolia Ave.
Riverside, CA 92505
(951) 353-4755

Support group open to members and non-members of Kaiser who have Leukemia or another blood disorder. Meets1st Tu of the month 6pm-8pm. Call, Elvira Pan, LCSW, for more info. SERVES: Riverside County.

LIFE CHOICE OF HEMET
475 W. Stetson PMB-T225
Hemet, CA 92543
(951) 652-3111

Counseling, adoption assist, abortion referral, phone referrals and resources, baby formula and diapers (limited). May add more srvs at later date. FUNDING: Donations, nonprofit. SERVES: Riverside County.

LIVING IN THE HERE AND NOW
Pomona Valley Medical Center
1910 Royalty Dr.
Pomona, CA 91767
(909) 865-9555
(909) 865-9697 FAX

Emotional support group for cancer patients, their families and friends to assist in coping with cancer. Meets 3rd Th at 10am in the professional library. FUNDING: Nonprofit, donations, grants. OFC HRS: M-F 7:30am-5pm. Free srvs. SERVES: Pomona Valley & Inland Empire.

LUNG DISEASE SUPPORT GROUP
See "American Lung Assn/..."

LUPUS FOUNDATION OF AMERICA, INC.
2000 L Street, NW, Ste 710
Washington, DC 20036
(800) 558-0121
(202) 349-1155
(202) 349-1156 FAX

Edu materials, seminars, and support groups. Call (800) number for literature. For Spanish, call (800) 558-0231. FUNDING: Nonprofit. OFC HRS: M-F 8:30am-5pm, EST. Spanish spoken. SERVES: U.S.A.

LUPUS FOUNDATION OF SO. CALIF
4699 Murphy Canyon Rd., Ste 104
San Diego, CA 92123
(858) 278-2788
(858) 278-2782 FAX

Conducts seminars, provides lending library for patients and their families on issues of lupus. Facilitates support groups. Supports research to treat & cure lupus. FUNDING: Nonprofit. OFC HRS: M-F 10:30am-4:30pm; 24-hr ans machine. ADM REQ: All ages served. Fixed fee schedule, $20 annual membership. SERVES: Orange, Riverside, San Diego and Imperial Counties, City of Ojai.

LUPUS INTERNATIONAL
Support Center & Lupus Library
17985 Sky Park Cir., Ste J
Irvine, CA 92614
(949) 833-2121
(888) 532-2322
(949) 833-1183 FAX

Edu materials, newsletters, etc. Quarterly symposium with panel of doctors providing up-to-date info on lupus (attendance ranges from 150-300 people). Rap session monthly. Call for time and location of support groups. Visit website for local helpline numbers (www.lupusinternational.com). FUNDING: Nonprofit. OFC HRS: M-F 9am-5pm. Spanish spoken. Fees: $25 per yr individual membership. Free general meetings & support groups. SERVES: So. Calif.

LUPUS SUPPORT NETWORK
P.O. Box 127
2026 N. Riverside Ave.
Rialto, CA 92377
(909) 874-9257
(909) 874-5312 FAX

Organization for lupus, fibromyalgia, arthritis, thyroid issues, diabetes and other autoimmune disorders. Partners with natl organizations to help patients and their families find srvs to help them live the highest quality of life. These srvs include, but are not limited to: support groups, self-help courses, edu, doctors, food, clothing and housing, when able. FUNDING: Nonprofit. OFC HRS: M-Sat 10am-5pm. SERVES: So. Calif.

METASTIC CANCER SUPPORT GROUP
Moments in Life
Kaiser Permanente/Park Sierra Medical
10800 Magnolia Ave.
Riverside, CA 92505
(951) 353-4755

Group meets 3rd W each month 2pm-4pm. Contact Elvira Pan, LCSW for more info. SERVES: Riverside County.

METH RESOURCES
www.methresources.gov
(916) 324-5523

Visit to find various resources and prgms in the fight against meth. FUNDING: Govt. SERVES: U.S.A.

MICHELLE'S PLACE
Women's Breast Cancer Resource Center
27645 Jefferson Ave., Ste 117
Temecula, CA 92590
(866) 304-1280
(951) 699-5455
(951) 699-3631 FAX

Education resources, community awareness, and support services for women with breast cancer. Support groups in English and Spanish. Volunteers welcome. FUNDING: Nonprofit. OFC HRS: M-F 9am-3:30pm; W evening by appt. Spanish spoken. SERVES: Riverside County.

MODEST NEEDS FOUNDATION
115 E. 30th Street, 1st Fl.
New York, NY 10016
(212) 463-7042

Visit (www.modestneeds.org) to learn more about the prgm and to apply for grant assist. Self-sufficiency grants, back-to-work grants, in-dependent living grants, nonprofit grants. FUNDING: Nonprofit. OFC HRS: M-F 9am-5pm, EST. Donations welcome. SERVES: U.S.A.

MOURNING STAR CENTER, THE
42600 Cook St., Ste 210
Palm Desert, CA 92211
(760) 836-0360
(760) 776-1612 FAX

Open-ended support groups for children and teens, ages 3-19 yrs, and their families, who are grieving due to a death. Trained volunteers and professionals facilitate groups. Also extended support, edu srvs, free grief camp and community outreach. Visit (www.mourningstar.org) for more information about srvs and locations. FUNDING: Donations, nonprofit. OFC HRS: Vary. Spanish spoken. Accepts donations. Free srvs. SERVES: Riverside County.

MULTIPLE SCLEROSIS GREATER RIVERSIDE AREA SELF-HELP PARTNERSHIP (GRASP)
10800 Magnolia Ave.
Riverside, CA 92505
(951) 544-1441

Support and education for patients, family and friends of Multiple Sclerosis. Meets 1st Sat each month 10am-12noon in conference room M-1C. Contact Gilbert Lopez. SERVES: Riverside County.

MULTIPLE SCLEROSIS SUPPORT GRP
Casa Colina Adult Day Health Care
P.O. Box 6001
255 E. Bonita Ave.
Pomona, CA 91769-6001
(909) 596-7733
(866) 724-4127
(909) 593-0153 FAX

Living Well With MS program: 3 hrs per wk for 12 wks. Call the National MS Society in Souhern CA for more info, (310)479-4456. FUNDING: Nonprofit. OFC HRS: M-F 9am-5pm. Payment plan available SERVES: Pomona, San Gabriel Valley, Inland Empire.

NAMI-CHINO VALLEY
2837 E. Tam O'Shanter Court
Ontario, CA 91761
(909) 923-7517

Family-to-family edu: a free, 12-week course for family caregivers of individuals with severe mental illnesses. Support group meets at Canyon Ridge Hospital, 2nd Tu each month at 7pm. FUNDING: Nonprofit. SERVES: San Bernardino County.

NAMI-COACHELLA VALLEY
P.O. Box 4015
Palm Desert, CA 92261
(888) 881-6264
(760) 902-5858
(760) 342-1898 FAX

Support group for family and friends of mentally ill. Meets 1st & 3rd M 7pm-8:30pm (except for August) to receive info about mental health issues and srvs. Meet at Hope Lutheran Church, 45900 Portola in Palm Desert (a half mile south of Hwy 111). Call to verify times and location. FUNDING: Nonprofit, dues, donations, fundraising. Yearly dues for NAMI members: $35 for individuals, $45 for families. SERVES: Coachella Valley.

NAMI-LOS ANGELES

Natl Alliance on Mental Illness
824 Moraga Dr.
Los Angeles, CA 90049
(310) 889-7200

NAMI is a natl organization that provides families of mentally ill persons with edu support and resources. Click the "Find Support" tab on the website for srvs in your area (www.nami.org). FUNDING: Nonprofit. OFC HRS: M-F 8am-6pm. Spanish spoken. SERVES: U.S.A.

NAMI-LOS ANGELES COUNTY

NAMI L.A. Co. Coordinating Council
P.O. Box 91206
Long Beach, CA 90809
(562) 435-2264

Natl Alliance for Mentally Ill (NAMI) support & info meetings monthly. NAMI is an edu, advocacy and support organization founded to help families struggling with severe neurobiological brain disorders and to eliminate stigma and discrimination faced by the mentally ill and their family members. FUNDING: Donations, grants, nonprofit. OFC HRS: M-F 9am-5pm. SERVES: Calif.

NAMI-MT. SAN JACINTO

National Alliance on Mental Illness
P.O. Box 716
San Jacinto, CA 92581
(951) 765-1850

Advocacy group formed to help combat stigma faced by the mentally ill and their family members. Provides educational prgms & promote awareness of mental issues in the community. Support group & info meetings 1st W each month, 6pm-8:30pm, in Hemet & San Jacinto Valley. Meetings held at the Camelot Retirement Community, 800 W. Oakland Ave., Hemet, CA, 92543. FUNDING: Nonprofit, dues, fundraising, donations. OFC HRS: M-Sat 9am-5pm. SERVES: L.A., Orange & Riverside Counties.

NAMI-NATIONAL OFFICE

National Alliance on Mental Illness
3803 N. Fairfax Dr., Ste 100
Arlington, VA 22201-3042
(800) 950-6264
(703) 524-7600
(703) 524-9094 FAX

Helpline provides info about mental illness & referral to community resources. NAMI is the country's leading grassroots advocacy organization dedicated solely to improving the lives of persons with severe mental illness, including schizophrenia, bipolar disorder (manic-depressive illness), major depression, obsessive-compulsive disorder, and severe anxiety disorders. More than 1,200 state & local affiliates, Calif office (916) 567-0163, fax (916) 567-1757. FUNDING: Nonprofit. OFC HRS: M-F 10am-6pm, EST. Spanish spoken. SERVES: U.S.A.

NAMI-SAN BERNARDINO

182 Jackson St.
San Bernardino, CA 92408
(909) 824-8060
(909) 252-4018 FAX

Support group meets 4th M at 6:30pm. In Dec, meeting is held on the 2nd M. Group meets at P.E.A.M. House. FUNDING: Nonprofit. SERVES: San Bernardino County.

NAMI-TEMECULA VALLEY

P.O. Box 186
30520 Rancho California Rd., Ste 107
Temecula, CA 92591
(951) 672-2089
(951) 695-0712 FAX

Self-help support and referral services for persons with severe mental illness, depression, panic disorders, etc. Address is for mailing only. FUNDING: Nonprofit. ADM REQ: Must have mental illness diagnosis or family member. SERVES: Temecula Valley.

NAMI-WESTERN REGION

Natl Alliance on Mental Illness
P.O. Box 4145
Riverside, CA 92514
(951) 369-1913

Support group for family and friends of the mentally ill. The group meets once or twice a month to receive info about mental health issues and srvs on 1st M of the month except in Aug or when a holiday lands on 1st M. Call for more info. FUNDING: Nonprofit. Free srvs. SERVES: Riverside County, Moreno Valley, Corona, Norco, Jurupa Valley/Rubidoux area.

NAR-ANON/FAMILY/HEADQUARTERS

22527 Crenshaw Blvd., Ste 200-B
Torrance, CA 90505
(310) 534-8188
(800) 477-6291

World srv office serves families and friends of drug addicts. Info & referral to self-help groups in local communities (12-Step support group for family and friends of drug abusers, similar to Al-Anon). Call for list of weekly meeting locations. 24-hr answering machine, calls returned. Additional Southern CA info at (888)297-9560. Additional helplines (714)647-7725 and (858)492-8720. FUNDING: Nonprofit. OFC HRS: M-Th 9am-5pm. Spanish spoken. SERVES: Internatl.

NARCOTIC EDU FNDN OF AMERICA

28245 Crocker Ave., Ste 230
Santa Clarita, CA 91355-1201
(661) 775-6960
(877) 775-6272
(661) 775-1648 FAX

Conducts an edu prgm revealing the dangers that result from the illicit and abusive use of narcotics and dangerous drugs so that youth and adults will be protected from both mental and physical drug dependency and harm. Prints and distributes an array of drug edu warning materials. Single copies of our various drug edu warning materials are free. A stamped, self-addressed envelope is appreciated. FUNDING: Donations, nonprofit. OFC HRS: Tu-Th 10am-5pm. SERVES: U.S.A.

NARCOTICS ANONYMOUS

So Calif Regional Serv Office, Inc.
1937 S. Myrtle Ave.
Monrovia, CA 91016
(626) 359-0084
(626) 305-0354 FAX

12-Step prgm referral to mutual NA groups. Regional helpline (800) TODAYNA. Spanish regional helpline (888) NAAHORA. FUNDING: Nonprofit. OFC HRS: Tu-F 2pm-7pm; Sat 9am-4pm. SERVES: So. Calif.

NARCOTICS ANONYMOUS

Inland Empire West Region
P.O. Box 9413
Ontario, CA 91762
(909) 622-4274

Self-help prgm with various meetings throughout the area. Helpline 24 hrs. FUNDING: Nonprofit. Spanish available upon request. Free srvs. SERVES: Pomona, Upland, Ontario, Chino, Claremont, Montclair, Rancho, La Verne, Chino Hills.

NARCOTICS ANONYMOUS

World Service Office
P.O. Box 9999
Van Nuys, CA 91409-9999
(818) 773-9999
(818) 700-0700 FAX

Internatl community organization of recovering addicts who meet regularly to help each other recover from the disease of addiction. FUNDING: Literature sales, nonprofit. OFC HRS: M-F 9am-5pm. Spanish, German & French spoken. Free srvs. Some publications available for a fee. SERVES: U.S.A. & Internatl.

NATL ALLIANCE ON MENTAL ILLNESS

See also "NAMI"

NATL ASSN FOR SHOPLIFTING PREVENTION

380 N. Broadway, Ste 306
Jericho, NY 11753
(800) 848-9595
(516) 932-0165
(516) 932-9393 FAX

Adult & juvenile home study & class prgms, self-help groups, info & referral to counseling for individuals with shoplifting problems. FUNDING: Client fees, nonprofit. OFC HRS: M-F 9am-5pm, EST. Spanish spoken. Some set fees, sliding fee scale. SERVES: U.S.A.

NATL ASSN OF ANOREXIA NERVOSA & ASSOCIATED DISORDERS

P.O. Box 640
Naperville, IL 60566
(630) 577-1330
(847) 831-3765 FAX

Works to prevent and alleviate the problems of eating disorders. Referrals to therapists, self-help prgms & groups, hotline counseling, extensive edu & prevention prgms. Early detection packets for schools and other groups, advocacy campaigns to protect potential victims of eating disorders. FUNDING: Nonprofit. OFC HRS: M-F 9am-5pm, CST. Spanish spoken. Free srvs. SERVES: U.S.A.

NATL BRAIN TUMOR FOUNDATION

22 Battery St., Ste 612
San Francisco, CA 94111-5520
(800) 934-2873
(415) 834-9970
(415) 834-9980 FAX

Raises funds for research to treat and cure brain tumors and provides info, edu and support to patients, family members and friends. Publishes brochures and quarterly newsletter. Some Spanish publications. FUNDING: Nonprofit. OFC HRS: M-F 9am-5pm. SERVES: U.S.A.

NATL CHILDHOOD CANCER FNDN

440 E. Huntington Dr., Ste 400
Arcadia, CA 91066-6012

(800) 458-6223

Organization dedicated to childhood cancer research. Patients, families and health professionals can locate info and assist by visiting (www.curesearch.org). FUNDING: Nonprofit. OFC HRS: M-F 8:30am-5pm. SERVES: U.S.A.

NATL FIBROMYALGIA ASSN

2121 S. Towne Centre Place, Ste 300
Anaheim, CA 92806
(714) 921-0150
(714) 921-6920 FAX

Dedicated to fibromyalgia, a chronic pain disorder. Develops and executes prgms dedicated to improving the quality of life. Efforts include patient edu and assistance, healthcare, provider edu, awareness outreach, advocacy and the facilitation of research. Visit (www.fmaware.org). FUNDING: Nonprofit. OFC HRS: M-F 8:30am-5pm. SERVES: U.S.A.

NATL HYDROCEPHALUS FOUNDATION

12413 Centralia Rd.
Lakewood, CA 90715-1653
(888) 857-3434
(562) 924-6666

Offers brochures, help guides, a reference library, videos & CDs on hydrocephalus. Several support groups and assist in starting new ones. Publishes quarterly newsletter: Life~Line. Visit (www.nhfonline.org) for more info. FUNDING: Nonprofit. Free srvs.

NATL SPASMODIC TORTICOLLIS ASSN

Also known as Cervical Dystonia
9920 Talbert Ave.
Fountain Valley, CA 92708
(800) 487-8385
(714) 378-9837
(714) 378-7830 FAX

Resources and info for physicians who treat this debilitating neurological movement disorder. Also offers support group contacts. FUNDING: Nonprofit. OFC HRS: M-F 8am-5pm. SERVES: U.S.A.

NATL STUTTERING ASSOCIATION

119 W. 40th Street, 14th Fl.
New York, NY 10018
(800) 937-8888
(212) 944-8244 FAX

Info & referral srvs regarding stuttering. FUNDING: Nonprofit. OFC HRS: M-F 8am-5pm, EST. SERVES: U.S.A.

NATL STUTTERING ASSOCIATION

Formerly Natl Stuttering Project
Riverside, CA 92522
(909) 790-2363
(909) 790-0074 FAX

Supportive, tension-free environment for people who stutter. Contact Ron Mitchell at the number above or e-mail: (ron.mitchell3@verizon.net). Group meets on the 2nd Sun of each month at 6pm in the edu trailers at Kaiser Hospital in Riverside. SERVES: Inland Empire.

NEW HOPE CRISIS COUNSELING

Crystal Cathedral
12141 Lewis St.
Garden Grove, CA 92840
(714) 639-4673
(714) 971-4327 FAX

24-hr phone counseling and online counseling in a pvt chat room for all types of problems: crisis intervention, suicide prev, info & referral. Srvs provided by trained & caring volunteers. Prospective volunteers call (714) 971-4123 or e-mail (quinnw@crystalcathedral.org). Hotline (714) NEW-HOPE. Teenline: M-F 4pm-10pm, (714) 639-TEEN. Visit (www.newhopenow.org). FUNDING: Church, donations, nonprofit. OFC HRS: M-F 9am-5pm. Crisis helplines 24 hrs, 7 days. Spanish spoken. Free srvs. SERVES: U.S.A.

NICOTINE ANONYMOUS/SO CALIF

(800) 642-0666

24-hr message refers caller to mutual self-help groups for smokers. Based on 12-Step prgm. FUNDING: Nonprofit. SERVES: So. Calif.

OPEN DOORS SUPPORT GROUPS

Riverside Co. Dept. of Mental Health
9707 Magnolia Ave.
Riverside, CA 92503
(951) 358-6858

Support groups for parents/caregivers who are raising a child with mental health, emotional or behavioral challenges. Meets 4th Th of the month at 6pm. Call for more details. Free srvs. Child care available for $2 per child, per hour. Call ahead for these srvs. SERVES: Riverside Co.

OVERCOMER'S OUTREACH

12828 Acheson Dr.
Whittier, CA 90601
(800) 310-3001
(562) 698-9000
(562) 698-2211 FAX

Referrals and worldwide Christian 12-Step recovery support groups dealing with addictive or compulsive behaviors for all of the family. FUNDING: Nonprofit. OFC HRS: M-F 9am-4pm. SERVES: U.S.A. & internatl.

OVEREATERS ANONYMOUS/HDQR

World Service Office
P.O. Box 44020
6075 Zenith Court N.E.
Rio Rancho, NM 87124
(505) 891-2664
(505) 891-4320 FAX

Referral to Overeaters Anonymous (OA) meetings throughout U.S. Info & literature for compulsive overeaters. 12-Step prgm deals with food and compulsive overeating. FUNDING: Donation, nonprofit. OFC HRS: M-F 8am-4:30pm, MST. No fees or dues. SERVES: Internatl.

OVEREATERS ANONYMOUS/I.E.

Inland Empire Intergroup
P.O. Box 56021
Riverside, CA 92517
(951) 715-2080
(951) 681-9713 FAX

Self-help group patterned after AA. Call for meeting locations, dates & times. Goal is to stop compulsive eating. FUNDING: Contributions, nonprofit. OFC HRS: M-F 9am-5pm. Free srvs. No dues, fees or weigh-ins. SERVES: Inland Empire.

P.A.D.R.E. FOUNDATION

Diabetic Support for Kids
455 S. Main St.
Orange, CA 92868
(714) 532-8330
(714) 532-8398 FAX

PADRE (Pediatric Adol Diabetes Research & Edu). Provides numerous edu & support prgms which are open to children with diabetes and their families regardless of medical provider or where they are located. Prgms include: Kids Klub (ages 5-12 yrs), Tadpoles (ages birth-5 yrs), and Parents of Children with Diabetes. Support groups meet the 2nd Tu of the month at CHOC. Also provides edu classes for caregivers, carb counting, pediatric edu, as well as family retreats, teen retreats and other events for children. For Kaiser Bellflower, RSVP to (562) 461-6184, meets 3rd Tu 7pm-8pm. DIR: Heather Speer. FUNDING: Fndn, corp, nonprofit. OFC HRS: M-F 9:30am-5:30pm. Spanish translators available. Free srvs. SERVES: L.A., Orange, Riverside & San Diego Counties.

PARENTS ANONYMOUS, INC.

675 W. Foothill Blvd., Ste 220
Claremont, CA 91711
(909) 621-6184
(909) 625-6304 FAX

Child abuse prev organization. Free weekly ongoing community-based support groups. FUNDING: Donations, govt, nonprofit. OFC HRS: M-F 8am-5pm. Spanish spoken. SERVES: U.S.A.

PARENTS OF MURDERED CHILDREN

Inland Empire Chapter
P.O. Box 9413
Alto Loma, CA 91701
(909) 987-6164
(909) 652-0188 FAX

Three meeting locations: 1st Th, Preciado Funeral Home 923 W. Mill St., San Bernardino; 2nd Th at St. Paul's Episcopal Church 242 E. Alvarado St., Pomona; 3rd Th at St. Mark's Episcopal Church, 330 E. 16th Street, Upland. All meeting times begin at 7pm. Spanish available at all meetings. Help available over the phone as well. FUNDING: Nonprofit. OFC HRS: Call anytime. Spanish spoken. Free srvs. SERVES: Inland Empire.

PARENTS OF MURDERED CHILDREN

National Headquarters
100 E. 8th Street, Ste 202
Cincinnati, OH 45202
(513) 721-5683
(888) 818-7662
(513) 345-4489 FAX

Info, advocacy & newsletters to survivors. Crisis calls taken 24 hrs. FUNDING: Donation, nonprofit. OFC HRS: M-F 8am-5pm, EST. Free srvs. SERVES: U.S.A.

PARENTS WITHOUT PARTNERS (ADMIN)

Internatl Headquarters
1650 S. Dixie Hwy., Ste 510
Boca Raton, FL 33432
(800) 637-7974
(561) 391-8833
(561) 395-8557 FAX

PWP serves single parents, of any age, who are divorced, widowed, never married or separated, whether or not they have child custody. Request literature by mail. FUNDING: Membership dues, nonprofit. OFC HRS: M-F 8:30am-5pm, EST. SERVES: U.S.A.

PEOPLE WITH DISABILITIES SUPPORT

Community Access Center
6848 Magnolia Ave., Ste 150
Riverside, CA 92506

(951) 274-0358
(951) 274-0833 FAX

Assists people with disabilities in living independently within the community. Info & referrals for wide range of needs including registry (interpreters for deaf), attendants, housing, advocacy, peer support and assistive technology. For TDD, call (951) 274-0834. OFC HRS: M-F 8:30am-5pm. Spanish spoken. ASL available. SERVES: Riverside County.

POINT OF GRACE CHRISTIAN FELLOWSHIP
9774 Hawthorne Dr., Ste 901
Rancho Cucamonga, CA 91730
(909) 944-9909
(909) 944-7789 FAX

Community closet, food pantry, learning center, behavioral support groups such as Celebrate Recovery, divorce care ministry based on demand, anger mgmt for kids & teens, Steps to Hope. FUNDING: Nonprofit, donations. OFC HRS: Tu-Th 12noon-4pm. SERVES: San Bernardino County.

POMONA VALLEY HOSPITAL MED CTR
Women's & Children's Srvs
1798 N. Garey Ave.
Pomona, CA 91767
(909) 620-6663
(909) 629-0890 FAX

Childbirth classes, baby express, CPR, boot camp for dads, safe sitter prgm, community resources, & physician referrals. Srvs include: labor, delivery, recovery suites, perinatal diagnostic/treatment ctr, lactation consultation and maternal/neonatal transport from other hospitals. FUNDING: Nonprofit. OFC HRS: M-F 9am-4:30pm. But hours vary depending on dept. Spanish spoken. SERVES: Inland, San Gabriel Valleys.

POMONA VALLEY HOSPITAL MED CTR
Family Education & Resource Ctr
1770 N. Orange Grove Ave.
Pomona, CA 91767
(909) 865-9858
(909) 865-9782
(909) 629-0890 FAX

Free referrals to support groups, physicians and community resources. Offers ongoing classes & support prgms. FUNDING: Nonprofit. OFC HRS: M-F 8:30am-5pm; Sat 8:30am-1pm. Spanish spoken. SERVES: Inland & San Gabriel Valleys.

POSSABILITIES PROGRAM
Loma Linda University Med Ctr
East Campus
25333 Barton Rd.
Loma Linda, CA 92354
(877) 558-6248
(909) 558-6384 FAX

A community outreach prgm for persons with physical disabilities. Peer mentoring, social and recreational activities, support groups, discount prescriptions, wheelchair sports, etc. Free membership. SERVES: San Bernardino County.

POSTPARTUM SUPPORT INTERNATL
706 S.W. 54th Avenue
Portland, OR 97219
(503) 894-9453
(503) 894-9452 FAX

Promotes awareness, prev & treatment of mental health issues related to childbearing. Provides resources to local social support networks and support groups, info on diagnosis & treatment of postpartum mood & anxiety disorders, postpartum chat rooms & edu. Professional memberships available. Visit (www.postpartum.net). Helpline: (800) 944-4773. FUNDING: Nonprofit. OFC HRS: M-F 9am-3pm. Free srvs. SERVES: Internatl.

PROJECT SISTER
Sexual Assault Crisis & Prev Srvs
P.O. Box 1369
Pomona, CA 91769-1369
(909) 623-1619
(909) 622-8389 FAX

24-hr sexual assault crisis hotline; personal accompaniment to hospital, police station and court; in-person counseling; support groups for rape. AMAC (Adults Molested As Children) and incest survivors, referrals to other agencies, community edu (including sexual harassment) and teen date rape awareness & self-protection classes. Srvs for seniors also available. 24-hr helpline (909) 626-4357 and (626) 966-4155. FUNDING: United Way, Office of Emerg Srvs, donations, CDBG grants, nonprofit. OFC HRS: M-F 8am-5pm. Spanish spoken. Free srvs, except for counseling & groups on a sliding fee scale. No one turned away for lack of funds. SERVES: East San Gabriel Valley, Pomona Valley & West San Bernardino County.

PROSTATE CANCER SUPPORT GOUP
Riverside Medical Clinic Foundation
P.O. Box 2605
7150 Brockton Ave., Ste 201
Riverside, CA 92516
(951) 682-2753
(951) 682-2755 FAX

Support group for prostate cancer meets 2nd Th 7pm-9pm. Doors open at 6pm. Walk in or call. Also have a non-lending medical library that can be reached at (951) 782-3783. OFC HRS: M-F 9am-5pm SERVES: Riverside County.

PULMONARY HYPERTENSION SUPPORT GROUP
St. Bernardine Medical Center
2101 N. Waterman Ave.
San Bernardino, CA 92404
(909) 883-5508

Meets 1st Sat every other month from 11am-2pm in the Matich Conference Center. Visit (www.PhAssociation.org). SERVES: San Bernardino County.

RAINBOW PRIDE YOUTH ALLIANCE
P.O. Box 312
985 Kendall Dr., Ste A
San Bernardino, CA 92407

Provides support for LGBT youth. Srvs include support group, outreach, wellness classes and recreational activities. Group for ages 13-20 yrs meets on F from 7pm-10pm. Group for ages 18-25 yrs meets M from 6:30pm-9:30pm. All events are helled at the Gabrielle Mulvane Community Center, 860 Gilbert St., San Bernardino 92404. Email (info@rpya.org) and visit (www.rpya.org). FUNDING: Nonprofit. SERVES: Inland Empire.

RANCHO COMMUNITY CHURCH
31300 Rancho Community Way

Temecula, CA 92592
(951) 303-6789
(951) 303-6066 FAX

Celebrate Recovery meets Th at 6:30pm, including large group worship, lesson time and small groups. Several support groups available. Groups include addiction recovery, grief, chronic pain, divorce/separation relief, and families of those with Alzheimer's. Call for dates and times. Groups open to the public and anyone is welcome at any time during the year. FUNDING: Nonprofit. OFC HRS: M-F 9am-4pm. Spanish spoken. SERVES: Riverside County.

RECOVERY, INC.
Grand Terrace
(323) 651-2170

Mental health, self-help support to help reduce nervous symptoms and fears such as depression, anxiety, social phobias, bipolar and anger. Voluntary participation. Program similar to cognitive behavioral therapy. See website or call for more info. FUNDING: Nonprofit. Spanish spoken. Free srvs, but donations accepted. SERVES: Riverside County.

REDLANDS COMMUNITY HOSPITAL
350 Terracina Blvd.
Redlands, CA 92373
(800) 367-8336

Visit (www.redlandshospital.com/support_groups.htm) for info and phone numbers for various support groups. Al-Anon, Alateen, AA, Alzheimer's, Compassionate Friends, eating disorders, caregiver of brain impaired, etc. SERVES: San Bernardino County.

REST MINISTRIES, INC.
Chronic Illness/Pain Support
P.O. Box 502928
San Diego, CA 92150
(888) 751-7378
(800) 933-1078 FAX

Christian organization that offers emotional, relational and spiritual support for people who live with chronic illness or pain. Offers monthly support newsletter, Bible studies, pen pal prgm, e-mail support list, etc. Resources for caregivers and/or spouses. Establishes chronic illness and pain support groups "HopeKeepers" in churches & communities. Provides churches with tools to effectively minister & outreach to people who live with chronic conditions. FUNDING: Donations, nonprofit. OFC HRS: Varies. ADM REQ: People who live with chronic illness or pain. Free srvs, resources such as books may have small fees. SERVES: U.S.A.

RESTLESS LEGS SYNDROME SUPPORT GRP
Coachella Valley
Rancho Mirage, CA 92270-5200
(760) 285-2231

Call or e-mail for meeting days and times. (charmaigne_menn@earthlink.net). SERVES: Coachella Valley.

RITA PROJECT, INC.
Mailing Address
2046 Hillhurst Ave.
Los Angeles, CA 90027
(866) 775-7482

Rita (Sanskrit for truth) is a global movement to stop suicide and celebrate life. Devoted to using the arts to help survivors of suicide connect with the power of creation, and in doing so, foster transformation. Prgms offered through studios, workshops & exhibitions. Assist with healing, suicide prev, edu and public awareness on the importance of the arts to mental health. Visit (www.ritaproject.org). Studios are held weekly at the Bergamot Cafe, 2525 Michigan Ave., #A-3, Santa Monica, CA 90404. Please call to register. FUNDING: Nonprofit. OFC HRS: 24 hrs. ADM REQ: Ages 18 yrs+. SERVES: So. Calif.

RIVERSIDE HOSPICE
6052 Magnolia Ave.
Riverside, CA 92506
(951) 274-0710
(951) 274-9551 FAX

In-home support and care for terminal patients and their families, assist with practical needs, personal care and edu, volunteer prgm, bereavement groups in English and Spanish, grief counseling referrals to hospices nationwide. Some printed materials in Spanish. Companion Connection for elderly. FUNDING: United Way, donations, grants. OFC HRS: M-F 9am-5pm. Spanish spoken. ADM REQ: Terminal diagnosis. Accepts Medi-Cal & pvt insurance. SERVES: Riverside, Moreno Valley, Corona, Norco, and parts of San Bernardino County.

SAFE HARBOR
Olive Branch Church
7702 El Cerrito Rd.
Corona, CA 92881-4295
(951) 279-4477
(951) 520-9797 FAX

Christ-centered, 12-Step recovery prgm. Support groups for all types of problems & addictions including: food, sex or relationship addictions, co-dependency and chemical dependency. Meets W at 7pm. Call for location. FUNDING: Nonprofit. OFC HRS: M-F 9am-5pm. SERVES: Riverside County.

SAN BERNARDINO COMM/WOMEN
Commission on the Status of Women
157 W. 5th Street, 1st Fl.
San Bernardino, CA 92415-0440
(909) 387-5543
(909) 387-8950 FAX

Monthly meetings on the 4th Tu 5:15pm, open to the public. Advisory to the Board of Supervisors. Increases awareness of women's issues through prgms and brochures offers referral srvs to women. OFC HRS: M-F 8am-5pm.

SEX ADDICTS ANONYMOUS (S.A.A.)
(213) 896-2964
(800) 477-8191

Natl 12-Step prgm encourages men and women participants to define their sexual sobriety through the boundaries of a "sex plan" which is evolved by working with other recovering members. Prgm for partners of sex addicts is called C.O.S.A. The (213) number serves L.A., Riverside, and San Bernardino Counties. Orange Co. (714) 254-7952. Santa Barbara (805) 961-2591. San Francisco (415) 364-1402. Outside Calif (800) 477-8191. FUNDING: Nonprofit. OFC HRS: 24-hr recording. Free srvs. SERVES: Calif.

SEXAHOLICS ANONYMOUS (S.A.)
Coachella Valley
(760) 837-7291

12-Step recovery prgm is for those who want to stop their own destructive behaviors. Recorded message states meeting locations in the Coachella Valley. FUNDING: Nonprofit. SERVES: Coachella Valley.

SEXAHOLICS ANONYMOUS (S.A.)
Central Office
P.O. Box 3565
Brentwood, TN 37024-3565
(615) 370-6062
(866) 424-8777
(615) 370-0882 FAX

12-Step recovery prgm for those who want to stop sexually self-destructive thinking and behavior. This prgm is also available to sexaholics in correctional institutions (literature srv; sponsor-by-mail srvs where inmates are linked with members outside who can help them work the 12-Step prgm; support for starting SA meetings at prisons; connection srv that helps parolees find the nearest SA contact). FUNDING: Nonprofit. OFC HRS: M-F 9am-5pm. SERVES: U.S.A.

SEXUAL COMPULSIVES ANONYMOUS/SCA
Old Chelsea Station
P.O. Box 1585
New York, NY 10011
(800) 977-4325

Internatl 12-Step prgm for those with a desire to stop having compulsive sex. Call for local meeting times and locations. FUNDING: Donations, nonprofit. OFC HRS: 24-hr recording. Callers leave a message for a return call. Some Spanish spoken. SERVES: San Francisco, L.A., Orange & San Diego Counties.

SIDS NETWORK
Website with up-to-date info and support for those who have experienced SIDS or infant death. Visit (www.sids-network.org). No direct srvs. FUNDING: Nonprofit, donations. SERVES: U.S.A.

SILVER LAKES COMMUNITY CHURCH
P.O. Box 1073
14766 Smithson Rd.
Helendale, CA 92342
(760) 952-1485
(760) 955-3797 FAX

Variety of srvs including: edu, resources, Bible classes, Christian counseling. FUNDING: Donations, Born Again Treasures (thrift store). OFC HRS: Tu-Th 9am-4pm. No fees. SERVES: High Desert.

SINGLE PARENT SUPPORT GROUP
Covina Valley Chapter
P.O. Box 1166
Covina, CA 91722
(626) 294-3211

Group and individual activities for parents who are divorced, widowed, single or separated. To become a member, call Trina at (626)332-9350. Many activities available. Dances held 2nd F at Elk Lodge in West Covina. FUNDING: Nonprofit. SERVES: San Gabriel Valley.

SMOKENDERS
P.O. Box 316
Kensington, MD 20895
(800) 828-4357
(301) 563-6192 FAX

Self-study prgms including: workbook, telephone support and CDs that teach how to quit smoking. FUNDING: Nonprofit. Fee $125 plus shipping cost. SERVES: U.S.A.

SMOKING CESSATION
See also "American Lung Assn/Inland Co."

SOS (SECULAR ORGANIZATION FOR SOBRIETY)
S.O.S. National Clearinghouse
4773 Hollywood Blvd.
Hollywood, CA 90027
(323) 666-4295
(323) 666-4271 FAX

S.O.S. is an alternative recovery method for alcoholics or drug addicts uncomfortable with spiritual content of the 12-Step prgms. Goal is to promote sobriety. More than 2,000 groups nationwide. Write to above address for a list of local groups. FUNDING: Nonprofit. SERVES: U.S.A.

STARLIGHT CHILDREN'S FOUNDATION
5757 Wilshire Blvd., Ste M-100
Los Angeles, CA 90036
(310) 479-1212
(800) 315-1212
(310) 479-1235 FAX

When a child or teenager has a serious medical condition, everyone in the famliy is affected. The Starlight Fndn has dedicated itself to helping seriously ill children and their families cope with pain, fear and isolation through entertainment, edu, and family activities. Starlight's prgms have been proven to distract children from their pain, help them better understand and manage their illness. Connects families facing similar challenges so that no one feels alone. Outpatient, hospital-based and web offerings. To learn more, visit (www.starlight.org). FUNDING: Nonprofit. OFC HRS: M-F 8am-5pm. Accepts donations. SERVES: U.S.A., Canada, Australia, UK & Japan.

STROKE ASSOCIATION OF SO CALIF
2125 Arizona Ave., Ste 205
Santa Monica, CA 90404
(310) 575-1699
(310) 575-1696 FAX

Support groups for stroke survivors and caregivers, phone helpline, home & hospital visitations, info & referral, literature available. Volunteers needed. FUNDING: Donations, nonprofit. OFC HRS: M-F 9am-5pm. Free srvs. SERVES: So. Calif.

STROKE INFO & REFERRAL
See "American Stroke Assn/Heart Assn"

STROKE REHABILITATION GROUP
P.O. Box 1135
Cathedral City, CA 92235-1135
(760) 322-3995

Support group for stroke victims. Call for meeting times/location. SERVES: Cathedral City.

STUMPS 'R US
2109 Skycrest Dr., Ste 1
Walnut Creek, CA 94595
(925) 952-4408
(925) 952-4427 FAX

Network of amputees & their friends & families offering support & info through humor. Social events, Gimpy magazine, newsletter. Also free flight instructions for every member who joins.

FUNDING: Nonprofit. OFC HRS: 24 hrs. SERVES: Internatl.

SUICIDE SURVIVORS

San Antonio Community Hospital
999 San Bernardino Rd., Ste 105
Upland, CA 91786
(909) 393-2563
(909) 263-7951

Support group for those who have lost loved ones through suicide. Meets the 1st & 3rd W each month 7pm-8:30pm at Pomona Valley Medical Ctr. SERVES: San Bernardino County.

SUPPORT GROUPS

Grove Community Church
19900 Grove Community Dr.
Riverside, CA 92508
(951) 571-9090

Offers a variety of support groups and classes including: chemical dependency, body image for women, grief, divorce, co-ed anger mgmt, sexual integrity for men and for women. Call for dates and times. Also recovery worship service F 7pm. Counseling available as well. FUNDING: Nonprofit. ADM REQ: Please call as groups and classes are subject to change. SERVES: Riverside County.

SURVIVORS OF TORTURE INTERNATL

P.O. Box 151240
San Diego, CA 92175-1240
(619) 278-2400
(619) 294-9405 FAX

Case mgmt srvs & referrals for psych, medical, & social srvs for survivors of torture and their families. For emerg, call (619) 278-2403; intake (619) 278-2404. Info provided for So. Calif, assist primarily for San Diego. FUNDING: Nonprofit. OFC HRS: M-F 8am-5pm. Chaldean, Kurdish, Arabic, Cambodian, Farsi, French & Spanish spoken. Interpretation for all languages available. Free srvs. Insurance utilized where applicable. Referrals to Medi-Cal providers. Accepts workers' compensation. SERVES: So. Calif.

SUSAN G. KOMEN BREAST CANCER FNDN

Orange County Affiliate
3191-A Airport Loop Dr.
Costa Mesa, CA 92626
(714) 957-9157
(800) 462-9273
(714) 957-9155 FAX

Natl organization working to eradicate breast cancer as a life-threatening disease through edu, research, screening and treatment. FUNDING: Grants, nonprofit. OFC HRS: M-F 8:30am-5:30pm. SERVES: U.S.A.

SUSAN G. KOMEN BREAST CANCER FNDN

Inland Empire Affilate
43397 Business Park Dr., Ste D-9
Temecula, CA 92590
(951) 676-7465
(951) 676-7211 FAX

Fundraising, community outreach & edu. Volunteers welcome. FUNDING: Nonprofit, donations, fundraising. OFC HRS: M-F 9am-4pm. SERVES: Riverside County.

TALK ABOUT CURING AUTISM (TACA)

3070 Bristol Ave., Ste 340
Costa Mesa, CA 92626
(949) 640-4401
(949) 640-4424 FAX

Info and connection to improve the quality of life of people with autism and their families. For families who have just received the autism diagnosis, TACA aims to speed up the cycle time that gets them from the diagnosis to the appropriate info that will lead to effective treatment and support. TACA builds the autism community by connecting people with each other & the professionals who can help them. FUNDING: Nonprofit. OFC HRS: M-F 9am-5pm. SERVES: So. Calif.

TALK IT OVER WITH MAMA

250 S. Grand Ave., Ste 402
Los Angeles, CA 90012
(323) 525-1393
(313) 932-8202 FAX

An online resource for parental advice and guidance in solving every day problems. Advice provided by seniors ages 60 yrs+ who share their experience and wit earned through raising children and grandchildren. Also, if you need advice from Papa, indicate that in the request. Visit (www.talkitoverwithmama.com). Spanish, Vietnamese spoken. SERVES: L.A. & Riverside Counties.

TEEN IMPACT

Children's Hospital of Los Angeles Center for Cancer & Blood Diseases
4650 Sunset Blvd., MS #99
Los Angeles, CA 90027
(323) 361-4660
(323) 361-7128 FAX

Psycho-social support for teens, pre-teens, and young adults undergoing post-treatment for cancer and their families. Self-referred or recommended by medical staff. Srvs include: twice-monthly support groups, 3-day retreats, adventure therapy getaways, social events, referral srvs & mentoring prgm. Can attend from any hospital. Call for days and times. FUNDING: Nonprofit. Spanish spoken. Free srvs. SERVES: Calif.

THE AMPUTEE COALITION OF AMERICA

(www.amputee-coalition.org)
900 E. Hill Ave., Ste 205
Knoxville, TN 37915-2566
(888) 267-5669
(865) 525-7917 FAX

Online community lists resources for amputees. Support groups, edu, advocacy, annual conference. For TTY, call (865) 525-4512 FUNDING: Nonprofit. SERVES: U.S.A.

THE COMPASSIONATE FRIENDS

See "Compassionate Friends/..."

THE GROVE COMMUNITY CHURCH

19900 Grove Community Dr.
Riverside, CA 92508
(951) 571-9090
(951) 571-9091 FAX

Celebrate Recovery, a faith-based, 12-Step support group dealing with anger mgmt, chemical dependency, co-dependency, eating disorders and sexual addictions, meets M at 7pm. Recovery worship service F at 7pm. Pre-marital, individual & family counseling and various support groups available. FUNDING: Nonprofit. OFC HRS: M-F 8am-5pm. Sat sessions by appt. Must call to register for counseling. Fees vary. $40 before 5pm, $50 after 5pm. No one turned away due to lack of funds. SERVES: Riverside.

THE JACQUELINE SIDMAN HEALTH FNDN

4199 Campus Dr., Ste 550
Irvine, CA 92612
(949) 251-9550
(949) 509-6599 FAX

An effective drug-free treatment for the recovery of behavioral and physical health from addiction, through the use of the subconscious mind. FUNDING: Nonprofit. OFC HRS: M-Sun 11:30am-6:30pm. SERVES: Calif.

THE OTHER BAR NATIONAL HOTLINE

(800) 222-0767

24-hr hotline for confidential counseling and referral assist for judges, lawyers, law students and other legal professionals affected by alcohol and drug abuse. Also offers support group meetings throughout Calif. FUNDING: Nonprofit, State Bar, donations. Free srvs. SERVES: Calif.

THE RELATIONAL CENTER

Formerly The Center for Relational Studies
5486 Wilshire Blvd.
Los Angeles, CA 90036
(323) 935-1807
(323) 935-1171 FAX

Affordable counseling/mental health srvs. Comprehensive assessment, resource coordination, individual, couple, family and group psychotherapy. All care srvs are designed and delivered in a way that is culturally senstive and respectful of differences. Assist consumers to organize self-advocacy groups. Harm reduction approach is used when dealing with addiction issues. FUNDING: Nonprofit. OFC HRS: M, Th 9am-8pm; Tu 9am-5pm; W 9am-8:30pm; F 9am-5:30pm; Sat 9am-2pm. Spanish spoken. SERVES: L.A. & San Bernardino Counties.

TOPS (TAKE OFF POUNDS SENSIBLY)

Headquarters
4575 S. 5th Street
Milwaukee, WI 53207
(800) 932-8677
(414) 482-4620

Non-commercial weight control organization. Weekly support groups. Call for local chapter. FUNDING: Nonprofit. OFC HRS: M-F 8am-4:30pm, CST. Annual membership fee of $24. SERVES: U.S.A.

TRINITY EVANGELICAL CHURCH

Pathways Support Group Ministries
1551 Reservoir Rd.
Redlands, CA 92373
(909) 335-7333
(909) 798-7096 FAX

Offers a variety of support groups including: divorce care groups for adults and children ages 5-12 yrs, grief share group, group for caregivers, struggling relationships. Also offers "Every Man's Challenge" prgm for men who battle sexually compulsive issues and special prgms for women who have gone through an abortion, struggle with sexual matters, or have been sexually abused. Child care available by arrangement for children ages birth-12 yrs. FUNDING: Nonprofit. OFC HRS: M-F 8am-5pm. ADM REQ: Some classes require pre-registration, call ahead. SERVES: San Bernardino County.

UMBRELLA MINISTRIES

Southwest Christian Church
77-701 Fred Waring Dr.

Palm Desert, CA 92255
(760) 775-0296

Support group for moms who have experienced the loss of a child. Call Diane Jacobson at (760) 469-3347 for meeting time and location. SERVES: Riverside County.

UNITED OSTOMY ASSN OF AMERICA
P.O. Box 512
Northfield, MN 55057
(800) 826-0826
(615) 799-5915 FAX

Moral support, emotional aid to those individuals who have had or will have ileostomy, colostomy, urostomy or continent procedure surgery. Will refer to local chapter. Please visit (www.uoaa.org). FUNDING: Nonprofit. OFC HRS: M-F 8:00am-4:00pm CST Chapter & national dues. SERVES: U.S.A.

UNO MAS! DOWN SYNDROME ONLINE
Mailing Address
40485 Murrieta Hot Springs Rd., Ste 207
Murrieta, CA 92563

Online sharing and support for parents of children born with Down's Syndrome: activities, bulletin & message board, share stories, etc. Visit (www.unomas21.com). Donations accepted to maintain the site. SERVES: Riverside County.

VINEYARD ANAHEIM
Recovery Solutions
5340 E. La Palma Ave.
Anaheim, CA 92807
(714) 777-4777
(714) 777-5423 FAX

Christ-centered, 12-Step prgm. Speaker's meeting in rm. 205 on M from 7pm-9pm, includes 15 minutes of worship and a weekly message on some aspect of Christ-centered recovery or one of the 12-Steps. Small groups are held following the speaker's meeting. Current groups: anger mgmt, CEA-HOW, chemical/alcohol dependency, co-dependency, Peace with the Plate, SA, S-Anon. Free child care. FUNDING: Nonprofit. OFC HRS: M-Th 8:30am-5pm. SERVES: So. Calif.

VITAS SUPPORT GROUP SRVS
1845 Business Center Dr., Ste 120
San Bernardino, CA 92408
(800) 394-6774

Support groups for children, adults and families. Please contact for info on types of groups and meetings times/dates. SERVES: Inland Empire.

VITILIGO SUPPORT INTERNATL
P.O. Box 4008
Valley Village, CA 91617-0008
(818) 752-9002

Offers vitiligo edu, research and awareness for those whose lives have been affected by the disease. Also sponsors support groups and advocacy. FUNDING: Nonprofit, donations. Free srvs. SERVES: U.S.A.

WELL SPOUSE ASSOCIATION
63 W. Main St., Ste H
Freehold, NJ 07728
(800) 838-0879
(732) 577-8899
(732) 577-8644 FAX

Volunteer-based natl organization focused on providing emotional support to husbands, wives and partners caring for spouses with chronic illnesses and/or long-term disabilities. FUNDING: Fees, donations, grants, nonprofit. OFC HRS: M-F 10am-3pm, EST. SERVES: U.S.A.

WOMEN AGAINST GUN VIOLENCE
8800 Venice Blvd., Ste 304
Los Angeles 90234
(310) 204-2348
(310) 204-6643 FAX

Edu on the dangers of firearms, advocacy for gun safety measures. FUNDING: Nonprofit. OFC HRS: M-F 9am-5pm. Spanish spoken. SERVES: Calif.

WOMEN FOR SOBRIETY
New Life Prgm
P.O. Box 618
Quakertown, PA 18951-0618
(215) 536-8026
(215) 538-9026 FAX

New Life Prgm is a self-help prgm that focuses on the special needs of female alcoholics. Send a self-addressed, stamped envelope to the address above or call or visit (www.womenforsobriety.org). FUNDING: Donations, nonprofit. OFC HRS: M-F 9am-4:30pm, EST. ADM REQ: Sincere desire to stop drinking. Donations requested. SERVES: U.S.A.

WOMEN HELPING WOMEN NEWSLETTER
www.femalegamblers.info

Online site designed by women gamblers for women gamblers in recovery from their addiction. Also visit (www.grippedbygambling.com). FUNDING: Nonprofit.

WOMEN HELPING WOMEN SRVS
543 N. Fairfax Ave.
Los Angeles, CA 90036
(323) 651-2930
(323) 651-5348 FAX

Callers receive emotional support and practical info on any issue. Support groups dealing with issues such as divorce, single parenting, domestic violence, self-esteem, individual counseling, case mgmt and volunteering. Talkline counselor training, specialized srvs for residents of CIPA3, including case mgmt, counseling, workshops & resources. Also offers edu scholarships. Talkline:(877)655-3807. FUNDING: Natl Council of Jewish Women, fndn, donations, nonprofit. Talkline hrs: M, Tu, Th 10am-12:30pm; W 6pm-8pm. 24-hr voicemail, calls returned. For srvs at this physical location, must have an appt. Spanish, Hebrew & French spoken. Free srvs or on low sliding fee scale. SERVES: So. Calif.

WOMEN'S CANCER NETWORK
www.wcn.org
230 W. Monroe, Ste 2528
Chicago, IL 60606
(800) 444-4441
(312) 578-1439
(312) 578-9769 FAX

Interactive website designed to educate the community regarding gynecologic cancers. Learn more about treatment options and clinical trials and understand the disease. Contact WCN for copies of brochures. FUNDING: Nonprofit, donations, fndns. SERVES: U.S.A.

WORTHWHILE REFERRAL SOURCES
13547 Ventura Blvd., Ste 374

Sherman Oaks, CA 91423
(818) 995-6646
(818) 995-4515 FAX

Referrals to a variety of srvs including legal, medical, psychological and many others. Also networking meetings, business consulting, workshops & seminars. FUNDING: Members, ad fees. OFC HRS: M-F 9am-5pm. SERVES: L.A., Ventura, Orange, Riverside & San Bernardino Counties.

WWW.AGING-PARENTS-AND-ELDER-CARE .COM
950 Tower Lane, 6th Fl.
San Mateo, CA 94404

Helpful website for caregivers. Free referral srv, newsletter. SERVES: U.S.A.

WWW.BEFRIENDERS.ORG

Offers anonymous, non-immediate, supportive email srvs for those having thoughts of suicide. This is not an emergency service. Trained volunteers answer emails on a daily basis and all go by the pseudonym "Jo." Email (jo@samaritans.org). Website also offers a directory of emotional distress centers throughout the U.S.A. and internatl. FUNDING: Nonprofit. OFC HRS: 24 Hrs, 7 Days. Free srvs. SERVES: Internatl.

WWW.GLBTNEARME.ORG
The GLBT National Resource Database

Website lists over 15,000 GLBT resources including social and support resources, community centers, and youth groups. FUNDING: Nonprofit. SERVES: U.S.A.

WWW.GRANDPARENTS.COM
589 8th Avenue, 6th Fl.
New York, NY 10018
(646) 839-8800

Info website to assist grandparents with kid-friendly activities, advice for new grandparents, long-distance grandparenting, etc. SERVES: U.S.A.

WWW.GRIEFNET.ORG
P.O. Box 3272
Ann Arbor, MI 48106-3272

Website (www.griefnet.org) with resources for adults dealing with grief or loss. E-mail support groups, bookstore. Companion site for kids (www.kidsaid.com). FUNDING: Nonprofit, donations. Donation of $5 per month for each support group; no one turned away due to lack of funds. SERVES: U.S.A.

WWW.HEALTHFINDER.GOV
U.S. Dept of Health & Human Srvs
P.O. Box 113
Washington, DC 20012

Website that offers a comprehensive encyclopedia of over 1,600 entries regarding conditions & diseases, tools to check your personal health, and ways to locate a doctor or health center. FUNDING: Govt. Spanish spoken. Free srvs. SERVES: U.S.A.

WWW.IMMUNESUPPORT.COM
ProHealth
2040 Alameda Padre Serra
Santa Barbara, CA 93103
(805) 564-3064
(800) 366-6056
(805) 965-0042 FAX

Website listing info and resources for those who suffer from chronic fatigue syndrome and fibromyalgia. FUNDING: Nonprofit. OFC HRS: M-F 7am- 5pm SERVES: U.S.A.

WWW.NARCOLEPSYNETWORK.ORG

110 Ripple Lane
North Kingstown, RI 02852
(888) 292-6522
(401) 667-2523
(401) 633-6567 FAX

Edu materials, resources, and advocacy for narcolepsy. Provides assist to support groups. Also visit (www.sleepcenters.org) to locate physicians. No direct srvs. SERVES: U.S.A.

WWW.NCTEQUALITY.ORG

1325 Massachusetts Ave., NW, Ste 700
Washington, DC 20005
(202) 903-0112
(202) 393-2241 FAX

Social justice organization for transgender equality. FUNDING: Nonprofit. SERVES: U.S.A.

WWW.TRANSPLANTLIVING.ORG

(888) 894-6361

Information and resources for pre- and post-transplant patients. State listing for support groups. Use website to contact through email. FUNDING: Nonprofit. Spanish spoken. SERVES: U.S.A.

WWW.YOUNGSURVIVAL.ORG

Young Survival Coalition
61 Broadway, Ste 2235
New York, NY 10006
(877) 972-1011
(646) 257-3000
(646) 257-3030 FAX

Advocacy and support resources. Network for breast cancer survivors and their families. Telephone networking sessions and one-to-one peer support. FUNDING: Nonprofit. SERVES: U.S.A.

YWCA/RIVERSIDE

8172 Magnolia Ave.
Riverside, CA 92504
(951) 687-9922
(951) 688-5270 FAX

Program offers parenting skills classes which meet or exceed current Calif guidelines governing parenting classes. Also offers numerous support groups for parents, and anger mgmt. Also women's sobriety, TOPS, & AA meetings. Twinges in the Hinges prgm for arthritis patients. Also offers teen pregnancy prevention classes. Sober living house. FUNDING: Nonprofit, class fees, donations, United Way. OFC HRS: M-F 8am-8pm; Sat 9am-1pm. Spanish spoken. Fees for classes. Y members $10 off. SERVES: Riverside County.

Senior/Home Care/Infusion Therapy

ADDUS HEALTHCARE
35-325 Date Palm Dr., Ste 235
Cathedral City, CA 92234-7015
(760) 770-9490
(866) 601-0163
(760) 770-9401 FAX

Homecare for seniors & disabled. Respite care, homemaker srvs, companionship, eldercare mgmt. FUNDING: Nonprofit. OFC HRS: M-F 7:30am-5:30pm; 24-hr srvs. Spanish spoken. ADM REQ: Srvs ordered by M.D. Accepts Medicare, Medi-Cal, pvt pay. SERVES: Riverside County.

ADDUS HEALTHCARE
2627 W. Flordia, Ste 103
Hemet, CA 92543
(951) 652-1000
(951) 658-9981 FAX

Homecare for seniors & disabled. Skilled nursing, respite care, homemaker srvs, companionship, eldercare mgmt. FUNDING: Nonprofit. OFC HRS: M-F 7:30am-5:30pm. Spanish spoken. ADM REQ: Call home support srvs for criteria (951) 413-5050. Accepts Medicare, Medi-Cal, pvt pay. SERVES: Riverside County.

ADDUS HEALTHCARE
1660 Chicago Ave., Ste N11
Riverside, CA 92507-2048
(951) 784-5222
(951) 784-5610 FAX

Homecare for seniors & disabled. Homemaker srvs, companionship, eldercare mgmt. FUNDING: Nonprofit. OFC HRS: M-F 7:30am-5:30pm. Spanish spoken. ADM REQ: Srvs ordered by M.D. Accepts Medicare, Medi-Cal, pvt pay. SERVES: Riverside County.

AGAPE HOME CARE
1004 W. Foothill Blvd., Ste 202
Upland, CA 91786
(909) 949-7666
(909) 949-7670 FAX

Homecare, home infusion, skilled nursing, PT, OT, speech therapy. OFC HRS: M-F 8am-5pm. Spanish, Tagalog spoken. ADM REQ: Srvs ordered by M.D. Accepts insurance, Medicare, Medi-Cal. SERVES: San Bernardino County.

BIO SCRIP
Formerly Intravenous Therapy Service
320 S. Flower St.
Burbank, CA 91502
(800) 584-0265
(800) 584-0635 FAX

Home care, home infusion, skilled nursing. FUNDING: Nonprofit. OFC HRS: M-F 8:30am-6pm, 24-hr srvs. Spanish, German, Farsi, Russian, Armenian, Greek and Japanese spoken. Accepts insurance for nursing, Medicare, Medi-Cal for pharmacy only. SERVES: So. Calif.

ELDERCARE LOCATOR
1730 Rhode Island Ave, Ste 1200
Washington, DC 20036
(800) 677-1116

Nationwide directory assist srv that helps older Americans & their caregivers locate local support resources that aid independent living. Visit (www.eldercare.gov) or (www.n4a.org). FUND-ING: U.S. Admin on Aging, govt. Spanish spoken. SERVES: U.S.A.

HIGH DESERT HOME HEALTH & HOSPICE
6601 White Feather Rd., Ste A-2
Joshua Tree, CA 92252
(760) 366-6424
(760) 366-9818 FAX

Home health & hospice srvs. FUNDING: Nonprofit. OFC HRS: M-F 8:30am-5pm. ADM REQ: Srvs ordered by M.D. Homebound. Accepts Medicare, Medi-Cal, SSI, insurance. SERVES: Morongo Basin.

HOMECARE WORKERS UNION
SEIU, Local 434B
195 N. Arrowhead Ave.
San Bernardino, CA 92408
(909) 373-3018
(909) 386-7739 FAX

Free referrals for in-home supportive srvs. Helps low income seniors and the disabled remain in their homes. Will match needs and find a worker in your area. FUNDING: Nonprofit. OFC HRS: M-F 8am-5pm. Spanish, Russian, Armenian spoken. SERVES: San Bernardino County.

KAISER PERMANENTE/HOME HEALTH
10917 Magnolia Ave.
Riverside, CA 92505
(951) 358-2600
(951) 358-2697 FAX

Homecare, home infusion, skilled nursing, PT, OT, pediatric care. JCAHO accredited. FUNDING: Nonprofit. OFC HRS: M-F 8:30am-5pm. Spanish spoken. ADM REQ: Srvs ordered by M.D. Accepts Kaiser, Medi-Cal, Medicare. SERVES: Riverside County.

LOMA LINDA UNIV MEDICAL CTR
Home Health Care
11265 Mt. View Ave.
Loma Linda, CA 92354
(909) 558-3096
(909) 558-3062 FAX

Homecare, home infusion, skilled nursing, PT, OT. JCAHO accredited. FUNDING: Nonprofit. OFC HRS: M-Th 8am-5pm; 8am-3pm. Spanish spoken. ADM REQ: Srvs ordered by M.D. Accepts insurance, Medicare, Medi-Cal. SERVES: San Bernardino County.

NATL ASSN FOR HOME CARE
228 7th Street, SE
Washington, DC 20003
(202) 547-7424
(202) 547-3540 FAX

Professional assn for home health care providers. Website offers guidelines for how to start a home health care agency (www.nahc.org). FUNDING: Members, nonprofit. OFC HRS: M-F 9am-6pm. SERVES: U.S.A.

NURSEFINDERS/SAN BERNARDINO
1832 Commercenter Circle, Ste B
San Bernardino, CA 92408
(909) 890-2286
(877) 466-8773
(909) 890-2346 FAX

Homecare & skilled nursing. FUNDING: Private for profit. OFC HRS: M-F 8:30am-5:30pm. Spanish spoken. ADM REQ: Srvs ordered by M.D. Accepts insurance, Medicare, Medi-Cal. SERVES: San Bernardino County.

RELIANT PROFESSIONAL SERVICES
Formerly known as CARE
104 E. State St., Ste R
Redlands, CA 92373
(909) 793-4011
(909) 335-8515 FAX

Senior srvs, including case mgmt, homecare and housing srvs. FUNDING: Nonprofit. OFC HRS: M-Th 8:30am-4:30pm; F 8:30am-1pm. SERVES: Redlands.

RIVERSIDE CO. COMM HEALTH AGENCY
Dept Of Public Health/Nursing
4065 County Circle Dr., Ste 305
Riverside, CA 92503
(951) 358-5438
(951) 358-4762 FAX

In-home srvs include assessment, guidance, counseling, teaching, intervention, referral & family case mgmt in the following categories: child health, senior health, perinatal, postpartum, family planning, parenting edu, high-risk pregnancy, high-risk infant, grief/loss, child abuse prevention, adult/elder abuse, communicable disease, tuberculosis, infant death, drug-exposed infant, birth/newborn screening follow-up, homeless, domestic violence, teen parenting. Group parenting edu classes are provided in many locations. TDD (951) 358-5124. OFC HRS: M-F 8am-5pm. SERVES: Riverside County.

RIVERSIDE CO. PUBLIC SOCIAL SRVS
In-Home Support/Child Protective Srvs
68-625 Perez Rd., Ste 2
Cathedral City, CA 92234
(760) 773-6700
(760) 770-2450
(760) 773-6793 FAX

IHSS provides frail elderly and disabled with outreach and in-home support srvs. Also CPS (Children's Protective Srvs). To report child abuse/neglect, call (800) 442-4918. FUNDING: County, state, fed. OFC HRS: M-F 8am-5pm. Spanish & Tagalog spoken. Free srvs. SERVES: Coachella Valley.

RIVERSIDE CO. PUBLIC SOCIAL SRVS
Adult Protective Srvs/In-Home Srvs
541 N. San Jacinto St.
Hemet, CA 92543
(951) 791-3250
(800) 331-6742
(951) 791-3255 FAX

24-hr emerg response, protective srvs for adults in danger of abuse, exploitation, neglect, etc. Call to report incidents or suspicions of abuse or neglect. Also provides frail elderly and disabled outreach and in-home support srvs. Hotline answered 24 hrs (800) 491-7123. FUNDING: County, state, fed. OFC HRS: M-Th 8am-5pm. Spanish spoken. ADM REQ: Varies per prgm. SERVES: Hemet, San Jacinto, Menifee & nearby.

RIVERSIDE CO. PUBLIC SOCIAL SRVS
Adult Protective Services
23119 Cottonwood Ave., Bldg. A, 1st Fl.
Moreno Valley, CA 92553
(951) 413-5050

276

(800) 345-6083
(951) 413-5107 FAX

Srvs for adults in danger of abuse, exploitation, etc. with full range of srvs from emerg shelter to investigation and in-home support srvs. Provides frail elderly and disabled with outreach and in-home support srvs. Walk in or call. Call, (800) 345-6083 to report any actual or suspected abuse. FUNDING: Govt. OFC HRS: M-Th 8am-5pm. ADM REQ: Varies with prgm. SERVES: Riverside County.

SAN BERNARDINO CO. AGING/ADULT

In-Home Supportive Services
536 E. Virginia Way
Barstow, CA 92311
(760) 256-5544
(760) 256-1435
(760) 256-1605 FAX

Social workers will make an assessment of need for in-home care and authorize payments for domestic and personal srvs in order to keep elderly, blind, and disabled in their own homes and thus avoid institutionalization. OFC HRS: M-F 8am-5pm. SERVES: Barstow area & Trona.

SAN BERNARDINO CO. AGING/ADULT

Senior Info & Assist
8572 Sierra Ave.
Fontana, CA 92335
(909) 829-8515
(909) 829-0313 FAX

Info & referral for legal, transportation, home repair, senior employment, ombudsman prgm, meals, home health care, emerg response, Med Alert and outreach srvs. Offices located throughout the county. FUNDING: Older American Act, Title 3. OFC HRS: M-F 5am-5pm. ADM REQ: Ages 60 yrs+ or disabled. Free srvs. SERVES: Fontana, Bloomington.

SAN BERNARDINO CO. AGING/ADULT

In-Home Supportive Srvs
1300 Bailey Ave.
Needles, CA 92363
(760) 326-9328
(760) 326-9340 FAX

Social workers will make an assessment of a need for in-home care and authorize payments for domestic and personal srvs in order to keep elderly, blind, and disabled in their own homes thus avoiding institutionalization. Hotline (877) 565-2020. OFC HRS: M-F 8am-5pm, closed alt F. SERVES: Needles.

SAN BERNARDINO CO. AGING/ADULT

DAAS/In-Home Supportive Srvs Prgm
686 E. Mill St.
San Bernardino, CA 92415-0640
(909) 891-3900
(909) 891-3919 FAX

IHSS is designed to enable eligible blind and disabled individuals to remain safely in their own home by paying someone to assist with those tasks needed for basic day-to-day home life. Tasks for the IHSS may include essential housekeeping, meal prep, non-medical personal srvs under a physician's supervision, paramedical srvs. Other locations: Barstow, Joshua Tree, Needles, Victorville, Rancho Cucamonga. FUNDING: County, state, federal. OFC HRS: M-F 8am-5pm. Spanish spoken. SERVES: San Bernardino County.

SAN BERNARDINO CO. AGING/ADULT

In-Home Supportive Srvs Prgm
17270 Bear Valley Rd., Ste 108
Victorville 92395
(760) 843-5100
(760) 843-5105 FAX

Social workers make an assessment of need for in-home care & authorize payments for domestic & personal srvs in order to keep elderly, blind, & disabled in their own homes & avoid institutionalization. FUNDING: County, state, fed, nonprofit. OFC HRS: M-F 8am-5pm. Spanish spoken. Low-income srvs available for those who qualify. SERVES: High Desert.

SENIOR COMPANION PROGRAM

600 W. 5th Street
San Bernardino, CA 92410
(909) 384-5430
(909) 889-9801 FAX

Personal in-home srvs to homebound adults. Respite care to caregivers. Also disabled, isolated adults ages 21 yrs+. Walk in. FUNDING: Federal, city. OFC HRS: M-Th 7:30am-5pm. ADM REQ: Ages 21 yrs+, low income bracket. Companions must be ages 55 yrs+ & have a low income. Free srvs. SERVES: Morongo Basin, Victor Valley, San Bernardino, Fontana, Rialto, Loma Linda.

VISITING NURSE ASSN/INLAND

Homecare/Hospice
264 N. Highland Springs, Bldg. 4, Ste A
Banning, CA 92220
(951) 769-1419
(951) 769-9873 FAX

Home health and support srvs, including nursing, PT, OT, speech therapy, respite care, medical social srvs, mental health, perinatal & pediatric care, enterostomal therapy, hospice srvs. For hospice, call (951) 845-3439 or fax (951) 769-1038. FUNDING: Nonprofit. OFC HRS: M-F 8am-5pm. Spanish interpreter available. ADM REQ: Physician's referral in need of homecare. Accepts insurance, Medicare, Medi-Cal. SERVES: Riverside & San Bernardino Counties.

VISITING NURSE ASSN/INLAND

222 E. Main Street, Ste 112
Barstow, CA 92311
(760) 256-2016
(760) 256-2302 FAX

Full range of health care srvs in the home. Nursing, assist with daily living activities, rehab therapies, OT, PT, nutrition counseling & medical social srvs. Free info & referral. FUNDING: United Way, nonprofit. OFC HRS: M-F 8am-4:30pm, nursing on call 24 hrs for high-tech. Spanish spoken. ADM REQ: Physician order, medical necessity. Accepts Medicare, Medi-Cal. Fees for srv. SERVES: Barstow & nearby.

VISITING NURSE ASSN/INLAND

42-600 Cook St., Ste 202
Palm Desert, CA 92211
(760) 346-3982
(866) 333-1424
(760) 779-9162 FAX

Full range of health care srvs in the home. Nursing, assist with daily living activities, rehab therapies, nutrition counseling and medical social srvs. Free info & referral, some professional srvs based on need. JCAHO accredited.

FUNDING: Fees, United Way, nonprofit. OFC HRS: M-F 8am-5pm, nursing on call 24 hrs for high-tech. Spanish spoken. ADM REQ: Physician order, medical necessity. Accepts Medicare, Medi-Cal, insurance, pvt pay. SERVES: Palm Springs, Coachella Valley to the Salton Sea.

VISITING NURSE ASSN/INLAND

12421 Hesperia Rd., Ste 11
Victorville 92395
(760) 962-1966
(760) 241-7055 FAX

Home health care professionals provide personalized health care to patients in their own homes. Teaches patients, family & friends about medications, injections, oxygen use, ostomy care, intravenous and tube feedings, special diets or other aspects of care. Wait: none. FUNDING: Srv fees, donations, nonprofit. OFC HRS: M-F 8am-5pm, nursing on call 24 hrs. Spanish spoken. ADM REQ: Physician order, medical necessity. Sliding fee scale. SERVES: Victor Valley area south & east of Lucerne Valley.

VISITING NURSE ASSN/INLAND

56300 Twentynine Palms Hwy., Ste 105
Yucca Valley, CA 92284
(760) 365-4271
(760) 365-1754 FAX

Home health srvs including nursing, PT, speech therapy, etc. FUNDING: Nonprofit. OFC HRS: M-F 8am-5pm. Spanish spoken. ADM REQ: Physician's referral in need of homecare. Accepts Medicare, Medi-Cal, insurance. SERVES: San Bernardino County.

WE CARE HOME CARE

826 Brookside Ave., Ste F
Redlands, CA 92373
(909) 792-5096

Homecare providers. FUNDING: Nonprofit. OFC HRS: M-F 8:15am-4pm. Spanish & Japanese spoken. SERVES: Redlands, Yucaipa, San Bernardino.

SENIOR/HOUSING

ABODE COMMUNITIES
701 E. 3rd Street, Ste 400
Los Angeles, CA 90013
(213) 629-2702
(213) 225-2805 FAX

Low-income housing throughout greater Los Angeles County. Mission is to open new doors in people's lives through creative and responsible design, dev and operation of service-enhanced affordable housing. Child care centers, community centers and computer labs are built into each facility. Provides an enriching resident services prgm. Abode encourages participation and leadership in our communities, and enhances children's academic achievement and self-esteem. Also helps adults to become confident and educated contributors to society. FUNDING: Nonprofit. OFC HRS: M-F 8:30am-6pm. Spanish spoken. SERVES: L.A., Orange and Riverside Counties.

APPLE VALLEY CARE CENTER
Skilled Nursing Facility
11959 Apple Valley Rd.
Apple Valley, CA 92307
(760) 240-5051
(760) 240-8150 FAX

99-bed facility, serves ages 50 yrs+; ambulatory, non-ambulatory. FUNDING: Nonprofit. OFC HRS: M-F 8am-5pm. Accepts Medi-Cal, Medicare, SSI. SERVES: San Bernardino County.

ASISTENCIA VILLA REHAB & CARE CTR
Skilled Nursing Facility
1875 Barton Rd.
Redlands, CA 92373
(909) 793-1382
(909) 798-6689 FAX

99-bed facility, ambulatory, non-ambulatory. Accepts Medi-Cal, Medicare, SSI. SERVES: San Bernardino County.

BANNING HEALTHCARE
Skilled Nursing Facility
3476 W. Wilson St.
Banning, CA 92220
(951) 849-4723
(951) 849-0972 FAX

64-bed facility serves ages 50 yrs+; ambulatory, non-ambulatory. OFC HRS: 24 hrs, 7 days. Spanish spoken. Accepts Medi-Cal, Medicare, SSI, HMO, pvt pay. SERVES: Riverside County.

BARKER MANAGEMENT, INC.
1101 E. Orangewood Ave., Ste 200
Anaheim, CA 92805
(714) 533-3450
(714) 533-8608 FAX

Affordable rental units for families & seniors. A property mgmt agent of the Community Redevelopment Agency of L.A. Call for availability. OFC HRS: M-F 9am-5pm. ADM REQ: Must meet income and/or age requirements. SERVES: So. Calif.

BEAUMONT CARE CENTER
Skilled Nursing Facility
1441 N. Michigan Ave.
Beaumont, CA 92223
(951) 845-1166

(951) 845-1791 FAX

86-bed facility serves ages 50 yrs+; ambulatory, non-ambulatory, Alzheimer's. OFC HRS: 24 hrs, 7 days. Spanish spoken. Accepts Medi-Cal, Medicare, SSI. SERVES: Riverside County.

BEAUTIFUL LIGHT INN
G & K Mgmt Co., Inc.
1365 N. Waterman Ave.
San Bernardino, CA 92404-5337
(909) 884-4033
(909) 381-6933 FAX

Affordable rental housing for seniors, Section 202. FUNDING: HUD subsidized. OFC HRS: M-F 9am-5pm. ADM REQ: Low income, ages 62 yrs+. SERVES: San Bernardino County.

BLYTHE NURSING CARE CENTER
Skilled Nursing Facility
285 W. Chanslor Way
Blythe, CA 92225
(760) 922-8176
(760) 922-0789 FAX

48-bed facility serves ages 40 yrs+; ambulatory, non-ambulatory. OFC HRS: 24 hrs, 7 days. Spanish spoken. Accepts Medi-Cal, Medicare, SSI. SERVES: Blythe & nearby desert areas.

BRADLEY GARDENS, THE
Skilled Nursing Facility
980 W. 7th Street
San Jacinto, CA 92582-3814
(951) 654-9347
(951) 654-6106 FAX

44-bed facility serves ages 50 yrs+; ambulatory, non-ambulatory, Alzheimer's. Spanish spoken. Accepts Medi-Cal, Medicare, pvt insurance. SERVES: Hemet, San Jacinto, Perris, Sun City, Beaumont, Banning.

BRASWELL'S COMM CONVALESCENT CTR
Skilled Nursing Facility
13542 2nd Street
Yucaipa, CA 92399
(909) 795-2421
(909) 795-5939 FAX

82-bed facility serves ages 70 yrs+; ambulatory, non-ambulatory, Alzheimer's. Accepts Medi-Cal, Medicare, SSI. SERVES: San Bernardino County.

BRASWELL'S HAMPTON MANOR
11970 Fourth St.
Yucaipa, CA 92399
(909) 790-2273
(909) 790-3333 FAX

99-bed facility serves serves ages 60 yrs+; ambulatory, non-ambulatory. OFC HRS: M-F 9am-5:30pm, 24 hrs. Spanish spoken. Accepts Medi-Cal, Medicare, SSI. SERVES: San Bernardino County.

BRASWELL'S YUCAIPA VALLEY CONV
Skilled Nursing Facility
35253 Avenue H
Yucaipa, CA 92399
(909) 795-2476
(909) 795-0458 FAX

59-bed facility serves ages 50 yrs+; ambulatory, non-ambulatory, Alzheimer's. Accepts

Medi-Cal, Medicare, SSI. SERVES: San Bernardino County.

BRIARWOOD MANOR APARTMENTS
Logan Property Mgmt Inc.
9656 Exeter Ave.
Montclair, CA 91763
(909) 624-5041
(909) 624-1423 FAX

Affordable rental housing for seniors, Section 8. Meals, housekeeping, transportation. Waiting list varies. FUNDING: HUD subsidized. OFC HRS: M-Sun 8am-5pm. ADM REQ: Low income ages 60 yrs+. SERVES: San Bernardino County.

BROOKSIDE HEALTHCARE CENTER
Skilled Nursing Facility
105 Terracina Blvd.
Redlands, CA 92373
(909) 793-2271
(909) 792-6477 FAX

96-bed facility serves ages 40 yrs+; ambulatory, non-ambulatory, Alzheimer's. Spanish, Chinese, Japanese, Tagalog, Indonesian spoken. Accepts Medi-Cal, Medicare, SSI, HMO. SERVES: San Bernardino County.

CALIF ASSN/HOMES/SRVS FOR AGING
1315 I Street, Ste 100
Sacramento, CA 95814
(916) 392-5111
(916) 428-4250 FAX

Represents more than 400 nonprofit providers of senior living srvs, including: affordable housing; continuing care retirement communities; assisted living; skilled nursing home & community-based care. CAHSAs advocacy, edu prgms, communications & other resources help its members best serve the needs of seniors. FUNDING: Nonprofit. OFC HRS: M-F 8am-5pm. SERVES: Calif.

CALIF NURSING & REHAB CTR
Skilled Nursing Facility
2999 N. Indian Ave.
Palm Springs, CA 92262
(760) 325-2937
(760) 322-7250 FAX

80-bed facility serves ages 18 yrs+; ambulatory, non-ambulatory, Alzheimer's. OFC HRS: 24 hrs, 7 days. Spanish, Tagalog spoken. Accepts Medi-Cal, Medicare, SSI. SERVES: Palm Springs & nearby.

CATHEDRAL CITY SENIOR HOUSING
Cooperative Srvs
34445 Corregidor Dr.
Cathedral City, CA 92234
(800) 500-7725

Affordable rental housing for seniors, Section 202. 13 So. Calif locations, waiting list 6 mos-2 yrs. FUNDING: HUD subsidized. OFC HRS: M-F 8am-5pm. Spanish spoken. ADM REQ: Seniors ages 62 yrs+, low income. SERVES: So. Calif.

CHAPMAN CONVALESCENT HOSPITAL
Skilled Nursing Facility
4301 Caroline Court
Riverside, CA 92506
(951) 683-7111
(951) 683-6826 FAX

59-bed facility serves ages 70 yrs+; ambulatory, non-ambulatory, Alzheimer's. OFC HRS: M-F 8am-5pm. Spanish spoken. Accepts Medi-Cal, Medicare. SERVES: Riverside County.

CHERRY VALLEY HEALTHCARE
Skilled Nursing Facility
5800 W. Wilson St.
Banning, CA 92220
(951) 845-1606
(951) 845-4152 FAX

132-bed facility serves ages 40 yrs+; ambulatory, non-ambulatory, Alzheimer's. OFC HRS: M-F 8am-5pm. Spanish spoken. Accepts Medi-Cal, Medicare, SSI. SERVES: Banning & nearby.

CHRISTIAN HERITAGE CARE CTRS
Skilled Nursing Facility
275 Garnet Way
Upland, CA 91786
(909) 949-4887
(909) 949-8476 FAX

Specializes in orthopedic care & rehab. Specific care srvs: skilled nursing, wound care, PT, OT, speech therapy, strengthening, mobility, & flexibility, ADL enhancing therapies, post-hospital care, pain mgmt, infection control, stroke & surgery recovery, injury rehab. FUNDING: Nonprofit. OFC HRS: M-F 8am-7pm. Spanish spoken. Accepts Medi-Cal, Medicare, SSI. SERVES: San Bernardino County.

CHRISTIAN HERITAGE GARDENS
Alzheimer's & Dementia Residence
1260 E. Arrow Hwy., Ste B
Upland, CA 91786
(909) 946-5757
(909) 931-3746 FAX

Residence devoted to the loving care of memory-challenged seniors. Secured facility & grounds, specially trained caregivers on site 24 hrs a day, nurse on staff, reasonable rates, memory stimulating activity & recreation prgm. FUNDING: Nonprofit. OFC HRS: M-F 8am-5pm. Spanish spoken. ADM REQ: Open to all. SERVES: San Bernadino County.

CITRUS NURSING CENTER
Skilled Nursing Facility
9440 Citrus Ave.
Fontana, CA 92335
(909) 823-3481
(909) 823-3829 FAX

99-bed facility serves ages 50 yrs+; ambulatory, non-ambulatory, Alzheimer's. Accepts Medi-Cal, Medicare, SSI. SERVES: San Bernardino County.

CLARK TERRACE APTS
So Calif Presbyterian Homes
2660 Clark Ave.
Norco, CA 92860
(951) 738-9712
(951) 738-9438 FAX

Rental housing for seniors, Section 202. Waiting list 15-18 months. FUNDING: HUD subsidized. OFC HRS: M-F 8am-5pm. ADM REQ: Low income, ages 62 yrs+. SERVES: Riverside County.

COMMUNITY CARE & REHAB CENTER
Skilled Nursing Facility
4070 Jurupa Ave.
Riverside, CA 92506

(951) 680-6500
(951) 680-6504 FAX

162-bed facility serves ages 40 yrs+; ambulatory, non-ambulatory. Spanish spoken. Accepts Medi-Cal, Medicare, SSI. SERVES: Riverside County.

CORONA COMMUNITY TOWERS
SK Mgmt Company
910 S. Belle Ave.
Corona, CA 91720
(323) 930-2300
(323) 935-3605 FAX

Affordable rental housing for seniors, Section 202. No waiting list. OFC HRS: M-F 8am-5pm. ADM REQ: Low income. SERVES: Riverside County.

CORONA COMMUNITY VILLAS/ELDERLY
Sk Mgmt Company
2680 S. Main St.
Corona, CA 92882-5967
(323) 930-2300
(323) 935-3605 FAX

Affordable rental housing for seniors, Section 202. No waiting list. FUNDING: HUD subsidized. OFC HRS: M-F 8am-5pm. ADM REQ: Low income. SERVES: Riverside County.

COUNTRY VILLA RANCHO MIRAGE HEALTHCARE CENTER
Skilled Nursing Facility
39950 Vista Del Sol
Rancho Mirage, CA 92270
(760) 340-0053
(760) 341-6523 FAX

99-bed, ages 60 yrs+; ambulatory, non-ambulatory, Alzheimer's, PT, OT, speech therapy. OFC HRS: M-F 8am-5pm. Spanish, Tagalog spoken. Accepts Medi-Cal, Medicare. SERVES: Riverside County.

COUNTRY VILLA REDLANDS
Skilled Nursing Facility
700 E. Highland Ave.
Redlands, CA 92374
(909) 793-2678
(909) 793-7390 FAX

50-bed SNF, 30-bed unit for Alzheimer's, serves ages 40 yrs+; ambulatory, non-ambulatory. Spanish, Tagalog spoken. Accepts Medi-Cal, Medicare, SSI. SERVES: San Bernardino County.

CYPRESS GARDENS REHAB CARE CTR
Skilled Nursing Facility
9025 Colorado Ave.
Riverside, CA 92503
(951) 688-3636
(951) 688-1507 FAX

120-bed facility serves ages 40 yrs+; ambulatory, non-ambulatory. Vietnamese, Spanish, Samoan, Italian spoken. Accepts Medi-Cal, Medicare. SERVES: Riverside County.

DASH, INC.
306 W. Colton Ave.
Redlands, CA 92375
(909) 798-1667
(909) 335-0236 FAX

Temporary and/or permanent residential care. Dementia waiver/dementia specific home in a residential neighborhood in San Bernardino Co. Not a live-in adult day care. FUNDING: Nonprofit. OFC HRS: M-F 9am-5pm. Spanish spo-

ken. Fee $40 per day. SERVES: San Bernardino County.

DESERT MANOR
Formerly Crescent Alzheimer's Care Ctr
8515 Cholla Ave.
Yucca Valley, CA 92284
(760) 365-0717
(760) 365-7127 FAX

58-bed facility serves ages 60 yrs+; ambulatory, non-ambulatory, Alzheimer's. Spanish spoken. Accepts Medi-Cal, Medicare, SSI. SERVES: San Bernardino County.

DEVONSHIRE CARE CENTER
Skilled Nursing Facility
1350 E. Devonshire Ave.
Hemet, CA 92544
(951) 925-2571
(951) 925-9739 FAX

99-bed facility serves ages 60 yrs+; ambulatory, non-ambulatory, Alzheimer's. Spanish, Chinese, Tagalog spoken. Accepts Medi-Cal, Medicare, SSI. SERVES: Riverside County.

DINO PAPA VERO SENIOR CENTER
Elderly Housing Development & Operations Corp
16707 Marygold Ave.
Fontana, CA 92335
(909) 350-0575
(909) 350-1903 FAX

Rental housing for seniors, Section 202. Wait: 1-2 yrs. FUNDING: HUD subsidized. OFC HRS: M-F 8am-4pm. Spanish spoken. ADM REQ: Low income ages 62 yrs+. SERVES: San Bernardino County.

EXTENDED CARE HOSP OF RIVERSIDE
Skilled Nursing Facility
8171 Magnolia Ave.
Riverside, CA 92504
(951) 687-3842
(951) 687-1690 FAX

99-bed facility serves ages 65 yrs+; ambulatory, non-ambulatory, Alzheimer's. OFC HRS: M-F 8am-5pm. Spanish spoken. Accepts Medi-Cal, Medicare. SERVES: Riverside & nearby.

FAMILY SELF-SUFFICIENCY
See "Riverside Co. Housing Authority"

FOUNTAINS AT THE CARLOTTA
Skilled Nursing Facility
41-505 Carlotta Dr.
Palm Desert, CA 92211
(760) 346-5420
(760) 341-7768 FAX

59-bed facility serves ages 50 yrs+; ambulatory, non-ambulatory. Skilled nursing. OFC HRS: M-F 8am-8:30pm. Spanish spoken. Accepts Medicare, SSI. SERVES: Riverside County.

GROVE APTS
Forest City Residential Mgmt
227 West H Street
Ontario, CA 91762-2748
(909) 983-3525
(909) 983-6062 FAX

Rental housing for disabled, Section 236 & seniors, Section 202. FUNDING: HUD subsidized. OFC HRS: M-F 9am-5pm. ADM REQ: Low income ages 62 yrs+ or disabled. SERVES: San Bernardino County.

HERITAGE GARDENS RETIREMENT

Skilled Nursing Facility
25271 Barton Rd.
Loma Linda, CA 92354
(909) 796-0216
(909) 799-6656 FAX

110-bed facility, serves ages 60 yrs+; ambulatory, non-ambulatory, rehab, independent living. Spanish & Tagalog spoken. Accepts Medi-Cal, Medicare, SSI. SERVES: San Bernardino County.

HERITAGE PARK CARE CTRS

Assisted and Independent Living
275 Garnet Way
Upland, CA 91786
(909) 949-4887
(909) 931-3746 FAX

Shared & private accomodations to seniors for either assisted or independent living. Srvs include: meals, activities, transportation to medical appts, special events, personal hygiene & grooming, beauty parlor, dressing assist, special worship needs, medication mgmt, continence mgmt, mobility assist, safety monitoring, etc. FUNDING: Nonprofit. OFC HRS: M-F 8am-5pm. Spanish spoken. SERVES: San Bernardino County.

HIGHLAND PALMS HEALTHCARE CTR

Skilled Nursing Facility
7534 Palm Ave.
Highland, CA 92346
(909) 862-0611
(909) 425-9611 FAX

99-bed facility serves ages 40 yrs+; ambulatory, non-ambulatory, Alzheimer's. Spanish & Tagalog spoken. Accepts Medi-Cal, Medicare, SSI. SERVES: San Bernardino County.

INLAND CHRISTIAN HOME

Skilled Nursing Facility
1950 S. Mountain Ave.
Ontario, CA 91762
(909) 983-0084
(909) 983-0431 FAX

59-bed facility serves ages 62 yrs+; ambulatory, non-ambulatory, Alzheimer's. FUNDING: Nonprofit. OFC HRS: M-F 8am-4:30pm; 24-hr facility. Spanish spoken. Accepts Medi-Cal, Medicare, SSI. SERVES: San Bernardino County.

INTEGRATED NURSING

Skilled Nursing Facility
2225 N. Perris Blvd.
Perris, CA 92571
(951) 657-2135
(951) 657-6145 FAX

109-bed facility serves ages 40 yrs+; ambulatory, non-ambulatory, Alzheimer's. Spanish, Tagalog spoken. Accepts Medi-Cal, Medicare, SSI. SERVES: Riverside County.

JAMBOREE HOUSING CORPORATION

17701 Cowan Ave., Ste 200
Irvine, CA 92614
(949) 263-8676
(949) 263-0647 FAX

Builds, preserves and maintains affordable rental & home ownership for low-income families and seniors. Helping Educate, Activate, and Respond Together (HEART) assists residents in maintaining self-sufficiency. On-site srvs may include: health & safety classes, computer learning centers with Internet access, after school tutoring, budgeting & parenting classes, home buying seminars, and referrals to local agencies. Senior resident srvs include transportation to appts & off-site events, also daily living assist. FUNDING: Nonprofit, govt, grants, donations. OFC HRS: M-F 7:30am-5pm. ADM REQ: Vary per location. SERVES: So. Calif.

LIFEHOUSE CARE CONVALESCENT

Skilled Nursing Facility
8781 Lakeview Ave.
Riverside, CA 92509
(951) 685-1531
(951) 685-1571 FAX

188-bed facility serves ages 40 yrs+; ambulatory, non-ambulatory, Alzheimer's. Spanish spoken. Accepts Medi-Cal, Medicare, SSI. SERVES: Inland Empire.

LINDA VALLEY CARE CENTER

Skilled Nursing Facility
25383 Cole Street
Loma Linda, CA 92354
(909) 796-0235
(909) 796-6366 FAX

83-bed, serves ages 65 yrs+; ambulatory, non-ambulatory, Alzheimer's. Spanish spoken. Accepts Medi-Cal, Medicare, SSI, HMO, pvt pay. SERVES: San Bernardino County.

LONG-TERM CARE OMBUDSMAN

Wise Senior Services
P.O. Box 769
Santa Monica, CA 90406
(800) 334-9473
(310) 395-4090 FAX

Accepts complaints regarding nursing home care. FUNDING: Nonprofit. OFC HRS: M-F 8am-5pm. Spanish spoken. SERVES: U.S.A.

LONG-TERM CARE OMBUDSMAN/CRISIS

Crisis Line
1971 E. 4th Street, Ste 200
Santa Ana, CA 92705-3917
(714) 479-0107
(800) 300-6222
(714) 479-0234 FAX

24-hr crisis line for people concerned about serious problems that may exist in a nursing home facility, such as abuse, diet, Medicare, etc. Local ombudsman speaks directly to residents concerning problems. (800) 231-4024 for crisis line. FUNDING: Govt. OFC HRS: 24 hrs, 7 days. SERVES: Calif.

MAYWOOD MANOR COOPERATIVE SRVS

4646 Slauson Ave.
Maywood, CA 90270-2936
(323) 773-5175
(626) 599-8463 FAX

Affordable rental housing for seniors, Section 202. 13 So Calif locations, waiting list 3 mos-3 yrs. OFC HRS: M-F 8am-5pm. ADM REQ: Low income, ages 62 yrs+. SERVES: So. Calif.

MID-STEP ASSISTED LIVING

See "Dash, Inc."

MIRAVILLA CARE CENTER

Skilled Nursing Facility
9246 Avenida Miravilla
Cherry Valley, CA 92223
(951) 845-3194
(951) 845-2064 FAX

59-bed facility serves ages 65 yrs+; ambulatory, non-ambulatory, Alzheimer's. Accepts Medi-Cal, Medicare, SSI. SERVES: Riverside County.

MISSION NURSING CENTER

Skilled Nursing Facility
8487 Magnolia Ave.
Riverside, CA 92504
(951) 688-2222
(951) 688-7659 FAX

40-bed facility ages 40 yrs+; ambulatory, non-ambulatory, Alzheimer's. Sub-acute unit. Spanish, Tagalog spoken. Accepts Medi-Cal, Medicare. SERVES: Riverside County.

MISSION VILLAS

Falkenberg/Gilliam & Assoc, Inc.
5870 Mission Blvd.
Riverside, CA 92506-4273
(951) 276-1952
(951) 276-1651 FAX

Rental housing for seniors, Section 202. OFC HRS: M-F 9am-12noon, 2pm-5pm. ADM REQ: Low income ages 62 yrs+. SERVES: Riverside County.

MOUNT RUBIDOUX MANOR

American Baptist Church of the West
3993 10th Street
Riverside, CA 92501-3574
(951) 684-3154
(951) 684-5615 FAX

Affordable rental housing for seniors, Section 202. Independent living, 188 apts. OFC HRS: M-F 8am-5pm. Spanish spoken. ADM REQ: Low income or disabled, ages 62 yrs+. Food prgm required, $116 per month, served M-F only. SERVES: Riverside County.

NEIGHBORHOOD PARTNERSHIP

Home Ownership Srvs
320 West G Street, Ste 103
Ontario, CA 91762
(909) 988-5979
(909) 624-9263 FAX

Home ownership edu & counseling, home maintenance classes, low-interest loans for homeowner's home improvement, neighborhood revitalization & housing rehab, workshops on home buying. Annual paint-a-thon for seniors, must apply before April. Also offers home ownership financial assist, & a HUD approved counseling center. FUNDING: Grants, fees, nonprofit. OFC HRS: M-Th 8:30am-4:30pm; F 8:30am-12noon. Spanish spoken. ADM REQ: Low to moderate income families. SERVES: Eastern L.A. County & Western San Bernardino County.

NURSING HOME HOTLINE

See "Long-Term Care Ombudsman."

OLIVE GROVE MANOR I & II

Triester International Mgmt
7858 California Ave.
Riverside, CA 92504
(951) 687-2241
(856) 795-4866 FAX

Rental housing for seniors. OFC HRS: M-F 8am-5pm. ADM REQ: Low income ages 62 yrs+. SERVES: Riverside County.

ONTARIO CARE CENTER

Skilled Nursing Facility
1661 S. Euclid Ave.
Ontario, CA 91762

(909) 984-6713
(909) 984-5254 FAX

59-bed facility serves ages 60 yrs+; ambulatory, non-ambulatory, Alzheimer's. Spanish spoken. Accepts Medi-Cal, Medicare, SSI. SERVES: San Bernardino County.

PALM GROVE HEALTHCARE

Skilled Nursing Facility
1665 E. 8th Street
Beaumont, CA 92223
(951) 845-3125
(951) 769-1582 FAX

57-bed facility serves ages 50 yrs+; ambulatory, non-ambulatory, secured Alzheimer's facility. Spanish, Tagalog spoken. Accepts Medi-Cal, Medicare, pvt insurance. SERVES: Riverside County.

PALM SPRINGS HEALTH CARE & REHAB

Skilled Nursing Facility
277 S. Sunrise Way
Palm Springs, CA 92262
(760) 327-8541
(760) 325-0289 FAX

99-bed facility serves ages 60 yrs+; ambulatory, non-ambulatory. Spanish spoken. Accepts Medi-Cal, Medicare, most HMOs & pvt pay. SERVES: Riverside County.

PALM SPRINGS SENIOR HOUSING

Vista Serena
1201 E. Vista Chino
Palm Springs, CA 92262-3345
(800) 500-7725

Affordable rental housing for seniors, Section 202. Thirteen So. Calif locations, waiting list 3 mos-3 yrs. FUNDING: Nonprofit. OFC HRS: M-F 8am-5pm. Spanish spoken. ADM REQ: Ages 62 yrs+, low income. SERVES: So. Calif.

PIONEER PARK PLAZA

AF Evans Mgmt
540 North F Street
San Bernardino, CA 92410
(909) 885-5773
(909) 885-1772 FAX

Rental housing for seniors, Section 202. Waiting list. OFC HRS: M-F 8am-5:30pm. Spanish spoken. ADM REQ: Low income ages 62 yrs+. SERVES: San Bernardino County.

PLYMOUTH TOWER

Skilled Nursing/Assisted Living
3401 Lemon St.
Riverside, CA 92501
(951) 686-8202
(951) 784-1508 FAX

38-bed facility serves ages 60 yrs+; ambulatory, non-ambulatory. 66 assisted living apts, 24 independent living apts. Skilled nursing & respite care prgms also available. FUNDING: Nonprofit. OFC HRS: 24-hr srvs. Spanish spoken. Accepts Medi-Cal, Medicare, SSI, pvt pay. SERVES: Riverside County.

PLYMOUTH VILLAGE

Memory Support
225 Priscilla Way
Redlands, CA 92373
(909) 793-9195
(909) 798-5504 FAX

10-bed assisted living facility with memory support. Alzheimer's, day care, respite care. FUNDING: Nonprofit. ADM REQ: Ages 62 yrs+,

ambulatory. Accepts pvt pay. SERVES: San Bernardino County.

PLYMOUTH VILLAGE ASSISTED LIVING

Skilled Nursing Facility
945 Salem Dr.
Redlands, CA 92373
(909) 793-1233
(909) 798-5504 FAX

30 apts, serves ages 62 yrs+; ambulatory. FUNDING: Nonprofit. OFC HRS: M-F 9am-4:30pm. Accepts Medicare. SERVES: San Bernardino County.

PLYMOUTH VILLAGE HEALTH CENTER

Skilled Nursing Facility
819 Salem Dr.
Redlands, CA 92373
(909) 793-9195
(909) 798-5504 FAX

Continuing care facility serving many levels of care, 48 beds, serves ages 60 yrs+; ambulatory, non-ambulatory, Alzheimer's. FUNDING: Nonprofit. OFC HRS: 24 hrs, 7 days. Spanish & Vietnamese spoken. Accepts Medicare. SERVES: San Bernardino County.

PREMIER CARE & REHAB/PALM SPRINGS

Skilled Nursing Facility
2990 E. Ramon Rd.
Palm Springs, CA 92264
(760) 323-2638
(760) 323-1723 FAX

99-bed facility serves adults, ambulatory, non-ambulatory, rehab & hospice. Spanish, Tagalog spoken. Accepts Medi-Cal, Medicare, SSI. SERVES: Riverside County.

RAMONA MANOR CONVALESCENT HOSP

Skilled Nursing Facility
485 W. Johnston Ave.
Hemet, CA 92543
(951) 652-0011
(951) 929-5924 FAX

104-bed facility serves ages 65 yrs+; ambulatory, non-ambulatory. Spanish spoken. Accepts Medi-Cal, Medicare, SSI. SERVES: Riverside County.

RIMROCK VILLA CONVALESCENT HOSP

Skilled Nursing Facility
27555 Rimrock Rd.
Barstow, CA 92311
(760) 252-2515
(760) 252-1572 FAX

59-bed facility serves ambulatory, non-ambulatory, Alzheimer's. German, Spanish & Tagalog spoken. Accepts Medi-Cal, Medicare, SSI. SERVES: San Bernardino County.

RIVER RANCH MOBILE HOME PARK

Jamboree Housing Corp. Project
15940 Stoddard Wells Rd.
Victorville, CA 92392
(760) 245-9831
(760) 245-6205 FAX

136 mobile home spaces for purchased/owned mobile homes for low-income seniors ages 55 yrs+. No rentals. Low monthly space fees from $140-$285 per month. Some assist to access local senior prgms. Contact Barbi Brooks for more info. FUNDING: State HCD MPROP. SERVES: San Bernardino County.

RIVERSIDE CO. HOUSING AUTHORITY

Housing Assistance Information
5555 Arlington Ave.

Riverside, CA 92504
(951) 351-0700
(800) 655-4228
(951) 354-6324 FAX

Housing prgms include: Section 8 tenant-based assist which provides rental assist to low & moderate income seniors and disabled. Tenants pay between 30% and 40 % of their adjusted income; a housing choice voucher is given to eligible participants. Affordable housing prgm allows families to live in selected HUD housing units. The Planning & Dev Dept is responsible for formulation, processing & implementation of new construction projects and maintenance of all the existing housing units. Also have a senior home repair prgm. Application is free. FUNDING: Govt. OFC HRS: M-Th 8am-5pm. Spanish spoken. SERVES: Riverside County.

SAN BERNARDINO CO. HOUSING AUTH

424 N. Lemon Ave.
Ontario, CA 91764
(909) 983-1318
(909) 381-3052 FAX

Housing choice voucher prgm. Assist for very low income families, seniors, & the disabled. TTY (909) 391-5058. FUNDING: County. OFC HRS: M-Th 7:30am-5:30pm; alt F 7:30am-4:30pm. ADM REQ: Low income, poverty level. SERVES: Fontana, Rialto, Pomona Valley, Unicorp Areas, West Side San Bernardino County.

SAN BERNARDINO CO. HOUSING AUTH

Administrative Office
715 E. Brier Dr.
San Bernardino, CA 92408-2841
(909) 890-0644
(909) 890-4618 FAX

Administers two rental assist prgms for low-income families, seniors, and disabled. Public housing prgm comprised of 2,500+ units owned or managed by Housing Authority, and scattered throughout 23 cities in San Bernardino Co. Housing choice voucher prgm provides rental subsidy to very low income individuals by providing subsidy payments directly to the owners on behalf of participant, who is required to pay at least 30% of their income toward rent. TTY (909) 388-9279. FUNDING: U.S. Dept of HUD. OFC HRS: M-Th 7:30am-5:30pm; alt F 7:30am-4:30pm. ADM REQ: Gross yearly income within HUD guidelines. SERVES: San Bernardino County, except the cities of Needles and Upland.

SAN BERNARDINO CO. HOUSING AUTH

15465 Seneca Rd.
Victorville, CA 92392
(760) 243-1043
(760) 243-2123 FAX

Housing choice voucher prgm. Assist for very low income families, seniors & the disabled. TTY (760) 951-7872. FUNDING: County. OFC HRS: M-Th 7:30am-5:30pm; alt F 7:30am-4:30pm. ADM REQ: Low income, poverty level. SERVES: High Desert, Mid Desert, Mountains

SOUTHPOINTE VILLA

Retirement Housing Fndn
302 W. Merrill Ave.
Rialto, CA 92376
(909) 874-9110

(909) 820-0670 FAX

Affordable rental housing for seniors, Section 202. Wait: 1 yr. FUNDING: Nonprofit. OFC HRS: M-F 8am-4:30pm. Spanish spoken. ADM REQ: Low income ages 62 yrs+. SERVES: San Bernardino County.

ST. BERNARDINE PLAZA

Falkenberg/Gilliam & Assoc, Inc.
550 W. 5th Street
San Bernardino, CA 92401
(909) 888-0153

Rental housing for seniors, Section 202. OFC HRS: M-F 8am-5pm. Spanish spoken. ADM REQ: Low income ages 62 yrs+. SERVES: San Bernardino County.

STEELWORKERS OLDTIMERS II

Oldtimers Housing Development Corp.
12855 Oaks Ave.
Chino, CA 91710
(909) 829-0384

Rental housing for seniors, Section 202. Wait: 1-2 yrs. OFC HRS: M-F 8am-4pm. Spanish spoken. ADM REQ: Low income ages 62 yrs+. SERVES: San Bernardino County.

STEELWORKS OLDTIMERS

See "Dino Papa Vero Senior Center"

SUN CITY CONVALESCENT CENTER

Skilled Nursing Facility
27600 Encanto Dr.
Sun City, CA 92586
(951) 679-6858
(951) 679-0399 FAX

99-bed facility serves ages 40 yrs+; ambulatory, non-ambulatory. Accepts Medi-Cal, Medicare. SERVES: Riverside County.

SYCAMORE TERRACE APARTMENTS

So. Calif Presbyterian Homes & Srvs
1301 San Bernardino Rd.
Upland, CA 91786-4927
(909) 946-2811

Affordable rental housing for seniors, Section 202. Waiting list. OFC HRS: M-F 8am-5pm. Spanish spoken. ADM REQ: Low income ages 62 yrs+. SERVES: San Bernardino County.

TELACU VILLA

Telacu Residential Mgmt
25105 Fir Ave.
Moreno Valley, CA 92553-2300
(951) 486-9842
(323) 485-1710 FAX

Rental housing for seniors, Section 202. Disabled, Section 236. Wait: 6 mos-1.5 yrs. OFC HRS: M-F 8am-5pm. ADM REQ: Low income ages 62 yrs+, or disabled ages 18 yrs+. SERVES: Riverside County.

U.S. ELDER CARE REFERRAL AGENCY

Corporate Office
1525 E. Mesa Verde Dr., Ste 210
Costa Mesa, CA 92626-5219
(800) 848-1008
(714) 424-6161
(714) 424-6162 FAX

Private nonprofit agency supported by the retirement industry. Assists families and professionals in finding care for the elderly. Also refers to residential care homes, assisted living & nursing homes, in-home care & incontinence supplies. FUNDING: Retirement industry. OFC

HRS: M-F 8:30am-5pm. 24-hr srvs. Spanish spoken. Free srvs. SERVES: Calif.

VALENCIA PALMS NURSING CENTER

Skilled Nursing Facility
82-262 Valencia St.
Indio, CA 92201
(760) 347-6000
(760) 775-6403 FAX

68-bed facility serves ages 50 yrs+; ambulatory, non-ambulatory, Alzheimer's. Spanish spoken. Accepts Medi-Cal, Medicare, SSI. SERVES: Riverside County.

VALLEY HEALTHCARE CENTER

Skilled Nursing Facility
1680 N. Waterman Ave.
San Bernardino, CA 92404
(909) 886-5291
(909) 882-4513 FAX

119-bed facility serves serves ages 60 yrs+; ambulatory, non-ambulatory, Alzheimer's. Spanish, Tagalog spoken. Accepts Medi-Cal, Medicare, SSI. SERVES: San Bernardino County.

VILLA HEALTH CARE CENTER

Skilled Nursing Facility
8965 Magnolia Ave.
Riverside, CA 92503
(951) 689-5788
(951) 689-9231 FAX

59-bed facility serves ages 50 yrs+; ambulatory, non-ambulatory, Alzheimer's. Spanish, Tagalog spoken. Accepts Medi-Cal, Medicare, SSI. SERVES: Riverside County.

VILLAGE HEALTHCARE CENTER, THE

Skilled Nursing Facility
2400 W. Acacia Ave.
Hemet, CA 92545
(951) 766-5116
(951) 766-5316 FAX

54-bed facility serves ages 50 yrs+; ambulatory, non-ambulatory. Spanish spoken. Accepts Medicare. SERVES: Riverside County.

VISTA PACIFICA CONVALESCENT

3674 Pacific Ave.
Riverside, CA 92509
(951) 682-4833
(951) 274-4696 FAX

49-bed hospital serves ages 60 yrs+; ambulatory, non-ambulatory. Accepts Alzheimer's, Huntingtons'. IV/wound care, respite, hospice, secure Alzheimer's unit, wanderer-alert system. OFC HRS: 24 hrs, 7 days. Accepts Medi-Cal, Medicare, SSI. SERVES: Riverside.

VOLUNTEER CENTER/RIVERSIDE CO.

Shared Housing/Riverside
2060 University Ave., Ste 201
Riverside, CA 92507
(951) 686-4402
(951) 781-2737 FAX

Shared housing is a give and take arrangement between participants offering alternatives to persons unable to afford or maintain safe and suitable housing, especially to the elderly who live alone. Alternative for single parents, displaced homemakers and young adults over age 18 yrs. Satellite office in Hemet (951) 652-3591. Wait: varies. Walk in. FUNDING: City, United Way. OFC HRS: M-Th 8am-5pm. Spanish spoken, language line available. Free srvs. SERVES: Western Riverside County.

VOLUNTEER CENTER/RIVERSIDE CO.

Ombudsman for Long-Term Care
P.O. Box 5376
2060 University Ave., Ste 212
Riverside, CA 92517-5376
(951) 686-4402
(800) 464-1123
(951) 686-7417 FAX

Investigates to resolve problems of older patients and residents of long-term care facilities in Riverside County, investigates adult abuse. FUNDING: Govt, United Way, nonprofit. OFC HRS: M-F 8am-5pm. Spanish translation srv. Free & confidential srvs. SERVES: Riverside County.

WATERMAN CONVALESCENT

Skilled Nursing Facility
1850 N. Waterman Ave.
San Bernardino, CA 92404
(909) 882-1215
(909) 881-2071 FAX

166-bed, serves ages 60 yrs+; ambulatory, non-ambulatory, Alzheimer's. Spanish, Tagalog & Vietnamese spoken. Accepts Medi-Cal, Medicare, SSI. SERVES: San Bernardino County.

WILDOMAR SENIOR LEISURE COMM

Assisted Living Community
32325 S. Pasadena St.
Wildomar, CA 92595
(951) 678-1555
(951) 678-1249 FAX

Section 8 housing assist prgm. 176 units for low income persons ages 55 yrs+. Independent living, affordable rent based on qualified income. 108 assisted living units. OFC HRS: M-F 9am-5pm. Spanish, Dutch spoken. ADM REQ: Total income under $23,000. SERVES: Inland Empire & Riverside County.

A & A HEARING AIDS

Formerly Internatl Hearing Aid Services
7720 Pacific Blvd.
Huntington Park, CA 90255
(323) 588-0742
(323) 588-6805 FAX

Answers questions about hearing aids: in-the-ear, behind-the-ear, earmolds, sound suppressors, assistive listening devices, batteries & repair srv. 100% digital technology available. Hearing Aid Assist Prgm. TDD assist. OFC HRS: M-F 9am-5pm. Spanish spoken. SERVES: U.S.A.

AARP/AMER ASSN/RETIRED PERSONS

200 S. Los Robles Ave., Ste 400
Pasadena, CA 91101
(866) 448-3615
(626) 583-8500 FAX

Non-partisan membership organization for people ages 50 yrs+. Info & resources, advocates on legislative, consumer, legal issues; offers a wide range of benefits. Additional office at 3200 E. Carson, Lakewood, CA 90712, (562) 496-2277. FUNDING: Nonprofit. OFC HRS: M-F 9am-5pm. Spanish spoken at the Lakewood ofc. SERVES: U.S.A.

AARP/AMER ASSN/RETIRED PERSONS

Riverside Chapter #237
3713 Tibbetts St.
Riverside, CA 92506
(951) 682-1416
(951) 682-2769 FAX

Volunteer community srvs. Tours & recreational activities for seniors ages 62 yrs+. Advocacy & insurance to members of the National AARP or Natl Retired Teachers Assn. Income tax assist, rental & homeowners for seniors. OFC HRS: M, Th 9am-12noon. Membership dues are $10 a yr per person. SERVES: City of Riverside & nearby.

AARP/PHARMACY SERVICE

Walgreens Health Initiatives
P.O. Box 2301
Muscle Shoals, AL 35662
(877) 422-7719
(800) 530-5014 FAX

Prescriptions and non-prescriptions at lower cost by mail. Srv not limited to AARP members. Allow 7 days for delivery. TTY (800) 925-0178. FUNDING: Nonprofit. OFC HRS: 24 hrs, 7 days. Pharmacist hrs: M-F 8am-4:30pm, EST. Spanish spoken. Accepts Medi-Cal. SERVES: U.S.A.

ADULT ABUSE REPORTING

Riverside Co. Public Social Srvs
(800) 491-7123
(951) 413-5815 FAX

To report any actual or suspected abuse, neglect or exploitation of elders or dependent adults, call the number shown above. FUNDING: County. Spanish spoken. Free srvs. SERVES: Riverside County.

ALARA ADVOCACY FOUNDATION

P.O. Box 3415
Culver City, CA 90231
(877) 292-5272
(818) 337-2181 FAX

Provides vital srvs for disabled persons and the elderly including: housing assist, medical devices, assist applying for Medi-Cal & Medicaid, food clothing, disaster kits, gifts for special occasions, bathroom equipment, pharmaceutical assist, & college entrance & financial worksops. Tailors srvs to the individual needs of client. FUNDING: Nonprofit. OFC HRS: M-F 9am-5pm. SERVES: L.A., Orange, & Riverside Counties.

ALS ASSOCIATION/NATIONAL

National Office (Lou Gehrig's Disease)
27001 Agoura Rd., Ste 250
Calabasas Hills, CA 91301-5104
(818) 880-9007
(818) 880-9006 FAX

Info, resource and referral srv for ALS patients & families. Public awareness and research support to find the cause and cure of ALS (Lou Gehrig's Disease). Support groups, patient srvs prgms. Patient hotline (800) 782-4747. FUNDING: Donations, nonprofit. OFC HRS: M-F 7:30am-4pm. Free srvs. SERVES: U.S.A.

ALZHEIMER'S ASSN/COACHELLA VALLEY

69730 Highway 111, Ste 202
Rancho Mirage, CA 92270
(760) 328-6767
(760) 328-2747 FAX

Info about Alzheimer's disease and related disorders. Referral to day care, diagnostic centers, support groups, legal srvs, case mgmt, home health agencies, physicians, nursing homes, etc. Literature, edu prgms. Edu events throughout the community for lay & professional people. Helpline (800) 272-3900. FUNDING: Nonprofit, donations. OFC HRS: M-F 8:30am-5pm. Spanish spoken. SERVES: Riverside County.

ALZHEIMER'S ASSN/NATIONAL

Natl Info & Referral Services
225 N. Michigan Ave., 17th Fl.
Chicago, IL 60601-7633
(800) 272-3900
(312) 335-8700
(866) 699-1246 FAX

Works to eliminate Alzheimer's disease through the advancement of research and enhance care & support for individuals, families & caregivers. Refers callers to their local chapters. Also provides literature on Alzheimer's disease. TDD (312) 335-5886. FUNDING: Nonprofit. OFC HRS: M-F 8:30am-5pm, CST. AT&T translators available. SERVES: U.S.A.

ALZHEIMER'S DISEASE EDU & REFERRAL

Natl Institute on Aging
P.O. Box 8250
Silver Spring, MD 20907-8250
(800) 438-4380
(301) 495-3334 FAX

Info, publications & referrals on Alzheimer's disease. Online order form for publications. After hrs recording accepts phone number and address for publications. TTY (800) 222-4225. Visit (www.alzheimers.org). FUNDING: Govt. OFC HRS: M-F 8:30am-5pm, EST. Spanish spoken. SERVES: U.S.A.

ALZHEIMER'S DISEASE RES/TREATMT CTR

UCI Institute for Memory Impairments

1100 Gottschalk Medical Plaza
Irvine, CA 92697
(949) 824-2382
(949) 824-3049 FAX

Specialized multidisciplinary assessment & treatment srvs for individuals with dementia or memory problems. Family conferences, ongoing support groups, and referral to other community resources as needed. Participation in ongoing univ research, including clinical drug trials and behavior studies. Testing available. The center is one of 11 state-designated ARCCs and operates at the UCI College of Medicine in Irvine. FUNDING: Nonprofit. OFC HRS: M-F 8:30am-5pm. Spanish & Vietnamese spoken. Accepts Medicare, Medi-Cal supplemental insurance and pvt payment. SERVES: So. Calif.

AMERICAN ASSN OF RETIRED PERSONS

See "AARP/Amer Assn/Retired Persons"

AMERICAN ASSN/GERIATRIC PSYCH

7910 Woodmont Ave., Ste 1050
Bethesda, MD 20814-3004
(301) 654-7850
(301) 654-4137 FAX

Free info and brochures, referrals and advocacy for the mental health needs of older people. FUNDING: Nonprofit. OFC HRS: M-F 9am-5pm, EST. SERVES: U.S.A.

AMERICAN SOCIETY ON AGING (ASA)

71 Stevenson St., Ste 4150
San Francisco, CA 94105-2938
(415) 974-9600
(800) 537-9728
(415) 974-0300 FAX

Works to enhance well-being of older individuals by enhancing the ability and commitment of those working with older adults. Offers 20 continuing edu opportunities per year, including an annual meeting and San Francisco summer series training prgm. Bestows awards, publishes "Aging Today," a newspaper, "Generations," a journal and several other topical newsletters on managed care, aging, etc. FUNDING: Donations, grants, dues, nonprofit. OFC HRS: M-F 8:30am-5pm. ADM REQ: Those who serve the elderly. SERVES: U.S.A.

AOK/ECOWAYS

10184 6th Street, Ste F
Rancho Cucamonga, CA 91730
(909) 477-6530

Supportive living srvs, supportive housing, work through Inland Regional Center, work with case worker, help to find jobs & budget money, maintenance of transition. FUNDING: Nonprofit. OFC HRS: M-F 9am-5pm. ADM REQ: Referral through IRC. SERVES: Rancho Cucamonga.

APPLE VALLEY SENIOR CITIZEN CLUB

13188 Central Rd.
Apple Valley, CA 92308
(760) 247-3155
(760) 247-1996 FAX

Social activites for seniors. Stop in for a list of current events. FUNDING: Nonprofit. OFC HRS: M-F 9am-4pm. Membership fees: $40 to start, $15 dues per year.

B'NAI B'RITH
Center for Senior Services
2020 K Street, NW, 7th Fl.
Washington, DC 20006
(202) 857-2785
(888) 388-4224
(202) 857-2785 FAX

Advocates for prgms for seniors and their families including subsidized housing and assisted living. FUNDING: Nonprofit. OFC HRS: M-F 9am-5pm. SERVES: U.S.A. & Canada.

BANNING SENIOR CENTER
P.O. Box 998
769 N. San Gorgonio Ave.
Banning, CA 92220
(951) 922-3250

Multipurpose senior citizen center offering recreational and social srv prgms. Info & referral srvs. Nutrition prgm site. Paralegal srvs, blood pressure check, crafts, bridge, sewing and needlework, quilting, Bingo, pinochle & notary srv. Advanced Spanish class, ESL, taxes, independent bus trips, special dances, etc. Cool center during 3-digit temperatures. M-F 8am-5pm. Walk in or call. Accepts donations. OFC HRS: M-Th 9am-2pm; F 9am-3pm. Fees vary. Many srvs are free. SERVES: Banning & the Pass area.

BARSTOW SENIOR CENTER
555 Melissa Ave.
Barstow, CA 92311
(760) 256-5023

Social activities, health screening & edu, legal assist, equipment loan prgm, Medi-Care counseling, postal alert, emerg response & volunteer opportunities. Meals on Wheels, lunch M-F 11:30am-12:30pm. FUNDING: United Way, govt, nonprofit. OFC HRS: M-Th 9am-3pm. F 9am-1pm. Spanish spoken. Fees under age 60 yrs $4.50, over age 60 yrs $3. SERVES: Barstow.

BEAR VALLEY SENIOR CTR
42651 Big Bear Blvd.
Big Bear Lake, CA 92315
(909) 584-0323

AARP income tax prep. Once a month distribution of USDA commodities. Lunches on M and W, breakfast on Th, line dancing, dominoes, Bingo, various classes and other activities. OFC HRS: M-F 9am-4pm. ADM REQ: Ages 55 yrs+. SERVES: Big Bear Valley.

BEAUMONT SENIOR CENTER
Senior Citizens & Community Services
1310 Oak Valley Pkwy.
Beaumont, CA 92223
(951) 769-8539
(951) 769-1372 FAX

Paralegal assist, outreach for seniors and persons with disabilities, exercise classes, tax assist, housing info, HICAP, fair housing referrals. Located in the Albert A. Chatigny Senior Community Recreation Center. FUNDING: City, Calif Dept of Rehab, ILC. OFC HRS: M-F 8am-4pm. Spanish spoken. SERVES: Beaumont & nearby.

BLYTHE SENIOR CENTER
445 N. Broadway
Blythe, CA 92225
(760) 922-8830

Senior citizens center providing a variety of social and recreational activities. Lunch served M-Th 11:30am. Call center for specific info. OFC HRS: M, Th 8am-12noon; Tu 8am-3pm. Spanish spoken. ADM REQ: Ages 60 yrs+ for nutrition prgm only. All ages welcome for all other srvs. Free srvs. Suggested lunch donation $3. SERVES: Desert area.

BONNIE BAKER SENIOR CENTER
149350 Ukiah Trail
Big River, CA 92242
(760) 665-2667
(760) 665-9475 FAX

Lunch served 8:30am-12:30pm during summer; by apt only during winter. Legal srvs, van transportation and various activities. Daily lunches M-F 11:30am-12noon. OFC HRS: M-F 7am-2pm Suggested donation of $3 per meal.

C.A.R.E. PROGRAM
See "Riverside Co. Public Social Srvs"

CABAZON COMMUNITY CENTER
See "James A. Venable Community Center"

CALIF ADVOCATES/NURSING HOME REF
650 Harrison St., 2nd Fl.
San Francisco, CA 94107
(800) 474-1116
(415) 974-5171
(415) 777-2904 FAX

Referrals to attorneys who specialize in elder law issues, including financial abuse, neglect & estate planning for long-term care. Provides statewide consumer info on Medi-Cal eligibility, pre-placement counseling & quality info on all nursing homes in Calif. FUNDING: Nonprofit. OFC HRS: M-F 9am-12noon, 1pm-5pm. ADM REQ: Call for appt, all ages served. Fees vary. Initial consultation is free. SERVES: Calif.

CALIF ASSN/HOMES/SRVS FOR AGING
1315 I Street, Ste 100
Sacramento, CA 95814
(916) 392-5111
(916) 428-4250 FAX

Represents more than 400 nonprofit providers of senior living srvs, including: affordable housing, continuing care retirement communities, assisted living, skilled nursing home & community-based care. CAHSAs advocacy, edu prgms, communications & other resources help its members best serve the needs of seniors. FUNDING: Nonprofit. OFC HRS: M-F 8am-5pm. SERVES: Calif.

CALIF COMMISSION ON AGING
1300 National Dr., Ste 173
Sacramento, CA 95834
(916) 419-7591
(916) 419-7596 FAX

Advocates for senior srvs, advisor to govt reps. Six meetings per year & public hearings. Refers callers to local Area Agency on Aging. FUNDING: Govt, nonprofit. OFC HRS: M-F 8am-5pm. SERVES: Calif.

CALIF DEPT AGING
Long-Term Care Ombudsman Prgm
1300 National Dr., Ste 200
Sacramento, CA 95834
(916) 419-7500
(916) 928-2268 FAX

Engages in advocacy for seniors and the disabled who are in long-term care facilities. Will refer callers to local ombudsman prgm district offices for further assist. 24-hr crisis line to report emerg situations that occur in long-term care facilities. TDD (800) 735-2929. FUNDING: Govt. OFC HRS: M-F 8am-5pm. ADM REQ: Seniors ages 60 yrs+. Free srvs. SERVES: Calif.

CALMA
Calif Advocates for Long-Term Care and Medi-Cal Assist
17130 Van Buren Blvd., Ste 181
Riverside, CA 92504
(877) 225-6202

Serves older adults and persons with disabilities at risk throughout Calif. Mission is to promote adult empowerment, prevent abuse and advocate for the rights and dignity of those experiencing health and aging issues. Dedicated to serving the needs of vulnerable adults. FUNDING: Nonprofit. Free srvs. SERVES: Calif.

CARE CONNEXXUS, INC.
Adult Day Srvs Center
4130 Adams St., Ste B
Riverside, CA 92504
(951) 509-2500
(951) 509-2578 FAX

Day care for adults ages 18-100 yrs with memory impairment. Support srvs include: counseling, family support groups, info & referral, case mgmt. Walk in or call. FUNDING: United Way, county, state, fees, nonprofit. OFC HRS: M-F 8am-5pm; prgm hrs: M-F 8:30am-2pm. Spanish spoken. ADM REQ: Must complete physician's health assessment form. Accepts SCAN, Medi-Cal, VA, pvt pay. Flat rate ADCP $51 per day, ADHC $77 per day; financial assist may be available. SERVES: Riverside County.

CARE CONNEXXUS, INC.
Adult Day Srvs Center
29995 Evans Rd.
Sun City, CA 92586
(951) 672-9536
(951) 672-0486 FAX

Day care for adults ages 40 yrs+. Specializes in caring for persons with memory impairment. Support srvs, counseling, family support groups, info & referral, and case mgmt. Walk in or call. OFC HRS: M-F 8:30am-2pm. Flat rate fee for half day or full day; financial assist may be available. Some insurance accepted. SERVES: Sun City, Temecula Valley, Lake Elsinore Valley and Perris Valley.

CARRIER ALERT PROGRAM
U.S. Postal Service

Prgm works with senior service agencies to alert you if the mail starts to build up in the mailbox of a residence which they identify by a sticker in the mailbox. OFC HRS: M-F 8:30am-5pm, varies with offices. Free srvs.

CASA BLANCA HOME OF NEIGHBORLY SRV
7680 Casa Blanca St.
Riverside, CA 92504
(951) 688-3043
(951) 688-3286 FAX

Senior prgms, Head Start prgm & emerg assist. Walk in. FUNDING: United Way, Riverside Co. Depts of Mental Health, Probation & Office of Ed, nonprofit. OFC HRS: Tu-F 8:30am-5pm. Spanish spoken. ADM REQ: Primarily for residents of the Casa Blanca community. Free srvs. SERVES: Riverside.

CATHOLIC CHARITIES/COMMUNITY SRVS

Administration
1450 North D Street
San Bernardino, CA 92405
(909) 388-1239
(909) 384-1130 FAX

Psychological counseling for individuals & family, case mgmt, emerg food, diapers, clothing, furniture (when available), utility assist, holiday baskets, transportation, advocacy, HIV/AIDS srvs, info & referrals. Emerg housing for needy transients with pre-arranged motel accommodations (as funds allow). Refugee & immigration srvs, parolee reintegration. FUNDING: Donations, nonprofit. OFC HRS: M-F 8:30am-4:30pm. Spanish, Chinese, Filipino, Vietnamese, Russian spoken. Sliding fee scale. SERVES: San Bernardino & Riverside Counties.

CENTRAL CO. UNITED WAY

Retired & Senior Volunteer Prgm
418 E. Florida Ave.
Hemet, CA 92543
(951) 929-0423
(951) 652-0064 FAX

Federally funded prgm recruits, trains and places senior volunteers ages 55 yrs+ and provides a variety of opportunities to participate more fully in the life of their community. RSVP currently has 60 prgms with over 850 volunteers. FUNDING: Fed, nonprofit. OFC HRS: M-F 8:30am-5pm. ADM REQ: Application process for volunteers. Free srvs. SERVES: Beaumont, Banning, Hemet, San Jacinto, Menifee, Perris, Sun City, Temecula, Murrieta.

CHINO COMMUNITY SERVICES

Human Services Division
13201 Central Ave.
Chino, CA 91710
(909) 591-9822
(909) 628-4093 FAX

Counseling srvs for children & adults. Community & school-based prevention & edu. Drug prevention, family treatment, teen and adult parenting classes, domestic violence, anger mgmt, community outreach, senior srvs, disabled srvs info & referral, PC-1000. For emergencies, call (909) 628-1010. FUNDING: State, county, school, city, govt. OFC HRS: M-Th 8am-8pm; F 8am-6pm. Spanish spoken. Free srvs or a nominal fee for some srvs. SERVES: Western San Bernardino County.

CHINO HILLS COMM SRVS DEPT

14000 City Center Dr.
Chino Hills, CA 91709-4868
(909) 364-2710
(909) 364-2725 FAX

The dept provides various types of programs and services for the community. Chino Hills advisory and mentoring prgm, youth accountability board, seniors assisted by visiting volunteers and youth, volunteer service prgm. FUNDING: Govt. OFC HRS: M-Th 7:30am-5:30pm; F 7:30am-4:30pm. Free srvs. SERVES: Chino Hills.

CHINO SENIOR CENTER

13170 Central Ave.
Chino, CA 91710
(909) 591-9836

Social activities, exercise, Bingo, income tax assist, case mgmt, info & referral. Brown Bag food prgm, Meals on Wheels, 5-6 frozen meals delivered on W, donation $2.50. Call (909) 628-0071. Business Hrs: M-F 8am-8pm; Sun 10am-6pm. FUNDING: Nonprofit. OFC HRS: M-F 8am-4pm. Spanish spoken. SERVES: San Bernardino County.

COACHELLA SENIOR CENTER

1540 7th Street
Coachella, CA 92236
(760) 398-0104
(760) 398-3712 FAX

Nutrition, recreation, arts and crafts, card games, etc. Walk in. FUNDING: County, city. OFC HRS: M-Th 7:30am-5:30pm. Spanish spoken. SERVES: Coachella.

COLORADO RIVER SENIOR COMM CENTER

HCR 20, Box 3408
Blythe, CA 92225
(760) 922-6133
(760) 922-6135 FAX

Senior recreation and activities, daily lunches, info & referral. Walk in. Lunches are $3. Center is 27 miles north of Blythe at Hidden Valley on Hwy 95. FUNDING: County, fundraising. OFC HRS: M-F 9am-3pm. Summer 9am-1pm. $5 membership fee. SERVES: Blythe & nearby.

COLTON NEIGHBORHOOD SRVS DEPT

670 Colton Ave.
Colton, CA 92324
(909) 370-6153
(909) 777-3351 FAX

City office offers 3 different types of srvs: child care, recreation prgm & community center activities, family srvs including a senior nutrition prgm. Info & referral for child care, health care, housing and other human srv prgms and assist with translations, interpretation, completion of forms, senior health screening and income tax assist for residents of the Colton area. OFC HRS: M-F 8am-8pm. Spanish spoken. Free srvs. Donation requested for senior nutrition prgm. SERVES: San Bernardino County.

COMMUNITY CARE LICENSING

Calif Dept of Social Srvs
3737 Main St., Ste 600
Riverside, CA 92501
(951) 782-4207
(951) 782-4967 FAX

Regulate residential care facilities for the elderly. Investigate complaints and conduct evaluations of the facilities. OFC HRS: M-F 8am-5pm. Spanish spoken. SERVES: Riverside, San Bernardino Counties.

COMMUNITY CENTER AT TIERRA DEL SOL

Cathedral City Senior Center
37171 W. Buddy Rodgers Ave.
Cathedral City, CA 92234
(760) 321-1548
(760) 321-0280 FAX

Outreach social services and health info and referrals, home visitations, social activities, senior health and nutrition programs. Also bridge, bingo, crafts, dance programs, etc. Transportation available for outreach clients. Utilities assist. FUNDING: Grants, donations. OFC HRS: M-F 8am-4pm. Spanish, French, German, Italian spoken. Free srvs, membership is

encouraged and donations accepted. SERVES: Coachella Valley.

COMMUNITY HOME HEALTH

1805 Medical Center Dr.
San Bernardino, CA 92411
(909) 887-6333
(877) 966-3066
(909) 806-1059 FAX

Skilled health care to homebound patients, RN, home health aide, PT, OT, speech pathology, medical social srvs, mental health, perinatal & pediatric care. JCAHO accredited. FUNDING: Nonprofit. OFC HRS: M-F 8am-4:30pm. Spanish spoken. ADM REQ: Physician order, medical necessity, homebound. Accepts Medi-Cal, Medicare, HMO, pvt pay, insurance. SERVES: East San Bernardino County.

COMMUNITY SETTLEMENT ASSOCIATION

4366 Bermuda Ave.
Riverside, CA 92507
(951) 686-6266
(951) 782-2337 FAX

Social & recreational activities for seniors. Drinking driving prgm (listed separately) and referrals for treatment of alcoholism. Free food for all ages in 92507 zip code only, M, W, F 10:30am-11am. Walk in or call. Senior nights TBA once a month for ages 55 yrs+. Summer camp TBA. FUNDING: Nonprofit. OFC HRS: M-F 8am-5pm. Spanish spoken. ADM REQ: After school & summer prgms for grades 1-7. Food prgm recipients must have photo ID, proof of residency, proof of income. Accepts donations. SERVES: Riverside metro.

CONGRESS OF CALIFORNIA SENIORS

1230 N Street, Ste 201
Sacramento, CA 95814
(800) 543-3352
(916) 442-4474
(916) 442-1877 FAX

Focuses on issues that affect seniors. Website has info on health/wellness and much more, visit (www.seniors.org). FUNDING: Nonprofit. SERVES: Calif.

COOPER-BURKHART HOUSE

See "Care Connexxus, Inc."

COPS FOR KIDS, INC.

P.O. Box 2001
333 Limited St.
Lake Elsinore, CA 92531
(951) 245-3389
(951) 245-3311 FAX

Outreach to community children ages birth-18 yrs. Also senior citizen assist prgm. FUNDING: County. OFC HRS: M-F 9am-5pm. Spanish spoken. ADM REQ: Must fill out request form in person at the sheriff's office. Free srvs. SERVES: Lake Elsinore.

CORONA PARKS/REC/COMM SRVS DEPT

400 S. Vincentia Ave.
Corona, CA 92882
(951) 736-2241
(951) 279-3683 FAX

Recreation prgms & srvs for all ages. Leisure activity classes. After school kids clubs for youth ages 5-12 yrs for a minimal cost. Senior citizens srvs, food prgms and specialty classes. Sports, swimming and many special events annually. Walk in or call. OFC HRS: M-F 8am-5pm. Spanish spoken. SERVES: Corona.

CORONA SENIOR CENTER
921 S. Belle Ave.
Corona, CA 92882
(951) 736-2363
(951) 736-6837 FAX

Senior info & referral, social prgms, health info, wide range of activities. FUNDING: Govt. OFC HRS: M-Th 7:30am-5pm, 6pm-9pm; F 7:30am-5pm; Sat 7:30am-12noon. Spanish spoken. ADM REQ: Ages 50 yrs+. SERVES: Corona, Norco, Riverside.

COUNTRY VILLA BELLA VISTA HLTHCARE
Skilled Nursing Facility
933 E. Deodar St.
Ontario, CA 91764
(909) 985-2731
(909) 985-1414 FAX

59-bed facility serves ages 60 yrs+, ambulatory, non-ambulatory, Alzheimer's. OFC HRS: M-F 9am-4pm. Spanish, Tagalog, Indonesian spoken. Accepts Medi-Cal, Medicare, HMO, SSI. SERVES: Ontario.

COUNTRY VILLA HACIENDA HEALTHCARE
Formerly Mountainside Healthcare Center
1311 E. Date St.
San Bernardino, CA 92404
(909) 882-3316
(909) 882-5126 FAX

99-bed facility serves ages 55 yrs+, ambulatory, non-ambulatory. OFC HRS: M-F 8am-5:30pm. Spanish & Tagalog spoken. Accepts Medi-Cal, Medicare, SSI. SERVES: San Bernardino.

CREST FOREST SENIOR CITIZENS CLUB
Leisure Shores Site
P.O. Box 0317
24658 San Moritz Dr.
Crestline, CA 92325
(909) 338-5036

Arts & crafts and special events for seniors ages 55 yrs+. Various classes and activities. Thrift store, craft fair. FUNDING: Nonprofit. OFC HRS: M-F 9am-3pm.

DALES SENIOR CENTER
3936 Chestnut St.
Riverside, CA 92501
(951) 826-5303
(951) 826-2005 FAX

Info & referral for senior srvs, recreation prgms and special interest classes offered. FUNDING: City. OFC HRS: M-F 9am-3pm. Free srvs. Breakfast is $3. SERVES: Riverside County.

DELMANN HEIGHTS COMM CENTER
2969 Flores St.
San Bernardino, CA 92407
(909) 384-5417
(909) 880-0809 FAX

Prgms include: senior nutrition, quilting, ESL, piano lessons, county health nurse and food distribution (USDA commodities). Open recreation. Free summer lunch for ages 1-18 yrs. Teen prgm, swimming pool (June-August) and Head Start preschool. OFC HRS: M-F 9am-6pm. Spanish spoken. SERVES: San Bernardino County.

DESERT HOT SPRINGS SENIOR SRVS
111-777 West Dr.
Desert Hot Springs, CA 92240
(760) 329-0222
(760) 329-5972 FAX

Outreach, info & referral, county nutrition on site, homebound meals, tax srvs, health screening. Meal served daily 11:30am. Walk in or call. FUNDING: City. OFC HRS: M-Th 8am-2pm; F 8am-1pm. ADM REQ: Ages 55 yrs+. Must reserve meal one day in advance. Free srvs, except nutrition. On-site meals $3 for members, $5 for non-members. SERVES: Desert Hot Springs, Painted Hills, North Palm Springs, Sky Valley.

DEVELOPING AGING SOLUTIONS/HEART
P.O. Box 8370
306 W. Colton Ave.
Redlands, CA 92374
(909) 798-1667
(888) 798-1667
(909) 335-0236 FAX

Srvs to elderly including adult day support center, Alzheimer's respite ctr, counseling, case mgmt, edu, info & referral, support groups, research, and professional consultation. Sponsorship may be available. FUNDING: United Way, donations, fees, nonprofit. OFC HRS: M-F 9am-5pm. SERVES: Redlands & nearby including Riverside area.

EDDIE DEE SMITH SENIOR CENTER
5888 Mission Blvd.
Riverside, CA 92509
(951) 275-9975
(951) 275-9745 FAX

Senior srvs, social & recreational activities, food prgms, trips and tours, crafts, painting, quilting, Bingo, ceramics, RSVP (Retired Senior Volunteer Prgm), transportation srvs. Walk in or call. FUNDING: County, EDC, nonprofit. OFC HRS: M-F 8am-3pm. Spanish spoken. ADM REQ: Ages 60 yrs+, live in area. SERVES: Riverside County.

EISENHOWER MED CTR FIVE STAR CLUB
Adult Day Program
42201 Beacon Hill, Ste A
Palm Desert, CA 92211
(760) 836-0232
(760) 773-2642 FAX

Social activities and personal care for the frail elderly and respite & supportive srvs for caregivers. Special prgms for those with Alzheimer's disease and other memory impairments. Free info, referral & support groups. FUNDING: Client fees, donations. OFC HRS: M-F 7:30am-5pm. Spanish, Tagalog spoken. ADM REQ: Transfer, minimum standby assist. Accepts SCAN, some long-term care insurance. SERVES: Palm Springs to Indio.

ELDER ABUSE
See "Riverside Co. Public Social Srvs" and "San Bernardino Co. Human Srvs Sy" (Adult Protective Srvs).

ELDERCARE LOCATOR
1730 Rhode Island Ave., Ste 1200
Washington, DC 20036
(800) 677-1116

Nationwide directory assist srv that helps older Americans & their caregivers locate local support resources that aid independent living. Visit (www.eldercare.gov) or (www.n4a.org). FUNDING: U.S. Admin on Aging, govt. Spanish spoken. SERVES: U.S.A.

EMMANUEL UNIQUE OUTREACH PARTNERS
P.O. Box 1861
Corona, CA 92878
(951) 279-0031
(760) 955-0007 FAX

Various prgms offered including: homework assist, literacy, enrichment for students, senior visits, summer food srvs, personal training, nonprofit creation. FUNDING: Nonprofit. OFC HRS: M-F 8am-5pm. SERVES: Riverside County.

EYECARE AMERICA
Seniors EyeCare Prgm
P.O. Box 429098
655 Beach St.
San Francisco, CA 94142-9098
(877) 887-6327
(415) 561-8567 FAX

Provides a comprehensive medical eye exam and up to one year of care for anything diagnosed at exam time at no out-of-pocket cost. Uninsured are seen at no charge for physician's services. FUNDING: Knights Templar Eye Fndn Inc., state ophthalmological societies, nonprofit. OFC HRS: 24 hrs, 7 days. Spanish spoken. ADM REQ: Ages 65 yrs+, a citizen or legal resident who has not seen an ophthalmologist in 3 yrs or more. Medicare and insurance are billed and accepted as payment in full. SERVES: U.S.A.

FAMILY SERVICE ASSN/WEST RIVERSIDE
Mead Valley Comm/Senior & Disabled Srvs
21091 Rider St.
Perris, CA 92570
(951) 657-0686
(951) 657-9208 FAX

Home-delivered meals, wellness center, advisory board meetings, senior meetings, AA & NA meetings, kinship meeting, summer school prgms, computers, Bingo, commodity food distribution, crafts, business network, congregate meals, THRIVE forums, food bank, postmaster's community srv. FUNDING: Nonprofit. OFC HRS: M-F 9am-5pm. Spanish spoken. ADM REQ: Depends on srvs. SERVES: Western Riverside County.

FAMILY SERVICE ASSN/WEST RIVERSIDE
Kay Ceniceros Center
29995 Evans Rd.
Sun City, CA 92586
(951) 672-9673
(951) 301-1923 FAX

Community and senior srvs, social and recreational activities, special events, workshops, food prgms, trips and tours, adult day care, info & assist, outreach to homebound frail. Walk in or call. Small donation requested (except trips). Room rentals available for wedding receptions, large birthday parties, etc. FUNDING: CDBG, donations. OFC HRS: M-F 8am-5pm. Classes are generally $1-2 per person. SERVES: Sun City, Menifee Valley.

FAMILY SERVICE ASSOCIATION
Mental Health Clinic
21250 Box Springs Rd., Ste 201
Moreno Valley, CA 92557
(951) 686-3706
(951) 686-7267 FAX

Full-srv marriage, family, child, individual and group counseling. Medi-Cal prgm for children.

Counseling office site in Riverside. Senior nutrition/home-delivered meals in Sun City & Mead Valley, San Jacinto, Hemet, Reno Valley, Cabazon, Banning, Calimesa, Desert Hot Springs. Child dev prgm with child care sites in La Sierra, Mead Valley, Rubidoux. Adult day srvs in Hemet, (951)791-3556. FUNDING: State, grants, contracts, United Way, donations, nonprofit. OFC HRS: M-F 8am-5pm. Clinic M-Th 8pm-9pm; F 8am-5pm. Spanish spoken. Sliding fee scale. SERVES: West & mid-Riverside County.

FIFTH STREET SENIOR CENTER
San Bernardino City Parks/Rec
600 W. 5th Street
San Bernardino, CA 92410
(909) 384-5430
(909) 889-0672 FAX

Center activities include crafts, Bingo, health screenings, food distributions (USDA commodities), HICAP counseling, legal counseling, free health edu, senior transportation, special events and adult classes. FUNDING: Nonprofit. OFC HRS: M-F 8am-4pm. Spanish spoken. SERVES: San Bernardino.

GENERATIONS UNITED
1333 H Street, NW, Ste 900
Washington, DC 20005
(202) 289-3979
(202) 289-3952 FAX

Online resource for educating the public & policy makers regarding improvement of the lives of children, youth, & older adults. Aim is to do so through intergenerational collaboration, public policies and prgms. Visit (www.gu.org) to find prgms in your area. SERVES: U.S.A.

GEORGE GIBSON SENIOR CENTER
250 N. 3rd Avenue
Upland, CA 91786
(909) 981-4501
(909) 981-3762 FAX

Social activities for seniors ages 55 yrs+. Legal assist, HICAP, support groups on M, food distribution on 2nd Tu each month. Senior meals M-F 11:30am. Suggested donation of $2.50. Senior health clinic 4th Tu 9am-12noon (appt required). Blood pressure check, vision, hearing, medicine check, blood sugar testing at various times during the year. FUNDING: Nonprofit. OFC HRS: M-F 8:30am-5pm; Sat 9am-12noon. Spanish spoken. SERVES: San Bernardino County.

GLEN AVON SENIOR CENTER
See "Family Service Assn/West Riverside"

GOLDEN RAINBOW SENIOR CENTER
611 S. Palm Canyon Dr., Ste 201
Palm Springs, CA 92264
(760) 416-7790
(760) 416-7786 FAX

Advocates for the unique needs of the GLBT senior community. Hosts a wide range of social, recreational, edu & service-oriented prgms, activities, and events. Volunteer opportunities available. FUNDING: Nonprofit. OFC HRS: M-F 8:30am-4:30pm. Evening and weekend programs as announced. SERVES: Coachella Valley.

GRANDPARENT INFORMATION CENTER
AARP
9750 3rd Avenue, N.E., Ste 450

Seattle, WA 98115
(866) 227-7457
(206) 517-9350 FAX

Info & referral, resources and policy efforts regarding grandparents raising grandchildren. Booklets available in Spanish or English. Free newsletter. FUNDING: Nonprofit. OFC HRS: M-F 9am-5pm, EST. SERVES: U.S.A.

GRANDPARENTS RAISING GRANDCHILDREN
Riverside Co. Office on Aging
1075 N. State St.
Hemet, CA 92543
(800) 303-0001
(951) 791-3575

This warmline was established to assist grandparents with issues they face when raising grandchildren. Childcare srvs (as funds are available) and case management available. FUNDING: County. OFC HRS: M-Th 8am-5pm. SERVES: Riverside County.

HEALTH GUARD INLAND
Adult Day Health Care
268 McArthur Way
Upland, CA 91786
(909) 920-1165
(909) 949-3800 FAX

Older adult day care. Nursing, personal care, exercise, social srvs, lunch, transportation and activities provided. OFC HRS: M-F 8am-4:30pm. Spanish spoken. ADM REQ: Ages 18 yrs+, medical diagnosis. Accepts Medi-Cal, SCAN, pvt pay. SERVES: San Bernardino County.

HEARING AID DISPENSER BOARD
Department of Consumer Affairs
1625 N. Market Blvd., Ste S-202
Sacramento, CA 95834
(916) 574-7990
(916) 574-8645 FAX

State agency that licenses individuals to fit and sell hearing aids. Provides info to consumers on licensed hearing aid dispensers license status and a 30-day warranty on hearing aids and other laws. Accepts and processes consumer complaints relating to hearing aids. Provides consumer info. TDD (916) 322-1700. OFC HRS: M-F 8am-5pm. ADM REQ: Ages 18 yrs+ & HS diploma or equivalent. Complaint & mediation srvs at no charge. SERVES: Calif.

HEARING AID HELPLINE
International Hearing Society
16880 Middlebelt Rd., Ste 4
Livonia, MI 48154
(734) 522-7200
(800) 521-5247
(734) 522-0200 FAX

Internatl source for general info on hearing aids and referrals to local hearing aid specialists. FUNDING: Membership, nonprofit. OFC HRS: M-F 8am-5pm, EST. SERVES: U.S.A.

HEART TOUCH PROJECT
3400 Airport Ave., Ste 42
Santa Monica, CA 90405
(310) 391-2558
(310) 391-2168 FAX

Compassionate & healing touch therapy provided by professional therapists & volunteers to persons with AIDS, non-ambulatory persons, senior citizens, persons receiving hospice care,

infants & children. FUNDING: Nonprofit. OFC HRS: M-F 10am-6pm. ADM REQ: Must have approval of primary health provider to ensure that the massage is allowed for the patient's condition. Accepts donations. Free srvs. SERVES: So. Calif.

HELEN WOODWARD ANIMAL CENTER
P.O. Box 64
6461 El Apajo Rd.
Rancho Santa Fe, CA 92067
(858) 756-4117
(858) 756-1466 FAX

Dog & cat adoptions, humane edu, AniMeals for pets of the homebound elderly, Pet Encounter Therapy for people in institutions, therapeutic horseback riding for the physically and mentally challenged, animal hospital, pet boarding. FUNDING: Nonprofit. OFC HRS: M-Sun 11am-6pm. SERVES: San Diego, Riverside & Orange Counties.

HESPERIA REC & PARK SENIOR CTR
9333 E Avenue
Hesperia, CA 92345
(760) 244-1680

Social activities, health screening & edu, food prgm, Meals on Wheels donation $2. Send mail to P.O. Box 401055, Hesperia 92340. FUNDING: Govt. OFC HRS: M-F 8:30am-3:30pm. SERVES: Hesperia.

HICAP
Health Insurance Counseling/Advocacy Prgm
1737 Atlanta, Ste H-5
Riverside, CA 92507
(800) 434-0222
(951) 697-6560
(951) 694-7980 FAX

Counseling & advocacy in Medicare-related issues, health insurance, HMOs, Medicare billing & LTC. Community edu to groups at no cost. FUNDING: Calif Dept of Aging. OFC HRS: M-F 8am-4pm. Spanish spoken. ADM REQ: Ages 60 yrs+ or Medicare beneficiary. Accepts donations. Free srvs. SERVES: Riverside, Inyo, Mono, San Bernardino Counties.

HIGHLAND SENIOR CENTER
P.O. Box 948
3102 E. Highland Ave.
Patton, CA 92369
(909) 862-8104
(909) 862-8196 FAX

Supportive srvs and recreational activities for older adults including: transportation and escort for medical, business, grocery shopping, etc. Friendly visitor prgm, senior info and referral, shopping assist for homebound, health edu & training, peer counseling and group activities. FUNDING: United Way, city, donations. OFC HRS: M-F 8am-4pm. ADM REQ: Ages 60 yrs+. Must live in service area. Must be able to get in and out of a car on their own. Free srvs. SERVES: Highland, San Bernardino & nearby.

HOME IMPROVEMENT PROGRAM
Economic Dev Agency/Riverside Co.
3403 Tenth St., Ste 500
Riverside, CA 92502
(951) 351-0700
(800) 655-4228
(951) 955-6686 FAX

Prgm designed to improve residential neighborhoods by assisting low and moderate income seniors and disabled persons with rehab financing. Currently two prgms available: Deferred loans and low interest loan prgm. 60 day escrow. TDD: (951)351-9844. FUNDING: CDBG, federal (HUD), govt. OFC HRS: M-Th 8am-5pm. Spanish spoken. ADM REQ: Income within HUD guidelines. Application is free. SERVES: Riverside County, except Riverside City, Corona, Palm Springs, Moreno Valley.

HOMEOWNER/RENTER ASSISTANCE
Calif Franchise Tax Board
(800) 868-4171
(916) 845-0484 FAX

Assists homeowners and renters who are ages 62 yrs+, blind or disabled, with low income. Eligible recipients receive annual refund. TDD (800) 822-6268. FUNDING: Govt. OFC HRS: M-F 8am-5pm. Spanish spoken. Free srvs. SERVES: Calif.

INDIAN HEALTH, INC.
Senior Services Morongo Clinic
11555 1/2 Potrero Rd.
Banning, CA 92220
(951) 849-4761
(951) 849-8259 FAX

Noon meals, nutrition counseling, supportive srvs. Physical, mental, dental srvs, health promotion. Sponsors senior nutrition prgms 11am-12noon at Morongo, Pechanga and Soboba Indian Reservations. Walk in or call. FUNDING: Title III, Title VI. OFC HRS: M-Th 8am-5pm; F 8am-2pm. ADM REQ: American Indian. Free srvs. SERVES: Riverside, San Bernardino Counties.

INDIO SENIOR CENTER
45-700 Aladdin St.
Indio, CA 92201
(760) 391-4170
(760) 391-6448 FAX

Multi-purpose senior center, info & referral srv. Recreational & socialization, edu & info prgms, health screening, Meals on Wheels, exercise classes, income tax assist, HICAP assist with property & renter rebates, home-delivered meals. Walk in or call. FUNDING: City, donations, nonprofit. OFC HRS: M-F 7:30am-5:30pm. Spanish spoken. Free srvs. SERVES: Indio area.

INLAND AGENCY
1737 Atlanta, Ste H-5
Riverside, CA 92507
(951) 241-8723
(951) 683-7980 FAX

Challenges of Youth. Adelanto Community Toolbox. HICAP (Health Insurance Counseling and Advocacy Prgm), Desert Sierra Breast Cancer Partnership. Part of a state and nationwide prgm for Medicare beneficiaries. FUNDING: Fed, state, county, fndn, donations, nonprofit. OFC HRS: M-F 8am-5pm. Spanish spoken. Free srvs. SERVES: Riverside, San Bernardino, Inyo, Mono Counties.

INLAND COUNTIES HEALTH SYSTEMS
See "Inland Agency"

INTER VALLEY HEALTH PLAN
P.O. Box 6002
300 S. Park Ave.
Pomona, CA 91769-6002
(800) 500-7018
(909) 622-2907 FAX

Healthcare for persons enrolled in Medicare Part B and entitled to Medicare Part A, and persons ages 65 yrs+ who are entitled to Medicare/Social Security disability benefits. FUNDING: Nonprofit. OFC HRS: Daily 7:30am-8pm. SERVES: Portions of L.A., San Bernardino & Riverside Counties.

INTERNAL REVENUE SERVICE (IRS)
Taxpayer Edu
P.O. Box 30210
24000 Avila Rd., Ste 3401
Laguna Niguel, CA 92677
(949) 389-4002
(949) 389-5023 FAX

IRS and the Franchise Tax Board co-sponsor two prgms to assist taxpayers with prep of their state and federal income tax returns. VITA (Volunteer Income Tax Assist) and TCE (Tax Counseling for the Elderly) volunteers offer free tax prep assist Feb 1-April 15 at many community locations. OFC HRS: Tu, Th, F 8:30am-4:30pm; closed from 1pm-2pm. SERVES: So. Calif, except L.A. County.

JAMES A. VENABLE COMMUNITY CENTER
Family Service Association
P.O. Box 349
50390 Carmen Ave.
Cabazon, CA 92230
(951) 922-1097
(951) 849-2961 FAX

Srvs, activities, referrals for home repair for seniors, recreation, after school prgm, Carol's Kitchen M & Th 11:30am. Walk in or call. OFC HRS: M-F 8:30am-5pm; summer 8am-5pm. Spanish spoken. Call for info. SERVES: Cabazon.

JAMES L. BRULTE SENIOR CTR
11200 Baseline Rd.
Rancho Cucamonga, CA 91730
(909) 477-2782
(909) 477-2787 FAX

Crafts, Bingo, commodity food distribution, info & referral, HICAP, blood pressure checks 2nd Tu, health edu, legal counseling, senior transportation and nutrition prgm. FUNDING: City. OFC HRS: M-F 8am-10pm; Sat 8am-6pm; Sun 9am-5pm. ADM REQ: Must fill out application and pay a $25 annual fee for transportation services. $12 fee for gym. SERVES: West End San Bernardino County, primarily Rancho Cucamonga.

JANET GOESKE CENTER
5257 Sierra St.
Riverside, CA 92504
(951) 351-8800
(951) 351-9731 FAX

Nutrition, phone assist, info & referral, ombudsman (other than nursing homes). Housing info, health eval, stroke and arthritis support groups. Line dancing, exercise, fitness and srvs for the disabled seniors, food sharing, estate planning and bridge tournaments. Walk in or call. FUNDING: City of Riverside. OFC HRS: M-F 7am-9pm; Sat 7:30am-4:30pm; Sun 1pm-5pm. ADM REQ: Ages 50 yrs+. Free srvs.

JEWISH FAMILY SERVICE OF THE DESERT
Palm Springs-Desert Area
801 E. Tahquitz Canyon Way, Ste 202
Palm Springs, CA 92262
(760) 325-4088
(760) 778-3781 FAX

Counseling, senior case mgmt, info & referral srvs for individuals, couples and families. Specialized support groups based on need (i.e. group for widowed persons, people in divorce process and resolving problems of everyday living), case mgmt srvs for frail, elderly adults. Project Outreach provides volunteer srvs to older persons in residential and skilled nursing facilities, including friendly visitors. Shabbat welcome and celebration of Jewish holidays. Wait: within one week. FUNDING: Jewish Federation, United Way, fndn, donations, fees, nonprofit. OFC HRS: M-Th 8:30am-5pm; F 8am-4pm. Spanish spoken upon request. Accepts Medi-Cal/Medicare combined and many insurance plans. Sliding fee scale for counseling & case mgmt. SERVES: Coachella Valley.

JOSLYN SENIOR CTR/COVE COMM
73-750 Catalina Way
Palm Desert, CA 92260
(760) 340-3220
(760) 568-9230 FAX

Meals on Wheels, info & referral srv, legal aid, 55 Alive classes, HICAP counseling, Spanish lessons, outreach. Bridge lessons, mah jong, table tennis. yoga and other activities, creative writing, various art classes. OFC HRS: M-F 8am-5pm; Sat 8am-1pm. Spanish spoken.

JOSLYN SENIOR CTR/REDLANDS
City of Redlands
P.O. Box 3005
21 Grant St.
Redlands, CA 92373
(909) 798-7550
(909) 798-7554 FAX

Singing groups, workshops, dance classes, walking & exercise groups, craft classes, sign language (ASL) classes, Bingo, movies, insurance counseling, monthly legal srvs, bridge groups, gardening, monthly dances, special events, trips and more. County nutritional prgm located at Lugonia Ave. Health clinic 2nd Tu 9am-12noon (appt required). Blood pressure, vision, hearing, medicine & blood sugar checks. Available for rent after hours. FUNDING: City, donations, nonprofit. OFC HRS: M-F 8am-5pm. Spanish spoken. ASL available. ADM REQ: Ages 50 yrs+. Free srvs. Some fees for specific activities. SERVES: Redlands.

JUST FOR SENIORS
Loma Linda University Medical Ctr
11406 Loma Linda Dr.
Loma Linda, CA 92354
(909) 558-6618
(909) 558-6669 FAX

Free community membership for ages 55 yrs+. Discounts, classes, seminars, events. Newsletter, fitness ctr memberships at nominal fees. FUNDING: Nonprofit. OFC HRS: M-Th 8am-5pm; F 8am-12noon. Spanish spoken SERVES: Inland Empire.

KAY CENICEROS SENIOR CENTER
See "Family Service Assn/West Riverside"

LA QUINTA SENIOR CENTER
P.O. Box 1504
78-450 Avenida La Fonda
La Quinta, CA 92253
(760) 564-0096
(760) 564-5004 FAX

Social and recreational activities. Legal and Medicare assist, adult edu, health screening, community resources. Info & referral. Call recommended, as most srvs require appt. FUNDING: Nonprofit. OFC HRS: M-F 8am-5pm. Many free srvs. SERVES: Coachella Valley.

LAKE ELSINORE SENIOR CTR

420 E. Lakeshore Dr.
Lake Elsinore, CA 92530
(951) 674-2526
(951) 674-7731 FAX

Info & referral, senior nutrition prgm daily (senior lunch connection), assist with forms, paralegal srvs, recreational activities, income tax assist, outreach, arts & crafts. Nutrition program (951)471-3571. FUNDING: City. OFC HRS: M-Th 8am-4pm; F 9am-4pm. Spanish spoken. ADM REQ: Ages 60 yrs+. Free srvs. Nutrition prgm $3 donation. SERVES: Lake Elsinore & nearby.

LIFE SERVICES, INC.

1111 N. Brand Blvd., Ste K
Glendale, CA 91202
(818) 547-0585
(818) 547-1093 FAX

Complete personalized care encompassing medical, financial, social, spiritual, and psych needs for seniors ages 60 yrs+. Srvs include: life care planning, personalized care, professional conservatorship (a guardian), trust mgmt, estate admin and referrals. FUNDING: Client fees, nonprofit. OFC HRS: M-F 9am-4:30pm; 24-hr srvs. Chinese and Spanish spoken. ADM REQ: Ages 60 yrs+. Sliding fee scale. SERVES: L.A. & adjoining counties.

LIFELINE SYSTEMS, INC.

111 Lawrence St.
Framingham, MA 01702-8156
(800) 380-3111
(800) 448-0107 FAX

Partnership project of state, community and pvt hospitals and health care affiliates using a communication device located in the home. Allows at-risk elders or disabled residents to electronically call for medical assist when a health crisis occurs and they are unable to use the phone. Local providers are identified by ZIP code to calling parties. OFC HRS: M-F 8am-8pm, EST. SERVES: U.S.A.

LONG-TERM CARE OMBUDSMAN/CRISIS

Crisis Line
1971 E. 4th Street, Ste 200
Santa Ana, CA 92705-3917
(714) 479-0107
(800) 300-6222
(714) 479-0234 FAX

24-hr crisis line for people concerned about serious problems that may exist in a nursing home facility, such as abuse, diet, Medicare, etc. Local ombudsman speaks directly to residents concerning problems. Crisisline: (800) 231-4024. FUNDING: Govt. OFC HRS: 24 hrs, 7 days. SERVES: Calif.

LUCERNE VALLEY SENIOR CENTER

10431 Allen Way
Lucerne Valley, CA 92356
(760) 248-2248

Social activities, food prgm, equipment loan prgm, congregate meal site, Bingo. FUNDING: Nonprofit. OFC HRS: M-F 9am-1pm. SERVES: Lucerne Valley.

LUQUE COMM & SENIOR CENTER

292 East O Street
Colton, CA 92324
(909) 370-5087

Social and recreational activities for seniors. Lunches for ages 60 yrs+ for a donation of $2. Lunch served M-F 11:30am-12:30pm. OFC HRS: M-F 9am-5pm. Spanish spoken.

MARY PHILLIPS SENIOR CENTER

Community Services
41845 6th Street
Temecula, CA 92590
(951) 694-6464
(951) 699-0373 FAX

Senior recreation. Exercise, oil painting, bridge, crafts, pool, caregiver support group, speakers, senior nutrition prgm, Alzheimer's support group, HICAP, income tax prep, citizenship class, Social Security, blood pressure, Spanish class, AARP, movies, Bingo, etc. Available activities vary throughout the year. Lunch served daily at 11:30am. Transportation available through ctr with reservation made 24 hrs prior. FUNDING: City of Temecula. OFC HRS: M-F 8am-5pm. Spanish spoken. ADM REQ: Must fill out application and make reservations for lunch. Lunch donation $3. Transportation $.50 roundtrip for residents and $1 for non-residents. SERVES: Southwest Riverside County.

MAYOR'S COMMISSION ON AGING

City Commission
3900 Main St.
Riverside, CA 92522
(951) 826-5372
(951) 826-2543 FAX

Provides senior advocacy, info & referral and community info. Meetings open to the public and held on the 2nd Th of every month at 1pm. (except for July & August). Walk-ins welcome. No direct srvs. SERVES: Riverside City.

MEAD VALLEY COMMUNITY CENTER

See "Family Service Assn/West Riverside"

MEALS ON WHEELS

See "Senior/Nutrition Services" chapter for addresses and phone numbers.

MEDIC ALERT FOUNDATION, INTERNATL

2323 Colorado Ave.
Turlock, CA 95382
(888) 633-4298
(209) 669-2450 FAX

Emerg medical info srvs, including ID bracelet or pendant, wallet card (updated annually) and 24-hr emerg response center. Multiple language translations. Membership is open to all, especially individuals with medical conditions, drug allergies or medications. Benefits include computerized confidential medical file. FUNDING: Donations, membership, nonprofit. OFC HRS: M-F 6am-7pm; Sat 8am-5pm. Translation srv for 141 languages. Fees are currently $39.95 to join with a $25 yearly renewal fee which provides free unlimited medical record updates. SERVES: U.S.A. & internat'l.

MEDICARE & MEDICAID INFO SRVS

Customer Relations Branch
75 Hawthorne St., Ste 408
San Francisco, CA 94105-3901
(415) 744-3602
(415) 744-3771 FAX

Info on Medicare-related questions. Call (800) Medicare or visit (www.medicare.gov). FUNDING: Govt. OFC HRS: M-F 8am-4:30pm. SERVES: Calif, Nevada, Arizona & Hawaii.

MEDICARE TELEPHONE HOTLINE

U.S. Dept of Health & Human Srvs
(800) 633-4227

General Medicare info & reporting of Medicare fraud. Srv of the Health Care Financing Admin, U.S. Dept of Health & Human Srvs. FUNDING: Govt. Hotline M-F 8am-8pm, EST. Spanish spoken. SERVES: U.S.A.

MIZELL SENIOR CENTER

480 S. Sunrise Way
Palm Springs, CA 92262
(760) 323-5689
(760) 320-9373 FAX

Meals on Wheels, outreach, info & referral, legal aid, recreational activities, tax assist, nutrition prgm, blood pressure checks and support groups. FUNDING: Donations, grants, fees. OFC HRS: M-F 8am-5pm. Some free srvs. Donations accepted. SERVES: Palm Springs.

MONTCLAIR COMMUNITY CENTER

City of Montclair
5111 Benito St.
Montclair, CA 91763
(909) 399-3173
(909) 625-9464
(909) 399-9751 FAX

Immunization, physicals, blood pressure screening, blood work twice a month. Women's clinic & other non-emerg med srvs. Senior info & referral, outreach, income tax prep assist. Senior nutrition prgm M-F 11:30am for ages 60 yrs+. Suggested donation: $1.75. Eggs and produce sold at reduced prices. Social & recreational activites for children and adults, excursions, after school prgm & edu classes. OFC HRS: Vary with prgm. Spanish spoken. SERVES: San Bernardino County.

MORENO VALLEY SENIOR CENTER

25075 Fir Ave.
Moreno Valley, CA 92553
(951) 413-3430
(951) 243-1400 FAX

Nutrition prgm, legal & medical assist, transportation, shared housing, outreach prgm and info & referral. Contact Joseph Jones. FUNDING: Tax supported. OFC HRS: M-F 8am-4pm. Spanish spoken. ADM REQ: Ages 50 yrs+, nutrition for ages 60 yrs+. Free srvs SERVES: Moreno Valley.

MORONGO BASIN ADULT HEALTH SRVS

P.O. Box 106
57121 Sunnyslope Dr.
Yucca Valley, CA 92284
(760) 365-9661
(760) 994-1337 FAX

Prgms include a senior center and pool to help keep our friends in their own homes by helping them stay healthy and fit. For applications and payment info, visit (www.mbahs.org). FUNDING: Client fees, grants, insurance, donations, nonprofit. OFC HRS: M-F 8am-4pm; F 8am-2pm. SERVES: Morongo Basin.

MOUNTAIN COMMUNITIES SENIOR CTR

P.O. Box 2
675 Grandview Dr.
Twin Peaks, CA 92391

(909) 337-1824

Line dancing, Bingo, exercise. Potluck lunch or regular lunches 3rd Tu per month (donation $5-$7). Travel club, prgm called "Do Your Own Thing" daily. Equipment loan prgm. Blood pressure screening 2nd W 10am-12noon. FUNDING: Nonprofit. OFC HRS: M-W, F 10am-3pm. ADM REQ: Must call for lunch reservation. SERVES: San Bernardino County.

NATIONAL CENTER ON SENIOR TRANSPORTATION

(866) 528-6278

Provides guidance to finding local transportation. Helps assist in finding transit agencies and providers of community transportation in your area. Offers resources, training, and technical assistance to service providers. For TDD, call (202) 347-7385 FUNDING: Govt. OFC HRS: M-F 9am-5pm, EST.

NATL AGING INFORMATION CENTER

1 Massachusetts Ave., NW, Ste 1200
Washington, DC 20001
(800) 677-1116
(202) 872-0057 FAX

Leadership, technical assist and support to senior srv providers, adult care centers, caregivers and volunteers. FUNDING: Nonprofit. OFC HRS: M-F 9am-8pm, EST. Spanish spoken. SERVES: U.S.A.

NATL ASSN FOR HISPANIC ELDERLY

234 E. Colorado Blvd., Ste 300
Pasadena, CA 91101
(626) 564-1988
(626) 564-2659 FAX

Info on srvs for low income Hispanic seniors ages 55 yrs+. FUNDING: Nonprofit. OFC HRS: M-F 9am-5pm. Spanish spoken. SERVES: U.S.A.

NATL ASSN/FOR HOME CARE

228 7th Street, SE
Washington, DC 20003
(202) 547-7424
(202) 547-3540 FAX

Professional assn for home health care providers. Website offers guidelines for how to start a home health care agency (www.nahc.org). FUNDING: Members, nonprofit. OFC HRS: M-F 9am-6pm. SERVES: U.S.A.

NATL COMM/PRESERVE SOCIAL SECURITY AND MEDI-CAL

10 G Street, NE, Ste 600
Washington, DC 20002-4215
(800) 998-0180
(202) 216-0420
(202) 216-0447 FAX

Advocates for social security & Medicare. FUNDING: Donations, nonprofit. OFC HRS: M-F 9am-5:30pm, EST. Spanish and Korean spoken. Annual membership fee $10. SERVES: U.S.A.

NATL COUNCIL ON THE AGING

1901 L Street, N.W., 4th Fl.
Washington, DC 20036
(202) 479-1200
(202) 479-0735 FAX

Info & publications on all aspects of aging, including topics such as family caregivers, senior employment and long-term care. TDD (202) 479-6674. FUNDING: Corp donations, non-

profit, govt grants, membership. OFC HRS: M-F 9am-5pm, EST. SERVES: U.S.A.

NATL INDIAN COUNCIL ON AGING, INC.

5997 Brockton Ave., Ste C
Riverside, CA 92506
(951) 369-8581
(951) 369-8565 FAX

Senior employment prgm. Title 5 prgms. E-fax (501)423-4429. FUNDING: Grants, govt, nonprofit. OFC HRS: M-F 8am-5pm. ADM REQ: Meet federal poverty guidelines, ages 55 yrs+. Free srvs. SERVES: Riverside, San Bernardino, San Diego, Imperial Counties.

NEEDLES REGIONAL SENIOR CENTER

1699 Bailey Ave.
Needles, CA 92363
(760) 326-4789
(760) 326-5643 FAX

Senior prgm includes Bingo M and Th 1pm, cards, line dancing, exercise equipment. Lunch served M-F 11:30am. Donation $3. Transportation within Needles $1. OFC HRS: M-F 9am-3pm. SERVES: Needles.

NEWBERRY SPRINGS SENIOR SRVS ASSN

P.O. Box 244
33383 Newberry Rd.
Newberry Springs, CA 92365
(760) 257-3284
(760) 257-3284 FAX

Services for ages 50 yrs+. Library, HICAP counseling, daily meals Tu-Sat 7am-2pm, monthly dinner, flu shots, loans of medical equipment, bi-monthly bereavement support group, Bingo games, weekly arts and crafts, annual health fair, business expo. Swap meet the 1st Sat of each month. Blood pressure checks 1st W 9:30am-11:30am. FUNDING: Nonprofit. OFC HRS: Tu-Sat 7am-2pm. SERVES: Newberry Springs.

NORTON YOUNGLOVE SENIOR CENTER

P.O. Box 1190
908 Park Ave.
Calimesa, CA 92320
(909) 795-2287
(909) 795-5204 FAX

Social and recreational activities. Nutrition prgm, monthly food sharing prgm, legal, Medicare assist. Outreach prgm and info & referral. Walk in or call. OFC HRS: M-Th 8:30am-4pm; F 8:30am-12noon. Spanish spoken. ADM REQ: Ages 60 yrs+. Must RSVP for lunch, call (909) 446-1071. Free srvs. Lunch donation $3. SERVES: Calimesa & nearby.

NURSING HOME HOTLINE

See "Long-Term Care Ombudsman."

OFFICE ON AGING/RIVERSIDE CO.

See "Riverside Co. Office on Aging"

OLD TOWN TEMECULA SENIOR CTR

See "Mary Phillips Senior Center"

OMBUDSMAN PROGRAM

See "San Bernardino Co. Ombudsman"

ONTARIO SENIOR CENTER

225 East B Street
Ontario, CA 91764
(909) 395-2021
(909) 395-2471 FAX

Senior multipurpose center. Daily lunch prgm, movies, Bingo, yoga, dancing, crafts, counseling, etc. Health screening 2nd & 4th Th

9am-12noon. Walk in or call. FUNDING: City. OFC HRS: M-F 8am-8pm. Spanish spoken Most all-day activities are free. SERVES: Ontario.

OPARC/ADULT DEVELOPMENT CTR

Passport Senior Srvs
8333 Rochester Ave., Ste 112
Rancho Cucamonga, CA 91730
(909) 948-5592
(909) 980-4682 FAX

Community life training for dev disabled adults. VTDD machines at each site for the hearing impaired. FUNDING: Pvt donations. OFC HRS: M-F 8am-5pm. Spanish spoken. ADM REQ: Dev disability. SERVES: Pomona Valley & Inland Empire.

PARTNERSHIP FOR PRESCRIPTION ASSIST

(877) 777-7815

Free or low-cost prescription srv for uninsured, underinsured or those with limited income. Call or visit (www.RXHelpforCA.org). SERVES: Calif.

PARTNERSHIP/PRESERVE INDEP LIVING

Seniors & Persons with Disabilities
6296 Rivercrest Dr., Ste K
Riverside, CA 92507
(951) 867-3800
(951) 867-3831 FAX

Info & referral srvs to existing srvs to seniors & persons with disabilities. Quarterly newsletter. Edu health videos. FUNDING: Nonprofit. OFC HRS: M-Th 7:30am-5:30pm. Spanish spoken. ADM REQ: Ages 18 yrs+ with disability. SERVES: Riverside County.

PERRIS HILL SENIOR CENTER

San Bernardino Parks/Rec/Comm Srvs
780 E. 21st Street
San Bernardino, CA 92404
(909) 384-5436

Senior lunch prgm, info & referral, arts & crafts, Bridge club, line dancing, periodic dances, travel prgm referrals, special events & senior access classes. Donations for lunch nutrition prgm. FUNDING: City, nonprofit. OFC HRS: M-F 9am-5pm. Free srvs. SERVES: San Bernardino & nearby.

PERRIS SENIOR CITIZENS CENTER

100 North D Street
Perris, CA 92570
(951) 657-7334
(951) 657-1671 FAX

Bingo, exercise, Bunco, cards, painting, trips, tax assist, health screening, local casino trips, food on-site, nutrition & outreach. Walk in or call. FUNDING: City. OFC HRS: M-Th 8am-5pm. ADM REQ: Ages 55 yrs+. Fees vary. SERVES: Nuevo, Perris, Romoland, Mead Valley, & Meadowbrook.

POINT OF GRACE CHRISTIAN FELLOWSHIP

9774 Hawthorne Dr., Ste 901
Rancho Cucamonga, CA 91730
(909) 944-9909
(909) 944-7789 FAX

Community closet, food pantry, learning center, behavioral support groups such as Celebrate Recovery & divorce care ministry based on demand, anger mgmt for kids & teens, Steps to Hope. FUNDING: Nonprofit, donations. OFC

HRS: Tu-Th 12noon-4pm. SERVES: San Bernardino County.

PROVIDENCE SPEECH/HEARING CENTER

1301 Providence Ave.
Orange, CA 92868
(714) 639-4990
(714) 744-3841 FAX

Mission is to enrich life through the gifts of speech and hearing. Strives to continually provide the highest standard of srvs in the identification, diagnosis, treatment and prevention of speech, language and hearing disorders for persons of all ages, races and economic backgrounds. Complete testing for speech and hearing problems for all ages. Hearing tests and speech therapy for seniors. Hearing aids & repairs, info & listening devices, newborn hearing screening, swim molds and musician's earplugs. Also licensed day care and Providence Therapeutic Preschool and clinical school for children ages 2-6 yrs. FUNDING: Nonprofit. OFC HRS: M-F 8:00am-5:30pm. Spanish spoken. Accepts Medicare, Medi-Cal, CalOptima, insurance, grants and financial aid. SERVES: L.A., Orange & Riverside Counties.

REDLANDS COMMUNITY CENTER

P.O. Box 3005
111 W. Lugonia Ave.
Redlands, CA 92374
(909) 798-7572
(909) 793-3569 FAX

Racquetball, gymnasium, tennis, game room, art, karate, room rental for clubs, groups, parties, help groups, computer lab, homework study, etc. Senior center (909) 798-7579. FUNDING: City. OFC HRS: M-F 10am-7pm; game room: 12noon-7pm. ADM REQ: Programs for youth and seniors. Fees depends on class, scholarships available. SERVES: Redlands.

REDLANDS COMMUNITY SENIOR CTR

Police Dept Community Services
P.O. Box 3005
111 W. Lugonia Ave.
Redlands, CA 92374
(909) 798-7579
(909) 793-3569 FAX

Classes & recreational activities for seniors. Insurance counseling, monthly legal srv, transportation, tax assist. County nutrition prgm. FUNDING: City, donations, nonprofit. OFC HRS: M-F 8am-5pm. Spanish spoken. ASL available. No membership fee. SERVES: San Bernardino County.

RELIANT PROFESSIONAL SERVES

Formerly known as CARE
104 E. State St., Ste R
Redlands, CA 92373
(909) 793-4011
(909) 335-8515 FAX

Senior srvs, including case mgmt, homecare and housing srvs. FUNDING: Nonprofit. OFC HRS: M-Th 8:30am-4:30pm; F 8:30am-1pm. SERVES: Redlands.

RENCK COMMUNITY CTR AT HUNT PARK

4015 Jackson
Riverside, CA 92503
(951) 351-6132
(951) 358-2750 FAX

Various activities for seniors and kids. Summer camp for kids. Disability services

(951)826-2000. Camp $80 per week. SERVES: Riverside County.

RETIRED & SENIOR VOLUNTEER PRGM

West Valley San Bernardino Co.
150 W. 1st Street, Ste 175
Claremont, CA 91711
(909) 482-0355
(909) 624-1294 FAX

Volunteer placements of seniors ages 55 yrs+ within community agencies and nonprofit organizations. Training provided as needed. FUNDING: Fed, VNA & Hospice of So. Calif, nonprofit. OFC HRS: M-F 8am-5pm. Free srvs. SERVES: Western San Bernardino County.

RETIRED & SENIOR VOLUNTEER PRGM

600 W. 5th Street
San Bernardino, CA 92410
(909) 384-5414
(909) 889-0672 FAX

Opportunity for seniors to volunteer throughout their communities at agencies and nonprofit organizations. Volunteers are provided with excess auto and liability insurance. Small transportation reimbursements on request and annual recognition & luncheon. Walk in. FUNDING: Fed, city. OFC HRS: M-Th 7:30am-4:30pm. 24-hr voicemail. ADM REQ: Ages 55 yrs+. Free srvs. SERVES: San Bernardino metro area, High Desert & mountain areas.

RIALTO RECREATION/COMMUNITY SRVS

214 N. Palm Ave., Ste 204
Rialto, CA 92376
(909) 421-4949
(909) 820-2554 FAX

Recreation & leisure prgms for adults and children including sports, social & cultural, neighborhood srvs, excursions, instructional classes, aquatics, senior prgms, karate, gymnastics, tap, and guitar. Also Tiny Tots prgm school age day care. Sponsor all types of recreational activities. FUNDING: City. OFC HRS: M-Th 7am-6pm. Spanish spoken. ADM REQ: Open to all. SERVES: Rialto.

RIALTO SENIOR CENTER

1411 S. Riverside Ave.
Rialto, CA 92376
(909) 877-9706
(909) 877-9962 FAX

Social activities (exercise, Bingo, music, crafts, etc), tax assist, info & referral. Free legal services. AARP driver safety monthly. Meals on Wheels, hot lunch M-F 11:30am (donations $2.50). FUNDING: Nonprofit. OFC HRS: M-Th 8am-5pm; F 8am-4pm. Spanish spoken. SERVES: Rialto.

RIVERSIDE CITY PUBLIC UTILITIES

3901 Orange Street
Riverside, CA 92501
(951) 826-5485
(951) 826-2074 FAX

WE CARE, Wise Energy Use Campaign to Aid the Retired and Elderly, is a free energy & water conservation prgm offered by the municipal water and electric utilities. Home survey and installation of water conservation kit, low-flow showerhead, weather stripping and door sweeps. Call for info. FUNDING: Rates & revenue bonds. OFC HRS: M-F 8am-5pm. Foreign languages available upon request. ADM REQ:

Ages 55 yrs+. Free srvs. SERVES: Riverside utilities service area.

RIVERSIDE CO. DEPT/MENTAL HEALTH

Administrative Office
P.O. Box 7549
4095 County Circle Dr.
Riverside, CA 92513
(951) 358-4500
(951) 358-4513 FAX

Overall planning, implementation, direction, coordination and eval of the Dept of Mental Health prgms in Riverside County. Treatment for adults: residential, outpatient, day care, socialization ctrs, crisis srvs, case mgmt, continuing care, etc. Children's prgms: outpatient, case mgmt, foster home placement, etc. Also main admin office for drug abuse and alcohol control prgms. No actual srvs available at this location. FUNDING: Govt. Spanish spoken. Accepts Medi-Cal SERVES: Riverside County.

RIVERSIDE CO. OFFICE ON AGING

Retired & Senior Volunteer Prgm
73750 Catalina Way
Palm Desert, CA 92260
(760) 341-0401
(760) 340-9585 FAX

Registers volunteers ages 55 yrs+, and provides nonprofit agencies with volunteers. Over 100 placement sites. Walk in or call. FUNDING: Govt. OFC HRS: M-F 8am-4:30pm. Spanish spoken. Free srvs. SERVES: Desert Hot Springs, Palm Springs, Cathedral City, Rancho Mirage, Palm Desert, La Quinta, Thermal, Coachella, Thousand Palms, Indio and North Shore.

RIVERSIDE CO. OFFICE ON AGING

6296 Rivercrest Dr., Ste K
Riverside, CA 92507-0738
(951) 867-3800
(800) 510-2020
(951) 867-3830 FAX

Office administers & implements planning, advocacy, prgm dev and coordination of senior srvs which include elder abuse edu & advocacy, info & assist, peer counseling, RSVP of the Coachella Valley, senior employment (for ages 55 yrs+) and nutrition srvs. Contracts for personal care and homemaker srvs, respite, adult day care, legal srvs, ombudsman, info & assist, outreach, congregate and home-delivered meals, phone reassurance, community edu and transportation. Senior HelpLink will make referrals to public and pvt agencies for srvs to seniors in Riverside County. TTY (951) 697-4699. FUNDING: Fed, state, county, pvt resources. OFC HRS: M-F 7:30am-5:30pm. Spanish spoken. ADM REQ: Ages 60 yrs+. Case mgmt for seniors and those with disabilities; can be under age 60 yrs. SERVES: Riverside County.

RIVERSIDE CO. PUBLIC GUARDIAN

Public Guardian & Public Conservators
P.O. Box 1405
3190 Chicago
Riverside, CA 92501
(951) 341-6440
(951) 341-6403 FAX

Public guardians, when appointed by the court, act as a guardian for persons legally incapable of administering their affairs and assets. Conservators investigate referrals for probate &

LPS. FUNDING: Govt. OFC HRS: M-F 8am-5pm. Spanish spoken. ADM REQ: Must meet legal requirements. SERVES: Riverside County.

RIVERSIDE CO. PUBLIC SOCIAL SRVS

901 E. Ramsey
Banning, CA 92220
(951) 922-7585
(951) 922-7180 FAX

Adult protective srvs. Accepts and responds to reports of dependent adult and elder abuse within Riverside Co. 24-hr hotline (800) 491-7123. FUNDING: Govt. OFC HRS: M-F 8am-5pm. Spanish spoken. ADM REQ: Low income. SERVES: Riverside County.

RIVERSIDE CO. PUBLIC SOCIAL SRVS

Adult Protective Services
68625 Perez Rd., Ste 2
Cathedral City, CA 92234
(760) 770-2450
(800) 582-9893
(760) 770-2260 FAX

Srvs for adults in danger of abuse & exploitation. Emerg shelter investigation and in-home support. Provides frail elderly and disabled with outreach and in-home support. To report elder abuse, call (800) 491-7123. FUNDING: County, state, fed. OFC HRS: M-Th 8am-5pm. Spanish spoken. SERVES: Coachella Valley.

RIVERSIDE CO. PUBLIC SOCIAL SRVS

Adult & Child Protective Srvs
505 S. Buena Vista, 3rd Fl., Ste 312
Corona, CA 92282
(951) 272-5564
(888) 877-3985
(951) 272-5583 FAX

24-hr hotline (800) 491-7123. FUNDING: Govt. OFC HRS: M-Th 8am-5pm. Spanish spoken. Free srvs. SERVES: Riverside County.

RIVERSIDE CO. PUBLIC SOCIAL SRVS

Adult Protective Srvs/In-Home Srvs
541 N. San Jacinto St.
Hemet, CA 92543
(951) 791-3250
(800) 331-6742
(951) 791-3255 FAX

24-hr emerg response, protective srvs for adults in danger of abuse, exploitation, neglect, etc. Call to report incidents or suspicions of abuse or neglect. Also provides frail elderly and disabled outreach and in-home support srvs. Hotline answered 24 hrs (800) 491-7123. FUNDING: County, state, fed. OFC HRS: M-Th 8am-5pm. Spanish spoken. ADM REQ: Varies per prgm. SERVES: Hemet, San Jacinto, Menifee & nearby.

RIVERSIDE CO. PUBLIC SOCIAL SRVS

Adult Protective Services
23119 Cottonwood Ave., Bldg. A, 1st Fl.
Moreno Valley, CA 92553
(951) 413-5050
(951) 413-5107 FAX

Srvs for adults in danger of abuse, exploitation, etc. with full range of srvs from emerg shelter to investigation and in-home support srvs. Provides frail elderly and disabled with outreach and in-home support srvs. Walk in or call. Call, (800) 345-6083 to report any actual or suspected abuse. FUNDING: Govt. OFC HRS: M-Th 8am-5pm. ADM REQ: Varies with prgm. SERVES: Riverside County.

RIVERSIDE COMMUNITY HEALTH FNDN

4445-A Magnolia Ave.
Riverside, CA 92501
(951) 788-3471
(951) 788-3589 FAX

Offers the S.H.A.R.P. prgm for seniors which provides monthly heath edu classes/screening assessments. Several prgms for at-risk teens including pregnancy prevention, STD edu, peer-to-peer groups, and support services. Also offers pediatric dental clinics. FUNDING: Nonprofit. Free srvs. SERVES: Riverside Co.

ROLLING START, INC.

570 W. 4th Street, Ste 107
San Bernardino, CA 92401
(909) 884-2129
(909) 386-7446 FAX

Independent living skills training, attendant referral, housing referral, info & referral, advocacy, deaf srvs, helpline, peer counseling for seniors and disabled. ADA tech assist, free workshops. Assistive technology, computer classes. For TDD, call (909) 884-7396. FUNDING: Govt, county, city. OFC HRS: M-F 8am-5pm. ASL available. ADM REQ: Ages 18 yrs+, county resident with disability. Free srvs except helpline. SERVES: San Bernardino County.

RSVP

See "Retired & Senior Volunteer Prgm"

SAN BERNARDINO CITY PARKS & REC

1350 South E Street
San Bernardino, CA 92408
(909) 384-5233
(909) 384-5160 FAX

Programs & services for all age groups. Activities include: trips, tours, community centers, park and playground prgms, youth & adult sports, adult classes, aquatics, workshops, tournaments, year-round lunch, nutrition prgms for youth & seniors, senior citizen prgms, human srvs, social srvs, etc. at various locations. FUNDING: City. OFC HRS: M-Th 7:30am-5:30pm. SERVES: San Bernardino City.

SAN BERNARDINO CO. AGING/ADULT

Adult Protective Srvs
536 E. Virginia Way
Barstow, CA 92311
(760) 256-1435
(760) 256-1605 FAX

For older adults or disabled and dependent adults in danger of abuse, exploitation, etc. Full range of srvs from emerg shelter to investigation of suspected abuse. 24-hr crisis line (877) 565-2020. OFC HRS: M-F 8am-5pm. SERVES: Barstow, Trona.

SAN BERNARDINO CO. AGING/ADULT

Senior Info & Assist
536 E. Virginia Way
Barstow, CA 92311
(760) 256-2834
(760) 256-1605 FAX

Senior assist and advocacy for needed srvs and prgms, senior employment, utility reductions, home repair or low-cost loan, legal, transportation, ombudsman, meals and home health care. FUNDING: Older American Act Title 3. OFC HRS: M-F 8am-5pm. Spanish spoken. SERVES: North Mojave Desert, Barstow,

Hinkley, Newberry Springs, Trona, Red Mountain and Baker.

SAN BERNARDINO CO. AGING/ADULT

Senior Info & Assist
8572 Sierra Ave.
Fontana, CA 92335
(909) 829-8515
(909) 829-0313 FAX

Info & referral for legal, transportation, home repair, senior employment, ombudsman prgm, meals, home health care, emerg response, Med Alert and outreach srvs. Offices located throughout the county. FUNDING: Older American Act, Title 3. OFC HRS: M-F 5am-5pm. ADM REQ: Ages 60 yrs+ or disabled. Free srvs. SERVES: Fontana, Bloomington.

SAN BERNARDINO CO. AGING/ADULT

Adult Protective Srvs
1300 Bailey Ave.
Needles, CA 92363
(760) 326-9274
(760) 326-9340 FAX

For older adults or disabled and dependent adults in danger of abuse, exploitation, etc. Full range of srvs from emerg shelter to investigation of suspected abuse. Hotline (877) 565-2020. OFC HRS: M-F 8am-5pm, closed alt F. SERVES: Needles.

SAN BERNARDINO CO. AGING/ADULT

In-Home Supportive Srvs
1300 Bailey Ave.
Needles, CA 92363
(760) 326-9328
(760) 326-9340 FAX

Social workers will make an assessment of a need for in-home care and authorize payments for domestic and personal srvs in order to keep elderly, blind, and disabled in their own homes, and thus avoid institutionalization. Hotline (877) 565-2020. OFC HRS: M-F 8am-5pm, closed alt F. SERVES: Needles.

SAN BERNARDINO CO. AGING/ADULT

Senior Info & Assist
1300 Bailey
Needles, CA 92363
(760) 326-9224
(760) 326-9340 FAX

Info & referral, eval & follow up, outreach, comprehensive assessment. IHSS (760) 326-9328; APS (877) 565-2020; CPS (800) 827-8724. OFC HRS: M-F 8am-5pm.

SAN BERNARDINO CO. AGING/ADULT

Senior Info & Assist
P.O. Box 75
111 W. Lugonia Ave.
Redlands, CA 92374
(909) 793-7707
(909) 793-4129 FAX

Info & referral, eval & follow-up, outreach, comprehensive assessment. Walk in or call. FUNDING: Govt. OFC HRS: M-F 8am-5pm. Spanish spoken. ADM REQ: Ages 60 yrs+. Free srvs. SERVES: Redlands, Loma Linda, Mentone, Yucaipa.

SAN BERNARDINO CO. AGING/ADULT

Adult Protective Srvs
686 E. Mill St.
San Bernardino, CA 92415-0640
(909) 891-3900
(909) 388-6718 FAX

Protects and supports the rights of adults. Social workers provide case work srvs to adults in danger of neglect, abuse, or exploitation to alleviate danger, correct hazardous living, prevent unnecessary institutionalizations. Referral srvs for domestic violence and sexual assault prgms. FUNDING: County, state, federal. OFC HRS: 24 hrs, 7 days. Spanish spoken. SERVES: San Bernardino County.

SAN BERNARDINO CO. AGING/ADULT

DAAS/In-Home Supportive Srvs Prgm
686 E. Mill St.
San Bernardino, CA 92415-0640
(909) 891-3900
(909) 891-3919 FAX

IHSS is designed to enable eligible blind and disabled individuals to remain safely in their own home by paying someone to assist with those tasks needed for basic day-to-day home life. Tasks for the IHSS may include essential housekeeping, meal prep, non-medical personal srvs under a physician's supervision, paramedical srvs. Other locations: Barstow, Joshua Tree, Needles, Victorville, Rancho Cucamonga. FUNDING: County, state, federal. OFC HRS: M-F 8am-5pm. Spanish spoken. SERVES: San Bernardino County.

SAN BERNARDINO CO. AGING/ADULT

Administration
686 E. Mill St.
San Bernardino, CA 92415-0640
(909) 891-3900
(909) 891-3919 FAX

Admin office only; administers prgms and funding to provide srvs to seniors and at-risk individuals to improve or maintain choice, independence, and quality of life. DAAS works to ensure seniors and adults with disabilities the right to age in a place with the least restrictive environment. Aging adult infoline (800) 510-2020, will direct caller to an agency in their area. FUNDING: Fed, state. OFC HRS: M-F vary. Spanish spoken. Translation srv available. SERVES: U.S.A.

SAN BERNARDINO CO. AGING/ADULT

Adult Protective Srvs
17270 Bear Valley Rd., Ste 108
Victorville 92395
(760) 843-5100
(877) 565-2020

For older adults or disabled and dependent adults in danger of abuse or exploitation, etc. Full range of srvs from investigation of abuse, emerg shelter, in-home assist. FUNDING: County. OFC HRS: M-F 8am-5pm. Spanish spoken. SERVES: High Desert.

SAN BERNARDINO CO. AGING/ADULT

Senior Info & Assist
17270 Bear Valley Rd., Ste 108
Victorville, CA 92392
(760) 843-5100
(760) 843-5105 FAX

Info & referrals for senior citizens to resources, eval, follow-up, outreach, and comprehensive assessment. Goal is to assist the senior with needed srvs. Also call hotline (800) 510-2020. FUNDING: Nonprofit, federal, county. OFC HRS: M-F 8am-5pm. Spanish spoken. SERVES: High Desert.

SAN BERNARDINO CO. BEHAV HEALTH

Agewise Program

850 E. Foothill Blvd.
Rialto, CA 92376
(909) 421-9470
(909) 873-4461 FAX

County-sponsored outreach mental health srvs for older adults using professionals and senior peer counselors, support groups and professional training. FUNDING: Dept of Behav Health, county, govt. OFC HRS: M-F 8am-5pm. ADM REQ: Ages 60 yrs+, in need of counseling. Free srvs. SERVES: San Bernardino County.

SAN BERNARDINO CO. BEHAV HEALTH

Managed Care-Access Unit
850 E. Foothill Blvd.
Rialto, CA 92376
(888) 743-1478
(909) 421-9272 FAX

Referral for Medi-Cal clients to county clinics or to a service provider for a fee. Clients without Medi-Cal may call for info & recommendations to nearby doctors & community clinics. After-hours crisis line. Mailing Address: 268 W. Hospitality Ln., Ste. 400. FUNDING: Govt. OFC HRS: 24-hr srvs. Translator srvs available. SERVES: San Bernardino County.

SAN BERNARDINO CO. BEHAV HEALTH

Patient's Rights Office
850 E. Foothill Blvd.
Rialto, CA 92376
(800) 440-2391

This office protects the patient, consumer and human rights of all recipients of psychiatric srvs. Consultation and training are available to providers of psychiatric srvs. Advocates investigate complaints concerning behavioral health srvs, monitor mental health facilities, provide training and edu regarding mental health law, and ensure that recipients of mental health srvs are notified of their rights. FUNDING: Govt. OFC HRS: M-F 8am-5pm. Spanish SERVES: San Bernardino County.

SAN BERNARDINO CO. HUMAN SRVS SY

HSS Administration
385 N. Arrowhead Ave., 5th Fl.
San Bernardino, CA 92415-0515
(909) 357-4717
(909) 387-5430 FAX

HSS is composed of the following depts: Aging & Adult Srvs, Behavioral Health, Children's Srvs, Community Srvs, Preschool Srvs, Public Health, Transitional Assist, and Veterans Affairs. OFC HRS: M-F 7:30am-5pm. SERVES: San Bernardino County.

SAN BERNARDINO CO. OFC/AGING

See "San Bernardino Co. Aging/Adult"

SAN BERNARDINO CO. OMBUDSMAN

686 E. Mill St.
San Bernardino, CA 92415-0640
(909) 891-3928
(866) 229-0284
(909) 891-3957 FAX

Investigates complaints, problems of long-term care facilities for the elderly and dev disabled adults in licensed facilities. FUNDING: Federal, state. OFC HRS: M-F 8am-5pm. Free srvs. SERVES: San Bernardino County.

SAN BERNARDINO CO. PUBLIC ADMIN

175 S. Lena Rd.
San Bernardino, CA 92415

(909) 387-2481
(909) 387-2335 FAX

Administers estates of persons who died in San Bernardino Co. where no executor or administrator was appointed. OFC HRS: M-F 8am-5pm. SERVES: San Bernardino County.

SAN BERNARDINO CO. PUBLIC HEALTH

Administrative Office
385 Arrowhead Ave.
San Bernardino, CA 92415-0120
(909) 387-7020
(909) 387-6228 FAX

Administers branch offices at various locations throughout San Bernardino Co., including: Barstow, Big Bear, Chino, Fontana, Joshua Tree, Needles, Ontario, Redlands, San Bernardino, Trona, Victorville & Twin Peaks. Edu, alcohol & drug prevention, animal control, birth & death certificates, Calif Children's Srvs, epidemiology, family planning, high-risk infant prgm, immunizations, nutrition, WIC, public health nursing, school health, senior health, VD control, TB, HIV/AIDS control. TDD (909) 397-6354. OFC HRS: M-F 8am-5pm; clinic hrs may vary. SERVES: San Bernardino County.

SAN BERNARDINO CO. PUBLIC HEALTH

Immunization Services
351 N. Mountain View Ave.
San Bernardino, CA 92415
(800) 722-4794
(909) 387-6521
(909) 387-6676 FAX

Immunizations to all persons ages 6 weeks+. Includes DTaP, polio, measles, mumps, hib meningitis, hepatitis B, varicella, and rubella. Travelers immunizations for yellow fever, polio, typhoid fever, hepatitis A & B, etc. Senior citizens can receive low-cost flu shot. Srvs are provided at clinics throughout the county. FUNDING: State, county, fees. OFC HRS: M-F 9am-11:30am, 1pm-4pm. Spanish spoken. ADM REQ: Open to anyone. Verification of parenthood. Fee $10 per person for pediatric immunizations (no child turned away for lack of funds). $15-70 for travelers. Administrative fees $15 per person per visit. SERVES: San Bernardino County.

SCAN HEALTH PLAN

P.O. Box 22616
3800 Kilroy Airport Way, Ste 100
Long Beach, CA 90806
(562) 989-5100
(562) 989-5200 FAX

Senior HMO health plan. Provides seniors with srvs not supplied by other area health and social srv agencies, including case mgmt, transportation, medical care and in-home assist. For member srvs, call (800) 559-3500. FUNDING: Nonprofit. OFC HRS: M-F 8am-5pm. Spanish spoken. SERVES: L.A., Orange, Riverside & San Bernardino Counties.

SEARLES VALLEY COMM SRV SENIOR CTR

Trona Community Center
P.O. Box 443
13187 Market St.
Trona, CA 93592
(760) 372-5889

Transportation for shopping and doctors appts for seniors & the disabled. Lunch 2nd & 3rd W at 12noon, breakfast Tu at 7:30am, dinner 4th

Th at 5pm. Meal times subject to change. OFC HRS: M-F 8am-12noon.

SENIOR CARE ACTION NETWORK (SCAN)

See "SCAN"

SENIOR COMMUNITY SERVICE EMPLOYMENT PROGRAM (SCSEP)

686 E. Mill St.
San Bernardino, CA 92415
(909) 891-3913
(909) 891-3919 FAX

Part-time community srv employment, on-the-job training, job search assist, job referrals, edu assist, referrals to other supportive srvs. Wait: depends upon available openings in area. FUNDING: Title V of Older Americans Act, Dept of Labor. OFC HRS: M-Th 7:30am-5pm; F 8am-5pm. Spanish spoken upon request. Otherwise, must allow time for an interpretor to be set up. ADM REQ: Ages 55 yrs+ and meet low income criteria and not employed. Free srvs. SERVES: San Bernardino County.

SENIOR COMPANION PROGRAM

600 W. 5th Street
San Bernardino, CA 92410
(909) 384-5430
(909) 889-9801 FAX

Personal in-home srvs to homebound adults. Respite care to caregivers. Also disabled, isolated adults ages 21 yrs+. Walk in. FUNDING: Federal, city. OFC HRS: M-Th 7:30am-5pm. ADM REQ: Ages 21 yrs+, low income bracket, companions must over be 55 yrs+ & low income. Free srvs. SERVES: Morongo Basin, Victor Valley, San Bernardino, Fontana, Rialto, Loma Linda.

SENIOR HOME AND HEALTH CARE

See "San Bernardino Co. Aging/Adult"

SENIOR INFO & ASSISTANCE

See "San Bernardino Co. Aging/Adult"

SENIOR MEALS

See "Senior Nutrition Services" chapter in this directory.

SENIOR NUTRITION SITE

Wonder Valley Community Center
80526 1/2 Amboy Rd.
Twentynine Palms, CA 92277
(760) 367-1678

Social activities, health edu, blood pressure checks 4th Tu 10am-12noon, food prgm, congregate meal site M-F 12noon. FUNDING: Nonprofit. OFC HRS: M-F 9:30am-1:30pm. Meal donation $2.50. SERVES: Wonder Valley.

SENIORS EYECARE PROGRAM

See "EyeCare America"

SIMON FOUNDATION FOR CONTINENCE

P.O. Box 815
Wilmette, IL 60091
(800) 237-4666
(847) 864-3913
(847) 864-9758 FAX

Info on incontinence, including a quarterly newsletter, books and video tapes. Free packets are mailed upon request. FUNDING: Nonprofit. OFC HRS: 24 hrs. SERVES: U.S.A.

SIMPSON CENTER

305 E. Devonshire Ave.
Hemet, CA 92543
(951) 765-2390

(951) 765-2398 FAX

Senior nutrition, info & referral srvs, tax assist, blood pressure testing, blood bank, homeowners and renters assist, senior activities, phone assurance, outreach. Walk in or call. FUNDING: Taxes, general fund, income from room rentals, nonprofit. OFC HRS: M-Th 8am-4:30pm. Spanish spoken. Most free srvs. SERVES: Hemet, San Jacinto.

SO CALIF EDISON/LOW INCOME PRGM

Low Income Programs Dept
12701 Schabarum Ave.
Rosemead, CA 91770
(800) 736-4777
(626) 302-8313 FAX

Low income customers should call about energy efficiency srvs to needy customers; efficient lighting, evaporative coolers & weatherization. Qualifying customers may also be eligible for a 15% discount on electricity rates. OFC HRS: M-F 8am-5pm. Spanish spoken. SERVES: L.A., Orange, Riverside & San Bernardino Counties.

SOCIAL SECURITY ADMINISTRATION

(800) 772-1213

The (800) phone number has info on all offices throughout the U.S. M-F 7am-7pm. Answers questions regarding social security and SSI benefits and sign-up. Provides earnings and benefits statement record for use in estimating retirement benefits, Medicare sign-ups and benefit info. Phone srv cannot process bills, issue SS cards, or handle benefits for survivors, disabilities, and supplemental security income. Give your ZIP code and they will tell you the office closest to you. TTY (800) 325-0778. FUNDING: Govt. OFC HRS: M-F 7am-7pm. Spanish spoken. SERVES: U.S.A.

SOCIAL SECURITY ADMINISTRATION

720 E. Main St.
Barstow, CA 92311
(800) 772-1213
(760) 256-9294 FAX

Info on social security and SSI benefits, SS cards, Medicare benefits & sign-up, survivor and burial benefits. For TTY, call (800) 325-0778. OFC HRS: M-F 9am-4:30pm. Spanish spoken by phone. SERVES: San Bernardino County.

SOCIAL SECURITY ADMINISTRATION

874 E. Hobson Way
Blythe, CA 92225
(800) 772-1213
(760) 922-5718 FAX

Assist with social security benefits including retirement, survivors' benefits, & disability, SSI for those blind, disabled and ages 65 yrs+. TTY (800) 325-0778. FUNDING: Fed, govt. OFC HRS: M-F 9am-4:30pm. Spanish spoken. Free srvs. SERVES: Riverside County.

SOCIAL SECURITY ADMINISTRATION

2191 Sampson Ave., Ste 105
Corona, CA 92879
(800) 772-1213
(951) 272-0423 FAX

Assists with social security benefits including: retirement, survivors' benefits, & disability, SSI for those blind, disabled and ages 65 yrs+. TTY (800) 325-0778. FUNDING: Govt. OFC HRS:

M-F 9am-4:30pm. Spanish spoken. Free srvs. SERVES: Riverside County.

SOCIAL SECURITY ADMINISTRATION

10668 Sierra Ave.
Fontana, CA 92337
(800) 772-1213
(909) 829-0119 FAX

Info on social security and SSI benefits, SS cards, Medicare benefits & sign-up, survivor and burial benefits. For TTY, call (800) 325-0778. FUNDING: Fed, govt. OFC HRS: M-F 9am-4:30pm. Spanish spoken. SERVES: Fontana, Colton.

SOCIAL SECURITY ADMINISTRATION

3095 W. Devonshire Ave.
Hemet, CA 92545
(800) 772-1213
(951) 766-1968 FAX

Assists the blind, disabled & seniors ages 65 yrs+, with social security benefits including: retirement, survivors' benefits, disability, & supplemental security income. TTY (800) 325-0778. OFC HRS: M-F 9am-4:30pm. Spanish spoken. Free srvs. SERVES: Riverside County.

SOCIAL SECURITY ADMINISTRATION

46845 Monroe St., Ste 2
Indio, CA 92201
(800) 772-1213
(760) 342-2972 FAX

Info on social security, SSI benefits, SS cards, Medicare benefits & sign-up, survivor and burial benefits. For TTY, call (800) 325-0778. FUNDING: Fed, govt. OFC HRS: M-W, F 9am-4:30pm. Th 9am-4pm. Spanish spoken. Free srvs. SERVES: Riverside County.

SOCIAL SECURITY ADMINISTRATION

1096 E. Broadway
Needles, CA 92363
(760) 326-4460
(760) 326-4029 FAX

Info on social security and SSI benefits, SS cards, Medicare benefits & sign-up, survivor and burial benefits. For TTY, call (800) 325-0778. FUNDING: Fed, govt. OFC HRS: Tu-F 9am-4:30pm. SERVES: Needles area.

SOCIAL SECURITY ADMINISTRATION

1533 E. Holt Blvd.
Ontario, CA 91761
(866) 331-2216
(909) 986-1369 FAX

Assists with social security benefits including: retirement, survivors' benefits, disability, SSI for those blind, disabled and ages 65 yrs+. TTY (800) 325-0778. OFC HRS: M-F 9am-4pm. Spanish spoken by phone. Free srvs. SERVES: San Bernardino County.

SOCIAL SECURITY ADMINISTRATION

4201 E. Ramon Rd.
Palm Springs, CA 92264
(800) 772-1213
(760) 327-8935 FAX

Assists with social security benefits including: retirement, survivors' benefits, and disability. Supplemental security income for the blind, disabled and ages 65 yrs+. Social security numbers and replacement cards. TTY (800) 325-0778. FUNDING: Fed, govt. OFC HRS: M-F 9am-4:30pm. Spanish spoken. Free srvs. SERVES: Riverside County.

SOCIAL SECURITY ADMINISTRATION
1449 W. Redlands Blvd.
Redlands, CA 92373
(909) 798-2669
(909) 307-9949 FAX

Info on social security and SSI benefits, SS cards, Medicare benefits & sign-up, survivor and burial benefits. For TTY, call (800) 325-0778. FUNDING: Fed, govt. OFC HRS: M-F 9am-4:30pm. Spanish spoken. SERVES: Redlands.

SOCIAL SECURITY ADMINISTRATION
7880 Mission Grove Park, South
Riverside, CA 92508
(866) 931-4495
(951) 789-7340 FAX

Info on social security, SSI benefits, SS cards, Medicare benefits & sign-up, survivor and burial benefits. For TTY, call (800) 325-0778. Phone hrs: M-F 7am-7pm. FUNDING: Fed, govt. OFC HRS: M-F 9am-4:30pm. Spanish spoken. SERVES: Riverside County.

SOCIAL SECURITY ADMINISTRATION
605 N. Arrowhead Ave., Ste 101
San Bernardino, CA 92401
(866) 331-7132
(800) 772-1213

Assists with social security benefits including retirement, survivors' benefits, disability, SSI for the blind, disabled and ages 65 yrs+. TTY (800) 325-0778. OFC HRS: M-F 9am-4:30pm. Spanish spoken by phone. Free srvs. SERVES: San Bernardino County.

SOCIAL SECURITY ADMINISTRATION
13955 Park Ave., Ste 110
Victorville, CA 92392
(760) 241-5009
(760) 241-2189 FAX

Info on social security and SSI benefits, SS cards, Medicare benefits & sign-up, survivor and burial benefits. Call (800) 772-1213 anywhere in the U.S. for info on srvs or local offices. For TTY, call (800) 325-0778. FUNDING: Govt. OFC HRS: M-F 9am-4:30pm. Spanish spoken. SERVES: Victorville area.

SOCIAL SECURITY ADMINISTRATION
57019 Yucca Trail
Yucca Valley, CA 92284
(760) 369-6535
(760) 369-6533 FAX

Info on social security and SSI benefits, SS cards, Medicare benefits & sign-up, survivor and burial benefits. For TTY, call (800) 325-0778. Local number (760) 369-6535. FUNDING: Fed, govt. OFC HRS: M-F 9am-4:30pm. Spanish spoken. SERVES: Morongo Basin.

SOUTH ASIAN HELPLINE & REFERRAL AGENCY (SAHARA)
17100 S. Pioneer Blvd., Ste 260
Artesia, CA 90701
(562) 402-4132
(562) 402-6093 FAX

Serves the South Asian community by providing them with info, referrals, skills dev and other culturally sensitive support srvs including mental health, health care, legal assist, transitional living ctrs, client advocacy, case mgmt, financial assist, job training and placement, community edu prgms, and senior srvs. FUNDING: Nonprofit. OFC HRS: M-F 8am-5pm. Hindi, Gujarati, Bengali, Urdu, Nepali, Tamil & Telugu spoken. Free srvs. SERVES: Southern California.

SPAN CALIFORNIA
Suicide Prevention Advocacy Network
P.O. Box 235260
Encinitas, CA 92023
(760) 753-4565

Creates awareness regarding suicide prevention. Advocates legislative policy. No direct srvs. Volunteers work throughout the state speaking at events & conferences. Visit (www.span-california.org). FUNDING: State. SERVES: Calif.

STEELWORKERS OLDTIMERS FNDN
8572 Sierra Ave.
Fontana, CA 92335-3840
(909) 829-0384
(909) 829-0313 FAX

Senior nutrition prgm, recreational activities, blood pressure check-ups, home-delivered meals, home maintenance prgm, Inland Counties Legal Srvs (every 3rd Th), Health Insurance Counseling and Advocacy Prgm (HICAP) on the 1st F of every month. OFC HRS: M-F 8am-4pm. Spanish spoken. SERVES: Fontana, Rialto, Bloomington, Chino, Ontario, Rancho Cucamonga, Upland.

SUMMIT PAYEE SRVS, INC.
1361 North E Street
San Bernardino, CA 92405
(909) 884-5299
(951) 263-9527
(909) 885-2859 FAX

Approved representative payee srvs through the Social Security Administration. FUNDING: Nonprofit. OFC HRS: M-F 9am-4pm. ADM REQ: Inability to manage financial resources. SERVES: Inland Empire. Srvs also available in limited areas throughout So Calif.

SUN CITY CONCERN, INC
Kay Ceniceros Community Center
29995 Evans Rd.
Sun City, CA 92586
(951) 679-2374
(951) 301-1923 FAX

Free info and referral srvs for seniors. Telephone reassurance prgm, gatekeeper prgm, friendly visitor prgm. Bus trips, Bingo. Volunteer opportunities. FUNDING: S.C. United Fund, nonprofit. OFC HRS: M-F 8am-12noon, 1pm-4pm. ADM REQ: Ages 55 yrs+. SERVES: Riverside County.

TEMECULA VLY SENIOR SERVICE CTR
Rancho-Temecula Valley Senior Srvs
41538 Eastman Dr.
Murrieta, CA 92562
(951) 600-9557

Senior service center with various food programs. Emerg food daily. Senior Brown Bag, senior SHARE, USDA commodities, bread. Paralegal srvs every three months, Social Security monthly, immunizations by Dept of Health when available. Walk in or call. FUNDING: United Way. OFC HRS: M-Th 8am-11pm; F 7:30am-11:30am. Spanish spoken. ADM REQ: Low income. SERVES: Temecula & nearby.

THE FRIENDSHIP LINE
Center for Elderly Suicide Prevention

3626 Geary Blvd.
San Francisco, CA 94118
(415) 752-3778

Free and supportive telephone counseling for seniors who are bereaved, depressed, isolated, or abused. Also offers srvs for their caregivers and advocates; grief support groups available in the San Francisco area. FUNDING: Nonprofit. OFC HRS: 24 hrs, 7 days. Free srvs. SERVES: Calif.

TWENTYNINE PALMS PARKS/REC
P.O. Box 995
74362 Joe Davis Dr.
Twentynine Palms, CA 92277
(760) 367-7562
(760) 367-5679 FAX

Recreational and leisure activities for adults and children including classes in the following: Tae Kwon Do, rubber stamp, guitar lessons, macrame, step interval serobics. Racquetball courts and leagues. Senior nutrition center. Numerous sports activities for both adults and youth. OFC HRS: M-F 1pm-6pm. Fees vary per class or prgm. SERVES: Morongo Basin.

U.S. DEPT OF HOUSING/URBAN DEV
451 7th Street, SW
Washington, DC 20410
(202) 597-1112

Natl website can help you locate a HUD office near you. Also info regarding family unification vouchers, home ownership, senior housing, welfare to work, Section 8, mgmt assessment, assist for people with disabilities, American Indian housing, etc. Visit (www.hud.gov). TTY (202)708-1455. FUNDING: Govt. SERVES: U.S.A.

U.S. RAILROAD RETIREMENT BOARD
858 Oak Park Rd., Ste 102
Covina, CA 91724-3674
(626) 339-9993
(877) 772-5772
(626) 339-8223 FAX

Benefits to the railroad employee & their families under the Railroad Retirement Act & Railroad Unemployment Insurance Act. FUNDING: Govt. OFC HRS: M-F 9am-3:30pm. Spanish spoken. Srvs to public are free. This is an agency in the executive branch of the federal govt. SERVES: U.S.A.

UCLA NEUROPSYCHIATRIC HOSPITAL
UCLA Div of Geriatric Psychiatry
760 Westwood Plaza, Ste 37372A NPH
Los Angeles, CA 90024-1759
(310) 825-8441
(310) 267-0376 FAX

Comprehensive eval and treatment for older adults suffering from depression, anxiety, confusion and memory loss. Day treatment and outpatient group therapy and inpatient srvs available. Wait: 2-3 wks. FUNDING: Nonprofit. OFC HRS: M-F 8am-5pm. Sliding fee scale. SERVES: So. Calif.

VICTORVILLE SENIOR CITIZENS CLUB
14874 S. Mojave Dr.
Victorville, CA 92392
(760) 245-5018

Center activities include: social activities, health screening (blood pressure, vision, hearing, blood sugar) & edu, yearly income tax assist, occasional lunches. FUNDING: Nonprofit.

OFC HRS: M-F 8:30am-4pm. SERVES: Victorville, Apple Valley, Hesperia.

VISTA PACIFICA CENTER
Skilled Nursing Facility
3674 Pacific Ave.
Riverside, CA 92509
(951) 682-4833
(951) 274-2742 FAX

108-bed, long-term care facility; locked gero-psych skilled nursing facility. FUNDING: Medi-Cal. OFC HRS: M-F 8am-5pm. Spanish spoken. ADM REQ: Ages 65 yrs+, mental illness diagnosis with behavioral problems (hitting, yelling, resistant to care, hallucinations, delusions). Accepts Medi-Cal, Medicare, SSI. SERVES: Riverside County.

WWW.AGING-PARENTS-AND-ELDER-CARE.COM
950 Tower Lane, 6th Fl.
San Mateo, CA 94404

Helpful website for caregivers. Free referral srv, newsletter. SERVES: U.S.A.

WWW.CALMEDICARE.ORG
Medicare info
5380 Elvas Ave.
Sacramento, CA 95819
(800) 434-0222
(916) 231-5114 FAX

Visit (www.calmedicare.org) or call for info on prescription drugs, Medicare coverage, counseling, fraud, low income help. FUNDING: Calif Healthcare Fndn, nonprofit. OFC HRS: M-F 8am-4pm. SERVES: Calif.

WWW.GRANDPARENTING.ORG
108 Farnham Rd.
Ojai, CA 93023

Website dedicated to grandparents raising grandchildren. Info, edu, research, networking. FUNDING: Nonprofit. SERVES: U.S.A.

YMCA/EAST VALLEY
San Bernardino Branch
808 E. 21st Street
San Bernardino, CA 92404
(909) 881-9622
(909) 886-3151 FAX

Active aquatics prgm with swim team. Twinges in the Hinges Prgm, Aquagym, swim lessons, gymnastics, Karate, Itty Bitty Sports, basketball, day camp for off-track elementary. Summer resident camp. Offsite after school care. Walk in or call. ACA accredited. FUNDING: Nonprofit. OFC HRS: M-F 5am-9:30pm; Sat 8am-6pm; Sun 1pm-5pm. Spanish spoken. SERVES: San Bernardino County.

YMCA/PALM DESERT
Lincoln Elementary School
74-100 Rutledge Way
Palm Desert, CA 92260
(760) 902-1748

Sports and fitness programs, aquatics. Family nights, programs for seniors. Child care for grades K-12. FUNDING: Nonprofit, donations. OFC HRS: M-F 7am-6pm. SERVES: Palm Desert.

FAMILY SERVICE ASSN/WEST RIVERSIDE

Mead Valley Comm/Senior & Disabled Srvs
21091 Rider St.
Perris, CA 92570
(951) 657-0686
(951) 657-9208 FAX

Home-delivered meals, wellness center, advisory board meetings, senior meetings, AA & NA meetings, kinship meeting, summer school prgms, computers, Bingo, commodity food distribution, crafts, business network, congregate meals, THRIVE forums, food bank, postmaster's community srv. FUNDING: Nonprofit. OFC HRS: M-F 9am-5pm. Spanish spoken. ADM REQ: Depends on srvs. SERVES: Western Riverside County.

HOME DELIVERED MEALS/ADELANTO

Adelanto Nutrition Site
11565 Cortez
Adelanto, CA 92301
(760) 246-7736

On-site meals M-F 11:30am-12:30pm. The donation for each meal is $3. Serves ages 60 yrs+, under age 60 yrs $5. Nutritious meals are delivered to seniors who are unable to cook for themselves. Call the main office in Victorville at (760) 245-7047. OFC HRS: M-F 7am-3pm.

HOME DELIVERED MEALS/LUCERNE VLY

Lucerne Valley Community Center
P.O. Box 1825
10431 Allen Way
Lucerne Valley, CA 92356
(760) 248-2248

Meals delivered to homebound seniors, lunch served 11:30am-12:30pm on site. Suggested donations $3 for ages 60 yrs+, $4 for under age 60 yrs. OFC HRS: M-F 9am-1pm.

HOME DELIVERED MEALS/TRONA

Trona Senior Center
P.O. Box 443
13187 Market St.
Trona, CA 93592
(760) 372-5889

Breakfast served on Tu 7:30am, lunch served on 2nd & 3rd W at 12noon. OFC HRS: M-F 8am-12noon. Suggested donation $5.

INDIAN HEALTH, INC.

Morongo Indian Reservation Nutrition Prgm
Morongo Senior Center
11555 1/2 Potrero Rd.
Banning, CA 92220
(951) 849-4761
(951) 849-5612 FAX

Lunch is served M-F 11:30am-12:30pm to ages 60 yrs+. FUNDING: Govt. OFC HRS: M-F 6am-12:30pm. Spanish spoken. Free srvs.

INDIAN RESERVATION NUTRITION PRGM

Pechanga Senior Nutrition
P.O. Box 936
12784 Pechanga Rd.
Temecula, CA 92592
(951) 676-6810
(951) 676-0744 FAX

Lunch & home-delivered meals for ages 60 yrs+, M-F 12noon. OFC HRS: M-Th 8am-5pm; F 8am-2pm. Tagalog spoken. ADM REQ: Must be Native American. SERVES: Riverside & San Bernardino Counties.

MEAD VALLEY COMMUNITY COMPLEX

Family Service Assn/Riverside
21091 Rider St.
Perris, CA 92570
(951) 657-0686
(951) 657-9208 FAX

Prgms for youth, families, and seniors. Health screening, dental & medical srvs, independent studies, counseling, parenting classes, Bingo, senior lunch and home-delivered meals, utility assist, commodities, etc. FUNDING: Nonprofit. OFC HRS: M-F 8am-5pm. Spanish spoken. Most prgms are free. SERVES: Mead Valley, Perris.

MEALS ON WHEELS/BIG BEAR LAKE

c/o Pine Summit
P.O. Box 2871
Big Bear Lake, CA 92315
(909) 866-5233

Nutritious meals are delivered to ages 60 yrs+ who are unable to cook for themselves including a lunch and dinner M-F. There is no set donation for each meal.

MEALS ON WHEELS/INLAND EMPIRE

1998 N. Arrowhead Ave.
San Bernardino, CA 92405
(909) 882-8466
(909) 886-1301 FAX

For a fee, a client will receive 7 complete frozen meals, low fat milk & pantry items. Meals are prepared specifically with minimal amounts of fat, salt and sugar. Volunteers deliver the good and friendship on regularly shceduled routes. FUNDING: Nonprofit. OFC HRS: M-F 8:30am-5:30pm. Spanish spoken. ADM REQ: Seniors or disabled. Cash, check & PayPal, credit cards accepted. SERVES: San Bernardino, Highland, Loma Linda, Rialto, Colton, Redlands, Fontana, Grand Terrace.

MEALS ON WHEELS/ONTARIO

1017 N. Glenn Ave.
Ontario, CA 91764
(909) 983-0203

Home-delivered meals to the homebound. Delivery areas include South to Philadelphia St., North to 6th Street/10 Fwy, West to Benson Ave, and East to Grove Ave. FUNDING: Nonprofit. OFC HRS: M-F 10:30am-12noon. Fees $2 per meal SERVES: Ontario.

MEALS ON WHEELS/PALM DESERT

Joslyn Senior Center
73-750 Catalina Way
Newport Beach, CA 92660
(760) 340-3220
(760) 568-9230 FAX

Home-delivered meals for seniors who are unable to cook for themselves. Seniors choose one or 2 meals and may request vegetarian or diabetic meals. Orders must be placed 24 to 48 hrs ahead. OFC HRS: M-F 7:30am-12:30pm. SERVES: Palm Desert, Rancho Mirage & Indian Wells.

MEALS ON WHEELS/RIVERSIDE

4845 Brockton Ave.
Riverside, CA 92506

(951) 683-7151
(951) 683-5911 FAX

All-volunteer, private nonprofit prgm providing M-F delivery of a hot lunch to people unable to cook for themselves because of disability, age, illness, recent hospitalization, etc. (have regular or special diets). OFC HRS: M-F 8am-2pm. ADM REQ: Unable to cook for themselves, regardless of age or income. Fees $4.99 per meal. SERVES: Riverside, excluding zip codes 92508 & 92509.

MEALS ON WHEELS/SUN CITY

(951) 679-0119

Nutritious meals delivered to seniors unable to cook for themselves including a lunch & dinner M-F. Donation for each meal is $3.

MEALS ON WHEELS/UPLAND

(909) 981-0377

Hot meals delivered to anyone unable to cook for themselves. OFC HRS: M-F 9am-5pm. Fee $3 per meal. SERVES: Upland.

MONTCLAIR HUMAN SRVS DIVISION

5111 Benito St.
Montclair, CA 91763
(909) 625-9460
(909) 399-9751 FAX

Senior activities and meals M-F 11:30am-1pm ($1.75 donation for ages 60 yrs+). USDA surplus food 3rd Th of each month to Montclair residents. Call (909)625-9483 or (909)625-9462 for info. Low-cost medical and immunization clinic. Weight room and racquet ball courts. After-school prgms and recreation activities. Also offers free parenting and nutrition classes. See website for more info on all srvs. FUNDING: DAAS, CDD, First 5, state after school edu & safety prgms, grants, Healthy Start Planning Grant. OFC HRS: Rec Office: M-Th 7:30am-6pm. Rec Facility: M-F 7:30am to 9:30pm & Sat 8am-5pm. Spanish spoken. ADM REQ: Proof of income/uninsured for clinic srvs. SERVES: San Bernardino County.

MORONGO INDIAN NUTRITION PRGM

See "Indian Health, Inc."

NUTRITION FOR SENIORS

See "Senior Nutrition Prgms" and "Senior Nutrition Site" in this chapter.

OLD TIMERS FNDN/FONTANA

Nuevo Nutrition Site
(909) 829-4543
(909) 829-0313 FAX

Home-delivered & congregate meal prgms. OFC HRS: M-F 8am-1:30pm. ADM REQ: Call to register for prgm M-F 8am-12noon. Fee $2.50 per meal.

RIVERSIDE CO. PUBLIC HEALTH DEPT

Nutrition Services
P.O. Box 7600
4065 County Circle Dr., Ste 207
Riverside, CA 92503
(951) 358-5311
(951) 358-5472 FAX

Food & nutrition info, edu, consultation srvs. Professional & paraprofessional edu & WIC Prgm srvs. Breastfeeding info (888) 451-2499. WIC appts outside the county, call (800)

455-4942. Riverside Co., call (951) 358-7200. OFC HRS: M-F 7:30am-5pm. Spanish spoken. SERVES: Riverside County.

SALVATION ARMY/HEMET
1779 E. Florida Ave., Ste D-2
Hemet, CA 92543
(951) 766-2020
(951) 925-5796 FAX

Emerg food. Senior food prgm once a month for ages 60 yrs+ who are residents of Hemet. FUNDING: Nonprofit. OFC HRS: M-F 9am-11:30am. ADM REQ: Call for more information. SERVES: Hemet & nearby.

SENIOR NUTRITION PRGM
Riverside Co. Foundation on Aging
6296 River Crest Dr., Ste K
Riverside, CA 92507
(951) 867-3800
(951) 867-3830 FAX

Senior nutrition at various sites throughout the county. FUNDING: Fed, state, county, pvt resources. OFC HRS: M-F 8am-5pm. Spanish spoken. SERVES: Riverside County.

SENIOR NUTRITION PRGM
San Brdo Parks/Rec/Comm Srv Dept
600 W. 5th Street
San Bernardino, CA 92410
(909) 384-5430
(909) 889-0672 FAX

On-site hot meals and other srvs for ages 60 yrs+ and spouses of any age, M-F 11:30am-12:30pm. No reservations required. Many locations in city of San Bernardino; call (909) 384-5430 for addresses. Proof of residence not required. Health screenings every Tu 8:30am-12noon, appt required. FUNDING: Nonprofit. OFC HRS: M-F 8am-4pm. Suggested donation $1.75 for seniors; non-seniors $3.75. SERVES: San Bernardino metro.

SENIOR NUTRITION SITE
Banning Senior Center
769 N. San Gorgonio Ave.
Banning, CA 92220
(951) 849-1920
(951) 849-0639 FAX

Lunch is served to ages 60 yrs+, M-F 11:30am. FUNDING: Nonprofit. OFC HRS: M-F 7:30am-1:30pm. Spanish & German spoken. Suggested donation $3. SERVES: Banning.

SENIOR NUTRITION SITE
Bonnie Baker Senior Center
P.O. Box 2071
Big River, CA 92242
(760) 665-2667
(760) 665-2667 FAX

Lunch is served to ages 60 yrs+, M-F 11:30am. Suggested donation $3. SERVES: Big River.

SENIOR NUTRITION SITE
Bloomington Senior Center
18317 Valley Blvd.
Bloomington, CA 92316
(909) 877-4310

Lunch served M-F from 11:30am-1pm. For home-delivered meals, call (909) 822-4493. Suggested donation $2.50 for ages 60 yrs+, under age 60 yrs $4.

SENIOR NUTRITION SITE
Colorado River Senior/Community Ctr
HCR 20, Box 3408
Blythe, CA 92225

(760) 922-6133
(760) 922-6135 FAX

Lunch is served M-F 11:30am-12:30pm. Located 27 mi north of Blythe on Hwy 95. OFC HRS: M-F 9am-3pm (Oct-May); M-F 9am-1pm (June-Sept). ADM REQ: Must call before 9am to RSVP. Suggested donation $3. SERVES: Colorado River Rural Community.

SENIOR NUTRITION SITE
Calimesa/Norton Younglove Senior Ctr
P.O. Box 1190
908 Park Ave.
Calimesa, CA 92320
(909) 446-1071
(909) 795-5204 FAX

Lunch is served M-F 11:30am-12noon. Homebound meals also served. FUNDING: City & county. ADM REQ: Ages 60 yrs+. Must have reservation for lunch, call (909) 446-1071. Suggested donation $2. Fee $5 for under age 60 yrs. SERVES: Riverside County.

SENIOR NUTRITION SITE
13170 Central Ave.
Chino, CA 91710
(909) 591-9836

Senior meals for ages 60 yrs+, M-F at 11:30am. Suggested donation of $2.50 per meal (if able). Home-delivered meals also available, call (909) 628-0071 for info. OFC HRS: M-F 9am-1pm. SERVES: Chino.

SENIOR NUTRITION SITE
Coachella Senior Center
1540 7th Street
Coachella, CA 92236
(760) 398-0104
(760) 398-3712 FAX

Lunch is served to ages 60 yrs+, M-Th 11am. ADM REQ: Call 24 hrs in advance to RSVP. Suggested donation $2. SERVES: Coachella.

SENIOR NUTRITION SITE
Pete Luque Senior Center
292 East O Street
Colton, CA 92324
(909) 370-5087
(909) 370-6157 FAX

Lunch is served to ages 60 yrs+, M-F 11:30am-12:30pm. Blood pressure checks 1st Th 10am-12:30pm. Suggested donation $2.50; non-seniors $4. SERVES: Colton.

SENIOR NUTRITION SITE
Desert Hot Springs Community Center
11-777 West Dr.
Desert Hot Springs, CA 92240
(760) 329-0222
(760) 288-0631 FAX

Lunch is served to ages 60 yrs+, M-F 11:30am. Suggested donation $3. SERVES: Desert Hot Springs.

SENIOR NUTRITION SITE
Neighborhood Center
305 E. Devonshire St.
Hemet, CA 92543
(951) 827-3613

Lunch is served to ages 60 yrs+, M-F 11:30am-12noon. Meals on Wheels prgm. ADM REQ: 24-hr advance registration required. Suggested donation $2. SERVES: Hemet.

SENIOR NUTRITION SITE
Highland Senior Center

P.O. Box 948
3102 E. Highland Ave.
Highland, CA 92346
(909) 862-8104
(909) 862-8196 FAX

Hot meal for ages 60 yrs+, M-F 12noon-1pm. No reservations required. You may order sack lunch for weekend; order M-Th, pick-up F 12noon-3pm, cost $1 per lunch (pre-paid when you order). OFC HRS: M-Th 8am-5pm; F 8am-4pm. Suggested donation $1.75. Bring younger guest for $3.75. SERVES: Highland, San Bernardino & nearby.

SENIOR NUTRITION SITE
Hinkley Senior Citizen Club
P.O. Box 185
35997 Mountain View Rd.
Hinkley, CA 92347
(760) 253-4677
(760) 253-4677 FAX

Nutrition prgm for seniors, M-F 11:30am-12:30pm. OFC HRS: M-F 9am-2pm. ADM REQ: Must register before 10am. Donation $2. SERVES: Hinkley.

SENIOR NUTRITION SITE
Joshua Tree Community Center
6171 Sunburst St.
Joshua Tree, CA 92252-0838
(760) 366-2471

Lunch is served to ages 60 yrs+, M-F 12noon-1pm. Also offers other srvs for seniors, including blood pressure checks 1st Tu. No reservations required. OFC HRS: M-F 8:30am-1:30pm. Suggested donation $2.50. SERVES: Joshua Tree.

SENIOR NUTRITION SITE
Lake Elsinore Senior Ctr
420 E. Lakeshore Dr.
Lake Elsinore, CA 92530
(951) 471-3571
(951) 471-1418 FAX

Lunch is served to ages 60 yrs+, M-F 11:30am. Also home-delivered meals. Referral & info, seminars, Bingo, pool, exercise, computer, arts, crafts, etc. FUNDING: Riverside Co. Office on Aging, Older Americans Act Funds. OFC HRS: M-Th 8am-4pm; F 9am-4pm. ADM REQ: Must make lunch reservation. Suggested donation $3. SERVES: Lake Elsinore, Wildomar, Murrieta, Sun City, Perris, Moreno Valley.

SENIOR NUTRITION SITE
Montclair Community Center
5111 Benito
Montclair, CA 91763
(909) 625-9462
(909) 399-9751 FAX

Lunch is served to ages 60 yrs+, M-F 11:30am-1pm. Suggested donation $1.75. SERVES: Montclair.

SENIOR NUTRITION SITE
Moreno Valley Family Srv
25075 Fir St.
Moreno Valley, CA 92553
(951) 247-1667
(951) 243-1400 FAX

Lunch is served to ages 60 yrs+, M-F 11am. Also homebound meals. ADM REQ: Must register. Suggested donation $3. SERVES: Moreno Valley.

SENIOR NUTRITION SITE

Norco Senior Center
2690 Clark Ave.
Norco, CA 92860
(951) 270-5638
(951) 371-1553 FAX

Lunch is served to ages 60 yrs+, M-F 12noon. Homebound srvs also available. OFC HRS: M-F 7am-5pm. ADM REQ: Reservations 24 hrs in advance. Suggested donation $3 for seniors 60 yrs+, non-seniors $5.

SENIOR NUTRITION SITE

Ontario Community Center
225 East B Street
Ontario, CA 91761
(909) 395-2010
(909) 395-3671 FAX

Lunch is served to ages 60 yrs+, M-F 11:30am. Suggested donation $2.50.

SENIOR NUTRITION SITE

Mizell Senior Center
480 S. Sunrise Way
Palm Springs, CA 92262
(760) 323-5689
(760) 320-9373 FAX

Lunch is served to ages 55 yrs+, M-F 11:30am. Homebound meals available. Also Meals on Wheels prgm. Suggested donation $4.

SENIOR NUTRITION SITE

Perris Senior Center
100 North D Street
Perris, CA 92570
(951) 943-4190

Lunch is served to ages 60 yrs+, M-F 11am. Also homebound meals. Suggested donation $3.

SENIOR NUTRITION SITE

Rancho Senior Nutrition
11200 Baseline Rd.
Rancho Cucamonga, CA 91701
(909) 477-2780
(909) 477-2781 FAX

Lunch is served to ages 60 yrs+, M-F 11:30am-1pm. Suggested donation $2. SERVES: Rancho Cucamonga.

SENIOR NUTRITION SITE

Redlands Community Senior Center
P.O. Box 3005
111 W. Lugonia Ave.
Redlands, CA 92374
(909) 798-7579
(909) 793-3569 FAX

Lunch is served to ages 60 yrs+, M-F 11:30am-12:30pm. Prgm administered through Community Action Partnership of San Bernardino. OFC HRS: M-F 8am-5pm. Spanish spoken. Suggested donation $2.

SENIOR NUTRITION SITE

Rialto Senior Center
1411 S. Riverside Ave.
Rialto, CA 92376
(909) 877-9706

Lunch is served to ages 60 yrs+, M-F 11:30am-1pm. Meal delivery to homebound, call (909) 829-0384. Suggested donation $2.50 for seniors, $4 for non-seniors. SERVES: Rialto.

SENIOR NUTRITION SITE

Eddie Dee Smith Senior Center

5888 Mission Blvd.
Riverside, CA 92509
(951) 369-7276
(951) 795-9745 FAX

Lunch is served to ages 60 yrs+, M-F 12noon. OFC HRS: M-F 8am-4pm. Suggested donation $2.

SENIOR NUTRITION SITE

Villegas Center
7240 Marguerita Ave.
Riverside, CA 92504
(951) 351-6142

Lunch is served to ages 60 yrs+, M-F 11:30am. OFC HRS: M-Th 10am-9pm; F 10am-6pm; Sat 12noon-5pm. Spanish spoken. ADM REQ: Reservation 24 hrs in advance. Suggested donation $2. Under age 60 yrs $5.50.

SENIOR NUTRITION SITE

Janet Goeske Center
5257 Sierra St.
Riverside, CA 92504
(951) 351-9163
(951) 688-9790 FAX

Lunch is served to ages 60 yrs+, M-F 12noon. OFC HRS: M-F 7am-9pm; Sat 7:30am-4:30pm; Sun 1pm-5pm. Suggested donation $3.

SENIOR NUTRITION SITE

Dales Senior Center
3936 Chestnut St.
Riverside, CA 92501
(951) 826-5303
(951) 826-2005 FAX

Breakfast served Th 9:15am-10:15am. FUNDING: City. OFC HRS: M-F 9am-3pm. Suggested donation $1. SERVES: Riverside County.

SENIOR NUTRITION SITE

Home of Neighborly Services
839 N. Mount Vernon
San Bernardino, CA 92411
(909) 885-3491
(909) 884-0181 FAX

Lunch is served to ages 60 yrs+, M-F 11:30am-12:30pm. Boxing, Boy & Girl Scouts, modern & jazz dance for youth. Sewing, emerg food & ESL classes for adults. OFC HRS: M-F 8:30am-5:30pm. Free srvs. Suggested meal donation $2.50. Under age 60 yrs $4.50. SERVES: San Bernardino County.

SENIOR NUTRITION SITE

Delmann Heights Community Center
2969 N. Flores
San Bernardino, CA 92407
(909) 887-2115

Hot meals and other srvs for ages 60 yrs+, and spouse any age M-F 11:30am. No reservations required. OFC HRS: M-F 8am-1pm. Suggested donation $2.50.

SENIOR NUTRITION SITE

Lytle Creek Community Center
380 South K Street
San Bernardino, CA 92410
(909) 384-5424
(909) 384-5160 FAX

Hot meals and other srvs for ages 60 yrs+ and spouse of any age M-F 12pm. No reservations required but must sign-in. OFC HRS: M-F 9am-8pm. Spanish spoken. Suggested donation $1.75. SERVES: San Bernardino City.

SENIOR NUTRITION SITE

Perris Hill Senior Center
780 E. 21st Street
San Bernardino, CA 92404
(909) 384-5436
(909) 384-5160 FAX

Lunch is served to ages 60 yrs+ and spouse of any age, M-F 11:30am. No reservations required. Suggested donation $1.75.

SENIOR NUTRITION SITE

Rudy Hernandez Community Center
222 N. Lugo Ave.
San Bernardino, CA 92408
(909) 384-5420
(909) 384-5160 FAX

Lunch is served to ages 60 yrs+ and spouse of any age, M-F 12noon-1pm. No reservations required. OFC HRS: M-F 9am-3pm. Suggested donation $1.75. SERVES: San Bernardino City.

SENIOR NUTRITION SITE

San Jacinto Community Center
625 Pico St.
San Jacinto, CA 92583
(951) 654-2054
(951) 487-6022 FAX

Lunch is served to ages 60 yrs+, M-F 11:30am. ADM REQ: Must register. Suggested donation $2.

SENIOR NUTRITION SITE

Kay Ceniceros Senior Center
29995 Evans Rd.
Sun City, CA 92586
(951) 679-0119
(951) 342-3057
(951) 301-1923 FAX

Lunch is served to ages 60 yrs+, M-F 11:30am-12:30pm. OFC HRS: 5:30am-1pm Suggested donation $3. If under 60 yrs, $5 charge. SERVES: Sun City, Menifee, Canyon Lake, Wildomar.

SENIOR NUTRITION SITE

Rummonds Center/Thermal Senior Center
P.O. Box 284
87-229 Church Street
Thermal, CA 92274
(760) 399-0081

Lunch is served to ages 60 yrs+, M-F 11:30am. Also homebound meals. OFC HRS: M-F 6am-2pm. ADM REQ: Call to reserve 24 hrs in advance. Suggested donation $3. SERVES: Imperial County.

SENIOR NUTRITION SITE

Wonder Valley Community Center
80526 1/2 Amboy Rd.
Twentynine Palms, CA 92277
(760) 367-1678

Social activities, health edu, blood pressure checks 4th Tu 10am-12noon, food prgm, congregate meal site M-F 12noon. FUNDING: Nonprofit. OFC HRS: M-F 9:30am-1:30pm. Meal donation $2.50. SERVES: Wonder Valley.

SENIOR NUTRITION SITE

Scherer Community & Senior Center
12202 1st Street
Yucaipa, CA 92399
(909) 797-1177

Hot meals and other srvs for ages 60 yrs+ and spouse of any age, M-F 11:30am-12:30pm. Homebound meals available. Suggested donation $3.

SENIOR NUTRITION SITE

Yucca Valley Senior Ctr
Community Action Partnership
57088 Twentynine Palms Hwy.
Yucca Valley, CA 92284
(760) 228-5453
(760) 228-5480 FAX

Hot nutritious meals are prepared and served to ages 60 yrs+ and spouse of any age, M-F 12noon-1pm. Reservations not required. Homebound meals are available. Donation $2.50 per meal. SERVES: Morongo Valley, Joshua Tree, 29 Palms, Wonder Valley.

SODEXHO

Home Delivered Meals
(951) 827-3613
(951) 827-3754 FAX

Seniors must call the Office on Aging for applications, (800) 510-2020. FUNDING: County. OFC HRS: M-F 8am-3pm. SERVES: Riverside County.

STEELWORKERS OLDTIMERS FNDN

8572 Sierra Ave.
Fontana, CA 92335-3840
(909) 829-0384
(909) 829-0313 FAX

Senior nutrition prgm, recreational activities, blood pressure check-ups, home-delivered meals, home maintenance prgm, Inland Counties Legal Srvs (every 3rd Th), Health Insurance Counseling and Advocacy Prgm (HICAP) on the 1st F of every month. OFC HRS: M-F 8am-4pm. Spanish spoken. SERVES: Fontana, Rialto, Bloomington, Chino, Ontario, Rancho Cucamonga, Upland.

THE WELL IN THE DESERT

555 Commercial Rd., Ste 10
Palm Springs, CA 92262
(760) 327-8577
(760) 327-8559 FAX

Congregate meal prgm M-F 11am-1pm. Also case mgmt and social srvs must have photo ID. Also grocery distribution (no case mgmt), Sat 7am-10am at 181 N. Indian Canyon, Palm Springs. FUNDING: Pvt nonprofit. OFC HRS: M-F 9am-3pm. ADM REQ: Sign guestbook Free srvs. SERVES: Cathedral City, Desert Hot Springs, Palm Springs, Thousand Palms.

AAA

See "Auto Club of So Calif (AAA)"

ACTS/ADVENTIST COMM TEAM SRVS

See "Adventist Comm Team Srvs"

ADVENTIST COMM TEAM SRVS (ACTS)

P.O. Box 477
24914 Barton Rd.
Loma Linda, CA 92354
(909) 796-8357
(909) 799-5653 FAX

Primary goal is to assist disadvantaged people, without regard to race or creed, in living as independently as possible. Info & referral, food for homeless, case mgmt, ACTS transit provides transportation srv to medical appts, markets, beauty parlor for a fee. Must be registered with ACTS. Also offer Meals on Wheels. FUNDING: Donations, nonprofit. OFC HRS: M-Th 8am-1pm; F 8am-12noon. ADM REQ: Appt needed. SERVES: Loma Linda.

AIRLINES SERVING ORANGE COUNTY

See "John Wayne Airport/O.C."

AMERICAN CANCER SOCIETY

Transportation to cancer treatment. Look in the Health Care/Medical chapter for a complete list of offices. Call the office nearest you for details.

AMTRAK PASSENGER STATION

Los Angeles Union Station
800 N. Alameda St.
Los Angeles, CA 90012
(800) 872-7245

Call for info and reservations. TDD (800) 523-6590. OFC HRS: 24 hrs, 7 days.

AMTRAK PASSENGER STATION

1170 W. 3rd Street
San Bernardino, CA 92410
(800) 872-7245
(909) 884-1307

Staffed station. Passenger train srv. TDD/TTY (800) 523-6590.

ANGEL FLIGHT WEST

3161 Donald Douglas Loop, South
Santa Monica, CA 90405
(310) 390-2958
(888) 426-2643
(310) 397-9636 FAX

Air travel via private aircraft for patients needing to travel for medical treatment or other compelling need. May also transport blood & donor organs. Patients must be ambulatory, medically stable and financially distressed or unable to use regular transportation. Flights covered to a maximum of 1,000 nautical miles. After hours emergencies, call (800) 413-1360, voicemail (310) 398-6123. FUNDING: Nonprofit. OFC HRS: M-F 8:30am-4:30pm. Spanish spoken. Free srvs. SERVES: 13 Western states.

AUTO CLUB OF SO CALIF (AAA)

Emerg srv, insurance prgms, referral for auto repairs, travel maps, info on lodging, DMV srvs except for U.S. driver's license, etc. Visit (www.aaa-calif.com).

AUTO CLUB OF SO CALIF (AAA)

Mature Driver Program
(877) 222-7868

Online 8-hr course. Teaches various techniques for coping with decreased vision, flexibility & reflexes. Provides strategies for the mature driver on how to predict, interpret & react to traffic around him/her. Also techniques for defensive driving, dealing with tailgaters, handling emergencies & what to expect when renewing driver's licenses. Visit (www.aaa-calif.com).

BARSTOW AREA TRANSIT

1612 State St.
Barstow, CA 92311
(760) 256-0311
(760) 255-3330
(760) 255-3006 FAX

Fixed route. General public transportation. TDD (760) 256-0311. HRS: M-Th 7:30am-5:30pm; F 7:30am-4:30pm. ADM REQ: Can make reservation day before or if same day pickup, wait time can be up to 45 minutes. Fee $1.65 each way. SERVES: Barstow, Lenwood and Grandview.

CALIF DEPT MOTOR VEHICLES

Authorizes Calif state driver's licenses, renews licenses, issues vehicle registration and official identification card if a person does not drive. The written driver's test is given in various languages, including Spanish and Vietnamese, in most offices. Appts are recommended to avoid waiting in line. Fee depends on srv requested. Visit (www.dmv.org).

CALIF DEPT MOTOR VEHICLES

1034 W. Ramsey St., Ste B
Banning, CA 92220
(800) 777-0133

Authorizes Calif state driver's licenses, registers motor vehicles, issues ID cards to those who do not drive. Appt recommended. For TTY, call (800) 368-4327. OFC HRS: M, Tu, Th, F 8am-5pm; W 9am-5pm. SERVES: Riverside County.

CALIF DEPT MOTOR VEHICLES

528 E. Virginia Way
Barstow, CA 92311
(800) 777-0133

Authorizes Calif state driver's licenses, registers motor vehicles, issues ID cards to those who do not drive. Appt recommended. For TTY, call (800) 368-4327. OFC HRS: M, Tu, Th, F 8am-5pm; W 9am-5pm. Spanish spoken. SERVES: San Bernardino County.

CALIF DEPT MOTOR VEHICLES

430 S. Broadway
Blythe, CA 92225
(800) 777-0133

Authorizes Calif state driver's licenses, registers motor vehicles, issues ID cards to those who do not drive. Appt recommended. For TTY, call (800) 368-4327. OFC HRS: M, Tu, Th, F 8am-5pm; W 9am-5pm. SERVES: Riverside County.

CALIF DEPT MOTOR VEHICLES

16499 Merrill Ave.
Fontana, CA 92335
(800) 777-0133

Authorizes Calif state driver's licenses, registers motor vehicles, issues ID cards to those

who do not drive. Appt recommended. For TTY, call (800) 368-4327. FUNDING: Govt. OFC HRS: M, Tu, Th, F 8am-5pm; W 9am-5pm. SERVES: San Bernardino County.

CALIF DEPT MOTOR VEHICLES

1200 S. State St.
Hemet, CA 92543
(800) 777-0133

Authorizes Calif state driver's licenses, registers motor vehicles, issues ID cards to those who do not drive. Also has commercial driving test office. Appt recommended. For TTY, call (800) 368-4327. OFC HRS: M, Tu, Th, F 8am-5pm; W 9am-5pm. SERVES: Riverside County.

CALIF DEPT MOTOR VEHICLES

44-480 Jackson St.
Indio, CA 92201
(800) 777-0133

Authorizes Calif state driver's licenses, registers motor vehicles, issues ID cards to those who do not drive. Also has commercial driving test office. Appt recommended. For TTY, call (800) 368-4327. OFC HRS: M, Tu, Th, F 8am-5pm; W 9am-5pm. SERVES: Riverside County.

CALIF DEPT MOTOR VEHICLES

1040 E. Broadway
Needles, CA 92363
(800) 777-0133

Authorizes Calif state driver's licenses, registers motor vehicles, issues ID cards to those who do not drive. Appt recommended. For TTY, call (800) 368-4327. OFC HRS: M, Tu, Th, F 8am-5pm; W 9am-5pm. Spanish spoken. SERVES: San Bernardino County.

CALIF DEPT MOTOR VEHICLES

3201 Horseless Carriage Dr.
Norco, CA 92860
(800) 777-0133

Authorizes Calif state driver's licenses, registers motor vehicles, issues ID cards to those who do not drive. Appt recommended. For TTY, call (800) 368-4327. OFC HRS: M, Tu, Th, F 8am-5pm; W 9am-5pm. SERVES: Riverside County.

CALIF DEPT MOTOR VEHICLES

950 N. Farrell Dr.
Palm Springs, CA 92262
(800) 777-0133

Authorizes Calif state driver's licenses, registers motor vehicles, issues ID cards to those who do not drive. Appt recommended. For TTY, call (800) 368-4327. OFC HRS: M, Tu, Th, F 8am-5pm; W 9am-5pm. SERVES: Riverside County.

CALIF DEPT MOTOR VEHICLES

8678 Archibald Ave.
Rancho Cucamonga, CA 91730
(800) 777-0133

Authorizes Calif state driver's licenses, registers motor vehicles, issues ID cards to those who do not drive. Appt recommended. For TTY, call (800) 368-4327. OFC HRS: M, Tu, Th, F 8am-5pm; W 9am-5pm. Spanish spoken. SERVES: San Bernardino County.

CALIF DEPT MOTOR VEHICLES
1659 W. Lugonia Ave.
Redlands, CA 92374
(800) 777-0133

Authorizes Calif state driver's licenses, registers motor vehicles, issues ID cards to those who do not drive. Appt recommended. For TTY, call (800) 368-4327. OFC HRS: M, Tu, Th, F 8am-5pm; W 9am-5pm. Spanish spoken. SERVES: San Bernardino County.

CALIF DEPT MOTOR VEHICLES
Riverside East Office
6425 Sycamore Canyon Blvd.
Riverside, CA 92507
(800) 777-0133
(951) 697-6786 FAX

Authorizes Calif state driver's licenses, registers motor vehicles, issues ID cards to those who do not drive. Appt recommended. For TTY, call (800) 368-4327. OFC HRS: M, Tu, Th, F 8am-5pm; W 9am-5pm. SERVES: Riverside County.

CALIF DEPT MOTOR VEHICLES
6280 Brockton Ave.
Riverside, CA 92506
(800) 777-0133

Authorizes Calif state driver's licenses, registers motor vehicles, issues ID cards to those who do not drive. TDD call (800) 368-4327. Appt recommended. For TTY, call (800) 368-4327. OFC HRS: M, Tu, Th, F 8am-5pm; W 9am-5pm. SERVES: Riverside County.

CALIF DEPT MOTOR VEHICLES
General Info Line
4700 Broadway
Sacramento, CA 95820
(800) 777-0133
(800) 921-1117

Receives complaints against new or used auto dealers concerning registration and sales or warranty repair problems. Send letter with copies of documentation. Questions answered about warranty responsibilities. Also call: San Bernardino (909) 383-4871; Rancho Cucamonga (909) 466-1008; L.A. (213) 744-7591; Culver City (310) 391-6268; Inglewood (310) 412-6416; Anaheim (714) 780-0560. FUNDING: Govt. OFC HRS: M, Tu, Th, F 8am-5pm; W 9am-5pm. Spanish SERVES: Calif.

CALIF DEPT MOTOR VEHICLES
1310 N. Waterman Ave.
San Bernardino, CA 92404
(800) 777-0133
(909) 884-5060 FAX

Authorizes Calif state driver's licenses, registers motor vehicles, issues ID cards to those who do not drive. Appt recommended. For TTY, call (800) 368-4327. OFC HRS: M, Tu, Th, F 8am-5pm; W 9am-5pm. Spanish spoken. SERVES: San Bernardino County.

CALIF DEPT MOTOR VEHICLES
110 W. Central Ave.
San Bernardino, CA 92408
(800) 777-0133

Authorizes Calif state driver's licenses, registers motor vehicles, issues ID cards to those who do not drive. Appt recommended. For TTY, call (800) 368-4327. OFC HRS: M, Tu, Th, F

7am-4pm; W 8am-4pm. SERVES: San Bernardino County.

CALIF DEPT MOTOR VEHICLES
27851 Diaz Rd.
Temecula, CA 92590
(800) 777-0133

Authorizes Calif state driver's licenses, registers motor vehicles, issues ID cards to those who do not drive. Appt recommended. For TTY, call (800) 368-4327. OFC HRS: M, Tu, Th, F 8am-5pm; W 9am-5pm. SERVES: Riverside County.

CALIF DEPT MOTOR VEHICLES
P.O. Box 936
3668 Adobe Rd., Ste G-J
Twentynine Palms, CA 92277
(800) 777-0133

Authorizes Calif state driver's licenses, registers motor vehicles, issues ID cards to those who do not drive. Appt recommended. For TTY, call (800) 368-4327. OFC HRS: M, Tu, Th, F 8am-5pm; W 9am-5pm. Spanish spoken. SERVES: San Bernardino County.

CALIF DEPT MOTOR VEHICLES
14855 Corta Dr.
Victorville, CA 92392
(800) 777-0133

Authorizes Calif state driver's licenses, registers motor vehicles, issues ID cards to those who do not drive. Appt recommended. For TTY, call (800) 368-4327. OFC HRS: M, Tu, Th, F 8am-5pm; W 9am-5pm. Spanish spoken. SERVES: San Bernardino County.

CALIF DEPT TRANSPORTATION
CalTrans
464 W. 4th Street
San Bernardino, CA 92401-1400
(909) 383-4631
(909) 383-6899 FAX

OFC HRS: M-F 7am-5pm. Spanish spoken. SERVES: San Bernardino County.

CALIF HIGHWAY INFORMATION
CalTrans
1120 N Street
Sacramento, CA 94273
(800) 427-7623

24-hr recorded message about highway conditions, wind advisories, storm conditions and other factors that will impede travel plans. Provides info about roads & freeways throughout the state. Visit (www.dot.ca.gov) for local office addresses. FUNDING: Govt. SERVES: So. Calif.

CALIF HIGHWAY PATROL/FWY SRVS
Freeway Service Patrol/Trans Mgmt Ctr
120 S. Spring St.
Los Angeles, CA 90012
(213) 897-7275
(213) 897-0519 FAX

Courtesy tow srv to motorists when their vehicles have become disabled on most L.A. Co. freeways. Cars will be towed free of charge to an approved CHP location. The CHP will notify an auto club or towing service.

CALIF PUBLIC UTILITIES COMMISSION
Consumer Protection & Safety Division
505 Van Ness Ave., 2nd Fl.
San Francisco, CA 94102
(800) 848-5580
(415) 703-2782

(415) 703-1758 FAX

Receives complaints about household goods carriers & passenger carriers within Calif. This includes movers, bus travel, limos, airport shuttles, etc. For passenger carrier complaints, call (800) 877-8867. FUNDING: Govt. OFC HRS: M-F 8am-5pm. SERVES: Calif

CALTRANS HIGHWAY INFORMATION
See "Calif Highway Information"

CARE-A-VAN TRANSIT SYSTEM
Prime of Life, Inc.
1075 N. State
Hemet, CA 92543
(951) 791-3572
(951) 791-3553 FAX

Transportation for seniors, disabled & needy 6 days a week by appt only. No Sun srvs. FUNDING: Govt, donations, nonprofit. OFC HRS: M-F 8am-4pm. SERVES: Hemet, San Jacinto.

CATHOLIC CHARITIES/COMMUNITY SRVS
West End Regional Center
9375 Archibald Ave., Ste 302
Rancho Cucamonga, CA 91730
(909) 481-7196
(909) 481-6305 FAX

Food baskets, assist with rental & mortgage payments, utility payments, pre-arranged motel accommodations, info & referral, transportation, medical referrals, clothing & furniture assist, tax prep & holiday baskets. Call for appt. FUNDING: Nonprofit. OFC HRS: M-F 8:30am-4:30pm. Spanish spoken. SERVES: Fontana, Etiwanda, Ontario, Montclair, Upland, Alta Loma, Rancho Cucamonga, Chino, Chino Hills.

CATHOLIC CHARITIES/COMMUNITY SRVS
San Bernardino Regional Center
1800 Western Ave., Ste 107
San Bernardino, CA 92411
(909) 880-3625
(909) 880-9847 FAX

Food baskets, assists with rental & mortgage payment, utility payments, transportation, info & referral, medical referrals, clothing, furniture assist (as funds are available). FUNDING: Nonprofit. OFC HRS: M-F 8:30am-4:30pm. Spanish spoken. SERVES: San Bernardino County except Morongo Basin & the west side.

CENTER FOR AUTO SAFETY (CAS)
1825 Connecticut Ave., NW, Ste 330
Washington, DC 20009-5708
(202) 328-7700

Info on auto defects & lemon laws. Send self-addressed, stamped envelope with request or complaint. Include make, model and year of vehicle. Agency compiles complaints to advocate recalls and regulation. Visit (www.autosafety.org). FUNDING: Govt. OFC HRS: M-F 8:30am-6pm, EST. SERVES: U.S.A.

CHARITY CARS
750 Miami Springs Dr.
Longwood, FL 32779
(800) 242-7489

Donated vehicles are provided to disadvantaged families who are working but cannot afford to purchase. Case workers or social srv agencies who would like to refer a client, please send info to (info@800charitycars.org) and someone will contact you. FUNDING: Donations, nonprofit. OFC HRS: Operators 24 hrs, 7 days. ADM REQ: Families, please do not contact Charity Cars directly. Contact must come from referring agency. Pre-screening process. Free srvs. SERVES: U.S.A.

COACH AMERICA

3333 E. 69th Street
Long Beach, CA 90805
(800) 642-3287

Group charter service, tours, airport shuttle. Also visit (www.coachamerica.com). OFC HRS: M-F 8am-5pm. Spanish spoken. ADM REQ: Call for rates. SERVES: U.S.A.

CORPORATE ANGEL NETWORK

Westchester County Airport
One Loop Rd.
White Plains, NY 10604-1215
(914) 328-1313
(866) 328-1313
(914) 328-3938 FAX

Free flights for cancer patients to treatment centers. The patients and family are flown on corporate aircraft flying on routine business. Volunteers and staff work to arrange the flights. FUNDING: Donations. OFC HRS: M-F 8:30am-4:30pm, EST. ADM REQ: Open to all cancer patients, bone marrow donors & recipients who are ambulatory and not in need of medical support while traveling. No fee and patients can travel as often as necessary. SERVES: U.S.A.

DEPT OF MOTOR VEHICLES

See "Calif Dept Motor Vehicles"

DESERT BLIND/HANDICAPPED ASSN

777 E. Tahquitz Canyon Way, Ste 200-28
Palm Springs, CA 92262
(760) 318-2882
(760) 770-1722 FAX

Transportation for blind, elderly & disabled. Info & referral srvs. FUNDING: Nonprofit, donations. OFC HRS: M-Sat 9am-4pm. ADM REQ: Member organization must fill out application and pay $30 annual fee. Must live in the serves area. Accepts donations from $2-$4 or coupons. Coupon books can be purchased from drivers or by calling. SERVES: Palm Springs, Cathedral City, Desert Hot Springs, Eisenhower Medical Ctr.

DIAL-A-RIDE/BANNING

P.O. Box 998
789 N. San Gorgonio Ave.
Banning, CA 92220
(951) 922-3252
(951) 849-5952 FAX

Curb-to-curb bus srv for seniors ages 60 yrs+, persons with disabilities, and ADA certified passengers. Call for more info, times and fees. OFC HRS: M-F 8am-3pm. Prgm Hrs: Non-ADA M-F 8am-3pm; ADA M-F 6am-7pm; Sat 8am-5pm; Sun 9am-5pm. Spanish spoken. SERVES: Banning, Cabazon.

DIAL-A-RIDE/BARSTOW

1612 State St.
Barstow, CA 92311
(760) 256-0311
(760) 255-3006 FAX

Curb-to-curb bus srv for seniors ages 60 yrs+, persons with disabilities, and ADA certified passengers. OFC HRS: M-F 9am-5pm. Spanish spoken. ADM REQ: Must make advance reservation. Fee $1.65 each way. SERVES: Barstow.

DIAL-A-RIDE/BEAUMONT/CHERRY VLY

550 E. 6th Street
Beaumont, CA 92223
(951) 769-8532
(951) 769-8531 FAX

Curb-to-curb bus srv for seniors and ADA certified passengers. Dial-A-Ride srv is also available for general public passengers who are outside 3/4 mile of the fixed route. FUNDING: Public, govt. OFC HRS: M-Th 8am-5pm; F 8am-4pm. Srv Hrs: M-Sat 6am-6pm. Spanish spoken. ADM REQ: Must call for pick-up. Fee $1.35 each way for seniors and the disabled. SERVES: Cherry Valley, Beaumont.

DIAL-A-RIDE/BIG BEAR LAKE

P.O. Box 1501
Big Bear Lake, CA 92315
(909) 878-5200
(909) 878-5207 FAX

Dial-A-Ride srv M-Sun 6am-8pm. Fixed route $2 for adults, $1 for seniors and disabled. SERVES: Big Bear Lake.

DIAL-A-RIDE/CORONA-NORCO

400 S. Vicatia Ave.
Corona, CA 92882
(951) 734-7220
(951) 736-2266
(951) 520-0681 FAX

Curb-to-curb transportation service. FUNDING: Public, govt. OFC HRS: M-F 6am-6pm; Sat 8am-5pm. Spanish spoken. ADM REQ: Must call one to 14 days in advance. Fee for the general public $3; seniors and the disabled $1.50. SERVES: Corona, Norco.

DIAL-A-RIDE/JURUPA

P.O. Box 59968
1825 3rd Street
Riverside, CA 92517-1968
(800) 795-7887
(951) 565-5000
(951) 684-1007 FAX

Curb-to-curb shuttle service. For seniors and persons with disabilities only. TTY (800) 369-3610. ADM REQ: Must call in advance for reservation. SERVES: Jurupa, Pedley, Glen Avon, Mira Loma and Rubidoux area.

DIAL-A-RIDE/LAKE ELSINORE

P.O. Box 59968
1825 3rd Street
Riverside, CA 92517-1968
(800) 795-7887
(951) 684-1007 FAX

Curb-to-curb shuttle. For seniors and persons with disabilities only. TTY (800) 369-3610. ADM REQ: Must call in advance for reservation. Fees senior and the disabled $2.50. SERVES: Lake Elsinore, Tuscany Hills and Wildomar area.

DIAL-A-RIDE/MORENO VALLEY

P.O. Box 59968
1825 3rd Street
Riverside, CA 92517-1968
(800) 795-7887
(951) 565-5005 FAX

Curb-to-curb bus srv for seniors ages 60 yrs+, persons with disabilities, and ADA certified passengers. TTY (800) 369-3610. FUNDING: Public, govt. OFC HRS: M-F 7am-6pm; Sat, Sun 8am-5pm. Spanish spoken. ADM REQ: Must call in advance for reservation. Fee $2. Regular fee $1 for seniors or disabled. SERVES: Moreno Valley.

DIAL-A-RIDE/MURRIETA

P.O. Box 59968
1825 3rd Street
Riverside, CA 92517-1968
(800) 795-7887
(951) 565-5005 FAX

Curb-to-curb bus srv for seniors ages 60 yrs+, persons with disabilities, and ADA certified passengers. TTY (800) 369-3610. HRS: M-F 6:30am-7:30pm; Sat 10am-5:30pm; Sun 8am-6pm. ADM REQ: Must call in advance for reservation. Fees seniors and the disabled $2.50. SERVES: Murrieta, Temecula and parts of Winchester.

DIAL-A-RIDE/PERRIS

P.O. Box 59968
1825 3rd Street
Riverside, CA 92517-1968
(800) 795-7887
(951) 565-5005 FAX

Curb-to-curb pick up of passengers in specific srv areas and provides transfers to fixed inter-city routes. TTY (800) 369-3610. FUNDING: Public, govt. OFC HRS: Call center M-F 7am-6pm; Sat 8am-5pm. Spanish spoken. ADM REQ: Must call in advance for reservation. Fees $2.50 for seniors and the disabled. SERVES: Perris & parts of Mead Valley.

DIAL-A-RIDE/RIVERSIDE METRO

Riverside Special Transportation
8095 Lincoln Ave., Ste A
Riverside, CA 92504
(951) 687-8080
(800) 795-7887
(951) 351-6192 FAX

Transportation for seniors and disabled anywhere within city limits via curb-to-curb pick-up. First come, first served. FUNDING: Public, govt. OFC HRS: M-F 8am-5pm. Srv Hrs: M-Th 8am-6pm; F 8am-8:30pm; Sat, Sun 9am-4:30pm. ADM REQ: Seniors ages 60 yrs+ or the disabled only. Must make reservations. Fee $2 each way. SERVES: Riverside Metro.

DIAL-A-RIDE/SOUTHWEST RIVERSIDE

P.O. Box 59968
1825 3rd Street
Riverside, CA 92517-1968
(800) 795-7887
(951) 565-5000
(951) 565-5005 FAX

Curb-to-curb bus srvs to and from designated areas on telephone request. Some cities have srv only for disabled and seniors but the following cities provide transportation for anyone: Canyon Lake, Corona, Hemet, Norco, Perris, Quail Valley, Romoland, San Jacinto, Sun City. (Must schedule trip 1-7 days in advance.) TTY (800) 369-3610. FUNDING: Public, govt. OFC HRS: Call center M-F 7am-6pm; Sat, Sun 8am-5pm. Spanish spoken. Fees: para-transit for residents in srv areas $2; seniors and disabled $1. SERVES: Most of Southwest Riverside County, from Banning to Temecula to Corona.

DIAL-A-RIDE/TEMECULA

P.O. Box 59968
1825 3rd Street
Riverside, CA 92517-1968

(800) 795-7887
(951) 565-5000
(951) 565-5005 FAX

Curb-to-curb pick up of passengers in specific srv areas. TTY (800) 369-3610. FUNDING: Public, govt. OFC HRS: Call center M-F 7am-6pm; Sat, Sun 8am-5pm. Spanish spoken. ADM REQ: Must call in advance for reservation. Fees $2.50 for seniors or disabled. SERVES: Temecula.

DIAL-A-RIDE/YUCCA VALLEY

Ready Ride
62405 Verbena Rd.
Joshua Tree, CA 92252
(800) 794-6282
(760) 366-2395
(760) 361-5013 FAX

Fixed route public transportation for the cities of Yucca Valley, 29 Palms and Joshua Tree. OFC HRS: M-F 9am-5pm. ADM REQ: Make appt 24 hrs in advance. Adults $5, seniors and disabled $4.50, students $5. SERVES: Yucca Valley, 29 Palms, Joshua Tree.

JOHN WAYNE AIRPORT/O.C.

Airport Terminal
18601 Airport Wy.
Santa Ana, CA 92707
(949) 252-5200
(949) 252-5178 FAX

Located at 405 Freeway & MacArthur Blvd. Airline srvs at this airport: Alaska (800) 426-0333; American (800) 433-7300; US Airways Express (Mesa)/US Airways (800) 235-9292; Continental (800) 525-0280; Delta, Delta Connection (800) 221-1212; Frontier (800) 432-1359; Northwest (800) 225-2525; Southwest (800) 435-9792; US Airways (800) 428-4322; United, United Express (800) 241-6522; American Eagle (800) 433-7300. Terminal Hrs: Daily 5:30am-11pm. OFC HRS: M-F 7:30am-5pm. SERVES: So. Calif.

L.A. INTERNATIONAL AIRPORT

Los Angeles World Airports
P.O. Box 92216
One World Way
Los Angeles, CA 90045
(310) 646-5252
(310) 646-1894 FAX

Internatl airport serving domestic and internatl passengers. Publishes guide showing srvs available for disabled and elderly. Parking Lot C provides a lift-equipped van. Call (310) 646-6402 or (310) 646-8021 for pickup. TDD (310) 644-0370. Srvs: 24 hrs, 7 days. SERVES: So. Calif.

MARTA BIG BEAR LAKE

P.O. Box 1501
Big Bear Lake, CA 92315
(909) 878-5200
(909) 878-5207 FAX

Fixed route public transportation for Big Bear area. Office at 41939 Fox Farm Rd., Big Bear Lake, CA 92315. RIM area (909) 338-1113. OFC HRS: M-Sun 5:30pm-7pm. Adults, students $4; seniors & disabled $1. SERVES: Big Bear Lake Area.

MERCY AIRLIFT

P.O. Box 90452
Los Angeles, CA 90009
(800) 637-2945
(714) 518-5980

(714) 518-5982 FAX

Disaster and humanitarian relief providing immediate transportation of food, medical supplies, medicines, and medical & relief personnel to disaster sites. Transports patients for medical srvs they are otherwise unable to reach. Emerg response (562) 209-2912. FUNDING: Nonprofit. SERVES: Internatl.

METRO TRANSIT AUTHORITY

One Gateway Plaza
Los Angeles, CA 90012
(213) 626-4455
(800) 286-7433
(213) 922-6395 FAX

Bus routes throughout L.A. Co. Also operates 3 bus routes into O.C., providing srv to L.A. Co. Call M-F 6am-8pm; Sat 8:30am-6pm. For Orange Co. transit, call (714) 636-7433, M-F 6am-7pm. Wheelchair lift (800) 621-7828. TDD (800) 252-9040. OFC HRS: M-F 6am-8pm; Sat, Sun 8am-6pm.

METROLINK

700 S. Flower St., Ste 2600
Los Angeles, CA 90017
(800) 371-5465
(213) 452-0200
(213) 452-0429 FAX

Regional train info for traveling from San Bernardino, Riverside, Oceanside, Lancaster or Oxnard to L.A. Union Station and for travel from San Bernardino to Irvine. Also info about connecting bus srvs to and from Metrolink stations. Speech/hearing impaired (800) 698-4833. Out of Southern Calif, call (213) 347-2800. Walk-up Union Station M-F 6:30am-6:30pm. OFC HRS: M-F 8am-5pm. Spanish spoken.

MO VAN FRIENDS-MORENO VALLEY

1400 E. Mission Blvd.
Pomona, CA 91766
(951) 358-9202
(909) 622-2173 FAX

Non-emerg transportation for seniors & disabled. No same day pick-up. FUNDING: Nonprofit. OFC HRS: M-F 8am-2:30pm. ADM REQ: Must call 5-7 days in advance for reservation. Fees vary within the city limits and outside the area limits. SERVES: South Riverside County.

NATIONAL CENTER ON SENIOR TRANSPORTATION

(866) 528-6278

Provides guidance to finding local transportation. Helps assist in finding transit agencies and providers of community transportation in your area. Offers resources, training, and technical assistance to service providers. For TDD, call (202) 347-7385 FUNDING: Govt. OFC HRS: M-F 9am-5pm EST

OMNILINK/YUCAIPA

1700 W. 5th Street
San Bernardino, CA 92410
(800) 990-2406
(909) 383-1681 FAX

Curb-to-curb bus srv for seniors ages 60 yrs+ and persons with disabilities, ADA-certified passengers. Call for more info, times & fees. Phone reservation hrs: M-F 6:30am-5:30pm; Sat 7:30am-4:30pm; Sun 7:30am-1:30pm. Spanish spoken.

OMNITRANS

1700 W. 5th Street
San Bernardino, CA 92411
(909) 379-7100
(800) 966-6428
(909) 379-7105 FAX

Fixed route public transportation for the cities from L.A. county line to Yucaipa area. TDD (909) 384-9351. Fees adults & students $1.35, seniors & disabled $ .50 cents. One way fares. Monthly and day passes available. All day pass: adults $3.50, seniors & disabled $1.60. Prices subject to change, call first. SERVES: East & West Valley of San Bernardino County.

ONTARIO INTERNATIONAL AIRPORT

1940 E. Moore Way, Rm. 200
Ontario, CA 91761
(909) 937-2700
(909) 937-2743 FAX

Airlines serving this airport include Alaska Airlines, American Airlines, AeroMexico, Continental, Delta, Great Lakes Airlines, Southwest, United/United Express, US Airways. For flight info, call airlines directly. TDD (909) 937-2163. For reservations, call (800) 237-6639. FUNDING: L.A. World Airports. OFC HRS: 24 hrs, 7 days. Spanish spoken. SERVES: Inland Empire Region, East San Gabriel Valley, North OC, L.A. Co.

OUR LADY OF VLY CATHOLIC CHURCH

Ministry to the Elderly
780 S. State St.
Hemet, CA 92543
(951) 929-6131
(951) 929-8009 FAX

Volunteer srvs provides transportation for seniors to medical appts, shopping, etc. Call ahead to schedule srvs. Direct line (909) 925-8382. FUNDING: Nonprofit. OFC HRS: M-F 8am-12noon, 1pm-4pm. Some Spanish spoken. SERVES: Hemet.

RIVERSIDE TRANSIT AGENCY

P.O. Box 59968
1825 3rd Street
Riverside, CA 92517-1968
(951) 565-5002
(951) 565-5005 FAX

Curb-to-curb bus srv for seniors ages 60 yrs+, persons with disabilities, and ADA-certified passengers. Call for more info, times and fees. FUNDING: Public, govt. OFC HRS: M-F 7am-6pm; Sat, Sun 8am-5pm. Spanish spoken. Fee $2. Regular fee $1 for seniors or disabled. SERVES: Calimesa.

ROAD CONDITIONS

See "Calif Highway Information"

SO CALIF ASSN OF GOVERNMENTS

See "Metro Transit Authority"

SUNLINE TRANSIT AGENCY

32-505 Harry Oliver Trail
Thousand Palms, CA 92276
(760) 343-3456
(800) 347-8628
(760) 343-3845 FAX

Fixed route transportation and door-to-door van equipped with wheelchair lift. OFC HRS: M-F 8am-5pm (srv from 4:40am-11:19pm). Spanish spoken. Adult fare $1; ages 5-17 yrs $.85; seniors, disabled or on Medicare $.50. Transfer $.25. SERVES: Coachella Valley.

TRANSPORTATION ACCESS PROGRAM

See "Volunteer Center/Riverside Co."

U.S. DEPT OF TRANSPORTATION

Aviation Consumer Protection Division
C-75, U.S. DOT
Washington, DC 20590
(202) 366-2220
(202) 366-3733 FAX

Contact this agency about commercial airlines and charter companies, lost luggage, reservation or ticket disputes, or similar problems. For safety questions or problems, contact the Federal Aviation Admin. TTY (800) 455-9880. FUNDING: Govt. OFC HRS: M-F 8:15am-4:45pm, EST. SERVES: U.S.A.

U.S. DEPT OF TRANSPORTATION

Auto Safety Hotline
P.O. Box NVS-216
1200 New Jersey Ave., S.E.
Washington, DC 20590
(888) 327-4236
(800) 424-9393
(202) 493-2833 FAX

Hotline provides info & literature on motor vehicle safety recalls, new car crash test results, safety defect investigations, etc. Also takes consumer complaints about possible safety defects that may help the Natl Highway Admin identify trends that could lead to a recall. Assists callers having difficulty obtaining repair work for existing safety recalls. 24-hr automated line. TTY (800) 424-9153. FUNDING: Govt. OFC HRS: M-F 8am-10pm, EST. Spanish spoken. Free srvs. SERVES: U.S.A.

VICTOR VALLEY TRANSIT AUTHORITY

ADA Complimentary Paratransit
11741 E. Sante Fe Ave.
Hesperia, CA 92345-8305
(760) 948-3030
(760) 948-4021
(760) 948-1380 FAX

Serves frail elderly and disabled only. Must be certified (takes 7-10 days). Must schedule the day before. TDD (760) 948-3990. OFC HRS: M-F 8am-5pm. SERVES: Victorville, Hesperia, Apple Valley, Adelanto, Phelan, Pinon Hills & Wrightwood.

VOLUNTEER CENTER/RIVERSIDE CO.

Transportation Access Program (TAP)
P.O. Box 5376
2060 University Ave., Ste 212
Riverside, CA 92517-5376
(951) 686-4402
(951) 686-7417 FAX

Bus & paratransit tickets to agencies for distribution to seniors, persons with disabilities, and needy clients. FUNDING: Transportation Comm, donations, nonprofit. OFC HRS: M-F 8am-5pm. Free srvs. SERVES: Riverside County.

YELLOW CAB COMPANY

1400 E. Mission Blvd.
Pomona, CA 91766
(909) 622-1313
(909) 622-3035 FAX

General public transportation. Metered rates. OFC HRS: 24 hrs, 7 days. Spanish spoken. SERVES: Fontana, Ontario, Pomona, Upland, Chino, Chino Hills, Covina, Claremont, San Dimas, Diamond Bar, Rancho Cucamonga.

VETERAN/MILITARY SERVICES

ABILITY AWARENESS
1440 E. 1st Street, Ste 107
Santa Ana, CA 92701
(714) 277-4330
(714) 277-3743 FAX

Natl organization dedicated to enhancing the quality of life for people with disabilities through housing, employment, edu, media and volunteer opportunities. Ability House, developed in partnership with Habitat for Humanity affiliates, is an accessible home built for low-income families in which one or more members have a health condition or disability. A unique aspect of this prgm is the outreach to volunteers with disabilities during all phases of construction. FUNDING: Nonprofit. OFC HRS: M-F 8:30am-5:30pm. SERVES: U.S.A.

AMERICAN LEGION

The American Legion has numerous locations throughout Calif for veterans who have served during a time of war and received an honorable discharge. Promotes good will towards veterans and veterans prgms. Many prgms for children and youth.

AMERICAN LEGION POST #106
820 W. State St.
Redlands, CA 92373
(909) 792-4523
(909) 792-0145 FAX

FUNDING: Nonprofit. OFC HRS: Vary.

AMERICAN LEGION POST #112
310 W. Emporia St.
Ontario, CA 91762
(909) 984-3811

FUNDING: Nonprofit. OFC HRS: M-F 1pm-9pm; Sat, Sun 1pm-7pm.

AMERICAN LEGION POST #14
732 N. Sierra Way
San Bernardino, CA 92410
(909) 885-4090

FUNDING: Nonprofit. OFC HRS: Vary.

AMERICAN LEGION POST #155
1401 Veterans Way
Colton, CA 92324
(909) 825-2985

FUNDING: Nonprofit. OFC HRS: M-Sun 12noon-5pm.

AMERICAN LEGION POST #200
P.O. Box 596
18871 Grand Ave.
Lake Elsinore, CA 92531
(951) 678-7777

FUNDING: Nonprofit. OFC HRS: Vary.

AMERICAN LEGION POST #229
P.O. Box 626
11382 Lawson Ave.
Adelanto, CA 92301
(760) 246-6054
(760) 246-6054 FAX

FUNDING: Nonprofit. OFC HRS: M-F 1pm-8pm; Sat 10am-9pm; Sun 8am-8pm.

AMERICAN LEGION POST #262
15840 Foothill Blvd.
Fontana, CA 92335
(909) 823-8061

FUNDING: Nonprofit. OFC HRS: M-Sun Vary.

AMERICAN LEGION POST #289
4151 Buchanan Ave.
Riverside, CA 92503-4814
(951) 520-8551

FUNDING: Nonprofit. OFC HRS: M-Th 12noon-10pm; F 12noon-1am; Sat 11am-10pm; Sun 10am-10pm.

AMERICAN LEGION POST #299
13759 Central Ave.
Chino, CA 91710-5526
(909) 628-2080
(909) 591-7397 FAX

FUNDING: Nonprofit. OFC HRS: Vary.

AMERICAN LEGION POST #324
2181 Armory Rd.
Barstow, CA 92311-5854
(760) 252-8369

FUNDING: Nonprofit. OFC HRS: M-F 2pm-12midnight; Sat, Sun 12noon-12midnight.

AMERICAN LEGION POST #328
P.O. Box 207
3888 Old Hamner Rd.
Norco, CA 92860
(951) 371-9108

FUNDING: Nonprofit. OFC HRS: M-Sun 10am-10pm.

AMERICAN LEGION POST #360
P.O. Box 816
Lake Arrowhead, CA 92352
(909) 336-7745

Visit (www.americanlegionpost360.com).

AMERICAN LEGION POST #421
P.O. Box 883
28309 Highland Ave.
Highland, CA 92346
(909) 862-8225

FUNDING: Nonprofit. OFC HRS: Vary.

AMERICAN LEGION POST #422
848 S. Lilac Ave.
Rialto, CA 92377
(909) 874-0433
(909) 874-1650 FAX

FUNDING: Nonprofit. OFC HRS: Vary.

AMERICAN LEGION POST #426
12167 California St.
Yucaipa, CA 92399
(909) 790-4030

FUNDING: Nonprofit. OFC HRS: Vary.

AMERICAN LEGION POST #466
P.O. Box 2385
150624 Del Rey
Big River, CA 92242
(760) 665-9308

FUNDING: Nonprofit. OFC HRS: M-Sun 11am-10pm.

AMERICAN LEGION POST #497
P.O. Box 215
9980 Cedar Ave.
Bloomington, CA 92316
(909) 877-9871

FUNDING: Nonprofit. OFC HRS: M-Sun 10am-10pm.

AMERICAN LEGION POST #500
9520 Mission Blvd.
Riverside, CA 92509
(951) 685-4257

FUNDING: Nonprofit. OFC HRS: M-Sun 10am-9pm.

AMERICAN LEGION POST #519
400 N. Bellardo Rd.
Palm Springs, CA 92262
(619) 325-6229

FUNDING: Nonprofit. OFC HRS: M-Sun 10am-8pm.

AMERICAN LEGION POST #574
13876 Old Hwy. 215
Moreno Valley, CA 92552
(909) 653-1590
(909) 653-6110 FAX

FUNDING: Nonprofit. OFC HRS: M-F 10am-9pm; Sat, Sun 9am-9pm.

AMERICAN LEGION POST #584
P.O. Box 555
41604 Big Bear Blvd.
Big Bear Lake, CA 92315
(909) 866-4845

FUNDING: Nonprofit. OFC HRS: Vary.

AMERICAN LEGION POST #650
1532 N. Church St.
Redlands, CA 92374
(909) 792-6783

Visit (www.calegionpost650.org).

AMERICAN LEGION POST #710
2181 W. Highland Ave.
San Bernardino, CA 92405
(909) 880-1336

AMERICAN LEGION POST #751
P.O. Box 247
30916 Newberry Rd.
Newberry Springs, CA 92365
(760) 257-3173

FUNDING: Nonprofit. OFC HRS: M-Sun 12noon-7pm.

AMERICAN LEGION POST #763
65-909 Pierson Blvd.
Desert Hot Springs, CA 92240
(760) 329-9332

FUNDING: Nonprofit. OFC HRS: Vary.

AMERICAN LEGION POST #772
16767 Spring St.
Fontana, CA 92335
(909) 829-9490

Visit (www.steeltownpost772.org).

AMERICAN LEGION POST #777
194 E. 40th Street
San Bernardino, CA 92404
(909) 882-3110
(909) 883-7902 FAX

FUNDING: Nonprofit. OFC HRS: Vary.

AMERICAN LEGION POST #797
P.O. Box 797
401 Knowles St.
Yermo, CA 92398
(760) 254-2545

FUNDING: Nonprofit. OFC HRS: Vary.

AMERICAN LEGION POST #800

P.O. Box 800
54360 Marian View Dr.
Idyllwild, CA 92549
(951) 659-3517

FUNDING: Nonprofit. OFC HRS: M-Sun Vary.

AMERICAN LEGION POST #848

P.O. Box 848
312 E. Main St.
San Jacinto, CA 92581
(951) 487-1664

FUNDING: Nonprofit. OFC HRS: M-Sun 8am-8pm.

AMERICAN LEGION POST #883

24907 Sunnymead Blvd., Ste H
Moreno Valley, CA 92553
(951) 243-8567

AMERICAN RED CROSS/29 PALMS

Marine Corps Air Ground Combat Ctr
P.O. Box 6043
Bldg. 1551 (Village Center)
Twentynine Palms, CA 92278
(760) 830-6685
(760) 825-8822 FAX

Armed forces emerg srvs. FUNDING: CFC, donors, nonprofit. OFC HRS: M-F 7:30am-4pm. SERVES: 29 Palms Marine Base.

AMERICAN RED CROSS/FT. IRWIN

P.O. Box 10047
Bldg. 565
Fort Irwin, CA 92310
(760) 380-3697

Emerg assist to families in disasters. Maintains communication between military families in an emerg, emerg leave, etc. First aid classes, including CPR, youth srvs. Call to confirm srvs. FUNDING: Nonprofit. OFC HRS: W 8am-3pm. SERVES: Ft. Irwin.

AMERICAN RED CROSS/HIGH DESERT

16248 Desert Knoll Dr.
Victorville, CA 92395
(760) 245-6511
(760) 245-3180 FAX

HIV/AIDS info, child care classes, water safety/lifeguard prgm, communication assist with military personnel, disaster prep and emerg assist for disaster victims, CPR, first aid prgm. FUNDING: Govt, donations, nonprofit. OFC HRS: M-Th 8am-5pm; F 8am-1pm. SERVES: San Bernardino County.

AMERICAN RED CROSS/MORONGO BASIN

58923 Business Center Dr., Ste H & I
Yucca Valley, CA 92284
(760) 365-5501
(760) 365-5505 FAX

HIV/AIDS info, child care classes, water safety/lifeguard prgm, communication assist with military personnel, disaster prep and emerg assist for disaster victims, CPR and first aid classes, food srv classes, food box once every 6 months, emerg prep classes, emerg food when available, family disaster assist, info & referral. Mailing address: P.O. Box 212, Joshua Tree, CA 92252. FUNDING: Govt, donations, nonprofit. OFC HRS: M, Tu, Th, F 12noon-5pm. SERVES: Morongo Basin.

AMERICAN RED CROSS/ONTARIO

Inland Valley West Chapter
9140 Haven Ave., Ste 115
Rancho Cucamonga, CA 91730
(909) 481-2835
(800) 951-5600
(909) 481-4629 FAX

Disaster assist & srv to military families, food assist for low-income families 2 W a month, senior food voucher prgm (must submit application), health & safety edu prgms, including first aid & CPR. FUNDING: United Way, donations, nonprofit. OFC HRS: M-F 8am-5pm. Free srvs except for health & safety classes. SERVES: Ontario, Upland, Rancho Cucamonga, Alta Loma, Chino, Chino Hills, Montclair, Mt. Baldy, Lytle Creek & Fontana.

AMERICAN RED CROSS/RIVERSIDE CO.

Morongo Basin Chapters
P.O. Box 55040
6177 River Crest Dr., Ste B
Riverside, CA 92517
(888) 831-0031
(951) 656-4329 FAX

HIV/AIDS info, child care classes, water safety, communication assist with military personnel, disaster preparedness and emerg assist for disaster victims, CPR and first aid classes. FUNDING: Donations, govt, nonprofit. OFC HRS: M-F 8am-5pm. Spanish spoken. SERVES: Riverside County.

AMERICAN RED CROSS/SAN BRDO

Inland Empire Chapter
P.O. Box 183
202 W. Rialto Ave.
San Bernardino, CA 92408
(909) 888-1481
(866) 330-9911
(909) 888-1485 FAX

Military emerg communication, disaster emerg srvs (edu, preparedness & assist). Health srvs: training in CPR, first aid, HIV/AIDS edu, new training for automated external defibrillator (heart attacks), pet first aid and babysitting training prgms. Nurse's assistant training, home health aide training, and state competency eval for nurse assistants. FUNDING: Contributions, United Way, grants, nonprofit. OFC HRS: M-F 8am-5pm. SERVES: San Bernardino, Redlands, East Valley & mountain region.

AMERICAN WOMEN VETERANS

1725 I Street, Ste 300
Washington, DC 20006
(202) 436-0678

Org developed to assist servicewomen and their families. Srvs include advocacy and awareness. FUNDING: Nonprofit. Free srvs. SERVES: U.S.A.

BARSTOW COMMUNITY COLLEGE

2700 Barstow Rd.
Barstow, CA 92311
(760) 252-2411
(760) 252-1875 FAX

Institution of higher edu offers counseling, testing, vocational edu & rehab srvs, financial aid, veteran srvs, servicemen's opportunity college srvs, extended opportunity prgms, disabled student prgm, scholarship awards, etc TTY (760) 252-6759. FUNDING: Govt. OFC HRS: M-F 8am-5pm. Foreign languages available upon request. SERVES: Barstow & nearby.

BLINDED VETERANS ASSN OF SO CALIF

11000 Wilshire Blvd., Rm. 5272
Los Angeles, CA 90024
(310) 235-6125
(310) 235-6110 FAX

Support & referral to blind veterans & their families. Leave name and phone number on voicemail for a return call. FUNDING: Govt, donation, nonprofit. OFC HRS: M-F 8am-3pm. Spanish spoken. Free srvs. SERVES: So. Calif.

BLINDED VETERANS ASSOCIATION

477 H Street, NW
Washington, DC 20001-2694
(800) 669-7079
(202) 371-8880
(202) 371-8258 FAX

Seeks out blind veterans, offers srv-enhancing employment opportunities, assists in procuring benefits offered by public and pvt agencies, edu info & scholarships. Membership not required. FUNDING: Donations, grants, nonprofit. OFC HRS: M-F 8am-4:30pm, EST. Spanish spoken. Free srvs. SERVES: U.S.A.

CALIF DEPT VETERANS AFFAIRS

CAL-VET Home Loans
1770 Iowa Ave., Ste 260
Riverside, CA 92507
(951) 774-0102
(800) 700-2127
(951) 774-0111 FAX

Cal-Vet home loans for eligible veterans. This is a Calif state agency. Walk in or call for brochures & info packets. FUNDING: Govt. OFC HRS: M-F 8am-5pm. Spanish spoken. SERVES: Calif.

CALIF DEPT VETERANS AFFAIRS

1227 O Street
Sacramento, CA 95814
(800) 952-5626

Administers benefits provided by the state of Calif to veterans and their dependents. Info for low-cost loans, rehabilitation, residential and medical care srvs. TDD (800) 324-5966. Outside Calif, call (800) 221-8998. FUNDING: Govt. OFC HRS: M-F 8am-5pm. SERVES: Calif.

CALIF PARALYZED VETERANS ASSN

5901 E. 7th Street, Bldg. 150, Rm. R-204
Long Beach, CA 90822
(562) 826-5713
(800) 497-0565
(562) 494-5140 FAX

Srvs to veterans include: research, sports, advocacy legislation, VA benefits, rehab. FUNDING: Nonprofit. OFC HRS: M-F 8am-4pm. Translation services by request. Free srvs. SERVES: Calif.

CLEANING FOR HEROES

221-B Hallene Rd.
Warwick, RI 02886
(401) 732-7856
(866) 389-3445 FAX

Provides free house cleaning srvs for disabled and elderly veterans and those employed with the police & fire dept. Must call or e-mail (info@cleaningforheroes.org) for more info. FUNDING: Nonprofit. Free srvs. SERVES: U.S.A.

CORONA VET CENTER

Dept of Veterans Affairs
800 Magnolia Ave., Ste 110
Corona, CA 92879

(951) 734-0525
(800) 523-7052
(951) 734-0063 FAX

Mental health counseling for all combat veterans, Vietnam era veterans, and for any victims of sexual harassment, or assault active duty. Also assist in filing a claim for srv-connected disability. Counseling for couples, children of veterans, substance abuse, and combat-related emotional trauma. Referrals for benefits, medical, employment, etc. FUNDING: Govt. OFC HRS: M-F 8am-4:30pm. Free srvs. SERVES: Riverside County.

DEPT OF VETERANS AFFAIRS

See "San Bernardino Co. Vet Affairs"

DEPT OF VETERANS AFFAIRS EDUCATION

GI Bill Helpline
(888) 442-4551

Recording gives info about VA edu & training, GI Bill assist. Visit (www.va.gov). SERVES: U.S.A.

DESERT HOT SPRINGS FAMILY RESOURCE CTR

14201 Palm Dr., Ste 108
Desert Hot Springs, CA 92240
(760) 288-3313
(760) 288-2854 FAX

Classes offered on parenting skills, family planning, adult edu. Healthy Children Connection, Healthy Families, Medi-Cal enrollment (through Catholic Charities), immunization info, utility assist clinic provided with Community Action Partnership, WIC info, job search, GED classes, veteran support group, individual, family, & group counseling. Referrals to emerg srvs. FUNDING: Nonprofit. OFC HRS: M-F 8am-5pm. Spanish spoken. ADM REQ: Must call first, except for job search srvs. SERVES: Bermuda Dunes, Cathedral City, Coachella, Desert Hot Springs, Indio, Indio Hills, North Palm Springs, Palm Springs, Rancho Mirage.

DISABLED AMERICAN VETERANS

National Headquarters
3725 Alexandria Pike
Newport, KY 41076
(877) 426-2838
(859) 441-7300

Helps with benefits assist from the Dept. of Veterans Affairs, provides a network of volunteers who offer rides to and from VA medical facilities for veterans, grassroots advocacy & srvs. Also offers special prgms for homeless vets and those suffering from substance abuse issues. Visit (www.dav.org) for more info and to find a chapter near you. Free srvs. SERVES: U.S.A.

EMPLOYMENT DEV DEPT/JOB SRVS

Rancho Employment Resource Center
9650 9th Street, Ste A
Rancho Cucamonga, CA 91730
(909) 948-6606
(909) 941-6500
(909) 941-1676 FAX

EDD offers employment srvs to employers & job seekers. Srvs include: employer recruitment, workshops & access to computers, fax machines & the Internet. EDD provides priority srvs to veterans & personalized assist to persons with disabilities & youth ages 15-21 yrs with employment barriers. FUNDING: State. OFC HRS: M-F 8am-5pm. Spanish spoken. Free srvs. SERVES: San Bernardino County.

GIVE AN HOUR

P.O. Box 5918
Bethesda, MD 20824

Matches volunteer mental health counseling providers with troops and families involved with current conflicts in Iraq and Afghanistan. Volunteers provide one hour of free therapy to client. For more info, e-mail (info@giveanhour.org) or visit (www.giveanhour.org). FUNDING: Nonprofit. Free srvs. SERVES: U.S.A.

HIGH DESERT VET CENTER

Dept of Veterans Affairs
15095 Amargosa Rd., Ste 107
Victorville, CA 92394
(760) 261-5925
(760) 241-7828 FAX

Provides individual and group counseling for veterans and their families. Also offers assessment and info & referral srvs for substance abuse, employment, various medical conditions, and VBA benefits. Bereavement counseling also offered to families of soldiers who have experienced an active duty death. FUNDING: Govt. OFC HRS: M-F 8am-4:30pm. ADM REQ: Must be a veteran or family member of a veteran. Free srvs. SERVES: San Bernardino Co.

HOMELESS VETERANS STAND DOWNS

Calif Dept of Veterans Affairs

Stand Downs are 1-3 day events providing free srvs to homeless veterans such as food, shelter, clothing, health screenings, benefits counseling, and info & referral srvs. Events are held throughout the year at locations throughout Calif. Visit (www.cdva.ca.gov/Resources/StandDown.aspx) to find the schedule of upcoming events and contact information for your area. SERVES: Calif.

MARCH A.F.B./FAMILY SUPPORT

1261 Graeber St., Bldg. 2313, Rm. 1A
March Air Base, CA 92518-1775
(951) 655-5350
(951) 655-4719 FAX

Info & referral. Assessment and referral assist to families in crisis, support during family separation, relocation assist, skill workshops as needed on family issues and job search skills. FUNDING: Govt. OFC HRS: M-F 7:30am-4pm (some weekends). ADM REQ: Military staff or family member. SERVES: March Air Reserve area.

MARINE CORP AIR GROUND COMBAT CTR

Career Resource Management Ctr
Bldg. 1438, POB 788105
Twentynine Palms, CA 92278-8150
(760) 830-7225
(760) 830-5955 FAX

Employment and transition counseling and assist. Monthly workshops include: skills assessment, career testing, resume prep, job interviewing and job search, completing fed applications and other special events. Career fair twice a year and quarterly recruitment days. Extensive computer lab with automated job search and career planning prgms that assist with job search worldwide. OFC HRS: M-F 7:30am-4:30pm. ADM REQ: Military ID. Free srvs. SERVES: San Bernardino County.

MARINE CORP AIR GROUND COMBAT CTR

Community Support

Bldg 1551, Village Center
Twentynine Palms, CA 92277
(760) 830-6540
(760) 830-6870
(760) 830-8323 FAX

Info and referral srv, career resource, relocation assist, edu, new parent support, child care etc. FUNDING: Nonprofit, govt. OFC HRS: M-F 7:30am-4:30pm. Japanese, Spanish, French spoken. ADM REQ: Active duty, family member, widow, retiree or DOD employee. SERVES: 29 Palms.

MARINE CORPS AIR GROUND COMBAT CTR

Navy/Marine Relief Core Society
P.O. Box 6041
Building 1551, MCAGCC
Twentynine Palms, CA 92278-0018
(760) 830-6323
(760) 830-7189 FAX

Emerg assist with food & other basic needs, including budget counseling, layettes, and visiting nurse srvs. FUNDING: Nonprofit, govt. OFC HRS: M-F 8am-4pm. ADM REQ: Military. SERVES: 29 Palms.

NATIONAL GUARD FAMILY PROGRAM

1411 Jefferson Davis Hwy.
Arlington, VA 22202
(703) 607-5411

Offers financial, emotional, and supportive assist to the families of National Guard members. Special prgms to help those who are dealing the deployment of a loved one. Visit (www.jointservicessupport.org). FUNDING: Govt. SERVES: U.S.A.

NATL CENTER FOR PTSD

U.S. Dept. of Veterans Affairs
810 Vermont Ave., N.W.
Washington, DC 20420
(802) 296-6300

Center aims to help U.S. veterans, professionals, and community members through research, edu, and training on trauma and PTSD. Website includes VA PTSD prgm locator. Visit (www.ptsd.va.gov). FUNDING: Govt. ADM REQ: Must be a veteran in order to obtain clinical srvs. SERVES: U.S.A.

NATL VETERANS FOUNDATION

9841 Airport Blvd., Ste 512
Los Angeles, CA 90045
(888) 777-4443
(800) 366-8823
(310) 642-0258 FAX

Crisis mgmt, referral & info hotline for all veterans and their families. Assists veterans in obtaining counseling, shelter, job training & placement, legal help, drug & alcohol addiction srvs, medical aid, claim processing, transportation & locator srvs. FUNDING: Donations, nonprofit. OFC HRS: M-F 9am-9pm. 24-hr message line. SERVES: U.S.A.

NAVAL HOSPITAL CAMP PENDLETON

Substance Abuse Rehab Program
P.O. Box 555191
Bldg. H-49 (Code 03A)
Camp Pendleton, CA 92055-5191
(760) 725-0063
(760) 725-1544 FAX

Outpatient & residential drug & alcohol treatment prgm. AA meetings, co-dependency, gambling, sexual addictions, smoking & nicotine srvs, info & referral, dual-diagnosis (including PTSD), counseling. Patient srvs center (760) 725-4357. FUNDING: Fed, govt. OFC HRS: M-F 6am-5pm. Spanish spoken. ADM REQ: Ages 18 yrs+, min stay 21 days, max stay 42 days; active military, retired or family of military. SERVES: U.S.A. & internatl.

NEW DIRECTIONS, INC.
11303 Wilshire Blvd., Bldg. 116
Los Angeles, CA 90073
(310) 914-5966
(310) 914-4045
(310) 914-5495 FAX

NDI has five residential treatment facilities on the westside of L.A. Serves men and women veterans who are homeless and suffering from the co-occurring disorders of substance abuse and mental illness. Specific facilities include those for veterans involved with OIF/OEF and female dependents of veterans. Also offers a non-residential facility in Pacoima. FUNDING: Grants, donations, nonprofit. Spanish spoken. SERVES: L.A., Orange, San Bernardino and Riverside Counties.

OPERATION HOMEFRONT
So Calif Chapter
P.O. Box 26747
San Diego, CA 92196
(866) 424-5210
(858) 695-6810

Assist & support provided to military families. Emergency aid, computer prgm, financial assist prgm, furniture, moving assist, social outreach, commissary gift certificates, Operation Drop Box (aid to deployed soldiers), etc. Typically serve ranks of E-1 through E-6 in all srvs including Reserves & Natl Guardsmen. For the Orange County office, contact Kim Farthing at (714) 864-0982. FUNDING: Nonprofit. OFC HRS: M-F 9am-4pm by appt only. ADM REQ: Service member deployment required for some prgms. Must have military ID. SERVES: U.S.A.

PARALYZED VETERANS ASSN/CALIF
See "Calif Paralyzed Veterans Assn"

PARTNERSHIP FOR PRESCRIPTION ASSIST
(877) 777-7815

Free or low-cost prescription srv for uninsured, underinsured or those with limited income. Call or visit (www.RXHelpforCA.org). SERVES: Calif.

RIVERSIDE CO. VETERANS SRVS
1075 N. State St.
Hemet, CA 92543
(951) 766-2566
(951) 766-2567 FAX

Info & assist with claims for VA benefits for veterans their dependents & widows. Common issues are: compensation, disability, death pension, burial benefit, grave site markers, edu benefits, vocational rehab, home loans, insurance, Cal-Vet info. FUNDING: Govt. OFC HRS: M-Th 8am-12noon, 1pm-4pm. Free srvs. SERVES: Riverside County.

RIVERSIDE CO. VETERANS SRVS
44-199 Monroe St.
Indio, CA 92201
(760) 863-8266
(760) 863-8478 FAX

OFC HRS: M-Th 8am-5pm. Spanish spoken. SERVES: Riverside County.

RIVERSIDE CO. VETERANS SRVS
1153-A Spruce St.
Riverside, CA 92507
(951) 955-6050
(800) 481-2101
(951) 955-6061 FAX

Serves veterans & their survivors & dependents through counseling, claims assist, info & referrals, advocacy, & special projects. Branch offices in Indio & Hemet, itinerant schedule, home visits for balance of county. TTY (909) 955-3098. OFC HRS: M-Th 8am-5pm. Spanish spoken. SERVES: Riverside County.

SALVATION ARMY/VICTORY PLACE
11301 Wilshire Blvd., Bldg. 212, 2nd Fl.
Los Angeles, CA 90073
(310) 478-3711
(310) 268-3669 FAX

100-bed shelter & medical care for veterans with an alcohol and/or drug addiction. Accepts single men and women ages 18 yrs+. Max stay is 90 days. State ID: 190023DN. FUNDING: Donations, nonprofit. OFC HRS: M-F 8am-4pm. SERVES: So. Calif.

SAN BERNARDINO CO. HUMAN SRVS SY
HSS Administration
385 N. Arrowhead Ave., 5th Fl.
San Bernardino, CA 92415-0515
(909) 357-4717
(909) 387-5430 FAX

HSS is composed of the following depts: Aging & Adult Srvs, Behavioral Health, Children's Srvs, Community Srvs, Preschool Srvs, Public Health, Transitional Assist, and Veterans Affairs. OFC HRS: M-F 7:30am-5pm. SERVES: San Bernardino County.

SAN BERNARDINO CO. VET AFFAIRS
13260 Central Ave., 2nd Fl.
Chino, CA 91710
(909) 465-5241
(909) 465-5245 FAX

Advises and assists veterans and their dependents with VA benefits available through fed, state and local agencies. Walk in. FUNDING: County, state. OFC HRS: M-Th 8:30am-4:30pm. Spanish spoken. Free srvs. SERVES: Western San Bernardino County.

SAN BERNARDINO CO. VET AFFAIRS
15900 Smoke Tree St., Ste 247
Hesperia, CA 92345
(760) 995-8010
(760) 995-8020 FAX

Files compensation claims and pension claims for veterans and their dependents. Also assists in filing claims for death benefits, welfare inquiries, dental and edu benefits. FUNDING: County. OFC HRS: M-Th 8:30am-4:30pm. SERVES: San Bernardino County.

SAN BERNARDINO CO. VET AFFAIRS
175 W. 5th Street, 2nd Fl.
San Bernardino, CA 92415
(909) 387-5516
(866) 472-8387
(909) 387-6090 FAX

Files compensation claims and pension claims for veterans and their dependents. Also assists in filing claims for death benefits, welfare inquiries, dental and edu benefits. OFC HRS: M-Th

8:30am-4:30pm; F 8am-4pm. SERVES: San Bernardino County.

SAN BERNARDINO VET CENTER
Dept of Veterans Affairs
1325 E. Cooley Dr., Ste 101
Colton, CA 92324
(909) 801-5762
(909) 801-5767 FAX

Provides individual and group counseling for veterans and their families. Also offers assessment and info & referral srvs for substance abuse, employment, various medical conditions, and VBA benefits. Bereavement counseling also offered to families of soldiers who experienced an active duty death. FUNDING: Govt. OFC HRS: M-F 8am-4:30pm. ADM REQ: Must be a veteran or a family member of a veteran. Free srvs. SERVES: San Bernardino Co.

SINGLE PARENTS OF POWER
Emlac Health Services
P.O. Box 452602
1620 Centinela Ave, Ste 202
Inglewood, CA 90302
(310) 753-7860

Counseling services include: mental health, sexual abuse, anger mgmt, parenting, alcohol and drug abuse. Advocacy and counseling for victims of violent crimes and post-traumatic counseling for veterans. FUNDING: Nonprofit. OFC HRS: M-F 9am-9pm; Sat 10am-3pm. Spanish, Swahili spoken. Free counseling for victims of domestic violence. All other srvs on a sliding fee scale. SERVES: L.A. & San Bernardino Counties.

SOLDIER'S ANGELS
1792 E. Washington Blvd.
Pasadena, CA 91104
(626) 529-5114
(626) 529-5446 FAX

Connects members of the armed forces (vets and those who are currently serving) with community civilians. Volunteers participate in letter writing campaigns, care packages, making quilts for vets homes, etc. Visit (www.soldiersangels.org) FUNDING: Nonprofit. OFC HRS: M-F 8am-5pm. Free srvs. SERVES: U.S.A.

SUICIDE PREVENTION LIFELINE
Veteran's Assistance
(800) 273-8255

Toll-free, 24-hr crisis hotline to assist veterans. TTY (800) 799-4889. FUNDING: Substance Abuse & Mental Hlth Srvs (HHS). OFC HRS: 24 hrs, 7 days. SERVES: U.S.A.

TEMECULA VET CENTER
Dept of Veterans Affairs
40935 County Center Dr., Ste A & B
Temecula, CA 92591
(951) 296-5608
(951) 296-0598 FAX

Provides individual and group counseling for veterans and their families. Also offers assessment and info & referral srvs for substance abuse, employment, various medical conditions, and VBA benefits. Bereavement counseling also offered to families of soldiers who experienced an active duty death. FUNDING: Govt. OFC HRS: M-F 8am-4:30pm. ADM REQ: Must be a veteran or a family member of a veteran. Free srvs. SERVES: Riverside Co.

TRAGEDY ASSIST PRGM FOR SURVIVORS (TAPS)
1777 F Street, NW, Ste 600
Washington, DC 20006
(202) 588-8277
(800) 959-8277
(202) 509-8282 FAX

Organization offers tragedy assist to anyone who has suffered the loss of a military loved one regardless of relationship. Provides srvs including peer-based emotional network, case mgmt, crisis intervention, and grief & trauma resources. Also offers Good Grief camps for children and teens to teach coping skills in dealing with death. Visit (www.taps.org) to participate in an active online community including real-time chats. FUNDING: Nonprofit. Free srvs. SERVES: U.S.A.

U.S. AIRFORCE
16960 Bear Valley Rd., Ste B
Victorville, CA 92392
(760) 245-7680
(760) 245-2506 FAX

Recruiting office. FUNDING: Govt. OFC HRS: M-F 9am-5pm. SERVES: High desert.

U.S. DEPT OF AIR FORCE
895 Baucom Ave SE (Bldg 317)
March Air Force Base, CA 92518
(951) 655-4137
(951) 655-2875 FAX

U.S. DEPT OF VETERANS AFFAIRS
Los Angeles Regional Office
11000 Wilshire Blvd., 5th Fl.
Los Angeles, CA 90024
(800) 827-1000
(310) 235-6199
(310) 235-7568 FAX

Administers all benefits handled by the Dept of Veterans Affairs. Edu, death benefits, compensation for srv-related disabilities, benefits for survivors, etc. Info about all kinds of srvs for veterans. The white pages of the phone directory will list local VA srvs under U.S. Govt. OFC HRS: M-F 8am-4pm. SERVES: So. Calif.

U.S. DEPT OF VETERANS AFFAIRS
Riverside National Cemetery
22495 Van Buren Blvd.
Riverside, CA 92518
(951) 653-8417
(951) 653-5233 FAX

OFC HRS: Daily 8am-4:30pm. Visitation: 6am-9pm. SERVES: U.S.A.

U.S. DEPT OF VETERANS AFFAIRS
San Diego Regional Office
8810 Rio San Diego Dr., Rm. 1160
San Diego, CA 92108-1688
(800) 827-1000

Administers federal benefits for veterans and dependents, including compensation, pension, medical, home loan, edu, death and burial benefits. Walk in or call. FUNDING: Govt. OFC HRS: M-F 8:30am-3:30pm. Spanish, Tagalog spoken. ADM REQ: Veterans of the Armed Forces of the U.S. Free srvs. SERVES: San Diego, Orange, Riverside & Imperial Counties.

U.S. DEPT OF VETERANS AFFAIRS
Veterans Assist Srv
810 Vermont Ave., NW
Washington, DC 20421
(800) 827-1000

Helps veterans obtain various benefits, including disability, pension, edu & training, vocational rehab, home loans, life insurance, health care and other fed benefits. Also check your local white pages phone book for Veteran Srvs offices (VA) under U.S. Govt. FUNDING: Govt. OFC HRS: M-F 8am-4pm. SERVES: U.S.A.

U.S. DEPT OF VETERANS AFFAIRS
Center for Women Veterans
810 Vermont Ave., NW
Washington, DC 20420
(800) 827-1000

Assists with matters relating to women veterans. FUNDING: Govt. OFC HRS: M-F 9am-5pm, EST. SERVES: U.S.A.

U.S. VETS
15105 6th Street
Moreno Valley, CA 92518
(951) 656-6892
(951) 656-6890 FAX

Back to work & housing prgm for homeless veterans and those at-risk of homelessness. OFC HRS: M-F 8am-5pm. Spanish spoken. SERVES: Riverside & San Bernardino Counties.

V.A. HEALTH ADMIN CLINIC
41-865 Boardwalk, Ste 103
Palm Desert, CA 92211
(760) 341-5570
(760) 341-5622 FAX

General medicine, immunizations, HIV/AIDS testing, lab srvs. FUNDING: Govt. OFC HRS: M-Th 8am-5pm; F 8am-2:30pm. Spanish spoken. ADM REQ: Veteran. SERVES: Riverside County.

V.A. HEALTH ADMIN CLINIC
28125 Bradley Rd., Ste 130
Sun City, CA 92586
(951) 672-1931
(951) 672-1935 FAX

Outpatient community clinic. Internal medicine only. FUNDING: Govt. OFC HRS: M-Th 8am-5pm; F 8am-2:30pm. Spanish spoken. ADM REQ: Veteran. SERVES: Riverside County.

V.A. HEALTH ADMIN CLINIC
1238 E. Arrow Hwy., Ste 100
Upland, CA 91786
(909) 946-5348
(909) 946-6598 FAX

General medicine, immunizations, HIV/AIDS testing, mental health, drug/alcohol treatment. FUNDING: Govt. OFC HRS: M-Th 8am-5pm; F 8am-2:30pm. Spanish spoken. SERVES: San Bernardino County.

V.A. HEALTH ADMIN CLINIC
12138 Industrial Blvd., Ste 120
Victorville, CA 92392
(760) 951-2599
(760) 951-5819 FAX

General medicine, immunizations. FUNDING: Govt. OFC HRS: M-Th 8am-5pm; F 8am-2:30pm. Spanish spoken. ADM REQ: Veteran. SERVES: San Bernardino County.

V.A. HEALTH ADMINISTRATION
Admin Ofc/Desert Pacific Network
5901 E. 7th Street
Long Beach, CA 90822
(562) 826-8000
(888) 769-8387

(562) 826-5987 FAX

Administrative office. No direct srvs. FUNDING: Govt. OFC HRS: M-F 8am-5pm. SERVES: San Diego, Long Beach, Los Angeles, Loma Linda.

V.A. MEDICAL CENTER/LOMA LINDA
Jerry L. Pettis Memorial V.A. Med Ctr
11201 Benton St.
Loma Linda, CA 92357
(909) 825-7084
(800) 741-8387
(909) 422-3106 FAX

200+ bed hospital. 24-hr emerg room with doctor on duty. General medical and some specialty srvs, surgical, rehab, psychiatric, primary outpatient care, STD testing & treatment, HIV treatments & therapies, extended and long-term care and homeless prgms. FUNDING: Federal. OFC HRS: M-F 8am-4:30pm. 24-hr srvs. Spanish, Vietnamese spoken. ADM REQ: Military srv veterans. Fees vary with eligibility. SERVES: San Bernardino, Riverside Counties.

V.A. MEDICAL CENTER/LOMA LINDA
Jerry L. Pettis - Addiction Treatment Unit
11201 Benton St., Ward 2 N.W.
Loma Linda, CA 92357
(909) 825-7084
(800) 741-8387
(909) 777-3226 FAX

Treatment for all types of chemical addictions. Outpatient treatment, dual-diagnosis, smoking cessation prgms. FUNDING: Govt. OFC HRS: M-F 8am-4:30pm. ADM REQ: Veterans. SERVES: So. Calif.

VA HEALTH CARE BENEFITS
(877) 222-8387

Info & referrals for VA healthcare benefits. Also enrollment assist. FUNDING: Govt. OFC HRS: M-F 6am-7pm, CST. ADM REQ: Veteran. SERVES: U.S.A.

VA MAMMOGRAPHY HELPLINE
(888) 492-7844

Info & referrals given to male & female veterans. FUNDING: Govt. OFC HRS: M-F 8am-4pm, EST. ADM REQ: Veteran. SERVES: U.S.A.

VARP, INC.
Harris House
907 W. Rialto Ave.
San Bernardino, CA 92410
(909) 885-8804
(909) 381-6845 FAX

State-certified peer group AA/NA-oriented social model recovery prgms, offering srvs for men only. Affiliated with veteran's hospital. 30-day prgm with 6-to 9-month aftercare. State ID: 360004AN. FUNDING: Nonprofit. OFC HRS: 8am-5pm. Spanish spoken. ADM REQ: Referral by any veteran's hospital. Men ages 18 yrs+, min stay 30 days. SERVES: San Bernardino, Riverside Counties.

VETERANS HOME OF CALIF/BARSTOW
100 E. Veterans Pkwy.
Barstow, CA 92311
(760) 252-6200
(800) 746-0606

Living environment for veterans to protect their dignity and help their feelings of self-reliance & self-worth. TDD (760) 252-6243. OFC HRS: M-F 8am-5pm. SERVES: Calif.

VETERANS HOME OF CALIF/CHULA VISTA

700 E. Naples Ct.
Chula Vista, CA 91911
(888) 857-2146

Long-term care provided for independent living. Licensed residential & skilled nursing care. FUNDING: State. OFC HRS: Varies. ADM REQ: Resident of Calif, disabled, ages 62 yrs or younger. SERVES: Calif.

VETERANS OF FOREIGN WARS

Social club for veterans. Visits to veterans in the hospital, assist with a wide range of srvs. Visit (www.vfw.org) to find a chapter near you.

VETERANS OF FOREIGN WARS

AMVets Post #1240
9190 Fontana Avenue
Fontana, CA 92335-4448
(909) 823-2600

Social club for veterans. Monthly visits to veterans in the hospital. Assist with a wide range of srvs. FUNDING: Nonprofit. OFC HRS: M-F 10am-9pm. ADM REQ: Veteran status. SERVES: Fontana.

WOUNDED WARRIOR RESOURCE CTR

U.S. Dept. of Defense
(800) 342-9647

Website and 24-hr hotline which provides wounded service members, their families and caregivers with info they need on military facilities, health care srvs, and benefits. To speak with a specialist, call the number above or send an e-mail to (wwrc@militaryonesource.com) or Visit (www.woundedwarriorresourcecenter.com). Free srvs. SERVES: U.S.A.

WWW.OEFOIF.VA.GOV

Resource website put up by the Dept. of Veterans Affairs for newly returning service members (OEF/OIF). Topics include health care eligibility, life insurance benefits, edu/training, and prgms that specialize in the treatment of PTSD. If you are an OEF/OIF veteran, and have not been contacted by VA about your health care benefits, call (866) 606-8216.

WWW.VETSPREVAIL.COM

P.O. Box 619101
Chicago, IL 60661

Website allows vets to connect with other vets through forums, blogs and multimedia. Also offers a 6-week mental health prgm to assist with life after deployment and transition back into civilian life. For more info, e-mail (team@vetsprevail.com). SERVES: U.S.A.

VOLUNTEERING OPPORTUNITIES

ABILITY AWARENESS

1440 E. 1st Street, Ste 107
Santa Ana, CA 92701
(714) 277-4330
(714) 277-3743 FAX

Natl organization dedicated to enhancing the quality of life for people with disabilities through housing, employment, edu, media and volunteer opportunities. Ability House, developed in partnership with Habitat for Humanity affiliates, is an accessible home built for low-income families to which one or more members have a health condition or disability. A unique aspect of this prgm is the outreach to volunteers with disabilities during all phases of construction. FUNDING: Nonprofit. OFC HRS: M-F 8:30am-5:30pm. SERVES: U.S.A.

AMERICAN RED CROSS/29 PALMS

Marine Corps Air Ground Combat Ctr
P.O. Box 6043
Bldg. 1551 (Village Center)
Twentynine Palms, CA 92278
(760) 830-6685
(760) 825-8822 FAX

Armed forces emerg srvs. FUNDING: CFC, donors, nonprofit. OFC HRS: M-F 7:30am-4pm. SERVES: 29 Palms Marine Base.

AMERICAN RED CROSS/FT. IRWIN

P.O. Box 10047
Bldg. 565
Fort Irwin, CA 92310
(760) 380-3697

Emerg assist to families in disasters. Maintains communication between military families in an emerg, emerg leave, etc. First aid classes, including CPR, youth srvs. Call to confirm srvs. FUNDING: Nonprofit. OFC HRS: W 8am-3pm. SERVES: Ft. Irwin.

AMERICAN RED CROSS/ONTARIO

Inland Valley West Chapter
9140 Haven Ave., Ste 115
Rancho Cucamonga, CA 91730
(909) 481-2835
(800) 951-5600
(909) 481-4629 FAX

Disaster assist & srv to military families, food assist for low income families 2 W a month, senior food voucher prgm (must submit application), health & safety edu prgms, including first aid & CPR. FUNDING: United Way, donations, nonprofit. OFC HRS: M-F 8am-5pm. Free srvs except for health & safety classes. SERVES: Ontario, Upland, Rancho Cucamonga, Alta Loma, Chino, Chino Hills, Montclair, Mt. Baldy, Lytle Creek & Fontana.

AMERICAN RED CROSS/SAN BRDO

Inland Empire Chapter
P.O. Box 183
202 W. Rialto Ave.
San Bernardino, CA 92408
(909) 888-1481
(866) 330-9911
(909) 888-1485 FAX

Military emerg communication, disaster emerg srvs (edu, preparedness & assist). Health srvs: training in CPR, first aid, HIV/AIDS edu, new training for automated external defibrillator

(heart attacks), pet first aid and babysitting training prgms. Nurse's assistant training, home health aide training, and state competency eval for nurse assistants. FUNDING: Contributions, United Way, grants, nonprofit. OFC HRS: M-F 8am-5pm. SERVES: San Bernardino, Redlands, East Valley & mountain region.

BEAUTY FOR ASHES WOMEN'S CENTER

Aftercare Program
9791 Arrow Route
Rancho Cucamonga, CA 91730
(909) 477-2781

BFA provides training, education, support and spiritual guidance for life following treatment and/or incarceration. 12-Step prgms, personal development courses, and job training. Volunteer opportunities available. Located at R.C. Family Resource Center. FUNDING: Nonprofit. Spanish spoken. ADM REQ: Adult women ages 18 yrs+, in crisis. SERVES: L.A., Riverside & San Bernardino Counties.

BIG BROTHERS/SISTERS/GTR L.A. & I.E.

Administration Office
800 S. Figueroa, Ste 620
Los Angeles, CA 90017
(213) 481-3611
(800) 207-7567
(213) 481-1148 FAX

Prgm matches boys ages 7-18 yrs and girls ages 6-16 yrs from single parent homes with volunteer Big Brothers and Big Sisters. Provides positive role models, friendship, companionship and guidance on a one-to-one basis. Each volunteer is trained to provide ongoing support to ensure that each mentoring relationship thrives. Also has an additional office at 5601 W. Slauson Avenue Ste. 130, Culver City 90230; (310) 338-0055. FUNDING: Nonprofit. OFC HRS: M-F 9am-5:30pm. Spanish spoken. Free srvs. SERVES: L.A. Co. & Inland Empire.

BIRTH CHOICE OF TEMECULA

27488 Enterprise Circle West, Bldg. 4
Temecula, CA 92590
(951) 699-9808
(951) 699-7268 FAX

Pregnancy counseling and testing. Right to life perspective. Maternity and baby clothes available. Walk in or call for appt. 24-hr hotline (800) 848-LOVE (5683). Volunteering opportunities available. FUNDING: Nonprofit. OFC HRS: M, W 10am-4pm; Tu, Th 10am-3pm. Spanish speaker on Tu. ADM REQ: Pregnant or suspected pregnancy. Free srvs. SERVES: Lake Elsinore, Perris, Hemet, Menifee, Temecula, Fallbrook, Murietta, Wildomar.

CALIFORNIA VOLUNTEERS

1110 K Street, Ste 210
Sacramento, CA 95814
(888) 567-7378
(916) 323-7646
(916) 323-3227 FAX

Volunteer matching network. Partners with nonprofits and public agencies to place volunteers. FUNDING: State. OFC HRS: M-F 8am-5pm. SERVES: Calif.

CASA YOUTH SHELTER

P.O. Box 216

10911 Reagan St.
Los Alamitos, CA 90720
(562) 594-6825
(714) 995-8601
(562) 594-9185 FAX

Emerg shelter care for runaway and homeless adols. Up to 2 wks temporary shelter. Individual, family & group counseling as well as parenting classes. Family reunification is the main goal. Outpatient counseling for children & families. Volunteer opportunities. FUNDING: Fed, United Way, fundraising, nonprofit. OFC HRS: Admin. M-F 8am-5pm. Clinical M-F 9am-9pm. Shelter 24 hrs, 7 days. Spanish spoken. ADM REQ: Ages 12-17 yrs. Free srvs for those lacking funds. Sliding fee scale. SERVES: So. Calif.

CENTER FOR NONPROFIT MGMT

1000 N. Alameda St., Ste 250
Los Angeles, CA 90014
(213) 687-9511
(213) 687-7159 FAX

Seminars on starting a nonprofit. Resource library to help with funding. Volunteer opportunities. FUNDING: Nonprofit. OFC HRS: M-F 8:30am-5pm. Free info. Fees based on sliding fee scale. SERVES: So. Calif.

CENTRAL CO. UNITED WAY

Retired & Senior Volunteer Prgm
418 E. Florida Ave.
Hemet, CA 92543
(951) 929-0423
(951) 652-0064 FAX

Federally funded prgm recruits, trains and places senior volunteers ages 55 yrs+ and provides a variety of opportunities to participate more fully in the life of their community. RSVP currently has 60 prgms with over 850 volunteers. FUNDING: Fed, nonprofit. OFC HRS: M-F 8:30am-5pm. ADM REQ: Application process for volunteers. Free srvs. SERVES: Beaumont, Banning, Hemet, San Jacinto, Menifee, Perris, Sun City, Temecula, Murrieta.

CHEMO ANGELS

P.O. Box 1971
Julian, CA 92036

Prgm matches people undergoing chemo or radiation treatment with "angel" volunteers who provide support during the process. Volunteers maintain weekly contact with their patient throughout the entire treatment process. Visit (www.chemoangels.net) for more info. FUNDING: Nonprofit. Free srvs. SERVES: U.S.A.

COMMUNITY HELPLINE

A Division of Helpline Youth Counseling, Inc.
P.O. Box 2503
Palos Verdes Peninsula, CA 90274
(310) 793-1415
(877) 541-2525
(310) 802-6164 FAX

Confidential listening, crisis intervention, info & referral toll-free hotline. Assist with loneliness, relationships, family violence, depression, grieving & losses, alcohol & drug abuse, anxiety, teen issues and suicide. Volunteering opportunities available. FUNDING: Nonprofit.

OFC HRS: Daily 7am-10pm. Free srvs. SERVES: Calif.

CORAZON DE VIDA FOUNDATION
14252 Culver Dr., Ste A-800
Irvine, CA 92604
(949) 476-1144
(949) 476-8715 FAX

Charitable organization provides support for the homeless children of Baja Calif and Mexico. Volunteers welcome. FUNDING: Nonprofit, donations. OFC HRS: M-F 9am-5pm. Spanish spoken. SERVES: So. Calif.

COURT APPOINTED SPECIAL ADV
Indio Center
P.O. Box 3008
44-199 Monroe St.
Indio, CA 92202-3008
(760) 863-7539
(760) 863-7431 FAX

CASA consists of trained community volunteers appointed by the juvenile court of Riverside County to act as advocates for dependent, abused or neglected children. Represents the child's needs, provides second point of view during the dependency process. Supportive & positive adult model for the abused or neglected child. The volunteer has weekly contact with the child. Walk in or call to apply. For Spanish, call (760) 863-7424. FUNDING: Nonprofit. OFC HRS: M-F 8:30am-4:30pm. Spanish spoken. Free srvs. SERVES: Riverside County.

COURT APPOINTED SPECIAL ADV
Southwest Justice Center
30755-D Auld Rd., Ste 1226
Murrieta, CA 92563
(951) 304-5220
(951) 304-5210 FAX

CASA consists of trained community volunteers appointed by the juvenile court of Riverside County to act as advocates for dependent, abused or neglected children. Represents the child's needs, provides second point of view during the dependency process. Supportive and positive adult model for the abused or neglected child. The volunteer has weekly contact with the child. Walk in or call to apply. FUNDING: Nonprofit. OFC HRS: M-F 8:30am-4:30pm. Spanish spoken. Free srvs. SERVES: Riverside County.

COURT APPOINTED SPECIAL ADV
437 N. Riverside Ave., Ste 10
Rialto, CA 92376
(909) 881-6760
(909) 881-6764 FAX

CASA recruits, screens and trains community volunteers to act as advocates for dependent, abused or neglected children. Volunteers represent the child's needs & provide a second point of view during the dependency process. Supportive and positive adult model for the abused or neglected child. The volunteer has regular contact with the child. Call to apply. FUNDING: Nonprofit. OFC HRS: M-F 8am-5pm. Spanish spoken. Free srvs. SERVES: San Bernardino County.

COURT APPOINTED SPECIAL ADV
Riverside Office
9991 County Farm Rd.
Riverside, CA 92503
(951) 358-4305
(951) 358-4302 FAX

CASA consists of trained community volunteers appointed by the Juvenile Court of Riverside County to act as advocates for dependent, abused or neglected children. Represents the child's needs, provides second point of view during the dependency process. Supportive and positive adult model for the abused or neglected child. The volunteer has weekly contact with the child. Walk in or call to apply. For Spanish, call (951) 358-4343. FUNDING: Nonprofit. OFC HRS: M-F 8:30am-4:30pm. Free srvs. SERVES: Riverside County.

COURT APPOINTED SPECIAL ADV/NATL
National CASA Assn
100 W. Harrison St., North Tower, Ste 500
Seattle, WA 98119
(800) 628-3233
(206) 270-0078 FAX

Supports a nationwide network of CASA prgms that train & support community volunteers to act as advocates for dependent, abused or neglected children. Represents the child's needs, provides a second point of view during the dependency process. Supportive and positive adult model for the abused or neglected child. FUNDING: Nonprofit. OFC HRS: M-F 8am-5pm. Spanish spoken. Free srvs. SERVES: U.S.A.

CRIME SURVIVORS
P.O. Box 54552
Irvine, CA 92619-4552
(949) 872-7895
(775) 245-4798 FAX

The mission of Crime Survivors is to ensure that the public knows of victim rights. Provides resources, support and information to empower crime victims to survive and thrive. Visit (www.crimesurvivors.com). FUNDING: Donations, nonprofit. SERVES: Calif.

CRISIS PREGNANCY CENTER
44750 San Pablo Ave.
Palm Desert, CA 92255
(760) 568-2200
(888) 956-4357

Pregnancy tests, ultrasound. Referrals for basic needs. Call or walk in. Volunteer opportunities. FUNDING: Nonprofit, donations. OFC HRS: M-Th 12noon-4:30pm; F 11am-3pm. Spanish spoken. Free and confidential. SERVES: Riverside County.

FAITH'S HOPE FOUNDATION
2271 W. Malvern Ave., Ste 382
Fullerton, CA 92833
(714) 871-4673

Assistance is provided to families experiencing financial hardship due to hospitalization of a loved one. Services provided to families facing homelessness and/or poverty. Volunteer opportunities available. Bilingual encouraged. Visit (www.faithshopefoundation.org) or e-mail (fhf@faithshopefoundation.org). FUNDING: Nonprofit, donations, fundraisers. OFC HRS: M-F 9am-5pm. ADM REQ: Must submit application. Parent or child in recent or current hospital stay. SERVES: Nationwide.

GAY, LESBIAN, STRAIGHT EDU NETWORK (GLSEN)
90 Broad St., 2nd Fl.
New York, NY 10004
(212) 727-0135
(212) 727-0254 FAX

Natl org focused on ensuring safe schools for all students. Hosts a wide range of prgms including Day of Silence, No Name Calling Week, and Gay-Straight Alliances. Chapters in Orange & San Diego Counties. Visit (www.glsen.org) for more info. FUNDING: Nonprofit. OFC HRS: M-F 9:30am-5:30pm, EST. Free srvs. SERVES: U.S.A.

GIVE AN HOUR
P.O. Box 5918
Bethesda, MD 20824

Matches volunteer mental health counseling providers with troops and families involved with current conflicts in Iraq and Afghanistan. Volunteers provide one hour of free therapy to client. For more info, e-mail (info@giveanhour.org) or visit (www.giveanhour.org). FUNDING: Nonprofit. Free srvs. SERVES: U.S.A.

GOLDEN RAINBOW SENIOR CENTER
611 S. Palm Canyon Dr., Ste 201
Palm Springs, CA 92264
(760) 416-7790
(760) 416-7786 FAX

Advocates for the unique needs of the GLBT senior community. Hosts a wide range of social, recreational, edu & service-oriented prgms, activities, and events. Volunteer opportunities available. FUNDING: Nonprofit. OFC HRS: M-F 8:30am-4:30pm. Evening and weekend programs as announced. SERVES: Coachella Valley.

HABITAT FOR HUMANITY/HEMET
328 N. State St., Ste D
Hemet, CA 92543
(951) 658-0235
(951) 658-3295 FAX

Christian-based organization that builds houses for low-income families living in poverty conditions who qualify for a Habitat Mortgage with a no-interest loan payable over a span of 20-25 yrs. Selected families must put in 500 hrs of "sweat equity" and make a down payment. Work is completed with volunteers, donated materials and monetary donations. FUNDING: Nonprofit, donations. OFC HRS: M-F 9am-4pm. ADM REQ: Low income. SERVES: San Jacinto Valley.

HABITAT FOR HUMANITY/PALM DESERT
P.O. Box 11738
Palm Desert, CA 92255
(760) 770-3723
(760) 770-3821 FAX

Christian-based organization that builds houses for low-income families living in poverty conditions who qualify for a Habitat Mortgage with a no-interest loan payable over a span of 20-25 yrs. Selected families must put in 500 hrs of "sweat equity" and make a down payment. Work is completed with volunteers, donated materials and monetary donations. FUNDING: Donations, nonprofit. OFC HRS: M-F 9am-5pm. ADM REQ: Low income. SERVES: Coachella Valley.

HABITAT FOR HUMANITY/RIVERSIDE
2180 Iowa Ave.
Riverside, CA 92507
(951) 787-6754
(951) 787-6750 FAX

Christian-based organization that builds houses for low-income families living in poverty conditions who qualify for a Habitat Mortgage with a no-interest loan payable over a span of 20-25 yrs. Selected families must put in 500 hrs of "sweat equity" and make a down payment. Work is completed with volunteers, donated materials and monetary donations. Habitat Store is open M-Sat 8:30am-4:30pm. FUNDING: Nonprofit. OFC HRS: M-Sat 8am-4:30pm. SERVES: Moreno Valley, Riverside, Jurupa, Corona, Belltown, Norco and Glen Avon.

HABITAT FOR HUMANITY/SAN GORGONIO

P.O. Box 269
Banning, CA 92220
(951) 922-3944
(951) 922-3934 FAX

Christian-based organization that builds houses for low-income families living in poverty conditions who qualify for a Habitat Mortgage with a no-interest loan payable over a span of 20-25 yrs. Selected families must put in 500 hrs of "sweat equity" and make a down payment. Work is completed with volunteers, donated materials and monetary donations. FUNDING: Nonprofit. OFC HRS: M-F 9am-12noon. ADM REQ: Low income. SERVES: Banning, Beaumont, Cabazon, Calimesa, Cherry Valley.

HADASSAH SOUTHERN CALIFORNIA

Administrative Office
9463 Gregory Way
Beverly Hills, CA 90212
(310) 234-8300
(310) 248-4944 FAX

Five area resource ctrs in L.A. & Orange Counties. Offers local programming to advocate for all women's health issues, promote literacy and edu, encourage social action and volunteerism, and strengthen Jewish growth and continuity. Long Beach & Orange County (714) 545-7162; Metro L.A. (310) 276-0036; Valley (818) 343-9316; San Diego (858) 547-9200; Desert (760) 327-7059. OFC HRS: M-Th 8:30am-4:30pm; F 8:30am-3pm. SERVES: L.A. Co.

HANDS ON INLAND EMPIRE

9624 Hermosa Ave.
Rancho Cucamonga, CA 91730
(909) 980-2857
(909) 980-2957 FAX

Brings individuals, families, teams and corporate groups together to strengthen communities through meaningful volunteer action within San Bernardino & Riverside Counties and the Pomona Valley. FUNDING: Nonprofit. OFC HRS: M-F 8am-5pm. Spanish spoken. Free srvs. SERVES: San Bernardino, Riverside and Pomona Valley.

HEMOPHILIA COUNCIL OF CALIF

Administration Office
1507 21st Street, Ste 206
Sacramento, CA 95814
(916) 498-3780
(916) 498-3782 FAX

Hemophilia edu & prevention, info & referral, outreach, support groups, home visits when needed. Volunteering opportunities available. FUNDING: Nonprofit. OFC HRS: M-F 9am-5pm. Spanish translation on call. ADM REQ: Persons at risk for HIV or have a family member, friend, or significant other who is at risk. SERVES: Calif.

INCREDABLES SPECIAL NEEDS PROGRAM

Rancho Cucamonga Civic Center

10500 Civic Center Dr.
Rancho Cucamonga, CA 91730
(909) 477-2782
(909) 477-2848 FAX

Recreational programs offered to residents and non-residents with special needs. Sports, singing, dancing, cooking, etc. Call for more info. Volunteers welcome. FUNDING: City. OFC HRS: M-Th 7am-6pm. ADM REQ: Ages 5-22 yrs, no one turned away. Fees for some activities. SERVES: Rancho Cucamonga.

INLAND EMPIRE UNITED WAY

Chamber of Commerce
7945 Vineyard Ave., Ste D5
Rancho Cucamonga, CA 91730
(909) 888-9011

Mission is to engage a caring community to respond to human need by: helping disadvantaged kids succeed in school, provide easy access to health and social srvs, develop opportunities for volunteers to create positive change, strengthen financial stability opportunities for low-income familes and individuals. FUNDING: Nonprofit. OFC HRS: M-F 8am-5pm. Free srvs. SERVES: Pomona Valley, Redlands/Yucaipa, Palo Verde Valley, Western San Bernardino County.

JEWELS FOR KIDS

560 Greenbrier Rd., Ste 210
Oceanside, CA 92054
(888) 770-7456
(760) 730-5437
(760) 730-5438 FAX

Accepts donations of unwanted jewelry in return for a free appraisal and 501(c)(3) tax credit. Items are redesigned and recreated, and auctioned at a yearly children's benefit concert. All proceeds go to support children's charities. Main goal is to work for the reunification of families. Four supervised visitation rooms available. Secure mailing address: 1835A South Centre City Pkwy., #323, Escondido, CA 92025. FUNDING: Nonprofit. OFC HRS: Varies. SERVES: U.S.A.

LITERACY NETWORK OF GREATER L.A.

6505 Wilshire Blvd., Ste 200
Los Angeles, CA 90048
(323) 761-8888
(800) 707-7323
(323) 761-8575 FAX

Prgm links volunteers, learners & teaching materials with 200 literacy prgms operating at more than 1,100 locations in So. Calif. FUNDING: Nonprofit. OFC HRS: M-F 9am-5pm. Free srvs. SERVES: So. Calif.

M-2 MATCH-TWO PRISONER OUTREACH

Southern Regional Office
P.O. Box 1350
15180 Euclid Ave.
Chino, CA 91710
(909) 606-5036
(909) 597-4824 FAX

Matches community volunteer mentors for supportive one-to-one visitation of incarcerated men, women and youth in Calif & Utah state prisons who receive few or no visits. Assists with basic needs and referrals. Wait: 30-60 days. FUNDING: State, donations, nonprofit. OFC HRS: M-F 8:30am-5:30pm. ADM REQ: Person receiving no visits while incarcerated. Free srvs. SERVES: Calif & Utah.

MERCY AIRLIFT

P.O. Box 90452
Los Angeles, CA 90009
(800) 637-2945
(714) 518-5980
(714) 518-5982 FAX

Disaster and humanitarian relief providing immediate transportation of food, medical supplies, medicines, and medical & relief personnel to disaster sites. Transports patients for medical srvs they are otherwise unable to reach. Emerg response (562) 209-2912. FUNDING: Nonprofit. SERVES: Internatl.

MICHELLE'S PLACE

Women's Breast Cancer Resource Center
27645 Jefferson Ave., Ste 117
Temecula, CA 92590
(866) 304-1280
(951) 699-5455
(951) 699-3631 FAX

Education resources, community awarenes and support services for women with breast cancer. Support groups in English and Spanish. Volunteers welcome. FUNDING: Nonprofit. OFC HRS: M-F 9am-3:30pm; W evening by appt. Spanish spoken. SERVES: Riverside County.

NEW HOPE CRISIS COUNSELING

Crystal Cathedral
12141 Lewis St.
Garden Grove, CA 92840
(714) 639-4673
(714) 971-4327 FAX

24-hr phone counseling and online counseling in a pvt chat room for all types of problems: crisis intervention, suicide prev, info & referral. Srvs provided by trained & caring volunteers. Prospective volunteers call (714) 971-4123 or e-mail (quinnw@crystalcathedral.org). Hotline (714) NEW-HOPE. Teenline: M-F 4pm-10pm, (714) 639-TEEN. Visit (www.newhopenow.org). FUNDING: Church, donations, nonprofit. OFC HRS: M-F 9am-5pm. Crisis helplines 24 hrs, 7 days. Spanish spoken. Free srvs. SERVES: U.S.A.

RANCHO CUCAMONGA VOLUNTEER PRGM

Rancho Cucamonga, CA 91701
(909) 477-2760

Volunteer prgms and activities provided by the City of Rancho Cucamonga. FUNDING: Nonprofit. ADM REQ: Ages 15 yrs+. Must complete application. SERVES: Rancho Cucamonga.

REBUILDING TOGETHER SO CALIF COUNCIL

P.O. Box 51088
Irvine, CA 92619
(714) 657-8174

Rehabilitates homes for low-income persons, the elderly & disabled, or anyone who is unable to do it themselves. Volunteer opportunities available. FUNDING: Nonprofit, donations. OFC HRS: M-F 9am-5pm. SERVES: So. Calif.

RETIRED & SENIOR VOLUNTEER PRGM

West Valley San Bernardino Co.
150 W. 1st Street, Ste 175
Claremont, CA 91711
(909) 482-0355
(909) 624-1294 FAX

Volunteer placements of seniors ages 55 yrs+ within community agencies and nonprofit organizations. Training provided as needed. FUNDING: Fed, VNA & Hospice of So. Calif, nonprofit. OFC HRS: M-F 8am-5pm. Free srvs. SERVES: Western San Bernardino County.

RETIRED & SENIOR VOLUNTEER PRGM
600 W. 5th Street
San Bernardino, CA 92410
(909) 384-5414
(909) 889-0672 FAX

Opportunity for seniors to volunteer throughout their communities at agencies and nonprofit organizations. Volunteers are provided with excess auto and liability insurance. Small transportation reimbursements on request and annual recognition & luncheon. Walk in. FUNDING: Fed, city. OFC HRS: M-Th 7:30am-4:30pm. 24-hr voicemail. ADM REQ: Ages 55 yrs+. Free srvs. SERVES: San Bernardino metro area, High Desert & mountain areas.

RIVERSIDE CO. OFFICE ON AGING
Retired & Senior Volunteer Prgm
73750 Catalina Way
Palm Desert, CA 92260
(760) 341-0401
(760) 340-9585 FAX

Registers volunteers ages 55 yrs+, and provides nonprofit agencies with volunteers. Over 100 placement sites. Walk in or call. FUNDING: Govt. OFC HRS: M-F 8am-4:30pm. Spanish spoken. Free srvs. SERVES: Desert Hot Springs, Palm Springs, Cathedral City, Rancho Mirage, Palm Desert, La Quinta, Thermal, Coachella, Thousand Palms, Indio and North Shore.

RIVERSIDE CO. PUBLIC HEALTH DEPT
Volunteer Srvs
P.O. Box 7600
Riverside, CA 92513-7600
(951) 358-5031
(951) 358-4457 FAX

OFC HRS: M-F 8am-5pm. Spanish spoken. SERVES: Riverside County.

RSVP
See "Retired & Senior Volunteer Prgm"

S.C.O.R.E./SMALL BUSINESS ADMIN
Service Corps of Retired Exec
1700 E. Florida Ave.
Hemet, CA 92544-4679

Info & assist in starting up a new business & dealing with specific areas in the operation of on-going business. Regular workshops, also members of SCORE will meet with people in or starting business & offer specific individual assist. Phone number no longer in service. E-mail (score503@netzero.net) for an appt. OFC HRS: Varies by location. By appt. only. French, Polish and Spanish spoken. Counseling is free. SERVES: Riverside County.

S.C.O.R.E./SMALL BUSINESS ADMIN
Service Corps of Retired Exec
200 W. Santa Ana Blvd., 7th Fl.
Santa Ana, CA 92701-4134
(714) 550-7369
(714) 550-0191 FAX

Info & assist in starting up a new business and dealing with specific areas in the operation of on-going business. Regular workshops, members of SCORE will meet with people in or starting business and offer specific individual assist.

Admin office operates 10 locations throughout O.C. OFC HRS: M-F 9am-1:30pm. Counseling is free. SERVES: Orange, Riverside & San Bernardino Counties.

SCORE/S.C.O.R.E.
See "S.C.O.R.E./Small Business Admin"

SOLDIER'S ANGELS
1792 E. Washington Blvd.
Pasadena, CA 91104
(626) 529-5114
(626) 529-5446 FAX

Connects members of the armed forces (vets and those who are currently serving) with community civilians. Volunteers participate in letter writing campaigns, care packages, making quilts for vets homes, etc. Visit (www.soldiersangels.org) FUNDING: Nonprofit. OFC HRS: M-F 8am-5pm. Free srvs. SERVES: U.S.A.

SUSAN G. KOMEN BREAST CANCER FNDN
Orange County Affiliate
3191-A Airport Loop Dr.
Costa Mesa, CA 92626
(714) 957-9157
(800) 462-9273
(714) 957-9155 FAX

Natl organization working to eradicate breast cancer as a life-threatening disease through edu, research, screening and treatment. FUNDING: Grants, nonprofit. OFC HRS: M-F 8:30am-5:30pm. SERVES: U.S.A.

SUSAN G. KOMEN BREAST CANCER FNDN
Inland Empire Affilate
43397 Business Park Dr., Ste D-9
Temecula, CA 92590
(951) 676-7465
(951) 676-7211 FAX

Fundraising, community outreach & edu. Volunteers welcome. FUNDING: Nonprofit, donations, fundraising. OFC HRS: M-F 9am-4pm. SERVES: Riverside County.

U.S. PEACE CORPS
Regional Recruitment Office
2361 Rosecrans Ave., Ste 155
El Segundo, CA 90245
(800) 424-8580
(310) 356-1125 FAX

Volunteers work in a developing nation for 27 mos. Must be ages 18 yrs+ Volunteers need a Bachelor's degree or 3-5 yrs experience in a skill or trade, be a U.S. citizen, no dependents under age 18 yrs. Living allowance, travel expenses and medical are covered. Year-round openings in a variety of work projects: edu, agriculture, environmental resources, business & health. Visit (www.peacecorps.gov). FUNDING: Govt. OFC HRS: M-F 8:30am-5pm. SERVES: U.S.A.

UNIV OF CALIF-RIVERSIDE
Student Life
229 Highlander Union Building
Riverside, CA 92521
(951) 827-7344
(951) 827-2439 FAX

Several prgms have a community outreach focus. Also have a prgm that connects student volunteers with nonprofit agencies for community srv work experience. FUNDING: Nonprofit. OFC HRS: M-F 8am-5pm. Spanish spoken. SERVES: Riverside County.

VICTOR VLY COMMUNITY SRVS COUNCIL
P.O. Box 1992
16692 Mojave Dr.
Victorville, CA 92393
(760) 243-9646
(760) 243-4762 FAX

Volunteer organization provides umbrella oversight to start-up organizations pending confirmation of nonprofit and charitable status. Encourages prgm formulation to serve unmet needs. Operates Volunteer Ctr of Victor Valley, including placing court referrals for community srv. "First Call for Help," a 24-hr info & referral srv. FUNDING: United Way, fees, donations, nonprofit. OFC HRS: M-Th 9am-2:45pm. Some Spanish spoken. SERVES: High Desert areas.

VOLUNTEER CENTER/RIVERSIDE CO.
Volunteer Connection/Community Srvs.
P.O. Box 5376
2060 University Ave., Ste 212
Riverside, CA 92517
(951) 686-4402
(951) 686-7417 FAX

Volunteer prgm, matches volunteers to agencies in need of volunteers, technical assist, volunteer recognitions, trainings. Court-ordered, probation ordered counseling & community srv. Monitors clients for court & probation. OFC HRS: M-F 8am-5pm. Spanish spoken, language line available. SERVES: Riverside County.

VOLUNTEER CENTER/VICTOR VALLEY
16692 Mojave Dr., Ste A
Victorville, CA 92392
(760) 245-8592
(760) 243-9646
(760) 243-4762 FAX

Recruits community members interested in giving their time and talent and then refers them to over 50 nonprofit agencies that have specific volunteer needs. Court referral prgm: an alternative prgm for court clients, in lieu of fines or jail time. Clients can serve community volunteer hours. Works with the courts of San Bernardino. Community Srvs Network: monthly meeting with nonprofit agencies, churches, schools to offer support, info & opportunity to network. Human Race: annual walk-a-thon to raise money for agencies. FUNDING: Nonprofit. OFC HRS: M-Th 9am-3pm. Spanish spoken. SERVES: High Desert area.

VOLUNTEERMATCH
Mailing Address
717 California St., 2nd Fl.
San Francisco, CA 94102
(415) 241-6868
(415) 241-6869 FAX

Connects individuals (including teens & seniors) or groups with volunteer opportunities at over 25,000 nonprofit agencies throughout the U.S. Visit (www.volunteermatch.org). FUNDING: Nonprofit. OFC HRS: M-F 9am-6pm. Free srvs. SERVES: U.S.A.

YOUTH/ANTI-GANG RESOURCES

AMER-I-CAN FNDN FOR SOCIAL CHANGE
269 S. Beverly Dr., Ste 1048
Los Angeles, CA 90010
(310) 652-7884
(310) 657-4838 FAX

Self-improvement & life skills facilitated by former gang members & ex-convicts. Promotes safe communities. FUNDING: Nonprofit. OFC HRS: M-F 9am-5pm. SERVES: U.S.A.

ANASAZI ORGANIZATION
1424 S. Stapley Dr.
Mesa, AZ 85204
(800) 678-3445
(480) 892-6701 FAX

Residential treatment center uses the troubled teen program as youth teen boot camp alternative. SERVES: U.S.A.

BOYS & GIRLS CLUB/INDIO
Indio Clubhouse
83-100 Date St.
Indio, CA 92201
(760) 347-5712
(760) 347-1192 FAX

Youth srvs for boys & girls, recreation, informal guidance, league sports, edu prgms, computer skills training, health & life skills, homework & tutorial srvs, after school child care, transportation, delinquency prevention prgm. FUNDING: Nonprofit. OFC HRS: Winter M-F 2pm-8pm. Summer M-F 7:30am-5:30pm. Spanish spoken. ADM REQ: Ages 7-18 yrs. Annual membership cost $20. SERVES: Indio.

CALIFORNIA MENTOR FOUNDATION
100 Main St.
Belvedere Tiburon, CA 94920
(415) 789-1007
(415) 789-1008 FAX

Information on mentoring prgms statewide. Visit (www.calmentor.org). SERVES: Calif.

CHINO COMMUNITY SERVICES
Human Services Division
13201 Central Ave.
Chino, CA 91710
(909) 591-9822
(909) 628-4093 FAX

Counseling srvs for children & adults. Community & school-based prevention & edu. Drug prevention, family treatment, teen and adult parenting classes, domestic violence, anger mgmt, community outreach, senior srvs, disabled srvs info & referral, PC-1000. For emergencies, call (909) 628-1010. FUNDING: State, county, school, city, govt. OFC HRS: M-Th 8am-8pm; F 8am-6pm. Spanish spoken. Free srvs or a fee of $26. SERVES: Western San Bernardino County.

CLEANSLATE, INC.
Gang Recovery Group & Tattoo Removal
12401 Slauson Ave., Ste G
Whittier, CA 90606
(562) 945-9111

CleanSlate is a gang violence recovery, rage resolution and tattoo removal prgm that helps to erase the visible signs of gang involvement while working with gang members to reconnect with their emotions. Individual counselors give one-on-one support. Gang recovery group every F 7:30pm-9pm at the So. Calif. Counseling Ctr. 5615 W. Pico Blvd., L.A. 90019. No appt needed for F groups. Tattoo removal prgm is at different locations one Sat a month. Address above is mailing address only. Visit (www.cleanslatela.org) for tattoo removal dates. FUNDING: Nonprofit. Spanish spoken. Groups $5 donation. SERVES: So. Calif.

CORAZON DE VIDA FOUNDATION
14252 Culver Dr., Ste A-800
Irvine, CA 92604
(949) 476-1144
(949) 476-8715 FAX

Charitable organization provides support for the homeless children of Baja Calif and Mexico. Volunteers welcome. FUNDING: Nonprofit, donations. OFC HRS: M-F 9am-5pm. Spanish spoken. SERVES: So. Calif.

DELANCEY STREET FOUNDATION
600 Embarcadero
San Francisco, CA 94107
(415) 512-5104
(415) 512-5141 FAX

Rehab prgm provides assist to ex-felons, substance abusers, gang members, perpetrators, and victims of abuse to assist them with skills to rebuild their lives. Literacy, homeless issues, anger mgmt, edu & voc mentoring. Does not accept people with mental disorders, people on medication or with disabilities, arsonists, or sex offenders. FUNDING: Nonprofit, donations. OFC HRS: 24/7. ADM REQ: Ages 18 yrs+. Free srvs. SERVES: Calif.

DRUG STRATEGIES
www.bubblemonkey.com
1150 Conneticut Ave., NW
Washington, DC 20036
(202) 289-9070

Internet site aimed at teens who want to learn more about the dangers of drugs and alcohol, but are afraid to ask. For Spanish, visit (www.changobomba.com). FUNDING: Calif. Endowment grant. SERVES: Internatl.

ETTIE LEE YOUTH & FAMILY SERVICES
P.O. Box 339
5146 N. Maine Ave.
Baldwin Park, CA 91706-0339
(626) 960-4861
(626) 337-2621 FAX

Family-style homes for severely emotionally disturbed young men ages 8-18 yrs. 24-hr care by trained staff. Individual & group therapy, gang intervention srvs, independent living skills training, case mgmt, family counseling, therapeutic recreation, 12-Step prgms, substance abuse treatment & on-site school. Licensed treatment foster family agency for boys & girls ages birth-18 yrs. Mental health therapy, case mgmt & family counseling. FUNDING: Nonprofit. OFC HRS: M-F 8am-5pm. Spanish spoken. ADM REQ: County referral for group home & foster care. SERVES: So. Calif.

FIELDS COMPREHENSIVE YOUTH SRVS
8780 19th Street, Ste 196
Rancho Cucamonga, CA 91701
(909) 945-1318
(909) 466-8685

Residential treatment, long-term foster care, emancipation prep, family reunification srvs. Individual, group & family therapy, parenting edu, self-mgmt training, gang intervention, drug abuse treatment, computer training. FUNDING: Private nonprofit. ADM REQ: Males ages 13-17 yrs, who are dependent and/or delinquent minors. SERVES: San Bernardino County.

HANDS ON INLAND EMPIRE
9624 Hermosa Ave.
Rancho Cucamonga, CA 91730
(909) 980-2857
(909) 980-2957 FAX

The alternative sentencing prgm acts as the referral agency for adult and juvenile residents of San Bernardino Co. who are assigned community srv work by the courts or probation depts. The prgm provides referral, follow-up, monitoring & reports on individuals referred to complete community srv hours. FUNDING: Fees. OFC HRS: M-F 8am-4pm. Spanish spoken. Prgm fee of $75 is charged for each referral payable by money order only. SERVES: San Bernardino County.

HOME OF NEIGHBORLY SERVICE
839 N. Mt. Vernon Ave.
San Bernardino, CA 92411
(909) 885-3491
(909) 884-0181 FAX

After school enrichment prgm for children in first grade and up. Recreation, youth skill building, counseling groups, gang intervention & prevention, homework assist/tutoring for youth, Boy & Girl Scouts, nutrition classes for adults, ESL for adults, children's clothes closet, Narcotics Anonymous meetings, parenting support groups, sewing for adults, boxing, hip hop dancing, aerobics & emerg food srv, resource & referrals. OFC HRS: M-Th 8am-5:30pm; F 8am-5pm. Spanish spoken. Free srvs & referrals. SERVES: San Bernardino County.

INLAND AGENCY
1737 Atlanta, Ste H-5
Riverside, CA 92507
(951) 241-8723
(951) 683-7980 FAX

Challenges of Youth. Adelanto Community Toolbox. HICAP (Health Insurance Counseling and Advocacy Prgm), Desert Sierra Breast Cancer Partnership. Part of a state and nationwide prgm for Medicare beneficiaries. FUNDING: Fed, state, county, fndn, donations, nonprofit. OFC HRS: M-F 8am-5pm. Spanish spoken. Free srvs. SERVES: Riverside, San Bernardino, Inyo, Mono Counties.

INTEGRATED LEARNING INSTITUTE
43-875 Washington St., Ste F
Palm Desert, CA 92211
(760) 772-9019
(760) 772-9610 FAX

Help for students of all ages to overcome learning problems and equip them for a lifetime of independent learning. Scholarships available. Agency has plans to move location, please call to confirm address. FUNDING: Nonprofit. OFC HRS: M-F 7am-5pm. SERVES: Coachella Valley.

JUVENILE JUSTICE CLEARINGHOUSE

Natl Criminal Justice Reference Srvs
P.O. Box 6000
Rockville, MD 20849-6000
(800) 851-3420
(301) 519-5212 FAX

A link between the Office of Juvenile Justice and Delinquency Prev (OJJDP) and the community at-large interested in juvenile justice, delinquency prev and missing and exploited children. The clearinghouse offers publications, references and referrals through an 800 number, conference support and attendance, online resources and other outreach activities. TDD (877) 712-9279 or (301) 712-9279. FUNDING: Govt. SERVES: U.S.A. & internatl.

PAL CAMP

Center for Drug Free Communities
14252 Culver Dr., Ste A-261
Irvine, CA 92604
(714) 505-4692
(714) 505-4887 FAX

Several times a year, advisors and students from elementary, junior high and high schools spend 3-4 days in the San Bernardino Mountains. The main objectives of the PAL Camps are to: (1) develop Peer Assistance Leadership (PAL) prgms on their school campuses; (2) prevention of alcohol and other drug abuse; (3) gang violence prevention; (4) resolve conflicts peacefully. FUNDING: O.C. Dept of Ed, Ctr for Drug-Free Communities, nonprofit. OFC HRS: M-F 8am-6pm. Spanish and Japanese spoken. Free or sliding fee scale. SERVES: So. Calif.

PERRIS VALLEY FAMILY RESOURCE CENTER

371 Wilkerson Ave., Ste L
Perris, CA 92570
(951) 443-1158
(951) 940-1964 FAX

Comprehensive srvs to families and children. Parents & teen classes, counseling, training workshops, food referrals, rental assist, ESL, anger mgmt, Healthy Families applications, college enrollment information. FUNDING: Govt. OFC HRS: M-Th 8am-5pm. Spanish spoken. SERVES: Perris Valley area, Moreno Valley, Lake Elsinore, Hemet and surrounding areas.

POLICE ACTIVITIES LEAGUE/PALM SPRINGS

The Palm Springs Boys & Girls Club
450 S. Sunrise Way
Palm Springs, CA 92262
(760) 318-1226

Local police officers working to provide activities and recreation to youth within the community. Prevention of juvenile crime, promotes youth leadership. FUNDING: City. SERVES: Palm Springs.

PROVISIONAL EDUCATIONAL SRVS

P.O. Box 7100
2450 Blake St.
San Bernardino, CA 92407
(909) 887-7002
(909) 887-8942 FAX

High school diploma & GED prep classes, Earn & Learn prgm, Upward Bound prgm, summer youth prgms & child care facility. FUNDING: Grants, donations, nonprofit. OFC HRS: M-F 8am-4:30pm. Spanish spoken. SERVES: San Bernardino County.

PUENTE PROJECT

Univ of Calif, Office of the President
300 Lakeside Dr., 7th Fl.
Oakland, CA 94612-3550
(510) 987-9548
(510) 834-0737 FAX

College prep prgm for edu disadvantaged students in Calif. Prgm made up of writing, counseling and mentoring components. Professionals are recruited & trained to serve as mentors. One-yr academic & leadership prgm co-sponsored by the Univ of Calif & Calif Community Colleges. FUNDING: Govt, nonprofit. OFC HRS: M-F 8am-5pm. Spanish spoken. ADM REQ: Must be enrolled in community colleges & high schools served by Puente Project. Free srvs. SERVES: Calif.

RESIDENTIAL TREATMENT CENTERS

Teen Options
(866) 495-8406

Online referral srvs for parents who need help with defiant teens. Referrals for boarding schools, treatment centers & prgms, therapists, etc. Visit (www.selectown.com). OFC HRS: 24 hrs, 7 days. Free srvs. SERVES: U.S.A.

SAN BERNARDINO CO. BEHAV HEALTH

9478 Etiwanda Ave.
Rancho Cucamonga, CA 91739
(909) 463-7624
(909) 463-7625 FAX

Juvenile eval & treatment srvs. Counseling srvs for minors in West Valley Juvenile Hall. Screening, assessment, brief psychotherapy, crisis intervention, medications, aftercare planning & referral. FUNDING: County. OFC HRS: M-F 8am-5pm. Spanish spoken. SERVES: San Bernardino County.

STRIVING TO REDUCE YOUTH VIOLENCE EVERYWHERE (STRYVE)

P.O. Box 6003
Rockville, MD 20849-6003

National Youth Violence Prevention Resource Center is now part of STRYVE. Info on prevention & intervention prgms, publications, research, technical assist & statistics on violence committed by & against youth. Visit (www.safeyouth.gov) for more info. FUNDING: Fed govt. OFC HRS: M-F 8am-6pm, EST. SERVES: U.S.A.

TEEN CHALLENGE INTERNATIONAL

Orange County Headquarters
P.O. Box 236
418 S. Main St.
Santa Ana, CA 92702
(714) 835-8822
(714) 835-8825 FAX

Free 1-year adult residential drug & alcohol rehab. Christian discipleship prgm. Learning center, computer lab, homework help M-F 2pm-5pm for jr. high & elem students; M-F 6pm-8pm for high school students. Call Frank Jimenez at (714) 836-7140. Gang & drug intervention & prevention prgm for teens Tu 7pm and for adolescents Sat 10am-12pm. TC New Creation Choir Outreach Prgm available for songs, testimonies & presentations in local churches. Anti-gang & drug presentations in local schools. Speakers for civil groups. FUNDING: Nonprofit. OFC HRS: M-F 8:30am-5pm. ADM REQ: Sign up & interviews required. Free srvs. SERVES: U.S.A.

THE ERIC ALLEN GROUP

P.O. Box 4975
Cerritos, CA 90703
(866) 217-0777

Leadership dev, college prep prgm, social skills prgms, life coaching & mentoring for foster care and at-risk youth and young adults. FUNDING: Nonprofit. OFC HRS: M-F 8am-5pm; Sat 9am-12pm. SERVES: Calif.

VICTORY OUTREACH/INLAND ADMIN

Administration Office
P.O. Box 5712
990 W. Mill St.
San Bernardino, CA 92410-2636
(909) 884-1921
(909) 383-9077 FAX

Christian prgm with two residential drug & alcohol recovery homes. Only spiritual methods are used in recovery without the assist of medication. Focus is to help the drug addict, gang member and/or alcoholic. Sponsors 350 homes internationally. FUNDING: Donations, nonprofit. OFC HRS: M-Th 9am-4pm. F 9am-3pm. Spanish spoken. SERVES: Inland Empire.

WE TIP CRIME HOTLINE

P.O. Box 1296
Rancho Cucamonga, CA 91729
(800) 782-7463
(909) 987-2477 FAX

Takes info from anonymous informants about all major crimes (drug traffic, arson, murder, rape, fraud, etc.) and passes it to law enforcement agencies. Callers remain anonymous. Calls taken 24 hrs a day. Additional phone numbers: (800) 78-CRIME, (800) 47-ARSON, (800) 87-FRAUD, (800) 47-DRUGS. Visit (www.wetip.com). See actual photos of criminals wanted in every state. See photos of missing and kidnapped children throughout the nation. Info can be provided on crime or criminals on WeTip-encrypted e-mail at (wetiphome@wetip.com). Possible reward of up to $1,000 upon conviction. SEEK prgm: Support Enforcement Enriching Kids, new prgm for O.C. available through any of the toll-free numbers. This prgm invites the callers to turn in parents not paying their child support. FUNDING: Nonprofit. OFC HRS: 24 hrs, 7 days. Spanish spoken. Free srvs. SERVES: U.S.A.

YOUNG VISIONARIES

Youth Leadership Academy
1616 North D Street
San Bernardino, CA 92405
(909) 881-3382
(909) 881-3385 FAX

Prgms provided to low-income, at-risk youth. Mentoring, leadership dev, after school tutoring. Youth violence prevention, healthy options for teens, youth employment dev, A.R.T.S. For Youth, C.U.T.T. (career, university, technology training). FUNDING: Nonprofit, donations. OFC HRS: M-F 1pm-7pm; Sat 9am-1pm. Spanish spoken. Accepts private pay. SERVES: San Bernardino County.

YOUTH/HIGH RISK

1736 FAMILY CRISIS CENTER
Admin Office
2116 Arlington Ave., Ste 200
Los Angeles, CA 90018
(323) 737-3900
(323) 737-3993 FAX

This location is one of the 21 Family Source Centers in L.A. County providing the One e-App system for financial assist, case mgmt, and high-risk youth/young adult employment and edu srvs. 24-hr srvs provided to runaway and homeless adols, including: counseling, food, clothing, advocacy and other basic needs. 2-week emerg youth shelter for adols ages 10-17 yrs who need short-term, crisis-oriented shelter. Also operates four shelters for battered women and their children (ages birth-17 yrs) for 1-24 months offering a comprehensive survival and job dev prgm to promote long-term safety, survival & success. 24-hr hotlines in South Bay (310) 379-3620, (310) 370-5902; Long Beach (562) 388-7652; South L.A. (213) 222-1237, (213) 745-6434. May call collect if needed. 24-hr drop-in center at 1736 Monterey Blvd., Hermosa Beach. FUNDING: Donations, grants, govt, CDBG, nonprofit. OFC HRS: M-F 8:30am-5pm. Spanish spoken. Free srvs. SERVES: So. Calif, Southwest L.A.

A HOME WITHIN
2500 18th Street
San Francisco, CA 94110
(888) 898-2249
(415) 621-6548 FAX

Pairs foster children and youth with private practice therapists who provide free long-term psychotherapy. Provides direct srvs & training and is active in public awareness and advocacy. Fostering art prgm seeks to provide an avenue for foster youth to express themselves through photography and writing. Branch offices located in various states. Visit (www.ahomewithin.org) for more info. FUNDING: Nonprofit. OFC HRS: M-F 9am-5pm. Spanish spoken. SERVES: U.S.A.

ACTION PARENT & TEEN SUPPORT
11372 Ventura Blvd., Ste 200
Studio City, CA 91604
(818) 763-9556
(800) 367-8336
(818) 763-9568 FAX

Weekly support groups for parents and teens. Support to families dealing with low self-esteem, drug/alcohol abuse, depression, runaways, teen pregnancy and other family-related issues. Low-cost drug testing, crisis intervention. FUNDING: Donations, nonprofit. OFC HRS: M-Th 12noon-9pm; F 9am-3:30pm. Spanish spoken. Accepts pvt insurance; individual & family therapy on a sliding fee scale. SERVES: So. Calif.

ADVENT GROUP MINISTRIES
90 Great Oaks Blvd., Ste 108
San Jose, CA 95119
(408) 281-0708
(408) 281-2658 FAX

Faith-based social service agency serving at-risk children and their families since 1986. Founded as a residential treatment program, they have since grown to include an outpatient recovery program, horse therapy, a comprehensive family counseling center and a foster care program for children of all ages. FUNDING: Nonprofit. OFC HRS: M-F 8:30am-5pm. SERVES: Northern Calif, San Bernardino County.

AGAPE GROUP HOMES
Mailing Address
1130 Clark, Ste 150-277
Santa Maria, CA 93455
(805) 937-5475
(805) 937-5473 FAX

Residential group home for boys, ages 13-18 yrs, and girls, ages 12-18 yrs. Life skills training, group, family and individual therapy. Parent support, family reunification, transitional planning, emancipation. GED support, vocational guidance. Drug & alcohol edu, goal setting, independent living skills. FUNDING: Nonprofit. OFC HRS: M-F 9am-5pm. Spanish and Italian spoken. ADM REQ: Must have court referral. Length of stay 6-9 months or longer. SERVES: U.S.A.

ALPHA LEARNING CENTERS
5053 LaMart Dr., Ste 104
Riverside, CA 92507
(951) 328-1020
(951) 784-4123 FAX

Through Riverside County Office of Education, the learning center provides free tutoring to foster children. Tutoring to non-foster children for a nominal fee. FUNDING: Nonprofit. OFC HRS: M-F 9am-5pm; Sat & Sun tutors only. Spanish spoken. SERVES: Riverside, Moreno Valley & Perris.

AMER-I-CAN FNDN FOR SOCIAL CHANGE
269 S. Beverly Dr., Ste 1048
Los Angeles, CA 90010
(310) 652-7884
(310) 657-4838 FAX

Self-improvement & life skills facilitated by former gang members & ex-convicts. Promotes safe communities. FUNDING: Nonprofit. OFC HRS: M-F 9am-5pm. SERVES: U.S.A.

ANASAZI ORGANIZATION
1424 S. Stapley Dr.
Mesa, AZ 85204
(800) 678-3445
(480) 892-6701 FAX

Residential treatment center uses the troubled teen program as youth teen boot camp alternative. SERVES: U.S.A.

APPLIED PRINCIPLES FOR SERVICE, INC.
P.O. Box 3751
San Bernardino, CA 92404
(909) 486-3775
(909) 863-9584 FAX

Offers mentoring prgms for at-risk youth, info & referral srvs, and a community computer lab. Also offers tech assist to those wishing to start a nonprofit agency. FUNDING: Nonprofit OFC HRS: M-F 9am-6pm. Srvs for youth are free; nonprofit work on a sliding fee scale. SERVES: San Bernardino Co.

ASSIST LEAGUE/FOOTHILL COMMUNITIES
P.O. Box 927

Upland, CA 91785
(909) 987-2813
(909) 484-0504 FAX

Three main areas of srv: (1) Operation School Bell is a prgm that provides clothing for needy children grades K-6 when referrals are made through the school districts; (2) Dental prgm is co-sponsored with San Antonio Community Hospital for children grades K-8 whose parents are not on welfare, do not have insurance and are low income. Referrals are made through the school district; (3) A-LUV prgm provides teddy bears to fire and police staff to give to victims of accidents, crimes, or trauma who need this special srv. Also ASK (Assault Survivor Kit) provides clothing, hygiene kits, and A-Luv Bear for assault victims through San Antonio Emerg Hospital. FUNDING: Donations, nonprofit. OFC HRS: Vary, this is a volunteer-staffed prgm. ADM REQ: Call first. Varies with prgm. SERVES: Upland, Montclair, Rancho Cucamonga, Alta Loma, Ontario, Fontana, Etiwanda.

ASSIST LEAGUE/HEMACINTO
180 N. Girard St.
Hemet, CA 92544
(951) 652-8307
(951) 927-6703 FAX

Operation School Bell prgm provides clothing to needy elem school children recommended by teachers in Hemet & San Jacinto school dists. Over 1,000 children clothed each year. Also food baskets at Thanksgiving, Christmas and Easter to families recommended by 23 schools. Usually 75+ families helped. Select scholarships offered to some eligible, returning women. Help for teen mothers. HAL BEARS, teddy bears provided to all law enforcement agencies for distribution to children in traumatic situations. Operates a thrift shop at the above location. FUNDING: Donations, thrift shop, nonprofit. OFC HRS: Thrift Store: M-F 9am-1pm; Sat 10am-2pm. Some Spanish spoken. ADM REQ: Must be referred by school nurse/teacher/etc. and live in the school districts of Hemet or San Jacinto. SERVES: Hemet & San Jacinto USDs.

ASSIST LEAGUE/PALM SPRINGS/DESERT
P.O. Box 3056
Rancho Mirage, CA 92270-2849
(760) 321-1990

Operation School Bell (clothing for needy elementary schoolchildren). Tutoring, bears for traumatized children, assault survivor prgm, senior srvs. Thrift store at 68-355 Ramon Rd., Cathedral City, 92234; (760)321-1990. FUNDING: Nonprofit. OFC HRS: M, Tu, Th-Sat 10am-4pm. Closed during summer (May 31st-October 1st). Spanish spoken. SERVES: Palm Springs, desert area.

ASSIST LEAGUE/REDLANDS
506 W. Colton Ave.
Redlands, CA 92374-3054
(909) 792-2675
(909) 798-0436 FAX

Operation School Bell (clothing for needy children in Redlands School District). Dental center for children in grades K-12 (must be referred by family srvs). Assault survivor kit and stuffed animals for traumatized children provided through the police dept. FUNDING: Nonprofit. OFC HRS: M-F 9am-3pm; Sat 10am-1pm. Spanish spoken. SERVES: Redlands & nearby.

ASSIST LEAGUE/RIVERSIDE
3707 Sunnyside Dr.
Riverside, CA 92506
(951) 682-3445
(951) 684-1703 FAX

Programs providing brand new clothing for referred, needy, elementary school children, SAT help, camp sponsorships for child burn victims, holiday essentials for a family, teaching scholarship, 2-day job seeking workshop for students, waiting room activity kits for children ages 3-10 yrs, teddy bears for child victims, help for community needs, snacks for homeless children, volunteer help for developmentally delayed children, SafeHouse for at-risk teens. Thrift Store, 3707 Sunnyside Dr., Riverside, 92506; (951)682-3445. FUNDING: Donations, nonprofit. OFC HRS: Thrift Store: Tu, 10am-6pm; W-Sat 10am-2pm. SERVES: Riverside metro.

ASSIST LEAGUE/SAN BERNARDINO
Children's Dental Center
580 W. 6th Street
San Bernardino, CA 92410
(909) 885-2045

Dental care provided to low-income children. Also Operation School Bell provides clothing to needy children. FUNDING: Nonprofit. OFC HRS: M-F 8:30am-4pm. ADM REQ: Must attend SBUSD and meet income guidelines. SERVES: San Bernardino County.

ASSIST LEAGUE/TEMECULA VALLEY
28720 Via Montezuma
Temecula, CA 92590
(951) 694-8018
(951) 694-8298 FAX

Alternatives to Domestic Violence, Operation School Bell (clothing for needy children in four local school districts), Heart & Hand meeting community needs. Assists teens, Kids on the Block puppet program, Operation Bookworm (for School Bell kids), Project Smile, college scholarships. FUNDING: Nonprofit. OFC HRS: M,W-F 10am-4pm; Tu 2pm-7pm; Sat 11am-2pm. Donate during business hrs. Spanish spoken. ADM REQ: Must be enrolled in local school dist. Must have referral from school personnel. Free srvs. SERVES: Temecula Valley.

ASSIST LEAGUE/VICTOR VALLEY
P.O. Box 39
Apple Valley, CA 92307
(760) 961-2468
(760) 961-2118 FAX

Operation School Bell provides clothing for needy children. I'm in Charge teaches kids safety skills, Operation Hug provides bears for traumatized children, Kids on the Block puppets, Project R.E.A.D., assault survivor kits. Common Cents Thrift Shop: 22021 Hwy 18, Ste A, Apple Valley, 92307, (760)961-1377. FUNDING: Nonprofit. OFC HRS: Vary. Office open infrequently. Call number provided for more info or to leave message. Thrift Store: Tu-Sat 10am-2pm. SERVES: San Bernardino County.

BIG BROTHERS/BIG SISTERS/DESERT
42-600 Cook St., Ste 110
Palm Desert, CA 92211
(760) 568-3977
(760) 568-2282 FAX

Adult role models and mentors matched to children & youth. Group mentoring. FUNDING: Nonprofit. OFC HRS: M-F 8am-5pm. SERVES: Palm Desert.

BIG BROTHERS/SISTERS/GTR L.A. & I.E.
Administration Office
800 S. Figueroa, Ste 620
Los Angeles, CA 90017
(213) 481-3611
(800) 207-7567
(213) 481-1148 FAX

Prgm matches boys ages 7-18 yrs and girls ages 6-16 yrs from single parent homes with volunteer Big Brothers and Big Sisters. Provides positive role models, friendship, companionship and guidance on a one-to-one basis. Each volunteer is trained to provide ongoing support to ensure that each mentoring relationship thrives. Also has an additional office at 5601 W. Slauson Ave., Ste. 130, Culver City, 90230; (310) 338-0055. FUNDING: Nonprofit. OFC HRS: M-F 9am-5:30pm Spanish spoken. Free srvs. SERVES: L.A. Co. & Inland Empire.

BILINGUAL FAMILY COUNSELING
317 West F Street
Ontario, CA 91762
(909) 986-7111
(909) 986-0941 FAX

County-funded center offers outpatient drug/alcohol and child abuse treatment. Prgms for adults, adolescents & children (including play therapy). Prevention prgms include: school & community presentations, and parent edu. Also crisis intervention, OTP Jag prgrm, individual, family & group counseling, referrals for suicide intervention and post-intervention srvs. FUNDING: Ofc of Alcohol/Drug Prgms, Human Srvs System, nonprofit. OFC HRS: M-Th 9am-8pm. Spanish spoken. Accepts Medi-Cal for drug/alcohol treatment, pvt fees. SERVES: San Bernardino County.

BOYS & GIRLS CLUB/CATHEDRAL CITY
32141 Whispering Palms Trail
Cathedral City, CA 92234
(760) 324-5844
(760) 321-2464 FAX

Latchkey, summer, Easter & Christmas vacation, special assist with homework, after school child care, some transportation provided. Walk in. FUNDING: Nonprofit. OFC HRS: M-F 7:30am-5:30pm. Spanish spoken. ADM REQ: Ages 6-19 yrs. Annual membership $10. Scholarships & free srvs to low-income families. Sliding fee scale. SERVES: Cathedral City, Rancho Mirage.

BOYS & GIRLS CLUB/DESERT HOT SP
Main Club Facility
P.O. Box 935
66150 8th Street
Desert Hot Springs, CA 92240
(760) 329-1312
(760) 329-8995 FAX

Youth dev agency with more than 70 prgms throughout the year. Camping, crafts, swimming, homework tutorial srvs, before & after school child care, mentoring prgms, sports,

computers, etc. FUNDING: Nonprofit. OFC HRS: M-F 2pm-6pm (summer hrs: May-Aug, M-F 12noon-6pm). Spanish spoken. ADM REQ: Ages 6-18 yrs. Membership fees are $10 per calender year, additional fees for extended day camp. SERVES: Desert Hot Springs, North Palm Springs, Painted Hills, Sky Valley.

BOYS & GIRLS CLUB/MTN COMM
P.O. Box 2228
607 Forest Shade Rd.
Crestline, CA 92325
(909) 338-0418
(909) 338-3949 FAX

Recreational activities including: volleyball, street hockey, basketball, arts, crafts, homework assist, mentoring. FUNDING: Nonprofit. OFC HRS: Vary by prgm, call for more info. Spanish spoken. ADM REQ: Ages 6-18 yrs. Membership is $20 per yr. SERVES: San Bernardino mountain areas.

BOYS & GIRLS CLUB/SAN BERNARDINO
1180 W. 9th Street
San Bernardino, CA 92411
(909) 888-6751
(909) 888-1474 FAX

Youth and family srvs agency. Youth dev, counseling, day camp, homework & tutorial srvs, before & after school child care, parent edu, employment srvs, physical and social recreation, community srvs, youth drug & alcohol counseling, ESL classes, GED. FUNDING: Donations, fundraising, United Way, nonprofit. OFC HRS: M-F 7am-7pm; Sat 8:30am-2:30pm. Spanish spoken. Annual membership $7. SERVES: San Bernardino metro area.

BOYS HOPE GIRLS HOPE OF SO CALIF
1041 W. 18th Street, Ste A101
Costa Mesa, CA 92627
(949) 515-8833
(949) 515-8844 FAX

Long-term, family-like residential group homes for capable, needy youth. Serves academically capable boys and girls who have been abused, neglected or abandoned or have come from dysfunctional families. Provides safe, stable, long-term alternative living environment; youth must be free of significant emotional or learning difficulties. This is a voluntary placement. Focus is at-risk children with academic-ability who are determined to go to college. FUNDING: Donations, grants, nonprofit. OFC HRS: M-F 9am-5pm. ADM REQ: Ages 10-14 yrs can remain through graduation from high school, clear need for long-term out-of-home placement, at least an average IQ. Free srvs. SERVES: So. Calif.

BOYS REPUBLIC
1907 Boys Republic Dr.
Chino Hills, CA 91709
(909) 628-1217
(909) 627-9222 FAX

Residential and day treatment for adjudicated wards or dependents. Residential prgm serves 212 boys and 8 girls, ages 13-18 yrs. Non-residential prgm is co-ed & serves 30 youth. FUNDING: Govt. OFC HRS: M-F 8am-4:30pm. Spanish spoken. ADM REQ: Primarily adjudicated wards or dependents. SERVES: Calif.

CALIF DEPT OF JUSTICE
Missing & Unidentified Persons Unit
P.O. Box 903387

Sacramento, CA 94203-3870
(800) 222-3463
(916) 227-3290
(916) 227-3270 FAX

Assists law enforcement and other criminal agencies to locate missing persons. Helps parents of missing children work with law enforcement. Distributes missing child posters, publishes a quarterly missing persons bulletin. Online bulletin updated quarterly. FUNDING: State, nonprofit. OFC HRS: 24 hrs, 7 days. Spanish, Japanese, Cantonese spoken. SERVES: Calif.

CALIF FAMILY LIFE CENTER

Empower Youth Program
930 N. State St.
Hemet, CA 92543
(951) 765-0917
(951) 652-8287 FAX

Work readiness skills, technology skills, work experience & career exploration, leadership dev, edu srvs for youth. FUNDING: Nonprofit. OFC HRS: M-Th 7:30am-8pm; F 7:30am-7pm. ADM REQ: Ages 16-21 yrs, from low income families. Must meet eligibility criteria. SERVES: Hemet, San Jacinto, Banning, Beaumont, Quail Valley.

CALIF YOUTH CRISIS LINE

Calif Coalition for Youth
P.O. Box 161448
Sacramento, CA 95816
(800) 843-5200
(916) 340-0505
(916) 340-0510 FAX

Statewide, 24-hr crisis intervention counseling for youth ages 12-24 yrs & their families on a wide range of mental health, drug & alcohol, peer, family and relationship issues. Youth-to-parent message srv, phone connections to srv providers & families, info & referrals. Rides provided to youth who cannot afford transportation home. FUNDING: Nonprofit, donations. OFC HRS: 24 hrs, 7 days. Spanish spoken. Translation srvs available. Free srvs. SERVES: Calif.

CALIFORNIA MENTOR FOUNDATION

100 Main St.
Belvedere Tiburon, CA 94920
(415) 789-1007
(415) 789-1008 FAX

Information on mentoring prgms statewide. Visit (www.calmentor.org). SERVES: Calif.

CANYON ACRES CHILDREN & FAMILY SRVS

1845 W. Orangewood Ave., Ste 300
Orange, CA 92868
(714) 383-9401
(714) 383-9300 FAX

Serves children & families through a comprehensive list of community prgms. The mental health clinic includes individual, family, & group therapy, psych medication support, and parent edu classes. The therapeutic afterschool prgm contains an array of structured group activities and a therapeutic horse riding prgm for children that have been identified as needing additional support for a mental health issue. The Creating Family Connections prgm works to find family or kin for dependent youth and engage them in the child's life. Foster care and adoption srvs prgm helps find kids forever families. FUND-

ING: AFDC-FC, EPSDT, County of Orange Health Care Agency, donations. OFC HRS: M-F 7am-5pm. Sat appts also available. Spanish spoken. Accepts Medi-Cal. Pvt insurance and cash pay for select srvs. SERVES: Orange Co (all prgms). Select prgms in L.A., Riverside, San Bernardino, & San Diego Counties.

CARE LEARNING CTR/PSYCH SRVS

27715 Jefferson Ave, Ste 112
Temecula, CA 92592
(951) 288-6835
(951) 506-9113 FAX

Edu & psych organization make up of professional educators, licensed psychologists, therapists, and counselors. Provides edu srvs including tutoring, edu therapy, counseling for individuals and families, and academic coaching for children. FUNDING: Nonprofit. OFC HRS: M-F 9am-9pm. Spanish spoken. SERVES: Temecula, Riverside Co, northern San Diego Co.

CASA BLANCA HOME OF NEIGHBORLY SRV

7680 Casa Blanca St.
Riverside, CA 92504
(951) 688-3043
(951) 688-3286 FAX

Senior prgms, Head Start prgm & emerg assist. Walk in. FUNDING: United Way, Riverside Co. Depts of Mental Health, Probation & Office of Ed, nonprofit. OFC HRS: Tu-F 8:30am-5pm. Spanish spoken. ADM REQ: Primarily for residents of the Casa Blanca community. Free srvs. SERVES: Riverside.

CASA YOUTH SHELTER

P.O. Box 216
10911 Reagan St.
Los Alamitos, CA 90720
(562) 594-6825
(714) 995-8601
(562) 594-9185 FAX

Emerg shelter care for runaway and homeless adols. Up to 2 wks temporary shelter. Individual, family & group counseling as well as parenting classes. Family reunification is the main goal. Outpatient counseling for children & families. Volunteer opportunities. FUNDING: Fed, United Way, fundraising, nonprofit. OFC HRS: Admin. M-F 8am-5pm. Clinical: M-F 9am-9pm. Shelter 24 hrs, 7 days. Spanish spoken. ADM REQ: Ages 12-17 yrs. Free srvs for those lacking funds. Sliding fee scale. SERVES: So. Calif.

CATHOLIC CHARITIES/COUNSELING

Caritas Counseling Srvs
1441 North D Street, Ste 4
San Bernardino, CA 92405
(909) 763-4970
(909) 763-4977 FAX

Professional counseling without regard to race, creed, sex, or age. Marriage, family, child counseling for a wide range of issues such as child abuse, anger mgmt, relationships, parent edu. Counseling provided days, eve & Sat in various locations. FUNDING: Nonprofit. OFC HRS: M-F 10am-4:30pm. Closed 1pm-2pm. Spanish spoken. Sliding fee scale. Some free srvs. SERVES: San Bernardino & Riverside Counties.

CENTRAL CITY LUTHERAN MISSION

1354 North G Street

San Bernardino, CA 92405
(909) 381-6921
(909) 884-5104 FAX

Transitional housing for homeless persons with HIV. Edu & prevention, info & referral, outreach srvs. FUNDING: Nonprofit. OFC HRS: M-F 9am-5pm. Spanish spoken. Free srvs. SERVES: San Bernardino County.

CESAR E. CHAVEZ FOUNDATION

634 S. Spring St., Ste 400
Los Angeles, CA 90014
(213) 362-0260
(213) 362-2065 FAX

Srvs include: learning tools for grades K-12, youth action prgm, sustainable communities prgm, civic engagement, culture, arts, nonviolence. FUNDING: Nonprofit. OFC HRS: M-F 8am-5pm. Spanish spoken. SERVES: Calif.

CHAFFEY COLLEGE/EOPS

5885 Haven Ave.
Rancho Cucamonga, CA 91737
(909) 652-6349
(909) 652-6342 FAX

EOPS offers support services to economically disadvantaged students who have experienced limited success in high school and/or college. Endeavors to ensure student retention and success through academic support and financial assistance. CARE is a special EOPS prgm for single parents (all ages) receiving govt financial assist & helps with child care, cafeteria food vouchers, books and supplies, etc. Also offers prgm for youth ages 16-21 yrs emancipating from foster care or seeking to live independent of their guardians. FUNDING: Govt. OFC HRS: M-W 8am-4:30pm; Th 8am-6:30pm; F 8am-2pm. Spanish, Vietnamese spoken. ADM REQ: Call or see website for eligibility req. SERVES: San Bernardino County.

CHARIS YOUTH CENTER

Admin Office
714 W. Main St.
Grass Valley, CA 95945
(530) 477-9800
(530) 477-9803 FAX

Residential education and day treatment provided to emotionally disturbed adol boys and girls. Support srvs for the families. FUNDING: Nonprofit. OFC HRS: M-F 8:30am-4:30pm. ADM REQ: Ages 13-18 yrs. Referrals from County, probation, school, mental health, CPS, AAP. SERVES: Calif.

CHILD FIND OF AMERICA, INC.

P.O. Box 277
New Paltz, NY 12561-0277
(800) 426-5678
(845) 883-6614 FAX

Registers & helps locate missing children (800) I-AM-LOST (Child Find Hotline). Helps to recover parentally abducted children through crisis mediation, and preventing parental abduction via (800) A-WAY-OUT (Parent Abduction Hotline). Dissemination of photos of missing children, safety info, Natl Missing Children's Day (845) 883-6060. FUNDING: Donors, corp, fndn, nonprofit. OFC HRS: M-F 9am-5pm, EST. Spanish spoken. ADM REQ: Child to be registered must be under age 17 yrs. Free srvs. SERVES: U.S.A.

CHILD QUEST INTERNATIONAL

1060 N. 4th Street, Ste 200

San Jose, CA 95112
(888) 818-4673
(408) 287-4673
(408) 287-4676 FAX

Search for missing children, including those abducted by non-custodial parents or guardians, and runaways. Also for recovery of abused and exploited children. Our Kids Are Safe Kids prgm provides on-site presentations to elem school children. FUNDING: Nonprofit, donations, fundraisers. OFC HRS: M-F 9am-4pm, 24-hr emerg sighting line. Spanish spoken. Free srvs. Sliding fee scale for some. SERVES: U.S.A. & internatl.

CHILDREN NOW
1212 Broadway, 5th Fl.
Oakland, CA 94612
(510) 763-2444
(510) 763-1974 FAX

No direct srvs. Advocates for children as top public priority—focusing on edu, health, parenting, child care, etc. Online newsletter, publications and reports available. For Talking with Kids program, call (800) 244-5344. FUNDING: Nonprofit. OFC HRS: M-F 8am-5pm. Spanish spoken. SERVES: U.S.A.

CHILDREN OF THE NIGHT
14530 Sylvan St.
Van Nuys, CA 91411
(800) 551-1300
(818) 908-4474
(818) 908-1468 FAX

Assist for children forced into prostitution. Natl 24-hr hotline; shelter home & school receives child prostitutes 24 hrs a day from every state. Structured prgm, includes transportation. FUNDING: Nonprofit, donations, grants. Spanish spoken. ADM REQ: Ages 11-17 yrs involved in prostitution. Free srvs. SERVES: U.S.A.

CHILDREN'S FUND
County Government Center
825 E. Hospitality Lane, 2nd Fl.
San Bernardino, CA 92415-0132
(909) 387-4949
(909) 383-9758 FAX

Provides for the needs of children (ages birth-18 yrs) who are at-risk because of abuse, poverty, neglect. Accessed through case mgrs of any of the 19 Children's Network agencies in the county. Other resources must be explored before requesting assist from Children's Fund, as its mission is to provide for those things that "fall through the cracks." FUNDING: Nonprofit. OFC HRS: M-F 8am-5pm. SERVES: San Bernardino County.

CHILDREN'S HOPE
1843 N. 2nd Avenue
Upland, CA 91784
(909) 949-8181
(909) 920-4230 FAX

Residential group home for boys who are emotionally disturbed or abused and wards of the court. Long-term care & mental health srvs, FUNDING: Nonprofit. OFC HRS: 24 hrs. Srvs are paid by the county. SERVES: San Bernardino County.

CHINO COMMUNITY SERVICES
Human Services
13271 Central Ave.
Chino, CA 91710
(909) 591-9822

(909) 628-4093 FAX

Professional counseling srvs to low-income children ages 5-18 yrs and their families. Youth & teen counseling srvs. Parenting classes, anger mgmt, court referrals and PC-1000 drug diversion prgm are offered throughout the year. Speakers are available for schools and other associations on a variety of subjects. Call for info. FUNDING: Chino Community Srvs Dept, Chino Valley USD, govt. OFC HRS: M-Th 8am-8pm; F 8am-6pm Family counseling is free. Fees vary per prgm. SERVES: San Bernardino County.

CHINO HILLS COMM SRVS DEPT
14000 City Center Dr.
Chino Hills, CA 91709-4868
(909) 364-2710
(909) 364-2725 FAX

The dept provides various types of programs and services for the community. Chino Hills Advisory and Mentoring Prgm, Youth Accountability Board, Seniors Assisted by Visiting Volunteers and Youth, Volunteer Service Prgm. FUNDING: Govt. OFC HRS: M-Th 7:30am-5:30pm; F 7:30am-4:30pm. Free srvs. SERVES: Chino Hills.

CHRISTIAN FAMILY COUNSELING
6117 Brockton Ave., Ste 100
Riverside, CA 92506
(951) 682-7138
(877)777-0755
(951) 686-2271 FAX

Marriage, individual, family, teen, adol, drug & alcohol counseling. FUNDING: Donations, nonprofit. OFC HRS: M-F 9am-8pm, Sat 10am-5pm. $45 per session. SERVES: Riverside, San Bernardino Counties.

CHRISTOPHER WAHL YOUTH CENTER
12401 Slauson Ave., Ste G
Whittier, CA 90606
(562) 693-2247
(562) 954-7264 FAX

Offers free HIV testing and prevention edu. Houses various support groups and 12-Step prgms including Celebrate Recovery. FUNDING: Nonprofit. OFC HRS: M-F 9am-5pm. Free srvs. SERVES: L.A. County, San Bernardino County.

CITY OF RIVERSIDE PUBLIC LIBRARY
Eastside Library Connection
4033-C Chicago Ave.
Riverside, CA 92507
(951) 684-8347
(951) 684-8347 FAX

Info learning center for children, ages 10-14 yrs, and their families. Free computer training, Internet, info literacy, homework assist, literacy & special presentations for adults. FUNDING: Riverside Public Library Project, grants, nonprofit. HRS: M-Th 11am-7pm; F, Sat 10am-6pm. SERVES: Riverside County.

CLEANSLATE, INC.
Gang Recovery Group & Tattoo Removal
12401 Slauson Ave., Ste G
Whittier, CA 90606
(562) 945-9111

CleanSlate is a gang violence recovery, rage resolution and tattoo removal prgm that helps to erase the visible signs of gang involvement while working with gang members to reconnect

with their emotions. Individual counselors give one-on-one support. Gang recovery group every F 7:30pm-9pm at the So. Calif. Counseling Ctr. 5615 W. Pico Blvd., L.A. 90019. No appt needed for F groups. Tattoo removal prgm is at different locations one Sat a month. Address above is mailing address only. Visit (www.cleanslatela.org) for tattoo removal dates. FUNDING: Nonprofit. Spanish spoken. Groups $5 donation. SERVES: So. Calif.

COLLEGE OF THE DESERT/EOPS
43-500 Monterey Ave.
Palm Desert, CA 92260-9399
(760) 773-2539
(760) 346-8041
(760) 776-0147 FAX

EOPS offers various counseling, financial aid for books, transfer fee waiver, laptops and graphing calculators on-loan, priority registration, long-term edu planning, tutoring, student ID card, assistance with health fee. CARE is a special EOPS prgm for single parents (all ages) receiving govt financial assist to help them go to college and obtain skills for meaningful employment. Helps with child care, gas cards & many other srvs. Also offer prgm for youth ages 16-21 yrs emancipating from foster care or seeking to live independent of their guardians. EOPS and CARE srvs subject to change. FUNDING: Govt. OFC HRS: M-Th 9am-5pm. F 9am-12noon. Spanish spoken. ADM REQ: Must be full-time COD student. Apply online or in person. Inquire about requirements. SERVES: Riverside County.

COLTON COMMUNITY SRVS DEPT
670 Colton Ave.
Colton, CA 92324
(909) 370-6153
(909) 777-3351 FAX

Recreation division, youth, family & seniors division. Senior outreach, counseling, tutoring, child care, summer youth, and youth intervention. Walk in or call. FUNDING: Govt. OFC HRS: M-F 7am-8pm; Sat 8am-5pm. Spanish spoken. SERVES: Colton, Grand Terrace & Bloomington.

COMMUNITY COUNSELING CTR/CSUSB
Dept of Psychology, Calif State Univ
5500 State University Pkwy.
San Bernardino, CA 92407
(909) 537-5040
(909) 537-7061 FAX

Graduate students in 2-yr M.S. counseling psychology prgm provide low-cost, long-term individual psychotherapy. Student therapists are supervised by Ph.D. level psychologists on CSUSB faculty. FUNDING: CSUSV, govt. OFC HRS: M, Th, F 8am-5pm; Tu, W 8am-7pm. ADM REQ: CSUSB student or connected to student; not suicidal, abusive, drug dependent or violent. Cost covered by tuition. SERVES: San Bernardino County.

COMPREHENSIVE YOUTH SERVICES
8780 19th Street, Ste 196
Alta Loma, CA 91701
(909) 466-8685
(909) 466-4815 FAX

Residential group home for boys ages 13-17 yrs. Long-term care, short-term emerg care, mental health srvs, family reunification, parenting edu, computer training, substance abuse prevention prgm. Serves abused children & wards of the court. Transportation to school. Counseling for individuals & groups. FUNDING: Nonprofit. OFC HRS: 24 hrs. Spanish spoken. Accepts insurance, Medicare, Medi-Cal, sliding fee scale. SERVES: Calif.

COPPER MOUNTAIN COLLEGE/EOPS

6162 Rotary Way
Joshua Tree, CA 92252
(760) 366-3791
(760) 366-5257 FAX

EOPS & CARE are state-funded prgms assisting the academically & economically disadvantaged student. EOPS srvs include, but are not limited to: academic counseling, book assist, tutoring, parking permits. CARE provides grants, food cards, parenting info, gas cards. All srvs upon availability or state funding. TDD (760) 366-3241. FUNDING: Govt. OFC HRS: M-Th 8:15am-5pm; F 8:15am-3pm. Spanish spoken. ADM REQ: Must be full-time student, less than 70 degree-applicable units, BOG waiver A or B, and academically disadvantaged. CARE students must be EOPS eligible, ages 18 yrs+, at least one child under the age of 14 yrs, and currently on CalWORKs/TANF & receiving cash aid. SERVES: Calif.

COPS FOR KIDS, INC.

P.O. Box 2001
333 Limited St.
Lake Elsinore, CA 92531
(951) 245-3389
(951) 245-3311 FAX

Outreach to community children ages birth-18 yrs. Also senior citizen assist prgm. FUNDING: County. OFC HRS: M-F 9am-5pm. Spanish spoken. ADM REQ: Must fill out request form in person at the sheriff's office. Free srvs. SERVES: Lake Elsinore.

COVENANT HOUSE NINELINE

461 8th Avenue
New York, NY 10001
(800) 999-9999
(212) 727-4000
(212) 989-9098 FAX

24-hr natl crisis intervention hotline for runaways, homeless, troubled youth & their families. Refers caller to help in his or her own community. Conference call capability & message relays to runaway youth. TDD/TYY hotline (800) 999-9915. FUNDING: Donations, nonprofit. OFC HRS: 24 hrs, 7 days. Spanish spoken. ADM REQ: Ages 18-21 yrs. Free srvs. SERVES: U.S.A.

CRAFTON HILLS COLLEGE/EOPS

11711 Sand Canyon Rd.
Yucaipa, CA 92399-1799
(909) 389-3239
(909) 794-2161
(909) 389-3621 FAX

EOPS offers info & referral, counseling, edu grants, financial aid for books, transportation assist, mentoring, student work prgm, emerg no-interest loans, transfer fee waiver. CARE is a special EOPS prgm for single parents (all ages) receiving govt financial assist & helps with child care, gas cards & many other srvs. Also offer prgm for youth ages 16-21 yrs emancipating from foster care or seeking to live independent of their guardians. OFC HRS: M-Th 8am-6pm; F 8am-1pm. Spanish spoken. ADM

REQ: CA resident, qualify for BOGW A/B, enrolled in 12 units unless in disabled student prgm, have less than 70 degree-applicable units & be edu disadvantaged. CARE: head of household, single parent receiving TANF/CalWORKS with a Welfare-to-Work plan & have a child under 14 yrs of age. SERVES: San Bernardino County.

DAVID & MARGARET YOUTH & FAMILY SRVS

1350 3rd Street
La Verne, CA 91750
(909) 596-5921
(909) 596-7583 FAX

Residential treatment prgm and specialized non-public school for girls ages 11-18 yrs. Shelter care for children ages 11-18 yrs. Foster family agency and adoption srvs serving children ages birth-18 yrs. Learning enhancement ctr for youth and adults with LD, ADHD, ADD. Community-based edu prgms including self-injury, alcohol and drug intervention, anger mgmt courses. Social srvs, probation and mental health agency referrals. Serves children and families. Provides transitional housing for youth ages 18-25 yrs who are at-risk of homelessness. Provides mentoring prgm for foster youth and pvt counseling on a sliding scale basis. FUNDING: State, county, donations, nonprofit. OFC HRS: M-F 8:30am-5pm. Spanish spoken. Accepts insurance, Medicare, Medi-Cal. Sliding fee scale. Set fee to public. SERVES: So. Calif.

DELANCEY STREET FOUNDATION

600 Embarcadero
San Francisco, CA 94107
(415) 512-5104
(415) 512-5141 FAX

Rehab prgm provides assist to ex-felons, substance abusers, gang members, perpetrators, and victims of abuse to assist them with skills to rebuild their lives. Literacy, homeless issues, anger mgmt, edu & voc mentoring. Does not accept people with mental disorders, people on medication or with disabilities, arsonists, or sex offenders. FUNDING: Nonprofit, donations. OFC HRS: 24/7. ADM REQ: Ages 18 yrs+. Free srvs. SERVES: Calif.

DRUG & ALC TREATMENT REFERRAL

Mental Health/Drug/Alcohol Abuse Hotline
(866) 716-3460

Referrals & help to those in crisis. Executive rehab, prescription addiction prgm, Christian-based prgm, teen & family rehab, intervention partners, gay & lesbian prgm, west coast adult rehab, east coast adult rehab, residential treatment, teen outpatient, 12-Step rehab. FUNDING: Nonprofit. OFC HRS: 24 hrs, 7 days. Spanish spoken. SERVES: U.S.A.

DRUG ENDANGERED CHILDREN PRGM

P.O. Box 1267
Riverside, CA 92502
(877) 955-6384

Multi-agency approach by Child Protective Services, District Attorney, Sheriff's Department, and other public health agencies to assist and protect drug-endangered children whose lives are jeopardized by families who have been involved with drug manufacturing, sales, or use. Srvs include: comprehensive medical screening, drug screening, mental and dental care,

background checks and home eval, removal from toxic chemical exposure and drug environments. Call the METH hotline (877) 955-METH if you suspect the manufacturing of methamphetamines. FUNDING: Govt. Spanish spoken. ADM REQ: Children who have been endangered due to familial involvement with drugs. Free srvs. SERVES: Riverside Co.

EAST VALLEY CHARLEE

440 Cajon St.
Redlands, CA 92373
(909) 307-5777
(909) 307-5776 FAX

County-funded prgm providing sexual abuse prevention for all minors accepted into the prgm. Also offers individual, family & child counseling. FUNDING: Dept of Social Srvs, San Bernardino Mental Health, nonprofit. OFC HRS: M-F 8:30am-5pm. Spanish spoken upon request. ADM REQ: Referrals by SSA or Dept of Mental Health. Accepts Medi-Cal, insurance. SERVES: San Bernardino metro.

EASTFIELD MING QUONG CHILDREN/FAM

Program UPLIFT
572 N. Arrowhead Ave., Ste 200
San Bernardino, CA 92401
(909) 266-2700
(909) 266-2708
(909) 266-2710 FAX

Residential group home for youth ages birth-18 yrs. Long-term care, short-term emerg care, family reunification, mental health srvs, srvs for abused children and wards of the court, substance abuse prgm, accepts emotionally disturbed children. FUNDING: Nonprofit. OFC HRS: M-F 8am-5pm. Spanish spoken. ADM REQ: Referral from Children's Srvs, Dept of Behavioral Health, or Probation Dept. Accepts Medicare, Medi-Cal, insurance, sliding fee scale. SERVES: San Bernardino County.

EDGEWOOD CTR FOR CHILDREN & FAMILIES

1801 Vicente St.
San Francisco, CA 94116-2995
(415) 681-3211
(415) 664-7094 FAX

Residential group home for youth ages 6-16 yrs. Long-term, short-term, & emerg care; non-public school on-site, mental health srvs, family reunification. Serves abused children and wards of the court; also accepts emotionally disturbed children. FUNDING: Nonprofit. OFC HRS: M-F 8:30am-5pm. Spanish spoken. Accepts Medicare, Medi-Cal, insurance, sliding fee scale. SERVES: Calif.

ETTIE LEE YOUTH & FAMILY SERVICES

P.O. Box 339
5146 N. Maine Ave.
Baldwin Park, CA 91706-0339
(626) 960-4861
(626) 337-2621 FAX

Family-style homes for severely emotionally disturbed young men ages 8-18 yrs. 24-hr care by trained staff. Individual & group therapy, gang intervention srvs, independent living skills training, case mgmt, family counseling, therapeutic recreation, 12-Step prgms, substance abuse treatment & on-site school. Licensed treatment foster family agency for boys & girls ages birth-18 yrs. Mental health therapy, case mgmt & family counseling. FUNDING: Nonprofit. OFC HRS: M-F 8am-5pm. Spanish spoken. ADM REQ: County referral for group home & foster care. SERVES: So. Calif.

FAMILY SERVICE AGENCY/SAN BRDO

Crest Forest Family Srvs
P.O. Box 4484
23406 Crest Forest Dr.
Crestline, CA 92325
(909) 338-4689
(909) 338-8230 FAX

Counseling and mental health treatment for child sexual abuse, dysfunctional families. Anger diversion classes, court-ordered batterer's intervention prgm, high-risk youth prgms, limited utility assist. 24-hr suicide and crisis hotline (800) 832-9119. Food bank available F 9am-12noon, 1pm-5:30pm; call ahead to get more info. FUNDING: United Way, client fees, nonprofit. OFC HRS: M-Th 8:30am-6pm. ADM REQ: Varies per prgm. Ages 5 yrs+. Accepts Medi-Cal, sliding fee scale. SERVES: San Bernardino County.

FAMILY SERVICE AGENCY/SAN BRDO

Outpatient Mental Health Srvs
1669 North E Street
San Bernardino, CA 92405
(909) 886-6737
(909) 881-3871 FAX

Info & referral, counseling & mental health treatment for child sexual abuse, domestic violence intervention counseling, dysfunctional families, parenting classes, anger diversion classes, high-risk youth prgms. S.N.A.A.P. (narcotics/alcohol abuse prgm for teens). State ID: 360044AN. FUNDING: United Way, client fees, nonprofit. OFC HRS: M-Th 9am-9pm. Spanish spoken. ADM REQ: Varies per prgm. Ages birth-21 yrs. Accepts Medi-Cal for youth only, sliding fee scale. SERVES: San Bernardino County.

FAMILY SERVICES OF THE DESERT

81-711 Highway 111, Ste 101
Indio, CA 92201
(760) 347-2398
(800) 536-4357
(760) 347-6468 FAX

Family, individual and group counseling. Locations in Indio, Desert Hot Springs and Blythe. FUNDING: United Way, donations, client fees, nonprofit. OFC HRS: M-F 9am-5pm. Eve & weekend by appt. Spanish spoken. SERVES: Coachella Valley.

FIELDS COMPREHENSIVE YOUTH SRVS

8780 19th Street, Ste 196
Rancho Cucamonga, CA 91701
(909) 945-1318
(909) 466-8685

Residential treatment, long-term foster care, emancipation prep, family reunification srvs. Individual, group & family therapy, parenting edu, self-mgmt training, gang intervention, drug abuse treatment, computer training. FUNDING: Private nonprofit. ADM REQ: Males ages 13-17 yrs, who are dependent and/or delinquent minors. SERVES: San Bernardino County.

FIND THE CHILDREN

2656 29th Street, Ste 203
Santa Monica, CA 90405
(888) 477-6721
(800) 843-5678
(310) 314-3169 FAX

Dedicated to the prevention and recovery of missing & abducted children. Srvs include photo & flyer distribution, contact with law enforcement, safety materials, school safety prgms, community outreach prgms & referrals. FUNDING: Nonprofit. OFC HRS: M-F 9am-4pm. Spanish spoken. Free srvs. SERVES: U.S.A.

FIRST CALL FOR HELP

Volunteer Center of Victor Valley
P.O. Box 1992
16692 Mojave Dr.
Victorville, CA 92393
(760) 243-9646
(760) 243-4762 FAX

Info & referral for people seeking srvs or info on community agencies. Interaction with individuals in crisis situations in order to reduce tension and stress, allowing that person to utilize available resources more effectively. FUNDING: Donations, grants, nonprofit. OFC HRS: M-Th 9am-2:45pm. Spanish spoken. SERVES: San Bernardino County.

FRIDAY NIGHT LIVE/ADMIN

Calif Friday Night Live Partnership
P.O. Box 5091
2637 W. Burrel Ave.
Visalia, CA 93278
(559) 733-6496
(559) 737-4231 FAX

This is the admin office that provides tech assist & training for Friday Night Live prgms in Calif. Most chapters are in public schools, but some are affiliated with community groups or faith-based prgms. Also directly responsible for "Teenwork" and "Calif Youth Council." FUNDING: State, govt. OFC HRS: M-F 8am-5pm. Spanish spoken. SERVES: Calif.

FRIDAY NIGHT LIVE/RIVERSIDE CO.

3525 Presley Ave.
Riverside, CA 92507
(951) 782-5004
(951) 682-3576 FAX

Community-based prgms to prevent or reduce alcohol, tobacco and other drug use among youth. FNL is for high school students and Club Live (CL) for junior high students, FNL Kids for grades 4-5. Youth join a chapter at school or community ctr & plan drug-free, fun activities. Prevention prgm has community srv projects, assemblies, etc. FUNDING: Grants, govt, nonprofit. OFC HRS: M-F 8am-5pm. SERVES: Riverside County.

FRIDAY NIGHT LIVE/SAN BERNARDINO CO.

351 N. Mountain View Ave. Rm. 305
San Bernardino, CA 92415-0010
(800) 387-6623
(909) 387-6348 FAX

Friday Night Live/Club Live is a peer prgm designed to prevent alcohol, tobacco and other drug use among teenagers. FUNDING: Govt. OFC HRS: M-F 8am-5pm. Spanish spoken. SERVES: San Bernardino County.

GAY STRAIGHT ALLIANCE NETWORK

National & Statewide
1550 Bryant St., Ste 800
San Francisco, CA 94103
(415) 552-4229
(415) 552-4729 FAX

Independent youth-led organization. Provides support, leadership and training to gay & straight students to end harrassment & discrimination in schools. FUNDING: Nonprofit. ADM REQ: Middle or high school. SERVES: Calif.

GAY, LESBIAN, STRAIGHT EDU NETWORK (GLSEN)

90 Broad St., 2nd Fl.
New York, NY 10004
(212) 727-0135
(212) 727-0254 FAX

Natl org focused on ensuring safe schools for all students. Hosts a wide range of prgms including Day of Silence, No Name Calling Week, and Gay-Straight Alliances. Chapters in Orange & San Diego Counties. Visit (www.glsen.org) for more info. FUNDING: Nonprofit. OFC HRS: M-F 9:30am-5:30pm, EST. Free srvs. SERVES: U.S.A.

GENERATIONS UNITED

1333 H Street, NW, Ste 900
Washington, DC 20005
(202) 289-3979
(202) 289-3952 FAX

Online resource for educating the public & policy makers regarding improvement of the lives of children, youth, & older adults. Aim is to do so through intergenerational collaboration, public policies and prgms. Visit (www.gu.org) to find prgms in your area. SERVES: U.S.A.

GLBT NATIONAL HELP CENTER

2261 Market St., PMB #296
San Francisco, CA 94114
(415) 355-0003
(415) 552-5498 FAX

Hotlines and online chat support for the GLBT population including emotional support with coming out, info on HIV/AIDS, relationships, andsafe sex. Gay & Lesbian National Hotline: (888) 843-4564, email (glnh@glbtnationalhelpcenter.org). Gay & Lesbian Youth Talkline: (800) 246-7743, email (youth@glbtnationalhelpcenter.org). FUNDING: Nonprofit. OFC HRS: M-F 1pm-9pm; Sat 9am-2pm. Free srvs. SERVES: U.S.A.

GUIDING LIGHT HOME FOR BOYS

24618 Ormista Dr.
Moreno Valley, CA 92553
(951) 485-0423
(951) 485-9164 FAX

Two, 6-bed residential treatment facilities for boys ages 14-17 yrs, who are drug/alcohol abusers, youthful offenders, have multiple placement failures or those who need a structured emancipation prgm. Also those who have severe psychological & emotional disturbances. Individual, family & group counseling, drug & alcohol prgm & psychiatric counseling. FUNDING: Nonprofit, govt, donations. OFC HRS: 24 hrs. ADM REQ: Must be referred by DPSS, Probation, CPS clients. SERVES: Imperial, Kern, Riverside, San Bernardino & Ventura Counties.

HANDS ON INLAND EMPIRE

9624 Hermosa Ave.
Rancho Cucamonga, CA 91730
(909) 980-2857
(909) 980-2957 FAX

The alternative sentencing prgm acts as the referral agency for adult and juvenile residents of San Bernardino Co. who are assigned community srv work by the courts or probation depts.

The prgm provides referral, follow-up, monitoring & reports on individuals referred to complete community srv hours. FUNDING: Fees. OFC HRS: M-F 8am-4pm. Spanish spoken. Prgm fee of $75 is charged for each referral payable by money order only. SERVES: San Bernardino County.

HANMI FAMILY COUNSELING CENTER

Formerly Korean American Counseling Ctr
12362 Beach Blvd., Ste 1
Stanton, CA 90680
(714) 892-9910
(714) 892-9927 FAX

Serves the Korean American community. Counseling, referrals, community edu, support groups for gamblers, parenting edu, alternative high school on site. FUNDING: Private for profit. OFC HRS: M-F 9am-5pm. Korean spoken. Sliding fee scale. SERVES: U.S.A.

HANNAH'S CHILDREN'S HOMES

1045 W. Katela Ave., Ste 330
Orange, CA 92867
(714) 516-1077
(866) 736-8434
(714) 516-1080 FAX

Foster and adoption agency provides out-of-home care for abused and neglected children, ages birth-18 yrs. FUNDING: Nonprofit. OFC HRS: M-F 9am-5pm. Spanish spoken. SERVES: L.A., Orange, Riverside, San Bernardino and San Diego Counties.

HANNAH'S CHILDRENS HOMES

9229 Utica Ave., Ste 140
Rancho Cucamonga, CA 91730
(909) 483-2552
(909) 483-2532 FAX

Foster and adoption agency that provides out-of-home care to abused and neglected children, ages birth-18 yrs. FUNDING: Nonprofit. OFC HRS: M-F 9am-5pm. Spanish spoken. SERVES: Riverside, San Bernardino Counties.

HART COMMUNITY HOMES

208 N. Lemon
Fullerton, CA 92832
(714) 526-2729
(714) 526-2653 FAX

Residential treatment for foster care youth ages 13-18 yrs. Treatment model is tailored to meet individual needs. Prgm focuses on emancipation and has a vocational center providing a life skills workforce dev prgm. Also offers Monkey Business Cafe which provides paid work experience in a cafe setting for foster care youth in and emancipating out of the foster care system. Visit (www.hartcommunityhomes.org). FUNDING: Nonprofit. OFC HRS: M-F 9am-5pm. Cafe open M-F 7am-3pm. Spanish, Korean spoken. ADM REQ: Abused and abandoned boys ages 13-18 yrs. SERVES: L.A., Orange & San Bernardino Counties.

HELEN HUNT JACKSON ALT SCHOOL

Hemet Unified School Dist
26400 Dartmouth St.
Hemet, CA 92544
(951) 765-5193
(951) 765-5195 FAX

Independent study prgm for students in grades 6-12. Students must be able to meet work deadlines while working independently. Parental involvement. OFC HRS: M-F 7:30am-3pm.

Spanish spoken. ADM REQ: Student & teacher meetings weekly. SERVES: Hemet USD.

HIGH DESERT CHILD/ADOL/FAM SRVS

High Desert Center
16248 Victor St.
Victorville 92395
(760) 243-7151
(760) 952-1432 FAX

Alcohol & drug prevention and treatment. Outpatient treatment for ages 12 yrs+. Group classes: anger mgmt, parenting, gang avoidance, shoplifting, smoking cessation. Delayed entry of judgement classes as scheduled. Wait: varies. State ID: 360030AN. FUNDING: County, nonprofit. OFC HRS: M-Th 9am-6pm. Spanish spoken. Accepts Medi-Cal. No charge for prevention srvs. Outpatient srvs on a sliding fee scale. SERVES: Victor Valley.

HIGHLANDER CHILDREN'S SRVS

Residential Treatment Program
10001 County Farm Rd.
Riverside, CA 92503
(951) 343-2536
(951) 729-3309 FAX

30-bed residential treatment prgm for sex offenders with on-site school. Prgm serves adjudicated males only, ages 13-18 yrs. Offers AA, NA, Pathways prgm, licensed therapist. FUNDING: Nonprofit. OFC HRS: M-F 8am-4:30pm, 24-hr care. Spanish spoken. SERVES: Riverside, Orange, San Diego, San Bernardino & L.A. Counties.

HILLVIEW ACRES CHILDREN'S HOME

3683 Chino Ave.
Chino, CA 91710
(909) 628-1272
(909) 627-1906 FAX

Residential home for wards of the state. FUNDING: Govt, donation, nonprofit. OFC HRS: M-F 9:00am-5pm. Spanish spoken. ADM REQ: All children must be referred by the Dept of Family Srvs. SERVES: Orange, Riverside & San Bernardino Counties.

INLAND AGENCY

1737 Atlanta, Ste H-5
Riverside, CA 92507
(951) 241-8723
(951) 683-7980 FAX

Challenges of Youth. Adelanto Community Toolbox. HICAP (Health Insurance Counseling and Advocacy Prgm), Desert Sierra Breast Cancer Partnership. Part of a state and nationwide prgm for Medicare beneficiaries. FUNDING: Fed, state, county, fndn, donations, nonprofit. OFC HRS: M-F 8am-5pm. Spanish spoken. Free srvs. SERVES: Riverside, San Bernardino, Inyo, Mono Counties.

INLAND BEHAV & HEALTH SERVICES

Westside Counseling Ctr
1963 North E Street
San Bernardino, CA 92405
(909) 881-6146
(909) 881-0111 FAX

Comprehensive health care, substance abuse, mental health and homeless support srvs. Offers crisis intervention, primary prevention edu, PC-1000 classes, anger mgmt, parenting STEP classes. Perinatal prgm for expectant and parenting mothers who are addicted to drugs with both pre- and post-natal srvs. Provides transportation as well as child care. State ID:

360015AN. FUNDING: Govt, contracts, grants, nonprofit. OFC HRS: M-Th 8am-6pm; F 8am-5pm. Spanish spoken. ADM REQ: Ages 13 yrs+, referrals & walk in. Accepts Medicare, Medi-Cal. SERVES: San Bernardino County.

INLAND VLY DRUG/ALCOHOL RECOVERY

Adolescent Srvs
934 N. Mountain Ave.
Upland, CA 91786
(909) 949-4667
(909) 931-3774 FAX

Outpatient drug and alcohol prgm, anger mgmt, truancy, shoplifting, family component srvs. Also offers domestic violence assist, anger mgmt, parenting edu, and smoking cessation classes for adults. Outpatient counseling srvs for adults, couples, and families. FUNDING: Nonprofit, Calif Dept of Probation. OFC HRS: M-F 8am-5pm; 24-hr facility. SERVES: L.A., Riverside & San Bernardino Counties.

JEFFEREY OWENS COMMUNITY CENTER

Mailing Address
5198 Arlington Ave., Ste 922
Riverside, CA 92504

Promotes the health and well-being of youth and adults by providing support, edu, and advocacy regarding sexual orientation and gender identity. For more information on how to get involved, email (jocc-info@jocc.org). Visit (www.jocc.org). FUNDING: Nonprofit. SERVES: Riverside and San Bernardino Counties.

JOB CORPS INFORMATION HOTLINE

Job Corps Admissions for Women
405 14th Street, Ste 401
Oakland, CA 94612
(510) 832-2549
(510) 832-4352 FAX

Voc & edu training for young women ages 16-24 yrs from low-income families. Dormitory facilities, food, health care, etc. are all free for those involved in the prgm. Women, call number above. Men, call (800) 733-5627. Chinese (415) 981-7835. FUNDING: Govt, nonprofit. OFC HRS: M-F 8am-5pm. Spanish & Chinese spoken. Free srvs. SERVES: U.S.A.

JOBS AND EMPLOYMENT SERVICES

Transition Assistance Service
1637 E. Holt Blvd.
Ontario, CA 91761
(909) 458-9700
(909) 933-6482 FAX

ESP is a special prgm for individuals receiving public assist. The prgm offers edu, training, skills assessment, job search assist, child care, transportation assist, etc. all intended to assist the individual to get off public assist prgm. FUNDING: Govt. OFC HRS: M-F 8:30am-4:30pm. Spanish spoken. Free srvs. SERVES: San Bernardino County.

JULIAN YOUTH ACADEMY

Teen Rescue, Inc.
P.O. Box 2167
Chino, CA 91708
(800) 494-2200
(909) 590-7030
(909) 590-7040 FAX

15-18 month accredited, private, nonprofit Christian residential boarding school prgm for teens in crisis. School is located in Northern California. Separate boys and girls prgms for ages 12-17 yrs. Problems addressed include: poor school peformance, drug and/or alcohol use, sexual promiscuity, defiance, anxiety, anger issues. Aftercare srvs are provided for 6-8 mos. after completion of prgm. FUNDING: Nonprofit, donations. OFC HRS: M-F 9am-5pm. Set fees. SERVES: U.S.A.

JUVENILE JUSTICE CLEARINGHOUSE

Natl Criminal Justice Reference Srvs
P.O. Box 6000
Rockville, MD 20849-6000
(800) 851-3420
(301) 519-5212 FAX

A link between the Office of Juvenile Justice and Delinquency Prev (OJJDP) and the community at-large interested in juvenile justice, delinquency prev and missing and exploited children. The clearinghouse offers publications, references and referrals through an 800 number, conference support and attendance, online resources and other outreach activities. TDD (877) 712-9279 or (301) 712-9279. FUNDING: Govt. SERVES: U.S.A. & internatl.

KNOTTS FAMILY AGENCY

1505 W. Highland Ave., Ste 19
San Bernardino, CA 92411
(909) 880-0600
(909) 473-1918 FAX

Residential care facility providing long-term srvs for pregnant & parenting teens & their infants/toddlers. Srvs to troubled adol girls whose lives are complicated by pregnancy or single parenthood. Also srvs to non-pregnant, abused, neglected or abandoned girls ages 12-17 yrs. Adol girls in juvenile probation or DPSS. Foster care agency, parenting prgm for parents with children ages birth-5 yrs. FUNDING: Private, nonprofit. OFC HRS: 24 hrs, 7 days. SERVES: Riverside, San Bernardino Counties.

L.I.F.T.

Life Is Forever Transitioning
8018 Santa Ana Cyn Rd. 100, Ste 169
Anaheim, CA 92808
(714) 749-4283
(267) 295-2533 FAX

Youth development organization to educate and mentor junior high & high school-aged youth. Basic life skills, college prep, career forums, community outreach. FUNDING: Nonprofit. OFC HRS: M-Th 9am-5pm; F 9am-2pm. SERVES: L.A., Orange and Riverside Counties.

L.U.N.A. RECOVERY

7007 Washington Ave., Ste 240
Whittier, CA 90601
(562) 693-0400
(562) 693-0422 FAX

Services provided to teens and adults. Group and individual sessions, drug testing, parenting, domestic violence, sexual assault & trauma, HIV awareness, STD prevention, parent support groups, family counseling. FUNDING: Nonprofit. OFC HRS: M-Th 9am-7pm; F 9am-5pm; Sat 9am-1pm. Spanish spoken. ADM REQ: Teens ages 12-18 yrs; adults ages 18 yrs+. Accepts Medi-Cal, sliding fee scale. SERVES: L.A. & San Bernardino Counties.

LAWS SUPPORT CENTER

Outpatient Alcohol & Drug Treatment Prgm
2707 W. 54th Street

Los Angeles, CA 90043
(323) 294-5204
(323) 294-4758 FAX

Six month to one year outpatient drug-free prgm. Edu classes; individual group, and family counseling. Based on 12-Step philosophy. Individuals are presented with the knowledge and skills necessary for their recovery. Their family and significant others are given info and guidance to understand and support continued recovery. FUNDING: Nonprofit. OFC HRS: M-F 9am-6pm. ADM REQ: Ages 18 yrs-. Referrals from Dept of Corrections, Dept of Health Srvs, and other community organizations. Free srvs for those with Medi-Cal. SERVES: L.A. & San Bernardino Counties.

LOMA LINDA UNIV PSYCH SRVS CLINIC

11130 Anderson St., Ste 117
Loma Linda, CA 92354
(909) 558-8576
(909) 558-0413 FAX

Specializes in the treatment of children, adolescents, students, adults, couples, families and seniors. Low-cost therapy and assessment srvs. FUNDING: Nonprofit. OFC HRS: M-Th 8am-6pm. Spanish spoken. ADM REQ: Ages 4 yrs+. Fee for srvs. SERVES: San Bernardino, Riverside Counties.

MCKINLEY CHILDREN'S CENTER

762 W. Cypress St.
San Dimas, CA 91773
(909) 599-1227
(909) 592-3841 FAX

Level 12 residential care and non-public school for 44 boys ages 7-15 yrs with serious behavioral and emotional problems related to histories of abuse, neglect and inadequate parenting. Specialized residential treatment prgm is designed to meet individual and family needs. FUNDING: State, county, govt. OFC HRS: M-F 8am-5pm. Spanish spoken. SERVES: So. Calif.

MENTORING PROGRAM

See "Big Brothers/Sisters/Inland"

MENTORING PROGRAM

See "Chino Hills Comm Srvs Dept," "Reach Out West End" and "San Bernardino Child Advocacy"

MENTORING PROGRAM

Turning Points Mentoring Program
21351 Yucca Loma Rd.
Apple Valley, CA 92307
(760) 240-5606
(760) 247-4300 FAX

Mentoring for grades K-5. OFC HRS: M-F 7:30am-5pm. Spanish spoken. ADM REQ: Must be a student at Yucca-Loma Elem. SERVES: Apple Valley.

MENTORING PROGRAM

Community Action Partnership
2038 Iowa Ave., Ste B102
Riverside, CA 92507
(951) 955-4900
(951) 955-6506 FAX

Project LEAD after school prgm for middle school youth offered through the YMCA. In-house pre-apprenticeship prgm for grades 11-12 who are actively enrolled in school. OFC HRS: M-F 8am-5pm. Spanish spoken. Free srvs. SERVES: Riverside County.

MENTORING PROGRAM

San Bernardino Parks & Recreation
555 N. Sierra Way
San Bernardino, CA 92410
(909) 885-1847
(909) 384-5160 FAX

Mentoring for ages 12-19 yrs. OFC HRS: M-F 7:30am-4:30pm. Spanish spoken. SERVES: San Bernardino County.

MENTORING PROGRAM

One 2 One Mentors
16245 Desert Knoll Dr.
Victorville, CA 92392
(760) 245-1997
(760) 245-9774 FAX

Mentoring prgm for at-risk youth. S.T.A.R., Supporting Teens At Risk, is an education program which includes: violence prevention, drug/alcohol prevention and family support services. Onsite and offsite 8- and 12-week programs. FUNDING: Nonprofit. OFC HRS: M-Th 8am-7pm. Spanish spoken. ADM REQ: Ages 10-17 yrs. Free srvs, $10 intake application fee. SERVES: San Bernardino County.

MESA COUNSELING CENTER

San Bernardino Co. Behavorial Health
850 E. Foothill Blvd.
Rialto, CA 92376
(909) 421-9200
(909) 421-9219 FAX

Coordinates srvs for severely emotionally disabled children ages 5-17 yrs who are in residential placement or require intensive treatment. Includes: hospital discharge planning, residential placement, intensive treatment, wilderness prgms, specialized case mgmt, AB3632, assessment and referral, OT & recreational therapy, individual, family and group therapy, medication eval & monitoring, and crisis intervention. Also, eval for conservatorship and residential placement. Continuing care srvs for minors in state hospitals also provided. FUNDING: County, nonprofit. OFC HRS: M-F 8am-5pm. Walk-ins accepted M-F 8am-10am. Outpatient hrs: M-F 8am-2pm. Spanish spoken. ADM REQ: Resident of Rialto or nearby. Accepts Medi-Cal, some insurances. Sliding fee scale used by all state-funded agencies: $0-full cost. Free referrals. SERVES: San Bernardino County.

METH RESOURCES

www.methresources.gov
(916) 324-5523

Visit website to find various resources and prgms in the fight against meth. FUNDING: Govt. SERVES: U.S.A.

MILHOUS CHILDREN'S SERVICES

24077 State Hwy. 49
Nevada City, CA 95959-8519
(530) 265-9057
(530) 292-3803 FAX

Residential group home for boys ages 8-17 yrs. Long-term care, family reunification, mental health srvs, serves abused children and wards of the court, accepts emotionally disturbed children. FUNDING: Nonprofit. OFC HRS: M-F 8am-4:30pm. Spanish spoken. County-paid services. SERVES: Calif.

MISSING CHILDREN INTERNATL, INC.

1905 E. 17th Street, Ste 110

Santa Ana, CA 92705-8628
(714) 542-8083
(800) 339-4357
(714) 210-1163 FAX

State-by-state search for missing persons. 24-hr hotline: (714) 323-6730. FUNDING: Nonprofit. OFC HRS: M-F 8am-5pm. SERVES: U.S.A. & internatl.

MOURNING STAR CENTER, THE
VNA of the Inland Counties
18169 Bear Valley Rd.
Hesperia, CA 92345
(760) 948-7249

Support center for grieving children, their families or caregivers. Also has locations in Palm Desert, Riverside, Banning, and Murrieta. FUNDING: Nonprofit, donations, fndns, corps, grants, fundraising. ADM REQ: Ages 3-18 yrs. Referrals from schools, hospices, hospitals, physicians, volunteers. Free srvs. SERVES: Inland Empire.

MT. SAN JACINTO CHILDREN'S SRVS
950 Ramona Blvd., Ste 2
San Jacinto, CA 92582
(951) 487-2674
(951) 487-2679 FAX

Info & referral srvs, intake assessments, psychiatric evaluations & treatment, case mgmt. In-home behavioral srvs, 5150 evaluations, transportation srvs, individual therapy, group therapy & family therapy to seriously disturbed children & adolescents. FUNDING: County. OFC HRS: M-Th 8am-5pm. Spanish spoken. ADM REQ: Ages birth-18 yrs. Must meet county criteria. Accepts Medi-Cal and Healthy Families. In a crisis, help is available. SERVES: Riverside County.

MT. SAN JACINTO COLLEGE/EOPS
1499 N. State Street
San Jacinto, CA 92583
(951) 487-3295
(951) 654-4812 FAX

EOPS offers info & referral, counseling, edu grants, financial aid for books, transportation assist, mentoring, student work prgm, emerg no-interest loans, transfer fee waiver. CARE is a special EOPS prgm for single parents (all ages) receiving govt financial assist & helps with child care, gas cards & many other srvs. Also prgm for youth ages 16-21 yrs emancipating from foster care or seeking to live independent of their guardians. Wait: approx. 3-4 wks. See website (www.msjc.edu) for more info. FUNDING: Govt. OFC HRS: M-Th 8am-5pm; F 8am-12noon. Spanish spoken. ADM REQ: See website or call for eligibility req. SERVES: Riverside County.

NATL CHILD SAFETY COUNCIL
P.O. Box 1368
4065 Page Ave.
Jackson, MI 49204-1368
(800) 222-1464
(517) 764-3068 FAX

Child safety edu materials & drug prevention provided to law enforcement agencies & schools. FUNDING: Donors, nonprofit. OFC HRS: M-F 8am-4:30pm, EST. SERVES: U.S.A.

NATL CTR/MISSING AND EXPLOITED CHILDREN
699 Prince St.
Alexandria, VA 22314

(800) 843-5678
(703) 224-2150
(703) 224-2122 FAX

Acts as a clearinghouse for missing & exploited children. Activities include assisting in the distribution of photos of missing children. Accepts calls from people who believe they have seen missing children. Families may receive tech assist. Training prgms are offered for law enforcement staff. Assists in locating children worldwide. Also provides an online location (www.cybertipline.com) for reporting Internet child pornography, prostitution, molestation, Internet-related exploitation & child sex tourism. FUNDING: Nonprofit. OFC HRS: 24 hrs, 7 days. Language line available. Publications & child safety brochures available free of charge by calling the hotline. SERVES: U.S.A.

NATL CTR/MISSING/EXPLOIT/CHILDREN
18111 Irvine Blvd.
Tustin, CA 92780
(714) 508-0150
(714) 508-0154 FAX

Safety edu prgm (promotes child safety & confidence), family srvs (advocacy for exploited children & their families), training & speakers. FUNDING: Nonprofit. OFC HRS: M-F 8am-5pm. Spanish spoken. Accepts donations. Free srvs. SERVES: Calif & Western U.S.A.

NATL NETWORK FOR YOUTH
P.O. Box 66492
Washington, DC 20036
(202) 783-7949
(202) 783-7955 FAX

Dedicated to ensuring that young people can be safe and lead healthy, productive lives. Network informs on public policy, educates the public and strengthens the field of youth work. Members provide safety, shelter, counseling, social, health, edu and job related srvs. Promotes positive dev of youth through community srv, peer edu, alcohol and drug free clubs, drama groups, etc. Emphasizes youth and adults working together. Networks with regional, state, community-based agencies and individuals. FUNDING: Members, fndn, donations, nonprofit, govt. OFC HRS: M-F 9am-5pm, EST. Spanish spoken. Free srvs. SERVES: U.S.A.

NATL RUNAWAY SWITCHBOARD
3080 N. Lincoln Ave.
Chicago, IL 60657
(800) 786-2929
(773) 880-9860
(773) 929-5150 FAX

24-hr hotline for youth ages 12-21 yrs and their families. Crisis intervention, info & referral, message delivery and conferencing srvs. Free bus rides home for qualified youth through the Greyhound "Home Free" prgm. FUNDING: Fed, nonprofit. OFC HRS: 24 hrs, 7 days. Access to language line. Free srvs. SERVES: U.S.A.

NEW HOPE/MORENO VALLEY
12818 Heacock St., Ste C-6
Moreno Valley, CA 92553
(951) 247-6542
(951) 247-9819 FAX

Christian counseling center. Serves as a training facility for those in the counseling profession. Psychological testing, child abuse counseling, crisis eval, parenting issues, school problems, teenage issues such as suicide, run-

away, depression, eating disorders and substance abuse, bereavement counseling, adult abuse issues, pain mgmt and a host of other adult counseling needs. FUNDING: Donations, fees, nonprofit. OFC HRS: By appt. ADM REQ: Low income. Accepts insurance in most cases, Victim-Witness Program, Recovery Assistance Foundation. Sliding scale basis upon request. SERVES: So. Calif.

OAK GROVE CENTER
Formerly Oak Grove Institute
24275 Jefferson Ave.
Murrieta, CA 92562
(951) 677-5599
(951) 698-0461 FAX

Residential treatment for children and adols, ages 8-18 yrs, experiencing social, emotional and behavioral disorders, neurological problems, chronic medical problems with concurrent behavioral difficulties, school problems, family dysfunction and secondary alcohol or substance abuse. Partial hospitalization & day treatment. Non-public school on grounds. Also offers an autism center for children with mild to severe autism. FUNDING: Dept of Children's Srvs, school districts, Regional Ctr, nonprofit. OFC HRS: M-F 8am-5pm. ADM REQ: Clinically appropriate for residential or day treatment & funding available. SERVES: So. Calif.

OLIVE BRANCH COUNSELING CTR, INC.
9033 Baseline Rd., Ste H
Rancho Cucamonga, CA 91730
(909) 989-9030
(909) 466-4594 FAX

Counseling services for individuals, families, couples & groups including: anger mgmt, eating disorders, grief recovery, domestic violence, sexual abuse, victims of crime. Pre-marital, divorce recovery, parenting classes. Court certified for anger mgmt, domestic violence, parenting & co-parenting classes. Certified visitation. All programs available for high-risk youth and adults. Locations in Claremont, Riverside, and Rancho Cucamonga. FUNDING: Nonprofit. OFC HRS: M-F 9am-8pm; Sat 9am-5pm. Spanish spoken. Accepts insurance, sliding fee scale. SERVES: San Bernardino County.

OLIVE BRANCH COUNSELING CTR, INC.
4041 Brockton Ave.
Riverside, CA 92501
(951) 369-8534
(951) 369-1145 FAX

Counseling services for individuals, families, couples & groups including: anger mgmt, eating disorders, grief recovery, domestic violence, sexual abuse, victims of crime. Pre-marital, divorce recovery, parenting classes. Court certified for anger mgmt, domestic violence, parenting & co-parenting classes. Certified visitation. All programs available for high-risk youth and adults. Locations in Claremont, Riverside, and Rancho Cucamonga. FUNDING: Nonprofit. OFC HRS: M-F 9am-5pm; Sat 8:30am-5pm. Evening counseling available by appt. Spanish spoken. Accepts insurance, sliding fee scale. SERVES: Riverside.

OLIVE CREST TREATMENT CENTER
555 Technology Ct., Ste 300
Riverside, CA 92507
(951) 686-8500
(951) 369-3037 FAX

Intense residential treatment prgm for adolescents experiencing emotional problems, using a medical model with nursing srvs. Centers are accredited and available to children through most health insurance plans. Occupational therapy, dietitian assessment, individual, group and family therapy. Residential care for boys & girls ages 13-17 yrs. Also licensed as a foster care and adoption agency; recruits, trains, provides respite care & network srvs for foster & adoptive families. This prgm places children ages birth-18 yrs in certified foster homes & provides placement srvs for adoptive families. FUNDING: Grants, nonprofit. OFC HRS: M-F 8:30am-5pm. SERVES: So. Calif.

OLIVE CREST TREATMENT CENTER

Corporate Office
2130 E. 4th Street, Ste 200
Santa Ana, CA 92705
(714) 543-5437
(714) 543-5463 FAX

Residential homes serving children, ages birth-18 yrs, victimized by neglect, abuse and/or abandonment. Full continuum of srvs, child abuse prevention & family intervention. Individual, residential treatment & family-style homes in residential areas. Licensed foster family agency recruits, trains, offers respite care & network for foster families. Also independent living prgm for youth emancipating from foster care prgms. FUNDING: Donations, grants, govt, nonprofit. OFC HRS: M-F 8:30am-5pm. Spanish & Vietnamese spoken. SERVES: So. Calif & San Diego County; also Seattle, Tacoma, Spokane & Las Vegas.

OPERATION SAFEHOUSE

9685 Hayes St.
Riverside, CA 92503
(951) 351-4418
(951) 351-8165 FAX

Short-term, 24-hr shelter for runaways and homeless youth ages 12-17 yrs. Individual, family & group counseling, academic assist, substance abuse edu aftercare, schooling. Transitional living prgm (951) 369-4921. Also operates Safehouse of the Desert in Thousand Palms, (760) 343-3211. FUNDING: Nonprofit. OFC HRS: 24 hrs, 7 days. Spanish spoken. ADM REQ: Max stay 14 days. SERVES: Riverside County.

OPTIMIST YOUTH HOMES/FAMILY SRVS

P.O. Box 41-1076
6957 N. Figueroa St.
Los Angeles, CA 90041-1076
(323) 443-3175
(323) 443-3264 FAX

24-hr residential mental health treatment srvs for male adolescents ages 12-18 yrs. Main campus in Highland Park. Four (2 male, 2 female) 6-bed group homes in L.A. County. Non-public school, foster family agency and adoptions prgms, mental health srvs, after care prgms. Referrals through the courts & probation. Limited pvt placements. Accredited by the Council on Accreditation (C.O.A.). FUNDING: Donation, grants, govt, nonprofit. OFC HRS: M-F 9am-5pm. Spanish, Vietnamese & Farsi spoken. Accepts Medi-Cal. SERVES: Calif.

OUTREACH CONCERN, INC

Counseling Srvs for School Children
2030 E. 4th Street, Ste 237
Santa Ana, CA 92705

(714) 547-1163
(800) 492-2731
(714) 547-4578 FAX

Counseling srvs to children and families in contracting schools in So. Calif. Counselors on-campus at these schools. Individual & family counseling at outreach community clinic, 24-hr crisis line for children, edu & psychological testing srvs. FUNDING: Donations, grants, stipends from schools, nonprofit. OFC HRS: M-F 8am-5pm. Spanish spoken. Sliding fee scale for clinic. SERVES: So. Calif.

PALO VERDE COMMUNITY COLLEGE/EOPS

1 College Dr.
Blythe, CA 92225
(760) 921-5402
(760) 921-3608 FAX

EOPS offers info & referral, counseling, edu grants, financial aid for books, transportation assist, mentoring, student work prgm, emerg no-interest loans, transfer fee waiver. CARE is a special EOPS prgm for single parents (all ages) receiving govt financial assist and helps with children, gas cards and many other srvs. Also prgm for youth ages 16-21 yrs emancipating from foster care or seeking to live independent of their guardians. FUNDING: Govt. OFC HRS: M-F 8am-5pm. Spanish spoken. ADM REQ: Must be full-time student, less than 70 units of college credit, low income and below average score on either English or math placement tests. CARE students must qualify for EOPS and also be receiving govt aid. SERVES: Riverside County.

PAPA DIDOS IDEALS FOUNDATION

1392 Spectrum Dr.
Irvine, CA 92618
(949) 500-3030

Promotes literacy, primarily to underprivileged and at-risk youth. Writes and donates their own books to the cause. Visit (www.papadidos.com) for more info. FUNDING: Nonprofit. OFC HRS: M-F 9am-9pm; Sat, Sun 10am-7pm. Spanish, Mandarin, Japanese, Cantonese, Vietnamese spoken. SERVES: L.A., Orange, and Riverside Counties.

PHOENIX SERVICES

See "San Bernardino Co. Behav Health"

PLANET YOUTH

400 W. Graham Ave.
Lake Elsinore, CA 92530
(951) 471-8415
(951) 245-7627 FAX

Work readiness skills, career exploration, leadership dev, job training & placement in entry level positions, internships, edu srvs for youth. FUNDING: Nonprofit. OFC HRS: M-F 8am-5pm. ADM REQ: Ages 14-21 yrs from low-income families. Must meet eligibility criteria. SERVES: Lake Elsinore, Wildomar, Lakeland Village, Murrieta, Temecula.

POLICE ACTIVITIES LEAGUE/PALM SPRINGS

The Palm Springs Boys & Girls Club
450 S. Sunrise Way
Palm Springs, CA 92262
(760) 318-1226

Local police officers work to provide activities and recreation to youth within the community. Prevention of juvenile crime promotes youth leadership. FUNDING: City. SERVES: Palm Springs.

POLLY KLAAS FOUNDATION

Missing Child Agency
P.O. Box 800
Petaluma, CA 94953
(800) 587-4357
(707) 769-1334
(707) 769-4019 FAX

24-hr hotline to assist parents and families of missing children. Public edu and info about child safety and Internet safety, child ID kits. Advocates for legislation supporting children & a safer community. FUNDING: Nonprofit, donations, corporations. OFC HRS: M-F 8am-5:30pm. Hotline open 24/7. Free srvs. SERVES: U.S.A.

PROVISIONAL EDUCATIONAL SRVS

P.O. Box 7100
2450 Blake St.
San Bernardino, CA 92407
(909) 887-7002
(909) 887-8942 FAX

High school diploma & GED prep classes, Earn & Learn prgm, Upward Bound prgm, summer youth prgms & child care facility. FUNDING: Grants, donations, nonprofit. OFC HRS: M-F 8am-4:30pm. Spanish spoken. SERVES: San Bernardino County.

PUENTE PROJECT

Univ of Calif, Office of the President
300 Lakeside Dr., 7th Fl.
Oakland, CA 94612-3550
(510) 987-9548
(510) 834-0737 FAX

College prep prgm for edu disadvantaged students in Calif. Prgm made up of writing, counseling and mentoring components. Professionals are recruited & trained to serve as mentors. One-yr academic & leadership prgm co-sponsored by the Univ of Calif & Calif Community Colleges. FUNDING: Govt, nonprofit. OFC HRS: M-F 8am-5pm. Spanish spoken. ADM REQ: Must be enrolled in community colleges & high schools served by Puente Project. Free srvs. SERVES: Calif.

RAINBOW PRIDE YOUTH ALLIANCE

P.O. Box 312
985 Kendall Dr., Ste A
San Bernardino, CA 92407

Provides support for LGBT youth. Srvs include support group, outreach, wellness classes and recreational activities. Group for ages 13-20 yrs meets on F from 7pm-10pm. Group for ages 18-25 yrs meets M from 6:30pm-9:30pm. All events are helled at the Gabrielle Mulvane Community Center, 860 Gilbert St., San Bernardino 92404. Email (info@rpya.org) and visit (www.rpya.org). FUNDING: Nonprofit. SERVES: Inland Empire.

RANCHO DAMACITAS

P.O. Box 890326
Temecula, CA 92589
(951) 302-2317
(951) 302-7015 FAX

Residential prgm providing treatment & srvs for juvenile victims of child abuse. Also operates a foster family agency which certifies, trains & supports foster families. FUNDING: State, county, pvt donations. OFC HRS: M-F 8:30am-4:30pm. ADM REQ: Ages 6-18 yrs.

Most children are dependents of the court. SERVES: Orange, Imperial, Riverside, San Bernardino & San Diego Counties.

REACH OUT WEST END

1126 W. Foothill Blvd., Ste 150
Upland, CA 91786-3768
(909) 982-8641
(909) 982-8642 FAX

Science-based drug abuse prevention edu for public schools. Mentoring for at-risk middle school students for pregnancy and drug abuse prevention. PC-1000 drug diversion edu prgm for court-ordered clients. Smoking cessation, parenting classes. FUNDING: County, grants, donations, nonprofit. OFC HRS: M-F 9am-4pm. Spanish spoken. SERVES: West end San Bernardino County.

RESEARCH & TRAINING CTR ON FAMILY FOR PATHWAYS TO POSITIVE FUTURES

Portland State University
P.O. Box 751
1600 S.W. 4th Avenue, Ste 900
Portland, OR 97201
(503) 725-4040
(503) 725-4180 FAX

Supports successful transition for youth and young adults with serious mental health conditions. Srvs include rigorous research, Focal Point (natl publication), and effective training and dissemniation. FUNDING: Govt, grants. OFC HRS: M-F 8am-5pm. Spanish spoken. Most publications free, some mailed at cost. SERVES: U.S.A.

RESIDENTIAL TREATMENT CENTERS

Teen Options
(866) 495-8406

Online referral srvs for parents who need help with defiant teens. Referrals for boarding schools, treatment centers & prgms, therapists, etc. Visit (www.selectown.com). OFC HRS: 24 hrs, 7 days. Free srvs. SERVES: U.S.A.

RIM FAMILY SRVS, INC.

P.O. Box 578
28545 Highway 18
Skyforest, CA 92385
(909) 336-1800
(909) 336-0990 FAX

Individual, group and family counseling, trauma recovery for victims of crime, domestic violence, etc. Community edu prgm. Info & referral; prevention & edu; outpatient counseling; DUI 1st offender & multiple offender (18-month) prgms; outpatient drug & alcohol treatment prgm. PC-1000, strengthening family prgm, mobile resource center, aftercare prgm. State ID: 360036AN. FUNDING: Nonprofit. OFC HRS: M-Th 8am-6pm; F 8am-5pm; Sat 8am-2pm. Spanish spoken. Interpreter as needed. ADM REQ: Counseling for all ages. DUI for ages 16 yrs+. Accepts Medi-Cal for drug/alcohol, sliding fee scale. SERVES: San Bernardino County.

RITA PROJECT, INC.

Mailing Address
2046 Hillhurst Ave.
Los Angeles, CA 90027
(866) 775-7482

Rita (Sanskrit for truth) is a global movement to stop suicide and celebrate life. Devoted to using the arts to help survivors of suicide connect with the power of creation, and in doing so, foster transformation. Prgms offered through studios, workshops & exhibitions. Assist with healing, suicide prev, edu and public awareness on the importance of the arts to mental health. Visit (www.ritaproject.com). Studios are held weekly at the Bergamot Cafe, 2525 Michigan Ave., #A-3, Santa Monica, CA 90404. Please call to register. FUNDING: Nonprofit. OFC HRS: 24 hrs. ADM REQ: Ages 18 yrs+. SERVES: So. Calif.

RIVERSIDE CO. DEPT/MENTAL HEALTH

Substance Abuse Prgm/Indio
83-912 Avenue 45, Ste 9
Indio, CA 92201
(760) 347-0754
(760) 347-8507 FAX

Srvs to substance abusers and their families. Outpatient treatment, edu, counseling & referral, prevention edu, detox. Wait: varies. Adol prgm. State ID: 330023EN. FUNDING: Nonprofit. OFC HRS: M-Th 8am-6pm. Spanish spoken. ADM REQ: Riverside County residents. Accepts Medi-Cal, sliding fee scale. SERVES: Coachella Valley.

RIVERSIDE CO. DEPT/MENTAL HEALTH

Administrative Office
P.O. Box 7549
4095 County Circle Dr.
Riverside, CA 92513
(951) 358-4500
(951) 358-4513 FAX

Overall planning, implementation, direction, co-ordination and eval of the Dept of Mental Health prgms in Riverside County. Treatment for adults: residential, outpatient, day care, socialization ctrs, crisis srvs, case mgmt, continuing care, etc. Children's prgms: outpatient, case mgmt, foster home placement, etc. Also main admin office for drug abuse and alcohol control prgms. No actual srvs available at this location. FUNDING: Govt. Spanish spoken. Accepts Medi-Cal SERVES: Riverside County.

RIVERSIDE CO. MENTAL HEALTH

Indio Mental Health Srvs
47-825 Oasis St.
Indio, CA 92201
(760) 863-8455
(760) 863-8587 FAX

Admin office for Desert Region Mental Health Srvs. Plans, coordinates & oversees several mental health prgms in Eastern Riverside County. Outpatient & residential prgms for severely mentally ill or severe crisis (suicidal). FUNDING: Govt. OFC HRS: M-Th 8am-6pm. Srvs for crisis or severely ill 24 hrs. Spanish spoken. Accepts Medi-Cal, sliding fee scale. SERVES: Desert & Eastern Riverside County.

RIVERSIDE CO. MENTAL HEALTH

Children's Treatment Srvs
9990 County Farm Rd., Ste 5
Riverside, CA 92503
(951) 358-4840
(951) 358-4848 FAX

Intensive prgms designed for children who need more intervention than a one to two hour outpatient prgm. Designed to increase coping skills and reduce their symptomology. FUNDING: Govt. OFC HRS: M-Th 8am-5:30pm. Spanish spoken. ADM REQ: Ages 5-18 yrs. Accepts Medi-Cal, Healthy Kids. SERVES: City of Riverside.

RIVERSIDE CO. MENTAL HEALTH

Children's Case Management
9707 Magnolia Ave.
Riverside, CA 92503
(951) 358-6858
(951) 687-3478 FAX

Case mgmt srvs for seriously emotionally disturbed adol & children ages 6-18 yrs. Includes screening, referral, placement and follow-up for minors in residential and hospital treatment. FUNDING: Govt. OFC HRS: M-Th 8am-6pm. Spanish spoken. ASL available. ADM REQ: Pre-eval required. Accepts Medi-Cal. Sliding fee scale. SERVES: Riverside County.

RIVERSIDE CO. OFFICE/EDUCATION

Student Prgms & Srvs
P.O. Box 868
3939 13th Street
Riverside, CA 92502
(951) 826-6436
(951) 826-6906 FAX

Counseling, mentoring and outreach component. 24 hrs of parent edu provided to males and females. Emphasis is on male responsibility; issues such as: health, birth, finances, incarceration, child abuse, foster youth srvs, tutoring, communication, discipline, employment prep. FUNDING: Nonprofit. OFC HRS: M-F 8am-5pm. Spanish spoken. Free srvs. SERVES: Riverside County.

RIVERSIDE CO. PROBATION DEPT

Youth Accountability Board
4168 12th Street
Riverside, CA 92501
(951) 275-8783
(951) 275-8784 FAX

Mentoring prgm is one of several youth prgms available. Team mentoring and one-to-one. OFC HRS: M-F 8am-5pm. ADM REQ: At-risk youth, and 1st time offenders. SERVES: Riverside County.

RIVERSIDE CO. PUBLIC HEALTH DEPT

Child Health & Disability Prev CHDP
P.O. Box 7600
10769 Holve Ave., Ste 210
Riverside, CA 92513-7600
(800) 346-6520
(951) 358-5481
(951) 358-5002 FAX

Well-child check-ups to children under age 21 yrs. Physical exam, dental assessment, nutritional assessment, vision & hearing screening, blood & urine testing, TB testing, immunizations, and health edu referrals for diagnosis & treatment. Children up to age 19 yrs who do not qualify for Medi-Cal may qualify for CHDP srvs depending on family size and income. Srvs offered at all county clinics and 120 CHDP providers. FUNDING: Govt. OFC HRS: M-Th 8am-5:30pm. ADM REQ: Children who have Medi-Cal and are not enrolled in a Medi-Cal managed care prgm. Free srvs. SERVES: Riverside County.

RIVERSIDE CO. PUBLIC HEALTH DEPT

Childhood Lead Poisoning Prev Prgm
P.O. Box 7600
10769 Holve, Ste 210
Riverside, CA 92503
(800) 346-6520
(951) 358-5481
(951) 358-5002 FAX

Community and school edu & presentations regarding the dangers of lead poisoning, sources of lead, importance of lead testing and case mgmt of lead-poisoned children. FUNDING: Govt. OFC HRS: M-Th 8am-5pm. ADM REQ: Directed to families with children ages birth-6 yrs and children diagnosed with lead poisoning. Free srvs. SERVES: Riverside County.

RIVERSIDE COMMUNITY COLLEGE/EOPS
4800 Magnolia Ave.
Riverside, CA 92506-1293
(951) 222-8045
(951) 222-8046 FAX

EOPS offers info & referral, counseling, edu grants, financial aid for books, transportation assist, mentoring, student work prgm. CARE is a special EOPS prgm for single parents (all ages) receiving govt financial assist & helps with child care, gas cards & many other srvs. Also offer prgm for youth ages 16-21 yrs emancipating from foster care or seeking to live independent of their guardians. FUNDING: Govt. OFC HRS: M-W, F 8am-4pm; Th 8am-5:45pm. Summer hrs: M-W 8am-4pm; Th 8am-4:50pm. Spanish, Vietnamese spoken. ADM REQ: Must be full-time student, less than 70 units of college credit, low income & below average score on either English or math placement tests. CARE students must qualify for EOPS and also be receiving govt aid. SERVES: Riverside County.

RIVERSIDE COMMUNITY HEALTH FNDN
4445-A Magnolia Ave.
Riverside, CA 92501
(951) 788-3471
(951) 788-3589 FAX

Offers the S.H.A.R.P. prgm for seniors which provides monthly heath edu classes/screening assessments. Several prgms for at-risk teens including pregnancy prevention, STD edu, peer-to-peer groups, and support services. Also offers pediatric dental clinics. FUNDING: Nonprofit. Free srvs. SERVES: Riverside Co.

RIVERSIDE RECOVERY RESOURCES
Admin Office
600 3rd Street, Ste C
Lake Elsinore, CA 92530
(951) 674-5354

Alcohol & drug abuse recovery prgms, parenting classes, DUI prgm, counseling & speaker's bureau. 38-bed residential facility for women with children in Hemet. 18-bed residential men's center & sober living in Hemet. Outpatient centers in Riverside, Lake Elsinore & Perris. Adol outpatient facilities in Lake Elsinore & Perris. State ID: 330009ON. FUNDING: Nonprofit. OFC HRS: M-F 9am-7pm; Sat 6am-12noon. Spanish spoken in Perris office. Accepts pvt pay. Sliding fee scale. SERVES: Riverside, Lake Elsinore, Temecula, Moreno Valley, Perris, Hemet, San Jacinto & nearby.

ROP/SAN BRNDO CO. SUPT OF SCHOOLS
Regional Occupational Prgm
144 N. Mt. View Ave.
San Bernardino, CA 92408
(909) 252-4550
(909) 252-4565 FAX

Guidance and instructional prgms for students to enter or re-enter the job market, change careers, or seek advancement. Career guidance, on-the-job internships and job placement assist. Certificates of competency in different employment areas. Walk in. FUNDING: State. OFC HRS: M-F 7:30am-4:30pm. Spanish spoken. ADM REQ: Ages 16 yrs+ and interested in career training. Free srvs, except for some materials fees. SERVES: San Bernardino County.

S.A.F.E./SUBSTANCE ABUSE/ED
Center for Drug Free Communities
14252 Culver Dr., Ste A-261
Irvine, CA 92604
(714) 505-4692
(714) 505-4887 FAX

S.A.F.E. (Substance Abuse For Educators) offers levels I & II of training for professionals & the community supporting the dev and implementation of successful drug & alcohol prevention & intervention prgms. Conducts PAL (Peer Assistance Leadership) camps. Focus is on conflict resolution, ATOD prevention. Call to arrange workshop. FUNDING: Nonprofit. OFC HRS: M-F 8am-6pm. Spanish spoken. SERVES: So. Calif.

SAFE KIDS INLAND EMPIRE COALITION
Loma Linda Univ Children's Hospital
11234 Anderson St.
Loma Linda, CA 92354
(909) 558-8118

Goal is to protect children ages birth-14 yrs from accidental injuries. Prgms include injury prevention prgms, child passenger safety events, legislative advocacy and professional networking. Also offers Drowning Prevention Network that meets the 4th W of each month from 9am-10am at various sites in the community. Email (kelly.donaldson@cityofrc.us) for more info about the Drowning Prevention Network and (kpatrick@llu.edu) for general info. SERVES: Inland Empire.

SAN BERNARDINO CHILD ADVOCACY
555 North D Street, Ste 100
San Bernardino, CA 92405
(909) 881-6760
(909) 881-6764 FAX

Recruits, screens and trains volunteers, CASA (Court Appointed Special Advocates), guardians advocate for the best interests of abused children in the court system. Volunteers provide advocacy srvs for abused children during court process. Mentoring prgms. Wait: varies depending on number of volunteers available. FUNDING: Grants, donations. OFC HRS: M-F 8am-5pm. Spanish spoken ADM REQ: Children must be in the juvenile court system. Free srvs to children. SERVES: San Bernardino County.

SAN BERNARDINO CO. BEHAV HEALTH
Phoenix Community Counseling
820 E. Gilbert St.
San Bernardino, CA 92415-0920
(909) 387-7200

Crisis and referral srvs, assessment, individual, family, group, psychological testing. Intensive case mgmt, home contacts, rehab training. Wait: max of 2 hrs for assessment. Walk in or call. FUNDING: County agency, pvt insurance. OFC HRS: M-F 8am-5pm. Assessment hrs vary on appt. Spanish spoken. Hearing-impaired interpreter. Other languages by request. ADM REQ: Some limitations based upon severity of problems. Must have ID. Accepts Medi-Cal.

Sliding fee scale. Free referrals to community resources. SERVES: San Bernardino County.

SAN BERNARDINO CO. HUMAN SRVS SY
Children's Srvs/Child Protective Srvs
56311 Pima Trail
Yucca Valley, CA 92284
(760) 228-5300
(800) 827-8724
(760) 228-5321 FAX

24-hr emerg response, protective srvs for children in danger of abuse, exploitation, neglect, etc. Call to report incidents or suspicions of child abuse or neglect. Full range of emerg srvs including shelter and investigations. OFC HRS: M-F 8am-5pm. Spanish spoken. SERVES: Morongo Basin.

SAN BERNARDINO CO. PUBLIC HEALTH
Administrative Office
385 Arrowhead Ave.
San Bernardino, CA 92415-0120
(909) 387-7020
(909) 387-6228 FAX

Administers branch offices at various locations throughout San Bernardino Co. including: Barstow, Big Bear, Chino, Fontana, Joshua Tree, Needles, Ontario, Redlands, San Bernardino, Trona, Victorville & Twin Peaks. Edu, alcohol & drug prevention, animal control, birth & death certificates, Calif Children's Srvs, epidemiology, family planning, high-risk infant prgm, immunizations, nutrition, WIC, public health nursing, school health, senior health, VD control, TB, HIV/AIDS control. TDD (909) 397-6354. OFC HRS: M-F 8am-5pm; clinic hrs may vary. SERVES: San Bernardino County.

SAN BERNARDINO CO. PUBLIC HEALTH
California Children's Srvs
150 Carousel Mall
San Bernardino, CA 92415
(909) 387-8400
(909) 387-8401 FAX

Assists families with payment of medical bills for children ages birth-21 yrs, who have serious injury, disability or illness. Also provides PT & OT. FUNDING: Govt. OFC HRS: M-F 8am-5pm. Spanish spoken. ADM REQ: Must meet medical financial and residential criteria. SERVES: San Bernardino County.

SAN BERNARDINO CO. PUBLIC HEALTH
Health Nursing
120 Carousel Mall
San Bernardino, CA 92415-0048
(800) 722-3777
(909) 388-0401 FAX

Services include: physical, psychosocial and environmental assessments with focus on capacity to meet own needs and needs of the child. Info & referral and dev of support systems. Call first and referral will be sent out. FUNDING: County. OFC HRS: M-F 8am-5pm. Spanish spoken. ADM REQ: High-risk for child abuse. SERVES: San Bernardino County.

SAN BERNARDINO CO. PUBLIC SOC SRVS
See "San Bernardino Co. Human Srvs Sy"

SAN BERNARDINO VLY COLLEGE/EOPS
701 S. Mt. Vernon Ave.
San Bernardino, CA 92410-2798
(909) 384-4412
(909) 888-6511
(909) 888-3071 FAX

EOPS offers info & referral, counseling, edu grants, financial aid for books, transportation assist, mentoring, student work prgm, emerg no interest loans, transfer fee waiver. CARE is a special EOPS prgm for single parents (all ages) receiving govt financial assist & helps with child care, gas cards & many other srvs. Also offer prgm for youth ages 16-21 yrs emancipating from foster care or seeking to live independent of their guardians. FUNDING: Govt. OFC HRS: M-F 8am-5pm. Spanish spoken. ADM REQ: Must be full-time student, less than 70 units of college credit, low income & below average score on either English or math placement tests. CARE students must qualify for EOPS and also be receiving govt aid. SERVES: San Bernardino County.

SOUTH COAST COMMUNITY SRVS
San Bernardino Co. Srvs Office
2930 Inland Empire Blvd., Ste 120
Ontario, CA 92764
(909) 980-6700

Provides life-essential srvs to troubled children, youth and families. Offers 4 group homes for abused, neglected and abandoned children ages 10-18 yrs and 2 group homes for young adults ages 18-25 yrs in need of short-term assist. Wraparound prgm offers family intervention srvs. Children's intensive srvs prgm provides outpatient counseling for individuals, children, teens and their families. Eval, assessment, testing, therapy, medication support, crisis intervention, case mgmt. Offers mental health clinics in Redlands, (909) 792-0747 & Yucaipa, (909) 790-0210. FUNDING: Nonprofit. Accepts Medi-Cal and pvt pay; sliding fee scale available. SERVES: San Bernardino County.

SPAN CALIFORNIA
Suicide Prevention Advocacy Network
P.O. Box 235260
Encinitas, CA 92023
(760) 753-4565

Creates awareness regarding suicide prevention. Advocates legislative policy. No direct srvs. Volunteers work throughout the state speaking at events & conferences. Visit (www.span-california.org). FUNDING: State. SERVES: Calif.

STARLIGHT CHILDREN'S FOUNDATION
5757 Wilshire Blvd., Ste M-100
Los Angeles, CA 90036
(310) 479-1212
(800) 315-1212
(310) 479-1235 FAX

When a child or teenager has a serious medical condition, everyone in the famliy is affected. The Starlight Fndn has dedicated itself to helping seriously ill children and their families cope with pain, fear and isolation through entertainment, edu, and family activities. Starlight's prgms have been proven to distract children from their pain, help them better understand and manage their illness. Connects families facing similar challenges so that no one feels alone. Outpatient, hospital-based and web offerings. To learn more, visit (www.starlight.org). FUNDING: Nonprofit. OFC HRS: M-F 8am-5pm. Accepts donations. SERVES: U.S.A., Canada, Australia, UK & Japan.

STARSHINE TREATMENT CENTERS
1255 E. Highland Ave., Ste 216
San Bernardino, CA 92404

(909) 882-7978
(909) 882-1282 FAX

Residential treatment for behaviorally and emotionally disturbed boys ages 12-17 yrs. Prgm designed specifically for sexual perpetrators. Emphasis on psychological treatment utilizing group & individual therapy modalities. FUNDING: Nonprofit. OFC HRS: M-F 8am-5pm, treatment ctr 24 hrs. Spanish spoken. ADM REQ: Most referrals are made by SSA or Probation Dept. SERVES: Calif.

STOMP OUT BULLYING
www.stompoutbullying.org
(877) 602-8559

Anti-bullying and cyberbullying prgm for kids and teens. Website provides info and prevention techniques regarding bullying. FUNDING: Nonprofit. SERVES: U.S.A.

STUDENT ASSISTANCE PROGRAM
Corona-Norco USD Pupil Srvs
2820 Clark Ave.
Norco, CA 92860-1903
(951) 736-5106
(951) 736-8202 FAX

Edu, prevention, intervention, support and referral srvs by trained school and community personnel for students in the Corona/Norco area. Prgms include: after school activities & clubs; parenting edu workshops; student conflict resolution and mediation; Healthy Families/Medi-Cal for Families application assist; school-aged parenting and infant care; peer assist; drug insight and general support groups; community prevention and edu efforts through U.N.I.T.Y. coalition. FUNDING: SDFSC & TUPE, general fund, donations, AB1113. OFC HRS: M-F 8am-4:30pm. Spanish spoken. ADM REQ: Must live in Corona or Norco school district area or your group must serve this area. Free srvs. SERVES: Corona & Norco school district boundaries.

SUICIDE PREVENTION CENTER
(877) 727-4747
(310) 398-5690 FAX

24-hr crisis hotline. AAS Certified. Crisis counseling & referrals to resources. Also Survivors After Suicide bereavement support groups to help cope with loss. Prevention speakers for schools & other community outreach. Toll-free (877) 727-4747 for L.A. & Orange Counties only. FUNDING: Govt, United Way, donations, nonprofit. OFC HRS: 24 hrs, 7 days. Free srvs. SERVES: So. Calif.

TEEN CHALLENGE INTERNATIONAL
Orange County Headquarters
P.O. Box 236
418 S. Main St.
Santa Ana, CA 92702
(714) 835-8822
(714) 835-8825 FAX

Free 1-year adult residential drug & alcohol rehab. Christian discipleship prgm. Learning center, computer lab, homework help M-F 2pm-5pm for jr. high & elem students; M-F 6pm-8pm for high school students. Call Frank Jimenez at (714) 836-7140. Gang & drug intervention & prevention prgm for teens Tu 7pm and for adolescents Sat 10am-12pm. TC New Creation Choir Outreach Prgm available for songs, testimonies & presentations in local churches. Anti-gang & drug presentations in lo-

cal schools. Speakers for civil groups. FUNDING: Nonprofit. OFC HRS: M-F 8:30am-5pm. ADM REQ: Sign up & interviews required. Free srvs. SERVES: U.S.A.

TEEN CHALLENGE INTERNATL/SO CALIF
5445 Chicago Ave.
Riverside, CA 92507
(951) 682-8990
(951) 682-3754 FAX

One-year residential drug and alcohol treatment prgm for men ages 18 yrs+, Christian structure. Wait: 1-2 weeks. Eight sites in So Calif. FUNDING: Nonprofit. OFC HRS: M-F 8:30am-5pm. ADM REQ: Sincere desire to change lifestyle. Free srvs. SERVES: So. Calif.

TEEN RESCUE, INC.
Family Advocate Counseling
P.O. Box 2167
11800 Central Ave., Ste 121
Chino, CA 91710
(800) 494-2200
(909) 590-7030
(909) 590-7040 FAX

Christian faith-based agency specializing in working with adols and their families. Offers child, adol, individual, couple, and family therapy dealing with issues like adoption, anger, communication, depression, divorce, family issues, and anxiety. FUNDING: Nonprofit. OFC HRS: M-F 9am-5pm, evenings by appt. Sliding fee scale from $5 to $100. Insurance not accepted. SERVES: San Bernardino, Riverside, and L.A. Counties.

THE 'I AM' FOUNDATION
7825 Fay Ave., Ste 200
La Jolla, CA 92037
(619) 297-7010

Gifts books and music to children and adults world-wide to build their self-esteem and promote literacy. Also works with children in private & public schools and hospitals within the U.S. FUNDING: Nonprofit. Free srvs. Donations accepted. SERVES: Internatl.

THE ERIC ALLEN GROUP
P.O. Box 4975
Cerritos, CA 90703
(866) 217-0777

Leadership dev, college prep prgm, social skills prgms, life coaching & mentoring for foster care and at-risk youth and young adults. FUNDING: Nonprofit. OFC HRS: M-F 8am-5pm; Sat 9am-12pm. SERVES: Calif.

THE OPHELIA PROJECT
The JFK Foundation
73-555 San Gorgonio Way
Palm Desert, CA 92260
(760) 776-1600
(760) 862-9898

Mentoring prgm matches middle & high school girls with successful women, who provide guidance and support. FUNDING: Nonprofit. OFC HRS: M-F 8am-5pm. Annual membership $35. SERVES: Riverside County.

THE TREVOR PROJECT
Trevor Helpline
8704 Santa Monica Blvd., Ste 200
West Hollywood, CA 90069
(866) 488-7386
(310) 271-8845
(310) 271-8846 FAX

24-hr toll-free helpline for gay and questioning teens. Counseling for youth ages 25 yrs or younger. Visit (www.thetrevorproject.org) for resources, suicide warning signs, events, etc. Ages 25 yrs and younger call, (800) 246-7743; for ages 25 yrs+ call, (888) 843-4564. FUNDING: Nonprofit. SERVES: U.S.A.

TRANS YOUTH FAMILY ALLIES

P.O. Box 1471
Holland, MI 49422
(888) 462-8932

Partners with educators, srv providers, and communities to develop supportive environments in which gender may be expressed and respected. Edu prgms, online forums, speaker's bureau, and support for parents of trans children. FUNDING: Nonprofit. SERVES: U.S.A.

UCLA PARENT TRAINING PRGM

Friendship Prgm
300 UCLA Medical Plaza
Los Angeles, CA 90095-6967
(310) 825-0142
(310) 267-0378 FAX

Teaches parents easy, effective techniques to increase cooperation and reduce conflict in the home and at school. Small classes or individual sessions. Also 12-week social skills training for youth in grades 1-6 who have difficulty making & keeping friends. FUNDING: Govt. OFC HRS: M-F 9am-5pm. Accepts insurance, regional center funding. Some free research studies. SERVES: So. Calif.

UPLAND COMMUNITY COUNSELING

934 N. Mountain Ave., Ste C
Upland, CA 91786-3659
(909) 579-8100
(909) 579-8149 FAX

Outpatient mental health srvs for all ages. Psychiatric evaluations, school-based prevention prgm, support groups. Walk-ins on Tu-Th 8am-10am for those with no insurance. For Medi-Cal, call and make an appt. FUNDING: Govt. OFC HRS: M-F 8am-5pm. Spanish, Vietnamese spoken. Accepts Medi-Cal, sliding fee scale. SERVES: San Bernardino County.

URBAN EDUCATIONAL PARTNERSHIP

1055 W. 7th Street, Ste 200
Los Angeles, CA 90017
(213) 622-5237
(213) 629-5288 FAX

Edu opportunities for students in high needs schools. Partners with teachers, principals, parents, edu & community leaders by providing training & dev in restructuring schools to create more effective teaching & learning. Separate prgm for children ages birth-5 yrs. Offers parent edu, assist, workshops, and support groups. FUNDING: Nonprofit. OFC HRS: M-F 8:30am-5pm. Free srvs. SERVES: U.S.A.

VALLEY STAR CHILDREN & FAMILY SRVS

1585 South D Street, Ste 101
San Bernardino, CA 92408
(909) 388-2222
(909) 388-2220 FAX

Mental health srvs for troubled children, adolescents and families. In-home, clinic-based & school-based srvs. FUNDING: County. OFC HRS: M-F 8:30am-4:30pm. ADM REQ: Referrals from SB County Dept of Behavioral Health, Children's Srvs, Probation, foster family agencies, schools, counselors, family. Accepts Medi-Cal only. SERVES: San Bernardino County.

VICTOR VLY COMM COLLEGE/EOPS

18422 Bear Valley Rd
Victorville, CA 92392-5849
(760) 245-4271
(760) 951-9225 FAX

EOPS offers info & referral, counseling, edu grants, financial aid for books, transportation assist, mentoring, student work prgm, emerg no-interest loans, transfer fee waiver. CARE is a special EOPS prgm for single parents (of all ages) receiving govt financial assist & helps with child care, gas cards & many other srvs. Prgm for youth ages 16-21 yrs emancipating from foster care or seeking to live independent of their guardians. FUNDING: Govt OFC HRS: M-F 8:30am-5pm. Spanish spoken. ADM REQ: Must be full-time student, less than 70 units of college credit, low income & below average score on either English or math placement tests. CARE students must qualify for EOPS and also be receiving govt aid. SERVES: San Bernardino County.

VILLAGE COUNSELING

Breaking Free
73302 Highway 111
Palm Desert, CA 92260
(760) 773-0669
(760) 773-0569 FAX

Outpatient drug & alcohol treatment prgm, parenting classes, marriage & family counseling, adol and individual counseling, anger mgmt, trauma & abuse counseling, life transitions, etc. State ID: 330052AP. FUNDING: Nonprofit. OFC HRS: Tu-F 9am-5pm. ADM REQ: Open to all ages SERVES: Riverside County.

WEST END FAMILY COUNSELING

Headquarters & Clinic
855 N. Euclid Ave.
Ontario, CA 91762
(909) 983-2020
(909) 983-6847 FAX

Outpatient mental health psychotherapy for adolescents, children and adults. Individual, family and group therapy. School-based counseling prgm, parent edu, elder outreach, info and referral. FUNDING: United Way, DBH contract, fees, nonprofit. OFC HRS: M 9am-8pm; Tu 9am-7pm; W 9am-6pm; Th 9am-5pm. Spanish spoken. Accepts Medi-Cal sliding fee scale. SERVES: West Valley of San Bernardino County.

WESTCARE FOUNDATION, INC.

Admin Office
900 Grier Dr.
Las Vegas, NV 89119
(702) 385-2090
(702) 658-0480 FAX

Various srvs offered for the edu, prevention and treatment of alcohol/drug abuse. Counseling, referrals, runaway youth emerg shelter, civil protective custody, detox, residential and day treatment. HIV/AIDS case mgmt. FUNDING: Donations, grants, contracts, nonprofit. OFC HRS: M-F 8am-5pm. Spanish spoken. Sliding fee scale. SERVES: Calif.

WESTSIDE CHILD/ADULT TRTMT CTR

See "San Bernardino Co. Behav Health"

WISR MINISTRIES, INC.

13800 Heacock St., Ste C242
Moreno Valley, CA 92553
(951) 897-5560
(951) 653-9084 FAX

WISR is an outpatient facility that specializes in spiritual recovery. Individual and group counseling for substance abuse, anger mgmt, domestic violence, sexual assault. Parenting edu. Intervention, prevention for teens. FUNDING: Nonprofit, donations. OFC HRS: W, F 12noon-8pm; Sat 10am-6pm. More hours likely to be added. Spanish spoken. ADM REQ: No one will be discriminated against based on disability, religion, sexual orientation, race or ability to pay. Counseling fee based on sliding scale. Accepts Drug Medi-Cal and Medi-Cal. SERVES: Riverside, Moreno Valley, Perris.

WWW.ADVOCATESFORYOUTH.ORG

2000 M Street, NW, Ste 750
Washington, DC 20036
(202) 419-3420
(202) 419-1448 FAX

Informational website aimed at teens on STDs, sex edu, and pregnancy prevention. FUNDING: Nonprofit. Free srvs. SERVES: U.S.A.

WWW.INCRISIS.NET

Online Behavioral Screening & Reports
965 NE Wiest Way, No. 2
Bend, OR 97701

Online mental health screening software that generates reports with analysis and treatment suggestions for teens who may have mental or addictive disorders. Reports are used to share with professionals in seeking help for troubled youth. Free public srv for parents, caregivers, educators, and youth professionals. Contact agency via website. FUNDING: Nonprofit, Mentor Research Institute. SERVES: U.S.A.

WWW.TALKINGWITHKIDS.ORG

(800) 244-5344

A natl initiative website in partnership with Children Now & the Kaiser Family Fndn to encourage parents to talk to their children earlier and more often about drugs, alcohol, violence, HIV/AIDS & sex. Guide booklets can be downloaded from the site (English & Spanish), also publishes a quarterly e-mail newsletter. FUNDING: Nonprofit. SERVES: U.S.A.

WWW.TEENGETGOING.COM

(866) 435-7999
(408) 918-2256 FAX

Teen website for teens to talk to other teens about drug/alcohol abuse. Help for teens who are using or considering using or who are in aftercare and need help with relapse prevention. Treatment srvs available through partnering facilities. Teens must have authorization from a parent or guardian. Visit (www.teengetgoing.com). SERVES: U.S.A.

YOUNG VISIONARIES

Youth Leadership Academy
1616 North D Street
San Bernardino, CA 92405
(909) 881-3382
(909) 881-3385 FAX

Prgms provided to low income, at-risk youth. Mentoring, leadership dev, after school tutoring. Youth violence prevention, healthy options for teens, youth employment dev, A.R.T.S. for youth, C.U.T.T. (Career, University, Technology Training). FUNDING: Nonprofit, donations. OFC HRS: M-F 1pm-7pm; Sat 9am-1pm. Spanish spoken. Accepts private pay. SERVES: San Bernardino County.

YOUTH CHANGE
Problem Kid-Problem Solver
275 N. 3rd Street
Woodburn, OR 97071-4705
(800) 545-5736
(503) 982-7910 FAX

Online info & resources for solving troubled youth problems & offering motivational materials, workshops. Toll-free number & online helpline for professional youth workers. Internet info & materials available for general public. Continuing edu workshops conducted for teachers & youth professionals around the country. Visit (www.youthchg.com). OFC HRS: 24 hrs. Some free resources. Fees for materials and workshops. SERVES: U.S.A.

4-H CLUB
Univ of Calif Coop Ext
777 E. Rialto Ave.
San Bernardino, CA 92415
(909) 387-2171
(909) 387-2179
(909) 387-3306 FAX

Sponsors clubs in city, mountain and desert communities of San Bernardino Co. Activities include: hands-on edu projects in camping, nutrition, crafts, science, animal care, etc. Call first. FUNDING: Fed, state, county. OFC HRS: M-Th 8am-4:30pm. Limited Spanish spoken. ADM REQ: Ages 5-19 yrs. Enrollment fees vary. SERVES: San Bernardino County.

4-H CLUB/RIVERSIDE COUNTY
Univ of Calif Coop Ext-Riverside Co.
21150 Box Springs Rd., Ste 202
Moreno Valley, CA 92557-8718
(951) 683-6491
(951) 788-2615 FAX

Community-based clubs offering a wide variety of edu projects and activities for youth ages 5-19 yrs. 4-H clubs are lead by adult volunteers who are screened and oriented. Annual prgm fee approx $25 covers accident insurance, newsletter, awards, incentives prgms & defrays the cost of camps & training prgms for leaders & youth. Additional offices in Indio (760) 863-8293, fax (760)775-0600; Blythe (760) 921-7884, fax (760) 921-7887. FUNDING: USDA, state, county. OFC HRS: M-F 9am-5pm. Spanish spoken. SERVES: Riverside County.

A.Y.S.O.
See "American Youth Soccer/AYSO"

ABILITYFIRST/CLAREMONT CTR
480 S. Indian Hill Blvd.
Claremont, CA 91711
(909) 621-4727
(909) 624-8388 FAX

Center offers after school prgms for children & adults with physical & dev disabilities. Prgms include: socialization, recreational, & dev activities. Weekend recreation prgm offered for adults ages 18 yrs+ on F nights & Sat mornings. Aquatic therapy available M-F. FUNDING: United Way, regional ctr, pvt, nonprofit. OFC HRS: M-F 9am-6pm. Spanish spoken. ADM REQ: Must be able to participate in prgms. SERVES: Claremont & nearby.

ACORN NATURALISTS CTR FOR SCIENCE
Environmental Education and Resources
155 El Camino Real
Tustin, CA 92780
(800) 422-8886
(800) 452-2802 FAX

Extensive science and environmental edu products and resources for students of all ages. Also teacher training facilities, conference areas, workshop lectures and large science and edu store. Thousands of hard to find specialty products. Catalog available thru website (www.acornnaturalist.com). OFC HRS: M-F 7am-5pm; Sat 10am-5pm. SERVES: U.S.A.

AMERICAN SOCIETY OF YOUNG MUSICIANS
6100 Wilshire Blvd., Ste 230

Los Angeles, CA 90048
(310) 358-8301
(310) 358-8304 FAX

Mentoring, scholarships, leadership, development, support, fund and drug/alcohol abuse referral prgm offered to musicians, music students, or others in the field of music. Also associated with the Multicultural Motion Picture Assn, which assists underprivileged students who seek entry into the film & television professions. FUNDING: Nonprofit. OFC HRS: M-F 9am-5pm. SERVES: U.S.A.

AMERICAN YOUTH SOCCER/AYSO
Riverside AYSO Region 187
P.O. Box 8416
Moreno Valley, CA 92552
(951) 242-2976

The goal of this group is to offer all children a positive experience in soccer. Call for sign-up dates, times and places. SERVES: Riverside County.

AMERICAN YOUTH SOCCER/AYSO
National AYSO Headquarters
19750 S. Vermont, Ste 200
Torrance, CA 90502
(800) 872-2976
(310) 525-1155 FAX

AYSO provides soccer for players ages 4-18 yrs, and for adults in some areas. Also provides training for coaches, referees and volunteer administrators. FUNDING: Fees, donations, nonprofit. OFC HRS: M-F 8am-5pm. SERVES: U.S.A.

APPLE CANYON CENTER
P.O. Box 35
56400 Apple Canyon Rd.
Mountain Center, CA 92561-0035
(951) 659-4609
(951) 659-4710 FAX

Facility available for camping, conferences, family reunions, retreats. Youth camp & edu, teamwork & challenge course, outdoor edu. FUNDING: Nonprofit. ADM REQ: Call for reservations and more info. SERVES: Calif.

AQUARIUM OF THE PACIFIC
100 Aquarium Way
Long Beach, CA 90802
(562) 590-3100
(562) 951-1629 FAX

Edu prgms for all ages, parent/child prgms, group sleepovers, jr. biologist class, volunteer opportunities. Edu infoline (562) 951-1630. OFC HRS: Varies. Call for fees. SERVES: So. Calif.

BEAUMONT-CHERRY VALLEY REC/PARK
Noble Creek Community Center
P.O. Box 490
390 W. Oak Valley Pkwy.
Beaumont, CA 92223
(951) 845-9555
(951) 845-9557 FAX

Serves children of all ages. Preschool classes, school-age child licensed daycare , cultural prgms, dance and art classes, gymnastics, senior prgms, special events and exciting trips. Adjoining regional park. OFC HRS: M-F

9am-5pm. Spanish, Hmong spoken. SERVES: Riverside County.

BIG BROTHERS/SISTERS/GTR L.A. & I.E.
Administration Office
800 S. Figueroa, Ste 620
Los Angeles, CA 90017
(213) 481-3611
(800) 207-7567
(213) 481-1148 FAX

Prgm matches boys ages 7-18 yrs, and girls ages 6-16 yrs from single parent homes with volunteer Big Brothers and Big Sisters. Provides positive role models, friendship, companionship and guidance on a one-to-one basis. Each volunteer is trained to provide ongoing support to ensure that each mentoring relationship thrives. Also has an additional office at 5601 W. Slauson Ave., Ste. 130, Culver City 90230; (310) 338-0055. FUNDING: Nonprofit. OFC HRS: M-F 9am-5:30pm. Spanish spoken. Free srvs. SERVES: L.A. Co. & Inland Empire.

BOBBY BONDS PARK/COMMUNITY CTR
Cesar Chavez Community Center
2060 University Ave.
Riverside, CA 92507
(951) 826-5746

Community center and park offering a variety of recreational activities. Walk in or call. FUNDING: Govt. OFC HRS: M-Th 8am-9pm; F 8am-6pm. Spanish spoken. Fees vary for activities. SERVES: Riverside County.

BOBBY SOX SOFTBALL-NATL HQTRS
P.O. Box 5880
7429 Orangethorpe Ave., Ste B
Buena Park, CA 90622-5880
(714) 522-1234
(714) 522-6548 FAX

No tryouts. Every girl is placed on a team and each girl plays & bats in every game. Parent-operated prgm. Seven divisions based on the age of the girl. Registration begins in Nov for practice beginning in Feb. For info, call (888) PLAY SOX. FUNDING: Nonprofit. OFC HRS: M-F 9am-5pm. ADM REQ: Girls ages 5-18 yrs. SERVES: Western U.S.A.

BOY SCOUTS OF AMER/INLAND EMP
Calif Inland Empire Council (CIEC)
1230 Indiana Ct.
Redlands, CA 92374-2896
(909) 793-2463
(877) 732-1450
(909) 793-0306 FAX

One-week resident camp for youth ages 8 yrs+. Activities include: archery, arts & crafts, camping skills/outdoor living, hiking, nature/environmental studies, riflery, instructional swimming, recreational swimming. Based on scout activities & ideals, prgm seeks to develop youth & prevent future social costs for rehab or detention. Adult volunteers provide youth with various prgms, club meetings, campouts, comm involvement, social & recreational activities. ACA accredited. FUNDING: United Way, donations, fundraising, nonprofit. OFC HRS: M-F 9:30am-5:30pm. ADM REQ: Boys ages 7-20 yrs and girls ages 15-20 yrs, adults all ages. Membership dues vary with unit. Cost for camp is $76-$200 per week. SERVES: Riverside, San Bernardino Counties.

BOY SCOUTS OF AMER/OLD BALDY

Old Baldy Council
1047 W. 6th Street
Ontario, CA 91762
(909) 983-4534
(909) 984-0064 FAX

Tiger Cubs, Cub Scouts, Boy Scouts and co-ed exploring prgms. Also summer camps and recreational activities that run throughout the year. Coordinates character dev, citizenship training and personal fitness prgms for males in 1st grade through age 20 and females ages 14-20 yrs. OFC HRS: M-F 9am-5pm, Sat 9am-1pm. Spanish spoken. Membership fee is $7 per year. SERVES: Fontana to Diamond Bar, Chino to Mtns.

BOY SCOUTS OF AMERICA

Boy Scouts of America promotes character building, citizenship & leadership in adol & pre-adolescent youth. Troop type organization. Offer informal edu, crafts & camping. Call local council for details.

BOYS & GIRLS CLUB/BARSTOW

P.O. Box 204
120 Avenue G
Barstow, CA 92312
(760) 255-2422
(760) 255-2422 FAX

Youth srvs for boys & girls. Recreation, informal guidance, league sports, edu prgms, computer skills training, health & life skills, homework & tutorial srvs, after school child care, parent edu. FUNDING: Nonprofit. OFC HRS: M-F 11am-6pm. Spanish spoken. ADM REQ: Youth ages 6-17 yrs. Membership: school yr $15, summer $30. SERVES: San Bernardino County.

BOYS & GIRLS CLUB/CATHEDRAL CITY

32141 Whispering Palms Trail
Cathedral City, CA 92234
(760) 324-5844
(760) 321-2464 FAX

Latchkey, summer, Easter & Christmas vacation, special assist with homework, after school child care, some transportation provided. Walk in. FUNDING: Nonprofit. OFC HRS: M-F 7:30am-5:30pm. Spanish spoken. ADM REQ: Ages 6-19 yrs. Annual membership $10. Scholarships & free srvs to low-income families. Sliding fee scale. SERVES: Cathedral City, Rancho Mirage.

BOYS & GIRLS CLUB/COACHELLA VLY

Coachella Clubhouse
85-350 Bagdad Ave.
Coachella, CA 92236
(760) 398-5287
(760) 398-8468 FAX

Youth srvs for boys & girls. Recreation, informal guidance, league sports, edu prgms, computer skills training, homework assist, health & life skills, homework & tutorial srvs, parent edu. FUNDING: Nonprofit. OFC HRS: Summer: M-F 7:30am-5:30pm. School yr: M-F 2pm-8pm. Spanish spoken. ADM REQ: Youth ages 7-18 yrs. Annual membership $20. SERVES: Coachella.

BOYS & GIRLS CLUB/COACHELLA VLY

La Quinta Clubhouse

49-995 Park Ave.
La Quinta, CA 92253
(760) 564-5555
(760) 564-5527 FAX

Youth srvs for boys & girls, recreation, informal guidance, league sports, edu prgms, computer skills training, homework assist, health & life skills, parent edu. FUNDING: Nonprofit. OFC HRS: Summer: M-F 7:30am-5:30pm; school yr: 2pm-8pm. Spanish spoken. ADM REQ: Ages 6-17 yrs. Annual membership $140 school yr, $120 summer. SERVES: La Quinta.

BOYS & GIRLS CLUB/COACHELLA VLY

Administration Office
42-600 Cook St., Ste 120
Palm Desert, CA 92211
(760) 836-1160
(760) 776-9111 FAX

Youth srvs for boys & girls ages 7-18 yrs. Recreation, informal guidance, league sports, edu prgms, computer skills training, homework assist, health & life skills, before & after school child care, delinquency prevention prgm, parent edu. FUNDING: Fundraisers, donations, United Way, nonprofit. OFC HRS: M-F 8am-5pm. Spanish spoken. Annual membership. SERVES: La Quinta, Indio & Coachella.

BOYS & GIRLS CLUB/DESERT HOT SP

Main Club Facility
P.O. Box 935
66150 8th Street
Desert Hot Springs, CA 92240
(760) 329-1312
(760) 329-8995 FAX

Youth dev agency with more than 70 prgms throughout the year. Camping, crafts, swimming, homework tutorial srvs, before & after school child care, mentoring prgms, sports, computers, etc. FUNDING: Nonprofit. OFC HRS: M-F 2pm-6pm (summer hrs: May-Aug, M-F 12noon-6pm). Spanish spoken. ADM REQ: Ages 6-18 yrs. Membership fees are $10 per calender year, additional fees for extended day camp. SERVES: Desert Hot Springs, North Palm Springs, Painted Hills, Sky Valley.

BOYS & GIRLS CLUB/FONTANA

Almeria Middle School Clubhouse
P.O. Box 3712
7723 Almeria Ave.
Fontana, CA 92336
(909) 822-4988
(909) 355-8663 FAX

Youth srvs for boys & girls. Recreation, informal guidance, league sports, edu prgms, computer skills training, health & life skills, homework & tutorial srvs, after school child care, delinquency prevention prgm, parent edu. Teen clubs, cyber cafe. FUNDING: Donations, nonprofit. OFC HRS: M-F 10am-5pm. Spanish spoken. ADM REQ: Ages 6-17 yrs. Annual membership $30 per yr per child. SERVES: San Bernardino County.

BOYS & GIRLS CLUB/HIGH DESERT

56525 Little League Dr.
Yucca Valley, CA 92284
(760) 365-5437
(760) 228-3017 FAX

Youth srvs for boys & girls. Recreation, informal guidance, league sports, edu prgms, computer skills training, health & life skills, homework & tutorial srvs, before & after school child care,

transportation, delinquency prevention prgm, parent edu. Mailing address: P.O. Box 402, Yucca Valley, CA 92284. FUNDING: Donations, nonprofit. OFC HRS: M-F 10am-6pm; summer hrs: M-F 10am-5pm. ADM REQ: Ages 7-17 yrs. Annual membership $50 during the school year. Summer $30 every two weeks. SERVES: Yucca Valley.

BOYS & GIRLS CLUB/INDIO

Indio Clubhouse
83-100 Date St.
Indio, CA 92201
(760) 347-5712
(760) 347-1192 FAX

Youth srvs for boys & girls, recreation, informal guidance, league sports, edu prgms, computer skills training, health & life skills, homework & tutorial srvs, after school child care, transportation, delinquency prevention prgm. FUNDING: Nonprofit. OFC HRS: Winter M-F 2pm-8pm. Summer M-F 7:30am-5:30pm. Spanish spoken. ADM REQ: Ages 7-18 yrs. Annual membership cost $20. SERVES: Indio.

BOYS & GIRLS CLUB/MTN COMM

P.O. Box 2228
607 Forest Shade Rd.
Crestline, CA 92325
(909) 338-0418
(909) 338-3949 FAX

Recreational activities including: volleyball, street hockey, basketball, arts, crafts, homework assist, mentoring. FUNDING: Nonprofit. OFC HRS: Vary by prgm, call for more info. Spanish spoken. ADM REQ: Ages 6-18 yrs. Membership is $20 per yr. SERVES: San Bernardino Mountain areas.

BOYS & GIRLS CLUB/MURRIETA

P.O. Box 892349
40550 California Oaks Rd.
Murrieta, CA 92562
(951) 698-3838
(951) 461-1774 FAX

Youth srvs for boys & girls. Recreation, informal guidance, league sports, edu prgms, computer skills training, health & life skills. Homework & tutorial srvs, before & after school child care, transportation, delinquency prevention prgm, guest speakers. FUNDING: Donations, nonprofit. OFC HRS: M-F 6:30am-7pm. Spanish spoken. ADM REQ: Ages 6-17 yrs. Annual membership $20. SERVES: Southwest Riverside County.

BOYS & GIRLS CLUB/PALM SPRINGS

450 S. Sunrise Way
Palm Springs, CA 92262
(760) 327-1304
(760) 322-7393
(760) 327-0101 FAX

Youth activities, game room, arts and crafts, swimming, teen center, girls unit, full size gym, camping and Keystone Club. FUNDING: Donations, grants, nonprofit. OFC HRS: M-F 10am-6pm. School hrs: M-F 2pm-6pm; holidays & summer M-F 8am-6pm. Spanish spoken. Membership fee on sliding fee scale, summer $45 per week. SERVES: Palm Springs & nearby.

BOYS & GIRLS CLUB/REDLANDS

P.O. Box 8416
1251 Clay St.
Redlands, CA 92374

(909) 798-4599
(909) 798-1684 FAX

Youth srvs for boys & girls. Recreation, informal guidance, league sports, edu prgms, computer skills training, health & life skills, homework & tutorial srvs, after school child care, transportation, parent edu, delinquency prevention prgm. FUNDING: Donations, nonprofit. OFC HRS: M-F 9am-6pm. Spanish spoken. ADM REQ: Ages 6-17 yrs. Annual membership $12. SERVES: Redlands USD.

BOYS & GIRLS CLUB/SAN BERNARDINO

1180 W. 9th Street
San Bernardino, CA 92411
(909) 888-6751
(909) 888-1474 FAX

Youth and family srvs agency. Youth dev, counseling, day camp, homework & tutorial srvs, before & after school child care, parent edu, employment srvs, physical and social recreation, community srvs, youth drug & alcohol counseling, ESL classes, GED. FUNDING: Donations, fundraising, United Way, nonprofit. OFC HRS: M-F 7am-7pm; Sat 8:30am-2:30pm. Spanish spoken. Annual membership $7. SERVES: San Bernardino metro area.

BOYS & GIRLS CLUB/TEMECULA

P.O. Box 892349
28790 Pujol St.
Temecula, CA 92589-2349
(951) 699-1526
(951) 699-4273 FAX

Youth srvs for boys & girls. Recreation, informal guidance, league sports, edu prgms, computer skills training, health & life skills. Homework & tutorial srvs, transportation, delinquency prevention prgm. Day camp, before & after school care for grades 1-8. Roller hockey, sports for toddlers, Tae Kwon Do. FUNDING: United Way, nonprofit. OFC HRS: M-F 6:30am-7pm; Sat 9am-2pm. Spanish spoken. ADM REQ: Ages 6-17 yrs. Annual membership $20. SERVES: Temecula, Murrieta.

CALICO GHOST TOWN

P.O. Box 638
36600 Ghost Town Rd.
Yermo, CA 92398
(760) 254-2122
(760) 254-2047 FAX

San Bernardino Co. Regional Park System owned and operated historic theme park. Flyers and town maps are available. Senior discounts available Sun-Th. Call (800) TO-CALICO or visit the website (www.calicotown.com) for info on upcoming special events. FUNDING: County, concessions. OFC HRS: M-Sun 9am-5pm. Maps available in several languages. Fees: $6 per adult, $3 for children 6-15 yrs. Camping hookups $22 per unit. Non-hookups are $18 per night per unit, cabins are $33 per night. Bunk house (sleeps 20) $60 a night. SERVES: Inland Empire.

CALIF ATHLETIC COMMISSION

2005 Evergreen St., Ste 2010
Sacramento, CA 95825-3217
(916) 263-2195
(916) 263-2197 FAX

OFC HRS: M-F 8am-5pm. Closed the 1st three F of each month. Spanish spoken. SERVES: Calif.

CALIFORNIA MENTOR FOUNDATION

100 Main St.
Belvedere Tiburon, CA 94920
(415) 789-1007
(415) 789-1008 FAX

Information on mentoring prgms statewide. Visit (www.calmentor.org). SERVES: Calif.

CHILDREN'S MUSEUM AT LA HABRA

301 S. Euclid St.
La Habra, CA 90631
(562) 905-9793
(562) 905-9698 FAX

Hands-on museum for children featuring a wide variety of exhibits, including a new dinosaur garden, child-size carousel and preschool play park. Offers special events, performances, hands-on workshops, and birthday parties. FUNDING: Grants, donations, nonprofit. OFC HRS: Tu-F 10am-4pm; Sat 10am-5pm; Sun 1pm-5pm. Admission fee: $6 for La Habra residents, $7 for non-residents. Children under age 2 yrs are free. Group reservations are required. SERVES: So. Calif.

CHINESE AMERICAN MUSEUM

425 N. Los Angeles St.
Los Angeles, CA 90012
(213) 485-8567
(213) 485-8238 FAX

Promotes Chinese American history and culture. FUNDING: Donations, fndns. OFC HRS: Tu-Sun 10am-3pm. Suggested donation $3. Seniors ages 60 yrs+ and students with ID $2. SERVES: So. Calif.

CITY OF FONTANA

Community Services Department
16860 Valencia Ave.
Fontana, CA 92335
(909) 349-6900
(909) 349-6911 FAX

City of Fontana recreation and leisure activities including: dance, gymnastics, karate, racquetball, bowling, Pee Wee and youth sports, ballet, guitar lessons, and much more. Variety of after school prgms for children and tiny tots. FUNDING: City. OFC HRS: M-F 8am-5pm. Spanish spoken. Fees vary. SERVES: Fontana & nearby.

CITY OF RIVERSIDE PUBLIC LIBRARY

Eastside Library Connection
4033-C Chicago Ave.
Riverside, CA 92507
(951) 684-8347
(951) 684-8347 FAX

Info learning center for children, ages 10-14 yrs, and their families. Free computer training, Internet, info literacy, homework assist, literacy & special presentations for adults. FUNDING: Riverside Public Library Project, grants, nonprofit. HRS: M-Th 11am-7pm; F, Sat 10am-6pm. SERVES: Riverside County.

COLTON COMMUNITY SRVS DEPT

670 Colton Ave.
Colton, CA 92324
(909) 370-6153
(909) 777-3351 FAX

Recreation division, youth, family & seniors division. Senior outreach, counseling, tutoring, child care, summer youth, and youth intervention. Walk in or call. FUNDING: Govt. OFC HRS: M-F 7am-8pm; Sat 8am-5pm. Spanish

spoken. SERVES: Colton, Grand Terrace & Bloomington.

COPS FOR KIDS, INC.

P.O. Box 2001
333 Limited St.
Lake Elsinore, CA 92531
(951) 245-3389
(951) 245-3311 FAX

Outreach to community children ages birth-18 yrs. Also senior citizen assist prgm. FUNDING: County. OFC HRS: M-F 9am-5pm. Spanish spoken. ADM REQ: Must fill out request form in person at the sheriff's office. Free srvs. SERVES: Lake Elsinore.

CORONA PARKS/REC/COMM SRVS DEPT

400 S. Vincentia Ave.
Corona, CA 92882
(951) 736-2241
(951) 279-3683 FAX

Recreation prgms & srvs for all ages. Leisure activity classes. After school kids clubs for youth ages 5-12 yrs for a minimal cost. Senior citzens srvs, food prgms and specialty classes. Sports, swimming and many special events annually. Walk in or call. OFC HRS: M-F 8am-5pm. Spanish spoken. SERVES: Corona.

DE ANZA COMMUNITY & TEEN CENTER

1405 S. Fern St.
Ontario, CA 91762
(909) 395-2030

A variety of classes & activities are held at the center for children, teens and adults. Homework assist, health & nutrition, sewing, cooking, etc. FUNDING: City. OFC HRS: M-F 8am-8pm; Sat 12noon-4pm. Each prgm has specific hrs, call for more info. Spanish spoken. Some free classes & activities. SERVES: City of Ontario.

DELMANN HEIGHTS COMM CENTER

2969 Flores St.
San Bernardino, CA 92407
(909) 384-5417
(909) 880-0809 FAX

Prgms include: senior nutrition, quilting, ESL, piano lessons, county health nurse and food distribution (USDA commodities). Open recreation. Free summer lunch for ages 1-18 yrs. Teen prgm, swimming pool (June-August) and Head Start preschool. OFC HRS: M-F 9am-6pm. Spanish spoken. SERVES: San Bernardino County.

DESERT RECREATION DISTRICT

Formerly Coachella Vly Rec & Park Dist
45-305 Oasis St.
Indio, CA 92201
(760) 347-3484
(760) 347-4660 FAX

This is not a day care facility. Preschool Tiny Tot Prgm M-Th 9am-11:30am. Prgms held at three community centers. Swimming, cultural prgms, summer day camp, kid's club, licensed after school care for grades K-6 in Indio, La Quinta and Palm Desert, two gyms with basketball, volleyball, racquetball. FUNDING: Nonprofit, donations. OFC HRS: M-F 8am-5pm. Spanish spoken. Low fees. SERVES: Palm Desert, Indian Wells, La Quinta, Indio, Coachella, Thousand Palms, Rancho Mirage, Bermuda Dunes, Thermal, Oasis, Mecca, and the Salton Sea.

DISABLED SPORTS USA
P.O. Box 10502
Fullerton, CA 92838
(949) 460-6969
(714) 526-8360 FAX

Recreation and socialization including monthly ski weekends at Mammoth (Dec-May). Serves blind, deaf, cerebral palsy, paraplegics, spina bifida, children and adults with any disability. FUNDING: Donations, dues. Annual dues are $15 (includes monthly newsletter). SERVES: So. Calif.

DISCOVERY SCIENCE CENTER
2500 N. Main St.
Santa Ana, CA 92705
(714) 542-2823
(714) 542-2828 FAX

Science edu museum with more than 120 hands-on exhibits, live and 3-D science shows, story time for children ages 3-6 yrs. Field trips, sleepover prgm, meeting & facility rental. FUNDING: Nonprofit. OFC HRS: M-Sat 10am-5pm; Sun 11am-5pm. Spanish spoken. Children ages 3-17 & seniors $9.95; adults $12.95; children ages 2 yrs and under are free. Annual membership offers significant savings. 1st M each month free for Santa Ana residents with ID. SERVES: Calif.

EDWARD-DEAN MUSEUM
9401 Oak Glen Rd.
Cherry Valley, CA 92223
(951) 845-2626
(951) 845-2628 FAX

A museum of European and Asian decorative arts and interpretive exhibits with collections of 17th-19th century art. Museum Hrs: F-Sun 10am-5pm. Admission fee $3. SERVES: Riverside County.

EF FNDN FOR FOREIGN STUDY
1 Education St.
Cambridge, MA 02141
(800) 992-1892
(800) 447-4273
(800) 590-1125 FAX

Internatl student exchange prgm. Sponsors high school foreign exchange students from around the world for a year-long exchange in the U.S. Students live with host families and attend local high schools. Also sponsors American students who wish to study in another country. Volunteers work to find interested families and coordinate exchange prgm. FUNDING: Nonprofit. OFC HRS: M-F 9am-5:30pm, EST. SERVES: U.S.A.

EMMANUEL UNIQUE OUTREACH PARTNERS
P.O. Box 1861
Corona, CA 92878
(951) 279-0031
(760) 955-0007 FAX

Various prgms offered including: homework assist, literacy, enrichment for students, senior visits, summer food srvs, personal training, nonprofit creation. FUNDING: Nonprofit. OFC HRS: M-F 8am-5pm. SERVES: Riverside County.

FEMA FOR KIDS
Resources for parents and teachers to teach disaster prep to kids. Visit (www.fema.gov/kids). FUNDING: Govt. SERVES: U.S.A.

FIRST BAPTIST CHURCH OF YUCAIPA
34784 Yucaipa Blvd.
Yucaipa, CA 92399
(909) 790-1971
(909) 797-5062 FAX

Youth and children's activities, including Blast, and a number of support groups for a range of different needs. The library has books and tapes for all ages. Also have a Christian preschool, and a school for children in grades K-6. Prgms for junior high, high school, college. OFC HRS: M-F 8am-5pm. SERVES: Yucaipa, Calimesa, Redlands & nearby.

GAY STRAIGHT ALLIANCE NETWORK
National & Statewide
1550 Bryant St., Ste 800
San Francisco, CA 94103
(415) 552-4229
(415) 552-4729 FAX

Independent youth-led organization. Provides support and leadership and training to gay & straight students to end harrassment & discrimination in schools. FUNDING: Nonprofit. ADM REQ: Middle or high school. SERVES: Calif.

GIRL SCOUTS OF USA
Spanish Trails Council
9525 Monte Vista Ave.
Montclair, CA 91763-2231
(909) 399-0808
(626) 331-7325
(909) 626-3639 FAX

Opportunities for girls in grades K-12. Life skills, personal dev, community srv & special prgms through informal contemporary edu. Also call (562) 693-0268. FUNDING: Nonprofit. OFC HRS: M-F 9am-5:30pm. SERVES: East L.A. & West San Bernardino Counties.

GIRL SCOUTS/SAN GORGONIO CNCL
Youth Organization/Camps
1751 Plum Lane
Redlands, CA 92374-4505
(909) 307-6555
(800) 400-4475
(909) 307-6526 FAX

Girl Scouts offers an informal edu prgm for girls. Prgms support self-worth, values and contributing to the community in an all-girl environment. Resident & day camps offered to girls throughout the summer in various areas. Camps include Camp Azalea Trails which is held in the San Jacinto Mountains near Idyllwild, and Camp Tautona. Summer hrs vary. FUNDING: United Way, donations, product sales. OFC HRS: M-W 8am-6:30pm; Th 8am-6pm. Spanish spoken. ADM REQ: Girls ages 5-18 yrs and believe in Girl Scout promise and law. $10 annual membership fee. Financial assist available. SERVES: Riverside Co. & most of San Bernardino County.

GIRLS CLUBS
Most of the clubs have after school recreational activities for children. The membership cost for one year varies per site, a positive option to latchkey children who are often left unattended in the afternoons. Many prgms are not licensed child care ctrs. Girls Clubs may be shown as "Boys and Girls Clubs."

GREENLEAF BATON TWIRLING ACADEMY
24971 Acacia Lane
Laguna Hills, CA 92653
(949) 768-4664

Teaches 1, 2 & 3 batons, rifle, flag, saber & fire (beginners & advanced). Youth perform at various community events and tournaments throughout the U.S. Contact: Lou Greenleaf. FUNDING: Nonprofit. OFC HRS: M-F 8am-5pm. ADM REQ: Ages 4 yrs+. SERVES: So. Calif.

GUIDED DISCOVERIES, INC.
P.O. Box 1360
Claremont, CA 91711
(909) 625-6194
(800) 645-1423
(909) 625-7305 FAX

Summer resident camps and school prgms. Visit (www.guideddiscoveries.org). FUNDING: Nonprofit. OFC HRS: M-F 8am-5pm. ADM REQ: Ages 8-14 yrs. Fees vary per prgm. SERVES: U.S.A.

HERNANDEZ COMMUNITY CENTER
222 N. Lugo Ave.
San Bernardino, CA 92408
(909) 384-5420
(909) 384-5160 FAX

Year-round youth recreation activities, summer pool parties. Teen workshops, ages 12-17 yrs; homework assistance Tu, W for grades 1-12; game room; teen club; fitness prgm. Spanish spoken. Some programs have registration fee, other srvs free. SERVES: San Bernardino County.

HESPERIA REC & PARKS DISTRICT
P.O. Box 401055
Hesperia, CA 92340
(760) 244-5488
(760) 244-2513 FAX

Recreational activities for adults and children including: swimming, special interest classes, equestrian events, youth & adult sports, preschool prgms. Sponsors the Mojave River Valley Special Olympics. OFC HRS: M-F 8:30am-5pm. SERVES: San Bernardino County.

HIGH DESERT YOUTH CENTER
15411 Village Dr.
Victorville, CA 92394
(760) 245-7103
(760) 245-9541 FAX

Various activities and programs for youth. OFC HRS: M-Th 10am-5pm; F 10am-3pm. SERVES: High Desert.

HOLLYHOCK HOUSE
Dept of Cultural Affairs
4800 Hollywood Blvd.
Los Angeles, CA 90027
(323) 644-6269
(323) 644-6271 FAX

Hollyhock House is open for public touring. Docent-led tours W-Sun: 12:30pm, 1:30pm, 2:30pm, 3:30pm. Reservations required for groups of 10 or more. Frank Lloyd Wright House museum located in Barnsdall Art Park. FUNDING: City, nonprofit. Adults $5; students & seniors $3; children under 12 yrs free. SERVES: Calif.

HOME OF NEIGHBORLY SERVICE
839 N. Mt. Vernon Ave.
San Bernardino, CA 92411
(909) 885-3491
(909) 884-0181 FAX

After school enrichment prgm for children in grades 1 and up. Recreation, youth skill building, counseling groups, gang intervention & prevention, homework assist/tutoring for youth, Boy & Girl Scouts, nutrition classes for adults, ESL for adults, children's clothes closet, Narcotics Anonymous meetings, parenting support groups, sewing for adults, boxing, hip hop dancing, aerobics & emerg food srv, resource & referrals. OFC HRS: M-Th 8am-5:30pm; F 8am-5pm. Spanish spoken. Free srvs & referrals. SERVES: San Bernardino County.

HOSTELLING INTERNATL/ADMIN OFC

American Youth Hostels
8401 Colesville Rd., Ste 600
Silver Spring, MD 20910
(301) 495-1240
(301) 495-6697 FAX

Opportunities for travel and outdoor recreation for all, but especially for young people, by providing hostels in scenic, cultural and historic areas. HI-USA hostels are also open to non-members for an additional fee with lower rates for children under age 18 yrs. Most urban hostels have 24-hr access; many hostels may be closed during some daytime hours. Visit (www.hiusa.org). FUNDING: Fees, grants, contributions. OFC HRS: M-F 8am-5pm. SERVES: U.S.A. & Internatl.

INCREDABLES SPECIAL NEEDS PROGRAM

Rancho Cucamonga Civic Center
10500 Civic Center Dr.
Rancho Cucamonga, CA 91730
(909) 477-2782
(909) 477-2848 FAX

Recreational programs offered to residents and non-residents with special needs. Sports, singing, dancing, cooking, etc. Call for more info. Volunteers welcome. FUNDING: City. OFC HRS: M-Th 7am-6pm. ADM REQ: Ages 5-22 yrs, no one turned away. Fees for some activities. SERVES: Rancho Cucamonga.

INDIO COMMUNITY CENTER

Desert Recreation District
45-871 Clinton St.
Indio, CA 92201
(760) 347-4263

Youth and adult recreation prgms. FUNDING: County. OFC HRS: M-F 6am-9pm; Sat 10am-2pm. Spanish spoken. ADM REQ: Must register. Fees vary per prgm. SERVES: Indio.

INLAND EMPIRE WEST CONSERV DIST

Resource Conservation
25864-K Business Center Dr.
Chino, CA 91710
(909) 799-7407
(909) 799-1438 FAX

Advise homeowners on types of soils and erosion control alternatives. Edu contests and scholarships for schools. Nature Discovery Prgm, an outdoor prgm for schools in San Bernardino County & portions of Riverside County. FUNDING: Govt, nonprofit. OFC HRS: M-F 7am-3:30pm. Free srvs. SERVES: Southwest San Bernardino & Western Riverside Counties.

JOSHUA TREE KID'S CLUB

P.O. Box 1245
6171 Sunburst Ave.
Joshua Tree, CA 92252
(760) 366-0378

(760) 366-0128 FAX

Summer edu & recreational walk-in prgm for youth ages 5-14 yrs, includes organized sports, crafts, youth dev activities, field trips. Environment enhances the opportunity for a child to develop self-esteem. FUNDING: Nonprofit. HRS: M-F 6:30am-6pm. Spanish spoken. SERVES: Morongo Basin.

JOSHUA TREE NATL PARK ASSOC.

74485 National Park Dr.
Twentynine Palms, CA 92277
(760) 367-5525
(760) 367-5583 FAX

Edu prgms and visitor ctrs for park info. FUNDING: Nonprofit. OFC HRS: M-F 8am-5pm. German & Spanish spoken. SERVES: San Bernardino County.

JUNIOR ACHIEVEMENT OF SO CALIF

6250 Forest Lawn Dr.
Los Angeles, CA 90068
(323) 957-1818
(323) 957-0585 FAX

Educates & inspires young people to value free enterprise, business & economics to improve the quality of their lives. Inspires kids to achieve in the business of life through a community-based partnership of educators, volunteers & businesses. FUNDING: Nonprofit. OFC HRS: M-F 8am-5pm. Spanish spoken. SERVES: L.A., Fresno, Kern, Kings, Orange, Riverside, San Bernardino, San Luis Obispo, Santa Barbara, Tulare and Ventura.

JURUPA MOUNTAINS CULTURAL CENTER

7621 Granite Hill Dr.
Riverside, CA 92509
(951) 685-5818
(951) 685-1240 FAX

Earth science educational facility & museum. Educational field trips and prgms for groups Tu-F (must pre-register). Public tours Sat only. Rock collecting at 9am. Fee $6 each. Fossil shack: 10:30am. Fee $7.50 each. Donation: Adults $3, children $2. FUNDING: Prgm fees & grants. OFC HRS: Tu-Sat 8am-3pm. SERVES: Riverside County.

KIDSAID

2 Kids 4 Kids by Kids
P.O. Box 3272
Ann Arbor, MI 48106-3272

Website with resources for kids dealing with grief or loss. E-mail support groups, bookstore. A safe place for kids to share experiences with other kids. Visit (www.kidsaid.com). FUNDING: Nonprofit, donations. SERVES: U.S.A.

KRISTIE'S PLACE

1747 S. Claudina Way
Anaheim, CA 92805
(714) 408-9781
(714) 956-1475 FAX

A place for children with life-threatening illnesses to come with their families for their So. Calif wish trip or for a short compassion stay. Wishland's Kid's Club and family support prgms bring joy and hope to all. FUNDING: Nonprofit. OFC HRS: M-F 8:30am-4pm; Sat 8:30am-10am. Spanish spoken. SERVES: L.A., Orange & San Bernardino Counties.

L.A. ZOO

5333 Zoo Dr.
Los Angeles, CA 90027

(323) 644-4200
(323) 622-9786 FAX

Visitors can view more than 1,200 mammals, birds, amphibians and reptiles representing more than 350 different species. Accredited by American Zoo and Aquarium Association. New red ape rain forest - home to the zoo's orangutans. FUNDING: Nonprofit. OFC HRS: M-Sun 10am-5pm. SERVES: So. Calif.

L.I.F.T.

Life Is Forever Transitioning
8018 Santa Ana Cyn Rd. 100, Ste 169
Anaheim, CA 92808
(714) 749-4283
(267) 295-2533 FAX

Youth development organization to educate and mentor junior & high school youth. Basic life skills, college prep, career forums, community outreach. FUNDING: Nonprofit. OFC HRS: M-Th 9am-5pm; F 9am-2pm. SERVES: L.A., Orange and Riverside Counties.

LA QUINTA COMMUNITY CENTER

77865 Avenida Montezuma
La Quinta, CA 92253
(760) 564-9921
(760) 564-5579 FAX

Youth and adult recreation prgms. Tiny Tots, Mommy and Me, etc. FUNDING: County. OFC HRS: M-F 8am-6pm. Spanish spoken. ADM REQ: Must register. Fees vary per prgm. SERVES: La Quinta.

LAZY CREEK RECREATIONAL CENTER

EDA Community Services
26500 Lazy Creek Rd.
Sun City, CA 92586
(951) 679-8092

Recreational prgm for children ages 2-11 yrs. Once a month Ladies Night Out. FUNDING: Nonprofit. OFC HRS: Vary. SERVES: Sun City, Menifee.

MEAD VALLEY COMMUNITY COMPLEX

Family Service Assn/Riverside
21091 Rider St.
Perris, CA 92570
(951) 657-0686
(951) 657-9208 FAX

Prgms for youth, families, and seniors. Health screening, dental & medical srvs, independent studies, counseling, parenting classes, Bingo, senior lunch and home-delivered meals, utility assist, commodities, etc. FUNDING: Nonprofit. OFC HRS: M-F 8am-5pm. Spanish spoken. Most prgms are free. SERVES: Mead Valley, Perris.

MENTORING PROGRAM

Community Action Partnership
2038 Iowa Ave., Ste B102
Riverside, CA 92507
(951) 955-4900
(951) 955-6506 FAX

Project LEAD after school prgm for middle school youth offered through the YMCA. In-house pre-apprenticeship prgm for grades 11-12 who are actively enrolled in school. OFC HRS: M-F 8am-5pm. Spanish spoken. Free srvs. SERVES: Riverside County.

MONTCLAIR COMMUNITY CENTER

City of Montclair
5111 Benito St.
Montclair, CA 91763

(909) 399-3173
(909) 625-9464
(909) 399-9751 FAX

Immunization, physicals, blood pressure screening, blood work twice a month. Women's clinic & other non-emerg med srvs. Senior info & referral, outreach, income tax prep assist. Senior nutrition prgm M-F 11:30am for ages 60 yrs+. Suggested donation: $1.75. Eggs and produce sold at reduced prices. Social & recreational activites for children and adults, excursions, after school prgm & edu classes. OFC HRS: Vary with prgm. Spanish spoken. SERVES: San Bernardino County.

MONTE VISTA PARK REC CTR

City of Chino Social Srvs
13196 Monte Vista Ave.
Chino, CA 91710
(909) 627-7577
(909) 591-0020 FAX

Park is open for recreation M-F 7:30am-5:30pm. Activities include: cooking classes, ping pong, weight room, board games, arts and crafts for all ages, movie club, summer day camp. OFC HRS: M-F 2:30pm-5pm, summer hrs may be extended. Spanish spoken. SERVES: San Bernardino County.

MURRIETA COMMUNITY SRVS DEPT

City of Murrieta Comm Srvs Dept
401810 Juniper St.
Murrieta, CA 92562
(951) 304-7275

Swim lessons, gymnastics, martial arts, senior exercise, etc. 25-yard outdoor swimming pool, one-foot wading pool for children ages 6 yrs and under. OFC HRS: M-F 8am-5pm. Spanish spoken. SERVES: Murrieta.

MUSICIANS WORKSHOP ARTS & MUSIC

Temecula Valley Cultural Music & Arts Ctr
27455 Tierra Alta Way
Temecula, CA 92589
(951) 678-2517
(951) 222-3009 FAX

After school performing arts & music prgm for ages 3-19 yrs. Various music classes offered. Private instrument & voice lessons. FUNDING: Nonprofit. SERVES: Temecula Valley.

NEWPORT SPORTS MUSEUM

100 Newport Center Dr., Ste 100
Newport Beach, CA 92660
(949) 721-9333
(949) 721-0999 FAX

Museum offering edu & entertainment about athletes & sports, sports memorabilia, visits from famous athletes. Athlete outreach prgm, career exploration, mentoring prgms and a venue for pvt functions. Call for hours. FUNDING: Nonprofit. OFC HRS: M-Sat 10am-5pm. Free admission. SERVES: So. Calif.

NORCO PARKS, RECREATION & SRVS

P.O. Box 428
2870 Clark Ave.
Norco, CA 92860
(951) 270-5632
(951) 270-5622 FAX

Activities offered at different locations in the city, including: swimming, karate, aerobics, dance, sports, arts and crafts, etc, for adults & children. Senior prgms: outreach, senior nutri-tion prgms. FUNDING: City. OFC HRS: M-Th 8am-6pm. SERVES: Norco.

NORTHTOWN HOUSING DEVELOPMENT

Northtown Housing College Scholarship
8599 Haven Ave., Ste 205
Rancho Cucamonga, CA 91730
(909) 980-0465

Community center offers free summer lunch prgm, ESL classes, GED, govt food commodi-ties, after school recreation & tutoring, immuni-zations, summer day camp, holiday toy giveaway, info & referrals, job skills workshops, affordable housing. FUNDING: Nonprofit. OFC HRS: M-F 8am-5pm. Spanish spoken. SERVES: Rancho Cucamonga & nearby.

ORANGE EMPIRE RAILWAY MUSEUM

P.O. Box 548
2201 South A Street
Perris, CA 92572
(951) 657-2605
(951) 943-3020
(951) 943-2676 FAX

Over 200 old trains and street cars to ride and see. Picnic area. Train & trolley rides $10 for adults; $8 for children ages 5-11 yrs, kids under age 4 yrs free. FUNDING: Nonprofit. OFC HRS: M-Sun 9am-5pm. Free parking. SERVES: So. Calif.

PALM DESERT COMMUNITY CENTER

43900 San Pablo Ave.
Palm Desert, CA 92260
(760) 568-9697
(760) 568-6847 FAX

Youth and adult recreational prgms. FUNDING: County. OFC HRS: M-F 6am-10pm; Sat 12noon-6pm. Spanish spoken. ADM REQ: Must register. Fees vary per prgm. SERVES: Palm Desert.

PALM SPRINGS PARKS & RECREATION

401 S. Pavilion Way
Palm Springs, CA 92262
(760) 323-8265
(760) 323-8279 FAX

After school prgm for grades 1-5 called "For Kids Only", provides recreational srvs and ac-tivities for all ages. Also coordination for major special events that take place in the Palm Springs community. Walk in or call. FUNDING: City, prgm fees. OFC HRS: M-F 7:30am-6pm. SERVES: Palm Springs & nearby.

POLICE ACTIVITIES LEAGUE/PALM SPRINGS

The Palm Springs Boys & Girls Club
450 S. Sunrise Way
Palm Springs, CA 92262
(760) 318-1226

Local police officers work to provide activities and recreation to youth within the community. Prevention of juvenile crime, promotes youth leadership. FUNDING: City. SERVES: Palm Springs.

RANCHO CUCAMONGA TEEN CENTER

RC Family Sports Center
9161 Baseline Rd.
Rancho Cucamonga, CA 91701
(909) 477-2760

Various activities and prgms for teens includ-ing: dances, video games, sports, crafts, etc. FUNDING: Nonprofit. Summer Hrs: M-Th 2pm-6pm; F 2pm-8pm. ADM REQ: Ages 18 yrs and under. Fees vary per prgm per age. SERVES: San Bernardino County.

RANCHO SANTA ANA BOTANIC GARDEN

1500 N. College Ave.
Claremont, CA 91711
(909) 625-8767
(909) 626-7670 FAX

86-acre native Calif plant garden open daily to public. Many community edu prgms, special events & volunteer opportunities. FUNDING: Endowment, donations, nonprofit. OFC HRS: M-Sun 8am-5pm. Spanish spoken. ADM REQ: must provide student ID in order to get student discount. Suggested donation: $8 for adults, $6 for students and seniors, $4 for kids ages 3-12 yrs. SERVES: L.A., Orange, Riverside & San Bernardino Counties.

REDLANDS COMMUNITY CENTER

P.O. Box 3005
111 W. Lugonia Ave.
Redlands, CA 92374
(909) 798-7572
(909) 793-3569 FAX

Racquetball, gymnasium, tennis, game room, art, karate, room rental for clubs, groups, par-ties, help groups, computer lab, homework study, etc. Senior center (909)798-7579. FUNDING: City. OFC HRS: M-F 10am-7pm; game room: 12noon-7pm. ADM REQ: Pro-grams for youth and seniors. Fees depends on class, scholarships available. SERVES: Redlands.

RENCK COMMUNITY CTR AT HUNT PARK

4015 Jackson
Riverside, CA 92503
(951) 351-6132
(951) 358-2750 FAX

Various activities for seniors and kids. Summer camp for kids. Disability services (951)826-2000. Camp $80 per week. SERVES: Riverside County.

RIALTO RECREATION/COMMUNITY SRVS

214 N. Palm Ave., Ste 204
Rialto, CA 92376
(909) 421-4949
(909) 820-2554 FAX

Recreation & leisure prgms for adults and chil-dren including sports, social & cultural, neigh-borhood srvs, excursions, instructional classes, aquatics, senior prgms, karate, gymnastics, tap, and guitar. Also tiny tots prgm, school age day care. Sponsor all types of recreational ac-tivities. FUNDING: City. OFC HRS: M-Th 7am-6pm. Spanish spoken. ADM REQ: Open to all. SERVES: Rialto.

RICHARD NIXON LIBRARY/BIRTHPLACE

18001 Yorba Linda Blvd.
Yorba Linda, CA 92886-3949
(714) 993-5075
(714) 528-0544 FAX

High-tech interactive presidential museum that chronicles the life and times of former President Richard Nixon and his 4-decade political ca-reer. HRS: M-Sat 10am-5pm; Sun 11am-5pm. SERVES: U.S.A.

RIVERSIDE CITY PARK/RECREATION

3936 Chestnut St.
Riverside, CA 92501
(951) 826-2000
(951) 826-2005 FAX

Recreation and leisure prgms for adults and children, including: concerts, family tours, sports tournaments and leagues, seasonal activities such as day camps. Walk in or call. Mailing address 3900 Main St., Riverside. FUNDING: Govt. OFC HRS: M-F 8am-5pm. Spanish spoken. SERVES: Riverside County.

RIVERSIDE CITY PUBLIC UTILITIES
Utilities Building/School Education Prgm
3901 Orange St.
Riverside, CA 92501
(951) 826-5816

Municipal utilities school edu prgm offers energy and water resource materials, audiovisuals, speakers and field trips for grades K-12 to all public and pvt schools in Riverside. FUNDING: Rates, revenue bonds. OFC HRS: M-F 8am-5pm. Spanish spoken. Free srvs & materials. SERVES: City of Riverside utilities service area.

RIVERSIDE CO. REGL PARKS/OPENSPACE
4600 Crestmore Rd.
Riverside, CA 92509-6858
(951) 955-4310
(800) 234-7275
(951) 955-4305 FAX

Quality recreation opportunities to Riverside Co. and other residents to include individual and group camping, fishing, boating, horseback riding trails, interpretive displays and tours. OFC HRS: M-F 8am-5pm. Spanish spoken. SERVES: Riverside County.

RIVERSIDE METROPOLITAN MUSEUM
3580 Mission Inn Ave.
Riverside, CA 92501
(951) 826-5273
(951) 369-4970 FAX

Exhibits of local culture and history, children's prgms in nature study, history, anthropology & geology. Nature lab with live animals. Nature lab open Tu-Sun 1:30pm-4:30pm. FUNDING: Govt. OFC HRS: Tu-F 9am-5pm; Sat 10am-5pm; Sun 11am-5pm. Spanish spoken. Accepts donations. Free srvs. SERVES: Riverside County.

RUBEN CAMPOS COMMUNITY CENTER
1717 W. 5th Street
San Bernardino, CA 92411-2463
(909) 384-5421

Arts & crafts, dancing, karate, youth soccer, wrestling, swimming, adult soccer league all day Sun, homework help, teen club, lunch prgm, etc. FUNDING: Nonprofit. OFC HRS: M-F 9am-8pm; Sat 10am-4pm. Spanish spoken. Fees for some activities. SERVES: San Bernardino County.

SALVATION ARMY/ONTARIO
P.O. Box 408
1412 S. Euclid Ave.
Ontario, CA 91762
(909) 986-6748
(909) 986-9979 FAX

Emerg short-term assist to resident families and transients including food and lodging assist. Case mgmt is also provided. Salvation Army Ontario Corps serves Western San Bernardino County. This regional office will provide referrals for needed srvs at various srv locations. Also provides youth prgms and women's srvs. Shelter when funding available, disaster relief, summer camp, scouting activi-

ties for children, and an after school prgm. FUNDING: FEMA, United Way, donations. OFC HRS: M-F 8:30am-4:30pm. Spanish spoken. ADM REQ: Photo ID, proof of income, address verification. SERVES: Ontario, Fontana, Upland, Rialto, Chino, Chino Hills & Rancho Cucamonga.

SAN BERNARDINO CITY PARKS & REC
1350 South E Street
San Bernardino, CA 92408
(909) 384-5233
(909) 384-5160 FAX

Programs & services for all age groups. Activities include: trips, tours, community centers, park and playground prgms, youth & adult sports, adult classes, aquatics, workshops, tournaments, year-round lunch, nutrition prgms for youth & seniors, senior citizen prgms, human srvs, social srvs, etc. at various locations. FUNDING: City. OFC HRS: M-Th 7:30am-5:30pm. SERVES: San Bernardino City.

SIERRA CLUB/SAN GORGONIO
4079 Mission Inn Ave.
Riverside, CA 92501-3204
(951) 684-6203
(951) 684-6172 FAX

24-hr hotline for all upcoming activities for youth and adults. SERVES: Riverside, San Bernardino Counties.

SOUTHERN CALIF YOUTH FOR CHRIST
3435 San Anseline Ave.
Long Beach, CA 90808
(562) 424-0775
(714) 776-1700
(562) 425-7934 FAX

Campus groups and clubs for Christian junior high and senior high students. Student leader training, support groups for teen moms, network events for church youth groups. Also call (626) 331-0066. FUNDING: Donors, nonprofit. OFC HRS: M-F 9am-4:30pm. SERVES: So. Calif.

TWENTYNINE PALMS PARKS/REC
P.O. Box 995
74362 Joe Davis Dr.
Twentynine Palms, CA 92277
(760) 367-7562
(760) 367-5679 FAX

Recreational and leisure activities for adults and children including classes in the following: Tae Kwon Do, rubber stamp, guitar lessons, macrame, step interval aerobics. Racquetball courts and leagues. Senior nutrition center. Numerous sports activities for both adults and youth. OFC HRS: M-F 1pm-5pm. Fees vary per class or prgm. SERVES: Morongo Basin.

UCR/CALIF MUSEUM OF PHOTOGRAPHY
3824 Main St.
Riverside, CA 92501-3624
(951) 827-4787
(951) 784-3686
(951) 827-4797 FAX

Photography & art exhibits and edu prgms. Group tours may be arranged for 10 or more people. Museum is open to public. FUNDING: Donations, grants, govt, nonprofit OFC HRS: Tu-Sat 12noon-5pm; 1st Th 12noon-9pm (free 6pm-9pm); 1st Sun 12noon-5pm (free select months). ADM REQ: Under age 12 yrs must be accompanied by an adult. Free to students,

members, staff & seniors. General admission $3. SERVES: So. Calif.

UNITED WAY/INLAND VALLEYS
Southwest Co. Regional Office
5109 Jefferson Ave., Ste 225-A
Murrieta, CA 92562
(951) 697-4700
(951) 656-8210 FAX

Partners with donors to support many nonprofit health & human srv agencies. Prgms include: srvs for battered women, child care, youth, low-cost counseling, medical srvs, senior prgms, homeless srvs, emerg assist, volunteer srvs, etc. FUNDING: Donations, grants, nonprofit. OFC HRS: Vary. SERVES: Inland Valley.

UPLAND RECREATION DEPT
Magnolia Recreation Center
651 W. 15th Street
Upland, CA 91786-2262
(909) 931-4280
(909) 931-4283 FAX

Physical fitness, trips, classes, gymnastics, tap dancing, and a wide range of youth activities as well as team sports and activities for adults. Walk-ins welcome. FUNDING: City. OFC HRS: M-Th 8am-6pm. SERVES: San Bernardino County.

WEB WISE KIDS
P.O. Box 27203
Santa Ana, CA 92799
(866) 932-9473
(714) 435-0523 FAX

Internet safety prgms provide to edu in the use of computers, e-mail, chat rooms. For kids, parents, teachers, law enforcement, caregivers, etc. Visit (www.webwisekids.org). FUNDING: Nonprofit. OFC HRS: M-F 9am-5pm. German spoken. SERVES: U.S.A.

WOMEN'S SPORTS FOUNDATION
Eisenhower Park
1899 Hempstead Turnpike, Ste 400
East Meadow, NY 11554
(516) 542-4700
(800) 227-3988
(516) 542-4716 FAX

Natl member-based edu org. that promotes and enhances sports and fitness opportunities for all girls and women. Founded in 1974 by Billie Jean King. Provides leadership, edu resources, recognition & advocacy prgms; financial support for the purpose of improving the physical, mental & emotional well-being of all females through sports and fitness. FUNDING: Nonprofit, donations. OFC HRS: M-F 9am-5pm, EST. SERVES: U.S.A.

WWW.GIRLSHEALTH.GOV
Website created by the Natl Women's Health Info Center to help young girls learn about health and various other topics that concern and motivate them. ADM REQ: Girls ages 10-16 yrs. SERVES: U.S.A.

YMCA/CORONA/NORCO
Youth Services
1331 River Rd.
Corona, CA 92880
(951) 736-9622
(951) 736-6759 FAX

A variety of prgms including: karate, swimming lessons, preschool, before & after school care (also evening child care), day & resident camp, sports, drama classes, Bingo, adventure guides, senior aerobics. OFC HRS: M-F 6am-6pm. Spanish, Portuguese, Tagalog spoken. Limited scholarships available. SERVES: Corona, Norco & Home Gardens.

YMCA/DESERT

43-930 San Pablo Ave.
Palm Desert, CA 92260
(760) 341-9622
(760) 779-9651 FAX

Recreation prgms, camping, licensed child care, youth sports, martial arts, yoga, aquatics, summer resident and day camps, teen prgms & special events. Walk in or call. FUNDING: United Way, donors, fees, nonprofit. OFC HRS: M-F 8am-7pm; Sat 9am-12noon. Spanish spoken. Sliding fee scale. Scholarships available. SERVES: Coachella Valley.

YMCA/EAST VALLEY

San Bernardino Branch
808 E. 21st Street
San Bernardino, CA 92404
(909) 881-9622
(909) 886-3151 FAX

Active aquatics prgm with swim team. Twinges in the Hinges Prgm, aquagym, swim lessons, gymnastics, karate, itty bitty sports, basketball, day camp for off-track elementary. Summer resident camp. Offsite after school care. Walk in or call. ACA accredited. FUNDING: Nonprofit. OFC HRS: M-F 5am-9:30pm; Sat 8am-6pm; Sun 1pm-5pm. Spanish spoken. SERVES: San Bernardino County.

YMCA/HIGHLAND

7793 Central Ave.
Highland, CA 92346
(909) 425-9622
(909) 864-4924 FAX

Sports and exercise options for all ages. Itty bitty prgms, Y-kid 1 mile, Y-kid 1/3 mile, 5k, 10k, 1/2 marathon. OFC HRS: M-F 5pm-9:30pm; Sat 8pm-6pm; Sun 1pm-5pm. Spanish spoken. SERVES: Highland area.

YMCA/ONTARIO/MONTCLAIR

215 West C Street
Ontario, CA 91762-3403
(909) 986-5847
(909) 984-5088 FAX

Cardiovascular center, weight room, aerobics, basketball court, shower facilities, adult and senior fitness prgm, volleyball, karate for kids, child care before and after school, gymnastics, swimming, dance. Walk in or call. FUNDING: Membership, donations, United Way, fees, nonprofit. OFC HRS: M-F 6am-9pm; Sat 8am-5pm. Spanish spoken. Member fees vary. SERVES: Ontario, Montclair & nearby.

YMCA/PALM SPRINGS

P.O. Box 9530
3601 E. Mesquite Ave.
Palm Springs, CA 92264
(760) 320-6430
(760) 320-1679 FAX

Focused on youth ages 5-16 yrs, with an emphasis on teens and young adults. Activities include: karate (4 styles), computer classes, summer & winter basketball, humanities classes. FUNDING: Nonprofit. OFC HRS: M-F 10am-8pm. Membership fees are $37 per year for individuals (ages 18 and under) and

$54-$74 for family membership. SERVES: Coachella Valley.

YMCA/REDLANDS

500 E. Citrus Ave.
Redlands, CA 92373
(909) 798-9622
(909) 335-2007 FAX

Youth sports, basketball, aerobics, swimming, fitness centers for men and women, indoor and outdoor pools, camping prgms, roller hockey rink, gymnastics circus, racquetball courts and teen & senior center. Full-day child care at this site, toddlers through middle school. Prime time afternoon prgm held at 16 elementary school campuses. FUNDING: Nonprofit. OFC HRS: M-F 5am-9:30pm; Sat 8am-6pm; Sun 1pm-8pm. Spanish spoken. SERVES: East Valley.

YMCA/RIVERSIDE FAMILY

4020 Jefferson St.
Riverside, CA 92504
(951) 689-9622
(951) 689-7543 FAX

Wide range of wellness and recreation prgms for youth and adults. Activities include: fitness eval, beginning to advanced aerobics classes, basketball, volleyball, wallyball, handball, racquetball, Nautilus/Cam II equipment, Paramount-Universal equipment, free weights, massage, lifecycles, stairmasters, martial arts, dance classes, senior exercise prgms, 25-yard indoor heated pool for lap swim, recreational swim, swim lessons, plus preschool and school-aged child care prgms. Day camp. ACA accredited. Walk in. FUNDING: Nonprofit. OFC HRS: M-F 5:40am-9pm; Sat 8:30am-6pm. Spanish spoken. ADM REQ: Open to all ages both members and non-members. Fees depend on class or activity. SERVES: Riverside.

YMCA/UPLAND

1325 San Bernardino Rd.
Upland, CA 91786-4930
(909) 946-6120

Child care & youth sports prgms. OFC HRS: M-F 8am-5pm. Farsi, Spanish spoken. ADM REQ: Members, ages 2 yrs+. SERVES: Upland.

YUCAIPA TEEN CENTER

12385 7th Street
Yucaipa, CA 92399-2236
(909) 797-3662

Drop-in center for teens ages 13-18 yrs. Activities include: pool, ping pong, video games, weight room, snack bar and TV lounge. Center also sponsors Hang With The Deputy and peer edu & teen court prgms. FUNDING: Nonprofit. OFC HRS: M-F 2:30pm-6pm. Summer Hrs: M-F 1:30pm-5:30pm. Spanish spoken. SERVES: San Bernardino County.

YWCA/RIVERSIDE

8172 Magnolia Ave.
Riverside, CA 92504
(951) 687-9922
(951) 688-5270 FAX

Program offers parenting skills classes which meet or exceed current California state guidelines governing parenting classes. The YWCA also offers numerous support groups for parents, and anger mgmt. Also women's sobriety, TOPS, & AA meetings. Twinges in the Hinges prgm for arthritis patients. Also offers teen preg-

nancy prevention classes. Sober living house. FUNDING: Nonprofit, class fees, donations, United Way. OFC HRS: M-F 8am-8pm; Sat 9am-1pm. Spanish spoken. Fees for classes. Y members $10 off. SERVES: Riverside County.

1736 FAMILY CRISIS CENTER
Admin Office
2116 Arlington Ave., Ste 200
Los Angeles, CA 90018
(323) 737-3900
(323) 737-3993 FAX

This location is one of the 21 Family Source Centers in L.A. County providing the One e-App system for financial assist, case mgmt, and high-risk youth/young adult employment and edu srvs. 24-hr srvs provided to runaway and homeless adols, including: counseling, food, clothing, advocacy and other basic needs. 2-week emerg youth shelter for adols ages 10-17 yrs who need short-term, crisis-oriented shelter. Also operates four shelters for battered women and their children (ages birth-17 yrs) for 1-24 months offering a comprehensive survival and job dev prgm to promote long-term safety, survival & success. 24-hr hotlines in South Bay (310) 379-3620, (310) 370-5902; Long Beach (562) 388-7652; South L.A. (213) 222-1237, (213) 745-6434. May call collect if needed. 24-hr drop-in center at 1736 Monterey Blvd., Hermosa Beach. FUNDING: Donations, grants, govt, CDBG, nonprofit. OFC HRS: M-F 8:30am-5pm. Spanish spoken. Free srvs. SERVES: So. Calif, Southwest L.A.

AGAPE GROUP HOMES
Mailing Address
1130 Clark, Ste 150-277
Santa Maria, CA 93455
(805) 937-5475
(805) 937-5473 FAX

Residential group home for boys, ages 13-18 yrs, and girls, ages 12-18 yrs. Life skills training, group, family and individual therapy. Parent support, family reunification, transitional planning, emancipation. GED support, vocational guidance. Drug & alcohol edu, goal setting, independent living skills. FUNDING: Nonprofit. OFC HRS: M-F 9am-5pm. Spanish and Italian spoken. ADM REQ: Must have court referral. Length of stay 6-9 months or longer. SERVES: U.S.A.

BOYS HOPE GIRLS HOPE OF SO CALIF
1041 W. 18th Street, Ste A101
Costa Mesa, CA 92627
(949) 515-8833
(949) 515-8844 FAX

Long-term, family-like residential group homes for capable, needy youth. Serves academically capable boys and girls who have been abused, neglected or abandoned, or who have come from dysfunctional families. Provides safe, stable, long-term alternative living environment; youth must be free of significant emotional or learning difficulties. This is a voluntary placement. Focus is at-risk children with academic ability who are determined to go to college. FUNDING: Donations, grants, nonprofit. OFC HRS: M-F 9am-5pm. ADM REQ: Ages 10-14 yrs can remain through graduation from high school. Clear need for long-term out-of-home placement, at least an average IQ. Free srvs. SERVES: So. Calif.

CASA YOUTH SHELTER
P.O. Box 216

10911 Reagan St.
Los Alamitos, CA 90720
(562) 594-6825
(714) 995-8601
(562) 594-9185 FAX

Emerg shelter care for runaway and homeless adols. Up to 2 wks temporary shelter. Individual, family & group counseling as well as parenting classes. Family reunification is the main goal. Outpatient counseling for children & families. Volunteer opportunities. FUNDING: Fed, United Way, fundraising, nonprofit. OFC HRS: Admin: M-F 8am-5pm. Clinical: M-F 9am-9pm. Shelter 24 hrs, 7 days. Spanish spoken. ADM REQ: Ages 12-17 yrs. Free srvs for those lacking funds. Sliding fee scale. SERVES: So. Calif.

CHILDNET YOUTH & FAMILY SRVS
Formerly Long Beach Youth Centers, Inc.
P.O. Box 4550
5150 E. Pacific Coast Hwy., Ste 365
Long Beach, CA 90804
(562) 498-5500
(562) 498-5501 FAX

ChildNet consists of 5 divisions: Vista Ridge & Zinsmeyer Academies, state-certified, non-public schools for severely emotionally disturbed and learning-disabled children; Foster Family Network recruits, trains, certifies and supports foster homes for children, with 24-hr counseling support; Behavioral Health Srvs provides mental health srvs to low-income youth; Wraparound prgm is aimed at keeping at-risk teens out of psychiatric and probation facilities; and adoption srvs. FUNDING: Donations, grants, govt, nonprofit. OFC HRS: M-F 8:30am-5pm. Spanish & Khmer spoken. ADM REQ: Ages birth-17 yrs. Family support srvs extend to entire family, regardless of age. Free srvs for those who qualify. SERVES: L.A., Orange, Riverside, San Bernardino, Kern & Fresno Counties.

COVENANT HOUSE NINELINE
461 8th Avenue
New York, NY 10001
(800) 999-9999
(212) 727-4000
(212) 989-9098 FAX

24-hr natl crisis intervention hotline for runaways, homeless, troubled youth & their families. Refers caller to help in his or her own community. Conference call capability & message relays to runaway youth. TDD/TYY hotline (800) 999-9915. FUNDING: Donations, nonprofit. OFC HRS: 24 hrs, 7 days. Spanish spoken. ADM REQ: Ages 18-21 yrs. Free srvs. SERVES: U.S.A.

DAVID & MARGARET YOUTH & FAMILY SRVS
1350 3rd Street
La Verne, CA 91750
(909) 596-5921
(909) 596-7583 FAX

Residential treatment prgm and specialized non-public school for girls ages 11-18 yrs. Shelter care for children ages 11-18 yrs. Foster family agency and adoption srvs serving children ages birth-18 yrs. Learning enhancement ctr for

youth and adults with LD, ADHD, ADD. Community-based edu prgms including self-injury, alcohol and drug intervention, anger mgmt courses. Social srvs, probation and mental health agency referrals. Serves children and families. Provides transitional housing for youth ages 18-25 rys who are at-risk of homelessness. Provides mentoring prgm for foster youth and pvt counseling on a sliding scale basis. FUNDING: State, county, donations, nonprofit. OFC HRS: M-F 8:30am-5pm. Spanish spoken. Accepts insurance, Medicare, Medi-Cal. Sliding fee scale. Set fee to public. SERVES: So. Calif.

HIGH DESERT HOMELESS SERVICES
14049 Amargosa Rd.
Victorville, CA 92392
(760) 245-5991
(760) 245-7513 FAX

55-bed shelter providing emerg and transitional housing. 1-90 day stay, srvs to in house residents only. Breakfast, lunch and dinner served, shower available daily 7:30pm-10pm. Laundry available for shelter residents only. Clothing, personal items, etc. Placement referral for drug/alcohol. Dental care provided in exchange for volunteer work. FUNDING: United Way, pvt, nonprofit. Free srvs. SERVES: Barstow to San Bernardino.

MARY MAGDALENE PROJECT, INC.
P.O. Box 8396
7136 Haskell Ave., Ste 125
Van Nuys, CA 91409
(818) 988-4970
(818) 947-3923 FAX

Residential prgm helps street prostitutes rebuild their lives and become contributing members of society. Medical and psychological eval, counseling, edu assist. FUNDING: Donations, grants, nonprofit. OFC HRS: M-F 9am-4pm. Limited Spanish spoken. ADM REQ: Prostitutes ages 18 yrs+ with a strong desire for lifestyle change. Free srvs. SERVES: So. Calif.

MCKINLEY CHILDREN'S CENTER
762 W. Cypress St.
San Dimas, CA 91773
(909) 599-1227
(909) 592-3841 FAX

Level 12 residential care and non-public school for 44 boys ages 7-15 yrs with serious behavioral and emotional problems related to histories of abuse, neglect and inadequate parenting. Specialized residential treatment prgm is designed to meet individual and family needs. FUNDING: State, county, govt. OFC HRS: M-F 8am-5pm. Spanish spoken. SERVES: So. Calif.

NATL RUNAWAY SWITCHBOARD
3080 N. Lincoln Ave.
Chicago, IL 60657
(800) 786-2929
(773) 880-9860
(773) 929-5150 FAX

24-hr hotline for youth ages 12-21 yrs and their families. Crisis intervention, info & referral, message delivery and conferencing srvs. Free bus rides home for qualified youth through the Greyhound "Home Free" prgm. FUNDING: Fed, nonprofit. OFC HRS: 24 hrs, 7 days. Access to language line. Free srvs. SERVES: U.S.A.

OPERATION SAFEHOUSE
9685 Hayes St.
Riverside, CA 92503
(951) 351-4418
(951) 351-8165 FAX

Short-term, 24-hr shelter for runaways and homeless youth ages 12-17 yrs. Individual, family & group counseling, academic assist, substance abuse edu aftercare, schooling. Transitional living prgm (951) 369-4921. Also operates Safehouse of the Desert in Thousand Palms, (760) 343-3211. FUNDING: Nonprofit. OFC HRS: 24 hrs, 7 days. Spanish spoken. ADM REQ: Max stay 14 days. SERVES: Riverside County.

1736 FAMILY CRISIS CENTER
Admin Office
2116 Arlington Ave., Ste 200
Los Angeles, CA 90018
(323) 737-3900
(323) 737-3993 FAX

This location is one of the 21 Family Source Centers in L.A. County providing the One e-App system for financial assist, case mgmt, and high-risk youth/young adult employment and edu srvs. 24-hr srvs provided to runaway and homeless adols, including: counseling, food, clothing, advocacy and other basic needs. 2-week emerg youth shelter for adols ages 10-17 yrs who need short-term, crisis-oriented shelter. Also operates four shelters for battered women and their children (ages birth-17 yrs) for 1-24 months offering a comprehensive survival and job dev prgm to promote long-term safety, survival & success. 24-hr hotlines in South Bay (310) 379-3620, (310) 370-5902; Long Beach (562) 388-7652; South L.A. (213) 222-1237, (213) 745-6434. May call collect if needed. 24-hr drop-in center at 1736 Monterey Blvd., Hermosa Beach. FUNDING: Donations, grants, govt, CDBG, nonprofit. OFC HRS: M-F 8:30am-5pm. Spanish spoken. Free srvs. SERVES: So. Calif, Southwest L.A.

AGAPE GROUP HOMES
Mailing Address
1130 Clark, Ste 150-277
Santa Maria, CA 93455
(805) 937-5475
(805) 937-5473 FAX

Residential group home for boys, ages 13-18 yrs, and girls, ages 12-18 yrs. Life skills training, group, family and individual therapy. Parent support, family reunification, transitional planning, emancipation. GED support, vocational guidance. Drug & alcohol edu, goal setting, independent living skills. FUNDING: Nonprofit. OFC HRS: M-F 9am-5pm. Spanish and Italian spoken. ADM REQ: Must have court referral. Length of stay 6-9 months or longer. SERVES: U.S.A.

CHAFFEY COLLEGE/EOPS
5885 Haven Ave.
Rancho Cucamonga, CA 91737
(909) 652-6349
(909) 652-6342 FAX

EOPS offers support services to economically disadvantaged students who have experienced limited success in high school and/or college. Endeavors to ensure student retention and success through academic support and financial assistance. CARE is a special EOPS prgm for single parents (of all ages) receiving govt financial assist & helps with child care, cafeteria food vouchers, books and supplies, etc. Also offers prgm for youth ages 16-21 yrs emancipating from foster care or seeking to live independent of their guardians. FUNDING: Govt. OFC HRS: M-W 8am-4:30pm; Th 8am-6:30pm; F 8am-2pm. Spanish, Vietnamese spoken. ADM REQ: Call or see website for eligibility req. SERVES: San Bernardino County.

COLLEGE OF THE DESERT/EOPS
43-500 Monterey Ave.

Palm Desert, CA 92260-9399
(760) 773-2539
(760) 346-8041
(760) 776-0147 FAX

EOPS offers various counseling, financial aid for books, transfer fee waiver, laptops and graphing calculators on loan, priority registration, long-term edu planning, tutoring, student ID card, assistance with health fee. CARE is a special EOPS prgm for single parents (all ages) receiving govt financial assis to help them go to college and obtain skills for meaningful employment. Helps with child care, gas cards & many other srvs. Also offer prgm for youth ages 16-21 yrs emancipating from foster care or seeking to live independent of their guardians. EOPS and CARE srvs subject to change. FUNDING: Govt. OFC HRS: M-Th 9am-5pm. F 9am-12noon. Spanish spoken. ADM REQ: Must be full-time COD student. Apply online or in person. Inquire about requirements. SERVES: Riverside County.

COPPER MOUNTAIN COLLEGE/EOPS
6162 Rotary Way
Joshua Tree, CA 92252
(760) 366-3791
(760) 366-5257 FAX

EOPS & CARE are state-funded prgms assisting the academically & economically disadvantaged student. EOPS srvs include, but are not limited to: academic counseling, book assist, tutoring, parking permits. CARE provides grants, food cards, parenting info, gas cards. All srvs upon availability or state funding. TDD (760) 366-3241. FUNDING: Govt. OFC HRS: M-Th 8:15am-5pm; F 8:15am-3pm. Spanish spoken. ADM REQ: Must be full-time student, less than 70 degree-applicable units, BOG waiver A or B, and academically disadvantaged. CARE students must be EOPS eligible, 18 yrs+, have at least one child under the age of 14 yrs, and currently on CalWORKs/TANF & receiving cash aid. SERVES: Calif.

CRAFTON HILLS COLLEGE/EOPS
11711 Sand Canyon Rd.
Yucaipa, CA 92399-1799
(909) 389-3239
(909) 794-2161
(909) 389-3621 FAX

EOPS offers info & referral, counseling, edu grants, financial aid for books, transportation assist, mentoring, student work prgm, emerg no-interest loans, transfer fee waiver. CARE is a special EOPS prgm for single parents (of all ages) receiving govt financial assist & helps with child care, gas cards & many other srvs. Also offer prgm for youth ages 16-21 yrs emancipating from foster care or seeking to live independent of their guardians. OFC HRS: M-Th 8am-6pm; F 8am-1pm. Spanish spoken. ADM REQ: CA resident, qualify for BOGW A/B, enrolled in 12 units unless in disabled student prgm, have less than 70 degree-applicable units & be edu disadvantaged. CARE: head of household, single parent receiving TANF/CalWORKs with a Welfare-to-Work plan & have a child under 14 yrs of age. SERVES: San Bernardino County.

DAVID & MARGARET YOUTH & FAMILY SRVS
1350 3rd Street
La Verne, CA 91750
(909) 596-5921
(909) 596-7583 FAX

Residential treatment prgm and specialized non-public school for girls ages 11-18 yrs. Shelter care for children ages 11-18 yrs. Foster family agency and adoption srvs serving children ages birth-18 yrs. Learning enhancement ctr for youth and adults with LD, ADHD, ADD. Community-based edu prgms including self-injury, alcohol and drug intervention, anger mgmt courses. Social srvs, probation and mental health agency referrals. Serves children and families. Provides transitional housing for youth ages 18-25 yrs who are at-risk of homeessness. Provides mentoring prgm for foster youth and pvt counseling on a sliding scale basis. FUNDING: State, county, donations, nonprofit. OFC HRS: M-F 8:30am-5pm. Spanish spoken. Accepts insurance, Medicare, Medi-Cal. Sliding fee scale. Set fee to public. SERVES: So. Calif.

EDGEWOOD CTR FOR CHILDREN & FAMILIES
1801 Vicente St.
San Francisco, CA 94116-2995
(415) 681-3211
(415) 664-7094 FAX

Residential group home for youth ages 6-16 yrs. Long-term care, short-term emerg, non-public school on-site, mental health srvs, family reunification. Serves abused children and wards of the court; also accepts emotionally disturbed children. FUNDING: Nonprofit. OFC HRS: M-F 8:30am-5pm. Spanish spoken. Accepts Medicare, Medi-Cal, insurance, sliding fee scale. SERVES: Calif.

ETTIE LEE YOUTH & FAMILY SERVICES
P.O. Box 339
5146 N. Maine Ave.
Baldwin Park, CA 91706-0339
(626) 960-4861
(626) 337-2621 FAX

Family-style homes for severely emotionally disturbed young men ages 8-18 yrs. 24-hr care by trained staff. Individual & group therapy, gang intervention srvs, independent living skills training, case mgmt, family counseling, therapeutic recreation, 12-Step prgms, substance abuse treatment & on-site school. Licensed treatment foster family agency for boys & girls ages birth-18 yrs. Mental health therapy, case mgmt & family counseling. FUNDING: Nonprofit. OFC HRS: M-F 8am-5pm. Spanish spoken. ADM REQ: County referral for group home & foster care. SERVES: So. Calif.

FIELDS COMPREHENSIVE YOUTH SRVS
8780 19th Street, Ste 196
Rancho Cucamonga, CA 91701
(909) 945-1318
(909) 466-8685

Residential treatment, long-term foster care, emancipation prep, family reunification srvs. Individual, group & family therapy, parenting edu, self-mgmt training, gang intervention, drug abuse treatment, computer training. FUNDING: Private nonprofit. ADM REQ: Males ages 13-17 yrs, who are dependent and/or delinquent minors. SERVES: San Bernardino County.

GUARDIAN SCHOLARSHIP PRGM

Cal State University Fullerton
P.O. Box 6828
800 State College Blvd., Ste C120
Fullerton, CA 92834-6828
(657) 278-4900

Srvs to young men and women ages 17-23 yrs emancipating from foster care or seeking to live independent of their guardians. Guardian Scholarship Prgm provides academic & living financial assist. Assists with on-campus housing, info & referral, counseling, mentoring, job search and professional networking. Helps youth navigate campus life and gives social support. OFC HRS: M-F 8am-5pm. ADM REQ: Foster youth admitted to Cal State Fullerton with FAFSA form, and no family or benefactor financial support. SERVES: Calif.

HART COMMUNITY HOMES

208 N. Lemon
Fullerton, CA 92832
(714) 526-2729
(714) 526-2653 FAX

Residential treatment for foster care youth ages 13-18 yrs. Treatment model is tailored to meet individual needs. Prgm focuses on emancipation and has a vocational center providing a life skills workforce dev prgm. Also offers Monkey Business Cafe which provides paid work experience in a cafe setting for foster care youth in and emancipating out of the foster care system. Visit (www.hartcommunityhomes.org). FUNDING: Nonprofit. OFC HRS: M-F 9am-5pm. Cafe open M-F 7am-3pm. Spanish, Korean spoken. ADM REQ: Abused and abandoned boys ages 13-18 yrs. SERVES: L.A., Orange & San Bernardino Counties.

HIGH DESERT HOMELESS SERVICES

14049 Amargosa Rd.
Victorville, CA 92392
(760) 245-5991
(760) 245-7513 FAX

55-bed shelter providing emerg and transitional housing. 1-90 day stay, srvs to in-house residents only. Breakfast, lunch and dinner served, shower available daily 7:30pm-10pm. Laundry available for shelter residents only. Clothing, personal items, etc. Placement referral for drug/alcohol. Dental care provided in exchange for volunteer work. FUNDING: United Way, pvt, nonprofit. Free srvs. SERVES: Barstow to San Bernardino.

HOMES OF HOPE FOSTER FAMILY

Foster Care
1107 S. Glendora Ave.
West Covina, CA 91790
(626) 814-9085
(626) 814-2276 FAX

Recruits and certifies foster families to care for boys and girls ages birth-17 yrs who are under the protection of Children's Srvs. Srvs include: PRIDE training, weekly social worker contact, KIDS fund, counseling, tutoring, transportation, and emancipation srvs, newsletter. 24-hr phone support. FUNDING: Nonprofit. OFC HRS: M-F 8:30am-5pm. Spanish spoken. SERVES: So. Calif.

LUGGAGE OF LOVE

295 Willis Ave, Ste E
Camarillo, CA 93010
(805) 804-5952
(805) 482-1665 FAX

Organization that is dedicated to providing children in shelters and foster care with a brand new piece of luggage so that their belongings are safe during transition. FUNDING: Nonprofit. SERVES: Calif.

MT. SAN JACINTO COLLEGE/EOPS

1499 N. State St.
San Jacinto, CA 92583
(951) 487-3295
(951) 654-4812 FAX

EOPS offers info & referral, counseling, edu grants, financial aid for books, transportation assist, mentoring, student work prgm, emerg no-interest loans, transfer fee waiver. CARE is a special EOPS prgm for single parents (all ages) receiving govt financial assist & helps with child care, gas cards & many other srvs. Also prgm for youth ages 16-21 yrs emancipating from foster care or seeking to live independent of their guardians. Wait: approx. 3-4 wks. See website(www.msjc.edu) for more info. FUNDING: Govt. OFC HRS: M-Th 8am-5pm; F 8am-noon. Spanish spoken. ADM REQ: See website or call for eligibility req. SERVES: Riverside County.

OPERATION SAFEHOUSE

9685 Hayes St.
Riverside, CA 92503
(951) 351-4418
(951) 351-8165 FAX

Short-term, 24-hr shelter for runaways and homeless youth ages 12-17 yrs. Individual, family & group counseling, academic assist, substance abuse edu aftercare, schooling. Transitional living prgm (951) 369-4921. Also operates Safehouse of the Desert in Thousand Palms, (760) 343-3211. FUNDING: Nonprofit. OFC HRS: 24 hrs, 7 days. Spanish spoken. ADM REQ: Max stay 14 days. SERVES: Riverside County.

PALO VERDE COMMUNITY COLLEGE/EOPS

1 College Dr.
Blythe, CA 92225
(760) 921-5402
(760) 921-3608 FAX

EOPS offers info & referral, counseling, edu grants, financial aid for books, transportation assist, mentoring, student work prgm, emerg no-interest loans, transfer fee waiver. CARE is a special EOPS prgm for single parents (all ages) receiving govt financial assist and helps with children, gas cards and many other srvs. Also prgm for youth ages 16-21 yrs emancipating from foster care or seeking to live independent of their guardians. FUNDING: Govt. OFC HRS: M-F 8am-5pm. Spanish spoken. ADM REQ: Must be full-time student, less than 70 units of college credit, low income and below average score on either English or math placement tests. CARE students must qualify for EOPS and also be receiving govt aid. SERVES: Riverside County.

RIVERSIDE CO. PUBLIC SOCIAL SRVS

10281 Kidd St.
Riverside, CA 92503
(951) 358-5650

(951) 358-5155 FAX

Independent living and transitional housing Placement prgms for youth ages 16-18 yrs. FUNDING: Govt. OFC HRS: M-F 8am-5pm. Spanish spoken. SERVES: Riverside County.

RIVERSIDE COMMUNITY COLLEGE/EOPS

4800 Magnolia Ave.
Riverside, CA 92506-1293
(951) 222-8045
(951) 222-8046 FAX

EOPS offers info & referral, counseling, edu grants, financial aid for books, transportation assist, mentoring, student work prgm. CARE is a special EOPS prgm for single parents (of all ages) receiving govt financial assist & helps with child care, gas cards & many other srvs. Also offer prgm for youth ages 16-21 yrs emancipating from foster care or seeking to live independent of their guardians. FUNDING: Govt. OFC HRS: M-W, F 8am-4pm; Th 8am-5:45pm. Summer hrs: M-W 8am-4pm; Th 8am-4:50pm. Spanish, Vietnamese spoken. ADM REQ: Must be full-time student, less than 70 units of college credit, low income & below average score on either English or math placement tests. CARE students must qualify for EOPS and also be receiving govt aid. SERVES: Riverside County.

SAN BERNARDINO VLY COLLEGE/EOPS

701 S. Mt. Vernon Ave.
San Bernardino, CA 92410-2798
(909) 384-4412
(909) 888-6511
(909) 888-3071 FAX

EOPS offers info & referral, counseling, edu grants, financial aid for books, transportation assist, mentoring, student work prgm, emerg no-interest loans, transfer fee waiver. CARE is a special EOPS prgm for single parents (of all ages) receiving govt financial assist & helps with child care, gas cards & many other srvs. Also offer prgm for youth ages 16-21 yrs emancipating from foster care or seeking to live independent of their guardians. FUNDING: Govt. OFC HRS: M-F 8am-5pm. Spanish spoken. ADM REQ: Must be full-time student, less than 70 units of college credit, low income & below average score on either English or math placement tests. CARE students must qualify for EOPS and also be receiving govt aid. SERVES: San Bernardino County.

SOUTH COAST COMMUNITY SRVS

San Bernardino Co. Srvs Office
2930 Inland Empire Blvd., Ste 120
Ontario, CA 92764
(909) 980-6700

Provides life-essential srvs to troubled children, youth and families. Offers 4 group homes for abused, neglected and abandoned children ages 10-18 yrs and 2 group homes for young adults ages 18-25 yrs in need of short-term assist. Wraparound prgm offers family intervention srvs. Children's intensive srvs prgm provides outpatient counseling for individuals, children, teens and their families. Eval, assessment, testing, therapy, medication support, crisis intervention, case mgmt. Offers mental health clinics in Redlands (909) 792-0747 & Yucaipa (909) 790-0210. FUNDING: Nonprofit. Accepts Medi-Cal and pvt pay; sliding fee scale available. SERVES: San Bernardino County.

THE CHILDREN'S VILLAGE OF SONOMA CO.
1321 Lia Lane
Santa Rosa, CA 95404
(707) 566-7044
(707) 566-7105 FAX

Provides nurturing, stable family homes in a multi-generational, enriched environment for children and their siblings in foster care. Goals: to establish stability for foster children, opportunity for siblings to remain together, allow children to develop healthy emotional attachments in a nurturing environment. FUNDING: Grants, donations, foster care system. OFC HRS: M-F 8:30am-5pm. SERVES: Nationwide.

VICTOR VLY COMM COLLEGE/EOPS
18422 Bear Valley Rd
Victorville, CA 92392-5849
(760) 245-4271
(760) 951-9225 FAX

EOPS offers info & referral, counseling, edu grants, financial aid for books, transportation assist, mentoring, student work prgm, emerg no-interest loans, transfer fee waiver. CARE is a special EOPS prgm for single parents (of all ages) receiving govt financial assist & helps with child care, gas cards & many other srvs. Prgm for youth ages 16-21 yrs emancipating from foster care or seeking to live independent of their guardians. FUNDING: Govt. OFC HRS: M-F 8:30am-5pm. Spanish spoken. ADM REQ: Must be full-time student, less than 70 units of college credit, low income & below average score on either English or math placement tests. CARE students must qualify for EOPS and also be receiving govt aid. SERVES: San Bernardino County.

THE FIRST PLACE TO LOOK FOR SOCIAL SERVICES

Turn to the Rainbow Guides when you need to quickly find help for your clients. Since 1979, the Guides have helped thousands of professionals refer clients to other social welfare organizations. All of the data in the Rainbow Guides is verified annually by telephone, with our staff making thousands of calls for each directory. Each of the over 25,000 listings contains the following information:

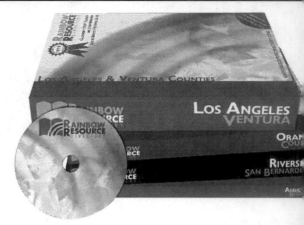

- 📖 Type of service provided
- 📖 Source of funding
- 📖 Admission requirements
- 📖 Languages spoken
- 📖 Address
- 📖 Phone and fax
- 📖 Office hours
- 📖 Region served

THREE TYPES OF DIRECTORIES ARE AVAILABLE

1. **Print directories by county.** Three county-specific guides are available: (a) Los Angeles and Ventura Counties, (b) Orange County, and (c) Riverside and San Bernardino Counties. Prices range from $49 to $69. Buyers of ten or more books receive a 10% discount
2. **CD-ROM.** Over 20,000 listings for the entire state of California are contained on one disk. The price for a single-user disk is $129. C 800-440-4780 for pricing if you need more than 10 CDs.
3. **Addiction Recovery Guide.** 4,000 listings of Southern California programs for treatment, sober living, child and adolescent programs, co-occurring disorders, DUI, eating disorders, education and prevention, gambling, professional certification, recovery and supp sexual addictions, and smoking. This is a free publication; the only cost is the shipping fee of $5.

ORDER FORM QUESTIONS? (800)440-4780	Quantity	Price	TOTAL
Los Angeles & Ventura Counties Rainbow Referral Guide Published every Spring with 10,000 listings and 800 pages		$69	
Orange County Rainbow Referral Guide Published every Summer with 5,000 listings and 450 pages		$49	
Riverside & San Bernardino Counties Rainbow Referral Guide Published in the Fall with 5,000 listings and 400 pages		$49	
California Rainbow Referral Guide on CD Published twice annually with 20,000 listings. One-year subscription (two CDs)		$129	
Southern California Addiction Recovery Guide Published in the Summer with 4,000 listings and 230 pages		Free	

PAYMENT METHOD (THREE OPTIONS, PLEASE CHECK ONE)	
☐ Check payable to James Publishing enclosed	**SUBTOTAL**
☐ Purchase order attached or faxed to 714-751-2709	10% Quantity Discount (10+ books)
☐ Credit card: ☐ Visa ☐ MasterCard ☐ AmEx	
Card #_____ 3 (or 4) digit security code_____	Add 8.25% sales tax
Exp. Date_____ Signature_____	Add $5 shipping per book/CD (including free Addiction books)
If a new edition is published within three months of your purchase, the new edition will be shipped to you at no charge.	**TOTAL**

Printed name:_____ Program/Title:_____

Agency/Organization:_____

Street Address, City, State, Zip:_____

Phone, Fax, E-mail:_____

KIDS Inc.

Helping kids around the world.

Every year James Publishing gives a portion of its revenues to its private charitable foundation. This foundation supports education and health projects for needy youth in the United States and less developed countries. For more information, visit our website (www.jamespublishing.com/foundation.htm).

Homes and support for street kids.

We are teaming up with **Arms of Love** to build additional homes and take in more orphaned, abandoned, and abused children in developing countries. Our first steps are to finish and furnish a home in **Bohol, Phillipines** and sponsor one child. Next we hope to build a home in Brazil or Nicaragua and support some children there.

Bohol is one of the poorest and most underdeveloped areas of the Philippines archipelago. To learn more about Bohol, and how Arms of Love is helping the region, visit their website, **www.ArmsOfLove.org**.

Bohol

Clean water in Indonesia.

We provided money for the **Sumba Foundation** (www.SumbaFoundation.org) to dig water wells and lay water pipe for the village of **Paholo** on the island of **Sumba**. Our well and pipe provide clean water for 145 students and 800 villagers.

A clean water source is important during the Indonesian monsoon months of December–March. The springs become polluted with runoff, causing dangerous outbreaks of diarrhea that kill many young children. Our wells will eliminate this cause of death.

Sumba

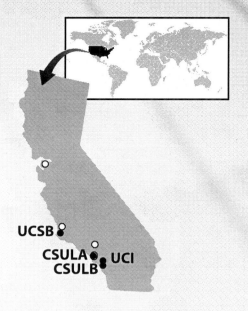

Full college scholarships in California.

We paid for tuition, books, and living expenses, and guidance to five inner-city students who were accepted to good universities, but could not afford to attend. Our scholarship recipients attended UC Santa Barbara, Cal State Long Beach, Cal State Los Angeles, and UC Irvine.

We also found sponsors for six additional needy scholars. Thanks to generous providers of full scholarships, these students attended UC Berkeley, USC, Cal Poly San Luis Obispo, Cal State Los Angeles, and Cal Poly Pomona.

UCSB
CSULA
CSULB
UCI

New elementary school in Afghanistan

New school in Afghanistan. We provided the startup money and most of the first several years' budget for the Helping Hands School in Kabul. Helping Hands began as an elementary and trade school for orphans and widows, and at its peak educated and fed over 200 students.

Kabul

For more information on

KIDS Inc.

visit our website: www.jamespublishing.com/foundation.htm